THE ENCYCLOPAEDIA OF INDIAN CULTURE

Edited by

DR. P. N. CHOPRA
DR. PRABHA CHOPRA

RELIANCE PUBLISHING HOUSE
NEW DELHI (INDIA)

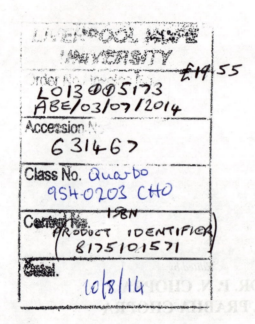

© Editor

First Published 2003

ISBN : 81-7510-157-1 ✓

Price : $22.00.

Published by
Dr. S.K. Bhatia (Life Member Common Cause HWF, ILA & INSA Lions Clubs Int.)
FEPI, FPBAI, DSBPA, RSH
for **RELIANCE PUBLISHING HOUSE**
3026/7H, Ranjit Nagar, New Delhi-110 008
Ph. : 25847377 / 25842605 Fax : 25846769

Composed by
Elegant Printographics
319, R. G. Complex, IIIrd Floor,
Sector-14, Rohini, Delhi-110085
Ph. : 27567413

Printed by : Printline, New Delhi.

PREFACE

India has made tremendous progress in almost every field since the attainment of Independence. Her advancement is all round and stupendous, her record in the creative activities in the realms of education, science and arts, is remarkable. Surprisingly enough, there is no standard internationally reputed and readable Encyclopaedia reflecting or interpreting this change or giving a full spectrum of knowledge or reference material for lay readers or experts. Well-known international Encyclopaedias of developed countries are woefully deficient in respect of facts about this fast developing and changing India. The current Encyclopaedias produced in Indian languages betray divergence in professional scope, quality and format.

The need for such a work had been felt for a long time. In fact, we endeavoured to take up this project about 40 years ago and planned it meticulously. We approached the leading industrialists in the country including the Tatas, Birlas, Aga Khan Foundation and others for financial support, but unfortunately there was no positive response. The only person who took interest was Mr. C. R. Irani, Managing Director of the Statesman, but the cost involved was so much that he too could not be of any help. To give the readers an idea we might mention that the total cost of compilation and publication of a 10-Volume Encyclopaedia on the pattern of Encyclopaedia Britannica was likely to be about rupees nine millions. About rupees six millions were required if five volumes were to be produced. So it was clear that it was beyond the reach of an individual and no government agency was coming forward to take up such a project. Under the circumstances we attempted this short Encyclopaedia of Indian Culture only.

An effort has been made in this Encyclopaedia to deal with all aspects of the country and the life of the people of India, its flora, fauna, physiography, fairs and festivals, arts, monuments, religions, literature, famous people in various fields, fine arts, such as music, painting, architecture, drama, dance. Most of the technical subjects have been written by specialists who have lent their name to enhance the value of this work. Our thanks are due to them.

Places of importance whether due to religious point of view or of historical interest have been taken note of. Many entries carry a bibliography to enable the interested reader to study the subject in more detail, if desired.

We do hope that this work will be of some help to the Scholars and the public in India and abroad. We would like to record here our deep appreciation of Dr. S. K. Bhatia, of M/s. Reliance Publishing House for the keen interest they took in the publication of this work.

P. N. CHOPRA
PRABHA CHOPRA

INTRODUCTION

CULTURE is the universal characteristic of human societies. Thus, even as civilizations are born, bloom and even die as did the ancient Greek and Egyptian Civilizations, the essence of the culture lives on in the heart of man. No human groups have ever been known that did not have language, traditions, custom and institutions.

There are numerous examples, in the long history of man, of cultural interactions which have fused not only customs and habits but the different races of man, so that most cultures have become composite.

A civilization is conditioned by geography, climate, temperament and habits of the people who inhabit the area, and many other factors. Attitude towards life of religious thinking, for instance, influences directly the works of art and architecture. The caves of Ajanta or Ellora are all evidence of efforts to incorporate and perpetuate religious ideals. That philosophy and art are interrelated can be viewed in the temples of Nara in Japan or the Banaras Ghats in India where the dedicated work communicates the inner perception of the artist.

India occupies a unique place in the world and has time and again shown a capacity for adjustment and comprehension. Civilization in India is at once more ancient and alive than in any other country in the world. "With its spirit of assimilation, comprehension and synthesis", says Dr. Radhakamal Mukerjee, "the Indian culture has stood at once for the inifinite expansion of the human community". The well known Indian poet, Rabindranath Tagore called the land *"Bharat Tirtha"* of the great concourse of humanity where everyone is welcome with its rich cultural heritage. Not only it has influenced the culture of many South Asian countires but assimilated whatever was good. Indian dance-forms tried to keep up the purity of *Bharatanatyam*, *Kathakali*, and Manipuri but at the same time many folk-dance traditions blended; they even brought, like the Himalayan *gaddi* dancers or Tibetan and Japanese mask-dancers' elements beyond the borders of India.

The cultural influence of India, as many articles in this book would reflect, today lies scattered in the numerous monuments and folk-tales rooted in Indian mythology. Though many of the South-East Asian countries subsequently changed their religion, the core of their culture remains ancient Indian in character. In many cases, Indians can discover their ancient culture in its true form outside their own country for there it has escaped the ravages of time. These regions were once seats of powerful Hindu kingdom and empires more than 1,500 years ago, and bore Hindu names such as *Champa. Yava-Dvipa, Suvarnabhumi* and *Suvarana-divpa.*

The ancient Indian epics, Ramayana and Mahabharata made the strongest impact on the Indonesian mind. Adapted into the Javanese language, as also in Baliness and Malaya and Thai, they became an intrinsic part of the literature and mythology in each of these countries. They remained a source of inspiration for the people through all the centuries and continued to be so even today.

Buddhism played a pivotal role in culture intercourse among various countries of Asia. In the field of sculpture, too, there is a great similarity in the images of Buddha produced in India and various other countries of Asia, such as Thailand, Sri Lanka, Korea, Japan etc.

The present work is an attempt to portray Indian Culture through the ages in all its aspects-political, social life, economic conditions, education and literature and arts and folk arts, music and architecture of different era's. This would help in assessing and focussing the role of cultural currents in different periods.

Most of the articles in this volume have been taken from authoratative journals such as India-Perspective published by Ministry of Information and Broadcasting, Cultural Forum published by Ministry of Education and Culture and Bharatiya Vidya Bhavan Journals which were contributed by well known authors and their names have been duly acknowleged.

P. N. Chopra
Prabha Chopra

CONTENTS

C

E

F

G

H

xii

L

M

N

O

P

R

S

T

U

V

W

Y

Z

"A"

A.R.RAHMAN

He has given a whole new *taal* to Indian music. With his synthesiser and his love for Western classical. A.R. Rahman has redefined popular film music by making the beat as important. as the verse. So much so, the films might flop but Rahman's music is always a hot - selling proposition.

The whiz Kid made his debut in Tamil cinema and won several awards (National and Filmfare) for his music compositions in Mani Ratnam's films. Incidentally, it was Mani Ratnam who catapulated him centre - stage in Hindi cinema with Roja, his first bi-lingual film.

Roja, Bombay, Dil Se, Kadalan, Thiruda Thiruda, Rangeela : Rahman has created an enticing 'oeuvre of songs that are essentially an oriental answer to occidental pop. Now, with prominent film makers like Subhash Ghai teaming up with him in *Taal*. Rahman has truly acquired pan - Indian popularity. Lately, he even teamed up with Michael Jackson in an international concert and provided the beats for the pelvic gyrations of the prince of pop.

AAMIR RAZA AND INDIAN THEATRE

There have been many adaptations of the epic Ramayana, on both stage as well as on screen, from time to time. But Aamir Raza Husain's "The Legend of Ram : Prince of India", has not only given a totally new look to its presentation but has lent an unparalleled dimension to English theatre in India. Expectedly it has evoked critical acclaim unheard of in the country. Aamir has, to quote a viewer, sent the audiences into " trance".

For translating his " The Legend..." dream into reality, Aamir created 22 sets on the empty hillocks of New Delhi's Diplomatic Enclave. The ambience here was lent a spiritual aura and design that was mind bogglingly nove. He erected the audience platform on a three-track rail line, controlled through a remote control. The size of audience platform was 42 feet by 62 feet, with a seating capacity of nearly 500 people. For that stunning and ultimate impact on the audiences, Amir brought together masters from different fields: For haunting and lilting music, he had Ustad Amjad Ali Khan whose folk and classical improvisations highlighted the moods of various situations; for set designing he had the famour Bijon Das Gupta who did a splendid job here; for chroeography, he had Tanushree Shanker whose team cast a spell on the audiences with their flowing movements. And then there was the magician, inllusionist and actor K.S. Ramesh for special effects that electrified the magic of the " Legend of Ram " Jattin Kochhar's costumes had novelty and innovation combining modern, glamour with traditional elegance.

To top it all, he had the best actors and actresses to play various roles. It is difficult to single out the performance of any one of them - since all of them were " living" their roles. Yet Zohra sehgal as " Manthra ", Jasbir Malik as " Dashrath" Shekhar Suman as " Ram", Ali Khan as " Lakshman " Archana Mehra as " Kekayi " and last - but not the least - Salim Ghouse as " Ravana" were outstanding.

But the real winner was the script of Aamir Raza, which sought to give contemporary relevance to the age - old epic.

Aamir had been working with the famous theatre personality Marcus Murch who was providing a new meaning to the English theatre in India since 1974. Marcus had with him an enthusiastic determined and diligent team of artists. But after the death of Marcus Murch in 1984, Aamir took up his mantle and has been coming out with quality presentations. But with his 'Legend of Ram' he has provided a new dimension to the concept of theatre presentation in the country.

NEELAM MAHAJAN SINGH

AGRA'S ARCHITECTURAL SPLENDOUR

There is something in the soil of Agra that several dynasties of great warriors and kings Rajputs, Lodhis and Mughals lay claim to have founded it. The earliest mention (about 1080 - 1081 A.D.) is by Khwaja Masud, who used to write poems in praise of Ghaznavide Kings - " The fort of Agra is built among the sand like a hill. No calamity had ever befallen its fortifications, nor had deceitful time dealt treacherously with it". Later, Father Monserrate, about 1580 A.D. recorded that " Agra is a magnificent city both for its size and its antiquity. Gold and silver are plentiful, as also horses from Persia and Tartary ".Whatever be the finality of history about its origin, Agra was adorned with the purple robes of royalty. Once Sikander Lodhi made it a royal seat, it became the Shiraz of India.

Babur, the first Mughal, was the first to build magnificently at Agra. Sighing for hill slopes, waterfalls, and the cool rippling climate of Samarkand, Babur introduced terraced water gardens in the heat of India. The meandering river Jamuna gave to him a perfect setting and Bagh Gul-i- Afshan or Rambagh Came about to be. Pleasure Pavilions, water tanks, canals, chutes, fountains and cascades were blended as carefully as parts of a flower growing on their own. The resultant effect was epochal.

The reign of his son Humayun was uneventful for architectures. His years were squandered, first, in maintaining himself as king, and later, in regaining his lost kingdom from Sher Shah Suri. His early death propelled Akbar to the throne of Hindustan in 1556 A.D. Akbar was truly the first Indian Mughal. Whether it be in architectural style, use of local resources, matrimony, art of governance, court procedures, or development of religious thought, Akbar revitalised the Indian traditions and arts. He built grandiosely and abundantly. The Red Fort assumed massive proportions. Delicate buildings were added to it, like Akbari Mahal and Jahangiri Mahal. Fortified gates to the fort - Delhi Gate and Akbar (later called Amar Singh Gate), are exceptional devices in strategic architecture. The material used was red sandstone and the universal use of beam - and - post (trabeate) method was established. Both Akbari and Jahangiri Mahals have courtyards, geomertical and areabesque patterns, ornamental arches, beautiful brackets, and an assemblage of rooms linked by galleries and corridors. The effect is profuse yet delicate.

The urge to build another palace city led Akbar to Fatehpur Sikri, close by Agra, where he laid out a palace cum fort complex. Rising out on a hill in red sandstone amidst the sprawling plains, Fatehpur Sikri is worth monumental praise. The choice of site was prompted by the blessings of Sufi Saint Khwaja Salim Chisti, which Akbar received here. A son was born to him, who would take the Mughal name into future centuries. So we hear in those days, of an emperor walking barefoot to seek blessings, and in an urge of gratefulness constructing a fine mausoleum over the Khawaja's grave. His palace came adjacent to the saint's tomb. Panch Mahal, Mariam's Palace, Jodha Bai's palace, Diwan-i-Am, Diwan-i-Khas, Abul Fazal's House, Hiran Minar etc. are all buildings which gave to Hindustan secular concepts and a tolerant thought. Religious discourses were held with clerics from a faiths. Even Jesuit fathers camped at Fatehpur Sikri. Din-i-Ilahi, a secular religious thought developed by Akbar, negated theocracy had made him the propagator of a national religion. Art flourished and Navarattans (the nine gems, as his countries were called) involved themselves in nation building and development of the finer aspects of humanism. Before he died, Akbar started the construction of his tomb at Sikandra.

When Jahagir ascended the Mughal throne, the empire had been consolidated by the mighty Akbar. He completed the tomb of his father and devoted himself to painting and gardening. To him is credited the building of his mother's tomb, know today as mariam's Tomb, at Sikandra. It has been skilfully done as a *baradari*, with *chhatris* capping the facade. Inlaid and embossed panels beautify the tomb with delicate motifs. The arts pleased him like no one else. The departure from red sandstone to white marble in architectural style came during the reign of Jahangir. Robustness was replaced by delicacy. This was the easence of his reign. It should be said to Akbar's credit that he laid the foundations of Hindustan strong on principles od secularism and equality of sexes. Nurjahan, the iron willed lady ruled Jahangir's heart and his Hindustan through him from 1612 to 1627 A.D.

A charmin monument, *Itmad - ud - daula*, the tomb of her father, was built in Jahangir's reign. It is the decorative aspect that first strikes then fascinates a visitor. On white marble has been exquisitely done an inlay work. Precious and semiprecious stones have been filled in carefully carved grooves and sockets. The patterns - sometimes geometirc, floral, and some times representative of fruits or delicate trees, accentuate in a certain finish the entire effect of the building. The inlay work here became the precursor of later embellishments to Mughal buildings.

Jahangir was a writer too and in his " Memories " has spoken of the city life thus - " in the number of its buildings it is equal to several cities of Iraq, Khurasan and Mawar - un - Nahr (Trans - oxiana) put together. Many persons has erected buildings of three or four storeys in it. The mass of the people is so great that moving about in the lanes and bazaars is difficult ". To the credit of the city intelligentsia, he further records, " the inhabitants of Agra exert themselves greatly in the acquirement of crafts and the search after learning. Various professors of every religion and creed have taken up their abode in the city". Such was the glory of Agra, the pride of Agra, and the lofty standing of Agra.

The golden age of the city of Agra began during the reign of Emperor Shahjahan, who ascended the throne in 1628 A.D. This King was a passionate man, and his passion led him to achieve many noble things. Apart from extending the frontiers of Mughal Empire, he built profusely inside the Red Fort combining magnificence with delicacy. The Khas Mahal with the Anguri Bagh in front, completing a concept, is a most charming presentation. The white marble building has been lavishly painted in different patterns. The cool effect, created by the river on one side and the water fountains of *Anguri Bagh* on the other, is unbeatable. As a concept it owes its origin only to kingly overtures. The Shish Mahal is decorated by glass mosaic work. Precision, Patience and artistry is at its best here. If you light a candle inside this chamber, the reflections from a thousand and more mirrors, quivering like emotions, approach you nudgingly. Dreams were not dreamt in slumber, but felt and seen here with waking eyes.

Administrative needs were satisfied in the *Diwan-i-Am* and *Diwan - i - Khas.* The arches of these buildings are works of mathematical accuracy and a paint brush delivery. The Diwan - i - Khas is ornate and is truly the preserve of kings. An octagonal towar, called the Musamman Burj, is a palace with a reiverine view. A sunk water basin in the courtyard in front, delicate pietra dura work all over leaves one starry eyed. History later recorded that Emperor Shahjahan died here viewing the Taj. In ornamentation, it is truly as beautiful as the sign of a king.

Religious longing gave birth to *Mina Masjid, Nagina Masjid* and *Moti Masjid* of all the three, it is the *Moti Masjid* that in its execution surpasses the others. The arches, pillars, *chhatris* and the perfect domes create a spectacular effect. It befits kingly worship. Grace, purity and sanctity combine in a harmonious relationship with the Creator. *Chini - ka - Rauza,* a mausoleum of Shirazi, a *vazir* of Shahjahan, 1639 A.D., is the test specimen of polychrome glazed tile decoration in India.

Life at Agra, as recorded by Francis Bernier in late 17th Century, was comfortable and lofty : "Agra having been a favourite and more frequent abode of the kings of Hindustan since the days of Akbar, by who it was built and named Akbarabad, surpasses Delhi in extent, in the multitude of residences belonging to *omrahs* and Rajas, and in the good stone or brick houses inhabited by private individuals and in the number of its *Karuanasserrahs"*.

The names of the then localities have stuck to the city encased in its history. Sikandara was named after Sikandar Lodhi. Phulatti was a residential locality where Peter Mundy, the contemporary historian, lived in 1631 A.D. *Kashmere Bazaar, Delhi Gate, Shah Ganj, Taj Ganj, Idgah Rui Ki Mandi* are some other old names that continues. The thin bylances of the old city acquired names and traditions of historical evolution that are still evident in the occasionally visible balustrade, chhatris, gates, and carvings on house exteriors.

Not many know that the legendary Mirza Ghalib, Urdu poet, philospher, litterature par excellence was born at Agra on December 27, 1797. Though Ghalib shifted permanently his home and hearth to Delhi, a year of two post marriage, Agra could not fade away from his heart. It was his birthplace and his childhood lay scattered in the bylanes of Agra. Ghalib has written a heartrending letter to his friend Ziya - ud - din Ahmad Khan, pining away for Agra like a lover for his beloved.

" Let no man look upon Agra as of slight account, but as he passes through her roads call on God's preserving and protecting power to hold her in its keeping. For she... was once the playground of my love - distracted heart.

There was a time when in her soil only the mandrake grew, and, save the heart, here tress would bear no other fruit, and the drunken breeze of morning ranged through her gardens to lift up and to bear away men's hearts so that the drunkard longed no longer for his morning draught, so that the pious bent his mind no more to prayer. To every grain of dust of that land in flower my body sends its message of love, and on every leaf in those fair gardens my soul calls benedictions to rain down. (excerpt from "Ghalib, Life and Letters, "translated and edited by Ralph Russell and Khurshidul Islam (Khurshidul Islam).

It was in the Taj Mahal that Agra fulfilled itself. The layout, the new concept of four square gardens running upto the plinth of the tomb instead of the mausoleum being in centre, the musical fountains erupting from the water channel, the four magical towers, the mysterious vaults and niches, the perfect bulbous dome, the whispering screens, the sacred light inside the tomb, the flicker of light inside the tomb, the flicker of light inside the transparent precious stones, the paint like inlay work, the effect of a dream realised, the whole atmosphere is one of something complete. It is an existence which is both human and ethereal. It is an emotion which is both common and kingly. It is art and poetry in stone.

SANDEEP SILAS

AJMER - ITS HOLY DARGAH AND OTHER ARCHITECTURE

Ajmer or *Ajmer Sharif* is the holiest city for Muslims in India, a great pilgrimage centre for people who plan their visit year in advance. It has the *dargah* of *Sheikh Muinuddin Chisti* a renowned saint who was among the first Muslims to arrive in India with the hordes of Muhammad Ghori in the 1190s, who, after sustained efforts, defeated the ruler of Ajmer, Prithvi Raj Chauhan III and made it a part of the Delhi Sultanate.

Ajmer was founded by Raja Ajai Pal Chauhan in the 7th century and remained the glorious center of Chauhan power till it was assimilated in the Delhi Sultanate and deteriorated into a mere provincial town. However, in the 16th century, after its annexation by the Mughal ruler Akbar, it acquired some strategic importance for the Mughal campaigns in Rajasthan and for their expansion plans towards the southern states of the Deccan.

Shaikh Muinuddin chose to stay in Ajmer and work towards the propagation of Sufism as he had a vision about his mission in Ajmer when he was in Medina. Gradually the people of other faiths were also drawn towards him. He lived upto 1235 AD. His fame had spread far and wide as a benefactor of the poor for which he earned the sobriquet *garibnawaz* (benefactor of the poor). Akbar visited the *dargah* of the saint, undertaking the

journey from his capital Agra to Ajmer barefooted, to invoke the saint's blessings for an heir to the throne. He made another journey, once again berefooted when his wish was fulfilled. He built a mosque at the dargah, a deliberately modest structure lest it overshadow the modest tomb of the saint. The dargah became famous as the shrine for wish - fulfillment.

The next Mughal emperor Shahjahan added another elegant mosque in marble at the *dargah*. Princess Jahanara is believed to have swept the floor with her hair and built the *Begami dalan* (Queens courtyard) around the tomb. In 1888 AD, the Nizam of Hyderabad added the *mehfil khana* (assembly hall). The simple grave of the saint now lies protected by a silver railing contributed by Jahangir, lattice screens and a grand dome, which beckons the faithful from across the seven seas

A little higher up the hilly climb is the *Adhai-Din-Ka-jhopra* (Shelter of Two - and - a half days). This is a mosque of great historical and architectural significance, built by Qutubuddin Aibak. It is the second mosque built in India in the Sultanate period, the first one being the *Quwwat - ul - Islam* mosque in Delhi. The present name for the mosque is perhaps attributable to the two - and - a half day encampment here of *fakirs* (mendicants) and the faithful celebrating the urs of Punjabi Sahib. Its architecture is more Islamic - chaste and correct - than that of the *Quwwat - ul - Islam* mosque. The arch screen, built by Iltutmish in 1213 AD, is a superb example of seculptured arabesque, multi-lobed arches and elaborate calligraphy. The interior contains some exquisitely carved ceilings raised on pillars, originally belonging to pre - Sultanate structures.

Within the city of Ajmer stands the *Daulatkhana* or residential palace of Akbar. It is now a museum housing Rajput and Mughal armoury, miniature paintings and sculptures. It was here that Sir Thomas Roe, the emissary from the court of James I of England, presented his credentials to Jahangir in 1616 A.D. The palace is an acknowldge specimen of Mughal architecture, built on a nine - fold plan. It has a central chamber surrounded by four corner rooms, with a grand portico connecting the rooms on all the four sides. Somehow, the walls and galleries are too close to the palace to allow a perfect view of the royal residence. The fortifications also appear to be insufficient. The reason perhaps is that Akbar used this palace only as a transit residence. Ajmer was not destined to vie with Agra, Lahore or Allahabad in architectural splendour, yet it attracted all the Mughal emperors.

Ajmer is also famous for Mayo College, originally founded for the education of the princes of various royal houses of Rajasthan to this day, it is a prestigious institution.

Aithing the hills, west of Ajmer, is *Chasma - i - noor* or *Nafiz - Jamal*. Built in 1615 by Jahangir on the original stepped structure constructed by Rao Maldeo of Mewar in 1535 to conduct water upwards, it stands in a defile between the sides of two hills, with a basin at its foot. The *Chasma - i - Noor* is a picturesque spot, still frequented by visitors. A grotto in the mountainside is approched through a gateway. "A place of much melancholy delight", as Sir Thomas Roe described it, the *Chasma- i -Noor* is certainly for the adventurous.

Within eleven kms. of Ajmer lies the holy spot for Hindus, Pushkar. The Brahma temple in Pushkar is among the few temples in India dedicated fully to this god of the Hindu Trinity. The sacred lake attracts thousands of devotees during the month of November when Rajasthan's biggest cattle fair is held here. Cultural shows organized during the fair showcase Rajasthan's mesmerizing dances and music.

SURENDRA SAHAI

AKAMARAL - BHARATNATYAM DANCER

Akamaral always felt she was an Indian in her previous birth. She could find no other reason for her feelings of closeness and love for this country, as she had been born and brought up in Kazakhstan. None of here relatives had ever been to India, but since here early years she had always felt that her second mother - land existed somewhere else.

During he childhood her grandmother used to read her stories of Rabindra Nath Tagore and the tales from Sri Lanka, which laid the foundation for the dream castle in her mind. Her mother, a singer, the soloist of the Kazakh Radio and TV, inculcated a sense of music and rhythm in the minds of here three adughters. Akamaral felt a desire to dance since her early childhood. But she could not dare ask her parents to send her to the dance school. She was afraid that her parents might seal her fate as they did of her elder sister, who wanted to be a ballet dancer. Instead, they sent her to learn the piano. Akamaral, therefore, was apprehensive about telling them of her dream to become a dancer.

Her secret fascination for India continued with watching of Indian films. Any information about India made her feel excited. If she heard some popular music from an Indian film she turned the volume to full, annoying her neighbours. Her fascination extended to the extent of collecting metal tea boxes and wall pictures depicting Indian dancers in different poses. She would make her younger sister hold such boxes while she tried to imitate the movements shown on the boxes.

As she grew up a bit more, she wrote letters to the only Indian cultural centre for the entire USSR in Moscow at that time. She received different manuals containing stories about here favorite country. Once Akamaral received an audio cassette with recordings of Bharatnatyam music. On hearing this fascinating rhythm, she burst into tears and cried, "This is mine, it is my own".

At the age of seventeen, Akamaral finished her schooling and entered the university to study journalism, as her father had wished. While she was at schools, Akamaral worked as a correspondent for a newspaper for children, and all her published works and artcles were exclusively dedicated to India. Her newspaper editor, an experienced journalist, wrote in the recommendation letter for her to enter the University : "A great expert in the field of Indian culture".

At the university, Akamaral found like - minded friends. Together with them she established an Indian Arts - lover Club, " Shanti ". She staged dances herself with the help of books and cassettes, but more often by her own intuition.

She organized the dresses for the concerts quite effectively. Indian students brought here cassettes containing dance music required by her. They also made ads in the Hindi language for performances. The dance group become very popular not only among the students but with others too.

In 1991, they were invited to the Festival of Indian Clubs in Moscow. There Akamaral happened to meet professional artistes from the field of classical Indian dance.

In 1992, after Kazakhstan became an independent country. Dipak Malik became the first Indian Consul to represent India. Akamaral rushed to meet him. A long talk followed. Malik listened to her attentively. They soon formed a team and Akamaral helped the young Consul find his moorings in the new country. They made a good team and popularized TV programmes about India. All this while Akamaral was nurturing a desire to learn Bharatnatyam in India.

However, the opportunity came just after she got married. Her in-laws were quite taken aback by the proposal that their newly- wedded daughter-in-law would have to spend four years in a foreign country to study dance. Luckily, she has a supportive husband who decided to continue working back home to support his wife's dream of learning Indian classical dance.

Akamaral studied Bharatnatyam at Kalakshetra, the famous institution in Chennai in India. She faced intitial language and communication problems in learning the dance form. But as she progressed in the learning process, she was able to get rid of the spectacles she had worn since her childhood as her health improved. Vegetarianism also influenced her in a big way.

The stint at Kalakshetra changed her life dramatically. Here, she had to opportunity to meet masters of the Indian classical art at the annual festivals. She utilized her stay to visit several holy places as well to enhance her understanding of the spiritual aspect of Bharatnatyam.

After returning to Almaty, Akamaral started working as a teacher of Bharatnatayam. Today, with one hundred and twenty students, aged six to fifty years, Akamaral is the only professional performer of Bharatnatyam in Kazakhstan, rendering valuable service to the cause for Indian classical dance. For her, this dance provides an opportunity "to manifest her love for God".

MARINA SAZONOVA

AKKINENI NAGESWARA RAO : DOYEN OF SOUTH INDIAN CINEMA

His unparalleled histrionic talent and abounding creativity have provided to millions of cinegoers wholesome entertainment through many a classic, mythologicals, historical and social films. These have carved a special niche in the hearts of moviegoers. Not many actors are fortunate enough to retain their charisma for over six decades in the Telugu film industry.

The Nageswara Rao saga makes a thrilling story indeed. Starting virtually from a scratch, he has come a long way and is still going strong at 74. It shouws his deep and abiding love for the film medium. His zest for acting lives on and he is currently acting in his actor son Akkinneni Nagarjuna's film. Born in a poor agricultural family of Krishna district of Andhra Pradesh, Nageswara Rao is a drop-out from the school only to eke out his livelihood on the stage. But when he was in his teens, the famous film-maker Ghantasala Balaramayya booked him for the lead role in 'Seetharama Jananam' (birth of Lord Rama). He never looked back after that.

In 1953, when "Devadas" was being planned, "I was already established as a romantic hero. But the role of Devadas, a psychological character (earlier played by K. L. Saigal in Hindi) brought me laurels, fame and recognition", reminisces Rao.

Nageswar Rao laments that films now glorify violence, obscenity and vulgarity. As if to prove that cinema can do without such gimmicks, Nageswara Rao's 'Seetharamayyagari Manuvaralu' has won critical as well as popular acclaim. Once against proving his class in this film, Nageswara Rao has bagged the Filmfare Awards for Best Actor.

He has held generations of Indian Film-goers, specially Telugu audiences, spell bound with his sterling performances as a tragedy of king and romantic hero in a variety of. For his lifetime contribution to the medium of cinema, Nageswara Rao was conferred the conveted Dadasaheb Phalke award for 1990.

K.R. SATHYAPRAKASH

ALAMPUR REPOSITOR / OF CHALUKYAN HERITAGE

Alampur is a charming little town nestling beside the river Tungabhadra - a tributary of the river Krishna, about 200 kilometres from Hyderabad. This place which abounds in antiquities of the Chalukyan times - 7th - 8th century AD - had made big news in the annals of archaeology in India a little more than a decade and a half ago.

That was the time when the Srisailam Hydel Project was under construction across the river Krishna, a few miles down - in the Srisailam river valley. The dam posed a threat to the valley's priceless heritage of antiquities which had to be moved from the site

In all, about 40 temples were dismantled from their original sites and reconstructed elsewhere in their original style and structure. It was a story of strife and struggle, of triump and pride. The skilled ancients carved them and with equal skill the modern engineers moved them, stone by stone and brick by brick, with utmost care, accuracy and precision of the watchmaker.

The Sangameswar temple newly located in the heart of the town is perhaps the largest salvaged. Dating back to the 6th century AD, this Chalukyan structure was originally existing about 30 kilometres away at the confluence of the river Krishna and the Tungabhadra. Hence the name Sangameswar or Lord of the Confluence.

About half - a - kilometre from the Sangameswar temple is a group of ancient structure (temples) called *Navbrahma* temples. Built in the northern style with wall decorations consisting of niches, latticed windows and superb figures, these temples resemble the other contemporary Chalukyan temples of Pattadkal and Aihole in north Karnataka.

The most important among the *Navbrahma* temples is the *Balabrahma* temple, the oldest and considered to be one of the eighteen *Shakti - peethiams* (Seats of the Goddess Shakti) in the country. The presiding deities are *Swayambhu* his consort *Jogulamba.*

RAMCHANDER PENTUKER

ALI AKBAR KHAN : THE GREAT MUSICAL GENIUS

Ali Akbar Khan, heir to the Seni Baba Allaudin Gharana and destined to become one of the greatest musical geniuses the world has ever known, was born in Shivpur, now part of Bangadesh, in 1922. The Khan family, originally Hindu, converted to Islam several generations ago. Today, Khan Sahib, whose religion is music, might be described as a Sufi, a distillation of many traditions, the quintessential world citizen. His music speaks to the soul wherever that may reside.

Ali Akbar Khan grew up in Madhya Pradesh, Being the only son of the legendary Baba Allauddin Khan, court musician to the Maharaja of Maihar, Ali Akbar's musical instruction began at the age of three. He was taught Sarod, Dhamar, Dhrupad and Khayal etc. under father and uncle. Aftabuddin in Uday Shankar's cultural centre) He practiced on different instruments untill he turned nine. Then his father singled out the Sarod for him.

For twenty years, the young Khan was made to practice eighteen hours a day by this temperamental and severe taskmaster who lived simply and dressed as plainly as a saint.

Still in his twenties, Ali Akbar Khan became Music Director for All India Radio in Lucknow. Then he was sent to Jodhpur as a substitute for his father who had been invited to become court musician for the Maharaja of Jodhpur. Six years later, upon the untimely death of the Maharaja, Ali Akbar moved to Bombay where to his father's distress, he composed film music.

"When my father heard that I was working in the movies, he sent me a telegram : " Form today you're no longer my son". Then one day my father went to the movie *kshudhita Pashan* (Hungry Stones) 'My goodness', he said, 'who composed the music ? He is great'. When told that the music was composed by me, he wrote a letter from Maihar : " You can compose film music. I withdraw my last telegram ". Then I sent him a telegram, " From today, I'm not going to compose film music ", he reminisces.

At his first concert in America, luminaries of the music world gathered to honour a star from the other hemisphere at New York's Museum of Modern Art'. Two more concerts followed. One at Rockefeller Center, and one in Washington D.C.

During the years followed, Ali Akbar Khan visited Europe and America many a time to play and to teach. In 1967, a little over a decade after his first visit, he founded the Ali Akbar College of Music in San Ragael, California. The School brought many of the greatest musicians from India as its full time faculty and / or as guest artists. Today, even at 73, Khan Sahib's international touring countinues with unabated energy, and he has taught in almost every country of the World. A branch of his college is established in basel, Switzerland to serve Europe.

Honours have been conferred upon Ali Akbar Khan both by his native country and in countries around the world. To cite only a few, Khan Sahib has twice been presented with the President of India Award, and holds the titles of Padma Bhushan and Padma Vibhushan. In the United States, he was invited to play at the inaugural ceremonies of President Kennedy and in 1991, he received America's most prestigious award, a MacArthur Foundation Genuis Fellowship.

In 1994. Khan Sahib founded the Ali Akbar Foundation to archive the music of the Seni Baba Allauddin Gharana. One of the projects is to create a series of CDs to preserve many of the thousands of compositions taught to him by his father, and the thousands that he has composed during the sixty years of his musical career.

JAAN HAAG

ALL-INDIA FINE ARTS AND CRAFTS SOCIETY, NEW DELHI

Registered under Societies Act, 1860; encourages and popularies Indian art in India and abroad; holds exhibitions, film shows and lectures on art and culture of India; publishes *Rooplekha* (bi-annual), *Art News* (monthly), etc., 2,000 books and 125 paintings.

References

Indian Council for Cultural Relations, Cultural Organizations in India, New Delhi, 1960.

Mohinder Singh, Learned Institutions in India, Ahmedabad, 1969.

Patel, H.S., Directory of Cultural Organisations in India, New Delhi, 1975.

____ World Index of Social Science Organisations in India, Paris, 1970.

____ World of Learning, London, 1972.

ALLAHABAD MUSEUM, ALLAHABAD

Autonomous body : sculptures, terracotta figures, miniatures, etc.; 2,500 books,

References

Baxi, S. J. & Dvivedi, V. P. Modern Museum; Organization & Practice in India, New Delhi, 1973.

Divedi, V.P., Brief Directory of Museum in India, New Delhi, 1969.

Patel, H.S. Directory of Cultural Organisations in India, New Delhi, 1975.

Rama Rao, V.V. Museum Guide, New Delhi, 1970.

Sivaramamurti, C., Directory of Museums in India, Delhi, 1959.

ALLARAKHA- MASTER OF TABLA

Ustad Allarakha Khan, the master of tabla, passed away in Mumbai on Feb 3, 2000. He was 81. He was an accompalished musician in both Karnatic and Hindustani styles.

Allegend in his lifetime, lovingly known as "*ABBAJI*" Ustad Allarakha Khan, the undisputed monarch of Tabla of the Punjab Gharana, had a significant following across the country. Tabla was the only language he knew.

Allarakha was born on April 29, 1919 at Phagwal Village of Jammu, and was the eldest of seven brothers. Most of his family members were either soldiers or farmers. But he was more interested in the performing arts.

At the early age of 11, he moved from his village near Jammu to Lahore, where he was trained in tabla by Mian Kadir Baksh of the famous *Punjab Gharana*. He was trained in vocals with Ustad Ashiq Khan. This exposure to vocal music gave him a deep insight into the melody and rhythm of music. This is reflected in the vocal inflexions and nuances that characterise Allarakha's performances on the tabla.

Allarakha came to Delhi where he started his career as a Staff Artist at the All India Radio, Delhi in 1940. After six years, he was transferred to Mumbai. Besides performing in classical concerts he also composed music for three films "Maa Baap" " Madari " and "Bewafa", between 1943 and 1948 under the name of A.R.Qureshi. He visited Japan in the late 1950's before embarking on a Middle Eastern tour. In the sixties Allarakha visited the US along with Sitar Maestero Pandit Ravi Shankar.

Allarakha' shot into fame in the sixties and the seventies with solo performances and took part in the Edinburgh Festival in 1965. He was part of the " Festival of India" team which gave several international performances to promote and project Indian Culture abroad. Some of his unforgettable performances included " Jugalbandis " with maestros such as Pandit Jasraj, Bhimsen Joshi, Pandit Ravi Shankar and Ustad Bismillah Khan.

Allarakha's control over *laya* was impeccable and he understood the intricate *layakari* of the instrumentalists he played with. He had a varied range of *bols* in his repertoire but excelled with *Tukras* and was free with the *tals* that he chose to play. The impact of his music was so powerful that many aspiring musicians used it as a reference point.

The Ustad's last performance on Jan 27, 2000, at the Nehru Centre, Mumbai is unforgettable. In the presence of about 400 students two of his students made their debut, Allarakha played with his students.

(Dr.) MRS. GEETHA RAVI KUMAR

ALLAUDDIN KHAN (ALAM)

(b. 1862) at Shibapore ; eminent sarod player and instrumentalist of Senia Gharana ; played various (indian) instruments (rabab, sarangi, flute, violin, surbahar, shehnai, clarionet, tabla, saxaphone, pakhawar, etc.; composer, pioneer in orchestration ; established Mahiar band (1924); toured Europe with Uday Shankar's dance troupe (1935); received Sangeet Natak Akademi award for Hindustani instrumental music (1952); elected its fellow (1954); received Padma Bhushan (1958) and Desikottama (Visva Bharati) (1961); composed new ragas ; disc recordings, recitals, etc. ; prominent students : Ali Akbar (son), Annapurna (daughter), Ravi Shankar (son-in-law),

Timir Baran, Sharan Rani, Bahadur Khan, Pannalal Ghosh, Nikhil Banerjee and others.

References

Jain, Naresh Kumar, Muslims in India : A biographical Dictionary ; Vol. I, New Delhi, 1979

The Muslim year book of India & Who's Who with complete information on Pakistan, Bombay, 1949.

Times of India Directory & Year Book, including Who's Who, Bombay, 1968.

Who's Who of Indian Musicians, New Delhi, 1968.

ALWAR : THE UNEXPLORED MARVEL

Alwar, a city carved out the jagged rocky Aravalli hills, upholds a fiery stand in the history. Historically, being strategically important and close to the Delhi Mughals, the jats of Bharatpur, the British as well as the Marathas — they all tried to gain control of it untill 1771 when Maharaja Pratap Singh, a Kuchawaha Rajput, won it back from the Mughals and founded a principality of his own.

The royal ambience of its illustrious rulers still pervades the city marked by a number of structures of historical and prehistorical importance. A visit to this town means going back into time, almost turning pages of a history book. Roots of Alwar city date back to the Mahabharata times when it was part of Matsyaya Desh, which is famous for being the home to the Pandavas who spent the last year of their exile here. Even today many relics of temples and monuments bear a testimony of it

The alwar fort, locally known as the Bala Qila, is a very old monument of the city. Even the first Mughal Emperor Babar is said to have spent a few days here in the early 16th century. It extends about five km from north to south and 1.6 k.m. from east to west. It has 15 large and 51 small towers around it which contain 446 loopholes for musketery. Eight towers around it are there to defend it. Though most of the structures within the fort are a reminder of its past glory, their historical significance cannot be over - emphasised.

The City palace, however, is comparatively of recent origin. It belongs to the 18th century and bears ample traces of the Rajput and Mughal styles of architecture. The ground floor of this palace has now been turned into the seat of power. Office of the District Collector. The upper floor of the city Palace, popularly known as Vinay Vilas Palace, houses the famous Alwar museum which probably has the richest collection of the Mughal and Rajput, paintings of the 18th and the 19th centuries. There are some priceless ancient manuscripts in Persian, Arabic, Urdu and Sanskrit. Prominent among these are the Gulistan (Garden of Roses), Waquiate Babari (autobiography of the Mughal emperor Babar) and Bostan (Poems)

It also has a copy of the Mahabharata painted by the artists of the Alwar school and the illustrated manuscripts of Koran. Another special feature of the museum is the collection it has of Indian armoury belonging to yesteryears 'great emperors and princes. The same complex contains the Durbar Hall and the Sheesh Mahal. When one enters the Sheesh Mahal, the grandeur of the mirrored walls and ceilings, the seat from where the king used to watch the dancing girls - all add wings the one's.

Rising almost 1000 feet into the sky from the city level, and thus completely dominating its skyline, is the Bala Qila Fort of Alwar. It has been so designed as to render it almost impregnable. No wonder the Fort is said to have never been conquered by any invader. The fort is now looked upon as a benign partriarch, who quietly oversees the goings - on down below in the city. It provides the best aerial view of Alwar making one almost feel as if one is floating in the clouds. This fantasy does become real in the rainy season when the fort is indeed engulfed by the clouds, giving it a quaint, fairytale dimension.

Behind the City Palace are many more monuments worth a visit. Many temples dot the " Coastline " of the Sagar, the artificial tank built by Maharaja Vinay Singh, who also built a cenotaph for Maharaja Bakhtawar Singh. Locally known as the Moosi Maharani ki Chhatri, it has a unique architectural style of sloping roof and arches.

A visit to Alwar will never be complete unless it is rounded off by a trip to Sariska, 37 km from Alwar. Nestled in a picturesque valley of the Aravallis, the forest literally comes to life here. The wildlife sanctuary here is one of the biggest game sanctuaries in India. Established in 1955 it offers an exceptionally unique opportunity to see a wide variety of animals from a close range. Tigers, dancing peacocks, cheetal four horned antelopes and wild boar are some of the animals that stalk the thick, deciduous forests of Sariska which have an area of 480 sq kms.

BHARAT BHUSHAN

AMIR KHAN (b. 1912)

Vocalist : Khayal (Indore gharana) ; studied with Shammir Khan ; Fellow, Sangeet Natak Akademi (1967) and Bihar Akademi ; concert tour to Kabul ; research conducted in Khayal and Tarana.

References

Sangeet Natak akedemi, Who's Who of Indian Musicians.

AMIR KHUSROW

(c. 1254 -1324 A.D.) - Muslim poet, musician, historian and mystic who flourished during the Delhi Sultanate, studied Indian music, and introduced changes that made it acceptable to Muslim society.

References

Abdul Kalam Azad Oriental Research Institute, Hyderabad, Amir Khusro : 17th Century celebration 11th - 13th February, 1972.

Gibb, G.W., History of Ottoman Poetry.

Mohammed Wahid Mirza, The Life & Work of Amir Khusro, Delhi, 1974.

National Amir Khusro Society, New Delhi, Life & Works of Amir Khusro, Delhi, 1977.

AMITABH BACHCHAN (b. 1942)

He bacame the 'Angry Young Man' because he got to articulate the predominant emotion of his times. Together, the trio of Salim, Javed and Amitabh Bachchan created a character that acquired cult dimensions because the 1970s was essentially a decade of dissent and anger.

A former stage actor, radio announcer and company executive, Bachchan knew his destiny lay in films. Hence he bided his time. Suffered rejection and continued to play a mute too (Reshma aur Shera), untill Hrishikesh Mukerjee cast him as the brooding Dr. Bhaskar in Anand (1970).

Therafter, there was no looking back for the actor who has to his credit the largest number of box office hits. It was this ubiquitous response of anger, visible in most of his films, which branded him the anti-hero in popular par lance.

For years, Amitabh was always angry, be it Deewar, Zanjeer, Trishul, Shakti, Sholay, Kabhi Kabhi, Sharabi, Agneepath. A controversial tryst with politics followed by a temporary retirement from the glare did not however blur his image from the collective memory. The superstar of the 70s has been trying to make a comeback in the 90's. But apart from Bade Miyan Chote Miyan, he has still to make an impact in his second innings after the debacle of Mritudata, Lal Badshah, Major Saheb and Kohraam.

AMJAD ALI KHAN

(b. 1947) - Instrumentalist ; sarod of Senia Gharana; studied with Hafiz Ali Khan ; concert tour of USA (1963).

References

Sangeet Natak Akademy, Who's Who of Indian Musicians.

ANANDA COOMARASWAMY : HIS LIFE AND GENIUS

Coomaraswamy was born at Colombo on August 22, 1877. He was the son of Sir Muthu Coomaraswamy and his English wife, Elizabeth Clay Beeby. Sir Muthu, who was a friend of the British Statesman Disraeli, was probably one of the first " Hindus" to become a Bar - at - Law and one of the first Asians to obtain a knighthood. He and his brothers, Sir P. Arunachalam and Sir P. Ramanathan - all residents of Jaffna, the stronghold of the Ceylon Tamils - played a notable part in the political and cultural life of the island. Lady Coomaraswamy took a considerable interest in intellectual pursuits. Thus, the young Coomaraswamy was brought up in a distinguished household and in an atmosphere that radiated culture and refinement.

He returned home when he was 25 and soon after took up an appointment as the Director of the Mineralogical Survey of Ceylon in the year 1903. He discharged the duties of his office with conspicuous ability and several of the reports which he wrote then continue to hold the field.

During his official career in Srilanka he had amassed a great deal of material on the arts and crafts of the country and he published it in 1908 under the title Mediaeval Sinhalese art - a monument of erudition and industry. In 1910, he organized an art exhibition at Allahabad where the Indian National Congress was holding its annual session. In this connection he travelled up and down the country and collected priceless art treasures which had been lying uncared- for....... Wherever he went he left many admirers who were deeply moved by his ideas.

1917 marked a turning point in the career of Coomaraswamy. That year his large art collection was bought by the Museum of Fine Arts in Boston, U.S.A. He was appointed there as a Fellow for research in Oriental Art and later became its keeper of Indian, Persian and Mohammedan Art.

He held charge of this department for 30 years and made it a repository of one of the largest and best collections of Asiatic art treasures in the world. He worked hard, acquired a mastery of six languages and published a large number of books and other writings which totalied about 500 at the time of his 65 the birthday. He had a devoted companion in his scholarly wife, Dona Louisa Runstein, an Argentine, and they had a son named Rama.

On August 22, 1947, his 70th birthday, Coomaraswamy was felicitated by his friends and colleagues at Boston. He expressed his desire to return to India, " thinking of this as an astam gamana, " going home". But this was not to be, for he died barely three weeks later, on September 10, 1947.

Coomaraswamy's main contribution lay in the elucidation and interpretation of Indian art and thought - forms. According to him, Indian and European art differed in method and intent. Indian art, particularly architecture and sculpture, did not aim at creating what has been called " aesthetic experience ". The main object of images was edification and an identification between the supplicant and the object of his veneration. " In the words of a well - known text ", wrote Coomaraswamy, " the deity can only be worshipped in so far as the worshipper becomes the deity ". Even in items containing a portrayal of nature, as at Amaravati and Ajanta, there was, he said, a complete identification of artist and subject.

Art, to him, was an " intellectual, not a physical virtue ; beauty has to do with knowledge and goodness, of which it is precisely the attractive aspect ; and since it is by its beauty that we are attracted to a work, its beauty is evidently a means to an end, and not itself the end of art ". Many objects of art, he added, dealt with God whose name was taboo in so - called " Polite Society " : The imparted not an " education in sensibility, but an education in philosophy, in Plato's and Aristorle's sense of the word, for whom it means ontology and theology and the map of life, and wisdom to be applied to everyday matters. "

Coomaraswamy held the view that natins were made by artists and poets, not by politicians and traders.

G. N. DAS

ANANT LAL

(b. 1932) - Instrumentalist, Shehnai, studied with Mahadev Misra and Raghu Nath Prasad.

ANDRETTA

Andretta is a quaint village in Kangra valley in Himachal Pradesh situated at 1100 matres above sea-level, the village has population of 800, with 80 odd houses. The village holds a special charm as it is taking shape of an " Artist's village. It is here that the famous cultural exponent, Narah Richards developed the village as an active cultural centre and it has been renamed as woodlands Estate. Subsequently theatre veterans like Prithviraj Kapoor, Freeda Bedi, Prof. Gaidayal, Zora Sehgal etc. stepped into this tiny village with their preformances. It was contemplated to develop the village as a full - fledged artiste's village with an actor, a poet, a painter, a writer, a potter to be all stationed under one roof. It gradually became a summer resort of the creative brigade. Only the famous painter Sardar Sobha Singh and master potter Gurcharan Singh set up permanent houses in this village and Andretta gained some of its recognition. (Condensed)

ANJANIBAI MALPEKAR
(1883 - 1974)

Born into a family of Kalavantins, Anjanibai was one of the most beautiful singers.

Anjanibai knew Sanskrit, Urdu and persian. She was under the tutelage of Nazir Khan, Khadim Hussain and Chhaju Khan of the Bhendibazar 'Gharana'. She had a phenomenal control over the breath. She earned lakhs of rupees through her concerts. Legendary painter Raja Ravi Verma chose her as one of his models. Aristocrats literally chased her which compelled here to give up the progession. Her last public appearance was in the famous Town Hall of Bombay, in 1923. She had lost her voice in 1902. She believed that the voice was restored to her through miracle by the godman Narayanbuva kedgaonkar. Anjanibai wed Visanjai Bhagwandas Ved, a rich businessman from Bombay. He died in 1927 leaving behind a stupendous debt of 10 lakhs.

Anjanibai repaid every single farthing of it. She taught a few disciples among whom was Kumar Gandharva.

ANNAPOORNA DEVI

Annapoorna Devi the daughter of Baba Allauddin Khan of the Moiher 'gharana'. Allauddin Khan produced disciples of the calibre of Ali Akbar Khan, Ravi Shankar, Pannalal Ghosh and Nikhil Bannerjee. Annapoornadevi supposed to have received authentic instruction from her father. She used to play the sur - bahar. Once upon a time she would play in duet with Ravi Shankar. She gave up performances over 40 years ago and concentrated on teaching. Her disciples include Hari Prasad Chaurasia, Pradeep Barot and Nityanand Haldipur.

ARATI ANKILIKAR - TIKEKAR

In all humility Arati Ankilikar__ Tikekar affirms that she has not really achieved much and has a long way to go. A warm homebody, though a hesitant conversationalist, Arati makes me feel right at home. Music is at the heart of the cozy little family (husband Uday Tikekar plays the table and was her accompanist during her college days). even her little daughter fancies a tune.

Arati attributes her introduction and initial encourage-ment to music to her father. She began taking lessons from Vijaya Joglekar, she trained for two years under the tutelage of Pt. Vasantrao Kulkarni before being taken under the wing of Kishori Amonkar from the Atrauli Jaipur 'gharana'. Recognition come to her in form of a national schoarship in 1980, where she was noticed as a youngster with potential. After almost 12 years of performing in public, Arati still feels that there is a lot she has yet to achieve.

Arati does keep her ear open to Western classical and jazz, " We can't just be tradition bound". The seven notes of music are universal. It is only the difference in composition and rendition that differentiates them.

SUNANDA SWARUP

ARCHAEOLOGICAL MUSEUMS : GENERAL SURVEY

Of the many museums that came into existence in India from the time of Lord Curzon mention may be made of the museums at Bijapur (1912), and Agra (1906), not to speak of those at Pagan, Mandalay in Burma, and Peshwar in Pakistan under the Imperial Government at the centre. During the regime of Sir John, local museums came to be established at Taxila (1928), Mohenjo-daro (1925), Harappa (1927), Sarnath (1909) and Nalanda (1917), besides a host of other museums under different authorities. Prominent among these were the site museums at khiching set up by the Mayurbhanj State in 1929 and that at Sanchi established by the Bhopal State in 1919. The Archaeological Survey to day has over 25 Archaeological or Site Museums under its charge. The following list up to 1965. indicates the order of the growth of Archaeological Site Museums in India. The List excludes the Central Asian Antiquities Museums which was formed in 1929 and is now merged with the National Museum, New Delhi. These consist of the Archaeological Museum, Sarnath (1904), Delhi Fort Museum, Delhi (1909), Archaeological Museum, Nalanda (1910), Archaeological Museum, Bijapur (1912), Archaeological Museum, Sanchi (1919), Fort st George Museum, Madras (1948), Archaeological Museum, Nagarjuna-konda (1949), Archaeological Museum, Anaravati (1951), Archaeological Museum, Kondapur (1952), Archaeological Museum, Khajuraho (1952), Archaeological Museum, Bodh Gaya (1956), Archaeological Museum, Hampi (1958), Tipu Sultan Museum, Seringapatam (1959), Archaeological Museum, Halebid (1962), Archaeological Museum, Goa (1965) and Archaeological Museum, Konarak (1965). Of these the Museum at Khajuraho was set up during the State regime in 1910 and named after Jardine, the then Political Agent in Bundelkhand. It was taken over a reorganised by the Survey in 1952, on the merger of Vindhya Pradesh with Madhya Pradesh and reorganization of the archaeological work of these States. The Museum at Sanchi was similarly founded by the Bhopal State Department of Archaeology in 1919 under the guidance of Sir John Marshall and it was taken over by the Centre in 1953. Seven more site museums may be mentioned : (i) Lothal, in District Ahmedabad, Gujarat, at the site of

Harappan settlement, famed for its dockyard; (ii) Vaisali, in District Muzaffarpur, Bihar, near the ancient site and *stupa;* (iii) Ratnagiri, in District Cuttack, Orissa, near the Buddhist site; (iv) Kodambalur in the former Pudukkottai State, now in District Tiruchirappalli, Madras, at the side of a group of early Chola temples of exquitie workmanship; (v) Deoghar, in District Jhansi, Uttar Pradesh, famed for its Gupta temple and a group of Jain temples within the fort on an adjoining hillock; (vi) Rupar, in District Ambala, Punjab, near the Harappan site, excavated by the Survey, and (vii) Burzahom, near Srinagar, Kashmir, where a neolithic settlement of great interest has been revealed by the excavations of the Survey.

ARCHAEOLOGICAL MUSEUM, AMARAVATI

The Museum with its own building exhibits mainly carved fragments of the *stupa* and railings obtained by the excavation at the famous site. These range in date from the second century B.C. to the third century A.D. and bear the decisive impress of the art of Bharhut in Central India. It may be recalled that the best pieces of carving recovered from the site are in British Museum, London, and the Government Museum at Madras contain a fairly large miscellany of the art reclaimed from the site.

ARCHAEOLOGICAL MUSEUM, BIJAPUR : (1912)

The Museum is located in the Nagarkhana in front of the Gol Gumaz and contains a wide miscellany of objects found in Bijapur and its neighbourhood bearing upon its history. These comprise mainly stone inscriptions in different scripts and languages, Brahmanical and Jaina sculptures, arms and weapons, manuscripts and ancient carpets from the Asar Mahal, besides fragments of brilliantly coloured mosaics from the Sat Manzil at Bijapur.

ARCHAEOLOGICAL MUSEUM, BODH GAYA; (1956)

The Museum was inaugurated by His Holiness the Dalai Lama of Tibet on the 28th December, 1956. It contains principally metal and stone images mostly of the Pala period, besides two *Yakshis* of the first century B.C.

DELHI FORT MUSEUM, DELHI: (1909)

Located since 1911 in the Mumtaz Mahal at the south-eastern end of the Archaeological Area, the Museum contains historical relics of the Mughal period of a wide veriety and poignant interests. The objects of display comprise inscriptions of the Sultanate and Mughal periods, sanads and farmans, carpets, arms and weapons, dresses, and relics of the rising of 1857.

ARCHAEOLOGICAL MUSEUM, GOA: (1965)

It is yet in formative stage and contains mainly relics of the rise of christianity in Goa under the Portuguese. The museum grew out of the collections of sculptural fragments and architectural members of temples displayed in the open-air Museum near the Temple of Hoysalesvara in the ancient capital of the Hoysalas.

ARCHAEOLOGICAL MUSEUM, HAMPI ; (1953)

The Museum contains mainly sculptural and architectural pieces collected from the extensive site of Hampi, the capital of the vijayanagara kings, studded with ruins of palaces and temples and remains of the old fortifications. The miscellany of collections include coins, terracottas, heads, copper-plate grants, and palm-leaf manuscripts, belonging to the Vijayanagara period.

ARCHAEOLOGICAL MUSEUM, KHAJURAHO; (1910)

At Present the exhibits comprising nearly 2,000 pieces of sculptures and architectural members, some containing inscriptions and sculptors names, and representing the Hindu, Buddhist and Brahmanical faiths respectively, are in an open-air museum adjoining the principal group of temples crowned by the Kandariya Mahadeva. These represent the Chandella art of the 10th-11th centuries. The Museum will shortly be shifted to a modern building in the village.

ARCHAEOLOGICAL MUSEUM, KONARK ; (1965)

The museum is yet in its formative stage and has a new building of its own near the Surya temple at Konarak. It will house the fragments of sculptures and architectural members and other objects found amid the structural remains on the site.

ARCHAEOLOGICAL MUSEUM, KONDAPUR: (1962)

The Museum contains the finds recovered from the site at Kondapur, dating mostly from the Satavahana period (200 B.C. 200 A.D.) and comprise pottery, beads, terracottas, bangles, coins and iron objects etc. Stone Age tools collected from the neighbourhood are also on display.

FORT ST. GEORGE MUSEUM, MADRAS: (1948)

The Museum located in a building built in 1792, which served as the Exchange, where traders and the officials of the East India Company met and settled their terms of business, within the premises of Fort St. George overlooking the Bay of Bengal, contains relics of the British connection with Fort St. George in particular and Madras in general. Amidst its numerous exhibits are arms and ammunition. Painting of the historical figures of the past, crockery of the days of the Company, etchings of the Daniel brothers recalling the long lost scenery and landmarks of the country in the changing perspective of the preset, and relics of the Church of St. Mary's.

ARCHAEOLOGICAL MUSEUM, NAGARJUNAKODA:(1949)

Though founded in 1949, it has grown into a unique museum of its kind, being shifter from the low depths of the valley, now submerged under water, to a hill top amid a recreated and self-same environment as in the valley, with the bathing ghats reaching down to the waters' edge. It is the first island museum of India and emulates the spirit and beauty of the Elephanta Caves which may in this context be described as open-air architecural museum. It contains the priceless relics of sulptural wealth mostly of the Ikshavakus and a wide miscellany of objects from the oldest days of the Stone Age to the last medieval period.

ARCHAEOLOGICAL MUSEUM, NALANDA: (1917)

The museum at the ancient university site of Nalanda merked by *Stupas,* large and small and monasteries and appurtenant structures, contain antiquities from the excavated sites at Nalanda and Rajgir respectively. They consists of sculptures representing both the Brahmanical and Buddhist faiths, of Pala workmanship and sundry objects comprising inscriptions, coins, pottery, seals, iron object and the like. The periods represented by the antiquities range from the times of the later Guptas to the times of the Palas.

ARCHAEOLOGICAL MUSEUM, SANCHI: (1919)

The museum, situated at the foot of the hillock upon which rises the famous group of *stupas* at Sanchi, is now housed in a modern building, and is enriched with the antiquities recovered from the site and its neibhourhood. They comprise antiquities from the Mauryan period to the medieval times, and consist principally of an Asokan lion capital, fragments of gateway and railings household objects of copper, bronze and iron and a relic casket.

ARCHAEOLOGICAL MUSEUM, SARNATH: (1904)

Situated in the sylvan settings of the Deer Park of Buddha's days, flanking the ruins of the stupas, temples and monasteries of old, it exhibits antiquities of the Maurya, Sunga, Kushana, Gupta and medieval periods. Housed in a modern building shaped after a monastery, it contains among others the famous lion capital of Asoka which has given Indian its official seal, a standing image of Bodhisattava of the period of Kanishka and the seated figure of preaching Buddha of the hey day of Gupta art, and many later works of art. It forms principally a centre for the study of Gupta art at its best.

TIPU SULTAN MUSEUM, SIRANGAPATAM: (1959)

The Museum at present located in Tipu Sultan's pleasure palace, called Daria Daulat Bagh, set in the centre of a sprawling garden of rare charm on the bank of the Kaveri, overlooking the historic fort of Srirangapatam, contains relics of the period of Haidar Ali and Tipu Sultan of hauntingly lingering memory.

V. P. DIVEDI

ARCHITECTURAL REMAINS OF SUJANPURTIRA

The historic town of Sujanpurtira is Kangra Valley of Himachal Pradesh is situated at a distance of 80 kms. from Dharmashala Via Yol-Maranda by road. The ancient remains at Sujanpurtira consist of a fort, a palace and a group of temples. The river Beas touches the feet of this historical town with clear and unsullied water. Sujanpurtira was the capital of Maharaja Sansar Chand and was founded by Raja Ghamand Chand (A.D. 1761), who belonged to the clan of Susarma Chandra mentioned in the Mahabharata. Sansar Chand, the grandson of Ghamand Chand, made additional constructions and tried to make Sujanpurtira an ideal capital. The strategic position of this town is quite unique. On the north-west, the river Beas serves as a permanent barrier. On the east, the regular and successive lines of hillocks, popularly known as the Qilas of Kamlah make one to have the glimpses of the Mandi State. On the south-west, the rivulet Pong, though having shallow waters, but, simultaneously, owing a great depth from the surface acts as a moat for the capital. The high gateway to the capital guarded by the statues of Hanuman and Bhairon is still in a good state of preservation. Across the river Beas on the north, one can witness the soul-moving panorama of the snow-capped Himalayas. The hillock on which lie the pile of architectural remains of the Baradari and Sheesh-Mahal has served as the pivot of this ancient principality.

NARMABESHWARA TEMPLE

The Narbadeshwara temple on the extreme end of the town, overlooking Beas, has paintings which were executed by painters of the court of Sansar Chand. Besides, this temple has its unique architecture. It is a square Baradari form and is modelled on a small outer palace. It has no sikhara on the top but a plain roof. The whole space of the wall behind the mandala in the shrine, as well as the door for circumambulation of all the four sides of the square building has a decorative array which arranges flowers, rectangular miniatures and square panels in a manner that creates delightful visual effects. Quite a few paintings in the Narbadeshwara temple are enlarged miniatures, but there are sufficiently large number of paintings in which colour energies are allowed to run freely on the walls. " However, the walls of this temple are galvanised by forms which show original creative impulses working on the old themes in bold curved lines and deeply felt brush strokes". The paintings vividly portray scenes from Ramayana, Mahabharata and Bhagvata Mahapurna. One can imagine that while Pandits were busy in excerpting anecdotes, the painters used their dextrous hand in executing murals on the walls of the temple.

Various scenes from the scriptures such as Siva's marriage, Gangavatarana, Indra apologising, Kaliyadaman, Rasamandala, meeting of the saints, various feats of Durga and the holy congregation of the Gods, are also painted in the Narmadeshwara temple. Depiction of animals such as elephants, antelopes, horses and cattle are, indeed, remarkable. The floral designs on the eves of the temple are done with a remarkable skill. With lingam in the garbha-griha and a standing Nandi in the courtyard, the temple has various sculptures of the deities, like Durga- Mahisasuramardini, Ganesa, and others on the gateway of the mandapa.

In the centre of the capital city is a vast maidan. To the southern corner of maidan is the Murli-Manohar temple which was built at the instance of the wife of Maharaja Sansar Chand. This temple has a tall sikhara. The back stone idol of Krishna along with Radha is enshrined in the temple. Just outside the gateway, the view of the massive maidan with lush green grass makes the area very picturesque. This ground was utilized by the king for the parade of the army.

BARADARI

The old residential palace of the Maharaja is just on the top of the hillock (known as Tira) which overlooks the town Sujanpur. A steep and serpentine approach road leads to the palace. The gateway which has balconied windows is flanked by seated elephants, one on each side. The palace is fortified and a massive wall girdles the place. Inside the gate is a big courtyard end on its right is the Baradari (Darbar Hall) with twenty-two-doors. The choice of this site speaks of the high aesthetic sense of the Maharaja. To the east, is the temple of Gauri Shankar, popularly known as Sansar - Chandreshwara which was meant for king's personal worship. Exquisite mural paintings exist only in the garbha-griha, the rest being completely whitewashed. The brasspanel in this temple has a unique kadamba tree and Krishna with his paraphernalia. A few yards to the south of the aforesaid temple is Chamunda Devi's temple. Though damaged by lightning, the temple enshrines Chamunda Devi in lingam form.

The sheesh Mahal which was once fitted with glittering mirrors is now in ruins and consists of dilapidated walls with hanging chhajjas. The fine white plaster imitating the finish of marble and the lakhori bricks bespeak of the architectural excellence of his Mahal which originally rose totwo storeys.Bleak flower designs are visible in the interior of the Sheesh-Mahal. This building suffered damage during the earth-quake in 1905. It is feared that the surviving remains of this Mahal will be obliterated if steps are not taken for its conservation.

GOLDEN AGE OF KANGRA

The reign of Sansar Chand was the golden age of Kangra. He was a devout Saivite. Seers like Bawa Swarup Gir and Bhikha Shah were adored by the king. Secular was his approach and democratic were his ways. During the Holi festival he used to mix with his subjects and share their joy by splashing colour. A small tank below the Darbar Hall was meant for storing coloured water for Holi. It still exists though in a ruinous state. Moreover, Muslims and Hindus owed equal fundamental rights. He respected talent and foreigners like O'Brien, an Irishman James a Britisher, were appointed by him in the army and were entrusted with the work of manufacturing ammunition.

Besides, versatile artists received his patronage in an abundant measure and he was the source of their inspiration. Each of craftsmen were assigned settlements within the confines of his capital. This tradition is still in vogue.

With Sujanpurtira is associated the rise and fall of Sansar Chand. Art flourished with the patronage of the king. In 1805 the Maharaja, popularly known as Pahari Badshah, was betrayed by sub-ordinate Pahari kings and was reduced to the position of a feuditory of the Sikhs. This downfall involved that of the other States also and from 1809 all of them owed allegiance to Lahore. (Condensed)

SHUBH DATTA DOGRA

ARCHITECTURE

Favoured material early Indian architecture, wood : the principle of wooden construction, played important part in determining, shape of Indian architecture, its varoius elements, components.

Baked or sun - dried brick has history as ancient as that of wood : earliest remains, buildings at excavated sites of Indus Valley Civilization. Use of brick evident from 6th century B.C : popularity undiminished in later centuries :

Traditions of some stone architecture more recent : the earliest examples not predating the 6th century BC. By 7th century AD, the use of stone for monumental buildings quite popular.

Surviving architecture, before Islamic period, religions in nature : consisting Buddhist shrines, stupas, temples.

From excavated remains, Indus Valley Civilization projects urban architecture, Mohenjo - daro, Harappa, Kalibangan, laid out a grid pattern, had provisions for advanced drainage system. Residential buildings, mainly of bricks, consisted of open patio flanked by rooms. Monumental architecture, little evidence : eg. the most important "the great bath" timber used with bricks : arches supported by brackets projecting.

State of Indian architecture between the Indus Valley Civilization and rise of Maurya Empire unknown : most work done on wood or brick, got perished away. Excavations at Rajgir, Kausambi, testify, existence of fortified cities with stupas, monastries : temples found at later Maurya sites of Nagari and Vidisa.

Considering power, extensive territorial control, architectural remains few. Most important stupa at Sanchi: the ruins of hall excavated at the site of Kumrahar in Patna : series of rock - cut caves near Gaya, interesting, because preserve some types of wooden buildings.

ARCHITECTURE - INDIAN, STYLES OF

India is perhaps one of the very few countries where a variety of magnificent architectural styles and trends had developed and flourished over centuries. This was mainly due to numerous invasions, conquests and domination by different foreign conquerors and rulers. There are richly carved and decorated relics of Buddhist, Muslim and Hindu Architecture in marble and stone, expressed in rock cut and free standing temples, mosques, tombs, palaces or fortresses. The Muslim ruler imported a new architectural style from the Middle - East and the Central Asia. In course of time is blended most beautifully with the details of Hindu and Buddhist Architecture and evolved a unique Indian - Muslim Architecture unlike any other architecture of neighbouring Muslim countries. The best examples to be found are in Fatehpur Sikri and Taj Mahal. While these grandiose, shrines, tombs and palaces gave visual delight and sense of awe to the people, the common man lived in mud huts with bamboo and straw thatched roofs - the real organic and native architecture of India - in villages scattered all over the country. Townships and urban area in the modern sense did not exist. The tradition of an urban house of middle class was practically unknown.

EMPIRE BUILDERS

The incidence of British colonial rule brought about a revolutionary socio - economic and technological changes in India. in their effort to knit together the vast Sub - continent of India where there had been divisions through feudal monarchy, the empire builders introduced a central Government to tax the people, built railways and roads to transport troops from one part of the country to another. For quick communication, postal and telegraphy systems were introduced. New types of buildings, previously unknown in India were required by the new rulers for their various activities to rule the country. New metropolitian centres such as Calcutta, Bombay and Madras gradually grew up as the seats of Government machinery and centres of trade and commerce more or less on the Western pattern. British architects, planners and engineers were commissioned to design, plan and build the important and monumental buildings. During this period, completely new and foreign types and styles of architecture were planted on the soil of India. The monumental buildings in most cases were poor copies of Greek, Gothic, Romanesque and Renaissance styles in vogue at that time in Europe. In district headquarters and moffusil towns, the British built civil lines and military cantonments. A new colonial type of bungalows were evolved for the white collectors and magistrates, sometimes designed by amateur British civil servants.

DISRUPTION IN CONTINUITY

This new socio - economic structure of urban India under the influence of Western technology completely disrupted the continuity and normal evolution of Indian Architecture as practised in the past. The "Master Builder" lost the patronage of the " High Priest ", the maharajas and the nobles. The craftsmen and sculptors associated with building construction also gradually lost and forgot their arts.

NEW ARCHITECTURE

Soon after Independence it was natural that a country, which has had such a rich architectural heritage but was denied self expression for a couple of centuries due to foreign domination, should have strong national sentiment wanting to express itself through an architecture that would look 'Indian'. Our architectural heritage, as already pointed out, was expressed in temples, mosques, tombs or fortresses built in stone and marble, richly carved and decorated - expressing the emotional, social, material and honest construction techniques of the times. Years and decades were required to complete some of the edifices. Under the pressure of such national sentiment to give 'Indian' look in our buildings, buildings like Ashoka Hotel in New Delhi, Vidhan Saudha in Bangalore - built in concrete and steel with veneering of stone or granite carved to resemble Indo - Muslim architecture of Rajasthan or Chola Temples were produced.

CHANGE IN SCOPE

Within the last hundred years or so the art and scope of architecture has undergone tremendous change. Architecture has emerged from the realm of narrow specialisation - such as religious buildings, tombs or palaces - to plunge into the realities of ordinary life.
(Condensed)

HABIB RAHMAN

ARCHITECTURE : KASHMIR

Style distinct, roof of Kashmira sanctum phamsana type, caves raised in two stages, e.g. ruined sun Temple at Martand, constructed mid 8th century, though Sikhara missing, gives idea of characteristic features. Temple placed on rectangular court, enclosed by a series of columns. Access to the court, through entrance hall, the walls have doorways with gabled pediments and trifoliate leaf shaped like recess. The Avantisvami temple, mid 9th century, now ruined, though richly ornamented style continued upto 12th century Eg Rilhanesvara temple at Pandrenthan, well preserved temple, of this period.

ARCHITECTURE - MEDIAEVAL SOUTH INDIAN STYLE

Also called, Dravida style, of Tamil Nadu State ; examples found all over southern India adjoining regions of Karnataka, Andhra Pradesh. Both developed variants; Karnataka evolved distinct style, basically South Indian but with some features of North India origin Karnataka style extended northward into Maharashtra; Kailasa temple at Ellora famous.

South Indian temple consists of a hall, square sanctum, has superstructure *Kutina* type. Pyramidal in form, Kutina consists of stepped storeys, each stimulating main storey conceived as having its own " wall" enclosed by a parapet. Parapet composed of miniature shrines strung together ; square called *Kutas* at the corners, rectangular with barrel vault roofs called Sales in the centre; the space between these connected by miniature wall elements *harantaras.*

On top a necking, supporting solid dome, crowned by pot or finial. The wall of sanctum rise above series of mouldings, constituting foundation block *adhisthana.* In Karnataka version, 10th century onwards, superstructure loaded with decoration obscuring composite elements.

Design of hall temple roofed by barrel vault, popular in centuries before after christ ; adopted in Southern India, Great entrance buildings ; or *gopuras* adopted it. Relatively small, inconspicious, by mid 12th century, outstripped main temple in size.

ARCHITECTURE - MODERN

Buildings initating contemporary styles, of European Architecture, blended with provincial flavour, known in India, 16th century onwards. Work of merit, the barsque architecture of Portugese colony, Goa ; splended buildings erected, second half 16th century. EG Church of Bom Jesus.

18th, 19th centries witnessed several buildings, no classic styles : initated by Indian patrons under European influence. Attempts by Britishers, to include no - Gothic, no - Saracemic styles to Indian architectural traditions. Buildings at metros, under European influence ; recent years attempts made to deal with problems of climate, urban development ; EG influence of Swiss architect Le Corbusier's work on Chandigarh Project early 1950's — led to modern architectural movement ; process adapting needs, traditions.

ARCHITECTURE : MUGHAL

Advent of Mughals, revival of Islamic architecture, northern India ; Persian, Indian, Various provincial styles fused together. EG the Humayun Tomb, begun 1564 ushers the new style; built of red sand - stone, marble, shows Persian influence. The Fort at Agra, 1565-74, city of

Fatehpur Sikri 1569-74, represent building activities of emperor Akbar. The Jami Masjid 1571, with colossal gateway, the Buland Darwazah, is one of finest mosques of Mughal period. Other notable buildings, palace of Jodha Bai, the Paneh Mahal, Diwan-e-Aam. Most buildings are of horizontal beam, arches used sparingly. The tomb of Sikandara, near Agra, of vast proportions, unique design, consists of series of stepped terraces on which rests tomb erected in honour of person, whose body buried below. Architectural undertaking during Jahangir's reign not ambitious; Shah Jehan's reign remarkable. He built the Red Fort at Delhi 1639-48, The Taj Mahal c 1632-49, masterpiece of his regin. Other buildings include Moti Masjid 1648-55, Jami Masjid at Agra.

Architectural monuments of reign of Aurangzeb represent a decone ; EG the tomb of Rabiat Begum, Aurangabad, 1679, poor copy of Taj Mahal ; Moti Masjid, Delhi, possesses early refinement. Tomb of Safdar Jang at Delhi 1754, among last important works, produced, under Mughal dynasty.

Mughal architecture, properly speaking, began in the the reign of Akbar. His buildings are noted for their massive proportions and solid construction. He mostly built in red sandstone, though towards the end of his reign white and black marble was also used as inlay pieces in the red sandstone. However, it was his son, Jahangir, who developed this art to perfection, first with marble inlaid in red sandstone and later with semi-precious stones inlaid in white marble.

The first important building of Akbar's reign is Humayun's tomb, the construction of which was personally supervised by his widow Hamida Begum. Who dedicated herself and her resources to the creation of this memorial. When Shah Jahan first contemplated the idea of his great conception at Agra, he turned Hazi Begum's production at Delhi for inspiration. The Tomb's immense dome of white marble dominates the landscape of Delhi towards the southeast. Standing on a square platform of red sandstone, the abiding impression of the tomb is one of size. It is positively enormous. The effect is enhanced by skilful juxtaposition of white marble and red sandstone. The whole conception not withstanding the typically Indian chhatris on the roof exemplifies the hitherto alien Persian element which was to make itself felt in the majority of Mughal art in the next three centuries. In spirit and in substance, Humayun Tomb portrays Persian architecture, and is reminiscent of the superb 14th century mausoleum of Il-khan Uljaytu at Sultaniyeh in north-west Iran. The dome, a typical Persian prototype, ranks with Khan-i-Khana's tomb as the best proportioned dome in India. Nevertheless, unlike the Persian use to bricks and glazed tiles, the Indian Builders of the tomb used stone and marble. The two significant features of Mughal architecture are also evident here the large gateways and the placement of the building in the midst of a large part. However, the most important of Akbar's contributions to architecture are the great fort at Agra and the capital city of Fatehpur-Sikri.

The construction of the Red Fort at Agra, on the bank of the Yamuna, was commenced in 1565 and was built under the instructions of Akbar by Qasim Khan, Mir-i-Bahr (the superintendent of Riverine Works.) In shape the fort is an irregular semi-circle with a straight base on the river front and the two sides joining at the Delhi Gate. The river front is nearly half-a mile in length and the total circumference of slightly over a mile and a half. The massive walls are of concrete and rubble, faced entirely with huge blocks of finely dressed red sandstone. The Delhi Gate of the fort on the west, forming the principal entrance, is an imposing structure consisting of an arched gateway between two massive octagonal bastions, each with one octagonal domed kiosk at the top. The other gateway is towards the south and is known as the Amar Singh Gate. This is the gate used by all visitors to the fort. The whole structure, with its charming facade in the back side, terraces, domed pavilions and finials, and the rich and varied ornamentation including white marble inlay, is architecturally a noble and dignified monument in itself. Within the fort, most of the extant buildings are those that were constructed in the reign of Shah Jahan. The only building of Akbar's period, preserved in its entirety, is the Jahangiri Mahal, a large square palace built in red sandstone in the usual palace-plan of double storeyed chambers enclosing an open courtyard. With the exception of a few arches appearing here and there in a subsidiary position, the entire palace is built in the Hindu trabeate style which also characterizes the profuse carving all over the building, but is particularly visible in the shape of the brackets.

Massive and magnificent in its proportions, the Red Fort of Agra has been witness to an eventful period of the Mughal dynasty-right from the lifetime of the great architect of the Mughal power to the condemnable imprisonment of a father (Shah Jahan) by his son (Aurangzeb) and to the final decline of the dynasty. In terms of architecture, what needs to be particularly noticed is the transition from red sandstone to marble. Akbar built in sandstone and his palaces done in stuucco plaster to resemble marble and also used marble inlay work in sandstone imperial buildings as in the facade of the Jahangiri palace and the gateway to Sikandra.

The most ambitious of Akbar's projects was his conception and creation of an entirely new capital city at Fatehpur Sikri situated 26 miles west of Agra. This was a great complex of palatial, residential, official and religious buildings, so designed and executed as to form one of the most spectacular structural productions in the whole of India.

The architecture of Fatehpur Sikri represents the art traditions of *'silpkaras'* who were requisitioned from two main sources: the Jamuna-Chambal region comprising of Delhi-Agra-Fatehpur-Sikri-Dholpur-Gwalior and Malwa-Gujarat-Rajasthan. They incorporated traditional Indian forms in their style and through them the classical touch reappeared at Fatehpur Sikri, as far as non-sectarian buildings were concerned. Thus, it was that various art traditions converged at Fatehpur Sikri to form the most creative style in medieval India.

The era of Akbar's successor, Jahangir, was relatively uneventful as far as the building art is concerned. The tomb of Itmat-ud-daulah, was built by his daughter and Jahangir's wife Nur-Jahan. Built wholly of marble and decorated profusely with exquisite inlay work, it forms a connecting link between the style of Akbar and Shah Jahan.

The Mughal style reached its zenith during the reign of Shah Jahan (1628-58) - a fact borne out emphatically by the existence of the world famous Taj Mahal. Shah Jahan is credited with the most graceful and best known buildings of medieval India. He beautified the capital cities of Agra and Delhi with splendid palaces and magnificent monuments, along with creating numerous elegant buildings at Ajmer, Lahore, Srinagar and other palaces. Consequently, the late Mughal style is also called Shah Jahan's style. The transition of style, is noticeable, for what was forceful and robust in Akbar's style was now dainty and elegant. Marble replaced red sandstone in most cases, and decorations took the form of artistic inlay of semi-precious and multicolored stones in marble, with a definite advancement in the artistic relief curving on sandstone and marble surfaces. Structurally too, the style changed. The arch was now curved in a multi-foil shape, the pillars had foliated based with either tapering or many-sides shafts and voluted bracket capitals, and especially the domes of Shah Jahan's buildings were remarkable for their extermely pleasing contours.

The most important of his building Projects were the Red Fort and the Jami-Masjid at his new capital of Shahjahananabad in Delhi. The completion of the Red Fort (1648) marked the transfer of the seat of government from Agra to Delhi. Although superficially similar and somewhat smaller than the Agra Fort, the Red Fort at Delhi is an imposing structure in itself, representing the late Mughal style at its best. The palatial buildings of the Fort are distinguished by a symmetrical planning along an ornamental marble water canal, with chutes and cascades. Workmanship is at its most perfect in the gorgoeous decorations in different styles and different colours. The pride of place, however, is captured by the Throne Seat-made of pure white marble (inland with precious stones) in a canopied form and set in a vaulted recess in the back wall of the Diwan-i-Aam; this was intended for the royal throne. Not far from the Red Fort is the magnificient Jama Masjid of Delhi- one of the most impressive mosques in India. Despite its vast size, the mosque is a remarkable piece of architecture and decoration. Both these buildings are a major landmark till date.

The study of the entire Mughal dynasty is incomplete-without the mention of the Dream in Marble of the Dream in Marble the Taj Mahal at Agra. The stuff that fantasies are made of........

Placed strategically on the banks of a huge river (Yamuna), the Taj stands out against the horizon and the blue sky beyond the very colour scheme with which this magnificent building merges into nature is breathtaking: the azure of the skies, the white of marble, pale-red of the sand-stone, and the lush green of the gardens. Every aspect of the Taj is a symphony in perfection that speaks of the tremendous effort that must have gone into the making of something so spectacular. The gardens were planned in a manner that a visitor could look at the Taj from varying distances and angles. The marble reservoir in the centre, as symmentrical as the Taj itself, is positioned for a memorable reflection of Taj, with exactly similar stairs and proportions on all four sides. All Mardan Khan, the designer of this world-famous Mausoleum, also planted Cypresses all along the pathway on both sides of the central water channels. These solemn sentinels of the Taj are supposed to represent mourners with sad gloomy looks and slender bodies. The wonder lies in the juxtaposition of the beauty of life as seen in the garden, with the perfect but lifeless marble structure which has, for centuries, stood as a shrine to the finally of death.

The artistic work at the Taj is all the more wonderful when one realizes that Indian marble is about the hardest quality of marble, and hence a very difficult medium to work in. There were three types of work done by Indian craftsmen in marble. The oldest was the intricate screen filigree work; the other was raised work where flowers or vases with flowers were carved in relief; and the third was inlay work in which precious and semi-precious stones were filled in tiny holes in marble that looked like beautiful blossoms and other decorative motifs.

The tomb of Queen Mumtaz Mahal, whose memory Shah Jahan created this wonder, is situated in the heart of the edifice. Now, after three centuries, the Taj still represents the ultimate act of love, " The grand passion of an Emperor's love", as Edwin Arnold wrote. It is as Tagore said," One solitary tear........ on the cheek of time".

In the tomb of Sadar Jung at Delhi (Circa-1753), we see the last notable monument of the late Mughal period. (Condensed)

ABHA KHANNA

ARCHITECTURE - RELIGIOUS

Through the ages, religious architecture has its own deep significance and influence on civilisations. India, one of the oldest civilisations of the world, is proud of being the land of great structures of various religions. The styles of architecture of all these religions have fused into one another in such a manner that it is difficult to visualise the origins of some of the religions. For instance, the richness of ornamentation of the Jain temples can easily be compared with the engraved figures of the Sun Temple, Konark, as well as with the beautiful carved paintings of Ajanta Caves. The architectural features of the famous Dilwara Temples of Jainism were later found in Akbar's mughal architecture. And then the Sikhism, whose architectural style has been influenced by the Mughal buildings. As an expert has commented, " The basic doctrines of Hinduism have been modified by the impact of Buddhism and Jainism which are both fundamentally non-conformist sects of Hinduism".

However, in spite of all these resemblances, each religion has its own symbolism. The role of symbol as the mid-point between the manifest or known and the unmanifest or unknown is of vital importance in human communication and understanding.

Symbols are extremely important in a country like ours where these are used to express the spiritual character of the building. One cannot imagine a temple without a *Sikhara*, a church without a cross, a gurudwara without a marble dome with *chhatri* and a mosque without a dome and minarets.

Today, there are no accepted religious standards as were prevalent in earlier times to guide and inhibit the architect. Modern efforts range from some abstract expression to some true complementary traditional forms.

They derive symbols from ancient conventions; yet their design expressions may exploit wholly contemporary materials and art concepts. A fine combination of the traditional and the modern, while scrupulously protecting the sanctity of each religion.

YASHINDER S. BAHGA & NAVNEET K. BAHGA

ART AND CRAFT MUSEUM

In Gurgaon, Haryana, the private art and craft collection of K.C.Aryan ranges from the bizarre to the down right common place. It contains a rare collection of art which are crammed into four rooms and 1000 items are still stored in chests. Museum pieces range from old locks and cattle bells from Madhya Pradesh and Punjab, Shiva heads and Ganeshas numbering more than 50 'from different parts of India, a water spout from Himachal Pradesh, large collection of *yantras* and *phulkaris* from Rajasthan, a tribal wedding pole from Bastar, etc. These collections date from the eighteenth century to the present some of the collections are priceless.
(Condensed)

ART FILMS CINEMA

What is an "Art Film" ? A film which is not consciously conceived for commercial consumption? A film which only critics and intellectuals claim to understand? A film which is not meant for philistine understanding? Or a film which is a deliberate antithesis of the 'so-called' commercial cinema ? All these are associated to some extent with the 'so-called' "Art films".

From the very time that cinema came into being, a time when this coinage "art film" did not exist, there have beenartists of immense statures completely dedicated to this medium. Right from the silent era there are glorious instances of remarkable artists exploring the height and depth of this fabulous medium, artists like Griffith, Flaharty, Eisenstein, Chaplin, Dryer, Renoir, Fritz Lang, Pudovkin, Rene Clair, De Sica, Bunuel, Bergman, Mizoguchi, Ozu, Kurosawa and others. These are the people who by their superhuman perseverance and their unstinted attachment to the mechanism of this medium, achieved the stupendous feat of giving a mechanical medium the respect of art. Unlike prosaic technicians these innovators tried to give creative personality to the machines (Camera, Sound Machine, Processing Machines etc.) which has helped cinema in seeking an exclusive identity. The process is still on. Artists like this all over the World are working with complete dedication, without succumbing to the corrupting cliches of the trade and some day it will be only these artists who will probably lift cinema along side the nine Muses. Paradoxically these artists never called their creations by the constructive term " Art Film".

Today the individual has become the highest form and the greatest bane of artistic creation. The smallest wound or pain of the ego is examined under a microscope as if it were of eternal importance. The artist considers his isolation, his subjectivity, his individualism almost holy.Thus we finally gather in one pen, where we stand and bleat about loner-liness without listening to each other and without realising that we are smothering each other to death. The individualists stare into each other's eyes and yet deny the existence of each other. We walk in circles, so limited by our own anxieties that we can no longer distinguish between true and false, between gangster's whim and purest ideal. (Condensed)

BASU BHATTACHARYA

ART OF BENGALI CINEMA

While the elders in the field of art remained resigned to their lot, the youngest-cinema, the Bengali cinema in particular, revolted against literature one day, and from then on, the visual image was liberated from the verbal image and cinema had its own language, its independence. This independence came in such films as Satyajit Ray's *Pather Panchali,* Rwittick Ghatak's *Ajaantrik* Mrinal Sen's *Baishey Sravan* and to a great extent, in Tapan Sinha's *Hansuli Banker Upakatha.*

The art of Bengali cinema is not its entertainment but its truth which is often lyrical-most of the films of Satyajit Ray are instances of this; sometimes bitter and violent-*Komal Gandhar* and *Subarnarekha* of Rwittick Ghatak are instances of this; sometimes experimental into the medium itself-Mrinal Sen's *Akash Kushum* is a brilliant instance of this, sometimes smooth and straight telling-most of the films of Tapan Sinha are instances of this.

It has now become clear from their subsequent works that these film-makers are essentially in agreement as to their view of the problems of realism and also of the diverging paths which each of them pursues in search of realism. In the whole field of creative film-making, there are no examples of such detailed, sympathetic and sensitive revelation of the beauty of works of art *Pather Panchali, Aparajito, Charulata, Aranyer Din Ratri, Baishey Sravan, Poonascha, Akash kusum, Ajaantrik Komal Gandhar, Subarnarakha, Khudhita pashan, Haatey Bazarey, Apan Jan* **etc.**

Such presentations of the art of cinema are closely linked with their humanist conception of the great task of creative film-makers, and illustrate their belief that truly great art must always be rooted to the soil. Truly great art reveals to man the things that make man truly human, reveals to him the great possibilities and faculties that slumber in him and that can be turned into reality by his own actions.

There is much of these film-makers themselves in their films (Cinema profits more by the experiments of the artist into himself than by the experiment in film), in the passion of th e artistes, and the passion of the thinkers, and in these two passions aesthetic and intellectual are the roots of their uniqueness as film-makers. In all their films they are consistently and persistently, artistes, artistes of the medium they serve, artistes of the life they live. Art, in any form, is to them a function of life, and as artistes, in all their films, they have employed the shaping hand of the artistes upon the raw material of experience.

The aim of the Bengali cinema is human relationship, a film about time and people, and now it affects human beings, and how one must reconcile himself to its working. To reach this aim these film makers are doing away with story; they are hunting down their material in the streets around them, they are taking the simplest of human situations and uncovering the elements contained within them; they are doing away with the professionals as far as possible; they are doing away with the kind of technical paraphernalia that gets in the way of the immediate contact with reality. (Condensed)

SAROJ K. SENGUPTA

ARTS AND CRAFTS OF KASHMIR

Besides its natural beauty, Kashmir has been the home of handicrafts since ages. It was during the reign of Sultan-Zain-ul-Ab-din, popularly known as Badshah or the Great king, who ruled kashmir from 1420 to 1470 A.D. that handicrafts were introduced in Kashmir. To improve the living standard and economy of his people he imported skilled craftmen from Central Asia and with their assistance got the local inhabitants trained in a number of handicrafts, which were till then altogether unknown to the people of the State.

The artistic ski''s of Kashmir have found expression in Parier Machie, Wood Carvings, Embrioderies, Carpets, Numdhas, Chainstitch and Gubbas, Constume Jewellery, Leather Embroidery and other such crafts. The production of crafts has had the distinction of having been able to offer something new all the time without sacrificeing their traditional character.

PAPIER MACHIE

Papier Machie is one of the handicrafts which Badshah introduced first in Kashmir with the help of experts imported by him from Samarquand. The craft if also known as kar-i-kalamdani or per case work, because in the initial stages it was usually used for ornamentation of pen cases and small boxes, generally used by feudal official dignitaries. But from the Mughal times it was extend to palnquins, ceilings, bed stands, doors and windows. The chief form used being floral and foliage. It was only later that papier machie came to be used on the numerous articles of household use.

The basic form for decoration work is made from waste paper, waste cloth, rice starch and copper sulphate, which is ground together by handpounding method into pulp. It is then coated to a requisite thickness on wooden moulds and dried. This basic form after dyring is smoothened and glazed and finally ornamented with colourful floral and other decorative motifs. The colours used for painting were earlier made from stones and minerals which do not fade. Although this type of colour is now difficult to find, yet there is still a certain clases of artisans who stick to this recipe for the manufacture of articles in Papier Machie. Pure gold and silver leaves are also applied to the ground to increase the richness and long life of the colour schme. A coat of locally made varnish with linseed oil is applied finally as a preservative against moisture etc. and this also gives a final finish and luster to the article.

The craftsman while drawing designs on the articles does not keep any drwaing before him. He draws the designs out of his imagination. The rich, varied exquisite floral designs include the chinar leaf, the it is the Persian rose, almond and cherry blossom, the tulip and the hyacinth, while bird form are represented by the kingfisher and the bulbul.

WOOD CARVING

The art of wood carving appears to have been born out of the most intimate needs of the local man. The expressions of this fact is readily available on the common use of wooden sandlas in every Kashmiri home. Be it as it may, the fact remains that the wood carvings flourished during the time of Badshah. This craft received great publicity both within and outside the country when a wooden carved gate was presented by Maharaja Pratap Singh of Jammu and Kashmir for the Delhi Durbar of king George V.

Carving work is a profound expression of flora and fauna in which kashmir abounds and which have an abiding effect on the minds of the artists who reproduce these motifs with admirable precision, in various articles manufactured by them. The Kashmir craftsmen, not content with their primitive expression, have efficiently carried it forward with technique and enriched it with the influence from neighbours. For instance the successful inclusion in wood carving of the famous dragon from Chinese Turkistan and latticed floral carving from Sassanid tradition are great achievement in the development of this craft. These influences exhibit a perfect assimilation and inclusion into the tradition of the indigenous form of ornamentation and galaxy of local motifs, such as chinar leafs, the grape bunch, the iris foliage or the water reed. Curiously the motifs carved in wood carvings are mostly from foliage and very seldom one sees flowers.

The articles produced in this craft now include a vast range of utility and decorative items from small bowls to bed steads, from cigarette cases and candle holders to cupboards and cabinets.

Walnut wood is the principal raw material employed in the production of wood carving articles. This wood is available at an elevation of 5,500 to 7,500 ft. and is known for its interesting grain and pleasant tint. Previously naturally seasoned walnut wood was used in the manufacture of wood carving items, but now as the seasoning centre has been set up by the State Government, scientifically seasoned wood is being used in this industry. The carving is done by locally made iron tools of numerous shapes and sizes. The carved surface is smoothened by sand paper and a gate stone and finally given a finish by wax polish.

SHAWLS AND EMBROIDERIES

The Persian word shal from which the English shawl is derived originally denoted a class of woven fabrics rather than a particular article of dress.

The origin of this crafts in Kashmir dates back to the time of Badshah whom the historians have called the Akbar of Kashmir. He is said to have introduced Turkistan weavers for this purpose.

The shawls were of two types, one is known as Kanishawal and the other Amli Work (Needle Embroidery).

The technique of Kanishawl has parallels in Asia and Central Asia. According to this, the wefts of the patte.ned part of the fabric are inserted by means of wooden spools without the use of shuttle. Weft threads alone form the patter; these do not run the full width of the cloth, being woven back and forth round the warp threads only where each particular colour is needed. In other respects, the Kashmir technique differs from tapestry weaving, the loom being horizontal instead of verticle, and its operation more like brocading.

Another important innovation introduced at the beginning of the nineteenth century was the Amli or needle-worked shawl, which was ornamened entirely with the needle on the plain woven ground. The type of shawl with an entirely needleworked pattern, however, was unknown in Kashmir before the nineteenth century. It was introduce at the instance of an American named kh-waja Yusuf, who had been sent to Kashmir in 1803 as the agent of a Constantinople trading firm.

The materials traditionally used for Kashmir shawl weaving was fleece derived from a Central Asian species of the mountain goat, Capra hircus. This was popularly known in the West either as Pashmina or Cashmere, from the old spelling of Kashmir.

In addition to shawls of different sixes, this embroidery is being done on dress materials, scarves etc. also. This craft industry employs the maximum number of craftmen, the total number being nearly 1,00,000.

NUMDHAS

Numdha is a kind of felt-rug made from coarse wool or wool mixed with cotton in various proportions forming different grades and qualities of the felt -generally termed as 100% wool, 70 % wool 30% cotton, 50% wool 50% cotton, 22% wool 78% cotton etc. indicating respective percentage of wool and cotton in the composition of the felt. Coarse wool or wool and cotton, as the case may be, in unspun and in original condition is spared evenly and by a process rolled and pressed constantly till the fibres intervine so as to form a felt. The felted Numdhas are made of different shapes and sizes. While there are round and ovel Numdhas, the commonest shape is rectangular and the general standard sizes are 2'X3" 4'X 6' and 6'X 9'- four by six being the most popular. Generally the embroidery is done on white Numdhas, but occasionally dyed Numdhas also from the base. Lately patchwork Numdhas of applique Pattern have also come up. The embroidery is done in woollen yarn and the motifs used are generally floral and occasionally geometrical.

CREWEL EMBROIDERY

Crewel embroidery is very commonly used for upholstery. It is a hook work embroidery done by the pointed hook resembling more or less the crochet, leaving the chainstitch type. The embroidery in thick yarn is done on hand-woven cloth. The hook work embroidery is not of indigenous type but came to Kashmir in the 13th Century through the Damascus traders from Asia Minor. The art has taken firm roots in Kashmir and developed to the extent that it has in certain fields replaced the needle embroidery in garments and costumes.

CARPETS

The art of carpet manufacture in India was introduced by Emperor Akbar after he ascended the throne in *1556*. But in Kashmir, the art had already existed much earlier.

So far as the development of the carpet weaving Industry in Kashmir is concerned, it has received set-backs on several occasions, before it was finally established.

Badshah was the first man to lay the foundation of carpet making in Kashmir and the carpets in attractive designs were produced for the first time in his regime. After his death the Industry deteriorated.

The art of carpet making in Kashmir is more or less identical to that which prevails in Persia, the only deviation being that in Persia, it is done by women, whereas in Kashmir, it is entirely done by men.

Of late, silk carpets, which were traditional in Kashmir but had become extinct due to depression of carpet industry, have been revived. They are known as much because of the use of silk yarn both for warp and pile instead of cotton and wool.

The Silk carpets are now coming up as a revival industry in Iran which enjoyed almost a monopoly in the manufacture of these rugs. It is a great compliment to the Kashmiri talent that the carpet weavers have succeeded not only in repruducing these rugs in designs and qualities as used to be woven by Persians but these carpets have also found export market and great possibilities.

Among the more recent innovations is the introduction of Amli effects in the carpets, which is derived from the famed Kashmir Shawls. One such Amli carpet was presented to Her Majesty Queen Elizabeth II as a gift from the Government of India.

Hand-made wollen carpets in traditional oriental designs of qualities 200 knots and above constitute the largest product with export potential.

CHAINSTITCH RUGS AND GUBBAS

Chainstitch Rugs have recently become popular as comparatively inexpensive but equally durable substitutes for carpets which are normally out of reach of the average public. Generally worked on soft jute-gunny thickly all-over, so much so that the just surface is comletely covered, the embroidery is in superior woollen yarn and the design and patterning mainly on the lines of carpets. After washing with soap the rug is lined with closely-woven and stronger variety of jute gunny.

Another variety of rugs commonly known as Gubbas is worked on old blankets, which are mended and dyed in a deep colour as black, deep chocolate or deep blue. In this case the whole base is not covered with embroidery but the patterning is generally linear leaving the black background of the blanket as a visible base.

TURQUDISE JEWELLERY

Kashmir, rich in the wealth of colourful precious and semi-precious stones, has provided a congenial atmosphere for the development of stone-craft also, but the use of rich and colourful turquoise blue stone in jewellery became popular for its naive crudity and folk character which go to make handicrafts what they are.

The basic article is made of brass, silver or white metal on which a layer of locally made black *lacquer* is laid. Small chips of the stone are embodied into the *lacquer* close to each other, the intermediate gape being filled by rubbing in blackened bees-was.

Real turquoise, having rarity in the Kashmiri market later, was replaced by white soft-stone which is being dyed in turquoise - blue colour. For dyeing, the stone is made absorbent first by a process of baking. The State Government run School of Designs has greatly improved the process of dyeing so that the dye remains fast and water-proof, and has introduced the application of a preservative on finish.

COSTUME JEWELLERY

The old ancient designs in jewellery are reproduced in silver and white metal. The articles are studded with precious and semi-precious stones. This type of jewellery has great demand and is exported to different parts of the world.
(Condensed)

J. M. MENGI

ATAL BEHARI VAJPAYEE (b. 1924)
(D/B in cert. is 1926)

Atal Behari Vajpayee was sworn in on October 13, 1999, as Prime Minister of India for the third time. Vajpayee, whose minority BJP-led coalition governments lost trust votes twice before once within 13 days of coming to power is his party's most celebrated face and among the nation's most admired parliamentarians.

Vajpayee entered Parliament for the first time in 1957, when he was one of only four Jan Sangh Candidates. Founder member of the Jan Sangh in 1951, Vajpayee led his supporters to the Janata Party in 1977 and became the first chief of the BJP after the Janata Party's split. Vajpayee was jailed along with all top Opposition during Emergency.

However, Vajpayee will be remembered most for having been the man to take India nuclear. Vajpayee authorised the nuclear tests at Pokhran in May 1998 and views them as a means of establishing India's independence and sovereignty.

A man with a taste for things apolitical, Vajpayee is a fairly accomplished poet. But these interests have not made him oblivious of his life's mission: " To see India take its place among the great nations."

ATTUKAL DEVI TEMPLE - (SIGNIFICANCE OF 'PONGALA' FESTIVAL

The city of Thiruvananthapuram is sanctified by temples dedicated to different deities, the presiding deity being Sree Padmanabha. The Attukal temple situated in sylvan surroundings attracts the maximum of devotees - women outnumbering men.

There are many stories concerning the origin of the Attukal Devi temple. But the once which is most believed is that Attukal Devi is an incarnation of Kannaki.

Over the last 50 years the temple had a phenomenal growth. The renovation of the temple in 1974 was a landmark in its development. This was the harbinger for the many developmental activities in the temple. The thrust was to provide maximum facilities to the devotees for darshan, offerings etc.

The sanctity of any temple vests with the Tantri of the temple. Due to the divine grace of Attukalamma the Attukal temple has a set of highly devoted and sincere Tantris. They are as well-versed in all the pooja rituals and enjoy absolute freedom in all religious matters.

The management of the temple is in the hands of a highly effective temple trust. The trust includes very sincere and committed persons whose main aim is to run the temple on most efficient lines. Already the temple can boast of two Kalyaṇa Mandapams, a medical centre and an industrial Training Centre. The Trust has a plan to add a super speciality hospital to their list of achievements.

The Pongala festival in the month of Kumbham can be compared to the Makaravilakku at Sabarimala. This is one of the greatest temple festivals in the whole of South India. Thousands of women irrespective of caste, creed and religion participate in this great festival. On this particular day, male devotees are not allowed to enter the temple premises simply because of the large number of women congregating to offer Pongala. Pongala symbolises 'Atma Samarpanam' to the Goddess. People believe that by offering Pongala they will be able to realise their wishes, shed their despair, purify their soul and absolve themselves of all sins.

Our Indian culture always gives lot of respect to the 'mother'. 'Devi Mahatamyam' and 'Syamala Dandakam' are great works in praise of the Mother. No wonder the 'Attukal Amma' is regarded as the mother who gives solace and succour to the millions of her devotees.

For offering Pongala an earthern vessel is used. Our body is transient and ultimately merges with the sand. By offering Pongala in an earthern vessel we are offering ourselves to the deity. The fire that is used destroys the ego in us and we surrender our body and soul to the great mother.

A story is current that the annual Pongala is offered to pacigy Kannaki Devi (Attukal Amma) whose anger was aroused by the unwarranted killing of her innocent husband, Kovalan. Whatever be the reason, the Pongala Mahotsavam of Attukal temple is an unparaled event which transforms Ananthapuri into Anandapuri.

PROF. P. GOPALARAMAN

AUROVILLE-INTERNATIONAL CRUCIBLE FOR SPIRITUAL EVOLUTION

Auroville is the materialization of an inner urge and a divine inspiration as expressed by The Mother (La Mere): " For millennia, we have developed outer means, outer instruments, outer techniques of life. And eventually these means and techniques are crushing us. The sign of new humanity is a reversal of perspective and the understanding that the inner means, the inner knowldge and the inner techniques can change the world and matter without crushing it. Auroville is the place where this new way of life is being worked out: it is a centre of accelerated evolution where man has to start changing the world by the inner spirit".

Located 150 South of Chennai and 14 km from Pondicherry. Auroville is situated in a rural setting consisting of over 80 settlements spread out over 25 Sq. km. The Auroville township is an eroded plateau in Tamil Nadu overlooking the Bay of Bengal. It is an expanding township because more land continues to be acquired to establish projects. Auroville was founded on 28 Februrary 1968 when about 5,000 young people as a symbolic gesture of human unity placed a handful of earth from 125 countries and from various States of India in a lotus shaped inaugural urn. The salient points from the Charter of Auroville given by the Mother say " Auroville belongs to nobody in particular. Auroville belongs to humanity as a whole....... Auroville will be the place of unending education.... Auroville is to be the bridge between the past and the future- Auroville will be a site of material and spiritual researches for a long embodiment of an actual Human Unity".

Auroville is also defined as the " laboratory of the new revolution". The Mother has further clarified that " humanity is not the last rung of terrestrial creation. Evolution continues and man will be surpassed. It is for each individual to know whether he wants to participate in the advent of this new species":

Auroville is also engaged in a long list of productive activities to achieve the aim of self- sufficiency, as also to promote village development programmes for the benefit of the poorer rural sector. Incense, clothing and gift items are made with the partcipation of the local people. Renewable energy systems like windmills and biogas plants are also manufactured here. The production of material for lowcost housing is yet another valuable contribution. The variety of products spans the vast range from peanut butter to shophisticated electronic components and computers. Auroville also provides a mosaic of community services.

The Mother had said that Auroville would emerge not because of human will and purpose but because of a subtle, divine inspiration. On 30 September, 1969, she observed: " Earth needs a place where men live away from all national rivalries, social conventions, self- contradictory moralities and contending religions, a place where human beings can devote themselves wholly to the discovery and practice of the Divine Consciousness that is seeking to manifest itself. Auroville wants to be this place and offers to all who aspire to live the truth of tomorrow".

World renowned anthropologist Dr. Margaret Mead of USA has said. " Auroville is a community dedicated to working - to develop living forms, both architectural and environmental, which will transcend our level of Community living which is fraught with such heavy penalties to human beings and to the global environment".

The Mother exhorts, "The true spirit of Auroville is collaboration and must be more and more so. True collaboration paves the way to divinity". In short, Auroville has been created to hasten the advent of a more luminous and harmonious future.

(Condensed)

PRAN NATH LUTHRA

"B"

BAADMERI PRINT
THE TRADITIONAL ART OF RAJASTHAN

The gentle pace of life in Indian villages has inspired its people, from time immemorial, to express themselves and their culture through various art forms. Baadmeri printing on cloth is one such folk art which, through the skilful hands of the artisans of Baadmer in Rajasthan, has not only become a symbol of their perception of life but also a medium through which they fulfil their aesthetic aspirations.

Rich, exotic and eye-catching colour combinations and a wide range of designs attract tourists, both in India and from abroad, to this age-old art of Rajasthan. Not only all kinds of outfits are made of Baadmeri prints, but household articles like tablecloth, curtains, bedsheets, cushion-covers etc. are also printed with this unique Rajasthani art. As the modern Indians choose to be more ethnic in their form and style, this art with its traditional and elaborated patterns accentuates the ethnic look.

The art of Baadmeri printing has come a long way, tracing a history of more than 300 years. In pre-independent India, mostly Hindus of Baadmer were engaged in this art. But it was the Muslim community which used this print more that anybody else. And gradually Hindus residing in the Sindh region also adopted it and eventually engaged themselves in the making of this art. After the partition o India, this cottage industry received a big jolt since Singh, which had become a big market of Baadmeri print products, became a part of Pakistan. Despite this, the Hindu families continued to make Baadmeri prints in the frontier provinces of Rajasthan and Gujarat, thereby keeping this precious traditional Indian art alive.

Like in any other art form, colours are important to Baadmeri printing also. In olden days, as there were no chemicals to produce a variety or shades, flowers and plants extracts were used as colours Wooden printing blocks were made by hand to create different designs. The depiction of auspicious symbols used to predominate. But today, besides these, geometrical combinations, trellis work, lozenges, chevrons and various other patterns are also used for printing.

Even to this day, before printing, people of Baadmer wash the cloth in an old pool of water named Nargasar. It is belived that this pool water has some natural chemicals which make the prints more lasting and more beautiful. Baadmeri designs on shawls, bedsheets and curtains have sizeable demand abroad.

Baadmeri artisans hold in their warp, weft and pile ages of tradition and cultural influences that can easily be recognized by their motifs, boldness of designs and strark colours.

SHALINI MITRA

BABA FARID
SYMBOL OF COMPOSITE CULTURE

The year was 1398, Timur was returning home after ransacking Delhi - light of mind but laden with gold, trampling corn, killing men and cattle alike. It was a typical Punjab winter and the air in the fields mingled with the blood of the innocents.

On the banks of the river Sutlej at a place called Pak Pattan his horse suddenly stopped. The horsemen whipped their animals, the stallion started bleeding but refused to move further. There was panic among the soldiers, hyseria among the officers, total confusion in the army. There was consternation and alarm writ large on every face. Not used to such unscheduled halts, the Turk chief leapt forward, roared like a lion and demanded answer.

Nobody replied. He shouted again. Everyone remained totally speechless. At last an old man came forward and said " Your honour, this place is sanctified"

"By whom?" the Chief asked, " By one saint whose ancestors had migrated from Iran to escape death at the hands of your ancestors", the old man replied. Everyone looked at everyone else. The General's hands reached for his sword but before they could go any further a miracle happened. As goes the legend, a voice came from somewhere and called, " Baba Farid, the king of kings." Every tongue felt that it had an ear on it. A vision came to the advancing marauder. He felt elated. The armies were ordered to spare the town.

Timur bowed low in the 'Khanqah', heard the Sufi hymns, spent the night in the 'dargah'. He ate the same austere foods, which the devotees ate, slept on the same mat and pledged not to kill any more innocents, only to break the pledge later.

Acknowledged by every literary authority as the first major poet of the Punjabi language, Farid was to Punjabi what Chaucer was to English. He made Punjabi poetry and poetry Punjabi. Later when Adi Granth (Sikh scripture) was complied by the fifth Guru of the Sikhs, Guru Arjun Dev, Farid's 'slokas' (sacred couplets) were given the place of honour along with those of Kabir, Ramdev and Guru Ravidas. They all sang in the people's dialect about the glory of India's culture, the greatness of Indian values and the supremacy of Indian thought.

Among the many social and religious movements in India or of the last two thousand years, the Bhakti movement of the middle ages from the 13th to the 17th centuries was the most pronounced as it cut across all distinctions of high and low birth, the learned and the unlettered, men and women and opened the doors of spiritual realization and salvation to one and all. Besides, it provided a base for common socio-religious culture in India.

One great characterstic of the Indian civilization is that more than its kings and warriors and generals, it is the saints and the sufis who realized the goals of the Renaissonce and Reformation. The cyclic tales recited by the lute players of ancient India, the songs of the wandering minstrels, the ballads and the 'Kathaka' (story-tellers) of medieval times provided a framework for the evolution and growth of the composite culture of India. They integrated the diverse elements of Indian society and knit them in a unified cultural necklace. It is these saints and sufis who bestowed a sense of Indianness on Indians down the ages. Baba Farid occupies a very high place in this cultural anthology.

Baba Farid lived in Punjab in the 13th century and composed hymns in Punjabi, the likes of which are yet to be composed. There was something in his poetry aking to prayers. He spoke of his people in the people's dialect and asked them to use Punjabi for religious purposes. He started a 'silsilah' at Pak Pattan and established a mystic organization, a 'khanqah' (Monastery) on the lines of European seminary upholding the rule of mind over matter in the ultimate analysis of human affairs.

Farid's 'Bani' (religious text) is small in volume but has moved mankind over the last eight centuries. The lyrical content and haunting melody of these 'slokas' has been so great that every visitor to Punjab has stopped to pay homage to the soul, which conceived them. In the true Sufi tradition Farid employed sensual imagery to convey mystical meaning. Regarding God as eternal beauty, the Sufi poets, both in Persia and India had set new trends in poetry. Its special quality lay in the fact that unless one knows the intentions of the poet, one cannot distinguish whether it is arode to human love or a hymn addressed to a deity. Take for example this love son of the Baba.

> The alleyway is muddy, O Farid,
> The Beloved's House is distant,
> if I go I would drench my cloak,
> And break my bond if stay.
> It's the Creator's ordinance, this deluge.
> Go I will to my Beloved to strengthen
> The links of love, and let my woollen sheet
> Be drenched with downpour."

Even the illiterate could understand, enjoy Farid's metaphos and imagery - rooted as they were in the soil.

K. K. KHULLAR

BADRINATH TEMPLE

In Garhwall (Uttranchal) on banks of Alaknanda; altitude 3,375 m.; one of the most sacred Hindu temples ; dedicated to Vishnu; 2 hot water springs issue (from mountainside) just below temple; the rawal (priest) must always be a Nambudri Brahmana from Kerala; visited by countless pilgrims and greatly venerated.

References
Brown. P., Indian Architecture, Vol. I (Buddhist & Hindu Period), Bombay, 1946.

Furgusson, J. & Burgees, J. The Cave Temples of India, Delhi, 1969.

Goetz, Hermann, India : 5000 yrs. of Indian Art, London, 1964.

Kramrisch, Stella, Hindu Temple, Vol. I & II, Calcutta, 1946.

Majumdar, R.C., The History & Culture of the Indian People, Vol. I-VI, Bombay, 1951-60.

BAIJNATH TEMPLE

Far from the deafening noises of the industrial towns the calm, still and picturesque valleys of Kangra, Kulu and Chamba give a becknoing call to the lovers of nature, the seekers after tranquility of mind and spiritual meditation. Lured by the beauty and repose of celestial mountains, great *rishis* like Manu, Vyasa, Vashishtha, Sukdev, Mandavaya, Shringi and Padam Sambhav etc., chose different places in Himachal Pradesh for meditation, Lord Shiva made Kailasha or Himachal as his eternal abode. No wonder, therefore, Shiva and Shakti have been the predominant cults of worship in Himachal Pradesh. This fact is borne out by the existence of a large number of ancient temples dedicated to these two deities in the interior of the State. Lord Shiva's temple at Baijnath is perhaps the most famous among such temples.

It is situated about 64 kms east of Kangra town on the Pathankot-Kulu road.

The site of the temple is most captivating. It stands on an elevated place in a walled enclosure. The snow-clad peaks of the mountains called Dhauladhar in the north at a short distance give an illusion of walls of silver to an Onlooker. Down below the temple flows in a crescent the serpentine Binwa Khad sporting like a child. Lush green fields, the verdure of the blooming meadows all around the grandeur of forests on the slopes of the Dhaulandhar and cascading waters of the mountain stream present a most delightful sight. Glittering golden Kalasha over the *Sikhara* of the temple becomes visible from a distance to incoming visitors from all directions. Pucca terra-cotta stairs lead from the Western gate of the temple to the Kshirganga- ghat on the bank of the Binwa Khad where the pilgrims take a dip. Quite nearby is the famous water-spring of Kathog the water of which is known to be rich with iron element. So not only for a religious devotee but even for a tourist also, Baijnath offers rich potentialities of an ideal place.

RAVANA AND THE SHIVALINGAM

The ancient name of the town in which the temple stands is kirgrama according to the stone inscriptions called Prashastis on either sides of the walls inside the temple.The modern name, Baijnath as it is know, has no doubt been derived from the Shivalinga called Vaidyanath. The name Baijnath is only a distortion from Vaidyanath which means the lord of physicians. Ravana, the great devotee of Lord Shiva is described to have sacrificed his tenth and last head at the altar of Shivalingam to please his Lord according to the Shivpuran. Just behind the temple there is a ditch called Ravan-Ka-Khola which is said to be the mark of Ravan's knee while paying reverence to the Shivlingam. As the story goes that Ravana regained all his lost heads here by the grace of Shiva, the Lingam was called Vaidyanath as no other physician could restore a head to the body once it had been separated from it.

Some people question whether the Vaidyanath Shivlingam at Kirgrama now known as Baijnath is the same where according to the Shivpuran, Ravan worshipped and sacrified his heads. This doubt has emerged mainly from the existence of some other Vaidyanath Shivlingams in Bihar, U.P. and Trichur in the South.

ARCHITECTURE

The architecture of the temple is so superb that it spontaneously appeals to the mind and pleases the eye. Great simplicity of outline, no repetitions of itself, elegant ornamentation,minute stone-engravings make this temple a masterpiece of Indian architecture. The smaller image of Ganesha at the entrance to the porch, the figures of Ganga and Yamuna on either side of walls near the shrine of the Shivlingam, the images of Ashtabhuja Kali, Kartikya Swami and Surya standing on marble pedestal on the recesses of outer walls have been neatly and precisely chiselled.

The temple consists of a mandapa 20 feet square inside and 28 feet square outside with massive pillars for the support of the roof and a shrine for the Lingam 8 feet square. The temple measures over all 51 feet by 31 with walls all around about 120 feet long and 60 feet wide in the east and 74 feet in the west. This contains some rooms for the priests with small temples on the north side.

Inside, the roof is divided into squares and oblongs which are closed in usual manner by large, flat overlapping slabs on the Exterior the straight lines of the walls are broken by projections and recesses enriched with pillared niches for statues. The upper part of the temple is covered with that amalka fruit which was so fashionable in the Indian temples of the ancient times. The stringecourses of the Shikhara have been tastefully adorned and it is well-proportioned. James Fergusson lays special stress on the two porticopillars in front of the porch.

In front of the porch just adjacent to the pillars that is a figure of Nandi Kishok under a canopy supported on four pillars. At a short distance further to the West there is the second figure of Nandi much larger than the other. The smaller one is the original which was set up at the dedication of the temple, the larger one was added by Raja Sansar Chand II in 1786.

Just beyond the pillars to the north, there was a very interesting temple of Jamadagni. But is has since fallen down.

PRASHASTIS

The main inscription or Prashatis are on two slabs on each side of the entrance to the porch, one on the south and other on the north wall, both inside the larger temple. The Prashastis are is Sharda alphabets. An average reader would, therefore, find it difficult to decipher the writing. As the Prashastis are perhaps the only written record on the history of the region of that period, these have tremendous historical value. Many attempts were made to decipher the writing of the Prashastis but at last Dr. Buhler succeeded in making an English translation.

One of the Prashastis has 34 lines and the other 33 lines. The upper half of the first is occupied with the praises of Shiva and Gauri. The lower half contains the names of the headman of Kirgrama and of the builder with the date in the hill cycle of Samvat 80. Two brothers, Manyuka and Ahuka sons of Sidha, have been described as the builders of the temple. The name of the ruling of Kirgrama is recorded as Lakshman Chandra.

The second Prashasti opens with the praise of Ganesha and Mahadeo. This is followed by praise of Jayach Chandra, the reigning king of Jalandhra and his Vassal, Rajnaik Lakshman Chandra with the names of latter's ancestors.

On the basis of the date in the Lokkala Samvat Sir A. Cunningham has arrived at the figures 726 of the Saka era, or equivalent 804 A.D.

The local traditions, no doubt, say that the present temple is the seventh restoration. But even if this be so why should it be assumed that the last restoration is of later date than 804 A.D.

Most of the people who ascribe the temple a date later than 804 A.D. argue that if it had been standing in 1008 A.D. when Mahmud Ghazanavi invaded Nagarkot, broke the idol and temple of the Vajreshwari Devi and looted its wealth, the bloody hands of the iconoclast would not have spared the Baijnath temple as well. But to believe that Mahmud Ghazanavi broke the Baijnath temple and it was restored in 1204 A.D. is to overtry a guess-work. Abu Rihan, meticulous in his description of the Nagargot invasion nowhere mentions the razing of the Baijnath temple to the ground. The facts is that the fame of enormous riches treasured by the Hindu rajas of Kabul attracted the free looter to invade Nagarkot. No such temptation was, however, held out by the Baijnath temple. It can, therefore be safely concluded that the temple was built in 804 A.D. and it existed when Mahmud Ghaznavi invaded Nagarkot.

HISTORICAL IMPORTANCE

The Prashasti have a great importance from historical stand point. Unlike many ancient temples of India, the builders of the Baijnath temple have not left us guessing as to who built it and when they built it. The Prashastis throw a search light on many aspects such as social moral, religious and political life of the people though of a small tract of territory, yet of a period of which we have no other information available with us.

We come to know from the Prashastis that Kangra was known as Trigarto even, at least, upto the beginning of the ninth century and that is was still being ruled by the Katoches as is evident from the names of Jaya Chandra and Lakshman Chandra. The Katoches of Kangra bear the family name of " Chandra" because they are Chandravansi Rajputs. The first mention of Trigarta is found in Mahabharata in which it is stated that its Raja Susaram Chandra who is considered to be the founder of Katoch dynasty took part in the Great War on the side of Kurvas.

It appears that the people enjoyed a measure of independence in all spheres of life. They were free to a mass as much wealth as they could. Defraying the expediture on the construction of such a big temple by two Baniya brothers shows that they might have been earning large profits by trading with far flung areas.

That the people were religious minded and munificent is apparent from the donations made to the temple according to the Prashastis. The achievement in the finearts of the times is demonstrated by the elegant sculpture and superb architecture of the temple and also by fine style of composition of the Prashastis. The architects and the poet all belonged to Trigarta.

Centuries have rolled on since Prashastis were composed.Time tends to change everything old. But the Baijnath Temple sands in spite of revanges of the Time. It has withstood the earthquake of 1904 A.D. which wrought havoc in many part of Kangra District. (Condensed)

JAYANTI DAS NAG

BALAJI TEMPLE IN RAJASTHAN

A magnificent south Indian style Balaji temple, complete with imposing temple towers, has come up in Sajjangarh in Rajasthan, some, 300 km from the pink city of Jaipur.

Ideally located near the Sajjangarh Railway and Bus stations, the temple, built in granite and marble, bids fair to become a major centre of attraction.

Sculptors, craftsmen, artisans and architects from the north and the south worked shoulder to shoulder for long months in raising this splendid edifice for the Lord of the seven Hills whose temple in Triputi draws the biggest concourse of devotees from all over India during all seasons.

The consecration of the main deities in the Rajasthan temple- Sri Venkatachalapati (Balaji) with Devi Padmavati and Sri Andal (Goda) on either side, carved in black stone and installed in the garbhagriha made of shimmering Italian marble - was held on February 21, 1994.

The ceremony, known as ' kumbhabhishekam' began on February 11 as part of which Vedic Pandits performed several Yajnas, and other elaborate rituals, watched by thousands of devotees. The atmosphere reverberated, for days together, with the recitation of krishna Yajurveda mantras and the sacred text of Divya Prabandha, famed as Tamil Veda.

The imposing temple towers, Gopurams, rising high into the sky with their exquisitely sculpted details, seem to beckon devotees from all directions to come to the Lord, dissolving all their differences in the greatest of all solvents, Bhakti.

The walls of the temple are embellished with eye catching panels depicting scenes from the Ramayana and **Dasavatara,** the ten incarnations of Vishnu.

A sea of humanity turned up on the temple consecration day, and the participation of a large number of Sikhs, Muslims, Jains and others was a tribute to the essential unity of Indian Culture.

The **"Utsavamurtis"**idols taken out during festivals wrought in *Panchaloha* (gold, silver,copper, brass and iron) were carried in a procession in a tastefully decorated vehicle, to the accompaniment of Nadaswaram and various musical instruments of the north.

Rajasthani women, attired in multi-coloured dress inlaid with mirror lace work, and gracefully carrying on their heads **decorated kalasas** (pots) topped with a coconut, and caparisoned elephants with their slow gait, lent additional charm to the procession.

The Balaji temple, which will be a new landmark in Rajasthan is the result of the devotion and philanthropy of the Sohanlal Jajodia family.

SMT. LAKSHMI KANNAN

BALAMURALI KRISHNA (1930-)

Balamurali Krishna was born in a family of musicians in a village in Andhra Pradesh. His father, Pattabiramayya, played the flute, violin and Veena and his mother, Suryakantamma was an excellent veena player. Balamurali took to such instrument as the Violin, Viola, Khanjira, Veena and Mridangam with ease. Giving his first concert at the age of eight, he became an enormously popular artiste by the time he was 15.

With songs composed in all the 72 melakarta ragas, Balamurali has enriched Carnatic music with varnams, kritis, javalis, devotionals and thillanas, which together number more than 400. He is the State Musician of Tamil Nadu and Andhra Pradesh, the Asthana Vidwan of Tirumala Tirupati Devasthanam, Sringeri Peetam and Adivyadhi Hara Baktha Anjaneya Swami Temple, Nanganallur. Some of the new ragas credited to him are Mahati, Smukham, Trisakthi, Omkari and Rohini. He also innovated the tala system by introducing new principles. His greatest asset, however, is his vibrant, wide-ranged, magnetic voice over which he has perfect control in all the three octaves. With his crystal clear enunciation of the Sahitya (lyric), the buoyant quality of his everfresh voice, and unpredictable swara-combination which flows with impressive ease, Balamurali has mesmerised audiences all over the country and abroad. Crowned by the Padma Vibhushan, the other awards bagged by him include the national award for the best music director for Madhavacharya (1987) and best playback singer for Hamsa Geetha.

BALASARASWATI, T.

(b. 1918)- vocalist : Karnataka; dancer, Bharatanatyam; studied with Kandappa Pillai, Chinnaiah Naidu, Vedantam Lakshmi Narasimha Sastry; received Sangeet Natak Academi Award for Bharatanatyam (1955), Padma Bhushan (1957), hon. doctorate of Rabindra Bharati University (1964); dance recital tours, Japan (1961), USA (1962), Edinburgh Music Festival (1963), Europe, USA (1965); conducted Bharatanatyam Summer School in San Francisco under auspices of drama Sarabendra Bhupala Kuravanji ; publication, Bharatnatyam (collaboration with V. Raghavan) ; Director, School of Dance, Madras Music Academy.

BALKRISHNA RAGHUNATH DEODHAR : A MUSICOLOGIST

Balkrishna Raghunath Deodhar, Padmashri, was born on September 18, 1901, at Miraj (then a princely State in the old Bombay presidency) in a highly respected family of Sanskrit scholars. His grandfather, pandit Vishnushastri, was a great Sanskrit scholar and a highly respected Sanskrit teacher. The then doyen of Hindustani classical musicians, Pandit Balkrishnabuva Lchalkaranjikar, used to direct his " Brahmin" disciples to Vishnushastri Deodhar to learn Sanskrit. Young Balkrishna was one of them.

Many members of the family of Deodhars dies in the severe plague epidemic of 1903, but little Balkrishna survived as he was destined to become a great musicologist.

The next door neighbour of Deodhar family at Mirja was one Sakhdeo family. Antaji and Bhikaji Sakhdeo were brothers. Antaji himself was a good singer and the also used to play the Sitar. Bhikaji used to play tabla. Once young Balkrishna attended a musical mehfil of the well-known musician, Abdul Karim Khan. He heard this mehfil with rapt attention. He tried to imitate Abdul Karim Khan's style with remarkable success. This was noticed by Antaji Sakhdeo and he gave initial lessons in music to Balkrishna.

Balkrishna took further lessons from Pandit Vinayakbuva Patwardhan with whom he came to Mumbai. He became, in Mumbai, a full timedisciple of Pandit Vishnu Digamber Palusakar. (The opera House Chowk in Mumbai has been renamed now as Pandit Vishnu Digamber Palusakar Chowk). Deodhar, while learning music, gardually also obtained his Bachelor of Arts Degree of the Mumbai University. He had, by this time, studied the Western style music also. Deodhar thus acquired a good deal of proficiency in both the styles of music, Hindustani as well as the Western.

It was in 1925 that Pandit Deodhar established the Deodhar's school of Indian Music which is now at Opera House, not very far away from the Bharatiya Vidya Bhavan. The school has now completed seventy-five years of its fruitful existence. The school has been imparting instruction in all the three branches of Sangeet Kala, namely, Music (Gaayan), instrumental music (Vaadan) and dance (Nartan) to thousands of students. Many students appear for the different examinations held by the Akhil Bhartiya Gandharv Mahavidyalaya and the school gives them coaching for this purpose. Many of them have acquired well-deserved reputation as musicians. The most famous disciple of Pandit Deodhar is Pandit Kumar Gandharv.

Some other well-known disciples of Deodharji are Hirabai Badodekar, Saraswati Rane, Manik Verma and Ashok Ranade.

How was Pandit Deodhar as a teacher? In the olden times, a music teacher (Guru) generally used to be a hot-tempered, whimsical person who would teach his disciple only when he is in a good mood and at his sweet will. And for that, in return, the disciple was required to serve the teacher. In case of any doubt the disciple dare not ask any question of his teacher. That would be construed as arrogance on the part of the disciple. But Deodharji was altogether a very different Guru. While teaching his students, he sought to maintain an atmosphere of freedom. Any student could talk to him freely to get his doubts cleared.

Pandit Deodhar, in 1947, started a journal called *"Sangeet kala vihar"* devoted to Sangeet. This publication contains scholarly articles written by prominent personalities on sangeet and allied subjects.

Pandit had visited several foreign countries including the United States of America. He studies in America the art and science of voice culture which would improve and regulate the human voice. He propagated this method successfully in India.

Many honours were conferred on Deodharji. He was Dean of the Music Faculty of the Banaras Hindu University and the Head of the Music Department of the Vanasthali University (Rajasthan). The Akhil Bharatiya Gandharva Mahavidyalaya conferred on him the honorary doctorate *"Sangeet Mahamahopadhyaya"*. The Government of India awarded him the fellowship of the Sangeet Natak Academy and also conferred on him very prestigious title " Padmashri".

Pandit Deodhar passed away on March 10, 1990 when he was 90. The Deodhar's School of Indian Music, established by him 75 years ago and which is still going strong, is a living monument to his memory. The chowk at Sukh Sagar near Opera House where the Deodhar's School of Indian Music is situated is now renamed is " Principal B.R.Deodhar chowk"

Principal Deodhar is one of the greatest Musicologists of the 20th century. As we celebrate his birth centenary, we remember our " Deodhar Master" and " Kaka".

SHRI SHRINIVAS B. BELVI

BANI

Bani, a small verdant village, some 215 kms away from Jammu, nestles at an attitude of 4,320 feet. What makes the people of Bani exceptional is their attitude to life. A mela, as a celebration of life, is held almost every month. Song and dance invoke love and laughter, there are no sad songs in Bani. This happy go lucky attitude is reflected in their personal relationship as well. An average resident can marry upto six or seven times. According to sociologists, one reason is that the first marriage occurs both the bride and groom are married at a very young age. After a few years as the girl matures both physically and emotionally her husband in the same group is still immature. She then usually succumbs to the charms of an elder man. The divorce proceedings are unique. A forked twig is found and two concerned parties pull from each end in front of the elders. Muslim divorces follow the normal Islamic patterns. It is always sought for by the woman and usually when another suitor is involved. He has to pay the ex-husband what he had spent on obtaining his wife and an additional amount to accout for inflation. The economy of Bani till today works on the barter system. Largely a self sufficient village the inroads and kind of currency has made it limited and used for dealing with the outside world. The household economy, which is the basis for the general economy, is contributed to more by the woman than the man of the house, which is one of the reasons why a woman calls a shots in the house.
(Summarised)

ARCHANA JAHAGIRDAR

BARODA MUSEUM AND PICTURE GALLERY, BARODA

Government sponsored; has art treasures, archaeological and numismatical collections, modern Indian paintings, objects of industrial art, Egyptian and Asian remains, specimens of European civilisation, etc., publishers bulletin.

References

Dvivedi, V.P., Brief History of Museums in India, New Delhi, 1969,

Patel, H.S., Directory of Cultural Organisations in India, New Delhi, 1975.

Sivaramamurthy, C., Directory of Museums in India, Delhi, 1959, W

World of Learning, London, 1972.

BARODEKAR, HIRABAI

(b. 1905)- Vocalist; Hindustani, Khayal of Kirana gharana, Marathi stage songs; studied with Behare Wahid Khan and Suresh Babu Mane; concert tours, East Africa (1948), China (1935); disc recordings.

Reference

Sangeet Natak Akademi, Who's Who of Indian Musicians.

BARVE, MANAHAR G.

(b. 1910) - Vocalist and instrumentalist: Hindustani, Khayal of Gwalior gharana; plays various (Indian) instruments; studied with Ganpatrao Gopalrao Barve; disc recordings; concert tour, Burma (1923), Sri Lanka (1926).

Reference

Sangeet Natak Akademi, Who's Who of Indian Musicians.

BASKETRY FROM PITHORAGARH

The exquisite Indian handicrafts are marked by a rich heritage, which dates back to primeval times. The traditional forms and symbols of each region bear a unique stamp of individuality. Passed down through generations, these artistic skills have been painstakingly kept alive. Rural and hill crafts are but an eloquent evidence of its vibrant tradition. Through a wide range of fascinating Products, blending beauty and utility, the artisans express their artistic and aesthetic aspirations.

The basketry of Pithoragarh, north west of Uttar Pradesh in the Kumaon Hills, is marked by a stamp of exclusivity, both in the raw material used and in the execution of forms. A young graduate of the National Institute of Design, Ambar Agnihotri recently prepared a research project on the study of basketry items in Pithoragarh district. He extensively toured the hilly terrains of this region at an altitude ranging from 2000 to 8000 metres above sea level. Says Agnihotri, " The region, particularly its upper tracts, is inaccessible because of steep slopes, climbs and thick jungles. These are infested with wild animals. " Agnihotri had close interaction with a large number of artisans of basketry, a dying art which has been partially revived in recent years through several Government and Voluntary organisations' schemes.

The tough, inaccessible terrian, which accounts for 32 percent of the total area of Uttar Pradesh, is punctuated by small and scantity populated village. These are cut off from one another and this, observes Agnihotri, imparts distinctive and varied styles of basketry which change every five Kilometers.

The raw material used in basketry is Ringaal Reed, found in abundance in the region. Agnihotri regrets that in recent years, young people from the region started showing dwindling interest in this traditional basketry craft. They migrated to plains in search of jobs, creating a situation polpularly described as " Money Order Economy".

Fortunately, organisations like OXFAM, Himalayan study Circle, the Handloom and Handicrafts Export Corporation, Mahila Haat and Gram Swarajya Mandal have been able to revive the dying art of basketry. Their plans have made a notable contribution to save a somewhat desperate situation. They have enrolled young and trained designers who have aptitude and toughness to work in this region.

A wide network of marketing centres has been set up by these organisations which has proved very helpful. There is a strong need for a well-equipped craft training centre to enlist and train young artisans. It will be beneficial to provide them innovative design inputs, while continuing the incorporation of local raw material and traditional techniques.

SHEFALI SAGGAR

'BASOHLI'
GITA GOVINDA

A TRIUMPH IN COLOUR

Among the most exalted expressions of the spirit of religion in the art of India is a set of paintings of the Gita Govinda from the Punjab hills, referred to generally by scholars as the 'Basohli' Gita Govinda. In this extensive set are illustrated with a rare depth of passion and understanding the mystic verses of the poet from Bengal, Jayadeva, who wrote in the twelfth century the last among the truly great **KAVYAS** of Sanskrit literature. The paintings succeed at places not only in capturing the mood of devotion, they also evoke the feeling of rythm of cadence that there is in the poem. Pictorially, they have been described as " a triumph in colour", as possessing " the intensity of mystic fervour". " Before a dark blackcloth", say Banett and Gray, describing the paintings, " lit by glimmering trees and a thin line of white sky the figures of Krishna and his lovers pose and cluster with grave, intent faces, as if arrested in the performance of some elaborate masque. The muted landscape and the glint of the dark green beetles' wings give an air of evening to the most successful pages."

The set is extensive and runs into more than a hundred leaves, and it is dispersed over several collections, private and public, spread all over the World. But it was the disco very by the late N.C. Mehta of the colophon of the set which created a great deal of excitement and, later, controversy. For the colophon in

Sanskrit mentions date which was first interpreted by Mehta as A.D. 1830 and later corrected by him to A.D. 1730. The verse in the colophon carried a slightly difficult syntax and was capable of being interpreted differently. Two names were clearly given in the verse, those of Malini and Manaku, and the controversy generally was on the point whether Malini or Manaku was the name of the lady patron for whom this set of paintings of the Gita Govinda had been executed. It was suggested by some scholars that Manaku was in fact the name of the artist who had executed this set of paintings, and Malini that either his patron or the meter in which the verse was composed. Other suggested almost exactly the opposite of this. Then the complications were added to by the discovery of precisely the same colophon in Sanskrit on one of the sheets of the set of illustrations to the Gita Govinda which was in the collection of the Maharaja of Tehri Garwal. This set stylistically could only be of a later date and in an obviously different hand, but by having the same colophon it did not make things very much easier for the art historian.

The matter seems to have closed with the publication of Dr. M.S. Randhawa's Kangra Paintings of the Gita Govinda in which W.G.Archer has dealt with brilliance and insight with the problem, and concluded by saying that Manaku cannot be taken to be anything else except the name of the artist of this set of paintings. The dates of this Manaku are not ascertainable with any degree of exactitude, but are fairly indicated by the fact that he was the elder brother of Nainsukh whose paintings of Balwant Singh of Jammu are dated and who is, thus placed in the forties of the eighteenth century. Manaku, being the elder of the two brothers, thus fits with perfect ease into this date, A.D. 1730, which appears on this set of paintings.

GULER NOT BASOHLI

The words " Basohli style" are, applied very loosely to paintings coming from regions very wide apart and are used mostly as synonymous with the " primitive" or early style of painting in the Punjab hills. The colophon of this set does not mention Basohli nor is there anything in the circumstances of the find of this set which should suggest a Basohli origin. If on the other hand we find paintings in this style in other areas also, the insistence on linking this set with the state of Basohli seems a little misplaced. The set could come from any of the other states of the hills, like Guler. Guler appears to have been an important centre of art even earlier than the time of Raja Goverdhan Chand with whose name the beginnings of Guler painting are generally associated. As early as A.D. 1703, during the period of Dalip Singh, the father of Goverdhan Chand, we find an explicit references to apinters living in Haripur, the principal town of the state of Guler. Added to this is the important fact that Manku and his family belonged without any question to Guler. There is in fact even an inscription in the hand of Majaku himself which ocurs in a register of pilgrims with a family of priests at Hardwar. This inscription is dated S. 1893 (A.D. 1736) and states clearly that Manaku came to Hardwar in that year from Guler. If Manaku was living in Guler in A.D. 1736, six short years after the Gita Govinda was painted, it raises a strong presumption in favour of Guler being taken as the place from which this set of paintings comes.

Dr. Coomaraswamy spoke of Jammu and Kangra as the two major centres of paintings in the hills because these were the two most powerful states politically in this region. Hence all early works could be neatly designated as Basohli and all late works as Kangra. The variations of the style may therefore be regarded essentially in a geographical context. Thus styles of painting could be associted with particular states rather than with particular artists or families. It is with references to this matter of styles that the Gita Govinda of A.D. 1730 needs to be looked at very carefully. In this set an important document of Pahari painting one finds coming to terms by the Pahari artist with the arrival of new influences from the plains.

While the Kangra style appears as a product of a process of evolution of style in the hills. One could in fact speak of a process of the adjustment by the Pahari painter to paintings of the Mughal style, elements from which he kept on borrowing over a period of time. The 'Basohli' Gita Govinda is a set which makes important departures in the direction of naturalism and, it affords avidence of the Pahari painter incorporating new elements into his work. It is possible to demostrate in fact that in this et, cast as it unsuspectingly is in the general style of the early period, the artist was making several experiments. For a traditional artist bound to inherited belief, this was a bold thing to do, but he went about it with some resolution considering that in painting after painting we find formulae or devices used which are new to painting in the hills.

RENDERING OF DASAVATARA

The set of paintings, generally believed to be belonging to the Gita Govinda theme, are prefixed ten paintings of the ten avataras of Vishnu. This is scrupulously correct from the point of view of the illustration of the Kavya of Jayadeva because he prefixes to his poetry of the love of Radha and Krishna a hymn in praise of the ten incarnations. The paintings of the avatars are exactly in the same format and manner and can only be regarded as a part of the set. What is a very interesting, and hitherto unnoticed, is that the painting shows Vishnu seated inside a loggia with the poet Jayadeva standing with folded hands and bent head in front of the Lord. On the grey wall at the back are drawn in an exteremely fine hand and in small squares of not more than an inch by an inch, sketches of all the ten avataras that Jayadeva sang of and that the artist of this set painted.

NEW CONVENTIONS: NATURALISM

In this set and one could draw attention to certain elements and conventions which be-speak of a spirit or influence which did not belong to the early art of the hills from the seventeenth century. The most noticeable thing of course is that in the faces of the figures, more especially in the eyes, is now a greater of naturalism, of a softness that is wrought by the delicate shading that the artist employs. The eyes are large but have lost a little of that forecity or predatoriness which characterized the paintings of the Rasamanjari from Basohli or the iconic paintings of so many manifestations of the Devi. The whole aspect of these paintings is in fact gentler that those that belonged to the predecessors of this et of paintings.

It is several new conventions, in this set. The treatment of mountains, for example. In a painting showing

Krishna in a grove with a group of gopis, in a painting in other words set in the same locale in which the entire poem is set, are introduced, rather redundantly in the background, high up and just below the horizon, some continuing wavy forms in mauve and green, that are the artist's manner of indicating mountains in the distance. These mountains look remarkably like the Persian style, dry-rock-piled-upon-dry-rock mountains which are so characteristic of Mughal painting.

EXPERIMENTS WITH A NEW TECHNIQUE

The foliage in a large number of the painting of the Gita Govinda shows a new tendency towards enrichment. The trees which in earlier paintings are almost like neat diagrammatic forms, generally isolated from each other and sharply defined outlines, acquire a new aspect in these paintings of the Gita Govinda by the addition of an occasional flowering creeper entwined around the trunk of the tree or of a spray of flowers that suddenly shoots forth from the crown. The effect is of a new gaiety and the trees lose a little of their ascetisism as it were in the paintings.

In another painting we find a very interesting architectural detail. Two sharp diagnols of walls are introduced meeting each other at right angles in the centre of the picture. A door opens out of the distant wall, and is cut by the wall in front with the aim clearly of creating the feeling of depth in space. This introduction of the walls outside the loggia is highly uncommon and, like the mountains noticed above, is deliberate, There are other matters, like, the introduction of short sweeping curves is the background separated from each other to mark the gentle undulation of the earth, or the highly distinctive manner of treating water, or the little shoots of grass in tiny tufts on the ground.

The Gita Govinda of 1730 becomes then, much more than a charming set of illustrations to a great poem; it becomes the vehicle for the introduction of newelements in the contained world of Pahari painting, and must be seen as such in the context of the history of Pahari painting, for much that followed flowed from the absorption of the new spirit seen in evidence here. (Condensed)

References

1. Kari Khandalavala, Pahari Miniature Painting. (Bombay, 1958)
2. Douglas Barrett and Basil Gray, Painting of India (Lausanne, 1963).
3. M.S. Randhawa's Kangra Paintings of the Gita Govinda.

B. N. GOSWAMY

BATUKAMMA

As in most parts of India, the month of October is considered to be the harbinger of festivity in Telangana region in the state of Andhra Pradesh. It is also the season when flowers of myriad variety blossom in full bloom on this plateau, spreading their fragrance far and wide. And what nicer way can there be to display the beneficial and generous aspects of nature than in a conical mound of bright coloured scented flowers:

Yes, that is how the people of Telangana worship mother nature with profusion of flowers and songs. This indeed is the *Batukamma Panduga* (festival) which the womenfolk here celebrate for seven days during *Dussera* with great religious fervour and piety.

Generally, Dussera is an auspicious occasion for the Indian women to display their artistic acumen. Be it a Gujrati **"Garba"** or Bengali **" Kali Puja",** this is an opportunity when the art instincts in women are given a free rein.

According to local legend, Batukamma festival is associated with the revival of goddess Uma (popularly known as Parvati, consort of Lord Shiva), who is thought to have stepped into a sacrificial fire over a tiff with her father. This festival of Batukamma is an attempt by her devotees to retrieve her from the ashes. Women make an image of the deity with turmeric paste and worship it with profuse decoration of flowers arranged in a bell shape-i.e. the Batukamma, to be precise- representation of the goddess herself.

For seven days, both young and old women sing and dance, glorifying the saga of goddess Gauri (another name for Parvati) and praying for the health and prosperity of their homes.

This festival is at is most colourful at the historic Bhadrakali lake in Warangal-the cultural capital of Andhra, where thousands of women dressed in rustling silks and decked in all their traditional finery converge, carrying Batukammas of various sizes with flowers of different hues. The songs of Batukamma have a folk tinge and possess an intrinsic musical dharm of their own. They are very popular with farm workers too who sing these songs (in chorus) while harvesting the crop. Thus Batukamma can also be seen essentially as a harvest festival.

Finally, at the end of the festival when singing and dancing is over, Batukammas are immersed in the waters of the lake-to be resurrected again the next year.

RAMCHANDER PENTUKER

BEGUM AKHTAR
PEERLESS GHAZAL QUEEN

A cherished wish of many renowned singers and performing artistes has been to leave this world while pursuing successfully their chosesn field of activity and while still riding on a high wave of popularity. It is, however, rare that such a wish is actually realized.

Begum Akhtar, the legendary ghazal queen of India, was amongst the selected few who had this wish fulfilled on October 30, 1974 - just a week after al stations of All India Radio had relayed her last *Radio Sangeet Sammelan* (Radio Music concert) listened to avidly by her countless fans throughout the Country. Even in her last moments, when the end came suddenly, she was engaged in planning to honour more of her singing commitments.

In the aforementioned swan-song concert of hers, which was indeed a fitting climax to her distinguished singing career, *ghazals* and other forms of popular light classical music burst forth from her gifted throat with an enrapturing exuberance. Her favourite disciple, Shanti Hiranand, as usual, gave her competent vocal support.

Only a few days earlier, Begum Akhtar had recorded a *ghazal* penned by *Kaifi Azmi* with such poignancy and emotional intensity that it appeared she had a premonition of the approaching end.

Some weeks earlier, she had suffered a mild heart attack and had been advised complete rest. But disregarding the well-meant advice of her physician, family and friends she went on to accept a string of singing assignments, asserting that she was not afraid of death and that she in fact nursed an ambition to die while singing beautifully.

Even in her sixties she enjoyed such an enviable popularity and the concomitant demand for her singing that she continued to be booked heavily and had to fly and hop from city to city to honour her numerous commitments.

She was born at Faizabad on October 7, 1910 (some reckon the year as 1914) and at the age of eight years started learning classical music from Ustad Imdad Khan of Patna. That highbrow teacher, instead of introducing her to the rudiments of classical music, took her straight to advanced lessons of intricate *raagas.* The young novitiate, however, found those lessons dry and difficult to learn and contemplated an escape from them. The teacher reprimanded her whenever she was caught singing *thumri* and *dadra* (lighter forms of popular music) in preference to what he sought to teach her.

Help came providentially when at that time she happened to listen to the singing of the much-admired Chandabai of Hyderabad at a touring theatre visiting Faizabad. She was so much fascinated by the style and quality of Chandabai's singing that she immediately decided to opt once and for all for light music rather than for the awesome and cumbersome *raagas.*

Thereafter, she learnt light classical music from Ustad Ata Mohammad Khan of Patiala and went on to sing beautiful *ghazal, thumris* and *dadras.*

Around that time, one evening, a theatrical company in Calcutta organized a musical conference. Several well-known singers had promised to perform at this event but failed to make their appearance. In such a challenging situation when *Bibli* (Begum Akhtar's childhood pet name) sang a few *ghazals* and *dadras,* the large, knowledgeable audience greeted her with thunderous appalause. Nationalist leader Sarojini Naidu, who was present in the audience that evening, was so impressed with her performance that she went backstage to congratulate and encourage her personally and later presented to her a hand-spun *Khadi* saree.

Years before the arrival of radio, television and tape-recorders in India, the gramophone records of Akhtari Faizabadi (her original name) had become popular in the Country. She recorded her first *ghazal* for the Megaphone Record Company of Calcutta in December, 1919, and followed it up with scores of other *ghazals, thumris* and *dadras.*

For some time, she also acted and sang in films such as *Ek Din Ki Badshahi, Mumtaz Begum, Naseeb Ka Chakkar, Roti and Thokar.* She also playbacked some songs for *Ehsaan, Daana Paani* and Satyajit Ray's *Jalsaghar.*

Deeply impressed by contemporary celebrities like Jaddan Bai, Malikajan and Gauharjan, she decided to dedicate the rest of her life to music and started devoting an assiduous twelve hours a day to her *riyaaz* (a musician's regular concentrated practice). She gave up working for films for good and responding to invitations, and sang in the courts of Hyderabad and Rampur. Around that time, Ustad Wahid Khan of Lahore formally accepted her as his pupil and worked to further mould and tone her style.

After her marriage to Ishtiaq Ahmed Abbasi, a well-known barrister of Lucknow, she stopped singing altogether in deference to her husband's wish, and settled down as a housewife. In the late 1940s, after nearly a five-year hiatus, she recorded a song at the Lucknow studio of All India Radio. This was at the coaxing of a family friend, L.K. Malhotra, a producer with the All India Radio, Lucknow. The song was recorded in the presence of only the instrumental accompanists and after the assurance that the recording would not go on air.

When the recording was played back to her, she was so emotionally charged that torrents of tears fell from her eyes and the suppressed longing for music spurted back. Theresfter, there was no bar on her singing. Her husband also supported her because after her mother's death, when she became hysterical with grief, the doctors recommended singing as an apt outlet for her pent-up emotions and as a sure step against any further damage to her health. Thus, her glorious comeback to singing was made and from then there was no looking back but only proceeding further with more and more of consummate and soulful renderings. Her fame touched new heights. She was honoured by the Sangeet Natak Akademi and awarded a Padma Shree by the President of India.

In December, 1994, the Begum Akhtar Academy of Ghazal (BAAG) organized a commemorative function in her honour. The Government of India issued a postage stamp to mark the occasion. Again, in 1999, on her 25th death anniversary, rich tributes were paid to her by her discilpes Shanti Hiranand, Rita Ganguli and Anjali Banarjee.

Begum Akhtar's repertoire which constitutes a veritable treasure trove includes such vintage numbers as "*Zara dheere se bolo*" (Speak in a hushed tone), " *oyaliya, mat kar pukar*" (Don't wail, O Koyal:) and " *Deewana banaana hai to deewana bana de*" (Make me mad if madden me you must).

She lent her richly-timbered and sonorous voice to several *ghazals* of distinguished Urdu poets such as Ghalib, Momin, Jigar, Dagh, Firaq, Faiz Ahmed Faiz, Shakeel Badayuni, Kaifi Azmi and Sudarshan Fakir.

Among the outstanding ghazals rendered by her in the second span of her singing career is " *Ae mohabbat tere anjaam pe rona aaya*" (O Love, your fate has made me cry). At one of her last private performance she sang, "*Mohabaat Karne wale Kam na honge, teri mehfil mein lekin hum na honge* (There will be no dearth of thosewho love you but alas; I shall be no longer present in your soirees). This was virtually an involuntary flash-forward of her soul's presentimen of the Final Exit.

B. M. MALHOTRA

BELL METAL BEAUTIES

Bastar produces certain exquisite works of art which include Kosa sarees, the best of its kind, and handicrafts. Bell metal toys and decorative pieces from Bastar are not only intricately designed, they also tell a story of their culture and lifestyle. They are fine pieces of art but they are finished in such a manner that they carry a raw look. Bell metal is an alloy of brass, copper and lead with nearly 75% of brass in it.

The process of moulding this alloy is quite intricate and even amazing. It is called lostwax process. Wax is available in abudance here and is used to carve out the design of the product. Initially soil is used to make a mould, thereafter beewax in the form of thread is used to make design on the mould. Molten alloy is then poured into the mould and allowed to cool for ten to fifteen days. Once the alloy sets in the mould, it is broken and soil removed. And what you have is a beautiful piece of art.

The favourite designs include the Muriya drummers, representing the local community. Animal figures are yet another popular theme. One of the most attractive pieces is of a warrior on a horseback. It is different indeed. Not only this, they also make utility items like jewellery box, ash trays, candle stands etc.

Ranging from extermely small pieces of bell metal their height can go upto nearly four feet and upto two to three feet horizontally. They may weigh as much as thirty Kilograms or perhaps only a few grams:

COL. K. J. CHUGH

BENGAL- NAGPUR RAILWAY AT PURI PRESERVING THE RAJ NOSTALGIA

Where the sun's flight is caged in an erotic art temple; where the silvery waves bemoan to the moon; where the temple lives in every heart; where words become whispers of pleasure, there in a time warp is eated the Bengal Nagpur Railway (BNR) hotel at Puri, on India's eastern coast.

It is a majestic structure. The facade, one could notice, was definitely colonial. Soft light lit up the garden. At vantage points stood voluptuous stone figurines in welcome, some displaying a dance pose or beating a drum. The rich Indian sculpture as flourished in this Mahanadi belt celebrated the female form with a Prominent bust, curaceous figure, rounded things and speaking eyes. In this part of the Country, she is always exhibiting a dance form, and as a rule never found engaged in mundane, meaningless activity. The higher are was closer to man than life itself.

Unfolding the yellowed powdery pages of history one discovers that this hotel was earlier titled Ashworth Villa. Dr. Elmes, the owner, sold the estate to the Company in 1922 for Rs. 50,000. BNR hotel opened with Mr. Stoner as its first British manager. Capt. Arnist A Fisk and Maj. A.J. Gowan followed. The salubrious climate and exciting atmosphere popularised it soon as a place to rejuvenate and enjoy its solitude. Elusive tranquillity, it brought near. No wonder it has now been declared as national heritage.

Being Part of history the BNR could not evade the fallout of world War-II. Chandipur-on-sea, on the same eastern coast, was bombed by Japanese. The fear of destruction gripped the place and the iron gates met to say 'no' to tourists. The British army officers enchated by the beauty of the place borrowed the BNR from the Campany and opened it as a resort for army officers above the rank of Captain. Only the brave could afford a holiday; The world War - II on the wane brought Indian holiday makers back to the hallowed precincts.

The building has a long verandah, curving as it progresses. Wide British arches on the front face mark its appearance. The top portion of each arch is covered with square glasses in a frame. The lower has a wooden perforated balustrade. This arrangement permits an ample share of light and wind, but at the same time safeguards against a direct sun or rain hitting a person. The structure was planned and designed with care. There extended verandahs stand as projections. Two are in use as relaxation canopies while the third is included in the dining room. As one sits in the projected verandah, one wonders whether the hustle and bustele of life is worthwhile at all. The strong breeze surely blows away the worries associated with existence. One feels as light as a bird in the wind. Here if one sits late in the evening, one hears the voices of sea becoming clearer as the waves run up to the rising moon.

The reception lounge is remarkable for its absolutely imposing British presence. It seems to peep from the pages of an Agatha Christie story, complete with its wooden staircase, ornate iron brackets and a Hercule Poirot hat stand placed two steps from the door, as one enters. Alas, there are no suspense stories to unfold but a taste of lingering romance.

Inside, " The Legend", is stylish, Simplicity combines with a touch of sophistication. The dining hall is divided into three pillared divisions. The front tables are close to the windows and one can see forceful waves leap up in the distance. A prominent attraction is a plastered ethnic presentation of Orissa life and culture. The welcome is represented by the dancer showeing flower petabls, the triumph of life by the robust prancing chariot, and the inherent beauty contained in the movement of life cycle by the procession of men and women in unison.

It is believed that Puri sky has the highest ozone content on the eastern coast of India. And the world famous Jagannath temple of Puri has its imposing presence upon the cityscape. A grandiose 65-metre high temple built in 12th century A.D. in Kalinga style by the Ganga King Chodagangadeva is topped by the circular solid stone mass. Lions frozen in time hold this pinnacle aloft.

Close on hand from BNR are enthralling excursions into the cultural and spiritual force of Mahanadi river belt. It would not be wrong to say that BNR serves as a gateway to witness the centuries old culture upsurge of this region. Konark, the Black Pagoda, now granted a World Heritage status, is just 35 km away. The sun temple, crafted as a chariot of sun god, symbolises the movement of the sun. In its effort to capture the strident force, it is unparalleled.

Dhaulagiri, on the outskirts of Bhubaneswar, some 52 km from Puri is the seat of Santi Stupa built by the

Buddhists. It is the same site where emperor Ashoka in 3rd century B.C. renounced war and bloodshed.

Whether one comes to discover, recuperate, reminisce, re-live the bygone era or just to relax, there is something strangely overpowering about this place; it holds one breathless and smug.

SANDEEP SILAS

BENGALI THEATRE

Bengali theatre, at its precise moment of birth, was more of Russian legacy than an English one. It was a Russian violinist-cum-cultural worker Gerasim Stepanovich Lebedeff who founded the Bengali Theatre at Calcutta to adapt an English play 'The Disguise' into Bengali Kalponik Song- badal and staged it as the first ever Indian proscenium-stage play in India: on 27 November, 1975. Thus was born the Indian theatre at the colonial capital with two other first to its credit: the first use of lyrics from a noted contemporary poet for its music and the first action of female roles by women. No mean achievement indeed;

The wind of English theatre was already blowing: the Play-House (1753), the Calcutta Theatre (1775) under the patronage of Warren Hastings and Sir Eliza Impay, the private Theatre (1789) of the irrepressible Mrs. Bristo and the Whaler Place Theatre (1797) for the British elite without entry for women were all staging vintage English plays with great gusto, - with the Chowringhee Theatre (1813), the Town Hall (1814), the Kiderpore Theatre (1815) and the Dumdum Theatre (1817) to follow.

But the Bengali theatre had its other tools as well struck deep into the indigenous soil. The devotional songs and dances, the ritualistic processions, fairs and festivals, the all-night performances of the thriving folk-theatre Jatra, and the evening soirees of Dhap-Kheur-Panchali-Akhrai were all precursor to the formal stage-setting that came later with the Baboo culture, for both English and Bengali plays.

The nascent cultural scene threw up its next Bengali gem a good 40 years later, - when Vidyasunder by the same lyric-poet Bharatchandra was staged at Calcutta in 1835 with female roles by women again, for a princely sum of Rs. 2 lakhs.

Another score of years- Rater came Abhigyanam Shkuntalam as an adaption from Kalidas's Sanskrit play. Almost simultaneously came the landmark production kulin-kul-Sarvashwa, an original play based on the social problems and the reformation movement- with the great reformer Ishwarchandra Vidyasagar among the appreciative audience. The playwright was Ramanarayan Tarkaratna who had the stellar honour of bringing out a dozen or more plays in the following decades. and being dubbed " Natuke Ramnarayan".

Woomesh Chandra Banerjee, who went on to become a Congress President, played the female role in Kalidas's Vikramorvashi, adapted by Ramnarayan- again 1857. But too many adeptations hurt the sensibility of the poet Michael Madhusudan who produced his mellifluous play Sharmistha (1857), enacted saveral times. Another landmark social- reform play was Bidhava Vivaha (1857) by Umeshchandra Mitra.

This phase was enriched a lot by the Tagore family who not only founded new theatre-halls but also encouraged new plays like adaptations, farce, verse-plays, social satires and epic-based plays, including Michael's Krishnakumari and Ekei ki Bale Sabhyata and a biting social play Naba Natak based on women's conditions and misrule of the Zamindars (Landlords)

Nildarpan, the explosive play of this age, came in 1867 based on the political subjugation by the British over the Indigo-farmers. It created a furore in the society and, by 1872, had introduced the first ever ticketed show (at Rs. 1.00 and paise 50) at the National Theatre. The same playwright Dinabandhu Mitra produced other satires like Jamai Barik and Sadhavar Ekadasi, all of which ushered in a new era for Bengali theatre, along with such stalwarts as Girish Kumar Ghosh and Ardhendusekhar Mustafi. At the suggestion of Michael, women came back to the stage to do female roles.

By 1876, the pyrotechnics of the political plays drew ire from the ruling classes. When the Prince of Wales visited Bengal in the year some members of the local aristocracy welcomed him effusively- a fact greeted with biting sarcasm in the theatre of the day. Play after play was banned by the police and the daring theatre-people retorted with such works as the Police of Piq and ship: to be immediately banned by the Drama Control Ordinance and, later, by the Drama Control Act of 1876. Many play-houses were consequently closed down.

Gopalsundari was one of the first actresses of the time to perform on stage and also happened to be the first woman playwright, Nati Binodini was another greatly telented actress with such a rare versatility that her donning the role of Sri Chaitanya on stage was felicitated by no less a person than Sri Ramakrishna.

A great event of this phase was the arrival of Rabindra Nath Tagore on the Bengali Theatre scene. The newly electrified Emerald Theatre presented his Bouthakuranir Hat and Raja O Rani. Tagore's was a striking presence on stage at the Jorasanko Theatre and, later, at Shantiniketan. Tagore's seminal influence on theatre continued till 1939- with 13 original plays and eight adaptations from his novels and short stories. The other fiery personality who blazed the trail of patriotism on the folk-stage was the writer-singer-actor Mukunda Das at the turn of the century, whose imprisonment for a few years did not dampen his ardour in the least.

In the wake of Bengal partition (1905) and the First World War (1914-18), the patriotic movement was at its peak. Bengal saw the advent of Sisir Kumar Bhaduri, a professor of English literature turnes into a most versatile actor and theatre-director, touched off by Basantaleela (1924) at the Alfred Theatre, presided over by the great patriot Chittaranjan Das and recitation by the rebelpoet Kazi Nazrul Islam. In a span of 38 years of Professional life, Sisir Kumar produced more than 50 plays and led to the contemporary Bengali theatre, as hailed by Tagore. Ahindra Chowdhury as Shah Jehan Manoranjan Bhattacharjee as Valmiki and Tagore himself as Raghupati as well as Jaisingh were some of the unforgettable characterisations of this era.

Three dominant trends were introduced by Tagore and Sisir Kumar. First, the Bengali stage was made accesible to women from the middle and upper middle-class families as distinct from the earlier women from the brothels. Second, in plays like Muktadhara and Raktakarabi, the great gap between the proscenium-stage and the more intimate folk-stage was substanitially reduced. Finally, and specially with Tagore, the liberation of stage-set and stage decoration from the straingling Western realism was achieved with the intervention of painters and sculptors, as in Falguni and Dakghar.

The volcanic eruptions in the Bengali theatre, stocked by the Second World War (1939-45) and fuelled by the great famine of Bengal, Bihar and Orissa (1943-44), saw the setting up of the Indian People's Theatre Association (IPTA) in 1943. The later's Nabanna (1943), based on the tortured, insulted and oppressed masses of Bengal, was a theatre event of the century and repeated many times. In his felicitations Sisir Kumar said " what they have done I could not achieve in my lifetime".

While IPTA continued in full flow for a couple of decades, many powerful theatre groups were formed rallying round some talented directors and actors, 1948 saw one of the best, " Bohurupee" coming up under the baton of Shambhu Mitra, who gave many a memorable production on the Bengali stage: Pathik (1949), Chhera Tarr (1950), Ulukhagra (1950), Char Adhyay (1961), Dashachakra (1952), Raktakarabi (1954), Dakghar (1957), Putulkhela (1958), Bisarian (1961), Raja (1964), Ghare Baire (1974), Pagla Ghora (1975), Malini (1986), Mister Kakatua (1987) and several others. Form Tagore to Ibsen, Sophocles to Eugene Ionesce:Bohurupee staged some of the best plays ever seen. Little Theatre Group under Utpal Dutta also produced some of the finest Bengali plays like the coalmine-based Angar (1959), refugee-centred Titas Ekti Nadir Nam (1963), naval mutiny-oriented Kallol (1965), Barricade and many more.

In the sixties and seventies came Theatre Workshop, Theatre Commune, Chetana, Sayask, Charbak and many other. Emanating from a voice of protest and self-assertion, theatre tried to articulate the common man's joys and despairs, ambitions and frustrations.

The emergence of Group Theatre has been a significant event today when the directors, actors and theatre-workers have formed many groups often transient in existence, but always vibrant in expressing aspirations and conducting experiments. They live outside the professional arena on a show-string budget and survive more on love for theatre than on largesse.

Street Theatre has been another variant often performed, on small play-grounds, street-corners, etc., on an impromptu basis and used for political propaganda, social messages or educational purposes. This has been a direct descendant of Poster Theatre, which flourished in the sixties to eighties. Badal Sircar propagated Third Theatre as a variation of Physical Theatre of Grotowsky and staged them, often based on improvisations, to appreciative audiences.

Professional Theatre has been providing staple fare on the commercial stage with paid artists (unlike the Group Theatre) and has taken an organised shape since the early sixties. Some memorable productions on this stage-often by the Group Theatre directors and actors from the silver screen working on a contract basis-have been Setu, Kshudha, Shyamoli, Saheb Bibi Golam, Anthony Kabial, Namjiban, Manjari, Barbadhu, Nahabat, and others.

Another important event was a through politicising of the folk-form " Jatra" with fares like Lenin Stalin. Hitler, Karl Marx and Utpal Duta's worthwhile contributions like Baishkhi Megh and Rifle to this genre.

The other branches of theatre that have flourished alongside are Mime Theatre under Jogesh Dutta's Padabali, Niranjan Goswami's Indian Mime Theatre; Children's Theatre under Samar Chatterjee and Puppet Theatre under Raghunath Goswami, Suresh Dutt and others.

Bengali theatre has been thriving, in fact, with the whole of India provinding its canvas. Allahabad holds festivals; Lucknow, Bangalore and Bombay have thriving groups and Delhi has been the scene of some of the best Bengali ouvre. What grew as an English legacy has become today the most dominant theatre (alongwith Marathi) of our subcontinent.

UTPAL BANERJEE

BEZBARUA, LAKSHMINATH

Born at Ahatagini in Assam in 1868; started his literary career through his journal Janaki in 1889; married to a descendant of Tagore family; give a fillip to Assamese literature by enriching it with all branches of Belles-Letters like essays, plays, fiction and poetry; author of Assamese national emblem O, Mor Aponam Desh.

References

Barua, B.K., Assamese Literature, Bombay, 1943. Bhuyan, S.K., Studies in the Literature of Asia, Gauhati, 1956. Gokak, V.K., Literature in Modern India, Language, New Delhi, 1957.

Kakati, B., Assamese, Its Formation & Development, 1941. Nagendra, M. (ed.), Indian Literature, Agra, 1959.

BHAGAVATHA MELA

Other classical, semi-classical dance forms are, bhagavatha Mela; performed annual Narasimha Jayanti festival in Melatur village, Tamil Nadu; uses classical gesture language; densely textured Karnatic music accompanied; Venkatarama Sastri (1759-1847), composed, dance-dramas, Telugu language.

BHAKTI

Doctrine of bhakti implies supreme faith, complete devotion and utter surrender to a personal God; cult started in 7th, 8th and 9th centuries A.D. with advent of 12 Nayanar (Saiva) and 63 Alvar (Vaishnava) saints of the Tamil Country (men and women from all walks of life) who went from place to place singing their devotional hymns in worship of their respective deities; best known of the first group were Appar, Sambandha, Sundaramurti and Mannik Vachaka and of the second, Nammalvar, Kulasekhara, Tirumangi and Godal (or Andal) a woman saint; other famous bhakti saints who preached and spread the doctrine were Jnanadev (d. 1296), Ramananda (1360-1470) and his followers, Chaitanya (1485-1534), Tukarama (b. 1608) and Ramakrishna Paramahansa

(1836-1886); bhakti must be unremitting and depends on an intimate, personal association between devogee and deity aided by chanting the latter's praises, hearing its praises, remembering it always and serving it by doing good works in its name; is a special feature of Vaishnavism.

Refrences

Bouquet, A.C., Hindustan, London, 1948.

Otto, R., India's Religion of Grace and Christianity Compared & Constrasted, London, 1930.

Sen, K.M., Hinduism, Penguin Books, 1961.

Sharma, C.A., A Critical Survey of Indian Philosophy, London, 1948.

Shastrey, B.K., The Bhakti Cult in Ancient and Medieval India, Calcutta, 1972.

BHANGRA

Most electrifying sound folk dance, Punjab, male harvest dance, punctuated by song, and on every line, drum thunders, last line, a chorus, taken up by dancers, spring, fellow, shout, gallap, in circle, wiggling shoulder, hips, men any age can join.

BHARATNATYAM

One of the classical forms of Indian dance done to accompaniment of musical instruments; originated in ancient times near Thanjuvur as temple dance of devadasis; usually performed solo; there are many postures, specified in the Bharatnatya Sastra, the Sanskrit treatise on dance; beautiful mudras (hand poses), facial expressions, 32 major hand positions, 12 hand movement, 13 symbolic gestures of the head, 9 of the neck, 9 of the eyeballs, 7 of the eyebrows, 6 of the chin, of the fingers, wrists and arms, etc., and million of minor variations, about 1,000 being described in dance manuals; employing the requisite number of these as well as mime, foot work, rhythm and other minor gestures are enacted, through the dance, carious roles, episodes, themes and stories (usually from the myths and religious legends); by symbolic gesture alone any given idea can be expressed; dancer has to express in dance movement the 9 traditional dramatic moods-passion, heroic sentiment, fear, anger, hatred, tenderness, laughter, amazement and peace; has been set to a classical pattern and purified; requires great technical skill, sense of timing and rhythm, subtle execution, sophistication and high quality.

Refrences

Ambrose, K., Classical Dances & Customs of India, 1950.

Banerji, P., Dance of India, Allahabad, 1960.

Raginidevi, Dance Dialects of India, Delhi, 1972.

Vatsyayan, Kapila, Classical Indian Dance in Literature & the Arts, New Delhi, 1960.

Traditions of Indian Folk Dance, New Delhi, 1976.

BHAVAI DANCES OF RAJASTHAN

Nagaji Jat's interest in dancing, singing was not appreciated by community who turned him out, but gave privilege of forming group of dancers for entertain them. This group, called *Bhavai* ; in which other jats who were interested in singing, dancing joined Nagaji resulting into the creation of a separate community of jat dancers.

Chief characteristics, of Bhavai : is fast speed of dances, extraordinary movements of body; a folk technique with qualities of classical dancing: dances in form of dance dramas; devoid of religious sentiments: themes on daily life of village community; women not allowed to participate ; female roles played by men. Main themes, **Bora and Bori,** depicting humorous caricature of village Bamya, his misery of life ;**Sudras,** life of blind **Sadhu,** romantic temperament, **Lodi Vadi,** life of man with two wives; **Dokri,** ill fate of old woman; **Shankaria,** caricature of village youth making love with young lady; **Bikaji,** life of Bikaji, founder of state of Bikaner **Dhola Maru** eternal love story of Dhola and Maru.

Bhavai dancers move in caravan; visits extended to distant parts of Gujarat, Saurashtra, beckward class people, economically well off; artistically dressed, adorned with gold ornaments; are hospitable, good natured;

Bhavai dance, a professional folk dance; has technical quailties; visit patrons (Yajmans) every year; style influenced by modern life; resorted to cinema tunes, cheap themes.

BHIMA DEVI TEMPLE
KHAJURAHO OF THE NORTH

On the road from Chandigarh to Shimla, a few km beyond Pinjore lies a temple in ruins. Its recent discovery from beneath wild vegetation and debris has unfoilded a 1000-year old temple architecture in Nagar, the northern style. The architectural membranes and sculptures worked out in grey sandstone take this temple close of Khajuraho and Konark group of temples in style and form.

It is the Bhima Devi temple. The scattered remains of the temple bear mute testimony to the vararies of man and nature.

The motif of the male and female locked into one is found in ancient sculptures all over India, be it in Konark, Ellora, Karli or Khajuraho, which particularly stands out in our minds more prominently, probably because there is a profusion of this motif.

Bhima Devi is somewhat different because there is a greater dominance of the icons of Shiva, Vishnu, Brahma, Surya, Ganesh, Ram, Parvati and so on. The amorous sculptures are executed in the niches of the pillars as well as on the friezes of the exterior walls of the temple.

The ornate vertical elements, perhaps balanced by horizontal panels found in the debris, depict the musical instruments such a drums, flute, veena, cymbals and wind instruments. The motifs depict scenes of hunting, feasting and dancing with a pronounced accent on the various aspects of sensual love.

According to Hindu philosophy, the ultimate aim of the human being is to achieve salvation. The erotic carvings are seen not only for what they are, but also as the transition from a worldly sensual plane to an absolute transcendentalism, via a chtharsis, when we look at them perhaps we are seeing not only the 'springs of love and passion' but also a way of liberation, the cessation of desire, ultimate realisation and finally 'Moksha' (salvation).

BRIG. D. M. BAHL

BHIMSEN JOSHI (1922-)

Grural Joshi of Gadag had compiled a Kannada-English dictionary. To a scholar of his stature, it was unacceptable that his son would want to become a *gavaiya* (professional singer). But Bhimsen, even at the age of 10, was sure that all he wanted to do in life was to sing. So he left his home and travelled to Gwalior, where someone directed him to Calcutta. In the culturally inclined city, he served in the household of actor Pahari Sanyal. From there he went to Rampur, where he found a *guru* in Mushtaque Husain Khan. It was during a Harballabh Sammelan that someone said: " Why are you going around the world when the best guru is just miles away from your home?"

The *guru* happened to be Sawai Gnadharva of the Kirana fold. Perhaps because of this eclectic upbringing in music, Bhimsen is considered to have gone beyond the repertoire of his *guru*. Raw energy is the distinguishing feature of both his looks and his voice. Depth, timbre, control, layered with warmth and sensitivity to the lyrics, make Bhimsen's khayal an unforgettable experience.

BHOLE, JYOTSNA

(b.1913) - Vocalist: Hindustani Khyal of Agra, Taurakshan gharanas; stage songs; studied with Khadim Hussain Khan; disc recordings; concert tour, China (1953).

Reference
Sangeet Natak Akademi, Who's Who of Indian Musicians.

BIDRIWARE- AN EXOTIC ART

Among the various enchanting arts unique to India, the art of Bidriware shines apart with its dazzle of silver inlay in intricate designs against the blackened backdrop of exotically shaped metallic objects.

Prominent among Bidriware are utilities like 'huqqas', boxes, bowls, bottles, pots, ewers, basins weights to anchor floor coverings and legs of cots. Presently, however, the bidri items are crafted basically as the objects of display.

Deriving their name from Bidar, the place of their origin in Karnataka, Bidriware undergo an elaborate process of making. The objects are cast in an alloy of Copper, lead and tin added in small amounts to the basic constituent zinc. A layer of wax and oil, boiled together and set in a casting of a dried mixture of clay and cowdung, on heating leaves a firm mould to receive the molten alloy. The grey surface of the objects is treated with copper sulphate to obtain a temporary black coating to enable a craftman to

each fine designs meticulously in free-hand with a sharp metal stylus. The designed area is then engraved with mini chisels, while the Bidri piece is held firmly on a waxed stone or in 'mangan ', a vice.

Engraved groves are then hammered carefully with fine wires or sheets of silver. Whereas copper replaces silver in economical substitutes, gold has also been used occasionally.

Common techniques used in inlay work are *'zarnishan'*, i.e. cutting inlay to fill in depression to level with the surrounding surface;'*zarboland*': inlaying silver on a lead pad to give it a bold appearance and '*aftabi*': where a design is cut out or silver sheet, giving it a silhouetted appearance against the body of the object. Finally, to brighten up the design in silver inlay, the object is applied and rubbed with a paste of amonium chloride, potassium nitrate, sodium chloride, copper sulphate and mud which reacts with the alloy to give it a permanent black colour. The object is then polished with a paste of groundnut oil and charcoal powder to obtain a glaze finish and lustre.

Designing of the arc-work is quite conventional and is mostly confined to certain oft repeated geometrical patterns, flowers, creepers and human and animal figures.

For Allauddin - II (15th Century AD), the ruler of Bidar in 'Deccan', it was the fascination for this art that led him to invite deft artisans from Bijapur to his state. Under his royal patronage the art flourished and became synonymous with Bidar. In Andhra Pradesh it is customary to gift the bride a complete set of utilities in Bidriware. But elsewhere, it has remained a part of the decorative realm of the rich, beyond the reach of commoners.

Salar Jung Museum, Hyderabad, in Andhra Pradesh has fantastic and outstanding collection of Bidriware. Also, there are sizeable and reputed collections with the Prince of Wales Museum, Mumbai, the State Museum, Hyderabad, and the National Mseum, New Delhi.

BIMAL SAIGAL

BIHU

Assam's spring festival; name derived from Sanskrit word for vernal equinox; originally a fertility ritual reflecting pastoral craving for increased fertility of crops, cattle and people; also heralds Assamese New Year; a secular and universal festival without any sectarian bias; groups of people go round houses singing benedictory songs without discrimination between high and low.

References
Buck, C.H., Faith, Fairs & Festivals of India, Calcutta, 1917.
Eliot, Sir Charles, Hinduism & Buddhism, 3 Vols., London, 1921.
Gait, E.A., History of Assam, Calcutta, 1926.
Gupta, B.A., Hindu Holidays & Ceremonials, Calcutta, 1929.
Underhill, M.A., The Hindu Religion's Year, Calcutta, 1921.

BIRD HOSPITAL IN DELHI (WORLD'S ONLY)

Delhi has the distinction of having the world's only bird hospital. Situated within the precincts of Shree Digamber Jain Lal Mandir at the entrance to Chandni Chowk opposite the Red Fort, it occupies an important place to see position on the tourist map of India.

If it is beauty that attracts people to Taj Mahal, it is compassion, love and care for the birds that brings hordes of people to its doorsteps. Foreign tourists, particularly, are perplexed to see the sight of birds being taken such good care of. The visitors books is replete with amazingly touching remarks from some of them. " Wonderful place. I wonder that the birds ever want to leave" writes Elizabath Forier of Phoenix, USA. Daniel Mermet ev Zoe Verier of Paris says, " A wonderful place where one would like to become a pigeon". And then there is Judith A plot of the Department of English. Washington University, who remarks "This is truly doing God's work for all creation. I feel priviledged and grateful to have come".

For several years the walls of the hospital proudly displayed the first write-up ever on it by a foreign journalist, Mr. A.M. Rosenthal, in The New York Times in March 1958 Instead, now on its walls are displayed such pithy slogans as, " Stop eating animals, love them". The hospital has been lucky to have dedicated and committed doctors who have been very kind both to the inmates and visitors.

The bird hospital was founded in 1930 about the same time when the temple was built by the Jain Community, followers of Lord Mahavir, who believed in the tenets of non violence (ahimsa) and respect for all beings, be they animals or vegetables. Originally set-up in a single room, it grew to cover two floors in 1957.

On any given day there may be "patients" suffering from broken limbs, eye diseases, pox, pecking injuries, diarrhoea, paralysis, cancer, malnutrition, pneumonia or exposure. During Delhi summer the hospital has a busy season when birds are hit by ceiling fans or birds that fall down the street due to exhaustion, when the sun is too strong to bear.

Birds once admitted are never returned to the owner. Along the wall is a 60 ft. row of 18 squareinch isolation cages in which they are kept till they get well. The owner gets a voucher. All birds are released as soon as they get well. The dead ones are released in the Yamuna daily, as Hindus do, by one of the employees. Nearly all birds are admitted in the hospital, except the owl, which is known to be carnivorous by habit and is a threat to small birds. Stray visitors are discouraged for they are tempted to steal birds.

What is very unique about the bird hospital is that it lives, thrives and prospers on charity.

R. K. RAJU

BISHNOIS
THE CRUSADERS OF CONSERVATION

For Bishnois, the unpaid crusaders of conservation for the last 500 years, protection of flora and fauna is not mere idle talk but a sacred duty entrusted by one generation to the next. They are so dedicated to this noble cause that no hunter or poacher dare sneak into their domain. Their villages constitute a haven for innocent animals and birds.

Chipko Movement (hugging trees to save them) attracted a lot of publicity some years ago. But it was something very insignificant as compared to the unmatched sacrifice and exemplary courage shown by Bishnoi community 300 years ago.

The story of their legendary sacrifice to save massacre of green trees dates back to the time when Maharaja Ajit Singh, then King of Marwar, was building a palace for himself. Since firewood was needed to run the kilns, his men started felling trees. In order to save the largest grove near their village, the Bishnois raised a strong voice of protest. The wood cutters did not have enough courage to face them and they stopped chopping the trees. When the news reached the King's minister, he became furious. He reached the site and ordered his men to start cutting the trees. In order to stop them, Amrita Devi, an exceptionally brave Bishnoi woman, embraced a tree trunk and her three daughters followed suit by clasping their hands around other trees. Fuming with rage, the minister ordered his axemen to cut the women along with the trees. Soon they were hacked to death, sending shock waves to the people gathered there. For a moment, other members of the community stood stunned, but then they emphatically declared that they would not let the minister have his way. Stepping into the shoes of Amirita Devi, each embraced a tree to save it; and within no time as many as 363 persons had laid down their lives for a noble cause. As soon as the king heard about it, he was appalled. He rushed to the spot and begged apology from the Bishnois. He also promised that their religious sentiments would always be respected in future.

It was a unique incident of human sacrifice to save the environment. No such thing has ever happened either before or after that incident. Form that time onwards, Bishnois from different parts of the Country congregate every year at Khejadli, 13 km from Jodhpur, to pay homage to the 363 martyrs.

Bishnoi sect was founded by Guru Jambheshwar. Born in a village called Peepasar in 1451, he led a simple life. However, people believed that God had gifted him with certain spiritual powers. When he was 25 years of age, a severe drought hit the region. Spanning over ten long years, it shattered the people and the economy. The young Jambheshwar was shocked to see indiscriminate felling of trees and killing of animals by humans. He realised that man must learn to live in harmony with nature. In order to create this awareness among his people, he enunciated 29 principles. Thus his followers came to be known as Bishnoi Bees meaning twenty and Noi meaning nine. Protection of environment became the central principle. Other principles were aimed at uplifting the community and cleansing it of all bad practices like alcohal, tobacco etc.

The Bishnoi women wear dazzling bright dresses and bedeck themselves with ethnic jewellery. The traditional dress of a Bishnoi women consists of a *Lehnga* (Long pleated skirt), *Choli* (short blouse tied with strings on the backside), and *odhni* (very long scarve covering head and shoulders, and wrapped around body) They wear typical chunky solid necklace, heavy crescent shaped *nath* (the nose ornament), anklets, and *rakhri* on the forehead.

However modernisation has affected their lifestyle too. Some women have started wearing salwar Kameez and school-going girls wear skirts. And Bishnoi men, on the other hand, are conspicuous by their white dress.

Bishnois pay special attention to cleanliness. Whether it is the mud-plastered hut with conical roof, rooms of the house or the courtyard every place is meticulously kept clean. In the arid deserts of Rajasthan where water is a scarce commodity, bathing daily and keeping oneself clean is really pariseworthy. They rear cattle, but do not keep goats or sheep. Reason: if they keep them they would have to sell them at one time or the other to butchers and this would violate their religious beliefs.

The importance of protection of environment cannto be over-emphasised. That is why they are held in high esteem by conservationists.

THAKUR PARAMJIT

BISMILLAH KHAN

(B. 1916) - At Dumraon; instrumentalist; Hindustani, shehnai; studied with Ali Baksh of Varanasi; vocal music with Ahmad Hussain; received Sangeet Natak Akademi Award (1956), Padma Sri (1961), Edinburgh Festival and Commonwealth Arts Festival, London (1965); Disc recordings; Received Bharat Ratna in 2000?

References
Garg, Laxmi Narayan, Hamare Sangeet Ratna, Hathras, 1969.
Indian Who's Who (INFA), 1976.
Muslims in India : A Biographical Dictionary, Vol.I, New Delhi, 1979.
Who's Who of Indian Musicians.

BISON-HORN DANCE

Muria tribe, Madya Pradesh, both men, women dance, men wear horned headdress, tall tuft of feathers, fringe of cowry shells over their faces, drum shaped log slung around their necks, women, heads surmounted broad, solid-brass chaplets, breasts covered, heavy metal necklace, carry sticks in their right hands, 50 to 100 dancers dance, " bisons", attack, chasing female dancers, dynamic interpretation, nature's mating season.

BRAHM KAMAL RARE HIMALAYAN FLOWER

The beauty of the mighty and majestic Himalayas has for centuries been a source of inspiration for travellers, researchers, saints, photographers and artist alike. Amongst its vast wealth of flora and fauna grow flowers of rare species and unknown beauty. One such flower is " Brahm Kamal ", The name of the lotus flower is rooted in the belief that Lord Brahma originated from this lotus. This rare beauty also finds mention in India's ancient scripts as the " Sugandhit Pushpa"- or fragrant flower. Unlike other lotus flowers which grow in water and marshy lands, Brahm Kamal (The Botanical name " Saussurea

obuallata") grows in snow and ice and is found in the world-famous " Valley of Flower" and along the banks of Hemkund lake in Garhwal Himalayas, at an altitude of about 15,000 feet. It appears in full bloom defying the freezing cold of the Himalayas. In pebble-ridden slopes they survive in terrible winds and bloom under the gaze of the warm and bright sun in the months of August and September, as they lie buried in the snow during winters from November to May. During the rainy season the snow melts and they make their appearnace. When ripe their colour changes from green to silky.

During their pilgrimage to Hemkund and other Himalayan shrines- Badrinath, Kedarnath, Gangotri and Yamnotri, pilgrims carry these rare flowers for offering in the temples. It is believed that the fragrance of these flowers, when kept on the threshold of houses, keeps away snakes and other poisnous creatures.

An Ayurvedic medicine made by grinding together the roots, stem, leaves and seeds of these lotus flowers is used for curing mental illnesses. Its oil is also used for other therapeutic purposes.

MULKRAJ SIDANA

BRAHM KUMARIS

A sect of Sadhus and non-Sadhus, men and women who have no prescribed scriptures and no Guru; it teaches its followers to worship Siva through Pita Shivji who became corporal medium of God in 1937; over 250 Brahma Kumari centres in world with main centre at Mount Abu; according to their belief Sahaj Rajyoga (yoga of intellect) is means of realization of God; their principles include vegetarianism, celibacy and abstinence from liquor.

References
Chopra, P.N., (ed.), Religions and Communities of India, New Delhi, 1982.
Farquhar, J.N., Modern Religious Movement in India, London, 1929.

BREATHTAKING HANDICRAFTS OF BANARAS

Banaras is more than an ancient religious centre. Over its long history, arts and artists have flourished here. The shops near the temples and ghats overflow with multicoloured religious pictures, flags, Paper-crafts, copperware, brass idols and brass and copper utensils for cooking, Washing and worshipping.

Banaras is famous for its beautiful handicrafts, expecially silk brocade and gold brocade sarees, cushion covers, wall hangings, bedspreads, scarves and dress material. The weavers of Banaras are so perfect in their art of weaving that they can creat wonders with their gold, silver and silk threads. They prepare elegant silk brocades with 'Jali ', 'tanchoi', 'Zamdani' and " Ganga- Yamuna" techniques. In Ganga- Yamuna 'style ' gold brocade has warp and weft of gold thread with patterns woven in silk and gold threads. Generally, the- background material is woven in silver 'zari ' and patterns in gold.

Gold stands for 'Ganga ' and 'Yamuna ' for silver.

The silk brocades of Banaras are very rich and varied. The pure silk brocades use a variety of multicoloured silk threads instead of gold and silver thread for creating numerous complicated patterns. The 'amru ' silk brocade of Banaras has beautiful 'butis ' (buds) in the background, a decoratéd border and a gorgeous 'pallu ' (hanging end of a saree) of flowering bushes and flowing mango patterns.

Banaras is also famous for its fine and delicate ivory and sandalwood work, attractive 'minakari ' 'enamel work) on silver jewellery and other decorative pieces, gold jewellery, fine softstone work, clay figures, bangles, wooden toys, brass and copper utensils and decorative pieces made from camel bone and the wood of the Kadamb tree.

The artistice inclination of its people is reflacted in the tasteful paintings that adorn the outer walls of the temples and houses. The themes are folk motifs, and are painted either by the lady of the house or by the priest. Sometimes people commission 'Chitaire ' (artists) to paint the house at the time of Childbirth or marriage.

DR. BIMLA VERMA

BRONZES

Tradition of Indian bronzes can be studied under two heads, folk and classical, both of which follow the tenets of the *Shilpa- shastra*; in classical bronzes greater emphasis was laid on proportion, perfection of form and features, elegance and finesse, folk bronzes were wrought without any regard for these qualities art of bronze-making had religious inspiration behind it; bronze images in classical or folk style were wrought for the purpose of worship; image-makers were also fully conversant with all the *shastras* and conformed to the tenets laid down in them; folk bronzes are facinating due to their spontaneous feelings and abundant vitality; in the history of Indian bronzes, it seems that the 6th century B.C. an important period when *Vedism* evolved towards *Brahmanism,* and two great new religions or movements, Jainism and Buddhism, were founded; gods of the Brahmanic pantheon became personalised and soon two of them, Shiva- form of the Vedic *Rudra -* and Vishnu, became, for their devotees, the supreme divinity; at the end of the 4th century B.C., kingdom of Magadha in the eastern valley of the Ganga (now in Bihar) under Maurya dynasty acquired importance; founder of Maurya empire, Chandragupta, reconquered the valley of the Indus from the Greeks; his grandson, Ashoka, brought this empire to the height of its power and achieved the first unification of India. Ashoka spread Indian culture outside the subcontinent, being a devout Buddhist, he got moral edicts- inspired by the Buddhist teachings on charity-inscribed on rocks and pillars throughout empire; in this period were produced superb terracotta figurines, which influenced the art of image- making to a large extent, as early as this period, the bronzes were cast by the solid casting process; during the early ages of Indian Buddhist art, the Buddha was represented by symbols only; later, like other Hindu deities, Buddha came to be anthropomorphised; a large number of bronzes representing the Buddha in sitting or standing postures were wrought; copper was used more commonly than bronze for the purpose of image-making; the art of the Guptas flourished for more than 200 years (4th century - 6th century A.D.); the bronzes wrought during this period are "classical" and are marked by superb elegance and classical perfection; in eastern India in the extended areas of Bihar and Bengal, the Pala dynasty ruled during the 8th century A.D.: after the Pala rulers, some kings of the Sena dynasty reigned over Bengal till the incursions of the Muslims in the 12th century; the images wrought during this period are known for the use of lost- wax process; this is illustrated by a study of the old schools of Nalanda, Kurkihar, Bodhgaya, Bhagalpur and Chittagong; from these places many Buddhist as well as Hindu idols in stone, copper, gift and bronze have been discovered; bronzes of Nalanda and Kurkihar have won wide acclaim for their elegance, gracefulness and masterly perfection, delicate features and proportionate bodies; each detail is worked out minutely. In 7th century A.D. under Kashmir ruler Lalitaditya (c. 720-756 A.D.), the Kashmir bronzes in a way continued the classical art traditions of the Guptas, and have a marked affinity with them; features of Kashmir art exercised a decisive influence on the lamaist art of western Tibet for some centuries, while the Buddhist culture diminished by the 14th century A.D., with the advent of the mediaeval period from 9th to the 16th centuries, the art of India lost much of its earlier creative impetus and the sculptor followed even stricter iconographical rules. In Bengal and Bihar, under the Pala and Sena dynasties, the Gupta rules were still applied but, having lost their former vigour, produced nothing but conventionalised types; the earliest works, those of the 8th and the 9th centuries, are free standing images set against a round- topped stele with plain backgrounds and are still very close to the post-Gupta style; there are a great many bronzes cast by the *cire perdue* (lost- wax) method, which apparently date from the 9th century and were made in Nalanda, an important Buddhist centre at that time; they are small in size and resemble stone sculpture; from 8th to 13th century A.D. a massive production of bronze and copper images was done in Madhya Pradesh and south India; the most popular image produced at this time in south India was that of the dancing Shiva, the *Nataraja*; with the advent of the Muslim rule in India, the Hindu classical sculptors lost their patronage but the folk bronzes continued to be wrought because they did not depend on external patronage; folk bronzes of India have often been ignored, perhaps because of their apparent crudity and weirdness; it was only with the introduction of modern art movement about 20 years, ago that these objects received appreciation.

K. C. ARYA

References

Brown, J.C. and Dey, A.K., India's Mineral Wealth, Bombay, 1955.

Ball, V., Economic Geology in India, n.a., 1881.

Munshi, K.M., Saga of Indian Sculpture, Bombay, 1957.

BUDDHIST ART IN INDIA
A BRIEF SURVEY

The early Symbols and Their Evolution

Buddhist are reflects very faithfully all the important aspects of Buddhism. In Primitive Buddism, Gautama Sakyamuni has been regarded as an ideal human being and quite naturally we find that the early Buddhist art of Bharhut, Sanchi, Bodh-Gaya, and Amaravati, and other places shows no anthropomorphic representation of the Master. His presence is indicated by means of an empty throne, or a Bodhi tree or a pair of foot-prints, or a dharmachakra, symbolizing one or the other event of his life. As the time passed, Buddhism acquired greater popularity and drew adherents from all sections of the people. The discipline and austerities of the early Buddhism were beyond the comprehension of the ordinary followers of the religion. A religion without a personal god in whom one can repose faith had but little appeal to them. The demand of the popular mind was met by the **Mahayanists** who defied, Budha and introduced the concept of Divine Boddhisattvas and several other deities. With the progress of time, the Boddhist pantheon was enlarged to include several hundred deities. Among the Male deities, the Bodhisattva Avalojiteshvara become the most popular because of his great compassion for the living creatures. He is an emanation of the Dhyani Buddha Amitabha and his **Shakti** Pandara (the Sukhavati-Vyuha or the Amitayus Sutra, translated into Chinese between A.D. 148-170, seems to refer for the first time to the name of Amitabha or Amitayus). Avalokiteshvara is the personification of universal compassion. As described in the Karanda-vyuha he refused or renounced Nirvana in favour of afflicted humanity. He is supposed to impart spiritual knowledge to fellow creatures so that all, by a gradual process, may advance on the pathn of salvation. Different forms of the Avalokiteshvara have been mentioned in the Sadhana-mala; of these the important ones are Shadakshari Lokeshvara. Simhanda, Khasharpana. Lokanath, Halahala, Nilakantha and few others.

THE BUDHIST PANTHEON

Side by side with the male deities, female deities (as well as Tantric Practices) were introduced in the Boddhist Pantheon. The Sikshasamuchchava of Santideva' (c. 800 A.D.) not only mentions the name of Akshobhya and Amitabha and several other male deities, but also contains dharanis for the female deities. Such as Chunda, Marichi, etc. The Buddhist pantheon saw important developments in the 8th-9th Centuries A.D. when yantras (magical diagrams) and mandalas (magical circles) were introduced and the vijamantras (gem - syllables) were assigned to the individual deities. With the introduction of this Tantrayana or Vajrayana system of worship, the Mahayana Buddhism developed a philosophy far removed in emphasis from the original teachings of Gautama Buddha. The main seat of Tantric Buddhism was the eastern parts of India- Bengal, Bihar, Orissa and Assam.

As Avalokiteshvara was the most popular among the male deities, so Tara and Prajna- paranitra were among the female deities. Although Tara has many forms, here common attribute is a lotus reminiscent of her origin from a lotus in the waters of a lake formed by a tear-drop of Avalokiteshvara. Prajna-paramita is the Buddhist-goddes of learning. She is considered to be the embodiment of the Mahayana scripture, which according to tradition, was rescued from the nether region by Nagarjuna.

ASOKAN MANUMENTS

The history of Buddhist art starts from the time of the Mauryan ruler. Asoka (3rd Century B.C.) As a zealous Buddhist Asoka is credited with the erection of eighty-four thousand stupas over Buddha's relice which he is said to have collected from stupas of the earlier period. It is held that the original brick-stupas at Sanchi (Main- Stupa) and Sarnath (Dhamekh Stupa) were constructed by him. The Stupa at Sanchi was however encased in stone during the 2nd Century B.C., and the other at Sarnath was so enveloped during the Gupta period. Asoka also erected a large number of monolithic pillars with capitals surmounted by animals, such as the bull, the lion or the elephant. These pillars bear an excellent polish characterstic of the Mauryan sculpture. Asoka engraved his edicts not only on rocks but also on these pilars with a view to preaching the principles of Buddhism in the language of the masses. Mauryan art, as represented by the animals of Asokan pillar capitals and also by the Yaksha and Yakshi figures of Patna and Didargunj is characterised by strength and massiveness. Carved in the round they are monumental and in size impressive.

THE BHARHUT STUPA

The Sunga-Andhra epoch (2nd-1st Century B.C.) was one of the most creative periods of Buddhist art. Though the sunga rulers were followers of the Brahmanical faith and Buddhism was deprived of the State patronage which it enjoyed during the reign of the Mauryan rulers, like Asoka and some of his successors, there was no set-back in the propagation or popularity of the Buddhist faith. Buddhist establishments flourished in Bodh-Gaya, Bharhut, and Sanchi in Northern and Central India, in Amaravati and Jaggayapeta in South India, at Bhaja, Nasik, Karle and Ajanta and at several other places in Western India. The art of this period consists mainly in the excavation of the rock-cut temples or viharas (some of which are embellished with paintings) and the erection of railings and toranas (gateways) to the Buddhist Stupas at different places. General Cunningham found remains of the reilings and one gateway of the Stupa at Bharhut (Madhya Pradesh) during the years 1872-74 and had them deposited in the indian Museum in the year following. The Stupa in question was built during the 2nd Century B.C. In the absence of the Stupa itself it is difficult to ascertain its shape and size. But it was probably similar to the Stupas represented on its panels and the almost contemporary stupas of Sanchi. All these Stupas consist of a hemispherical dome with a harmika above supporting the umbrellas.

One of the main interest of the Bharhut sculptures consists in the representation of the birth-stories of Gautama Buddha. These stories (or the Jatakas) are of two main classes, those relating to the previous births of Buddha as a Bodhisattva (a Buddha potentia), and those of his last appearance as Gautama Shakyamuni when he attained Englishtenment or Buddhahood. The Jatakas represnted on the Bharhut panels include Manakapi-

Jataka. Latuva-Jataka, Miga-Jataka, Sujata-gahuto-Jataka, Mahayanka-Jataka and Vidhurapandita-Jataka, Chhadanta Jataka, etc.

The scene on the Bharhut sculptures, relating to the life of Gautama Shakyamuni include, among others, the dream of Maya (illustrating the descent of a Bodhisattva in the form of an elephant into the mother's womb), the defeat of Mara, Gautama's Enlightenment under the Bodhi tree, the worship of the Bodhi tree, the worship of Gautama's hair-locks by celestial beings, the visits of king Ajatashatru of Magadha and of Prasenjit of Koshala, etc.

The worship of the Bodhi tree, seems to have been widely prevalent, as there are many representations of it on the sculptured panels of Bharhut, Sanchi and Amaravati, Again, in the Divyavandana it is related that the Bodhi tree was Asoka's favourite object of worship. The lowest architrave of the Eastern Gateway, Stupa 1, Sanchi (1st Century B.C.) depicts the ceremonial visits of King Asoka and his queen, Tishyarakshita to the Bodhi tree. In the centre of the panel are the tree and the temple of Bodh Gaya. On the left is seen a crowd of musicians and devotees carrying water vessels. On the right are the king and the queen descending from the elephant and paying homage to the Bodhi tree.

THE SANCHI STUPA

In addition to Bharhut, the other important centres of Buddhist art and religion in north Indian during this period were Sanchi (Madhya Pradesh) and Bodh Gaya (Bihar). The main interest of the art at Sanchi centres round the Great Stupa. Originally buil of brick, during the reign of Asoka (3rd Century B.C.), it was encased in stone and brought to its present dimension about a century later. The other additions, such as the erection of the toramas and the ground balustrade were done still later, probably about 50 B.C. of all the four gateways, the south gateway seems to be the oldest. On one of its architraves, there is an inscription showing that it was the gift of Ananda, the foreman of the artisans of king Sri Satakarni (1st Century B.C.), who was evidently the son of Simuka, the founder of the Satavahana family of the Ceccan. Of all toranas or gateways, the best preserved is the northern gateway, which enables the visitor to have a complete idea of the appearance of all the gateways. Each gateway is composed of two square pillars with capitals at the top. These capitals of standing dwarf or elephants support a superstructure of architraves. Finally, on the summit of the gateway is the dharma-chakra sympol in the middle. The pillars and superstructures are elaborately decorated with representation of Jataka legends (stories of Buddha's past lives) as well as important events relating to the subsequent events of the Buddhist religion. There are also representations of the sacred trees, stupas and other motifs to indicate the presence of Gautama Buddha symbolically. As in Bharhut art, here also in conformity with the tradition of early Indian art, there is no anthropomorphic representation of Buddha.

JAGGAYAPETA STUPA

A stylistic equivalent of the panels of Sanchi is to be found in a carving from a Jaggayapeta stupa near Amaravati on the Krishna river. This will show how little differences existed between different regions in the field of art. A monument to be ascribed to the early Sunga period is the old Vihara at Bhaja, which is situated in the hills of the Western ghats to the south of Bombay. It is a rectangular chamber with several cells. The decoration of the Bhaja monastery includes among others the representation of Yakshas, a sun god on a four-horse chariot and Indra riding his vehicle, i.e. Airavat.

Although there are innumerable references in the Jatakas and other Buddhist literature to the painted decorations, the earliest surviving examples of Buddhist paintings are met with at the oldest Chaitya Halls at Ajanta in the Deccan, dedicated in the 2nd century B.C. The principal wall painting in cave 10 is devoted to the illustration of the Shaddanta Jataka

AMARAVATI STUPA

The Buddhist art in South India during this period is best illustrated by the remains of the Maha-Chaitya (or Stupa) of Amaravati. As the earliest Buddhist sculptures found here are primitive in style resembling those of Bharhut, it can be presumed that the Maha Chaitya was built during the 2nd Century B.C. The sculptures of Amaravati fall into four different periods from 200 B.C. to 250 A.D., its earliest pieces as noted above, show affinities to Bharhut art. The images of Buddha were introduced here about the 1st-2nd Century A.D. The Amaravati art of this period is highly elegant and sensitive.

GANDHARA ART

Buddhist art entered upon a new phase with the rise of Mahayana Buddhism during the 1st Century B.C. to 1st Century A.D. The period is remarkable in that it gave for the first time the figure- art or the anthopomorphic representations of the Buddha. Under the patronage of Kushana rulers (1st-2nd Century A.D.) a new school of art flourished in the Gandhara region i.e. Peshawar and its neighbouring districts. Because of its strategic geographical position the region became a meeting place of various races and cultures. As a result of this, the art of the region shows mingling of both Indian and foreign ideas and motifs. Gandhara art is a hybrid product; though Buddhist in theme it is Graeco. Roman in style or technique as is evident from the physiognomy and drapery of the images. The artists of this region have produced a large number of Buddha and Bodhisattva images along with other Buddhist deities. Gandhara art flourished for about four to five hundred years and to a great extent it influenced the idigenous art of Mathura, Amravati and Nagarjunakonda. It exercised a profound influence upon the art of Afghanistan and Central Asia. The Buddha and Bodhisattva images of many sites in Central Asia show affiliations to the Gandhara style. The main centres of Gandhara art were the cities of Peshawar and Taxila, and also Afghanistan where a large number of stupas, monasteries and sculptures have been unearthed by the archeologists.

MATHURA - A GREAT CENTRE OF ART

Mathura also was a great centre of art and culture during this period. Here flourished side by side all the important religions of India, such as Brahmanism, Jainism and Buddhism, It is believed that the first Budha images were carved at Mathura simultaneously, if not earlier, with the Gandhara school. Mathura has produced Buddha images of various dimensions. The Kushana Buddha or Bodhisattva images of Mathura served as the Prototypes of the more beautiful specimens of the Gupta period. The workshop of Mathura exported several Buddhist images to various other places, such as Sarnath, and even as far as Rajgir in Bihar. It is well known that friar, Bala, an inhabitant of Mathura had several Bodhisattva images set up at different places. Two of them were found at Shravasti and Sarnath. The Kushana art of Mathura is some what heavy. The style and technique which the Kushana artists were trying to evolve were brought to perfection during the Gupta period. But the art of South India during this time is more elegant and sophisticated. The sculptured panels of Amaravati and Nagarjunakonda, Goli, Ghatasala, belonging to the 2nd-3rd Century A.D., are characterised by delicacy of forms, and linear grace.

THE GUPTA ART

The main centres of Buddhist art during Gupta period (4th - 6th AD.) were Mathura, Sarnath and Nalanda in the north. The Buddhist images of Mathura and Sarnath are some of the best specimens of Indian art, never equalled by any art creations of later periods. The swiicate folds of the transparent garment adorning the Gupta figures were done in a beautiful style. The profusely decorated halo is another special feature of the art of the Gupta figure. The delicate modelling of forms with meditative repose has rendered the Buddha and Budhisatva figures of the Gupta period most attractive. The Gupta artists showed an equal ingenuity in the carving of metal images also, like the bronze Buddha image from Sultanganj and also one from Dhanesar Khera.

This period is also known for excavations of several rock-cut viharas and temples at Ajanta and Ellora, in Maharashtra, under the patronage of the Vakataka Kings. Cave 16,17,19 and 26 at Ajanta are excellent examples of pillared halls with usual cells with shrines in the back containing Buddha figures. The beauty and variety of the pillars are remarkable. The mural paintings in the Ajanta caves of the Vakataka period contain representations of scenes from Buddha's life from the conception to enlightenment. Ajanta paintings both in composition and technique are characerised by a delicacy and depth of feelings. Several Buddhist caves are to be found also at Bagh (Madhya Pradesh) and Ellora (Maharashtra), containing numerous Buddha and Bodhisattva figures (5th-6th Century).

POST-GUPTA DEVELOPMENTS

The Gupta art tradition was followed in later period also. The art of Nalanda, Kurkihar, Sarnath, Orissa and other places during the mediaeval period is based upon the Gupta art idion. The north Indian Buddhism of the mediaeval period (8th-11th Century A.D.) is a peculiar synthesis of the Mahayana ideals and trantric elements. The concept of the Adi-Buddha. the Dhyani-Buddhas, the divine Bothisattvas as well as the concept of Shakti or the female energy figure most prominently in the Buddhist art of the period. One anachronism of Buddhist art in mediaeval period is the introduction of the crowned Buddhas with jewelleries. Though incompatible to the idea of renunciation which Buddha followed and Preached, such images were made probably to lay emphasis on the concept of Buddha as a Chakravartin, the supreme universal monarch.

NALANDA

The art of Nalanda shows very high standard of stone carving as well as metal casting. The minute execution of the bronzes specially of the smaller ones, has excited the admiration of all art lovers of the World. Several Nalanda bronzes were exported to Nepal and Tibet and also to Java. Equally interesting are the palm leaf illustrations of the Buddhist manuscripts of the Pala period. The Pala style of painting, as Pala sculptures and bronzes, very much influenced the art of Nepal, Tibet and the further East. The most important centres of mediaeval Buddhism in North India were Bengal and Bihar under the patronage of the Pala Kings.

NAGAPATTINAM

A flourishing centre of Buddhism in South India during the period was Nagapattinam, near Madras on east coast. There existed here in the mediaeval period a colony of the Malaya Buddhists who, patronized by the Cholas erected here two temples in the 11th Century A.D., with the aid granted by the Sailendra kings of Java and Sumatra. One of the temples was called Rajarajaperumpalli and the other Rajendra-cholaperumpalli. Since 1856 about 350 bronzes have been found in these vihara sites. Some of them are of the early chola times while the rest belong to the later Ghaola period. The Nagapattinam bronzes are some of the finest metal works of South India.

P. BANERJEE

BUDDHIST MONASTERIES IN LAHUL AND SPITI

Through generations of religious upheaval in India, the cradle of Buddhism, gradually lost hold over this religion though it has yet to vanish completely. The border bastion of Lahul and Spiti District of Himachal Pradesh has still the indelible imprint of Buddhism. It is the land of lamaism in India. The natural beauty of this district is fascinating in its own way and few parts of the Himalayas can compare with it in awe inspiring splendour and regged grandeur.

BUDDHIST PATTERN OF LIFE

Lahul & Spiti has much in common with the neighbouring Tibet including language, dress, social customs and religion. Before the Chinese occupation of Tibet in 1959 the inhabitants of this part looked towards Lhasa for religious and educational training and inspiration. Buddhism originallly entered this area in the 8th century and the credit for this rightly goes to the celebrated Buddhist missionary of that era, Padma Sambhava. During his brief sojourn here he is said to have founded the renowned monastery of Guru Ghantal which depicts the original Buddhism, differing from the shrines established after 12th century under the Tibetan influence in their pyramidal roofs and carved wood work. People are so mechanically devoted to Buddhism that prayer in this area has been reduced to a sort of reflex action and the prayer wheel is a common sight. All lamas and fervid votaries carry prayer wheels, metal cylinders of brass, copper or silver, containing a long roll of thin paper in which are prayers, printed or written. A small pendant chained to the cylinder, causes it to revolve easily round a long metal pin attached to a wooden handle. At the approaches to villages, on the tops of the passes, near river beds, are seen numerous constructions of mani, long walls built of dressed stones which carry the unvarying formula of the Buddhist prayer, " Om Mane Padme Hum". The literal translation of the formula · is " hail, thou possessor of the jewel lotus". The construction of these walls is regarded as the panacea for all ills and the votarise in order to appease the Lord and thereby secure His blessing, take recourse in building them. It is also believed that the donors cf these mani walls earn merit at the hands of the heavenly powers.

THE GONPAS

The most interesting and distinguishing feature of the district is the location of Buddhist monasteries in almost every hamlet or village. Some of these gonpas (Shrines) as pronounced in local dialect are objects of architectural interest. These are usually perched in picturesque situations high on the hill side, only to be reached by rough and steep paths. The reason for constructing these monasteries on such declivities was seemingly to provide solitude and aloofness to the monks from the din and noise of the villages. The ordinary · *gonpa* of Lahul is a large and irregular building with a flat roof, the lower stories are closed and ill ventilated but the upper ones are more open with balconies leading out to the flat roofs. These monasteries are the abodes of Lamas and Chomos, some of whom are married and posses their own houses and fields. They visit the monastries to take their turn of duty.

GURU GHANTAL MONASTERY

The monastery of Guru Ghantal is one of the oldest having been established some 800 years ago and has the distinction of housing wooden idols as distinguished from the clay idols which are a common feature of the *gonpas* in the district. This monastery is situated on a hill top about four kilometres above Tandi, the confluence of the Chandra and the Bhaga rivers. It is said to have been constructed by one Lama Tashi Tamphel on the pattern of Tashigong *gonpa* in Tibet. It is a wooden struture with pyramidal roofs and have eye catching wood carvings. Whistler has mentioned in his travelogue entitled in the High Himalayas that Padma Sambhava visited this area personally and consecrated this monastery in the 8th century. To this day the monastery preserves the idols of Padma Sambhava, Lord Buddha, Nawans, Namgial, Brajeshwari Devi, etc. It is still the centre of cultural and social life for the local inhabitants. The head lama of this monastery imparts education to the lama and chomo initiates as well as to the children and the general public of the area. This monastery owns revenuefree grant of land measuring about 117 bighas scattered throughout the surrounding kothis. Every year on the 15th lunar day (full moon night of Ashada) a festival called ghantal is held when the lamas and thakurs feast for one day. During this festival a number of votaries launch a pad yatra, around Drilburi, the holy mountain, which involves a walk of about 28 km. The interesting feature is that on this occasion the lamas go into trance and solve riddles for their devotees. They converse in Bhoti language. Side by side half a dozen lamas are seen engaged in continuous prayers in the sanctuary throughout the day.

KARDANG MONASTERY

Kardang village is situated on the left bank of the river Bhaga, just opposite to and about 1.5 km. from Keylong, the headquarters of the district. Local lore aver that Kardang was once the capital of Lahul though now it is mainly famous for this monastery situated at a distance of abour 4 km. on declivity overlooking the Kardang village. The monastery is believed to have been founded about 900 .years ago, but is lay in till 1912 when it was reconstructed by revered Lama Norbu of this village. Having renounced things of the world and pleasures, he braced mendicancy and travelled on foot to distant places like Bhutan, Tibet, Lhasa, Kham, etc. and made a deep study of the holy books. It is said that he acquired the power of freeing his soul from his body at will and attained the status of a true saint. On his return home he preached the gospel of dharma throughout the district. In 1946, he abandoned his mortal body. Later, through the occult power of lamas, it was revealed that Norbu Lama had incarnated at Lhasa. The local lamas fervently desire to bring him back to this monastery.

The interesting and worth noticing features in this magnificen, white-washed, flag-bedecked monastery are the huge barrel-like prayer drums, revolving to the touch. These are rotated by lamas as they preamulate the lobbies. This sanctuary houses the images of Buddha and numerous other religious heroes and monks. The inner-walls are decked with fresco paintings of various hues depicting Buddha in various postures with other attendants. It has a small library containing valuable books on Buddhist philosophy written in Bhoti language. There are twelve lamas and thirteen chomos in this *gonpa*, who lead the celibate monastic life. The villagers are from birth to death under the impact of these lamas. All good and evil happenings are attributed to the pleasure or wrath of these lamas. When a member of a family falls seriously ill, the lama is immediately sent for. He by performing a special ceremony called *tanamana* in local parlance, cures the ailment. It is also believed that the faithful propitiation averts deaths. On the death of an individual, funeral offerings are made to the monastery on behalf of the family and comprise money, clothes, pots, grain and butter. At each harvest the monks adorned in their traditional dresses form themselves into parties and go from house to house in each village in turn, chanting verses mean " we are men who have renounced the wordly pleasures, give us in charity food and other necessary requisites to sustain our lives". Annually during the month of June, a sort of miracle play is enacted by the lamas of this monastery in which monks are seen attired like devils, demons and in other queer and astonishing robes. At this festival senior lamas dressed in ceremonial robes perform dexterously, devil dancing and buffoonery. The dancing etc., eating and drinking sometimes continues up to twenty six days.

SHASHUR GONPA

It is situated on a hillock, about 1.5 km. away from keylong. This monestery is built on a similar and familiar pattern and its importance shoots into a prominence during a fair usually held in the months of June/July when the visitors in their multitudes converge. Women, bedecked in thier quaint finery and jewellery and sprightly dressed boys and men with tufts of artificial or dried flowers on their caps mix in gaiety on the festival days. The unique feature of the preceedings at this *gonpa* is the abrupt emergence of the Abbot of the monastery along with his satellites from the dove of the *gonpa*. The scene transcends the crowd to a mystic world and the on-lookers bow their heads to exhibit their reverence to the Abbot and party. This is followed by a group dance in which the local orchestra constantly remains in attendance. The onlookers eagerly look forward to the commencement of breath catching feats. The dancers hidden behind white masks, with quick and nimble feet all in unison, disappear with a lighteening speed leaving the crowd spell bound. Next scene follows with a band of lamas wearing varying and different types of masks. Their masks are the main attraction and are of various hues and designs. Some wearing yak horns yet others in a cloak of sheep skin present a fiesta of unrivalled dimensions. The tanleau thus presented at the gonpa of Shashur sends the visitors to peals of laughter and outsider look forward to visiting this monastery at festival time.

KYI MONASTERY

Kyi in Spiti stands most picturesquely on the top of its conical shaped mountains approachable from Kabir, a halting stange. This is the biggest monastery of the district and is the cultural centre of the two valleys. The monastery consists of some large rooms with narrow corridors. On entering the courtyard are seen two trumpets, about nine feet in length, resting on a triangular block of wood. Through a side of the courtyard the terraced stone steps lead you to the inner rooms. Horns of ibex nailed above the door way lend distinction and dignity to the entrance. In the inner sancturary is a raised dais on which are rested idols of Lord Buddha and Goddess Tara. An effigy of a snow leopard, in a rampant posture, stands snarling at another effigy of a panter. The walls of the room are beautiful painted depicting scenes from Lord Buddha's life. Added to these are quaintly drawn figures of demons, gods and goddesses.

The annual fair of this monastery takes place in the month of November every year, when about one thousand people inhabiting the surrounding villages, congregate here. The fair lasts three days during which the people attired in their best dresses, indulge in all sorts of fun, frolic and merry making. As in other monasteries, a masked dance to the accompaniment of local orchestra, is performed. The dance is in the form of a ballet and depicts the legendry tale of the invasion of the virtuous by the evil forces. The two sides are represented by Gods and demons respectively. The battle royal ensues in the customary manner in which the demons succumb and the Gods come out triumphant. The Masks donned by the rival actors are so skillfully prepared that they give an illusion of reality.

TABO MONASTERY

Tabo is yet another monastery in Spiti valley and is quite pristine. Its antiquity can be traced from the stone inscriptions inside the shrine. Its unique fresco paintings furnish proof of the supreme patience and skills of the devoted artist. This sanctuary though standing in a desolate and obscure place, is the beautiful and rare example of an artist's creation.

M. D. MAMGAIN

BUNDI
SHOWPIECE OF RAJASTHAN'S HERITAGE

Bundi, a small city in east Rajasthan, is reminiscent of India's rich cultural heritage. The elegantly carved architecture of its ancient monuments points just towards that. Situated in the lap of Aravalli hills and nestled in a narrow valley, Bundi is enclosed by huge walls fortified by four gateways. Besides having rich treasure of magnificent historical monuments, nature has endowed it with enchanting scenic beauty too.

Among the palaces of Bundi, Chhatra Mahal or the Palace of Towers holds the most important position. Built by Rao Raja Chhatrasal in 1631, it is full of ancient astronomical instruments called Yantras which were used to observe the movements of the sun, the moon, the planets and the stars. A steep paved carriage-way leads up to this monument. It has a beautiful pavilion with breathtaking wall paintings of the Bundi School. The Hazaripole, or the gate of the thousand, the beautiful Hathipol (elephant gate) with curious old water clock are some of the other places of interest here.

Badal Mahal or the palace of clouds was the residence of queens. It has some very beautiful and charming miniature wall murals. The Bundi fort, known in history as Taragarh, was considered invincible. It is said to have been constructed by Rao Narpal in 1372. The entrance to this fort is through two huge gateways in the south and the west directions. There are four big water tanks which, in the days of yore, were used as the palace reservoirs.

The Chitra Mahal exhibits some of the finest Bundi mural paintings which attained world fame. The subjects of paintings are processions, cour life and lovers meeting each other. The skillful shading, the reddish brown colouring of the face and the sober and harmonious application of colours gives special depth and relief to facial expressions.

Just outside the Bundi city, on the Kota-Bundi highway, the eighty-four pillared cenotaph welcome the visitors. It is a unique memorial, the ceiling of which is embellished with beautiful paintings of wild animals, beautiful dancers and damsels.

Phool Sagar, or the lake of flowers, is a typical 20th century architecture and is the residence of the former ruler now.

Sukh Mahal is the summer palace built in the Sukh Sagar (Ocean of Joys) lake which is surrounded by rambling gardens. The shadow of this palace on the shimmering and lazy waves of the lake inspires poets to write immortal poetry.

Bundi is also known for its colourful festival of Teej. It is celebrated on the third day of the second half of the month of Sravana which usually falls in July-August. To celebrate the advent of monsoon, girls and young women dressed in traditional finery sing songs and offer puja to Goddess Parvati for conjugal bliss and everlasting happiness. A big procession is taken out on this occasion and a fair is also organised which lasts for three to four days.

It wouldn't be an exaggeration to say that Bundi is a showpiece of Rajasthan's rich culture.

TASNEEM F. KHAN

BURMAN, SACHIN DEV

(b. 1906) - Classical, folk and light music composer and director of films; studied with Badal Khan, K.C.Dey and Bhisham Dev Chatterjee; received Sangeet Natak Akademi award for music direction (1958), Film fare award (1958), Asian Film Society (London) award (1959) and Swami Haridas award (1965); concert tours, UK (1959), USSR (1961) and Finland (1962), disc recordings.

"C"

CALCUTTA : BUSTLING HERITAGE OF THE RAJ

In 1947, when India gained independence and the Britishers left, they unknowingly left behind an immeasurable wealth of tradition, a legacy that the waves of time could not wipe out. Calcutta bears ample testimony to that. A very important metro of India, there is a reminder of the old world charm right from the old Howrah Bridge itself. A uniqueness and a certain amount of dreaminess about the city pervades.

There is a lot that the city has inherited from its colonial past. Calcutta retains much of the splendour for yesteryears with a presence that is regal, imposing and memorable, making the city worth one's admiration and love. The city in fact was born in August, 1690, following the midday halt of Job Charnock, chief of the British East India Company, on the eastern banks of the river Hoogly, overlooking the bustling village of Sultanati and the adjoining villages of Govindpur and Kalikata, the site of the famous Kali temple. Over the next 250 years, Calcutta grew into a leading city east of Suex and the second biggest city of the British Empire. Inextricably interwoven into its history are the river Hoogly and the port (Kidderpore docks) both witnesses to the first time visitor, Calcutta is indeed overwhelming. It presents a unique blend of 19th century Europe and the throbbing vitality of a metropolis teeming with millions.

Calcutta has indeed changed, but what is noticeable is the incline of the present towards its past, a benign till towards the rich heritage of yesterday. The buildings the housed the British officials and served as palaces are today's major landmarks of the city, such as the original tank (Lal Dighi), the silver domed General Post Office, the adjacent Collectorate, Writers' Building, seat of the state government, the Reserve Bank Building and St. Andrew's Church, the Governor's house, now known as Raj Bhawan modelled along the Kedleston Hall of England, the High Court and the Legislative Assembly adjacent to it. Nothing has been done to the buildings, apart from renovations, to alter their original plans, as the citizens of Calcutta have great regard for all that is old and capable of speaking for itself. At the southern end rises the imperial majesty of Victoria Memorial, known as the " Taj Mahal of the British Raj " and of course the omnipresent Howrah Bridge, the cantilever wonder that has just completed 50 eventful years. One still sees and uses quaint trams trundle down narrow streets amidst jostling crowds and the city still has the hand drawn rickshaws, an antique concept that lives on.

Beside the physical characteristics, Calcutta boasts of an amazing array of activities that owe their origin to the colonial upbringing. Calcutta was the first Indian city to enjoy the fruits of Western education. As a result, the city provided new and modern ideas on almost all aspects of life. Besides the first newspaper, Hickey's Gazatte, arts and crafts, literature and folk theatre (Jatra) left a rich and varied tradition whose effects are evident to this day. This can be seen at the " Academy of Fine Arts', the 'Government College of Art and Craft' , that came up in 1845, 'Birla Academy of Fine Arts' , and Birla Academy of Art and Culture' , 'Ashutosh Museum of Indian Art' , 'Rabindra Bharati Museum ' and the 'State Archaeological Gallery '. What is commendable is the undying spirit of every Bengali to pursue the arts and crafts, even if it is done on a small scale. The concept itself is ingrained in the Minds and is an important part of the basic education for every student.

The sporting tradition of Calcutta also owes its origin to the pre-independence days; the 1000 acre Maidan houses several clubs and stadia. These include Eden Gardens, Race course, Royal Calcutta Turf Club (RCTC) and Tollygunge Club.

The South Club, once the 'Wimbledon of the East', has switched to hard court tennis. Besides, there are clubs that were started years ago but are as alive as ever before like clubs for Rowing, Polo, horse riding and squash.

The " adda " culture of Calcutta owes its origin to the English family system. The city still offers and extended participation system by way of having one's family and friends over, and generally the day culminates into grand social evenings. There are also clubs in the finest British tradition such as the Bengal Club, Calcutta Club, Calcutta Cricket and Football Club and Saturday Club to name a few. The 'adda ' culture has today been distilled and refined and further extended to clubs where people relax and enjoy with like-minded people.

Even from the culinary point of view, the old traditions prevail. The famous " Kabiraj Cutlet " is a blend of the Bengali and the English cuisine. The food and the menu is reminiscent of the good old days. The roast Turkey, for the 'Xmas meal. the club's " Pomme Fondants' , roasts with mint sauce, and the very famous X-mas pudding with brandy sauce are still relished by the Calcuttans.

There is certain peace and tranquillity, so subtle yet so imposing, so quiet yet so vociferous, that one cannot but help envy the city for a touch of romance with a whiff of the yesteryears...............

ANJU MUNSHI

CARNATIC MUSIC

"Others abide our question but like the bard of Avon Thyagaraja is free. There are, too, some half a dozen illumined souls like Bhardachalam Ramadas and Purandara Dasa, whose lives are known in great detail. Several others, not so well known, have made rich contribution peripherally and at the base to the grand design that is Carnatic music. And it is the work of some of them that we propose to chronicle in this series". It is in these words that India's national newspaper, " The Hindu ", introduced a series of 65 biographical essays on Carnatic music composers authored by distinguished scholars and musicologists, published one on every Sunday during the period from December 21, 1959 to March 21, 1971.

One of the oft-repeated critical remarks about classical Carnatic music it that it is too much'Kirtan'-orientated to the detriment of adequate and free 'raga ' delineation. The 'Sahitya ' is said to interfere with melodic presentation of the 'raga '. Now if that were true, there is no need to delve into the biographical and other details about our Carnatic music composers. Hence this criticism must be examined in some detail.

Western orchestral music is built upon pure melody and rhythm But once the composer sets the blue-print of the composition, he leaves no scope for 'mano-dharma' to the performer- 'mano-dharma', as we understand in Carnatic music. On the other hand, Hindustani classical music gives little importance to the composition or the composer. It is all 'mano-dharma' pure and simple unless one is singing a '*bhajan*' or a '*thumri*'.

The rendering of a 'kirtana' undoubtedly enhance the aesthetic impact of a 'raga' by embellishing it with poetic and emotional over-tones. We owe much to our composers, particularly the 'Trinity ' who have given us in their compositions exquisitely structured melodic and intensely poetic phrases full of 'raga ' and 'tala ' *bhava*. It is truly said that while Hindustani music proceeds from note to note, Carnatic music proceeds from phase to phase. Each 'raga ' let alone a song, has its own specific phrases which gives it an individuality. That is why a novice identifies a 'raga ' using a known 'kirtana ', as a model for comparison.

In fact 'bhakti ' has been such a compelling preoccupation in classical Carnatic music, that even apparently erotic compositions are explained away as expressions of 'madhura bhakti '.

The fact that 'bhakti is the principal theme of Carnatic music is further exemplified if one considers the many anonymous composers who composed beautiful songs without an eye on publicity just for their own fulfilment. They sang them during their daily 'pooja '. They taught the songs only to their children so that the tradition is kept up.

Not that there were no other themes in Carnatic music other than 'bhakti ' 'padama ' are not always godly and 'Javalis ' never. But they are mostly meant for dance and dancers. Even then such is the excellence of their musical appeal that these composers cannot be down-graded. They have stood the test of time and find a place not only with the dancers but also with performing vocalists and instrumentalists of Carnatic music.

In fact, classical Carnatic music is unique in that there is hardly anything in the world of music for which it has no answer. It ranges from highly devotional to highly erotic, from songs with an abundance of 'sahitya ' to compositions with minimal or no 'sahitya ' as 'tillanas ' and 'tanams', from sweet musical phrases in words to rhythmic 'chittaswaras ' interspersed with telling effect here and there, from strict adherence to tradition and 'sampradaya' to boundless 'mano-dharma' as in 'neraval ' 'swarakalpana 'and 'Pallavi ', from intricate 'tala puzzles ' to 'tala ' devoid 'slokas ' usually sungs as 'ragamalikas '. Indeed, Carnatic music is a many-splendoured empire worthy of an Alexander to conquer but not many of our Alexanders are worthy of such a conquest, 'sahitya ' being the first casualty.

DR. D. DAYANANDA RAO

CENTRAL MUSEUM, INDORE

Government sponsored; acquires, displays and studies antiquities of Malwa and Nimar regions; organises cultural activities; publishes bibliographies, mss., guide books, picture postcards in Hindi and English, etc., 3,000 books.

References

Dwivedi, V.P. (ed), Brief Directory of Museums in India, New Delhi, 1969.

Patil, H.S. (ed.), Directory of Cultural Organisations in India, New Delhi, 1975.

Sivaramamurthy, C., Directory of Museums in India, Delhi, 1959.

Times of India, Directory & Year Book including Who's Who, Bombay, 1972.

World of Learning, 1969-70, London, 1970.

CENTRAL MUSEUM (LA CHUMIEVE), SHILLONG

State Government owned; district museums at Ziro, Bomdila, Along, Tezu, Khausa and Pasighat; acquires, preserves and displays objects of cultural interest; publishers Arts and Crafts of NEFA.

References

Dwivedi., V.P., (ed.), Brief Directory of Museum in India, New Delhi 1969.

Kothari, Hemraj, Professional & Trade Organisations in India, Calcutta, 1963.

Patil, H.S. (ed.) Directory of Cultural Organisations in India, New Delhi - 1975.

Sivaramamurthi, C., Directory of Museums in India, Delhi, 1959. World of Learning, 1960-70, London, 1970.

CENTRAL MUSEUM, NAGPUR

Government sponsored; mulipurpose with sections on archaeological, crafts, arts, anthropology, natural history and geology; picture gallery; published albums, catalogues, guide books, bulletins, history, etc.; 3,000 books including rare art books.

References

Dwivedi, V.P., Brief Directory of Museums in India, Delhi, 1969. Patil, H.S., (ed.) Directory of Cultural Organisations in India, New Delhi, 1975.

Rode, V.P., Short Guide to the Central Museum, Nagpur, 1960_____, Catalogue of Coins in the Central Museum, Nagpur, Bombay, 1969.

Sivaramamurthi, C., Directory of Museums in India, Delhi, 1959.

A CENTURY OF INDIAN ARCHAEOLOGY

In 1861 Alexander CUNNINGHAM, An army engineer, who had already acquired renown by his antiquarian activities, made a blod bid to end the stalemate by impressing upon Lord Canning, the Governor-General, the necessity of undertaking a systematic programme of exploration in the country. Canning accepted the proposal and established the Archaelogical Survey of India, with Cunningham himself as the Archaelogical Surveyor.This was the first time that the Government unequivocally recognised its responsibility in regard to the monuments and remains of the country. At the same time, the preservation of monuments was not to be a function of the Survey or of any other organisation.

From November 1861 to January 1865, Cunningham covered large parts of North India, following the accounts of the ancient Chinese pilgrims Fa-Hien and Hiuen Tsang. He surveyed and enormous number of monuments and remains and fully reported on them with elaborate illustrations. Unfortunately, the Government, for reasons unknown, decided to abolish the Survey in 1865.

During the next five years some attention was paid to the photographing of monuments and preparation of casts of architectural pieces, but no real work was done. In 1870, Lord Argyll, the Secretary of State for India in the British Government, realised that something more substantial should be undertaken and that could be possible only by a Central organisation. As a result, the Archeological Survey of India once more came into being, with Cunningham as its first Director General. He was this time helped by two (later on three) Assistants.

During the next fourteen years, up to 1885, Cunningham and his Assistants travelled up and down the whole of north and east India, discovering monuments and remains, revisting old ones and bringing to light coins, inscriptions, sculptures and other antiquities. These achievements were summed up by Cunningham himself in the following words: 'I have identified the sites of many of the chief cities and most famous places of ancient India, such as the rock of Aornos, the city of Taxila, and the fortress of Sangala, all connected with the history of Alexander the Great. In India I have found the sites of the celebrated cities of Sankisa, Sravasti and Kausambi, all intimately connected with the history of Buddha. Amongst other discoveries I may mention the Great Stupa of Bharhut, on which most of the principal events of Buddha's life were sculptured and inscribed. I have found three dated inscriptions of king Asoka, and my assistants have brought to light a new pillar of Asoka, and a new text of his rock edicts in Bactrain characters, in which the whole of the 12th edict is complete. I have traced the Gupta style of architecture in the temples of the Gupta kings at Tigowa, Bilsar, Bhitargaon, Kuthera, and Deogarh, and I have discovered new inscriptions of this powerful dynasty at Eran, Udayagiri and other places.'

Considering the extent and fruitfulness of the work done by Cunningham, this is a jejune estimate of his achievements.

Cunningham's survey covered only north and east India. To cover west India, an Archaeological Survey of West India was constituted in 1873 under James Burgess, to whose charge was added the Archaeological Survey of South India in 1881

In 1873, the Supreme Government of India issued instructions to the local governments to preserve monuments. In 1878, however, Lord Lytton, the Governor General, realised that the preservation of monuments should be the responsibility of the Supreme Government itself, for he 'Could not conceive of any claims upon the administrative and financial resources of the Supreme Government more essentially imperial than this'. This resulted in the appointment of H.H. Cole as the Curator of

Ancient Monuments in 1881. During the next two years Cole did satisfactory work, but the post was abolished in 1883, and preservation of monuments once more became the vague responsibility of the local governments.

Cunningham himself took great interest in the collection and decipherment of inscriptions but, at the same time, felt that the available inscriptions should be systematically published according to the dynasties to which they beloged. Accordingly, John Faithful Fleet was appointed Government Epigraphist in 1883 for a period of three years. In 1886, E. Hulzsch was appointed Epigraphist for south Indian inscriptions.

Cunningham finally retired in 1885, to be succeeded in the following year by James Burgess as Director General. But the functions of the Director General were to a very large extent decentralised as there were now three local Surveyors in north and east India, with Burgess in direct charge of west and South India. The system was too complicated to be effective.

Burgess retired after three years, and the Government decided to abolish the Archaeological Survey of India as a Central organisation. All archaeological work developed on the local governments, with the result that hardly any progress was recorded. An attempt was even made to transfer the work to the Asiatic Society of Bengal, which, however, refused to undertake the responsibility; the Society's decision was undoubtedly wise, for then (as now) any country-wide co-ordinated work could only be done by a well-knit Central organisation.

This state of affairs continued till 1898, when the Government woke up to its responsibilities once more and proposed to divide India into five Circles for the purpose of preservation of monuments, each under an Archaelogical Surveyor. The scheme was approved for a short period of five years.

Period of Decision (1899-1903)

Soon after his arrival in India in 1899 as Governor General, Lord Curzon realised the chaotic condition into which Indian archaeology had fallen in the absence of any Central leadership. He noticed that hardly any local government was interested in archaeology, with the result that 'not merely are beautiful and famous buildings crumbling to dacay, but there is neither principle nor unity in conservation or repair'. 'Were Germany the ruling power in India', he stated, 'I do not hesitate to say that she would be spending many lakhs a year on a task to what we have hitherto rather plumed ourselves on our generosity in devoting Rs. 61,000, raised only a year ago to 88,000'. In his famous address to the Asiatic Society of Bengal on the 6th February 1900, he declared: 'Epigraphy should not be set behind research any more than research should be set behind conservation. It is, in my judgment, equally our duty to dig and discover, to classify, reproduce and describe, to copy and decipher and to cherish and conserve. His conception of archaelogy was therefore comprehensive: it included exploration, excavation, research, epigraphy, publication and preservation of monuments and establishment of museums.

Curzon lost no time in giving shape to his ideas, with the result that a new era soon dawned on Indian archaeology. In 1900, he proposed to the British Government the revival of the post of Director General for the supervision and co-ordination of the work of the Archaeological Surveyors. He also proposed that the Central Government should give grants-in-aid to the local governments to the extent of a hundred thousand rupees per year for archaeological work. This was no doubt a compromise between Curzon's ideal of total centralisation (which, as we shall see below, was achieved two decades later) and the prevailing situation.

The British Government having accepted the proposals, John Marshal came to India in 1902, at the age of twenty-six, as the first Director General of the reconstituted Archaeological Survey of India.

1902-21

JOHN MARSHALL succeeded in organising the archaeological activities of the country in a remarkably short period. Within a few years of his arrival, important monuments, such as those at Delhi and Agra, were thoroughly overhauled, excavation was undertaken at a few important sites and museums received a fillip. In 1904, the Ancient Monuments Preservation Act, steps about the framing of which had been taken in 1898-even before Curzon and Marshall was passed 'for the preservation of ancient monuments, for the exercise of control over excavation in certain places, and for the protection and acquisition in certain cases of ancient monuments and of objects of archaeological, historical or artistic interest'

Five Circles had been sanctioned in 1899 for a period of five years. Marshall insisted on the retention of the Survey on a permanent basis, for 'the work of the archaeological officers is of a kind which cannot be discharged by any other existing agancy and it can only cease if the Government cease to admit their responsibility for the preservation of the ancient remains of the country'. In 1906, the Survey was placed on a permanent footing: it was to consist of the Director General, Government Epigraphist and officers for six Circles, to cover the whole India (including Burma but excluding Mysore, which had its own organisation).

Thus placed on a permanent footing with well-defined policies to guide it, the Survey continued its work with greater vigour and confidence. Hundreds of monuments and sites were declared protected and brought under the purview of the Ancient Monuments Preservation Act. Extensive repairs to monuments and excavations were undertaken. Amateurishness was superse-ded by professional zeal byapre and technique

In 1911, the fact that the Survey was almost exclusively in British hands was severely criticised at a conference of Orientalists, with the result that in the following year the Government decided that competent Indians should be appointed to the Survey.It may be mentioned in this connection that in 1921 the Government laid down that forty percent of the service should be European and the rest Indian. It is needless to say that this rule died out long ago, and the Archaeological Survey of India is now entirely manned by Indians.

In 1921, under the Government of India Act, 1919, archaeology was made a Central subject, so that the Survey became entirely a Cenral organisation, the Provinces being left merely with the power of declaring monuments and sites protected under the Ancient Monuments Preservation Act. Even this power was transferred to the Centre by the Government of India Act, 1935.

A brief mention may be made here of the excavations carried out by the Survey up to 1920.Under Cunningham, there was a preference for Buddhist sities: Sarnath, Rajgir,Sravasti, Kusinagara and Nalanda, all in the central Ganga valley, Sanchi in central India and the remains in the North-West Frontier Province received adequate attention: knowledge of Buddhist architecture, art and iconography advanced enormously. Of the city-sities, Bhita and Patna, again in the central Ganga basin, and Taxila in the north-west were excavated. The first place proved to be a commercial twonship of pre-Christian origin. Near Patna, the remnants of the Mauryan palace of Pataliputra were laid bare; it was believed that the palace consisted of a wooden structure resting over eighty or more stone pillars. The prolonged excavations at Taxila, started in 1913 and continued till 1934, brought to light remains of three successive cities: the earliest, Bhir Mound, orginating in about the fifth century B.C., must have witnessed the invasion of Alexander; the second, Sirkap, was established under the Indo-Greeks and had a most systematic town-planning during the days of the Indo-Parthians; and the third, Sirsukh, was established in Kushan times.

1921-28

A monumentous event took place, viz., the discovery of an ancient civilisation at Harappa in Montgomery District of Punjab and at Mohenjo-daro in Larkana District of Sind, both now in Pakistan. Excavation at the first site was started in 1921 and at the second 1922. It was realised at the outset that the relics of the culture exposed at these two places (now known as the Indus Valley Culture or, more appropriately, the Harappa Culture) were beyond the common range of Indian antiquities till then known. When brief results of the discoveries, which included steatite seals with strange writings on them, were published in London in 1924, foreign scholars at once noticed that similar seals had been found at some sities in Iraq in levels belonging to the third millennium B.C. The archaeology of India was thus at once pushed back by two thousand years, for till then there was hardly anything which attedated Buddha (Sixth-fifth century B.C.). Expensive excavations were conducted at both sites till 1931 and the remains of two large cities laid bare. A comprehensive exploration of Sind and Baluchistan was undertaken between 1925 and 1931. In Sind, apart from the discovery of a large number of smaller stations of the Harappa Culture, an outstanding discovery was an earlier culture at Amri and a later culture at Jhukar and Chanhudaro. In Baluchistan were discovered a large number of sities belonging to various dates, some earlier and others later than the Harappa Culture.

The other excavations during the period included the Buddhist sites of Nalanda, Paharpur and Nagarjunakonda.

Since 1928

MARSHALL retired from the office of the Director General in 1928. In 1932, the Exploration Branch was done away with due to shortage of funds.

In the same year, to encourage outsiders, including foreigners, to undertake excavations, the Ancient Monuments Preservation Act was amended. Taking advantage of this, the American School of India and Iranian Studies and the Boston Museum of Fine Arts jointly excavated at Chanhu-daro in 1935-36. In 1935, the Yale and Cambridge Universities sent a geological cum prehistoric expedition to India under the leadership of Helmut De Terra. The expedition did most valuable work in the country, particularly in the north-west.

In 1939, the excavation technique and policies of the Department came under severe criticism from a distinguished British archaeologist,Sir Leonard Woolley, who had been invited by the Government to advise on the future policy on exploration and excavation. The Indian archaeologists had not kept in touch with the techniques of excavation improved in Europe and America, with the result that the methods followed by them were antiquated. The archaeology of large parts of the country had remained in the dark.

Between 1940 and 1944, the Department undertook ex-tensive excavations at Ahichchhatra in the upper Ganga valley and established for the first time a cultural sequence of the region from the second half of the first millennium B.C. to about A.D. 1100.

In 1944, Dr. Robert Eric Mortimer Wheeler was appointed Director General and under him the Survey witnessed an allround progress. His excavations at Taxila, Arikamedu near Pondicherry on the east coast, Harappa, and Brahmagiri in the lower deccan. Brought forth significant results. Thus, in Sirkap the second city of Taxila, the stratigraphic relationship between its defences and the habitation inside was established. At Harappa was laid bare a tremendous defensive wall unnoticed before; also was identified and excavated a cemetery of the Harappa Culture. At Brahmagiri a chacolithic culture of the first millennium B.C. was brought to light and the chronology of the great South Indian Iron Age megalithic complex, till then an enigma, was placed on a sound footing.

In 1950, the Constitution of India made far-reaching changes in the official position of archaeology: it prescribed

(1) ancient and historical monuments and archaeological sites and remains declared by or under law made by Parliament to be of national importance should be in charge of the central Government:

(2) ancient and historical monuments not belonging to the first category should be in charge of the State (Provincial) Government; and

(3) both the Central and State Governments will have jurisdiction over archaeological sites and remains not belonging to the first category.

In pursuance of this, Parliament, in 1951, passed an Act declaring to be of national importance all the monuments and sites which had been previously protected under the Ancient Monuments Preservation Act, together with a large number in pre-Independence days called the princely states, over which the Government of India had till then no archaeological jurisdiction before.

ARCHAEOLOGY IN STATES

Following the disappearance of all princely states with the Independence of India and the taking over. their important monuments by the Central Government as monuments of national importance, a large part of the staff of the Departments of Archaeology of those states where such Departments had existed was taken over by the Central Survey in 1953. In 1959, the staff and important monuments of Jammu and Kashmir were similarly taken over.

The States have a great archaeological role to play. No central body, however large, can effectively take care of all the monuments that stud the large countrysome of them the focous of local pride and sentiment. Even if they are not of any outstanding historical, archaeological or architectural importance, they are nevertheless worthy of preservation for posterity. Some State Government have not only taken, within a short time, steps in this direction but have also undertaken important explorations and excavations.

INTERNATIONAL COLLABORATION

India has been intimately connected with the archaeological and museological organisations of UNESCO almost from their very inception. (condensed)

A.GHOSH

CHAMPAWAT : ITS HISTORY & MONUMENTS

Champawat, a city 76 kms. southwest of Pithoragarh, on the main road from Tanakpur toward the hills is very ancient. It was the " first capital of the Kings of Kumaon".But the Chand dynasty Kings who lived here, seem to have had control over the isolated and fiercely independent settlement in Kumaon only for short periods of time. Somachand was the legendary founder of the dynasty. The last ruler of the local royal family was said to be cruel and greedy. The suffering people got together and threw him off a precipice. The elders then went searching for a suitable king. The fame of the ruler of Kannauj attracted them to a young prince from this " Chandravanshi" family, who was living in Jhusi, across the Ganga from Allahabad. They brought him back to Champawat, where he was married to a princess of the previous ruler's family, and became the King.

One of several alternate versions of the story claims that he was a prince from Kannauj who came to the hills on a pilgrimage. An elderly local ruler found him so charming that he gave him his daughter's hand in marriage, and the area around Champawat as dowry.

If there is anything in today's Champwat that might date back to the time of this possibly legendry figure, it would probably be the massive gateway and wall that are all that remain of the old Royal Fort.

"The temple of Nagnath is a point of attraction", a U.P. Tourism pamphlet claims. This is an architecturally unimposing shrine near the Fort. Iron trishulas (tridents) fill the small enclosure. More interesting to those interested in art, however, would be the Baleshwar temple complex in the heart of the city.

Baleshwar is a form of the God Shiva. It is quite possible that Baleshwar was worshipped by the early Chand Kings here- or even the rulers before them - but shrines are always being "modernized" by worshippers and patrons. The present group of buildings seems to date from the 13th century, at the earliest estimate.

It is believed that a Gujarati Brahmin was invited to consecrate the temple, to suggest that he must have brought along some Gujarati masons also, because the design and ornamentation of the temples is so much like that favoured by the Gujarati Solanki Kings. The larger surviving dome of the main temple, for instance, has the same basic design as Tejpal's famous temple at Mt. Abu. Clearly, there was a free exchange of artistic ideas, if not actually of artisans, between the plains and the hills even in that distant era.

"Hearsay history " seems to have had serious consequences for the Baleshwar temple. Early historian Ferishta repeated the story that the kings of the hills has " gold, copper and ealth" , and each king preserved the treasure of his father. By his calculation the hills hid 56 separate royal treasures. This fabled wealth was enough to send Rohilkhand cheiftains charging off into the Himalayas in 1570, and again in 1734, when a Chand ruler had also offended them for killing a rival while he was under their protection.

Each one of the images in the Baleshwar temples was defaced in one of these raids, people say. By the time of the second raids,people say. By the time of the second raid, though, the Chand çapital had been moved to Almora, to be nearer to the centre of their growing kingdom. Neglect and lack of royal partonage may have contributed a lot to the crumbling of these grand monuments, of which only a small corner, locally called " Rani ka chabutara" , remains.
(condensed)

LUCINDA DHAVAN

CHANDIGARH : BEAUTIFUL GARDEN CITY

When India became independent in 1947, the Indian state of Punjab lost its original capital of Lahore to the newly-born Pakistan. It had not to look for a new capital.

It was at this juncture that Pandit Jawaharlal Nehru, the first Prime Minister of independent India, suggested to the first Chief Minister of the state, Partap Singh Kairon, that he should build a brand new town, which would be a symbol of free India - unfettered to the past. The Chief Minister of Punjab, who was very close to the Prime Minister, readily accepted the idea and the first completely planned new city of Chandigarh, surrounded by majestic Shivalik hills and Sukhna Lake, came into being. It is now the state capital of the two most prosperous Indian states- Haryana and Punjab.

It is a well known fact that the city of Chandigarh was planned by the great French architect, Le Corbusier, but waht is little known is that a lot of pioneering work was done by two American architects called Albert Mayer and Mathew Nowicki who were approached for the planning of this project by the Chief Minister of Punjab, before the arrival of Le Corbusier.

Albert Mayer was the founder of the well-known architectural firm of Mayer and Whittlesey and Glass of New York who had worked in India during World-War-II in the US army and was involved in building airfields in Bengal and Burma.

Planning a completely new city to house more than a couple of million people, with all the modern urban amenities, was an enormously challenging job. After the location of the city was finalised with the Shivalik Hills in the background and Sukhna Lake on the periphery, Mayer planned to have a lot of greenery around, a city which would provide all the modern facilities to its inhabitants with a look of the countryside. The American architect was greatly influenced by the romantic Garden City movement of England of the nineteenth century. It was after the tragic death of the brilliant Mathew Nowicki in a plans crash that Albert Mayer found himself helpless to carry out a project of this magnitude and abandoned it. A former chief architect and perhaps the only surviving Indian associate of the Chandigarh Capital project, Mrs. Eulie Choudhary, was of the opinion that Mayer was creating a city more similar to an Indian city than a modern one created by Le Corbusier.

Although the present day Chandigarh is entirely different in essence than what Mayer- Nowicki team had conceptualised, but Corbusier cleverly blended the traditional with the modern and used some Indian motifs selectively while discarding some, like the use of *Jaalis,* which not really fit into modern architecture.

Some very distinguished Indians were also involved with the Chandigarh project from its inception. They were ICS officers P.N. Thapar and E.N.Mangat Rai and an extremely talented and jovial architect Piloo Mody, who incidentally married an American girl who had come to work on this project. Another ICS officers M.S. Randhawa is responsible for the beautifully laid-out avenues of flowering trees all over Chandigarh.

Chandigarh is not only famous for its majestically imposing buildings, clean wide roads, posh houses, rose gardens, transquil environment, huge population of top retired civil servants but also for the world famous rock garden which attracts hundreds of tourists everyday from all over the country and abroad. Along with sprawling bungalows surrounded by vast expanses of greenery and neatly laid-out flats, it caters to any and every conceivable need of its inhabitants. A huge university with several colleges, a high court, club with swimming pool (Press Club of Chandigarh is the best and cleanest in the whole country), hotels to cater to every pocket, huge office complexes and shopping malls, Post-Graduate Institute of Medicine which is attracting students from several foreign countries and newspapers of its own. It has practically everything one can think of.

Chandigarh is certainly not a concrete jungle like so many other big cities but is a great experiment in comfortable urban living.
(condensed)

N. K. SAREEN

CHANDRA MAHAL : THE CITY PALACE OF JAIPUR

Jaipur is a charming city. It did not grow over the centuries; it was built to order. Sawai Jai Singh-II, Raja of Amber, realised that his ambitions had out-grown the small hill capital north of Jaipur. He ordered the building of a new city where his imagination could create architectural splendours to equal in grandeur the Mughal cities of Agra and Delhi where he had served Aurangzeb and Muhammad Shah II. Sawai Jai Singh was a multi-faceted genius-architect, engineer, astronomer, mathematician, connoisseur of art and a lover of beauty and elegance. Jaipur was to be the realisation of his dream city fortified bastions, magnificent gateways, splendid palaces, long wide avenues laid on grid pattern to form eight squares with the central royal palace in the auspicious ninth square. The *Shilpa Shastras* were consulted by architect Vidyadhar to build this most elegant and spectacular of cities of Rajasthan.

Jaipur wears the stamp of Sawai Jai Singh's genius. Legend has it that when he was 13, he was presented before the Mughal Emperor Aurangzeb who dispensed with courtesy and rudely asked his young visitor; " Your ancestors gave me much trouble. Now say· what you deserve of me before saying what you desire". And to confound the lad's wits further, he held both his hands and lowered over him; "Tell me, what use are your arms now ? "The Prince answered: "Your Majesty, when · a bridegroom take his bride's hand in one of his own during the wedding, he is bound by duty to protect her all his life. Now that the Emperor of India has taken my· hand in his right hand, what have I to fear ? With your Majesty's long arms to protect me, what other arms do I need ? Aurangzeb was stunned at this smart repartee. The prince had clearly outwitted Aurangzeb but the Mughal Emperor was pleased. He admitted Jai Singh as "Sawai" (one and a quarter) over his contemporaries. All subsequent rulers of Jaipur bore this title.

Chandra Mahal, the city palace of Jaipur, is the most splendid showpiece of the city. It stands surrounded by a host of various small and multi-purpose structures-indispensible accoutrements of a royal residence, offices and guest houses, kitchens and stables.As with the Mughal cities, particularly Fatehpur Sikri, which seems to have much inspired the Sawai, the private residential apartments are concealed behind high curtain walls and heavily guarded imposing gateways. Life in royal palaces as in humble houses centres around the courtyard which drwas the inmates aut of their chambers.

There is a vast courtyard surrounded by rows of double-storeyed rooms with balconies. At the centre stands Mubarak Mahal, an excellently designed guest house with the elegance of jewel box. Mubarak Mahal is a lovely double-storyed structure with exquisite ornamentation in white marble.

On the northern side stands *Sarhad ki Deorhi*, a lovely gateway to the inner precincts. Its central arch is guarded by two elegant marble elephants. At the centre stands *Sarvatobhadra* or *Diwan-i-khas* on a podium. It is a simple but functional hall of a double row of columns supporting scalloped salman-pink arches. Ministers and high officials met here for higher consultations. On display here are two huge pure sterling silver urns which in 1901 Madho Singh-II carried with him to London in a specially chartered ocean linear. These contained Ganga water enough to last his stay abroad. Each urn can contain 1800 gallons (8181 litres) of water; 242.7 kilograms of silver· was required to cast each urn. The Guinness Book of World Records takes a due note of these urns.

Ridhi Sidhi Pole, a four-storeyed grand portal, separates the Diwan-i-khas area from the palace. Framed within a long ornamental triple-storeyed facade of wall with window openings covered with decorative jali work, Ridhi Sidhi Pole is simply magnificent. Two staggered door lead into *Pritam Chowk*. Pritam Chowk is really likes courtyard designed for the exclusive use by royal family. On the eastern and western walls are four marvellously frescoed doorways supporting romantic balconies. These frescoes depict moods of four Indian seasons. The door used for entry from the Ridhi Sidhi Pole is the peacock door, most exquisitely decorated with gorgeous peacock motifs in turquoise blue, amber and acquamarine.

Chandra Mahal stands on the northern side of Pritam Chowk, It is a grand pile in seven storeys, quiet and majestic. The pyramidal structure of the palace has received additions from many a Maharaja of Jaipur. The engrailed arches, now closed, with fabulous jali screens and projected balconies are rather reminiscent of the Panch Mahal at Sikri. In a daring architectural experiment some remarkable features of both Rajput and Mughal styles have been fused to create an imposing royal residence to suit the climatic conditions in a dry country and privacy required by the seraglio. Only the ground floor hall admits visitors. It displays portraits of Jaipur rulers. Gold work on the ceiling is extermely attractive. The doors at Chandra Mahal are superb examples of fastidious craftmanship, particularly the brass door depicting scenes from Lord Krishna's life. The upper floors of the palace were subsequent additions by later rulers whose individual tastes dictated the style. Mukut Mahal, the crowing pavilion, is in white marble with an attractive curvilinear roof. The city palace provides ramps in place of regular stairs. This was to facilitate easy climb for the palanquin bearers and wheel chairs. A particular Maharaja was afflicted with rheumatism, hence the arrangement.

The Diwan-i-Amm, a grand hall is now used as a museum. It is virtually a treasure of rare art objects-carperts from Herat, Lahore and Agra; exquisite miniature of the Jaipur, Kishangarh, Bundi and Kota schools of paintings; manuscripts of Sawai Jai Singh's work on astronomy; Abul Fazl's translation of the Mahabharata in Persian called *Razmnamah* besides a grand collection of palanquins used by the Maharaja of yesteryears. Here Queen Elizabeth II was accorded a grand reception befitting the heritage of Jaipur.

The most fanciful *zenana* (for females) palace, part of the Chandra Mahal complex, is *Hawa Mahal*, built by Sawai Pratap Singh (1778- 1803). Here from behind 953 niches on its five- storeyed facade, ladies could watch processions on the street below. This pyramidal structure was meant for the enjoyment of breeze. Surely, as Edwin Arnold extolled its beauty; "Alladin's magician could have called into existence no more marvellous abode. "It is Jaipur's landmark famous the world over.

SURENDRA SAHAI

The Encyclopaedia of Indian Culture

CHARIOT FESTIVAL OF LORD JAGANNATH

The chariot festival of Lord Jagannath of Puri presents a grand spectacle, with thousands of deveotees in a frenzied ecstasy pulling and pushing the chariots of the holy Trinity......

The grand chariot festival of Lord Jagnnath takes place in the month of June-July. The festival is celebrated to mark the sojourn to the garden-house of Lord Jagannath from his own abode in the temple complex at Puri. The holy deities, Balabhadra, Subhdra and Jagannath are taken out of the sanctuary and placed on three separate chariots. Thousands of people lay their hands on the sturdy ropes of the chariots and drag the massive structures along the grand road or *Bada Danda*. The chariots are led towards Sri Gundicha temple with usual fanfare in a spectacular procession called *Pabandi*. In a frenzied ecstasy the devotees pull, push and draft the chariots of the holy triad to the accompaniment of the beat of cymbals, drums and chanting of their names in chorus. The chariots move forward slowly untill they reach the Gundicha temple. But it is the custom that deities instead of entering the Gundicha temple on that very day stay overnight on the chariots and the next morning they enter the temple and stay there for seven days.

The chariots of the deities are made by a special team of carpenters who have hereditary rights of this. Jagannath's chariot is called 'Nandighosha' which is decked with red and yellow cloth coverings. The chariot of Balabhadra, known as Taladhwaja' is covered with red and blue cloth, while the chariot of Subhadra, called 'Darpadalana', is covered with red and black.

The colossal wooden images of the holy triad are adorned with giant floral crowns called 'Tahias'. The deities are seated in their respective chariots. Before these are drawn by the people the ritual called *Cbera Pabandra* or the sweeping of the chariots with a golden broom by the king of Puri, starts. This is symbolic rite which proclaims that the king like all others, is but a humble servant of the real sovereign, Lord Jagannath.

PROF. PRANAB RAY

CHENGANNUR RAMAN PILLAI

Born 1884 in Chengannur, Central Travancore; developed in early boyhood interest in Kathakali, his father Parameswaran Pillai a Chutti (make-up) artist; uncle Nanu Pillai a Kathakali actor; received early training under Takashi Kesava Panikkar; and later under Ambalapusha Kunhukrishna Panikkar; balance between acting and dance has a rare aesthetic appeal; in him Kathakali tradition preserved with classic fulness; only Asan of note in South Kerala; enjoys topmost position among Kathakali dancers.

CHHATH PUJA

Chhath is the most popular festival of Bihar, as important in this state as *Pongal* is in Tamil Nadu and *Durga Puja* in West Bengal. *Chhath* is the sixth day after Diwali. *Chhath* is observed with solemnity. There is no pomp and show, there is no wasteful expenditure, no room for any hooliganism and rowdyism. Only a pure sense of humility and sacrifice. According to Hindu tradition, Chhath has been performed from the time of the Aryan invasion of this part of the country. Its most important element is the worship of the sun god, on the bank of a river or tank. The celebration starts from the fourth day of *Diwali*, which is known as *Nahakha*. On that day, the whole house is meticulously clearned. After a ritual bath, family members sit down to eat a vegetarian meal. Curd is an obligatory item on the menu, and the price of this vegetable shoots up to Rs. 15 per kilo during festival days. Central to the *Chhath* festival is the *Parvati*. On the fifth day, the *parvati* observes a dawn to dusk fast, traditionally broken with a *kheer* made of *gur*, or with rice and *dal*. No vegetables are served on this day. After the fast is broken, the *parvatis* eat nothing till the break of dawn on the seventh day. After sunset on the sixth evening the *Parvati* performs a puja, standing kneedeep in the water of a river or tank. The *parvatis* are supposed to crawl on their hands and knees from their houses to the river bank. The most important *puja* is performed on the dawn of the seventh day after *Diwali*. The main *puja* starts at the crack of dawn, but people rush in large numbers to the river banks as early as 2 a.m. just to corner a place. The turn out on the bank of the Ganga in Patna crosses two lakh, most of them women. After the *Puja,* the *parvatis* fast is broken with a *sherbet*.

(Summarised)

SOROOR AHMED

CHHATTISHGARH AND ITS HISTORIC TEMPLE

The Chhattishgarh region is a quiet place where nature is at its best. Vast open fields of red earth and pockets of jungle thick with sall trees greet a visitor. Here the greet of the nature is more intense. Set among these pristine environs are neat village houses; the gentle villagers placidly go about their daily chores. The discovery of ruins of an ancient temple excavated in a village in 1976-77 near Bilaspur is revealing.

What have been excavated are the complete ruins of two temples. The only thing that exists is part of the foundation of a half constructed temple with the entry pillars and some statues. The material used is locally available red coloured stone. The upper portions may have been made of brick but have totally withered away.

The main attraction is an eight-foot high statue of Rudra Shiva. It was found in a horizontal position below the temple near the steps. What is exteremely interesting is that this representation has not been found anywhere else in India in the myridads of sculptures that exist of Shiva.

The features on the face have been given animal forms. Coils of a serpent form the hair. A lizard forms the nose with hind limbs as the eyebrows. Peacocks are ears, two fish facing each other are moustache and the crab is the mouth. Nine faces are carved on the rest of the body; two on the chest, a massive one covers the entire stomach region, two on each thigh and two on the knees. The penis is a tortoise's head. One wonders, what could have been in the mind of the sculptor when making this representation.

On the gateway of the temple are several carvings of amorous couples surrounded by floral borders. There is also a demon like figure carved with a profusion of swirls on the entrance pillar. On the beam is a pot bellied seated figure with elaborate carvings of faces and figures around. These complex sculptures are belived to date back to the 5th or 6th century A.D. during the reign of Dakshin Kaushal rulers and experts believe additions were made in the 8th or 9th century A.D.

Next to this temple of Shiva, there is a much larger ruin. This temple is unique in its style of construction and the originality of its sculptures. The temple faces south. There are two more entry doors facing east and west.

Lying around are several carved pillars. The intricate carvings of floral motifs, fluted columns, very modern sculpted figures quite unadored, but elegant. Although not by design, the manner in which the structure had fallen apart surprisingly creates a pleasing composition.

The ruins stand completely by themselves. Nothing else exists nearby that has a connection with them except the stony banks of the river Miniari which have a natural sculptured beauty.

(Condensed)

JAHAR KANUNGO

CHHAU

Chhau : unique form masked dance, preserved by royal family of farmer state Saraikela, Bihar, dancer impersonates god, animal, bird, hunter, rainbow, night, flower, acts short theme, performs vignettes annual Chaitra Parva festival, April, Chhau masks, predominantly humand features, Modified to suggest, what pertraying dancer's body communicates, total emotional, psychological of character, feet, gesture language, toes agile, dancer mute, no song sung, instrumental music accompanied.

Another form, Mayurbhanj district, Orissa actor do not wear masks, stiff and immobile faces; movements vigorous, acrobatic.

CHICKANKARI OF LUCKNOW

The very mention of the city of Nawabs conjures up an image of regal splendour. It is only appropriate that the highly creative art of *Chikankari* found a niche here and became the established craft of this historical city.

The word *chikan* stems from a persian word and means " to raise". *Chikankari* is said to have been brought to Awadh (Lucknow) from Persia. It flourished under the patronage of the nobility and the Nawabs of Lucknow. The art was developed and promoted and it reaches a high degree of finesse catering to a highly appreciative clientele not only in India but in other parts of the world as well.

The origin of *chikan* work, however, is romanticised. The legend has it that a 19th century Nawab had in his large harem a princess of Murshidabad (one of the main centres of *Chikankari*). A skilful seamstress, she embroidered an exquisite cap for him out of an old piece of muslin. This so delighted him that she became his favourite Begum (queen). The other princesses vied with each other to produce yet more delicate patterns to win the favour of the Nawab.

Another school of thought establishes Empress Nurjahan as a great patron of *chikankari*. Fascinated by the Turkish architectural embellishments on marble edifices, she tried to execute them on cloth.

Her ladies in waiting taught *chikankari* to the other women in the harem.

In Bengal, *Chikankari* was executed on an off-white tusser woven from the fibres of the Indian wild silkworms, or the legendary Dacca Muslim which was renowned for its softness and finesse. In Lucknow, the material used was the local muslin called *Tanzeb*.

Here the craft was passed on from generation to generation and bacame a hereditary vocation. Faiz Khan's family has been in this trade for the last 200 years. Ustad Moammed Shair Khan one of his forefathers, was perhaps the first of master the craft when a passing traveller taught him the intricacies of the stitches, as he gave him a drink on a hot summer day.

Chikankari embroiderers even today believe that he was God incarnate.

Traditional *chikankari* is embroidered onto muslin with a white thread.First the pattern is drawn on the cloth. The embroidery is then done on the underside of the cloth to appear as an opaque pattern. The lace like effect of the design depends largely on the variety of stitches employed and also on the ranging grades of thread. Open work is very often combined with shadow work to emphasise the details. The outlines are either subtle or bold. Earlier, colour was more or less avoided so that the minute stitches by their sheer excellence provided the ornamentation. The love for pastel hues relates to the era where any show of blatant extravaganza was considered gauche. However, modern fashions incorporate all colours and patterns.

Today almost 50,000 craftsmen work zealously trying to eke out a living from this art. A large number of Muslim women are engaged in the trade. And with the passage of time *chikankari* has been modernised. The embroidery is not just confined to shadow work, but a variety of designs have been evolved. Each design is identified by a particular name, which describes the different stitches used, like *Bakhia Tepchi, kamdani* etc.

Many organisations have now come up to give an impetus to this art. As a result, its annual production has now reached worth Rs. 70 million. Of this, exports to countries like the USA, Italy, Canada, Australia, France and England account for about Rs. 45 million.

(Condensed)

ARCHANA SINGH

CHILDREN'S FILMS IN INDIA

It has been accepted by the educationists all over the world that audio-visual methods are the best means of educating persons, more so children. Certain films do at times create in the minds of children a sense of wrong values and an unbalanced view of life, capable of producing harmful and undesirable results and a lopsided personality. Adult films with such themes as crime and sex have a harmful effect on a child's mind which is not yet enough to be able to discriminate between good and evil and to discard what is evil and accept that what is acceptable.

The late Pandit Jawaharlal Nehru once said: "... the cinema, let us remember, is one of the biggest influence in the modern world. There are many other things which influence people; books, newspapers and so on. But I think it is perfectly correct to say that influence of the films in India is greater than the influence of newspapers and books combined."

R. P. AGNOHOTRI
R. K. CHATTERJEE

CHILDREN'S MUSEUMS

It is an undisputable fact that the museums make a remarkable impact upon the receptive faculties of a child, and so also in the realm of education. In India the children's section of the Amreli Museum (Gujarat) made a pioneering effort to introduce and establish children's museums in the country under the patronage and encouragement of Pratap Roy Mehta. It was inaugurated in the year 1955 by Morarji Desai. This brings up a number of new methods to suit the requirements of the child. Amreli Museum houses a wide range of exhibits that are interesting to children as well as adults. The objects are intended to impart knowledge and to create interest on the subjects ta ght in the classes to the children.

In the year 1956 a children's section was added to the main sections of the Salar Jung Museum, the exhibits of which come from the bulk of the collection of Nawab Salar Jung - III.

Some of the state museums have now taken considerable interest in setting up and developing the children's sections. The Government Museum, Madras has a beautiful children's section which was recently opened to the public. Likewise children's section have been started at few other regions.

NATIONAL CHILDREN'S MUSEUM

According to the recommendations of the Central Advisory Board of Museums. National children's Museum has been started at New Delhi in 1955-56 which was inaugurated by Dr. Shrimali, the then Minister for Education. Devoted to elucidation of scientific principles, problems of natural history, arts and crafts, history and culture. It was hoped that this institution would serve as a model and give impetus to establish more children's museums throughout the country. Museum has started functioning with limited material and now the staff of the museum is actively engaged in collecting the material and exhibiting them to suit the requirements of children.

To sum up, it can be said that the children's museums play a vital role in the realm of education for children by stimulating and developing the hidden power of the child. Education can be made easy it we impact education through the material evidences for which the meseums are best institutions. It is therefore, necessary that the central, state Governments and public should give sufficient support and encouragement for starting and developing the children's museums throughout the country at least one in a district, Schools, and colleges should be encouraged to develop their own museums on such subjects that are taught in their institutions to make themselves colplete.

G.G. KRISNIAH

Reference
Govt. Of India, India- A Reference Annual, 1984, New Delhi.

CHILKA : LARGEST SALT WATER LAKE OF ASIA

Bordered by the Bay of Bengal on the east coast of the Deccan penisula lies the Indian State of Orissa. Unique and fascinating, it is both a fusion of art, craft and holy temples on one hand and bountiful nature with lush green forests on the other. Known also as the green jewel state of India, as more than one-third of her land is under forest cover, Orissa is home to the three mighty rivers and the largest fresh and salt water lake of Asia-Chilka.

Covering an area of over 1100 sq. Kilometers, Chilka Lake is separated from the sea by marginal strips of fragile land which have actually resulted into the creation of the vast marshes, lowlands like islands. Nalabarra island with a circumference of approximately eight kms. is extremely scenic. Also called the Island of Reeds, it attracts a very large variety of migratory birds from November to March from as far as Siberia and the Persian Gulf. Flamingoes, teals, bar-headed geese, a variety of ducks including the Brahminy ducks, coots, shovellers and white-bellied sea eagles can be seen in plenty at Chilka.

The picturesque setting of the lake with thousands of birds chirping and playing on the waterbed of the lake, infact transports one into a different world far away from the madding crowds. An early morning cruise on the lake reveals a large variety of birds, the most impressive and striking being the delicate pink flamingoes, the huge stately cranes and one could also have an occasional glimpse of the Gangetic dolphins and of course the majestic brown-necked white sea eagles in flight.

The spectacular sight of innumerable ducks and other birds taking off from the lake and then suddenly diving back into its cool waters.

RAJ MITTAL

CHITA MURALS

In a prolonged worship of four to five weeks in the month of *Marqasira* (November 21- December 21) Goddess Laxmi is feliciated. Cleanliness is the first prerequisite. Homes are repaired, plasttered and cleaned and a typical decorative mural locally known a *Chita* is drawn on walls, doorways, Courtyards and around the " Tulsi Manch ". The medium is a watery mixture of rice flour. No brish is used, only the fingers.*Chita* may not be assured of the status of an accepted art form, but it embodies in its form and strictures all the basis

characteristic of traditional Indian art. *Chita* finds its origin in mythology and ritual. Like all art it is "concept" in image form through its images, it seeks to represent the ultimate universal force. That is precisely why, like all other ancient Indian art forms, *Chita* brings to the beholder, a touch of serenity and mystical pleasure. A typical portrayal of *Chita* represents many and varied images, that of flowers and birds vines and animals, paddy sheafs and Laxmis feet. The diversity suggests movement. It portrays the restlessness, the intensity of felling of the artist. The inherent rhytham, symmetry, order and balance. The symmetry order and balance coverage a sense of harmonious integration. From this results a feeling of purity, and tranquility which is the basic purpose of the ritualistic *Chita*.
(Summerised)

MANIPADMA JENA

CHITRASALA OF VARINDAVAN

Indians by nature are extermely fond of the art of painting. They consider it as art supreme. A verse in the *Vishnu Dharmottra Purana* says: " Of all the arts the art of painting is the greatest. It is giver of *dharma*, *artha*, *kama*, and *moksha*, the four goals of human exitence. It is very propitious to decorate the house with paintings. Thus says the *Purana:* "

In his celebrated work, the *Kamasutra*, author Vatsyana has given the blueprint of citizen's house. He says that the Man-of-the-town or *Nagaraka* should keep in his bedroom the palette, colours, brushes, canvas to paint pictures whenever he feels like painting. Also, in classical Indian poetry and plays there are several references to the art of painting.

We know about the heroes of the dramas who fall in love with the heroines on seeing their paintings, or take to drawing the pictures of their beloveds when separated from them.

In the world-famous Sanskrit play, the *Abhijnan Shakuntalam*, there is reference to king Dushyanta, the hero, doing a beautiful painting of the heroine, Shakuntala, when he was separated from her by the quirk of fate. So striking was the likeness that the courtiers felt that it was not the painting of the heroine but Shankuntala herself was standing before them;

In the palaces of yore a separate, spacious hall used to be marked for keeping such paintings and they were known as *chitrashalas*,In ancient literature we find several references to *Chitrashalas* or art galieries. They were precursors to modern day private and public art galleries.

There was a practice of illustrating the walls of the *Chitrashalas*. As we know in India there was a tradition of painting specially treated walls of the caves as is evident from the famous cave paintings of Ajanta. In ancient India there was a practice of painting the walls of the theatre halls as well.

Modern India too witnessed the rise of public art galleries for the display of works of art of contemporary artists. One such famous art gallery in the national capital of New Delhi is that of Lalit Kala Akademi, known as Ravindra Bhavan Art Gallery.

However, most of these arts galleries are located in big cities. But recently a magnificent are gallery has come up in the small temple town of Vrindavan.

About 150 kilometers from the national capital of New Delhi, Vrindavan is situated on the banks of river Yamuna in the Indian state of Uttar Pradesh.

On the outskirts of the city of Vrindavan, situated by the side of the road leading to the village Chatikara, is a lovely tourist complex named *Nandanvan* spread over ten acres of land, well endowed with beautiful gardens. In this complex is a magnificent building named as *krishna Mahal* or the Palace of Krishna. This building belongs to the family of traditional artists of Vrindavan, the Chitrakars.

Keeping in mind the tradition of Indian palaces having *Chitrashalas* or art galleries, the *Chitrakars* constructed a spacious *Chirtashala* in the basement of the Krishna Mahal.

Rectangular in design, the floor area of the *Chitrashala* is about five thousand square feet. The unique feature of this *Chitrashala* is that it is exclusively devoted to the display of gold paintings created by the *Chitrakar* family of Vrindavan.

The tradition of using gold in the form of ink or thin sheet, Varkha, is quite old. We find specimens of gold paintings since 12th century A.D. Various schools of Miniature paintings including Mughal, Pahari and Rajpur used gold in some form or the other.

The tradition later spread to South India and we find gold being used lavishly in the Tanjore School of Painting. So profuse was the use of gold and semi-precious and precious stones in the paintings of this school that they almost looked like huge ornaments rather than paintings.

Under the British rule the tradition or making gold paintings declined and almost went out of vogue.

Around fifty years ago Kanhai, *Chitrakar* of Vrindavan, made serious efforts to revive this art. He started making gold paintings studded with semi-precious and precious stones in his studio situated in Vrindavan. Later he was joined by his sons, Krishna and Govinda, and with their help he could enlarge his artistic activity.

The *Chitrakar* family felt the need of establishing a permanent art gallery, the Chitrashala, for the display of gold paintings created by them in an effort to revive the tradition of yore. In 1995, they constructed Krishna Mahal or the Palace of Krishna and devoted its spacious basement portion to house the gold paintings.

There are about fifty gold paintings of various sizes and dimensions displayed on the walls of the *Chitrashala*. A portion of it is used as studio where you can see various gold paintings being made by artists under the guidance of *Chitrakars*.

The subject of these gold paintings is Lord Krishna, the hero of the epic *Mahabharata*. Lord Krishna spent much of his childhood years in the cowherd settlement of Vrindavan. The pastoral land of Vraja, of wich Vrindavan is a part, is known as the playground of Krishna.

Vrindavan is a great cultural centre of North India. Old traditions of dance, drama Dhrupad music still linger in the city. It also has a great tradition of painting the temple-walls depicting the childhood of Lord Krishna. To this, Chitrakar family added a new chapter by reviving the old tradition of gem-studded gold paintings based on Krishna theme.

The Vrindavan Art Gallery of Chitrakars is the only art gallery or *Chitrashala* devoted to the display of gold paintings of Kanhai style.

M. L. VARADPANDE

CINEMA ABROAD AND INDIANS

The Indians are everywhere abroad in science, literature, computers, arts, politics and even in cinema. The 31st International Film Festival of India has as many as 16 films in which Indians figure as producers, directors, actors. Some of them were born and brought up abroad while others migrated in search of new pastures. Even resident Indian stars have found their way into films made abroad Om Puri (East is East), Anjalee Deshpande and Ajay Naidu (Once We were Strangers), Roshan Seth, Rajindera Jayasingh (Iqbal), Nandana Sen and Mohan Agashe (Seducing Maarya). But all of them are making ripples in the world of cinema.

The trail blazed by Ismail Merchant is now being followed by a number of others, like krutin Patel whose ABCD (meaning American Born Confused *Desi*) made quite an impact at the IFFI-2000, Rohin Poddar (STORM in the Afternoon), Vishal Bhandari and Kuldip Singh Kasuri (A Pocket full of Dreams), Deepak Nair (Buena Vista Social Club), Udayan Prasad (My son the Fanatic), Mira Nayar (Salaam Bombay), Deepa Mehta (Sam and Me), Warris Hussein (Sixth Happ'ness), Jigar Talati (Fly), Shri Nivas Krishna (Forever), By on Shah (The Mischievious Ravi), Anula Shetty (Paddana), and Ashim Ahluwalia (Thin Air). Ismail Merchant's two films, Room With a View and Custody (Hifazaat) were also screened.

CINEMA IN INDIA

When the Lumiere Brother's first films were shown at Bombay's Watson's Hotel in 1895 or when Dadasaheb Phalke released his epochal feature film *Raja Harishchandra* in 1913, it is unlikely that either the exhibition or the pioneer film maker realised they were unleashing a mass entertainment medium that would hold millions in sway for the next hundred years; that they were spawning an industry that in years to come would overtake the rest of the world in film production.

For most Indians, cinema is integral to their lives, it is not a distant, who to three hour distraction, but a vicarious life-style for them. The large screen provides an alternative, an escape from the realities of day-to-day life. The protagonists are totally identified with, the hero is applauded, the virtuous is worshipped and villain is condemned. the actors and actresses are household names; there is no escaping their omnipresence, from the Paanwala (betel vendor) to the most revered Indian painter-they are all caught up with the magnetism of screen personalities.

A study of the vicissitudes of Indian cinema would throw light on the progress of technology, especially cinematography, and the changing political scene and social mores and attitudes. The silent films launched by Phalke, which had titles in English, Gujarati, Hindi and Urdu by and large related to myths and legends. The stories were familiar to the audience and required minimum commentary. Historicals also proved very popular; Harsh, Chandragupta, Ashoka and the Mughal and Maratha kings strode the silver sceen amidst cardboard pillars and it tinsel costumes. Strangely enough, while in the nineties we are still arguing over whether or not 'kissing' should be shown on screen, in the first decade of Indian cinema, with the British paying scant attention to censorship except when the Establishment was attacked in any wa; leading men were without innibitions, like Lalita Pawar in *Pati Bhakti* (1922).

With the advent of Gandhiji came the plea for according a better status to women, the removal of untouchability and a cry for religious harmony. The silent era of Hiralal Sen, Baburao Painter and R. Nataraja Mudaliar came to an end when Adershir M. Irani produced his first talkie, *Alam Ara* in 1931. If Phalke was the father of Indian cinema, Irani was the father of the talkie. The classic Hollywood musical singing in the Rain exemplifies the cynicism with which people first regarded the talking movie and this holds good for India too. There were too many gargantuan problems to be tackled; there were no dialogue writers, no lyricists; songs had to be sung during the filming as prerecording facilities were yet unknown. Minimum instriments were used as the instrumentalists had to be camouflaged behind the singer. A quaint story goes that during the filming of a song the actress was too fast. Finally the shooting had to be stopped and a hapless *table* player was pulled out of the pool where he had been hidden. "What can I do", he cried, "a fish got into my dhoti (Loin cloth).

But the talking film had come to stay. Considering that even the silent film had a prepondrance of songs, the talkie came to be more of a singie; the heroes and heroines sang their way through the three-four hour movie. Historionics and appearances counted less; a singing talent was all the mattered. To this day the Indian film song has a unique thrall. The music director, the song writer and the playback singers have an unparalleled status in India's cinema.

If Bombay was the hub of early cinema the other centers were not far behind; Calcutta and Madras with their own patriarchs were also making path-breaking films. *Chandidas* a film glorifying the Bhakti movement and castigating casteism, directed by Debaki Bose in 1932 for New Theatres, was lauded for its use of background music and dramatic narrative. K. Subrahmanyam's *Thyaga Bhoomi* (1939) and *Seva Sadan* both advocated women's rights and self-dependence. *Seva Sadan* also introduced to the world through the Silver screen, the great singer M. S. Subbalakshmi, who came to be imortalised for her role in and as the poet-saint Meera both in Hindi and Tamil.

While it is almost impossible to even list all the luminaries of Indian cinema over ten decades, the Wadia Brothers deserve special mention, before going into the different generes. JBH and Homi Wadia were the forerunners of the stunt film the thirties was a period in Indian cinema when 'Wadia' and 'Nadia' were synonymous. Australian by birth, Mary Evans came to India with a dance troupe. She was asked to do a number of JBH's *Noor-e-Yman;* she changed her name to Nadia. "besides being a lucky name, it thymes with Wadia", she is reported to have said, and through various circumstances she became stunt actress for the Wadias, earning the sobriquet "Fearless Nadia". The Wadias had a fixation for trains and made a number of films titled, *Toofan Mail, Flying Ranee, Punjab Mail* and so on. Nadia got so used to sitting on roof top of trains for her stunts that she became reluctant to step off and even demanded herelunch be sent up; the True stunt woman, she grappled with a lion, did the trapeze, carried a calf and a man over running trains. It is unlikely there could ever be a other actress like Nadia. She married Homi in 1960, and breathed her last a few years ago.

The forties was a tumultuous decade, the first half was revaged by war and the second saw drastic political changes all over the world. Film-makers delved into contemporary themes. V. Shantaram, the doyen of lyrical films, made *Dr. Kotnis Ki Amar Kahani* - tribute to Dr. Dwarkanath Kotnis who went out with a medical team to China and died there. Shantaram's other films were reformist but visually appealing, like, *Do Aankhan Barah Haath, Pinjra, Chaani*. But there were films where pure artistic merit supercedes social message as in *Jhanak Jhanak Payal Baaje* and *Geet Gaya Pattaron ne.* south Indian films also gained great footing. AVM and Gemini were two of the most prolific producers turning out social drama in the South Indian languages as well as in Hindi. While the the spian actor Shivaji Ganesan delivered mind boggling soliloquies on screen, many of the politically inclined writers and actors of the south Indian screen began to use the medium for reaching out to people. the DMK stalwarts Annadurai, Karunanidhi and MG Ramachandran did not even resort to subtlety. *"Naan anaittal adu nadandu vital"*... sang MGR, (if I could be the decision maker, the poor of this world will not suffer....") The very titles of the films were chose with care; *Rickshaw-karan* (Rickshaw Driver), *Muttukara Velan* (Cowherd Velan) and *En Kadamai* (My Duty) to convey his identification with the masses. No wonder he was hailed *Makkal Thilagam* (Gen amongst people). How effective was the use of the medium was amply proved with the party coming to power and MGR getting voted Chief Minsiter of the state.

The other star who used the screen image to great advantage was N.T. Rama Rao of Andhra Pradesh. The veritable screen god, NTR played the role so often that he began believing in his divinity. Apparently so did a lot of other people in Andhra, which is why then was a second screen here from the south as Chief Minister.

While the south was busy wooing the public for votes, Bombay was either turning out escapist fare, light, happy, musical films with Dilip Kumar, Raj Kapoor, Deva Anand, Shammi Kapoor, Kishore Kumar, Nargis, Madhubala, Nutan, Geeta Bali, Mala Sinha and others or gave the audience absolute tear jerkers with social melodrama. This was the golden era of music. Shankar-Jaikishan, O. P. Nayyar, Madan Mohan, C. Ramachandra, Salil Choudhury, Naushad, S. D. Burman - all had their distinctive sway. Each vied with the other to produce some of the most unforgettable melodies Indian has ever known. This was also the age of innocence; the screen was black and white, the vamp and the heroine did not merge, they had their domains, there were no shades to the hero, a man was all good or rotten to the core. No double

entendres were woven into the songs and even the vamp was decently attired on the screen. This was the era of Raj Kapoor, of *Shree 420, Awara, Boot Polish, Jagte Raho, Chori-Chori* and of course his magnum opus *Mera Naam Joker* - he was still making and acting in enduring films, the tramp who is not able to cope with the pace of the world. He caught up with times and his films changed with *Sangam, Jis Desh Mein Ganga Behti Hai, Satyam Shivam Sundaram* and *Ram Teri Ganga Maili*. Dilip Kumar and Guru Dutt were excellent foils to the chocolate-faced heroes as tragedy kings. So were Meena Kumari and Bina Rai amongst the heroines. But such was their versatility that they could also carry off comedy effectively. Two outstanding Hindi films of the fifties and deserve mention are K. Asif's *Mughal-e-Azam* (took 14 years to make and is one fo the most lavishly produced historical of Indian cinema) and Mehboob Khan's *Mother-India* which is said to have gaine the status of *Gone With the Wind.*

In the meantime in Bengal, the man who was to take Indian cinema to the international arena and win accolades from the greatest film-makers, Satyajit Ray, released his first film, *Pather Panchali* (1955). After his triology there was no looking back for him or for cinema from Bengal. Mrinal Sen conveyed his quiet commitment to socialism through films like *Calcutta, Oka Orie Katha* (Telugu) and *Bhuvan Shome*. Director Ritwik Ghatak gave us memorable films *Megha Dhaka Tara* and *Subaranarekha*, Although Bengal also came up with films that asked for a willing suspension of disbelief, these were exceptions rather than the rule as in bombay films, where the Mukherji's, Sippy's, Chopra's Chakraborty and Manmohan Desai produced one bonanza after another for the masses and laughed all the way to their banks. There was no market for serious films, i was felt, and the classics that failed to break even like Guru Dutt's *Kagaz Ke Phool* and Raj Kapoor's *Mera Naam Joker,* only strengthened the convinction. The former committed suicide and the later resorted to the populist fare with Bobby.

It was only after the Govenrment set up the Film Finance Corporation (FFC, which in 1980 came to be known as NFDC i.e. National Film Development Corporation) that several small but serious film makers got the wherewithal to make films, notable among them being Mani Kaul, Kumari Shahani and G.V. Iyer (with his maiden venture in Sanskrit), *Adi Sankaracharya)* The Corporation also partnered the making of Attenborough's *Gandhi* and financed Satyajit Ray's *Ghare Baire* which was to be one of the last films of the master.

Like cinema in Bengal, Malayalam cinema too was meaningful but it took a longer time to get noticed. In fact it was Ramu Kariat's melodious tragedy *Chemmeen* winning the President's gold medal in 1965 that drew attention to Malayalam cinema. Adoor Gopalakrishnan *(Swayamvaram)* and others all gained similar recognition in the years to come. With actor Prem Nazir doing stellar roles in a record breaking 600 films, Malayalam films have come to be characterised by simple narration of powerful stories, authentic locales and low cost production.

The Karanth (BV)-Karnad (Girish) combine have produced two milestone Kannada films *Vamsa Vriksha* and *Samskara,* both essentially iconolast in treatment. Though much talked about, the critique of caste brahmins, the theme of both films was later seen to be rather extreme. In this context it is worthwhile to mention two films made in Tamil on the same subject. *Vedam Pudithu* directed by P. Bharatraja and *Ore Oru Gramathile* by K. Jyothi Pandyan. Both carried strong indictments against caste hierarchy and the common man's struggle to overcome it, but retained as balance-rather unusual for Tamil films.

With Government funds availabel for making films, the seventies saw an unhealthy divide between the existing commercial or mainstream cinema and the new parallel cinema or art films. The former was condemned unequivocally by the critics but continued to fill the coffers while the latter got rave reviews, bewildered the masses and created deep dents in Government resources. Fortunately this situation did not last long, for soon there came a crop of film makers who realised that meaningful films need not necessarily incur heavy losses. Shyam Benegal, *(Ankur, Nishant, Manthan)* proved that there was an audience for films without frills but with a strong story and interesting narration. Govind Nihalani Jabbar Patel, Mahesh Bhatt, K. Balchander, Bharati Raja, Adoor Gopalakrishnan, all fell into this category. Around this time, the singular phenomenon, the angry young man with his dark looks, smouldering eyes and mesmerising voice, Amitabh Bachchan, began to stride the scene like a colossus. He introduced to cinema for the first time as cult, the negative or the anti-hero. Special screen plays were written for this hero seeking vengeance and taking on single-handed an unsympathetic establishment and inadequate legal system.

The eighties was the advent of women film makers, Vijaya Mehta (*Rao Saheb*), Aparna Sen (*36, Chowringhee Lane, Parama*), Sai Pranjpye (*Chashme Baddoor, Katha, Sparsh*) Kalpana Lajimi (*Ek Pal*) and later the much acclaimed *(Rudali)* Prema Karanth (*Phaniamma*) and Meera Nair (*Salam Bombay*). The most commendable thing about these directors is their individuality. Their films have strong content and are told with passion, (only Sai has tackled light hearted subjects).

In the nineties and twenties Indian cinema faces tough competition from television; the cable network gives viewers any number of channels and though the. most popular channels continue to be the film based ones, the cinma halls have taken a beating. Nevertheless, films like Aditya Chopra's maiden effort, *Dilwale Dulhaniya Le Jayenge* and Suraj Barjatya's *Hum Aapke Hain Kaun* have broken all records, because they recall the innocence of the fifties, a novelty in this age of sex and violence. This gives hope.

JAYA RAMANATHAN

CLASSICAL DANCE

India evolved through classical and folk traditions, type of dance drama that is total theatre; actor dances out story through complex gesture, language, form that cuts across multilanguage barrier. Some classical dance-drama forms e.g. *kathakali, kuchipudi, bhagavatha Mela* exact statues from Hindu mythology.

Chief source classical dance Bharat Muni's

Natya-Sastra

Natya-Sastra, covers period 1st century B.C. to 1st century A.D., comprehensive treaties on origins, functions of *Natya* (damatic art also dance), types of plays, gesture, language, acting, miming, theatre, architecture, production, make-up, acting, miming, theatre, production, makeup, costumes, masks, various *bhavas* ("emotions"), *rasas* ("sentiments"); A book of exhaustive study of dramaturgy.

In *Natya-Sastra* dancer actor communicates meaning of play through four kinds of *abhinaya* (historic representations); *angika,* transmitting emotion through stylized movements of parts of body; *vacika,* speech, song pitch of vowels, intonation; *aharya,* costumes and making; *Sattvika,* entire psychological resources of dancer actor.

The actor equipped with complicated repertoire of stylized gestures; conventionalized movements prescribed for every part of the body, eyes and hans most important. There are 13 movements of head, 7 of eyebrows, 6 for nose, 6 for cheeks, 7 for chin, 9 for neck, 5 for breasts, 36 for eyes; 32 movements of feet, 16 on ground, 16 on air; various positions of feet shrutting, mincing, fromping, beating worked out; 24 single hand gestures (*asamyuta hasta),* 13 for combined hans (*Samyuta-hasta*) One gesture (*hasta*) may mean 30 different things unrelated. For each of different meanings a *hasta* given different body posture.

The asthetic pleasure of Hindu dance and theatre determined by how successful artist is in expressing *Bhava* and evoking *Rasa*. Literally *rasa* means "Taste" or flavour" i.e. exalted sentiment. The critics concerned about *rasa* of particular work. There are 9 *rasa:* erotic, comic, pathetic, furious, heroic, terrible, odious, marvellous and spiritually peaceful. There are 9 corresponding *Bhavas :* Love, laughter, pathos, anger, energy, fear, disgust, wonder and guietude.

The *Bharata-natyam* (also called *desi-attam*) survived till present through the *devadasis,* i.e. temple dancing girls, devoted their lives to go through this medium. Muslim invaders destroyed powerful Hindu kingdoms in South, could not destroy arts which took shelter in temples. After 16th century when Muslims overpowered South, it was a set back to dance. Institution of *devadasis* fell into disrepute, temple dancing girls synonymous; with prostitutes. Late 19th century in Tanjore, Chinniyah, Punniah, Vadivelu and Shivanandam, four talented dancers, brothers, revived purity of *dasi attam* by studying, following, the ancient texts, temple friezes; missing links supplied by *deva dasis.* Their popularised form of dasiattam was *bharata-natyam.*

Performance lasts 2 hours, consists 6 parts; beginning allarippu (Telugu language, "to decorate with flowers"); devotional prologue shows elegance, grace of dancer; second part *jatisvaram,* a brilliant blaze of *jatis* ("dance phrases") with *svaras* ("musical sounds"); followed by Shabdan, singing words that prepare dancer to interpret throguh *abhinaya* ("gesture language") interspersed with pure dance); fourth part *varnam,* a combination of expressive and pure dance fourth party *vannan,* a combination of expressive and pure dance, then follow *padamas,* songs, in Telugu, Tamil or Karnarese, that the dancer dramatizes by facial expression and hand gestures; the accompanying singer chants the line repitatively, dancer exacts clashing and contrasting meanings. Performance ends with *tillana,* pure dance, accompanied by meaningless musical syllabus chanted to punctuate the rhythm.

During last 50 years *Bharata-natyam* attained world recognition, aspirants go to Tamil Nadu to learn from gurus who live in villages, performing artists women because of *tasya* character, teachers are old men, chant lines to tiny symbols, controlling comples rhythm without dancing themselves.

Major 20th century performers are T. Balasaraswathi, especially known for her *abhinaya* of *padams,* Rukmini Devi, popularised *bharata-natyam* among upper classes 1930's Yamini Krishnamurthi, Shanta Rao, Sonal Mansingh, Vajayantimala, Hema Malini.

COINS OF INDIA

As basic material for the re-construction of history, coins of India have their own importance. Numismatic issues of ancient India provide the grounds for a study not only of the political vicissitudes through which this country has passed but allow a glimpse into the art endeavour of the contemporary people through the ages. Nay, they provide almost a complete cultural background of the land in general, In the medieval period in the Islamic series of royal issues the coins are emblems of royalty and symbolic of their mint-names and precise dates of issue inscribed on the coinage. The metals, the motifs, the portraits and the dresses as well as other accompanying details of the faiths followed and the customs adopted are evidenced in the numismatic issue in every age and for every individual monarch. These details provide the very foundation of the edifice of the country's heritage-political, social, economic and artistic.

Literary references to certain weights of gold or silver are very old in India leading back to be Vedic age about 1500 B.C. These lent their names later to actual coins of the respective measures, though the extent earliest coinage known as the Punch-marked, can be dated not much before the 6th Century B.C.. These coins, either circular or square silver flat cut-out pieces, are believed to be issue of the trading community and are punched with various symbols, and animal and other figures a large proportion of which are secular. Copper pieces are rarer and gold is almost unknown. While the Punch-marked coins were in use probably upto the beginning of the Christian era, sometime from about the 5th Century B.C. die-cast copper coins manufactured by pouring molten metal into a cavity formed by joining two moulds together were issued by a number of ancient States, most of the extant die-cast coins being, however, dateable from after the disruption of the Mauryan empire, in the 3rd-2nd Century B.C. Some issues of the cast coins were also undertaken as the 3rd Century A.D. by the Kingdoms of Kausambi, Ayodhya and Mathura, bearing names of local kings in Brahmi script. A system of double-die was also introduced, and one of the types was even imitated by a few Greek princes in India in the middle of the 2nd Century B.C.

In the South, the Andhras whose period of reign starts sometime about 230 B.C., had issues of various types, some of the early devices being elephant, chaitya and bow. Mostly in bullion or lead, their issues reveal a few very unusual designs including the figure of a ship with two masts.

INDO-GREEK SERIES

In the 2nd Century B.C. (between 190 and 150 B.C.) the Bactrian King, Demetrios, extended his kingdom as far as the Punjab in India and issued coins. The two Greek rulers, one ruling over Kabul, Qandahar and Gandhara, and the other over east Gandhara and the Punjab, issued coins with the portrait of the king on the one side and that of a Greek deity on the other, based on the Greek prototype. An important innovation made in the Indo-Greek series was the use of the Kharoshti script on the reverse with a Prakrit rendering of the Greek legend on obverse giving the appellations of "King of Kings", "'Saviour", etc. and the name of the moneyer. The postrait-and-deity type of the Indo-Greek series remained the model for coins in India in the north for quite a few centuries.

The coins of the Sakas who conquered Bactria in 135 B.C. and whose three important rulers are Maues, Azes I and Azilises, use the royal titles, Basileos Basileon "King of Kings". Apart from the Greek gods, and goddess, like Zeus, Herakles, Pallas and Poseidon, the Indian goddess Lakshmi also appears on the Saka Kharosthi on reverse as was usual with the Indo-Greek.

Sakas were closely related to the Pahlavas whose earlier rulers like Vonones, Spalahores and Spelirises ruled in Seistan and Qandahar (Arachosia). The most important of the later Pahlava kings was Gondophares or Gondopharnes, famous as the "Kind of India" in traditional lore, whose coins have all a "King-on-horse-back" obverse uith a solibary type showing the Indian God Siva. All of his successors and contemporaries Abdageses, Orthagnes and Pakores, closely follow his coin types.

About 115 A.D. a saka chieftain, Chashtana, ruling originally over Western Rajputana extended his kingdom over Malwa and struck hemidrachms on the Greek model. The successors of Chasttana, known as Western Kshatrapas, with their dominions on the west coast of India continued to issue Hemidrachms, though the portraits on obverse are typically Scythian. On the coins of the fifth Kshatrapa of the dynasty, Jivadaman, dates in Saka era appear as part of the legend.

The Kushanas, one of the tribes of the Yue-chi horde, who came from the north and drove the Sakas out, had five powerful Princes, Kujula Kadphises, Vima Kadphises, Kanishka, Huvishka and Vasudeva, who ruled in succession in India and issued coins from about 25 A.D. The commoner type of Kadaphes' coins has head on the obverse persumably copied from one of the ealry Roman Emperors. The coins of Kujula Kadphises are all of copper, some of which are struck in the Green style and others according to the Saka, The gold issues of his successors used only Greek legends and introduced Iranian royal title, Shaonanoshao, in place of the corresponding Greek. On the reverse of the gold and copper coinage of Kanishka and Huvishka are portrayed the Hindu god Siva (Oesho), and Greek and Iranian deities. Buddha figures also appear on these coins, the earliest occurence being on a copper of Kadphes, Kanishka's coins generally show standing royal figure, while Kanishka's coinage is well-known for half-length or merely the face-head portrait of the king, though a seated and an elephant-riding royal figure are also known, as rarities.

GUPTA INNOVATIONS

With the rise of the Guptas about 319-20 A.D. the Indian indigenous coinage takes a very interesting turn. For, though it adopts in general lay-out- the Kushsn, and ultimately back, the Indo-Greek type of portrait coins, the use of contemporary Brahmi in the legends, which give in chaste classical Sanskrit an eulogy of each ruling king together with distinctive titles, mostly in delightful poetic couplets, is an important step towards Indianization of the coin-devices. The earlist types of Gupta coinage bear the impress of the Kushana proto-type of the standing king with the royal figures still wearing Kushana dress, and with a Kushana symbol on the reverse. The gold coins issued by Samudragupta include a posthumous issue in the name of his fater, Chandragupta-I, and an Asvamedha and a Lyrist type, apart from the more common, Archer, Standard, the Tigerslayer, Battle-axe and Kacha types. Chandragupta-II (375-413 A.D.) continued his father's Archer Standard and Lion-slayer (Tiger Slayer) types in addition to a few new and rare ones, like the *Chhatra* type, the Horseman, Tiger-slayer with sword, the *Couch* type and the *Chakravikrama* type. While the silver coinage of the Gupts started by Chandragupta II after the overthrow of the Western Kshtrapas closely follows the latter's types, those in copper are almost closely follows the latter's types, those in copper are almost confined to this ruler and are more original in design. Kumaragupta-I (413-455 A.D.), his successor, is known for his revival of the Asvamedha, Lyrist and King-and Queen types and introduction of the Apratigha, Kartikeya, Swordsman, Elephant-rider and Rhinoceros-slayer types in addition to the more well-known earlier ones like the Archer, Horseman, Lion-slayer and the Tiger-slayer. Skandagupta, his successor and last of the imperial Guptas, continued the few favourite types like the Archer, the *Chhatra* and the Horseman but also introduced a new type with the king in fron of Lakshmi. He effected a change in the gold standard in the currency with a corresponding depreciation in metallic purity. The successors of Skandagupta whose relationship and duites are somewhat disputable struck the usual Archer type with a marked decline in purity of metal and design.

LATER HINDU COINAGE

During the early medievel period between the decline of the Guptas and the rise of Islamic power in India in the 12th Century A.D., the coinage is marked by sporadic symbolism of the different clans coming into power in the different regions. The Gadhaiya Paisa and the Adivaraha Silver coinage struck on Sassanian models mark the medieval currency in circulation in Rajputana and Gujarat for a long time. The Kalachuris of Dehala (11th Century A.D.) struck coins with four-armed Lakshmi in outlines on bverse withold Nagari inscription of the king's name on the reverse. This was closely followed by the Chandellas of Mahoba (1055-1280) A.D., Tomaras of Ajmer and Delhi (978-1128 A.D.) and Rathors of Kanauj (1080-1193 A.D.). Later Rajput kings adopted the Bull and Horseman device originally started by the Brahman kings of Gandhara (Ohind) during 860-950 A.D.

In the Deccan, the Chalukyas ruling in the 7th Century used in their early coins a lion device and a Telugu legned. A type of pagodas fanams and copper coins with boar symbol belong to dynasty. To the eastern Chalukyas in the 11th Century also belongs the boar symbol on coins in large flat gold pieces. The cup-shaped *padmantankas* were struck by the Kadambas. The Hoysalas who succeeded the Western Chalukyas issued coin with a maned lion. The Kakatiyas (1110-1323 A.D.) issued coins with couchant bull on copper, pagodas and fanams; Kalachuris of Kalyana (1126-75 A.D.) with old Kanarese inscriptions : Yadavas of Devagiri (1187-1311 A.D.) pagoda and silver coins with kneeling figure of Garuda. The Ganga dynasty that settled in Kalinga (6th-11th Century A.D.) also issued fanams with a recumbant bull, couch ad crescent; the Kadamba chief of Goa released gold coin with special Kadamba symbol and the lion passant. In the South proper were the Pandyas, the cholas and maned lion, appears on their coins, while an elephant on obverse. The early Chola coin (985-1035 A.D.) portray a tiger seated under a canopy along with Pandya fish, the later device being a standing figure on obverse and a seated figure on reverse.

MUSLIM NUMISMATICS

One of the earliest Muslims issue was by Mahmud of Ghazni whose bilingual coins in Arabic and Sanskrit are famous. A very important change in coin-devices introduced by the Muslim rulers was the Kalima, i.e. the Muslim cread, specially from after Illtumish (1210-1235 A.D.) who in addition, had a horseman type in silver and perhaps also in gold. His predecesor, Muizz-ul-din Muhammad bin Sam, one of the earliest to issue coins chose to adopt an existing indigenous type with Lakshmi on obverse.

A remarkable moneyer in the Sultan period was Qutbuddin Mubarak who used a variety of titles for himself and threw off spiritual allegiance to the Khalif. The first issue in spare coinage under the Muslims is also due to him. But perhaps the largest number of varieties in coins issued by any Muslim Sultan in India was by Muhammad bin Tughluq (1325-51 A.D.) whose token bullion coins with legend urging people to accept them still remain unique. The Lodis, who preceded the Mughals, do not appear to have issued gold or silver, and it was Sher Shah, who followed, that put the currency on a satisfactory footing.

In the provincial Sultanates in Malwa, Jaunpur, Gulbarga, Kashmir and Bengal, distinctive types in coinage are notices in regard to calligraphy, shape and designs. Special mention may be made of the style of writing adopted in early Jaunpur coins and a lozenge-shaped issue of Nasir Shah Khiliji of Malwa.

MUGHAL COINAGE

The earliest Mughal currency is in general fabric, based on the Central Asian coinage of the Timurids, with Kalima, on the observe and names of the four Khalifs at the corners. The 'rupee' adopted from Sher Shah's currency is the most famous of all Mughal coins, the name 'rupee' occuring on a coin of Akbar from Agra. Mughal coins in a large proportion give the names of the mints from which they are issued and also the date in the Muslim era and in the regnal year. Akbar's most imporant innovation on coins was the use of the *Ilahi* era (Divine era) based on solar system. And while Akbar, the most illustrious of the Mughals, is noted for a few interesting types like the *mihrabi* type, the duck variety and also as having initiated the verse-couplets on coinage, Jahangir, his son and successor, is remembered for his portrait coins, one with couplets, and the series of Zodiac coins in gold and silver. The association of the queen, Nurjahan, in coinage is also due to him. Square and founded types started from Akbar's time but continued in Jahangir's. One of the peculiar mints from which Akbar used to issue coins was the "Victorious Camp" (Urdu-e-zafar qarin), while one of Jahangir's mints, *Urdu kah-i-Dakan'* (Camp on roads to the Deccan) is still more interesting. Solar months introduced by Akbar were continued by Jahangir and also Shahjahan, for a few years. The use of the *Kalima* is revived by Shahjahan enshrining it in endless varieties of geometric patterns. Large *muhars* in gold and tiny *nisar* pieces for gifts coined in his period still remain unique monetary novelties introduced by this monarch.

The story of Indian coins from after Shahjahan is sordid. They reveal a monotonous formula and a few only show stray artistic outward designs.

The Mughal coins bear a few ornamental marks which atleast in earlier issues are not mint-makrs and were probably mere ornamentals, though a few on Shah Alam II's issues may be taken to be marks of ditinctive mints. The decorative field for the legend on coins adopted specially by Shahjahan recall the exquisite patterns on monuments of his times, notably the Taj.

The successors of the Mughals, more particularly the East India Company and the provinces under the Native rulers with Mughal Suzerainty, continued the later Mughal types though from about the end of the 18h Century has emergence of a distinctive type in copper under the East India Company marks a completely new phase in Indian coin devices.

A. K. BHATTACHARYYA

COMPOSITE CULTURE OF INDIA

Popularly called the Composite culture of India, it is the 2nd millennium's greatest gift, the hallowed heritage, the finest legacy which has not been erased in spite of the ravages of time and vicissitudes of history. According to Jawaharlal Nehru. "some kind of a dream of unity has occupied the mind of India since the dawn of civilization. That unity was not conceived as something imposed from outside, a standardisation of externals or even of beliefs. It was something deeper and, within its fold, the widest tolerance of belief and custom was practised and every variety acknowledged and even encouraged".

When Raja Anang Pal of Shahia dynasty gave a clarion call to the chieftains of northern India to resist the foreign invasion of Mahmud of Ghazni, his call was more cultural than political. History records that many a Prince responded to the call and sent forces. But after the conquest, Mahmud's soldiers settled in Punjab and there was a great deal of social fusion by inter-marriage and common living. No invader interfered in teh basic customs of the Indians. The result was that they were admitted into the broad spectrum of India's cultural train which movs on and helped strengthen the process of synthesis and growth.

The millennium broadly covers the whole of middle ages and goes upto the modern times. The period is marked by open conflict between reason and blind faith, between science and religion, between tradition and modernity and between tyranny and tolerance. The highlights of the millennium are the advent of Islam and the rise of Sufism, the birth of Sikhism and the evolution of the Khalsa, the establishment of British rule and the spread of Christianity. It must be remembered that India was already a land of many religions which included Buddhism and Jainism, apart from Hinduism. Christians, Nestroians, Jews and Zorastrians were already settled in south India. Even Muslims were there in Sind and on the west coast. The Millennium, therefore, presents a unique mosaic of culture, a cultural kaleidoscope which attracted people of other countries as no other country did. Coupled with its economic prosperity it earned the title of a "golden sparrow".

The central theme of the Indian civilization is *"Dharma"* which is something much more than a religion or creed. It is a moral law governing the functioning of the universe and the conduct of mankind. Charity, compassion, generosity and humility are the main features of the combined culture of India as practised through the ages. When Shaikh Moinuddin Chisti, a Sufi saint, was asked what was the highest form of devotion to God, he replied "It was nothing but redressing the misery of those who are in distress, fulfilling the needs of the helpless and feeding the hungry, both man and beast". He asked his disciples and followers who are still many in India and abroad, to develop river-like generosity, sub-like affection and earth-like hospitality. The saints and bards of India from 12th to 17th centuries, from Baba Farid to Shankaradeva, all preached freedom from all religious Prejudices and dogma and superstitions. The Bhakti movement strengthened the cultural continuity of the country. It stood for equality not only between man and man but also between sexes as it existed in the vedic age where no ceremony was considered complete without the presence of women.

According to A. L. Bashma, "No land on earth has scuh a long cultural continuity as India. There are four main cradles of culture from where elements of culture have spread to other parts of the world, viz, China, India, Greece and Italy. Of these four areas, India deserves a larger share of credit than she is usually given, because, on a minimal assessment, she has deeply affected the religious life of most of Asia and has provided very important elements in the culture of the whole of South-East Asia, as well as extending her influence directly or indirectly to other parts of the world". This is testified by foreign travellers to India, particularly Alberuni, who visited India many a time with the invading forces of Mahmud of Ghazni from 1017 to 1030 AD. Although he found Indians intellectually conceited, but he is the first Muslim observer who found unity underlying India's vast cultural diversity.

Alberuni thought the Hindus were excellent philosophers, good mathematicians and extraordinary astronomers. The estatement coming as it does from the greatest astronomer of the times is a great tribute to Hindu astronomy. According to him, the Hindus believe that there is no country like theirs, no nation like theirs, no science like theirs, no religion like theirs. According to them there is no race on earth like theirs, and no created beings besides them have any knowledge or science like theirs whatsoever. Although he calls them naughty, he found them proud and patriotic. Describing the beauty of Indian sculpture, he says : "In this they have attained a very high degree of art so that our people when they see them wonder at them and are unable to describe them much less to construct anything like them". Five hundred years later Babur did not find anything exclusively Muslim, and in his Tuzuk-i-Babari, he talks of the 'Hindustani ways of life', which indeed is the essence of the composite culture of India. The process was accelerated during the time of Akbar - the *"Suleh-i-Kul"*.

Love of one's country is the most essential part of this culture. The 19th century social and religious movements such as Brahmo Samaj, Arya Samaj, Theosophical Society, Prarthna Sabha, etc. inculcated a sense of morality and patriotism among Indians. They also inspired among the people a sense of unity and solidarity about India as a nation. Sometime it went even beyond nationalism. "I love India", said Rabindra Nath Tagore, "not because that I cultivate the idolatory of geography, not becuase I had a chance to be born in her soil, but because she was saved through the tumultuous ages the living words that have issued from the illuminated consciousness of her great ones.

But the greatest exponent of Indian culture after Adi Shankara was Swami Vivekananda. In his famous address to the *Parliament of Religions* at Chicago in 1893 he said: "I am proud to belong to a nation which has sheltered the persecuted and refugees of all religions and all nations of the earth. I am proud to tell you that we have gathered in our bosom the purest remnants of the Israelites who came to southern India and took refuge with us in the very year in which their holy temple was shattered to pieces by Roman tyranny. I am proud to belong to the religion which was sheltered and is still fostering the remnants of the grand Zorasterian nation. I will quote to you, Brethern, a few lines from a hymn which I remember to have repeated from my earliest childhood, which is everyday repeated by millions of human beings:

"As different streams having their sources in different places All mingle their waters in the sea, So O lord, the different paths which
men take through different
tendencies
various though, appear crooked or
straight
All lead to Thee".

This is perhaps the greatest statement of the millennium. This is the essence of Indian culture. It is this spirit of universal tolerance and universal acceptance which has enabled Indian culture to survive and prevail.

Mahatma Gandhi summed up the spirit of Indian culture when he said : "I do not want my house to be walled in from all sides and my windows to be stuffed. I want the cultures of all lands to be blown about my house as freely as possible. But I refuse to be blown off my feet by any". He led the destiny of India for nearly half a century. Indian to the core, he believed in its distinct cultural identity. 'India is to me the dearest country", he

wrote, "not because it is my country but because I have discovered the greatest truth in it. I cling to India like a child to its mother's breast because I feel she gives me the spiritual nourishment I need. She has the environment that responds to my highest aspirations". A man like Gandhi is born once in a thousand years.

The partition of India in which millions of people died was a great setback to the Indian concept of secularism and its composite culture but the country quickly recovered itself and adopted a constitution based on socialist, secular and democratic principles, where identiy of the Indians was not to be based on relgion but on a single and uniform citizenship for the whole of India. The Preamble of the Constitution is so inspiring that it deserve to be reproduced in full :

"We, the people of India, having solemnly resolved to constitute India into a Sovereign, Socialist, Secular, Democratic Republic and to secure to all its citizens :
Justice : Social, economic and political
Liberty of thought, expression, belief, faith and worship;
Equality of status and of opportunity; and to promote among them all
Fraternity assuring the dignity of the individual and the unity and the integrity of the nation:
In our Constitution Assembly this twenty-six day of November, 1949, do hereby adopt, enact and give to ourselves this Constitution".

This heralded the birth of a new, free India. The Constitution came into force on January 26, 1950,. By far the best, finest, the grandest document of the millennium, it is the sum total of India's composite culture.

The next fifty years have been spent in an earnest effort to fulfil these commitments, both constitutional and cultural, through legislation, successive Five Year Plans, people's participation and governance. India thus enters the next millennium with courage · and confidnece to become a haven where the mind is free and the head is held high, where the strong are just and the weak secure, where no child is out-of-school, no adult illiterate and nobody is without employment and a roof over his head. That would be the greatest triumph of our culture.

K. K. KHULLAR

CONTEMPORARY INDIAN ART - STYLES

Contemporary Indian art may be a recent phenomenon - the beginning being recorded from the trauma of partition days of 1947. It is yet to evolve into a movement of specifics in terms of history, civilisational evolution and technological revolution. Painting is not only the inter-play of brush-stroke and colour over canvas, It is also a process wherein the technological aspects of the exercise play an important role. Modern Indian painting is a juxtaposition of ideas, images, symbols, traditions and value structures of the vast expanse of India that can only be understood in continental terms. From the South Indian to the vastness of oceanic cultural contours of Bengal with Baroda, Bombay and the Sandy dunes of Rajasthan intermixing with the grandeur of creative impulses in Orissa and the North-east, the contemporary Indian art scene is an the move accepting, rejecting; assimilating, owning and remodelling a movement within the cultural specifies of Indian Sanskara - the life - blood of Indian civilization evolution.

If Raja Ravi Verma and K.C.S. Panikar endowed the Indian Art scene with a freshness of images, Rabindranath Tagore, Amrita Sher-Gil and Gaganendranath Tagore put the authentic Indian imagination into the works to set it apart from what was perceived as European at that time. Rabindranath Tagore, Nandlal Bose and Jamini Roy took over to carry forward what was initiated by the early masters of Bengal. From Calcutta to Bombay and little farther in Baroda, the contemporary Indian art evolved after going through a long period of experimentation and assimilation. The preceding four and a half decades of the Indian Art Scene may be broadly assessed as a transitory period moving from traditional values to the modern yet, preserving the oriental competence of technique and presentation. K. K. Hebbar, M. F. Hussain, F. N. Souza, S. H. Raza, Bal Chhabel, K. G. Subramaniyam, Tyed Mehta, Babri Narayan, Reddeppa Naidu and Paritosh Sen have gone through various phases of creativity but seldom detached themselves from the Indian idiom and the distinct legacy of Indian spatial arrangement. In contrast, there is a group of artists who have chosen non-representational expensive means. Ram Kumar, V. S. Gaitanda, Akkitham Narayanan, Kudalur Achuthan and many others belongs to this group. (Summarised)

JAY RAINAI

CORBETT PARK BIRDS

The Corbett National Park has a special place amongst all the National Parks in India. Nestled in the midst of Kumaon foothills, it preserves the rich wealth of flora and fauna that attracts visitors from all over the world.

The majestic Saal forest, hills clothed with mixed vegetation right upon their crest, vast stretches of grassland interspersed with dusters of trees and shrubby patches, wide open glades with luxuriant growth of lush green grass, trees and scrub jungle dotted with patches of light green foliage; sparkling water channels winding through, velvet green meadows, narrow ravines running deep into hills, glistening pastures and pictureseque waterfalls lend unique grandue to the serene wilderness of this forest country. The diversity of the scenery is fully reflected in its rich birdlife. Many of the most beautiful and characteristic birds, such as wood peckers pigeons, owls, minivets, cuckoos, pheasants, drongos, babblers, tits flycatchers etc. are found in forest areas of foothills. Indeed, the variety of attractive species makes bird-watching in the park a most enjoyable pastime, with the added pleasure of walking amidst beautiful scenery.

The vast water reservoir formed by the construction of dam across Ramganga at Kalagarh provides shelter to many species of birds that visit the Indian sub-continent in winter. The spectacular flocks of wintering water-birds are one of the special attractions.

It is a treat to watch a baya building its next or seen with a long thread, torn off a leaf or a blade of grass; or a flock of thrushes, robins, bulbuls and shamas pouting out melodious songs to welcome the newborn dawn; or a group of mynas and babblers warning the jungle folk of the approaching danger; or a solitary peacock emitting its piercing call to attract hens; Large flocks of migratory birds (winter visitors ducks, geese, cormorants etc.) landing in Ramganga to rest and feed on way to distant places in the Indian sub-continent, perform exicting acts in the Nature's garden here. Visitors here perhaps cannot imagine that the 'world of birds' could be so vast, so varied, so colourful and so beautiful.

BHAGAT SINGH

COSTUMES OF INDIA

Costume may be defined as anything appended to the body out of a sense of natural deficiency. This sense may be promoted by a need of protection against the rigours of the climate, supernatural influence and natural enemies or by propensities for imitation of the fur and feather coats of the creatures of the earth and the air, or by aesthetic impulses or tendencies to display physical charm, rank and wealth. Thus costume combines in itself all the motives of attraction, concealment, exhibition and functional distinctiveness. It is, however very difficult to identify and distinguish them categorically in each individual case. The best that can be done, for a scientific analysis, at the present stage of our knowledge to find the main purpose or purposes of each item of costume of a given people at a given period of time. An attempt has been made below on this principle and for the sake of convenience, costume has been classified in two sorts:

Apparel proper : It includes such articles of personal attire as are used mainly for the purpose of covering.

Ornaments : By these are meant articles which are used for adding to the attractiveness of the personal appearance of the wearer.

India through the corridors of time preserved her traditional costumes and travelled a long way to perfect, through ages and experienee, the costume style. with an aesthetic sense, suited to its climatic conditions and socio-economic pattern. It is true that Indian costume to some extent underwent modifications here and there through invasions of influx of population from other countries but in due time India moulded the alien style into her traditional mode of costume.

It is with this background of tradition in costume that the subject of the existing Indian costume is discussed here.

India with diverse types of population abounds in numerous varieties of costumes; yet the apparel proper can broadly be classified under a few major heads.

APPAREL OF INDIGENOUS MATERIAL

The simplest of the costume is made out of indigenous material. People living in an isolated area try to keep as close to nature as possible and utilise natural products surrounding them. The first in this series is the costume produced out of the indigenous material like bark, leaf, etc. The usual costume of the Onge men of the Little Andaman island until very recently was almost nothing except a plain belt made of bark fibre. They have very recently started wearing between the legs a strip of cloth only three inches broad tied to the belt in front and at the back. This type of costume for men is not very uncommon among the people of the Orissa hills, viz., Bondo, Saora, etc. The Onge women still wear nothing but a belt about two inches in breadth made of Pandanus leaf from which is suspended a small tassel made of young unopened palm leaf. It is not long ago that Gond women used to wear bunches of twigs around the waist. The Juangs of the Orissa hills until very recently used to wear leaf dresses. Example of a very short skirt produced out of the fibre of trees are still very common among the Bondo women of Orissa. These skirts are only eight to ten inches wide and about two feet six inches to three feet long. None of these people usually has, any upper garment.

UNSEWN AND DRAPED APPAREL

A small strip of cloth of about four to six inches in breadth is an under garment one end of which is tied in front with the chord used as belt and the other end passed between the legs and tied with the chord at the back. The upper garment in most cases comprises of an open front sleeveles coat or jacket. This simple type of costume is distributed over a vast area in India. It is very common among the people of the North-East Frontier Agency, parts of the Assam hills and among the hills and Gond, etc.

An un-tailored skirt of moderate breadth (2'— 2½") without upper garment or with blouse is common costume among the women of the NEFA, Nagaland, Kachari and Garos of Assam among the Riang and Tripuries of Tripura and in abundance among the hill people of Orissa and Madhya Pradesh.

There are skirts touching almost up to the ankle with an upper garment, either blouse or jacket, also a common costume with an addition of a third piece used either as a scarf ar Odhani. The women Misos of the Mizo Hills, Manipuris of Manipur, Todas and the majority of Kerala people still use this type of costume.

Next in order in this group of untailored costume is the different length of *dhoti* used by the men of our country. The length of the dhoti varies with the style. When the dhoti is put on with *kachha** the usual length is from four to five yards in length. The upper garment used with the *dhoti* varies. In the South the *dhoti* is put on without any sewn upper garment and is usually accompanied with a *chaddar*. The upper garment in other parts of India comprises of sewn type of *banian, kurta, mirzai,* shirt, *angadi* or *angrakhi*. The distribution of kachha style with sewn upper garment or without upper garment is common almost in all states of India wheres the dhoti without kachha is commcan in Madras, Kerala, parts of Punjab, Rajasthan Mizo Hills and Nagaland.

The last important item of the costume of women in the un-tailored category is the *sari* which reigns supreme among the beautiful costumes. The most common style in the *sari* group is the '*gather*' and '*Nivi*' style without *kachha*. The length for this style varies fram five to six yards and is accompanied by a *choli* and petticoat. The loose decorative end of the *sari* is either left loose over the back (South India and Eastern India) or is brought forward over the right shoulder and tucked in the waist (Gujarat, Bihar and Uttar Pradesh). Another style is to fasten a bunch of keys as weight at the upper end of the border of sari and is then left over the left shoulder, the main portion of the border is visible in front (Bengal and Orissa). The style in this category is to bring the less decorative end of the sari from the back and is fixed over the breast portion giving an impression of a skirt. A second piece is necessary in this style to over the head. This style is predominant among the Coorgs of Mysore and people of the hill areas of Kerala. Yet another style is to wear the whole length of the *sari* like a skirt tied on the waist, with a blouse and a second piece of cloth to cover the head. This style is very common among the Nepalese women of the Darjeeling area.

Another widely distributed style in the *sari* is with *kachha*. The length in this case cannot be less than nine yards. The kachha style also varies from state to state. The distribution of this style is fairly wide and is common in the States of Madras, parts of Kerala. Madhya Pradesh, Maharashtra and Andhra Pradesh.

CUT AND TAILORED COSTUMES

Pyjama and *ghaghra* or *Lahenga* are the two important lower garments in this group used by the men and women respectively in a widely distributed area. The Indian *pyjama* can broadly be divided into three categories viz *salwar dhilla* type and *churidar* or narrow cut. The upper garment of sewn type like *banian, kurta, mirzai,* skirt, *angadi* or *angrakhi* is invariably put with any of the three above mentioned types of *pyjamas*. The distribution of these three different types of *pyjamas* is common among the Nepalese Bhutias and Lepehas of Bengal, Uttar Pradesh, part of punjab, Himachal Pradesh, Jammu and Kashmir and part of Gujarat. The women's costume with salwar and two other pyjamas is completed with *kamiz* and *dupatta*. This dress is in vogue in parts of Uttar Pradesh, Punjab, Himachal Pradesh and Jammu & Kashmir a special type of *Kamiz (Fhiran)* reaching midway between knee and ankle is a common costume without the addition of *dupatta* and *salwar*.

The tailored type of skirt or *ghaghra* or *Lahenga* for women is a very common costume of Northern, Central and parts of Western India. The *Lahenga* is put on with a blouse or *choli, kurta* or, *kamiz* and a *dupatta* or *odhani*. There are two types of *ghaghra*. The first type is sewn with an enormous amount of cloth, the upper end having loop to pass the cord (*nara*) for tying in the waist with frills and the lower end is free with an enormous gather. The second type of Lahenga is tailored almost in the same fashion with much less cloth and consequently with less of a gather.

FOOT GEAR

The foot gear and head gear are as varied as the apparel proper and needs special attention. In short the foot gear may broadly be divided into three distinct types. The most widely distributed type is the *sandal,* the second in importance is the Nagra type and the last is the Hill type. Leather is the main medium used for the foot gear but use of wood, straw, and cloth is not so rare. A large percentage of people in India, both men and women, move about bare-footed.

HEAD GEAR

The use of head gear is not very common in Eastern and Southern India. The head gear can broadly be classified under ceremonial and non-ceremonial types. A discussion of both the types requires considerable space.

In short, the head gear for non-ceremonial purpose can be classified under turban type, cap type and hat type. The distribution of that type is very restricted in the hill areas of Bengal. NEFA and parts of Assam — the cap type on the other hand is distributed over Bihar, Uttar Pradesh Himachal Pradesh, Jammu and Kashmir. The turban with an ancient tradition is distributed over a wide area, Its size and style are available. The turban as head gear is most common in Gujarat, Rajasthan, Punjab; Maharashtra, Mysore, and among the non-Christian Khasis. On ceremonial occasion the turban is an essential head gear in Uttar Pradesh, Assam and Manipur.

SACHIN ROY

COTTON LACE OF ANDHRA

Best known, crochet lace of Andhra Pradesh; craft has Irish origin; introduced by Christian missionaries in 1863. Lace sent as gifts abroad, an effort to collect donations.

Extensively practised Narsapur, Palakol, Tanuku of west Godavari District; also found in Krishna, East Godavari Districts of Andhra Pradesh.

Thread combined with crochet needle; craftsmen produce finest laces in the world. Products like table cloths, luncheon sets, bedspreads, curtains made, marketed in the United Kingdom; West Germany; Norway, Sweden; Australia, Middle East.

Unique features of craft, provides employment, large number of people majority of women, children.

CRAFTS MUSEUM, NEW DELHI

Set up in 1956 under the aegis of All India handicrafts Board; aims to collect and preserve "outstanding speciments of Indian handicrafts as source material for initiating study, research, documentation, reproduction and development", further objective "disseminating information about the history of crafts as well as their production techniques", well stocked library, photo library and well catalogued slides, displays entire range of Indian handicrafts, textiles, embroidered fabrics, would and metal carvings and sculptures, paintings and terracotta objects; regional offices at Okhla (New Delhi), Bombay, Calcutta, Lucknow, Bangalore and Madras.

References

Dwivedi, V. P. (ed.) *Brief Directory of Museum in India,* New Delhi, 1969.

Patil, H. S. (ed.) *Dictionary of Cultural Organizations in India,* New Delhi, 1975.

Sivaramamurthi, C., *Directory of Museums in India,* Delhi, 1959, *World of Learning,* 1969-70, London, 1970.

CRAFTS OF MIZORAM ; A RICH REPERTOIRE

Mizoram - literally meaning the highlander's land, is the 23rd State of India covering a total area of 21,081 sq. km. Geographically, it is landlocked and has Myanmar in the east and the south, Bangladesh and Tripura in the

west and Assam and Manipur touch its northern borders. With an enviably pleasant climate, where the skies are as blue as the water in the streams flowing below, with the misty mountains, lush green valleys and plethora of flowers, the state also boasts of a rich tradition of crafts.

Since Mizoram has an abundance of bamboo, its bamboo is used in all walks of life, from making houses, fashioning bridges, furniture et al. It is also an inherent part of its dances.

A unique object from mizoram's treasure trove of bamboo products if the *Khumbeu.* This is a cap woven or plaited out of cane. It is then lined with leaves which are dry or smoked dry. The leaves make the cap waterproof. It is considered a fooproof protection against wind, sun and rain. The top portion of the hat has circular designs; the circular areas and rim sport the typical *'jhala'* symbol. While the shape of the hat used earlier was functional, this slowly gave way to a more up market version, now resembling a cap with an extension hood. So beautiful and environment friendly is this cap that it can any day give the major brands a run for their money.

The basket used for carrying are also distinct. The baskets carried by women only have the hand support to hang on the head, while those of men have a yoke attached to it. The band is hung on the head and the yoke fits in at the neck. The former is called Paikwang with Hnam and *latter Emping with Nghwang-Kawl.* The former basket is not densely plaited while the latter is. Bamboo pouch called *Paihper* is used to carry seeds to be sown. The rice seeds for sowing are carried in this bag to the fields. Though the use is functional it can any day pass for a sophisticated hand purse. *Thlangra,* which is essentially a babmoo tray, is used for winnowing grains. It is characerized by an oblong shape. *Thul,* a large distinctive basket made to store clothes, stands on four legs; it hs a conical-shaped lid to keep things safe. This is, however, very rarely used and serves more as a decorative piece.

Today, many design variations have been introduced in bamboo items, thus producing attractive beds, sofa sets, bookstands and other types of furniture as also trays, pot holders and bread baskets. The list of contemporary use of bamboo is endless.

Bamboo also comes in handy for the popular bamboo dance known locally as *Cheraw.* Bamboo poles are held in horizontal position. Equal sized poles are then held by the dancers vertically of these horizontal poles. They then tap the bamboo open and shut in a rhythmic beat. The dancers dexterously step into open spaces, thus creating a unique mixture of rhythm and grace. Drummers and gong men invariably accompany the dancers. Wooden drums are used to provide the rhythm along with metal gongs called *Darbu.* Another metal gong used is the Darkhuang. The metal gong is usually used to announce the death of an important person.

The dresses worn during the dances are also indicative of the crafts used in making them. The headgear of the dancers is usually a combination of leaves, dried flowers and dyed feathres of birds.

Loin looms are predominantly usd for weaving, which is done in cotton, wool and silk. *Puans,* cloth, eye catching shawls are all woven at the handloom. *Puan* is a traditional garment of the Mizos, worn below the waist. The length of the *puan* varies from 55-60 inches with the breadth being

48 inches. The garments worn by the ladies are of full length, touching the feet, while that of men are of knee-length only. The blouse to top the *puan* is called *Kwarchei*. Together it forms a stylish, chic and elegant ensemble.

The *puan* is very colourful and beautifully woven. In its entirely it brings out a wealth of motifs, designs and symbols encompassing the rich fauna and flora of the place. The designs used in weaves are simplistic depiction and derivation of the nature surrounding the areas. A very common motif used is that of Fanghmamu, the cucumber seeds, while *Harzhai* represents an oblong shape. All types of colours are used to weave the *puans* right from bright clours like red, green and yellow to basic black and white stripes.

Most of the *Puans* are made of handspun cotton. Current variations are also being tried using man-made fibres like acrylic or synthetic yarn. Woollen shawls are incredibly striking and impressive; in a host of colours and designs. Silk is also woven into attractive *stoles* and *puans*. These again stand out for their subtle and elegant combination of colours.

The hallmark of Mizoram's crafts is the cubtlety and under-stated elegance. Though the colour combination may striking and vibrant, the overall impact is subdued and not showy or gaudy.

No account of Mizo crafts is complete without the mention of the amber bead necklaces. Called *Thihna* and *Thival*, they are worn by the wealthy or the upper class women. These are esentially stones in gorgeous shades of orange and ochre. No occasion is complete without wearing it. Other items include ivory earrings and small smoking pipes made of wood.

CHITRA BALASUBRAMANIAM

CUISINE OF SOUTH INDIA

India, it is often said, is an experience, complex and fascinating, it is ablaze with traditions, people, crats, colours, wildlife and food. A veritible kaleidoscope -- with every little detail of life so startlingly different, so uniquely its own.

Take South India, tucked away snugly below the Vindhya and Satpura mountain ranges, which roughly divide India into two. This chunk of land that extends across the Deccan peninsula, a remnant of a once large and stable plateau, is nothing like its northern counterpart. Fringed by coastal plains, traversed by rocky plateaus, fertile river valleys, lush trophical forests and hardy mountainous terrain, it has an entirely different story to tell. Its four States and one Union Territory - Tamil Nadu, Karnataka, Andhra Pradesh, Kerala and Pondicherry - have their own language and culture, customs and heritage, architecture and handicrafts. In fact, it is not even very wise to club these states together since ethnic variations are so apparent that even with each State, every little community has its own way of doing things, totally at variance with another.

Yet, one preceives a common heritage, a discernible unity, especially in the vegetarian cuisine of the four states. Of course, there are innumerable area specialities. For example, the little town of Udipi is the home of the golden brown, crisp *Masala Dosai*, which is justly renowned the world over. Today, of course, every single self-respecting South Indian will swear by her or his own family recipe for the scrumptious *dosais*. Almost every household will tell you about a secret ingredient - a great grandmother's legacy - for almost any dish. Despite native diversities, the pattern of eating is much the same in the whole of the South.

A typical meal consists of three courses - rice with *sambar, rasam* and *yogurt* (Indian curd). The rice is generally served steaming hot and pearly white.

Ranging from greetings cards to small wall calendars; rice straw pictures however have only three ingredients used in their making. A straw board, black poplin cloth and straw sticks. The cloth is mounted upon the board on which the master cratsman would draw sketches with crayon pencil; followed by pasting of chiselled straw pieces on the already drawn sketches. "It takes four to five days to create one such big picture", informs Josaf, winner of the national and state level awards for his dedicated effort to promote this extraordinary art.

Although concentrated mainly in Kerala, these pictures are even exported abroad. "It is the USA and Germany where these picture are in great demand", says Josaf. "Even North India holds a big market for the business. Sometimes it is difficult to meet the overwhelming demand".

May be because straw pictues are less costly but equally attractive and appealing, if not more, than the oil or colour paintings.

CULTURAL CONTACTS BETWEEN INDIA AND INDONESIA

Extending like a chain of emeralds for about a thousand miles, Indonesia, the largest archipelago in the world, is an interesting land full of scenic diversity. Among the thousand islands forming this archipelago, largely volcanic and clothed in tropical verdure, full of high mountains and plateaus, beautiful lakes and waterfalls, Java and Bali are indeed the gems.

EARLY INDIANS IN INDONESIA

Indians began to settle in Indonesia during the first centuries of the Christian era. The actual process of acculturation was effected by the newly arrived immigrants following the footsteps of merchants and princes, Brahmins and Sramanas. The earliest data of more tangible character are the 4th-5th century A.D. inscriptions of purnavarman and Mulavarman from West Java and Borneo respectively. Similarly the oldest Buddha images found in Indonesia, Indo-China, Siam, Malaya and Burma were obviously inspired by the Krishna region of South Indian belonging to the 3rd and 4th centuries at the latest.

Throughout the course of Central and East Japanese history, between the 7th and 14th centuries, Indian teachers visited Indonesia. On his way to China one of the great teachers of Buddhism, Prince Gunavarman of kashmir passed Suwarnadwipa, as the archipelago was called in the 5th century A.D. and spread Buddhism here according to Chinese text. Other distinguished teachers were Dharmapada, in inhabitant of Kanchi and a Professor of Nalanda in the 7th century. Kumarghosa, the preceptor of the Gauda royal family in the 8th century, Vajrbodhi, a

South Indian monk and his disciple Amoghavajra who came via Ceylon on way to China and stopped for five months in Sri Vijaya; and last but not the least Dipankara Atisa, the Bengali Acharya of Nalanda in the 11th century. The names of some of the teachers, Buddhists and Brahmins are given in text and inscriptions. In order to build highly complicated monuments such as Boro-budur, Sewoe or Lara Jonggrang or to conceive iconographical systems such as that of mendut, a through knowledge of Buddhist and Saivite texts and familarity with Indian ideas, symbolism and some of the monuments in India were considered indispensible. The facts that such monuments and systems were actually found in Indonesia may partly have been due to the co-operation of Indian masters and master artists of the type just mentioned. In this way, Indonesia developed to be a great centre of Budhistic studies. Universities rivalling that of Nalanda and Vikramsola grew up in Indonesia itself.

As early as the 7th century Chinese pilgrims are reported to have sojourned in Indonesia in order to prepare themselves for their visit to the Holy Land of India. For example, studied Buddhism in Sri-Vijaya identified by some with Sumatra at the end of 5th century to India. There is no reason to doubt the existence as early as the 7th century of Buddhist centres of study in Indonesia, which led to the remarkable afforesence of art during the following centuries specially in Central Java.

MEDIAEVAL PERIOD

Intimate cultural collaboration between India and Indonesia in the early mediaeval period is further attested by the Nalanda charter of the 9th century Devapala granted five villages for the upkeep of an Indonesian monastry at Nalanda at the request of his friend Sailendra King Balaputradeva of Yava-bhumi. Similar direct relationship is envisaged in the Leiden Grant of 1005 A.D. which speak of the assignment of a village by the Chola emperor Rajaraja the Great, for the upkeep of a Buddhist Vihara at Negapatam built by another Sailendra King of Srivijaya, Sri Maravijayattungavarman. These interesting records bear historic testimony to the fact that in both the cases an Indian King granted villages to a Buddhist sanctuary, created in India by a Sailendra King, undeniably proves that Indonesians visited different parts of India in considerable numbers and the Indian Kings were always happy to offer them warm hospitality.

Of all the vestiges of the cultural contact between India and Indonesia, ranging for about fifteen hundred years beginning from the dawn of the Christian era, the most visible and exciting records are furnished by the works of art and architecture. Both in form and content, style and inconography, design and pattern, Indonesian art recall the forms and the concepts of Indian Art enriched by indigenous fancy. The main inspiration of the growth and evolution of Indonesian art came "from the contact with one of the greatest civilizations of the ancient world. Buddhism, Hinduism and the social atmosphere surrounding the idea of Kingship provided the creative impulses for the new evolution".

The magnificent sculptural wealth of Indo-Japanese art are housed in the Jakarta Museum. Some of the newly discovered sculptures and inscriptions, throwing new light on Indian art and culture abroad were found invaluable in so far as they provided interesting source materials missing in India itself.

MONUMENTS IN CENTRAL JAVA

Boro-budur, the world famous monument - the terraced mystic temples - adorned with more than 500 Buddhas profoundly significant, covering a low hill like a lily blooming in water. Chandi Mendut another Buddhist shrine oriented vest towards India, the holy land, is eqully notable for the divine trinity of Buddha, Avalokitesvara and Vajrapani of unsurpassed beauty and elegance. The Siva Temple, Prambanan which fell in utter ruins, has recently been completely restored by the Government of Indonesia, its tower reaching to a height of 200 feet. In the Archaeological Museum at Sorokarta and Jogyakarta many new sculptures of extraordinary significance and of an early period unknown before, indicative of a strong Indian influence were noted and photographed. The Department of Archaeology had also recently discovered a few inscriptions specially in Western and Central Java and excavated some archaeological sites which would necessitate the revision of history and chronology of the Sailendra dynasty and monuments of the 8th-9th century.

Japanese dance drama (Wayang Orang) the Ramayan-Mahabharata is very impressive. Although the Javanese have embraced Islam, their cultural flavour is still predominantly Indian. They would gladly sit up at night to witness performances of Wayang-Orang and Wayang Kulit. On the other hand the Javanese pre-historic bronze antiquities, preseved in the Djakarta Museum betrayed indelible Chinese influence, before India emerged on the scene in the easly historic period. This alternating cusrents of Indian and Chinese influence on the cultural pattern of Indonesia throughout the ages, is indeed a fascinating phenomenon.

LOVELY BALI

Wesakhi temple of the 10th century A.D. perched on the lap of the sacred Volcano of Gunnung Agung and other notable archaelogical sites and excavations are thrilling to have a glimpse of ancient Indian life current one thousand years ago, in the living cultural of Bali today, in her temples and edifices, rituals and customs, art and dances. The Indonesians are surprised to know that the popular Indonesian cult of Siva-Buddha (where Buddha is considered as a younger brother of Siva) emanated from India as attested by the fine bronze image of Siva-Buddha of the 11th century A.D. preserved in the Asutosh Museum, Calcutta University.
(Condensed)

D. P. GHOSH

CULTURAL HERITAGE OF JAMMU AND KASHMIR

Composed of three principal cultural units, namely, Jammu Kashmir and Ladakhs, Jammu and Kashmir State has a further variety of sub-cultures, languages and dialects. The Constitution of the State recognises as many as seven Regional Languages while the Census of 1961 lists 103 mother tongues spoken by the people of the State. The speakers of at least 22 of them are in thousands.

Jammu and Kashmir is the only Muslim majority State of India. It has also the largest concentration of Buddhists. For Ladakh is the only Buddhist majority district of the country. Other religious followers include Hindus, Sikhs, Christians and Jains. There are only a few Parsis.

Apart from the known ethnic and cultural influences on Kashmir like pre and early Aryan, Dardic, Tibetan, Mughal, Afghan, Punjabi some writers trace it ancestry to ancient Jews, Sir Walter Lawrence and Sir Francis Younghusband - known for their authoritative writings on Kashmir have admitted the decided Jewish cast of faces among men, women and children. It is even assested by some that Kashmiris are the lost Tribe of Israel, mentioned in the Bible, Such beliefs, known and unknown, and upto a bewildering variety of the cultural components of the heritage of the Jammu and Kashmir State. Some of them are arranged in a geographical order while other are chronological, which combine to form a colourful horizontal and vertical design.

THREE MAIN CULTURAL STRANDS

With Jammu, Srinagar and Leh as the focal points, the innumerable cultural strands of the State, resolve themselves into three broad meaningful entities. On borders they intermingle. Thus Kashmiri culture overfollow the high Pir Panchal range into the border areas of Jammu region and gets mixed up with the local culture. Likewise the predominant polulation on the periphery of the Kashmir Valley is non-Kashmir speaking, mostly of Gujars with their own distinct ethnical and cultural entity, perhaps closer to the mainstream of Jammu.

The three cultural units of the State were brought together under one administration by Maharaja Gulab Singh in 1946 when Kashmir Valley was ceded to him by the disintegrating Sikh Empire in lieu of Rupees seventy-five lakhs. His General Zorawar Singh had already subdued Ladakh a few years earlier. But as geographical neighbours, the three units had been in close contact with one another, politically as well as culturally, earlier also. Kashmiri Kings like Sultan Zainul Abdin had domain and the first Muslim King of Kashmir, Rinchen, was a Ladakhi who embraced Islam. Again, Jammu's Raja Daya Karan, grandon of Jamboo Lochan the founder of Jammu city, is believed to have been invited by the feuding Brahmin Kingdoms of Kashmir to restore order and rule over there about a thousand years ago.

Kashmiri kings have often sought refuge in Jammu to escape the wrath of the invading armies. In fact the last Kashmiri King, Yusuf Chak, after being defeated by the Mughal Emperor Akbar, fled to Kishtwar, the northern most part of Jammu and lies buried there.

JAMMU : DOORWAY TO STATE

At present Jammu provides one only land route to Kashmir and Ladakh for not only the rest of Indian but also to the rest of the world. It is the vital doorway of the whole State. Traditionally also access to the valley was through Bhomber Rajouri Mughal Road and Kishtwar-Chamba Road, that passed through Jammu. The latter was also a link with Ladakh.

Before Independence and annexation by Pakistan of a part of the territory of the State, Jammu was the most populous province of the state with 19,81,433 inhabitants. In area-26,087 square kilometers - it is still almost double than that of the Valley but is smaller in population which 16 lakhs population against 19 lakhs in the latter.

Rising from the right bank of the rivers Ravi near the plains of the Punjab, Jammu extends to the Pir Panchal range, some of the peaks of which are as high as 16,000 feet. Cultural characteristics of the region tend to vary with geographical variations.

DOGRA INFLUENCE

The predominant influence on the personality of Jammu is of course of the Dogra community concentrated mainly in the central belt of the region, around the Kandi, rocky plateau of two to four thousand feet high. On its South and West the Dogra cultural mainstream gets mixed up on its borders with cultural currents overflown from the East and the West Punjab. Towards the north, it merges into cultural currents like that of Kashmir, Gujars culture is also discenible in the adjoining areas of Chamba and Kangra in the Himachal Pradesh.

Much further research is needed to identify various cultural and recial layers which comprise the foundation and components of the modern Dogra culture.

GUJARS AND TAKKS

One of the earliest settlers in Jammu were perhaps the community of Gujars. They are believed to have entered India in 6th Century B.C. and first settled on the Shiwalik ranges which run through Jammu. Dr. R.D. Bhandarkar is of the view that Gujars first inhabiting Shiwaliks were an noited by Brahmins as Kshatriyas for their Kshatiya like qualities. In this guise they clamped down on what is now Rajasthan and founded the State of Rajputana and emerged as Rajputs. Their pastoral bretheren who stayed behind later embraced Islam. Some of the fighter Gujar-Rajputs, fled back, after centuries, due to political vicissitudes to their former abode and were successful in carving out for themselves big or small principalities. The story of return and conquest of Jammu by Rajput princes is not older than four centuries, But common ancestory and ksnship between Gujars, Rajputs and Jats is established by other evidence also.

Another ancient community of Jammu to which references have been made in the old scriptures as also in Rajatarangni is what was called takks who are believed to be the ancestors of modern Thakkars and who invented Takri the original script of Dogri. It is difficult to identify the descendants of the Khash tribes who inhabited Jammu even before Takks and Gujars. Perhaps they were driven away or reduced to low caste status. Khash is still a word of contempt in dogri to describe simple hilly people. A large Harijan population over 30% of the Hindu population in Jammu, further suggests the existence of some pre-Aryan aborigines in Jammu. Comparatively recently Brahmins from Uttar Pradesh, Jains and Khatries from Punjab and Arorvanishis from Multan came to settle in Jammu.

Except for small principalities on the periphery of Jammu, it has never been ruled by a Muslim. But Muslims constituted a majority of the population of the undivided Jammu. Even after the occupation of certain areas by Pakistan in 1947 Muslim percentage in its population is around 40%. Apart of it migrated from Punjab and Kashmir due to compulsions of political events or natural clamities and attracted by generous treatment they received from Dogra rulers like Ranjit Dev. Others are converts under the influence of Sufi preachers like Sayyid Faridud Din and his son Israrud Din who lie buried in Kishtwar, Budhan Shah, a contemporary and friend of Guru Nanak, and Roshan Shahwali both buried near Jammu city. These saints are revered by Hindus and Muslims alike. Their ziarats are attended by a large number of Hindu devotees also.

Likewise Muslims participate in some of the semi-regilious Hindu festivals. Kud, Phumni and Bhangra are main seasonal dance-festivals of Pahari region, Kandi and the plains respectively. Like most of the cultural currents of Jammu, Phumni style is just in between the other two dances of the flanking areas.

Jammu's immortal contribution to the national culture, however, is in the fields of Pahari music and Pahari Art. Soul stiring Pahari Music - and ragas like Jhanjoti and Durga based on it - is an extremely precious heritge of Pahari region which includes Jammu. In recent times also Jammu has produced outstanding singers and musicians, like Malika Pukhraj and Allah Rakha.

PAHARI PAINTINGS : JAMMU KALAM

The Jammu Kalam has made a distinct contribution to the gallaxy of Pahari paintings, which constitute on the richest chapters in the history of Indian art and have already been accorded a place of honour in the artistic heritage of the World. From sixteenth century to the dawn of the present century, Shiwalik ranges had been the abode of the art of painting in India. Among the Pahari schools of painting, at lease four centres flourished in Jammu viz: Jammu proper, Bosohli, Ramkot and Poonch. There were minor centres at Jasrota, Bandralta and Kishtwar also. Most of the authors of the internationally renowned masterpieces of Pahari or Dogra Art are annonymous. However, the painter of the celebrated complete series of colourful illustrations to the great Sanskrit love poem, Gita Govinda, has been identified as Menaku (1730 A.D.) who must rank as one of the greatest painters of his age.

It is also known that Nain Sukh, Vajan, Didi and other talented artists adorned the court of Raja Balwant Dev of Jammu around mid-18th century.

Kangra style was transplanted on the local soil when Nandlal migrated to Jammu in the durbar of Maharaja Ranbir Singh. His grandson Harichand rose to further fame. Harichand's pupil Jagat Ram kept alive the classical trandition. "With his death in 1922 the last knell of the Pahari art was sounded". almost unnoticedly.

SCULPTURE AND ARCHITECTURE

Painting was preceded by plstic art. "The vast sculptural treasures of Jammu pose a serious challenge to the archeologist and the historian". Special mention must be made of terracotta pieces recently unearthed in Akhnoor, sculptures in Babor, Billawar and Kiramchi. Sculptures are closely linked with are architecture of the age. Some of them are the idols installed in the temples. Others are human and animal figures or decorative pieces in the places. Vigne, the French traveller who visited Basohil between 1835-39, describes its places as "The very finest building of the kind I had seen in the East". While most of the monuments of Basohli were constructed

in 18th century, other master-piece of sculpture and architecture mentioned above belong to the late Gupta period of eight to eleventh century.

"The intense, highly charged feeling of the folk sought expression in multifarious forms of clay and brass images, ritualistic drawings and paintings". The folk poet, however, who has not to depend upon the court patronage as the sculptor and artist do, provide a more uninhibited, spontaneous and genuine expression to the folk aspirations. Songs singing glory of saints and heroes, songs sung by peasants in the fields, shepherds on hill tops, by men and women on festivals, marriages and other ceremonies give a turner insight into the life of Jammu than chronicles and artists of the Durbar.

CURRENT DOGRI RENNAISANCE

Drawing upon the rich folk tradition - in content and melody-current Dogri rennaisance has thrown up quite a number of writers of merit. In the last quarter of a century Dogri literature has been enriched by almost three hundred books in prose and poetry. Writing a foreword to Padma Sachdeva's book of poetry, Ramdhari Singh Dinkar, the noted Hindi feels like throwing away his pen on hearing her poems and "seeing the amazing spiritual wealth scattered in Dogri.

KASHMIR VALLEY : SEAT OF CULTURE AND LEARNING

If basic human urges are universal, the people across Pir Panchal in the fabled Valley of Kashmir, or across Zojila in esoteric Ladakh, must have stirrings similar to those in Jammu, alibeit articulated by their own saints, heroes, artists, poets and lovers, History, geography and countless other factors snape the forms of manifestations of and put a stamp of uniqueness on each culture.

Kashmir is the largest valley in the lap of the largest mountains in the world. Its culture is as unique as its geographical situation and as fascinating as its physical beauty.

As observed by Pandit Jawarharlal Nehru : 'It has been one of the biggest seats of Indan culture and learning throughout history for about, 2000 years". There is no branch of knowledge in which a Kashmiri scholar has not distinguished himself. The great ancient celebrities like Patanjali, author of Sanskrit Grammar, Charka, pioneer of Ayurvedic system of medicine, Koka, the foremost authority on sex, Nagarjun, the leading exponent of Mahayana Buddhism, Abhinav Gupta, the renowned Shiva Philosopher Kshamendra and Bilhana, the great Sanskrit poets, Bhaskracharya and Aryabhat the great Astrologers, Vama Bhatt, and authority on poetics, Mani, the painter and Kalhana, the great historian, flourished in Kashmir and are some of the brightest stars ever shone on the Indian firmament. We may add to this illustrious list the names of greatest poets of all ages like Bhavabhuti who came from Kannauj to adorn the court of Lalitaditya (725-753 A.D.) and Kalidas who is claimed to have been born in Kashmir (though controversy o the issue is far from settled.) This intellectual phenomenon lasting till about a thousand years after Christ is comparable to the intellectual explosion in ancient Greece.

"Although itself remote, Kashmir lies within that part of Central Asia which at one period was the clearing house of several separate civilizations and the influence of these found their way into this natural retreat". The special genius of Kashmir lies in its ability to assimilate diverse influences.

"It can be maintained that the present population of Kashmir is an admixture of aborgines with slight Jewish, large Aryan and some other foreign elements. The original Dardic language has supplied the skeleton of Kashmir language, Sanskrit has given it flesh and Islam (which brought Persian and Urdu influence) has given it life".

HABBA KHATOON

Real genius of the Kashmiris perhaps expressed itself in Kashmiri poetry, which is almost six hundred years old. Just as poets of Bhakti movement all over the country were popularising spiritual knowledge through common man's language, religious poetry of Sufis and Rishis of Kashmir like Lalla and Nund Rishi - provided the pioneering impulse of Kashmiri poetry. It acquired a secular and human touch in the melodious love songs of Queen Habba Khatoon - wife of the last Kashmiri King Yusug Shah Chak (16th Century). Arani Mal and Prakash Bhat also belong to the same age. In the latter part of the 19th Century Mohammad Gami and Aziz Ullah Haqqani further enriched Kashmiri poetry. Pirzada Ghulam Ahmad Mahjur led its modern phase. His tarana became the clarion call of the freedom movement in the forties of this century.

LOL LYRICS

If Kashmir breathes poetry, music is also in its air. It lol-lyric-lil is an untranslatable Kashmiri word signifying complex of love longing and a tugging at the heart - particularly lends itself to musical recital. Sarangadeva, the famous author of Sangita - Ratnakar, in the first half of the 13th century, is believed to be a Kashmiri. Later Irani and Turani musicians influenced and introduced new melodies into Kashmiri music. Mulla Udi and Zafran were renowned musicians of the 15th century. But is was Habba Khatoon, a century later, whose sweet melodies filled the valley and continue to resound.

KASHMIRI ARCHITECTURE

Another filed in which Kashmir has earned distinction is that of architecture. Sir Alexander Cunningham observed : "The superiority of the Kashmirian architecure over all other Indian buildings would appear to have been known to the Hindus themselves, for one of their names for the people of Kashmir is Shastra-Shilpina or architects". Martand temple, constructed by Lalitaditya in 8th Century, which we may take as the representative or rather the culmination of all the rest, is "Built on the most sublime site occupied by any building in the world".

During Zain Ul Abidin's reign, a novel wooden style was introduced. The first example of wooden architecture and Kanquahi Moulla and Jama Masjit, Mughal contribution to architecture of Kashmir is the series of gardens they constructed. "There are no other gardens in all Asia which nature and men have combined to make so lovely".

Grecian pillars and columns, Buddhist style of Stupas and Viharas, Hindu architectual decoration and relief sculptures, Islamic simplicity and massiveness have left their mark on Kashmiri's architectural landscape.

It is the same genius that Makes Kashmiris" the most expert handicraftsmen of the East". Their products still adorn the drawing room of the men of taste all over the world.

In assessing Kashmiri's contribution to the cultural heritage of India, it would not be out of place to make a mention of those luminaries - scholars, literatures, statesmen and administrators - who moved out of Kashmir and made their mark at the national level.

LADAKH : CITADAL OF BUDDHISM

Ladakh, the third partner of the State and the State and the only surviving citadal of Buddhism in India, is another world in more than one sense. Less than ninety thousand persons live at what may be called the roof of the world ranging between, 12000 ft. to 25,000 ft. above sea level in an area of almost one lakh square kilometers i.e. less than one person in a square kilometer.

Ladakh which comprises 70 percent of the area of the State, has 800 miles of common border with China - 350 miles with Tibet and 450 miles with Sinkiang.

The people of Ladakh are a mixture of the Mongolian and the Aryan races. The Aryan settlers included Buddhist from Kashmir and the Dards from Gilgit. The Mongolian stock consisting of shepherds and nomads, descended from Tibet. The original settlers (200 BC) were Mars. They built the ancient irrigation system of Ladakh and erected fine pieces of sculpture. They were also the first to introduce the art of music and later adopted it as a profession. Dard, who subsued the Mars and the earlier Tibetan settlers, introduced the art of rock carving and drawing figures of animals. The last of settle were the Mongols.

Buddhism spread in Ladakh during the reign of Asoka. The Buddhists, owe their allegiance to Lamas who have their own discipline and hierarchical order. Most of the cultural life of the people in the Buddhist areas centres around Gumpas the Ladakhi monastery. One of the notable cultural activity is the famous mystery play performed with the advent of spring. It comprises of a series of dances spread over most part of the day.

A little less than half the population of Ladakh lives in Kargil Tehsil separated from Kashmir by Zoji la Pass (11,530 ft.) and from Leh, the District headquarters by Faty la Pass (13,400 ft.) Belonging mostly to Shia sect of Muslims, people of Kargil are a distinct cultural linguistic entity within Ladakh. (Condensed)

References
1. Lost Tribe Lay, Dr. Jill Cossley, Batt and Dr. Irvine Baird.
2. Gulab Nama by Kripa Ram
3. Basohli Painting by M.S. Randhawa.

BALRAJ PURI

CULTURAL HERITAGE OF LADAKH

MONASTERIES

Ladakh is the only considerable territory in this land of the Buddha that is still predominently Buddhists. And as is only to be expected, it is interspersed with monasteries or gumpas, as they are locally known. So numerous are they that Ladakh may well be called the Land of Lames and Gumpas, or the "Land of Monks and Monasteries."

Except in its Kargil area, the people of Ladakh follow mainly the Buddhist faith. But, as in many other parts of the Buddhist world today, it is not the pure unadulterated doctrine propounded by the Buddha. Ladakhis follow what is unusally termed as Lamaism.

Lamaism, as the form of Buddhism prevalent in Ladakh and Tibet may well be described as a combination of Mahayana and Tantrism, not unmixed with traces of Bon. the pre-Buddhist faith of Tibet.

Buddhism came to Tibet in the time of the powerful native ruler, Srontsan Gampo in the middle of the seventh century A.D. He adopted the new faith under the influence of his two Buddhist wives - princesses of China and Nepal. But despite royal patronage, it did not make much headway because of the stiff opposition of the native Bon faith. But the new faith got firmly implanted in the time of his fourth successor about a century later. This was through the pious exertions of Padmasambhava whom Shantarakshita, a prominent Indian monk then working in Tibet, brought from Nalanda to help him.

Though Tibet got its Buddhism mainly from India yet Ladakh got its faith mainly from Tibet. Accordingly we find the same sects of Buddhism in the territory as in Tibet and the people following the same ritual and religious practices, etc. The Red Hats, however, predominate in Ladakh. Accordingly Padmasambhava, the main importer of Tantrism into Tibet, is held in very high esteem. Padamasambhava is also known as "Guru Rimpoche". or "The Precious Teacher". So long with the images and representations of the Buddha Shakya Thuba, Avalokitisvara (Chenrazik), Amitabha, Maitreya (the future Buddha) and Tara, the Buddhist goddess, we find images of Padmasambhava and Tsong-ka-pa in the Ladakhi monasteries. But the recipient of the greatest worship and devotion of Chenrasi or Avalokitesvara who is also known as Padma Pạni, or "The Lotus Born". According to some the omnipresent prayer, OM MANI PADME HUM! (Obeisance to the Jewel in Lotus) is also, in the main, addressed to him.

Religion has been a dominating factor in the life of the simple, un-sophisticated Ladakhis and monks and nuns were fairly numerous. This necessitated the founding of a large number of monasteries or gumpas to house them. In fact every village has a monastery of its own.

The gumpas or monasteries are the most conspicious building in Ladakh. The word gumpa signifies a solitary place and in this connection it need to be remembered that monasteries were orginally intended to be built in palce far from the bustle and disturbing influences of the populace. Perched on cliffs or in the side of mountains, they look both picturesque and impressive. Though somewhat difficult of access, a visit to one of them is a rewarding experience. They all contain exquisite images of the Buddha and other divinities and dignitaries of the Buddhist pantheon. The images in some of the gumpas are of such colossal dimensions that one wonders how they were made and carried to the lofty pinnacles on which some of the gumpas stand.

The gumpas are spacious building. In addition to the main prayer hall or worship room, they contain a large number of rooms for the lamas to live in. The sacred images are placed at the further side of the chapel or prayer room while the sacred books or pothis lie in front in two rows. The lamas sit behind and read them at the time of the service several times in the day. A butter-fed lamp is kept constantly burning and this has given a sombre look to the exquisite paintings on the walls of the room.

The presence of a monastery hearlded by Manis, Chortens, and prayer cylinders. The Mani is a massive stone wall, usually more than six feet in height, with the top sloping down from the centre towards either side. They are six to ten feet broad and in length may vary from a few feet to well over a thousand or more feet. The flat-surfaced stones on top bear the sacred inscription, Om Mani Padme Hum. Occasionally a mani-stone may contain a coloured figure of a Buddhist God also. The Manis are sometimes found in palces other than the vicinity of the Gumpas. The devout walk around them whenever they happen to pass them believing that this confers on them the merit of the recitation of the number of mantras inscribed on their countless stones.

The prayer-cylinder is another such ingenious device to multiply one's prayers many-fold. Moade to metal the prayer-cylinder is filled with scrolls of prayers and charms, expectially Om Mani Padme Hum. As a devotee walks, he sets them in motion with a gentle motion of the hand, believing that he is adding to his prayers by the number of prayers inside multiplied by the number of rotations.

Besides the Manis and prayer-cylinders, what immediately attracts the attention as one approaches a gump as is the chorten. The word appears to have been derived from the chaitya, but instead of a sacred image it houses the ashes of a revered lame, mixed with clay and moulded into a tablet. This table is then placed, in the peculiar pagoda-like structure known as the chorten.

The monasteries, as also the people's houses in Ladakh, are mounted with prayer-flags printed with the highly venerated and popular mantra, Om Mani Padme Hum. Occasionally a pole or two may be found mounted with a long bushy yaktail or the figure of a horse, apparently in thanks giving for the safe return of a caravan.

Besides containing the sacred images and the holy texts, the gumpas are the repositories of the best in Ladakh's art and culture.

Apart from the sacred images some of them golden, the gumpas also contain paintings and murals of great worth. Above all, they contain the thangkas, or scroll paintings which excite the wonder and admiration of all who see them. Not all of them are indigenous in origin; some exquisite ones seem to have come from beyond the border of the territory in the east.

The gumpas are also the places where the famous mystery-plays of Ladakh are staged. Every monastery has its own festival which, besides the ceremonial puja, is celebrated with music, dance and drama. The plays, enacted on the occasion represent the fight of the forces of good and evil, with the former triumphing in the end. The actors are lamas wearing elaborate brocade costumes, masks of animals, skeletons, etc. The orchestra comprises huge trumpets, giant cymbals, drums, etc. The puja offered on the occasion of these festivals is looked upon as a safeguard against likely calamities on the land and its people.

Before bringing the brief account of the monasteries of Ladakh to a close it may not be out of place to give a brief description of some at least of the principal monasteries.

Hemis : The biggest and by far the best known monastery of Ladakh is the Hemis gumpa, situated at a distance of 40 kms from Leh along the Leh-Manali road. The road to Hemis leaves the main road at about the 35 kms from Leh, and crosses the Indus. The monastery is not visible from the road as it is located in a side valley. There are a number of gold statues decorated with precious stones in it. Among the thangkas, there is a very big one, which is displayed once in eleven years.

The Hemis gumpa is known far and wide for the annual fair which attracts tourists from different parts of the world; the main pull being the mystery plays, interspersed with lama dances, enacted on the occasion. The festival takes place in the month of June.

Thiksey : On the way to Hemis is the famous monastery of Thiksey, situated on a hill-top. It has a beautiful location and one can enjoy an enchanting view of the green Indus Valley from its rooftop. The Monastery has a number of chambers full of statues, stupas and thangkas of all kinds. There are sixty lamas in the monastery and it is supposed to have a nunnery also. Wall-paintings are very interesting.

Shey : About 15 kilometers from Leh, on the way to Hemis is the Summer place of the Old Raja of Leh. The place is situated on top of a hill and houses the largest victory stupa with a golden top. The monastery has a two-storey high statue of the Buddha in a sitting position. The statue made of copper and gilded with gold is worth seeing. The Monastery remains closed and it is advisable to make prior arrangements with the Lama to see it.

Sankar : About 3 kilometers from the town of Leh is this Gumpa headed by Kushak Bakula, a former Minister in Kashmir Government. The Gumpa is electrified. There are innumerable small statues of pure gold and a number of interesting paintings. The Gumpa can be visited in the evenings also as it is well-lighted.

Spituk : A few kilometres short of Leh, on the Srinagar-Leh road on top of a small hill overlooking the Indus, is the Spituk monastery. There is a new Gumpa within the monastery. The old Gumpa has been-renovated. Some very interesting Thangkas are the pride possessions of the monastery. This Gumpa too is electrified. Higher up on the hill is a chamber housing enormous statues of Goddess Kali with faces covered. The faces are exhibited only once in a year on the occasion of the annual Mela (festival) which occurs in January. This chamber also contains a very old collection of face masks. It is interesting to visit the Gumpa on the day of the Puja.

Phyiang : This Gumpa situated on the left side of the road from Srinagar to Leh, 20 kilometers short of Leh, is the monastery of the Red-Sect of Buddhists. The monastery has some beautiful statues and Thangkas.

Alchi and Likir : These two monasteries are to be found near Saspol on the Srinagar-Leh road. They house a great deal of gignatic clay statues of the Buddha in various forms. The primary attraction of these monasteries is, however, their 1,000 year old wall paintings which make a visit more than worthwhile. Alchi, in particular, is regarded as a treasure of art and artists and art-lovers do not consider their visit to Ladakh complete without a visit to Alchi.

The founding of the Alchi monastery is ascribed to the celebrated Tibetan monk, Rinchenzangpo, who spent a number of years in Kashmir, studying the sacred Buddhist texts with the masters in the valley. Kashmiri influence in the construction of the monastery and its rich artistic embellishment is un-mistakable.

Lamayuru : The next important monastery that we come across on the Leh-Srinagar road is that of Lamayuru. Situated some distance short of Futo-la, the highest point of the road, the monastery is built on the low hills at the far end of a valley. It consists of a number of buildings and contains a wealth of sacredimages, paintings, and thangkas. This monastery also houses a colossal image of Chenrazi or Avalokitesvara, with eleven heads had a thousand hands.

The great Kashmiri monk, Naropa, is credited with the founding of this monastery, which belongs to the Yellow Hat sect.

Mulbeck : The first village on the Srinagar-Leh road to have a monastery is Mulbeck. Mulbeck comes after Kargil and is just short of the second highest pass on the road, Namikala. The monastery has a bizzare location. It is perched on a high, solid rock over-looking the village and commands a grant view of its surroundings. It is a nice excursion to climb to the monastery to see its relics.

The village of Mulbeck has a unique possession. It is a colossal image of Maitreya Buddha, carved on a high, solid rock on the rightside of the road.

Leh Gumpas : Leh, the headquarter town of the Ladakh district, has always enjoyed a pre-eminent position among the villages of the district. Accordingly it contained a number of sacred temples, Chorten, and Mani walls. The conspicuous Raja's Place contains a huge image of Maitreya Buddha. Some years ago, a new gumpa has been built in the heart of the town. A school of Buddhist Philosophy was also set up as part of it to teach the children seeking admissing to the order of monks. The monks earlier rounded off their education with a visit to Lhasa. But Tibet's incorporation by China, they can no longer do so. Now-a-days the monks visit Sarnath and Both Gaya to round off their monastic training and education.

Among the other important manasteries of Ladakh, mention must be made of the Samur and Diskit gumpas in Nurba Valley, across the Ladakh range and Sani, Padam and Rangdum monasteries in the cold bleak Zanskar valley, which remains cut off from the rest of the world for the greater part of the year.

J. N. GANHAR

CULTURAL HERITAGE OF NORTH-EAST INDIA

Culturally the north-eastern region of our vast sub-continent is the least known to the outside world. It is inhabited by people who still live in their pristine grandeur. As in the culturally-rich Himalayan region, no systematic archaeological excavations had been carried out in the north-east region and its ancient past remained unknown. The sole credit for placing the early history and culture of this areas, particularly Manipur, Nagaland and Meghalaya, on the artistic and the cultural map of our country goes entirely to A.K. Sharma, a noted archaeologist, undertook excavations at numerous sites such as Sekta near Imphal in Manipur, Vadagokugiri (Bhaitbari) etc.

The artfacts due up from diverse sites viz. wheel-turned pottery (a sure sign of civilized society), kaolin jars and carnelian beads necklaces have significance all their own. They date from the pre-chiristian ears and give clue to trade relations existing between these areas and Kutch in Gujarat. Besides, a large number of religious objects have been found that inform about the religious affiliations of the local populations with Hinduism, mainly Shaivism, Shaktim and Buddhism, which were equally popular in the neighbouring Bengal, Bihar and to some extent parts of Orissa. At Vadagokuiri on the west Garo hills have been excavated fortified towns that came into existence in Pre-christian era and flourished under Hindu rulers till about the twelfth-thirteenth centuries A.D.

Tanks dating from ancient periods, paved roads, Hindu temples of the *shikhara* variety, i.e. the *Nagara* style temples like those found all over northern and western India, huge lingam and *yoni pithikas,* architectural fragments, terracotta plaques having striking thematic and stylistic affinities with those from Bengal, at times reminiscent also of Napalese sculptures in addition to the sanctity attached to the *peepal* trees, red and saffron flags, etc. furnish strong evidence of the indigenous populations being Hindus. Hinduism was the dominant religion as it still is in Manipur. Majority of the temple are datable to the early medieval and medieval periods, i.e. 7-11 century A.D., and have remarkable affinities with the Pratihara architectural tradition. It comes as a surprise indeed that the sphere of Pratihara artistic influence extended as far as the east of the Brahmaputra in the north-eastern India. More intensive research needs to be done by art historians and political historians into this aspect.

The Buddhist vestiges comprise stupas. The use of baked and unbaked bricks relates these structures with those from Bengal which has a full-fledged traditionof erecting terracotta temples. So also of terracotta plaques featuring Hindu deities like Shiva and Ganesh. The sculptural reliefs have a strong tantric flavour. The tradition of enclosing the figures of the deities within trefoliated arch is common to Bengali terracottas as well as those from *Molela* in Rajasthan. A peaculiat characteristic of north-eastern terracotta plaques are stepped stages of temple spires seen behind the arches. These stepped pyramidal spires are common in Orissa. These archaeological finds followed by more extensive and intensive excavations and researches by interested scholars adds a great deal to the knowledge of these neglected regions and shed a reveling light on India's glorious ancient past. The picture which emerges is one of a culturally unified India. Besides artistic and architectural links with the mainstream· of Indian culture, there were trade relations between the north-east region with other parts of the country as well as with the outside world. In more ways than one, the ancient past of the region under study has far more to offer in artistic and cultural terms.

SUBHASHINI ARYAN

CULTURAL HERITAGE OF ORISSA

India is the epitome of the world at large. It is as well a museum of races, languages, customs, creeds and religions. Geographically viewed, it is a vast sub-continent traversed by high mountain ranges and long navigable rivers, dotted with thick forests and densely populated area. But, in the ultimate analysis of national culture, Indian is essentially one and undivided. The differences of languages and religious faiths, social customs and moral practices are but the manifold expressions of Indian culture. Hence, in the context of the life and thought of the people of the various States of India, it is to be remembered that "unity in diversity". is the basic principle of the Indian way of life. Orissa with her high traditions of racial integration. Social equality, economic prosperity, religious catholicity, literary excellence and artistic splendour demands to be properly assessed in a symposium either on Indian Culture or on World Civilisation.

In olden days, Orissa comprised of four regions known as Kalinga (Southern) Udra (Middle) Kosala (Western) and Utkala (Northern) of which Kalinga was the most famous and there were periods when Udra, Kosala and Utkala formed parts of Kalinga.

The name Orissa (or rather, Odisa, more correctly spelt) came. into use from the 15th century onwards. According to some scholars, it is a corruption of Odra (Udra)-desa, meaning, the land of the Odra people who constituted a powerful section of cultivators of the Central and North-Western Orissa. But, others maintain that the word Odisa is derived from Odra-Vishaya, through its corrupt from Odi-Visha. As Vishaya in Sanskrit means a part of the country the words signifies the region inhabited by the Odras. Whatever might be the origin of the name, Orissa gained usage during the· British rule, but even today, the enlightened people of the State feel glorified to call it by its puranic name, Utkala.

It is learnt from the Mahabharata the king of Kalinga played an important role in the battle of Kurukshetra. Even more significant is the evidence of the famous Hatigumpha inscription of Kharavela (near Bhubaneswar, Orissa's new Capital) belonging to the 2nd century B.C. It is definitely known from it that a king of the Nanda Dynasty of Magadha conquered Kalinga much earlier no doubt but it was retaliated by Kharavela, the famous Kalingan emperor. Prior to this, Chandra Gupta Maurya, the farfamed emperor of the 4th century B.C., had driven out the Greeks from India and extended his territory to the far South but Kalinga did not form part of his empire. Thus undoubtedly. is a reliable testimony to the valour and heroism of the people of Kalinga. It remained for his grandson Asoka to conquer Kalinga, in 261 B.C. The loss of life and property in the battle, due to the most stubborn resistance of the people of Kalinga to maintain their independence, was so terrible that Asoka, the victor, had practically to admit a Spiritual defeat in as-much as he was transformed into Dharmasoka from Chandasoka.

Three great ruling dynasties known as the Bhauma-Kara, the Somavansi and the Ganga dynasties, having cultural affinities with the North-eastern India, Central India and Southern India respectively are memorable for their lofty achievements in the domain of art, architecture, religion and military glory. It is particularly noticeable that during the Bhauma Karas of the 8th and 9th centuries, some of the rulers of Kalinga were women. The Somavansis of the 10th and 11th centuries were great builders and the Ganga dynasty that succeeded them maintained the glorious tradition of bringing about the all-round development of the people. The names of the three Suryavansi Kings, the most renowned of the Orissan rulers who ruled after the Ganges-Kapilandra, Purushottam and Prataprudra- are even today the household names thoughout Orissa.

Several ruling dynasties of Orissa with their distinct and diverse cultural patterns manifested through social customs, afforded opportunities to the people of the land to be immensely benefitted by them in the evolution or in the making of what may be termed as Orissan Culture. Socially and economically viewed, Orissa was a land of plenty and prosperity until the 16th century when one-half of it passed into the hands of the Mughals and the other half came under the administrative control of the Bhamani Kingdom of the South. For several centuries past, it had maritime commerce with the East Indies and even today, there are remnants of the culture of Kalinga in the Java and Bali islands-a fact which testifies not only to the spirit of adventure of the people of Orissa, generally speaking, are hale and healthy and are simple in their dress and deportment. Their social structure is bejewelled with the brilliant gems of feasts and festivals, conducive not only to aesthetic enjoyment but also to the tightening of the social ties among individuals and institutions. The literary, artistic, sculptural and dramaturgical developments of ancient Orissa as preserved in the extant literary works and as reflected in the temple art and traditional dramatic styles reveal beyond doubt in their ultimate analysis that they were founded on the bed-rock of a very resourceful economic system of a prosperous country.

The Oriya language is spoken by over twenty million people, and has a script of its own. Odra-Vibhasha finds mention in the Natyasastra of Bharata and it is also maintained by some scholars that one of the 64 scripts learnt by Budhadeva at the initial stage of his education, was the Urdilipi or the script of the Odra people.

The people of Orissa deserve special recognition for their ancient literature. The Oriya Mahabharata, composed by the middle of the 15th century, the Oriya Ramayana and the Bhagvata written about half a century later are glorious achievements for the Oriya-speaking people. Some of the important Sanskrit purana were rendered into Oriya with additions or eliminations and they catered to the religious needs of the people. The 16th, 17th and 18th centuries in particular, witnessed the evolution of the embellished style in poetry. Scores of ornate Kavyas were written under the patronage of the runing princes all over the State and the poets of these Kavyas, boldly and successfully too, accepted the challange of the Sanskrit Pandits who were proud of their own scholarly attainment.

Modern Oriya literature is progressing along the lines of the other literatures of India from the middle of 19th century. Prose, poetry, drama, literary criticism, biographies, travelogue, juvenile literature etc. have developed remarkably under the influence of western education. From a desire for national amancipation in the 19th century, the general trend of Oriya literature is seen moving towards Humanism through a scientific and systematic process of social reformation and economic reconstruction, based on a sympathetic study of the common man with regard to his physical, mental, moral and material well-being.

One of the greatest expressions of Indian culture in Orissa is the Jagannatha Dharma or the Cult of Jagannath. Even in a multi-religious country like India torn as under sometimes with diverse castes, cults and creeds, Jagannathism positively decries un-touchability. While proclaiming the Oneness of God it does not forbid the worship of the numerous deities of the Indian pantheon in as much as all men and women are not of the same intellectual standards. People belonging to different religious cults such as Saivaism, Vaishnavism, Saktism etc. which are found at times to be diametrically opposite to one another have their spiritual confluence in Jagannathism.

Why is it so and how has it been possible to bring about such a synthesis of religions here? It is an admitted fact that originally Jagannathan was worshipped by the Savara belonging to an aboriginal tribe dwelling in Orissa in those days. Gradually, the deity drew the attention of the Aryan Princes and gained wide popularity as the supreme centre of worship in Orissa.

In course of centuries, Kings, devoted to the worship of Maheswara, Vishnu, Bhairava, Durga etc. sought spiritual refuge at the lotus feet of the deity and thus paved the way for the evolution of the celebrated Jagannath Dharma. Monarchs and religious preachers came and went, each trying to see and show that Jagannath was his "own". But, despite all their attempts, the deity carried the thumb impression of no particular cult or creed, no single path of worship or individual school of philosophy.

The temples of Orissa have gained worldwide popularity. For centuries past, they have withstood the ravages of time and the onslaughts of the inconoclastic hands of religious fanatics who made many attempts to demolish them totally. It would perhaps be no ordinary introduction for the Orissan temples to say that they themselves constitute one of the four schools of temple architecture, found in the whole of India known as the Kalinga School of Architecure. They have their own literature with regard to their structual peculiarities, external engravings, architectural designs and other technological specifications. Apart from the engineering skill displayed in the construction the dexterity of the sculptors in engraving images on the body of the temples also exhorts the most profound admiration of the spectators.

There is a consensus of opinion among historians with regard to the antiquity of Orissan Sculpture which (with its crude beginnings in the Pre-Asokan age) culminated in the construction of the Konarka temple in the 3rd century A.D. The earliest dated engravings go down to the 3rd century B.C. and form part of the monolith adorned with the historic edicts of Emperor Asoka on the Dhauli hill near Bhubaneswar. The elephant engraved on a boulder at the foot of the Dhauli found a fuller and more artistic expression in the Udagiri hill, famous for the Hati-Gumpha inscription of Kharavela of the second century B.C. It is surmised that one of the several engravings found in the

Queen's caves of Udayagiri is a scene from the story of Vasavadatta, animated with the expression of delicate, feelings of lovers. The magnificant carving on Udayagiri,- apart from their historical significances, constitute a must for every visitor to Orissa even after more than two thousand years of their first appearance.

The countless stone image of Buddhistic deities and Gurus recently unearthed from the site of the famous Pushpagiri Vihar in the district Cuttak bear the indelible stamp of wounderful mastery over · the plastic art Gradually, the skill of the sculptors found more concentrated expression in the temples that grew up under royal patronage during the next six centuries.

The Parasurameswar temple, the Mukteswar temple, the Rajarani temple, the Lingaraj temple, the Paravati temple, the Jagannath temple and the Konarka temple constructed between the 7th and the 13th centuries are the nummied specimens of Orissa's glorious àrt-culture. Even to this day the temples of Orissa capture the imagination of thousands of spectators from all quarters of the globe. The sublime superstructures of the temples, the fine decorations from the plinth to the zenith, the lively poses of beasts and human beings, the scenes of the various social ceremonies, the display of artistic engravings and architectural designs present a most charming picture to the visitor. The huge image of Lord Ganesh found on the body of the Lingaraj temple, the engravings of scenes from the. Ramayana and the Mahabharata found on the same temple at a height of about twenty feet and the caparitiobed horses of Konarka are objects of great artistic dexterity even for the most competent connoisseurs of art.

It may not be out of place to mention here that two images of Lord Vishnu in the pose of Ananta-Sayana (32 feet and 42 feet in length respectively) discovered some decades ago on the river-bed of Brahmani in the district of Dhenkanal, carved on stone, may, with the availability of communicational facilities, be the objects of additional attraction for visitors to Orissa.

In the field of dance, drama and music, Orissa holds out her own against the other States of India. The temple of Jagannath which attracts numerous ilgrims from all parts of the country afforded wide scope to the musicians and dancers of Orissa to study and accept the best of the systems of music and dance prevailing in the different parts of India. Recitation of the Geeta Govinda and presentation of the Devadasi dance in the dancing hall of the main temple daily by about midnight form part of the regular "Seva and Puja" of Lord Jagannath, Famous musicians who visit Puri during their Pilgrimage in Orissa consider it to be a great fortune to display their art within the inner compound of the temple as a mark of devotion to the lord of the Universe. This has been going on for several centuries.

Some works on music and dance written in Sanaskrit in the preceding centuries contain details of the special characteristics of Orissi music and Orissi dance. The Natya-manorama, the Abinayadarpana Prakasa, the Sangeeta-narayanam, the Geetaprakasa and some other works lend additional weight to the claims of classicality adduced by artists in the field.

Closely associated with the expression of Indian Culture in Orissa is the Orissi type of painting. The marvellous paintings found within the Jagannath temple, the Pata-painting of Puri, the palm-leaf paintings and the diverses type of paintings done proficiently by the women folk all over the State, fresco painting sitabinji, to mention only a few, furnish us with material for a proper assessment of the high standards of art culture in Orissa.

GOURI KUMAR BRAHMA

CULTURAL RELATIONS BETWEEN INDIA AND THE PHILIPPINES

The inhabitants of the Philippines first became aware of their early relationship with India back in 1887 when Dr. Trinidad Pardo de Tevera published in Paris a monograph entitled "E1 Sancrito En La Lengua Tagalog" Dr. Parado de Tavera, a creole who was considered as the foremost Filipino scholar of his time, listed some 300 words in Tagalog, the principal ethnic group in the Philippines, as having been derived from Sanaskrit.

For example, the Sanskrit word bandu or ally has become bantay in Tagalog, which means sentinel or guard. Wana is Sanskrit has become baha in Tagalog, and the meaning slightly changed from ride or water current to flood or a stream. Hantu or the dead in Sanskrit has become the popular word anito in Tagalog for images of the dead and idols. And so on.

Eight years earlier, in 1880, Prof. H.Kern of the University of Leider had printed a paper with a similar but smaller list. Both of these scholars deduced that sometime before the Spanish conquest of the Philippines in the 16th Century, the natives of the archipelago had contact with India. Just what these contacts were, they were not prepared to state, but hinted that the Hindu influence on the Filipino probably came indirectly through Malaya and Indonesia, rather than by direct contacts with the Islanders.

Then in the 1920's Philippine archeaoiogists led by Prof. H. Otley Beyer, discovered several artifacts in various islands which undoubtedly originated or ware influenced by Indian craftsman. These were : a golden image of Buddha in the province of Agusan, in northern Mindanao, the second largest island of the Philippines; a Buddhist Tara with Tantric connections; a clay medillion from Calatagan, Batangas in the south-western part of Luzon, the largest island in the archipelago; a Garuda pendant of gold from the island of Palawan, which faces the China, Sea; and a bronze statue of Lokesvara found in Mactan island in the Visayan central group, where Ferdinand Magellan met his death in 1521. These archaeological artifacts are dated, and scholars now believe that they reached the Philippines sometime between the 12th and 14th centuries, or from two to four hundred years before the arrival of the Spaniards in the archipel-ago.

Evidence of direct contact between India and the Philippines are not existent, or at least they cannot be found today in either the archives of India or the Philippines or in any of the historical account that we know of today. If there were such a records, it was destroyed during the first fifty years of the Spanish regime when overzealous Spanish friars burned native accounts and artifacts because they were inimical to the implantation of Christianity. Nevertheless, it is highly doubtful if direct relations ever existed between these two countries prior to the Spanish regime in the Philippines : whatever Hindu culture that influenced the Philippines was made indirectly, and these through the various Philippine languages, on literature and on religion.

In the last few years, a brilliant young Filipino scholar Dr. Juan R. Francisco who took his doctorate's degree at the University of Madras, had made a thorough study from available materials on the relations between Indian and the Philippines. A study of the relationship between Indian and the Philippines is comparatively new for scholars of both countries. Despite the fact that initial attention to our relation ship was started in the 1880's, not until the past few years have these contacts been clearly defined by Prof. Francisco. He believes, for example, that Hindu influence was felt directly in Malaya and Indonesia and that, in turn that residents of the two countries exerted their own influence on the Philippines as early as about a thousand years ago. Students who are well-versed on the impact of Hindu culture on Malaya and Indonesia will tell you that the coming of Islam checked or changed the form of the cultural waves emanating from the Indian continent. Never the less, the Hindu elements that reached the Philippines percolated into the islands for a period of roughly four hundred years at different stages of its history. These Indian influences may be seen today in the use by Filipions of words derived from Sanskrit and even some Dravidian or Tamil words which exist in a dozen Filipino languages today. I need not add that there are over a dozen different tongues spoken in as many as different regions in the Philippines today and one of our vexing problems is to have a common national language.

The other field where Hindu influence is felt the most is in our native literature. There is no material evidence today to show that Indian influence is present in the Philippines; by this I mean that there are no inscriptions, no architecture, etc., that can be found today or have been found in the past to show actual Indian influence on our literature; but in the development of folktale motifs in the popular and tribal stories throughout many parts of the Philippines, the similarity with that of India is well marked, and it might be said that some connections must have existed earlier. The absence of actual translations of Indian literature into the Philipinne languages may be due to the fact that these stories were carried to the Philippines by Islamized Malays or Javanese and that, therefore, changes in the varsions took place through the centuries, For example, the influence of Indian literature in Malaya, Java and Bali is obvious, for here literary themes and styles flourished; but by the time these cultural influences reached the Philippines via Malacca and Indonesia, only a paralielism of elements and incidents and in the motif indices remain. You will find indirect influences only in the folk literature of Philippines, for as I have stated before, written pre-hispanic record and artifacts were destroyed shortly after the arrival of the Spaniards.

To quote Prof. Francisco : "While no recensions or translations of Indian literature have been discovered in the Philippines, the use of folktale motifs in popular stories may be an evidence of Indian influence. The recurrence of motifs in Indian tales, and the migration of these to various localities show that the motigs of tales in the country may have had their origins in India".

As an example of the similarity in folktale motifs is the Indian story of Mayilira-vanankatai, Rama and Laksmana were captured by the ruler of the Netherworld named Mayiliravana. Hanuman comes to the rescue of the brothers and fights the demon, who is defeated many times but cannot be killed. Hanuman later finds out that demon's life is lodged in the bodies of five bees to be found in five different caves of the Netherworld. So he searches for the caves and kills the bees, and thus Mayiliravana dies. The similarity of motif is used in the Maranaw legend called Bidasari. It is the story of a second wife to a king who could not be killed by the jealous first wife because her soul resided not in her body but in a golden fish. There are many other tales throughout the Philippines where similarities with Indian motifs can be found, leading us to conclude that somewhere in the distant pass philippine tales were derived from India.

Prof. Francisco concludes that "the Hindu elements tended to blend with the native elements in the intervening regions (that is in Malaya and Indonesia) so in reahing the Philippines they were no longer in their pristine forms. Moreover, whatever percolated throughout the intervening regions were not carried by Indians themselves, but by Hinduized Malaysians". As a corolary to this, the rather sketchy evidence of these influences lead to the inference that the percolation of Indian culture into the Philippines have been sporadic and far between. If you will take a look at our archipelago in any map, divided as it is into nearly 8,000 islands, you realize the reason for the preceding statement. But we can safely conclude that the enrichment of Philippine culture in ancient times was due in part to the spirit of Indian culture that managed to reach the Philippine archipelago.

CARLOS QUIRINO

CULTURAL RELATIONS WITH SOUTH-EAST ASIA

The present geographical region of South-East Asia includes India, pakistan, Nepal, Ceylon, Burma, the peninsula of Indo-China (excluding Tonkin and North-Vietnam) and all the islands known as East Indies. Eastern Asia, with which this region had long cultural associations, comprises China, Tibet, Sinkiang, Mongolia, Korea, Japan, Tonkin and Not-Vietnam.

From the point of view of the cultural study, South-East Asia offers many common points. This is on account of the fact that the countries of South-East Asia, enumerated above, had long and abiding religious, social and commercial contacts among them. Notwithstanding their local natural traits, these regions in the past were bound together with a common cultural link. From about the beginning of the Christian era till the end of the early Medieval period this link remained quite strong. India, no doubt played a significant role in binding together the different regions. The good will and cooperation that could be sustained among these countries for such a long period was mainly due to sustained among these countries for such a long period was mainly due to the cultural relations, beased on the ideals of love and peace, rather on any political domination.

The studies in the past history of South-East Asia during the last one hundred years have been amply rewarding. Thanks to the endeavours of a host of scholars, much valuable light has been thrown on the political and cultural history of the region. The cultural and commercial relations of India with her neighbouring countries of the South-East for a period of more than a thousand years are clearly known now. The previous theory of ancient India's "splendid isolation" has been exploded.

The sources for the study of this extensive region are numerous indeed. Apart from the Indian, Chinese and native literary sources, the number of inscriptions, mostly written in Sanskrit, is pretty large, similarly the vast material in the form of ancient temples, stupas, monsteries and sculptures, discovered in various parts of the region, has been immensely helpful in this regard. Recent archaeological explorations an excavations conducted in various parts of Sri Lanka, Malaya, Indo-China and Indonesia have shed welcome light on South-East Asia's past.

Recent archaeological researches in Malaya, Indo-China and Indonesia have brought forth some evidence to indicate that before the Hindu advent in these lands, their original inhabitants had developed their primitive cultures. Besides hunting and fishing, they knew the cultivation of land and produced sugarcane, bananas and other fruits and probably rice also. Domestication of animals was also known to them. They were good navigators and prepared boats of various types, like the wooden houses which they built to live in. They knew the use of Iron and other metals. They had a social and political set-up with their chiefs to control and protect them.

It is to be conceded that the native of these regions learnt the advanced civilized life, as understood even in those days, after they came into contact with Indians. It is also noteworthy that beginning from the first century A.D. to the early Medieval times there were several waves of immigrants from India, who settled in the south-eastern foreign lands from time to time. The early settlers hailed from Bengal and kalinga and from the southern coastal regions. Afterwards, people from Gujarat and Saurastra also made their long voyages to the south-eastern lands. The controversy regarding the superiority or dominant role of one particular region of India over the other in regard to the colonization in South-East asia is to be given up in view of the fact that during the early centuries of the Christian era the entire country was culturally one integrated whole, with a composite culture prevading almost the entire Indian sub-continent.

Indian merchant class, no doubt, played the main role in the discovery and eventual colonization of several parts of South-East Asia. The traders were helped by the Ksatriya and the Brahmanas alike. The Ksatriyas, many of them disgruntled at home or too enterprising, must have been persuaded by the Vaisya traders to seek their fortunes in distant lands. The Sastropajivi Brahmanas did not lag behind their Sastropajivi brethren in this respect, like the Kastriyas, as section of the Brahmans might have found their homeland's atmosphere rather uncogenial to them. Some of them were perhaps finding it quite difficult to depend on the Sastras for their livelihood. They were probably led to believe that "hungry men cannot eat grammar, thirst cannot be quenched by the juice of poetry, by prosody nobody has been able to uplift his family. It is, therefore, good to concentrate on earning fold only, as all the qualities of a learned man are fruitless (without it). The craze for the yellow metal and the prospects of a superior position in the foreign land must have influenced a good number of Brahmanas who, for their sake, left their kith and kin. Their Siddhayatras were highly successful, because a large number of them settled themselves in the new colonized lands and did not think of coming back to their mother-land. They married the local girls and adopted themselves to the local circumstances. A contented household life, respect and dominating position in society and the gaysome religious celebrations of the new place were sufficient causes for this.

It must be admitted that the Brahmanas more than any other class of the Indian settlers, worked with a missionary zeal to propogate Sanskrit language and Indian culture among the South-East Asia people. The other sections had great faith and regard for the learning and generosity of the Brahmanas and gave them all necessary help to propagate Indian culture. In the task of cultural propagation the broad Hindu outlook of Vasuddaiva Kutumbakam ('the entire world is a family') (was followed.)

The respect for Sanskrit became so great in Malay early in the 6th century A.D. that Malayan prince, called Bhagadatta, in 515 A.D. wrote to his contemporary Chinese ruler that "the precious Sanskrit is generally well-known in his land. The walls and places of his imposing cities are high and lofty as the mountain Gandhamadana".

As regards the nature of Indian religion propounded in the South-East Asian countries, a controversy has been raised by some scholars. It has been resumed by one section that Budhism had the upper hand in this region and that 'the aristocratic Brahmanism' failed to carry conviction among the masses. This view does not seem to command itself. It may be remembered that during the Sunga-Satavahana rule it was the Vedic religion, in the form of several developed cults, which was popular in the north and south India. This fact is borne our by the contemporary literary and epigraphic sources. It is corroborated by a large number of monumental remains. Relics of the plastic art, coins, seals and sealings on which the Vedic symbology, in its varied form, is noticeable. Side by side the vedic cults were developing the Jaina and Buddhist pantheons in an atmosphere of good will and toleration.

The early relics so far discovered in "various parts of Burma, Malaya, Indo-china and Indonesia leave doubt in an objective mind that it was Veica religions, in the form of developed cults of Saivism, Vaisnavism and other Puranic sects, which was predoment right from the beginning of the colonization of these regioins. Numerous temples and statues of Vedic and Purnaic deities found in almost all the parts of South-East Asia, depictional or scenes from the Indian epics, inscriptional and literary evidences and the Vedic sacrifical posts (Yupas), discovered in Borneo and other islands, constitute an eloquent testimony to prove this. Kalidasa, the great Indian poet, alludes to the installation of Vedic Yupas in the eighteen island of the region". Kings of Kambuja (Ancient Cambodia), Funan, Champa, Borneo and other kingdoms seem to have vied with each other in performing Vedic Yajnas. As in India so also in the South-East Asia Siva-worship was quite popular. Temples of Siva with various local names, such as Bhadnesvara Swami, Chandesvara, Randaparvatesvara, were constructed. Fetivals, with great pomp and show, were held in these temples which were attended not only by the local people but also by a large number of persons coming from far off places. Some of the new towns founded in Kambuja, named Bhavapura, Isanapura, Ugrapura, etc., are significant in this connection. Worship of Vishnu, Surya, Ganesa and Devi was also quite popular, looking to all this an bearing in mind the fact that the Vedic-Puranic religion had a great appeal among the masses and was adopted by them in their popular beliefs and rituals for centuries together, the theory of the limited effect of the so-called arstocratic Brahmaism on the masses had to be rejected.

Buddhism did play its significant role. The literary and archaeological evidence at our disposal is a proof positive to indicate the popularity of Buddhism not only in Ceylon, Burma and Malaya but also in Indo-china and Indonesia. The rulers of Tamradvipa (Ceylon), Burma and Srivijaya made great efforts to popularise Buddhism.

It may be stated here that there was a continuous spirit of amity and toleration among the followers of the Vedic-Puranic faith and the Buddhists. This was resposible for the development of their different sects smoothly side by side in tis region till the Indian culture was eclipsed by the Muslim domination.

No plausible evidence has, however, been obtained to indicate that Buddhism has an upper hand over the Vedic religion.

A critical and comparative study of the rich Sanskrit literature obtained in a variety of records all over the region is still a desideratum. Similarly the Monkhmer and Cam groups of languages require a thorough study. The valuable work so far done by the Dutch, French and Indian scholars in this connection has been very fruitful. The Academy of Indian culture at New Delhi, which has already done commendable work in this field, deserves all encouragement.

The study of the historical geography of the region is equally important. In our ancient literature references to the oceangirdled South-East Asian countris are found in the terms like dvipantara, Sagarantaradvipa, Ashtadasadvipa, etc. With the Hindu colonization of the region, several big and small kingdoms, bearing Indian names, were established. Their names were Kambuja, Gandhara, Malaya, Dasarna, Srikshetra, Kalinga, Utkala, Vanga, etc. The names of some of the twons in this area were Ayodhya, Mathura, Vaisali, Taksasila, Kausambi, Kusumanagara, Dwaravati, Vikramapura, Amaravati, etc. Some of the rivers of this region bore the names of Gamati, Sarasvati, Iravati, Chandraghaga, etc.

Indian river-names were also adopted for several of the rivers in the region. Some of the rulers here founded new towns either after the names of the Vedic-Puranic gods or after their own Indian names.

The names of Raktamrittika occuring in the well-known Brahmi inscription of the great navigator Buddhagupta, discovered in the Northern district of Malaya, baffled the correct identification the past. The recent excavations by the University of Calcutta at village Rajbadidanga, Dist.

Murshidabad, have yielded a large number of inscribed clay seals and sealings. Several of the sealings bear the Buddhist Dharmachakra symbol of Jetvana and the Brahmi inscription 'Sri Raktamrittika-mahavai-harikary abhikshu-sanghsya (i.e. seals of the celebrated Bhikshusangha of the great monstry of Raktamrittika'). The Brahmi script of these sealings is of about 400 A.D. and tallies well with the inscription of Buddhagupta in point of time. There is no doubt now to locate Raktamrittika of the Malaya inscription at Rajbadidanga, where the old town and great vihara of Raktamrittika (now called Rangamati), was situated. Buddhagupta, a resident of this palce in Bengal and gone to Malaya, where, after the completion of his Siddhayatra, he dedicated a stone tablet, bearing the symbol of a Buddhist stupa and the text of a Buddhist Sutra.

Like the literary evidence, the architectural and sculptural material in South-East Asia is amply rich. A good deal of work has already been done in this field, but much still remains to be accomplished. The archeological explorations and excavations in several parts of this vast region have brought forth new material and, alongwith it, some new problems. A comparative and detailed study of south-East Asian art particularly with reference to iconography, is badly needed. The study of ancient architecture of this region, on the basis of the Silpa-texts, and its comparison with the extant Indian monuments is indeed a great necessity.
(Condensed)

K. D. BAJPAI

"D"

D. K. PATTAMMAL

D. K. Pattammal has carved in niche for herself in music due to her incredible singing, her melodious voice and her mastery over the technical aspect of classical music.

When D.K. Pattammal was placed at the feet of Ramana Maharishi at the age of three months, he put a few drops of honey into her mouth. She firmly believes her immense talent is indeed a result of many prayers and blessings - a gift from the gods.

She was born in Kancheepuram in a religious arthodox family, from the age of seven onwards she was often taken to the temple where she sang many 'solkas' in the esteemed presence of the Sankaracharya of Kancheepuram. Her father D.Krishnaswamy Dikshitar, a Sanskrit scholar, had a great influence on her - and so education became a priority. She passed the government technical examination in music which was a rarity amongst women those days.

Later she blossomed under the futelage of Sri Ambi Dikshitar, grandson of Sri Muthuswamy Dikshitar of the Musical Trinity of the South. The learning process continued with one of his disciples. T.L. Venkatraman Iyer. Over the years she learnt many songs from the disciples of great 'vidwans' like Naine Pillai of Kancheepuram, Ariyakudi Ramanujam Iyengar, etc. She has had the rare privilege of learning directly from great composere like Papanasam Sivam and Kotiswara Iyer.

Today she regrets not having learnt Sanskrit from her father. Though primarily a Carnatic music exponent, she sings in other languages too. She says, "I consult pundits of various languages before I sing, so as to give a perfect rendering of the 'solkas'. "Pattammal reminisces on those bygone days when dedication was complete - it was "Sadhna", a devotion. She says, "Recitals today last for one and a half hours with an interval in-between. Those days there were no intervals and recitals sometimes went on for six hours continuously. I remember singing for hours at a stretch without a break in Vishakhapatnam, Delhi and a small town in Tirunelveli".

She married R. Iswaran in 1940 and later had two sons. Her husband, an electronic engineer, gave up his job and career in 1942 and devoted himself to managing her career which according to him, was a full time job. The title of "Gyana Saraswati" was conferred on her soon after in 1943. This was followed by several awards including the Sangeet Natak Academy Award in 1962, the Sangeet Kalanidhi Award, the padma Bhushan, the 'Isai Peraringnar' by Tamil Isai Sangam, Madras and the Fellowship of the Sangeet Natak Academy.

Pattammal is a remarkable woman. Apart from her incredible singing, her sweet melodious voice and her superb mastery over the technical aspect of classical music, she is a woman of many 'firsts' She was the first housewife to sing in public - in thos days it must not have been easy breaking an age old male - dominated tradition. But Pattammal apparently faced no discrimination problems of any kind either. "I was treated with respect and reverence," she says. She was also the first woman to give a public performance of the difficult "Ragam Thanam Pallavi"

In addition to that, she was the first woman playback singer who lent her voice way back in 1938 in a film "Tyaga Bhumi". But she had her reservations on this, due to which she ultimately stopped singing film songs. Her husband Iswaran says, "it was fine singing for abstract or patriotic songs, but she drew a line to lending her voice for romantic songs or for dances".

Pattammal has been singing for 58 years without a break. She was honoured by the Music Academy, Madras, recently for having given 58 recitals, one each year in every music festival creating a world record.

N.C.

DAGAR, NASIR AMINUDDIN

(b. 1924) - Vocalist : Hindustan, dhrupad; flute; studied with Nasiruddin Khan Dagar, Riyazuddin Khan Dagar, Ziauddin Khan Dagar; concert tours, Nepal (1960), Europe (1961 and 1964) ; disc recordings.

Reference

Sangeet Natak Akademy, Who's Who of Indian Musicians.

DAGAR, RAHIM FAHIMUDDIN KHAN

(b. 1927) - Vocalist : Hindustan, dhruped of 'Dagar bani'; studied with Rahimuddin Khan Dagar, Ziauddin Khan, Immamuddin Khan, Hasinudding Dagar; Lecturer, Rabindra Bharati University, Calcutta.

Reference

Sangeet Natak Akademy, Who's Who of Indian Musicians.

DAGAR, RAHIMUDDIN KHAN

(b. 1901) - Vocalist : Hindustani, dhrupad of 'Dagar bani'; studied with Alla Bande Khan (Father), Zakiruddin Khan, Ziauddin Khan and Nasiruddin Khan; received Sangeet Natak Akademi award for Hindustani vocal music (1964).

Reference

Sangeet Natak Akademy, Who's Who of Indian Musicians.

DANCE - DRAMAS OF RAJASTHAN

Rajasthan has developed several varieties of dance-dramas known as khyals. These dramas have been helpful to the historians in recording the history of the state and they have maintained cultural and social traditions for more than 400 years. More than 200 khyals have come to the notice of Bhartiya Lok Kala Mandala and it is in possession of quite a number of them. The first Khyal was written and played 400 years back. These khyals have been a powerful medium of free entertainment to thousands of our people. In remotest parts of Rajasthan where no medium of modern entertainment has reached, this popular style has been a great source of cultural and social education till today.

The following styles of khyals are existing in Rajasthan today: 1. The khyals of Kuchaman Marwar, 2. The khyals of Shekavati, 3. The Tutu Kalgi of Chittor, 4. The Rasdharies of Mewar and 5. The Bhawai dances of Rajasthan and Madhya Bharat.

THE KUCHAMANI KHYALS

Lachiram the originator of this style and a great exponent of khyals evolved his own style in collboration with the existing ones. The common features of khyal styles are (i) drama in the form of dances, (ii) Predominance of singing, (iii) difficult technique of instrumental music, (iv) playing and dancing on a big platform known as manch. The characteristic features of Lachiram's style are (i) simplicity of language used in songs, (ii) use of new and refreshing tunes, (iii) intricate facial expressions while acting and (iv) the use of new themes for drama.

Lachiram himself was a good dancer and a writer of repute. He has composed nearly ten khyals, prominent among them being "Chand Milagari" "Ridmal" and "Meera Mangal". He had his own team of dancers, which he used for professional performances. The performance starts from evening till morning and hundreds of people assemble from distant villages to witness this great open air show. Though Lachiram died 25 years ago, his khyals are still played all over Rajasthan. The female roles were invariably played by the males. The musical accompaniment is given by drummers, shahnaiwala and the dholak and sarangiwala. The songs are usually very shrill and are also sung by the dancers themselves. The musicians in the background give support to the dancers in singing the rest of the lines for them.

The manch (platform) is elaborately decorated and the cost of the construction is borne by the hosts themselves. These Kuchamani dancers used to visit almost all parts of Rajasthan. But now the people are not very enthusiastic about their shows because of their length and monotonous themes.

THE KHYALS OF SHEKHAVATI

Nanu ram, the greatest exponent of this style, died a few decade back leaving behind a legacy of a few popular khyals of great beauty. Some of the important ones are (i) Heer Ranjhah, (ii) Harichand, (iii) Bharathari, (iv) Jaydev Kankali, (v) Dhola Maru, (vi) Ahaldeo.

He belonged to Chidawa and was a Muslim by caste. He was loved by all and even now he is remembered by people with respect and love. His greatest desciple these days is Dulia. The main characteristic of his plays are as follows : 1. Intricate foot work. 2. Difficult style of singing. Elaborate orchestral music consisting of harmonium. Sarangi, Shahnai, flute, nakkara and dholak. 4. Low height of the stage and absence of elaborate decoration.

Dulia had his own party of performers and played for almost eight moths in the year. He was nearly 70 years old in 1964 but played the role of a female very effectively. He was also the author of many khyals and took great pride in staging them. Dulia's khyals are very popular in the whole of Shekavati and the play-songs have great literary value. Hundreds of people witness his shows almost free of charge. The main host who invites Dulia's mandli bears all the cost of his show and remunerates the artists. The participants of these khyals are generally from Mirasi, Dholi and Sargara communities. but there is no restriction for others who wish to make khyal dancing as their profession.

Nanu's and Dulia's khyals are also played by other non-professional groups who undertake such plays only for self expression and fun.

THE TURA KALGI OF CHITTOR

Shah Ali and Tukun Giri were two great saints, 400 years back, who gave birth to this cult of Tura Kalgi. Tura was considered to be the symbol of Shiva and Kalgi that of his Shakti (Parvati). Tukun Giri belonged to Tura sect and Shah Ali to Kalgi. Both these cults propagated the philosophy of Shiva and Shakti respectively in their own way. The chief medium of their propagation was poetic composition popularly known as Dangal, where the followers would solve intricate philosophical problems through the medium of poetry. These dangals have produced the best poetry of the time.

The Tura Kalgi sect became very popular at that time and spread all over the border of Rajasthan and Madhya Pradesh.

The centuries old dangals of Tura Kalgi gradually turned into stage shows first in Ghosunda nearly 70 years back. Inspired by the khyals of Shekavati and Rasdhari the Tura Kalgi Dangals composed and produced some dance drama on the style of the popular khyals. The first composer of this style belonged to Ghosunda in Mewar. These dance-dramas had nothing to do with Tura Kalgi and Dangals and were written on altogether different subjects already prevalent that time. The style of singing the poetry was of course taken from Tura Kalgi.

The rest of the charactristic of Tura and Kalgi being the same as those of other khyals, the following are some of its main features : 1. Its non-professional nature, 2. Elaborate stage decorations, 3. Simplicity of foot steps, 4. Predominance of poetic singing, 5. Quality of community entertainment.

The chief centres of activities of Tura Kalgi are ghosunda, Chittor, Nimbhahera, and Neemach. These places have given birth to some of the best Tura Kalgi composers like Chain Ram, Mamid Beg of Ghosunda, Jaydayal Tara Chand and Thakur Onkar Singh. Among these, the most out-standing one is Soni Jay Dayal. He was really a saint. His khyals are most popular even now. After his death people remember his works with great esteem.

THE BHAVAI DANCES OF RAJASTHAN

Nagaji, a Jat, had great interest in dancing and singing. He acquired proficiency in this art, which unfortunately the jat community, as a whole, did not encourage and approve. They turned him out of their community after giving him the privilege of forming his own group of dancers for entertaining them every year. This group was known as Bhavai and many other Jats interested in dancing also joined him. This creation of a separate community of dancers among Jats had very bad influence on other communities, with the result that every community superior or inferior exterminated all those interested in the art of dancing and induced them to form their separate community for entertaining them on special occasions. Gradually all these Bhavai groups from different communities formed into one seperate community irrespective of any caste or creed.

Bhavais of the following communities exist in Rajasthan these days : Jat, Dhakad, Bola, Bhil, Dangi, Mina, Kumhar, Nayak, Teli, Chamar, Balai, Gujar, Malis and Lodha. Their headquarters are at Chittor, Nimbhahera, Ghosunda, Jhintia and other neighboring villages on the border of Madhya Pradesh and Rajasthan.

The chief characteristics of their dances are : Fast speed of their dances and extraordinary movements of the body. They practice dancing from their very childhood and ecquire great proficiency in their art. Bhavai is a folk technique but it has all the qualities of classical dancing. The dances are presented in the form of dance-dramas and are devoid of any religious sentiment. The themes are based on the daily life of a village community. They are very humorous though sometimes obscure. Women are not allowed to take part in the dances. The female roles are played by men. The Main themes which the Bhavai dances centre round are as follows :

1. Bora and Bori- depicting a humorous caricature of a village Baniya and his misery of life.
2. Surdas- depicting the life of a blind Sadhu with a romantic temperament.
3. Lodi Vadi- depicting the life of a man possessing two wives.
4. Dokri- depicting the ill fate of an old woman.
5. Shankaria- The caricature of a village youth making love with a young lady. 6. Bikaji- depicting the life of Bikaji the founder of the state of Bikaner. 7. Dhola Maru- depicting the eternal love story of Dhola and Maru.

Immediately after the rainy season, the Bhavai dancers move out of their villages for earning the livelihood. They move in the form of a caravan of camels gorgeously decorated.

The Bhavai dance is a professional folk dance and many technical qualities. The Bhavais visit their patrons (Yajmans), every year and are received by them cordially. The influence of modern life has not spared his style also. The Bhavai, due to their contact of the city have taken to cinema tunes and cheap themes.

THE RASDHARIS OF RAJASTHAN

The Rasdhari originally dealt with Lord Krishna and depicted the different phases of his life. But, later on it included other themes also. The first Rashdhari drama was written by one Motilal Jat of Mewar nearly 40 years ago.

The style is altogether different from the other khyals prevalent then. This particular technique is prevalent in Udaipur and its neighbourhood, and has spread in Marwar alsi. Some of the Rasdharies in Marwari were composed by Marwari composers.

The Rashdhari differs from other are vairagi sadhus but there is no restriction on others joining it. Rasdhari originally was a community folk-dance-drama in which all used to take part for joy and mirth, but later on it became the monopoly of a selected few, who took it up as a means of livelihood and formed their own group for professional earning.

The Rasdhari differs from other styles in many ways. One main difference is that no stage is required for the display of this dance-drama. Most of the themes like Ramlila, Harishchandra, Nagji and Mordhwaj are religious ones. The technique adopted for the depiction of the themes is mostly through singing and dancing. The dancing is technically superior to that of the khyals prevalent in Rajasthan.

The lyrics generally sung with this drama are all unpublished and have been handed down to us from mouth to mouth. Hundreds of village folk gather round the village choraha to witness this fascinating dance-drama almost free of any charge. The village community has to contribute at least Rs. 20 for these artists and arrange free meals by inviting them individually.

THE DANCES OF THE GANDHARAVAS

The Gandharvas are vaishyas by caste and enjoy all the privileges of that community. They originally blongged to Marwar and move out for nearly eight months for the performance of their dance-drama "Ajana Sundari" and "Mena Sundari". These are well known Jain themes and almost all the Jain followers witness these dramas with great interest.

This particular style has not much dancing in it but is prominently a musical drama. It is also an open air drama, but it is a bit modernized in the sense that painted curtains are used for their display.

The Gandharavas have become very rare these days and it seems the advent of the modern entertainment has had an adverse influence over their traditional occupation.

The Gandharavas play their drama form monetary gains but they have religious motives also. The artists are generally cultured and educated and do this work as a mission of their life.

D. L. SAMAR

DANCE : THREE EVENTUAL DECADES

"There are no schools of dancing in India and it is an art which nobody is interested", lamented Victor Dandre in 1922, when he and his wife, the great Russian ballerina Anna Pavlova visited India and failed to find any trace of the art of dance of this land of which they had heard so much. And not long ago when I asked Ted Shawn. "Father of American Dance", as to what he and his equally celebrated wife, Ruth St Denis, had encountered by way of dance when they visited India in 1925-26, he wrote: "As you know, under British rule dancing was frowned upon and there was very little to be seen. Entertained by highly society and officialdom, whenever they asked what they could do for us, they were begged to show us dancing of India; by they were all embarrassed, and many said they had never seen any dancing in their lives, and this included Hindu and Mohammedan people, as well as American and English:"

THE FOUR CLASSICAL FORMS

Such, then, was the state of the dance in India in the first quarter of this century. Then in the thirties came the revival, the immediate outcome of which was that four major forms of traditional dance, suppressed for a while by the vagaries of history, were resurrected and prombly accorded their rightful place in the scheme of Indian art and life. So rapid was the rehabilitation of these dances and so firmly did they establish themselves that for a long time people continued to maintain that these - Bharata Natyam, Kathakali, Kathak and Manipuri - were the only forms of classical dance in the Indian tradition. For years practically all writing on Indian dance referred, pointedly, to "the four classical forms", and it is only now, during the last ten years or so, that it is coming to be increasingly realised that India is the home not only of these but also of at least a dozen other equally rooted modes of dance, each of which has its own distinct tradition, its own manner, it own following.

REVIVAL OF OTHER FORMS

The Orissi dance, for instance, is today much in prominence; yet hardly six years ago, few outside Orissa were aware even of the name of this art. Then forms like the Bhagavata Mela Nataka of Tanjore and the Krishnattam of Kerala, which for centuries were performed only in temples, have for the first time been brought to the professional state. In the case of Bhagavata Mela Nataka the achievement has been of even greater significance, for this dance has for the first time been presented by performers who are not within the exclusive hereditary fold with which the art is associated. Certain other classical dances, such as the Satriya of Assam, the ottan Thullal and Koodiyattam of Kerala, the chhau of Mayurbhanj and purulia and the Mysore school of Bharata Natyam, have for the first time in their history been seen in regions other than the onces to which they belong. And then there are traditional dance forms like the Kuchipudi and Mohini Attam which are now much more commonly and much more extensively performed than even before.

TECHNIQUE

The technique of some of the classical dances has suffered, and this has largly been done by unscrupulous teachers and performers to make their work easier. For example, some items in the traditional repertoire of Bharata Natyam, such as the Kavitam and Virutam, are rarely, if ever, performed today, and others like the Varnam have been much abbreviated endeavouring, presumably, to be original, a number of dancers have borrowed poses for temple carvings and indiscriminately incorporated these in their work. In Kathakali, attempts have been made to present new themes, such as David and Goliah, Salome and Tagore's chitrangada and the result has not always been flattering. Some dancers have done away with the conventional and highly stylised Kathakali make-up and also simplified the cumbersome Kathakali costume, but in doing so they have also relieved the art of its quaint and other-wordly character. In Kathak unlike other, when it was incumbent on a dancer to be an accomplished musician as well, the present it is quite common to see a dancer rendering expression to words sung by another.

FOLK AND TRIBAL DANCES

Folk and tribal dances have gained an added importance. Since 1954, year after year, the Folk Dance Festivals held in the capital at the time of annual Republic Day celebrations have presented a variety of dances drawn from the different parts of the country. Even if the renderings have not always been rigidly authentic, the Festivals have helped to bring into focus the immense wealth of dance that is our. The Festivals have also prompted visiting teams to bring them which are purposely made stage-worthy. For instance, the Dummy Horse and Kummi folk dances of Tamil Nadu have been presented with Bharata Natyam steps and movements and strictly sacrosanct ritual dances such as the Karamgam, Kavadi, and Therayattam have appeared as stage pieces.

BALLET

The art of ballet in India, a produce of the revival of Indian dance, which was ushered in some forty years ago, has made considerable headway. Time was when only mythological themes were considered proper in Indian dance, but we now have ballets and dance-dramas on topical and sociological subjects. Again, while the early ballets in India were mostly creative in the sense that they did not depend upon any recognised technique of Indian dance, ballets and dance-dramas have in recent years been composed using any one or more of the different classical modes of dance.

In the cinema, the dance has come to be recognised as one of the most handy ingredient to ensure success at the box-office. In the early days of the film in India dancing was occasionally included to provide diversion and the technique used was a version of the decadent Nautch, but in recently years classical dance forms like Bharata Natyam and Kathak have been freely used in Indian films. On the whole, however, it can be said that it is rare that one see good and chaste dance in an Indian film, for what is generally presented is an adulteration of hybridisation of various Indian dance techniques, and more recently. There has also been a tendency to incorporate and ape dances and rhythms of the West in Indian films.

STATE ENCOURAGEMENT

The State has also contributed its share of enhance the prestige and popularity of the art. It has recognised meritorious work in the field through honours betwowed at the time of Republic Day each year. Cultural scholarships are awarded to deserving talent to receive advanced training with gurus or institutions of rnown. Cultural delegations, including dancers, regularly go from India to countries with which India has a cultural agreement and similar delegations from those countries are received in India, leading to healthy exchange of thoughts and ideas. The films Division has prepared and extensively exhibited documentaries, in colour, on some of the classical dances and also on Indian folk dance. The Sangeet Natak Academy of Music, Dance and Drama in India, has substantially aided the development and promotion of the art through grants to institutions and organisation all over the country. It has also built up sizeable archives of documentary material on Indian dance in the form of photographs, films and tape-recording.

All in all, the last three decades or so have been very eventful in the history of Indian dance. And, though there has been to some extent a lowering of standards brought about mainly by charlatans and dabblers in the art, one is at the same time happy to find the art of dance gain a new and more honoured place in popular esteem and also the emergence of Indian dance as an art with an international status.

MOHAN KHOKAR

DANCE AND THE BODY LANGUAGE

India is preoccupied with time, the West, with space. Music and dance are time arts to India. They are space arts to the West, with space. Music and dance are time arts to India.

To India, dance is sublime. At its highest form, it is said to be attuned to the cosmic rhythm. The artist enjoys bliss. The great Sufi mystic poet Rumi says dancing is the "nearest way to God".

Shiva is the patron of both music and dance. He taught music to Narada, the celestial messenger, and dance to Bharata, the author of Natyashastra, a treatise on drama.

The ancient Greeks, like the Indians, had a composite form of drama with music and dance. While they used the chorus to tell the tale, India has its songs. The Vidushaka (compare for want of a better expression) explained the nuances.

Dance is a coordinated movement of the whole body and mind. Abhinaya Darpana explains that a dancer must sustain the song in the throat, depict meaning by hands, the mood (bhava) through eyes and keep time with feet. Again, "where the hands go, there the eyes must follow; where the eyes go, there the mind; where the mind goes, there the feelings; where the feelings go, there the mood". Gesture is said to be the soul of Indian dance.

Drama (natya) was created by Brahma (one of the Indian Trinity) for the education and entertainment of all people. It was a "mimicry of the ways of the World". The four elements of Natya-II recitation, singing, acting and rasa - were taken from the four Vedas. Hence it is called Natyaveda. The Rig Veda provided the recitation, sama the method of singing, Yajur gave abhinaya (acting including gestures) and Atharva gave rasa (aesthetics).

Gestures are among the oldest forms of communication. There is a powerful instinct in man to imitate. And the first imitate (in drama) were the fights between demons and gods. And many of these sign languages are common to mankind - for example, signs for come, go, eat, sleep, why, what, etc. But dance gestures can mean many things. This is why the song became important. The Vachika (spoken) abhinaya supplements the angika abhinaya (body language). And, let us not forget, gestures add grace and beauty to the dance.

How do words find their equivalent mudras (postures)? It is said that words and here in the limbs. This expresses the principle underlying the language based on natural and expressive movements, says Ananda Coomaraswami, the great authority on Indian art.

To give a few of such "natural" expressions; eyeball going round expresses wrath; lingering glance expresses love; raising eyebrow doubt; widening of nostrils expresses anger, drooping cheek, sadness; drooping lip, envy, and so on. The body can express itself in so many ways.

The dancer tries to achieve the perfect pose and convey a sense of the timeless. The dance technique is, therefore, integrated with sculpture. Beryl De Zoete, a European student of Indian dance, says about European dance compared to the expressive culture of the body" of Indian elementary" of Indian dance.

There are three forms of dances: Tandava (male, vigorous), Lasya (feminine, gentle), and Pindibandha (a combination of both) Tandava (the cosmic dance) came from Shiva and Lasya from his consort Pravati. Dance was added to Natya by Shiva to give it "splendour and beauty", dear to the people. So there is pure dance without abhinaya, as also dance with acting.

Pure dance has evolved out of an alphabet of 108 perfect postures, upon which are based the techniques of movements known as Karanas. Each Karana consists of the movement of several limbs - in other words of much of the body. Similiarly, a comprehensive system of language signs (hand gestures) has evolved out of an alphabet of basic hand poses (bastas) in the same manner as the spoken and written language has been established. Hands became the chief vehicle of expression. They translate words into signs. Adjectives, nouns, verbs, proper nouns, adverbs, conjunctions, prepositions, abstract nouns - all these are expressed though gestures and facial expressions. Each school of dance (and there are six major schools - Bharatnatyam, Kathakali, Manipuri, Kuchipudi, Oddissi and Kathak) has used the basic getures. And each gesture can mean many things - as many as 85 in the case of the Pathaka (flag) gesture. Hence, the need for the explanatory song.

A great deal of the details is left to the imagination of the audience because the Indian stage is not naturalistic. The atmosphere is described through gestures. For example, picking flowers suggests a garden.

In Western ballet reliance is on broad gestures and minimum expressions on the face. In fact, the face of a ballet dancer carries little expression. The Indian dancer, on the contrary, expresses a thousand fleeting emotions through his face. He is expected to rouse the emotions of the audience so that they can become one with spirit of the drama or dance. No such task is placed on the ballet dancer. Ballet is a mere "spectacle" no doubt an attractive one. Aristotle says of drama that its Dance in India evolved out of Vedic ritual dances. The ritual also contained the seeds of drama.

No other dance from has given so much thought to the body language as the Indian dance. Every gesture is thought out in great detail. From very early times the Language of the hand" (akhara-musbtika) became an important study. And some of the gestures became universal, for example, the gesture for "Protection" (abhaya mudra). Similarly the folded hands (anjali) with which every Indian greets another Indian reminds them of the divinity of man. By the way, you raise your folded hands above head to greet gods, hold them before your face to greet your guru (teacher) and against the chest to great a brahmin or a respected person.

With that I say "pranam" - almost a universal gesture.

M. S. N. MENON

DANCE FESTIVAL (KONARK)

The festive season in Orissa begins soon after the monsoon clouds have vanished from the sky. The days are warm and the nights are cold. The people of the state are in a gay mood, be ready to celebrate and enjoy, exchange and share.

The floodlit Konark Temple provides an ideal backdrop to the festival reviving a scenario of regal splendour and flourishing art forms. This festival has assumed a kind of distinctive significance and importance for the timely endeavours it has made towards the revival, preservation and continuation of hte unique temple dance tradition of Orissa. The typical Odissi style of dance and music worship offered to God by the dancer through a medium no other than the speed or movements of music. This form of dance and music, in course of time, gained popularity and approval. Different aspects and nuances of the Odissi dance form were studied in greator details by the celebrated performer-dancers and teacher-gurus. It was then that the figures on the walls of the dance temple at Konark served as items of reference. It appeared as if the dance temple itself was conceived as a systematic documentary on stone of various poses and gestures of this dance form.

This winter Festival has already become a meeting ground of various classical dance forms of India for several days and nights. The audience, comprising both domestic and foreign visitors, is offered a package that is a lavish feast for the eyes and ears. The physical atmosphere of Konark dazzles with bright lights, costumes and ornaments; reverberates with a variety of musical notes and vocal renderings. When a series of distinctive dance forms is presented in quick succession, comparison becomes all the more convenient and appreciation instant.

This Festival provides not only a platform to the performing dancers and musicians but also an occasion for mutual interaction resulting in better understanding and wider exposure.

Various dance forms, such as Bharatnatyam, Kathak, Kathakali, Kuchipudi, Mohiniattam and Odissi are in vogue in India. These dance forms, when presented by consummate artists, acquire a kind of grace and cadence that is just poetry in motion. Adherence to the rigid mould of the great sage Bharata's exquisite technique does not allow new-fangled innovations or gimmicks. The forms, styles and gestures demonstrated by the sculptors in the flowing lines of temple sculptures come alive in the flowing lines of temple sculptures come alive in the movements of dancers to establish the fact that great traditions do not wither away.

Classical dance forms of India require long periods of disciplines practice bordering on a kind of surrender of the self. The vocabulary and grammer of these forms can only be retained through uncorrupted presentations on occasions such as the Konark Festival, of which the dancers' nights are the most glaring points of attraction. These nights serve the essential purpose of highlighting an important facet of our composite culture.

SHUBHA

DANCE INSTITUTES OF CALCUTTA : EVOLVING NEW IDIOM

Calcutta is the most happening place culturally and dance occupies an eminent position in its culture. In the present scenario, the variety of dance institutes in Calcutta and the dancers who are running them offer an insight into their contribution to the new realm of fusion-dance. Some changes just crept into the classical dance forms and some have been introduced to woo the youngsters.

But this has not been an easy task. The connoisseurs have been both innovative and compromising and have worked very hard to achieve a kind of appeal and popularity amongst all age groups. Some of the major institutes involved in this exercise are as follows:

PADATIK DANCE CENTRE

Chetna Jalan of the padatik Dance centre fit into dance. Which she feels is inspirational for the present day youth. She says, "Today's generation is like a ranging storm. Modern choreographi creations can be a powerful vehicle of coordination, interaction, teamwork, concentration and imagination with rhythm". The toddlers exercise for fitness and flexibility. Awareness about music is created by fun and games supported by music finely choreographed to "Macarena" and "Going to Ibitza".

Here, teenagers are given lessons in exercises for body conditioning and body movement with music. They are taught jazz and ballet postures and formations as well as coordination with their beats.

Some of the padatik creations widely appreciated have been "Ardha Shatabdi" and Shravan Sandhya". The former is a fusion of three definite streams- Kathak- ballet and theatre. The latter is an innovative Kathak composition set to Rabindra Sangeet.

TANUSHREE SHANKAR AND HER NEW AGE DANCE

A dancer of international repute and the late Ananda Shankar's wife, Tanushree shankar is the choreographer of this troupe now. She trained for seven years under Ananda's mother Amala Shankar. Her compositions are based on the creative style started by Ananda's father, the late Uday Shankar, a pioneer in popularizing Indian dance and music all over the world. Tanushree's choreography is an outstanding as its is creative and contemporary and is known as the "New Age Dance".

It was Ananda, who, as early as the early 1970s, started combining Indian and western instruments to create a new kind of "fusion music" long before it became a trend. Today, Tanushree conductes classes at the Ananda Shankar Centre for performing Arts in Calcutta and the Udai Shankar Academy of Creative Dance in New Delhi where students train in the Shankar technique of New Age Dance.

New Age Dance is a modern interpretation of the rich cultural heritage India has in the world of dance. The dances are based on the creative style, a kind of coming together of the old and the new, the traditional and the contemporary. The style is Indian, the presentation is modern and has a universal appeal. It is demanding indeed, says Tanushree. A sense of aesthetic fulfilment is inculcated in the students with enough fun and entertainment.

Tanushree has choreographed fashion shows, films and several ballets like "Atmoday", "Mrignayani", "Frangrance", "Temptations", "Ahimsa", "From Darkness to Light", "Budhi Vijay" and "Legends of Rama", etc.

KALAMANDALAM

Kalamandalam Calcutta had its humble beginning way back in 1968 and has been the pioneering organization for classical dance forms in the eastern region of India, promoting Bharatnatyam, Mohiniattam and Kathakali. The founders of this institution, Guru Govindan Kutty and Guru Mrs. Thankamani Kutty, are both alumunus of Kerala Kalamandalam and have been composing several new items for the repertoire of the dance forms. Under the guidance of the Kuttys, dance classes are being held in several places in the United Kingdom. Kalamandalam has now started the constuction of a performance arts complex in Calcutta which shall soon be able to host workshops, audiovisual shows, library, students' hostel, auditorium etc.

Recently they held a show in Qatar featuring the classical Indian dance forms. Another show held at Kuwait was also a resounding success.

The Kuttys have developed a style of their own, blending the southern classical style of dance with the notes of Rabindra *Sangeet*. They have successfully choreographed, perfected and performed Tagore's dance dramas in the *Kathakali* style.

AMITA DUTTA : TALKING DANCE

Amita is visiting professor in *Kathak* at the University of Burdwan and also an examiner for Ph.D. at the Rabindra Bharati University, Calcutta. She has taught *Kathak* under the aegis of the University Grants Commission at the Indira Fine Arts University, Madhya Pradesh, and the Punjabi University at Patiala.

Groomed in the strictest classical traditions under Pandit Birju Maharaj and other leading maestros of the premier Kathak *gharanas* (traditional families), Amita dances with a hyphotic force and subtle sensitivity combining rhythmic virtuosity with delicate expressiveness, commendable '*taiyaari*' (preparedness with mastery in '*Abhinayanga*') acting out of emotions). In her art we find a successful blend of tradition and talent, environmental totality as well as breathtaking dynamism. Her innovative mind has encouraged her to experiment with new ideas, thus expanding vistas of *Kathak*.

Having her root in Calcutta, Amita has performed far and wide, across three continents. Among her memorable dance recitals in major music and dance festivals one can recall the Khajuraho Dance Festival, Konark Dance Festival, Vishnupur Dance Festival, and the annual *Kathak* festivals of the Kathaka Kendras at Delhi and Jaipur. To her goes the credit of popularising *Kathak* not only in India but in different parts of the world.

ANJU MUNSHI

DANCE JUGALBANDIS

New experiments are being conducted in music and dance. In the realm of dance, experiments are being carried on by blending Indian Classical dance with a foreign dance and it is termed as dance Jugalbandi. In 1990, such a their daughter Asavarinath with all their virtuosity and grace in Kathak when dancing with their equally accomplished Flamenco counterparts from Spain - Jose and Juanigarcia with their well planned themes like the spanish Bull (flamenco) and the Indian Archer (Kathakali) and the joint ballet entitled "Dream of Mughal prince", these carefully rehearsed dances revealed not only the high standards of the well matched dancers but also the similarities and the differences between the two lovely styles of dancing. Kathak is perhaps the only Indian classical dance that has close links with foreign dance forms like dances of Uzbekistan and the Flamenco of spain. One recalls the "Aroha" programme jointly presented by Kumudini Lakhia with her lovely troupe of young Kathak dancer from the Kadamba school (Ahemdabad) and the highly trained "Bakhar" ballerinas under Madame Ravasono Sharipova in Tashkent and their joint presentation of 60 dancers in the grand finale of closing function of the festival of India in erestwhile Soviet Union.

DANCE OF CHHOTANAGPUR (TRIBAL)

Folk-dance and music of the tribals of chhotanagpur area in the state of Madhya Pradesh are the dominant feature of their culture. Be it Munda dance, Oraon dance, Santhal dance or any other, these performed during every religious celebration of any other social occasion of significance. For all the religious or socio-religious ceremonies, the tribals have an appropriate set of songs and dances.

Their dances which are vigorous, colourful and stimulating present an amazing array of rhythy and folklore. They are not mere entertainment; they are part of their way of life. Most tribal languages are unwritten but are highly musical and contain a large number of symbols. And most of the songs are handed down from one generation to the other through word of mouth.

MAJOK K. JHA

DANCE TRADITION OF INDIA

Dance pleases even the Gods. The Gods themselves are the supreme dancers. Brahma, Vishnu and Shiva, the Creator, the preserver and the Destroyer of the Universe, are the eternal trinity. Vishnu, the presserver, seeks, from time to time, to redeem the world as an "Avatar" (incarnation).

Shiva, the Destroyer, is the king of dancers, Nataraja. His beautiful spouse, the daughter of the Himalayas, Parvati, was the first teacher of dancing.

In the art of dancing, drama and music, Bharata was the first guru. His 'Natya Sastra' (an encyclopaedia on drama and music) explains the origin of the art. "When the world had become steeped in greed and desire, resulting in confusion and disharmony, in pain and pleasure, Brahma, the creator, was asked by the people to create an amusement which could be seen and heard by all, for the scriptures were not enjoyed by the masses, being too learned and ambiguous".

Bharata having composed the first drama, went to seek the help of shiva for the steps of dance. Shiva taught the steps to his disciple Tandu and that is how "Tandava" or the masculine style of dancing came into existence. The 'lasya' or the feminine style of dancing was initiated by goddess Parvati.

VIJAY SHANKAR

DANCE TRAINING CENTRES

Dance training, small academics, local Kala Kendras, available all over India, most universtities introduced dance as subject, gurus impart training to pupils, villages, many state run public financed training centres, attract students from all over world, important are, Kerala Kalamandalam (Kerala Institute of Arts), near Shoranur Kalashetra at Adyar, Tamil Nadu; Kathak Kendra; a dance branch of Bhartiya Kala kendra in New Delhi; Triveni Kala Sangam (centre of Music, Dance, Painting), at New Delhi; Darpana Academy, at Ahmedaba l, Gujarat; Visva-Bharati, at Santiniketan West Bengal; Jawaharlal Nehru Manipuri Dance Academy, Imphal; and many more.

DANCE VILLAGE (NRITYAGRAM), WITH A DIFFERENCE

When the history of this century of Indian dance is written, protime Gauri Bedi's name will be etched as the most dynamic dancer to have created an institution which outlived her.

It all started innocuously some twenty-five years ago, when bored with her bohemian Bombay life, she took to Odissi, triggered by a chance performance when saw she guru Kelucharan Mahapatra. Learning and perfroming was not enough, not for protime whose appetite free gurukul for dance. In 1989, the then Prime Minister of India, V.P.Singh, inaugurated the Nrityagram gurukul, simply called Nrityagram, a dance village or a village for dance.

Recalls Daksha Sheth, India's leading contemporary dancer, who with her Australian husband Devissaro left Delhi to help protima set-up this dance village : teachers came, students trained and the national press supported this unique dance village. Gurus (Kelubabu for Odissi, Kalanidhi Narayanan for Bharata Natyam, Mumudini Lakhia for Kathak and Bharati Shivaji for Mohiniattam) came and taught there.

Protime soon realised what she had to offer was far more than any guru could- and environment to learn. Slowly she shifted the focus to create ensemble (group) works, short ballets and train new students herself. She arranged smashing debuts for her prized pupils Surupa Sen, Bijayini Satpathy, Bharat Rao and showed the world what was possible.

More importantly, Nrityagram became a must for every visitor from abroad, dance companies, choreographers and researchers in the tradition. Nrityagram was on road to becoming not merely a dance-training place but a meeting point for world dance communities. It took the shape of becoming the Hacob's pillow of India (Ted Shawn and Ruth St.Dennis, the pioneering dance-duo of America, nay its founding figures, took a barn outside New York and created jocob's pillow in 1940s).

And soon a woodstock too. For protima hit upon the idea of holding an annual dance-music festival featuring the best names in the country. Done on first Saturday of February to coincide with the arrival of spring, it is called Vasanthabba. The Who's who of the dance and music world have performed for this festival. Its ultimate test and tribute came in 1999 when after protima was no more, major gurus, artists and performers performed for free. So Protima's dream for dance lives on at Nrityagram.......

ASHISH KHOKAR

DANCES OF HIMACHAL PRADESH (FOLK)

The land or snow-elad mountains and emeraldine valleys, the Himachal Pradesh is famous for its colourful folk dances. Secluded in their almost inaccessible mountain vastness, Gods and the people have lived together in Himalayan villages sharing their sorrows and happiness alike. After the hard toils of the day the people gather in front of the temple and sing and dance away their fatigue. No festival is without a dance and the festivals are numerous. Often enough the Gods also dance with the people.

The widely known annual fairs of the state, such as Lavi Fair of Rampur- Bushair, Shivratri Fair of Mandi Dussehra Fair of Kulu and Minjar fair of chamba are occasions when people from remote villages come with their gods, singing and dancing along the tortuous mountain paths. The few days they spend together are occasions when they display their skill in dances in a spirit of healthy competition. Besides these annual fairs there are any number of festivals connected with religious and social observances in different regions when dance and music play an important part. Thus, Himachal Pradesh has preserved in its far flung regions an amazing variety of colourful folk dances. It is one of the few States that has sent authentic Folk Dance parties consistently for all these years of Republic Day Folk Dance Festival in Delhi.

KINNAUR

Kinnaur is situated in a region which is snow-bound for about six months in a year. It is said to have been the abode of the Kinnaras and Gandharvas, the celestial musicians and dancers. Whatever the case may be, it is certain that the present day descendants of these heavenly beings have kept up the tradition of dance and music alive. Kinnaras living in lovely villages bordering on Tibet follow Buddhism and Hinduism and their cultural tradition is based on the happy fusion of these two religions. While they celebrate Diwali, Dussahra, Makar

Sankranti, Shivratri, Beesh etc., they follow with equal verve the celebrations of Dungyur Jaal of the Buddhist tradition when the Lamas perform Devil-Dance.

Besides these they have their own seasonal festivals like Ukhyang (fading of the flower) and Dakhrain (on-set of rain) etc. On all these occasions they indulge in dances. Main dances popular in Rareng village in this region are Panas, Chamik, and Champa. Whereas the Panas, Champa are mixed dances the Chamik dance is performed only by women during Holi festivals. The dancers move first clock-wise and then anti-clockwise with lyrical steps, singing songs of love.

Sangla Valley nestles in the lap of the lofty Kinnar Kailash. Like the people of Rareng they too observe both Hindu and Buddhist rituals. To eke out a living they have to work hard against the rigours of nature and during the winter they are forced to keep indoors or migrate to warmer regions. Naturally the onset of spring makes them rejoice and thus the gaily attired people, particularly the women decked in silver fineries. gather in the temple courtyard and dance with gay abandon. Some of their well-known dances are : Bakyang, Dakyang, and Kayang. The songs they sing while dancing describe natural beauty, love of youth and on occasions religious sentiments.

The people of the village pooh perform Khar dance on Diwali and Dussehra festivals and Shabroo dance on all other occasions while the youth of the village have a particular preference for Jogshan, the dance of love performed in a fast tempo.

Sarpara, situated across the Sutlej in the lap of the snow-clad Srikantha Mountain, has a harvest dance in praise of Lord Siva. The dance is called Khera Ka Nach. But the most popular dance of this region is Srikhand Naati which girls and boys dance with wild enthusiasm, lustily singing love songs of their choice. All dances and in Bhamanu and Dohey when boys and girls in pairs perform vigorous dance and go out of the area hand in hand.

Other dances popular in various parts of Mahasu and Ghugati, Laoli-Bagoli and Diwali which are performed during Dussehra and Diwali celebrations. A peculiar feature of these dances is that dancers sing songs from Ramayana.

SIRMOUR

In Sirmour region most popular dances are Burah dance performed during Diwali, Rasa and Crossa dance performed during Bisu fair and Magh Sankranti and Naati dance on all other occasions.

The Burah dance has a circular motion from right to left with men leading and women following. The Tempo is fast from the very stary. With a prayer to Goddess Durga dancers start singing about the story of Sidhu and his Tikri (Fort) which the Raja of Nahan wanted to acquire for his Rani.

The Rasa and Crossa dances are performed in circular formation with men and women standing in alternate positions holding hands. The steps closepy follow the songs and the intrumentalists stand in the centre of the circle.

The Naati dance is also a mixed dance performed in a circular formation with a man and a woman dancing in the centre of the circle depicting the theme of the love song which they all sing.

CHAMBA

Chamba region of the state is famous for fine arts as well as for music and dance. One may hardly find a person in Chamba who may not sing or play on flute. But the dances of Chamba are confined to the distant villages like Churaha. Pangi, Chhatrar etc. Inhabitants of these villages are eigher Gaddis (shepherds) or agriculturiests and their dances are colourful and infectious. The Churaha people dance party was adjudged the best in the 1954 Republic Day Folk Dance Festival held in New Delhi and the Sangeet Natak Akademi Trophy for the first time was awarded to the party.

Pangi, situated in the North of Chamba, is snow-bound practically for six months in a year. Before the snow-fall begins the people of Pangi celebrate Phool Yatra and on that occasion women dance to their hearts content. Their dance beings with a movement called Ghurei when the dancers in two batches enter the area in a diagonal way and then make a circle with arms, inter-locked. Then they take a step forward and backward with the bend of the knees in between and then take a step side-ways, repeating the forward and backward steps again.

In Chhatrari village the women-folk dance Dangi on the occasion of Jatras and Depak when their Gaddi men-folk migrate to Kangra with their flock during winter. However, men and women join in dancing Jhanjar, a vigorous dance when they form themselves in two concentric circles executting pirousettes simultaneously in opposite directions.

The greatest dance event in this region takes place during the annual Minjar Fair held in Chamba where people from distant villages across the snow-capped mountains converge to take part in the rituals of consigning the Minjar to the river Ravi. The spacious Chougan in Chamba offers them a large ground for dancing to their hearts content.

LAHOUL-SPITI

Lahoul-Spiti region is inhabited mainly by Buddhists and there are many famous Gompas (Monasteries) there. Once a year the Lamas in these monasteries celebrate a festival called Goithur and on that occasion Chham (Devil) Dance is performed with weird mask called Bag. The people in general dance during festival like Lo Sar (New Year) Da Chang, Thon, Namgan etc. When there are abundant feasting and dancing.

KULU VALLEY

The picturesque Kulu valley is famous for its scenic beauty and colourful dances. Kulu is proud of its ancient tradition of Naati, which is the slowest dance one could think of. It is said that in olden days it used to take an hour for the dancers to make a round of the circle. The Naati has various parts based on the tempo of the movements, such as, Dheeli, Pheti, Basahari, Luddi, Bantha, Laldi, Ujagjama, Gharghareekar, Kartha, Khandait etc. The two traditional fairs held in this region are Dussehra in Kulu and Shivratri in Mandi when the people from far away villages come with their Gods and spend their time singing and dancing and making merry. Even Gods dance in these festivals which attracts people from all over India.

Besides, the people dance in their villages on all main festivals such as Jetha Birsu in Baisakh. Kappu Saja and Shadi Naach in the month of Jeth, Shayari Saja in Asauj, Trayan Saja in Magh, and Larayan Saja in Phalgun.

Modern times with its speed and pace would have by passed the slow Naati but for the poineering efforts of eminent leaders like Shri Prarthi, who reorganised the dance to suit the modern times. Their efforts have now borne fruit and to-day every village, every school and college in the region echoes with the strains of music and steps of dancing.

The dances of Himachal pradesh have many things in common such as their spontaneity and abandon, their essential formations etc. At the same time they carry the distinctive features of the locale which are different from each. Each region, almost each village has its distinct costume and jewellery which are strikingly beautiful.

ACCOMPANYING MUSIC

The dances are always accompanied by songs, songs which again carry local colour and traditional background. The people of Chini region in Mahasu sing of Locha Ramabocha and Chavai Lama along with the songs of Ramayan and Mahabharat. They also sing of fading flowers and the story of Thakurmoni. In sirmour region the songs describe the highhandedness of local Rajas, infidelity of a wife or the hazards of forest journey. In Chamba they sing of Vanjaras who carry merchandise and of emerald mines of Padar, while in Kulu they sing freely of love and of legendary heroes

The musical instruments used in dances are mosre or less the same every where. They are Narsingha, Kannal, Buggal (Jhang), Sannai (Shehnai), Dhol, Bhan (Thali), Dumag are Nangar except in Sirmour where Hulak and Turi are also used. In Lahoul Spiti the instruments used by people in their dances are Dao (Duff), Daman (Nagara), Surnai (Shehnai) and Kopor (a sarangi type instuments of five strings played with how). The Lamas of Rareng and Lohoul Spitis use instruments common with their counterparts in other places, such as, Dhung-chen, Gyaling, Ser-Gna, Rolmo, Dhun-Kar etc.

GOVIND VIDYARTHI

DANCING CLASSICAL (SOLO)

The very mention of Indian classical dance conjures an image of a solo dancer, beautifully attired, performing an entire programme, be it Bharata Natyam, Kathak or Odissi. There is a long deep-rooted and unique tradition of solo classical dancing in India.

What is mentioned in Bharata's Natya Shastra (treatise on dance) as an embellishment or ornament to drama or theatre has, over the centuries, evolved to acquire a separate identity. and status as an art form all its own. The reason lies in the very nature of the art.

Indian classical dance combines in it abstract dancing (Nritta or pure dance as it is commonly called), a story line or theme communicated in a narrative form through abhinaya (mime and expression) and an abundance of grace. The solo dancer uses her body as the instrument to communicate and create the atmosphere and effect without any kind of props.

What distinguishes Indian classical dance from other dances the world over is the important role played by every part and contour of the face. As the body assumes a posture and moving hands depict an appropriate gesture (Mudra), the face and eyes reflect the inner feelings and emotions of the character portrayed, however subtle they may be (bhava).

This art of communication through bhava and abhinaya by the dancer and the resultant aesthetic enjoyment by the audience is dealt in detail in the Rasa theory, which is the creation of the Indian genius, The analysis of the human mind, the range of emotions that a person is capable of and the detailed discussion of the manifestation and development of Rasa in the Natya Shastra and other subsequent texts leave us completely spellbound.

The temporary identification of the dancer with the character she portrays, along with the depiction of the actions and facial expressions of that character, make an effective impact on the spectator. It involves the spectator also, who is temporarily involved with the and the theme. This two-way involvement results in the savouring of rasa, which literally means juice. Here, it is the essence of aesthetic pleasure.

What distinguishes a great artiste is that she is able to cast this magic on the audience every time she performs. According to Ananda Coomaraswamy, the celebrated authority on Indian arts and aesthetics, in Indian acting or dancing nothing is left to chance, since it is the action and not the actor that is important, there is no scope for amateurs on the stage.

Today, we live in a world where the blitzkrieg of information teachnology has resulted in quick interaction and free flow of ideas between groups and communities. The West, which its economic supremacy and advanced technology, has made a tremendous impact on us in many ways. The impact in the cultural field has been quite overwhelming. Modern dance with never stage and presentation techniques has a tremendous appeal especially for modern educated youth. The consequent effect on our dancers and choreographers is noticeable. New and bold themes are being attempted. Experiments are being made with more abstract dancing by introducing group compositions and adopting emerging stage techniques. However, the traffic is not just one way, our dance has also made an impact on the Western choreographers and teachers who have adopted our techniques of body and gesture language, ideas of communication etc. Many of them evince interest in the Rasa theory and are exploring possiblities of adopting the abhinaya and bhava techniques to their creations. Some collaborative efforts have also come up.

In this changed scenario, the soloclassical performer is somewhat bewildered by the challenge the faces. Many attempt to imbibe never themes hitherto considered unsuitable for the stage. Some have been very successful. But ultimately, the intense appeal and intrinsic worth of Indian classical dance will enable the dancer to continue to enthrall audiences as human emotions remain unchanged over the millennia.

If Krishna's Radha waited for him in the bower, today's Nayika (heroine) may wait at a bus-stand or at a coffee shop. The emotions experienced during the wait - the surging feeling of love, the expectation, the doubt, the disappointement and the disapproval of the delay, the anger or the pretence of it all these remain the same and will remain the same for all times to come.

The human eye and mind being capable of concentrating only on one thing at a time, the solo dancer has an advantage. In a group dance presentation, the alignment and realignment of the dancers and the patterns they weave are intresting and engaging, but there is no focal point in such abstract presentation. In a dance drama, each dancer represents one character and in a given scene, they will be dancing or miming one at a time. The audience has to watch each one by turn.

In a solo dance, the dancer being the narrator and communicator, is the focus of attention of the audience, which concentrates particularly on her face and facial expressions. She instantly establishes a rapport with the audience and dances her way into their hearts.

KAMALA VARDAN

DANDA NATA

Danda Nata of Orissa is a tribal way of welcoming the New Year which begins with the month of Vaishakh. It is a festival of ritualised performance believed to fulfil the desires of participants. It took shape of performing art with ritual overtones during 9th - 10th century in the tribal belts and in course of time it has embraced non-tribals, even Brahmins, into its fold. Verbal and non-verbal symbolic enactments in Danda Nata performanced have inspired a few playwrights to adopt its style in modern plays. Danda Nata has elements of both Desi and Margi Styles (little tradition and great tradition). The theme of Danda Nata is at times taken from Sanskrit literature; the style of performance has a tribal and folk accent. Danda Nata is celebrated during the month of Chaitra marking the end of one agricultural cycle and the beginning of another. Lord Siva and Goddess Kali are worshipped. Some say that the period from *Chaitra Purnima* to *Vishuva-Sanskranti* is the proper time for Shiva and Shakti worship. The festival is celebrated for 12/18/21 days as per their convenience, but it ends on Vishuva Sankranti.

LAXMIKANTA

DECORATION (FLOOR)

Decorating the floor, a tradition that is alive throughout India, is called Alpana in Bengal, Sathia in Gujarat, Rangoli or Rangavalli in Maharashtra and Gujarat, Mandna in Rajasthan and Madhya Pradesh, Jhunti in Orissa, Kalam in parts of South India, Muggulu in Andhra Pradesh, Likhnu in Himachal Pradesh, Aripan in Bihar, Chank Purna Aipan and Rangoli in Uttar Pradesh and

Pakhambha in Manipur. All these Popular terms for floor decoration mean the art of making embankments.

Usually floor decoration is done in the north with rice paste mixed with water. It is done with the fingertips on the floor which is first smeared with red clay (gehru) or cow dung or cleaned just with water. The execution is swift, direct and simple and the surface of the floor is kept moist so as to enable smooth and swift painting. Wheat and barley flour, coloured rice and saw dust, earth colours, pulses, flowers etc, are also used for creating patterns on the floor.

Floor designs in some parts of India, particularly in the southern regions, are imaginatively drawn to link an array of dots which vary in numbers, combination and forms. In Maharashtra and certain parts of U.P. and Madhya Pradesh, patterns are prepared by joining the dots whereas in the South, patterns are drawn around the dots and that is why dots are visible in their patterns.

Floor decoration, according to the style or preparation, can be devided into three categories: Akriti Pradhan, Vallari Pradhan and Akriti Vallari Pradhan. The patterns of floor decoration in U.P., Rajasthan, Haryana and Gujarat are known as Akriti Pradhan. Here patterns are prepared with the help of geometrical shapes like dots, lines, squares, triangles, circles etc. Vallari Pradhan patterns are popular in Bengal, Orissa and Bihar. Here the stylised forms of birds, animals, lotus, fisth, butterfly, Conch with other auspicious symbols are used. In the south, both these styles can be seen in their floor or wall decorations and that is why these are known as Akriti Vallari Pradhan patterns.

All religious festivals are popular social events. On these occasions, women spend a great deal of time and expertise in decorating their homes. It is a spontaneous expression of their joy and that is why it flourishes even today despite the onslaught of modernisation.

DR. BIMLA VERMA

DELHI - ITS HISTORICITY

The history of Delhi is wreathed in hoary antiquity. That it was the capital of the Pandava's kingdom more than five thousand years ago has already been attested not merely by the literary allusions in the Mahabharata but also by specimens of pottery from Purana Qila, (old fort) in Delhi. The excavations carried out by the central Archaeological Survey push back the history of Delhi to prehistorice times. The excavation site of Anangpur to the south of Delhi has yielded a wealth of prehistoric tools that have enabled the archaeologist to reconstruct the history of Delhi from prehistoric times onwards.

Valuable light has been thrown on the changeds that have taken place in the climate of Delhi due to countless reasons. The changing courses of the sacred drivers Yamuna and Ganga, the role played by the Aravalli ranges that terminate in the southern Delhi and parts of which are still visible, the geological factors, the paleochannels of the river Yamuna, the flora and fauna have all been taken into account. That stone Age finds are available from the excavated site is impressive in itself.

From Stone Age and prehistoric period to the tenth century AD is a big leap indeed. Really significant is the discovery of the vestiges of the fort and masonry dam erected by Raja Anangpal Tomar at Anagpur, his capital palaces have also been unearthed. These discoveries will go a long way to demolish many myths fabricated by the western scholars that the Hindu rulers did not build palaces and forts that could stand comparison with those erected by the Mughals.

In fact, the general impression created by them is that these architectural and engineering skills were possessed only by the Mughals who brought in Perisian masons to errect their forts and palaces : That all the Rajput forts and places were built in imitation of the Mughal buildings. It is forgotten by all such writers that Raja Man Singh's palace "Manmandir" pre-dates the Mughal Babar's invasion in 1526; that Rajput king Anangpal Tomar had got twenty-seven temples, sumptuously decorated goregeous temples, built at Mahrauli. Their remnains can still be seen in the pillared arcades which are intact, besides sculptural reliefs scattered there.

There is authentic information about the diverse types of tools used and made at Anangpur, which again date back to Stone Age. The raw materials and techniques employed in the making of these tools will interest archaeologists as well as others who are interested in the history and evolution of mankind.

The historicity of Delhi is well established. Much more needs to be done by way of excavations, How would it be possible, considering the expanding boundary lines of Delhi due to ever growing population, is difficult to say. But there are countless sites, inhabited ones, that have a vast treasure lying buried underground. A lot more remains to be done in order to know more about Delhi's historical past. (Dr. Subhashini Aryan, India Perspectives, March, 1995).

As if a natural sequence to the story of Delhi's antiquity, the glorious site of Indraprastha of the great epic Mahabharata is not confirmed to have been part of this region. Findings of the stone age tools earlier in the vicinity of Anangpur area had conclusively indicated that prehistoric man lived in Delhi and its surrounding areas, vaster than what forms the part of southern Delhi. The excavations carried out by Archaeological Survey of India (ASI) in 1991 revealed many such tools. The information available through literary and archaeological sources, though small, confirms Delhi's antiquity and continuity.

It is significant that until the beginning of present century, a village called Indrapat, obviously derived from Indraprastha, lay within the precincts of purana Quila (Old Fort). In fact till late forties, the area within the boundaries of this fort presented a village - like appearance and the surviving accommodation was used by the villagers as well as refugees after partition of the country in 1947. The villagers till then called it as Pandava's Quila. The discovery of an Ashokan epigraph in Lajpat Nagar in South Delhi in 1966 seemed to have furthered the keen interest in the search of antiquity of Delhi and the location of the site of Indraprastha. Since the site near Anangpur has been confirmed as the site of prehistoric man, the reasons for its choice were attributed to the easy availability of water, raw material for tool-making and thick forest for game.

But more than that, this region has inherent magnetism since time immemorial. It is this pull which seems to have drawn even Pandavas. After the division of their ancestral estate, Pandavas were offered the densely-forested area of Khandavaprastha; they accepted even that. This area was also known as Yoginipur. Other places called Baghpat, Sonpat (Sonepat), Tilpat and Panipat were the other "Pats" which were demanded by Pandavas from the Kauravas (Mahabharata). Significantly all these places have yielded the painted grayware associated with the so-called Mahabharata sites which have emerged after the excavations at Hastinapur in 1950.

Before beginning the digging into the past eras, the archaeologists tap the literary sources. To go deeper, in this case, they looked extensively into Buddhist texts and Jatakas to find a definite direction. Epics and Puranas (ancient sacred scriptures) are the other sources taken into account. As mentioned in the Buddhist text, the present Delhi kingdom was known to have had many towns, villages and cities and Indrapatta was the most important of them all. Since these sources, as well as legends refer to events and conditions of much earlier times, these have been relied upon to a reasonable extent. Though the exact dating of the literary sources is not possible their chronological sequence has generally been agreed upon. The Buddhist text has described the Indrapatta in much precise detail and glowing terms. This town, as described therein was well connected by roads to all the main cities of which Benaras received a special mention.

An eminent archaeologist A. Cunningham asserted the probable date of occupation of Indraprastha as 1511 B.C. No direct evidence to support the theory of the indentity of Indraprastha with Delhi was found till date, though plenty of circumstantial evidence was there. The assumed location of Indraprastha was between the present Ferozshah Kotla and Humayun's Tomb along the banks of Yamuna (when it flowed in that area). But it had remained a vague guess till the excavations were carried out by the Archaeological Survey of India 1955 and the site fixed to be in the lower mound in Purana Quila. Extensive excavations were carried out in 1966 and the following four years. Painted greyware, an offering stand in red and few other objects found there confined the and encouraged further probes.

According to the accounts in Buddhist texts and other scriptures, Indraprastha included the present Meerut region in the north-east and parts of Kathiawar in the south-east. According to some scholars Indraprastha was bounded by Meerut in the north, Goddavartha in South, Mathura in the east and Dwaraka in the West. Suruchi Jataka (a Buddhist text) also mentioned into be a city of great fame.

URMILA VERMA

DEV ANAND

Through the 1960s he held his own as one of the mighty triumvirate of heroes in Indian cinema. His image as the dashing reckless romantic combined with his good looks made him the heartthrob of millions. Dev Anand gained stature with his roles in his home productions by Navketan Films, and proved his acting prowess in his double role in Hum Dono, Guide and Tere Mere Sapne under the able baton of brother Vijay Anand.

The evergreen hero, whose zest for life shines undiminished despite the series of flops he has made over the past few years, still makes young hopeful's hearts flutter. To him, after all, goes the credit for discovering two major heroines, Zeenat Aman and Tina Munim.

A vegetarian, teetotaller and eternal optimist, Dev Anand's popularity has spanned three generations. And his going is still good.

DEVDASIS : DANCING TO THE GODS

The association of dance with religion, and therefore with temples in India, can be traced to very ancient times.

The sacred Hindu texts list the offerings that should be made to the Supreme Being during religious rites. These include incense, water, lamps, flowers as well as something considered very auspicious-music and dance.

The system of devadasis (maids of God) emerged in order to perform these duties. The main responsibility of these young girls, consecrated to the deity of the temple, was to dance in its honour, carry out certain rituals such as the Arati, in which camphor is burnt and offered to the god in order to drive away negative forces, as also to perform in the big annual festivals held at these temples.

According to the Puranas, the Indian chronicles of ancient times, consecrating devadasis to the temples was considered an auspicious deed. The girls who dedicated their lives to this mission started their training at a very early age, generally between seven and nine years. Once her admission was approved by the temple authorities, the young girl, on an auspicious day, was taken with a lot of pomp to the shrine and a special ceremony was performed whereby she was weded to God, who was represented in one of his aspects by the local deity. Subsequently, she received her first lesson in dance and continued her studies of the art and other subjects for several years. When the learning period was over and the young girl was suitably trained, she devoted herself to the service of the temple.

The day the new devadasi danced for the first time in public in honour of the deity to whom she had been consecrated, was considered very important and was accompanied by lavish celebration to mark the event. The dancer, richly dressed in silk, and bedecked with jewels and flowers, received the blessings of the priests and teachers, who also blessed the bells that she would wear from then onwards around her ankles whenever she danced.

Thereafter, the young girl, accompanied by her musicians, performed her dances in a deeply artistic and devotional atmosphere.

The devadasis were considered extremely auspicious. They were called Nitya Sumangalis, or the ones that eternally portended good fortune because they were wedded to God, and so could never become widows. Because of their beneficial portent, they were always invited to important events, such as the coronation of the kings, the signing of political pacts, wedding, etc., and were accorded places of honour.

The devadasi system has continued in India through the centuries, although it faced some ups and downs owing to certain social, religious and political factors. Though the system of dedicating young girls to temple deities was legally abolished in 1947, in some temples they have managed to continue the tradition, for example in the Jagannath temple of Puri, Orissa.

After independence in 1947, the movement that had started some years earlier to revive the ancient arts, was intensified. Along with other arts, the 2000 year old classical Indian dance was once again allowed to occupy the place of honour that it deserved, thanks to the efforts of artists, scholars and art lovers.

Nowadays, these classical dances that earlier were performed by the devadasis, are taught in prestigious institutes and universities and presented on stage in big theatres by professional dancers.

It is interesting to note that although dance stopped being an integral part of the daily life of temples quite a long ago, it has once again gone back to them, albeit in another equally beautiful and auspicious form. Every year dance festivals are organized on stages set up outside some of the most important temples, relics of India's past, such as those in Khajuraho, Konark, Mahabalipuram and Chidambaram.

Dance has been associated not only with the Hindu religion in the Shaivaite and Vaishnava cults, but also with Jainism and Mahayana Buddhism. Exquisite sculptures of dance poses can be seen in some of the very old caves and temples of all these religions.

There is a spiritual message in the dance of the devadasis of yesteryears and of the classical dancers of today, besides in the stillness of the dance captured in stone, marble and brass : "God created beauty and since dance in beauty, it should be performed as an offering to God."

MYRTA BARVIE

DEVADASIS OR NAUTCH GIRLS

Dance and music, according to Indian tradition, are divine creation. The story goes that one day, Indra, lord of the firmament and some other gods grew bored and implored Lord Brahma, the creator, to find them a pastime that could be both seen and heard. So Brahma inspired the saga Bharata to compile the Natya Shastra, the sacred treatise on dance and music. While codifying the dance art, Bharata realized that the graceful lasya dance could be performed only by women. He informed Brahma about his problem, whereupon the supreme Lord created the Apsaras, the first performing women artistes, to entertain the gods. Poets have composed songs extolling the beauty of Apsaras and how they delighted the gods as they danced merrily to the accompaniment of music by the Gandharvas, the mythical divine singers. Mythological stories refer to Apsaras being commissioned by Lord Indra to seduce the sages whose austere penance caused tremors in Heaven. Thus it was that the great sage, Vishwamitra, was captivated by Maneka's charms that led to the birth of Shakuntala, the heroine of Kalidasa's famous drama by that name.

Urvashi, peer among the Apsaras, who is said to have been born on earth, imparted divine knowledge of dance and music to human beings. Devadasis, as temple dancers, were the first recipients of this art, and over the centuries, their devotional dances became an essential part of the temple service. Devadasi system was prevalent all over India which is evident from glimpses of social and cultural life in the Mauryan period, provided by Kautilya. As time passed, the exchange of devadasis between the temple and the court became an established practice.

In ancient India there were also Ganikas, accomplished in 64 kalas (arts) which included dancing and singing. known for their physical charm, they entertained the rich and the famous who vied with each other to win their favours. To be seen with a Ganika was considered a status symbol. The encouter between the Ganika and the ascetic is stockmotif in Sanskrit literature. In the course of time, dancing grew more and more popular and every kind and chieftain had his own troupe of professional artists accomplished in dance and music.

With the advent of Islam, the Devadasi institution disintegrated in north India but it continued to flourish in the South. For the Mughal rulers, dancing was an essential component of royal entertainment and they brought to India persian dancing girls know as Domnis, Lolonis, Horokenis and Hentsinis with their own distinctive style of dancing. The interaction of persian dancing style with that of the traditional Hindu form brought a glorious fusion of Hindu-Muslim arts and a new kind of alloyed dance form was evolved, popularly known as "Kathak". The wealth and prosperity of the Mughals the cultivation of all art forms and with royal patronage, "Kathak" came to be regarded as a sophisticated form of entertainment, The high class dancing girls were conferred the title of Kanchanis (gilded) by Akbar.

During the later Mughal period, singers and dancers with lavish royal patronage began to wield great influence in the court, Jahandar Shah married the famous dancing artist, Lal Kunwar and gave her the status of a queen with the title of Imtiaz Mahal (chosen one of the palace). She came to be known as the "Dancing Empress" of India. Another colourful ruler, Mohamad Shah Rangila, also married a dancing girl, Uttambai, known as Qudsia Begum. After the decline of Mughal power, Delhi lost its former glory and the scene shifted to Lucknow, the seat of Oudh Nawabs, where the leading dancing girls found a new home. Repositories of art, culture and refinement, they occupied a respectable position in society. Wajid Ali Shah, the last Nawab of Oudh, whose reign is remembered as the golden age of music and dance, went to the extent of establishing an institution called the Parikhana (Fairy-house) where young girls were taught dance and music.

Meanwhile, in South India, the institution of devadasis had continued but after the decline of kingdoms and gradual impoverishment of the great temples, devadasis were forced to seek patronage of Indian princes and landlords. Those who could not secure regular employment with them travelled around in search of patronage of the upcoming English masters.

Under the Sahib's patronage, the classical dance forms of Kathak in north India and Dassi-Attam in south India were given the common appelation of Nautch and the performing artist in her new incarnation emerged as the Nautch girl - delicate in her person, soft in her feathers, perfect in form - and captivated the hearts of the English sahibs by her song and dance and enthralled the more sophisticated among them by her conversation and wit.

The nautch girls and their earlier counterparts, the ganikas, devadasis and nartakis belonged to a class of professional artists who were accomplished singers and dancers and also well- versed in literature. They provided stimulating company and the elite usually sent their sons to their salons to learn refinedmanners and social etiquette. The Nautch girl institution dominated the entertainment scene until the end of the nineteenth century when its decline began in the wake of an anti-nautch campaign mounted by the missionaries and the Western-educated Indian social reformers. This moral censorship dealt a deathblow to the traditional Indian dance art nurtured and preserved by these women artists through the ages. The reformers succeeded in denigrating the dancing profession and its practitioners. The great teachers and disciples of classical arts of dance and music were forced to find other avenues for a living.

However, while nautch and its exponents - the nautch girls carrying different appelations as Baijis, tawaifs, devadasis and naikins - were languishing - Indian classical dance witnessed a revival. In the twenties and thirties of the 20th century some dancers from abroad, including the legendary ballerina Anna Pavlova from Russia and Ruth St. Denis and Ted Shawn from the United States, contributed to this awakening in no small measure. Among the Indian pioneers or revival were Gurudev Tagore, Uday Shankar, Menaka from north India and E. Krishna Iyer, Rukmini Devi and Ragini Devi from South India. They sought to make their compatriots aware of the ancient spiritual glory of Indian dance. Both dance and music were thus liberated from the yoke of the social stigma attached to them and acquired a new dignity. The surviving great masters and gurus of dance art all over the country were sought after and they began teaching dance and music to young educated girls from respectable families.

PRAN NEVILE

DHYAN CHAND (1905-1979)

A man of few words, Dhyan Chand could make a hockey stick talk as no other player could. He was called the "wizard" of hockey, and each time he played, he mesmerised the world with his astounding ability to score goals at will. He made scoring a goal look like the easiest thing in the world, but it required a true hockey mind to appreciate the skills that lay behind the dexterity. And yet, the explanation behind the genius was simple : whatever he did, he did it in the shortest possible time and with the least fuss. This simple trait however led many to erroneously believe that Dhyan Chand's prowess was a gift from heaven, and few realised the enormous intellect that lay behind it. Hockey writers waxed eloquent about his wizardry. He was variously called 'a legend', his game was described as a 'juggling turn, it is splendid', 'full of finesse and to watch him was ecstasy'. The greatest tribute was paid to him by none other than Adolf Hitler, who watched as India decimated Germany 8-1 in the Berlin Olympics. When Dhyan Chand told him he was a sepoy in the Indian army, Hitler replied : "If you were a German, I would have made you at least a major-general." In the event, he retired as a major and continued to serve hockey to the best of his ability.

DILIP KUMAR : THE COLOSSUS AMONG ACTORS

Dilip Kumar - the colossus who has stalked the silver screen in India since the 1940s has become a legend in his life time. Though he is generally regarded as the thespian The King of Tragedy - he is a versatile actor whose range is infinite. Be it a tragedy or a comedy, he is equally at home with both. Now that he has grown in years, he plays the 'don' (as in Vidhata) with the same elan as he played the role of Leader - in Yesteryears. For his lifetime contribution to the medium of cinema, the Government of India conferred upon him the 1995 Dadasahed Phalke Award.

Strange though it may seem, Dilip Kumar had no ambition to become an actor. Imagine, this young boy, fresh from college wanted to own a mobile tea stall. But the fate had willed otherwise. A chance meeting in Nainital with Devika Rani of the Bombay Talkies changed the course of his life. She asked him to see her in the film city, Bombay (now rechristened Mumbai).

It was she who gave Yusuf Khan - that was his real name the nom de plume Dilip Kumar. In those days it was common to rename actors and actresses for the screen.

Yusuf Khan (b. December 11, 1922) was one of the 13 children of Sarvar Khan who had come to Bombay from Peshawar. The man was in the fruit business. Yusuf who studied upto B.Sc in Bombay, was a shy, introvert and rather nervous young man. Once he took part in a college chess competition while he was playing, a pretty girl came and stood near him. Yusuf lost the game.

He was shy even when the shooting began for the first film he signed Jawar Bhata (1943), released the next year. On the first day he was told to run and rescue the heroine (Mridula) who was about to commit suicide in the scene. A keen hockey and football player, Dilip ran faster than the scene required. In fact, it was not until four retakes that the shot was okayed. However, his trouble was not yet over. The hero had now to hold the girl in his arms and mumble sweet nothings, which he did in an embarrassing manner. No wonder the film critics praised Mridula, also a newcomer, and not Dilip Kumar. This was not the sort of start one expected from an actor who within a few years, was to play memorable romantic leads in film after film.

Then followed Jugnu (1947, opposite Noorjehan, a top star of the day), Nadiya Ke Paar and Shaheed (opposite Kamini Kaushal) and Mela with Nargis.

Dilip Kumar has had many hits to his credit. These include Babul (1950), Deedar (1951), Dang (1952), Uran Khatola (1955), Naya Daur (1957), Madhumati (1958), Kohinoor (1960) and Ganga Jamuna (1961).

His Devdas (1955) and Mughal-e-Azam (1960) were outstanding movies. While Devdas epitomises tragedy of a lover, Mughal e Azam introduced hitherto unknown splendour and opulence in moviemaking. K.Asif took many years to create this ever-greem classic which had the best of photography, the best of music and the best of performances.

What made Dilip Kumar a tragedy king? Perhaps more than anything else it was his voice. It conveyed in the right tone, with the right expression, his mood or plight - sad, lonely, brooding, gloomy and heart-broken.

In moments of intensity he often reduced his voice to a mere whisper, He also put his pauses to good use. In other words, he made his silence speak - effectively. In fact, he chose to speak as few words as possible.

He played light - hearted roles in films like Azad, Gopi, Bairag, Leader and Ram Aur Shyam. Later, he played the angry man in pictures like Vidhaata, Shakti, Karma and Saudagar. All these speak of his versatility.

For a career that spans half a century, Dilip Kumar has not many films to his credit. The average comes to a little more than one a year. This is not because he was not offered more roles, but because he was choosy.

Hist acting potential has been duly recognised by both the connoisseur and the commoner alike. He bagged the prestigious Filmfare Award for the best actor no less than eight times. These were for his roles in Daag (1952), Azad (1955), Devdas (1956), Naya Daur (1957), Kohinoor (1960), Leader (1964), Ram Aur Shyam (1967) and Shakti (1982). In 1994 he was also given the special Filmfare Award for his lifetime's achievements.

He was also awarded the Padma Bhushan in 1991 by Government of India for excellence in the field of performing arts. Earlier in 1980, he had served as the sheriff of Bombay.

Then, in a befitting manner, came the Phalke Award in 1955, in the Centenary year of the Cinema.

Now in his seventies, this 'living legend', as he is fondly referred to, is in good health. Acting being his first love, he is likely to continue till his very last. And there is hardly an actor of the past two generations who has not been inspired or influenced by him.

O. P. BHAGAT

DILWARA TEMPLES : PRIDE OF MOUNT ABU

Nature never ceases to surprise us. More so in Rajasthan where on the one hand we have long stretching sands of the Thar and on the other, high mountain ranges of the Aravallis. Mt. Abu stands towards the south-east corner of the desert state, part of the Dharwar system of Indian geology, 4000 feet above sea level, with its highest peak at Guru Shikhara at 5650 feet. With an enchanting lake at the centre, surrounded by picturesque hills, Abu is one of the most charming hill stations of India.

The most memorable aspect of Mt. Abu, however, is a visit to the Jain temples at Dilwara, earlier known as Devakulapatak or Devalapatak (city of temples). Standing within the confines of a deceptively modest exterior, these temples contain a magnificent treasure-trove of splendid sculptures in white marble; Vimal Vasahi, Luna Vasahi, Chaumukha Vasahi and others have an astounding embellishment of the highest quality.

Vimal Vasahi, dedicated to the first **Jain Tirthankara** Adinath was built in 1031 by the Dandanayak of Bhima I, inspired by a devine vision. It was designed by the famous contemporary architect Kirtidhar who put his heart and soul into the work. Built at a staggering cost, the Vimal Vasahi has an elaborate architectural compactness with a sanctum and 52 cells around the courtyard, screened with a double arcade of carved pillars and amazing ceilings depicting scense from Jain scriptures. More than 120 artisans worked for fourteen years to complete this dream-like vision in marble.

The circular ceiling in the Rangamandap added afresh or substantially altered by Prithvipal in 1150, is an engineering and sculptural marvel supported on eleven concentric circles and a circular arcade of dwarf pillars joined by cusped arches. "Boldly superimposed athwart the lower of these circular rings is a series of sixteen brackets consisting of female figures representing Vidyadevis or goddesses of knowledge, each contained within an aureole, their semi detached projection giving them the appearance of supplementary braces supporting the vault", as observed by the noted art critic Percy Borwn. The ethereal translucence of the white marble appears like some "marvellous underwater formation in coral an and mother of pearl".

The Hathishala, a stable of elephant statues in front of the porch at Vimal Vasahi, is a rather uncanonical addition to the temple by later day rulers.

Luna Vasahi, dedicated to the 22nd Tirthankara Meninatha, was built in 1231 by two brothers Vastupal and Tejpala as a wish fulfilment for their brother. It is smaller than Vimal Vasahi but no less grand, and certainly embellished in a richer and more varied sculptural idiom. The fluted columns, vaulted interior and thematic panels have been carved with an astonishing ingenuity. The ceiling, here again, is the piece de resistance a fantastic marble lotus hange down in amazing weightlessness, a shimmering filigree of marble, an indisputable claimant to a place "among the architectural wonders or curiosities of the world".

The tiple-storeyed Chaumukha, gift of the artisans, contains images of Parsvanatha, the 23rd Tirthankara. The female figures are carved with indulgence but the impure quality of marble does injustice to excellent craftsmanship. The four metric ton brass image of Lord Adinatha is in-stalled at Pittalhara shrine, latest addition to Dilwara group.

Behind the famous Dilwara temples stands the Kanya Kumari temple dedicated to the virgin with whom sage Valmiki fell in love. His unfulfilled love, thwarted by the girl's mother, is remembered by three status for mother, daughter and the sage. An inscription dates its construction to 1395 A.D.

The shrine of Achaleshwar Mahadev, Abu's presiding deity, stands amid enchanting natural surroundings below the ramparts of ana Kumbha's fort at Achalgarh. Achaleshwar Mahadev temple carries an inscription of its builders - Vastupal and Tejpal.

The 1722 m. (5653 feet) high crest of the summit preserves footprints of the 14th century Vaishnava preacher Ramananda. The heavy bell carrying an inscription dated 1411 is installed on this wind swept top which is the highest point in Rajasthan Section of the Aravalli Ranges. The views are simply breathtaking.

SURENDRA SAHAI

DINDI AND KALA DANCE

Dindi and Kala Dance: religious folk dances; Maharashtra; dancers revolve, circle; beating short sticks (dindis), time with chorus leaders, drummer in middle; rhythm accelerates, two rows of dancers formed; advance, geometric formations; Kala dance features pot symbolizing feindity; group dancers, form, double riered circle; other dancers on their shoulders; top man breaks pot, splashes curds, then twirl sticks, swords, feverish battle dance.

DIPAVALI - INDIA'S POPULAR FESTIVAL

Unique as the most popular festival in India, Dipavali, also known as Diwali, is celebrated by all Hindus, irrespective of caste or creed. This important festival after the monsoon presents a fresh outlook. It consists of different forms of worship and celebration.

In South India, it is celebrated for a day, while in other parts of the country it is a five-day affair and each day has a special significance, like the worship of the Goddess of Wealth, killing of Narakasura, Vishnu's victory over bali, and above all the expression of affection among the members of the family.

In Tamil Nadu, the festival starts the previous night, when children start lighting crackers and sparklers, parents too join the fun.

The mother starts preparing lighting of the sparklers and crackers continues till day-break.

The neighbours start visiting each other inquiring "Ganga Saanam Aacha?" Which means "Did you have your oil bath in the Ganges?" Men and women visit from house to house accepting whatever refreshment is offered. On the Dipavali day medicine, known for its digestive qualities called "Marundu" - is also prepared. An oil bath on the Dipavali day is considered equivalent to a bath in the Ganges according to Hindu belief. In the noon there is a feast and the festival ends at night.

Worship of the Goddess of Wealth is most popular among businessman. After the usual early morning oil bath the merchants begin the day by opening new account books. They decorate the office premises with gay coloured cloth and flowers. Then they pile up all account books and heap silver coins. Over these coins are placed flowers and a paste of turmeric, kumkum and sandalwood. This heap is worshipped. Silver coins are supposed to be the incarnation of wealth and thus represent Goddess Lakshmi. No business is transacted on that day and the guests are well received.

The story of Dipavali tells us that demon Narakasura was harassing people. They prayed to Lord Krishna, he killed the demon with the help of his death, Narakasura asked for a boon, the people should celebrate his death like a festival. Krishna granted it. Hence the festival is celebrated to commemorate the deliverance from the clutches of the demon.

Another legend is that king Mahabali, a devotee of Siva, who was granted many boons, began to torment his people. Unable to bear it, the people complained to Lord Vishnu, who came in the form of a dwarf, Vamana and approached Mahabali for gift of land that would measure three feet.

Mahabali made light of request and granted him his wish. The Lord took his "Viswaroopa" - Giant size - and measured the earth with a foot, and the sky with another. He asked the king space for third foot. The king bowed low before him, and the Lord crushed him to Pathala. He however was granted a boon that he would be the king there and could reign on earth on the Dipavali day when there was no light. That is why every place is illuminated, so that the demon king may not come to earth again to rule, even on Dipavali day.

In the five-day celebrations the first day is for Lakshmi Puja, the next day for Krishna's victory over Narakasura called Naraka Chaturdasi. The bathing festival is on the fourth day and on the last day yama is worshipped. Jumuna is considered to be sister of yama and so every boy is expected to dine with his sister. If one has no sister, a cousin is substituted. He is substituted. He is expected to present jewellery to his sister. Elders offer prayers to Yama, Lord of Death at noon and bathe in the Jumuna and offer prayers to their ancestors.

Diwali is celebrated in different ways in Rajasthan mud vessels are replaced, and metal vessels are cleaned and polished. The artistic docoration of the floors, roofs, and courtyard is the highlight. The ladies of the household take their special baths, prepared in almond powder and barley, which is said to enhance the smoothness of the skin and complexion. They decorate their palms with colourful lines with the help of henna leaves. They dress themselves gaily in attractive clothes and move about in groups.

Yama is known as Dharamaraja and dogs believed to be the incarnation of Yama, are fed. Lamps made of flour paste are lighted after filling them with ghee. This is done on the previous day, and the next day is the Amavasya Day (new moon) on which the Diwali festival is celebrated. Temple worship is reserved for this day.

The Bhils of Rajasthan send gifts and prased to their friends and relatives. The prasad is said to cure any illness. The animals are bathed, and their horns coloured. Pen and ink pots are worshipped probably because they are used for opening new accounts.

Jains observe this festival as the death anniversary of Mahavira, founder of Jainism, who attained Nirvana on Diwali day. There are historical references to show that even Muslim rulers celebrated Diwali on a grand scale. The Sikhs observe the festival by illuminating the Golden Temple at Amritsar. Their sixth Guru, Hargovind, was released on the Diwali day during the reign of Jahangir.

In Maharashtra people celebrate the festival on a grand scale as it is said that Shivaji went on an expendition against the rulers on on that day. Children build small mud forts and illuminate them. In Bengal, Kali is worshipped instead of Lakshmi. Young girls light and float lamps in the river. The lamps should not sink or change their course for, if they do, it is considered a bad men. If they sail smoothly the whole year is supposed to be smooth according to the general belief.

King Vikramaditya observed Diwali as his New Year Day. Rama of Ramayana, returned to Ayodhya after killing Ravana and crowned himself king. People celebrate the occasion by bursating of crackers and lighting of sparklers. There is a popular legend that Siva and Parvathi played dice and gambled on Diwali Day. Hence gambling is prevalent on Diwali nights. Results of this gambling are taken as the shape of things to come in the year.

Similarly, celebrations in Gujarat, Rajasthan, Uttar Pradesh, Bengal, Bihar, Punjab and other parts of the country are lively.

Even the hill tribes celebrate Diwali in their own way. They have many superstitious beliefs. Not only in India but also in far off Malaysia, Bali, Java, Indonesia, Sinam, Philippines, and Japan, this festival of lights is celebrated. In Nepal it is dedicated to birds and animals and rangolis are drawn.

N. RAMAKRISHNA

DRAMA (SANSKRIT) : A REAPPRAISAL

Dr. I.D. Shastri's recent publication Sanskrit Drama : Its Origin and Decline seems to establish the non-Aryan patronage as the stimu, ator for the growth and development of Sanskrit Drama. The traditional belief in the Aryan patronage as the cause of the flourish that Sanskrit drama enjoyed has received a severe jolt by the well-documented researches of Dr. Shastri. It has been pointed out that the development in drama and allied arts received very little incentive from vedic culture. The MohenjoDaro and Harappa excavations went to show the close proximity between the Indus Valley Civilization and the Dravidian culture in the south. These Dravidians, according to Dr. Shastri, were mainly responsible for the growth and development of sanskrit drama. In fact, Bharata, the celebrated author of Naryasastra was patronised by Nahusa, the 'detestable' Dasyu king of the Vedic days. Nahusa constructed a theatre hall for Bharata and his troupe for the performance of Sanskrit dramas and this enabled our traditional dramatic art and dramaturgy to flourish. Against this historical background there is conspicuous absence of any reference to Vedic traditions regarding dramatic art in Bharata's Natyasastra. Natyasastra, the greatest ancient work on dramaturgy presents a comprehensive study of stage, stage-craft and the art of acting. It has been claimed that there is no such knowledge, no such art, no such science and no such conceivable thought that has been left undiscussed in the Natyasastra, popularly known as the Fifth Veda. It is believed that Brahma, the Lord of creation gave to Bharata, the author of Natyasastra this precious gift while he was in meditation. The trasures of Sanskrit literature not only nurtured great dramas but also some outstanding works on dramaturgy. But Western scholars took no note of the vast treasures that were lying unredeemed in the store-house of Sanskrit literature and that is how prof. Knight could lament of the supposed lack of abstuse writing on the nature of art and asthetics in Indian languages, particularly in Sanskrit.

The classical Sanskrit drama reached the high watermark of perfection at the hands of Kalidasa. There are some other playwrights such as Bhasa, Bhavabhuti and Sudraka. Many of the great ancient dramatic works are lost but what remains of the priceless treasures evokes the interest of the discerning connoisseurs.

Our alamkarika differentiated between Natya, Rupa and Rupaka i.e. representation of emotions, presentation of individual situations and a regular drama. Rupaka or regular drama has been further sub-divided into Nataka, Prakarana, Bhana, Prahasana, Dima, Vyayoga, Samavakara, Veethi, Anka and Ihamriga. Dhananjaya's Dasarupaka elaborately discusses these different forms. Visvanath's Sahityadarpana makes clear and elaborate presentation of certain intricate issues relating to the above classification. The Sanskrit drama opens with a benedictory stanza (Nandi sloka). Then there is a prologue (Prasthavana) to follow. This prologue presents a description of the author, his works and indicates the types of characters that are to enter the stage. The hero, according to the classical Sanskrit conception, must be 'Dhirodatta' i.e. he should be heroic, noble and notable. The prevailing rasa is generally taken to be sringara or love and vira or heroism. There are other rasas contributory to the main. Sanskrit dramas have been prescribed five acts. These acts have been prohibited to exhibit battle, crude amorous acts such as kissing of the stage; some have been prohibited on moral grounds and others on technical grounds. A Sanskrit drama usually ends with Bharata-vakva or prayer. Amongst the other rapakas, prakarana and prahasana deserve special mention. Real life provides the plot for prakarana. It resembles life though it does not copy life in its details. It were a mere copy it would have lost all its charm and freshness. The concept of 'Niyatikrita niyamarahita' enjoins on every kind of work of art not to be sub-servient to nature. Art imitates nature and at the same time transcends it. So in prakarana life is represented no doubt but not imitated. Prahasana is a farce. Its main object is incongruity, suddenness and unexpectedness; they make a situation comic. Our ancient Sanskrit aestheticians prescribe that every drama must have a plot (vastu), a hero (Neta) and sentiment (Rasa). They clearly lay down the stages through which the plot should proceed from its commencement to its finish (Karya).

Sanskrit drama is nearer in spirit to the modern romantic drama than to the classical drama. The ideal for this type of romantic drama was 'soaring individualism' which sought to blend the finite and the infinite. The concept of 'Dhirodatta' type of heroes is a close approximation to this 'soaring indiviualism'. Sanskrit drama had a preference for rich profusion of adornment and herein they resembled the modern drama. Sanskrit dramas lacked the self-restrained simplicity of Greek dramas. Romantic art is careless about the unities of time and place and only cared about the unity of action. This distinctive characteristic of romantic art was also present in Sanskrit dramas and the two agreed in this respect. The benevolent and benign touch of nature made the dramatic theme in romantic art lit up in a glorious blaze and this happened in Sanskrit dramas as well. The treatment of love in the Sanskrit dramas was mostly pure, lofty and noble. Tagore this characterised Kalidas's treatment of love in his dramas.

"The ancient poet of India refuses to acknowledge passion as the supreme glory of love. Truly in Sakuntala there is one Paradise Lost and another Paradise Regained.

This treatment of love has been criticised by some as inspired by a didactic mission of art. If art claims to be a teacher of mankind, it ceases to be art qua art. But this objection does not hold goods because of the tacit acceptance of the identity of the true, the beautiful and the good. The order of beauty is not a different order and as such the law of Karma has been shown to be operative in the Sanskrit dramas. The characters and events in the drama follow a cause-effect sequence and this nexus ultimately leads to the conclusion. The concept of a gracious Lord capable of overruling the natural and causal order has been freely used in the Sanskrit dramas. The Lord links the natural with the super-natural in his acts of grace and the Sanskrit drama makes use of his law of Karma and the Abode of Grace more freely than the Greek idea of Nemesis or the modern idea of the defect of will or the evolutionary taint or the social malformation. This has contributed largely to the excellence of Sanskrit dramas and thus many of them, though written centuries back, are still read, rehearsed and appreciated all over the world. Its inherent excellence satisfactorily solves the problem of communication; and the hurdles of language, age and clime do not deter its universal acceptance.

S. K. NANDI

DRAMA FOLK

The history of Indian folk drama as back to the years before christ. The ancient Indian epics Ramayana and Mahabharata contain references to the art, and later they were themselves propagated through this medium. A farce staged by Greek solidors and traders on the west coast in association with local folk artistes in the second century A.D. is on record.

ART TRADITIONS

Because he laid so much stress on religion and tradition, the indian village artists went for his themes to the great epics and the Puranas which yielded so much romance relition, mystery and morality, all at the same time. Dance, song and gesture went to make the theatrical unity that was the hallmark of the Hindu dramatic art. The village play highlighted the most ancient theartical principle which would regard the players and the audience as a single entity, which the audience obligingly making way for the actors as they walked up to and from the green room, and joining those on the stage in community singing and the like.

In the emphasis they placed on deities that governed natural phenomena and human fate, Indian folk plays bore a resemblance to the Greek concept. It was the people's belief that the change of season of the fall of rain had to do with the divine will, which operated these elements as a blessing or as a curse to reward or punish humanity according to its deserts. On festival days or at harvest time or one the occasion of religious ceremonies the coarse but deeply felt portrayals of Krishna and Rama and all the rest of the pantheon made a great impact on the rustic people, purifying their emotions and turning their eyes inward upon their souls. There was no stage equipment to speak of, no stage even-only some kind of raised platform - and only the crudest makeup and consume: but all this was irrelevant to the appreciation of the show by those present. The language employed by the characters was uncouth though vigorous; and Krishna or Rama behaved like a villager, only one somewhat higher in rank. Yet the lesson went home.

PUPPET SHOWS

Puppet shows and shadow plays were other forms of rural histrionics. In the first, two or three foot- high doll made of wood and cloth performed on the stage, human like, while unseen hands from over the curtain adjusted their movements with the master touch by means of strings. Episodes from the epics that pointed a-moral and adorned a tale were rendered realistically by these puppet players. Playing the roles of traditional heroes and villains, the inanimate dolls danced, gesticulated, displayed their passions and emotions, sang, and even entered into long discourse, thanks to the human voices behind the curtain that synchonized so admirably with the puppets' gestures. Before his very eyes the spectator witnessed the triumph of good over evil, of life over Dealth, and thereby the himself gained immortality.

SHADOW PLAYS

Shadow plays were of two kinds. One was the art of projecting on a white screen silhouette shadows of dolls acting and dancing. This seems to have been mostly in the hands of itinerant troupes who travelled from village to village, gave their shows in street corners and were rewarded with what aims the village spectators chose to give. A number of dolls, an earthen lamps, a white upper cloth and a drum were the paraphernalia of these wandering artistes. This kind of shadow play is now all but extinct.

The type that is still current is the Andhra shadow play, in which Puranic characteres ornamentally painted on flat leather strips are thrown against a white screen from behind a well-lit stage and manipulatd to move, act and dance by means of ling, thin bamboo sticks. Though the back-ground music is rather crude, the rhythmic sense is strong and unerring. The story is interspersed with long interludes of boisterous fund and racy anecdotes which send the audience roaring with laughter and later others took it up by turns.

YAKSHAGANA

The Yakshagana provided the basis of a Bailata, from that is part opera, part ballet, and part straight dialogue. "Bailata" means "field play", and it is staged in the open field after the crop has been harvested, the players having mugged up the dialogue during the slack season. The show is financed by contributions from the local bigwigs, sometimes by just one or two of them, but is open to all, and is in fact the highest of village entertainment.

All eyes are turned towards the rought and ready platform that goes for the stage where the Bhagawata or the director introduces the evening's theme. Now comes dancing on to the stage, right from the green room some distance away, and scattering the audience on his way, a guadily costumed character who goes on dancing until he is stopped by the Sarathi who demands to know who he is, "I am Bhima", he cries in stentorian tones,"slayer of Duryodhana, destroyer of the kauravas, strong man of the pandavas". And he proceeds to rattle off, in words of learned length and thoundering sound, a lengthy list of his titles, his deeds, his merits and his valovous plays. Only then does the character, having duly impressed the audience and been formally introduced by the sarathi, establish himself on the stage. The Bhagawata or the stage director is the main singer and the songs are sung not only by the character concerned but in chorus by the entire troupe seated in the wings of the theatre. Song and dance and dialogue go on till morning when the audience returns home in high ecstasy.

Variations of this form were common to all parts of India because of the fundamental unity of ideals and the universal reverence for the epics through out the country. Moreover, hands of wandering players carried the traditions of one province to another. The Rasadharis of Mathura in Northern India, whose theme was the exploits of the Krishna, beloved of the young and old alike, were a picturesque institution. Two boys played the roles of Krishna and his consort Radha, and others of cowherds and milkmaids, whom the young Krishna made it his occupation to tease and to please. The performance culminated in a merry-of-round when the fascinating cowherd Krishna with a peacock crown and perfumed garland danced and san with the chorus. The devout spectators were so sensitive that for the time they often worshiped the boy as the actual deity.

RAMLILA

Another North Indian feature is the Ramlila or the festival of Ram, which is said to have originated in the famous version of Ramayana by Tulsidas in 1574. The Ramlila celebration signifying the victory of god Rama over the demon king Ravana of Lanka, was marked by exceptional splendour. Nearly the whole of the Ramayana was read through in the course of 20 or 30 days and whatever incidents were capable of being acted or displayed were simultaneously depicted in pantomime.

Yet another North Indian form is the Nautanki, kind of folk opera, mainly recalling medieval romances and tales of heroes. Then there are the Nakal and the Soung, which are popular types of farce and burlesque, probably modern versions of the ancient Indian Bhana and Prahasana.

YATRA

Foremost among the folk plays prevalent in Bengal was the Yatra (or Jatra), described as a "sacred opera" connected with the religious processions or carnivals got up by devotees of Sri Krishna. The exploits of Krishna, Rama or Siva, some selected popular medieval tales, or even imaginary situations and characters could be the subject of these Yatras, but Krishna, stealer of curds and despair of the gopis, with his romantic background and slapdash antics, was an easy favourite. "Yatra" literally means a pilgrimage, procession, or carnival. Crowds celebrating the festival of a deity marched in a procession singing his glories to the accompaniment of simple musical instruments, and danced in temple, courtyard or street. In the early stages the Yatravalas used to improvise the music and the words of the plays to suit the occasion, literary composition being rather at a discount. Even so, however, there was a method in their madness, if so it was, for certain conventions had been set up. Thus, in the case of the Krishna Yatra, Jayadeva, author of Gitagovinda, laid down the method of presenting the Krishna love-story.

Only men took part in the acting of the Yatra. The performance took place on the bare ground, without any scenic representation. A long piece of cloth in the rear served to make some space for the gree room. The players sang in chorus with the leader lingering behind and occasionally tweaking the ear of an errant youth in sight of the audience.

Bearing a close resemblance to the Bengali Yatras were the Jatras in vogue in the Marathi - specaking region encompassing Goa and the adjacent area of the Konkan. The Dashavatari Khel (ten incarnations of God vishnu) was another popular variation of the same theme. The play took place in temple halls or inns with the aid of a curtain or two, the sutradhara or manager serving as a Greek chorus and the vidushaka or clown being the privileged ready - witted man coming in and going out as he pleased. The play started with a prayer; then Ganapati, the auspicious deity came in with his elephant trunk, and the manager sang his praise and received his blessings. The goddess of learning, Saraswati, rode in her peacock. The whole story was told in action, and as the Mahrattas are a warlike people, they were fond of demonstrating their fighting skill on the stage.

TAMASHA

Because of this warlike quality, and because Mahratta power was still a dominant feature of Western India till the middle of the 19th century, the Marathi stage was particularly imbuid with the sense of national awareness. Historical plays about the famous Mahratta heroes from Shivaji downwards were written and presented. As these were banned by the alien Government, the Marathi dramatists invented more subtle devices to put their ideas across in allegorical fantasies or farcical comedies. One of these was the tamasha, an indigenous form of folk dance-cum-drama, which being exempt from precensorship came to be resorted to as the medium to convey what was prohibited on the conventional urban stage. Inforrned by subtle political propaganda, it fired the heart of rural India with a longing for freedom.

It would be no exaggeration to say that these early rural performances held the seeds that were later to blossom out into the plays of the present day. There is freshness of fancy here, a free treatment of materials, a rich fund of humour, and at times a true sense of the profound and the tragic. The banishment of the sweet and virtuous Sita in the Ramlila, the sufferings of Draupadi in the Mahabharata plays, and the heroic self-sacrifice of king Harishchandra in the cause of righteousness, are instances in point. Although lacking in refinement and standards of artistic production, these plays possessed a tremendous amount of vitality and exercised a profound impact on the emotions of the masses.

The classic theatre in India has been created and developed by masters who were of the people and not freaks isolated from the community; which means that as the highest forms of art expression have come from the community as a whole, their cultural level must have been high. Whatever the economic divisions might have been, the vast masses were not so completely divorced from culture influences. Had not the people been the repositories of the nation's culture, all or most of it would have been lost. From generation to generation, at least some of the great truths that the ancient discovered, the philosophies they founded, the arts they evolved, these treasures reverently nurtured in the unsophisticated bosom of the vast concourse, have been saved for posterity.

FOLK ARTISTES AND THEIR ART

Today Indian folk drama, moving with the times, is taking note of the changing face of India and the vast development activities in the shape of the Five-Year Plan and other projects such as the defence of India from foreign aggression. The folk artiste by carrying the story of the plan through the medium of his art to the villages, where throbs the hearts of India, is helping to make it a real, living, dynamic thing to the villagers. The Government for its part is doing all it can to revive and develop folk drama and to create a consciousness among the more sophisticated sections of the country's population of the value and glory of village arts. Folk forms forgotten during the recent years of foreign rule are being brought again to the notice of the urban population through documentary motion pictures produced by the Government. The Government is also giving financial grants and other forms of aid to drama troups operating in the villages. Use is being made of number of surviving folk forms in different parts of the country. For, when all is said and done, the village show is good, and the show must go on.

BINOD RAO

DUNGARPUR : QUITE A SURPRISE

"Dungarpur is quite a surprise.... it contains one of the most carefully preserved of the older generation of Rajput Palaces and one the most extravagantly unusual of the newer creations." The reference is to the old palace called the Juna Mahal. While the newer creation is the Udai Bilas, now part of the legendary Heritage Hotels of Rajasthan.

The Dungarpur State was founded in the thirteenth century and its Sisodia Rajput rulers traced their ancestry to the elder branch of the famous house of Mewar at Chittorgarh. For about a hundred years, the seat of authority was based at a place known as Vatpadrak or Baroda. It was in the middle of the fourteenth century that the capital was shifted to where the present township of Dungarpur stands. Apart from other reasons, the site was surely chosen for strategic reasons as it lies in the midst of hills and appropriately called Dungarpur which literally means "the city of hills". After its establishment as the state capital, Dungarpur retained that position for the next six hundred years or so until 1947, when with the merger of states in the Union of India, it was made the headquarters of the present Dungarpur district.

Dungarpur is easily accessible by road from Udaipur to Ahmedabad and is almost equidistant from both these places. As one approaches, the sight of the old palace, the Juna Mahal, looming out of the hillside above the town is striking and impressive. It is virtually as ancient as the township and has grown steadily over the past six centuries under the command of several rulers. The visible part of the massive structure is seven-storied, but there are two more storeys below the ground floor level. The basement also has provision for storage of ample water, ·very essential in such traditional fort palace, which had to withstand enemy attacks and long sieges. Above the surface, there are the crenellated walls and narrow passages, turrets and watch-towers, peep holes and weapon slits, rising storey by storey in graduated form, so typical of an olden time structure such as this.

The real attraction of the Juna Mahal lies in its interior art and decor, which is very colourful, intricate and remarkably intact despite the vicissitudes of time. Right at the top is a lovely Sheesh Mahal called the Fateñ Prakash, which has intense glass and mirror inlay work. The decorative designs are large and generous which, along with the profusion of colour, have a very pleasing effect. At the lower levels, the Durbar Hall and the Am Khas are worth seeing. Both have richly painted decorations and plenty of glass inlay work. Then, there are delightful miniature wall and ceiling frescoes, which are remarkably fresh. The ceilings are supported by beams resting on corbels and pilasters and, at places, on free standing columns of the temple sort, while the doors and windows are mostly in cusped arch form. The fine lime plaster on the walls and floors looks like polished marble.

Throughout the massive structure, there is a profusion of balconies and Jharokas. A very striking feature is the selective use of a local bluish-gray stone called Pareva, which lends itself to very fine and intricate working. Many of the balconies and Jharokas are made of this stone. It has been used also for decorative carved tablest embedded in the walls or serving as balustrades in the balconies. In effect, it is a rather unique example of this kind of temple decoration built into palace architecture.

The Juna Mahal is still owned by the royal family and has lately been converted into a private museum. It is open to special guests and visitors staying at the Udai Bilas, the construction of which was started in the late 19th century by Maharawal Udai Singh II and hence, was named after him. Its location by the side of the lovely Gaipsagar lake, facing the township, is idyllic. The original design conceived and executed by the local artisans, known as Silavats, was of a full-fledged palace wing overlooking the lake, made of the indigenous Pareva stone, and a marvellous structure called the Ek Thambia Mahal, which is literally the one-pillared palace. With its intricately sculptured arches, pillars and panels, ornately bracketed canopies, windows and balconies, finely worked marble carvings and friezes as well as marble inlaid with semi-precious stones, this is one of its type and certainly an architectural piece de resistance.

In 1898, Maharawal Udai Singh passed away and was succeeded by his grandson, Maharawal Bijay Singh. He had an artistic and literary temperament and was responsible for starting the construction of a lovely Shiva Temple on a small island on the lake adjacent to Udai Bilas. This is the Vijairajrajeshwar temple, which is easily approchable from the palace premises in a paddle boat.

The next important phase in the evolution of the present day Udai Bilas was in the 1940s during the time of the late Mahrawal Lakshman Singh. He carried out extensive additions by building three new wings around the Ek Thambia Mahal and creating a very attractive courtyard, which encircles it on all sides and enhances its aesthetic appeal, apart from providing much needed protection. The walls of the courtyard are made of the soft Pareva stone, which has been rendered into very fine friezes, engravings and filigreed balconies. For the floor and some tastefully placed platforms, white marble has been used liberally, In effect, the courteard is so well designed that it merges beautifully with the original architecture of the palace and has virtually emerged as the centrepiece, with access to all the main parts of the premises.

Maharawal Lakshman Singh was a versatile personality and had an eye for details. He established the banquet hall, the private dining room, the sitting rooms for different occasions and the various living rooms. Each received his personal attention and was done up tastefully and elegantly. With attractive marble staircases added and modern amentities provided in the living rooms, the outcome was a grand and comfortable palace. In a sense, this set the stage for converting the premises into a heritage hotel.

Yet another interesting feature of Dungarpur district is that it is the home and heartland of the Bheel tribals, who are the original inhabitants of this whole region covering south Rajasthan and the adjoining tracts in the states of Gujarat and Madhya Pradesh. Their traditional customs and mode of living, including their music and dance, are fascinating indeed. So also are their fairs and festivals, which invariably attract large gatherings of these tribals from far and near. The most notable is the Baneshwar fair held at the confluence of the Mahi and Som rivers in the month of February. Other important fairs are the Kartik Poornima fair held during November at the temple border and the Gokul Ashtami fair held at Aspur during the monsoon period.

SAMAR SINGH

DUSSEHRA CELEBRATIONS IN KULU

Dussehra celebrations in Kulu have a unique quality of their own. While celebrations of this festival in different parts of the country conclude, these begin here for a seven-day long ritual which attracts tourists not only from different parts of India but also from abroad.

Kulu is a picturesque town of the Indian state of Himachal Pradesh and easily accessible by road and air. It is sandwiched between two hills and the enchanting river Beas runs parallel to it. The whole Kulu is swept by the religious fervour. The people here strongly believe in their local gods and goddessess. More than hundred temples and a very large number of "Devtas" (deities) can be encountered here. In fact, every village in the valley has its own deity. The most powerful among them all, however, is said to be Lord Raghunath (Lord Rama).

The seven-day Dussehra festival begins with the Rathyatra of Lord Raghunath. Deities from different villages are also taken out in colourful palanquins.

During the celebrations a trade-fair is also organised. It provides ample opportunity for the locals as well as people from higher reaches to purchase goods they need for the rest of the year.

Folk dances from every district of the state are also performed at an open air theatre in the evenings to jampacked audiences.

However, with the passage of time, religious character of the fair is giving way to trade and entertainment. That perhaps explains the popularity kulu Dussehra is gaining with every passing year.

RUBY THINDA

'DWARKA' OF SOUTH INDIA

Guruvayur is one of the most important pilgrimage centres in India and is also referred to as the Dwarka of South India.

Legend goes that the temple dedicated to Lord Krishna was destroyed when the holy city of Dwarka was submerged under the sea. Guru, the Preceptor of gods and Vayu, the god of wind, were entrusted with the task of finding an equally holy place for a new temple. At the end of a long quest for an appropriate site, they entered Kerala and met Parsurama, the legendary creator of Kerala. He led them to a beautiful lake ful of lotuses, the present temple tank, Rudratiratha. Here, Lord Shiva and His consort Parvati welcomed them and the idol of Shri Krishna was duly installed at this spot, lovingly called Guruvayurappan, or Lord of Guruvayur.

The main entrance to Shri Krishna temple is called Eastern Nada or Bhooloka Vaikuntam. In the outer enclosure called Chuttambalam stads the tall 33.5 mt high gold-plated flag-post called dhwajastambam and the 7mt high deepastambba or pillar of lamps, whose thirteen circular receptacles provide a truly gorgeous spectacle when lit. The entrance to the inner precincts lies just beyond this. Within are ten exquisitely carved pillars on two raised platforms, one on either side of the passage. Bhattatiti, the devoted bhakta of Guruvayurappan believed to have sat here, composing the famous Narayaniyam, the great Sanskrit poetical work comprising 1035 slokas in praise of the Lord.

The sacred sanctum sanctorum of the temple is the square, two-storeyed Srikoil where the main deity is housed. Made of a particular stone called Patala Anjanam, this beautiful idol of Sri Krishna with four arms carrying the conch, the discus, the mace and the lotus is adorned with a tulsi garland and pearl necklaces. The deity is well known for its healing powers.

Within the temple are also the images of Ganapati Lord Ayyappan (the son of Shiva by Mohini) and Edattedattu Kavil Bhagavati (Goddess Durga).

The temple opens at 3.00 a.m. for the Nirmalayam darshan to the melodious strains of the nadaswaram and the devoted chanting of "Narayana, Narayana". For this darshan, considered especially auspicious, the Lord is adorned with folowers and garlands from the previous day.

The idol is then ritually bathed and dressed to represent Balagopala or Krishna as a child. The important Uchoha Pooja take place at mid-day. During the dirapradbana, the elaborately bedecked idol glows in the warm light of the temple lamps. The temple closes at 10.00 pm after day-long Poojas, rites and processions.

Besides the famous Sri Krishna temple, Guruvayur also has other famous shrines, which attract crowds of pilgrims. Lord Shiva's shrine at Mammiyur, just half a kilometer away, is believed to be of greater antiquity than the Sri Krishna temple. The Parathasarathi temple, close to the Sri Krishna, deifies Lord Krishna as Arjuna's charioteer. Half a kilometer to the north-east of the Parathasarathi temple is a shrine of Venkatachalapati of Tirupati. Other shrines are Perunathatta Shiva Temple and Tamarayur Vishnu temple.

PRIYANKA

"E"

ELEPHANTA FESTIVAL

More than 13 centuries old Elephanta caves come to life when the pegeant of music and dance is presented every year in the month of February when the Maharashtra Tourism Development Corporation organises the Elephanta Festival. Some of the finest Indian artistes drawn from various fields perform during the Festival.

The history of Elephanta cave temple is lost in the hoary mist of time. Crowning the island's eastern hill, where the temple is situated, and commanding a panoramic view of woodland, marsh and sea are the Buddhist 'stupas' or burial mounds and cistern. Once known as Puri, later Gharapuri, this island was the proud capital of a coastal kingdom and the seat of this great cave shrine set up in praise of Lord Shiva, excavated in the sixth century. Several centuries later the Portuguese took possession of the island. They found a monlithic stone elephant at the place where they landed and so named this as 'liha do elephanta', island of the elephant.

There is no outer elevation to the temple, only natural contours of the hill. The architect sculptors, in a feat of unmatched skill, penetrated deep into the solid basalt rock to create a representation of the heavenly mountain residence of 'Shiva'. The cave temple opens out on three sides, letting in light from various angles so that the sculptures seem to move and shift in the transition from light to shadow. Inside the temple is a large pillared hall, with rows of columns, that seem to hold up the roof of the cave. The plan of the temple is symmetrical with important focal points worked out in a geometrical 'mandala' - the magical design that represents an energy field.

At the western end of the cave is the quiet, serene centre of Elephanta, the sanctuary of the 'linga'. Two smaller shrines flak the eastern and western entrances to the main cave. The northern entrance, opening out to the sea, is the one that is easily accessible and used today. The eastern entrance leads straight to the sanctuary of the 'linga' and was probably used when the cave temple was an active centre of worship.

These world-famous caves also house the awe-inspiring 18-foot high Maheshmurti (Shiva's statue). This amazing figure captures the essence of Hindu philosophy with its portrayal of the three eternal forms of Shiva : Creator, Preserver and Destroyer. Even older than the caves are the island's Buddhist burial mounds.

So as to focus the attention of tourists, from both home and abroad, this Festival is organised annually here so that one can see the marval called Elephanta Caves.

L. K. BAKHSHI

ELLORA CAVES : (4TH TO 13TH CENTURY A.D.)

North-West of Aurangabad (Hyderabad), 16 Brahmanical, 12 Buddhist and 5 Jain rock-cut cave temples range along-side each other at the foot of a cliff about 33 m. high, hewn down-wards out of the living rock into temples with many sculptured ornamentations of gods, goddess and other figures and much carved ornamentation, decoration, etc. The most magnificent expression of architectural splendour is the Brahanical Kailas temple (c. 8th century) which is a complete temple in mixed Dravidian and northern styles, on a stupendous scales and took a century to be completed. Through made in the rock itself, has all the features of a Hindu temple- including a double-storeyed gate house flanked by stone pillars about 17 m. high standing in front of the edifice, pillars, collonades, side chambers, small shrines, flying bridges, etc., all beautiful sculpured. It is dedicated to Siva, Kailas being his eternal heaven in the Himalayas. The sculptured grandeur, the sublimity of execution and the deep religious feeling accompanying the complex, make it the final example of rock-cut Indian architecture.

References

Acharya, P.K., An Encyclopaedia of Hindu Architecture, Calcutta-1946.

EMBROIDERY : THE CRAFT OF GYPSIES

The normadic Indian gypsies, Banjaras or Lambadis, belonging to Andhra Pradesh, Gujarat, Rajasthan, Madhya Pradesh, etc. are well known for their picturesque appearance; their embroidered garments are embellished with large mirrors, tussles, coins and cowrie shells. The patterns and colours are bold and bright, the stitches varied and the work extremely fine. In fact so fine that both the sides look alike.

Women of this community generally wear a full length skirt (Ghagra) generally in blazing red or maroon or black colour with borders embroidered in mustard, green, yellow and red threads, The odhni which covers the head, is long enough to drape down their backs almost touching the feet. Their cholis (blouses) are also eleborately embroidered and studded with little mirrors in striking colour scheme.

The tribals of India, especially from Gujarat, are also very fond of decorating their houses, household articles, mud walls and floors and doorways.

The inhabitants of the Kutch region of Gujarat try to compensate their dull environs by spreading colours all around through their garments. embroideries, jewellery, mirror work, tie and dye and applique work.

Embroidered toran, decorated doorway, tiny mirror studded kothi (a kind of box) and tiny mirror - embedded mud-plastered walls enhance the beauty of their houses. They also decorate their mud- plastered walls with folk motifs in many colours. Gujarat probably produced a greater wealth and variety of embroidery than any other Indian state. Kutch is famous for its rich variety of embroidery work in varying techniques and styles. It is a traditional craft, handed down from generation to generation.

The most popular and famous embroidery of the needle work of Kutch is known as "Mochi Bharat", It is also called "AAri Bharat". The artists never draw a design on paper or cloth in advance before starting embroidery; they just reproduce it from their memory. Their patterns are full of leaves, fruits, flowers, birds and animals and human figures.

'Kanbi Bharat' is another styles of embroidery which is extensively practised by the cultivating caste of Kanbi. It is mainly done in chain stitcht and in bright yellow and orange colours. "Banni Bharat" with its intricate minute designs in gorgeous colours, is considered to be the most outstanding and exquisite among the different type of Kutch embroidery. The Jats, a sub-caste of Bannis, are known for their refined embroidery here is the execution of architectural designs known as "Hear Bharat".

The tribals of Rajasthan execute embroidery but in a different style. They do it by counting threads. The use of double stitch methods results in creating an effect on both sides, giving a semblace of dancing figures, flowers, peacocks and Mandala, the tree of life, as these are popular motifs.

The best of their embroidery can be seen on their religious ceremonies, weddings and festivals. It is on these occasions that each caste proudly establishes its identity by wearing its own highly distinctive and original embroidered garments.

DR. BIMLA VERMA

EMBROIDERY OF CHAMBA RUMALS

The charming valley of Chamba lies in Himachal Pradesh, which has been given the staturs of a full-fledged State since 25th January, 1971. It covers an approximate area of 3,216 sq. miles. the picturesque town of Chamba was the capital of ancient Brahmaputra on the bank of river Ravi and derives its name from Champawati, a daughter of Raja Sahilla-Varman (A.D. 902). The Chamasni temple there is also named after her. Brahmor (ancient Brahmapura), the capital of Chamba, not only continued to be the seat of political power till the 10th century A.D., but also as a centre of artistic activity which produced several splended temples, magnificent seculpture, and intricate wood-carvings, These are datable to about the 7th to the 17th century A.D. Even in the centuries that followed, a fascinating school of minature painting flourished in the region, which occupies a place of pride among the Pahari School of miniatures.

Another artistic field in which Chamba is famous is embroidery, popularly known as Chamba rumals. This craft in which the hill artists engaged themselves during their leisure seems to the quite old, but the extant examples are datable only to the 18th century. This needle-work of a ground artistic nature developed into a special kind of textile with patterns embroidered in silk threads of different lively colours. The rumal was hand-spun (cotton), usually square in shape, and used generally as covers or decorative pieces. Mainly, two kinds of hand-spun cloth is used for these rumals, viz., mal-mal, a fine twin fabric and khaddar, a coarse thick fabric. Hand-spun yarn is used in the manufacture of these special varieties of cloth, which is generally unbleached.

PAINTINGS TRANSLATED INTO EMBROIDERY

The origin of these rumals, their designs, themes and their techniques of embroidery are interesting studies.

"These rumals", as Dr. Kramrisch observes, "are paintings translated into embroidery, like Guler, Nurpur, Kangra, Basholi and Chamba. The soft flowing lines of both the flowers and figures, of background vegetation, hills, trees, and shrubs, all recall the miniature composition in the Pahari styles". A Kangra painting depicting the Brahamin's wives carrying offerings to Krishna shows a casket covered with an embroidered rumal. The painting is presserved in the State Museum, Lucknow.

The technique employed in the embroidery of rumals can also be seen in the embroidered cholis or blouses, scarves, fans, caps, pillows, dice-cloth (Chaupads), bedspreads, celling-covers (chandoas), etc.

First the outline of the pattern was drawn in black, normally with a fine charcoal stick. The embroidery, a double satin stich carried forward and backward alternately, was done on both the sides of the cloth. The untwisted and dyed silk thread of a variety of pleasing colours was used in these rumals. The colours frequently used were blue, green, orange, yellow, red, etc. No Chamba rumal embroidered with a single colour has yet come to light.

Some of the Chamba rumals were influenced by the technique of the phulkaris of Punjab. In these examples the entire field is covered with floral and geometrical patterns. Horizontal, vertical and diagonal stitches are employed to bring out various motifs, a distinctive one being that of Bagh, or the garden, rectangular in layout.

DESIGNS AND MOTIFS

The main designs, motifs and subjects of these rumals are (1) Geometrical designs (2) Floral designs (3) Religious scenes from the Ramayana, Krishna-lila and other mythological stories and (4) Secular scenes of marriage, hunting, musicians and courts, nayaka-nayika, bheda, Ragas and Raginis, etc.

The geometrical designs consist of horizontal or vertical lines, squares, rectangles, circles, crosses, dots etc. The vegetative designs include creepers, scrolls, trees, guldasta, etc.

RELIGIOUS FIGURES

The central space of the rumal is generally occupied by religious figures, such as dancing Radha and Krishna, four-armed Vishnu and his various incarnations, Krishna-lila, Rasamandala, Rukminiharana, Ganesha worshipped by women, Rama and Sita enthroned, Lakshminarayana, Uma-Maheshwara, various forms of Durga, etc. These themes tell us about the religious beliefs of the people and provide a peep into their devoted hearts. Of these, the Rasamandala is depicted where Radha and Krishna are dancing in the centre within a circle having a floral band. This is enclosed by a dancing circle composed of five gopinis with five figures of Krishna. Four figures of seated musicians, one at each of the four corners, keep the rhythm. Along the edges, there is a border of flowers and creepers.

In another rumal in the centre is a round face of Surya with prominent moustache and a third eye with flames radiating on all sides. This is framed by alternate figures of Radha and Krishna forming the Rasamandala scene. The entire composition is enclosed within floral designs and creepers.

SECULAR SCENES

The secular subjects depicted on these rumals provide a running commentary on the contemporary social life of the people, their customs, their manners, their pastimes, etc. A favourite subject was the marriage procession with all its fanfare, dance and music. Similarly, various kinds of heroes and heroines (Nayaka-nayika-bneda), musical modes and melodies (ragas and reginis), the hunting in hilly land-scape (shikargah), the game of dice (chaupad) are all picturesquely emboidered on these rumals. The court scenes and palaces, with their architectural forms, reveal the contemporary taste.

Although the charming ladies of Chamba, who patiently embroidered these beautiful rumals did not usually inscribe their names on their words yet occasionally we come across a specimen with the name of the embroiderer.

The contemporary dresses, musical instruments, architecture, trees, animals and birds, in all their variety, are depicted on these rumals. The head-dress and the lower garments for the male figures are interesting. In the Rasmandala scenes, Krishna is shown with a conical headgerar with protruding folded ends at the sides, typical of Chamba painting. The lower dress is short with a flowing band and a knot at the waist. Some male figures wear tight fitting Churidar-pyjama, The folowing chaddar draped from the back invariably flows on the two sides flappant with the movement of the figures. The dress of the women performing the dance or in attendance, is equally peculiar. The dupatta covering the back of the head falls apart in front. The ghagaras have horizontal or vertical bands of various colours with a contrasting border. The Kamaraband or waist-band is also known.

The characteristic musical instruments of the hill States are also depicted on these rumals. They include a flute called ranasinga, ramtula which is a curved blowing instument of copper, kahal, various kinds of drums and dholak or dholki, nagara, kartala (cymbals) sitara and the tanpura, etc.

Some rumals show various palaces, the architectural form of which is straight trebeate type with small minarets and typical arched niches.

FLORAL DESIGNS

A variety of trees, such as the willow, cypress, plantain, often with flowers and fruits, are also found embroidered in magnificent colours.

A large number of animals and birds have also been depicted. They include running deers, prancing horses, running boars, fleeting rams, leaping tigers, all dynamic and vivacious. The birds include ducks, swans, peacocks, parrots, single or in pair.

The Chamba rumals have been essentially a product of the household industry. The women in the house, whether the mother, the wife or the daughter, fruitfully spent her leisure in creating these beautiful specimens of folk art having the charm of miniature paintings. In all probability, these were used on festive occasions, and they formed an important item in the bridal dowry. At times, these may have been used as gifts or as furnishing and decorative articles. Unlike any other art, these rumals have an intimate touch of life of the common people.

References

Anand, Mulk Raj, "The Chamba Rumals", Western Railway Annual, Bombay, 1952.

Bhattacharya, A.K. Chamba Rumals, Indian Museum Calcutta, 1968.

French, J.C. "Art in Chamba", Art and Letters, Vol. 25 No : 2.

Ganguli, K.K. "Chamba Rumals", Journal of the Indian Society of Oriental Art, Calcutta, 1943, Vol. XI.

Singh, Puran, "Some Rumals from Chamba", Rupam, 1927, No.2.

Marg Publications, "Textiles and Embroideries of India", 1965.

SUJIT KUMAR BHATTACHARYA

"F"

FAIRS AND FESTIVALS OF ORISSA

Orissa is not only a land of magnificent monuments, golden beaches, precipitous waterfalls, sprawling lakes, healing hot springs, luxuriant forests, intricate handicraft, etc., but also a land of colourful fairs and festivals. Every season Orissa has a variety of occasions to celebrate. In fact, the festivals are as numerous as the days in the year, each with a difference. They open up a vista of age-old traditions and customs, rites and rituals, dance and delicacies. The mood of the people is up-be-at. They put in the best of their attire and ornaments and exhibit the way they lead their lives. There is no better occasion to see the people in their true costumes and pageantry.

These fairs and festivals are also occasion to see a large congregation of people from far and near including people from within and outside the country. Most of the festivals are associated with the innumerable shrines or family traditions. Almost every village or town has its own presiding deity. During the festivals the deities and the shrines, etc., are colourfully decorated and painted in the traditional way.

On many festive occasions, fairs are invariably a part of such festivals as exhibit the local craft and cuisine. Amidst such festivities the visitors also get a chance to learn about the legends, folk lores and stroies of the past and present through dance, music and drama performances by artistes.

Given below are glimpses of important fairs and festivals of orissa.

MAKAR MELA

Makar Sankranti is celebrated with gusto in mid-January when the Sun enters the zodiacal stretch of Capricon. The Sun God is worshipped with great fervour and enthusiasm by one and all. The festival can be best enjoyed at Kalijai (an island in Chilika), Atri, Ghatgaon, Keonjhar, Jashipur and Jagatsinghpur.

PARAVA : A TRIBAL DANCE FESTIVAL

With 62 tribes Orissa is rich in tribal culture. The simple tribes have developed a host of dance forms to enjoy their life after a day's hard work. With a view to unfolding this aspect of the tribal culture a festival of tribal dances known as Parava is organised in Koraput during january every year. Tribal dancers with their traditional costumes and typical head gears ammuse the visitors. Also, a large exhibition of tribal crafts and cultural programmes is held at Bhubneswar as a part of the Republic Day celebrations.

FOLK DANCE FESTIVAL AT SAMBALPUR

Besides the classical Odissi dance, a festival of the rich folk dances of Orissa is organised at Sambalapur from January 4 to 6 to present glimpses of folk dances like Karama, Dalkhai, etc. The scintilating dances accompanied by rhythmic music-vocal and instrumental-keep the visitors spell-bound.

MAGHA MELA

The most popular and colourful festival of Konark, an occasion for a grand congregation of Indian pilgrims and enthusiasts from abroad, falls on the 7th day of the bright half of Magha (January-February). The pilgrims take holy dips in the Chandrabhaga Tirtha near the sea and welcome the rising Sun with prayers. Also a grand fair is held at Khandagiri near Bhubaneswar and continues for about a week.

MAHA SHIVARATRI

The festival of "Shiva's Great Night" falls on the 14th day of the dark half of Phalgun (February-March) and is celebrated by devotees from all over the country who keep fast and perform puja throughout the night. They keep a vigil to witness the sacred lamp on the temple-top. The festival can be best enjoyed at Mahendragiri, Gupteswar, Kapilas, Puri, Bhubaneswar, Huma, Khiching and Akhandala Mani, near Chandabali in the district of Bhadrak.

DOLA : (FAGU PANCHAMI)

Dola, popularly known as Holi is a colourful festival of Orissa, celebrated on Phalguna Purnima (March-April) and a day succeeding it. People converge on the streets with the idols of Shri Radha and Shri Krishna on gaily-decorated Vimanas (chariots) singing devotional songs in their praise and throwing gulal (Abhira) (colour powder) on each other.

TARATARINI MELA

The Taratarini Mela, one of Orissa's biggest fairs, takes place on each Tuesday of the month of Chaitra (March-April), at Taratarini Pitha, 30km. from Berhampur. A grand congregation takes place on the 3rd Tuesday.

JHAMU YATRA

In March-April the Jhamu yatra is celebrated colourfully at Kakatpur and Banki. The special attraction of the festival is walking of the devotees over a narrow trench filled with burning embers.

ASHOKASHTAMI

Rath Yatra (car festival) of Lord Lingaraja at Bhubaneswar, Ashokashtami, is held in the bright half of chaitra. The idol of Lord Lingaraja is taken in a chariot from the main temple to Rameswar Temple and is returned after a four-day stay.

CHAITRA PARBA

The Chaitra Parba or Chhow Festival commences from April 10-11 every year and continues for three days concluding on "Mahavishuva Sankranti Day" at Baripada. Chhow dances presented by Uttara Sahi and Dakshina Sahi, two leading institutes at Baripada are the highlights of the festival besides an exhibition.

SITALASASTHI

The celebration of marriage ceremony of Lord Shiva with Goddess Parvati starts with the untying of the wedding knot of the divine couple. Devotees act as their parents to perform the marriage. The bridegroom's procession popularly known as Barat beings on the 5th night of the bright half of Jyestha (May-June) and the marriage is performed in the traditional manner. The festival is celebrated in Sambalpur and Barpali in a gorgeous way.

RATH YATRA

Rath Yatra, known as car festival, is the grandest of all festivals in Orissa. It is the sacred nine-day journey of Lord Jagannath with brother Balabhara and sister Subhadra from the main Jagannath Temple to another shrine called Gundicha Mandir. It beings from the 2nd day of the bringht half of Asadha (June-July) every year. It is celebrated at every place where there is a Jagannath Temple but the most spectacular place is Puri where about five lakh devotees from all over India and abroad throng on that day to pull the sacred chariots.

DURGA PUJA

Durga Puja symbolises the victory of good over evil. Clay images of Goddess Durga are made and worshiped in gorgeously decorated pandals (tents) for four to five days (in September-October). On the day succeeding Vijayadashami, the last day of Durga Puja, the images are taken out in a spectacular provession for immersion in the rivers.

LAKSHMI PUJA

Observed with much pomp and ceremony in Dhenkanal town, it commences from the full mood day of Ashwina (September-October) and continues for a week.

BEACH FESTIVAL (CHAPA KHEL)

Puri, the abode of Lord Jagannath, is a wonderful beach resort for leisure tourists. It is known for its thirteen major festivals of Lord Jagannath celebrated every year. But the new Tourist Festival known as Puri Beach Festival, held in January, is an additional attraction.

BALI YATRA

To commemorate the glorious past of maritime trade voyages to the islands of Bali, Java and Sumatra, a big fair called Bali Yatra is held on the bank of the Mahanadi at Cuttack on the full-moon day of Kartik (November-December).

KONARK FESTIVAL

A festival of classical dances presented by celebrated danseurs of the country in the open air auditorium (December-1-5) is set amidst the casuarina grove against the back-drop of the Konark Sun temple, a world Heritage Monument. It is a memorable event. The atmosphere is surcharged with rhythmic dance beats and melodious tunes.

DHANU YATRA

Dhanu Yatra, relating to the episode of Lord Krishna's visit to Mathura and Krishna's killing of the demon king kansa is colourfully observed at Bargarh. Different episodes from the Puranic literature are also enacted here in December-January. It is the largest open-air theatre of the world, spread over a five-kilometre radius. The fairs and festivals reveal to the tourist the various rites, rituals, dances and music- the colourful way of living of the people of Orissa.

BIRANCHI MISHRA

FAYYAZ HUSSAIN KHAN

Padma Bhushan; Fellow of Sangeet Natak Akademi (1963); concert and lecture tours, Sri Lanka (1949 and 1951); publications : Tan Sangraha, Geet Manjari, etc. research papers; formerly principal, Bhatkhande College of Hindustani Music, Lucknow; disc recordings.

FILMS IN INDIA
PHALKE : FATHER OF INDIAN CINEMA

On April 30, 1870 a son was born unto a poor, priestly family in Tryambakeshwar, near Nasik, in Maharashtra. No astrologer could have predicted that this boy, named Dhundiraj Govind Phalke, would later come to be acknowledge as the "Father of the Indian Cinema". More familiarly known as "Dadasaheb" Phalke in later life, this shastri was responsible for launching the cinema in India. His forbears, the brahmins, for centuries had been responsible for the origin, the flowering and the sustenace of literary and other arts in india. But it was the priviledge of this particular brahmin to grasp the fundamentals of cinema, the 20th century art and to launch this "Seventh Art" and the "Tenth Muse" in India. In doing so, Dadasaeb Phalke also laid the foundations of the Indian film industry, which ranks the third largest in the world, and second in India among medium-size industries in terms of capital investment.

Like all great pioneers, Phalke was a genius, During his childhood and youth, he was more interested in painting, play-acting, and strangely in magic. When his father moved to Bombay, Phalke joined the Sir J.J. School of Arts and he had a good grounding in the graphic and plastic arts. He was intrigued by the "magic box", the camera, and soon he mastered it. He joined the Department of Archaeology as a photographer-cum-print-maker. As luck would have it, this enabled him to go to Europe and England to specialise further in printing processes. By then, the Lumiere Brothers, the earliest popularizers of the cinema, had come to India and had shown films- "the marvel of the century, the wonder of the world, living photographic pictures". Inspired by them and their films, a few Indians had already fallen for the magic spell of the cinema. Sawe Dada of Bombay and Hiralal Sen of Calcutta were pioneers in making short on Indian subjects- wrestling matches, the training of a monkey, Poona races, Indian stage plays and so on. But it was left to Phalke to make the first Indian feature film- Raja Harischandra, which was 3,700 feet long. Phalke, the showman, described it as a picture "three miles long, with 57,000 moving photographs, which can be seen for only three annas".

But I have jumped ahead of the story of Phalke, which deserves to be recapitulated for he and his films launched the Indian film industry. It was after his return from the West that two important events happened. One was that he lost his eyesight for a while and if he had not regained it, his birth centenary would not have been celebrated now, And, the other was that one day in December 1911, he went and saw The Life of Christ. He was spellbound by this film and he decided to make a film on the life of Lord Krishna. The next day he took his wife with borrowed money and explained his project. From then on, he was like a man possessed. He quit his job. He mortagaged his policy. He sold his wife's few jewels. He sailed again to London to learn the theory and practice of film-making and to buy equipment - a Willismson camera, a perforator and a developing and printing machine.

But by the time he returned to India, the idea of a film on Lord Krishna got shelved. Indstead he decided to make a film based on the mythological tale of Harishchandra, that great upholder of Truth. He wrote the script, perforated the film, hand-cranked the camera, directed the actors, developed the film, in the kitchen and printed it. He faced a major problem when some, even prostitutes, refused to act in his film. Ultimately, he picked up a hotel boy called Salunke to portray the role of Taramati, Harishchandra's wife.

RAJA HARISHCHANDRA

It was in May, 1913 that Raja Harishchandra was released in Bombay. It was a sensation. The theatre was continuously mobbed. Three-anna tickets were sold for three rupees in the black-market. The people who saw the moving images were so mesmerised that they prostrated before the screen. Tears were shed in profusion when the hero faced various hardships. There was laughter galore when now and again there was a humorous scene. This film became popular in other parts of India too. A South Indian exhibitor testified that he had to take the collections of the shows, held from seven in the morning to mid-night, in a box so heavy that it had to be carried in a bullock cart.

Phalke took his films to London later and he got favourable notices and offers of good business. But he preferred to return home. He made over 100 films (Lanka Dahan, Krishna Janma, Kaliya Maradhan, Bhasmsure Mohini, Setu Bandhan, etc.) during the next 30 years, except for a short break when he decided to leave film-making and retire to Banaras. And, his films were replate with magic and miracles. Gods and Goddesses rode on chariots in clouds. Heads were severed and later joined with body. Arrows turned into flames. Locations changed with the flicker of the eyes. Phalke, like Georges Melies, the French fantasy film-maker, knew the full potentialities of the film. The dream factories of the Indian film industry started with him.

Puranic legendary and mythological tales that belong to "the collective unconscious of the race", have been the favourites of our film makers till some time ago. These stroies were known to the young and the old to the rich, the middles class and the poor, and to the majority community. Even the minority communities could identify themselves with the stories, the characters and the situations. Miraculous events, lavish sets, fabulous costumes, stylized acting and camera as well as optical tricks became part and parcel of Indian films.

ACTING OR "STUNT" FILMS

Apart from this genre of films, in the Silent Era, other genres began to emerge. Puranic, legendary and mythological tales got exhausted or came to be repeated adnauseum adinfinitum. The fast-paced American and British "action" or "Stunt" Films, which found their way to India and which attracted large crowds, provided inspiration to film-makers, actors and cameramen, who unashamedly imitated the foreign versions for quite some time. Miss Frmeline was the Indian counterpart of Pearl white of the famous perils of Pauline series much later-came Nadia, the "Stunt Queen" In those days, strong men like Nandaram Pahlewan, and Raja Sandow were popular. And so were tall, fair and handsome men like Master Vithal, the Bullimoria Brothers, Gul Mamid, Jal Merchant and Jal Khambatta. The women to whom they paid court either in the heavens or in Ruritanian setting were "enchantresses temprtesses and vamps" like Sulochana, Madhuri Zubeida, Zebunissa, Rampiyari, Gohar and Patience Cooper. This was also the period when Prithviraj Kapoor, Jairaj, Nyampalli and other made their debut.

In the early days of the Silent Era (1913-31), J.F. Madan was the monarch of the film trade in Bengal, making films and distributing and exhibiting them in his own theatres. In Bombay, Abdullally Essofally was his counterpart. They were great showmen. Between Phalke. Madan and Baburao Painter of Kolhapur. They formed a Triumvirate and they dominated the early films.

PURPOSIVE SOCIAL FILMS

Two other developments during the silent Era of Indian films were the steady expansion and wider sidpersal of the industry and the production of "purposive social films". Economic factors compelled the industry to spread. Bombay and Calcutta could not remain for long as the only two centres of film production. Kolhapur, Poona, and Madras were added to the list. And, thanks to come individuals with imagination and social conscience, purposive films broke through the prevailing parttern of mythological and stunt serials. Madan Theatre discovered filmic potentialities in the novels of Bankim Chandra Chatterji like Krishna Kanta's will and Kapal Kundala. Naval Ghandy was inpired to make a film out of Tagore's Sacrifice. Mohan Bhavanani adapted the Sanskrit classic, Mrichakatika and made Vasantasena, in which "society ladies" like Enakshi Rama Rau and Kamaladevi Chattopadhyaya, were featured. The Punjabi legend, Heer Ranjha, was turned into a film Shantaram made Udayakal, in which he portrayed the lead role of Shivaji. R.S.Chowdhury's The Wrath, full with nationalist sentiments, was banned. It had in it an actor impersonating Mahatma Gandhi. And Ram-Rahim was made to promote communal harmony.

ALAM ARA : THE TALKIE

And then came the next major landmark in Indian films. On March 14, 1931 Ardeshir Irani of Imperial Films released Alam Ara, the first indian talkie, which was described as "all living, breathing 100 percent Talking Film" that added "Indian words to Indian images". Ardeshir Irani, in his own way another pioneer like Phalke, was obsessed with the "Talking Film" ever since he saw and heard Universal's Molody of Love, two years earlier. So he acquired the Tanar system of sound recording and made this film featuring Zubeida, Master Vithal, Prithviraj and Jagdish Sethi. This film became so popular that the police had to be called to control the crowds. Ardeshir Irani added fresh laurels to his name seven years later when he produced India's first colour film Kisan Kanya.

From that day in 1931, the sound barrier was broken and the regional language films began to emerge. Alam Ara was followed by Madan Theater's Shirin Farhad and Jamaisashthi, the first Bengali talkie. H.M.Reddy produced the first Tamil talkie, Kalidas, and followed it up with the first Telugu talkie. Bhakta Prahalad. A. Narayanan produced the first Tamil talkie in Madras (Reddy's first Tamil talkie having been made in Bombay), with his wife helping him as a sound recordist. The same year, 1934, the first Kannada film, Dhruva Kumar was released. Ayodhyecha Raja, featuring Durga Khote, was the first Marathi talkie. And Narsinh Mehta was the first Gujarati talkie.

THE SONG

The Talkie came to stay and the Silent Film was on the way out. In 1931, 300 silent films and 28 talkies were produced. Four years later, the number of talkies soared up to 233 and the number of silent films dwindled down to a bare seven. It was inevitable that the Silence Film should extinct. For, when the sound strip was added to the celluloid, a new dimension was added to the Film as such and an ancient tradition of India was incorporated into the Indian film. The song, which is associated in our incorporated into the Indian film. The song, which is associated in our country with birth and death, with seasons and festivals, with love and marriages, now became an indispensable part of the Indian film. The operatic tradition of our plays got a fresh lease. Our films, which were based on the state plays, were now replete with songs. (Madan Theatres' Indra Sabha and as many as 59 songs). The dance sequences of the silent films, which only had visual appeal till then acquired new value with music and dance added to them. And, the song-and-dance spectacle became a national characteristic of the Indian films.

GOLDEN AGE

During the short period between 1932 and 1940, we had what we can rightly claim as the "Golden Age" of the Indian Films. New Theatres, Prabhat, Ranjit Films of Chandulal Shah, East India Films of B.L.Khemkha, Bombay Talkies of Himansu Rai and Devika Rani and others produced some outstanding films. (It is to be recalled that Himansu Rai had earlier made The light of Asia and Karma with foreign collaboration and won international acclaim for Indian films).

During the Golden Age, New Theatres Produced the unforgettable film like Puran Bhakta, Chandidas, Devdas, Vidyapati, Mukti, President and Kapal Kundla. Through these films, P.C. Barua (a prince turned film-maker and actor), Debaki Bose and Nitin Bose emerged as directors, who understood the medium of the film. Actors like K.L.Saigal, K.C.Dey and Pahari Sanyal became household names through their histronic talents and songs. Jamuna, Kannan Devi, Kamalesh Kumari and Molina Devi were the favourites of the public.

Prabhat under the direction of Shantaram, Fatehlal and Damle put out memorable films like Amrit Manthan, Amarjyoti Dharmatma, Duniya Na Mane, Sant Tukaram, Admi and Padosi. These films were characterised by deft direction and social content. Master Vinayaka, Chandramohan, Durga Khote, Shanta Apte and Jagirdar were great exponents of the Thespian art.

East Indian Company gave Seeta and Milap. Devika Rani, the First Lady of the Indian Screen, and Ashok Kumar became a famous pair under the banner of Bombay Talkies, which produced films like Achut Kanya and Naya Sansar. Ranjit contributed Gunsundari and Secretary. Sohrab Modi made Pukar, the lavish period piece, and Kidar Sharma made a name with Chitralekha. Kardar made Bag-e-Sipahi and Mehboob turned Our Aurat. Even Mushi Premchand strayed into films with hist story for the Mill, which was about workers and strikes. The Bihar earthquake provided the theme of After the Earthquake.

FILMS FROM SOUTH

In the South, devotional on the lives of saints and reformers like Pattinathar and Nandanar were popular. Thyagaraja, the saint composer, was the subject of a memorable Telugu film. Dance films like Jalaja, socials like Two Brothers and Sati Leelavati and box office hits like Chintamani and Ambikapathi (these two films ran continuously for more than a year in some cinemas) cannot be easily forgotten. M.K.Thyagraja Bhagawathar, T.P.Rajalakshmi, N.S.Krishnan and T.A. Mathuram (The husband-and-wife comedy duo), Kanhamba, S.D.Subbulakshmi, M.S.Subbulakshmi, (in Seva Sadan and Shakuntala and Nagiah were the most popular stars of this period. K.Subramanyam. H.M.Reddy. C. Pulliah and a few others did their best to keep the South Indian film industry on a par with the Bengali and Bombay film industries. But South India came to recognised as a vital factor only after the emergence of S.S.Vasan, the editor-publisher turned film-maker. With his lavish spectacle, Chandralekha, he set the trend for the conquest of the Hindi film by the South, Vasan, A.V. Meyyappan, Prasad, and others began specialising in making two-language versions and Hindi films in the South.

The Second world war affected the Indian film Industry with its restrictions on the raw stock and length. The pattern of film-making changed with the entry of people from other lines, more interested in money than in the art. The only benefit that came out of the War period was that the Documentary Film was introduced by the then British rulers. And, it has stayed since then.

POST-WAR PERIOD

After the war was over, and after Independence, a fresh chapter in the history of the Indian Cinema was started. Bimal Ray's Hamrahi and Do Bigha Zamin, Jagirdar's Ramshastri, K.A. Abbas's Dharti-ke-lal (produced under the auspices of the IPTA), Uday Shankar's Kalpana and Chetan Anand's Neecha Nagar were some of the outstanding films. Sohrab Modi's Jhansiki-Rani, Raj Kapoor's Awara, Abbas's Munna, etc. signified a new trend. Big box office hits like Mehboob's Mother India, Shantaram's Jhanak Jhanak Payal Baje and K.Asif's Mughal-e-Azam represented another trend. In contrast to them of - beat films like Hrishikesh Mukherjee's Anuradha, Guru Dutt's Sahib Bibi aur Ghulam, Krishna Chopra's Heera Moti, B.R.Chopra's Dharamputra and Shantaram's Do Ankhen Bara Haath deserve mention.

A NEW TRAIL

But the miracle that occured in the last fifty years of Indian Cinema was the emergence of Satyajit Ray. An artist of rare calibre and scholor with wide interests, he blazed a new trail for the Indian film. With his film, he put India on the world map. His Apu Triology, consisting of Pather Panchali, Aparajito and Apur Sansar, was so rich in conception and so fresh in its approach that it has been hailed as a contribution to world cinema. During the last 14 years, Satyajit Ray has earned a score of award from the leading film festivals of the world, apart from national awards and honours.

At an international convention of filmologists, he has been hailed as one of the 20 significant film directors in the history of the Cinema along with the "Greats" like Eisenstein, Pudovkin, Chaplin, Orson welles and others. His individual style is so evident in the Apu Triology and other films like Chavulate and Mahangara and so different from what has come to be known as the typical Indian film that a whole thesis can be written. Satyajit Ray was a maker of only Bengali films and he has consistently refused to make films in Hindi. He was such a towering pastmaster that none can easily imitate him. But because of his emergence, other film makers have had better chances, greater freedom and easier sponsorship. Thus Ritwick Ghatak and Mrinal Sen were able to make their individual contributions because Satyajit had cleared the way. In Bombay too if Kantilal Rathod is able to make Kanku and Basu Chatterjee has been provided the facilities to make Sara Akash, it is partly because of the trend that Satyajit Ray started. Partly it is also because of the Film Society movement, which has been responsible for the refinement of tastes and for bringing into the country the contemporary language of the World Cinema. The major contribution of Ray has been that one could make a thoroughly and truly Indian film without resorting to the "Stars", the black-market operations, song-and-dance spectacles, foreign locations, playback singers and lavish settings.

The Indian film Industry today is in doldrums. Aged and ageing stars who refuse to pay income-tax and who demand fabulous amounts, for acting in "white and black" money, still dominate. Music directors, who copy and imitate and who synthesise in an unholy manner Indian and foreign music, are doing thriving business. Absurdstories with incredible twist and turns provide the escapist fare of today's films. Costly ventures turn out to be flops. All the latest equipment and technical gimmickry have not been able to rescue the Hindi and Tamil film from the morass into which they have sunk. The only hope is in the low-budget, off-beat films, which have been made by Mrinal Sen, Basu Bhattacharya and others with the help of loans from the Film Finance Corporation, in the documentaries of Sukhdev and in the films of lone fighters like K.A.Abbas.

A new chapter is about to be started in the history of Indian films. One can only wait and see how the portents join up and gather momentum. Learning from past experience, will the Indian film industry regulate itself and improve? Or will it sink further? Or will nationalization rescue it in the interests of the country?

JAG MOHAN

FILMS OF INDIA – ABROAD

It took a good deal of persuasion on the part of numerous people to convince the Government of India that the West Bengal Government had been responsible for the production of a film which would change the status of the Indian cinema in the eyes of the world. The fact was that the history of the Indian cinema was such that a great many responsible people in and out of the Government turned away in disgust or boredom from Indian films. They stubbornly believed that India was incapable of making films which could rank with major films of other film producing nations.

But *Pather Panchali* was finally sent to the 1956 Cannes Film Festival where it won a special award for its great human interest. It had been conceived of as the first film of a trilogy. The second film of the trilogy, *Aparajito,* or as it is called in English, *"The Unvanquished",* won the highest award at the Venice Film Festival of 1957. Less obviously popular in appeal than the first film with its two captivating children, the second film was to the critical mind a more maturely directed film was to the definitely proved that the director, Satyajit Ray, was not, as some sceptics had predicted, "a one-film director".

The next year, 1958, the Hindi film, "Jagte Raho", or "Keep Alert" starring Raj Kapoor and Nargis, won the major award at the Czechoslovak Film Festival. The same year a documentary award went to the Films Division-Bimal Roy picture, "Gotama the Buddha", a picture made entirely with sculptural images interspersed with some shots of the Ajanta frescoes. Recently, another documentary award was given at the West Berlin Film Festival to another Films Division art film, one made from the paintings of the Krishna and Radha love story.

Thus, during the period of four years international juries in several countries have recognised that India produces major films even if the general run of films are bound down by the conventions that producers insist upon as an essential ingredient of a commercially successful picture in India. As an immediate practical result of the foreign success of Pather Panchali and Aparajito, foreign distributors in the West are now interested in any Indian film that is of a high calibre.

It should be said here that there is a very distinct difference in taste regarding the Indian Film that is likely to appeal to the Western European countries and America, and those appealing to Eastern Europe. Pather Panchali has not been released in the Soviet Union, and also in China, the most successful foreign ever released in either of these countries is said to be Raj Kapoor's popular film "Awara", which has not received general distribution in the West.

There is, of course, a quite rational explanation for this difference in taste. The Soviet Union, has been producing social problem pictures for a very long time and the Soviet audience have seen relatively few entertainment films. They rushed to "Awara" because it is the kind of entertaining film which was a great novelty to them. Moreover, there has never been the cultivation of what can be called an elite audience for better films in the Soviet Union. But in the West there has grown up an ever increasing audience for the best films produced by any country, whether in Asia or Europe. The same thing applies to the United States, where there are special theatres catering for more critical audience than those who patronize the large chain cinema houses.

The prospects for the Indian film of the highest calibre is distinctly good abroad. But against this positive picture of foreign reaction there is unfortunately a rather negative picture within India in regard to India's outstanding films. Incredible as it may appear, Pather Panchali, which either headed the list, or appeared in the list of the ten best films of the year (1957) which is drawn up by each of the major newspapers in England, has never been given a general release in India outside of West Bengal ! The same thing applies to Aparajito.

These films, which are now ranked abroad as in the category of 'film classics' which ensures them a very long life, have only received special Sunday morning showings at Delhi and Bombay. Thus, great numbers of people who have heard and read about these films have never been able to see them. The cause of this extraordinary situation is that India has, as yet, no special cinemas catering for the public interested in 'better films'.

The situation is even further complicated by the fact that distributors and exhibitors in India are most unwilling to take risks. They are stubbornly convinced that they dare not give general release to films in local languages which are outside the framework of the conventionalized style of popular Indian film. The convention is that films must be many reels longer than those of other countries; they must include numerous songs and dances, even if songs and dances are not an inherent part of the plot; and they must be something of a hotch-potch to appeal to the diverse tastes among the audience.

The result of this dictum is extremely well illustrated by the film "Sujata", directed by Bimal Roy, and acclaimed by mass support all over the country as probably the most successful film of the year 1959. "Sujata" is "the story of an untouchable girl" and it is perfectly clearly intended to be a serious film raising one of the deepest of all social and psychological problems. Here is a film intended to stir people to think and feel intensely about "untouchability".

Coinciding with the successful commercial release of "Sujata" came the completion of the third film of Satyajit Ray's trilogy - Apu Sansar, or as in English, "The World of Apu". While the film was included in the Venice Film Festival it did not gain an award there.

MARIE SETON

FIRAQ GORAKHPURI

Asked what had influenced him most in life, Firaq Gorakhpuri who bestrode the scene of urdu poetry for more than four decades and brought a new freshness to Urdu muse, relied : "I am influenced neither by heredity nor by environment, nor by circumstances. I have influenced myself. The stars and the sky have influenced me more than the books. I have brought the original Aryan mind to Urdu poetry".

Born on 28 August, 1896, at Gorakhpur in U.P., Firaq Gorakhpuri, whose original name was Raghupati Sahey,

had his schooling at Gorakhpur and graduated in 1917 from Allahabad University. A student of English literature and philosophy, he was known for his originality of expression and tenderness of thought. Rejecting the Indian Civil Service which was the highest ambition of the times, he joined the freedom struggle and served a term in Jail. In the early thrities he joined the Department of English at Allahabad University and taught there for nearly thirty years as an outstanding Professor of English.

But he wrote in Urdu. He challenged every tradition, destroyed every myth and rescued Urdu poetry from the thraldom of 'Jaam' (cup) and 'Saqi' (cup-bearer). He wrote endlessly, incessantly and got the highest literary awards, the loudest applause at the 'Mushairas' (poetical symposiums). He died in 1982 leaving behind a rich volume of poetry which will continue to enthrall the readers in agony and ecstasy. He used "Khari Boli" and weaved it in the layers of Urdu diction. "I tried to plumb the basic layers of Urdu. In the language of all great poetry there is something like anti-language. My language has been anti-language, bereft of deceptiveness of its outer layers".

Sham bhi thi dhuan dhuan
Husn bhi tha udaas udaas
Dil ko kayi kahanian
Yaad si aa ke rah gayeen
(The pensive evening
Her plaintive looks
Unfolded many tales....)

His *'Gul-e-Naghma'* which won him the coveted *Jnanpith* Award in 1969 is the culmination of what keats has described as 'the heightened sensibility'. It is a collection of 90 *ghazals* and *nazms* known for their tenderness and fragrance. Firaq's poetry is highly suggestive. Half of the things he says are unsaid. Even at a 'mushaira' he would recite the first line of the couplet and expect the audience to ccomplete it with the other one. Thus he talks of music of the midnight- the luckewarm responses, *'Neem Nigahi'* (half-glances), dreamy or half-sleepy eyes or, more appropriately, half-bent eyes. He never talks of the full circle- he just refers the reader to the semi-circles and leaves him there. He is a great poet of early hours (pichli raat), of dusk, of twilight. He is a poet of half-bent eyes, half-bent glances and half-bent looks.

The past was a great resource for Firaq. He is most evocative when he talks of the past. On of his earliest work is Hindola (Cradle) in which he brings the haunting melody of the past against the inertia of the present. Firaq's poetry has a dream-like quality, his idiom is chiselled, his imagery is colourful, his thought is full of feelings and the feelings are surcharged with tenderness. But he is also a poet of sorrow, A tender melancholy permeates his life. His thought is basically elegiac, yet he is not a Marsiya (elegy) writer, like Anees and Dabir.

In his poetry on nature, he is better than the best, for he finds in nature more than a soothing balm, more than a friend, philosopher and guide, Nature, he feels, has no preferences, or prejudices. She treats all her children alike. Man, on the other hand, is a creature of prejudice and passion. Man creates false barriers and falls into factionalism. Nature knows no such passions and believes in no barriers. Nature, therefore, is the best example of tolerance and goodwill.

Taine's famous remark that literature is the consequence of the moment, the race and the milieu is very relevant in the context of Firaq's poetry. Another remark by Taine, that survival alone is the test of creative literature, is equally relevant in the same context. Putting the two together the question which arises is very simple. Will Firaq be read after fifty years?

The answer must be attempted with an eye on the poetry of another great Urdu poet, Faiz Ahmed Faiz. The two managed the affairs of Urdu literature between themselves in the present century the way Tennyson and Browning did in the Victorian age. Firaq represented the lyrical aspect while Faiz concentrated on the philosophical issues. Firaq's place is with Mir Taqi Mir. According to "Baba-e-Urdu", Niaz Haider: "Firaq takes the top position among his contemporaries. The grace and texture of his verse are so pure and pleasing that we can rate it as the ultimate intellectual delectation".

As amply illustrated in his own verse, Firaq will not only be read after fifty years but read with pleasure and passion :

Aane wali naslain tum par
Rashk Karaingi hum asro
Jab ye dhyan aeyaga un ko
Tum ne
Firaq ko dekha tha
(The coming generations will envy you,
O my contemporaries,
That you had
Seen Firaq in flesh and blood.)

K. K. KHULLAR

FLUTE SONG AND DRUM

Tribal people have their own mode of living and therefore they always prefer to live a little away from the Medding crowd undisturbed and unhampered by external influences. That is why hilly tracts, valleys and river beds have found favour with them for purposes of habitation. They derive their inspiration from nature and depend on its products for their livelihood. Because of their deep association and affinity with nature, they develop extraordinary Faith in supernatural powers and dedicate their lives to their worship. They have a strong belief that their life is guided and guarded by these forces and that it is their duty to keep them pleased through offerings of several kinds. Almost all their fairs, festivities and festivals are connected with there deitie in some way or the other and all their dances, songs etc. are meant mainly to keep them pleased. The birth of a child, his normal growth, marriage and other land marks of his domestic life are spposed to depend on the pleasure of these powers, The ceremonial hunt, the community singing, the dance, the performance of a folk drama, the ceremonial night-vigils, and the huge gathering of the tribals in fairs and festivals are all for keeping their deities contented so that they may give them a peaceful life with plenty of sun and rain and save them from calamities and catastrophies. That is why the tribal dance, song, ceremonial hunt and rich in intensity, colour and rhythm. When the individuals, other than tribals, are constantly inventing new ways for comfortable and economic living, the tribals are devoting all their energies in making costumes for their dances, tattooing their bodies to look attractive and preparing drums and flutes. The preparation for such rejoinings, as evident in the hairdressing of girls, making of flower-venies and ornaments, decorative arrows and spears for ceremonial hunts, from the most important activity of their life. They do not care to adopt advanced methods of cultivation or' for better houses for their living. All they desire is to possess a good drum, a colourful costume to wear for the festivities and necklaces, headgears and waist-ornaments made of conch shells for their dances. The articles of rejoining are more essential for them than the food that keeps them alive.

That is how the tribal dances have developed. They are not intricate and varied. They are lengthy and repititive. The songs do not have much of musical and lyrical quality and the rhythmic variations are few. The colour, rhythm and forceful rendering of their dances and songs are the result of their deep faith in the deity, who is supposed to be fond of songs and dances.

IMPACT OF NATURE

Keeping this in view, we have not to find out how nature has influenced these dances and songs and provided colour and gaiety to them, and also how their dresses and other decorations depend on the conditions prevalent in their natural surroundings. For example, the songs and dances of tribal living in the forest region of Madhya Pradesh, particularly those of Bastar, Sarguja and Abujamad region, are quite different from those living in the hilly tracts of Himachal Pradesh, Mainpur and Tripura. It is terribly hot in these areas in summer and there are plenty of flowers and greenery all round them. The Tribals do not have to put on much of clothes on their bodies. They are almost naked even when they dance, but the girls do a lot of tattooing on their bodies for decoration and the males put on plenty of conch-shell ornaments to look attractive. Besides, there are plenty of teak wood and other materials to make drums with and several types of bisons and wild boars for making head dresses out of their teeth and horns.

The dances of these forest regions are circular and have varied patterns because nature has provided them with plain fields for even big groups to dance at a time. They are more varied and choreographically well composed because of the ingenuity of the tribals who have all the time to devote on this. That is why dances like Karma, Puskolang, Dandara, Cherta, and Damkaeh have developed so wonderfully in these attractive surroundings. The richness of nature and the sober effect of the valleys these dances, are huge and profusely decorated with heads and shells. The bison born, the teeth of the wild boar and conch shells and seeds, twigs and flowers and dried up grass are profusely used in the ornaments of the dances.

The dances and songs of the tribals living in the Himalayan region of Himachal Pradesh. Assam, Manipur and Tripura are quite different from those of the plains. Because of scarcity of food material and the extreme cold, these tribes have to labour hard for their livelihood. But dancing and singing, as in the case of the other tribes, is essential for the worship of their deities and they also have evolved several dances and songs. Lacking the flat ground, they have to dance on the sloped and narrow footpaths of the hills. Their dances, therefore, are more or less in straight lines or serpentine in formation. Their pace is also slower because of the heavy costumes they to put on account of the extreme cold. This however is compensated for the colourful costumes and ornaments of the cancers. Their songs too are slow and are mostly based on huming and whistling because of the influence of stormy winds and fast breezes.

The dances of the tribes, living on river banks and sea shore, as in Orissa and some parts of Maharashtra and Malabar coast, have their own speciality. The songs too have acquired wavy and sweeping effects like those of the sea waves. They vary in musical modes and the rhythms are fast. The movements of the dancers, as seen in Surhul and Dalki dances or Oraons of Orissa, are fast and jerky. They have a very rich range of steps and are colourful and spectacular in their effects. Because of several types of birds, perching near these rivers and sea shore, their head dresses too carry feathers of birds like, Bhrangraj and swans.

The dances and songs of the tribes of the western parts of Rajasthan and Punjab have their own characteristics. These regions do not have much of greenery and rains. The weather conditions too are different from those of forests and hills. The tribes, living in these areas, have to work hard for their livelihood and therefore they do not have much leisure. The little time they get devoted to the worship of their deities. Since they do not have the opportunity of living in comparatively secluded and sheltered places like forests, they are more akin to the other inhabitants of the area. Their ladies cover their bodies with skirts and odhnies and sometimes even cover their heads and faces also as other ladies of the area do. Their dances and songs too are colourful and varied because of external influences. They have acquired several habits and customs of their non-tribal neighbours. Their songs therefore have more of the spoken word and meaning. Their deities too, on account of this association, are less connected with supernatural powers. The dance-dramas like the Gouri of the Bhils- of Rajasthan and the Gour Puja of Garasias are the products of this impact. Very few tribes in India have such rich festivals and dance-dramas as the Rajasthan tribes have. The Gouri dance-drama of the Bhils of Rajasthan has become a subject of study for research scholars because of its dramatic value. So is the case with the Gour Puja of the Garasias of Rajasthan. Several dances and musical patterns, used in these dance-dramas, are unique and spectacular. The Bheru Puja, the Ger, the Ghumra dances of the Bhils and the Valar and Ghumra of the Garasias also have a very attractive rhythmic pattern and they are superb from the choreographic point of view. The drum, the nakkara, the thali, the madal, the algoza (flute) and the ghodayoun (an instrument made of bamboo reed) too have their own story to tell. The effect they produce can outshine any other tribal instrument in India.

All these dances and songs, as mentioned above, are influenced by the topographical, geographical and natural conditions of the regions they are found in. They are connected with some sort of ceremony or the other. These occasions and ceremonies also provide colour and distinction to these dances and songs. As for example, the

songs and dances used in the night vigils, Popularly knows as Ratijaga songs and dances, are sober and soothing. The dances and songs like the Karma. Phaskolong, Dandara of Madias and Mundias of M.P. and the Ghumara and Gammets of the Bheels and Garasias of Rajasthan performed on festive occasions, are known for their richness in movements and rhythm. The dances and songs, connected purely with rituals performed compulsorily for the elimination of horror and devastation caused by the wrath of the supernatural powers, do not have much of gaiety and colour. They are a little crude, elementary and mostly repetitive. Such dances are the Bharon Puja of the Bheels, Parong and Dhol Nacha of the Madeas and Mudias.

Some mention may also be made here of the games and hunts prevalent in the Indian tribes. These games and hunts are not for entertainment only but have a purpose to serve. The ceremonial hunts of the Madias, Mudias and some age tribes have in them several dances of a virile nature to mark a particular occasion. One such festivity is known as Surul in the tribes of M.P. There are several gemes, particularly in the tribes of M.P. and Rajasthan, which are followed with special dances like Nakdodi Karsana, Khora Karsana, Dhur Padadi Karsana, the Byah Karsan Karsana of the Madia and Mudias and the Khil Natya of the Bhils of Rajasthan. All these dances, connected with these ceremonial games, do not have much dance value. Musical instruments like the Dhol, Madal, Ganga, etc, are played not purely for giving rhythm but for inspiring the participants. The games too have rhythmic patterns and are mostly accompanied with songs.

As mentioned above the musical instruments used for dances and songs are regional in nature. In those areas, where lots of bamboos are grown, flute is abundantly used. Where goat leather and suitable wood are available in abundance, drums have a prominent place. Where conch shells and other materials for blow pipes are available, pipe instruments are most prevalent. Where no such material is available, as in the cold mountanous regions of the Naga Hills and the Himalayan hills, clapping and whistling take the place of musical instruments.

While concluding it must be mentioned that the tribal dances and songs are governed by the community spirit. Their pattern or rhythm, movements and musical compositions too expresses the inner feelings of the tribes and their pattern of life.

D. L.SAMAR

FOLK ART OF MADHYA PRADESH TRIBALS

A peep into the world of tribal and folk art and craft of Madhya Pradesh is a fascinating journey back into time. The artists and craftspersons inhabiting the tribal areas of the state are keeping alive the rich tradition of their past. This is to be seen in the way they mould clay, wood, stone, metal etc into mindboggling shapes, froms and designs which are attractive and alluring. Equally captivating tribal and folk paintings and fabric designing.

Art and craft are a documentation of time, society and culture. The tribal and folk artists and craftspersons give concrete expressions to their thoughts, ideas and imagination and sense of beauty is at work even while making objects and artefacts of daily use. Their tradition of ritualistic artistic offerings to propitiate their gods and goddesses has kept their art alive and vibrant down the centuries. Art, in fact, is part of their very existence.

In Madhya Pradesh, the tribal-dominated districts of Bastar, Raigarh, Surguja, Mandla and Jhabua, as also the districts of Betul, Dhar, Hoshangabad and Tikamgarh have a long and rich tradition of folk art. For instance, the Muria, Maria, Bhatra, Gond, Baiga, Oraon, Korku, Saharia, Kol and Kamar tribals have been engaged in making terracotta objects and figures since ancient times. They make utilitarian and ritualistic objects which are used in festivals and religious ceremonies.

The terracotta art of Bastar has a rich and diverse tradition. Decorated elephants horses, bulls, figures of various gods and goddesses of Maria and Muria tribes are well known. Huge figures of terracotta horses, cows, bulls and goats are made in Dhar and Jhabua region.

Metal objects also form an integral part of the craft tradition of these tribals. Brass, silver, iron and lead are used in making various figures of gods and deities, objects of daily or occasional use and decorative pieces. Baster is famous for its bell metal works. In the world of metalcraft, artists let their imagination run riot to make various mythical forms and figures of gods, supernatural powers, animals, birds and trees.

The tribal woodcraft of M.P. is also extremely rich in variety and form. Beautifully carved wooden doors, pillars, canopies, windows, hangers, seals, musical instruments, ritualistic wooden figures of animals and birds, bows and arrows, toys and dolls are part of this craft. In Bastar woodcraft has reached its pinnacle in the ghotuls, a dwelling place built on the edge of village where all the young boys and girls come to chat, dance and sleep.

Mask making is as prevalent in the tribal areas of M.P. as it is in all tribal societies, whether of India or anywhere else. In M.P. the tribals make masks depicting gods and goddesses.

Apart from these there is a long tradition of tribal and folk paintings in the state. The tribals keep alive ancient memories passed from generation to generation. As such, the subject-matter of their paintings are drawn from their ancient beliefs and customs. Paintings of primitive tribes mostly depict the primary evolutionary process of human beings. In folk painting, however, various developments in human life and society are depicted along with their mythical beliefs.

The tribal society is also famous for its hoary tradition of tattooing. It is a form of adornment and is popular among womenfolk. In some tribal groups tattooing serves as a mark of identity. Symbols and motifs employed vary from one tribal group to another, ranging from the Sun, Moon, Stars, Peacock, Flowers to ornamental designs and animals.

DINKAR SHUKLA

FOLK CULTURE OF INDIA

As the dancer throw up their hands towards the sky, the drums beat louder and exuberance transcends human

imagination. The colour and vibrance of such a dance is escriptive of almost any part of India. Travel into the dense forests on the upper reaches of the Himalayas in Arunachal Pradesh or sit by the rocks and boulders of Bastar in Madhya Pradesh hold your breath as you watch it in Tamil Nadu or join the the fun in Gujarat, folk dances are captivating and infectious in their vugour and spontaneity.

Of course it needs to explanation to the support the statement that every region or small community in India has its own dance from devised and choreographed to suit local practice and this form of joyous expression is unrestiricted both in participation and content. Yet, one can discern a common rhythm through all the folks of India.

Folk dances can be broadly classified into the occupational dances, seasonal dances, martial, devotional and ritualistic dances. Generally every society has a share of all these types of dances, with some overlapping which becomes inevitable. For example the dance at a wedding may be both ritualistic as well as devotional. A pre-harvest dance will be both seasonal and occupational. It may even be reitualistic. But the essence of the matter is that folk dances too have their significance.

They also have an important role to play in communication and functioning as records of history. Take the Adis, the largest tribe in the state of Arunachal Pradesh, for instance, relate the story of their ancestors.

A careful record of the songs can reveal their entire history. The same is true of the Kunbi songs and dances in Goa. The Oldest settlers in Goa, the Kunbis, tell the tradition of their land in their songs. The best example is the Gigi Pada dance of Karnataka. It involves a question and answer session between the men's and women's teams too.

Occupational dances generally depict the entire process of harvest or hunting as the occupation of the people may be In Nagaland, for instance, the dancers in leaps and jumps are forever simulating a hunt and how they capture the wild animal. It is said therefore that even a child will be able to defend himself from a wild animal because he has seen the dance. On the other hand in Tamil Nadu, the dance describes the process of harvesting.

On a full moon night in the month of February-March, when spring is just there, go to Manipur and you will be thrilled to see the dance called Vasanta Ras celebrating the season, as the gentle swaying captivates you, switch to another scene in the south. In Kerala, particularly at the end of March, the Velakali dance is performed. Hear the war cry as it finds men performing this martial art with swords and shields; they are telling the story of the victory of good over evil.

If it is a story that you want to hear then you could go to Maharashtra and watch the Powda or the Dasavata. Powda is a term which means narration of a story in glorious terms and sure enough it is the story of a hero that is told to you. Dasavata is the story of the great epic Mahabharata. Yakshagana of Karnataka tells of mythological stories just as burra katha of Andhra Pradesh.

Watch closely as this tribe of Arunachal tells a story. The earth and sky were lovers and they loved each other very much. Of them was born their son, a bison. The Bison (mithun in local parlance) got so jealous that he tossed the two apart. And each time the earth rose to join her lover, the sun came shining out and the shy maiden stopped short. That is how mountains cam into existence.

Another fantastic similarity one finds is in the content of the stories. Even though folk dances belong entirely to the people and not to the scholastic tradition, one finds the exchange of ideas between different parts of India has been constant and at all levels. Take one epic like the Ramayana and you will find so many versions of it that it is amazing.

Each version is adapted to the people of that region and therefore presented in folkfore similarly. Even in Buddhist communities one finds a similar story. Along with the story comes the symbolism which too is retained intact through the length and breadth of India. Mythological figures are identified with a particular area completely and so some difference in the story told becomes. inevitable.

Stories, as one can see can be religious, explain nature or deal with history and even social theme. Religious theme are generally aimed at appeasing a deity and that is why we find in all the regions of India a dance devoted to Kali or Durga. Sometimes she is worshipped as Draupadi since Draupadi is also considered to be an incarnation of Shakti, that is Durga. The regional variations give an interesting insight into the surroundings of the people, their climatic conditions as well as their eating habits.

Drop the inhibition and join the dance if you really want to get a feel of the local rhythm. It is easy to pick up. Generally there are specific formations of the dancers. They are in a ring with the sutradhar (story teller) in the centre. This may be varied to find one ring of men and another of woman. Semi circles and concentric circles are other formation Another interesting formation is the linear one where they may be in a single file or facing each other as in the bamboo dance from Mizoram.

At once striking in the diversity is their costume. Folk dances are always performed in the traditional attire of the people and that again is common to all folk dances. The joy and celebration of life is perhaps the most common feature of all and their expression of it, the most diverse of it all.

SUDHAMANI REGUNATHAN

FOLK DANCE

Indian folk dances, inexhaustible variety of forms, rhythm, differ, region, caste, occupation; difficult to categories, generally four types, social (concerned with such labours as tilling, sowing, fishing, hunting); religious; ritualistic (to propitiate an angry goddess or demon with magical rites); masked (appears in all above categories).

Music and dance have long been used to communicate with God. From the temples to the fields, each area of activity has evolved an identifiable form of step and rhythm to convey love, thanks giving and devotion. Each dance is performed to propitiate a particular god or goddess. Most are in prayer for or in gratitude of the gifts. They bestwo upon us.

The Karma dance of Madhya Pradesh is a dance to propitiate Lord Karma or action, since that is the essence of life.

In pondicherry there is the Garadi dance, whose origins are traced back to the days of the Ramayana. The Vanara (monkeys) were said to have danced these steps in celebration of the victory of Lord Rama. Since Rama is believed to be the incarnation to Lord Vishnu, all Vaishnavite festivals in the area incorporate this dance as part of the festivities.

The Ramayana motifs is evident in many dances around the country as it occupies a very central position in the life of the people and is not necessarily community specific as it reiterates universality of the victory of good over evil. Another variation of this theme is the Mathuru Koppu dance of Andhra Pradesh which is performed during the Krishnashtami (birth of Lord Krishna) celebrations.

The Gidda of Punjab is performed by the women and it is in celebration of child's birth and the teej (monsoon) festival, or on any such occasion when you let go your spirits. It is in fact an integral part of the Punjabi way of life.

The phag dance from Haryana again celebrates the month of Phagun or spring. The dance amply reflects the soaring spirits of the people and is dedicated to all things bright and beautiful.

Not only to these dances signify happiness, they also are performed as rituals to please the gods who guard against ill health, disease or misfortune. An example of this is the Kargam (Kargam) dance of Tamil Nadu which began as a tribute to Goddess Mariamma, considered to be the protector of health and harbinger of rain.

The Puja Kunitba of Karnataka is a dance for Goddess Shakti. It is performed on festive occasions by dancers to fulfil their vows.

LAVANYA REGUNATHAN

FOLK DANCES OF KARGIL

KARGIL, the second largest urban centre of Ladakh, is situated on the bank of Suru river. It is also the headquarter of Kargil district. Although the entire area is rendered inaccessible in winter due to heavy snowfall, its fields watered by streams from the surrounding mountains produce a rich crop of wheat, barley, peas, a variety of vegetables and other cereals. Fruit such as apricot, apple and mulberry are also grown aplenty here. Thick plantations of poplar and willow trees give the area a lushness rare in other parts of Ladakh.

In such an invigorating atmosphere, people belonging to different religions and faiths live together in peace and harmony. The Brokpa and Purik tribes are also living here since ages. About the Brokpas, it is said that they are the descendents of the soldiers or Alexander of Macedonia. They can be recognized by their dress- an un-dyed wollen tunic, with its edges adorned with geometric designs. They always wear a hat heavily decorated with colourful dried flowers, rows of needles, ribbons, etc. Their features are pure Indo-Aryan and they have preserved their racial purity down the centuries. Their ladies adorn themselves with many types of head and neck ornaments made of silver, coral and the semi-precious stone firoza (turquoise). They are fun-loving people and love to sing and dance on festivals, especially at the time of the Bono-na, a festival celebrating the harvest.

The other tribe known as Purik also celebrates the advent of Spring with dance and music. Their costumes are different from those of the Brokpa tribe. Woman dancers wear the traditional long black kurta (shirt) with orange, green or yellow cuffs, a white chunni (long scarf) and a salwar or paijama (trousers). Their men wear white or off-white traditional dress, a shawl (a wraparound), belt and a cap. While dancing, both men and women carry a flower in their hands.

Both the tribes dance in a group. Their dance styles are very gentle, comprising light, swaying movements in slow tempo, with an interwining of arms. The dancers are graceful and charming and their postures are very delicate. Generally, they dance in a circle or semi-circle. All the musicians sit on one side to play their instruments and sing songs.

DR. BIMLA VERMA

FOLK DRAMA

The history of folk drama lates back to years before Christ; Epics Ramayana and Mahabharata contain references; later they were propagated through this Medium.

Indian folk drama, grew out of innate instinct in Man; his capacity to impersonate and represent apparent; the consciousness of his talent emboldened to experiment, improve his techniques; he took resort to entertain, to moralize, to satirize........... to discuss vast array of complex\and elusive problems to make up human life.

Man stressed on religion and tradition; village artists went for themes to the great epics, puranas; these yielded romance, religion, mystery and morality. Dance, song, gesture made theatrical unity...... hallmark of Hindu dramatic art.

Village play highlighted ancient theatrical principle; players and audience regarded as single entity; audience making way for actors as they walked from green room; joining those on stage in community singing.

There was no stage equipment; some kind of raised platform; crudest making and costume; language employed by characters uncouth but vigorous; Krishna, Rama behaved like villagers; yet the lesson went home.

FOLK DRAMAS (RAJASTHAN)

Fok drama in Rajasthan, as in other States, employ song and dance as their chief medium of expression. Their impact on the audience is stronger than that of the prosaic spoken word. The audience understands the different symbols and the gestures of the actor so well that no explanation is required. They are so much engrossed in the music and dance of the drama that all other formalities of the theme, stage, decor, costumes and presentation do not matter to them at all. This traditional outlook and approach of the audience to the dramatic art has evolved distinctive styles of acting in Rajasthan, some of which are described in this article.

THE ACTING IN TURRA KILGI KHYALS

Turra Kilgi is known for its poetic contest between the two Shivait sects, believing in the cult of Turra (Shiva) and Kilgi (Parvati). Nearly 80 years ago it developed into a stage play in some parts of Rajasthan and Madhya Pradesh. Its stage consists of a main platform with two towers (Attalikas) on both its extremeties. Singing of lyrical dialogues, from the top of the towers, is the speciality of this style. The actors, standing on the towers in gorgeous dresses, lend a special colour to the whole show. This device is used not only for the visibility of the actors but for creating an impact on the audience at the very outset. Their gestures and movements become conspicuous in the absence of a clumsy and meaningless background. The actors, ultimately, descend down the towers to the main stage with the help of the artistically built ladders and continue dancing along with their lyrical renderings. The distance, thus traversed, is synchronized with their singing in such a way that they are in their correct position at the end of each couple. The actors are unmindful of their actions, as they have to do free with their dancing and singing modes. The audience too does not bother about their actions as the lyric itself conveys everything that they went. The accuracy of expressing every mode of emotions, through their dance-steps and singing modes has to be maintained at every step. They have to act in such a way that they are visible to the audience seated all round. One significant activity to be noted in this style is the holding of sticks in hands with bunch of flowers on the top. These sticks move along with the limbs of the actor, creating an impression of enlarged movements for better understanding of the motives he wants to express.

THE CURCULAR ACTING STYLE OF RASDHARIS

The Dasdhari dramas are enacted on plain ground with the audience seated all round. While entering the arena they move round and round with spears in their hands and stop at the rhythm point, thus creating a thrill and sensation in the audience at the very outset. They stand opposite to their counterpart with their co-singers standing by their opposite to their counterpart with thier co-singers standing by their side. While one group of actors sing, their counterpart on the opposit direction goes on giving rhythm with their foot. When the recitation of that couplet is over both the groups start dancing in circular fashion, forming a chain and allowing the audience a clear view of their gestures and intricate movements. Their communicative power of the verse thus sung is also enhanced by this spectacular rendering. The stylized actions and expressions of the face are also highlighted because of the high tension created by singing and the dancing tempo crated at the culmination of each lyrical dialogue.

THE ACTING STYLES IN GOURI

The Gouri dance-drama of the Bhils of Rajasthan has a very fantastic and unusual acting-style. The drama is enacted on plain ground with the audience seated in a circle around. The troupe consists of three specific units.

(1) The group of actors, (2) The musical accompanists (3) The divine Bhopa and the Kutakdia (Commentator).

The main actors enter the arena from their dressing enclosures in two different directions. The divine Kutakdia (Commentator) intercepts their movements and asks for the purpose for which they had come. The answer comes from the Kutakdia himself, thus eliminating speeches from the masked and veiled actors. The dialogues, which are invariably in Prose, are specially designed in series of questions involving answers as well.

In response to each question the actor says "Oh" and Kutakdia finds a solution out of it.

The Gouri is like a big pageant in which several episodes, correlated with the central theme, are displayed with goregous constumes and acrobatic feats. The acting part of the whole drama, through the medium of the Kutakdia is an extraordinary device, almost unknown to any other dramatic form. The Kutakdia is a man of extraordinary talent and possesse high sense of humour.

THE SELF INTRODUCTORY STYLE OF RAMMATS

The Rammats of Bikaner and Jaisalmer are enacted on raised platform during nights and have a wide mass appeal. There are several types of Rajasthani Rammat out of which the "Hindaumari Rammat" is the most popular one. The actors at first introduce themselves on the stage in musical dialogues, after which they occupy their seats at some prominent place on the state. The narrators of the drama are also seated on the stage, on whose narration the actors have to show their skill of acting through intricate gestures and mime. The actor's display of his acting and dancing-skill is supported very prominently by the skilful vocalist and accompanists seated along with them. The impact of the accompanists and the vocalists on the audience is so great that it easily drawns their attention and eliminates all external disturbances in the plays.

THE RHYTHM OF CHIDAVA KHYALS

The khyals of Chidava and Jhunjhunu are known for their intricate stepping and the mode of high pitched singing. The complicated meteric system of tals, used in singing and dancing, gives it a special colour. The high literary quality of the text and the intricate rhythmic system adds to the charm of the show. Because of this predominance of the rhythm and the high lyrical quality of the song, the thematic value of the drama is minimized tc a considerable extent. The fast tempo of the music fascinated and overpowers and temper the actors take recourse to intricate footsteps and fast and the personality of the singer does not matter to them at all. In a khyal performance of 'Heer-Ranjha' the female role of the beautiful Heer used to be played most creditably by the 75 year old Dulia Rana. He had his beard covered with his long veil and his withering age concealed by his superb acting. The text, as in Rammata is best rendered by the narrators seated on the stage, whose impact on the audience is extraordinary. The entry of the actor on the stage is accompanied with highly intricate foot work and cleverly played musical instruments. The audience is thrilled by their spectacular entry followed with the collective singing of the actual text by the actors and the accompanists all at a time. The actors face the audience on the three sides of the stage with their musical dialogues and intricate foot work. The Chidava form of khyals does not lay any emphasis on facial expressions. The female characters, having their faces veiled and the male characters, with their faces thickly covered with big beards and moustaches, have almost no scope for facial expressions. Even the spoken work plays a secondary role because of the intricacies of singing and dancing, which invariably form the main part of their acting. Some of their moods are expressed through this medium. The tense situations are expressed through highly intricate footsteps and shrill singing in 'chaubolas' and 'bols'. For tense situations of anger and temper the actor take recourse to intricate footsteps and fast movements on the accompaniment of nakkara.

THE ACROBATIC STYLE OF BHAVAIS

The Bhavais of Rajasthan adopt quite a curious methos of acting in their plays. They are perhaps the most accomplished performers of Rajasthan with highly proficient acting styles. No formal stage is required in their performances and no curtains and stage decor are used. Their mastery over their art can produce any spectacular effect on the audience without resorting to any external help. The delicate looking Bhavai takes extra care of his form from his very childhood. Right from his daily wear to his personal upkeep he is an artist in the right sense. When he is a child he undertakes several difficult exercise to keep his body supple and agile. He puts on fine clothes of feminine interest and wears all sorts of gold ornaments to look attractive and handsome. His singing and dancing proficiency, besides being hereditory, is also acquired through years of practice.

Their play starts at the premises of their family patron (yajman) right from evening till morning. The dholak and the harmonium play the most important part. The actors enter the area with somersaults and acrobatic jumps and at every beat of the dholak, he gives curious bodily jerks to create a fantasy in the audience. The musical dialogues are sung collectively and enacted by the artists in a very impressive manner. In fact, this is the only form of drama in Rajasthan in which the musical verses are explained so accurately by the artists through facial expressions and bodily movements. The Havai himself is an accomplished singer and dancer and therefore he does not require any support from his co-singers. While acting he moves round the arena approaching almost every spectator, making them speak and participate in the drama directly or indirectly. The average Bhavai drama is full of satire on several social evils. The Bhavais are immensely imaginative and are capable of crating new situations according to circumstances. They are perfect in improvising dresses and producing effects with almost nothing. One Bhavai plays several roles without taking much time in change-over. Any plain chadar wrapped round his body and a lathi in his hand with a peculiar bend in his body, will make him look like an old woman.

The most important aspects of his acting are his acrobatic feats which start at the culmination of every emotional and dramatic situation. The dholak at that time becomes intricate, the music becomes extraordinarily fast and his footsteps almost like whirlwind.

D. L. SAMAR

FOLK PAINTINGS OF VRINDAVAN

Situated on the banks of river Yamuna, Vrindavan is a beautiful tiny city in the Mathura district of Uttar Pradesh. This famous centre of pilgrimage is hallowed by its association with Lord Krishna, the hero of the epic Mahabharata, who, according to scriptures, spent his eventful childhood here. It was here, it is believed, he frolicked with the cowherd girls, fair as Champak flowers, danced with them on the white sands of river Yamuna, stole fresh delicious butter from their pots and also killed many menacing demons who were deputed to destroy him by the king of Mathura.

It was here the great musician saint Swami Haridas sang melodious songs to Krishna and it is here a grand temple of Govind Dev (synonym of Lord Krishna) was built in the 16th century. Considered as the largest extant temple of North India, it is described as the "most eclectic building of the world, having a Christian groundplan, a Hindu elevation, and a roof of modified Saracenic character".

Among many other things Vrindavan is known for its art tradition. Some art critics believe that in the 16th century a number of artists from the Vrindavan region joined stelier of Emperor Akbar who is considered as one of the early founders of Mughal school of paintings. They contributed significantly to the evolution of the new school of painting that took shape in Emperor's stelier.

In the form of temple frescoes and wall-paintings some paintings of old school have survived in the Vrindavan region. However, during the last couple of years, thanks to the creative efforts of a young local artist, a new style of contemporary folk art is emerging in this tiny city of temples. Being on the bank of Yamuna, the new style came to be known as Yamunaghat painting, meaning painting style that flourished on the bank of river Yamuna.

India has a very rich folk and tribal art tradition which detes back to mesolithic rock art. By maintaining its independant existence it continued to nourish the elite art from time to time. For instance when the elite schools of painting declined around 19th century the visual arts continued to flourish with very little loss of vigour. It was this folk art which nourished the elite art of modern painting, as folk art has always played a significant part in the history of visual arts in India. Considering this, the emergence of Yamunaghat painting is quite significant event in the contemporary art history.

The main theme of Vrindavan paintings always remained Krishna and his divine sports. Around fifty years ago local ingenious artists brought from Rajasthan the art of gold paintings. Here a painting is embellished with real gold leaf and semi-precious stones making it shine luxuriously.

However, a young member of the traditional chitrakar family engaged in making gold paintings started looking beyond his traditional skill for inspiration and themes. And because of his creative efforts the new genre of contemporary folk paintings emerged on the bank of river Yamuna. His name is Krishna Chitrakar.

One day while moving in the countryside Krishna Chitrakar saw a village woman moving on the lonely road with water pots on her head and child and a bucket in her hand, face covered with a veil. It reminded him of the lines of a famous poetess which said:

Full are my pitchers
and far to carry
way is lone and long.

Inspired Krishna made a beautiful painting on the theme which later brought him much fame and recognition.

Since then he started painting village scenes on the canvas with oil paints in a very realistic manner. The cows, the river, the wandering mendicants, birds and trees, people engaged in their daily chores became the themes of his canvases.

Among his folk paintings the painting of women after bath or in the process of taking bath figure again and again, may be because he lives on the bank of the river. He has also painted a young women milching a buffalo. In yet another painting he has shown two young women looking over curiously through their veils.

The figures of the Yamunaghat folk paintings are well intergrated with their natural habitat; in fact they form an integral part of their rural landscape. The natural landscape and the figures merge into each other, as in lyrical poetry words and music are integrated beautifully.

M. L. VARADPANDE

FOLKLORE OF INDIA

The folklore of a country consists of the tales, customs traditions and superstitions of its peoples. While folklore probably emerged independently in each nation, exchanges between peoples have always been made. Some authorities believe that the folktales and folklore of the world have their prototypes in India. Although India has lent lavishly, She has also borrowed from her neighbours. Islam, for instance, brought with it much of the lore now existing. It is generally acknowledged however, that India and the East have provided the nucleus of the world's folk literature.

It is almost impossible to deal with every branch of Indian folklore; the difficulty lies not in any lack of material but in its selection.

The sun enters into the folklore of all peoples. In England people still pass the decanters round the dinner table in the way of the sun. In Ireland, when in a graveyard, it is customary to walk as much as possible with the sun, with the right hand towards the centre of the circle. In India there are similar revolutions round the sacred fire, and bride and bridegroom move round the central pole of the marriage shamiana, following the course of the sun. A bride, because of the belief that the sun has power to impregnate her, to salute the rising sun on the morning after she goes to the house of her husband. In England there is a survival of the same belief -

"Happy is the bride on whom the sun shines." In all folklore the same belief in the power of the sun is shown in the principle that to show a certain object to the sun is sufficient to summon an absent friend.

The moon, too, is a generous source of curious beliefs. In India the moon, like the sun, is always treated like a minor god and in the rural areas it is the minor gods and receive special attention.

In the West, the moon was inhabited by a man with a bundle of sticks on his back, which he had to carry as a punishment for a crime - murder, theft, or a peccadillo. In parts of India the place of the man is taken by a hare and hence the moon is called "Sasadhara" or "he that is marked like a here". In Maharashtra the patch on the moon is explained by saying that one day Lord Ganesh fell off his stead, the rat, and the moon laughed. Ganesh was very angry and ordained that no one should ever again see the moon. The moon asked to be forgiven and Ganesh was very angry and ordained that no one should be disgraced only on his birthday, the Ganesh Chaturthi. On this day, no one should look at the moon.

Ganesh is the god who blesses all beginnings. The author who begins to write a new book, the banker who opens a new ledger, the traveller who starts on a journey, all invoke the kind blessings of Ganesh.

To return to the moon, we find that is credited with powers over disease, with the title of "Lord of the Medicinal Plants".

In every country there is the ideal that roots and simples, if there they are to be used for medicinal, magical or mystical purposes, should be gathered by moonlight. At the first sight of the new moon, people in England turn a piece of silver and take care not to catch the first glimpse of it though a piece of glass. Hindus hold one end of a turban in their hands, take from them seven threads, and offer the threads to the moon. They then exchange the compliments of the season. Mohammadans on the new after the New Year sprinkle the blood of a goat on the thereshold of their dwellings.

Eclipses are ominous. A pregnant woman will do no work during an eclipse because if she does, she fears that her child will be deformed. During an eclipse a Hindu should not eat or drink. The most effectual way to ward off the evil influence of the eclipse demon is to bath in the sea or in some sacred stream.

Throughout India the sancity of the earth is believed in. The Hindu uses earth with which to clean his pots and pans. Jains, after the funeral, rub their hands with earth and water to remove the impurity of death. Paris cover the parings of the nails with earth to prevent disaster. Similar ideas exist in Europe, where the earth has always been part of many old remedies for disease. In Ireland they take a pinch of earth from the grave of a pious priest and drink it in water. In Europe it is a pious act to throw a handful of earth in the coffin of a friend or relation. Water, too, is sacred, hence the bathing in many holy streams.

Rain-making in India has its parallel in Europe. Among the serbs, in times of drought, a girl was stripped and covered with flowers. She danced from house to house. and the mistress of each dwelling poured a jar of water over her. Bhimsen is held by the Gonds in Madhya Pradesh to be a rain god. At the festival held at the end of the monsoon, two poles are erected with a rope attached to the top of each. Boys climb up the pole by the rope and then slide down the poles. representing the fall of rain. In Punjab, village girls pour down from a window some cow-dung dissolved in water, on any old woman unlucky enough to pass by.

England has some interesting old rituals for curing various ailments. In Chesire, in order to get rid of warts, one has to rub them with a piece of bacon, cut a slit in the bark of an ash-tree and put the bacon under the bark. The warts will disappear and grow on the tree. At berrkhamsted, in Hertfordshire, there used to be certain oak-trees which were long celebrated for the cure of ague. A lock of the suffer's hair was pegged into the oak. A sudden wrench, and he left his hair and the ague in the tree.

In Europe cats were always regarded as the companions of witches, and were often burnt along with their mistresses. But the ancient Egyptians worshiped the cat, and decreed death to anyone who killed a cat even by accident. They had good reason to value the cat, for it prevented their granaries from being overrun with vermin. The cat, say some jungle tribes in India, is the aunt of the tiger, and taught the tiger everything except how to climb a tree.

The rat is considered an unlucky animal, and to call a rat a rat is to invite disaster. It is better to call it "Uncle Rat".

Crows personify departed souls in some parts of India. The cawing of a crow is bad sign when beginning a journey. If a cow caws on a roof, a guest may be expected. To some extent it takes the place of a magpie in England. "One for sorrow, two for joy, three for a girl, and four for a boy".

RUSKIN BOND

FOLKLORE OF JAMMU AND KASHMIR

Kashmir has an inexhaustible fund of folk-tales. They are, as folklorists have it, as old as the rocks. Many of the folk-tales of Kashmir like 'Himal and Nariray', "Zohra Khotan and Haya Bund", "Gulala Shah" etc. are distinctly Kashmiri in origin.

Gunadhya of Kashmir (1st or 2nd century AD) has been called the earliest story-teller of the world. He complied his monumental collection of stories, Brihat Katha, in Paisachi. The collection was recomposed as Brihat Katha Manjari by a great Kashmiri poet, Kshemendra (11th century). It was then rewritten in beautiful Sanskrit verse by another Kashmiri scholar, Somadeva, under the title Katha-Sarita-Sagar (Ocean of the stream of stores). Divided into 124 chapters and 315 sub-chapters, it contains hundreds of tales and at least three novels. It is no doubt the largest single collection of tales in the world, twice as voluminous as the Iliad and the Odyssey put together.

In Zohra Khoton and Haya Bund, a purely Kashmiri tale, Zohra Khotan-Pursued relentlessly by a rich tyrant of a merchant-collects earth, shapes it into a clay head and invokes god to transform it into her own head. God grants her prayer, to preserve her chastity. The clay changes into Zohra's head, dripping with blood. "Take this", she tells the soldier, "and give it to the merchant". The soldier departs with the head. This anecdote is typically Kashmiri, where occultism has deep roots.

A king whose charity is unflagging even in the most trying circumstances can be found in Kashmiri stories, as in Many other Indian and Asian tales. Self-transformation is the essential theme of the "swan maiden" stories in Katha-Sarita-Sagar. As in Asian tales, the protagonist dons a cap to make himself invisible to execute his plans. The prose of Kashmiri folktales is picturesquely colloquial. Nature's bountiful charms of the "vale of Cashmere" add not a little to the beauty of the figure and the aptness of the diction.

In the Elysian habitat of Kashmir, with its abundant beauties of nature and man, it was but natural for some unknown folk-bard to have started the trend of folk-songs, that was destined to become immortal. Folk-songs in Kashmir, as elsewhere, reflect the myths, customs, traditions and way of life of the bygone era.

Kashmiri folk-songs are current in almost every Kashmiri home particularly in the rural areas. The songs present considerably variety in theme, content and form. The broad classification of the songs is : 1) Love songs Lol-gevun, 2) Ruf-dance songs, 3) Pastoral songs, 4) Boatmen's songs, 5) Spring songs, (sont genun), 6) Harvest songs (Lok-nuk gevun), 7) Children's sporting songs (Gindan gevun), 8) Wedding songs : (Vanvun), 9) Sacred Thread Ceremony songs: (Yagnopavit gevun) 10) Semi-mystic songs (current among the village holly men), 11) Opera songs (Band Jashan), 12) Dancer's songs (Bach Nagma Jashan), 13) Ballads (called Bath or Kath, literally meaning stories) 14) Cradle songs (lullaby, mursery rhymes called Lalavun, meaning, to lull), and 15) Dirges (Van).

The predominant theme of folk-songs is a women's poignant plaint about her lover who has deserted her. A typical love song runs like this :

O, you must tell me,
Where my boy has gone.
Is he a fountain in life's garden,
Or, a well of nectar, sweet and delicious?

The serpentine and calm, the flowing river of the Happy Valley, the Jhelum, forms the theme of most songs, like :

O thou slow-motioned Jhelum
For thee, let me devote my all, O
Jhelum;

Saffron of Kashmir is well known in song and legend. The Saffron fields of pampore, in the vicinity of Srinagar are famous. While picking the saffron flowers, peasants men and women sing :

Towards Pampore went away my darling,
Saffron flowers caught him in fragrant ambrace.
O, he is there, and ah me; I am here,
When, Where, O God, would I see his face?

There is a rich variety of pastoral songs which are simple and chaste, and acquire a singular charm when sung in chorus. The Himalayan Muse sings through the folk-songs of Kashmir, fresh, lucid and chaste, and rich in rhythm and vitality. The tender footed Kashmiri belles, singing the dance-songs at harvest time or on festiv occasions, and dancing the Ruf in rhythmic movement with interlocked arms, are the expression of the inner joy of Kashmirs over the beauty of nature around them.

Rooted in the soil and reflecting accurately the life and aspirations of the common folk, the Dogri folklore has not only provided the predominant means of creative self-expression of the people but has preserved their expreiences, values and beliefs (myths, customs etc.). It epitomises the chequered history of the Dogra Desh, which has stood like a rock through the vicissitudes of time.

Dogri folk-tales present an interesting spectrum. But these are basically connected with the exploits of the heroes like General Zorawar Singh (who has been described by some historians as the greatest General of 19th century) and his associates, Wazir Ratno and Basti Ram, Raj Singh etc. These have strong appeal in the Jammu and outlying districts. These ballads, called 'bars' recount the thrilling episodes of Dogra heroes who sacrificed their all to uphold the honour of their family and country.

The Dogri folklore is closely connected with religious shrines in Jammu and Kangra. Each Bheta, containing parises, prayers and descriptions of deities, is pegged on a particular shrine, telling the story of each deity and its association with the sacred place.

The folk-songs of Dogra Desh represent Dogri life in all its aspects, musically and more fully than any other type of folk literature. There are songs from birth to death, called samskar geet, songs connected with rituals. In a well-known Dogra lyric, O Dagebaz Manuan ("O, my deceitful love"), the frustrated beloved takes her lover to task for his indifference, but, as is typical of folk-songs of Jammu and Kashmir, there is no exhibition of unrestrained emotion or passion. Dogri folk literature has provided entertainment and sustained means for creative expression to the Dogras for hundreds of years. It offers immense possibilities for research to the philologist, the historian and the linguist.

The magic land of legend and love, Ladakh, is inhabited by an essentailly mirth-loving people. In the land of incongruities, that is Ladakh, the harsh, barren terrain remarkable for its climatic rigours, the people of Ladakh are full of life, fun and gay abondon. The smallest event here becomes an occasion for a feast and a song session. They consume huge bowls of chhang, their own country liquor, and sing and dance.

On such occasions, chong-g-lu, that, is, drinking songs are sung, fun and laughter abounding and continuing until the last drop of chhang, served in huge bowls, is consumed; The singer of the merry or drinking songs is often accompanied by a fiddler and sometimes by a drum. The vast repertoire of Ladakhi folklore contains songs, overflowing with consonants and unmusical expressions. At the other end of the scale are songs that lend themselves easily to slow, dancing movements.

PROF. SOMNATH DHAR

FOLKLORE TALES AND SONGS OF KASHMIR

ASSOCIATION WITH SERPENT WORSHIP

Folklore generally respects geo-cultural boundries, but there are important exceptions in Kashmir. Traditions, myths and legends associated with the Nagas or serpentworship are alive in the valley of Kashmir with its numerous springs or lakes named after serpent deities, Sheshnag or Susramnag, Karkotnag, Anantnag, Konsarnag, Verinag, etc. Even where the suffix Nag is missing from the name as in the case of Ailapatri, near the Apharwat Pass above Gulmarg, the association with the serpent is inalienable. This cult seems to have dominated the southern region of the valley known as maraz and is still alive in Kishtwar and Bhadarwah tehsils in Jammu, and beyond in Chamba and adjoining areas of the Himachal Pradesh. It seems to have left the Tawi and the lower Chenab basins untouched. In Bhadarwah the most important local festival, Kailash Yatra, centres round the legend of the naga deities and people of Chamba and Kangra also participate. The festival has nothing to do with also participate. The festival has nothing to do with Nagpanchami as celebrated in some parts of India. In the Basdeo temples of Bhadarwah the head of the deity is surmounted with a hood of seven serpent heads. There are many such idols hewn out of wood in remote villages and forests, a testimony to folklore and folk-art alike.

Apropos of the nag or serpent cult, it may be mentioned, that it has practically petered out of the valley of Kashmir except in a few cases where some Hindus offer worship at an important spring on the occasion of the 'birth anniversary' of naga deity. It has been held, however, that the valley was once inhabited by a tribe or people called nagas who have left their impress on our place-names. More than once has Kalhana referred to naga individuals in the Rajatarangini, describing their appearance, dress or habits. Whoever they may have been, their immortality is assured in the well-known romantic tale of Himal ta Nagrai which has exercised the imagination of the people for centuries. This tale has, however, been influenced by other legends familiar in India, as those associated with nagpanchami.

Nagas remind us of another stock of people who are believed to have lived here before the Aryans, viz., paisacas (goblins). The dialects of Dardistan are supposed to be akin to paisaca language which, some scholars aver, has made a lasting impact on Kashmiri language itself. A choice dish is offered to the goblins even now on a dark December night by Kashmiri pandits out of gratitude to the paisaca king Nikambhu who in the remote antiquity, permitted the Aryan Brahmins to settle in the valley.

MYTHS AND LEGENDS

The more well-known myths and legends widespread in India naturally swept over Kashmir also but in many cases a shift in emphasis introduces the Kashmiri local colour. In the Kashmiri version the traditional narrative of the wedding of Shiva with Parvati finds emphasis on heavy snowfall. The tales about Hebrew prophets and saints of the earlier phase in Islam retain their exotic flavour even in their Kashmiri garb, but anecdotes sprung round holy men, either Hindu or Muslim, of local origin, have a peculiar kingship. The phenomena in Kashmir of the waxing and waning of the ice-lingam in the cave of Sri Amarnath has a soul-stirring call for the faithful all over India. Few are, however, aware that the magnificient lake that rewards their eyes on their pilgrimage their is not known after sheshanag, the lord of the serpents but is actually sustamnag, the lake of the 'father-in-law'. A most fascinating legend in Kalhana's chronicle narrates how the lake come to be transported along with its naga denizens from its original position near Srinagar to its remote isolation beyond Pisughati.

STUFF OF FOLKLORE

The myth and the legend shot through and through with primitive reaction to natural phenomena and superstition are the very stuff of folklore.

As in ancient greece, there is hardly a lofty peak, a mountain tarn, a stream or a spot of topographical significance which has not an important bearing on the beliefs or religious practices of the people of Kashmir. Thus, Konsarang bears the impress of the foot of Vishnu who struck his plough and dessicated the Satisar; Shiva and Parvati have their abode on the myriad-domed Harmukh above Gangabal Lake and adopt the form of a pair of pigeons on Sawan Purnima when pilgrims enter the cave of Shri Amarnath; the Vitasta or the Jhelum is but Parvati in the waterine form and must be worshipped. Fertile imagination has furthur been stimulated in this sphere on account of some peculiar geographical phenomena : water streams out of Srinagar on the eighth day of the bright half of Bhadun in the morning and dries up in the evening for the next 364 days; water changes colour at the sacred springs of Tulamula, Baramulla etc; the lingam of ice in the Amarnath cave waxes and wanes with the moon.

THE ORAL TRADITION

A political revolution took place in India during the eleventh century and in Kashmir itself the ruler adopted Islam two hundred years later. Persian and Arabic gained more importance and the Kashmir language was cast into a form akin to its present one. Literary works, now extinct, came to be composed but the vast majority of the people hugged the oral tradition and enjoyed it. Tales known originally in Sanskrit or Prakrit were cast unconsciously into Kashmiri and have been passed on from grandmother to grandchild ever since. Without recourse to the written word, generations of Kashmiris have thus enjoyed tales like those of Bombur ta Lolre, Akanandun, Himal to Nagrai, Zin Mozur, Lalmal Pari, Hayabandh ta Zohra, Khotan and Soni Kesar. A diffesion of tales and motifs takes place continuously and since the development of Kashmiri language in its present form, the influence of romances in Persian and Arabic, or of collections like the Tales of Mulla Nasirud- - Din, a book of practical philosophy and moral instruction like the Panchtantra, could not be excluded. Several collections of folklores in Kashmir have been published since the pioneering work of Rev. J.H.Knoles in 1893. Close variants of many of these tales are found in different parts of India, the Middle East and Europe.

FOLK SONGS

Kashmiris love to sing songs. The house wife doing here chores, the shepherd tending his flock on the uplands, the boatman paddling his way to his destination, peasants in their back-breaking toil and lasses at the spring will be found bursting with song, and in most cases they have anonymous folksongs on their lips.

Kashmiri folksongs are unique for their rich variety; harvest songs, marriage songs, lullabies, hymns, Id and roh songs, spring songs, etc. Ceremonial songs during bereavement are no longer in vogue. Marriage songs show a surfeit of sentiment and conceit:

qadman wathrie mushki kofuro, ashka bomburo laili aakho (I,II stream musk for thy feet to tread on; tho moth of love hast come to wed thy darling)

There is hardly any item in the prolonged ceremonial of a Kashmiri marriage for which a number of songs are not bubbling on every tongue.

FOLKLORE IN JAMMU

The area forming the adminstrative division of Jammu comprises over 15,000 square miles of mountainous and sub-mountain land. Unlike the valley of Kashmir, which is geographically an integral entity, Jammu Division is a conglomeration of sub-units : Ramban, Kishtwar, Bahadarwah, Basohli, Reasi, Udharnpur, Poonch, Chenani, etc. There is a well-know saying : bayees raj pahar de beech Jammu sardar, meaning around their sovereign Jammu there are twenty two states spread over the hills Most of these 'dukedoms' have distinctive cultural characteristics. As pointed out earlier, the Dod District has had ancient contacts with Kashmir and the prevalence of the naga myth in its peculiar form from Kashmir to Kangra via Kishtwar, Bhadarwah and Chamba is significant. Central Jammu has had little contact with Kashmir politically. During the eighteenth century when Sukhjewan Mal of Kashmir sought his assistance against the alicn Afghans in 1762 A.D. Raja Ranjit Dev of Jammu sided with the trans-khyber invader.

Jammu has provided a fertile soil for the growth of graphic arts, especially painting, and distinctive qalams or styles named after their area sub-units as Basohli qalam, Jammu qalam, Poonch qalam, Bhadarwah qalam have been indientified. There varying styles have close links with Kangra, Garhwal, Mandi and similar efflorescence of the Pahari art. Painting has been so popular in Jammu as almost to have attained the basis of a folk art.

In folk literature also, in spite of variations peculiar to distinctive administrative sub-units or localities, there is a basic unity of theme, genre, conception and idiom. As hinted earlier, many folk tales and songs in Kishtwar and Bhadarwah hover round naga myths and legends. The folk literature in Poonch betrays a stronger influence of it counterpart in Punjab. With all that, important characteristics of the region prevail. (condensed)

S. L. SADHU

"G"

G. N. BALASUBRAMANIAM

Born in 1910, G.N. Balasubramaniam, (G.N.B. for short) could perform wonders in music, even though his lifespan was only 55 years. His was a great new bani .(G.N.B) and both purists and commoners listened to him with care and attention. Musicians have labelled his musical skill as one of the highest calibre. Blessed with a God-given powerful and sonorous voice, G.N.B. could captivate all with his wonderful presentation of Ragas as well as Kirtanas. His imagination was poetic and, coupled with his unimaginable brain-work, he proved himself to be the greatest among the greats.

G.N.B. was one among the few who had a good academic career. He completed his Honours-course in English Literature with a first rank. His father, shri G.V. Narayanswamy Iyer, though himself a connoisseur of music and also the headmaster of Hindu High School in Chennai never wanted his son to pursue the music profession. But Narayanaswamy Iyer played host to top-ranking musicians and musicologists. So much so, his house was always echoing with music. G.N.B. was brought up in such an environment and no wonder he had the yearning to learn this wonderful art. He used to listen to the music sessions at his house, as well as in the house of karur Chinnaswamy Iyer, a violinist of repute, where Budalur Krishnamoorthy Sastrigal (Gottuvadyam), Palladam Sanjeeva Rao (Flute) and others used to gather. He had the opportunity to take lessons from Karur Chinnaswamy Iyer and Madurai Subramania Iyer.

He used to sing in a high pitch and his sruti was about 61/2 Kattai with tremendous speed. Ariyakudi Ramanuja Iyengar, a great musician heard G.N.B. singing and gave him all encouragement G.N.B had a very high regard for Iyengar and though he developed a style of his own, one could notice how faithfully he followed Iyengar's Madhyama Kala Bani. He gave middle tempo (Madhyama Kala) special importance. He was of the view that the Madhyama Kala gave endless scope for improvisation and manodharma to the performer. He gave colour to his Raga essays with majestic ease to make them glitter and sparkle. Several features combined to make G.N.B's performances wholesome and complete.

G.N.B.'s system of Raga alapana had the imprint not only of his originality but also of his critical and analytical approach to music. He chose his kritis in such a way that every composition was worked out to such fineness that further improvement seemed well-high impossible. His svara elaboration marked uncommon endings with unconventional eduppus. Eg. Tapatraya in "Subramanyaya Namasthe" and Sumati Tyagaraja in "Nitisala Sugama".

G.N.B.'s technical skill and astute judgement kept him in good mettle. He would handle any Raga with ease, thanks to his captivating masculine voice which served him like a slave. His approach in rendering Ragas was full of imagination and originality, filled with brikas and flashes. Undoubtedly, G.N.B. was the most creative, most original and the most attractive performer among the maestros of the past.

G.N.B. was one of the prominent composers of recent decades with about 250 compositions to his credit. Well-versed in Sanskrit, Telugu and Tamil, he could bring our songs without any deviation from tradition. The Ragas Chandrahasila, Sivasakthi, Amritha Behag, Saranga Tharangini were his creations. Two books of his compostions have already been released. He very rarely sang his compositions in his concerts and he left it to his disciples to do the job of propagating his kritis. He was a great teacher and had no equals. He imparted the best in music, which he had imbibed from the stalwarts of the past, to his disciples.

G.N.B. was in touch with modern trends without sacrificing the essentials prevailing over traditional music. An educated practising musician, as he was, eminent among the peers, though soaring high in the field, G.N.B. had high regard for elders and fellow musicians. To sum up, he was a universally accepted musician who brought glory and fame to Carnatic music.

G.N.B. spent his last days in Thiruvananthapuram when he was serving as Principal of Sri Swati Tirunal College of Music. He passed away after a brief illness on the first day of May, 1965, leaving behind his wife and children and a host of disciples and rasikas to mourn his loss.

G.N.B. had very high regards for Maharani Sethu Parvati Bai and was appreciative of her deep knowledge in Carnatic music. During the forties and the fifties, the Maharani used to invite G.N.B. to the Adyar Palace for discussions on various aspects concerning music. G.N.B. used to tell me that his meetings with the learned Maharani were of immense value.

It was the time when the former Travancore Broadcasting Station was functioning at a place a few miles away from Thiruvananthapuram. G.N.B. had come there for a broadcast and the day happened to be the Maharaja's (Sri Chithra Tirunal) birthday. Violin Vidwan Sri T.K. Jayarama Iyer and Mridangam maestro Sri Tanjore Vaidyanathier were the accompanying artistes. I had the good fortune of going along with them in the conveyance provided. During the short drive towards the Radio Station, G.N.B. told me that the day being the birth-day of the Maharaja, he would feel it as a good gesture if he paid some tribute to the Maharaja and he kept it at that. After a few kritis he sang an elaborate kalyani with all beauty, which was taken up for the Ragam-Thanam-Pallavi. I was greatly and agreeably surprised to note the words of the Pallavi which ran like this "Vanchi Bhoopala Ranjitha Canalola". Spontaneously came these words and the tribute to the Maharaja, as desired by him was rightly paid.

Once a great critic approached Ariyakudi Ramanuja Iyengar with a request to sing and popularise some of the kritis of Mysore Sadasiva Rao which he had brought out with considerable effort. Iyengar immediately told him, "you have come to the wrong man. Instead of asking me, you please approach Mani (G.N.B.) to do the job and I am confident the kritis will become popular overnight if he includes them in his concerts". Such was Iyengar's appreciation and confidence in G.N.B.

Just after his debut in the cine field through the mythological story "Bhama Vijayam" (G.N.B. has appeared as Narada in the film) at the instigation of Mridanga Vidwan. T.K.Murthy, who had heard G.N.B., Tanjore

Vaidyanathier, his Guru, invited G.N.B. to sing at a Hanuman Temple in Tanjore. But Vaidyanathier was not happy at the prospect of an English-educated youth- a film star too- singing in a place where veterans like Maharajapuram Viswanatha Iyer and Ariyakudi had figured. Senior accompanists too were reluctant to accompany the vocalist. By God's grace, Tanjore Sankara Iyer on the violin and T.K.Murthy on the mridangam saved the situation and provided accompaniment. The senior vidwans who had gathered there were exhibiting a light-hearted approach with indifference. But their impressions changed and they started listening with utmost attention when the young G.N.B. astonished them by providing captivating music.

G.N.B. had occasion to sing before the Maharaja of Mysore. Veterans like Gayakasikamani Muthiah Bhagavathar and Vidwan Vasudevachariar were also present when the concert was going on. After giving a captivating kamas, G.N.B. sang "Brocheva" in the same Raga. Vasidevachariar, the composer of this piece, was in raptures and was seen shedding tears of joy and went up to the extent of remarking, "Have I really composed such a wonderful piece? You are really great. This humble piece of mine has gone upto high levels, thanks to your wonderful rendition. May God bless you with long life". A Shanmughapriya sung by G.N.B. that day was so lively that the Maharaja complimented G.N.B. and patted him on the back- a rare gesture, because in those days Royal hands rarely touched a commoner.

On another occasion, G.N.B. sang an elaborate "Gowda Malhar" a creation of Muthiah Bhagavatar. It was followed by "Sarasamuki". Bhagavatar's own composition. Dhagavatar was not able to control his joy of appreciation and embraced G.N.B. Taking G.N.B. to his quarters, the magnanimous Bhagavatar presented him a Thambura called "Bharatha".

Bade Gulam Ali Khan was introduced to the Madras audience by G.N.B. during the early fifties of the last century. Gulam Ali Khan requested G.N.B. to sing the Raga "Andolika" twice or thrice with the ardent desire to learn it. Later, he could sing the Raga to perfection in his performances in Delhi, Mumbai and Calcutta.

S. UMAMAHESWARAN

GALLERY CHEMOULD

It all started out as early as 1946 with the opening of Chemould Frame Shop at Princess street. Encouraged by the likes of schlessinger it made definitive forays into the art world, framing and displaying the works of Raza, Ara, Gaitonde, Alnelkar and Raval among others. It caught the eye of the early buyers amongst who were several Swiss including the Volkart family. At that time Homi Bhabha collected several works. With a gradual rise in art awareness came the need for a full-fledged gallery, which was professionally managed. In 1963 Gallery Chemould was opened at Jehangir Art Gallery complex. The Gandhys now followed their natural instincts providing the many artists they had grown to know over the years with a centrally located space, where they could exhibit their work, meet the viewing public and stock their paintings.

Gallery Chemould became a Stammplatz, a meeting ground for artists, writers and connoisseurs to interact articulate ideas and critically view styles and trends that emerged with the use of diverse media. Gallery Chemould has come a long way from its tentative forays into promoting contemporary Indian art. Today, both nationally and internationally, it is respected and has an impecable image, which puts it at the vanguard of the Indian art's scene.
(Summarised)

SUMITRA KURAM SRINIVASAN

GANAPATI BAPPA FESTIVAL

Ganapati Bappa festival is the leading festival of Maharashtra Ganapati Bappa the elephant headed one is panipered like no other god in the Hindu pantheon. For ten days the reigning diety of western India is spoilt silly by men, women and children alike. All his whims and fancies pandered to on the tenth day he finally bids adieu. A curious excitement grips the city. Traditionally, the king of Lalbaug, the tallest of the Ganapatis from the predominantly Maharashtrian area in Central Bombay leads the procession. The main street is aflutter with saffron flags and scores of loud-speakers compete with each other to break the sound barrier with " I love Ganapati" hymns and bhajans. The Ganapati-worshiphers arrive in thousands and take up vantage positions. A faint sound of tashas, dholaks and assorted drums penetrate the amplified cacophony. As the procession turns the corner, the 32 feet lord emerges and an endemic frenzy grips the crowd. One after the other the numerous ganapatis on trucks, trailers, carts, bullock-carts, on heads and shoulders fend their way to Chowpatty beach where the noise level reaches a crescendo. Seething masses smeared with gulal and haldi take a break for the concluding aarati. The traditional ritual of leave-taking done, Lord is hoisted on shoulders and taken to the water where he is dunked with the chants "The Ganapati Bappa Morya"
(Abridged)

GANDHARVAS DANCES

Gandharvas vaishyas by caste professional dancers, command respect among their community, belong to Marwar, out for eight months for performance, dance-dramas on Jain themes, e.g. "Ajanta Sundari" and Mena Sundari".

Prominently a musical drama, not much dancing, an open air drama, painted curtains used for display.

Gandharvas rare, advent of modern entertainment, an adverse effect over traditional occupation.

Drama played for monetary gains, have relgious motives took artists cultured, educated, do this work as a mission of their life.

GANESH CHATURTHI

A Hindu festival (specially popular in Maharashtra and Rajasthan) occurring on 4th day of bright fortnight of Bhadrapada (August-September) celebrated in honour of the birthday of the elephant-headed god, Ganesa (son of Siva and Parvati) is god of beginnings, prudence, policy and patron of letters, is propitiated and worshipped at the beginning of any undertaking; his name is inscribed by his devotees at the beginning of literary works; clay figures of Ganesa are made and worshipped from one to nine day, the images first being brought into the house with great pomp and rejoicing; after the conclusion of the puja, they are immersed into water.

References

Sastri, N., Hindu Fasts and Ceremonies, Madras, 1903.

Sivananda, Swami, Hindu's Fasts and Festivals and Their Philosophy, Rishikesh, 1947.

GANGA : IN INDIAN MYTHOLOGY & SCULPTURE

The most holy of rivers, the best known and most honoured, is the Ganga or Ganges. She is personified as Goddess Ganga. The river rises from an ice bed, 13, 800 feet above the sea level in the Garhwal Himalayas.

There are various legends associated with Ganga's descent from heaven to earth in the epics and Puranas such as the Mahabharta, Devi Bhagavata and the Bhagawata Purana etc.

According to the Bhagavata Purana, Ganga had its origin during the incarnation of Vishnu as Vamana. When Varnana measured the three worlds in three steps, the nails of his left feet were raised high. They caused a pore on the upper side of the universe. Ganga, starting from the finger of Vishnu's feet, fell in heaven and is therefore called Vishnupadi.

Taming of the Ganga by mythical figure Bhagiratha is beautifully depicted in the famous Besnagar sculpture, now in the Museum of Fine Arts, Boston, This sculpture belonging to the Gupta period is of about 500 A.D., from lintel of a temple at Besnagar. Here Ganga stands gracefully on the back of a makara whose mouth is held open by a small male figure who is depicted as taming the monster, symbolizing the taming of the Ganga by Bhagiratha. As always, she is portrayed as a beautiful maiden with lower half of her body resembling flowing water which reflects the myth that formerly the Ganga was a celestial river. The story of Ganga's descent to the plains should be viewed in this context.

The Ganga is often identified with Parvati, consort of Lord Shiva, or one of the other forms of mother goddess like Annapurna, goddess of food and plenty. Ganga's form varies according to local tradition. Thus in South India she is represented as mermaid, swimming in water with folded hands, wearing a crown, and bearing on here forehead the Saiva mark in sacred ashes. In Bengal she is depicted as a woman, coloured white (denoting here cleansing and purifying qualities), crowned and seated on her vahana, a makara. In her right hand she holds a lotus, in her left a lute.

Ganga has always remained a symbol of purity and holiness. Even the rememberance of her name purifies devotees, a look at the river and bath in her waters assure sanctity. According to legend, the waters of Ganga flow into every river in India at a certain time each year; these streams then assume the great holiness of Ganga herself and the power to purify pilgrims.

The story of Goddess Ganga is one of the most important themes in Indian mythology which has inspired the artists and sculptors. The doorway of every temple in India is guarded by an anthropomorphic representation of river Ganga. In the South, Ganga usually appears on the both jambs, but in the North, Ganga is represented on one jamb and Yamuna on the other. On these portals Ganga is represented as a damsel holding a water vessel and standing on her mount, the tortoise. The celestial guardians are seen most frequently on sanctuaries dedicated to Siva. They are also often present in shrines to other deities and even appear in the Vakataka caves at Ajanta.

One of the most beautiful representations of Ganga and Yamuna flanking a doorway is from a Gupta temple in Dah Parvatiya in Assam. Indian museums have several such representations of Ganga and Yamuna personified on door jambs. Each river goddess is shown on her mount and is accompanied by attendants, one of whom raises a parasol over her head. The swans that flutter above, with garlands of lotuses or lilies in their beaks, suggest the cool fragrance of an aquatic environment.

Ganga has been represented in art and sculpture in various forms. She is seen as the celestial stream and as the celestial stream and as the triple stream, as a damsel, pride incarnate, who rushes down on Siva's head, and as the river mother feeding the children of the soil with her water of plenty.

At Elephanta, Ganga is seen on the locks of Siva Gangadhara, at Paattadakal she is depicted as a mermaid dancing on the locks of Siva which swirl as her performs the virile tandava dance. A beautiful sculpture of Sena period shows Ganga standing by the wish fulfilling tree, which is a symbol of heaven, with a pitcher in her hand, indicating prosperity through abundance of water.

Ganga acquired many names indicating her various incarnations, the geographical regions through which she flowed and personages with whom she was associated. These are : Vishnupadi (flowing from the foot of Vishnu), Haimavati (flowing on Himavan), Alaknanda (from the 'locks of Siva'), Abharaganga or Akasaganga (the celestal Ganga), Devabhuti (heaven born), Mandakini (gently flowing, the milky way), Bhagirathi or Bhagirathasuta (from Bhagiratha), Pataiaganga and many more.

PRABHAKAR BEGDE

GANGA : THE HOLY RIVER

To an Indian, the river Ganga is not a mere inert mass of moving water : it is the perennial source of sustenance, both material and spiritual. No other river in the world has a history as rich in myths and legends as the Ganga, and no other river anywhere has become so inextricably integrated with the terrestrial, cultural and religious life of a whole nation.

The origin and meaning of the word "Ganga" is wrapped in mystery. According to one authority the word Ganga etymologically signifies that which leads you to 'Brahman', the Ultimate Reality. In other words, she liberates people from the magic spell which the world of sensual experiences. Casts on them. Etymologists differ over whether "Ganga" is a Sanskrit word. Some hold it is derived from the Tibetan "Tsong" which means "flowing water". The Nobel Laureate poet Rabindra Nath Tagore envisioned the Himalayas as a serene and serious sage in deep meditation, holding on his chest (or the heartland of India), a rosary of a river, namely the Ganga. She is reckoned as divinity in the form of water. To touch it, to drink it, to bathe in it when alive, to be washed in it when dead, is to be cleansed within and without for life and beyond.

Ganga evokes a mixture of feelings in the mind of its devotees Feelings of reverence emerge because of her divine origin for which she is reckoned as a sustajning mother. Her water is "amrit" or nectar that quenches the people's thirst and irrigates the vast expanse of agricultural crops. She is the cradle of our civilization and culture because ancient settlements and towns sprang up upon her banks as far back as the Aryan kingdoms before 500 B.C. Pandit Jawaharlal Nehru observed that "the story of the Ganga, from her source to the sea, from old times to the new, is the story of India's civilisation and culture".

In his will, he poetically opitomised the binding national symbol of the Ganga in the following words: "The Ganga, especially, is the river of India, beloved of her people, round which are interwined her racial memories, her hopes and fears, her victories and her defeats. She has been a symbol of India's age long culture and civilisation, ever changing, ever flowing and yet ever the same Ganga". No wonder then that the mendicant, the merchant, the prince, the preceptor and the conqueror have, over the ages, been drawn to the Ganga. And so it was in recent history when the Danes, the Dutch, the French and the British who coveted the riches of the east, sailed up the Ganga, the principai focus and core of the sub-continent.

The Ganga is one of the ten mighty river of the world. It meanders across the length and breadth of India for some 2525 miles covering the entire area north of the Vindhayas till she merges with the ocean in the Bay of Bengal. Its origin lies 4000 metres above the sea level in the Western Himalayas, to the north of Uttar Pradesh amidst a deep icy cavern resembling the mouth of a cow. This is known as Gaumukh which attracts a large number of pilgrims. The Ganga basin which spreads across eight states, sustains some 37 per cent of India's population. The Ganga basin is extensively cultivated and forms 47 per cent of the total irrigated area in the country.

The Ganga has been a major channel of communication since ancient times. During the British rule, one the favourite pastimes of the Europeans was to cruise along the Ganga to beat of the unbearable heat. The Viceroy, Lord Wellesley, had a special boat which was "richly ornamented with green and gold and it could carry 20 people with ease".

Today, the Ganga is in trouble it is polluted by three main pollutants: The domestic waste and sewage and lastly, poisonous garbage, animal carcasses and the run-off of chemical fertilisers and pesticides from the agricultural fields surrounding the river.

The river has been known to possess-self-purifying capacity due to the natural chemicals inherent in its water. But the excessive volume of man-made pollutants consigned into the Ganga each day has proved to be beyond its capacity. Besides the river has silted and become shallow because the dense forest cover on its watershed is vanishing with each passing day. Even so, the Ganga has not lost an iota of her sanctity deeply set in the minds of her countless worshippers. The challenge before the country today is to balance city growth with environment so that the river, which gave rise to India's cities and its civilisation, is not ravaged by the wastes thrown into.

In 1984, a scientific assessment was made of its pollution problem. In 1985, the Government of India's Environment Ministry set up the Central Ganga Authority as a separate wing. Its charter was to undertake a project to restore the pristine purity of the Ganga. On 14 June 1986, the then Prime Minister Rajiv Gandhi launched the Ganga Action Plan at Varanasi and resolutely affirmed that : "We shall see that the waters of the Ganga become clean again".

PRAN NATH LUTHRA

GANGA MAHOTSAV FESTIVAL

The very fact that Ganga Mahotsav (festival) is held in Varanasi the oldest living city in the world, lends an aura of mysticism, antiquity and tradition. This festival seeks to reveal an entire culture of a people, their confluence, their lifestyle, history, religion, customs and crafts - all in a span of five days; The festival also aims at projecting Varanasi as an ideal tourist destination where one can savour the famous woollen carpets of Uttar Pradesh, the silk and zari sarees of Banaras (Varanasi), black pottery and chunar terracotta of Azamgarh, chikan work of Lucknow and much more.

The sightseeing during the festival takes you too among other famous spots, Emperor Ashok's Edicts carved on rocks in Brahmi scripts; sarnath, a Buddhist pilgrimage centre, and the four-Lion stupa, which is India's National Emblem.

Ganga Mahotsava commences with a melee of activities and culminates in a grand finale, with the lighting of over 1,00,000 diyas (earthen lamps) by thousands of devotees. Indeed, quite literally, all the ghats come alive at night in a golden glow, as though the celestials have descended on earth to praticipate in the joyous occasion. A bright, full moon illuminates the vista below-the river Ganga bathed in an aureate hue with diyas, the reflections of which render her richer than a woman clad in ornate gold jewellery. The slow motion of the boats on the waves, as though keeping up with the rhythmic swaying of people in ecstasy, and religious fervour at the ghats; beautiful, soulful music filling the air- all this creates a tranquil feeling. It is a memory worth taking home.

MEETA SANGHVI

GANGAUR - THE FESTIVAL OF WOMEN

Gangaur is one of the most famous festivals celebrated in Rajasthan. Although it is celebrated throughout India, but in Rajasthan it has a distinct flavour.

A festival of women, Gangaur is celebrated specially by the unmarried girls, besides the married ones. Unmarried girls celebrate this festival to wish for a good husband and the married women pray for perpetual marital bliss.

In earlier times Gangaur was celebrated by the Rajput rulers of Jaipur with great pomp and show. This tradition has been kept alive by the people of Rajasthan, as this festival continues to be celebrated in great style. In similar fashion it is celebrated in Udaipur and Bundi too. Villagers from different parts of the state flock to see this festival. A large number of foreigners also participate in it.

PRERNA SHARMA

GANJIFA

Ganjifa, though made for use as playing cards, is a very unique art form. It synthesises a whole range of art forms and an entire heritage of thought, feeling and creativity. It is inspired by gods, demons, sages, country life, fauna and flora, Ganjifa cards look very beautiful like miniature paintings and their history goes back to centuries.

Ganjifa is a Persian word which means a treasure and in India, Nepal, Iran and other Arab countries it signified "playing cards". It is said that the game of Ganjifa was a favourite pasttime of the founder of the Mughal empire, Babar, and his daughter Begum Gul Badan. The celebrated chronicle of Babar's time - the Babarnama - introduced the game to India in the summer of 1527 when he sent Ganjifa cards as a gift to his friend in Sindh. Over the years, the game itself developed into many types. By the end of the 16th century, a standard form was evolved with the new game of 96 cards with eight suits consisting of 12 cards each. This has been mentioned in Akbar's biography written by Abul Fazal. This particular set of which no card is now available remains the standard for all Ganjifa games even to this day.

The Mughal Ganjifa is known as Changa Kanchan in Maharashtra's Sawantawadi region and Changarani in Andhra Pradesh. The game is also popular in Orissa where the cards are painted with images of Hindu deities though one can discern Mughal influence on them. In Orissa, the local name for Ganjifa is Navagunjara and visitors to Puri can find groups of people spending their leisure hours in playing Ganjifa. It is difficult to describe the Oriya's fascination for the game.

"Bishbar" is the name given to the first four suits of the Mughal Ganjifa cards. The Taj or crown symbolises the imperial court. "Safed" or white represents a silver coin. "Shamsa" or sabre stands for the palace guard and "Ghulam" is retinue. The weak suits are "Chang" (musical instrument), "Suraj" (sun), "Barat" (the king's chancery) and "Quimash" (emperor's stores).

With the Hinduisation of the game, new cards got evolved and this helped spread the game and made it popular in North India and the Deccan. Both the ruling classes and commoners were attracted by the game and the artistry of the cards themselves. The most popular among the cards belonged to the Dashvatara series - depicting the ten incarnations of the Hindu god Vishnu. There are Navaragraha Ganjifa representing the nine planets. Then there are those depicting Ramayana scenes.

In Karnataka, the Ganjifa cards received a great stimulus during the reign of Mummadi Krishnaraja Wadiyar, who was a great connoisseur of the arts. The game in Karnataka came to be known as Devara Aata - the game of the gods. Mummadi is said to have commissioned several artists to paint the cards - locally known as Chadas - and he himself compiled an encyclopaedia in Kannada called Shritatwanidhi that described 13 different Ganjifa games, some of which required packs of an many as 320 or 360 cards.

There is no standard pattern for Ganjifa. Every card is a masterpiece, hand-made and hand-painted and every pack an original creation. The traditional cards are circular in shape with diameters ranging from 22 mm and 32 mm to 120 mm in the larger cards. The larger cards are used only by the nobility and are called Darbar Kalams.

These are superb pieces of miniature art with exquisite details and made of expensive materials such as ivory, tortoise-shell, mother of pearl and enamelled precious metals. The inexpensive Bazar Kalams are made from papier-mache, palm leaf, waste paper and cloth. Many artists today make Ganjifa cards from layers of paper and cloth glued together, stretched and burnished.

There are rigid conventions for playing Ganjifa. Only used packs must be used for play with the cards placed face down at the centre of a clean white rectangular piece of cloth. The play moves in an anticlockwise direction with three, four or even five players participating.

The best-known Ganjifa artist of today is Karnataka's Raghupathi Bhatta of Mysore who has brought a fresh and original approach to this traditional art. Most of the illustrations for this text are by him. This 39-year old National Award Winner for 1993 draws on epicthemes that have stirred the imagination of people both in India and abroad. The most celebrated of Bhatta's cards for the Victoria and Albert Museum in London in 1992. Bharatiya Vidya Bhawan has sponsored his shows abroad and Bhatta is frequently invited to demonstrate his art at the Art in Action, Oxford, when artists from all over the world participate.

Ganjifa cards are precious heirlooms. By virtue of their delicate sensitive art, they provide windows into the past, as well as intimation of immortality, on just a little card.

T. S. SATYAN

GARABHA DANCE

Garaba dance; religious dance; Gujarat, danced by group, 50 to 100 women, in nights, in honour, goddess Amba-Mata, also known, Durga or Kali, women, move in circle, bending, turning, clapping their hands, songs, praise of goddess, accompanied.

GARDENS OF INDIA

Gardens in India are at least as old as those of Persia, and Hindu mythology contains many reference to them. The first of the great Indian gardens of 4 to 3 BC was that of the Mauryan King Chandragupta at Pataliputra, near present-day Patna, described as having fish tanks, peacocks and pheasants, plants parterres and shade trees as well as splendid building. Similar accounts of the gardens of king Ashoka, a few centuries later, also exist.

The early gardens of Buddhist seminaries and monasteries were devoted to retreat and meditation but remain today, as at Sarnath and Sanchi, only as archaeological sites. Then there were the numerous gardens of rulers and merchants, as well as a large number of gardens created by the early Muslim Emperor Feroz Shah in and around Delhi 600 years ago.

The Mughal gardens of the 16 c and 17 located on the Plains and in Kashmir are those which have justifiably attracted attention on the most. The first of these was possibly the Ram Bagh at Agra established by Emperor Babur. Their most creative phase peaked under Emperor Jahangir as at Shalimar Bagh. Kashmir, and perfected under Shah Jahan, as at the Taj Mahal and Red Fort, Delhi. There was also a strong Hindu garden tradition most noticeable in the 16 c garden at Vijayanagar and in the 18 c garden at Deeg; or in combination with the Mughal tradition which resulted in the Rajput style, exmplified in the Amber Palace gardens at Jaipur.

The Taj Mahal (1630-53) was built by Emperor Shah Jahan as a mausoleum to memory of his favourite wife Mumtaz Mahal. It is set majestically on a raised platform at the end rather than, as is more usual, at the centre of the classic Char Bagh (Quadripartite garden), based on the paradise garden described in the holy Quran. As is customay, the garden is enclosed on three sides by a wall and on the fourth by the river Yamuna.

A long north-south water course with fountains leads from the platform of the main entry gateway to a raised marble tank half way along its length. Here it meets canals on the east-west axis before finally leading to the tomb whose splendour is reflected in the water. The geometry of the gardenis reinforced by sandstone pathways that flank the canals as well as further subdivide the four quadrants. There are stone and marble benches but no water chutes or chadars, and fountains are only located within the main canal that leads to the mausoleum.

Originally, water was drawn from the Yamuna by a system of buckets and then collected in rooftop reservoirs located over rooms in the middle of the walls that bound the garden.. a system that has since been replaced by electric pumps. The garden is directly irrigated by overflow from the canals and for this reason the causeways are slightly raised. The constant stream of visitors is charged a nominal entry fee and the more frequented parts of the garden are well-maintained.

The Amber Palace, built by Man Singh and Jai Singh I during the early 17 c is located within the fort on a steep rocky hill 11 km from Jaipur. There are two gardens; both exhibit the influence of the Hindu and Muslim traditions and the result is a fine example of Rajput style. The first garden is set like a raft within the lake at the foot of the hill, and the best view of it may be obtained from the windows of the zenana quarter for women's residence of the palace above. The second garden is within the zenana quarter itself. A remarkable integral feature of both gardens is a precise interlacing pattern of stonework, and the result is that regardless of any subsequent variation of flowers or shrubs, the original form and layout of the garden remains clearly discernible.

The garden within the zenana quarter is small, its boundaries firmly defined by buildings of the palade complex. Occupants of the palace and their attendants once came here to find respite from the heat, enjoying from the marble platform and surrounding terrace the sound of water trickling over small carved chadars as well as the water-cooled air. The garden's stone paths form the shape of a star, once taken as a symbol of both life and intellect. These paths divide the sunken garden in a formal geometric manner and link to bridges that in turn lead to a central octagonal platform.

The Hindu palace gardens at Deeg, 98 km west of Agra, were laid out by the Maharaja of Bharatpur. Suraj Mal, in the first half of the 18 c. The formal char bagh plan is formed by four canals that start with a cascade and lead to a central tank. Flowers supply a great range of colour and together with flowering trees, shrubs and herbs provide many scents. Stone-flagged footpaths lead to the various buildings via ramps and steps.

Most gardens are designed to provide pleasure in one form or another and this was certainly the case at Deeg. For example, a swimming pool was designed with a swing that passed through cooling jets in the heat of the summer. In fact, water in this garden is fully exploited. Fed from a large raised tank located at the south end of the garden, there are canals, pools and chadars; many fountains are located within the canals as well as within the pavilions that flank the main building, the Gopal Bhawan. This building is fronted by gardens and at the rear, kiosks and balconies overlook the Gopal Sagar reservoir. A further pavilion, the Keshave Bhawan, overlooks the Rup Sagar reservoirs or the east side of the main garden. A unique feature of this latter pavilion is a double roof with a device that was once operated by water forced through hollow columns to rorate lithic stone balls; when these balls rolled along water channels, the thunder of the monsoons was simulated.

Adimittedly, it may well be assumed that the majority of today's visitors could be more interested in a garden's potential to afford pleasure and enjoyment than in its scholarly authenticity. Nonetheless, it is instructive to compare the present state of these gardens with what is known of their original condition, bearing in mind that trees and shrubs grow, died and are replaced, and that successive head gardners and private owners, followed later by government departments with responsibilities to the public, have all exerted their ideas and influence over time.

For its part, the garden of the Taj Mahal has been well-documented, and in fact, detailed descriptions of the planning of their gardens was often recorded in journals by the Mughal emperors. Originally there could have been fruit trees in this garden whose produce helped pay for its upkeep. Such trees would have long disappeared and photographs taken in the last centry show masses of other trees on either side of the central canal. This planting was subsequently cleared, but from the standpoint of authenticity, today's informal layout of large trees, though familiarly accepted and pleasant, is equally removed from the Mughal tradition. However, the char bagh layout and the canals exist virtually unaltered and the Taj Mahal itself remains supreme.

At Amber, the basin in the zenana garden that surrounds the platform was once filled with water; this is now for the most part dry, but since a small fee is charged for entry to the palace complex, which itself is now undergoing restoration, it is possible that sufficient amount of water will be made available to reveal the full glory of this sheltered garden. Indeed, water plays a majore role in the design of all three gardens described here. Its attractions are universal, and its characteristics of reflection of stillness, or of movement, together with its cooling effect, invariably make it the focus.

The historic Indian gardens still provide a strong measure of continuity with the past. Besides the quiet and fresh air that these supply, in contrast to the noise from traffic and dust outside, their designs possess a unity and simplicity that remains of fundamental relevance even today.

JONAS LEHRMAN

GAUHARJAAN (1870 -1929)

Gauharjan was born in Lucknow. She learnt from Moujuddin, the uncrowned king of 'thumri'. She was also adept at singing the 'teppa', the 'hori', etc. She had an astonishingly flexible voice which could easily traverse three octaves. Her numbers 'Radhe-krishna mukhase' and Krishna Murari have become immortal.

GEETA CHANDRAN : PRIMA DONNA OF BHARATANATYAM

A classical dancer who is a top-ranking performer, a teacher, founder - President of "Natya Vriksha", a writer, an activist who believes that atrists must articulate social concerns... there are several dimensions to Bharatanatyam dancer Geeta Chandran.

Hailed as a contemporary legend in the classical dance of Bharatanatyam, the art of Geeta Chandran traverses the twin universes of pristine tradition and modernity. Though she is an artist trained by a galaxy of eminent gurus in the Taanjavoor bani (tradition) of Bharatanatyam, yet Geeta is a women of today. Her dance reflects her contemporary concerns: the need to protect the environment, urging gender equality, evoking national pride and building societal bridges.

To watch her dance is an aesthetic experience where competence of technique is further imbued by the dancer's creative spirit and her entire persona. Geeta is especially known for her fluid abhinaya (expressions) which bring the ancient dance of Bharatanatyam alive to audiences today. She has visited many countries and enthralled her audiences.

Geeta is firmly of the view that "all art must reflect the artist; all true art is deeply imprinted by the person who creates it. My dance must be true to me. I am a deeply spiritual person and my dance reflects this". She further says that "we have to make relevant statements through

the grammar of our art. If, I feel environment is relevant and a very dear cause, or if peace is the vortex of my "wish terrain", then those are the themes that get reflected in my dance".

Dance, she says, fulfils her at several levels; it is a vital mechanism for her in her search for beauty. Beauty of the body as it carves space and beauty of the mind as it seeks serenity. Bharatnatyam enables her to find both external and internal solace. "My dance is a beautiful bridge between past and present, it slices through time, it enables me to create".

Geeta founded "Natya Vriksha" to make her students understand India's complex and vast cultural heritage. This institute conducts classes in Bharatanatyam dance and Carnatic music.

Geeta encourages her world-wide students to visit her website at http:/tripod.members.com/geetachandran/and query her on all cultural issues at geetachandran hot-mail.com.

BHARAT BHUSHAN

GHALIB, ASSADULLAH KHAN (1779-1869)

Of Turkish descent; born at Agra (December 27); studied classical Persian (prose and poetry) in local maktab; has little education but acquired much knowledge in many fields because of his deep and sedulous studies; his uncle, Nasrullah Beg Khan's wife was sister of Ahmad Baksh Khan, ruler of Loharu, whose niece, daughter of notable Urdu poet, Ma'roof he married (1810); left Agra and settled down at Delhi (1812); connection with ruling family of Loharu gained him entree to highest circles of Delhi which was literary centre of Urdu and Persian letters where many illustrious poets, scholars, savants, learned religious men, Sufis and other famous people were (probably) his uncle's and father-in-law's friend's, with many of whom he also made life long friendship; at Ahmad Baksh Khan's recommendation (1806), British authorities granted Nasrullah annual pension of Rs. 10,000 through Ahmad Baksh but somehow only Rs. 5,000 was received by family of which Ghalib got Rs. 750 as well as some additional monetary help from Ahmed Baksh; could not make ends meet on this amount; learning that his family had been deprived of half the pension because of Ahmed Baksh, he went to Calcutta to fight his case (1828) but was unsuccessful; Ahmad Baksh's help also ceased; Bahadur Shah II (Zafar), last Mughal emperor, lover of Urdu poetry and himself a poet and great patron of poets, commissioned him to write history of house of Timur on salary of Rs. 600 per month, presented him with a robe of honour and some titles (1850); gave him appointment as his literary consultant and his literary adviser; with outbreak of struggle of 1857, his pension was stopped; received allowance of Rs. 110 per month from Yusuf Ali Khan, Nawab of Rampur, his literary disciple and at whose instance his portion of family pension was restored (1860); expenditure on his style of living far exceeded his income; last few years were spent in difficult financial circumstances; became victim of physical ailments; died of brain haemerrhage; buried in Nisamuddin (West), New

Delhi; marble mausoleum on his tomb created by Ghalib Society (1956); greatest Urdu poet of India; of his Urdu diwans (5,000 couplets) he selected and published 2,000 poems, which made him famous; his letters (in Urdu) were collected (2 volumes) in his lifetime and after his death a large number of his letters were included in various collections; wrote voluminously in Persian (11,000 couplets), prose works, a grammar and vocabulary, letters, history of Mughal dynasty, Dastanboo (accounts of events during struggle of 1857) and Qati-Burhan (literary criticism); his letters in Persian are valuable being simple, full of wit, clever turns of speech and biographical detail; blazed trail in Urdu poetry by introducing new outlook and atmosphere and writing on problems of philosophy of religions, philosophical ideas, God, man's problems in life, etc.; language used is elegent and beautiful, ideas have mystical quality, realism and great depth of meaning.

References

Freeman-Grenville, S.S.P., The Muslim and Christian Calendars, London, 1963.

Russell, Ralf and Islam, K., Ghalib : Life and Letters, London, 1969.

Spear, Percival, Twilight of the Mughals, Cambridge, 1951.

GHOOMAR

National folk-dance, Rajasthan, women in full skirts, colourful chuneries dance, spectacular, kacchi gheri dancers, equipped with shields, long swords, upper part of bodies, arrayed, traditional attire of a bridegroom, lower part concealed by coloured papier-mache horse, built on bamboo frame, enact contests, marriages, festivals, Bawaris, criminal tribe, experts in this dance form.

GINGEE FORT - ARCHITECTURAL SPLENDOUR

About 150 kilometres from Madras in the north-western corner of South Arcot district, rising out of a plain extending about fourteen to fifteen kilometres or rather more, one can see a range of hills. With jagged summits they are covered with huge rounded boulders. All of them look precariously balanced and a feeling grips you that any moment you may witness them tumbling down. But then, stand still and you are convinced that they have remained so for ages, and there is no chance of their coming down. These rocks tempt you and pep your spirits so that you clamber over them and certify the massive strength and unshakable solidity of the fortifications of Gingee, the last signature of history in terms of forts.

As is the case with many names, Gingee is anglicised name of the place locally known as Sengi. Historical research shows that this name was traced to Sangaram - A Vaishnavit shrine close by, whose God is supposed to be the guardian deity of this place.

Long back it was known as Krishnapura - the name was probably goven by the first ruling dynasty who traced their lineage to a shepherd clan. When the Bijapur rulers held this fort they called it Badshahbad and as Marathas took it, they called it Chandry or Chindy. Then later on the Mughals called it Nasrat Gaddah - the name of the commander who besieged it.

The fortress of Gingee embraces a triangle formed by three high hills namely Krishnagiri, Rajagiri and Chandradurg which are enclosed by an outer wall, Rajagiri, 600 feet high, is the highest of the three and aloft its summit stands the citadel. It is perched on an overhanging bluff of a ridge, which on three sides is surrounded by three walls 20-25 feet high, and on the fourth side by a narrow but steep ravine. It is these high-rising rocks and the steep ravine that makes escalations or access to the ditadel extremely difficult. The only access to the citadel from the north is by way of timber drawbridge over the ravine at a certain point. One of the most striking features of the Gingee Fortifications is the abundant water supply and the system of reservoirs which ensured that in case of a siege the defenders could have easy access to this vital necessity of life. History tells us that the Marathas captured this fort under the kingship of Shivaji and after his death the Mughals took possession of it. It was not an easy task and the battle went on for seven years. Though the Mughals had come with a strong force, the architectural solidity and strength of the fort made their task difficult as a smaller force inside could withstand the onslaught. This speaks volumes of the arrangements inside the fort that kept the defender's spirits high. It ultimately fell because is became a prestige issue for the Mughals who were ready to suffer any amount of casualties to take charge of Gingee.

Gingee is a tourist attraction, as it is an exquisite example of architectural splendour.

N. CHANDRAMOHAN NAIDU

GIRISH KARNAD : ICON OF THE INDIAN THEATRE

Girish Karnad- an icon of the Indian theatre - has worked throughout his life for the enrichment of theatre in India, particularly Kannada theatre in the Indian state of Karnataka. A playwright and an actor par excellence, Girish Karnad also is a film-maker and novelist "who has sought to promote the benefits of moderation without resorting to shrillness or stridency". The most coveted "Jnanpith award" for 1998 was conferred upon him in recognition of his artistic sensitivity that has upheld the virtues of democracy, pluralism and decency in public life.

Theatre and tales of popular heroes have always fascinated Girish Karnad from the very beginning. He recalls that "as children, we grew up in the town of Dharwar (in Karnataka) and were extremely fond of beguiling stories, folk tales, lores and legends drawn from the epics Mahabharata and Ramayana and the Panchtantra tales. We would witness and enjoy the weekly Byalu Nataka (Open Stage Theatre) as well as the Janara Nataka (People's Theatre). It was a milestone in our impressionable minds, a vital element in our regular regimen. The evenings would often stretch into late nights, and our parents, elders or guardians had to vitrually herd us back home from the open grounds. Though sleepy and dog-tired, we were still awe-struck and misty-eyed over the litany of tales and fables of heroes, heroines, villains and buffoons...."

Explaining his overwhelming interest in the theatre, Dr. Karnad goes on, "Our parents and elders would visit the weekly or fortnightly travelling theatre companies to witness and enjoy the popular versions of plays by Ibsen, Molliere, Proust, Shakespeare, Elliot, George Bernard Shaw and so on - such was the literary - mad and theatre - conscious cultural town of Dharwar. They equally enjoyed the theatrical productions based on Indian classics. We, the school boys and girls, would go day-after-day to dramatic performances at the Byalu Nataka (Open Stage Theatre), and go into raptures over the renderings of many a tale excerpted from the classics....."

In the wake of his splendid scholastic credits at the University of Karnataka (in Dharwar) and subsequently at the University of Bombay, Girish Karnad in his early twenties won the Rhodes scholarship to pursue his studies at Oxford University. According to him, he did his "PPE - Philosophy, Politics and Economics" at Oxford.

The young Girish Karnad tried his hands at many literary and artistic pursuits and excelled in most of them. But he has a regret : "My efforts (to be a poet) came unstuck. But, dialogue-writing is his forte. "I don't know how I took to penning down appropriate dialogue."

As a novice playwright, he wrote Yayati in 1961. The theme was drawn from the Mahabharata, and centres around the Hindu concept of responsibility. The play is considered to be a tour de force of Hinduism. Hindu ethos, life-style and psyche. It is the story of young puru pledging to sacrifice his youth so that his aging father can prolong his own youth. Puru considers it his duty to his father, his "creator". The play was an instant success with mesmerized audiences, and won him the Karnataka State Award for the Best Drama of the Year (1961). Exactly ten years later, he was confered the Natya Sadhna Award for the "Best Play of the Year 1971" for his play Hayavadana.

It was his second play Tughlaq which catapulted the playwright into national, and indeed international, fame. Originally written in Kannada, it was translated into English by Dr. Karnad himself. It has also been translated into Hindi. The virtuoso of Indian theatre, Dr. Al Qazi staged it long ago. Since then, it has been staged innumerable times to packed houses all over India, to everyone's critical acclaim. The play won for him the Sangeet Natak Academy award in 1964. It has also, undoubtedly, made him an icon or cult personality of the Indian theatre.

Spurred on by the success of Tughlaq, Dr. Karnad wrote several novels from 1970s to 90s, such as Anjumallige (Frightened Jasmine, 1977), Hittina Hunja (The store House in the Backyard, 1980), Nagamandala (The World of Snakes, 1988) and Tale Danda (Death by Beheading, 1990.). He also wrote another of his most popular plays, Hayavadana (The Face of the Horse) in 1971.

Dr. Karnad, a man far beyond the confines of the theatre, has always displayed a natural flair for the cinema and television. He has acted in many feat re films. Swami, Manthaan and Nishant are films that will always be remebered by his fans for his powerful roles. In Kannada cinema, his roles in Samskara, Ghatta Shraddha, Vamsa Vriksha and Ondanondu Kaladalli bring him out as an actor of depth and preception.

All literary works of Dr. Karnad are originally in evocative Kannada. Most of them have been translated into English by him, and published by Oxford University Press.

Several awards have been conferred on Dr. Karnad for his outstanding achievements and contribution to the world of literature and theatre. President's Gold Medal for the script of Samskara (1970), Padma Shree for his first play Yayati (1974), Padma Bhushan for his play Hayavadana (1922), the Sahitya Academy award in 1994 for his historical play Tale Danda (Death by Beheading), and the Janapith Award (1998) are some examples from a long list.

Dr. Karnad was the Chairman of the Karnataka Natak Academy (Karnataka Theatre Academy) from 1976-78, and Chairman of the Sangeet Natak Academy (Academy of Music and Theatre) and the National Academy of Performing Arts from 1988-93. He has been a visiting Professor and fulbright scholar in residence at the university of chicago from 1987-88. He is currently the President of the Film and Television Institute of India.

D. R. RAJAGOPAL

GIRJA DEVI

(B. 1938)- Vocalist : Hindustani, Khayal of Senia Gharana, thumri, tappa; studied with Shri Chandra Misra.

Determined to popularise classical music, Girijadevi is planning the set up an ashram in Varanasi to teach poor children music and etiquette besides formal studies.

She has remained the reigning queen of the Benaras 'gharana' for decades and at 65 she has still not been called upon to abdicate, because Girijadevi sings almost just as well now as she did in her heyday.

However, she feels that while Varanasi has the maximum number of 'gharanas' to offer, she is like a solitary figure holding onto them. So she is planning to set up an ashram near the Ganges at Varanasi where she could teach even poor children.

"They would serve the ashram and I would ensure the best education for them", says Girijadevi. "The lessons would include not just music, but studies, etiquette and running the home (for girls)".

She has already created a trust in her own name for the purpose, totally out of her own funds because she does not want "Government involvement and interference". Grants are welcome but she wants to set up the trust and run it in her own way.

"Set it up I will, even if it is in a hut," she adds' laughing.

And "set it up" she will, because she is a person who has not only been obsessed with this form of music since the age of five but has tenaciously pursued it through a busy married life.

"My father was a teacher and interested in music, but my mother was a village girl", informs Girijadevi. "When my father realised that I was interested in music even at an early age (may be it has something to do with my previous birth), he arranged for my music lessons under the late Pandit Sarju Prasad Misra".

It continued till the age of 16 when her guru died. By this time, however, she had received her training in 'tappa', 'thumri' and 'Khayal'. She was married off at 17 and for a while her learning was interrupted. But then she resumed it after a year under the Late Pandit Sree Chandra Misra.

"I was taught old traditional music by him like 'dhrupad', 'chandprabhas' and 'khayal' as well as many others which nobody knows now", says Girijadevi.

In 1949 she gave her first programme over AIR. In 1951 she participated in a conference for the first time and after that there was no looking back for her. She went on to become what she is today. Girijadevi stands out among her contemporaries because she does not specialise in only one genre of classical music. She sings everything and excels in all of them.

Although her husband had no objection to her pursuing her career in music (excepting for performances at private parties, which she never did), it has not been an easy life for Girijadevi.

"I used to get up at 3.30 in the morning and practise till 5.30, after which I did my housework and cooking. From 11 a.m. to one p.m. I practised again because by two o'clock my family would be back home. Then my guru came in the evening and taught me from seven to nine", she says.

Her only daughter, Sudha Datta, is an Oddissi dancer and has learnt from Pandit Kelucharan Mahapatra.

Based in Varanasi, her birthplace, Girijadevi went to Calcutta for a five-day workshop that was organised by the West Bengal State Academy of Music and dance (a brainchild of the then State Minister for information and Public Affairs, Buddhadev Bhattacharya).

"It is not possible to learn much in such a short period, but at least such workshops will give the participants some idea about Girijadevi's style. She will be able to guide them", says Jaya Biswas, well-known sitarist, who is on the academy's panel of management.

Girijadevi conducted a 25-day workshop in Shantiniketan and had been a visiting professor at the Benares Hindu University.

She, however, seems to feel that the younger generation is increasingly going in for "rap and other forms of modern music" (instead of classical) as compared to the old times.

"Once I was performing in Calcutta and people who could not be accommodated in the auditorium, sat on newspapers outside and listened all night", recalls Girijadevi. "Classical music was much more respected then. The interest is more in names now".

Perhaps, it is partially with this motive of popularising classical music, that Girijadevi is planning her dream ashram, and as one of the greatest torchbearers of her own 'gharana', she is bound to succeed.

GOA'S CARNIVAL SPIRIT

"Let there be merry-making, Let there be rejoicing and dancing for three days. Let men and, women enjoy themselves the way they like - but only for three days. After this period come back to your original routine." This is what the legendary King Momo is said to have told his subjects during the earliest carnival in Goa.

King Momo is just a folktale king of Portugal without having any bearing in the history. But it does not matter. Because the carnival he referred to is celebrated every year in February for three days.

The exact dates are fixed every year according to the Catholic calendar, though the Catholic Church has disowned the carnival. They feel it is not in consonance with the Christian tenets. But no problem. The tourist industry, private companies and organizations have stepped in with their floats and dancing groups to keep the carnival going.

The carnival is celebrated in the big cities of Panaji, Margaon and Vasco. Big, beautifully floats on educational themes are organised. Different dancing groups with their bands and music parties enthral the people. When the carnival is on, every roof-top, balcony and footpath is full of people wearing colourful dresses, masks and hats. Even foreign tourists participate and enjoy the celebrations.

Although the festive mood is infectious, but nothing indecent is allowed to happen. This indeed is creditable for the people of Goa of all castes and creed who are basically sober, honest and God-fearing.

JOGINDER CHAWLA

GOLCONDA : THE INVINCIBLE CITADEL OF THE DECCAN

Golconda Fort is one of the most famous of the medieval forts of the Deccan. It was first built by the ancestors of the Rajas of Warangal in 1363 AD. It was ceded to the Behmai kings (1346-1518). After the defeat and fall of the Behmais it became the capital of the Qutub Shahi kingdom (1518-1687AD.) Aurangzeb annexed it to the Mughal empire from the last of the Qutub Shahis, Abul Hasan Tanasha. Later on when Asif Jah was appointed by Aurangzeb as the Mughal subedar (governor) of the Deccan, the Golconda fort passed under the Asif Jahi dynasty in 1713 AD. The Fort was extended and strengthened from time to time the Qutub Shahi kings with fortified walls, bastions and battlements.

The remains of this magnificent citadel are located on the outskirts of the city of Hyderabad. But it must be borne in mind that a short, hurried tour followed by the light-and-sound show is not enough to do justice to the architectural delights hidden in the ruins of Golconda. If your really want to feel the pulse of this magnificent Fort, even a full day in the company of a knowledgeable guide may not be adequate.

When the Qutub Shahi dynasty ascended the throne and occupied Golconda, it was more or less a mud and clay brick settlement established by the herdsmen (Gola Cunda) from whom the Fort, derives its name. The first three qutub Shahi rulers are largely responsible for shaping it into a formidable citadel by constructing in stone on the rocky mountain foundation. The construction work continued for 62 years, from 1518 to 1580 AD.

The Fort has an elevation of 120 meters; it has three protective boundary walls, the outer wall has a circumference of seven kms, has eight gates and 87 bastions. There is a ditch around the outer fortified wall. Each bastion was mounted by guns, rendering it one of the strongest medieval forts of the Deccan. Golconda town came to be established within the boundary wall and was sell known for its extensive trade in diamonds and large gems.

The layout of the Golconda fort shows unique planning. There are numerous instances of stellar architectural wonders incorporated into its design. For instance, just inside the main entrance, Balahisar Gate, there is a point from where the echo of a handclap is audible on top of the citadel located on the peak of the hillock. This extraordinary, medieval telephone is believed to have been deliberately constructed to communicate to the palace guards any messages regarding visiting persons. Also, the mountainous terrain compelled the builders to adapt the foundation laying to an extraordinary system. A number of marvellous structures have been built on solid rocks without any dug up foundations. The building is simply resting on rocks. Nails hewn out of solid rock were hammered into boulders to guarantee stability and moor the structure. These nails are sais to have pierced upto a foot inside the rock and can be seen in the fringes of several buildings. Yet another feat of architectural ingenuity is the method of creating an artificial cooling effect in the palaces by channelling the outside hot air through increasingly narrower, moist passages to ensure cool breeze inside. The cooling effect is comparable to an air conditioner's cooling, without any energy consumption.

There are many structures and buildings inside the Fort complex and each has it own story to tell. As you start the upward climb, near the main gate is a beautiful park known as the Nagina (uncountable) Park. Folklore has it that an old faithful subedar, Abdulla Pani, attained martyrdom at this place, defending the Fort against Aurangzeb's third assault in 1684 AD. The valiant subedar was injured so grievously that the injuries afflicted on his body could not be counted, leading to the Park's name.

To overcome the Perennial water scarcity, underground clay pipes were laid, covering an incredible distance of 16 kms to bring water from Hussein Sagar reservoir. A system of four water storage tanks inside the city, each tank at a successively higher level, was constructed. The lowest tank for instance is 40 feet deep, measuring about 150 feet by 75 feet. The water for the tank was brought through the pipes and lifted with the help of lift pumps. These tanks effectively solved the water problem. Each tank was covered and was further made safe by constructing a 40-ft high facade to confuse and thwart the enemy's design to poison the water supply source from outside through a poison laden missile;

There is ample evidence of very advanced drainage systems in other parts of the Fort as well. As remarkable network of concealed drains and the brackets to secure them to the walls are still visible amongst the ruins. The original fountain in Rani Mahal (still in working condition) was similarly fed by these types of concealed clay pipes. The queen's attached toilet in Rani Mahal is in fact a beautifully carved pit latrine with the pit at least 180 ft deep. A swimming pool for the exclusive use of the Royal family measures 200-ft by 200 ft and is 10 ft deep. It was filled with rose water. Smaller baths were provided within the living quarters and palaces of the queen and royal family members.

As one climbed towards the top of the hillock, one comes across the Ram Das Bandighar or jail. This is in fact a grain store of substantive dimensions which was converted into a makeshift cell. It was used to imprison a revenue officer named Kancherlu Gopanna who allegedly misappropriated a princely sum of six million and used it for constructing a Ram temple in Bhadrachalam. The erring official was imprisoned by Sultan Abdul Hassan Tanasha and kept in confinement for 12 years (1671-1684). During this time Gopanna or Bhakta Ramdas as he later on came to be called, carved 16 stone sculptures on the walls of his makeshift prison. Folklore says that at the end of 12 years, the Sultan was visited in his dreams by two strangers of divine bearing, interpreted to be the Gods Ram and Laxman, who returned the embezzled money and ordered him to release the captive. Ramdass was thus set free by the Sultan.

Near the Bhakta Ramdas jail is the Ambar Khana or the granary from where the Sultan used to distribute grains to the poor (Khairat). Slightly further up are the remains of the Qutub Shah, commemorating the completion of thirty years of his rule (1550-158) A.D. The architecture and design of this mosque formed the blueprint for construction of the Char Minar by Sultan Mohammad Quil Qutub Shah later (1580-1612 AD.)

At the top of the hill are two notable structures, the first being an 850-year-old temple dedicated to the Goddess Maha Kali. This temple has two huge stone boulders, which dwarf it. One is shaped like a bull's head. An annual festival dedicated to the Goddess is celebrated during July-August.

The second is the Baradari, a two-storey building with a commanding view of the surrounding countryside, used as a meeting hall where the Sultan met with his people, held conferences and settled disputes. This is the place where the echo of a handclap can be clearly heard about 420 meters from the Balahisar gate - a truly remarkable feat; A secret underground tunnel from Baradari provides a secret passage or escape route to the Gosha Mahal near Char Minar. The tunnel is reported to be 30 feet deep, 12 feet wide and 8 kms long, large enough for horsemen to ride through. The entrance to this tunnel is now sealed. The unique colling medhanism ensures a cool breeze blows across the terrace. Just behind the Baradari is a massive bastion on which were mounted the most powerful guns.

As you start the descent from the opposite side of Baradari, a moment should be spared to enjoy the bird's eye view of the ruins of the city. The ruins of the three prominent Palaces meant for the royal woman viz. Taramati's Mahal, Rani Mahal and Baghmati's Mahal, along with the Zanana Palace, meant to house the royal women folk's bodygurds (mostly eunuchs) can be clearly outlined. The imposing triple storey structure meant for the Armoury can also be seen. The palaces meant for the royal women had beautifully planned dressing and bathing areas and numerous artistic alcoves meant for shrinagar still remain. The best-preserved are found in the Rani Mahal ruins, which was originally a three-story structure.

At Ranga Mahal, the original fountain and stages meant for performances by the various artists and entertainers are intact and this is where the audience for the light-and-sound shows are seated.

Golconda under the Qutub Shahi dynasty thrived as an important trade centre and merchants from Afghanistan, Persia and Iran crowded the streets of this magnificent City Fort. Golconda was an important producer of diamonds and other gems; the Koh-i-noor diamond being one of the impressive possessions of the Qutub Shahis, plundered by the Mughals when the Fort fell.

Golconda Fort was built as an invincible citadel. The might of the Mughals could not pierce even the first line of its defence. Aurangzeb's first assault (in 1653) was repulsed at the outer wall itself; in 1665 AD he attacked a second time but realizing the futility of a frontal assault, laid siege to the fort and cut off its supply line. At that time the Sixth Qutub Shahi ruler, Sultan Abdullah Qutub Shah, was on the throne. In the sixth months of the siege, the Sultan's mother arranged a meeting with Aurangzeb and as a result one of the Sultan's two daughters was given away in marriage to Aurangzeb, ending the siege. The third and final assault by Aurangzeb was in 1684 AD when the enemy gained entry into the Fort through treachery. A traitor subedar Abdulla Razak Lahiri betrayed the seventh and last Qutub Shahi ruler, Sultan Abdul Hassan Tanasha, and allowed Aurangzeb and his army to enter the. Fort from the till then insurmountable Balahisar gate. The traitor, who was promised the mansabdari of Aurangabad, was killed at the gate itself as soon as Aurangzeb entered the Fort. Against odds and heavily outnumbered, the other valiant subedar, Abdulla Pani, fought the invading army and put up a stiff last ditch attempt to push back Aurangzeb from the Fort. Wounded and ounnumbered, this brave soldier was martyred at the 'Nagina Park' and with him fell the Fort. The Sultan was captured when the Mughal forces reached Baradari. He was detained first at Aurangabad and later at Daulatabad where he breathed his last 14 years later. He is buried there. Aurangzeb gave the subedari of the Fort of Asif Jah, a soldier in Auranzeb's army who abandoned the Fort and decided to develop instead the city of Hyderabad.

The fall of Golconda Fort brought to an abrupt end its golden age and of the Qutub Shahi dynasty. The incomplete tomb of the seventh and last Qutub Shahi king is a sad memorial to the treacherous end of a secular, magnanimous and prosperous reign. Perhaps the poetess Sarojini Naidu has composed the most eloquent eulogy to this dynasty :

Though centuries falter and decline
Your proven strongholds shall
remain
Embodied memories of your line
Incarnate legends of your reign
(Form The Royal Tombs of Golconda)

AJAY KASHYAP

GOURI : A FASCINATING : TRIBAL DANCE - DRAMA

The Bheels of Rajasthan have the same cultural traits as other tribals of India have but Gouri, the dance-drama of vigour and thrills, performed by them has no parallal any where. It is the only dance-drama in India, which is perfromed in the day time and has no commercial and profiteering motives. Its perfromance in the nights is considered as a serious breach of religious faith and may bring calamity to the Bheel community at any time and of any magnitude. The ban on its performance at night is also due to several rituals and ceremonies that the performers have to perform in the night immediately after the performance in the day time is over.

Gouri cannot be performed on invitation and on payments. It is purely a religious drama performed as a part of duty. The village in which any of the girls belonging to the performers village is married, invariably becomes the venue of their performance. The play is initiated by beating of drums and fixture of the holy Trishool in a prominent place of the village. This event announces the arrival of the Gouri group in the village. The village girl, from whose ancestral home the Gouri group hails, perfroms the inaugural ceremony by offering coconus, a piece of red cloth and a sari to the Rais, to the two heroines of the play. The play starts early in the morning and ends at sunset. Hundreds of the people from neighbouring villages gather round the Trishool and witness the show.

The Gouri Dance-drama commences from the second day of Raksha Bandhan. The performers have to be away from their families for more than a month and are given a ceremonial send off at the time of their departure from the village. During this period the performers have to observe strict celibacy and refrain from non-vegetarian diet, liquor and green vegetables. They pass vigilant nights in the village and sing devotional songs in the worship of their deity Bhairav.

The origin of Gouri dance is linked with the story of Mohini and Bhasmasur. The Demon Bhasmasur was a great devotee of Shiva. He sat in penance for an indefinite period and succeeded in getting a promise from the Lord for the award of the much coveted anklet that Lord Shiva wore in his arm from times immemorial. The anklet was known for its power of emiting tremendous fire, which he had to part with most reluctantly. This unusual event created confusion in the minds of Gods and was received with dismay and shock all over the universe. It caused havoc and destruction when the anklet started emiting fire when moved by Bhasmasur indiscriminately. Lord Shiva and his wife Parvati too had to take shelter in a cave. When Lord Vishnu, the God of preservation, heard of this unfortunate plight of Lord Shiva and Parvati, he came to their rescue in the garb of Mohini, the heavenly apsara of enormous beauty. Bhasmasur got enchanted with the beauty of Mohini and started flirting with her. Mohini, by her magical powers, was successful in making Bhasmasur dance in such a way that the anklet was on his head for a while. This was the specific posture when the anklet emits fire on the holder of the anklet himself. Bhasmasur, thus, was enveloped in fire and was on the verge of death. Taking pity on the sad plight of the devil, Bhasmasur, Mohini offered to fulfill his last wish if any. At wihich Bhasmasure expressed his wish that his name may be immortalized by retaining his devilish face and imbibing some of Shiva's powers in him. His wish was ultimately fulfilled and from then the Gouri started functioning with Bhasmasur as its Chief deity and Bheels as its participants.

The Gouri dance-drama is performed to keep the memory of this devil deity alive, The Bheels are its chief performers. The Gouri commences with a group dance termed as Gammat. The circular gammat is also known as Gai and symbolizes the universe in its extreme ecstasy. Budia, behaving himself as the creator of the universe, controls the Gai while moving in anticlock wise direction. The dancers clad in loose and flying costumes are at their best when they are allowed to dance freely. The Jhalar and Madal, the chief accompanying instruments, are played in varied styles to inspire the dancers and enable them to creat extraordinary movements. The culmination of the Gammat follows with the ultimate surrendering of the artist in the hands of their deity. They feel relieved from all the troubles of life.

The Gouri has very few spoken words and is mostly based on gestures, body movements and songs. The chief Bhopa, the producer and the controller of the drama also known as Kutakdia, forms the main link between one episode and the other and interprets the drama in a vocabulary best known to the Gouri dancers themselves. Women characters are performed invariably by male members because of the vigour and strength that every character of Gouri is expected to posses.

The costumes are fantastic and the emotions produced by the artists are superb and perfect. The first episode is the fight between Kalka, the Goddess of destruction and Sankothri, the witch. The Sankothri makes all kinds of efforts to kill the Goddess but fails, because Budia with his two consorts Parvati and Mohini comes to their rescue and kill her.

The second episode is of Hatia Ambay. Hatia is the king of Hativardesh located some where near Mansarovar. The Ambay who is a lady of immense power comes to take bath in the lake every day and polutes the water. The maids of Hatiavardesh, who come to fetch water, are greatly disturbed complain to their king, Hatia, about this nuisance at which the king and his brother waged war against the lady Ambay in which they were ultimately killed.

The third episode is about the two robbers trying to rob the treasures carried by Banjaras for their deity Lord Budia (Bhasmasur) and his two consorts. But they are ultimately killed. The Banjara episode is the most picturesque event of the whole drama. The dance, songs and the dramatic effects produced are spectacular and moving.

Some details about the audience of Gouri require special mention. As it is purely religious drama and cannot be performed on invitation and payment the audience too has to be of a particular type. They are usually imbibed with the same spirit as the performers are. They are to be emotionally attached to the Gouri cult and have to be totally free from disbelief and doubts. Any reason or logic put forward by the audience for any aspect of Gouri will be strongly objected by those who are believers in this cult. Almost all the Gouri performers, while in action, are supposed to be inbibed by supernatural powers and the audience is absolutely in tune with them. The ladies, in the audience, are under a spell all the time because of the tense atmosphere that the Gouri drama creates. All the sick, particularly the children, sitting in the audience are anxiously awaiting the soothing touch of the performers for their permanent cure. The most auspicious and coverted touch of the feet of the Budia is considered as a rare privilege.

The Gouri has been performed from times immemorial and it has still not lost its charm. The modern film and all other modes of entertainment have not been able to influence these Bheels even today. No training in the art of Gouri-technique is necessary for any of the Bheels, because he is brought up in this particular environment from his very childhood. The Gouri cult comes to him as a part of his life.

DEVI LAL SAMAR

GREEK AND ORIENTAL ART : BEAUTY AND PLEASURE

When Paul Valery (1871-1945) says that Greek art is concerned with attaining Beauty and Oriental art only with giving Pleasure, he ignores the realisation that Beauty which cannot give pleasure which is not beauty which cannot give pleasure is not beauty, and pleasure which is desireless to beauty is no pleasure; and both these activities (giving of pleasure, and desiring beauty) when iustful, becomes rapes. If at all any distinctions can be made these have to be among Greek, Indian and Chinese arts, because these approaches cover all the representative (or directly representational) arts of the Eurasian continent with local derivations till the rise or non-representational art of abstraction, expression, and transfiquring distortion.

Greek art's objective was imaging the perfectibility of the human estate in its here-ness by physical human action which can best be observed in the ideal male musculature and female curvaceouseness that one can aspire for by right exercise and diet. The faces show an expression which possessors of such bodies would have in action or at rest. Greek representation of gods is that of a perfected physical man or women. Greek art of nature does not rise beyond mere surface verisimilitude.

Indian art sees human perfectibility as a return to a divine state from which man descends to earth to work for a higher divine state progressively ending in God-head, for which work here-on-earth is a necessary preparation in which nature and other living beings are also aids. In Indian art, attention is not given to the human form as a body having life for human exertions, but as a vehicle reflecting the possible godly state and pleasures. Male forms are relaxed in movement of an even harmony, and the female has a form of melodious allure which is reposeful. This nature is seen as decorous and designful. Faces of gods in Indian art are not of great men; but of a divinity superior to humanity and which must exact unsolicited reverence. The idiom of European aesthetics is not able to account for this thrust of Indian art because it has not incorporated the concept of Sadhana for a Yoga as a generator of art; of enlarged and transcedent vision. It is worth nothing that the face of Christ in European art never rises beyond being the face of a very good man with an expression of manly compassion- even in Michaelangelo it is so. In iconic and Byzantine depictions, intimations of divinity are nuted and even this is possible due to decorous design.

The Chinese art aims at repose which it sees as possible by man being non-instrusively harmonious with nature. Hence its meticulous rendition of the significant details of the natural forms. Human forms for the Chinese art are creations of nature for clothing souls which merge back into nature after the soul has used them for its advancement. But such charecterisations should not be taken to be more than mere indications of genuine impressions.

Blanket and unsustainable assertions like Valery's occur because they are infertile poet's leapint thoughts without the exercise of logical rigour based on direct observation, or dispassionately intercalated introspection.

Valery has made many remarks like the one cited at the start, during his 20-years period when hibernated away from poetry which he tried to fill with what he thought was the immersion in creative process by way of conscious witnessing of the operations of his own consciousness, and which he, in itself, took to be a creative activity.

This is a mistake, as once the creative process is commencec from the moment of inspiration it always ends in a created object or a creative act unless deliberately interrupted. Thoughtful observation of the product or act can be done after its accomplishment by remembrance. But it such observations reviving the feeling states leading to accomplishment is virtually impossible as the intromission into them of sub-conscious and ab-conscious ego-states becomes unavailable to the maker and doer. So the poet after making the poem is its first reader always thereafter. For his next poem he has to await the next moment of inspiration to agaii become a poet who is different from the poet of the previous poern though his personality is the habitat of these two poets. Here again the anology of fertility comes in handy. Offspring is possible only when one is fertile; otherwise knowledge and experience are alike rendered useless.

Only the descent of the Muse, by whatever name described, enables the creator to actualise his potency. Here is the curious twist. It is the descent of the Muse which is both the seed and the womb. Artist/Poet's potency is maintained by his art and craft; which can also desert him. Then he becomes a critic. It must have been in such a state that Valery could have written his remarks about beauty and pleasure.

One wishes that poets like Valery could have kept in view the categoric triads of being and becoming generally acceptable in all Indian philosophies, i.e.,

Being : Existence- consiousness-bliss

Becoming : Truth(ful)-Good(ness)- Beauty(ful)

Then he would have seen that becoming is a moral order where agent and action are the middle terms leading to the state of bliss resulting from beauty which proceed from the property (truth) of the source (existence).

I have the greatest regard for the major poetical works of Paul Valery. However, in his remarks about beauty and pleasure, Valery did not do enough justice to his own high intellect.

C. S. VISHWANATHAN

GUDI PADVA : A NEW YEAR BEGINS IN THE SOUTH

Chaitra is the first month of the Hindu calendar and the very first day of this month begins the new year in Maharashtra, Andhra and parts of Karnataka. This festival is valled Gudi Padva or Ugadi. The people of these states follow the Shalivahan Shaka, one of the two eras used in the lunar calendar. Gudi means a banner raised to announce victory and joy and padva is the first day of lunar month. The victory banner in Maharashtrain families is made with a wooden or metal pole at the top of which stands an upturned metal water pot. The pot is edged with gathers of silken cloth, garlands of marigold and new mango leaves. The gudi is raised at the entrance of a house and is reminiscent of the valiant Marathas returning home from their successful conquering expeditions of war. This auspicious day also means good eating. Melons, jackfruit, mangoes, sprouted gram and a variety of sherbets such as mango panha, are served.

Since Gudi Padva is considered one of the four most auspicious days in the year, people start new ventures on this day. It is believed that India. Brahma created the world on this day- hence he is worshipped specially at this time. Vishnu is also said to have been incarnated as Matsya, the fish, on this day.

VIMLA PATIL

GURAZADA : PIONEER OF MODERN TELUGU DRAMA

Gurazada Appa Rao, popularly known as Gurazada, can be considered as the pioneer of modern Telugu Drama. Not that there were no original plays in Telugu before his epoch-making work 'Kanyasulkam' (literally Bride Price) was written, over a century ago. It was not only his magnum opus, but it marked a watershed between the traditional and the modern; between the historical- my- thological and the social-realistic; between the Granthika (bookish-classical) style and the Vyanvaharika (spoken form of language). His output was comparatively limited, but its impact was significant and lasting.

Not only in drama, but also in other genres was Gurazada accepted as a trend-setter-in poetry and short story in particular, irrespective of the quality of the content. Opinions may differ on the poetic imagination and the literary standard of his "Neelagiri Paatalu" (Songs of the Blue Hills). But they are written in a new metre, known as "Mutyala Saralu" (garlands of pearls), which marked a blod departure from the traditional Marga Chandas.

A striking difference between Gurazada and the older writers of his time is that he had drunk deep at the invigorating springs of English literature and Western knowledge. This hand inculcated in him a rationalist outlook and a scientific temper on the one hand; and on the other lent support to his belief in the efficacy of the spoken language as the medium of expression in literature. To him as to wordsworth and to Burns there need be no difference between the language of literature, so called, and the language of real life.

True to the Indian tradition of uncertain chronology, we can't be 100 per cent sure about Appa Rao's exact date of birth - November 30, 1861, according to some; and

September 21, 1862, according to some others. He was born in a village near Vizianagaram. He died in Vizianagaram in 1915 on April 19, according to some; and November 30, according to some others. But he lived most of the time in Vizianagaram, but for the visits to Madras and Ooty. He took his B.A. degree from the Maharaja's College in 1886, with English and Sanskrit as his special subjects. After a false start as a clerk, he started his career as a Junior lecture in the College, which he did fairly well, because of his wide reading and flair for teaching.

The real opportunity in his life came when he was drawn into the court of the Prince Maharaja Ananda Gajapati, who was to Vizianagaram what Pericles was to Athens, or Bhoja was to Ujjain. The Prince was a man of culture, and accomplished linguist and a patron of the arts, besides being a sportsman. His generosity was proverbial, as could be seen in his liberal contribution to Prof. Max Muller's project of the Sacred Books of the East, among other things. He encouraged Appa Rao in all his literary endeavours, including his play on the social problems of the day, like child marriage and enforced widowhood. That was "Kanyasulkam", in its first edition, which was prepared and presented around 1992. The author was seriously considering its revivion. Meanwhile, there was bolt from the blue in the sudden death of the Prince at a comparatively early age in 1897.

The second edition had necessarily to be delayed, because of the author's preoccupation with court matters, relating to adoption and succession. At that time, he was working as private secretary to the Maharaja's sister, the Maharani of Rewa. While the first edition was in five acts, the second published in 1909 was in seven. But the main improvement was in shaping some of the main characters.

Gurazada wrote two other plays 'kondu Bhatteeyam' (centering on the nautch girls); the 'Bilhaneeyam' (depicting some petty intrigues in a Prince's court). They are not only shorter but inferior in quality. Though a contemporary of Tagore, he should not be compared by his uncritical admirers to him either in volume, variety or quality.

Though serving in a Prince's Court, Gurazada was a democrat, who believed inequality and human values. He stressed the need for a readjustment of our social ideas and a more rational understanding between the seses. "Modern Women will rewrite human history", he wrote in 1909 and we now realise the truth of his prophetic words. "My cause is the people's cause", he declared. He was ahead of his times by atleast a century, as his readers would be glad to recognise.

(Condensed)

DR. D. ANJANEYULU

GURCHARAN SINGH SACHDEV : THE INCREDIBLE FLUTIST

The Friday night concert scheduled at Beall Hall in the Oregan district had begun late. Crowds were still sneaking into the hall when the first notes of his instrument began. It was music with a difference. It was classical in origin and dated back a good two thousand years, absorbing into its structure the strains of a myriad cultures and distilling it into an Indian essence. It was artist Gurcharan Singh Sachdev performing on his "bansurf or flute and his music was of virtuoso Indian classical content, encompassed in a framework of ragas and destined to touch the inner chords of the individual spirit. Having tenaciously furthered the cause of Indian classical music in the American situation, he has refrained from the tendency to fuse his music with western inclusions, popularly termed as fusion. Awards, like the prestigious Billboard Music Award, in the worlds music category, are yet another recognition of this artistry and calibre. Aptly termed as "Flights of improvisation, the table accompaniment for this winner has been provided by Ustad Zakir Hussain and together the twain have made the work a celebration of what is core music and genuine appeal.

But all this recognition did not come the way of this artist for the asking. He had arrived in this land (United States) a good twenty years ago, as a teacher of proven ability at the Ali Akbar College of Music, in Marin Country.

But before entering its portals there was an uncanny link of his flute with his land. Author Carolyn North Strauss was in search of a flute player who could play the long flute. She had almost given up hope when radio director Charles Amirkhanjan of Berkely, who had earlier played Sachdev's music on the air, introduced the two. Not only did the appointment to the College follow but even a two-hour long monthly demonstration on radio, spelling out the historical aspect of this music was its fallout.

Though the American episode had taken off on a smooth and steady keel, Sachdev often recalls the years of Hardship that the learning years had entailed. While searching for a guru he had chanced upon Pandit Vijay Raghav Rao, who himself was a disciple of the famed sitar maestro, Pandit Ravi Shankar, Rao himself had ennobled the humble. 'bansurf' as this read instrument is termed, to concert dimensions in the Ravi Shankar style. Sachdev's eleven year discipleship under him, therefore, was a further reiteration and continuation of this style. When he came out, the name of Ravi Shankar had become synonymous with Indian music and Sachdev was given chance to show his worth almost immediately. In the beginning, the halls were small and the tours meant travelling exhaustively along the west Coast to keep up with concert schedules. But the listerners at these places were inclined to listen further on and by and by the crowds began to swell. Sachdev has now matured into an independent, senior performer who is regarded by fellow music lovers as a foremost exponent of a form that the world now finds likeable and understandable.

Within this ambit, Sachdev has helped the rising popularity of this music by a series of cassette releases. These map out a sampling of Indian ragas with the title numbers that appropriately respect the time cycle of raga playing, in their arrangement. Whether his audiences are in the city halls of metropolitan New York or European cities of Holland and England, they echo with one accord; 'Incredible'. Sachdev has never been known to disappoint them. With his hand sized reed instrument with its seven holes, through which he blows out sound with incredible control, that transcends all boundaries of form presentation, to reach the cloud nine experience of indescribable purity.

SUBHRA MAJUMDAR

GURU DUTT : INTENSE AND HYPERSENSITIVE FILMMAKER

Guru Dutt Padukono, one of the most intense and prodigious creators of meaningful films during the Hindi Cinema's golden era of the 1950s and 1960s, is best known for his all-time classics Pyassa (1957), Kaagaz Ke Phool (1959) and Sahib Bibi Aur Ghulam (1962), besides his much-applauded money-spinner Chaudhvin Ka Chand (1961).

Born near Banglore on July 9, 1925 of educated middle class parents, he received his education in Kolkata (Calcutta), where the family had moved when he was only five. Attracted dance, he trained under Uday Shankar at his Dance Academy at Almora and in 1944 made his debut as a choreographer, assistant director and actor in Lakharani, a film produced by the Prabhat Film Company at Pune. Here he made friends with Dev Anand and Rehman, both of whom also made their first appearance as actors in the same company's Hum Ek Hain (1945) of which also he was assistant director and in which too he played a small role. After completion of that movie Dev and Guru parted with a promise to help get each other work in the future.

Later, in Mumbai, Guru Dutt worked as an assistant to directors Amiya Chakraborty and Gyan Mukherjee in Girls School and Sangram, respectively. Redeeming his promise, Dev Anand invited him to direct Baazi (1951), produced by Navketan Pictures, which had been set up jointly by Dev Anand and his elder brother Chetan. Baazi, an urban crime thriller based on a story by actor Balraj Sahni, with S.D. Burman's music and Sahir Ludhianvi's lyrics and starring Dev Anand and Geeta Bali was a big hit.

Impressed by his work Geeta Bali asked Guru Dutt to direct her next film Jaal (1952) in which he got inducted Dev Anand as the hero opposite her (now Guru kept his word to Dev). The same year he was signed for Geeta Bali's sister Hardarshan Kaur's film Baaz not only as its director but also as hero opposite Geeta Bali.

Later, he launched his own Guru Dutt productions with his debut film Aar Paar (1954) with shyama and himself in the lead roles. Then followed Mr & Mrs. 55 (1955) in which he appeared opposite Madhubala and C.I.D. (1956), directed by his assistant Raj Khosla, with Dutt's discovery Waheeda Rehman, Shakila and Dev Anand playing lead roles. All these films which had lively music by O.P. Nayyar succeeded at the Box office. While the first two forthy comedies, the last mentioned was a crime thriller.

Pyassa, his first classic, unfolded the story of an idealist poet disillusioned with the world and the selfishness and falsehood of its inhabitants. The film was inspired by the life of poet Sahir Ludhianvi, who had loved and lost and carried deep pain in his broken heart. He vented all his grief through lyrics like "Yeh duniya agar mil bhi jaaye to kay hai" (There is no point in getting this worthless world), "Jalaa do ise, phoonk dalo yeh duniya, mere saamne se hata lo yeh duniya" (Burn and destroy this world and take it away from my sight). He dwelt on the miseries, injustices and excesses in this world and tickled the consciences of those who were proud of India, urging them to mend matters.

Incidentally, all art to a degree is autobiographical, as is borne out by Shair's couplet "Duniya ne tajurrubat-o-hawadas ki shakal mein / Jo kuchh diya mujhe wohi lauta raha hoon main" (I am only returning what this world gave me in the form of experiences and accidents).

Sahir's lyrics were effectively set to music by maestro S.D. Burman and deftly integrated into the film's structure by Guru Dutt. As a result of this happy confluence of the talents of three creative artistes, the songs acquired great significance.

Guru Dutt's next classic, Kaagaz-Ke-Phool, was India's first cinemascope film in black-and-white. It reflected through a prism of cynicism how a director viewed the tinsel world and nostalgically recalled his experience as a once much-adulated film-maker and now cast aside as a failure and spent force by those very people who had earlier fawned on him. Even his upper-class in-laws and wife discarced him.

As suggested by the film's title, Kaagaz Ke Phool (Paper Flowers, which are artificial, without fragrance and are often used in films for decoration), Guru Dutt sought to expose the ubiquitous artificiality and hypocrisy of humans including those in the film world.

The director in Kaagaz-Ke-Phool, like the poet in Pyassa reckoned himself as a social reject. Old and Poorly attired, he was irresistibly drawn by his former film studio. Goaded by his unfulfilled ambitions, he went there and occupied, amidst vast emptiness, the director's chair to which he was no longer entitled, and anti-climatically, just died while sitting there.

Besides its lyrical quality and narration, the film stood out for its beautiful visuals by V.K. Murthy, bestowing on him the Filmfare Award as the best cinematographer. In tandem with Guru Dutt he created an artistic chiaroscuro using the black-and-white tones to emphasise sadness and joy.

The film was, however, a colossal failure at the box office and devastated Guru Dutt. Disappointed and dejected, he never again took directional credit for any of his subsequent films. He produced and acted in Chaudhvin Ka Chand (1961), ostensibly directed by Sadiq. It was a romantic drama with a Muslim background, set in the decadent era of the Nawabs of Lucknow. The film bagged three Filmfare awards - M.R. Achrekar (best art director), Mohd. Rafi (best playback singer) and Shakeel Badayuni (best lyricist).

Encouraged and psychologically rejuvenated by this film's success, Guru Dutt went on to produce another ambitious film, Sahib Bibi Aur Ghulam, for which he gave directorial credit to Abrar Alvi. Based on Bimal Mitra's insightful Bengali novel, the film dealt with the gradual disintegration of feudal nobility at the turn of the last century. The pivotal role of a wife was competently played by Meena Kumari, the sharp focus being on how she takes to drinking liquor to deter her husband from seeking company elsewhere. Dutt acted as her factotum, in empathy with her but unable to offer any crucial help. The film was much appreciated and earned four Filmfare awards for best film, best director, best actress and best cinematographer.

Having been exposed to the great K.L. Saigal's memorable classic Devdas and the trends of the times, nihilistic and abnegative thoughts got embedded in Guru

Dutt's Pysche and found expression through his above discussed biographical films. Like Shakespeare's King Lear, who faced two simultaneous storms- one, physical, blowing around him with all its sound fury and the other, internal, which engulfed and gripped his mind- Guru Dutt, too, faced a dilemma as a public performer and a private person.

A parallelism could be traced in the professional and personal lives of Guru Dutt and Raj Kapoor. Both as producer-director-actors made classics of great dimensions. Both spent a good part of their childhood in Kolkata where they were charmed by Saigal's soulful yet melancholic songs. After a time, Raj could, however, cut himself loose from the Devdas syndrome.

Both Raj and Guru were shattered by the failure of their most ambitious and semi-autobiographical films (Mera Naam Joker and Kagaaz Ke Phool). While Guru Dutt sank deeper with shock and grief, Raj rose from the ashes like a phoenix and with a vengeance made a hugely successful Bobby. Both employed a similar stratagem to show a wife trying to dissuade her husband from seeking pleasure outside : Guru by making Meena Kumari sip whisky in Sahib Bibi Aur Ghulam and Raj by having Vyjayanthimala perform a sort of strip-tease in Sangam. Both favourite heroines whom they had specially groomed for long and who had contributed in a big way to the success of their films.

While any shocks of Raj's behaviour, reflecting his exteriorized frustration and anger, were absorbed by his understanding family, in the case of Guru Dutt, the situation got compounded as his words and actions rebounded with equal if not great force, leaving him more dejected and despondent. While the resilient Raj survived all odds against him because of his extrovert nature and positive attitude, Guru being a hypersensitive introvert and an inveterate pessimist, remained mired in misery and wallowed in unending grief.

Thus, driven to the extreme by his failures and matrimonial incompatibility, Guru Dutt reportedly ended his life on October 10, 1964 by consuming an overdose of sleeping pills. Those close to him, however, felt that the cause of his untimely death was not a deliberate suicide (he did not leave behind any note) but an accident resulting from another of his several efforts at diluting his grief. Only this last time, the intake of an excessive quantity of barbiturates proved fatal.

B. M. MALHOTRA

"H"

HABBA KHATOON

(16th century A.D.) - Kashmiri woman poet; husband, Yusuf Shah, who ruled Kashmir for a time, was taken away captive by Akbar and never allowed to return; broken hearted, she became an ascetic; poured out heart in most moving and beautiful Kashmiri lyrics and songs which take highest place in Kashmiri literature.

Reference

Chopra, P.N. (ed.), Gazetteer of India Vol. II

HAFIZ ALI KHAN(b. 1880)

Instrumentalist; Hindustani, sarod of Bangash and Senia gharana; studied with Nanna Khan (father); studied dhrupad with Ganeshilal Chaube of Brindavan and dhrupad and surisingar with Wazir Khan of Rampur; court musician of Gwalior; received Padma Bhushan (1960); professor of instrumental music, Bharitiya Kala Kendra, New Delhi; received Sangeet Natak Akademi award for Hindustani instrumental music (1953) and elected its fellow (1954); disc recordings.

Reference

Sangeet Natak Akademy, who's who of Indian Musicians.

HALEBID ARCHITECTURE

One of the most outstanding examples of Hoysala architecture is found in the temple of Halebid, which is among the most striking in South India. The Hoysalas ruled over vast Kannada spaking regions during 11th-14th Centuries and were the first rulers to organise the area into a ruling dynasty during the reign of Vinayaditya 1047-1100 A.D.

The most famous among the Hoysala Kings was Bittideva who was initiated as Vaishnavite under the influence of the great Saint Ramanujacharya. The annexation of Talakand to the Hoysala Kingdom in 1116 gave occasion to several temples which were erected to commemorate the victory.

HOYSALA OR CHALUKYAN

The Hoysaleswara temple was constructed by Ketamalla who was in the service of Vishnuandhana Hoysala during 1121. While there are numerous theories regarding the temple by Vinayaditya in 1047, Professor Furgusson has opined that the temple even though incomplete in the strict sense of the term is the foremost example of Hindu architecture. There are also many theories regarding the styles of the temples at Belur and Halebid. To quote Furgusson again "The architecture of these temples is of the Chalukyan style, though Rao Bahadur Narsimachar holds that the style is essentially Hoysala".

ARTISTIC TIMES

The temple at Halebid is a veritable paradise of beautiful stone images which breathe with life. It appears as though the figures have been freezed in particular poses and could return to life at any moment. What makes the stone carving even more spectacular is the fact that such character and depth have been instilled into a medium which is perhaps one of the most difficult for artistic expression. Almost 1,000 years old, the temple at Halebid retains a remarkable freshness, which stands a favourable comparison to creations of a much later date. Salient feature of the Halebid temple, is the artistic combination of horizontal and vertical lines and the interplay of light and shade which highlights the effectiveness of the sculpture. The Hoysaleswara temple is dedicated to Lord Shiva who is considered as the symbol of the origin, preservation and destruction of the Universe.

At Halebid there are actually two temples which are almost identical and house two large Nandis under an intricate canopy.

While one is bound to admire the craftsmanship of the temple and the labour of love that has gone into it to make it such a lasting monument, it is particularly satisfying to view the carvings of the outer walls which display an exuberance of skill and finesse of line, and depth of character.

The temple has four door ways with exquisitely sculptured lintels portraying the figures of Tandeswara in the centre and flanked with Makara on which Varuna and his consort are seated.

Among the well-known Gods and Goddesses of the Hindu pantheon that are exquisitely sculptured with lasting mastery are the figures of Ganesh, Subaramanyam Vishnu, Indira and Mohini. The entire temple is constructed with soft soap-stone which becomes hard when exposed to the elements; while selecting the material the sculptors have taken advantage of the inherent quality of the soap-stone which lends itself superbly to intricate carving.

The Kendareswara temple, which belongs to the Santo family as Halebid, resembles the Keshava temple at Somnathpur. A fine example of Chalykyan architecture, the temple was built by Viraballala in 1219 A.D. The terrace on which the temple stands is supported at the angles by elephants. The friezes on the outer walls are similar to those at Hoysaleswarra with the exception that there are horses here instead of lions. The figures in this temple are smaller and sharper in outline and probably executed better. The principal dome of the central shrine and many beautiful images and friezes are missing which would otherwise make the temple even more striking.

The entire place breathes history and bears testimony to the artistic genius of a great people. Replete with historic remains, Helebid is full of mounds containing many ruined or destroyed temples. A highlight of the topography is Bennegudda, a low hillock running north to south. A Panoramic view of the beautiful countryside and the idylic setting of the great temples is possible from here. It is said that the east of the place contained the fort wall of the Hoysala Kings. While one feels elated with these magnificent structures which have been handed down as symbols of genius of Indian craftsmen and the great aesthetic conception they represent, it seems pitiable that even the bares minimum facilities for the tourist do not exist. It is difficult to imagine how we can make these temples popular with neither rest houses nor any other facilities attached to these sites.

M. N. UPADHYAYA

HANDICRAFTS

India, with a rich cultural heritage is well know for her deep-rooted tradition in arts and crafts. In the distant corners of this vast land, in the remote village, among the peasants and artisans, flourish a rich tradition of handicrafts, handed down from time immemorial, from father to son and mother to daughter.

It is evident in variety of forms with brilliant colour, panoramic splendour of Indian life finds expression equally through pomp and pageantry of festive occasion as also in the daily usages of the folk people. What atonce fascinates is the ranges of variation in treatment and effect though which once can watch a progression and designs and shapes elaborately though organically, ornamented by generations ahead of us.

India's arts and crafts can fully be apreciated in the significance they draw from perennial vitality, encompassing the conscious and subconscious, emotion and thought. Symbolic of the universal urge, the hertiage springs from the deepest sources of the unchanging inner life, coming down from the past through the present to the future.

To understand how closely integrated with life and how expressive of a way of living crafts can be, India offers rich and significant forms which reveal some of the deepest satisfaction known to man.

It is not the unique individual who speaks through handicrafts, but the anonymous collective mind with millennia of traditional knowledge. The form of expression, ranging from realism to abstraction, simplicity to fantasy, is as modern as it is timeless.

That the Indian tradition has survived innumerable vicissitudes though the ages is due to the fact that the social organisation was based on the village community, in the corporate life of which artists and craftsmen played the assigned roles. The potter, for instance, was given plots of land in fixed quantities of grain or amount at harvest time by village people in exchange for which he supplied them their requirements, dolls and toys included. The blacksmith functioned in the same way. The system meant security, without which the artists and artisans could not have developed their crafts in close touch with tradition. Under such conditions, the craftsman worked out age-old forms, and countless recapitulations resulted in a state of mind in which he could produce the most abstract without any conscious effort. Even where he made a significant change, he was perhaps unaware of it. He could introduce new patterns, give the old a new look, but the possibilities of a radical assertion of his individuality in the modern sense were very much limited because of the total impact of a social and religious structure extending from the joint family to the panchayat.

The professional artist or craftsman is normally a member of a small and closely knit community. Under ordinary circumstances he works for his own community, with the requirement of which he is thoroughly acquainted. As he carves out paints, all other members of the same group, though not equally proficient can also do it. In their attempt to make similar forms, they experience the same mental conditions, thus identifying themselves with the matter craftsman, the significance of whose products can readily be assessed by his fellow folks.

The producer is almost invariably the consumer and all the family members participate in the productive activity. A home thus becomes a small family workshop in which the old, the adult and the child perform one or the other duty in accomplishing a job to his or her capacity and aptitudes. The complete infusion of group emotion is characteristic of their art.

The Indian handicraft is therefore not meant to serve an aesthetic end. It is rigidly controlled by the age-old conventions in which the meaning of each motif has been unalterably fixed. If his works appear naive, it is only because the details, either unimportant or taboo, are avoided.

Many of the art forms are results of deep spiritual experience, the innate meanings of which cannot be clearly understood in terms of our own aesthetic reactions. In particular areas, however, there may be a key design which unlocks the secrets of the origin of other designs. But the mass of significance attached to these designs had been the product of an age-old emotional contact conditioned by the environment and social behaviour of a people and does not easily reveal itself to the uninitiated.

That is why the underlying primitive character upsets the norm because it throws up realities and symbols that are far removed from the common place and the conventional. It charges the apparent, the insignificant, with strangely evocative ideas and associations. It is drawn from a life that has retained its ancient simplicity despite time variations, like the mind of a child, which simultaneously lives both in the present and the primordial.

Myths and legends prevalent among the Adivasis form another important factor in their art. These stimulate dramatic intensity resulting in distortions and exaggerations and the use of strongly contrasting colours A village potter can made a tiger without any story element, but a tiger for the folk people must have some association with a legend or rite. The women of the Rani Paraj area in Western India make terracotta votive offerings which are bold examples of such form and fantasy. This form is however not a isolated phenomenon in Rani Paraj alone but the same typical form of the votive cow can be found in the deer-rattle, recently discovered in all likelihood may be of prehistoric origin. Here is an example of how significant forms have survived in the handicraft through centuries, nothwithstanding their use either as votive offerings or as toys. It is, however, difficult to say when a toy becomes a votive offering or a votive figure turns a toy, but undoubtedly the form is the same.

The tradition of Indian handicraft is capable of epitomising the character of an age and we treasure those things in whose forms and designs a way of life is expressed.

AJIT MOOKERJEE

HANGAL GANGUBAI (GANDHARI)

(b. 1913) - Vocalist : Hindustani khayal of kirana gharana; studied with Sawai Gandharva; disc recordings; concert tours, Nepal (1958), Pakistan (1962).

Reference

Sangeet Natak Akademy, Who's Who of Indian Musicians.

HEADDRESS CULTURE OF INDIA

Few years back, the author attended a royal marriage in Rajasthan. Apart from the food and drinks, the pugrees (headgear) of myraid shades, colours and sizes are what he recalled most. The style and shape of each pugree was different and for princely families was a matter of regal pride. In one corner a man was tying a pugree to a young prince who had been educated in the States. The man who was tying in belongs to the profession called dusterbandi, now almost extinct as most modern people prefer to sport a readymade 'pug' to get away with the cumbersome tying process.

No matter how modern one may be, on occasions like marriages or royal get-togethers the pugree is a must, expecially in Rajasthan. It not only symbolically tells the position and status of the person but also tells about the geographical location of that family.

Though called by different names in different parts of India-such as Pagri, Safa, or Pagote in Punjab, Kashmir and Maharashtra respectively, pugree or turban first found its mention in the fifteenth and sixteenth century, especially in the Persian language where it was prounced as 'dulband'. Its etymology is apparently from 'dul' (pronounced by Arabs as 'tul') or 'volvere'. Or its origin could be from Turkish tulipant, tolliban, turbant. In seventeenth century French dictionary 'Cotgrave', we find the explanation 'toliban' as a Turkish has of white colour which was sometimes ornamented. It is possible that the word turban originated from Persian and subsequently entered the English language.

The first record of headdress we find in the pre-historic rock arts or murals at Bonampa, Mexico, of Maya civilization or in the ancient sites of Bhimbetka, Jhiri, Kumaun Himalayas in India. These pre-historic rock arts depict varied headdresses from animal symbols to flower and foliage. Thus we find that long before men could start weaving and sewing they had evolved their headdress and considered it a symbol of pride.

Form archaeological evidences of Harappan and Mohanjodaro civilization one come across the fanlike headdress, perhaps made of stiffened cloth mounted on a frame like object. There were variations on this basic shape as the headgears were sported by both sexes. However, archeologists have concluded that in those times, pugree was the prerogative of persons of high strata as deities were also given the same-importance.

The Vedic era also mentions about the Ushnisha- a crossbind headdress which was generally white and bright and tied with the tilt. Moreover, the ancient Sanskrit literature referred to headdresses as Ushnisha, Kirita, Patta, Vestanapatta and Sirovestana. In Banbhatta's famous Kadambari we find ample references to it.

Ancient Indian literature reveals that the form, shape and its symbology altered according to the changes in the hierarchical structure of society. In the post Vedic period, Brahmins were higher than the king in the scheme of things and were respected by others by removing their headdress before them. From this era onwards, the removal of one's headdress was viewed as a mark of respect and veneration and continues in different forms till today.

From third century B.C. to third century A.D. headdress evolved in different styles and shapes and was made of different materials. Interplaying pugree with hair also came into vogue. Roshak Alkazi, a specialist in ancient Indian costumes, says that hair itself was often twisted into headdress. "Thetwisted braid being then arranged to form protuberance at the front or side of the head, but never at the centre top, as this style could only be used by priests. Over the turban a narrow band was used to hold it in place". This style is yet to be revived by modern fashion designers.

The headdress continued even in South India where Pallava Kings sported the conicol headdress which later came into vogue among the Vijaynagar nobility. In later years this was adopted by Tamil nobles as well. During the rule of Vijayanagar dynasty, the royallty continued to sport high headdress. Dr. G.G. Ghurye refers to a Portuguese account of Deccani headdresses: "The traveller Vasthema recorded that the King wore a cap of gold brocade, two span long, while Nuniz has described it as caulae and its material as brocade. Durate Barbosa refers to the use of small turbans and brocade caps by ordinary males".

With the advent of Islamic rule, influences from persia and Central Asia were soon observed in the country's fashion. Jamila Brijbhushan, an authority on medieval fashion, writes that" caps worn were of may shapes pointed with a boss at the tip, conical and with a broad upturned brim, triangular or pointed. Sometimes it was downward sloping with seams visible in the middle. It can also be observed that while the Muslim influence was enveloping northern India, the east and south or Deccani India tried to improvise old Indian headdresses. The commoners sported freshly folded pugrees which developed in the later sapha or patka".

In Mughal era the headdress became the most striking symbolism of culture and glory. European traveller Fancois Bernier wrote that Jahangir's headdress "was composed of diamonds of extraordinary size and value, besides oriental topaz which may be pronounced exhibiting lustre like the sun".

Amir Khusru wrote that the dandies of Delhi wore the type of headgear which were "short turban and oblique caps".

After the Mughals the most prominent headdress we find is that of Rajputana whose legacy is awe-inspiring. During the 17th century, in and around Jaipur, we find mention of cotton pugree called chira and phenta. Some headdresses were of dyed and printed cotton fabric sometimes 25 mts. long and 20 centimetres wide.

Today each community in each district of Rajasthan sports a different type of pugree. The Udaipur pugree has a flat surface while the Jaipur one has knot on the top. Regality sport the lepata, sort of narrow piece of ornate material, usually with intricate gold embroidery.

On Rajasthani pugree we find an interesting analysis by Coomaraswamy. He wrote: "The Rajput pugree appears to have been adopted at the Mughal court in the time of Akbar, and remained the typical headdress of both Musalmans and Hindus as represented in the paintings of the seventeenth and eighteenth centuries."

The tradition of headdress continued during India's freedom struggle as well, as we find many leaders sporting some headgear or the other. Gandhiji, unconsciously gave Indians the Gandhi Topi (Cap) to bring about a pan Indianness at least at the political level.

In modern India pugrees is very much in vogue in rural areas. And a village name without a pugree is unthinkable as it reflects his socio-religious status. One can see glimpses of pugree in ritual dance, folk dresses and theatrical forums. In urban India though pugree has taken a back seat but as social symbolism pugree comes back whenever festivity and auspicious ceremonies take place.

DR. GAUTAM CHATTERJEE

HEMKUND : THE SACRED SIKH SHRINE

In the Zanskar Range of the Great Himalayas lies the Heimkund (Shri Hemkund Sahib), a cobalt - coloured lake, surrounded by seven peaks of Saptrashringa Parvat and on the bank is located the Gurudwara (Sikh shrine) dedicated to the tenth Guru of Sikhs, Shri Guru Gobind Singhji, the founder of the Khalsa Panth who, as the legend goes, meditated on the bank of the lake in his earlier incarnation as Rishi Bishala and was also known as Rishi Medhasa and Madhakta.

As per an older legend, the other names of Hemkund are Lokpal and Lakshman Kund. According to the local belief, Shri Lakshman, the younger brother of Lord Rama, medidated on the banks of this lake. A temple dedicated to Shri Lakshman has also been constructed a few yards from the Gurudwara.

In 1932, Bhai Sohan Singh, who was a priest in the Golden Temple at Amritsar, was fascinated with the study of the Vichitra Natak, the autobiography of Shri Guru Gobind Singhji. In this treatise, the Guru has alluded to his meditation at a glacial lake surrounded by seven peaks. Bhai Sohan Singh was so inspired by this account that he set out in search of this place to have a memorial built for others to visit. After difficult trek of many days with enormous hazards like uncongenial climate, inhospitable terrain and adverse effects of altitude, he reached a lake called Lokpal. He found the place to be exactly in accordance with descriptions in Vichitra Natak. It is believed that while he was continuing his search for the exact spot where the Guru sat in meditation, he met an old man who pointed towards at a flat piece of rock next to the lake as the place where the tenth Guru sat in meditation. Later on that old man was nowhere to be seen. In 1933, the foundation stone for the Gurudwara was laid at the exact spot indicated by the mysterious old man. The

Gurudwara was completed in 1936. Bhai Sohan Singh spent remaining 25 years of his life in the service of this shrine.

The shrine is open to the pilgrims for four to five summer months starting from June to October and is covered by snow for the remaining months. The roadhead for Shri Hemkund Sahib is Gobindghat at a height of 1670 metres which is 12 miles north from Joshimath in the Alaknanda Valley on the Badrinath road. The Gurudwara at Gobindghat provides relief to the pilgrims having travelled the tough mountain terrain, providing them free accommodation and food, before they start their Hemkund journey on foot. Private lodges are also avialable for the tourists apart from the accommodation in the Gurudwara.

The onward journey of 19 kilometres uphill from Gobindghat to Hemkund is a challenging trekking route for the adventurous pilgrims. Though mules and civil ponies are also avialble, potters carrying the pilgrims and their baggages is also a common sight during this journey. The first part of the journey of 13 kilometres terminates at Gurudwara Gobind Dham, also called Ghagaria, which is at a height of about 3400 metres. In Ghagaria the pilgrims take a night's halt before embarking on the final climb of approximately six kilometres to the shrine the following morning.

The final climb is a gradient of nearly 1555 metres in a distance of about six kilometres of Hemkund. One kilometres ahead of Gobind Dham the track bifurcates to the left for the Valley of Flowers. The uphill path is paved with stones ascending in a interminable series of steps. Set amidst the green forest, jagged peaks and glaciers as a backdrop is some of the grandest scenery. There is a profusion of lowers wearing elaborate costumes of swirling colours. Huge chunks of ice are seen in shaded books and corners.

On reaching the destination, one finds the crystal clear expanse of holy Hemkund lake measuring 200 metres by 150 metres and the Gurudwara, an imposing star-shaped structure of stone and concrete. The Kund reflects in iridescent beauty of the peaks and glaciers. In spite of the water being freezing cold devotees take dip in the holy kund.

PRITI

HIMALAYAN MOUNTAINEERING INSTITUTE

Tenzing Norgay's ascent of the Everest (29,028 ft.) along with Sir Edmund Hillary, in 1953 provided a great impetus and fillip to mountaineering as a sport in India, and it was to commemorate that success that the plans to start a mountaineering school were drawn up, at the instance of Prime Minister Shri Jawaharlal Nehru and the former Chief Minister of West Bengal the late Dr. B.C. Roy. It was in November 1954 that the foundation stone of the Himalayan Mountaineering Institute was laid at Darjeeling by the Prime Minister. Though the constructional work took a long time to complete, the instructional wing started functioning and the first Basic Mountaineering Course was conducted in Nov./Dec. 1954.

The year 1956 saw the completion of four more Basic courses, training 84 more students in mountaineering. In the same year second Advanced course was conducted which went to Karakoram as an expendition led by Major Jayal. They attempted Saser Kangri (25,170 ft.) and climbed a virgin peak named Sakang (24,150). Again 1957 four Basic courses and one Advanced course were organised. This time the advanced course had envisaged an expedition to Nandadevi (25,646 ft.) under the leadership of late Major Jayal. It was a good attempt and they reached within 600 feet of the summit, when they were forced to abandon it due to bad weather.

Since the construction of essential buildings was nearing completion, it was planned at the end of 1957 to move the Institute to its present location. On 25th December, 1957 the Prime Minister performed the inauguration ceremony.

In February 1958, Brigadier (then Lt. Col.) Gyan Singh took over the Institute as Principal from Major Jayal. During that year too, the Institute organised four Basic courses and trained 89 students.

As the fair sex did not like to be left behind, many requests for conducting regular courses for women started coming. The result was that in April 1961 the Institute organized the first ladies Basic mountaineering courses, which proved a great success as the course was cent per cent subscribed.

The Advanced course is designed to give further experience to those who have already done the basic course with the high grading. It helps to organize climbs on peaks over 20,000 feet or, alternatively, to explore hitherto unvisited or scientifically unexplored areas in the Himalayas and to bring back information of scientific value. The Advanced course aims at producing potential leaders and members of expeditions, training in advanced techniques of mountain climbing, particularly on an ice-fall, acclimatisation for high altitudes by staying out in camps about 17,000 feet and academic exercises in the organisational planning of major expedition.

Achievement in the field of mountaineering in the country within last nine years have been very encouraging. Upto the middle of 1962, many Indian Expeditions to the Himalayas were organised, including two to the highest peak of the world, "Everest", Out of these expeditions more than 16 were successful and most of the mountaineers who participated in these expeditions were ex-students of the Institute. (Condensed)

B. N. JASWAL

HIMROO

Himroo consists of cotton yarn for warp silk, art silk elaborately woven, in spotted, striped, floral designs. The Kairi or mango design; the Kishti or boat design more popular; the cloth an extra weft figuring fabric, with solid coloured ground of satin; makes exquisite stoles, furnishing fabrics, dressing gowns, ladies coats and other accessories.

Weaving of Himroo, a complex process; managed by young boys. Initially design prepared, Jala made; Jala represents design in terms of yarn; this, then arranged on loom; operated by two boys. On attends to design, other manages the shuttle.

Himroo fabrics, inherited, part of cultural heritage of the Deccan; synonym for cultivated taste; gracious living, part of Moghul tradition. Exquisite in texture, design; popular all over the country, abroad, Himroo adopted to tastes of present generation; retained its colour, charm. Used by saree, dress overs.

Himroo ranks with Benaras Brocode, known for luxurious sophistication. Brought to India by Mughals, made in Hyderabad, Aurangabad, derived from ancient style of wearing, Jamaiwar Impetus provided to industry by settlement; many Kashmiris in the Aurangabad area. Probable estimation, 15000 Himroo looms operated under patronage of Emperor Aurangzeb.

Himroo fabrics used by nobility. Another fabric, Mashroo', a mixture of cotton, silk came in use this time. Used as apparel during prayers by the Quran. 'Himroo' meant alike, on both surfaces. Term used till today. Other noted fabrics of Brocade family, Mushajar, Kinkhwab (from Benaras, Surat), present dazzling spectacle of colour, delicacy of form.

G. R. SUNDAR

HOLI – THE FESTIVAL OF SPRING

Holi, a festival composite in nature celebrated in many parts of India on more days than one, in origin, is more than a spring festival. It is mostly celebrated in the Phalguna month on Poornima or Full Moon day.

Holi or Holika is a festival of unmixed gaiety and frolics, the common feature being bonfire. There are some local variations in some parts of the country. In particular, in Bengal, the image of Krishna is worshipped in putting it in a swing on that day. Another item which is more or less common in many parts of the country is the sprinkling of coloured water from bamboo or metal syringes or smearing of coloured powders on friends. This merriment is indulged in even to the day in many families whether high or low, accompanied by music and dance, sometimes obscene though with a tinge of religious element, In some parts of the country people produce sounds by beating their mouths with their hands on the celebration.

This festival seems to have comedown to us from a very ancient period. In some of the ancient texts references are made to a festival called Holika. Sabara's Bhasya on the Purva Mimamsa Sutra refers to this festival mostly prevalent in the eastern parts of India. Jaimini, another ancient author holds that this festival was observed by all the people in Aryavarta. According to Devapala, a commentator on Kathaka Grihiya Sutras, an ancient text, "Hola" is a special rite performed for the Saubhagya of women and in that rite "Raka" (Full Moon) is the deity. There are other interpretations too. Vatsyayana in his Kamasutra says that among the twenty Kridas prevailing in the whole of the country and restricted to certain provinces, only is the festival of Holaka.

The commentator or this work Jayamangala explains that in this festival on Phalguna Full Moon day the people celebrate it by sprinkling coloured water discharged from a horn or the like and throwing performed coloured powders on one another. Hemadri another well-known commentator on Kala quotes from an ancient text that Holika Purnima is also called Hutasani. He further quotes from Lingapurana, the Phalguna Full-Moon day is said to be known as "Phalgunika", as full of boyish pranks and tending to the prosperity of people and Varaha Purana qualifying it as "patavasa vilasini" meaning containing pranks with powder". According to Bhavishyottara Purana, Krishna, when asked by Yudhishthira as to why in each village and town a festival is held on Phalguna Full Moon day and the boys become boisterous in each house an kindle Holika and what God was worshipped therein, said that in celebration of the death of an orgress (rakshasi) named Dhonda, who had troubled boys by day and night, on that day, God Kama is worshipped to symbolise the death of the tormentor, Further adding that on the 15th day of Phalguna, season of cold vanishes and summer season starts, and the people enjoy at the advent of the Spring, when the trees bloosom and the entire nature gets decorated with colours and sweet smell pleasing to eyes and nostrils.

The bonfire on the occasion is a symbol of the expiry of the season of frost and cold and heralding of the warmth and love-making of spring. The ribald songs, dance and music form the further accretions due to the joy felt on the advent of spring. The sprinkling of coloured water and powders is to mark the celebration of the delight of Spring. In many parts of the country this festival is celebrated as Sasantotsava in which God karma is worshipped and yellow coloured water sprinkled lavishly in which adults both men and women participate uninhibitedly. The medieval works like Nirnayasindhu, Smriti-Kaustubha, Purushartha cintamani and other works also discourse on this festivel.

This festival is celebrated thoughout the country in various forms at the dawn of he Spring Season in gaiety and joy to this day. Thus Holi festival is a great tradition inherited by us from times immemorial.

G. R. SUNDAR

HYDERABAD PALACES

Hyderabad is known for its imperial opulence and a stunning range of its architectural styles. Be it any palace here, the splendour /speaks volumes for those who created them. The seventh Nizam of Hyderabad, Osman Ali, was reputed to be the world's richest man. His father Mahaboob Ali Khan, on the other hand, was lavish in his spendings and his generosity was legendary. While the well-known structures like the Charminar, Mecca Masjid and the historic Golconda fort were built by the Qutab Shahis, the fascinating palaces of Falaknuma, Chowmohalla and the Purani Haveli were built during the reign on Nizams, the Asaf Jahis. They are renowned for their imperial richness and architectural grandeur. These palaces in their heyday were legends unto themselves, and were looked upon by people with awe and wonder.

Mukarram Jah, the eight Nizam of Hyderabad, lifted the veil on the life-style of the Asaf Jahis and offered to the public revealing glimpse of the dynasty that ruled the Deccan for 224 years. On October 6 last year his 62nd birthday- Jah played host to a veritable who's who of Indian glitterate at the sprawling Chowmohalla Palace complex, south-west of the Charminar. And the following day, the complex's giant wooden gates opened to the public for the first time- for two weeks till October 20- even as other family gems like the magnificent Falaknumma Palace and the Purani Haveli welcomed descendants of royal subjects.

The showpiece is the Chowmohalla complex itself. It remains a monument of imperial opulence, a riot of palatial buildings, gateways and pavilions, the earliest of which date from 1750 and the rule of the first Nizam. Former state architect Raghukul Prasad enthuses:

"The Chowmohalla is symbolic of centuries of architectural styles found in Hyderabad. It ranges from the purely European to the highly ornate composite Islamic-European style of later building like the Khilwat".

Among the complex's best preserved buildings are the Afzal Mahal at the southern end, the Khilwat- where the Nizams were crowned - and the Durbad Hall. Of these, the first is the most spectacular, built during the regin of the fifth Nizam, Afzal-un Dowla (1857-1869) as a direct copy of the Shah of Iran's palace, but considerably finer architecturally.

If the Chowmohalla complex is a testament to the taste of the fifth Nizam, then the hill-top palace of Falaknuma, five km south of the Charminar, is the expression of executive rather than imperial power. An Italian- designed extravaganza, combining classical and Islamic features and constructed in Italian marble, it was conceived by Sir Vicar UI Umra, a Paigah noble and prime minister of the Nizam's dominions, and was presented to sixth Nizam in the form of nazar, the customary offering presented by nobles to their ruler.

Under the Nizams, the palace became a royal guest lodge. Visitors included King George V and Queen Mary, King Edward VIII, the first Governor-General, Sir C. Rajagopalachari, and the first President Rajendra Prasad. With its spacious verandah, stained glass doors and chandeliered waiting halls, it is clear that the guests were well received.

The entrance of the palace leads to an imposing marble stairway with carved balustrades, rising to he first floor where a series of oil paintings of the Asaf Jahi family, their ministers and guests constitutes a unique portrait gallery. But none of this prepares the visitor for the banquet hall on the same floor which extends the length of the palace. The dining table itself seats 108 and runs under five colossal chandeliers, unparalleled anywhere in the world. In its heday, this room had a leather ceiling. Dinner was served on monogrammed China and eaten with crested gold cutlery.

Falaknuma Palace has many more firsts, which included the largest chandeliers which are Venetian. It is said that it took six months to clean a 138- arm Osler chandelier and the palace has 40 Osler chandeliers adorning the hass; Besides, it had one of the finest collections of the holy Quran in India. The famed ballroom here houses a two-tonne, manually operated music organ, said to be the only one of its kind in the world.

In finer fettle is the Purani Haveli, the third royal complex. This 11- building complex, built by the second Nizam, has been partly preserved by the schools and training institutes which operate there, funded by Mukkaram Jah and his brother Mufakkam. The Haveli owes much of its interest to the French-style extensions made by the sixth Nizam, who was popularly known as Mahbub Ali Pasha. One significant interior addition designed to satisfy the Nizam's demand is the longest wardrobe in the world, a 240 ft long corridor.

The Purani Haveli is also home to the Jubilee Pavilion, which houses the gifts of gold and silver presented to the seventh Nizam for the silver jublee of his accession to the throne, as well as the crested golden chair specially commissioned for the occasion. Silver models of the Hyderabad railway station, the high court building and the Osmania University Arts College also form a part of this rich collection.

RAMCHANDER PENTUKER

"I"

ILYAS KHAN (b. 1924)

Instrumentalist : Hindustani, sitar of Senia gharana; studied with Karamat Ullah Khan, Abdullaham Khan, Yusuf Ali Khan; head of department of instrumental music, Bhatkhande Sangeet Vidyalaya, Lucknow.

IMAMBARAS OF INDIA
FUSION OF FAITH AND GRANDEUR

Certain values attached to religious monuments are peculiar to them and to them alone. Three of these values, which may be called spiritual, aesthetic and cultural, are of particular importance, because each one affects the ways in which religious monuments can be explained and interpreted to those who wish to see' or understand them.

The Imambara is an Indian institution more popular with the Shias who assemble here during Muharram, the first month of the Islamic Calendar. Unlike a mosque, there is no set pattern for an Imambara. Its style, architecture and unity varies with local cultural influence. In south India, for instance, it is called an Ashurkhana.

As soon as the moon of Muharram is sighted, Shias abandon their festivities and prepare for the Azadari (as period of mournining for two months and eight days) by attiting themselves in black. They assemble at the Imambaras for Majlis (congregations) where Marsiya (elegies) on the tragic martyrdom of Imam Hasan and Imam Hussain are recited in prose and poetry.

The month of Muharram revives the memory of the battle of Karbala fought between the forces of Yazid and Imam Hussain. The succession of Yazid as the Khalifa of the Muslims was challenged by Imam Hussain who refused to submit to his authority, which would tantamount to acquiescence in the abominations let loose during his reign. Yazid on the other hand demanded Bait (total submission). Imam Hussain with is band of 72 fought to the bitter end, Finally the Imam was slaughtered and his head. transfixed on a spear, was carried to Damascus.

Shias in particular perform Matam (beating their chest), recite Marsiyas and shed their blood by inflicting knife wounds. Processions are taken out with Tazias (huge bamboo structures decorated with paper and tinsel representing Imam Hussain's mausoleum) and Alams (replicas of the ensign of Imam Hussain during the battle of Karbala). Taimur is believed to be the founder of the Tazia ceremony. As a devotion to Imam Hussain he erected the first Tazia and carried it on his military pursuits. Gradually the Mughals, though they were not Shias, perfected and promoted this art.

The pivotal point for the Muharram activities is the Imambara literally "enclosure of the Imams". In India Imambaras or Ashurkhanas are more prominent in places partonized by the Shias. The earliest kingdom to declare Shiaism as state religion was Bijapur, followed by the Qutb Shahis of Golconda. The ancestors of Wajid Ali Shah or the rulers of Lucknow and some of the nawabs of Bengal were devoted Shias who observed Muharram with due sanctity.

Mohammad Quli Qutb Shah, the founder of Hyderabad, was a keen composer of Marsiyas in Deccani Urdu. Alams during the Qutb Shahi rule were made out of gold and silver with jewels studded in them. As they symbolised the martyrs of Karbala, royal privileges like armed escorts, naqqarkhana and chattar were accorded to them. Little remains of the numerous Ashurkhanas that once dotted the Deccani Kingdom. One of the best preserved it the Badshahi Ashurkhan a not far from Hyderabad's world-famous monument Charminar. It was erected soon after the completion of Charminar in 1592. This Ashurkhana has an impressive height and is noted for its profusion of Chinese tiles. Once it boasted of 14 gold Alams and 10,000 lamps that spoke of the grandeur of the Sultan. With the fall of the Qutb Shahis, the Alams vanished and so did the countless lamps. In fact, the Ashurkhana was converted into a prison camp by the Mughal emperor Aurangzeb. However, during the Asaf Jahi period efforts were made to revive the glory by introducing new Alams and European lamps.

Most of the Ashukhanas of Hyderabad are gifted with proud historic Alams or some piece of memorabilia. Koh-e-Moula Ali on the hillocks of Secunderabad is reputed for its Nishan (hand impression of Hazrat Ali): others have preserved the historic swords, fragments of the armour cap, etc. One such proud possession is Hazrat Fatima's chaddor. The box in which this relic is kept bears the seal of several emperors. Hazrat Fatima was the daughter of Prophet Muhammad and one of the Alams in Hyderabad was made out of the wood from the bed on which her funerary both was performed.

Oudh was another Nawabi kingdom with Lucknow as the capital where numerous Imambaras mushroomed under different nawabs. There hardly used to be any mohalla in Lucknow that did not boast of a couple of Imambaras. The three best know Imambaras of the city - the Asafi or Bara Imambara in the old city, the Chota Imambara in Hussainabad and the Shah Najaf Imamabara near Hazratganj-are famous for their architectural beauty and European chandeliers.

The Asafi Imambara was undertaken in 1748 with a view to provide relief to people from a severe famine. The basement of this Imambara is now closed as no one is sure about the utility of the dark rooms where it is easy to get lost. This Imambara is an architectural feat, considering the fact that it is the largest vaulted hall in the world. It requires merit to build a 50-feet high roof, sparining 162 feet in length and 53 feet in breadth, without a single beam. In fact, Nawab Asaf-ud-Daulah had made it a point that his architecture should be original in conception. From the terrace at the top one can have a fine view of the City with a striking skyline. Adjoining the Imambara is the mosque and on the other end are the tombs of the nawab and of his begum.

Chota Imambara, not far from the Bara Imambara, was the work play of the third king of Oudh, Nawab Muhammad Ali. Between the Imambara and the gareway is a large courtyard with a rectangular raised tank spanned by a bridge. Within the Imambara is the burial place of the king and on the sides of the courtyard are buried his daughter and son-in-law. This edifice is noted for its golden dome, calligraphy at the arched entrance, exquisite chandeliers, huge mirrors, silver pulpit and of course a very colourful interior.

Shah Najaf Imambara entombs the first king of Oudh, Ghaziuddin Haider, together with his three gives. The Imambara, resembling the tomb of Hazrat Ali ata Najf (Iraq), is a huge masonry structure with a large dome having an equally impressive interior replete with various chandeliers and mirror work.

On the eastern front there are three grand Imambaras worth visiting. An extension of the Nawabi Lucknow concluded at Metiaburj in Calcutta where the last of Nawabs, Wajid Ali Shah, was laid to rest within the Sibtainabad Imambara built in 1864. The imposing gateway with double mermaids - the emblem of the royal family - lies acorss the busy road. The building evokes memories of happier times when flowering plants and fountains almost recreated a mini Lucknow. Not far from Calcutta is Hoogly where Hajee Mohammad Mohsin's Imambara is a landmark. Hundreds of European chandeliers reflecting on the Italian marble speak for themselves. The inside walla of the Imambara are profusely worked upon with inscriptions from the Holy Quran. The sun dial and the mighty clock from Black & Murray, London, have tall tales to tell. One has to climb to see the three enormous iron bells of the clock together with a room full of machinery. The spacious courtyard, gilded doors, water talks with goldfish add to the beauty of the scenic Imambara. The backyard wall of this building is inscribed with the fairly long will (dated 1806 A.D.) of Hajee Mohammad Mohsin who dedicated this grand Imambara, besides schools and hospitals, for the needy.

Murshidabad, along the Bangladesh border, houses the world's biggest Imambara rebuilt in 1848 at a cost of 600,000 Rupees in those times. The new building was erected when the old one caught fire during a party organised for the Europeans. In front of the Imambara is the old Medina which is filled up to a depth of six feet with earth brought over from Mecca. The Imambara in its hey days stocked hundreds of Alams ad other relics, besides chandeliers, lamps, girandoles and other means of illumination. When the relationship between the nawab and the English took a bitter turn, the Begums melted their jewellery to create the new Alams.

SHAHID AKHTAR MAKHFI

IMRAT HUSSAIN KHAN

Instrumentalist : Hindustani, Surbahar, sitar; studied with Vilayat Hussain Khan; disc recordings; concert tours, Europe (1958) and (1961).

INDIA : A MICROCOSM OF RELIGIONS AND PHILOSOPHIES

Without freedom (of thought, word and action), there can be no change. Without change, there can be no diversity. If India's diversity is without parallel, it is because India has always been free to think.

There were other favourable factors, too. For example, the spirit of accommodation, which led Hinduism to become "a mass of philosophies, religions, mythologies and magics". (Dr. S. Radhakrishnan) and India's modesty: Ashoka never claimed pre-eminence for Buddhism, although he was an ardent missionary, an attitude rare in religious history.

Unfortunately, India took its freedom to extremes. "The process of god-making in the factory of man's mind cannot be seen so clearly anywere else as in the Rig-Veda." (Dr. Radhakrishnan). In fact, the Rig-Veda is the only document in the world, were one can see the evolution of the concept of God (Max Mueller). But the quest for truth took India to other conclusions, too. "How many gods are there really. O Yagnyavalkya?" asked his disciples. "One", replied the Master. (Taitariya Upanishad). The real is one; the learned call it by various names, say the Vedic seers. But it is the spirit of diversity which triumphed in India.

Diversity prevented conflicts. And diversity led to compromise. The discovery that all gods are one brought about the great reconciliation of the Aryans with pre-Aryan tribes. The Aryans accepted the cults of Shiva and Krishna, while the natives accepted Sanskritisation A similar accommodation can be seen in Mahayana Buddhism, which absorbed many Central Asian myths and beliefs brought by the Sakas into India.

The Indians were the first to realise that truth has many facets They, therefore, never fell into the error of imagining, as some people do, that they had the ultimate truths and that no further enquiry was required. Says Dr. Radhakrishnan: "The Aryan did not possess the pride of the fanatic that his was the true religion".

Uniformity can give strength to a polity. But it can also weaken it. A people who hanker after uniformity become intolerant of dissent and diversity. They turn against the spirit of enquiry. Their life becomes repetitive.

True, diversity can also weaken a polity. But it also gives strength. India's strength lies in its diversity. It has become a major element of its destiny. The spirit of enquiry has given India the most wide-ranging systems of thought. No amount of dissent can weaken India. It can take everything in its stride. There is nothing that India has not already thought of from negation to affirmation, from atheism to pantheism to monoism.

The genius of India is assimilative and receptive. It never opposed scientific enquiry: while all the Semitic religions banned scientific studies, India's has been an open mind. In the shaping of Indian thought so many streams have combined: Aryan, pre-Aryan, Central Asian (Pre-Islamic and Islamic), Chinese, Greek, Arab and so on. And India, in turn, has given generously to all. It was like the Sun giving its light.

There is much logic and reason in the evolution of Hindu gods, And irrationality, too. The Aryan offered his prayer to the bright ones of nature (sun, air, rain) in gratitude when these natural forces came to be personified as devas (gods), the Aryan offered them sacrifices. Men and gods existed close to each other. As the gods became witness to human actions, sense of mortality was born. Belief in the existence of fathers after their death turned into belief in immorality, and recognition of the rhythm of nature was raised into the highest principles.

the "law of nature" (Rta). It was soon found that the same law governed to Conscience of man. Conscience told man "what was right". This is Dharma, a force above the gods. "As the one fire, after it has entered the world, though one, becomes different according to whatever it enters..." This is Vedanta- the final teaching of the Vedas. It also explains India's diversity.

There are 108 Upanishads, of which ten are very important. These express many speculative ideas. So varied, are the guesses on the nature of God that anybody may get here the answers he seeks.

In the Vedas, the Indian sought communion with the outer world. In Upanishads, he explored the inner world of man. In the Vedas, the Indian sought prosperity. In the Upanishads, he sought deliverance from sorrow.

The transcendent nature of the Indian thought, its main distinguishing feature, acquired complete supremacy in the Upanishads. No other people have given as much thought as Indians to the nature of Being (Max Mueller).

Today India is home to Hinduism, Jainism, Buddhism, Christianity, Islam, Zoroastrianism, Sikhism, many reformist sects and tribal beliefs But a student of comparative religions will find that they are all influenced by each other. It may be intersting to examine very briefly how they contributed to the diversity of beliefs.

Jainism (derived from Ji: to conquer oneself) traces its roots to the Vedas and acknowledges Mahavira as the last of the sages of Jainism. What distinguishes Jainism from Brahmanism is the absence of ritualism and sacrifices, strict adherence to ahimsa and opposition to castes. The philosophy of the Jains called Anekanta-Veda (unity in multiplicity) exemplifies India's outlook.

Before Buddha's birth, religion consisted of observance of rituals and sacrifies. Naturally, the Buddhist revolt was against meaningless forms. In fact, Buddhism was the logical development of the Upanishads, although it did not accept the authority of the Vedas.

Buddhism contributed a great deal to ethics and psychology. It did not try to satisfy metaphysical curiosity (of the Beyond), and laid stress on personal striving for spiritual experience. Budha was neither for worldliness nor for asceticism.

Christianity and Islam are Semitic religions, not native to India. They influenced Hinduism and have, in turn, been influenced by Hinduism, Islam's belief in equality, and Christianity's mission of service to men had powerful influence on Hinduism. In turn, about Hindu influence on Islam Dr. Akbar Ahmad, a Pakistani scholar, says that he is proud of india's past achievements and its tolerance which "provided space for Islam to flourish". He asserts that the greatest contibution to Muslim thinking in this century has been made by South Asia. But this would not have been possible, he says, "without the deepest synthesis with Hinduism".

Hinduism has also added to the mystic dimension of islam. Identification of man with God, a fundamental postulate of the Upanishads, was anathema to orthodox Islam, but the Sufis made it a chief tenet of their beliefs. The "infatuation for god", common to Sufism and the Bhakti movement, made Islam more acceptable to India. Thus in the spirit of give and take, Hinduism, Christianity and Islam have mutually enriched each other. Had they exhibited a more fundamentalist spirit, this give and take would not have taken place.

Reformist religions of India like Sikhism have no fundamental disagreement with Hindu philosophies. The disagreements were with the social accretions of religion (caste system) and rituals. Sikhism was basically a peasant religion. It was influenced by both Islam and the Bhakti cults. One distinguishing feature of Sikhism is the importance given to the Guru. In this it is closer to Islam and Christianity. Sikhism did not have a specific identity till Guru Gobind Singh gave it one in the form of the panch pyaras.

The vicissitudes of india's history did not permit India to develop absolutist doctrines or faiths. Instead, an eternal quest for truth became its way of life. In the process, it created an immense diversity.

India today is a microcosm of the world, of races and religions, philosophies and ways of life, interacting with each other. This has creasted anxieties among some Indian people about the destiny of India Perhaps this is justified, because not all people are aware of their role in a society like that of India. But history seems to have chosen India for a great spiritual mission. Says Father Peter Hans Kolvenbach, Superior General of the Jesuit Order: "How in India people with many languages, religions and cultures live together is a lesson to learn. India has an important role to play in shaping the destiny of mankind. "The point is not other country in the world can undertake this role. This task belongs to India, for it is only India which saw humanity as one single family. If India finds a way for diverse peoples to live in amity, it will have set an example to the world.

M. S. N. MENON

INDIA AND CAMBODIA

Two great cultures - India and Chinese - affected the life and culture of East and South-East Asia in the past and regions of their cultural influence are well known. Indian influence is apparent in Afghanistan, Burma, Thailand, Cambodia, a part of Viet-Nam, Malaysia, Java, Sumatra and Borneo and the Chinese one can be noticed in Turkistan, Korea, Japan and Viet-Nam (ancient Taonkin and Annam). In certain cases Indian and Chinese influences crossed each other as, fcr instance, in Chinese Turkistan (Central Asia) and Tibet. From the beginning of Christian era India had a particular inclination towards South-East Asia, and one of the countries in that part is Cambodia where Indian cultural influence is remarkably evident.

In ancient Indochinese inscriptions the country of Cambodia is called Kambujadesa and sometimes simly Kambuja. In their own legends the country was known as Kok Tholk (land of tree) and later on Sruk Khmer. We learn of an Indian Brahman, Kaundinya, who sometime in the 1st century A.D. landed in Cambodia and married a princess named Soma and became ruler of the country. The later kings, specially of Chen-la and Angkor periods, claimed descent from the lunar dynasty of koundinya and Soma. This legend seems to be a fact as the countries situated to the east of Bay of Bengal were famous in India by the name of Suvarnabhumi (land of gold) or Suvarnadvipa (island of gold) and Indian traders were tempted for the voyages to acquire gold from these regions.

The expansion of Indian culture to Cambodia was not a political colonisation but it was mainly the result of commercial enterprise of Indian traders and missionary zeal of Brahmanic and Buddhistic savants. Arikamedu, Kaveripatinam and Tamralipti were the important ports from where traders must have sailed abroad. In the beginning they established small settlements on the southern shores of Indochina, Malaysia and Annam. Thus, indiginous Indo-chinese came in contact with Indian life and culture. They came to know a number of this and their social, political, religious and artistic conditions were tremendously affected. The first and foremost revelation to them was the Indian script through which they could write their language.

Prior to the introduction of European influence, the history of Combodia upto 15th century A.D. is divided in three main periods: Funan (1st century A.D. to 550 A.D.) Chen-la (550-802 A.D.) and the Kambuja or Angkor (802-1431 A.D.) Throughout all these three periods the impacat of Indian religion, society, language and art can be seen though in varying degrees. Funan seems to have started a new political and cultural phase based on Indian values and Chen-la and Kambuja or Angkor periods continued to illustrate Indian influence mixed with native tendencies.

Names of the kings having Varman (protector) as suffix, for instance in Mahendra - varman, Isanavarman, Jaya-varman and several others, point out the Indian tradition according to which Kashtriyas and kings should be styled as Varma or Varman. Similarly names of several places and Sanskritic in origin as Indrapur, Hariharalaya, Mahendraparvata etc. As in India all political activity centred round the personality of a king but he was guided by Purohita, guru (teacher) and ministers.

Vashpayamano balimanniketamalekhyaseshashya piturvivesa (xiv-15)

In compodia the society was divided into four castes as in India, though its regulations were not so rigid. The princes were educated in different systems of philosophy, Sanskrit language, Dharmasastras and Vedic studies. The Ramayana, the Mahabharata and the Puranas enjoyed considerable popularity and respect as in India. The extent of understanding and prevalence of Sanskrit language can be noticed through a number of inscriptions written in pure Sanskrit. It played more or less the same role as latin did in Mediaeval Europe.

In the sphere of religion, Indian faiths like Saivism, Vaishnavism and Buddhism attained a privileged position among the kings and their subjects alike. From the 5th century A.D. to the decline of Angkor period the cult of Siva occupied the status of a state religion, at times with Vaishnavism and Buddhism. The cult of Devaraja (royal god) bears testimony to this fact. From the 9th century A.D. Mahayana Buddhism came into prominence and it received the patronage of kings like Suryavarman - I (1011-1050 A.D.) and Jayavarman VII (1181 - 1220 A.D.) and shared the royal favour with Saivism. Suryavarman-II was a follower of Vishnu and the magnificient temple of Angkor Vat was very probably devoted to Vishnu. In khmer inscriptions we come across a number of references to the images of Krishna, Uma, Lakshmi, Ganga and Sarasvati etc. and most of them find representation in sculptures as well.

In the field of art and architecture the influence of India is as promient as in other fields. The architecture of Funan period, particularly in ornamental details, resembles the contemporary Pallava architecture. Later important architectural remains from the 7th to the 9th century A.D. are directly inspired by Magadhan temple architecture, specially by the temple of Bodhgaya. So far the ideology behind the temple architecture is concerned, Cambodians like Indians, considered a temple as a house of god. The main sanctuary was erected in the centre of the temple area and it symbolised the sacred Mount Meru situated in the centre of the universe.

It is quite likely that Indian influence penetrated into Cambodia through the ancient Indianised kingdom of Davaravati in Siam (Thailand). In the Cambodian sculptures of the 6th and 7th centuries A.D. the influence of Gupta art of India is conspicuously remarkable. Door-lintels with Makar motif, windows with peeping human head, finials and little columns, massive architectural effect of temples serene facial expression and idealised physical built up are some of the charcteristics which can be noticed equally in Indian and Cambodian art. The popularity of the cult of Harihara (combined form of Vishnu and Siva) is evident from a number of marvellous Harihara figures. In this form the deity combines the qualities and attributes of Siva and Vishnu. One half of the deity represent Siva with Jatabhara (tangled locks) over the head and the trident (Trisula) in his hand, while the other half wearing mukuta over the head and holding the wheel (Chakra) in his hand stands for Vishnu.

During the 7th and 8th centuries A.D. the powerful dynasty of Sailendras of Sri-vijaya emerged as a great force to control the destiny of South-east Asia for some time. They conquered Malayan peninsula, Java and Sumatra and built the great monuments of Central Java culminating in Borobudur. For a long time they transmitted Indian culture into Cambodia and even after Cambodian independence under Jayavarman II the glorious achievements of the Sailendras proved to be a guiding inspiration which resulted in the birth of a new epoch of Angkor. In the reign of Suryavarman-II (1113-1150 A.D.) the temple of Angkor Vat, the crown-jewel of Khmer art, was produced. It represents the culmination of the pyramid temple style based on the concept of Mount Meru, the legendary abode of gods and centre of the universe. Most of the subjects carved in the temple are drawn from the epics- the Ramayan and the Mahabharata- and other sacred textes like the Hari vamsa and other puranas. In the technique of execution, local tendencies merged in such a way with Indian ones that Cambodian art appears to be lovingly original.

The last powerful king of Khmer was Jayavarman VII (1181-1220 A.D.) who founded a new city named as "Nagarajayasri (city of the goddess of victory) just to the north of Angkor them to commemorate his victory over neighbouring state of Champa. The art of this period is known as the art of Bayon. It was in this period that smiling Buddha images were made. Budhha figures standing or seated on the Nagas were also introduced in this period. The drapery of Buddha figures reminds us particulary of the garment of classical Gupta times.

After a brief survey of Cambodian history in all its aspects one can realise what a great similarity exists in India and Cambodian cultures. Khmer and other neighbouring regions were so highly Indianised that Arab travellers in the 10th century A.D. considered them as an inseparable part of India. It is not a matter of mere Indian influences which travelled abroad but it is virtually a complete migration of Indian culture and ideology with all its characteristic details. Regarding the Indian influence in Indochina, the opinion of Mr. B. Ph. Groslier, an authority in the field of Indochinese studies, seems to be quite true. "It was one of the most important civilising movements of ancient times, worthy to compare with the Hellenisation of the Mediterranean world. And India can be justly proud to have spread the light of her understanding over such distant lands, lands which without her might have remained in darkness". (Art of the world-Indochina; P. 47).

R. D. TRIVEDI

INDIA AND MALAYSIA ANCIENT HERITAGE

India's ties with Malaysia are closer than is generally recognised. There is evidence of intercourse between the two countries in pre-historic times, and of vigorous contacts for millennium and a half, from the beginning of the Christian era until circa A.D. 1500. For the next four centuries, during the western colonial era, their relationship was eclipsed but the impact of a long association was impaired only superficially. The threads of friendship were picked up again when both regions began the struggle to re-establish their identity as independent nations. A stocktaking of the past has now begun in order to have a clearer view of their respective histories.

Going back to the Stone Age, Malaya's earliest pebble artifacts discovered form Kota Tampan in the Perak valley have affinities with similar objects from Pleistocene terraces in India, Burma, and Java.

India and Malaysia have a common ethnic and linguistic element through the migration of the Proto-Australiods from the west to the east. The peoples were modified within India and beyond by admixture with the Negritos and the Mongoloids. As a result the Kol or Munda, the Monkhmer, the Malay-Indonesia, the Melanesian and the Poleynesian peoples have common linguistic traits. Under the general tem Austric, this group of languages is further divided into the Austronesian which include among others Malay-Indonesia, and the Sustro-Asiatic which embrace the Kol or Munda, Nicobarese and the Mon-khmer speeches of India (Assam), Burma and Indochina. It is also a fairly well established fact that after the Proto-Australoids had become charcterised in the malay Archipelago, some of them backwashed to India bringing with them some local products and customs.

Very important evidence proving contact by sea between India, Malaysia, Indonesia and the Philippines was brought to light through the archaeological discoveries by Prof. Beyer, mostly in the province of Rizal in the Philippines during 1926-30. From the Iron Age strata were found pottery; iron implements and weapons such as knives, axes, daggers and spear points; glass beads and

bangles both green (by contact with Iron; found in the earlier Iron Age strate) and blue (by contact with copper); and finally beads of semi-precious stones such as agate, cornelian, amethyst and rock crystal.

Both the iron and glass objects are similar to and in some cases identical with the prehistoric glass and iron objects found interred in the dolmen tombs and urn burials in southern India. Similar glass beads and bangles have been found on the Malay Peninsula, in Java and in northern Borneo. Recently, the habitation area at Hallur in the Dharwar District of Mysore, a site connected with dolmen activities, has been dated at circa 1000 B.C. by the radio- carbon method (T.F. 573: 945 - 100 B.C. and T.F. 570: 1005 + 105 B.C.). Apparently Indians and Malaysians were in contact with each other way back in the first literary sources also contain a few references to typical Indian products reaching China in the seventh century B.C. by way of sea. The thesis of extensive maritime activity on the part of the people of the Malay Archipelago has been strengthened by a recent study entitled Africa and Indonesia by A.M. Jones which demonstrates the existence of Indonesian-type zylophone in western Africa prior to the establishment of Indonesia's first great empire.

The bead-trade continued to link the important harbours of Asia. Arikamedu, near Pondicherry in India, Kota Tinggi in Johore were eighty out of a collection of 600 beads are classed as "early Indian stone beads". Kuala selinging in Perak, and Oc Eo in Funan (Cambodia), testify to the existence of this connection.

Commercial interests intensified the contact between India and Malaysia around the beginning of the Christian era. Indian merchants were interested in gold, scented woods, spices and herbs, camphor etc. Interesting but brief and casual references regarding Indian association with South-east Asia, in the form of Sanskrit or Tamil names for local islands, regions and cities, and their products etc., occur in Indian literature such as the Ramayana, the Niddesa, a Pali cononical text of the late B.Cs. or early A.Ds., the Jatakas, the Ceylonese Maha-vamsa, the Milinda-panha, the Tamil poem Pattinppalai in the Pattupattu, the Silappadikaram, the Puranas, the Raghuvamsa of Kalidasa, the Kaumudi-Mahot-sava, the Katha-sarit-sagara, etc. Chinese sources, however, provide us with the greater bulk of information on Indian influences in the area and more specially on the dates and location of Indianised architectural and cultural remians found on the archipelago and above all in the living cultural traditions of the people. The latter comprises many walks of life; customs and beliefs, laws, religious history and present day attitudes (the character of Islam in Malaysia and more specially in Java) language and literature, theatre, arts and crafts, etc.

It will be best to talk of Malaya in the ancient times, not as a political unit but in terms of the Malay Peninsula as a geographical entity. Regulations regarding travel were politically not so restrictive in those days and sailors and traders naturally frequented spots that suited them best from the view point of navigation.

On the west coast of Kuala Selinsing in Perak a site has been unearthed the history of which stretches from the Negrito times to the days when Sung celadon was imported. Apart from the beads with Indian affinities, a cornelian seal of circa sixth century A.D. in southern India characters bearing the Sanskrit inscription "Sri Vishnuvarmmasya", and a gold ring bearing a group including Vishnu on Garuda have been recovered from Kuala Selinsing. Motifs similar to that on the ring are also to be found in Indonesia and the Philippines. A Gupta style bronze Buddha figure of about fifth or sixth century A.D. and a bronze asana for a figure of the Buddha were dredged up at Pangkalan near Ipho in the Kinta Valley. Another small bronze Buddha of about sixth century was found in a tin mine at Tanjong Rambutan. From Bidor comes the eight-armed Bodhisattva Avalokistesvara in Pala style belonging to the eighth or ninth century and from Sungei Siput two more Avalokitesvara figures as well as a pottery jar containing some gold ornaments.

In Ligor, at one time a vassal state of Sri-vijaya, a bronze Ganesa has been discovered with a Tamil inscription, in modern characters, which reads : Ma-jha-pi-chi-de-sa, the country of Majapahit. The most important inscription from the political point of view comes from Wat Sema Muang in Ligor on the Isthmus of Kra. Dated A.D. 775 on one face, it reveals that a king of Sri-vijaya with his capital in Sumatra had by that time established his supremacy over parts of the Malay Peninsula. The other face of the stele with an incomplete inscription varved no earlier than 782 A.D. states that king Vishnu "bore the title of Maharaja to indicate that he was a descendant of the family of the Sailendras" (of Java). The Sailendras, who in the latter half of the ninth century united Java and Sumatra under the gegemony of Sri-vijaya were, a century earlier, aiming at the same political strategy as the Sri-vijayas of Sumatra by attempting to control the northern parts of the Malay Peninsula.

At Takua-pa, also on the Isthmus a stone carrying a Tamil inscription of the ninth century A.D. has been found. It is a record of the construction of a tank which was placed under the protection of the members of a merchant guild, the residents of the cantonment and one other group.

The earliest inscriptions on the Archipelago have been found in Borneo at Kutei and Muara-Kaman on the R. Mahakam. In sanskrit verse and the so-called "Pallava" script of the late fourth century A.D., they commemorate the acts of a king named Mula-varman who "conquered kings in the battle-field, (and) made them tributaries, as did King Yudhisthira". The Indian principles of polity and the theme of the Mahabharata were, thus, known to eastern Borneo as early as 400 A.D. The process of Indianisation in Borneo must have begun many decades prior to the date of these records. Somewhat later than Mula-varman's inscriptions are eight epigraphs with Buddhist formulae discovered from the Kapusa region of western Borneo.

Indianised ornaments and statuary too have been discovered from various parts of Borneo. Some of them are: a pendant showing a four-armed Vishnu attached to a back piece of two birds tail to tail and a small gold tortoise from Muara-kaman, a small Nandi and a linga from a spot where the Rata meets the Mahakam, a Pallava inscription from Sangbetrang, a bronze Buddha image from Kota Bangun, Buddhist and Saiva images from Mt. Kombeng, all from eastern Borneo; a sarvamukha-linga from Sapaoek, a linga and a yoni from upper Malawie both from western Borneo; and an image of Ganesha and the Santubong Buddha from Sarawak.

The designs and methods of Malay arts and crafts bear the impress of Indian mythology and motifs.

The hilt patterns of the Malay dagger, the keris, often depict characters from Indian tales, Hindu and Buddhist. Hanuman and Garuda, for their superhuman qualities, are some of the favourit figures fashioned to shape. The keris blade may have become wavy to represent the nagas, the goes of Garuda whom he overpowered.

In the textile designs both countries are likely to have influenced each other; the exporter catering to the tastes of the importer and in the process acquiring some of the latter's preferences. The word for silk in Malay is of Sanskrit origin. Both the Indochinese and Indian methods of "tie and dye" are is use, the warp threads being tied before dyeing according to the former method and the cloth stitched firmly in puckers before appying the dye according to the latter method. Malay bronze, silver and gold work are reminiscent of Indian shapes and patterns The lotus blossom and the side view of the lotus appear in repouses work on jewellery, bowls and caskets. The filigree, sometimes jewelled on broaches, betel boxes, keris sheaths etc., show strong Indian influence. The foliation on the old type of large water-bottle stands, pedestals etc. often carries figures from the Ramayana. Bronze kitchen utensils popular in India are also used in old Malaya households and the general name for all bronze, copper and brass were is the Sanskrit gangsa.

In few countries of the world, theatre is as popular a mass medium as in Malaysia and Indonesia. The favourite themes for dance, drama, puppet-shows (wayang orang) and shadow-play (wayang kulit) are taken from the Indian epics, the Ramayana and the Mahabharata. The shadow play version of the epics was always preferred to their writtenform but some literary works of this genre have survived.

With the coming of Indian Muslim traders to Malacca, the Muslimised folk-lore of Hindu India, a mixture of Hindu, Persian and Arab stories, flooded Malaya. The Hikayat Indra Bangsawan was a result of these influences. With the coming of Islam Malaya also become familiar with the three world famous cycles of tales, the Persian Tutinameh, or the Original Sanskrit Suka-saptati, the Kapila dan Damina derived ultimately from the Panchatantra (known earlier to Malaya and Java) and the Bakhtiar cycle. The Malay version of the first cycle is known as Hikayat Bayan Budiman; of the second, three recensions were made, one from Tamil in 1835 by Munshi Abdullah; while the third cycle has two translations; the Hikayat Puspa Wiraja and the Kkayat Ghulam.

The fifteenth-century Malay author of the Sejarah Melayu or Malay Annals knew, among other languages, words from Sanskrit and Tamil and shows his familiarity with the Ramayana, the Gita and the cycle of Panji tales. The Kedah annals or the Hikayat Marong Mahawangsa are full of local folk-lore and myths from the Ramayana and the Jataka tales.

Words from Indian languages, Sanskrit, Tamilised Sanskrit, Tamil and Hindustani, came to Malaysia directly; or indirectly through Javanese with which Malay has a lot in common.

When examining ancient Malay religious beliefs, animistic, Pantheistic and monotheistic; civil and criminal law, birth, wedding and burial customs; government organisation, the King's rights, duties and status; economic life and social pastimes, it becomes abundantly clear that the Malays acquired much that was Indian but none which was at cross purposes either with their temperament, geographical or historical realities, or indigenous custom. Among other reasons this is to be explained by the lack of a traumatic element in the coming together of two civilisations.

When Islam came to Malaya with its specific religious beliefs, social and political institutions, the change, far more significant quantitatively then qualitatively, was smooth and easy in consonance with Malay tradition. It was also conditioned by the background of Islam, Indian and Arab, and the nature of its penetration in to the Archipelago. It is not a matter of surprise that the two great Malay (Achinese) thinkers, Hamzah of Barus and Shams-al-din of Pasai, of the seventeenth century should show such a fine grasp of Sufi mysticism.
(Condensed)

D. DEVAHUTI

INDIA AND NEPAL : OUR COMMON HERITAGE

उत्तर हिमवत् पार्श्वे पुण्ये सर्वगुणान्विते ।
पुण्यः क्षेभ्यश्च काम्यश्च स परो लोक उच्यते ।

A Himalayan Abode for Saints

The above sloka occurs in the 'Shanti Parva' of the Mahabharata. The entire 129th Chapter of the same deals in the praise of this region. The Himalayas have been the abode of the ancient saints. In order to obtain mental peace and enter meditation, saints and kings used to go to the Himalayas. All our scriptures bear testimony to this fact. Besides the voluntary exodus, whenever there has been turmoil in the plains of the peninsula - be it in the nature of foreign invasion, religious persecution or socio-political convulsions, the Himalays have been the haven for refugees; specially the Nepal Himalayas. To this category fall the Sakyas sacked by Birudhak, the King of Kosala; the Vedic Aryans persecuted by the Buddhist Zealots and subsequently the Buddhists when the revived Brahmanism took revenge on the Buddhists; the persecuted Hindus during the fanatic expansion of the Muslims; and as late as 1857 and 1942, the nationalist leaders persecuted by the British rule. In Nepal itself fall the tallest of the Himalayan peaks like Sagarmatha (Everest), Makalu, Lhotse, Nuptse, Kanchenjangha, Annapurna, Dhavalagiri and Gouri-shankar. Except for K2 of the Karakorum Range, which stands second in the world, first, third, fourth and fifth tallest peaks of the world are in Nepal or on its border.

Nepal nestles on the lap of the Himalays or Himavanta. Its name first occurs in Kautilya's Arthasastra, the age of which has been ascribed 300-100 B.C. by Bharatratna Shri P.V. Kane. Later we find the mention of Nepal in the Pryag inscription of Samudra Gupta, in which Nepal has been placed as a frontier kingdom. The mention of the country Nepal is found in several Puranas viz Skanda, Varah, Garuda, Aristhanemi etc., and also in Brihat Samhita of Varah Mihir. In the stories of Gunadhya, one of the stories gives account of Raja Yashketu of Nepal. The Buddhist and the Jaina Gathas too have on several occasions described Nepal. Thus we find Nepal to have held an independent existence since time immemorial.

LOCATION OF NEPAL

What had been its exact geographical location and extension in the ancient time is a matter of conjecture only. In the ancient period, the whole of the Indian sub-continent was divided into several kingdoms or small republics and it seems that Nepal has been expanding and contracting from time to time, as did the other kingdoms in the hinterland of the sub-continent. There is also no doubt that it existed on the north-eastern region of the peninsular sub-continent, as it does today. Whenever it has been mentioned, it has been with Pundra, Kamrup, Dawak, Pragiyotisha and Samatata.

In ancient times, the domain of Bharata also expanded and contracted in the reign of different kings and emperors. During the first Aryan expansion the eastern limit was the Sarayu and Sadanira (Gandak?). Both these rivers have their origin in the Nepal Himalayas. Incidentally, we have in our country a district, just on the western bank of the Gandak, called Parasi, which definitely to my mind, is derived from Prachi (the Prasi of the Greek writers). The eminent saints of the ancient time like Vishwamitra, Valmiki, Rishya Shringa, and Yagnavalka and a host of others had their abode in today's Nepal. Then the Jatakas, the saint kings also were in Nepal. The Nepal Vamsavali (history) mentions about the reign of Kushadwaja, brother of Janaka and father-in-law of Bharata and Shatrughan, in the Kathmandu valley or near about. The common name of the villages on its eastern part are Sankhu, Sunkhu, Visankhu, Sanga etc. which could have been derived from Sankasya, the kingdom of Kusadhawaja. The present day Tukuha rivulet flowing though the centre of the valley had its older name Ikshu or Ikshumati. The other rivers on the east of the valley too, bear names sounding almost the same viz., Zhikhu, Likhu etc. Of the several Mallakies most of them were in Nepal. We have an area on the hills north of Kapilvastu known as Malebum. The name is derived from the word Malla-Bhumi. Even in the later period many Nepal kings bore the surname Malla. Besides these were the small republics of the Sakyas and the Kolyas. Exact location of the Moriya clan and other small republics of that time have not yet been ascertained. Since the same were close to the Sakyas and Mallas, they could have been in Nepal or very close to it; so the Bethadwipa could be Bethari of Nepal.

IN THE CRADLE OF NEPAL

Sita, the spouse of Rama of the Ramayana, was nurtured on the soil of Nepal; and Gautama Sidhartha the enlightened and the light of Asia, had his birth in Nepal. Of the sixteen Mahajanapadas of the ancient time a very considerable portion of Kosala, Videha or Vajji, and Anga lies in today's Nepal. Of the several Mallakis most of them were in Nepal.

The history has yet to locate the original places of the Haryanka-kula Shreniya Bimbisar, the Saisunagas, the Nandas, the Mauryas, the Guptas and the Palas, the great empire builders. We do not know, however, that Samudra Gupta's mother, Kumar Devi, the most heroic and remarkable lady of our history, was a daughter of Nepal. Every student of Indian history knows that the credit for the birth of the Gupta Empire goes mostly to this great lady. The Videhas and the Vajjies have produced a number of eminent women, who gave birth to the famous characters of our cultural hertiage. In this list fall-Ilbila, Rishi Pulastya's wife and grand mother of Ravana; Trisala, mother of Tirthankar Mahavira; Vaidehi, mother of Ajatsatru. Even a Vaishalik Nagarsobhini gave to the society such eminent personage as Sisunaga.

THE KIRATS OF THE KIRATESWARA

Even earlier than the name Nepal, we find the word 'Kirat'. In Nepal we have several tribes bearing the name 'Kirati' and regions known as nearer Kirat, central Kirat and farther Kirat. The Yakhas, the Limbus, the Khumbus, the Rais of thirteen sects called Thulung, Chamling, Bantawa etc. are all Kirats. This region extends on the eastern part of Nepal hills and comprises area drained by the tributaries of the Kosi. The Kiranties, as they are called in the Nepali parlance, were pushed eastwards from the west. In the Kirati language the word 'Kira' means Kirati. Most probably the latter is derived by adding the suffic 'Anta' (as Sanksrit Gujaranta, Simanta etc.) to Kira. That is why it may be Kiranta or Kiranti in Nepali. We have a few pockets of this tribe in so. ie of the western districts too. The Kirats have ruled Nepal in the ancient time and the Vamsavali of Nepal consists of a genealogical description of the Kirat kings.

Of the three Gods of the Hindu trinity, Shiva, Shankara or Mahadeva has been given the name Kirateswara among many others. The story of Arjun's fight with the Kirat and subsequent obtaining of the "Pashupat Astra" is too common to be recounted here. I believe, Pasupatastra was nothing but the Nepali Khukuri, which did strike terror in two great world wars of modern time, equally with the Germans as well as the Japanese.

The older name of the Shaivaite cult of the Hindu faith has been Pashupat Dharma vis-a-vis the Bhagwat Dharma of the Vaisnavites, the only temple consecrated to Lord Pashupati is in Kathmandu; for the pilgrimage to which millions of Hindus from Kashmir to Kanyakumari have been coming every year from time immemorial. This temple has been in existence long before the advent of Shri Sankarcharya (Adi). This is supported by recorded evidence of his visit to the temple and laying down rules of worship and the appointment of the priests, who to this day hail from Karnataka.

On the language and the literary aspect of our heritage, Nepal has Devanagari characters for writing. It is true that the original Nepali speech is 'Khas-Kura', the language of the Khasas, but it has been so overlapped by the Indo-Aryan vocabulary and grammer that it is very difficult not to call it a branch of the same. The older Newari language of the Kathmandu valley too, which is mono-syllabic in nature, has assimilated lots of Sanskrit words and the earlier character and alphabets of the sub-continent.

HINDUISM PRESERVED IN NEPAL

The Madhya Desa (called Madhes in Nepal) or the Indian plains, due to various impacts of alien cultures, has lost most of its earlier Hindu values and rites, which Nepal has been able to preserve intact. For example, the system of marriages which exist in Nepal to date like Anuloma, Brahma, Prajapatya, Gandharva, and Asura.

Nepal has been the nourishing ground for the Shakta cult too with its different branches like Tantrism etc. The Vajrayana too flourished here for many years. We find lot of literary and iconographic evidence of the same. In the Shakta and Vajrayana sects of both the Hindu and the Buddhist faith, we find a triangle with Vajji or Mithila and Bengal as the two corners of the base and Nepal as apex of the same.

In the shaping of culture and history, geography and geo-physical conditons play a vital role. All the rivers which have their sources in the Great Himalayas, the Outer Himalayas, the Ladakh Range from the Sindhu to the Lohit flow southwards. Even the rivers that flow out of the Hindu-Kush eastwards drain through this very sub-continent. The sea on the three sides have helped maritime activities and sea trade in the distant past. No wonder the culture from Iran to Irian and further beyond to the Pacific Islands bears the common stamp.

THE ASIAN CULTURE

Many nations belong to this group now. The Chinese, the Korean, the Japanese, the Mongolian cultures too have been greatly influenced by the same culture or vice versa. It is high time we call it Asian Culture, rather giving it a narrower and parochial name. The ancient Greek, Roman, Slay, or Anglo-Saxon cultures have fused into one and has been given one name, the Western or European culture. So the Austric or Mon-Khmer, Dravidian or Iranian, Mongols or Tartars, Buddhist or Tao, Aryan or Asur, Hindu or Muslim cultures fused into one should be named now Asian Culture. If we insist to be more particular, we could name it South Asian Culture.

MATRIKA PRASAD KOIRALA

INDIA AND PHILIPPINES

Contemporary Filiopinos-both the rural and the Sub-urban as well as the urban-view India and the Indian in the Philippines with an air of mysterious regard. To the rural Filipino, he is one with turbanned head, long flowing beard, carrying with him his bundle of merchandise, for he is an itinerant peddlar, one who has become the symbol of esacting obedience from truant children in the outlaying areas. (The Bombay will carry you off in his bag, so goes the syaing.) To the suburban and the urban Filipino, he is the ubiquitous watchman in every commercial establishment (particularly during the early years of American Occupation) as well a the peddlar who now rides the motorcycle or the institutionalized American army jeep. To both these levels of Filipions, he is the Bombay, the appealation being an unnecessary misnomer. For in the past, the Indian who came to the Philippines necessarily embarked from the port of Bombay, hence the name. Even a Filipino who looks like an Indian is addressed Bombay, and at the same time assigned to a place of origin, that is Cainta in the province of Rizal, east of Manila.

The results of extensive studies of scholars on the pre-hispanic relations of the Philipines with lands across the seas revealed that India, through the intervening regions, e.g., primarily Malaya and Indonesia, had very intimate contacts with the Philippines. These contacts are indeed significantly seen in the enrichment of Philippine culture, particularly in the languages and literatures, the system of writing, and archaeology. Perhaps, it can be said that there may be traces of Indian customs, manners and traditions in the Philippines society.

There is a body of Sanskrit as well as Tamil terms in the languages of the Philippines which in one way or another had contributed to the enrichment of concepts and ideas of the Filipino.

The literatures of the early Filipinos had been substantially influenced by the Indian, particularly the pre-Islamic literatures of the now Muslim Filipinos. This is clearly illustrated by the discovery of episodic borrowing from the Rama story, like the episode of the abduction of Sita by Ravana, which lead to the war between the army of Rama and that of Ravana in Lanka. This is, however, traced through the Malaya Hikayat Seri Rama and its folk-story version in Malay literature. Some portions of the Panchatantra had been also discovered among the literatures of these Muslim Filipinos. Apart from this episodic borrowing, there are many motifs and themes which may be trced back to the Indian. However, it could not be entirely Indian in provenance, but it is also possible that certain South-East Asian cultural elements may have found their way to India through the process of intercultural encounter and stimulus.

The system of writing of the early Filipinos had been equally traced back to India through the Sumatra (according to one view) or through the Buginese (according to another). But the present writer is inclined to the former view. However, this inclination is still tentative because of the many factors relative to the movements of cultures in the past. One of these factors, perhaps a very imortant one, is the distance in time between the Philippine developments of this system of writing and the assumed origin and the forms through which the former had been derived. The ultimate Indian origins, nevertheless, are seen in the Pallava Grantha script made famous in the inscriptions of the Pallava kings of South India, on the coast fronting the Bay of Bengal.

Archaeological evidences of Indian contacts with the Philippines in proto-historic times appear to be very meagre in contrast to those found in other Southeast Asian regions- the mainland, the peninsula and archipelago. The few evidences may be described briefly. From the 14th - 15th century sites at Calatagan, Batangas (on the south-western portion of Luzon Island) was recovered by the Philippines National Museum archaeologists a clay medallion fied to represent the likeness of a Mahayana Buddhist, the Boddhisattva Avalokidha Amitabha represented in the oval nimbus of the image's headdress. It is related to the artistic tradition that prevailed in Siam during the 12th-13th centuries.

Perhaps the most spectacular archaeological find in the Philippines is the famous Agusn (Mindanao) golden status also belonging to the Mahayana group and related to the concept of a female Boddhisattva, and at the same time the counterpart of the Hindu goddess (Sakti) as a Tara (or wife of a Buddhist god), which is a peculiar development of Buddhism in Southeast Asia. Moveover, its probable connection with the Tantric development of Buddhism in South East Asia would put it in the late 13th or early 14th century A.D. The statue is now deposited in the gold room of the Chicago Natural History Museum, U.S.A.

Another very important find is the golden garuda pendant from Brookes point, Palawan. It is a finely executed piece. The identification as garuda is drawn from the representation of Vishnu's weapon, the Filipino's view of India and the Indian is even more lucid and has become sharper in terms now of his broader understanding of India and the Indian. The post-colonial and independence period brings to the Filipino a much more different perspective of the Indian and India. This is indeed manifested in the opening of diplomatic as well as trade and cultural relations between the two countries. More and more Filipinos had travelled through India - either as tourist or students or businessmen or diplomats - and therefore, giving the former a much broader view of the country and her people. On the other hand, more and more Indians had come to the Philippines as scholars, students, businessmen and diplomatic personnel, hence the Filipino has had not chance to travel to India had now a new image of the Indian apart from that which he was made to see in the past. The Indian who had come to settle in the Islands has acquired a singularly high status in the community because of his integrity in dealing with the Filipinos. To that extent, he had been relatively if not absolutely, integrated into the Philipine society, excepting his participation in the political field, if he had not yet acquired citizenship. This is best illustrated in the increased inter-marriages between the Indians and the Filipinos in most cases between the Indian male and Filipines female.

In the field of foreign diplomatic relations, India and the Philippines "started on a note of unenthusiastic cordiality, almost devoid of warmth and certainly lacking in intimacy". To elaborate this further I would like to cite an Indian scholar, who is now connected with the Asian Centre of the University of the Philippines and who has devoted some years in the study of India-Philippine relations in contemporary times. He writes - "Philippine-India relationship started on a low key and continued to grow in an atmosphere of mutual indifference and mistrust. There was no eminent clash of national interests nor were they involved in situation where direct confrontation was inevitable. However, as a consequence of their diametrically opposed positions in cold war politics, their ideas and view often came into direct conflict with each other. Despite these developments, the basic necessity of their Asian existence and the inevitable needs of cultural cooperation gradually improved their working relations. With the change in international climate and reduction in cold war tensions, it brought a marked change in Philippine - India relations. India's reassessment of her attitude towards Asian countries eventually brought a reapprochment between India and the Phillippines resulting in extended cooperation, lessening of irritants and broadening of political and cultural cooperation".

While there are still isolated instances of distorted view of India and the Indians by Filipinos, the changing patterns of relationship between the Philippines and India on all levels have given the Filipino a broader base for understanding the Indian and his country. The mystery behind the flowing beard and in the turbanned head, as well as in the majestic sari has cleared up with this sharper focus brought upon the culture of India through all the means of contact between two nations, who in the past had regarded each other with mutual indifference, and at times distrust because of the accidents in history, e.g., India having been under the tutelage of British imperialism and the Philippines under the rising banner of American colonialism, both having taken diferent counrses in their relations with other countries in the world of cold war politics.

JUAN R. FRANCISCO

INDIA AS IT IS KNOWN TO THE PEOPLE OF INDONESIA

Although the people of Indonesia were converted to Islam since the end of the 13th century, the high civilization of India, which once stimulated the birth of a new civilization in Indonesia, is still living in the memories of millions of Indonesians. The Indian heritage is not only proved by the remnants of ancient monuments, like the Buddhist Borobudur and the Shaivatic temple complex of Prambanan, both in Central Java, and others, but it is also proved by the present civilization of Indonesia, in particular by Bahasa Indonesia, i.e. the national language of present Indonesia. Despite the discontinuation of the cultural relations between India and Indonesia as the result of foreign dominations in both countries during three centuries, the spiritual link between India and Indonesia still exists up to present times.

The Borobudur monument together with the Chandi Mendut and pawon is making a tripartite union, because the three temples have been built in one axial line. In the times when the archaeological studies in Indonesia were still in its infancy, the Chandi Mendut and Pawon which are situated rightly to the East of the main Borobudur monument, were considered as two preliminary stages through which any visitor of the Borobudur should prepare himself to enter the holy sphere of Shunyata or the sphere of the void i.e. the highest ideal in Mahayana Buddhism.

But at present, based on the reading of the bilingual inscription of Karangtengah, (using Sanskrit and Old-Javanese language) found in the village of Karangtengah in Central Java, it can be concluded that the Chandi Mendut and which is mentioned in the inscription as the Venuvana-temple was built by the Shailendra King Indra. The pious deed of this king was in accordance with the teaching of Mahayana Buddhism, which laid the strees on mahadaruna or great love for other human beings who were still suffering and needed the knowledge through which they could reach salvation. The sanctuary of the Chandi Mendut contains three monolithic images of big size- Buddha Gautama with the Dharmachakramudra (the handpose of turning the wheel of the religion) and his spiritual son the Bodhisatava Avalokiteshvara, the saviour of the present world, whereas the third image represent Vajrapani, the guardian of the Buddhist religion. All the three images have been carved according to the famous Gupta heritage of Northern India, the common denominators of which are the in-look or yoga eyes, the curly hair, the more or less oval face, a fleshy body, a broad breast and the soft flowing lines of the contours of the body.

As far as the Chandi Pawon is concerned, it can be mentioned as to be the place of cremation of king Indra as suggested by the Karangtengah inscription. In fact, in Javanese language pawon means the place of ash; according to the Javanese grammar the prefix pa and the suffix an are denoting a locality, whereas in the word Pawon the noun awu is found, which means ash. But what is very important for the interpretation of these tripartite monuments is the passage in that inscription which mentions that King Indra who built the Venuvana temple after his cremation in the temple (of Pawon) should march through the Dashabodhisatvabhumi or the ten stages of Bodhisatva. The Dashabodhisatvabhumi was one of the very important tenets in Mahayana Buddhist religion (7). This religion taught that anyone who reached bodhi or the true knowledge should make a vow to become a Bodhisatva and, after having marched upwards through the ten stages of Bodhisatva, he reached the sphere of Shunyata or the sphere of the void; then he was entitled to become a Budha himself and which was the ultimate goal of the Mahayana Buddhist religion.

The above mentioned passage is very important for the interpretation of the Borobudur monument which from the architectural point of view consists of ten stages. These stages should be nothing but the material representation in stone of the spiritual ideas of the Dashabodhisatvabhumi doctrine.

Another centre of ancient monuments in Indonesia which represents another branch of the heritage of India is the temple complex at Prambanan, to the East of present Jogjakarta in Central Java. This temple complex which should have been built in the 9th century A.D. is more or less of the same age as the Borobudur monument which should have been built in the first quarter of the 9th century. This Saivatic temple complex is also known as the temples of Lara Djonggrang means the Javanese word Lara Djonggrang means the slender maid. The name of the whole temple complex has been named after the slender image of Parvati, the consort of Lord Shiva and who is depicted in the form of Durga Mahisasurmardini or Durga, the killer of the demon Mahisa.

One of the decorations of this temple complex which desrves fully the attention is the sequence of reliefs showing a story of Rama (13). The story has not been based on the Ramayana version by Valmiki, but on one of the so many versions of the Rama stories known in India. The part of the Rama story on the balustrade of this Shiva temple ends with the story of setubandha, i.e. the story which is connected with the effort of King Rama to build the bridge between the Indian peninsula and Lanka, the Kingdom of Ravana.

In this connection it is worthwhile to mention that on another balustrade of the same Shiva temple there are 62 panels with dancing figures which correspond with the Tandava of Shiva as described in the Natyashastra, the manual on the art of dancing ascribed to Bharata-muni. More or less the same dances have been depicted on the walls of temple at Kumbhakonam in South India and also on the wall of the Rajrajeshvara temple at Tanjore.

The main Shiva temple is flanked by two smaller main temples, namely the Brahma temple to the South and the Vishnu temple to the North of it. The first one is called the Brahma temple, because in its sanctuary a beautiful four-headed image of Lord Brahma is placed, whereas the other one is called Vishnu temple, because a chatur bhuja (four-armed) Vishnu is adorning its sanctuary. On the balustrade of the Brahma temple the story of Rama is continued and depicts the Mudha-kanda, among others dealing with the story of the death of Ravana and the journey of Rama and Sita to Ayodhya. As far as the balustrade of the Vishnu temple is concerned it is decorated with the story of Krishnayana or the story of Lord Krishna as the incarnation or avatara of Lord Vishnu.

From the brief description of the Prambanan temple complex as mentioned above, it can be made out that the Indonesians in the past were continuing the traditions of the Indian heritage more or less in its purest form.

As far as the sculptural peculiarities of the reliefs which decorate certain parts of the temples of the Prambanan temple complex are concerned, the human figures like Rama, Lakshmana, Sita, Hanuman, Krishna and the like still follow the Indian classical traditional school of art; it means that the human figures are highly naturalistic and if classified according to the language of art they have been executed according to the three dimensions tradition. But in the development of the history of sculpture in Indonesia, it can be observed that only in the times of strong Indian influence on the native civilization in Indonesia this classical Indian tradition of art could be preserved. Because as soon as the Indian cultural influence was waning since the 13th century A.D., the sculpture which was inherited from India underwent a modification, and indigenous Indonesian art traditions which were used to execute sculpture according to two dimensions tradition came to the fore; According to the two dimensions tradition the angular shape of the body of the human figure is seen from the front, whereas the head and feet are turned sideways. Since this type of tradition of art is still applied by artists in present Bali and Java, in particular in the art of shadowplay which is called wayangplay, this special style of art is mentioned as the wayang style.

Since the temple complex of Panataran in East Java, as well as the Shaivaitic Prambanan and the Buddhistic Borobudur both in Central Java still attract thousands of visitors, it means that despite the conversion to Islam, the Indonesian people are still proud to preserve the heritage from Indian civilization. This peculiar phenomena is only due to the fact that the type of Islam which was integrated in the pattern of Indonesian civilization was in the beginning not the kind of Islam with its rigid legalistic system, but the one which could make compromise with the existing Indonesian civilization which was the result of the acculturation between pre-Indian indigenous Indonesian civilization with the one of India. The effort of introducing the type of true Islam did not take place in Indonesia until the opening of the Suez canal, which opened the possibility of frequent contacts between the holy land of Islam and Indonesia.

That the type of Islam which spread to Indonesia in the 15th and 16th centuries was as eclectic form of Islam and which could be adjusted to the local civilization in Indonesia, was among others proved by the development of architecture and are in the 15th and 16th century which were nothing but a continuation of the indigenous Indonesian and Indian traditions.

That the art of Islam in Indonesia in the 15th and 16th century was adjusted to the Indo-Indonesian civilization is proved by a painting on wood preserved in the court of the Sultan of Cheribon in West Java and which shows Ganesha standing on a lion. Both the figures of Ganesha and the lion have been decorated with Arabic characters mentioning the name of Allah (God) and the prophet, Mohammed with other phrases from the holy Quran. The above mentioned example is only one of the so many proofs of acculturation which took place in the development of the present Indonesian civilization.

The Indonesian word bahasa in the meaning of language is derived from Sanskrit bhasa; the change of bhasa into bahasa is due to the fact that according to its sturctural system the Bahasa Indonesia does not know the use of aspirates. So the Sanskrit aspirates can only be pronounced with the inverted a in between the respective sound and the. Thus bhasa becomes bahasa, Sanskrit bhaya (fear) becomes bahaya, Sanskrit phala (fruit) becomes pahala etc. From these examples it is clear that the Sanskrit loanwords in Indonesian language are adjusted to the pattern of the last mentioned language.

The acceptance of Sanskrit loanwords in Indonesia did not take place only in ancient Indonesia, when the cultural impact from India was very strong and in which period many of the Indian literary products like the Puranas, the Kavyas, the epics Ramayana and Mahabharata etc. were translated into Old-Javanese, one of the very important local languages in ancient Indonesi, but also in present modern Indonesia. The Bahasa Indonesia which was accepted as the national language in 1928 during the emergence of national movement in Indonesia, was in origin the Malay language, which was used as lingua franca in the whole of Indonesia during Dutch colonial times.

In this connection it can be mentioned that there are many adeas and institutions which are derived from Western civilization but the words have been substituted by newly coined Indonesian words derived from Sanskrit. Say for example, the words derived from Sanskrit. Say for example, the word for a Catholic Priest is pendeta, which is undoubtedly derived from Sanskrit pandita, whereas the word for a Catholic monastery is piara, derived from Sanskrit vihara. Accordingly a Catholic nun is in Indonesian language biarawati. The formation of this last word should have been inspired by the use of the Sanskrit ending van, vati or vat which can be added to any noun, and which form an adjective of possession. So Biarawati which should be the equivalent of Sanskrit viharavati means the one which possesses the monastery.

Of late, the Indonesians are embracing Islam, but despite this fact, the Indonesians, in particular the ones from Java, still retain their Sanskrit names. The Christian name of the author of this paper is Sutjipto which is in fact nothing but the Indonesian form of Sanskrit suchitta, meaning the good (su) minded (chitta) one. As far as my surname is concerned, namely Wirjosuparto, it consists of Sanskrit virya or vairya (heroic) and supartha the well-behaved (su) Partha (Arjuna). So any Hindu Indian in present time will be surprised to know that common Indian names like Krishna, Lakshmana, Indrajit, Bhima and the like are still used by Muslim Indonesians. The more surprising is the knowledge of the average Indonesian, even of the illiterate villager in Java and Bali who knows by heart the innumerous names of the heroes of the Indian epics Ramayana and Mahabharata. Through its adaptation in the Old-Javanese language, and through its modern versions in Javanese, Malay, Sundanese, Balinese and other loval languages in Indonesia the stories of the Indian epics are becoming part and parcel of the modern Indonesian civilization. It is no exaggeration when it is mentioned, that the average knowledge of the Indonesian concerning the stories of these epics is more comprehensive if compared with their brothers and sisters in present India, i.e. the land of origin of these stories.

From the brief discussion of the civilization of Indonesia one will have the impression, that the heritage of Indian civilization is deeprooted in Indonesia and this fact is also acknowledged by the Government of Indonesia which tries to maintain the good relationship with its neighbours, in particular with India which once had strong ties in the past and which should be continued in present time for the sake of their mutual benefits. Therefore it is not surprising to know, that in the secondary school, in particular for those who are studying arts, have to learn the history and culture of the Indian people, whereas the students in the universities who are taking the course of Indonesian language, history and classical archaeology of Indonesia, have to study Sanskrit and the archaeology of India for two years. Facts, that reveal that the cultural link between India and Indonesia is continued.
(Condensed)

SUTJIPTO WIRJOSUPARTO

INDIA IN THE EYES OF THE PEOPLE OF THAILAND

Indians have long been familiar to the Thai people. Ages ago, Indian merchants and traders travelled to the Golden Peninsula, as we call it, bringing with them not only merchandise but also many other facts of Indian civilization and culture, such religious doctrines, legendary lore, sculpture, music and dances. From India, first directly and later by way of Sri Lanka. Thailand received the greatest of all gifts from overseas the teaching of Lord Buddha, which moulded the Thai character and thus shaped the destiny of the Thai nation.

Those ancient traders from India settled in Thailand. As they grew in number and prosperity, more and more of them made it their permanent domicile and became part of the thread of Thai life. Many of their descendants became Thai citizens, being the offsprings of mixed marriages. Today, the Indian or Thai or Indian ancestry has become an indispensable segment of the social scene in Thailand.

An affectionate regard has developed for the "khaek", as we call them whether they are the turbaned merchants of cloth, the ubiquitous night-watchmen with their canvas beds (on which they are sometimes found asleep in duty) or those who have risen to high positions in officialdom or the community. Contemporary society in Thailand would not be complete without them.

Ancient Indian culture made a deep impression on the comparatively younger Thai culture. The Buddhist Sutras and Jataka Tales form part of the fabric of our religious and moral life. The Ramayana in its Thai version called Ramakein has become a great epic of Thai literature, and the characters of Rama, Sita and Hanuman are as much loved by Thai playgoer as by the Indian; the Thai "khon" or masked play having been evolved from the Ramlila. The hierarchy of Hindu gods and goddesses provided inspiration for our artists, and some of them have assumed symbolic significance, such as Ganesh the patron of fine arts and Saraswati whose gilded statuette is awarded to winners of Thailand's top cinematic honours (far more aesthetic than Hollywood's Oscar).

The Thai love festivals, and some of these are undoubtedly derived from Indian inspiration. The ceremonial bathing and water-throwing of Songgran (the Thai midsummer festival) approximate Holi, while the Loy Krathong, floating of lights along Thai rivers and canals is an aquatic version of Diwali.

Thai poetry, music and dance are similar to the Indian in form as well as in them. Those who have seen the folk dances of both countries have commented on the similarity of Thai dance movements of those of Manipuri and Assam. The latter is hardly surprising as the Assamese and the Thai come from the same racial stock.

Indeed, many Thai and Indians share the same facial characteristics. Our names, too, having a Sanskrit base, are quite Indian, as also many words in our language; we largely resort to the ancient Sanskrit and Pali roots in coining brand-new words to meet the impact of modern technological terms.

In view of these racial, hostorical and cultural affinities, it is hardly surprising that the peoples of India and Thailand have achieved a high degree of homogenous association. Today, this is refelcted not only in personal relations such as by way of intermarriage but also in other ways; turbaned young Indians have gained scholastic honours in Thai Universities while young Thai footballers have won their place on Indian college teams, an Indian professor has gained fame in Thailand while a Thai citizen was recently elected chairman of a bank in India.

Perhaps the only divergence between the two countries has been in the political field. This is the result of fairly recent history. While India like most Asian countries fell under the colonialist yoke, Thailand became the only country in South-East Asia to remain independent. Hence our relations with the western imperial powers assumed quite a different footing from that of most of our immediate neighbours. Circumstances compelled us to adopt a new way of life with new modes of thought, dress and behaviour patterns. This inevitably brought about difference which caused a temporary rift between us and our near neighbours.

This, however, did not lessen our sympathy for our neighbours under alien rule, and we were hopeful that they would regain their freedom. One instance of this was when, during World-War II Netaji Subhas Chandra Bose organised his Indian National Army in South-East Asia with a view to striking a blow for India's freedom, he received encouragement and support from the Thai Government and much of his organisational activities took place in Bangkok. Although his efforts did not meet with success, the sympathies of the Thai people for the Indian independence movement continued until India regained her freedom. Thailand, which has previously maintained a consulate-general in Calcutta, became one of the first countries to open a diplomatic mission in New Delhi, sending here a succession of distinguished diplomats one of whom was Thailand's Minister of Foreign Affairs, Dr. Thanat Khoman.

Since 1871, when our great King Chulalongkorn personally came on a tour of India, most of our national leaders have at one time or another visited the sub-continent and became acquainted with its varied peoples. In the eyes of the Thai people, India is a vast conglomeration of races, religions and languages. This, to begin with, is not easily comprehended in a land where one religion predominates and one language prevails. Then there are other factors not readily understood such as the caste system, for ours has always been a casteless society. These and some others of India's problems have perhaps not been given the due consideration they deserve. All these factors led to the shaping of India's domestic and foreign policies. Non-alignment, adopted by India as a modus vivendi following the legacy of Mahatma Gandhi and Jawaharlal Nehru, was never properly understood in Thailand because the conditions facing the latter were totally different. The Buddhist doctrine enjoins its adherents to adopt "The Middle Path", and Thai Budhists generally followe this. But the stark realities of contemporary power politics militate against negative compromise. The Thai are, if anything, a realistic and practical people, inured by centuries of perseverance for survival as a free nation. They are apt to regard non-aligment as the idealistic dream of a philosopher, too unpractical in the context of present-day materialism. This perhaps has been the widest gulf between Thai and Indian thinking to date.

The time has come, however, for India and the fast-developing nations of South-East Asia to draw closer-together for their mutual interest and benefit. In the economic sphere, especially, there are promising prospects for greater co-operation. Thailand, currently the most prosperous South-East Asian country, is looking to India as a potentially important trade partner. There is reason to believe that official thinking is the same in this regard both in New Delhi and Bangkok. This could mean yet another new and improved bridge of understanding and friendship built on the solid foundations of the old. (Condensed)

PRINCE PREM PURACHATRA

INDIA THROUGH THE AGES

No country has been at the centre of such mystery and obsession as India, It still is. Love and hate, fear and fervour -these have been the West's responses to India. The pattern has not changed in all these years.

It was perhaps Herodotus (484-430 BC), the Father of History, who first referred to India. The Persian conqueror Darius brought the Greeks and Indians together. The contact continued for a thousand years, from 5th century BC to 5th century AD. Alexander's invasion (326-324 BC) brought Greece and India into intimate contact as never before. He was in touch with Indian ascetic philosophers (the Greeks called him Gymnosophists). But writers on the Alexander saga turned the story into a fabulous romance, which persisted well into the 16th century.

Megasthenes, who spent five years in India (317-312 BC) as envoy of Seleukas Nikator (the Greek king of Syria) at the court of Chandragupta, left a more realistic picture: of a happy people, of simple manners, frugal, seldom going to law, leaving their doors open and holding truth and virtue in high esteem. Popular images, however, persisted. Virgil, the great Latin poet (70-19 BC) still referred to Indians as "Ethiop of the East". Strabo did much to correct the errors.

Indians were present in Antioch and Alexandria by the second century BC. We owe them the picture of India as a country of religions and speculative philosophies.

Pliny the Elder, author of "Natural History", found the image of India rather "incredible". But people believed in them, which is why St. Augustine wrote that God might have created "fabulous races so that monstrous births among Christians should not be attributed to lapses in His wisdom". (He thought India was a country of Christians.)

To Appolonius of Tyna (1st century AD), a neo-Pythagorean philosopher, who was the first Greek to travel all over India, the "wise Brahmin" was more Greek than Indian. This tradition of the "good and wise Brahmin" was internalised by Christianity.

Thus, different images of India emerged in the West: that of a "black" people who lived on the borders of Ethiopia; of a people east of Persia, who were highly advanced; and of the "fabulous India of Homer" located at the end of the world. "From Antiquity to Renaissance, the ordinary European drew his conception of India mainly from the stories attahced to the fictional biography of Alexander the Great",. writes Donald Lach in his monumental study of Asia. It was both positive and negative.

It is not known how many books were written on this "Romance Alexander", but they increasingly showed Alexander as a demi-god and India as a country of surprises. With the advent of Christianity Alexander became the first soldier of the Cross, determined to suppress the idolatory of India.

But the image of the wise East also persisted. There is the story of Dandamis, the "oldest and wisest Brahim". In Germany a manual was brought out in which Dandamis was shown as a princely exemplar. Abelard Lauds Dandamis as one of the four Pagan kings, who foresaw the advent of Christ.

The Alexander romances of the Middle Ages created other images of India as a land of opulence, golden palaces and beautiful amazons clad in silver armour. But the Gymnosophists themselves lived in simplicity and isolation, we are told.

With the advent of the crusades, Alexander became the archetypal hero of the Crusaders. On the popularity of Alexander, Chaucer writes:

Alisander's storie is so commune. That everie wight that has descretionne Hath herde somewhat or all of his fortune. But is also meant that "everie wight" had also heard somewhat of the fabulous stories of India, As Alexander's fame spread, so did that of India.

The romance of Alexander was almost over by the 16th century when European explores came into direct contact with Asia. They came in search of its wealth and spices. But they-were also curious about the mysteries.

Since ancient times, India has been the "ocean" of stories, didactic and heroic. They travelled all the way to Europe. Take the story of Barlaamand Josaphat, Christianised life of the Buddha. It was so popular that Josaphat was declared a Christian saint and a day was set aside for his festivities. Only in the 19th century it was recognised that Josaphat was none but the Buddha.

Something similar happened to the famous Panchatantra stories of India. As these stories travelled beyond recognition. Only the morals remained.

Christian Europe wanted to hide the parentage of these Indian stories for one major reason: it did not want to appear to be learning its morals from Pagan India.

Asian visitors left more realistic images of India. Hiuen Tsang (600-654 AD), a chinese pilgrim found Indians "high-minded, upright and honourable". "I have seen races not seen before, heard sacred words not heard before, witnessed spiritual prodigies exceeding all wonders of nature, "he wrote on his visit to India. A third of the Chinese classics are translations of Sanskrit and Pali works.

Al-Biruni (12 century), one of the greatest scholars of Islam, who spent several years in India marvels at the religious tolerance and lack of theological disputations in India. Of the irrigation work constructed in the south of India by Chola king Rajendra I, Al-Biruni writes:

"Our people are unable to describe them, much less construct anything like them".

On the city of Vijayanagar, Farishta, a soldier-scholar of Persia, writes: "The city is such that eye has not seen or ear-heard of any place resembling it upon the whole earth". A Portuguese traveller found it "the best provided city in the world". And an English historian tells us that the city was "splendid", with "a wealthy and industrious population in the plenitude of prosperity".

Even in 1495, on the advent of Vasco da Gama's visit to Calicut, Europe still thought of India (or part of it) as a Christian country. Writes Guilano Dati:

Oh, India, blessed and wallowing in the glory,

May God Preserve the in His Christian faith.

It was the story (no doubt apocryphal) of Presster John, a legendary Christian king, who ruled over a part of India, which attracted the Portugue. They wanted to seek his help against the Moors. Of course, the spice trade was no "culture shock". They found the cities thickly populated, with fine buildings. And they visited Hindu temples and thought that the natives were worshiping Mother Mary.

Utopia of Sir Thomas More was inspired by the Gymnosophists. And Shakespeare made twenty-four allusions to India in his works.

But those who came to rule over India or convert the natives into Christianity saw India with a different eye. Lord Curzon, who saw the British empire as the greatest instrument for good, had no good word for orientals. Lord Willingdon never met a Hindu, he says, with a single good quality. He thought Muslims were worse. Others who came to rule over India saw it as the home of depotism and violence, venality and indolence. They were all fed on James Mill's book "History of British India".

But there were other men, greater than these rulers, like Sir William Jones, who became the pioneer of Indology. This is what he had to say of Sanskrit: "More perfect than Greek, more copius than Latin and more exquisitely refined than either". Of the Hindus, he says, they were "People with a fertile and inventive genius", who "in some early age, were splendid in arts and arms, happy in government, wise in legislation and eminent in various branches of knowledge".

As for missionaries, they were here for conversion, and to give "light" to the natives. As for "light" to the natives. As Tagore says "The torch of Europe's civilisation was not meant to give light but to start fires". Perhaps, missionaries are not to be blamed entirely They could not have spoken in praise of India's religions and philosophies and yet got converts. So, to Bishop Heber, one of the advocates of conversion, India was a country "where every prospect pleases and only man is vile". "I could not endure this abuse of Hinduism", said Mahatma Gandhi.

Bacon had an explanation for this. He says that "what really animates the imperialist is the firm belief, even if mistaken, that the race to which he belongs is the noblest, and the civilisation and ideals for which it stands are the highest".

Sir John Marshall, the excavator of Mohenjodaro, tells us that there was nothing comparable to the well-built baths and commodious houses of Mohenjodaro (3500-3000 BC). And of the cotton textiles he found there, he says, "the use of cotton was exclusively restricted to India at this period and was not extended to the western world until 2000 or 3000 years later". Of the Mauryan architecture (4th, 3rd century BC) he said that it surpassed even the finest workmanship of Athenian buildings.

Europeans who visited India between 15th and 18th centuries all testified to the superiority of India over Europe in manufacturs and to the high degree of India's prosperity.

Two British writers stand out as image makers of India - Kipling, the imperialist, and E.M. Forster, the scoffer. But Maugham (Razor's Edge) shaw, Huxley, Wells - all of them helped to improve the image. Why, even the founder of the British empire in India, Warren Hastings, was not sure whether the empire would last, but he was sure that the translations he ordered from Sanskrit "will survive when the British dominion in India shall have long ceased to exist". And he was in the habit of quoting from Gita, perhaps to spite the missionaries.

But we must leave the last word to Thomas Munroe, the British governor of Madras. He says that "foreign conquerors have treated the natives (Indians) with violence and often with great cruelty; but none has treated them with contempt and so much scorn as we". Malcolm Muggeridge, editor of "The Statesman" an Indian daily pioneered by the British, agreed with Munroe. He says: "An alien culture, itself exhausted, trivial and shallow, was imposed on them (Indians); when we went, we left behind... a spiritual wasteland".

To creat this image of the wasteland, American writers also made some contribution. Katherine Mayo's "Mother India" (1927) saw nothing but "loathesome eroticism" in India. Mahatma Gandhi called her book a "drainage inspector's report".

But what did the greatest Americans think of India? Emerson Thoreau and Whitman, the makers of the American renaissance and members of the Transcendental group, found in Indian thought what they had missed in Greek philosophy.

Through the ages, India has sought to arrive at an inner perfection of the spirit. In the process, it has perhaps cared less for outward adornments. Gandhi was the supreme example of our times. He was a "naked fakir'; but the world bowed before him.

India cannot be measured by its snake-charmers, cows and godmen. As Max Mueller said: "As we measure the Himalayas by the height of Mr. Everest, we must take the true measures of India from the poets of the Vedas, the sages of the Upanishads, the founders of Vedanta and Sankhya philosophies and the authors of the oldest law books".

India is not an ordianry country.

M. S. N. MENON

INDIAN ART : BRITISH CONTRIBUTION
TO ITS STUDY

Until the twentieth century, the British in India did much to preserve Indian art, but it was only the rarest of scholars and administrators who honestly admired it or investigated its principles. The Archaeological Survey, under a series of British directors, salvaged temples and monuments and their work, preserved in thorough and recondite reports, shows how deeply moved by antiquity was this small band of careful observers. Fergusson, Cunningham and Burgess patiently described architecture and Griffths, a British principal of the School of Art in Bombay, recorded through his students the ancient murals of Ajanta. A number of other workers also made contributions and in this way vast reserve of archaeological and historical facts was built up.

It was left to an Indian Civil Servant, Vincent A. Smith, however, to achieve a gigantic dual task - to write not only a comprehensive history of all India from the earliest times to 1911 but to present the first full account of fine art in India and Ceylon. In this book, published in 1911, Smith set out in plain and simple English most of the main facts which research had then brought to light. He described important types of Indian sculpture and architecture, arranged them into periods and also discussed ancient wall-painting and the miniature art of Kangra and the Mughals. Throughout, his attitude was one of warm and lively interest. Wherever possible, he commended 'excellent' work and his book, as a whole, is remarkable for its broad understanding and stalwart common sense.

In some important way, however, Smith was of his times. As a late Victorian, he was unaware of all those trends in Europe which have since revolutionised artistic criticism and ultimately led to modern art. He knew what he approved-but also what he disliked-and he avoided any serious attempt at defining the expressive qualities of Indian sculpture or at explaining its greatness Certain aspects-the glamorous treatment of the female form and the un-abashed portrayal of loving couples-acutely embarassed him and, confronted with their presence at such famous sites as Karla, Khajuraho and Konark, he did the only thing possible for someone of his training and temperament-he either turned, like Nelson, a blind eye and quietly omitted any mention or brusquely dismissed them as too indecorous for serious discussion. Certainly, a modern visitor, if nurtured only on Smith's History, would have no idea of what sculptural glories awaited him at these centres and might innocently visit the 'Black Pagoda' at Konarak expecting only to see fine horses and a splendid sun-chariot. Smith's greatness-and greatness is the term which he most clearly merits-lies rather in his quiet enthusiasm for a vast subject, his power of reducing intricate material to an orderly whole, his basic respect for Indian Culture and conviction that historical facts would alone lead to its proper understanding.

Smith's History of Fine Art in India and Ceylon was a landmark in British studies and the fact that it has since been superseded suggests how far-reaching has been its influence on later writers. By the general public, on the other hand, it is E.B. Havell whose name will be cherished as the first and most vigorous British champion of Indian art. His books - Indian Sculpture and Painting (1908), The Ideals of Indian Art (1911), Indian Architecture: its psychology, structure and history (1913) set out to expound in clear and vivid terms the Indian artistic achievement. His aim was to shake India and the West out of their seeming in-difference to Indian art and to impress on the civilised and cultured public of his time the fact that Indian sculpture was of great spiritual and ethical value. He considered Indian renderings of the Buddha as of special importance, but throughout his writings runs the constant theme that Indian religion and spirituality demand high respect and that the greatness of Indian art is connected with the greatness of Indian religion. This view was expressed in trenchant terms and could not be lightly disregarded. Indeed, in the circumstances of his day, it was probably the only approach capable of arousing interest and of winning support. Today, so biassed a defence or so polemical a challenge are no longer needed and it is noteworthy that even Vincent Smith thought much of Havell's pleading 'extravagant'. Yet the example of his passionate devotion remains and as an Englishman who loved India and her culture and fought for her art, his work deserves abiding respect.

Between the two world wars, British studies of Indian art were mainly archaeological and although Sir William Rothenstein had argued that, by world standards and quite irrespective of religion, Indian sculpture was among the world's greatest art, constructive appreciation was on the whole wanting. It was rather in the sphere of miniature painting that important strides were taken. In 1912, Coomaraswamy had published his pioneer work, Rajput Painting and thereby brought to world attention the poetic art of the Punjab Hills. By them, Mughal painting was already famous and much admired but it was Arnold and Binyon's Court Painters of the Grand Mughals, published in 1921, to be followed by Percy Brown's Indian Painting under the Mughals (1924) which provided the first detailed surveys and fostered among British scholars that special interest in Mughal art which had never waned. A very different but none the less important contribution was J.C. French's Himalayan Art. French was all Indian Civil Servant whose interests had been fired by Coomaraswamy's classic treatise. He spent a number of vacations touring the Punjab Hills, visiting palaces of rajas and inspecting family collections of pictures. His book describes with modest charm his dogged travels and proved how important for writers, critics and historians of painting were visits to actual spots.

With the coming of Indian Independence, British contributions entered a new phase. The winter exhibiton of the Royal Academy, London (1947-48) led to the production of a monumental catalogue, The Art of India and Pakistan (1950) and it is possibly to this great assemblage of Indian masterpieces that the rapidly growing enthusiasm for Indian sculpture can be traced. At no previous time, in fact, could it be said that Indian sculpture has been so widely or so greatly admired and although the spate of books which reflect this admiration are important mainly for their plates, and their texts are by non-British writers, British interests can justifiably take credit for much of their production and publication.

It is possibly in the field of painting, however, that the most revolutionary advances have been made. The acquisition by the Victoria and Albert Museum and the British Museum of several important private British collections, the appearance of much new materials in India, the exhibition by the Arts Council of Great Britain - Indian Paintings from Rajasthan - as well as visits to India by British scholars have enabled many styles of Indian miniature painting to be identified for the first time and a wholly new essessment of Indian painting in all its marvellous variety has been arrived at. In this task, British art-historians have worked in close co-operation with their Indian colleagues and indeed it would require a separate article to do justice to the great contributions made by Indians to the study of Indian art. Besides art-history, and essential feature of recent British activities has been the attempt to secure wider appreciation of Indian painting among the public at large and thus to make belated restitution for former neglect. The poetic charm of Kangra and Rajasthani painting, its great artistic qualities, its human and emotional appeal as well as its reliance on poetic symbolism have been emphasised and, as a result, a much larger public than ever before has come to understand and value this expression of the Indian genius. It is possibly through further work in this direction - enlarging of taste, the broadening of appreciation -that British art critics can still make contributions to the study of Indian art.

W. G. ARCHER

INDIAN BRIDES : SYMBOL OF PRISTINE BEAUTY

A bride in any part of the world is an epitome of beauty and the brides in India are no exception. Decked up in their fine jewellery and clothes they look extremely charming and radiate pristine beauty.

Being a vast country, not only the rituals and ceremonies for the holy union of two souls differ from state to state, but the bridal attire also has characteristivs of its own. Even within the same state, the customs, customers and ceremonies differ among various communities. But one ornament, the nath, or the glorious nose ring, be it of silver or gold, is a must for a bride in northern India. A traditional embellishment of the female face, it is a favourite subject of many folk songs where the poet wishes to be one of the pearls on the nose ring so that he could always be near the lips of his beloved!

The Indian brides have had centuries' old tradition in shingar. Jewellery was, and still is, her main beauty accessory with which she embellishes her body, face and hair. The bridal ornaments are made not only of silver and gold but also in copper, brass, wood, ivory, pearls and lac.

Some typical brides from different parts of India Himachal Pradesh: Besides the nose ring which is the prominent ornament, the brides of Himachal Pradesh adorn their heads with an ornament called cbuk. This dome shaped ornament has two small hooks for the multi-coloured thread used to tie the ornament around the head of the bride. The ornament for the forehead is called cburi-dora or shringa-path, and is worn over the forehead on other side of the face. The ornament for the cars is the bali, a circular erring worn around the outer edge of the ear. Satlari, seven strings of pearls inter-woven with enamel work motifs, is the ornament for the neck. It is also called Chandan-haar when made of seven chains of silver.

PUNJAB : The Punjabi bride wears a brilliant pink or a bright red salwar-kameez or an embroidered saree and adorns herself with most elaborate jewellery, lone ear-rings or balis and a wide necklace. The red and white bangles made of ivory and bone are a must for the punjabi pride. Known as chura, these bangles of ivory consist of plain red ones flanked by decorated white ones, at least five on each wrists. The tikka a glittering pendent-shaped jewel adorns the center of her forehead. She drapes the richly embroidered phulkari over her head and a part of her face with gold jewellery glittering against her forehad ears, nose and neck peeping out of this makes a pretty picture indeed. The prominent nose ring is always there to adorn her nose. It is about one and a half inch in diameter, strung with multi-coloured pearls, mostly red, white and blue. The nath, supported by a chain, is clipped to the hair so as not to strain her nose. Her hands are decorated with beautiful floral designs created with henna. Arsi is an ornament for the fingers and is to be worn on the thumb. It has a small mirror encased in it to enable the bride to steal a look at herself.

HARYANA : The Harayana bride traditionally wears a long ghagra stiched from 15 to 20 meters of cloth, preferably of red, green or yellow colour. She wears a full-sleeved shirt similar to a man's shirt on top of this. Her head is covered with an odhani or duppatta adorned with gota and small shining stars made of nickel. A belt of silver called tagri tied to her waist, keeps the odhani and ghagra in shape. A heavy hansli made of solid silver adorns her neck. A flower-shaped tikka decorated with pearls of different colours adorns her forehead. The tikka is clipped to her hair with a silver chain. A hollow silver kara or bangle with small ringlets fixed all around it is worn above the anklets, which jingle and produce a melodious sound when the Haryanavi damsel walks!

RAJASTHAN : Green and red glass as well as ornamented lac bangles are worn by every bride in Rajasthan. In some areas, such a Barmer and Jodhpur, the Chura (wedding bangles) made of ivory or bone, is of graduated sizes to cover the entire forearm, from the wrist to the elbow. Bangles for the bride are considered auspicious. The Rajasthan bride also wears a lehanga-choli embroidered with colourful disigns and small round pieces of mirror. She wears a small round or conical piece of silver or gold on her forehead called boria or tikka (similar to that of the bride from Haryana), held similarly with a silver chain tucked around her ear. Around her neck, she wears a heavy silver hansli and a silver chain of three or four strings. A small nose ring called nathni adorns her nose, supported by a golden chain clipped to her hair. She gets her palms and feet decorated with intricate henna patterns.

LADAKH : Colour reigns supreme in the bridal dress of this otherwise arid snow desert area. The most beautiful head-gear of the Ladakhi bride is a turquoise-studded perak. Only the wealthy Ladakhi women can afford the full length perak. The family's wealth and the matriarch's individual worth can be calculated by one glance at her peraks. The peraks are passed on from mother to daughter as dowry. They resemble the flayed-hood of a cobra, with a wide band of turquose trailing down the back. From a distance, the serpentine analogy is further enhanced by the placement of the pieces of stone which resemble the scale on a snake's skin. Ladakhi society is polyandrous, and a woman's disposable income goes to accummulate items to adorn her peraks. The Ladakhi bride also wears long robes called bak made of goat skin. Around her neck she wears a necklace with corals and pearls. In the centre of this necklace hangs a golden amulet box. There maching bracelets and rings. She wears sturdy footwear made of sheep skin and embroidered with colourful traditional patterns on its upper part, into which yak hair are woven to protect her feet from frost bite. Although forced to cover her feet thus, the bride from Ladakh makes up for it by her colourful costume.

SOUTH INDIA : The brides in South India wear jewellery similar to that which Bharatnatyam dancer adorns herself with. Her hands and feet, decorated with red colour, are adorned with anklets, bangles and a hath phul consisting of a bangle and several rings attached to a central gold plate resting on the back of her had. She wears a jewelled band on her head with a pendant tikka. Two circular pieces of jewellery are worn on either side of the parting in her hair, one representation of the sun and other of the moon. She wears gold as well as green and red glass bangles. To ward off the evil eye, a single hair from an elephant's tail bent into a frame of silver or gold is tied to the wrist in some southern areas. The Mangal Sutra (string symbol of matrimony) which is offered to the bride by her husband is the most precious ornament of the South Indian bride and she never parts with it.

MULK RAJ SIDANA

INDIAN CIVILIZATION : ITS TWO STREAMS

Two streams - one of senses, the other mind; one of form, the other of thought - this had been the way the indian civilization grew from times we know. They met and left, and met again. One was Dravidian, the other, Aryan. One attained its highest reach in the form of the dancing god, Nataraja, a symbolish of the cosmic dance of the dynamic universe. The other rose to the abstract concept of monism - in Shankara's advaita. One created music and dance, painting and sculpture, art and architecture- in short, the sights, sounds and smells of our civilization; the other created the world of the intellect- our philosophies, our world of thought.

"The metaphor of the cosmic dancer has found its most profound and beautiful expression in Hinduism in the image of the image of the dancing Shiva," says Fitsjoff Capra. The dancing Shiva is the most sublime artistic attempt to capture the mystery of the universe in form. Perhaps the only symbol of its kind in the world. And, who but Shankara could have followed the logic of monism to its inevitable conclusion-to a God without form and attributes?

The Vedic Aryan had no temples or idols or images. Each patriarch lighted the sacrificial fire in his house and invoked the bright gods for their blessings. But their invocation was in rather poor poetry because Vedic rituals failed to inspire the poets. Great poetry, music and architecture had to wait for the Puranic age and the advent of the more colourful gods and goddesses.

The Manusmriti talks of idol worship among the Dasyus (Dravidians). But the Aryans were also quietly taking to idol worship. Which is why Manu, the Hindu lawgiver, threatened them with ostracism. He says, "A Brahmin who attended idol worship should be shunned". But at the same time he did not want to suppress idol worship. In fact, he advocated punishment to idol breakers.

In Vedic rituals, the functions of the deity are described, but nothing of its physical appearance. But in Tanstrism (supposed to be anterior to the Aryan advent), the description is concentrated on the physical beauty of the deity. The Aryan mind was bound to go from form to formlessness. Max Mueller, one of the greatest authorities on the Vedic age, says that if he were to define in one word the distinguishing feature of Indian character, he would put it as 'transcendence' - a tendency to transcend the limits of empirical knowledge. Most people are happy with the empirical, but for all that there is a beyond. Max Mueller says: "The transcendent temperament acquired, no doubt, a more complete supremacy in the Indian character than anywhere else".

The quest went beyond name and form. God became a principle. The Indian image of the divine was not that of a ruler who directed the world form above, but of a principle that controlled everything from within. The identification of the Atman (soul) with Brahman (Creator) was the end of this quest. It became a central doctrine of the Upanishada. Motion and change, according to Indian thought, are assential properties of things, but the forces causing the motion are not outside the objects, as in Western thought, but are intrinsic to matter. With the first explosion of matter in 1945, we discovered that matter contains light, heat, sound and motion - a confirmation of the Upanishads.

The Buddha had little to say on God. So the first idol among Buddhists was made in the image of the Buddha himself, not of God. It was made by a Greek artist attached to the court of Emperor Kanishka (first century AD. The Kushans carried the image of Shiva on their coins). Thus, Buddhism, perhaps unwittingly, made a major contribution to India's idolatry. The Buddhists installed thousands of Buddha idols in the Viharas they built. But, then this was a Greek and Central Asian weakness. In Central Asia, Buddhism was simply engrafted to Shamanism of the Turanians and it transformed itself into some of the grossest forms of Scythians indolatry.

Tanstric literature, however, admits that idol worship was designed for the lowest human personality type, for those who were incapable of comprehending the higher truth without concrete props (Woodroffe). Tanstrism advises people to take to silent meditation.

Shankara took the same position. Although his monism admitted no personal god, he introduced Ishwara for the sake of the lower orders of men.

Most scientists, when referring to the mysteries of the universe, its vast forces and its origins, tend to avoid using the world 'God! Yet when they accept the idea of evolution, they also accept the idea of a remote goal, an intelligence, a transcendent will. Vedanta, the most intellectual school of Hinduism, emphasizes Brahman as a non-personal, metaphysical concept, free from any mythological content. What was Einstein's concept of God? On this Einstein had said; "My religion consists of a humble admiration of the illimitable superior spirit who reveals himself in the slight details we are able to perceive with out frail and feeble minds. That deeply emotional conviction of the presence of a superior reasoning power, which is revealed in the incomprehensible universe, forms my idea of God". Sounds almost like the faith on the Greeks in human reason. Einstein's was not a personal God.

But we cannot visualize this God, just as we cannot visualize an electron. The idea of God cannot be concretized. But....

If the Indian mind went beyond form to the formless, it also revelled in a riotous feast of forms- in a world of imagination. Sir William Jones writes of the Hindus that they are "a people with a fertile and inventive genius". It flourished in exuberance. Anthropomorphism came naturally to the people. More so to the ordinary people. They wanted to please their deity, to worship him, not to contemplate over his nature. A synthesis of the Aryan and non-Aryan cults became inevitable. This is the vast system of idolatry dealt with in the Puranas (mythologies) and for this reason it may be called Pauranic Hinduism, to which the majority of Hindus belong.

The cardinal principle of this type of religion is Bhakti (worship). Vaishnavism is its most developed form, and one of its doctrines is of avataras (incarnations of the divinity), which became the richest field for the imagination of the artist and poet.

How can we please a deity conceived in **human form** with eyes, ears, nose, mouth and feeling? There is only one way: we must create the most beautiful things for him to see (painting, seculpture), poetry and music for his ears,

fragrance and flowers for small, finest savories for his palate and dance and drama for his feelings. And how else can you express your awe for his majesty except by housing him in the most magnificent temples? It is this desire to please a very human god, which led men to seek perfection in all that they did. Thus, the entire civilisation of India is a feast of sounds, colours and sights, of tastes and smells of beautiful temples and sensual pleasures. Had this God no eyes, why should the painter paint? Had this God no ears, why should the poet sing? Had this God no feelings, why should one dance? Anthropomorphism determined the course of indian civilization'. There can be no art without idolatry, says Ananda Coomaraswamy, the first to discover the greatness of Indian art. Thus, no civilization is possible without idolatry of some kind, in its broadest meaning.

The Indian artist never copied from Nature. All that he wanted to suggest was the idea behind sensuous appearance, not to give the details of a seeming reality. The purpose of his art was sacramental. It was an accessory to worship.

The art of fresco painting at Ajanta and Ellora reached perfection, unsurpassed anywhere else. Here religious piety fused with architecture, sculpture and painting into a happy harmony.

It is by its art and literature that a society is judge by history. In his "Lectures on the Philosophy of History", Hegel says: "India is the land of dream". India had always dreamt - more of the Bliss that is man's final goal, and this had helped India to be more creative in history than any other nation. Hence the efflorescence of myths and legends, religious and philosophies, music and dances and the different styles of architecture.

But man must go beyond the gratification on the senses. He must progress in thought. This cannot come, says Aurobindo, "if we chain the spirit to some fixed mental idea or system of religious cult, intellectural truth, aesthetic norm, ethical value, practical action.... and declare all departure from that a peril and a disturbance... We must free our consciousness from its fetters. That is what the world, and we have failed to do. We are bound by varied fetters.

We are like pilgrims on a long march. Some are in the lead. They have lighted torches in their hands. They are nearer to Bliss. Some are in the rear. They are somewhat in the dark. They are still in the thrill of the senses. And this is how it is going to be for ages. Before us is a great goal- the progressive divination of men. Those who are at the rear will seek to gratify their senses and those who are in the lead will raise their consciousness.

The two streams of our civilization are like Ganga and Yamuna. Both will continue to water our lands, Praise be to both;

M. S. N. MENON

INDIAN CULTURE : CONCEPTS OF TOLERANCE

From the very beginning, spiritual aspiration was the governing force of Indian culture. It made spirituality the core of its thought, the highest aim of life and made every endeavour to turn the whole life towards spirituality. The predominance of the spiritual aim as the guiding spirit of life necessitated a casting of thought and action into the religious mould for, religion occupaied the highest position in people's psyche. Consequently, the Indian mind became indifferent to relitious dogma. To it spirit mattered not the theological credo.

Indian religious thinkers realised that the supreme truth is neither the rigid conclusion of the logical reasoning nor the affirmation or credal statement, but the fruit of man's inner experience. Intellectual truth is only one of the entrances to the outer precincts of the shrine, and since intellectual truth turned towards Infinite must be in its very nature many-sided, the most diverse intellectual beliefs can be equally true because they reflect different facets of the Infinite. Therefore, there are no true or false religions, but rather all religions are true in their own way, each one of them being one of the numerous paths to the Eternal, the One without a second.

When people elsewhere were indulging in mindless bloodshed to establish the superiority of their favourite god or gods, the Rigvedic seers boldly proclaimed, "Ekam Sat vipra bahudha vadanti" Truth is one, wisemen call it by various names". Later, the same tenet was reiterated by Krishna in the Bhagvad Gita when he declared, "Ye yatha mam Prapadyante tamastathaiva bhajamyam; mama vartamanuvartante manusyah Partha Sarvasah" - "Through whatever Paths men come to me, I receive them through those very paths; all paths O' Partha, ultimately come to me only'. It is not that this mind elevating massage of great wisdom and unparalleled profundity which became the backbone, the essence of national existence in this ancient land, was enunciated by these two scriptures alone though undoubtedly they have a pervasive impact on the Indian mind. Every scripture, the teachings of every saint and seer conveyed this noble sentiment, may be their languages differed. The simile often cited has been, just as several rivers emanating from different mountains and traversing their separate courses eventually meet the ocean, in the like manner all the diverse paths taken by men of different tendencies various though they may appear, ultimately lead to the same Brahman.

Not only was the greatest spiritual truth seen in India with the boldest largeness, and approached from all sides, but it was consciously made the grand uplifting idea of life, the crore of all thinking, the foundation of all religion, the secret sense and declared aim of human existence. Thus, Indian culture succeeded in infusing religion with the essential ideal of a real spirituality thereby making an indelible imprint of this basic truth on the general mind of the people. The Spiritual reality which it reflects, the profound experience to which it points, has permeated the religion, the literature, the arts, even the popular religious songs of a whole people. The verses of Tukaram, Kabi and Mirabai to cite but a few examples, with their profound spiritual thinking have, therefore, found so speedy an echo among the general public.

The Indian mind has thus perceived right from its Vedic origins that the Infinite must always present itself in an endless variety of aspects. Therefore, the idea of one religion, one set of dogmas and one ecclesiastical ordinance which has led to so much intolerance, cruelty, obscurantism and aggressive fanaticism elsewhere, has never been able to take a firm hold of the free thinking mind of the Indian people. Men everywhere have common human failings; Indians are no exception but these things have never taken the proportions which they assumed in other cultures.

The Indian religion-philosophical culture, which grants liberty of thought and of worship to the individual in his approach to the infinite, has always shown readiness to acknowledge and even accept new ideas from whatever quarters they came. Consequentiy, Sahishnuta or Kshanti mentioned in the Bhagavad Gita as a divine virtue has been its constant tradition, in fact its intrinsic constituent. Whoever first translated these Sanskrit terms as tolerance had done injustic to the underlying lofty concept. Tolerance has an air or patronage with a hint of disdain in it. Rightly, therefore, Swami Vivekanand once declared in disgust, 'I do not believe in it (tolerance). I believe in acceptance. Why should I tolerate? Toleration means that I think that you are wrong and I am just allowing you to live'. In socio-religious context tolerance as acceptance meant giving up the demand that others change in order to conform to one's liking, expectation or belief, and accommodating them with fortitude. This is not a sign of cowardice or timidity but of maturity and understanding of the nature of people and their conditionings. Tolerance in this sense, therefore, is willing acceptance of a differeing point of view based on understanding and sympathy even respect, and not something that conceals pride or indifference leading to contempt or sufferance.

The persistent emphasis, right from the formative period of the Indian civilisation, on the spiritual unit of all existence and religious pursuit gve rise to the concept of unity in diversity. The Indian mind-set did not believe in uniformity of type either in religion or in culture, in fact even in social norms which govern human interrelationship. They developed a firm conviction in the philosophy of a variety of expressions held together by a central thread of unity so much so that their concept of tolerance interpreted as acceptance embraced not only groups professing different religious streams and beliefs but also those who doubted or denied the concept of God. This liberal attitude which accommodated and showed understanding towards people holding disparate and divergent views on religious matters has allowed place to every individual in this splendoured land without his having to gorego or suppress any of his beliefs or convictions. As a natural consequence, this accommodative spirit has instinctively, almost imperceptibly fostered in him a sense of belonging, a sense of allegiance to this land and its people. Inevitably, therefore, unity in diversity has become the sheet-anchor and the hallmark of the Indian nation, its culture, its civilisation.

Acceptance of the reality that others may have a different point of view, a different set of beliefs, a different religio-cultural background influencing their attitudes and overt behaviour, and their accommodation-even assimilation where assimilation was considered worthwhile - in social norms and behaviour, can have some unsavoury consequences. The very people who are accommodated, or whose mode of behaviour and beliefs are accepted as true for them and hence deserving of equal consideration, are likely to misunderstand this noble gesture as indicative of timidity or cowardice especially if their own cultural traditions are riveted to uniformity and conformity in matters of religion and hence bereft of such considerateness. They may, therefore, look down with disdain upon the people they should be grateful to, and take liberties with or poke fun at what their benefactors venerate or hold in high esteem as fundamental to their heritage, their culture, their religion, their spirituality.

When this happens conflict ensues and as a consequences sectarianism, obscurantism and even militant zealotry raise their ugly heads where none existed before, to influence the thinking and imagination of a few volatile elements, thus bringing ridicule to the whole community as being shame and hypocritical that conceals below a thin veneer of professed highmindedness a debased and perfectly condemnable character. It has to be realised that these are mostly reactive momentary aberrations which soon die down like a ripple for want of a sustained support from the people at large. This monster of human unreason which beges narrowmindedness, cruelty and parochialism has never been able to take firm hold of the free and receptive mind of India. And the rein lies the greatness of its eternal culture.

VASANT K. SARAF

INDIAN MUSIC

The music of India is perhaps one of the oldet in the world. It is also a major system of music that is essentially melodic; and what is of great significance and interest is that it has retained this character to this day. This is in contrast to European culture, for example, where the early melodic music has changed into the current harmonic music.

The social pattern of India today is the result of many ancient ones and the way of life on this land has been woven of fibres of different hues and textures. It is supposed that the Negrito races, the remnants of which are still with us, were the most ancient in India. The Dravidians, Mongoloids and Aryans were later cultural incursions. And the music of India today shows this cultural admixture.

The tribal people in various parts of the country- the Pulayans, the Oraons, the Santhals, the Savaras, the Chenchus, the Bhils and others - have their own characteristic music and dance. This tribal music has contributed to a large degree to the general mould our music. Another ancient form of Indian music was that of Tamils and related cultures. This was also a melodic style fused with Aryan music, eccelsiastical styles of which are sung in the Rigveda and Samaveda. Slowly all these forms have come closer and become amalgamated into one another, a later strain coming from Central Asian regions; and, of course, the latest is coming from the West. It is therefore essential to free oneself of the many preconceptions about this music. First is of the monolithic origin of not only the music, but the general culture of India. But what then is India? One cannot accept only the political borderlines, for cultural patterns overflow these walls and lines on the maps. There can also be no rigid cultural barricades, for one social group passes into another, sometime imperceptibly. And this subcontinent

with its enormous extension in space has also a hoary past. The material and mental products of various cultures which were quite distinct in ages gone by - and this variety is evident even to this day - have had time to flow and dissolve into one another. This music of India ranges, then, from the grunts and shrieks of the Nagas in the far eastern border and the Todas in the southern hills, to the most sophisticated concert ragas and talas. The result of such a give and take is the present day Indian art music with its two major areas - the Hindustani and Carnatic. In general they have the same basic, being melodic and governed by rules of raga and tala structure. The Carnatic system is the art form of southern India (Tamil Nadu, Kerala, Andhra and Karnataka). The rest of India follows the Hindustani musical dialect.

The Hindustani and the Carnatic systems are only the highly grammarized music of the simpler art of the country. Naturally the basis and foundations of the art music have to be sought for in this soil of tribal, folk and borderline areas. And almost non-musical, yet with a 'musical' feeling, are the gruntsand shrieks of the Todas and the Nagas. But then these are the seeds out of which the complicated concert music has blossomed out. The flour - grinding songs of rural women grow into various folk songs, more or less intricate. Music in and out of the temple is a other tributary to the mainstream. Vedic music which commenced as a recitation of three tones ended as a seven-toned chant. In the temples and maths (monasteries) music was, and stull is, a vital part of meditation and worship. Through these simple bhajans, abhangis (devotional songs) and keertans group musical chants) the most profound mystic truths and socially reformative ideas were conveyed to all the populace. Thus Indian life is filled with music at all strata and levels. Classical music has, them grown out of this fecund earth and in its turn flowed back into that soil. This is true not only of musical elements and forms but also of instruments. After all, the concert rudra veena is another version of the kinnari and jantar. The table might well have been a progeny of a village pot covered with hide. The elaborate cross rhythms and drum mnemonics heard in the mehfils (musical gatherings) have been developed long ago among the tribal Santhals.

In essence, a raga is a melodic scheme governed by certain traditonal rules, but providing a great freedom for improvisation. These rules define and determine the notes of a scale that should be used, their order, prominent and necessary melodic indioms which give a particular 'colour' to the scheme. Based on these more or less strict limitations, the musician is free to create and herein lies his genius. The raga has, of course, to the pleasing: "A raga is called by the learned that kind of sound composition which is adorned with musical notes in some peculiarly stationary, or ascending, or descending, or moving values, which have the effect of colouring the hearts of men".

The tala is a rhythmic arrangment of beats in a cyclic manner. Each cycle is complete in itself and is repetitive. The cycle is dividided into sections which may or may not be equal. It is formed by the addition of time units in a defined manner. But what is of real significance is the closed or cyclic arrangement. This is the essential difference between tala and rhythm.

Within this framewor, there are many styles of creating music. These very according to their emphasis on rhythm, extent fornamentation, lyrical qualities,etc. Some of such formal structural dialects are the dhrupad, the kheyal, the Thumri and so on of north India, the kriti, the varnam, the padam, the javali, etc of south India. In the more serious styles of music, the elaboration of a raga starts with a slow exposition called the alap, followed by a composition (a cheea or a kriti) in a given tala, incorporating well designed melodic phrases and libretto, and faster phrases. Instruments in north India play rhythmic pieces known as gat, whereas south Indian instruments generally follow vocal patterns and compositions.

The most ancient instruments known to us are the venu (flute) and veena (harp) mentioned in the vedic texts. As old as these are the drums. But a matter of great interest is the migration of instruments of India and Central Asia. The rabab is one such. The kinnari, a finger-board folk-instrument of India, is suggestive also of the kinnor of the Bible and the ancient Chinese khin. The shehnai of our country and the surnai of Central Asia are similar, obove-like instruments.

Instruments (vadya) are considered to be of four types - tata vadya (stringed), sushira vadya (wind), avanaddha vadya (drums and ghana vadya (bells, plates, rods, etc.) Among the tata vadya are the veena, the sitar, the tamboora, etc. (plucked), the sarangi, the dilruba (bowed); the wind instruments are the flutes, the shehnai, the naferi and the nagaswaram (Indian oboes); the drums comprise the tabla, the pakhawaj, the mridang, and so on; bells, rods, etc. are common, though not generally used in concert music.

Thus the music of India is not only the proud legacy of this subcontinent but of the whole world. For without doubt it is one of the most highly developed and sophisticated musical systems of human society. Particularly, its microtonal pitch differences (srutis as they are called) its melodic scheme (ragas) and the rhythmic subtleties of its tala are amongst the most cherished artistic contributions of India to the world culture.

B. C. DEVA

INDIAN THEATRE

Classical Sanskrit Theatre; flourished first nine centuries, Christian era; Apporisons on acting appear writings of Panini, Sanskrit grammarian, 5th century B.C.; references to actors, dancers, theatrical companies, academics, in Kautilya's Artha-Sastra (4 century B.C.); classical structure, form, style of acting, production, consolidated Bharat Muni's treatise on dramaturgy, Natya-Sastra; classified drama, ten types; two important are, Nataka ("heroic"), deals exalted themes gods, kings, draw from history, mythology; Eg Kalidasa's Sakuntla. Prakarara ("social"); dramatist invents plot; dealing ordinary human beings, such as a courtesan; eg Sudrakas Mrcchakatika

Classical theatre, three structural types; oblong, square, triangular; each divided into large, medium, small sizes; Bharata Muni, disapproved, large playhouse; recommended medium-sized structure.

Ancient Hindus insisted small playhouse; drama acted, stylized gesture language; subtle movements of eyes, hands.

Two types; the lokdharmi, stylized drama; using gesture language, symbols, considered artistic.

Classical play opened with nardi, 8-12 lines of praise of gods; sutradhara entered with wife, described place, occasion of action; last sentence of his prologue, a bridge leading to action of play.

Only surviving Sanskrit drama, Kudiyattam; performed by Cakkayars of Kerala; principles of Natya-Sastra evident in presentation.

Most acclaimed dramatist; Kalidasa. Other important playrights succeeding him, Harsak Mahendravikramavarman; Bhavabhuti, Visakhadatta; exception is king Sudraka, work most theatrical.

First developed Bengal, beginning 18th century; other regional theatres followed Bengal's pattern; British conquered Bengal 1757; influenced local arts, clubs performed Shakespeare, Moliere, Restoration comedies, Golak Nath Dass, a local linguist, Gerasim Lebedev, Russian bandmaster, produced first Bengali play, Chhadmabes in 1795, on Western style stage; Bengali actors of both senes acted. Growing social consciousness, theatre a platform for social reform, propaganda against British rule. Important playrights, Michael Madhu Sudan (1824-73), Dina Bandhu Mitra (1843-87); Girish Chandra Ghosh (1844-1912), D.L. Roy (1863-1913).

First elements of realism introduced 1920s by Sisir Kumar Bhaduri, Naresh Mitra, Ahindra Choudhuri, Durga Das Banerji, actresses Probha Devi, Kanka Vati.

Rabindranath Tagore (1861-1941); steeped in Hindu classics, indigenous folk forms; responsive to European techniques O/production; evolved dramatic form quite different. Used music, dance as essential elements; created opera-dance form; chorus sat and sang on stage, players acted roles in dance, stylized movements.

In northern, western India, theatre developed late 19th century; the Bombay Parsi companies; based on dramatic structure of five acts; songs, dances, comic scenes, declamatory styles, copied by regional threatres; toured all over. Acting style in Maharashtrian theatre, Melodramatic.

In South, dance-dramas popular; not allowed realism to flourish. Tamil commercial companies; dominant Andhra Pradesh, Kerala, Mysore, song, dance extravaganzas.

Urdu, Hindi drama, production began with Indrasabha by Nawab Wajid Ali Shah, 1855.

Actor Prithvi Raj Kapoor; founded Prithvi Theatres, Bombay, 1944; brought robust realism to Hindi drama.

Centres for theatrical training 20th century; important are, the National School of Drama and the Asian Theatre Institute in New Delhi; Sangeet Natak Academy (National Academy of Music, Dance and Drama) in New Delhi, and the National Institute for the Performing Arts in Bombay. Bhartiya Natya Sangh; the union of all Indian threatre groups, founded 1949, in New Delhi. Affiliated with UNESCO's branch of International Theatre Institute, organises drama festivals, seminars; centre for information.

INDO-ROMANIAN CULTURAL CONFLUENCES

Lying at the crossroads that link the Orient and the Occident, Romania claims to belong to both. If modern Romanian literature is the offspring of Romanian culture grafted onto Western culture trends, the old Romanian legends and beliefs lie under the sign of another spiritual zodiac, that of myth and ancient sages.

Since time immemorial, the Getae, a branch of the Thracians, believed in the immortality of soul and considered the body an obstacle which should destroy itself at the moment of death. According to them, humans should aim at freeing themselves from the body so that the soul could lead its life in the kingdom of Zamolxis (a god similar to Varuna of the Vedic mythology). This is similar to the Hindu concept, according to which when the body dies, the human soul returns to the infinite spring of life, to Brahma. The history of the Dacian-Getic invasion by the Roman conquerors is somewhat similar to that of India's invasion by the Aryans (a theory now in dispute). In both cases, there was a native background, characterized by a passive, dormant resistance to the new spiritual forms imposed by the conquerors, whose traces are extremely difficult to identify at present.

Similarities do not stop here. "Miorita", the most widespread Romanian myth, has been found to practice a doctrine resembling ahimsa - non-violence. Folk books like "Alexandria", "Sindipa" or "Panchtantra" helped Romanians become familiar with Indian literary philosophical and moral values.

Interestingly, in Romania religious art - in Voronet monastery, for instance - we can see saints sitting on lotus flowers just as Buddha and some mythological characters are represented in the Indian sculptures and miniatures. All this made Lucian Blaga, one of the greatest poets and the philosophers of the Romanian culture, state: "Taking into account the level, dimensions and internal proportions of the Romanian culture, I think that nowhere else in Europe has the Indian thought had a greater influence than in Romania." It may not come as a surprise then that some of the greatest names of the Romanian literature - Eminescu, Hasdeu, Cosbuc, Brancusi, Blaga, Mircea Eliade - have been deeply marked by the encounter with the Indian thought, an initiation experience that was bound to reflect in their works.

The continuity of the archaic thought made India preserve the symbolic dimension of the spirit and of the world. India's greatest masterpieces, both artistic and theoretical, must be related to the dialectics of symbol. We deal here, as Eminescu so nicely put in a famous line, "with a world that thought in terms of legends and spoke in rhymes."

Except for old Romanian literature - which came to a close with Dimitrie Cantemir - before the early 19th century, and before Romanticism reached Romania, the Romanian spirituality was deeply rooted in the universe of folk culture, which was loaded matter emerging from the remotest archaic springs. Romanticism, which marks the transition from the ancient to modern culture, does not contradict other cultural ideas; on the contrary, it unveils the tradition it claims itself from and takes farther on. Under the circumstances, India's reception was made in a space related to it in its very core. This explains why with Eminescu, India became, as Blaga puts it, "the inalienable presence of our culture", the cosmic and cosmogenic pathos - with its symbolic and sacred significance. It can be simultaneously related both to the Indian view of the world and to that of the Romanian national folklore.

After Eminescu, Lucian Blaga discovered the magic of the Indian symbolical forms. One can certainly state that Romainan literature has two kavis - poet-sages- to use the Indian term. Like all great Indian poets, from the Vedic sages to Rabindranath Tagore, they clothed their philosophical view in the veil of poetry. Mircea Eliade, the reputed historian of religions, has also stated that India taught him what symbolism meant. By discovering the archaic roots of Indian culture, he came to understand the deep structures of his own national folklore. Mircea Eliade emphasized that what is characteristic to Romanian culture and differentiates it from the European one is, in fact, its affiliation to the ancient background of universal values.

In 1937, the same year when Mircea Eliade was trying to highlight the importance of India in the context of symbolical thought in Romanian folklore, Constantin Brancusi, the Romanian sculptor, left for India, to Indore. This is where his artistic works, inspired by Romanian folklore were to be a part of a funeral monument, a fact in perfect harmony with the sacred traditions of Indian architecture. Brancusi's sculptures display primeval cosmogenic symbols - The Egg, The Bird, The Pole/Column, The Couple- which diminish eventually the manifestation of forms to their essence. What can be more relevant than his "Endless Column" which is also found in the Vedic texts as the World Pole that separates the Heaven from the Earth? The entire work of Brancusi, inspired from the endless source of ancient Romanian folklore, represents the reiteration of India's cultural ethos through the centuries. It is an attempt at conceiving the new in compliance with the old and which becomes richer and richer owing to the ever more fresh torments of creation. This similitude reveals the undeniable affinities between the two cultures, owing to the similar manner in which they perceive the sacred.

As Lucian Blaga said about Romanian spirituality: "Through a total assimilation, the motifs of Indian origin have so deeply penetrated our being that they can be taken away only by tearing off vital tissues." The Indian values which reached Romania directly or indirectly have represented for the Romanians a world in which they have re-discovered their own cultural vitality.

DANIELA TANE

INDUS CIVILISATION

When Charles Masson first saw the mounds at Harappa, in the summer of 1826, a sleepy town situated on a trade route from Lahore to Multan on the banks of river Ravi, hardly did he realise that the ruined brick castle on which he stood hid in its bosom a civilisation order and richer than almost all the known civilisations of history.

Nor did Lieutenant Alexander Burns, the British King's emissary, feel the pulse of this civilisation when he came to Punjab, during the spring of 1831, to present king William's special gifts to the Punjab ruler, Maharaja Ranjit Singh. Burns stopped for a while at Harappa, gazed at the ruined citadel, gave a long look to the river whipped his Scottish horses and left for Lahore. In 1849 Punjab was annexed by the Britishers and a new district with new canals was carved .out and named Montogomery. Harappa is presently located in this district. It is here that General Alexander Cunningham, the Archaeological Surveyor to the Government of India, in 1862, during his search for the Buddhist relics, accidentally found extraordinary antiquities. Being indifferent to prehistory and proto-history, Cunningham ignored the 'find' and lost a life's opportunity to bring to light a civilisation that had no parallel in civil life and utilitarian planning.

In his archaeological survey report in 1875 Cunningham stated: "I made several excavations at Harappa but the whole surface had been so completely cleared out by the Railway contractors that I found very little worth preserving. My chief discovery consisted of a number of stone implements. They are all made of dull cream coloured stone but a few of these are really black in colour... My excavations also brought to light numerous specimens of ancient pottery. The most curious object discovered at Harappa is a seal, belonging to Major Clark, which was found along with two small objects like chess pawns, made of dark brown jasper. The seal is a smooth flat stone without polish. On it is engraved very deeply a bull without hump looking to the right, with two stars under the neck. Above the bull there is an inscription in six characters which are quite unknown to me. They are certainly not Indian letters and as the bull which accompanies them is without a hump, I conclude that the seal is foreign to India". Thus began the discovery of the remains of the greatest civilisation of the world of which Cunningham was not aware at that point of time. Harappa was, therefore, neglected for quite some time.

In 1902 John Marshall was appointed as the Director General of Archaeology. It was he who organised from 1912 onwards systemtic excavations of city-sites of pre-historic as well as proto-historic times. The excavations work at Harappa was taken up in 1921 on regular basis. In 1922, one Mr. R.D. Bannerji, who had an uncanny gift of spotting buried cities and ancient sites, while excavating the ruins of a Buddhist site at Mohenjodaro in Larkana district of Sind, chanced upon certain inscribed seals which were earlier found at Harappa. The study of the seals of these two sites revealed that a highly sophisticated urban civilisation, with a flourishing economy and a vibrant outlook existed in India during the 3rd B.C. (2500-2000 B.C.) covering an area bigger than the combined area of Mesopotamia.

The discoveries startled the world, stimulated public interest in India resulting in the increase of Government grant for explorations and excavations. For the next about ten years each new discovery was accompanied by an element of surprise and drama.

Seventy-five years ago it was thought that the history of India began with the advent of Aryans who came on a civilising mission to a country inhabited by abrriginals, primitives and savages. The discoveries at Harappa and Mohenjodaro dispelled this myth and added 2500 years of a glorious period to India's history. The credit for shedding light on this long forgotton civilisation of India goes to men of vision such as Sir John Marshall, Daya Ram Sahani, Madho Sarup Vats and others who did important

excavations from 1926 to 1934. In 1931 Mackay published the results of these excavations while G.R. Hunter researched on the Indus script. Writing on the old civilisation thus laid bare, Sir John Marshall says: "One thing that stands out clear and unmistakable both at Mohenjodaro and Harappa is that the Civilisation hitherto revealed at these two places is not an incipient civilisation, but one already age-old and stereotyped on Indian soil, with many milenniums of Human endeavour behind it. Thus India must henceforth be recognised alongwith Persia, Mesopotamia and Egypt, as one of the most imprtant areas where the civilising processes were initiated and developed. Never for a moment was it imagined that five thousand years ago, before even the Aryans were heard of, the Punjab and Sind were enjoying an advanced and singularly uniform civilisation of their own, closely akin, but in some respect even superior to that of contemporary Mesopotamia and Egypt". The piece de resistance at Mohenjodaro, however, is the Great Bath. This seems to be the work of a genuis. Carleton in his book "Buried Empires" syas that the Great Bath discovered at Mohenjodaro is a swimming bath on a scale which would do credit to a modern sea-side hotel. The Indus people also knew the principle of 'Hammams' and Turkish Baths or Hot-Air baths. Dr. Mackay, however, is of the view that the ablution places were meant for the eclesiastical classes while the Great Bath was for the common people and was open to all.

Men and women of the Indus civilisation were fashionable. They wore ornaments and were toilet and cosmetics conscious. Women wore earings, necklaces and pendants. They were made of gold, silver, copper, bronze, shells and pottery. Around the waist they wore girdles. Men wore long hair, grew shorft beards. Chairs and stools decorated their drawing rooms. There were candlestands and lamps of shells and pottery. Carts driven by oxen were the chief mode of communication. The Harappans used the 'Ekka' (tonga) which is still used in those areas.

The Indus people, as is evident from the numerous seals knew reading and writing. They knew arthmetic as well, as is evident from the weights and measures in vogue in the cities and the villages. The civilisation has not revealed all its secrets because its script is yet to be deciphered. As it stands it runs from right to left, and when there is a second line it runs from left to right. The experts call to Bustrophedon: It is an ancient mode of writing where lines run form right to left and from left to right.

When Marshall published the results of excavations at Mohenjodaro and Harappa in 1931, Jawaharlal rushed to Mohenjodaro to have the first hand knowledge of India at the dawn of its history. This is what he recorded in the "Discovery of India": "It is surprising how much there is in Mohenjodaro and Harappa which reminds one of persisting traditions and habits - popular ritual, craftsmanship, even some fashions in dress. Much of this influenced western Asia. It is interesting to note that at this dawn of India's story, she does not appear as an infant, but already grown up in many ways. She is not oblivious of life's ways, lost in dreams of vague and unrealisable supernatural world, but also made considerable technical progress in the arts and amenities of life, creating not only things of beauty, but also the utilitarian and more typical emblems of modern civilisation - good baths and drainage system".

The discovery of a few seals of this civilisation in West Asia helped in dating of the civilisation to the later centuries of the third millennium B.C., thereby establishing the antiquity of the Indian civilisation. These excavations have added new dimensions to the civilisation.

The most striking feature of the Indus Valley Civilisation is its town planning, sanitation, public baths and an elaborate drainage system which are a puzzle even to the modern engineering experts. Similar finds have been discovered at Harappa which is an older site and is located at a distance of 400 miles. The streets are as wide as from nine feet to thirty four feet and run straight as far as half a mile. They interesect at right angles forming squares and rectangles. Then there are lanes studded with wells. The houses are made of burnt or sun-dried bricks. They are mostly rectangular in shape and are of the same size in all the sites in two cities. There are seven lamposts in the streets, serais for the caravans and the transient traders with excellent watch and ward system. Encroachment on publicland and buildings was rare, civic laws strictly enforced. At Harappa a huge granary has been found measuring 169 feet by 135 feet, the like of which is not found in any contemporary city. Another remarkable find at Harappa is the workmen's quarters, each house having two rooms and a countyard.

Gadd, Smith and Langdon are the earliest analysers of this script. Hunter has listed 400 symbols and distinct signs including birds and animals. The day this script is deciphered revolutionary discov ies will be made of this civilisation which has already made headlines. Its seals have already revolutionised the ideas on early Indian art. As and when the script is deciphered it is likely that the history of India may be pushed further back and fresh light thrown on Indian writing. It has not been possible for to determine whether the script is Sanskrit, Dravidian or any other, particularly in the absence of bilingual seal or inscription like Rosetta Stone.

To quote Pusalkar again: "No buildings have so far been discovered in the Indus Valley which many be definitely regarded as temples, and even those doubtfully classed as such have yielded no religious relics. There are no shrines, altars or any definite cult objects. It is indeed curious that the Indus finds do not include any positive religious material, for religion has always played a dominant part in ancient cultures, and especially in India, where it was the prime factor moulding the lives of people for ages".

As a result of the partition of India in 1947, both Harappa and Mohenjodaro are now located in Pakistan. But new sites have been discovered in post-independence period in India. These excavations have extended the coverage of Harappan culture to a vast area which runs from Desalpur and Dholavira in Gujarat in the west, Manda in the Jammu hills in the north, Daimabad in Maharashtra and Hulas in Uttar Pradesh in the east. Almost all these sites are located on the banks of rivers, a large number of them on the lost river Sarasvati, the dried-up beds of river Ghaggar. "In the Sarasvati-Hakra system there are at present 931 pre-Harappan. Harappan and late Harappan sites out of which 721 beong to mature Harappan and late Harappan cultures", says J.P. Joshi, former Director General of the Archaeological Survey of India. He is of the view that the existence of such a large number of sites of the Sarasvati-Hakra system indicates that the Harappa civilisation was flourishing more vigorously in the river system than in the Indus basin itself.

Major sites in India which have thrown new light on this most sensitive civilisation of the world include Kalibangan on the left bank of river Ghaggar (lost Sarasvati) in Rajasthan; Banwali and Kunal in district Hissar in Haryana on the dried-up beds of Sarasvati; Manda in the Jammu hills on the banks of river Chenab; Surkotada, Dholavira in Kutch in Gujarat; Padri near the Gulf of Cambay; Lothal in district Ahmedabad in Gujarat near the junction of the rivers Sabarmati and Bhogavo; Diamabad in Maharashtra on the banks of Pravara, a tributary of river Godavri; Bhagwanpura in Kurukshetra and Hulas in District Saharanpur of Uttar Pradesh on the dried-up tributary of river Yamuna. Covering an area of 1.3 million square Km, these excavations and the new finds have changed not only the canvas but also the content of the Indus civilisation requiring re-assessment and re-evaluation.

At Kunal a painted jar has been discovered which contains two silver crowns, stone necklaces and silver and gold jewellery. So far no regal item has been found in any of the sites in India. The housing pattern at Kunal is the same as that of Harappa. However, a sanitary jar has been found outside in the street for draining the waste water of the household. As in Harappa and Mohenjodaro drains are provided with manholes for periodical cleaning.

The excavations at Kalibangan have yielded one of the richest archaeological harvests. There is a fortified citadel, a lower town also fortified, six massive platforms for rituals or ceremonials, grind-iron planning of streets and a cemetry with grave-pit and pot burials. The greatest discovery, however, is a ploughed field showing furrows at the pre-Harappan levels. Situated outside the townhall it is the earliest ploughed-field excavated so far.

Inside the houses there were 'tandoors'. The discovered pottery offers a fascinating range: ringstands, cup-on-stand etc. Between the massive platforms and the residential complex there is a wall. The ladies of Kalibangan used bangles of shells and terracotta.

Located on the right bank of the invisible Saravati river the excavations have yielded pre-Harappan, intermediate Harappan, mature-Harappan as well as post-Harappan occupations. All the elements of Kalibangan occupation are present at Banawali. In addition in has a Harappan Moat. The new finds here include an apsidal structure with a fire-place and a terracotta plough, a complete clay model the like of which is not found anywhere except Kalibangan.

Situated near Akhnoor on the banks of river Chenab, Manda represents the northern-most site of Harappan civilisation. The finds include Indus pottery, copper pins and terracotta cakes shaped artistically as a triangle. The three phases of Harappa are reflected in the three-fold cultural sequence.

Like Kalibangan in Rajasthan, Dholavira is regarded as a major Harappan city with all its typical features. The water management of the city has baffled many experts. In its prime days the whole city might have looked like a lake-town. Not a drop of water was wasted. The city measures 771 metres in length and 616.80 metres in width. The city is divided into three parts, the citadel, the middle town and the lower town. Besides it had a ceremonial ground. Tanks and reservoir are engineering marvels where the walls became bunds. To study Dholavira from a small settlement to a big metropolis in all its seven cultural phases is to study the whole civilisation in miniatrure. The most valuable find of Dholavira is an inscription of ten king-sized signs of Harappan script. In the words of J.P. Joshi who discovered Dholavira, "this is the oldest sign-board of the world".

Another important site in Harappan civilisation, Lothal has yielded an ancient dockyard connected through Bhogavar river with the Gulf of Cambay. Besides it had a granary, a warehouse an acropolis and a lower town. The excavations have laid bare five phases of continuous settlements. Besides its maritime activity Lothal was known for its bazaars and commercial areas. Blades and copper fish-hooks are among the numerous finds. Above all lothal is known for its double burials which are not found anywhere else in the Harappan context.

At Bhagwanpura in Kurukshetra in Haryana, we have a 13 room house made of mud walls with a corridorrunning between the two sets of rooms with open courtyard. At Daimabad in Maharashtra the Chief discovery is a bronze chariot pulled by a pair of bullocks and driven by a man in the nude. There more bronze sculptures of an elephant, a rhino and a bufallo are also the prize discoveries reminding us of the exquisite Indus toys already discovered at Mohenjodaro.

A large number of toys discovered at Shanhudaro are suggestive of a toy-making centre or a toy-manufacturing factory there. Pottery carts yoked to humped oxen are in plenty. The toys depicting monkeys with whistles in their throats are perhaps for the amusement of children. On some of the toys there are finger-prints of the tiny tots' suggesting that these toys were made not in factories or workshops but in schools by children themselves as a part of the curriculum.

Indus seals like the Indus toys are a thing of beauty and a joy to look at. Thousand of seals have been discovered during the excavations in the last 75 years in hundreds of sites. These seals speak for themselves and the times they belong to, keeping to themselves the mystery of language and the secret of the script.

K. K. KHULLAR

THE INFLUENCE OF INDIAN SANSKRIT EPICS IN JAPAN

Geograpically, India and Japan are placed very far apart. In ancient times virtually no direct contact existed between the two countries, though today the advances in communication have broght them appreciably nearer so that they enjoy a close relationship politically, economically and culturally. Even in the old times, however, Japan was affected in many ways by Indian culture, which entered the country in the form of Buddhist culture by way of China. It is a matter of common knowledge that Indian thought, particularly Buddhist thought, has exerted a great influence upon Japanese thought and culture.

Now that more Japanese have come to understand the Indian languages, including ancient Sanskrit and modern Indian vernaculars, there is much activity in the translation and introduction of Indian literature, but in ancient times the Japanese had no opportunity of encountering any works of Indian literature because of the lack of communication with India and on account of the language barrier. The only manner in which Japan was affected by Indian literature was through the medium of Chinese translations of Buddhist canons. Classical Indian literature other than such Buddhist works exerted practically no direct influence.

As regards Sanskrit, the Japanese language contains many words of Sanskrit origin. This is because the Japanses Buddhist priests who went to China transmitted an elementary knowledge of Sanskrit writing and grammer as so-called Shittan or Siddham and brought back many Chinese Buddhist canons. Buddhist literature that was introduced through Chinese translations included many Buddhist adaptations of Hindu literature. Especially the Buddhist folk tales such as Jataka Avadana contained many legends and folk tales that had been orally passed on by the Indian people and appeared in Panchatantra, Kathasarit-sagara and the like. Consequently, such Indian themes were adapted to Buddhist and included in Chinese Buddhist canons. Thus they were eventually introduced in Japan.

The Chinese collections of folk tales contain brorrowing from Buddhist canons and Chinese versions of stories of Indian origin. Tao-shih's Fa-Yuan-Chu-lin, which appeared in the seventh century, in the days of the Tang Dynasty, is an outstanding compilation of this type. Likewise the Japanese drew upon such collections of folks tales. Shasekishu and Hobutsu-shu are purely collection of Buddhist folk tales, but Konjaku-monogatari-shu and Ujishui-monogatari are collections of folk tales, which bring together stories from Japan, China and India.

A considerable number of stories from Jataka were introduced into Japan by way of China. Such stories were adapted to this country and have become widely spread. In this paper I have discussed the influence in Japan of the two great Indian epics Ramayana and Mahabharata.

ISKCON : KRISHNA TEMPLE AT VRINDAVAN

International Society for Krishna Consciousness (ISKCON) is a spiritual organisation dedicated to propagate the message of the Bhagvad Gita. It was founded by Bhaktivedanta Swami Prabhupada, born in Calcutta in 1896. Determined to spread the message of Krishna consciousness throughout the West, Prabhupada arrived in New York in 1965 at a ripe Old age of seventy years.

With firm faith in the teachings of Lord Krishna, Swami Prabhupada soon started attracting adventurous American youth into his fold, trained them as his disciples and sent them all over the world for propagating the Krishna Consciousness.

With a humble beginning, the next decade witnessed opening up of more than 100 Hare Krishna tamples in all major cities of the world: New York, London, Los Angeles, Rome, Paris, Berlin, Tokyo, Washington etc. Soon ISKCON became a worldwide movement.

Upon his return to Vrindavan, 15 kilometers from Mathura near Agra, in 1977 Prabhupada attained

"Samadhi" (spiritual term for death). His disciples erected a beautifully engraved white marble Samadhi Mandir over his tomb, located in the premises of the Krishna Baldev Temple. Beautiful paintings depicting the life of Lord Krishna adorn the galleries leading to the main temple, which houses superb marble statues of Lord Krishna and Baldev (His elder brother) besides those of Lord Krishna and Radha. ISKCON devotees from various parts of the world can be seen here, manning the library or ISKCON bookstalls, besides partaking in various temple rituals with gay abandon.

Besides the excellent marble carvings and paintings, what strikes a visitor is the serenity and the ambience of the temple.

ANIL MEHROTRA

"J"

JAGANNATH'S RATHA YATRA

Orissa is known as the land of Lord Jagannath. The world-famous Ratha Yatra (Car Festival) of Lord Jagannath at Puri is the most spectacular event of the State that attracts pilgrims from far and wide. Otherwise known as Sri Gundicha Jatra or Ghosha Yatra, this festival is observed on the second day of the bright fortnight of Asadha (June - July) every year. On the day, the wooden images of Lord Balabhadra, Goddess Subhadra, Lord Jagannath and Lord Sudarsana are taken out from the main temple in a ceremonial procession called Pahandi Bije. They are placed in their respective Chariots, kept in front of the Simha Dwara (Lions Gate) of Shri Jagannath Temple. While Lord Balabhadra and Lord Jagannath have separate Chariots, Goddess Subhadra and Lord Sudarshan are placed together in the middle Car. Traditionally, the Chariot of Lord Balabhadra moves first. The Chariot of Subhadra and Sudarshanna follow and at last the Chariot of Jagannath moves. They cover a distance of nearly three kilometers to a place known as Gundicha Ghar, where the deities stay for a period of seven days. On the tenth day of the same fortnight, the deities are carried back to the main temple.

Preparations for the festival, however, start months earlier. Every year new chariots are constructed. Only the Charioteers (sarathi), Horses (Ghoda), Crowning element (Kalasa), side deities (Parshva devatas) are not made new. They are prepared in the year of Navakalebara (New body Ceremony). As per the provisions laid down in the Puri Car Festival code, it is the responsibility of the Forest Department of Orissa Government to supply the required timber for construction of the Chariots free of cost every year. As a matter of practice and principle, the Divisional Forest Officers of Nayagarh and Khurda have been supplying 72 Fasi logs, 790 Asan, Dhaura timber and 274 Green timbers every year. Besides the D.F.O. Nayagarh has also been supplying 3 of Sinuli timbers for the last couple of years. As per the traditon, the D.F.O. Nayagarh sends first truckload of timber before Vasanta Panchami day and the remaining timbers reach in a phased manner.

The construction of the Chariots starts from the day of Akshaya Trutiya (Baisakhya Shukla Trutiya). The progress of construction is monitored regularly by a team of officials The Executive Engineer, R & B, Puri Division and Administrator, Shri Jagannath Temple, Puri supervise the progress of the construction works from time to time. Total numbers of 92 carpenters (Maharana), 81 Bhois, 22 Kamars (native smiths) and 22 Rupakaras (Painters & idol makers) are engaged in the construction work of the three chariots. To cover the chariots, 14 number of darajis (tailors) prepare the Ratha Mandani.

Allied materials in connection with the Car Festival are collected by the Temple Administration well in advance. Ropes are supplied by Kerala Coir Corporation. The 1200 meters of different colours (Green, Red, Black & Yellow) clothes for Rathamandani are procured from the O.T.M., Orissa and Century Mills, Mumbai. The lagi cloth of the deities is prepared by the traditional weavers whereas Basunga patta (Silken thread) are arranged by the State Tassar and Silk Co-operation Society. Salresins are procured locally.

Arrangement for the Car festival is reviewed in the Temple Co-ordination Committee and time-table for this great festival is approved in the Shri Jagannath Temple Managing Committee meeting. As specified in the Puri Car Festival Code meetings of the District level co-ordination Committee under the Chairmanship of the Revenue Divisional Commissioner (RDC) meets in three times, wherein arrangements of all the concerned Departments are held. The Collector, Puri takes the meeting of a group of dedicated officers very often who are kept in charge of supervision of allied arrangements viz. Sanitation, drinking water, light arrangement, temporary shed, distribution of essential commodities, transport arrangements etc. The Superintendent of Police takes care of the security arrangements. On the specific day, after the completion of all rituals of the Lords both in the temple premises and on the Chariots, thousands of devotees wait eagerly to touch the 250 feet holy coir cables. Thus the chariots are pulled along the three-km long Grand Road to the terminal point at the Gundicha Mandir. All the three Chariots after being constructed and decorated traditionally are dragged to the Lions Gate in the afternoon of the day preceding the Yatra.

BHASHKAR MISHRA

JAGU BHAI SHAH - THE PAINTER WHO LOVE⁻ MAHATMA GANDHI

Jagu Bhai Shah - the famous artist from Gujarat - has revelled in teaching art to students, both in villages and cities. In his almost 40 - year teaching career, Jagu Bhai treated all his students as if they were future Michaelangelos. They were ecouraged to paint walls of their classrooms with murals so that they could hone their skills.

But above all, like the saint poet Tulsi Das who loved to praise Lord Rama, Jagu Bhai genuinely enjoyed praising Mahatma Gandhi and his ideology of non-violence and constructive activities. He got involved in Gandhian ways when he worked for the Swarajya Ashram of Vedchhi near Bardoli in South Gujarat in 1941. There he made many paintings on walls that would communicate Gandhiji's teachings to villagers and tribals visually. Since then he has been making narrative paintings, some very large and complex, based on the eventful life and activities of the Mahatma, using various madiums.

JAHANGIR : THE NATURALIST EMPEROR

As the young Prince Salim, Jahangir accompanied Akbar on his campaigns in Kashmir and fell in love with the enchanting natural splendour of the mountains, streams, trees and flowers. Jahangir's personal memories, Tuzuk-i-Jahangiri, contain ecstatic accounts of the charms of the happy valley: "Kashmir is a garden of eternal spring..., a delightful flower-bed and a heart - expanding heritage for dervishes. Its pleasant meads and enchanting cascades are beyond all description". This was the beginning of a life-long affair. Nurjahan encouraged Jahangir by laying out gardens in different parts of Kashmir. It also kept the mind of Jahangir unburdened by affairs of the kingdom.

Jahangir shared with Babar, his great-grandfather, a special bondage with nature. Jahangir was a naturalist, gifted with powers of keen observation of detail even in the tiniest flower. It did not invoke any spiritual mood or inspire him towards unseen forces of the cosmos. He had an irrepressible urge to preserve for posterity the splendours of nature in miniatures. Ustad Mansur and Abu'l Hasan, two renowned specialist Painters, were entrusted with the task of painting the likeness of flowers. Mansur is believed to have painted nearly one thousand specimens of Kashmir blooms, of which only a few have survived. Still a fair idea of the work of these painters can be obtained from the paintings of flora and fauna on the borders of many royal portraits, where often their grandeur overshadows the presence of royalty. Perhaps the inspiration to paint the flora came from the 16th century herbals such as those of Gerard, which had reached the Mughal court. Jahangir was the first Mughal emperor to initiate depiction of flora and fauna to form a distinctive category of paintings based on observation by him and his atelier.

Jahangir provides some detailed descriptions of flowers in his memoirs: "Strange flowers that grow in this country (Kashmir) come to view. Among these flowers I saw an extraordinary one-it had five or six orange flowers blooming with their heads downwards. From the middle of these flowers came out some green leaves, as in the case of the pineapple". This is Crown Imperial, as Jahangir describes it. The flowers depicted in miniatures and inlay work appear extremely stylized and sometimes barely identifiable. These are stylistically Persian-cyclamen, iris, tulips, crown imperials, lilies, roses, poppies and peonies. Kashmir provided a wide variety of 'strange' flowers - carnation, delphinium, hollyhock, jasmine, lilac, lotus, narcissus, saffron, stocks and wallflower. The great artists infused these flowers with a rarefied glory and charm. Jahangir's account of these flowers form a botanical study of its own kind, sans the incomprehensible scientific jargon and dissection of bloosoms. Today if might look simplistic but in the early 17th century it was rare and surprising. Chempa "is a flower of exceedingly sweet fragrance; it has the shape of the saffron flower, but is yellow, inclining to white. The tree is very symmetrical and large, full of branches and leaves and is shady. When in flower, one tree would perfume a garden. Surpassing this is the keora flower (Pandanus odoratissimus). Its shape and appearance are singular, and its scent is so strong and penetrating that it does not yield to the odour of musk", Jahangir recorded. He adds jasmine, maulsiri and ketki to the list of flowers with an enchanting overpowering fragrance.

Among the trees typical of Kashmir are cypress, pine, chinar, white poplar and bid mullah (willow). Some on the list are not native to Kashmir: "The sandal tree, which once was peculiar to the is lands (Java and Sumatra) also flourishes in the gardens."

Jahangir's fame as a naturalist rests on the pictorial studies of birds and animals which appealed to his imagination for their gorgeous plumage and unique physical features and habits. Jahangir nursed a pair of infant cranes for five years and took these birds with him on his journeys to watch their amatory habits. He was excited when the birds laid eggs and chicks were hatched. He was the first Mughal emperor to have ringed birds and fish for future observations, a hint well picked up by modern ornithologists.

Like an inspired naturalist, Jahangir was keen to probe the secrets of nature. He was sceptical of myths about the strengths and physical features of animals. Once, when he shot a great lion, Jahangir ordered that its intestines be extracted. He records: "it appeared that in a manner contrary to other animals, whose gall bladder is outside their livers, the gall bladder of the lion is within its liver. In occurred to me that the courage of the lion may be from this cause". Jahangir also noted that an Abyssinian elephant's ears, trunk and tail are larger than those of its Indian counter-part, the first recorded comparison between these two species.

For some of his nature studies, Jahangir ordered dissection of animal bodies. His findings on a bustard' dissection are quite revealing: "It is a strange thing that the wind-pipe in all animals which the Turks call balq is single, running from the top of the throat to the crop (china dan) while in the case of the bustard it is different. It is of a breadth of four fingers from the top of the throat and then it divides into two before reaching the crop. At the place where it divides, there is a stoppage (sarband) and a knot (girih) is felt by the hand. In the kulang (crane), it is still stranger. Its wind-pipe passes in a serpentine manner between the bones of the breast to the rump and then turns back from there and joins the throat". Similar keen observations fill many a page of the naturalist emperor's memoirs Tuzuk-i-Jahangiri.

Jahangir's observations on elephants are quite interesting when he records that their calves are born with feet emerging out first and how the mother throws dust on the calf before it struggles to rise on its feet. Jahangir's words show his immense coruosity and delight at the beauty of nature's creations. A particular turkey cock fascinated him: "larger than a peahen and smaller than a peacock. When it is in heat and displays itself, it spreads out its feathers like a peacock and dances about. Its back and legs are like those of a cock".

His description of the Abyssinian zebra is simple and correct: "One might say the painter of fate, with a strange brush had left it on the page of the world. As it was strange, some people imagined that it had been coloured. After minute inquiry into the truth, it became known that the Lord of the World was the creator thereof".

The imperial albums contained masterpieces of nature studies by accomplished artists like Mansur, Abu'l Hasan, Manohar, Inayat and Murad. Mostly depicted in Profiles, these bird studies from the most impressive section of miniatures of the Jahangir period. Jahangir could easily recognize the work and special features of his chosen painters and conferred on Mansur and Abu'l Hasan the title of Nadir-ul-Asr (Wonder of the Age), a rare honour for the artists.

Whereas Babar's copious jottings about his observations on events, life and nature had to be pieced together into a proper authobiography at a later date, Tuzuk-i-Jahangiri contains a day-by-day account of the emperor's perceptions of nature, science and art, combining a rare aesthetic response to life. It is however, Jahangir's empirical rationalism combined with an almost esctatic response to simple facts of nature that is of incalculable value to us after nearly four hundred years. As the noted art historian Bamber Gascoigne observes, "The emperor would have found himself much in sympathy with the scientific gentlemen who, thousands of miles away and some thirty years after his death (1627), gathered together in London to form the Royal Society". Not too high a compliment for India's first naturalist emperor.

SURENDRA SAHAI

JAINA ART AND ARCHITECTURE

Jainism has been a vital inspiration for multifaceted developments in Indian Art, architecture and literature. However, it would not only be difficult but also unrealistic to segregate Jaina creations from the mainstream of Indian art and architecture. The Jaina mythological and religious concepts evoked splendid sculpture and wall paintings, adding to the spirti of Indian art.

Jainism is said to be one of the oldest religions of India. According to the Jaina inscriptions, as many as twenty-four holy saints. "TIRTHANKARAS" - have significantly contributed to the evolving of their religion. The twenty-fourth and the last one was VARDHMANA MAHAVIRA, the chief proponent of Jainism. He was born in 557 B.C. at KUNDAGRAMA, a suburb of VAISALI in north Bihar, bordering Nepal. His nirvana (salvation) took place at Pawa (commonly called Pawa Puri) in Patna in Bihar. Although, like Buddhism, Jainism spread in every direction in India, at present the Jains are more concentrated in the western part of India, i.e. in Gujarat, Rajasthan and a portion of south India.

In all historical probability, Jainism had the ingenuity as well as leadership in various forms of art such as wall paintings, frescoes and carving of images. The Tirthankara image found at Lohanipur (Patna) belonging to the Mauryan period, establishes this fact very well. Images of Yakshis (female folk deities) and Tirthankars from the subsequent period, known as the Mathura period, are also very typical expressions of the then Jaina art. Jainism differs from Hinduism and Buddhism only in the form of worship. But, the temples of all these religions have no specific religion based structural or architectural differences. Temples of all these religions have elegant decorative elements of various human and animal figures in addition to symbolic floral and other elementary decorative motifs.

Female decorative figures of apsaras (divine ladies), surasundaris (women wine servers) alas-kanyas (languid women), nayikas (heroines) and help-rendering attandants are placed singly or in pairs as temple sculptures. These are also depicted with their male counterparts in various mithuna (amorous) postures. Such sculptures have an artistic proportion, melodious curvature of body-lines in dvi-bhanga (two fold) or tri-bhanga (three fold) mudras (postures), elegant ornamentations and vivid dresses eye-catching drapes. From very early times, art based on Jainism depicts copulate artistic figures in places of worship. On sculptured stupas (pillars) and railing posts of Mathura period even nude sura-sundaris are to be found. such erotic figures appear mostly in medieval Jaina temples such as those at Khajuraho and Arang in Chhattisgarh district of Madhya Pradesh. There is an undoubted Tantric influence as well on such figures. They are also to be found in Hindu and Buddhist temples of the medieval period.

Jaina art and architecture relies foremost on religious faith and various religious inscriptions. Among all the Jaina sculptures, the images of Jains or Tirthankars are most vital and prominent. One such sculpture is that of Gomteshwara at Sravanbelagola in Karnataka. This colossal monolithic sculpture, 57 feet high, is said to be the tallest and most elegant statue in the world. It is carved out of a rock on the summit of the 143-meter high Indragiri hill. A flight of five hundred stairs cut into the hill leads the devotees to the foot of the statue. Believed to have been erected in the 10th century A.D., the intricate workmanship as well as the expression of compassion depicted on the face of the statue is testimony to the artist's splendid thought and creation.

Between the 5th and 12th centuries AD, Jaina monks built some of the cave temples at Ajanta and Ellora. Unlike other religious sects of those times, the Jains invariably selected secluded picturesque sites for their temples and cave-temples for meditation and other related rituals. As per Jaina religious incriptions a devotee is just like a perfect pilgrim, who is journeying though life as a stranger in this world". He is required to perform the journey on the path of truth, knowledge and perfect conduct.

Unlike Buddhism, Jainism has been associated from the very beginning with idol - worship. Jaina Tirthankaras were idolized to that the people could remember their preachings. With the passage of time, the process of idol-worship became rather complex in nature as well as in forms of expression, leading to idols of Acharya (teachers), Siddhas (Enlightened Ones), Navdevatas (Nine Gods), Sarvalobhadra (four faced Adinath, the first Jaina Tirthankar), Sruta Devi (Goddess of Learning), Yakshi (Female folk deity) and their various attendants being sculpted. The idols of the various Tirthankaras came to be associated with unique symbols like Neminatha with a mark of a sea-shell, Rishabha with a bull and Mahavira with a circle.

DILIP BHATTACHARYYA

JAIPUR KATHAK GHARANA

Jaipur Kathak Gharana is struggling hard for its existance especially after the death of Durga Lal, considered as the Guru of Kathak, in March 1991, Durga Lal was probably the most charismatic and talented performer of this gharana. In a peculiar quirk of fate, the gharana finds itself today without a national level representative, on the pantheon of great dancers. The problem of patronage is an old one. During the time that Kathak received royal support, the rulers revealed themselves to be true counoisseurs, with quality and not gharanas being the operative concern. In pre-independence period, while the best dancers were sought after, even the lesser dancers were spared the uncertainity of a struggle for living, for there were enough feudal states, for whom having dancer in residence was a matter of status. After independence, when princely rule and Zamindari came to an end, while classical music found a ready patron in Akashvani and the gramophone companies, dance, being a visual art, could look towards none but government for support, Some of the government policies also contributed to the alienation of Jaipur Kathak Gharana. The Kathak Kendra established in 1953 showed its predisposition towards Lucknow Gharana. In comparison, Jaipur Kathak Kendra specialising in this Gharana was established as late as in 1979 and there had been no prominant products of it because it continues to function without a senior Guru who could provide right direction. Another factor that has contributed to this gharana's decline that all provincial eg. Jaipur Kathaks have fanned out in the absence of any premier institute where any of the legendary Gurus could have stayed for a length of time to preserve and propagate Jaipur Kathak. (Adapted)

ARSHIYA SETHI

THE JAMALI-KAMALI MOSQUE & TOMB HOMAGE TO SAINTS

The area around the Qutb Minar in Delhi has been the playground and the graveyard of empires for several centuries. Five of the seven cities of Delhi built by the Sultans of various dynasties in the medieval period, and once the capitals of large empires, were located within a redius of ten kilometers from the Qutb Minar. Most of these cities have vanished because almost every Sultan, while building his own capital destroyed the earlier cities. For example, nothing remains of the legendary palace of One Thousand Pillars built by Sultan Alauddin Khiliji. Portions of boundary walls, huge gates standing in splendid isolation, broken ramparts, fortifications pock-marked with shells are all that remian.

The sultans who thought they were building for eternity are long dead and gone. Some like Alauddin Khiliji, Balban and Iltutmish are buried in this area. Also buried here are those unfortunate Sultans who were executed after they were dethroned and their continued existence was considered dangerous by their successors as well as Princes who lost the battle of succession. It is an irony of fate that not many visit their tombs, while the tombs of saints, who lived hundreds of years ago and the mosques they built, continue to be objects of reverence even today. People visit them regularly to offer prayers, to seek blessings and to get their grievances righted. The stream of visitors is unending. The piety of the visitors moves even those who do not believe in the existence of God. It was easy for kings, Princes and the rich to build magnificent tombs and large mosques, but a saint had of necessity to depend on the munificence of his followers for erecting a large mosque and a final resting place for his own remains. One such Complex in the Qutb Minar areas is the Jamali-Kamali mosque and tomb, some 200 meters to the south of the world famous monument. The mosque,

built in 1528-29, is a fine example of Lodi architecture. The mosque must once have been surrounded by a wall. Only a part of it and the gate now remain. There are several tombs in the courtyard of the mosque but the names of those buried there are not known. The prayer hall of the mosque is divided into five bays, with a five-arched facade without cloisters, gateways or other paraphernalis. These bays are entered through five openings, all almost of the same size though of greater width than is warranted by their height. The entrance to the central bay is through a seven-cornered arch. It is because Hindu artisans and masons were employed to build many buildings erected during the Muslim rule. The "satkonamihrab", or The Arch of Seven Points, was not used merely for ornamentation but had a symbolic meaning and was considered auspicious.

The entrance to the central bay on both sides, at the top of the arch, has the six-pointed star, formed by the imposition of an equilateral triangle on another reversed equilateral triangle. This figure called the Sri Chakra in Hindu mythology represents the two primal forces of creation and is worshipped as the harbinger of prosperity. The lotus motif is liberally used in the mosque. Verses from the Holy Quran are inscribed on the walls. On either side of the prayer chamber are stairs leading to the top. The back of the mosque is pierced by three window, which have bracketed balconies. Along the whole length of the front, but broken in the center by the projecting bay is a deep freeze of red sandstone, divided into a variety of panels containing niches.

Who were Jamali and Kamali, who built the mosque and are buried in the tomb near the mosque? Shaikh Fazalullah, also known as Sheikh Jamal Khan or Jamali, was a saint, traveller and poet who lived during the period of the last Lodi Sultan, Sikandar Lodi, and the founder of the Mughal dynasty Babur and his son Humayun. He was widely respected for his piety and saintliness. The tomb built by his followers after his death is modest in comparison to the tombs of the Sultans, but is a compact structure beautiful in its simplicity. The ceiling and the walls of the burial chamber are covered by coloured tiles. The colour of the tiles is breath takingly bright and so are the geometric patterns on them. The wall also bears an inscription of a compositon by Sheikh Jamal himself. What is surprising is that the tiles, except in a part of the dome where rain water has seeped in, have retained their colour and brightness even after nearly 500 years.

Nothing is know about Kamali who is buried by the side of Jamali. He was obviously a man of some eminence and must have been close to Shaikh Jamal to be given the honour of being buried by his side.

K. G. JOGLEKAR

JANMASHTAMI (KRISHNA JAYANTI)

Vishnu, the preserver aspect of the universe and one of the Hindu Trinity, takes birth in this world whenever it is overburdened with evildoers and sinners, who by their wicked actions upsed the equilibrium of the earth.

One such incarnation is his birth as the son of King Vasudeva and his wife Devaki Devi of bygone ages as Sri Krishna, and his story is recorded in Bhagavatam.

Born to rid the world of the wicked, he was secretly brought up by the chief of the Yadavas (cowherds) to whom he was taken as soon as he was born, sicne his uncle Kansa considered him an enemy and wanted to get rid of him as soon as he was born, by killing him.

The birthday of this marvelous child Is celebrated as a festive and sacred day on the eighth day of the dark fortnight in the month of Sravana called Avani in Tamil which corresponds to the English months of August-September.

The festive day is known by different names. Some call it Krishna Jayanti day, while a good many call it Janma Ashtami day, A few call it Gokula Ashtami and Sri Jayanti also.

The story relating to the advent of this mighty soul on earth is as sketched below:

Mother earth brought to the notice of god Vishnu that the population of the earth had enormously increased, that virtue was being trampled down by the tyrannical wicked and that she felt the burden unbearable. Vishnu thereupon consented to rid the earth of the superfluous population by destroying the wicked. To accomplish this, he took birth as the son of a king who was under the persecution of his brother-in-law, Kansa, a veritable demon in human shape. But he had to be secretly brought up by others to avoid being put to death by his cruel uncle.

He accomplished the main object of his incarnation on this earth by having punished the wicked and helped the virtuous. He fixed the Dharma of each individual on a permanent basis, and proper arrangements were made for the protection and guidance of the world.

This avatar or incarnation of Vishnu is a typical one since he had combined in his divine personality the three aspects of creation, preservation and destruction to demonstrate world the oneness of the cosmic deity.

That he was typical child and his boyish pranks and escapades demonstrate ideal child described in prose and verse and read and sung by thousands of people. His adventures with the gopis and the manner in which he made all love him, shows that he was a youth or marvelous beauty and an ideal lover.

The destruction of the wicked and the masterly manner in which he conducted military operations shows that he was a warrior to the core, unparalleled in the annals of any history. A wise counselor he assuredly was, and it is demonstrated by the decision by the Pandavas under his instructions. The teachings imparted by him to Arjuna on the battle field, graphically described in Bhagavad Gita, reveal him as the greatest philosopher of all ages and times, and a yogi of the highest order.

The various forms in which Sri Krishna is worshiped are, (1) the Bala Gopala Krishna or the baby Krishna, (2) the crawling Krishna or Krishna as a child on all fours, (3) Govardhana Uddhara Krishna or Krishna who lifted up the mountain, (4) Venugopala Krishna or the cowherd Krishna with the flute, (5) Kaliyamardana Krishna or Krishna in the posture of dancing on the head of a serpent to punish the same for its wickedness and (6) Radha Krishna and Rukmani Krishna or Krishna in company with Radha and Rukmani.

In the great Mahabharata war, Sri Krishna acted as a charioteer to Arjuna, also called Partha. Hence he derived the name Parthasarathy or the charioteer of Partha A temple is dedicated to him in this aspect at Triplicane in Madras, known as Sri Parthasarathy temple and it is one of the important temples in southern India. There is also a temple dedicated to Sri Krishna in Conjeevaram and it goes by the name Pandavadhoothar temple or the temple of Krishna who went as a messenger of the Pandavas.

The temple in Mannargudi in the Tanjore district is known as Rajagopalaswami temple and it is dedicated to the memory of Vishnu's incarnation as Sri Krishna. There are also temples of this god in the holy place called Udipi in the South Canara district and at Trivanjikolam near Iringalakuda on the Shoranur-Cochin railway line.

P. V. JAGADISA AYYER

JATRA
(RESILIENT FOLK-THEATRE OF BENGAL)

India is such a richly multiethenic and multicultural country that every region has its distinctive traditional performing arts. Bengal is no exception; its folk theatre "Jatra" is synonymous with Bengali rural threatre. But it is not the only performing tradition in Bengal. Theatrical elements can be found in many localized entertainments scattered across West Bengal's various districts: Kabigan (a dramatic mode of recitation) Kirtan and Baul songs (devotional music), Gajan and Gambhira (ritualistic dances), Chhau (a tribal dance-drama), Panchali and Kathakata (solo actor-singers' art), Jhumur (performing duets) and Putul Nach (puppetry).

Many of these can lay claim to a hoary past. Though their origin is clouded by the lack of documentary evidence, but definitely these go back, in one form or another, to very ancient times. Most scholars of theatre accept that different folk styles existed thousands of years ago (parallel to the courtly Sanskrit theatre) and gradually evolved into the forms we know them today. We can even discover a Jatra-like format in the famous Gita-Govinda of the 12th century, while the Srikrishna Kirtans in praise of Lord Krishna contain many characters conversing through songs - an uncannily theatrical presentation. Jatra could have developed from these early poems, songs, dances and puppet techniques, though historically we can only say for certain that it is continuously being perfored from the 16th century onwards.

Nevertheless, Jatra has itself changed over the last five centuries. Very broadly speaking, we can view it in three separate avatars. The clue to its original incarnation is in its name. The word Jatra (or "Yatra") means "journey" or "procession", obviously religious in source, associated with physical movement of a Hindu deity from one place to another by devotees, as in the case of the celebrated annual "Rath Yatra" of Jagannath Temple in Puri.

It seems that during the lifetime of the saint Chaitnya (1485-1533), his disciples began evolving dramatic representations of events from Lord Krishna's life. Chaitanya's followers thus started off what came to be known as Krishna Jatra, Ras Jatra (Ras being Krishna's dance), Jhulan Jatra ("jhulan" referring to the swing used by Radha and Krishna) and Kaliya Daman Jatra (about Krishna defeating the devil Kaliya). Chaitanya himself is thought to have encouraged and participated in these plays taking a keen interest in costumes and makeup. His performance as Rukmani, Krishna's wife, in Rukmini Haran ("Abduction on Rukmini") is legendary.

Spurred by the success and appeal of these Jatras, other sects such as the Shaktas, worshippers of the Shakti cult also began presenting dramatization like Chandi Jatra, Manasar Bhasan Jatra ("Immersion of Manasa") and so on, but with far less success. Plays on episodes in Lord Rama's life also appeared. The influence of religious Jatra spread to tribal areas as well; in our own time we find Krishna stories interwoven with the traditional tribal lore of southwest Bengal in Lalita Pala, a folk drama discovered only about 20 years ago.

It is now abundantly clear that in its early stages, Jatra was devotional and belonged to the oral, not written, heritage. Typically, it consisted of a loose, unstructured chain of scenes and was exclusively musical in nature, as lyrical exchanges were the order of the day, instead of normal dialogues This style still survives in Balak Sangeet, delivered by young village boys and girls. Some Jatra features have stood the test of time - the presence of abstract allegorical figures like the Vivek (or "Conscience", a favourite even today), who forewarns other characters or stops them from committing evil, and also fills the role of a commentator. Performances were staged on roughly circular, open ground with viewers surrounding the players on all sides - a practice still followed in the countryside.

Gradually, the Jatra entered its second phase and by the late 18th century, it had turned into a secular art. An important landmark was the long poem Vidyasundar, composed in the mid-18th century by Bharat Chandra Ray (1712-60), which was adpted for the theatre. It told the spicy tale of Princes Vidya and Prince Sundar - full of royal intrigue and romance, murder and passion - and became an immediate crowd - puller, convincing many of the newly-established intinerant Jatra troupes to include it as their top attraction. Soon, Jatra plays began to depict various common stereotypes - lovers and reformers, villains and saints - while prose dialogues along with comic passages were inserted slowly but surely.

It became the norm that shows should go on all night, ending at or near dawn, and that spectators should sit segregated-men and women separately. The "orchestra" comprised cornets, clarinets, harmonium, violin (clear proofs of British inspiration), flutes and assorted percussions. The instrumentalists played lengthy overtures (to draw people to the show, perhaps) and mood music during the performance. There was also the juri (duet or double), a vocal chorus who sang on behalf of the actor, a rare sight nowadays.

However, vulgarity and sensationalism gradually increased and by the 19th century, there was a backlesh from the sophisticated city-bred educated class. Renowned authors like Michael Madhusudan Dutt and Bankim Chandra Chatterjee severely castigated Jatra for its vulgarity.

Towards the close of the century, the famous Jatra dramatist Motilal Ray went back to the epics with a successful play on Yudhisthira's coronation at the end of the Mahabharata. Then, in the early 20th century, the man who personified Jatra of the last one hundred years, Mukunda Das, used the form to propagate a political message: resistance to the British Raj: A very simple device of costume - trousered sahibs against natives in dhotis - sufficed to convey the theme. In such adaptable garb, Jatra actually returned to its oldest purposes, inherent in all folk theatre: to moralize and to educate. Even the greatest literary genius of modern India, Rabindranath Tagore, appears to have been influenced by the outdoor ambience of Jatra in his season-plays, where he pioneered the modern concept of humanity living in perfect harmony with nature.

Ironically enough, the city that rejected Jatra in the 1860s became the cradle of its latest incarnation a hundred years later, in the 1960s, with the birth of contemporary urban Jatra in Calcutta. Of course, artistic connoisseurs continued to look at it condescendingly, but amidst the usual melodramatic love stories and pseudo-historical plays, objectively speaking, Jatra had just changed with the times. The plays were comparatively shorter, not more than four hours, and dealt with figures like Hitler or Stalin; spectacular opening scenes were devised to grip the viewers' attention.

Above all, Jatra became a big business, the only truly professional segment of Calcutta theatre today. These Calcutta - based "companies" and "operas" arrange impresario - agents to book dates for them all over West Bengal, and even parts of Bihar, Orissa, Assam and Tripura. They tour strenuously from industrial townships to tea estates, for about eight months in the year.

It is quite apparent that Jatra indeed is resilient. If past history is any guide, it will always adapt to the changing mores of society.

ANANDA LAL

JEWELLERY

Indian jewellery can be traced back to the period of Indus Valley Civilization when gold and semi-precious stones were in use for necklaces, armlets and ear-rings. The close of the Vedic period witnessed for the first time the introduction of pearls in the making of jewellery. The unbroken continuity of the trend is further corroborated by archaeological and literary evidences of later dates. Excavated materials from Rupar, Taxila and many other palces, and references in the Indian epics, Kautilya's Arthasastra, Bharatamuni's treatise on drama or accounts left by Megasthenes, Arrian and others amply bear that out.

The technical skill acquired by the Indian Jewellers has not been stated by anybody in a more systematic manner at such an early date than in the Arthasastra, a text of about the first century A.D. The jeweller, during the time of Kautilya's Arthasastra, had already become conversant with the technique of shaping various stones and of inlaying stones on gold surface and the like. The progress in the gradual attainment of technical knowledge and experiment with various shapes find widely depicted, though in an indirect way, in the ancient monuments of Bharhut, Sanchi, Amaravati, Mathura and numerous terracotta figurines found at different places. But ornaments were nowhere more faithfully represented than in the monuments of the Gupta Age specially in the murals of Ajanta. These representations are remarkable evidence of improvement, almost a revolution that had been achieved in not only the form of the ornaments but also the conception of adorning the body with jewels.

With the advent of the Muslims in India, jewellery may be said to have had new lease of life. The synthesis of the Hindu and Muslim culture, both inherently decorative, reached its peaks in the era of the Mughals. It was in this period of history that the art of enamelling reached its zenith, the enamelled jewellery of the age taking of many of the attributes of the delicate beauty of the painted miniatures of the Mughal School. Ornaments were superbly enamelled with beautiful design, floral and geometrical with birds and beasts, trees and flowers, exhibiting the finest technique and skill.

The decorative motif of the Mohammedan period was chiefly floral. The Mohan Mala, consisting of gold beads formed in the shape of melons, was a special favourite. The Champakali or necklace of the buds of the Champaka flowers, though evidently a Hindu design, was equally popular with the Mohammedans. They found plain bracelets or karas, generally terminated in the heads of elephants or lions while Jhoomer, and ornament for the head ended in the representation of a peacock's head.

But the most important feature of Muslim jewellery is a combination of the star and crescent; for example, ear-rings were made with a tiny star at the top and a crescent below from which hung the emblem of a fish, the whole terminating in a bunch of pearls or tiny precious stones.

Paintings done in the Mughal Court and later under the aegis of the Rajput princes show the full evolution of a fashion of wearing ornaments and the types of ornaments that came to be in vogue. These ornaments, chaste and elegant to the extreme, were mostly simple, composed of pearls and gold showing decorated suraces. This was essentially a style which could be patronised by a rich and prosperous court. But the ornaments worn by the folk people are the heritage of bygone centuries which changed little with the passage of time.

The Indian goldsmith's apparatus for heating and melting consists of the furnance, a crucible, a blow pipe and a small carved blow pipe. The furnance is made of an ordinarily large earthenware waterpot and the crucible is a small cup of clay. Leather bellows instead of bellow pipes is used by the goldsmith in India. His other common tools are the anvil (nihai) and the hammer (hathaura), tongs (chimta), pincers (sansi), filed (reti) and various types of small chisels or engravers (cheni). As in other countries of the world, gold wire is formed by drawing thin strips of metal through a steel draw-plate bearing holes of different sizes, or by the use of various thappas or dies.

A few chemicals used by goldsmith may also be mentioned viz., borax (suhaga) is universally used as a flux in hard soldering; the ornaments when made are successively polished with mango parings, salt, sal ammoniac (nausadar), alum and a form of iron oxide or rough called manikret.

The common hair-ornament are the shishphul (floral boss) and the sur mang (pendant chain) and a boda (silver hair-platings) used especially for children. Other ornaments consists of the heavy bala (ring) the karnaphul

(bell-shaped ear ornaments) and a few others in the form of a fish or a peacock. Neck ornaments include sat-lari (seven strings), jugnu (jewelled pendant) hansli (silver or gold collar), etc. For the arm are: the bazuband (armlet for upper arm), and kangan (bracelets), kara (enamelled bracelet) and ratanchur (decorated gold plate for the wrist.) Different kinds of head ornaments are sarpach (jewelled front ornament) and kalgi (jewelled plume) and ornaments for waist and anklets are ghangru (silver-beaded ring), chanja (large hollow ring), etc.

The Adivasis of India wear necklaces of various kinds like, for instance, necklaces of rupees and eight anna pieces, hansli or a silver neck-ring, chandi-ka-sutiya, a silver necklace, guriya or red and black glass beads and necklace of multicoloured beads is called latka. Adivasi women have their ear pierced at various places. The common ear-ornament is called har (shield), a large circular silver ornament. Their hair ornament over the forehead is called bindia. It consists of two borad silver chains of bands, reaching from the middle of the head down to the temples while they wear in the nose a small flower-like stud which is called loong. On the wrists they sometimes wear churi or gujri, their toes are decorated with brass rings.

Muria girls still use hair pins of carved wood. The Baiga hair ornament of plaited needs is attached in a bundle to the back of a girl's head; Muria ear-rings with pendants of red, white and blue beads are both exceiting and artistic. Elaborate brass fillet is worn by the Bison Muria woman of Bastar. The hill Murias make beautiful necklaces of while beads with bells. Sometimes the mass of necklaces is so great that it serves as a sort of breast-cover. Bangles, armlets and rings are also used by the adivasis.

It may rightly be said that ornaments worn by the adivasis of different regions of India are exotic if not nostalgic. One is struck by the variety in these ornaments. And it is a real charm to see a adivasi woman decked with jewellery. Whether she is a heavily bejewelled village belle of hill areas of Bastar with her silver coin necklace, damsel from Rajasthan with her typical heavy chains by the sides of the face and a pendant hanging on the forehead, a manipuri woman with her pith necklace, Khasia girl with her multi-pattern jewellery or a dame from Garhwal with her massive silver circle round her neck, they all look charming, serene and natural. In the physical forms and physiognomical characteristics represented in the sculptures of Bharhut, Sanchi, Bodhgaya, Bhaja, Karle, etc. in their dress and ornament, one can have a glimpse of artistic prototypes of the present day adivasis, the Bhils, the Muria, the Gonds, the Baigas, who have been, through the ages inhabiting the regions where these monuments were built.

Jewellery unearthed from Indus Valley Sites consists fanlike plumes for head, V-shaped fellets of gold with holes for hanging pendants, hollow gold coins, animal headed, carnelian-studded hairpins, ivory and bone pinheads, gold and bronze ear-rings, leab-fiddle and coueshaped blue and yellow faience eardrops; steatite ear-studs bearing divided circle and lotus, designs, necklaces of several strings of different coloured beads of carnelian, agate, jasper, chalcedony, gold, etc. with spacers and dome-shaped terminals of metals, coloured bangles of pottery, hollow bangles and bangles of gold, silver and bronze, finger rings of bronze, silver and gold; girdles of beads on bronze wire interspersed with decorated disks; round and elliptical anklets. The Indus jewellers appear to have acquired knowledge of melting, refining and miring of metals; moulding, chiseling; cold setting of stones, designing, casting, colouring and glazing of faience pieces; of hardening steatite, carising, fitting colour in depressions to give enameled effect glazing the stone; of shaping beads, making facets.

The Aryans; The Rigveda (c. 1500 B.C.) asserts Aryans decorated themselves with gold fillets; found crowned, crowns with horus; gold breast plates, necklaces of gold beads; earrings; armlets; bangles; girdles. The Yajurveda testifies magical power of gold. The Rigveda describes brides, with ornaments; symbolic of married bliss.

Jewellery found Piprawa, Nepal, relics of Buddha also found, consists, beautifully designed flowers of gold; thin gold pieces bearing different ancient symbols; beads of semiprecious stones; corals; pearls; testifying belief, relics be protected from evil eyes.

Jewellery; found Taxila; influenced later Indian designs; includes, ornamented gold fillets; gold and ivory hairpins with decorated heads; thin gold chain necklaces of long cubical pieces, of round gold beads, of twisted gold wire representing coiled serpants; necklaces of beads of various shapes of crystal jade, amethyst, carnelian, etc; gold crescent shaped pendants; an ivory pendant with two philosopher's heads carved on it; gold decorated ear-tops with dome-shaped pendants hung with chains; oval gold earrings with decoration on the thick middle portion; ivory earrings; hollow bangles with decoration near the ends; bracelets with cut-out work; gold and silver finger rings with engraved designs; gold safety pins; amulets and engraved gears.

Jewellery; found different sites; consists of round disks attached to fillets; long eardrops; flat torques; necklaces of various shaped beads, some carved in the form of animals; broad ornamented armlets; bangles of gold bronze, glass; finger rings of gold and bronze with bezel tops bearing symbols, designs; beautifully designed girdle pieces; foot bangles and anklets.

People begun to wear light jewellery; excavations yielded earrings like wheel tires; ear studs bearing flower designs; bead necklaces; armlets; round bangles; finger rings of gold, of stones aglapis lazuli.

Jewellery includes fillets with round decorated pendants; decorated discs for the buns; elaborate earrings, probably worn, attached, to locks of hair; torques studded with gems, having pendants in form of rats' teeth; necklaces of beads; elaborate armlets; bangles with jewels; girdles of several strings of beads in loops with chains, used to hang over thighs; oval anklets; silver foot bangles;

Muslim invaders from north averse to wearing jewellery; contact with Indians, hot climate, discarded heavy cloaks; lighter jama, ornaments used. Eg Akbar (reigned 1556-1605); wore double strings of pearls on Indian turban; a plume or simurgh; two strings of pearls with garnets of neck; finger rings studded with emeralds et en caboclion. Jahangir (1605-27) wore earrings of two pearls, a garnet; a long necklace of pearls with garent,

emerald beads. Shah Jahan (1628-66) wore a plume of Surkhab on turban, adorned with Kohinoor diamond; added heart-shaped pendant, studded rose-cut diamonds, backed by silver foil, to pearl neclaces; wore armlet, with central piece of knives, swords, scaffards, jade handles of knives, swords, embellished with jewels; famous peacock throne, costliest throne ever made. Jewellery enameled on Persian pattern, set with precious stones, chiseling a hollow place; backing stones with white, coloured foils; covering edges with gold. Later Mughls started wearing bangles, jewelled kalgi.

Ladies, mostly Rajputs, in jares, wore on foreheads a round star-shaped pendants with rose-cut diamonds; emeralds, rubies, attached to a string of pearls on ears; earrings with pearls, on upper lobes of ears; nose ring; choker of three-four strings of pearls, a pendant in centre; armlets of gold set with emeralds or garnet; or horizontal piece with big jewel beautifully enameled at back; bangles with elephant or alligator form of ends; finger rings with precious stones; girdles, anklets of cheseled gold. The Persian, Mogul princesses wore a cap with plume; bracelets; long pearl necklaces; finger rings; strings of pearls on ankles.

The commoness wore jewellery; made of silver, cheap stones.

Contact with Europeans influenced Indian Jewellery; move towards simplicity, lightness, perfection of forms; designs now westernized; trend for revival of ancient designs, noticeable mid 20th century. Men ceased wearing jewellery; except finger rings, button, tiepins; chains occasionally.

References

R.G. Chandra, Development of Ornaments and Jewellery in Prehistoric India

J. Evans, A History of Jewellery, 1100-1870

JOG, VISHNU GOVIND

(b. 1922) - Instrumentalist: Hindustani, violin; studied with V. Sastry, S.G. Atharle, G. Purohit and S.N. Ratanjankar; concert tours, East Africa (1948); publication, Bela Siksha; disc recordings; music producer, All India Radio.

Reference

Sangeet Natak Akademy, Who's Who of Indian Musicians.

JYOTIRLINGAS : THE TWELEVE LIGHTS OF SIVA

Jyotirlinga is a Sanskrit expression consisting of two words, namely "Jyotir" meaning light and "Linga" signifiying the "Brahmand" (comos). Jyotirlingas are the sacred places where Lord Shiva Manifested Himself to his various devotees down the ages in different parts of India. There are a large number of Shiva temples in India but the Jyotirlingas are held in the highest veneration. They are the greatest "Tirathas" (Pilgrimages) prescribed in Hinduism for enlightenment, for intellect, for "Gyan" (knowledge), for purification of the self and for 'Moksha'

(Salvation). Besides Pilgrimages, they are places of beauty: to visit them is a joy forever.

The original source of information in respect of Jyotirlingas are the Puranas compiled by Sage Vyasa. According to Shiva Puran, there are twelve Jyotirlingas identified from Somnath in Gujarat to Guwahati in Assam, from Kedarnath in the Himalayas in the north to Rameshwaram in Tamil Nadu in the South. Their geographical location signifies not only the cultural unity of the country but also a sense of sancity to the Motherland. Millions of devotees visit these sacred sites every year, every month, everyday thereby strengthening the religious and cultural foundations of this ancient land.

In their present locations, the Jyotirlingas have been identified at Somnath at Prabhas Patan on the western coast in Gujarat. Mallikarjun in Sreesaila mountain in Andhra Pradesh. Omkareshwar on the banks of river Narmada in the island of Mandhata in Maharashtra: Kedarnath in the Garhwal Himalayas; Bhimashankar in Neral in Maharashtra; Viswanath in Varanasi in Uttar Pradesh; Trimbakewar near Nasik in Maharashtra; Vaidyanath at Parli near Hyderabad; Nageshawar between Dwarka and Bet Island (i.e. Krishna's Dwarka); Rameswaram at Sethubandh in Tamil Nadu; Ghushmeshwar and Mahakaal in Ujjain in Madhya Pradesh.

Although different ceremonies are prescribed for different Jyotirlingas they all revolve round the worship of Shiva in His particular manifestation at a particular Jyotirlinga. If, at Kedarnath, the waters collected at Gangotri and Yamunotri have to be poured on the Shivling, at Mahakaal in Ujjain it is the "Ash" ceremony which takes precedence. Likewise, during the journey form Dwarka Its bet Dwarka the pilgrims take the shells and the coconut to the Jyotirlinga. Following are brief sketches of these Jyotirlingas:

SHRI VISWANATH KASHI

This is the holiest of the holy places for the Hindus. Situated between the river Varuna and Asi, it is known as Varanasi. According to Skanda Purana unique light shines here in this abode of Lord Shiva. The Jyotirlingas is also known here as "Avimukta", i.e. free from sins.

It is still the greatest centre of Hindu civilisation, and an equally great centre of Indian classical music and dance. Tulsidas performed his first dance-drama Ramlila here.

Kashi Viswanath Temple is also known as the Golden Temple. A tonne of gold plating covers the fold spire of the temple. The gold was gifted by the Punjab ruler, Maharaja Ranjit Singh. Varanasi can be reached from Delhi both by air and rail, as well as by road.

KEDARNATH

Kedarnath is an ancient shrine situated in the Himalayas at height of more than 11,000 feet above the sea level. The range of mountains of which this Shiva temple stands is known as Panch Parvata i.e. Five Mountains.

There are two routes from Delhi to Kedarnath. The pilgrims first go to Hardwar and Rishikesh to Gaurikund from where they trek a distance of 14 kilometers to Kedarnath. The total distance from Delhi to Kedarnath is 464 Kilometres. The other route to Kedarnath is via Kathgodam (Nainital).

"MAHAKAAL" AT UJJAIN

According to Skanda Purana, Ujjain stands for the victory of Lord Shiva over the Tripura Asura (demon). Situated in the modern Madhya Pradesh, it was the site of an ancient university, a great centre of arts and music and the capital of Malwa once known as Avanti. The best time to visit the temple is the evening. The temple of Mahakaal is a very powerful Jyotirlinga of Lord Shiva. The shrine is situated close to a lake and has, five storeys in underground. The path leading to the Sanctum Sanctorum is dark but is kept illuminated by the lamps which keep burning forever.

NAGESWAR JYOTIRLINGA

It is believed that this Jyotirlinga exists at two places; one in the temple of Nageswar At Audhagram near Hyderabad, the other on a 20 mile stretch of sea between Dwarka and Bet Dwarka in the Bay of Cutch. On the day of Mahashivaratri in February-March every year, thousands of pilgrims visit the Jyotirlinga for darshan.

OMKARNATH JYOTIRLINGA

About ten kilometres from a place called Mortakka in Mandhata island situated between rivers Narmada and Kaveri there is a famous temple of Omkarnath which is worshipped by devotees as a Jyotirlinga of Shiva. The place is also called Sivapuri. Every year a religious festival is held here on the full moon day in the month of Kartika. Tradition and legend account for two Shivalingashere, one at Omkarnath or Omkareswar and the other at Amareswara. It is about 90 kilometres from Indore in Madhya Pradesh.

TRYAMBAKESWAR JYOTIRLINGA

Thirty six kilometers south west of Nasik in Maharashtra is located the Jyotirlinga not far from the river Godavari which rises from the Brahmagiri Hill situated by the side of village Tryambak. There is a water tank in which the pilgrims must take a bath before entering the temple of Tryambakeswar. The shrine is reached by a thousand marble steps.

GHUSHMESWAR JYOTIRLINGA

About 29 kilometers from Ellora Caves in Aurangabad district is identified the Jyotirlinga at Ghusheswar or Grishneswar temple dedicated to Lord Shiva. Ellora is situated only about 20 kilometers from Aurangabad city. There are 12 Buddhist caves, 17 Brahamical caves and five Jain caves at Ellora. There is a Kailash temple around which there are 16 caves each on the south and the north of it. The Kailash Temple at Ellora is regarded as the most exquisite cave temple in India.

RAMESHWARAM JYOTIRLINGA

Rameshwaram is an island in the Gulf of Mannar at the Land's End of India, where the Arabian sea meets the Bay of Bengal. The island is about 39 kilometers long and about ten kilometers wide. Deriving its name from Lord Rama installed the Jyotirlinga of Shiva here, Rameshwaram symbolises the cultural unity of India.

SOMNATH JYOTIRLINGA

About 120 kilometers from Ahmedabad, the town of Patan is situated on the banks of river Saraswati. Old Patan was known as Anhilvad where the Shiva temple of Somnath stands. As per the excavations carried out here, there existed in ancient times about a thousand Shiva temples in this area.

MALLIKARJUN JYOTIRLINGA

Sreesailam is situated about 220 Kilometers from Hyderabad. It is located on the banks of river Krishna. A temple was built here during the days of Vijayanagara Empire in the 15th century on the site believed to be one of the twelve Jyotirlingas. The special feature of the temple is that it is open to all communities, all castes, every body. The easiest way to reach this Jyotirlinga is through Warangal, 140 kilometers from Hyderabad. In January, a festival is held here in honour of Lord Shiva. Not very far from the Jyotirlinga there is a shrine devoted to Adi.

Shankaracharya. There is also a temple of Ma Saraswati, the Goddess of intellect and knowledge, at Basar about 50 km. away. There are only two temples of Saraswati in India, the other being in Kurukshetra.

BHIMASHANKARA JYOTIRLINGA

This Jyotirlinga is claimed at two places, one in Assam on Brahampur Hill near Guwahati and the other at 122 km. from Pune near Neral Railway Station. Here the Jyotirlinga is situated at the source of Bhima river at a height of more than three thousand feet above the sea level. On the Mahashivaratri day a big fair is held here. Pilgrims come from far and near.

VAIDYANATH JYOTIRLINGA

Like Nageswar and Bhimashankara, the Jyotirlinga of Vaidyanath also is believed to exist at two places, viz. at Parli near Hyderabad and Chittabhoomi in Santhal Pargana.

According to traditional accounts, besides the 12 Jyotirlinga, there are five Shivalingas representing the five elements which constitute life. All these are located in South India at Kanchi (Earth Linga), Jumbukeswar (Water Linga), Tiruvananamalai (Fire Linga), Kalahasti (Vayu Linga) and Chidambaram (Ether Linga).

PRANAV KHULLAR

"K"

K. K. HEBBAR

Described as 'the master of the line', Shri K.K. Hebbar evolved from being a painter of the Ravi Varma School into an artist of abstract art, relying on his own individual talent. He struck out a path for himself.

Following is the reproduction of his introduction to his book "An Artist's Quest".

After matriculation, with great enthusiasm, I went to Mysore and jonied the Drawing and Painting section of the Chamarajendra Technical Institute. But the atmosphere in the class was uninspiring. I decided to give up studying from model and began composing from Memory. I tried to absorb the finer quality in the minature paintings. The decorative forms and bright colours of the Jain minatures fascinated him.

One of the works of this period, "To Maidenhood",

Won me the then coveted gold medal of the Bombay Art Society (1974) Critics hailed me as the inheritor of Sher-Gil. All the works of this period were sold. Reproductions of my work were brought out in a large-size deluxe edition by an admiring publisher (1948).

K. L. SAIGAL : THE MUSICAL GENIUS

Recognized as the greatest singer of the century, K.L. Saigal was a musical genius who became a legend in his life time. He brought music to the masses and with his God-gifted voice and unique style gave a totally new dimension to the music of his time. His unforgettable melodies continue to enthrall millions of listeners and have become a part of our heritage.

As an actors-singer, Saigal attained unprecedented fame and popularity through New Theaters' productions, beginning with 'Chandidas' in 1934, and followed by a number of other box office hits. However, he had already won acclaim from knowledgeable music lovers after the release of his first recording 'Jhulna Jhulao' by Hindustan Records of Calcutta in 1932.

It is as the 'Ghazal King' that Saigal is remembered most by connoisseurs of music who seldom went to cinema. The first ghazal he sang and which created a countrywide sensation was Ghalib's "Nukta-chin hai game-dil" in 'Yahudi Ki Ladki' released in 1933. Not belonging to any gharana (school) and without any formal training, Saigal stunned the music meestros of his time with his instinctive knowledge of the ragas and his regal and resonant voice. He mesmerised his audiences with his rhythm which had a touch of the divine.

Saigal loved Urdu poetry and the created a new fusion of the music and the poetry. His musical interpretation of the ghazal gave a new form and content to the meaning of the verse. He played with words in a singular manner, producing an amazing array of emotions and sentiments. He seemed to share the joys and sorrows as spelt out in the words. In fact. like a magician, he succeeded in striking similar chords in the listeners' hearts. Many Urdu poets like Zauk, Seemab, Bedam, Arzu and Hasarat became famous, thanks to Saigal's rendition of their poetry.

The great Mirza Ghalib was, however, the most favourite of Saigal. In his own inimitable way, Saigal immortalised Ghalib by singing his verses with his heart and soul, interpreting the deep meaning of every syllable. It is through Saigal that Ghalib gained vast popularity even with the non-Urdu knowing audiences. Again, it is Saigal's choice of Ghalib's ghazals which found place in the famous movie "Mirza Ghalib" produced by Sohrab Modi in 1954. Sung by Saigal, these ghazals continue to enchant listeners all over the subcontinent and abroad even to this day. Many other singers, both male and female, have sung "Ghalib" but no one has been able to match Saigal, who identified himself with the poet's thoughts and feelings. No wonder, the most popular ghazals of Ghalib till today are those which Saigal sang during the 30s and 40s.

It is a little known fact that Saigal himself was a poet and is said to have recited his own compositions. No recordings are, however, available except the one "Main baithi thi phulwari mein". In this song, written and composed by him, Saigal highlights the divine presence within every human being and points out that it is the inner voice which reveals this to us when we are frustrated with our search in the outer world. He speaks about the closing of one's outer eyes in order to awaken the inner vision for self-realisation. As a poet, Saigal knew how to give life-like imagery to his words. Music was his life and soul. He sang for himself, more like a Sufi Saint, finding in music the most effective instrument for sublime communion with the Ultimate. A great artist, a great man, Saigal belongs to the class of human beings who defy death. He is immortal.

Born in Jammu in April 1904, and after an uninteresting schooling and working as a typist, a time-keeper in the railways and a salesman of sorts, Saigal reached Calcutta, then considered the home of music, to cave a career in films.

Sircar perceived gold in Saigal's sonorous voice when they first met and cast him in film after film (Mohabhat Ke Aansoo, Subah Ka Sitara, Pooran Bhagat, Chandidas, Yahudi Ki Ladki, Devdas, Street Singer, My Sister, et al.)

His ghazals and melancholic songs had a cathartic effect on the audiences drenching their spirits with the agonising ecstasy it evoked in them.

After migrating to Mumbai in 1941 Saigal acted and sang in Bhakta Surdas, Tansen, Tadbir, Bhanwara, Kurukshetra, Omar Khayyam, Shahjehan and Parwana. In all he acted in three dozen films - 29 in Hindi and seven in Bengali.

He was 43 then and was at the pinnacle of his glorious career spanning nearly a decade-and-a-half, during which he had recorded hundreds of songs in films in which he acted, as also non-film compositions comrising ghazals, Rabindra sangeet etc.

It was almost in the wake of the advent of talkies in our country in the early 1930s that Saigal joined the B.B. Sircarowned New Theatres in Calcutta and started acting and singing in Hindi and Bangla films. His excellent talent and its applications to the then just emerged talkies synchronised so propitously that the resultant synthesis was a pure audiovisual bliss.

Kundan Lal Saigal, this legendary soulful singer endowed with a golden voice and a keen perception of music, took his final bow from this world on January 18, 1947. He breathed his last at his ancestral home in Jallandhar where he had gone from Mumbai to recuperate from persistence illness.

B. M. MALHOTRA

K. S. NARAYANASWAMI -
VEENA VIDWAN

Sangeetha Kalanidhi K.S. Narayanaswamy, was one of the eminent veena vidwans of the Thanjavur School. He was the Principal of the Sangeetha Vidyalaya of the Shanmukhananda Fine Arts & Sangeetha Sabha, during 1970.

He developed a unique technique in Veena-playing, on the 'Sampradaya', mould, akin to the vocal style. He was a musician, musicologist and a dedicated teacher of all aspects of Carnatic music. As research - minded musician, he had studied many works on music. He had considerable knowledge of the grammar of music.

Possessed of 'Swara Janana', he was an expert in setting others' songs to music, writing the notation. He had the rare capacity to approach the raga from different angles. He could develop it step-by-step or just cover it in a sweep, bringing its 'jeeva' to the fore. He was particularly an adept at playing Dikshitar's kritis like "Sri Mathrubhutam" in Kannada, 'Ananda Nadana Prakasham" in Kedaram "Sri Subranabyaya Namasthe" in Kambodi, "Thyagarajaya Namasthe" in Begada and "Balagopala" in Bhairavi; Thuagaraja's kritis like 'Gripai' in Sahana, and 'Geetharthamu' in Surati; Shyama Sastri is kritis like 'Mari Veragathi' and 'O Jagadamba' in Ananda Bhairavi "Palinchukamakshi" in Madhyamavati and "Durusukha" in Saveri.

KSN's concert performances were a delight to connoisseurs and students. Mostly he welt a lot of ragalakshanas. He believed in the brevity of the gamaka and never approved of excessive. He attached importance to Sukhabhava and avoided frills. Vidvan Palghat Mani Iyer used to enjoy the 'Sukhabhava' of raga in Veena while playing mridangam for him. His raga alapana was rich with deep gamakas or graces. His 'bani' was more of the gayaki style. He maintained grandeur and purity of rendition.

A dedicated teacher, his method of teaching was unique. He would try to repeat the sangati of the kriti as many times as possible without feeling tired unless it was crystal clear in the minds of the students, many of whom later distinguished themselves.

Born on September 27, 1914, at Koduvayur in Kerala, he received intensive training under his parents, koduvayur Sivaram Iyer and Narayani Ammal from his seventh year and later learnt music from his brother K.S. Krishna Iyer. He was in the first batch of students of the Music College at the Annamalai University, Chidambaram. He learnt vocal music under Maha Vidwan Sabesa Iyer and Sangeetha Kalanidhi Tanjore Ponniah Pillai, a descendant of the famous Tanjore Quarter. He learnt Veena under Vidwan Desamangalam Subramania Iyer; also learnt Mridangam under Sri Ponniah Pillai. He was a Lecturer in Veena in his alma mater from 1937 to 1946. He also assisted in publishing the Tamil kritis of Gopalakrishna Bharati, Nilakanta Sivan and Arunachala Kavi.

He was a Lecturer in Veena at the Swati Tirunal Music Academy when Sangeeta Kalanidhi Semmangudi Srinivasa Iyer was the Principal. He also assisted him in editing (with notation) and publishing the kritis of Swati Tirunal. Subsequently, he was the Principal of the Academy till 1970. He was Principal of Sangeetha Vidyalaya of Shanmukhananda Fine Arts & Sangeetha Sabha, Mumbai in 1970.

KSN was the recipient of several titles and awards including Padma Bhushan in 1977. He passed away on December 12, 1999 in Chennai at the age of 85.

Dr. (SMT.) GEETA RAVIKUMAR

KALAMKARI

Process complex; industry depends, favourable weather conditions; process involves two months. Rains inconvenient, as damage vegetable colours. 15 steps; first bleaching of cloth with buffalo excreta; next, soaking cloth 'Myrabhylane juice', dying in sun; outlines of designs printed in blacks; colours used red, black; black colour derived iron filings, jaggery, red obtained from gum, alum cloth allowed to remain, two, three days; washed in water. Boiling process makes red black colours permanent; cloth bleached again; starched, stiffens cloth, facilitates application of wax. This process important, cloth dipped in it for application of blue colours. Entire cloth covered with wax, except places where blue is to be applied. Latter done by hand, with iron tipped pens. Other processes, indigo vat dyeing; wax removing, bleaching, starching, application of yellow, green colours, alum, bleaching with soap.

Chronologically these fabrics of Masulipatnam (Andhra) oldest; unique in many respects.

In existence since 6th century B.C.; supplied cloth all over country; abroad. The Puranas mention Kalamkari fabrics as being qualitative, durable, rich vegetable colours.

The Kalamkari process - blending of colours on a piece of cloth in striking designs; liquid wax, brushlike pen used. Colours - primarily vegetable; derived from herbs, plants, banks and flowers.

Used as temple drapes, depicting mythological themes. The fabric has - longevity; eg specimens of hundreds of years old - still remain a freshers. Ancient fabrics used in exciting new ways, makes exquisite sarees; house wats; skirts; evening coats, matching accessories also possible.

Prehistoric and protohistoric periods

Paintings; perishable nature, little survived. Nothing earlier 8th century B.C. and as late as 10th century A.D. Faint idea of painter's art, Indus Valley Civilization, found from pottery, decorated elaborately with leaf designs, geometric patterns.

KALIDASIAN

Dramas (Natya), operas, dances and musical dances, ballet (dances by Apsarasas) or Natyarasaka, puppet-plays (puttali), mimetics, chorous songs and a variety of cultural competitions highlighted the special festivals of Gods in the temples or palaces of Kings at the time of Kalidasa. It is no small wonder to note that all our modern representations of artistic talents had a due place in the age of Gupta Kings, remarkably in the reign of Vikramaditya Chandragupta - II for his magnificent court was studded with 'Nine Jewels' when the art of Kalidasa fully bloomed.

THE THEATRE

The play-house was simple structure rather oval shaped and was built carefully with due consideration to sound effects. It was divided into two parts, the largest part in front of the stage (Rang-Manch) was marked well with seats arranged in rows and the smaller rectangular piece formed the stage. It was sufficiently high for the full and complete view of the spectators. All the sides of the stage, including the back portion, were used as green-rooms (Nepathyagrha) or retiring rooms. These grhas made no distinction between males and females, so much so that the sexual aspect had no place on or near about the stage. In these days measurements were done in hands and the stage is said to be four hands high. The nepathyagrha was further used as a place for actions which could not be displayed on the stage, such as voices of animals, superhuman voices, uproar and akashvani etc. It was also a place for orchestra.

The orchestra included a lot of instruments such as drums of various kinds - Mridanga, nagaras, tabala, stringed - instruments ranging from one wire to twelve wires; blowing or wind organs such as flute, conches, trumpets, shahnai and quite a number of iron and brass instruments such as iron triangles, tongs, Brass-plates. Tanpura is our most ancient and scientific instruments, without which the character of Narada could not be presented on the stage with chiplis in hands. Most of these instruments are being used to this day. It would be no exaggeration to say that the modern Indian orchestra pales into insignificance before the mighty array of musical instruments used in the Kalidasian period.

A permanent painted curtain (pat or apati) was hung behind the stage in a cross-wise direction. Nearly five or six curtains were used with painted scenes required for particular performance and in harmony with chief sentiment of the action to be produced. These sentiments were well classified viz. erotic, heroic, comic, fury (rudra) etc. A treatise known as Natyasastra is a classical work dealing with all the details of a dramatic performance. Our Vedic hymns also represent the beginnings of the dramatic art. Kalidasa followed most of the priciples enunciated in the Vedas and Natyasastra, with suitable modifications, to fit in with his dramatic art.
(Condensed)

VAMAN H. PANDIT

KAMALINI - NALINI : REINTERPRETING KATHAK

Kathak - that graceful dance form of north India - had originated more than 500 years ago in the temple precints where its exponents used to dance before the Lord to Propitiate Him. Later on, however, this bewitching dance form was hijacked by the rulers of the day who were so enamoured by it that they not only extended patronage to it but also debarred it from the courtyards of temples. And now after five centuries, this temple tradition has been revived at no less a place than the Bankey Behari mandir (Lord Krishna's temple) at Mathura - Vrindavan.

The credit for doing so goes exclusively to the sisters duo Nalini and Kamalini and their Guru Jitendra Maharaj. They have diligently worked to give a new dimension to the Mandir Shaili (temple tradition) by creating new paradigms through innovative idioms. This they have done by relating this ancient dance to human aspects of our daily life as is evident "in my non-mythological compositions like Kala aur Vasna (art and lust), Kaal aur Manav (Time and man) etc." says Guru Jitendra Maharaj.

Speaking later about their experience of performing in the Bankey Behari temple, the sisters said they felt ecstatic about having performed before the lord; the whole atmosphere was electrifying and even the response of the audience was different, as if they were in a trance;

Being strong votaries of the Guru-Shishya Parampara (teacher-taught tradition), the sisters feel that one has to rise above one's egocentric problems to imbibe the intricacies of the dance form; mere graphic demonstration by the Guru will not help. One has to completely surrender before the cosmic dancer (personified by the guru) and only then can one learn any dance form.

The sisters are blessed with rare artistic qualities of expression, grace, clarity and perfection. Known for their refined sensibilities and subtlety, their style pleases both the aesthete and the purist. With an immaculate footwork, their style is marked by an elegant ease and a sensuousness that can only come with a complete understanding of the idiom.

While on stage, the two sisters have perfect synchronisation, as if they are two bodies but one mind. Their sincerity and total dedication to the dance is absolutely transparent. Whether they perform on the shores of the Mahabalipuram or in the Chidambaram temple or before the connoisseurs both in India and abroad, they never fail to cast a spell that is difficult to shake off.

TEEVRA SHARMA

KANCHI MAHASWAMI : GREATEST MORAL MONARCH

The venerable Paramacharya of Kanchi was the greatest Moral Monarch, with the longest spiritual reign, extending to 87 years, not only in the 20th century but perhaps in the annals of history of mankind.

His demise during the concluding phase of the world-wide celebrations of his centenary is a glorious culmination of a life solely consecrated to protect, preserve and foster the Majesty of the Moral Law.

By precept and practice, he gave meaning and purpose to the lives of several thousands, transcending religious and national boundaries, in all stations and segments of life. He was rare and unique Divine Integrator.

His mission in life, in his own words, was to "somehow save from destruction, the principal source of universal peace and prosperity - Dharma, as enunciated in the Vedas". Sanatan Dharma is the Eternal Law of righteous conduct, he always stressed.

(Condensed)

S. RAMAKRISHNAN

KANGRA MINIATURE PAINTINGS

Pahari miniature paintings were commonly confused with Mughal paintings till Dr. A.K. Coomaraswamy recognized Rajput painting as a distinct entity in 1916. Rajput paintings he classified into two main categories viz., Rajasthani and Pahari. Under the term Pahari paining was included the paintings which were done in the hill areas, formerly known as Punjab Hill States and now called Himachal Pradesh. These paintings too are classified into two categories. An early school which flourished in the 17th century is called Basohli School and the second which became current about the middle of the 18th century is known as Kangra School.

Kangra style developed at the State of Guler which has the longest tradition in the art of painting. The ruler connected with this art movement was Dalip Singh (1645-1743). In the later part of his reign, artists were working at Baripur Guler. Partraits of Dalip Singh exist and these can hardly be later than 1720. There are a number of portraits of his eldest son, Bishan Singh which can be dated to 1730. Bishan Singh died during the life time of his father and in 1743, his brother, Govardhan Chand became the raja of Guler. It is Govardhan Chand who was the main patron of art and a large number of his portraits which were formerly in the collection of Raja Baldev Singh of Haripur Guler are now in the Chandigarh Museum. Raja Govardhan Chand can be called the main patron of this new style of painting which combined the grace of the late Mughal Art with the beauty of the Hindi poetry and the elegance of the environment in which art itself grew.

GULER : BIRTH PLACE OF KANGRA STYLE

The role of Gular in the evolution of Kangra style is thus summed up by Dr. Archer: "The State of Guler played a decisive part in the development of Pahari painting in the eighteenth century. Not only did it develop a local art of greatest delicacy and charm, but the final version of this Guler style was taken to Kangra in about 1780, thus becoming the 'Kangra' style itself. Guler is not merely one of thirty-eight small centres of Pahari art. It is the originator and breeder of the greatest style in all the Punjab Hills". Subsequent research has fully confirmed Dr. Archer's thesis, and if any place can be called the birth palce of Kangra paintings. It is Guler. The research which has been carried on from 1952 onwards has proved that the paintings in early Guler style were by the artists, Manak and Nain Sukh. These persons belonged to Haripur Guler and their sons and grand-sons who were also great artists worked at Guler, Basohli, Chamba and other places. It is this great family which is responsible for most of the finest products of the Kangra School.

SANSAR CHAND'S PATRONAGE

The next great patron of the paintings in the Punjab Hills was Maharaja Sansar Chand of Kangra. Sansar Chand was born in 1765 at Bijapor, a village in Palampur Tehsil. In 1786, he occupied the Kangra fort and became the most powerful raja of the Punjab Hills.

In 1794 he defeated Raja Raj Singh of Chamba and annexed a part of his territory. Later on he defeated Raja of Sirmaur, Mandi and Suket Raja Parkash Chand of Guler also became his vassal. Sansar Chand when he became the paramount ruler of Kangra also attracted artists from Guler. It was for Sansar Chand that the great series of Kangra paintings were executed. The most famous in this series is a series of paintings of the Gita Govinda, a Sanskrit poem by the great Bengali poet, Jai Dev, which speaks of the love of Radha and Krishna. Another great series to be refered is that of Bihari Satsai. Bihari, the poet, wrote 700 verses on the love of Radha and Krishna which are now famous in Hindi poetry. All these poems were transmuted into paintings by the artists and this series is also regarded as very great in the Kangra School of paintings.

The third set of paintings relate to Ragamala or garlands of musical modes. These paintings were discovered very recently and are connected with the other two series referred in style. There is another set of paintings in the Bhagvata Purana which is also similar in style to the paintings of Gita Govinda. The sixth series relates to Rasikaprya of Keshav Das, as well-known Hindi poet. All great art owes its existence to religion and here Kangra paintings are no exception. It is Krishna worship which is the main theme of these paintings and also the source of their inspiration.

RHYTHMIC GRACE AND BEAUTY

The central theme of the Kangra paintings is love. The sentiments of love are expressed in a lyrical style in these pictures and the Kangra artists, many of whom preferred to remain anonymous, have created pictures of rythmic grace and beauty, which are a sheer delight to look at. As Coomaraswamy states: "What Chineses art achieved for landscape, is here accomplished for human love". Whether it is Shiva and Parvati, or Krishna and Radha, the theme is the same; the love of man for woman. In a number of paintings we see the Rajas in dalliance with their consorts; they are seen smoking hukkas and admiring the bloosoms of shrubs and trees in the garden, or watching white Sarus cranes against the background of slate-coloured curly clouds, Monsoon clouds bring happiness not only to the farmers, but also to young lovers who look forward to the coolth which the showere bring after the not winds of June have parched the countryside. Lonely love-sick women whose husbands are away, are shown standing in balconies of palaces, watching flashes of lighting in dark curly clouds at the dead of the night. In one of the Guler pictures a young lady is shown clinging to the smooth stem of a plantain eagerly wacthing the horizon for the return of her lord master. Toilet of Ranis and princesses in portrayed with a sense of realism and the young ladies are shown watching their faces in mirrors, while their female attendants are washing their feet and combing their hair, and on the branch of a tree a pair of birds is shown making love to each other. Birds as messangers of love commonly shown in these pictures. The expectant heroine asks the black crow, who is cawing in the balcony, to fly away and to tell her when her beloved would be back home? The male peacock spreading the iridescent tail feathers in a fan-shaped array reminds her of her gallant husband. In Hindu romanticism, it is the woman who is the lover and she expresses ardours of her love for her beloved, the man, by gestures and symbols.

The women of these paintings are ideals of feminine beauty, with gazelle - like eyes, tresses of jet black hair, firm and rounded breasts, slender waist and delicate hands dyed red with mehndi. One can see passion and modesty welling in their eyes and their erotic appeal is unrivalled. In their faces one sees the sentiments of love and devotion mingled with exuberant joy of life. In the delicate rendering of the female figure and in the portrayal of the sentiments of love these pictures stand unrivalled. (Condensed)

M. S. RANDHAWA

KANGRA VALLEY RAILWAY
SILVER LINING

The prominence of the white ranges - the Dhauladhars - in the Kangra Valley is singularly attractive. They surprise and over-awe at the same time.

Be as menacing as they look, they are conquered each day by a tiny soldier that climbs the rising altitude with determined jaws. This is the Kangra Valley Railway, that runs from Pathankot, at 333m, to Jogindernagar which is 1139 m high. The majestic Dhauladhar, almost with a found indulgence, lets this tiny conqueror partake in this game of climb, roll, unfurl and win. It is an unusual situation when both the conqueror and the conquered are not just favourably inclined towards each other, but almost in love. Because on this journey, landscape has not been altered or spoilt to let the railway come. Instead, the alignment has been laid through a maze of hills, valleys, long bridges over rivers, and adapted to suit and nurtue the environment. The result is absolutely marvellous sights and picturesque delights all through the journey.

The first 100 miles of the line came through on April 1st, 1929. There are only two tunnels on this railway, one about 250 ft. long and the other 1,070 feet long. Easy curves make the journey quite heart-warming. It is said that one must cross a bridge when it comes. This trains does so 971 times during a single journey of 164 Kms. An interesting point about its history is that a portion of this track was closed in April, 1942 and the material sent to aid British war efforts. Lal Bahadur Shastri reopened the railway in 1954 as Minister for Railways. Realignment continued as late as 1976, before it took its present shape.

The journey begins at Pathankot, and in an hour comes Nurpur a town named after Nurjehan, the royal consort of Emperor Jehangir. An ancient fort stands as a mute witness to a faded royal ambience. However, since royalty always patronized arts and crafts, the tradition lives on in Nurpur in the weaving of fine Pashmina shawls.

The train, passes through terraced fields, orchards laden with fruit, tea gardens and sprawling green pastures stretching unto the horizons - all appearing to be in tumultuous revelry. The mountain streams which sing song their way through gulleys and underwood, pamper these pastures.

This train journey provided some of the most beautiful sights that could be seen during a hill train journey. The train moves on leisurely.

Past Jawanwala Shahar and Guler, comes Jwalamukhi Road, for the pilgrims, this is the place. The famous Jwalamukhi temple is here, built in a style which is an amalgamation of Hindu and Sikh architecture. The dome is popularly believed to have been gilded by the Mughal Emperor Akbar. The sanctum snactorum is aflame with a fire that burns eternally. This flame is the manifestation of the goddess. Sometime later comes Kangra station. At 686 m. Kangra is gateway to a valley of pleasantries. The town of Dharamsala is just 18 km. away, where history and art combine in tradition and artefacts. The Pahari style of miniature painting that flourished during the regin of Raja Sansar Chand (1775-1823) has made this place famous. The use of fine brush strokes, in gold, red, blue and a combination of colours in various themes, speaks volumes about the creativity and imagination of the locals. Tibetans inhabit Mcleodganj, where His Holiness The Dalai Lama resides. Tibetan artefacts that flood the market place impart a faestive look to the narrow street. The most attractive are the bright wall hangings, painted with dragons or other designs.

Moving ahead on the train, there is Palampur at 127 km. Stone. The place is a trekkers' paradise.

The devout have a still more powerful attraction on this line, that of Baijnath Paprola, at 943 km above sea level. There is an ancient Shiva temple here that dates to 804 A.D. It is built in Shikhara style. The linga enshrined inside the sanctum sanctorum is one of the 12 Jyotirlingas in India. The domestic tourists flock here during Shivratri, when a colourful fair is organised.

After this 143 km journey, the train now pulls itself silently almost devoutly across the Bhir Gorge till it finally arrives at Jogindernagar, 1139 km, and almost 164 km. away from the starting point. (Condensed)

SANDEEP SILAS

KANKANA BANERJEE

Music to Kankana is more than an expression, it is her purpose in life.

"Music for me is a "sadhana". She would say. After her husband expired she sued to sit up the whole night with the 'tanpura'. Music gave her strength and solace. Her affair with music began when she was four years old. She learnt from her mother, Mandira Devi, then from the age of nine onwards she was groomed by Ustad Amir Khan of the Indore 'gharana' and at the age of 14, Mohua (as Kankana was lovingly called) gave her first public performance.

Kankana's tutelage varies from the Indore gharana (Ustad Amir Khan) to Mewati 'gharana' (Pd. Pratap Narain), but by her own opinion she is from the Kirana 'gharana'.

Kankana is basically a traditionalist but enjoys an occasional fling with semi-classical - 'thumri', 'dadra', 'thappa' and 'bhajan'. She even scores background music (strictly classical) for movies as she has for Raj Kapoor's "Ram Teri Ganga Maili", and Chetan Anand's 'Hathon Ki Lakereen!.

The 'guru-shishya Parampara' she feels inculcates that diligence into the artist. "An academic approach might get you a degree in music, then what? You become a teacher, but you cannot become a Bhimsen, Joshi, Good music is what comes from within and touches the audience".

With Kankana's music the experience lingers on "long after it was heard no more".
(Condensed)

S. SWARUP

KANTHA EMBROIDERY OF WEST BENGAL

Ancient literature, Buddhist sculptures of the second and first centuries BC, Kushan sculptures of second century AD and the frescoes of Ajanta from fifth and sixth centuries AD provide vital clues about the hand embroidery which has been widely practised in India sicne very early times. However, the examples that survive are only from sixteenth century onwards due to their perishable nature.

Indian emboroidery, with the exception of Kashmiri and Zardozi, remained a feminine preserve. Indian craftsmen have used various media such as cotton, silk, wool, velvet and leather to embroider upon. Every region in India has its distinctive style, motifs and colour schemes. The most popular Indian hand embroideries are Phulkari of Punjab, Chikankari of Lucknow, Toda embroidery of Tamil Nadu, Kasauti of Karnataka, Crewel embroidery of Kashmir Meo embroidery of Rajasthan, Chamba Rural of Himachal Pradesh. Applique work of Rajasthan, Gujarat and Orissa and Kantha of West Bengal.

The Kantha is unique more creative and artistic as it is done on used cotton saris. Women of Bengal prepare Kantha in leisure time. A number of worn-out and old saris are layered and sewn together. To keep the layer uniform and straight weights are placed on the four corners and the layers sewn together using close running stitch. Motifs are traced on the surface. The ground of the motifs is filled up with close, long and short running stitiches, using thread drawn out from the border of old saris. The entire field is then quilted into small blocks of different shapes and sizes using simple running and darning stitches. This gives a rippled effect to the cloth. At times, the design appears the same on both sides and it is almost impossible to distinguish the right side from the reverse. The colour scheme is very sober and artistic. The most popular colours are blue, yellow, red and black. Kantha has limitless designs.

Every woman who prepares Kantha can make any innovation that she has in mind. Traditional motifs originate from epics and legends. Birds and animals are also popular themes, as well as flowers, trees and creepers, Wedding scenes, procession of musicians, local folk arts scenes from village life or from particular periods in history - all can be found in Kantha motifs. Sacred symbols such as fish. conch-shell, lotus flower, 'mandala' 'Kalash' are also widely used.

Traditionally, women prepare seven different kinds of Kanthas. The thickly quilted warm wrap for winter; the Sujni is used as a bed cover or as a blanket for small children on ceremonial occasions, the Bayton is a wrapper for books and valuable articles, the Pillowcase, the Arsilata is a wrap for combs and mirror, the Durjan/Tbalia holds a wallet and the Rumal is a hankerchief. Rumals generally have a lotus design in the centre, with other artistic motifs around it. Arsilata has the motifs of trees with birds, lotus flowers and creepers whereas the Pillowcase has a series of straight border lines or conventional trees and birds. Though Kanthas have endless motifs and designs but the 'mandala' and 'kalasha' designs are especially made of festive occasions, in fulfilment of certain vows.

Many Kanthas items are now prepared with cotton of different colours, silk, 'tusser', Monga silk, cambric, semi-cotton material, terrycotton blends and even synthetic fabrics. The schemes are artistic and colourful Embroiderers use both traditional and modern designs. The outsanding feature of Kantha is its elegant and sophisticated look due to which it has became popular all over the world. Modern fashion designers are also using Kantha embroidery in their garments, with a combination of applique, mirror or sequin work.

USHA JOHN

KAPIL DEV

Kapil Dev Nikhanj emerged on the cricket scene just when the era of great Indian spinners was in its twilight. The country needed wicket-taking pace bowlers more than ever and the sturdy Haryanavi answered prayers when he landed on the international cricket scene with a bang in 1978. Kapil never looked back and left an indelibel mark on the ciricket world after a 16-year-long career.

One of the greatest all-rounders of the modern era, Kapil reached the pinnacle when he led his underdog team to an improbable World Cup victory in 1983, surely India's greatest sporting achievment till date. Among his many feats is the record of 434 Test wickets, more than anyone in history. Kapil lent a refreshing air to everything he did on the cricket field. With an instinctive talent, he had the knack of changing the course of matches in a jiffy. Whether bowling, batting or fielding, Kapil had a mercurial presence and was one of the biggest international stars of the game in his playing days.

His influence on the game was immense as can be gauged by the emergence of several quality pacemen who have followed in his footsteps. Today, Kapil has not turned his back on the game and has been associated with it in more ways than one.

KARMA

His Holiness the Dalai Lama observed that Hinduism and Buddhism are siblings born of the same mother. Their views of the nature of ultimate reality are similar to each other. The Buddhist view of Shunyata is very close to those propounded by the Advaitya schools of Hinduism. It is from this that they both derive belief in Karma and Reincarnation.

Karma very often, due to early misunderstanding of Western scholars, is understood to be passive, impotent, helpless and defeatist. This view is a misleading, and is the very opposite of the real import of Karma. Karma is dynamic, ever-changing, self-actualising and self-transcending. Rather than being a helpless pawn of Kismet wafted about by an arbitrary God, karma allows one to recreate oneself in one's own image and aspirations. Rather than being arbitrarily moulded and slave driven by another, Karma puts the responsibility of your destiny on yourself.

In the traditons that believe in eternal rest, in either heaven or hell, the question as to why people are born in extreme diversity - of fortune, riches, physical beauty, in the supper rich countries of the west or the living hells of Africa and Siberia under totolitarianism - are not adequately answered. Except by blind faith and belief in a mysterious and inscrutable God that works in inexplicable ways that can neither be questioned or answered, they offer no acceptable explanation.

Karma literally means action, work, and activity. We act as form in a physical body; and we also act as mental continums of the wisdom of our feeling, perception, actualisation and accomplishment, within a world view of the nature of ultimate reality. The results of these acts leave imprints that ripen into future results.

Buddhism postulates four laws that govern Karma.
1. Karma is definite in that good karma will yield happiness and afflicted karma will produce suffering.
2. Karma always increase Just as multiple fruits come from a single seed, karma too multiplies. A small act of virtue blooms manifold as does a small act of meanness.
3. The results are similar to the cause. Or you can not make silk out of a sow's ear;
4. Like the laws of energy that govern the external world, in the inner space of one's mental continuum karmic causes once created cannot be lost or denied.

Karmic acts leave imprints (vasanas) in our mental continuums whose results will bear fruit - both bitter and nectarine - into inexorable ripening. Like a minor humiliation to another fertilises vast fields of resentment, spite and hatred, a single karmic seed gives birth to a vast tree of fruit. Like a seed of spinach will not yield a tree of guavas, an act of compassion will not produce hatred; an act of abuse will not produce love. Similar seeds will give similar fruit.

It is a universal experience that 'luck' or 'destiny' or 'Kismet' can make a suden about-turn. Gain turns to loss, fame to disgrace, profit to loss, and happiness to sorrow in a single instance. Glowing radiant health can find itself being silently eaten by cancer or heart disease.

The Buddhist view of impermanence observes that objects give the illusion of appearing solid and permanent due to a dependence on various causes and conditons. They exist when the causes exist and cease when the causes cease.

The causes and conditons of our physio-psychological aggregates of form, feeling, perception, volition and consciousness are the results of our karmic actions. And in turn every act we perform every moment impacts upon the subsequent moments of our being and consciousness. All phenomena are in an intransigent state of dynamic flux, and changing from moment to moment. Nothing is permanent and forever, including misery and suffering.

It is possible to abandon this endless cycle of conditioned existence by one's own efforts and without the intervention of some superior Being. We ourselves create the causes and conditions of our own misery. And it is we alone that can get us out of it. Our acts must create those causes and conditions that can give us happiness and liberate us from suffering. By creating deserts of hatred and greed we cannot harvest groves of love and kindness. To eliminate suffering you have to uproot the roots of the causes and conditions of suffering. This wisdom is available to every being, for as the Shakya Muni said every sentient is a potential Buddha. Our negative karmas obfuscate us from seeing this profound truth.

SURESH JINDAL

KAROKON DANCE

Karokon; dance of Tamil Nadu, performed, annual festival, in front of image of Mariyammai to defer her from unleashing an epidemic, Tumbling, leaping, dancer retains pot of uncooked rice on head, surmounted by tall bamboo frame, people ascribe this feat, to spirit of deity, which enters his body, dancers arrayed awe-inspiring costumes, hideous masks, enact wierd rituals before shrine.

KARTIK FESTIVAL

From November 15 through 24, during the bright and auspicious autumnal month of Kartik (Indian Calender), Nahar Singh's splendid 18th century palace at Ballabgarh comes alive for the annual Kartik Cultural Festival. This year thousands of visitors turned up to witness a spectacular performance of dances, fashion and magic shows, puppets and firework displays, folk theatre, general festivities amidst the traditionally decorated camels and elephants and live demonstrations by master craftsmen.

Nahar Singh, the king of Ballabgarh came to power in 1829, at the age of four, During his childhood, intrigues by courtiers led to financial disaster and Ballabgarh was put under the management of British. But as soon as Nahar Singh entered his youth, he convinced the British to return control of Ballabarh to him. However, in May 1857 when the first war of independence broke out, Nahar Singh jumped into the fray against the British. As a result, he was over-powered by the British army and hanged in Chandni Chowk, Delhi, on January 9, 1858, for refusing to acknowledege British supremacy. Thereafter, Nahar Singh's palace and fort faded into oblivion.

Although today the palace and the fort complex lie in the centre or thickly-populated area, its beauty and grandeur remained unknown until a few years ago when

the Government of Haryana undertook its restoration. Now, restored to it pristine glory, the palace complex has become the venue of an annual performing arts festival in an aunthentic royal ambience.
(Condensed)

MEENA BHANDARI

THE KATHAK

Kathak, birth, a culmination of Hindu and Muslim culture, flourished North India under the Mughal influence, Kathak dances retain 17th century costumes, steeped in Radha and Krishna love-lore; this spiritual relationship deeply passionate, with erotic love-play, slowly dance degenerated, found shelter in bawdy houses, nautch girls practised the art to make themselves more tantalizing. Beginning 20th century, reclaimed, received through efforts of Kalkaprasad Maharaj, his sons Achchan, Lachchan and Shambhu perfected the art.

Kathak popular with both males and females because of its mixed Lasya and tandava temperament, has no rigid technique, takes movements from life, stylizes them, add complex rythemic patterns, the mathematical precisivion in doubling; quadrupling the beat with quick transfers and shifts makes the onlookers dizzy.

Female Kathak dancer wears a brocade blouse, a long, wide, shimacesing silk skirt, a transparent tissue scarf of gold threads, a heavy cluster of silver bells; A musician, the guru sits beside the drumancer on floor, vocalizes complicated syllables of the drum, dancer beats out with her feet, the muscial refrain, tehra provides lase of which the drummer and dancer execute rythmic patterns, important elements of the dance are chakkars, torahs and tihais. Chakkars denotes whirling with great speed, stopping for a faction of time after each whirl within prescribed beat; torah is the compostion of rhythmic syllables; Tihai, a repitition of a phrase of rhythmic syllables used to adorn the concluding part of the torah.

Two styles of Kathak - The Jaipur Gharana specializes in brilliance of footwork; The Lucknow Gharana excels in bhava.

Major performers in 20th century, Shambhu Maharaj, specialized in bhavapradarsan ("display of emotion"); Sunder Prasad, concentrated on tala and layakari aspects of dance; Birju Maharaj, Gopi Krishan, Sitara Devi, Damayanti Joshi, Uma Sharma, Shobana Narayan, all excelled and have important reputation in India as well as abroad.

THE KATHAKALI

Kathakali (Katha "story", Kali, Performance") originated 17th century in Kerala; devised by Raja of kottarakkara, who angry over refusal of neighboring prince to allow his dancers to perform Sanskrit dance drama in his court, decided to create own dance through using Malyalam; this dance school has own hastas; based on religious text, influenced by Natya-Sastra and later treatises makeup has roots in Dravadian demon masks of pre-Hindu period; themes taken manly from the Ramayana, the Shiva-

Purana the Bhagvata-Purana, the Mahabharata and other religious texts; superhuman characters present primal forces of good and evil at war; men play all the roles because of terrifying vigour.

Principal characters specified 7 types :

1. Pacca ("green"); noble hero, face painted bright green, framed in white-bow shaped sweep from ears to chin; Heroes, et, Rama, Laksmana, Krishna, Arjuna, Yudhisthira fall in this category.

2. Katti ("knife"); haughty, arrogant but learned, exalted character; fiery upcurled moustache with silver piper, white mushroom knob at tip of his note; two walrus tusks protude from corners of mouth; headgear is opuluent; skirt is full. Duryodhana, Ravana, Kichaka belong to this type

3. Chokannatadi ("red beard"); power drunk, vicious; painted jet black from nostrils upwards; both cheeks semi-circular stripes of white paper run from upper lip to the eyes; has black lips, white warts on nose and forehead, two long curved teetch, spiky silver claws, blood red beard.

4. Velupputadi ("white beard") represents Hanuman, son of wind god; upper half face is black, lower red, marked by a fracery of whiteliner; lips are black, nose is green, black squares form the eyes, two red spots decorated forehead; feathery grey beard, large furry coat, bell shaped headgear give illusion of monkey.

5. Karipputadi ("black beard"); a hunter or forest dweller; face is coal black with crisscross lines around eyes; white flower sits on nose; peacock feather closely woven into cylinder rise above his head; carries a bow, quives and sword.

6. Kari ("black"); intended to be disgusting, gruesome, witches, ogresses this category; have black faces, marked with queer patterns in white, huge, bulging breasts.

7. Minnukku ("softly shaded"); represents sages, brahmins, women; men wear white or orange dhotis; women have faces painted light yellow sprinkled with mica, heads covered with sarees.

Well known performers include Guru Chandu Panikkar, Guru Kunju Kurup, Ramunni Nair, Kalamandalam Krishna Nair; Guru Gopi Nath, Krishnan Kutty, emphasised simplification of use of towering headgear, thick crusted elaborate making, for the dance to be more commonly understood.

KEDARNATH - THE ABODE OF LORD SHIVA

Kedarnath in the Garhwal Hills, Uttar Pradesh (now in Uttaranchal), is on of the foremost shrines in India dedicated to Lord Shiva. Unlike in other Jyotirlinga shrines, the idol here is made of a rough black rock in the shape of the trunk of a buffalo.

According to a Puranic story, after the Mahabharata war, the Pandavas were told by the pandits that they could get rid of the sin of killing their kinsmen only if they have a darshan of Lord Shiva. So the Pandavas went to the Garhwal Himalayas in search of Shiva.

The Mahayogeshwar eluded the Pandavas at many places. At Guptkashi he disappeared altogether. So the place came to be known as such. But the Pandavas continued the search. When they reached the small plateau at the bottom of the Kedar peak, they were told that Kailasapti was there in the garb of a buffalo. It was a problem to recognise him amidst so many grazing buffaloes. Bhima finally recognised the Lord.

It is believed that the worship of Shiva is complete only if one also visit the Pasupatinath temple in Kathmandu (Nepal) as the idols in these temples are believed tobe parts of one whole. The head portion is in Pasupatinath. With this faith a large number of pilgrims from India and Nepal visit these two religious palces every year.

The Kedarnath temple is situated at an altitutde of 3,584 mtrs. Therefore, it is snow-bound for almost six months in a year. The temple closes after Diwali and reopens in Mid-May. Sometimes the priests who go there in early May to open the door find the temple submerged in snow and have to clear it before opening the door.

The gateway to Kedarnath, as for the other three shrines in the Garhwal Hills, is Rishikesh.

For the nature lovers there is a surfeit of scenic beauty. The dark green hills, the Kedar Valley with the yellow tinge of ripening Kharif crops, the emerald waters of the Mandakini flowing gently in its downhill course, the silvery peaks of the Garhwal Himalayas shining in the mist-free autumn sky are all breathtakingly beautiful.

Starting from Rishikesh in the morning, one reaches Soneprayag in the evening. On the way one passes through Srinagar, Rudraprayag and Guptkashi three important pilgrim centres dedicated to Lord Shiva. Those who break journey at Guptkashi get an opportunity to see the ancient temple built at the spot where the ascetic god is said the have disappeared to the disappointment of Pandavas. From Soneprayag many pilgrims visit Trijunginarayan, 4 km away, after negotiating a steep climb. It is here that Lord Shiva and Goddess Parvati are said to have been married. Those who proceed further stay at Gaurikund, 5 km. from Soneprayag, for the night.

The real yatra begins from Gaurikund. The pilgrims have to trudge a distance of 15 km. in which they climb from 1981 metres to 3,584 metres. But the incline is gradual. Only at a few places it is as steep as 60 to 70 degrees. The track is quite wide. Those who cannot walk, hire ponies and dandis. Old and frail pilgrims are carried in kandis.

There are many Chattis on the way where the pilgrims stay for a while to take rest.

Ram Bara is the largest Chatti, half way on the journey. The Mandakini flows nearby where those staying here overnight take bath. Even those arriving here tired after walking seven km from Gaurikund are tempted to take a quick dip in its emerald water. It refreshes them to proceed further.

The stretch beyond Ram Bara right up to Kedarnath is a steep climb. At places, however, the ascent is not very steep which serves as a breather. There are two more chattis, Garurh Chatti and Dharnur Chatti, before Kedarnath where the tired plodders halt to get back the strength to reach their goal.

It is in this part of the journey that one comes across old men and women, past 70 and bent with age, trudging their way to the shrine. With only a stick to support them, they move up panting; their will to go to the holy place before departing from this world keeps them moving. Their fortitude encourages others much younger to them to continue walking on the ever-rising trail. It is they who are

the real embodiments of pilgrims. The pains they take to reach the abode of God gives an idea of what tapas is.

The tiresome ascent ends just about one and a half km. before the Kedarnath temple. Suddenly the pilgrims find themselves on a plain land and are relieved to read a signboard: ' you are now in the land of God'. They will be happy to see the township and the temple situated amidst it. All round are barren rocky hills with a coat of green grass. The snow-capped Kedar peak peeps from behind them. The devotees areenchanted by the scenic beauty and forget the travails of the journey.

The Mandakini flows skirting the hamlet. The pilgrims have to cross a bridge to enter the temple area. Just below the bridge is the bathing ghat. The temple is situated at the end of the small bazar. It stands on an elevated ground from the surrounding area. The visitors have to climb a few steps to reach its courtyard. It opens for worship and darshan both in the morning and evening. Even in mid-June fresh snow is visible on the adjacent hills and those not well covered with woollens and wind-proof jackets are seen shivering. This long wait in the biting cold itself is a tapasya.

Before entering the temple, the worshippers pay homage to Nandi, which keeps guard in front of the shrine. Just at the gate is the statue of Ganesha where priests chant mantras invoking God's blessings on the devotees.

After a few steps they enter the sanctum snactorum. Unlike in other famous temples, there is no restriction on entering it. And instead of Jyotirlinga the devotees see a rough black rock in the shape of the trunk of a buffalo. And as oblation, water is not offered as in other Shiva temples, but the idol is anointed with ghee. Then a piece of cloth and gram dal are offered. After that devotees perform arti and pray, some silently, some by reciting slokas and mantras and a few by a loud appeal. Everyone comes here with his or her cherished wishes and prays to Lord Shiva to fulfil them.

Just, near the temple, above the bank of the meandering Mandakini, is the samadhi of Adi Shankaracharya, who is said to have achieved nirvana here. His marble statue in a serene pose arouses reverence for that great exponent of Advaita philosophy and reviver of the Hindu religion. By establishing four dhams in the four corners of the sub-continent he laid the foundation of unity of the country.

From here Mandakini is seen descending from the hill overlooking the township. It gives an enchanting view of a placid lake, with its bluish water so transparent that the pebbles at the bottom are clearly visible. Sitting by the side of the lake at an altitide of about 3,900 metres in that earie silence one feels as if one has had a vision of God. (Condensed)

VIKRAM BIST

KEOLADEO SANCTUARY A WORLD HERITAGE SITE

Keoladeo National Park popularly known a Bharatpur Bird Sanctuary in the Rajasthan state of India, has more than 300 species of birds in an area of 29 sq.km. of which

11 sq.km. are marshes and the rest scrubland and grassland.

It is much more surprising that this unique ecosystem is man-made. Bharatpur town used to be flooded regularly every monsoon. In 1760 an earthen dam (Ajan Dam) was constructed to save the town from annual vagary of nature. The depression created by extraction of soil for the dam was cleared and this became the Keoladeo lake. At the beginning of this century, this lake was developed and was divided into several portions. A system of small dams, dykes, sluicegates etc. was created to control water level in different sections. Shooting butts, hides and pevements were constructed. This became the hunting preserve of the Bharatpur royalty and one of the best - duck shooting wetlands in the world. Hunting was stopped here by mid 60s. The status of this avian haven was upgraded to a National Park in 1981.

Keoladeo is a paradise for migratory birds. More than 100 species visit the Park due to hostile climatic conditions and shortage of food back home. They come from as far off as Russia, Europe, China, Mongolia, South-West Asia, Tibet etc. Many of them even overfly highest peaks in Himalayas. September onwards, species start arriving here one after the other. By December the Park is kaleidoscopic.

Migratory birds at Keoladeo include as large a bird as Dalmatian pelican, which is slightly less than two meters, and as small a bird as Siberian dusky leaf warbler, which is the size of finger.

These migrants include many species of cranes, pelicans, geese, ducks, eagles, hawks, shanks, stints wagtails, warblers, wheatears, flycatchers, buntings, larks and pipits etc. Most of these species are present in their thousands packing the marshes like hordes at Kumbh Mela (a religious festival occurring every 12 years when millions of pilgrims assemble to take a dip in the holy Ganga river).

Geese come in large skeins probably from Central Asia. These include greylage goose and barheaded goose.

Ducks include strikingly coloured common shelduck which is chiefly black, white and chestnut with bright red upturned bill and pink legs; mallard with conspicuous glistening metallic dark green head and neck, yellowish - green bill, orange legs and two black upcurled central tail feathers; wigeon with head and neck chestnut and distinctive cream coloured patch on the forehead, and squat and tubby common pochard with chestnut-red head and neck. Coot from China is uniformaly coloured black.

Osprey and marsh harrier are migratory birds of prey. It is a strange peculiarity in most of the raptors that the female is bigger than male.

Migratory waders include the large black-tailed godwit with long slender bill, peewit with glistening green long slender upstanding pointed crest and sparrow sized temmick's stint.

If one hears low musical group song passing from one tree to another and see the flash of rose-pink and black, one is sure they are the krosy pastors probably from South-West Asia.

And in how large flocks can spanish sparrow, a part of whose population comes from Turkestan, congregare?

More than a million birds; Salim Ali, the great ornithologist, once estimated.

One of the major attractions of Keoladeo, the Siberian crane or the great white crane, occasionally visits the Park. Siberian crane, numbering only few hundreds, is on the verge of extinction. There are two races - western and eastern. It is birds from the western race which used to visit Keoladeo - migrating from the Obriver basin region in the Aral mountains in Siberian, after a journey of more than 6000 km.

According to official records, since 1969, when 76 Siberian cranes visited the Park, there was consistent decline in their number every season, till 1992-93 winter when only five visited. In 1993-94 six Siberian cranes visited Iran, another known destination of this race. This is too small a number to be viable population. Extinction of this western race seems inevitable. The reasons are complex, but the more obvious one had been the persistent hunting of this crane, enroute, in Afghanistan and Pakistan. Locals in Iran too hunt these birds.

International Crane Foundation (USA) had been fearing this for quite some time. They launched a massive high-tech global effort to augment the western race by releasing the captive-reared juvenile and sub-adults among the few wild ones left at Siberia in 1991 and 1992 and at Keoladeo in 1993. They were banking on the basic instinct of the Siberian cranes to migrate. The great effort, unfortunately, did not succeed though the ICF scientists have not given up as yet.

The unique mix of marsher, pastures and woodland and the floral communities at Keoladeo is suitable for high density and diversity of macro and micro fauna. This richness suits about 100 species of resident birds to breed here while a similar number of species visit the Park but breed elsewhere.

Terrestrial birds like redwattled lapwing, grey partridge, black partridge, common quail, pea fowl, jungle fowl etc nest on the ground in summer. Had they been breeding in monsoon, their nests would have run the risk of getting flooded. Aslo when the chicks arrive it is monsoon and there is ample supply of insects and vegetation for feeding young ones. Doves, kingfishers, mynas, woodpeackers, orioles etc. breed in summer.

Onset of monsoon brings a sea change in the Park. The drying lakes are recharged. Parched habital turns green once again. Waterlily blooms all over the lake and other hydrophytes grow spontaneously. A canal from Ajan dam brings more water to the Park, along with which come millions of fish fry and other micro organism. Aestivating turtles come to life once again. Frogs start crocking. Sarus cranes dance. Monsoon is the time when another major development takes place in the Park: it is the formation of the world-famous heronry.

Seventeen species of birds, namely, grey heron, purple heron, night heron, large egret, median egret, little egret, cattle egret, large cormorant, Indian shage, little cormorant, darter, painted stork, openbilled stork, blacknecked stork, whitenecked stork, white ibis and spoonbil are known to breed at Keoladeo heronry. Talking about the heronries of the world, Roger Tony Peterons wrote, "Perhaps the most impressive spectacle of all is the great assemblage at Bharatpur, near Agra, India, where half a dozen species of herons and egrets nest in association with painted storks, spoonbills, ibises and cormorants...".

The heronry is almost exclusively built on modest sized Acacia trees submerged in the marshes or on islands in their lakes. Openbill stork, not so commonly found otherwise, breeds here in large number. They are quiet and concentrate in one part of the heronry. White ibis too does not make much noise but breeds in lesser number and is more widely distributed. Painted stork needs fresh tender stems from three tops. The Indian shage breeds here in the largest number. the drab black shage in provided by nature, during breeding, a white mark on the cheek to look handsome for the occasion. The spoonbill is by far the most beautiful and conspicuous.

The heronry extends to a small part of the Park, where each tree is crowded with 80 to 100 nests. To a layman, it might seem strange that so many birds of so many species breed in such a small area of the Park. It there no other suitable place in the Park for the birds to be more comfortable? The fact is that it is not the lack of suitable area in the Park which results in crowning but these birds find security in numbers. Whenever a bird of prey flies low over the heronry to rob a nest, all adults jointly create such a din that the raptor even if not afraid of the birds would leave them alone.

Keoladeo heronry is full of life, action and activity.

Besides the avian fauna, many species of mammals and reptiles are also common in the Park. Blue bull and sambar feed on hydrophytes at the lake. Black buck and spotted deer herds graze in the extensive grasslands. Wildhoar and jackal roam around in the scrubland. Fishing cat frequents the lakes to scoop away fish or steel a duck. Pythons are present in the Park in large number. In Winter they are invariably found basking near their hole.

With all these features and many more, it is not surprising that Keoladeo is a site recognised as Waterfowl Habitats under the Convention on Wetlands of International Importance.

Besides, it is a World Heritage site too.

PUSHP K. JAIN

KERALA - INDIA'S EXOTIC SOUTH

The southernmost state of India, Kerala is a long, thin, coastal strip cut off by the jagged teeth of the Western Ghats. This region is full of mindblowing landscapes capped with a benevolent climate. After all, this region is believed to have emerged from the sea when the god threw an exe into the deep waters and commanded it to retreat. Fertile peddy fields, sheaths and sheaths of water, at times flanked by laterite cliffs, stretches ahead to merge with the horizon. Red tiled homes, groves of coconut, palm swaying gently to the call of the light breeze, water hyacinths and screw pines are some of the unusual sights in Kerala. Consider no less than 40 rivers criss - crossing their way across the hill to join the palm-frigned backwaters, lagoons and on to the sea.

Trivandrum (now called Triruvannathapuram is the state capital. The city boasts of antiquity dating back to King Solomon whose ship landed around this place. However, it was not until the 18th century when the Tranvancore king shifted his capital here from Padmanabhapuram (now in Madras or Chennai). The Tranvancore kings took the title of Padmanabha Das (servant of the lord) while dedicating the kingdom to the Lord and the king remaining the mere executive of the trust.

The 16th century Padmanabhapuram Palace near Trivandrum, the seat of former rulers of Travancore is one of the world's largest wodden palace and for sure a typical example of Kerala architecture. The well preserved palace reveals several things like the hidden murals, the unique flooring finished in a secret formula that imparts cooling effect, etc.

Cochin (Kochi) is Kerala's largest city built on a cluster of islands famous as the queen of the Arabian sea, with one of the finest harbours in the world. It was here that traders and travellers from around the world vied for a place in the spice trade-cardamom, nutmeg, ginger, pepper - for which Kerala is still famous. Nearby is the famous Vasco da Gama church and the Bishop's House. Other things of interest in the town include the synagogue and the nearby Mattancherry Palace exhibiting the architectural influences of various European powers.

Further north is Thrissur, best known for its temples and the Poorm festival held in the month of April where the decorated elephants dance to the tune of temple orchestra. Nearby is Guruvayoor, famous for its Krishna temple. En route is Kodungalloor that houses India's earliest mosque.

The most important town in the north is Calicut (Kozhikode), center for spice trade, the old University and the Calico. The world 'Calico' for a kind of cotton fabric, now adapted into the english language, comes from Calicut. At the extreme north is Bekal where the remains of a 15th century fort have been guarding the coastline for years and are now being developed into one of the largest resorts in South East Asia.

To all appearances, Kerala is a racial and religious medley. The Namboodiris, the first intruders from outside, were originally of Aryan stock. The Nairs and the Thiyas were Dravidian. Between the Nairs and the Namboodiris, howevere, there has been extensive inter-mixture. For centuries there had been a custom under which only the eldest member of a Namboodiri family married a Namboodiri girl. All the others married Nair girls. The Nairs used to think, though they no longer do, that it was an honour for their girls to be married by the aristocratic Nomboodiris. For the Nambodiri this was highly convenient, because he could have the joys of married life without paying for them or having to maintain their children who under the matrilineal system, belonged to and were looked after by their mother's family. The result is that today the Nairs have as much Aryan as Dravidian blood in them.

All the principal religions of India have their adherents in Kerala, Here the minorities are more prominent than elsewhere. In India, as a whole, the Hindus account for 83.5 per cent of the population; in Kerala, 63.88 per cent. In India, only 10.69 per cent of the population are Muslims; in Kerala the percentage is 17.29 rising to 33 per cent in the Malbar region. Christians in India come to only 2.44 per cent; in Kerala they form 21.22 per cent rising for 27.22 per cent in Travancore and 32 per cent in Cochin.

Yet, no matter if a Malayalee is of Aryan or Dravidian stock, a Hindu, Muslim, Christian or Jew, he is easily distinguished wherever he may be, as a Malayalee.

Not only did Kerala assimilate Sanskrit culture, but it has made a substantial contribution to it. In the 6th century A.D. one Bhaskara wrote a ι authoritative Sanskrit treatise on astronomy. In the 16th century the theory and practice of law were elaborated in two treatises, Vicharamala and Vyavaharamala, and these remained as the recognised legal codes until they were displaced by the Indian Penal Code and the Evidence Act.

The most majestice contribution of Kerala to Indian culture was the philosophy of Sankara in the 8th Century. Here human though transcended all limits in its ultimate quest for truth "renouncing all thought of the enjoyment of reward here or here-after". Hinduism was cleansed of all subsequent accretions such as ritualism, tantrism and excessive anthropomorphism. Indeed Sankara's philosophy proceeded even beyond God, though in his humanism and in his recognition of the limitations of the human mind, he gave a place for God or Iswara in his system. His life, like Jesus Christ's covered a span of 32 years only. Within that period he travelled all over India and formed monastic centres in Puri in the east, Dwarka in the west, Sringeri in the south and in the north Badrinath, where the Poojari is still always a Keralite. No one has done more to integrate India than this great son of Kerala.

Kerala has not only contributed to a synthesis of Aryan and Dravidian cultures but has tried to reconcile differnt seats of Hinduism. As history has shown, conflicts between sects, as, for instance, between Catholics and Protestants, can cause as much havoc as conflicts between religions. Under the Chera dynasty, Saivaism and Vaishnavism flourished side by side. King Kulasekhara, the founder of the dynasty, was a Vaishnavite; his successor, Rajasekhara was a Saivite.

The attitude towards Christianity and Islam, too was one of benevolent tolerance and often active patronage. Christianity entered Kerala in 62 A.D., with St. Thomas, the Apostle of Christ, who lies buried in St. Thomas Mount, Madras, and flourished under the patronage of the local rajas on the West Coast. Christians, while adhering to their religion, took an enlightened interest in Hindu thought and philosophy. The fanatical Portuguese, however, looked askance at this tendency. Fortunately, Portuguese rule in kerala - and in India - proved to be a mere interregnum. Thereafter the Christian community was free not only to benefit from, but to benefit Indian culture, to which Christian scholars have made a substantial contribution. As examples may be mentioned I.C. Chacko's monumental book of Panini's Grammar, the Index of Puranas compiled by V. Mani, Mundasseri's Synthesis of Aristotle and Abhinava Gupta in poetics; and Katakkayam's Kavya in 21 cantos and 3700 stanzas, called the Triumph of Jesus.

The earliest Muslims are said to have come to India soon after the passing of the Prophet. The spice trade for which Kerala had been famous from time immemorial and to which there is reference in Herodotus in the 5th century B.C. was, after the fall of the Roman Empire, mainly in the hands of Arab traders.

Iban Batuta, the Arab traveller who visited India in the middle of the 14th century, has written ; "The Muslim merchants of this place (Calicut) are so wealthy that anyone of them can purchase the entire cargo of the vessels put in here and fit others like them".

Kerala Muslims played a redoubtable part in the Hundred Year War between India and Portugal. Malayalam writers like Basheer and K.T. Mohammed have been enriching Malayalam literature. At the same time, Hindu poets like Vallathol, Ulloor and G. Sankara Kurup have used Muslim themes in their poetry with great effect.

The Kerala genius for synthesis found superb expression in the development of the Ayyappan legend. Originally Ayyappan was a deity of the forest at Sabarimala, which overlooks the plains of Tamilnadu from which there were occasional incursions of criminal tribes like the Maravars into Kerala. He was a great hunter who kept tigers instead of dogs at his pack. When Buddhism entered Kerala, Ayyappan was worshipped as Buddha. Subsequently, when there were rivalries between the Shaivaite and Vaishnavaite sects, Ayyappan tried to reconcile them. Thus arose a charming though fantastic, legend that Vishnu took the female form and captivated Siva and that Ayyappan was the offspring.

With the persistent Chola invasions from Tamil Nadu, Ayyappan became warrior leading armies against the intruders from the east. He had to deal with intruders from the west as well, the Arab pirates infesting the Arabian Sea. At a fierce encounter between their leaders Babar, who in Malayalam is called Vavar and Ayyappan, both fought so magnificently that they developed mutual respect and admiration and formed a friendhsip which is perpetuated in the shrine for Vavar adjoining Ayyappan's; and pilgrims to the temple of Ayyappan have also to worship at the Vavar Shrine. In Sabarimala there are no distinctions of caste or class. All devotees hail one another, saying "Ayyappa Swami; Be Blessed";

In the fight against caste Kerala was in the forefront. There used to be no caste under the Chera dynasty. Caste was one of the offshots of the advent of Aryan culture. In Kerala the caste system was elaborated to such an extent that, according to the census of 1931, there were 271 castes and 473 sub-castes in Kerala. No wonder Vivekananda called Kerala "a lunatic asylum".

It was in Kerala that the crusade against caste gathered strength. It expressed itself in the great Vaikom Satyagraha of 1924-25, the result of which was that all approaches to temples, which had hitherto been closed to the untouchables, were thrown open, and the Guruvayur Satyagraha of 1931-32, led by Kalappan and K.P. Kesava Menon. Ultimately, the compaign against caste culminated in the Temple Entry Proclamation of 1936, under which all temples in Travancore were thrown open to Hindus of all denominations. Mahatma Gandhi called this "miracle of modern times".

In the sunthesis of Carnatic and Hindustani music, too, Kerala has played a part which is by no menas negligible. The greatest of Kerala's composers was Maharaja Swati Tirunal (1813-1847), comparable to Tyagaraja himself. Of his 500 compositions 300 are extant in different languages, Malayalam, Tamil, Telugu, Kannada, Hindi and Sanskrit. His electicism was reflected in his court, to which apart from Carnatic musicians, he invited Lakshmana Das from Gwalior, Mansari from Maharashtra and Sulaiman and Allauddin from Delhi.

Kerala has contributed immensely towards the enhancement of Indian culture. (Condensed)

K. P. S. MENON

KHAJURAHO - A WORLD HERITAGE SITE

Khajuraho is now one of the sixteen world heritage sites in india. But over a thousand years ago, the beautiful landscape of Khajuraho village must have been extraordinarily enchanting and mesmerising, to have drawn chandella rulers to undertake an enormous temple complex. And the complex itself must have changed drastically over the last thousand years, as it now lies in the midst of fields and lakes. The site represents one of the finest examples of Indian architecture and craftsmanship. Perfect in execution and sublime in expression these breath taking sculptures capture life in every form and mood, present every shade of human desire including erotic details and yet transcending it, to be one with every element,.. earth, fire, air, space... and that too without being abstract.

According to historical inscriptions, Chandellas ruled over the area till about 1200 AD when the last Chandella king lost to the Delhi ruler Qutab-ud-Din Aibak.

After that there is a paucity of information for the period from 1203 to 1838, till Captain T.S. Burt of the Bengal Engineers heard some interesting details about a place called Khajuraho. He travelled to see the complex. Captain Burt thought that "the sculptor had at times allowed his subject to grow rather warmer than there was any absolute necessity for his so doing; indeed, some of the sculptures here were extremely indecent and offensive....". But he also notice that he was not allowed to enter one temple, where people still worshipped.

What Captain Burt felt, down the century, hordes of others including experts, scholars and artists opined not very differently. But, a noted art historian and scholar Dr. Shobita Punja's research developed a theory, of a different class alto-ther, which viewed the orgins of Khajuraho away from what the earlier..... experts thought. In fact, it very convincingly projecte that this world heritage site had a base in a deeply religious, ritual and philosophical attitude. And on this, Dr. Punja feels, the Khajuraho temple scheme was founded. She has explained that the sculptures of Khajuraho, far from being pornographic in intent, are symbol of deep philosophical meaning. Her theorry revolves around the divine marriage of Shiva and Parvati. And when it took place, the beauty of their union was so splendid that anyone who was doing anything, be it feeding a child or engaged in love-making, had the compelling urge to see the event. At the Matangeshwara temple in Khajuraho - it was here that Capt. Burt was refused entry - this divine marriage is celebrated every year at the Maha-Shivratri festival.

Once this landscape had 85 temples, perhaps more, as the legend goes, of which only 20 remian. Of these excellently sculpted temples, the Kanderriya Mahadev is the grandest, followed by temples of Devi Jagdambi, Chitragrupta, Lakshmana, Vishvanath, Nandi, Brahma, Parshvanath, Adinath and Chaturbhuj.

The vibrancy of life and the range of the emotions depicted through the pale yellow and warmer brown tones of Viṅdhyan sandstone, the intricacy of carving and delicate handling by the sculptors enthrall everyone visiting this cherished heritage site. And one cannot but agree with Dr. Punja that these temples represent the process of birth, life and death... an unending continuum.

KAMAL SAHAI

KHAMBA THOIBI DANCE

Khamba Thoibi dance, also known as Lai Haroba dance is performed all over the valley in Manipur. The focal point of this dance is moirang town which is dated upon the Manipuri as the meeting place of two besotted lovers who have become the substance of legend. Kamba and Thoibi. The two were united under the trying circumstances only to face an abrupt, poignant, shared end. An integral part of the dance is the duet purporting to represent that of Khamba and Thoibi. The number has become so popular and pervasive that it by itself has come to be identified by the name of Khamba Thoibi. In this dance there is nothing in the movements, gestures or facial expression to suggest the emotion of love. There is no song and the only music provided is a lachreymose melody played relentlessly on the pena, a stranged instrumental native to Manipur. (Condensed)

MOHAN KHOKAR

KHAN, USTAD ALLAUDDIN

Born in 1862 in village Shivapur (Tripura); Disciple of Guru Nanu Gopal who taught him vocal music; from Nandlal he learnt Tabla and Mridang; later on was a pupil of Ustad Amjad Ali, famous Sarod player; outstanding Sarod player; recipient of Sangeet Natak Akademi award for Hindustani instrumental music (1952); awarded Padma Bhushan in 1958 and Desikottama (Viswa Bharati) in 1961; composed new ragas like Hemand, Prabhat Kali, Hem Behag, etc.

KIRAN VERMA : SYMBOL OF AESTHETICS IN PAINTING

Kiran Verma, born in Marwar Junction, has been greatly inspired by the state in which she spent her youth. Her paintings reflect the immense contribution that Rajasthan has made in choosing here themes and colour schemes.

Kiran's interest in art evolved during her childhood. She was especially fascinated by the colourfully-dressed women working in the fields whose faces radiated happiness. While returning from school Kiran would inevitably stop and watch the women for hours and sketch their activities in her exercise books. Her weakness was to sketch beautiful, attractive women because, as she says, "I am fascinated by real beauty". Her interest led her to choose drawing as one of the subjects in the higher secondary board examination and while her formal education included a double M.A. (English, Music) she never dreamt of becoming a formal painter.

After her marriage to a goverment officer, she came to Delhi, and worked under a famous painter S. Krishnan during the 1970s.

Later, she studied Fine Arts and Painting at the Barrow's school of Art in Georgetown, Guyana. Here she was able to learn the Western style of art. As Kiran puts it, "it was here that I gained knowledge of the anatomy, perfected my teachnique and also took a realistic approach to nature which helped me improve my style of art"

Kiran spent nearly four months at the Ranthambore Tiger Sanctuary in Rajasthan. She spent an average eight hours of day watching the tigers and sketching them. It was here that she honed her skill in drawing tiger portraits. She has depicted various facets of tiger's activities - with its mate and cubs, staling its prey, at work and play, in the jungle, making love, drinking water, calm visage, by the riverside and so on. "The tiger is truly a royal animal and I am fortunate to have had this great experience to study the tiger and its lifestlye". Says Kiran.

Kiran have also done a number of paintings in the wash technique on "Women". "I decided to depict the woman as a strong, essential and intrinsic part of society. Because the 'woman' has proved herself more capable in administrative, academic and manual spheres," she avers.

The woman she has portrayed in her paintings are strong characters, from traditional lore, including Saraswati, Dampati, Urvashi, Mahakali etc. When asked why the faces look similar, she answers, "The model used in these paintings is a field worker in Rajasthan. Just as M.F. Hussain's paintings of horses are instantly recognised as uniquely his (due to his personalized style of drawing'painting them), I want people to recognize my paintings on women instantly by looking at the face".

While wash paintings, as the name implies, requires washing with water frequently after painting, Kiran washes her paintings eight times. The advantage of using this technique is that the colours become permanent and fixed and the paintings last for a longer period besides being aesthetically alluring. Due to an intricate process involved, not many Indian artists have adopted this technique.

She also plans a series on the customs and costumes of India through her paintings. "I strongly believe that the rich culture and powerful heritage of our country is preserved and stays alive through traditional paintings". (Condensed)

KALPANA CHITTARANJAN

KIRTI MANDIR : A UNIQUE TEMPLE

Kirti Mandir is an amalgam of two Hindi words "Kirti" (renown) and "mandir" (a place of worship). It is, therefore, the most befitting name for a place that is renowned the world over as the birthplace of a man who laid down his life for ahimsa (non-violence) and eternal truth or satya as he called it. He was none other than Mahatma Gandhi.

Bapu or Mahatma, had himself reiterated his quest for truth. "In my search after truth", he wrote, "I have discarded many new things. Old as I am in age, I have no feeling that I have ceased to grow inwardly or that my growth will stop at the dissolution of the flesh. What I am concerned with is my readiness to obey the call of Truth, my God, from moment to moment." This lean and frail looking man associated God with truth.

A visit to Porbandar virtually compels every Indian and foreigner to make a detour towards Kirti Mandir. Porbandar is a coastal town in the Indian state of Gujarat. This well planned city, besides having a busy port, also boasts of a mind-boggling variety of avian life.

Amongst the hustle and bustle, Kirti Mandir stands in the old and congested part of the city. A palatial building that stands as a memorial to Bapu.

The memorial was constructed by Nanaji Mehta in 1947. He built this specimen of modern architecture around the ancestral house of Gandhiji. After Gandhi's assassination on 30th of January 1948, it was thrown open to the public by Sardar Vallabhbhai Patel on 27th of May, 1950.

As one enters Kirti Mandir, a spacious open area with life-size statues of Mahatma Gandhi and Kasturba Gandhi, his wife, greet us. These are strategically placed under a dome in the shape of an open book. Below these statues, the two most prominent faiths of Bapu, "Truth" and 'Non-violence', are inscribed in bold letters. An unimportant aspect is the absence of any deijying symbols like incense lamps or garlands of flowers near the statues. The whole idea is to focus on the convictions and philosophy of Bapu, on the piousness of his teachings and the zest with which he strived to make society a better place.

The Serenity of the place is striking and its grandeur lies in its simplicity. The twelve feet high 26 marble pillars are adorned with the doctrines of Bapu in the devanagari script. Besides, his favourite bhajan (devotional song) and the main events in his life are also inscribed on the pillars.

The monument has six rooms made of the famous Porbandar stone. These rooms contain the writings of Gandhiji and his other memorabilia. There is also a library and an office that sells literature pertaining to Bapu's life.

The height of this memorial is 79 feet and an equal number of lighted clay lamps have been thoughtfully arranged on its summit. The number denotes the life span of Bapu and the lamps themselves denote the enlightenment that society received from his struggle to eradicate the vices of poverty and superstition.

The kirti Mandir Management which runs the Committee frequently orgnizes special prayer meetings where equal importance is given to all religions. Leprosy eradication programmes are also organized by the Committee. (Condensed)

NEERA

KISHAN MAHARAJ

(b. 1923) - Instrumentalist : Hindustani, Tabla of Poorab gharana; studied with Kanthe Maharaj; concert tours, Europe (1954); disc recordings.

KISHORE KUMAR : THE MULTIFACETED ENTERTAINER

Parallel to the triumverate of matinee idols Raj Kapoor, Dilip Kumar and Dev Anand ran the trio of top-notch singers Mukesh, Mohammad Rafi and Kishore Kumar, who playbacked for these and other actors from the late 1940s till after the mid- 1970s. Although other playback singers such as Hemant Kumar, Talat Mahmood and Manna Dey also playbacked for these heroes, it were the voices of Mukesh, Mohd. Rafi and Kishore Kumar that came to be identified with Raj Kapoor, Dilip Kumar and Dev Anand respectively.

After Mukesh and Rafi passed away in August, 1976, and July, 1980, respectively, the mantle of rendering a variety of outstanding songs for the new superstars such as Rajesh Khanna and Amitabh Bachchan, including, of course, Dev Anand, fell on Kishore, He covered himself with glory till October, 1987, when he also joined eternity.

Unlike Mukesh and Rafi, Kishore acted in a good number of movies too, produced both by himself and others, in which he himself sang his songs. He also wrote some lyrics and scored music for a few of his films. Besides his comedies such as Jhumroo, he made some serious films as well, like Door Gagan Ki Chhaon Mein (1964) and Door Ka Raahi (1972), which he himself directed.

Following the example of his eldest brother, the senior thespian Ashok Kumar, who was then an established hero in Mumbai, Kishore also migrated from Khandwa (in the Indian state of Madhya Pradesh) to the tinsel town with a dream to become a singing hero. Born in 1929, he had just stepped out of his teens when he made this move. Endowed with a melodious voice, he had started singing from an early age. He was encouraged to sing like the great K.L. Saigal, whom he revered as his idol and guru in absentia.

In Mumbai, he tried his luck as a singer at the All India Radio where, interestingly, for his audition he was assisted on the tabla by none other than the future cine genius Raj Kapoor. Kishore's first solo under maestro S.D. Burman, under who tutelage he achieved great heights later, was indeed recorded for Raj Kapoor in Pyar (1950).

Earlier, he had sung his debut song "Jagmag jagmag karta nikla chaand poonam ka pyara" (Shining and glowing the full moon has come out) for Dev Anand in Ziddi (1948) under the baton of Khemchand Prakash.

His early films- between 1949 and 1952 - included Rim Jhim, Andolan, Baazi, Bhai-bhai, Naujawan, Chham Chhama Chham and Kafila.

His playback and on-screen singing was often marked by his unique style of yodelling, inspired by the European singer Jimmy Rogers. He also exhibited an expertise in effecting voice modulations to mimic male and female protagonists of all ages, including cherubic children, ebulient youth and coughing foggies. He gave ample proof of such singing in movies like Half Ticket, Pehli Tarikh, Adhikar, New Delhi, Bahar, Ladka-Ladki, Manmauji, Naya Andaz, Dilli Ka Thug, Bawarchi and Padosan.

On the first of every month the External Service of Sri Lanka Broadcasting Corporation relays its 30 minute programme of old film songs at 7.30 a.m. The programme inevitably opens with Kishore's evergreen number "Khush hai Zamana aaj pehli tarikh hai" (The world is happy today as it is the first of the month - a payday and a gay-day).

The music of this song, written by Qamar Jalalabadi was scored by Sudhir Phadke for the film Pehli Tarikh.

In his evergreen comedy Chalti Ka Naam Gaadi, all three brothers- Ashok, Anup and Kishore - featured along with Madhubala. The film directed by Satyam Bose, had its music scored by S.D. Burman and was a roaring hit.

S.D. Burman's refreshingly innovative music in Aaradhana (1969) not only catapulated Rajesh Khanna to superstardom but also established Kishore Kumar as India's numero uno playback singer. There was no looking back thereafter and Kishore continued to captivate his listeners with a variety of songs for almost all the leading heroes and sang under the baton of all the leading music maestros.

He was a natural actor who converd a wide range of human emotions through his rib-tickling comedy on one hand and poignant roles on the other. However, he regarded singing rather than acting as his real passion. In fact, it was for his singing that he won eight Filmfare awards from 1970 to 1987 and the Lata Mangeshkar Award of the Government of Madhya Pradesh in 1985.

Kishore Kumar was indeed a multifaceted entertainer. Besides being a splendid singer, he was an actor, lyricist, music director, script-writer, producer and director- all rolled into one. His multi-dimensional contribution to the Hindi cinema will endure perenially.

B. M. MALHOTRA

KISHORI AMONKAR

Kishori Amonkar is the tallest singer on the contemporary scene

KISHORI was groomed by her mother Mogubal Kurdikar. She is known mainly for her velvety-soft voice. Though she was taught the Jaipur-Attrauli style, she has strayed away from its rigidities. In the Jaipur- Attrauli 'gharana', the 'swara' and 'laya' are intertwined. Kishori has consciously deviated from this principle and incorporated leisurely 'alaaps'. in the exposition of the 'raag'. Kishori has been a major influence for the female singers of the young generation. Many youngsters are content imitating her style of voice projection as well as 'raag'-elaboration.

KITE - FLYING FESTIVAL

India is fast becoming a venue of international kite flying. From 10-11 August 1993, an international kite flying Festival was held at at the majestic Umaid Bhavan Palace Jodhpur. This festival attracted aficionados from seven countries including India, U.S.A., Canada, Germany, Singapore, Malaysia and Japan. The festival started with Banu Shah of India flying 400 kites fitted on the cords one by one. Soon they were joined by various trends, some flying at a safe height, while Indian kites are made exclusively of paper, the foreign kites are made of nylon, the material used for making parachutes.
(Adopted)

C. P. RAJENDRAN.

KODAIKANAL : A RESORT WITH A DIFFERENCE

Known variously as the "Princess of Hill Stations" and the Switzerland of the East, Kodaikanal is the sole hill station in India to have been founded during the British Raj by Americans. In fact as History has it, it was only by sheer accident that Kodaikanal ever became a hill station. The American Madura Mission was founded in 1834 in the temple city of Madurai. Within ten years of its founding its missionaries were looking for a hill station for health reasons. They finally chose Kodaikanal on the advice of an Englishman, Mr. Fane, who also helped them build their first houses. By 1850, 20 members of the Madura mission were well ensconsed here and thriving. The first fabulous structure which was constructed here was the church.

Although built in 1916, the Law's Ghat Road in Kodaikanal is exceptionally attractive, passing through plantations of citrus fruits, coffee, black pepper, vines and tapica and overlooking waterfalls and reservoirs. On the way one also comes across in plentiful yield Kodaikanal oranges and avocados.

Eight kilometres before Kodaikanal is the Silver Cascade, a spectacular waterfall in the rains and one of the important spots in this hill station, Kodaikanal's pride is its lake, with a 8 Km circumambulatory promenade. During the holiday season the lake is dotted with boats filled with raucous crowds enjoying the pleasures of an otherwise placid lake. Kodaikanal is at its spectcular best in May when its boughs are laden with fruits and flowers.

The best flower show on earth is laid out by nature when the Kuriniji blooms here once in 12 years, carpeting the hillside with its pale blue. A one-km climb from the main bazaar brings you to Coaker's walk, cut from the hillside in 1867 by Lieutenant Coaker of the Royal Engineers. The footpath offers glorious view of the tallest mountain in the area, the volcano shaped Perumal Malai standing at 8,005 feet. There are several 'walks' which are really paths cut into the mountainside. One of them leads to Levin's stream and waterfall and one can look over the 656-feet high Snake Falls. Then there is the Dolphin's Nose and the Echo Valley.

The hill station also boasts of 18 - pole golf course. (Condensed)

RAMCHANDAR PENTUKAR

'KOH-I-NOOR' : THE CHEQUERED JOURNEY OF

Koh-i-Noor, the ever sought after glittering diamond, changed hands from ruler to ruler, as is evidenced by the history of India. This diamond was taken away by the East India Company as part of the Treaty of Lahore after the Punjab armies had surrendered. The Treaty was signed on March 29, 1849, by Maharaja Dalip Singh from the Punjab side and Lord Dalhousie representing the East India Company.

An inch-and-a-half in length and an inch in width an regards the antiquity and the ownership of the Koh-i-Noor, the Mountain of Light. It is believed that the diamond was the eye of a Hindu god. Legend has it that Karna (of Mahabharata) wore it on his right arm in the battle of Kurukshetra. The next historical reference to it is that the Mughal ruler Babur acquired it from the Raja of Gwalior as a result of victory. Babur's son, the luckless Humayun, gifted it to the Shah of Iran for giving him asylum. Shahjehan either acquired it from the Shah on payment or he purchased it from a diamond merchant Mir Jumla when he was the Governor of Dakhan (Deccan). The general belief was that Koh-i-Noor was mined in Golconda, near Hyderabad (Andhra Pradesh). According to the French traveller Tavernier, himself a jeweller, the diamond weighted 420 carats in the reign of Aurangzeb when he saw it embedded in the Peacock Throne. Surprisingly, no harm came to the Koh-i-Noor during the battle of succession between the four sons of Shahjehan to which Tavernier is an eye-witness. The French traveller also states that the diamond was cut in a rose-from and weighted 900 carats when rough.

The Koh-i-Noor thus remained with the Mughal dynasty till Nadir Shah invaded Delhi when Mohammad Shah Rangeela, an incompetent and a weak ruler ruled Delhi. Nadir Shah had already decided to possess the great diamond but he could not know where exactly it was. It was certainly not embedded in the Peacock Throne at that time which he had already acquired. His spies told him that Rangeela kept the diamond in his turban. Nadir Shah forced Rangeela to give his daughter in marriage to the former's son. After the nuptials, Nadir Shah said: "Now we are brothers, According to Iranian ritual, brothers must exchange turbns". And without waiting for Rangeela's response, he removed the Mughal Emperor's turban and put his own turban on his head. This happened in 1739.

Ahmad Shah Abdali in a battle in 1747 removed the diamond from the dead body of Nadir Shah. Thereafter, he took it away to Kabul and ultimately Shah Shuja happened to possess it.

When Maharaja Ranjit Singh established his empire in Punjab, Koh-i-Noor was with Shah Shuja. From his very boyhood, Ranjit Singh had two ambitions: one to acquire the Koh-i-Noor and the other to get back the Gates of Somnath temple taken away by Mahmud of Ghazni. When Shah Shuja faced rebellion, his wife Wafa Begum pleaded with Ranjit Singh to rescue her husband. She said that she would surrender the Koh-i-noor if her husband was delivered to her safely in Lahore. The Maharaja agreed and sent Dewan Mokham Chand, his ablest general, to free the Shah from Shergarh fort. The Shah was rescued from a dungeon and brought to Lahore where he joined his wife at Mubarak Haveli, a special Guest House for the Afghan refugee family.

Koh-i-Noor was its Persian name. The Afghans called it "Shah Heera". Ranjit Singh's court historian also called it by the same name. When Shah Shuja was reminded of his wife's promise he was first reluctant to talk on the subject. Then he said that he had pawned the diamond to a banker in Kabul, and that he would take about two months to deliver it. Ranjit Singh granted him the time.

Two days before the expiry of the two-month deadline, Shah Shuja invited the Maharaja to Mubarak Haveli. The Maharaja went-in-state and a document was signed on June 1, 1813, and the diamond was presented by the exiled Afghan ruler to the Maharaja of Punjab. According to some historians, the Maharaja paid a huge amount to Shah Shuja as a token of goodwill. The diamond remained in the custody of Ranjit Singh from June 1, 1813, to June 27, 1839, when he died. The last wish of the Punjab ruler on his death-bed was that the "Shah Heera" be longed at the Temple of Juggunnathji at Puri in Orissa. But that was not to be. Soon thereafter, Ranjit Singh slipped into a coma never to regain his consciousness.

Dalip Singh was the seventh son of the Maharaja and the last of the survivors in his family. He was proclaimed the Maharaja of Punjab in February, 1844, when he was under six years of age. At the time of annexation of Punjab by the British, he was not even eleven. In lieu of the vast kingdom of Punjab which yielded a surplus revenue of 500,000 Pound Sterling a year, according to a signed letter by Maharaja Dalip Singh in The Times, London dated September 8, 1862, His Highness was given a compensation of 400,000 of the Company's Rupees. Koh-i-Noor was surrendered and Fatehgarh in Uttar Pradesh was chosen as the temporary residence of the young Maharaja who was allowed to retain the title of Maharaja Dalip Singh Bahadur. An English tutor Victor Logan was chosen to indoctrinate the young mind. Within six months, he was converted to Christianity. When his long beautiful hair were cut, they were presented to Mrs. Logan. In the words of Lord Dalhousie, the country was conquered and dynasty destroyed.

The Koh-i-Noor reached London through the British Warship HMS Media on June 29, 1850, while Dalip Singh reached London by a special boat in 1854. When the 15-year old Maharaja was presented to Queen Victoria who was then 35, she liked him at first sight. An entry in the Queen's diary records:

"After luncheon we received the young Maharaja Dalip Singh, the son of Ranjit Singh who was deposed by us after the annexation of Punjab. He has been carefully brought up chiefly in the hills, and was baptised last year, so that he is a Christian. He is extremely handsome and speaks English fluently and has a pretty, graceful, dignified manner. He was beautifully dressed and covered with diamonds. I always feel so much for these poor deposed princes".

The Maharaja became a frequent visitor to the Buckingham Palace. One day the Queen suddenly took him by the arm and said:

"Maharaja, I have something to show you".

Before he could understand what was happening, he found the Koh-i-Noor was once again in his grasp and the Queen was asking him if he thought it was improved and if he would have recognized it again.

The Maharaja looked critically at the reduced diamond and turned it over and over again. After a thoughtful few moments and nostalgia for the old days, he moved very respectfully towards the queen and said:

"It is to me, Ma'am, the greatest pleasure, thus to have the opportunity, as a loyal subject, of myself tendering to my sovereign the Koh-i-Noor".

Dalip Singh was sanctioned an allowance of Rs. 15,000 a year against the advice of the British Government. He was also given the staus of a European Prince and a title of "His Serene Highness". There are some historians who believe that the Queen always felt guilt whenever she wore the Koh-i-Noor. And as such she persuaded the Maharaja to formally present the diamond to her.

K. K. KHULLAR

KOKKARE BELLUR BIRD PARADISE

The small village of Kokkare Bellur in the Karnataka State of India is a paradise for bird watchrs where they can research and investigate the behaviour of the Painted Storks and the Grey Pelicans.

The Painted Storks and Grey Pelicans are migratory birds and about 2000 of them come to this village in December every year, making about 1000 nests on trees. They nest here, lay eggs and look after their young until they are old enough to fend for themselves. By June, this cycle of procreating and rearing their young is completed and the birds fly away from the village.

The Stork is called "Kokkare" in the local language and the village took its name after these birds. Mahadev, an elderly villager, says, "From time immemorial, these birds have been coming to this place, and we have been living together amicably". It was as natural for Mahadev as having cows, goats or hens in his village.

Interestingly enough, these birds build their nests only within the jurisdication of the village and they inhabit not a single tree outside the village. Says Mahadev, "The villagers consider these birds as friends and do not disturb them. Nobody climbs these trees or uses them for any other purpose during the nesting period. At the slightest sign of danger, these birds vomit fish and water which they store in their long necks and bellies and fly away". Peaceful co-existence.

Perhaps the fish in the Shimsha river, which flows nearby, attracts these birds. Yet, even when there is no water and fish in the Shimsha river, the birds fly off to distant places to look for water and fish bring it back to fed their young in Kokkare Bellur.

It is a real treat to see the gliding and hovering of these birds over the trees, which are literally crawling with their young ones. When the huge pelican makes a landing, all of its young ones open their beaks for a feed of water and fish. The colourful Storks have pink, black and white feathers, which form, at the top of their neck to create a beautiful bow. It is a sight to see these birds slightly spread their wings to protect their young from the burning sun. The young storks sit under their mother's shadows and blissfully play as the mother calmly bears the brunt of the scorching heat.

The village lies between Bangalore and Mysore in southern India. There are about 300 huts with a population of over 2000 people. Their main crop is paddy, maize and sericulture. The Indian government compensates the owners of the trees where birds nest.

JOGINDER CHAWLA

KOLYACHA

Social folk dance, fishermen's dance, indigenous, Konkan coast, western India, Kolyacha, enactment, rowing of a boat, women hand handkerchiefs to their male partners when move, sliding steps, for wedding parties, young Kolis dance, streets, carrying utensils for newly wed couple, join dance at climax.

KOMKALI, SHIVAPUTRA SIDDHARAMAYYA (KUMAR GANDHARAVA)

(b. 1924) - D. Mus. (Hons.); vocalist : Hindustani, Khayal of Gwalior and Bhindi Bazar gharanas; studied with B.R. Deodhar, Anjanbai Malpeker; concert tours Nepal (1967), East Africa (1961); disc. recordings.

KOMALA VARADAN A MULTI - FACETED PERSONALITY

A child progidy in Bharatanatyam, a classical dance form of South India, Komala Varadan is an artist of many facets. She has not only performed in different parts of the country but in different Indian languages too, integrating its people and culture.

Komala has choreographed many new and rare pieces in the Bharatnatyam idiom. Special mention can be made of two mono ballets on the Buddha theme and the more recent, Ram Charit Manas. Stages in 1990, it was a full Bharatnatyam recital based on selected verses from the priceless work by Tulsidas, a great Indian poet who wrote Ramayana. In this dance recital Komala traced the history of Lord Rama from his birth to Pattabhishekam (his being crowned king). "If I were to write on my art and choose one most satisfying creation, I would choose the presentation of Ram Charit Manas", she says candidly.

She selected different verses from different poems of great poets in different Indian languages.

Born in Tamil Nadu, she was intiated into this art by Cheyyoor Thhiruvengada Natuvannar. She later became the student of Guru Vazhuvoor Ramaiah Pillai. Since then, she has not looked back. Widely appreciated and honoured, she reminisces foundly, "My dance has inspired another form of expression within me - the urge to paint".

From portraits to landscapes and figures, Komala has evolved a distinct style of her own. "as a dancer, I saw and felt the need to make a statement", say Komala. And her paintings too are bold statement on her perception of various dance movements. Many of her dance numbers are also her paintings. For example, Krishna's dance on Kalinga, Shiva as Natraja, Durga etc. Her first painting Nartaki (dancer) was executed in 1974. Exploring dance movements, at first those of classical styles and later of folk and other movements, Komala has to her credit numerous solo shows all over the country.

A part from presenting dance, both as a performing and visual art, Komala is also a photographer or international repute. Provoked by beauty she clicks all hues of nature. She recently used her nature slides while performing for 'Prakriti'.

More than her desire to dance, paint and photograph, it's her compulsion to write which draws out her inherent quality of understanding the human relationships. She writes both in English and Tamil. All her stories are simple and down to earth. "I am moved by what is heppening around me. But my stories are not message-oriented", she says softly.

Komala, who writes novels too, is more involved in writing short stories. She has to her credit more than a hundred short stories.

ASHIMA KAUL BHATIA

KONARK SUN TEMPLE

Orissa, unlike many other parts of India, has the unique destinction of possessing innumerable temples illustrating the history of a well-defined Kalinga order from its very inception to decline. The Sun Temple of Konark Marks the highest point of achievement of that order. Even in its present ruined state - it lost its searing tower long ago - it stands in majestic dignity in the midst of a vast stretch of sand which further emphasizes its grandeur.

The word "Konark" is composed of two word elements: "Kona" meaning corner and "Arka" meaning the sun. This corner on the east seacoast houses the ruins of this Sun Temple exquisitely built to resemble a gigantic chariot with intricately carved wheels, columns and panels.

The legend has it that King Narasimha Deva-I of Ganga dynasty had ordered this temple to be built as a royal proclamation of political supremacy of his dynasty. Built by 1200 master architects, sculptors and craftsmen of Orissa, symbolising the Orissan temple architecture and art, the Sun Temple of Konark has drawn the attention of art lovers the World over and finds a place in the World Heritage list.

The temple appears as a massive pyramidal block of stone standing distinctively tall amidst all other structures nearby. As one enters one faces the now roofless dance hall on a raised platform, next to which is the audience hall. The main temple is in the ruins.

The temple was conceived to resemble a giant-sized chariot with 24 wheels attached to the base and seven horses harnessed in front of the entrance hall. It was nothing but a symbolic representation of the abode of the Sun god, whose movements are marked by division of time into months, weeks, days, hours, minutes and seconds. Each of 24 wheels has eight spokes and one axlehead, bearing scenes of daily life.

An annual cultural festival is held at the site of the temple. This festival has already become a meeting ground of various classical dance forms of India.

PREM KAPOOR

KONDAPALLI WHERE WORLD FAMOUS TOYS ARE BORN

Toys belong to the genre of never fading away treats. It is something that no grown-up ever outgrows. It can still bring back a smile on many a matured, professional face. This probably reflects the child in every man. Though, traditionally, wooden toys are made in several parts of the country, but one of the very famed such toys are the Kondapalli toys.

These toys derive their name from the village where they are made, Kondapalli, near Vijayawada in Andhra Pradesh. Beautiful objects are carved from locally available softwood. The unique feature of these toys is that they are incredibly light and are very simplistic in their portrayal; they depict things commonly found in villages - animals, birds, trees, places of worship, woman folk in villages, playing children, etc.

Though the origin of the toys is somewhat obscure, some people believe that the craft was brought to Kandapalli by craftsmen from Rajasthan or Madhya Pradesh. These craftsmen in all probability migrated from their lands and made this place their home. The patronage provided by the kings and noblemen helped their craft to flourish.

The wood used to carve these toys is called "ponikki Wood". It is basically a soft wood which is available locally. The wood of a young tree is referred to as "tella ponikki" while that of older trees is referred to as "nella ponikki". And it is the "tella ponikki" that is used for the toys.

The sap within the tree has to be dried before it is ready for carving. In the drying process the wood is first cut and then slowly dried in the heat of paddy husk and saw dust; only then it is ready to be carved. The carving is done with instruments known as "Bhavadhar". First the figure is carved; each limb of the toy is carved separately and joined together with gluey tamarind seed paste. Any defect of the toy is also rectified with this. Once the toy is carved it is then coated with a solution of lime paste and gum resins. The toy is now ready to be painted. The coating of lime paste solution ensures that the wood does not absorb the paint. Painting is done using chemical paints. Earlier, vegetable dyes were used to give an everlasting coat to these toys. The prohibitive cost of vegetable dyes and their not being available readily has resulted in these craftsmen switching to cheaper chemical options. When a sheen is required on the toys, enamel paint is used. The toy is now ready for sale. The entire process is not very time consuming. The craft can be best described as a domestic enterprise in which all members of the family participate. A craftsman can carve as many as one dozen toys in a day. The carving is done by menfolk while the painting is taken care of by women and children.

One of the most well-known Kondapalli toys is the Ambari elephant. This blue coloured traditional elephant is the distinct feature of these toys. Elephants are also made in traditional black colour. N. Sridhar, a craftsman residing in Vijayawada, says old wood "nella ponikki" is preferred for these elephants. Other themes include Krishna playing the flute, cows grazing, houses, trees, kings atop an elephant being taken in a ceremonial procession, omnipresent dashavataara, and women performing household chores. Apart from these traditional pieces, new ones have also been included like temples, man collecting toddy from palm trees, etc. N. Sridhar proudly displays a bust of three freedom fighters made in softwood. He also made an astounding replica of the Assembly Hall. It had been given a finish with enamel white paint and the wood alone weighed approximately 35 kgs. The whole piece was further encased in a glass cover.

Younger craftsmen are now experimenting with newer styles while continuing to produce age old traditional toys. These toys are also being exported, though there is a large domestic demand as well.

CHITRA BALASUBRAMANIAM

KUCHAMANI KHYALS

Lachiram originator: exponant of Khyals, evolved own style in collaboration with existing ones. Common features are, drama in form of dances; predominance of singing; difficult technique of instrumental music; playing, dancing on big platform, i.e. manch.

Characeristic features of Lachiram's style, simplicity of language used in songs; use of new refreshing tunes; intricate facial expressions while acting; use of new themes for dramas. Lachiram composed ten khyals; prominent being "Chand Milagari", "Ridmal", Meera-Mangal".

Performance starts from evening till morning; people from distant villages assemble to witness great open show; female roles played by males, musical accompaniment given by drummers, shahnaiwala, dholak; sarangiwala, songs shrill, sung by dancers; musicians in the background give support to dancers in singing.

Kyhals of Lachiman still played; people not very enthusiastic of shows because of length, monotoneous themes khyals of Shekhavati:

Manu Ram greatest exponent; left legacy of popular khyals, eg, heer Ranjah; Harichand, Bharthari, Jaydev Kankali, Dhola Maru, Ahaldeo.

Nanu Ram belonged to Chidawa; Muslim by caste; main characteristics of his plays, intricate foot work; difficult style of singing; elaborate orchestral music of harmonium, Sarangi, shahnai, flute, nakkara, dholak; low height of stage; absence of elaborate decoration. Dulia, his greatest disciple participants from Mirasi, Dholi and Sangara communities; however no restriction for others.

Nanu's, Dulia's khyals played by other non-professional groups; play undertaken for fun, self expression.

M. N. UPADHYAY

KUCHIPUDI

Kuchipudi owes orgin, small village of Kuchipudi (Kuchelapuram) Andhra Pradesh, from originated 17th century by Sidhyendra Yogi, creator dance drama Bhama Kalapani. Story of Satyabhama, jealous wife of Lord Krishna, taught art to brahmin boys of Kuchipudi, performed 1675 for Nawab of Golconda, pleased, granted Kuchipudi to Brahmin Bhavathas for preservation of this art. Even in 20th century, every Brahmin, Kuchipudi, expected to perform, once, role of Satyabhama, as an offering to Lord Krishna.

Dance begins with worship rituals, male dancer moves, sprinkling holy water, incense burned, Indra-dhuaja (flagstaff of God Indra) planted on stage, women sing, dance with worship lamps, worship of Ganesha followed, the bhagavatha sings invocations to goddesses Sarasvati (learning), Lakshmi (wealth), Parasakti (parent energy); in between chanting drum syllables.

It is based on stories from the Mahabharata, Puranas and other epics. Being a dance drama, it incorporates elements of both tandava (strongly masculine) and lasya (graceful and feminine movements) elements.

The element of abhinaya, or facial expression, is very strong. Compared to Bharatanatyam and odissi, it is a more realistic and contemporary dance form.

Major dancers 20th century, Guru Chinta Krishnamurthi, Vadantam Satyanarayana, Yamini Krishnamurthi, and Radha and Rajareddy.

The inspiration for the Kuchipudi style of dancing is found in the realms of Bharata Natyam which has become a vital component of Indian cultural heritage. Though fountains from which both the styles have sprung are common, Bharata Natyam is more ritualistic as compaired to the romantic under currents in Kuchipudi. The Natya Sastra of Bharata dating back to 500 B.C. was a condifation of the techniques and philosophy of dancing in India.

The temple was the centre of dancing and the Devdasis were dedicated women who danced in the temple-yard to please the Lord. With the passage of time the instirution of Davdasis did not live up to the noble traditions it had set up. To arrest the degeneration in dancing and to promote dance in its highest sense, a number of scholars attempted to organise institutions for the preservation of Indian dancing. Such a movement started from Kuchipudi situated near Masulipatnam in Andhra Pradesh. The place was renowned for its cultural traditions and was the centre of music and dance. Inspired by Nagarjunakoda and Amaravathi and thriving under royal patronage, the fine arts of Andhra reached remarkable standards and were admired all over the country. Treatises on dance were also written and the contributions of Jaya ba Nayaka and Vennalakanti Suramatya have remained mile-stones in the realm of Indian Dance.

In 1502 A.D. a troupe of dancers from Kuchipudi performed at Vijayanagar. The Males of Kuchipudi dramatised mythological stories particularly from the Puranas, Ramayana, and Mahabharatha.

With the decline of the Vijayanagar empire, the Natya Acharyas and other learned men found encouragement under the royalty of Tanjore.

Siddhendra Yogi of Kuchipudi adopted the Parijatha Harana into the form of a dance-drama and it became one of the better known items of the Kuchipudi school. To ensure continued interest in dancing, Siddhendra Yogi asked the males of Kuchipudi to continue to practise dancing during their lives. True to the pledge, the Kuchipudi School of Dance was handed down from generation to generation.

The following items compose, the repertoire in the Kuchipudi School of Dance:

Bhamakalapam, Golla Kalapam, Prahlada Charithram, Usha Parinayam, Sashirekha Parinaya, Mohini Rukamangada, Haris Chandra, Goyopakhyanam, Rama Natakam and Rukmini Kalyanam.

The result of this admixture was the change of Parijathanataka into Bhamakalapam. In effect this resulted in enlarging the character of Satyabhama.

The art of make-up was simplified for Kuchipudi performances. A single coloured paint was used and was prepared from herbs, gums and stones. The leading characters, however, wore elaborate jewellery made of wood and coloured paper.

Kuchipudi is eminently suited for the exposition of the beauty and techniques, involved in Natya Shastra.

Kuravanci, dance-drama; lyrical beauty, Tamil Nadu; performed by four to eight women; gypsy fortune teller initiater; story, lady pining for lover; mixture, folk, classical types of Indian dance.

M. N. UPADHYAY

KULDIP SINGH JUS

While the contemporary Indian art definitely got its impetus from contemporary movements of art in Europe, it grew out of this stage fast enough by tying up its future with the National Movement, and consequently with the myriad of living folk-traditions that survived in India.

This was only to be expected as it was the peasantry that was the backbone of the anti-colonial movement. So its aesthetics too were likely to find a place in it. And artists like Nandalal Bose and Ramkinkar Baij (the son of a rural barber and masseuse) emerged as larger that life figures whose vision broadly dominates our art to this day.

However, once India became independent, its forms too evolved less self-consciously. A robust marriage between our folk expression and European expression took their place.

Along with this other trends emerged, taking the cue from our ritual arts, both in the evolution of abstract symbols as of icons. If the National Movement had helped our folk art attain a global importance by linking it with contemporary expression, independence has helped various other trends, drawn from our ritual arts and classical artistic expression to evolve a new life as well.

In this process, tantric art with its contemplative and dialectic symbolism has been replaced by neo-tantric - abstracts and the sign language of gaze and gesture. If the peasantry and its folk tradition gave the lead during the National Movement it was the new industrial classes that, with the bureaucracy not only revived old classical forms but linked our classical tradition with modern expression.

Paintings of Kuldip Singh Jus belong to this trend in our art. But it is interesting to not that he approaches the visual metaphor from the perspective of music rather than religious iconography, with the gesture taking over from the gaze and a sequence of gestures in the work of Jus to be remainded of his family's close connection with Ustad Amir Khan, the noted Khayal singer.

The Khayal concerns itself with structure and then pursues nuances of the basis of the original compositional framework, so it is with Jus' images. The main stress in on composition with the gestures highlighting nuances. It is interesting, how, just as in khayal, different clours begin to lose themselves in tones and we are drawn to the surfaces and textures which he has evolved over the years through his study of our traditional art.

But there his reliance on tradition ends. Tradition demands that the gaze has a primecy over the sign or the mudra. Jus challenges that with works in which he refuses to give to his figures heads or eyes. But it is interesting that Jus has been working on these forms for over ten years. This origin clearly lies in the importance gestures have as a means of communication in Indian society,

whose complexity demands a certian level of sophistication so that, as the saying goes, a wise man is one for whom a gesture is warning enough. And one who understands sign-language does not need to be told anything in plain speech. So Jus' paintings are statements of their own existence and reality which are to be understood directly. And they are produced in India, steeped in Indian reality and traditon.
(Condensed)

SUNEET CHOPRA

KUMUDINI LAKHIA - KATHAK DANCER

For a first time viewer, the Kathak form of classical Indian dance is an eyeful. The elegant swirling movements of the dancer, her gossamer like costume, the lightning pirouettes and the sudden statue-like friezes at the right moment of the rhythmic beat, appears surreal and entertaining. Only later, when one has watched a few more exposes, does the true meaning seem to sink in. Even later still, one begins to understand that Kathak as a dance form, if not about body movements but an emanation of energy that is spiritual and cohesive. Essentially a solo performance, some, like Kumudini Lakhia, have devised Kathak into a contemporary art form, to be danced by a highly trained and superbly coordinated group of dancers who have received their grooming and execution as a single unit, under a sigular guru or teacher. The best example of such an achievement in India is the Kadamb Centre of Dance and Music at Ahmedabad city, which is founded, nurtured and developed by guru and dancer, Kumudini Lakhia.

Established in 1963, the Kadamb Dance Centre, which Kumudini Lakhia runs, has on roll over three hundred dance aspirants. Their approach to the dance form is not one of stolid rigidity but of relevant innovations. They are spurred on by a desire to be creative, without tampering with the essential idiom of Kathak. Their themes are not strait jacketed apical and legendary in erpretations but veer around contemporary issues. At the same time, these manipulative poses and forms on stage do not deteriorate into crass gyrations, for each movement is intrinsic to the art. All this is strictly according to the instruction that the young dance use Kumudini Lakhia had herself received at the feet of her revered guru, Shambhoo Maharaj. In her art, which has had imbibed in totality, the dancer is suggestive, rather than explict.

More than all else, Kumudini and her troupe at Kadamb impress by the power of their art. On stage there is not a moment when the affair gets restive. This gives off a charismatic appeal so profound that it implies the entire personality and teaching style of Kumudini behn. This powerful approach to dance gives the lyrics being danced to, a myriad interpretation. It is not vigour alone that is used by the dancers for at times, a slight and subtle movement is enough to convey a world of meaning.

The very first venture into a creative group innovation, for Kumudini behn, dates back to the seventies. It was with her production, 'Dhabkar' a dance choreography involving a set of three performers, who had danced to the music of Atual Desai. The essential solo movements of Kathak were, for the first time, synchronised into a three fold unison and the presentation brought with it rave reviews from an electrified Ahmedabad audience. By the time 'Gat Gati' burst upon the scene, the unblemished classicism had been incorporated with rhythmic combinations of twos, threes, even eight multiples. The dancers executed this rhythm marvel through formations on stage and while one watched the amazing footwork of the dancers, one was struck by the precise coordination of the steps. Not one ankle bell was heard to sound askew as they depicted the gait of a graceful elephant or the shy, yet provocative ways of a velied woman in front of her lover.

It was not just dry footwork and formative stances that Kumudini behn had perfected. The art of narrative, that is intrinsic to Kathak, which is really a derivative from Katha or story, is also her forte. Her expressional dance number 'Chodo Chodo Bihari' is a highly interpretative piece. A lyric duo presentation of the thumri style, enacts a complaint being made against the pranks of Krishna to Mother Yashoda by a pair of distressed gopis. Besides traditional themes, Kumidini behn has also explored the depicition of topical issues through her dances. An outstanding work is "Setu" dealing with the physically and mentally handicapped. It was first brought on stage in 1987.

An even greater challenge to her dancing acumen is the manner in which she has sloughed off the dancer's chief tool, a glamorous appearance of stage. Instead of the conventional Kathak dancer's costume of lehenga or embroidered skirt and veil, the customary attire of the erstwhile courtesan, she has opted for a sleek unisex kurta and pyjama suit for her dance troupe. The clean lines and the single colour of the dress allows a clarity of dance lines. Even dancers are left free to expand and create on stage, uncluttered by frills and flounces.

Though she claims that Kathak is something to be perceived, it is not an illustrative form of perceiving that is central to her art. Kathak dance has to grow is the motto of this dancer.
(Condensed)

S. MAJUMDAR

KURAVANCI

Kuravanci, dance-drama; lyrical beauty, Tamil Nadu; performed by four to eight women;gypsy fortune teller initiater; story, lady pining for lover; mixture, folk, classical types of Indian dance.

KUTTAYATTAM : SANSKRIT THEATRE OF KERALA

A rich and flourishing tradition of staging classical Sanskrit plays has survived in its local variation in the picturesque state of Kerala, a narrow strip of bountiful land-running along the west coast of India adorned with numerous rivers, lush green fields and tall coconut palm trees.

Known as "Kutiyattam" its recorded history dates back to tenth century A.D. "Kuti" means together and 'attam' refers to acting, dancing rhythmic and stylized movements.

In short dramatic performances. "Kutiyattam" thus means ensemble acting.

Though Indian dramatic tradition is very ancient, the earliest extant dramatic works in Sanskrit belong to fourth century B.C. and Bhasa, their author, is the earliest known sanskrit dramatist. It is quite significant to not that though Bhasa's plays went into obvlivion in other parts of the country they survived in Kutiyattam performances in Kerala.

After Bhasa, a number of playwrights contributed to enrich Sanskrit dramatic literature. Prominent among them were Ashvaghosha, Kalidasa, Shudraka, Vishakhadatta, Shri Harsha and Bhavabhuti. After Bhavabhuti who was the last of the giants belonging to the eighth century A.D. the decline set in.

When exactly Sanskrit dramatic tradition reached Kerala is of known, however it is certain that in the tenth century king Kulashekhara Varman, who himself was a dramatist, with the help of his scholar friend named Tolan introduced a number of innovations in the mode and technique of staging Sanskrit plays. Out of their efforts arose a highly localised tradition of presenting Sanskrit plays on the stage.

They confined the performances of Sanskrit dramas to the theatres built in the temple premises, delegated the responsibility of enacting the plays to the members of Chakyar and Nambyar castes, introduced and encouraged the use of local Malayalam language by the jester figure Vidushaka to explain Sanskrit and Prakrit passages in the play. They also laid down the procedure of producing a number of popular plays and allowed the actors the liberty of introducing narrative material other than the actual text of the play.

Incorporating all these innovations, a local style of producing Sanskrit play emerged in Kerala in the tenth century A.D. under the name "Kutiyattam".

Apart from the plays of the authors mentioned earlier including Bhasa, the Chakyars took up for enactment other plays too like Ashcharyachudamani of Tapatisamvarana of Kulashekhara, Kalyanasaugandhika, Kalyana-saugandhika and Srikrishna charita by Neelakantha, Mattavilasa by Mahendra Vikram Varman and Bhagavadjjukiya of Bodhayana.

But the technique of presenting a play is so elaborate a and time consuming that never a full play is taken up for enactment. A single act of the play is selected for production and even then it takes several days for the play to come to an end. Even a Chakyar actor, with his stupendous mastery over translating every single word of the text into visual acting, if given sufficient scope, will take more than a month to complete the stage presentation of a single act.

Since ancient times Chakyars are known for their acting skills. They are mentioned in early Tamil epics. The male members of the Nambyar community are excellent musicians and instrumentalists, and provide musical score. The women folk of the community, known as Nangiar, enact female roles, sing songs on the state and play on small cymbals. When they present a solo performance enacting the Krishna story it is known as Nangiar Kuttu.

Chakyar, Nambyar and Nangiar come together to produce a play in Kuityattam style which is very elaborate and moving.

The specially designed and constructed Kuitiyattam theatre is known as Kuttambalam. They are raised in the temple premises. There are about sixteen such temple theatres in Kerala. The very well preserved one out of these is located in the premises of Vadakunatha temple at Trichur.

Kuttambalam, usually rectangular in its ground plant is a building with a huge sloping roof. The inner area is divided into two.

M. L. VARADPANDE

KUTTI KRISHNAN OF BOMBAY - KATHAKALI & BHARAT NATYAM ARTISTE

Shri Kuttikrishnan's is the story of an artiste who made his way up in the world of art in Bombay through hardwork and perseverance.

Coming to Bombay at the age 22, with nothing but his knowledge of and training in Kathakali and Bharata Natyam, Shri Kuttikrishnan started his Nritya Niketan in 1959 in Santacruz as an academy of dance. Simultaneously, he improved his own equipment by getting trained under Guru Kuppiah Pillai, Guru Mahalingam Pillai & Guru Kittappa Pillai.

During the last 35 years, Kuttikrishnan, besides giving solo performances himself, has trained up to 'arangetram' stage about 60 students, including one from Australia.

Born in a village near Badagara in North Malabar of Kerala, Kuttikrishnan has his early training in Kathakali under Asan Ramuni Nair who was attached to the Kathakali troupe of Kadattanad Kovilakam. After eight years of training he moved to Madras and joined the Natana Niketan of the late Guru Gopinath. Kuttikrishnan stayed in Thanjavur for three years for training in Bharat Natyam under Smt. Lakshmikantam.

Kuttikrishnan believes in the traditional gurukula system of instruction and hopes to develop his Nirtya Niketan of traditional lines.

(Condensed)

"L"

LAC JEWELLERY

Perhaps nowhere in the world people have loved to adorn themselves with ornaments and jewellery so much as in India. Of whatever material it may be, jewellery must be provided to women. Jewellery of different sorts of glass, or lac, or ivory or shell or gold or even silver, is worn in profusion by women of all classes.

LAC OR LAKH

Lac or lakh - a natural resin produced by crimson red tiny insects, is an important ancient Indian commodity. Two prominent products of these insects viz. the resin and the crimson-red-dye (lac-dye), have been well-known as raw materials used for decorative purposes, from time immemorial. The dye has been used by Indian women as alta, a decoration for hands and feet. It has also been used for dyeing silks to obtain a beautiful sparkling scarlet shade. In Ain-i-Akbari (1590), mention is made of the use of lac in varnishing public buildings, chicks, and as an inlaying material for glass chatons, beads and pearls on chariots, jewellery, furniture pieces and in brass artwares. The traditions have since then continued to this day when the use of lac in jewellery and in other handicrafts such as in wooden lacquerwares, brass artwares, needs appreciation and revival on a better scale, particularly in view of the recent increase in the aesthetic urge of the common man. Today's womenfolk, whose taste for colourful dress and jewellery is fast developing, can certainly find ample place for lac-jewellery.

DECOR AND OUSPICIOUSNESS

Lac jewellery besides providing a decorative appeal and lending a touch of charm and delicacy to the apprearance of women folk also has some mythological significance in certain regions. For instance, lac-bangles and necklaces are used by women in Rajasthan, Madhya Pradesh Uttar Pradesh, Hyderabad and Bihar in India, and Multan, Lahore, Gujranwala, Hyderabad in Pakistan, which are also the chief manufacturing centres for lac jewellery. It is said in these regions that wearing of lac-bangles by women of every caste and status is essential not only for decoration but also for the well-being of their husbands. The cost varies greatly according to the quality of the bangles. One can have a pair of lac bengles say from 25 np. to Rs. 25.00 depending upon whether the bangles are of plain colour designs or studded with beautiful multicoloured glass chatons, beads or pearls. In local village markets in these regions one often come across a bangle maker making lac bangles on the spot with simple but colourful and attractive designs.

THE CRAFTSMENSHIP

Making of lac-bangles and other items of lac-jewellery is a hereditary craft mostly practised by Mohammedans popularly known as 'Lakheras' in Rajasthan and also by Hindus, known as 'Lakshakars' in Madhya Pradesh. Craftsmen in lac jewellery in other regions come chiefly from these two places, besides a few local ones. The materials used in making lac-bangles are generally lac or shellace, soapstone powder, white pigment (lithopone), various shades of water soluble dyes and glass chatons, beads, pearls etc. Lac is mixed with siapstone powder, while melting it, and a rubber-like brown mass is obtained. This brown mass while hot is mixed with lac colour (rung) mattis (Lac + White pigment dye) to obtain coloured sticks in various sizes which are then moulded into suitable sized bangles by means of most ordinary tools. In case of bangles with simple designs, a number of such sticks are joined together and made to size. In the case of more complicated designs, glass chatons etc. are treated and arranged in one, two or three lines on the plain bangles, when lac melts and fixes the chatons on them. All this requires a great deal of skill and experience on the part of the craftsman. As this is a hereditary craft, a visit to a craftsman's home reveals the fact that almost every member of his family, whether young or old, receives thorough training and participates in the manufacture of some or the other item of lac-jewellery in the house which serves as a living place as well as a workshop-cum-showroom.

In the manufacture of gold-like jewellery, such as necklaces and bracelets etc. mostly from Madhya Pradesh, lac is used alone or in a mixture with yellow or red dyes and is coated on aluminium foils which are pasted on rods made out of a mixture of resin and certain clay matter. Designs are imprinted by pressing these rods, while still warm, against specially prepared wooden moulds. The imprinted rods are then cut into beads of suitable sizes. Colourful threads are later on put through these beads to make necklaces and other pieces of jewellery. Such lac-jewellery items are quite cheap and at the same time, have the advantage of looking like gold-jewellery.

The attractive and colourful desings in lac jewellery are not only in demand in different parts of this country but some of the items find ready market in European and Far Eastern countries thus contributing to the livelihood of thousands of craftsmen engaged in this industry.

O. P. RATRA

LADAKH'S CULTURE HERITAGE

Inspite of its extreme weather conditions, long distances and inadequate means of communication, Ladakh has always been a land of gay festivals and crowded fairs. Most of the festivals, no doubt, revolve round religious themes. The exuberance, make them great occasions of rejoicing and joy.

Losar, "The New Year Day' is the most well-known festival of the Buddhists. The celebrations are spread over a period of fifteen days. Surprisingly, the new year celebrations begin in the tenth month of the Bodhi calendar, which falls sometime in December. Formerly the Losar festival commenced on the first day of the Bodhi New Year. But during the 16th century Chewang Namgyal, a Raja of Ladakh, decided to celebrate it two months earlier in view of an imminent battle. Since then that date is being adhered to. However, Mr. S.S. Gergan, a renowned Historian of Ladakh, differs with this view and holds that since times immemorial Ladakhis have been celebrating this festival on the same dates.

The celebrations begin with the extensive illumination of houses. The Losar also coincides with the birthday of Chonkhapa, the Buddhist reformer of the 15th century. It is essential for all the members of the family to be present at home on this occasion. The important feature of the celebration is the mock-fights of boys who go out in groups brandishing burning torches and conduct mock battles in open place outside the village area. This event has great attraction for the children. They make bonfire of dry grass and burning sticks. Then one of the boys relates some traditional folk tales which have been passed on from generation to generation. This event goes on till the first date of 11th month. During these days the local musician called 'Mon' keeps fast and goes around with a drum playing a very special tune at all the holy places and also the houses in the village. In return, the zamindars provide him with flour and other eatables.

From the first of the 11th month onward the ritual of the replacement of the 'Lhato' the seat of the family deity, is performed. 'Lhato' is a bundle of juniper branches erected on a small square platform on the roof of the chapel. Horns of ibex, sheep, deer and a number of arrows and scarves are tied around the branches of juniper. In some cases two or three families may have on 'Lhato' in common. The process of the replacement of 'Lhato' with a new one is called 'Lhasol'. It is done early in the morning by the male members of the family. A he-goat and she-goat are selected and washed thoroughly. Then, they are carried to the roof near the 'Lhato' where their ears stitched with small pieces of ribbons and red colour is applied on their bodies. The goats then are made to drink a bit of 'Chang' (Local bareley wine) and their faces are put to smoke of incense burnt for the purification of 'Lhato'.

Immediately after the 'Lhasol' a male member goes to the family cemetry with a big semi-circular cake of flour. He lights a lamp on the grave and places thereon small pieces of cake, meat and other eatables. He then loudly calls the names of the deceased members of the family invoking them to take the meal. This ritual is called 'Mesol'. Having completed it he joins a festive gathering where chang and cakes are served. On the first day of 11th month a horse race is arranged in the village. A small target is set at some distance and each horseman galloping his horse tries to hit it. Whosoever hits it first is honoured by the ladies who offer them chang. Two clowns known as 'Lama Zigu' amuse the people with their jokes and antics. They put on quaint dress and smear flour on their faces. At the end, they entertain people with dances and songs. Then, to the accompaniment of the musicians, they start visiting the houses in the villages and perform certain rites to ward-off evils. This continues for nine days. During this period the houses are decorated with flour painting of sun, moon etc. This custom is attributed to Bon religion, which was professed by people of Ladakh before the advent of Buddhism. The entire villages wears a new look and the people are in a festive mood. On the 9th day the horse race is repeated in the same fashion. Then the flour images of an old man and an old woman symbolising evil are thrown at a distant spot. Finally people gather in a field, where they sing and dance. The two clowns after taking bath in cold water of the stream put on their best

clothes and join the crowd at the field. The elderly men and women spend the night exchanging visits while others busy themselves in singing and dancing. The mode of celebration of the festival varies from village to village but the basic features are the same.

Two dances are specially associated with Losar Shondance and Koshen-dance The Shon-dance was formerly performed before the Raja of Ladakh by the members of some high specialised familes - one member generally representing one family. Koshendance was presented at Leh bazaar led by 'Lardak' head of horseman at the end of the horse-race.

At Leh the festival is characterised with exchange of greetings and giving feasts to Muslims and Christians. Two decades back, events were market by a 15-day long festive programme at Leh palace where women performed dances. The horserace followed for a week preceded by a procession of horse-riders led by the Raja of Ladakh.

Id is celebrated by Muslims of Ladakh with the traditional enthusiasm and reverence as in other parts of the country but one distinguishing feature of the celebration is that every Muslim house is visited by his Buddhist friends to offer Id greetings.

The festivals and fairs of all the monasteries are celebrated in winter months except Hemis festival popularly known as Hemis Chhishu. These not only provide fun and frolic to the people but cater to their religious needs as well. Two-day Hemis festivals is celebrated on the 10th and 11th date of Bodhi 5th month (which generally coincides with June or July) in the 350 year old famous Hemis monastery on the birth-day of great Indian Tantrik and scholar-critic Acharya Padsasambhava. The Acharya is known as Guru Ringhochhey in Ladakh. The saint had visited Tibet and Zanskar in Ladakh in the 7th Century AD. It is said that had there been no Padmsambhava, there would have been no Buddhism in Tibet. The dance-drama of the festival depicts some important aspects of Padmasambhava's life. The eight crucial events of his life are reflected in the dance-drama. The gods and goddesses wearing masks and elaborate brocade and silken clothes receive him accompanied by orchestra, composed of trumpet, cymbal, shawm, drum, horn, clarioned, gong, bell, shell, bigule and flageolet. The gods and goddesses dance and sing in his praise.

Besides, numerous oxen-headed, serpent-headed, three-eyed, dragon-faced variously masked figures present dances in regulated movements, which symbolise the victory of truth over evil. Shaven-headed Lamas (monks) move swinging censers. The festival culminates in the destruction of devil, which is personified by barely dough.

People come from far-off places of Ladakh to see the festival. In the past, they used to come on foot travelling ten to fifteen days. It attracted some European travellers also. Now, Hemis is linked by vehicular road and most people cover the journey by buses, taxis and jeeps. The balconies, roof-tops, galleries etc. of the monastery are over-crowded by spectators clad in ceremonial dresses. Since Ladakh was thrown open to tourists, Hemis monastery is the centre of tourist attraction. It is the largest monastery of Ladakh and 500 red-sect monks live in it. The monastery has a rich treasury of art and antiques. In 1977 about two thousand foreign tourists witnessed the Hemis festival according to official figures. After every eleven years the largest Thangka (Religious painting on cloth) in Hemis is exhibited, which attract a huge crowd.

In each monastery the Lamas wearing masks presents dances representing different personalities associated with the monastery. Each monastery has its own orchestra. The war between forces of good and evil is dramatised leading to the triumph of the former. The dancers have to undergo rigorous practice to avoid any lapse in movement of steps. A final rehearsal is conducted one day before the festival starts.

The first winter festival is celebrated in the 360 year old Chemray monastery, situated at a distance of 40 kms from Leh. The Lama dances are performed in conjunction with Angchog festival. The fair concludes with the hurling of votive offering to ensure peace, prosperity and health. There are 300 monks in this monastery. This is followed by Spituk Gustor festival in yellow sect Spituk monastery seven kilometers from Leh. The style of the dance-drama is similar to that in the Hemis monastery but the items of the programme vary. A large crowd assembles on the occasion. Exactly one month after this, the fair of the Thiksay monastery known as Thiksay Gustor is celebrated. The monastery lies at a distance of 19 kilometers from Leh. Sacred dances associated with the festival of Gustor are held wearing dance masks accompanied by the usual orchestra of musical instruments. This is followed by Dosmochhey festival at Leh. The monks of different monasteries participate alternatively for performance, in this festival. A large thread-cross model is set up near Leh, after which the festival is named. It is the most ancient festival in Ladakh. Dough images are taken through the main bazaar of Leh followed by Lamas dancing to the tune of musical instruments. People follow the procession. The dough images which symbolise evil, are cast outside Leh and the great thread cross-model is over turned. The Buddhists frantically fall upon it to collect a piece of thread, which is considered suspicious to retain in grain-store. The prominent feature of the Dosmochhey festival is a big gathering of people in colourful dresses, which crowds the bazaars and streets of Leh. The shopkeepers make good profit during the festival.

The Dosmochhey festival is celebrated simultaneously at Likir. Shachukul and Diskit monasteries of Ladakh and attract large crowds from adjoining villages. The 1000-year old Lakir monastery is one of the oldest monasteries of Ladakh and lies at a distance of 52 kms. from Leh. Shachulkul monastery is situted in Changthang in Ladakh on the Tibet border. The 600-year old Diskit monastery lies in Nubra valley beyond the snow clad 18,000 feet high khardong pass. The peole of Nubra who cannot come to Leh, owing to the blockade of snow-bound road, assemble at Diskit. The war between forces of good and evil is dramatised through the medium of mask dance and dough images which are thrown to ward-off disaster and ensure prosperity and health.

In January the festival of Ghagon Chhiruk is celebrated in the 450-year old red-sect Phiang monastery which lies at a distance of 17 Kms. from Leh. One peculiar feature of the fair is that the Lamas wearing masks present folk dances to the tune of Ladakhi drum and pipe.

One renowned festival is Matho Naghrang of the Matho monastery which is also held in January. Besides the performance of sacred dance-drama, two monks known as the 'Rong-Tran' appear and brandishing swords run blind-foldedly on the roof-tops of the monastery. They make prophesies and people seek their or acular statements. They also give names of the newly-born babies. They are considered holy by the people and their oracular statements are relied upon. To attain this super-natural power these two monks remain in meditation for two months in a hermitage prior to the festival. Matho monastery lies at a distance of 26 kms. south of Leh on the opposite bank of River Indus.

In February, on 28th and 29th dates of the second Tibetan month the festival of so-called 'Yuru Kapgyat' is celebrated in Lama Yuru monastery during which usual masquerade is held. The monastery was founded by Naropa, the Buddhist saint and thinker in the 11th century. It lies at Leh-Srinagar road at a distance of 126 kms. from Leh.

In Zanskar of Ladakh besides Losar, religious festivals are celebratd in the Stongde and Skurun monasteries. The Lama dances are performed in conjunction with the festivals. Rituals of votive hurling is strictly observed. People from all parts of Zanskar assemble in these monasteries on the occasion of the festivals.

At sani shrine of Zanskar a festival is held in summer. People from all parts of Zanskar and adjoining villages assemble there to have pilgirmage. It is the oldest shrine of Ladakh, which was visited by Padmasambhava. In Sani a stupa known as Kanika is attributed to the Kanishka period.

The religious festivals have great significance for the people of Ladakh. The monasteries are the pivot of society and the centre of socio-economic activites. The halls and shrines with priceless statues, exquisite paintings and arts of treasure are thrown open to the people on the occasion of festivals and fairs. The Buddhists offer butter to the butter lamps and burn incense. They prostate before the images of Buddha chanting saired hyms. They circumambulate around monastery, long stupas and Manis. Blessings of the head Lamas are sought. Rare and gigantic size thankas are exhibited during the festivals.

People belonging to other religions also mix freely with the Buddhists. Many eating houses and shops spring up during the festival in the premises of monastery. The festival creates mood of festivity among people. It breaks the humdrum of long monotonous wintry months. Dramas are staged by different dramatic clubs and feasts are arranged. The people living near the monastery have to face the onrush of guests during the festival period.

The festivals not only have an element of sanctity but have also a humurous aspect. In every monastery two masked clowns popularly known as grandfather and grandmother amuse the spectators with their humourous remarks and antics.

In all festivals and fairs women are conspicuous in their bright colourful costumes. In the past many persons with turning prayer wheel was a common sight. Nowadays a magician or a juggler hailing from down areas occasionally attract crowds at Leh on the eve of Hemis festival.

There are two seasonal festivals, though these are confined to particular villages. 'Shey Rhupla' festival synchronises with the harvesting and farmers offer their first fruits of their corn harvest to God at Shey monastery. One special dance known as 'Rhupla dance' meant for the occasion is performed by two men assuming the guise of tigers. This is followed by other folk-dances. A chariot and a pair of royal horse are interesting items of the programme which are applauded by the spectators. Two oracles make their appearance and give oracular statements.

Stoq Guru Ghhishu is the harbinger of the close winter season. It is celebrated in February at Stoq village 14 kms. from Leh across river Indus. The festival has a touch of religion.

Song and dance are indispensable items of all the festivals. Special songs popularly know as 'SHON-LHOO' are sung during harvest festival, Losar and tournaments of archery are held.

The German scholar Dr. A.H. Francke, who has written several scholarly books on Ladakh, writes "The people of western Tibet)Ladakh) possess a natural genius for poetry. But the high standard of western Tibet folklore shows plainly what a high position the literary genius of the people would have taken had it been given free fair play". According to Dr. Frankke the old regimes of Ladakh did not allow the poetry and national literature to develop properly.

Dance is the breath of the life of the people of Ladakh and is an indispensable item of all festivals. As mentioned above all great religious festivals are observed through the medium of dance. The folk dances are performed with a gusto and abandon to the tune of drums and 'Shahnai (pipe)'. These dances include two steps dance, three-steps dance and mixed dance, in which both men and women participate. Men, Women, old and young, prince and priest all take part in dancing.

In the words of a non-Ladakhi writer, "Any occasion is good for feasting and dancing. Someone born into a family in the village? The Chhang flows. The whole village is fed. Someone getting married? The formalities are prolonged so that the feasting can continue.... The main idea is merry-making. At work, the people whistle and sing songs of epic heroes and religious events".

In Changthang and Rong 'Jabso' dance is very popular. It is performed on the occasion of Losar and other festive occasions. In this dance the males and females form two separate rows and hand in hand confronting each other sing and dance to the tune of 'rubah'.

Archery festival is held in many villages at the advent of spring season. The archery festival of Leh is famous. Many people from surrounding villages come to Leh to witness it. It lasts several days and nights. In the past it continued for a fortnight or more and was held with great enthusiasm. Many musicians participated in it. The participants put on their best clothes. A target is set at some distance and the participants stike arrows in pairs accompanied by the beat of drums and tune of pipes. Whosoever hits the target is honoured with traditional white scarf. At intervals, folk dances and recreationary programmes are arranged. Dancing and singing programmes continue till late night in the light of patromax

lamps and bonfire. In the past entertaining programmes included tall man, the chicken, the lion, the English hunter, the Kashmiri Pandit, the old man with his son, the sword dance, the dragon dance and the 'boat and Amban'. The latter two items and the Lion dance have come down from China when Leh was all important trade centre of Central Asia. Three days the English hunter, the Chicken and lion dance are presented. Folk dances of Himachal Pradesh, Kashmir, Srnkiang, Tibet and Gilgit are also presented in their national costumes. The crowd is regaled by a clown occasionally.

A festival known as 'storlog' is observed every year at Leh. A figure symbolising the enemy of religion and the country is taken out in a procession to the outskirts of Leh. This is preceded by recitation of 308 volumes of religious books by 400 Lamas in four days. Jawans of local army garrison shoot volleys of fire to the figure from a considerable distance before it is cut down into two pieces with a sword and buried.

Diwali, Holi and Dussehra festivals are also celebrated at Leh by Punjabi shopkeepers, non-local government officials and defence personnel. Local people also participate in the rejoicings. On Diwali shops and many houses are illuminated. The streets and main bazaar are thronged by noisy urchins and sweets are distributed among them.

ABDUL GHANI SHAIKH

LADDAN KHAN

(b. 1934) - Instrumentalist: Hindustani, Sarangi; studied with Jhallan Khan; concert tour, Burma (1961); disc recordings.

LAL BAGH : INDIA'S FLORAL PARADISE

The booming South Indian hill city of Bangalore is today Asia's fastest growing urban conglomerate endowed with a uniform, temperate climate all through the year. Because of its cornucopia of vegetation, Bangalore is the greenest metropolis of India. Moreover, this city beautiful with its gorgeous gardens in their myraid hues, scintillating parks rich in floral splendour and the cool, shady walks deserve the sobriquet "Garden City of india". While nature has endowed the city with a salubrious climate and a fertile soil, man has utilised these bounties to enrich its beauty, by giving horticultural expression to his aesthetic sense.

The Lal Bagh, a pleasure garden of great dimension, is by far the loveliest among the city's gardens. Conceived as a royal retreat during the reign of Hyder ali and expanded by his son Tipu sultan over 200 years ago, it has blossomed over the years.

The founding of Lal Bagh is one of the most exciting episodes in the history of Bangalore. Fascinated by the delightful appearance of French gardens in Pondicherry, Hyder Ali decided to raise a similar one in Bangalore. Located ideally at the south-eastern corner of the city, it sprawls over 240 acres of landscape. The park acquired the appellation of Lal Bagh, owing to a profusion of roses and other red flowers.

A great lover of flowers and gardens that he was, Hyder Ali imported rare and exotic varieties of plants and fruit trees from far off places for the ornamentation of this garden. A little tank situated to the extreme south of the garden was its main source of water.

Tipu Sultan enlarged and enriched the garden by adding many more varieties of flowers by procuring seeds from Kabul, Persia, Mauritius and Turkey. But after the tragic fall of Tipu in a bloody battle, the garden suffered grievous neglect for a long period, till it was made over to the newly formed horticultural society in 1836.

Six years later, the government assumed control of the garden and transformed it into a horticultural garden. The credit for making it a botanical garden goes to Dr. Clerghan, Chief Conservator of forests in South India.

Lal Bagh now underwent remarkble changes. Many rare species of flora were imported from places as far away as North and South America, Africa and the South Sea islands, Australia, China, Britain, etc.

Within a few years, the garden could boast of some 250 varieties of roses, 160 kinds of ferns and 122 varieties of crotons, besides countless varieties of ornamental flowering shrubs, brilliant foliage plants, gay annuals and gorgeous blossoming creepers and colourful orchids.

Recording his impressions of Lal Bagh in his fascinating book, "Eastern Experiences", Mr. Lewis Bowring, who succeeded Sir Mark cubbon as Commissioner, says "In the public garden called Lal Bagh, the foundation of which is attributed to Hyder Ali, the visitor might at first imagine himself transferred to a purely European pleasure ground till, advancing, he sees the gorgeous creepers, the wide-spreading mango, and the graceful betelnut trees which characterise the East. The Garden is a beautiful retreat, and is frequented by all classes".

The horticulture shows held every August and January have lent Lal Bagh a global reputation. During these shows, the garden turns into a paradise of beauty, a floral pageant.

RADHAKRISHNA RAO

LAL KOT - THE FIRST CITY OF DELHI

According to mythology Delhi was once known as Khandav Prastha founded by King Sudarshan of the Chandra (lunar) dynasty. It was here that Indra, the king of gods, performed a yajna attended by all the gods and sages. Thereafter, Khandav Prastha was named Indraprastha. As narrated in the great epic Mahabharata, when the relationship between the Pandavas and Kauravas soured, the former were granted Indraprastha by king Dhritarashtra - father of the Kauravas - for a conciliation. Purana Qila (old fort) has traditionally been identified by popular belief as the site of the city of Indraprastha developed by the Pandavas. Archaeological excavations at Purana Qila have unearthed remains of several successive settlements dated from as long as one millenium B.C. to the sixteenth century A.D. Ironically, the historical origin of the city of Delhi as Indraprastha has not been established. On the other hand, archaeologists have reasons to believe that much earlier settlements, perhaps

from the days of the Neanderthal men of the stone age, existed in and around Delhi. It is also certain that between 8th and 11th century A.D. a small kingdom called Anangpur flourshied in the south of present day Delhi which was founded by king Anang Pal I, a chieftain of the Tomar Rajputs. Excavations in Anangpur village and the nearby Suraj Kund, an ancient water reservoir, support the view.

However, the first of the seven fortfied cities of Delhi was in fact founded in 1052 A.D. by the Tomar king Anang Pal - II who chose the Mehrauli area as his new capital and named HIS citadel as the Lal Kot. The raised fortifications of Lal Kot with its meandering ramparts, now mostly in ruins are visible from the tomb of Adham Khan in Mehrauli village. Anang Pal chose an oblong area of Mehrauli, then a rocky, barren land as the site of his fort. In slecting the spot he must have excerised great foresight, since the immense strategic significance of its location had been realized by the later kings and some Sultans who never shifted too far from Lal Kot; they extended the area of Lal Kot whenever needed and tried to contain the growing population over the years into the coming up village settlement called Mehrauli, adjoining the citadel. The area of Lal Kot can best be viewed in its entirety from the balconies of the towering Qutb Minar. As far as the eyes can seen it is a stark landscape spread over a long stretch of undulated land strewn with stones, debris and wild growth of thorny bushes. Recent excavations of a high mound behind the ancient Yogamaya Temple have exposed the foundations of Lal Kot, the core of the first fortified city of Delhi. King Anang Pal had developed a low lying area within the zone as catchment lake of rain waters. Known as Anand Tal, the lake that once served as the water source of Lal Kot has now dried up and changed into a grassy playground for the children.

The Tomars were later succeeded by the Chauhan clan, the most powerful amongst whom was king Prithviraj Chauhan, popularly called Rai Pithora. Prithviraj built his Qila Raj Pithora extending Lal Kot in the 12th century. Many Hindu and Jain temples were built during the reign of the Rajputs. Legend has it that Prithviraj raised a it that Prithviraj raised a tower for his dauhter to view and worship everyday the holy Yamuna from its top. In 1192 Prithviraj died in a battle fighting Muhammad Ghori, the Afghan invader.

The Following year Ghori's slave and Viceroy in India. Qutb-ud-din Aibak captured Qila Rai Pithora and in celebration of the victory further raised the height of the tower and developed it into the beautiful Qutab Minar that was completed by his successor Shamsuddin Iltutmish. The tower also served for the muezzine's summons to prayers. In the spacious courtyard of the Qutb Minar's complex stands the ageless marvel - the non-rusting iron pillar whose origin some authorities place in the 4th century. The deeply etched Sanskrit inscriptions on its western face read that the "Pillar was' arm of fame' (Kirtibhuja) of Emperor of Chandraja (Whose identity remains uncertain) who defeated the Vahlikas and drove them across the river Indus winning for himself uninterrupted sovereighty over entire India". It is believed that from some Vishnu temple of Vihar the pillar was brought there by Anang Pal whose name is also found etched on it with the year Samvat - 1109 (1052 A.D.).

The periphery of Prithviraj Chauhan's Qila Rai Pithora including Lal Kot extended to about six kilometers. Built in stone, the long boundary wall with its many gates had been subjected to gradual disintrigration by the Muslim Sultans in search of building materials for their palaces, built around the Qutb Minar at different times. The coronation of Muhammad-bin-Tughlag as the Sultan of Delhi had taken place at Qila Rai Pithora, ignoring his father's imposing fortress at Tughlaqabad, further south.

P. K. DE

LAL KUNWAR : THE DANCING EMPRESS

The Mughals were found of a good life and lively entertainment, dancing being one of their principal diversions. They even brought troups of professional dancers from Persia with their own distinctive style of dancing and singing. The interaction of Persian and Hindu styles of dancing brought about a glorisous fusion of the two and new music and dance forms were evolved.

In her heyday of popularity and power in Mughal India, the professional dancing girl, torchbeearer of the performing arts, humbled many a mighty man of the realm. She rose to the status of celebrity, wooed by kings and princes who could not resist her physical charm, lively company and high accomplished in dance and music. They fell madly in love with her, risking their thrones and very lives. She figured as the heroince of royal romance, some of which have been immortalised in folklore. There are several ascinating accounts of loyal romances with dancing girls. Akbar was a great patron of arts and high class dancing girls were conferred the title of Kanchani (the gilded one), Rupmati, a dancing girl of Saharanpur, 'more beautiful than the moon, the tulip and the early dawn of the spring, became famous all over North India. After hearing about her alluring beauty, vivacity of her singinging and her passionate affairs with Baz Bahadur, the ruler of Malwa, Akbar wanted to have her. So he invaded Malwa and captured Rupamati. However, she ended her life by drinking poison rather than be caught alive. Jahangir fell in love with the beautiful but unfortunate Anarkali, a dancing girl who became a legend. During the reign of Shah Jahan, dancing girls were invited to all state fairs and festivals and allowed into the seraglio. Once, according to Manucci, Shah Jahan himself fell in love with one of his dancing girls and took her in his herm. His son Dara Shikoh was charmed by a danging girl called Ra-no-dil and married her, giving her the same status as other princess. Even the puritanical Aurangzeb is said to have been infatuated with a celebrated countesan Zainabadi, who captivated him with her unrivalled melody and exqusite physical beauty. It was her sudden demise that ended the affairs but love tales of Aurangzeb and Zaninabadi have been handed down to prosperity in song. Later, he married another dancing girl and gave her the status of a queen with the titled of Bai Udaipuri Mahal.

The later Mughal period saw a remarkable flowering of the performing arts - music and dance - through generous royal patronage. The most colourful and dazzling romance, which surpasses every other royal romance, was that of Lal Kunwar and the Mughal Emperor Jahandar Shah, the grandson of Alamgir (Aurangzeb). A descendent of Tan Sen, the great musical genius and one of the gems of Akbar's court, Lal Kanwar, the most glamorous and yet the most notorious dancing girl emerged as the 'Dancing Empress of India. She belonged to a family of Kalawants (musicians) and had captivated Jahandar Shah with her bewitching beauty and charm at a very early age. A consummate singer, she had a melodious voice, sparkling wit and vivacious dance movements that endeared her to one and all. A contemporary writer has described her beauty and grace in a long Persian poem that concludes:

Lal Kunwar, her very name is most befitting,
Sweet in speech, her body was white as silver

Lal Kunwar was so deeply attached to Jahandar Shah that she kept his company even in the battlefield. After his victory in the fratricidal struggle, when Jahandar Shah ascended the throne in Delhi, he raised his favourite Lal Kunwar to the status of a queen. He made her the Empress with the title of Imtiaz Mahal (the chosen one of the palace) She was even provided with the royal insignia and granted an annual allowance of twenty million rupees for her household expenses, exclusive of clothes and jewels. Five hundred troops followed in her train. She enjoyed great influence on Jahandar Shah in the matters of state and got high official appointments as well as jagirs for her family members.

The entire court was indeed given over to the pleasure of music, dance and wine. The courtesans and other public entertainers had their heyday now. Pubs and other public taverns sprang up everywhere and the sound of music and dance was heard all over Chandni Chowk. The Emperor drank in the company of musicians at his palace to please Lal Kunwar, thus losing his prestige and dignity in the eyes of both high and low. But the Emperor and Lal Kunwar were so deeply attached that they are said to have visited saints and medicants together to seek their blessings. Jahandar Shah was so keen to have an offspring from her that acting on popular belief, he bathed every Sunday with her in the tank at the shrine of Shaikh Nasir-ud-din-Oudhi called the Chirag-i-Delhi (the light of Delhi) in the hope of getting blessed with a son.

Jahandar Shah was overthrown after a brief reign of 11 months by Farrukh-Siyar in a battle at Agra. It was Lal Kunwar who came to the rescue and took away Jahandar Shah to safety on her elephant to Delhi. There is a moving account of their journey to Delhi where they reached after five-day ordeal by hiding in daylight and travelling after dusk. Soon thereafter, through the treachery of his Wazir Zulfikar Khan, Jahandar Shah was taken prisoner and lodged in the Red Fort. At his fervent appeal Lal Kunwar was allowed to Join him. Later, when he was being taken for execution under the orders of Farrukh-Siyar, the new Emperor, Lal Kunwar shrieked clasped her lover round the neck and refused to let go. Violently forced apart from Jahandar Shah, she was dragged away and then sent to the Suhagpura settlement where widows and families of deceased Emperors lived in retirement.

Jahandar Shah was buried in the vault of Humayun's tomb at the side of other members of the family. Not far away from there, near the entrance to the present-day Golf

Club on Zakir Hussain Road, there is a red sandstone mausoleum known as 'Lal Bangla' supposed to contain the tomb of Lal Kunwar.

PRAN NEVILLE

LALBAGH PALACE

Situated in the heart of Indore in Madhya Pradesh and spread over an area of nearly 72 acres is the majestic place of the Holkar Kings, popularly known as Lalbag Palace and Garden, it was built in three different times. The palace was constructed and furnished in western style over an area of four acres and is surrounded by lush green trees and gardens.

The palace was first conceived by king Tukoji Rao II (1844-86), who actually made a plan for his elder prince but shelved it for lack of water and trees. His successor Shivaji Rao Holkar (1886-1902) however constructed the main Lalbag Palace as a small garden house. But it was Tukoji Rao III (1902-25) who gave the Palace the final shape. And even after his abdication in favour of Yashwant Rao II in 1926, Tukoji Rao III lived in the Palace from 1938 till his death in 1978.

Lalbag is an exclusive blend of renaissance, palladian and baroque elements in architecture, rococo and neoclassical elements in its furniture fittings and decorative use of stucco and marble. The awe inspiring paintings on the ceilings are an integral part of interior decoration in architecture. An eclectic proximity to the classical past, allusions of Greek and Roman mythology, literature and music are all evident here.

The Garden harmonises French, English and Mughal concepts of landscaping in midst of straight avenues and winding curves of art and nature. Numerous varieties of roses, dahlias and gladioli, chrysanthemum and cannas, papaya seeds, lilium and thuja orientila were introduced and propagated after due acclimatisation in the three Lalbag nurseries, Flower beds were bordered with upatorium odoratium and an orchard of grape fruit and peaches was planted. The Palace and Garden constituted a living testimony to cultural assimilation.

In the year 1987 the palace was taken over by the state directorate of archaeology and museums for protection.

Dedicated to the comprehensive spirit of Jawaharlal Nehru, the Lalbag Palace and Garden now houses Nehru Centre for Ideas, museum of science and technology and arts of different kinds.

The palace is also one of the main tourist attractions of Indore. While the Palace is immaculately arranged and gives a clear glimpse of the lifestyle of the Holkar Kings, the sprawling gardens are a favourite picnic spot for the nature loving denizens and visitors. It is also the right choice for the admirers of architecture, sculpture, painting and crafts.

COL. K. J. CHUGH

LALESHWARI (LAL DED)

(b. 1335) - Kashmiri mystical poet; Saivite; had great religious leanings to which her husband never reconciled himself; poems (in Kashmiri) recount her spiritual experiences; became a preacher and ascetic; sang songs of Siva, her beloved; had Hindu and Muslim followers.

References

Chopra, P.N., (ed.), The Gazetteer of India: History and Culture, New Delhi 1973.

Walker, Benjamin, Hindu World, Vol. 1, London, 1968

LALIT KALA AKADEMI (AKADEMI OF ARTS), NEW DELHI

Established by Government of India in 1954; is autonomous organisation; promotes understanding of Indian art in country and abroad; carries out this objective through publications of art, journals, etc., has published monographs on ancient Indian art, results of new research in Indian arts, makes reproductions of paintings copies frescoes, murals, etc., in caves, palaces, forts, temples, archaeological sites, etc., which are deteriorating or are in danger of being spoilt or lost; organises lectures, seminars, artists' meets and camps; gives grants to recognised art institutions and organisations in India; holds annual exhibitions and every 3 years Triennale-India (international exhibition); makes eminent artists fellows of Akademi, 16 having been so honoured uptill now; and gives awards to artists when national exhibitions are held.

References

Agarwal, V.S., Heritage of Indian Art, New Delhi, 1976.

Government of India - India - A Reference Annual, 1984, New Delhi, 1984.

Winstedt, Richard (ed.), Indian Art, New Delhi, 1969.

LATA MANGESHKAR : THE ETERNAL

It is not very often that a person with prodigious talent is born in the ambience particularly conducive to the flowering of that talent. But this is exactly what happened to Lata Mangeshkar, the reigning melody queen, the "First Lady of Film Music" and "indisputable and indispensable queen of India's playback singers", as the Times magazine described her.

Several other honorifics, appellations, honorary University doctorates, Padma Bhushan and the Dadasaheb Pahlke Award, besides having been elected a Fellow of the Sangeet Natak Akademi also adore her.

In her honour the Government of Madhya Pradesh, the state of her birth (She was born at Indore), has instituted a Lata Mangeshkar Purskar which is conferred every year on some distinguished musician or singer. Notable recipients include maestros Anil Biswas, Naushad and Lata's own sister, Asha Bhosle, and brother Hridyanath Mangeshkar - a music director in his own right.

Whenever she sings the national song "Saare Jahan se accha Hindustan Hamara" (East or West, India is the the best) or the dirge. "Ai mere watan ke logo" (O, my compatriots) or the devotional song "Allah tero naam, Ishwar tero naam" (God: Allah and Ishwar are among Your names), she never falls to stir the patriotic and secular chords of millions of Indians across the globe.

Born September 28, 1929, she was initiated into music by her classically trained father Master Dinnath Mangeshkar, who was a celebrated singer-actor of the Marathi stage.

While only six, Lata could detect and correct a flawless note being rendered by one of her father's students, whom he used to teach classical music at his residence within the earshot of Lata. Noticing his daughter's astute perception of music, Dinnath started appreciatly her talent at that tender age and recommended to her the signinging style of the great K.L. Saigal. It is since then that Lata has been nursing an avid admiration of for Saigal whose style, she says, has accompanied her throughout her singing career.

Half a centry later, she brought out a two volume audio-cassette titled "Shraddanjali" or her 'tribute' to the immortals of Hindi film music, giving pride of place to Saigal by signing the maximum numbers of his hauntingly nostalgic music.

When she was nine, she was giving singing performances on the stage and at eleven she topped in a music competion organised at Kolhapur by Pancholi Art Pictures of Lahore to spot talent and worn two medals.

Master Dinanath gravitated from the stage to film making, but suffered huge losses in his very first celluloid venture. This broke his heart and he fell ill and died in 1942, leaving behind wife, Shudhmati, eldest daughter, Lata, who was not even thirteen then, and her younger siblings Meena, Asha, Usha and Hridyanath in a state of deprivation.

Thus, complelled to seek some job to keep the family's kitchen fire burning, Lata offered to act and sing in films as she thought that was the only thing she could possibly do.

Through a friend of her father's, she was introduced to Master Vinayak (father of actress Nanda) in whose Marathi production Pabili Manglagaur, a hilarious comedy, she made her debut as an actress in the role of mischievious teenager. She also sang a song in that film under the music direction of Dada Chandekar.

Her first Hindi song, which was picturised on her was a patriotic number for a Marathi film Gajabbau in 1944, but the first mainstream Hindi film for which she sang was Aap Ki Sewa Mein, also directed by Vasant Joglekar, for whom she had sung as a playback artiste for the first time in Marathi.

Lata also acted in Master Vinayak directed Marathi film Chimkula Sansar (1943), and Hindi pictures, Badi Ma (1945) Jeewan Yaatra (1946) Subbadra (1946) and Mandir (1948).

When Master Vinayak moved from Kolhapur to Mumbai, the Mangeshkar family also shifted there. It was in Mumbai that Lata learnt further music from Ustad Amal Ali Khan Bhendibazarwale, Amanat Khan Dewaswale and Pandit Tuslidas, a disciple of the famous classical vocalist, Bade Ghulam Ali Khan.

Badi Ma in which the then reigning singing heroine Noorjehan (later known as 'Malka-e-Tarannum' of Pakistan) starred, was a war-effort film made during the Second World War as per a stipulation of the then British rulers requiring all producers to make one such popaganda-oriented picture. Lata acted a young girl in this film and came in close contact with Noorjehan whom she intinctively adopted as her model female singer.

With the partition of the country in 1947 Noorjehan migrated to Pakistan, leaving the signing areana open for Lata with virtually only Suraiya as the singing actress. But other female playback singer Amirbai Karnatak, Johara Begum of Ambala, Shamshad Begum, Raj Kumari, Sitara of Kanpur, Getta Dutt, Meena Kapur etc. too were rendering some memorable melodies.

According to Lata, she was discovered as a singer by Master Ghulam Haider of Khazanchi fame who discerned a great promise in her singing and visualized her as the most resplendent star of the future in the subcontinent's music firmament. He even recorded a duet of Lata and Madan Mohan from Filimstan's Shaheed in 1948, but producer S. Mukherji did include that number in the film.

However, in 1949, three of her films - Mahal, Andaz and Barsat - which had lilting number scored by Khemchand Prakash, Naushad and Shankar Jaikishen respectively, zoomed her to gereat hiehgts. Then there was no looking back and gradually all music directors wanted only Lata to sing for them.

Lata continued to sing in the Noorjehan vein music directors of the period like Anil Biswas, C. Ramachandra and Shyam Sunder also cast her songs in the Noorjehan mould for quite some time. It was only a few years later that Lata freed herself from that syndorme and shone on her own steam.

The first quarter century of independence India was the golden era of Hindi film music and Lata was its most popular female singer. Music directors vied with each other to present their best from them by employing her vocal skills. dexterously and interpreting music through her songs, many of which became immortal gems.

Talent was in born and ingrained in Lata but she was not metamorphosed into a sweet and consummate singing artiste overnight. It was after a prolonged and sustained earnest effort, marked by vigorous practice, that took her to the very pinnacle of excellence and glory where she has reigned supreme for five and a half decades now.

Lata got so engrossed her single-minded pursuit that the thought of marriage never received priority in her scheme of things. Today Lata dotes on her nieces and nephews.

She is religious, secular and charitable by disposition and has donated large portions of earnings for laudable social causes. She has founded two schools and a college in Maharashtra and takes active interest in running them.

As she was getting the Filmfare's Best playback Singer Award every other year since its inception in 1969, she declined to accept the award any more, abdidicating it in favour of young and up-coming singers. She was, however, awarded the Filmfare Difetime Achievement Award in 1994.

Lata is the world's most prolific recorded female singer ever with the highest percentage of hit songs from her formidably rich repertoire. She has also recorded a largue number of non-film compositions. Her fan following spans not olny her contemporary three generations in Indian but also music-lovers of every hue and clime the world over.

including special record Introducing Indian Music; publications: various articles on music, etc.

B. M. MALHOTRA

LATHMAR HOLI OF NANDGAON

The Holi group from Nandgaon consists of boys as young as 10 years and men of 60 years old. Then in great revelry Holi is played between the huriharas and the Gopikas of Barsana. This is the prelude to Lathmar Holi and is usually referred to as Thitholi Holi (Holi of fun and frolic).

Then follows the much-awaited Lathmar Holi. The Gopikas dress up in brightly coloured traditional attire and bedeck themselves profusely with ornaments. They have their mantles drawn over their faces and are armed with long bamboo sticks with which they strike the huriharas. The Gopikas blows are really deadly. Not unfrequently, blood oozes out of the wounds. But this is rather considered a good omen and has never given rise to any ill-feeling.

The day after the Lathmar Holi of Nandgaon, Holi is played in almost all the temples of this region with coloured powder, rose water etc. Tableaus depicting various moods of Radha and Krishna are also taken out on this day. (Condensed)

SUBHRA MAJUMDAR

LAVANI

Lavani is a popular theatre form of tamasha in Maharashtra. Part drama and part song and music, tamasha single handedly preserves what remains of the famed Lavani the song and dance routine that has an older tradition which the waves of Bhakti movement swept through India between the fourteenth and seventeenth centuries, there emerged a form of sangeet - song, music and dance that synthesized erotica with mysticism, mostly using the matically "Madhurya Bhakti" for Krishna described as Radha's dance. Even today Radha dances survive in the dance of Muralis and Vaghyas in Maharashtra where they have a ritualistic significance. However, their more popular version is the Lavani - closely associated with the Tamasha these days. The purpose of Lavani was always to stir the emotions of Bhakti and rabi being two sids of the same coin. This movement from the metaphysical to the sensual, the imprint of history and patronage is clear. During the times of Shivaji, Lavanis were adopted to stir the emotions of the soldiers for valour. During the Peshwa period, Lavani had its hey days and with the end of Peshwa's rule there followed decline of Lavani. And emphasis shifted from spiritual to sensuous. The Lavani moved to public platform and it also encouraged the more somewhat bawdy lyrics and burlesque dancing.

ARSHIYA SETHI

LOBO ANTSHER (b. 1905)

Musicologist, instrumentalist and vocalist: Hindustani, khayal of Jaipur gharana; western, violin, guitar, composer; studied with Alladiya Khan; disc recordings

"M"

M. F. HUSSAIN (b. 1915)

When dust settles on the history of Indian art in the 20th century, what will Maqbool Fida Husain be remembered for? For his silver-haired looks, oversized brush, barefoot strides that often took him into the heart of controversy? Or the oeuvre that began with paintings of cinestars on billboards to Ramayan, Mahabharat and subsequently to the icons of our times - Gandhi, Indira Gandhi, Amitabh Bachchan, Sachin Tendulkar, Madhuri Dixit....

Style has been the essence of this self-taught artist, whose work has become the buzz of every art-circuit cocktail. In life, as in art, Husain has left a stamp of originality. When he married off his daughter, the receiption was held in a Girgaum chawl. When he picked up his pen, the bold portrayal brought before people his love for women that had not waned after seven decades. And when he painted, his bold expressionistic sweeps gave life not only to oils and acrylics, watercolours and silkscreens but also to celluloid experiments like Gajagamini.

Dipping his brush in the palette of personal life, Husain has not stopped short of projecting the absurdities he witnessed for six years as member of the Rajya Sabha. All this has acted as fodder for the chatter mill. Harmless gossip started to hurt when his experiments and departures in arts started being seen as gimmicks to keep the bids going at Sotheby's. Installations like Swetambari and Theatre of Absurd were seen as publicity stunts and nothing more. When he wiped out paintings of goddesses as a protest against the commercialisation of art, it was considered an Islamic affront. And when he painted Madhuri and Saraswati with as much felicity as his mother and Muharram, it was dubbed as a rape of Hinduism. Hurt, but not to be subdued, the Padma Vibhushan awardee continues to paint events that are topmost on contemporary minds, be it the solar eclipse, the cricket mania or the victory at Kargil.

M. S. SUBBALAKSHMI

M.S. Subbalakshmi was born in a home where music was truly valued and where musicians often gathered;impressing on her mind and bestowing on her the richness of a great tradition. Her mother, Veena Shanmukhavadivu of Madurai, was herself highly acclaimed by stalwarts like Tirukodicaval Krishna Iyer, Venkatraman Das and Veena Senshana of Mysore. Before she was 10 years of age M.S. Subbalakshmi began accompanying her mother at recitals and by the time she was 17, she started giving major performances at prestigious institutions like the Music Academy, Madras.

She married T. Sadasivam in 1940 who was also her friend, philospher and guide. She became a disciple of the Paramacharya, who greatly influenced her life. Her complete devotion is reflected in her singing.

Apart from her voice and the exquisite power of rendering verses suffused with feeling, was her stunning beauty which catapulted her to fame with her very first film, "Savitri". Then came "Meera". It was a film that mesmerised million of viewers. Sarojini Naidu was so moved, she said "Subbalakshmi's performance is not a performance that merely gives the illusion of the reincarnation of the princess and poetess lover of Sri Krishna. For those two hours that we heard her singing the verses of Meera, we felt that it was Meera herself who had come to life". It is said she is one of the rare human beings on whom the gods have smiled. That's not all, the gods have designed to appear both in the serenity of her devotional songs as well as in the high octaves - when she transports her audiences to spiritual heights. The emotional exuberance of her voice has a great impact on the listener.

It was indeed a golden era where audiences often comprised luminaries like Nehru, T.T. Krishnamachari, Rajendra prasad and Dr. Radhakrishnan. After hearing one of her recitals, Gandhiji once remarked; "Her voice is exceedingly sweet; she loses herself in a 'bhajan'. During prayer one must lose oneself in god. To sing is one thing; to sing it by losing oneself to god is quite different". Later she sang for him 'Hari tuma haro' which Gandhiji heard on the evening of his last birthday - 2nd October 1947. This song was aired on radio after the Mahatma was assassinated hearing which M.S. Subbalakshmi collapsed with grief.

M.S. was paid a tribute by Nehru when he called her "Queen of Songs". M.S. Subbalakshmi and husband Sadasivam had the privilege of being his house guests for nearly 10 days in 1955. They recollect warm memories of the hospitality extended to them by his daughter Indira then a young girl.

M.S. as she is fondly called, has received so many awards, it would be impossible to list all of them. The title 'Isai Vani' was conferred on her in 1940 in Kumbakonam. She received the Padma Bhushan in 1954 in the very first year that the National awards were instituted. In 1956, she received the President's award and is the first receipient of Bharat Ratna in perfuming arts.

Although a living legend in the world of Carnatic music, she is widely known as a humanitarian who has given over a 100 recitals for charitable causes. Both M.S. Subbalakshmi and Sadasivam were seen very often in various cultural gotherings in Madras. Still beautiful, she has acquired over the years, a humble grace and beauty that seem to emanate from somewhere deep down, a spiritual serenity that continues to suffuse her soul and breathe into the pristine glory of her music.

NANDITA CHAUDHURI

M.V. DHURANDHAR : A LEGENDARY PAINTER

Rao Bahadur Mahadev Vishwanath Dhurandhar (1867 - 1944) was a doyen of artists of his time. A product of J.J. School of Art, Bombay, he was the first Indian to be appointed as Director of the School, a premiere art institution in the country. The artistic genius who embodied the virtues of an academic artist explored every possible medium for his creative talent. He could draw, paint, illustrate, compose, portray and design murals with equal facility. He painted over 50,000 works during his lifetime and did an equal number of drawings. Considered as one of our turn-of-the century legends, Dhurandhar's paintings are on view are many museums in India and also at the Buckingham Palace and Kensington in London.

Dhurandhar's autobiography is Marthi "Kalamandirati 41 Varshe" (Forty-one Years in the Temple of Art) presents an insight into his magnanimous Personality, his devotion to art and the progress of art education in his time and the changing tastes of art lovers and connoisseurs. He recounts a number of anecdotes and the social mores of the times. He describes how his encounter with European art at the Bombay Art School inspired him to become an artist. He writes : "Standing in front of huge plaster of Paris statues of the Venus di Medici, Apollo Belvedere, Apollo Sauronchthonos and the Discholos, I felt as if in a dream. I went round and round the statues and yet I was not stated.... Even out on the street I felt like one possessed and kept seeing them appears before me".

There was hardly any exhibition of art in the country in which he had not participated and won an award. He was the first Indian artist to be awarded a gold medal by the Bombay Art Society in 1895. His "greatest moment of glory", according to his daughter Ambika Dhurandhar, also an eminent artist, was when he was awarded a prize for a painting shown at the Wembley Empire Exhibition in London in 1923.

Dhurandhar was a graphic portrayer of nature and man. He had only one pastime, diversion or recreation : painting. A pencil and sketchbook where his constant companions wherever he went. A keen observer with an artist's eye, he recorded everything he saw. While busy with his pencil or brush, he would get totally lost in his work and nothing could distract him. The romantic aura created by him about his characters was something unique and different than ever seen before. His mythological figures, Rama and Sita and others were different from the earthly folks and yet real and refined. His series of water colour paintings on music show scholarly understanding of Indian mythology, Sanskrit literature and history.

Dhurandhar had an eye for female beauty with all its grace and charm. His portrayal of women shows the awe and rapture with which he regards the womanhood of India as worthy of worship. All artists, at some time or the other, must have made sketches of their wives, but Dhurandhar excelled every peer in this field. He made 175 water colour sketches of his two wives, Bapubai and Gangubai. The former died a bare two years after their marriage, and Dhurandhar wed Gangubai a second time. He imparted life to his figures by infusing emotions with every line or drop of paint. They became alive as if stepping out of the pictures and coming right at us. They are note mere images but symbols of pure emotions.

Dhurandhar's Paintings of Indian women at temples, weddings, festivals and rituals show his mastery in sketching figures in movement and engaged in different activities. They also throw light on the social, religious and ritualistic customs of the age gone by. Perhaps his most outstanding work in this field is a series of paintings of women from different parts of India which serve as illustrations in Otoo Rothfield's classic work, "Women of India", published in 1924. Here, the women with their charming physical forms appear lively, attractive and natural. Their ornaments, costumes and graceful

movements are so authentic that these paintings are a visual documentation of our social history nearly a century ago.

PRAN NEVILE

MADAN MOHAN
THE MASTER MELODY MAKER

Ironically, some createive geniuses get their well-deserved success and recognition only after their death. Such has been the case with Madan Mohan, the melody maker of many outstanding film songs in general and of *Ghazals* in particular. His versatile talent was better recognized only after his death on 14 July, 1975, when he was just fifty.

Among his incomparable creations are the two *ghazals* from the film "Anpadh (1962) - "Aapki nazron ne samjha pyar ke qabil mujhe" (I am heartened that your eyes have deemed me worthy of your love) and "Hai isi mein pyar ki aabroo, woh jafa karen main wafa karon" (Love's honour demands that I be faithful to my lover even if he is unfaithful to me). The maestro Naushad was so impressed by these two compositions that he offered to exchange them for his own musical oevvre.

Both these compositions were sung with consummate artistry by our national nightingale, Lata Mangeshkar, who has also rendered with similar skill and fervour, a number of other Madan Mohan Melodies. To Lata Mangeshkar, he was indeed a "*Rakhi*" Brother and many an outstanding composition resulted from their collaboration. In 1948, Lata sang a duet with him for the Kamini Kaushal - Dilip Kumar starrer *Shaheed* under music director Master Ghulam Haider. Howerver, this song was omitted from the film, His fans could, however, listen to his voice in his self-composed tune of "Maai ri, main Kaase kahon pir aapne jiya ki" (O Mother, whom shall I tell of the pain in my heart) in *Dastak* (1970).

Interestingly, Madan Mohan initially tried his luck as a film actor. His first assignment was Rasik Productions' "Parda". Although a son of Rai Bahadur Chuni Lal, once the General Manager of the now defunct Bombay Talkies and later one of the founder partners of Filmistan Studios, Madan Mohan never used his father's clout to promote his career.

Almost all famous playback singers of the Indian film industry of his times have sung for Madan Mohan, but resounding commercial success and the concomitant awards dodged him. The song of *Laila Majnu* and *Mausam* emerged as great hits only after his demise. There was seldom anything much to celebrate after his first great commercial break of *Bhai Bhai* (1956) except the *ghazals* of *Adalat* and the success of *Woh Kaun Thi* (1964), which was his first jubilee hit.

The immortal *Ghazals* of *Adalat* firmly established Madan Mohan as "Ghazal King" and offeres from big producers and directors for songs of other genres were hard to come by. He thus remained under-rated while he lived. Deluded and frustrated, he took to heavy drinking which caused him the fatal cirrohsis of the liver from which he never recovered.

Madan Mohan was one of the Pillars of Hindi film music during the two fine decades from the mid - 50s to mid- 70s, when melody was reigning supreme. he invested his scintillating melodies with rare softness and sweetness and a plaintive stain which evoked sublime human emotions. He created a vertiable rainbow with the hues of the seven notes of his music.

As his son Sanjeev Kohli tells us, his father often had as many as ten different tunes for his special songs. On Madan Mohan's sixth death anniversary, Music India brought out an album of his ten rare solo songs, which, though recorded in the voices of Mohd Rafi, Talat Mahmood, Lata Mangeshkar, Asha Bhonsle and Kishore Kumar, had remained in limbo as the films for which they were recorded were never completed. Undoubtedly, these and his other popular melodies constitute a vintage treasure of ever lasting value.

B. M. MALHOTRA

MADARAM FAIR : PRESERVING TRIBAL TRADITIONS

The three day *Jatra* (pilgrimage) is just about to begin. Lakhs of pilgrims have already arrived, some of them entirely on foot. They have begun setting up their makeshift tents. Hundreds of merchants have laid out their merchandise all along the paths leading to the *Jatra* altar. Thousands of gaily decorated bullock carts, hundreds of buses, trucks cars etc. continue to bring in devotees from far the wide, raising clouds of orange dust that hangs in the air all over. Trees, shrubs, rocks and even people on either side of the roads look reddish as the red dust, characteristic of the soil here, covers them all. With people streaming in endlessly from all corners the whole area has turned into a sea of humanity. All roads leading to the *Jatra* site appear to have disappeared under unbroken streams of people and their encampments, stretching to the horizons.

This is *Madarm's Sammakka Saralamma Jatra*. This biennial festive fair known for its sheer size and statistics attracts more than three million people, predominantly from the tribal areas who undertake this pilgrimage in prayer and penance to Madaram village to pay homage to the legendary Sammakka and Saralamma, the two tribal woman who became martyrs fighting the imperial armies of the Kakatiya king Prataparudra. That was eight hundred years ago. But people strongly believe that the spirits of these women still visit Madaram every two years to bless them with peace and prosperity. Hence the rush to Madaram for three days, during January-February. It is the largest tribal fair in the country drawing people from Andhra . Pradesh, Orissa, Maharashtra and Madhya Pradesh states. For three days this remote, obscure village of Madaram transforms itself into an immense pilgrimage centre that reverberates with the ballads immortalising the illustrious story of Sammakka and Saralamma.

Tucked in the Tadwai reserve forest., 104 km away from the historic Warangal town of Andhra Pradesh, Madaram is a small village amid undulating afforested landscape and inhabited by tribals, chiefly belonging to the Koya community. In olden days, it is said, this *Jatra* used to be a tribal affair as very few people outside aware of it. But over the years its popularity amongst non-tribals too incresed tremendously. Today for lakhs of people the names Sammakka and Saralamma are household names. Devotion is strongest among rural folks, as many suppliants travel scores of kilometres on foot to reach Madaram. But what surprises visitors here is that there is no temple structure nor idols of the deities at the site of the altar. Instead, there is only a simple platform where devotees place their votive offerings like coins, coconuts, turmeric etc. before a couple of bomboo sticks wrapped in pieces of cloth which people worship as Sammakka and Saralamma. These images are ceremonially brought to the platform by trial priests, from a nearby hillock called the "Hill of Gods".

This festival has indeed done a lot to preserve tribal traditions in this part of the country.

RAMCHANDER PENTUKER

MADARSAS
EMINENT MEDIEVAL SCHOOL OF LEARNING

Rulers of medieval India are remembered for the cities and citadels they created, mausoleums, mosques and minarets they built and *Madarsas* (schools) they establihed. Islamic education through *Maktabs* and *Madarsas* had permeated the Indian society way back in the 12th century. With political stability, the rulers extended their patronage to these institutions (*Madarsas*) and gradually their number grew. A traveller's account of the 14th Century would have us believe that Delhi alone had no less than a thousnd *Madarsas*. Whereas this rounded figure may be somewhat exaggerated, but it certainly reveals the popularity and growth of these schools.

Vestiges of bygone days have been swept away by the deep abyss of time, together with its students and professors, but still something remains to be admired. The glorious ruins of some of the *Madarsas* are still tempting enough for a student to carry his books there and spend some time in solitude.

A *Madarsa* roughly corresponds to a college for higher studies in various subjects. The curriculum, in the medieval times, revolved around the Holy Quran and scholastic theology but the final choice of subjects depended on the fancy of the ruling monarch. The Tughlaqs had a distaste for fiction, Humayun was inclined towards astrology and astronomy whereas Aurangzeb stressed upon the study of Muslim law. Neither examinations were held, nor any certificates awarded by these *Madarsas*, but to have studied in a reputed *Madarsa* under a famous scholar was in itself the greatest qualification. The teachers and the taught resided within the premises of the *Madarsa* as emphasis was laid on constant communion between them. Stipends, allowances and scholarships for the inmates were fixed by the rulers. Separate apartments were available for travellers and guests who arrived frequently to attend the lectures or just to have a glimpse of the grand edifice.

Prior to the Tughlaqs, the early slave kings promoted education through the *Madarsas* but nothing remains to be seen of the *Madarsa-i-Muisi* founded by Iltutmish, or the *Madarsa Nasiriya* built by his illustrious daughter, Razia, in 1237 AD.

Alauddin Khilji (1296-1316), although an illiterate like Akbar and always busy in campaigns and conquests, did not neglect the education of his citizens. A *Madarsa* started by him can be seen in the shape of ruined halls around tomb, close to the Qutab Minar in Delhi. In the same complex is the *Alai Minar*, with an inscription extolling Alauddin as the patron of colleges and places of worship.

Inspired by the Seljuk tradition, the concept of combining a tomb, mosque and *Madarsa* gained ground quite fast. One such ideal institution from pre-Mughal times can be seen at Hauz Khas in New Delhi. Literally meaning "Special Tank", it was a water tank built by Alauddin Khilji for the use of the inhabitants of Siri, the second city of Delhi founded by him. Later, when it fell into disuse, the Tughlaq monarch, Firoz Shah, repaired it. The *Madarsa* came to be associated with him, and was henceforth called the *Firoz Shahi Madarsa*. There are several other *Madarsas* to his credit, but little remains of them, save for historical accounts constructed from fragments in books. Like Mohammad Ghauri, he had a peculiar fancy for imparting to his long retinue of slaves, numbering around 18,000, technical education in different trades through a system of appreticeship.

Madarsa Firoz Shahi's architectural magnificence has been compared to the lofty palaces of Babylonia and its academic reputation competed with those at Samarkand and Bukhara. Mutahar, an eminent poet of the age, records his impression. "The moment I entered the building, I saw an even space as wide as the plain of the world blooming with beautifully arranged flowers as far as the eye could reach. The court yard was soul animating and its expanse was life-giving."

Amid such floral surroundings stood the double-storeyed *Madarsa*, as can be seen even today, with halls and chambers overlooking a water tank. The walls of the buildings were once coated with mica and its dome lavishly embellished with gold. Carpets came from Shiraz and Yemen and the doors were of sandalwood. Its dazzling reflection into the placid water of Hauz Khas can best be left to imagination! The *Madarsa* was headed by a reputed scholar, Jalaluddin Rumi, who knew fourteen sciences, could recite the Quran according to the seven known methods of recitation and held a complete mastery over the four schools of Muslim law.

In the *Madarsa* complex can be seen the tomb of Firoz Tughlaq, along with those of his son and grandson. A tomb in the courtyard is believed to be that of the *Mutawwali* or the Chancellor of the institution. The surrounding wilderness is the dormitory of the soldiers who laid down their lives at this very site to bring the Tughlaqs to power. The place was worthy of a visit by Taimur and Babur. Taimur is said to have comped here after winning the battle for Delhi and granted audience to the local princes and leading *amirs*.

Another *Madarsa* of Firoz is associated with the tomb of his son, Fateh Khan. At Paharganj in Delhi, it is easy to locate the shrine known as *Qadam Sharif*. An inscription here perpetuates the memory of the builder, "Glorious is

the *Madarsa* the pupil and the house in the midst of which is ready the praise of God."

Other *Madarsas* in this period were at Turkman Gate (Kalan Masjid), Khirki village(Khirki Masjid) and Begumpur (Begumpuri Masjid). a mile beyond Adilabad is an isolated structure on a hill popularly known as Nai's fort (Barber's Fort). Hardly anything remains of this *Madarsa*, save for the walls and doorways dating back to the Tughlaqs.

Subsequent rulers did not confine their building activities to Delhi and hence the growth of *Madarsas* in Jaunpur, Malwa, Bidar Bhagalpur, Badaun and other provincial capitals. Some of these are still extant and worth a visit. Jahangir awarded a jagir (land endowment) in Bhagalpur (now in Bihar) for the upkeep of the *Madarsa* founded by Maulana Sahbaz, a scholar and a saint who was an authority on Muslim law and tradition. This *Madarsa*, called the *Khanqab-i-Sahbazia* 'hospice of Shahbaz) became a rallying point for scholars and men of learning. One of the five men invited to the Mughal court by Aurangzeb for compiling his famous *Fatwa-i-Alamgiri* was Mir Mohammad Radhi, a proud alumni of Shahbaz's Madarsa. Shah Johan, as a rebel prince, turned to this *Madarsa* seeking benediction. The saint was busy with his pupils and did not take notice of the prince despite his royal, flamboyant robe. Later the prince was reprimanded for the extra long robe that was against the Islamic tradition. The extra cloth was cut off and gifted to students for making of their caps. The library of this *Madarsa* is still rich in manuscripts dating back to Maulana Shahbaz.

Akbar's seat of administration was Agra and hence there was little activity in Delhi. Though an illiterate himself, he constructed several *Madarsas* in Agra. Akbar himself presided over the *Ibadat Khana* (house of Worship), where a variety of subjects, including religion and philosophy, were debated. However, one *Madarsa* from his period can be seen in Delhi. This is the *Khairul Manzil* (Blessed among Houses), opposite the Purana Qila (Old Fort). It was built by Maham Anga, Akbar's wet-nurse. The *Madarsa*, although in ruins, displays fragments of the original decoration, coloured plaster and glazed tiles. Built of rubble and plaster, its mosque has a single dome with arched openings in its prayer hall. The main prayer hall is in the west and double-storeyed colonnades, serving as room for the *Madarsa*, enclose the other three sides. This "blessed house" would have gone down in history as the most inauspicious had an assassination attempt made on the life of Akbar succeeded when he was passing this place at the age of just twenty.

Jahangir maintained the tradition and passed a regulation providing for appropriation of properties of the heirless deceased or travellers by the state and to utilize the wealth thus acquired for the upkeep of *Madarsas*. We don't hear much about *Madarsas* newly built by him but certainly records indicate that the renovation of several *Madarsas* was carried out by him. Shah Jahan's imperial *Madarsa* that once stood to the Jama Masjid in Delhi was destroyed in the civil disturbances of 1857. Both Shah Jahan and Aurangzeb remained generous towards the noble cause of education.

One of the *Madarsas* that has continued to live to this day is the old building of Zakir Hussain College at Ajmeri Gate. Founded by a leading amir, Bhaziuddin Bahadur Firoz Jung, at the court of Aurangzeb in 1710. It served as his tomb as well. There is a mosque and an arcade of apartments around the courtyard. Another *Madarsa* that lives upto its name is Safdarjung Madarsa dating back to 1754 when Safdarjung, the viceroy and Wazir (Prime Minister) of Emperor Ahmad Shah, died. Sunehri Masjid in Chandni Chowk of Delhi, from where Nadir Shah ordered the massacre of the inhabitants of Delhi in 1739, also served as Madarsa Aminiya. It was founded in 1897 and gradually shifted to Masjid Panipatian near Kashmiri Gate. It continues to function as a typical Madarsa with several students still working to master the theological science.

SHAHID AKHTER MAKHFI

MADHAVI MUDGAL

Born into a famous musical family, Madhavi's musical tastes are of high standard which is only natural because her father Pandit Vinay Chandra Maudgalya, a prime disciple of late Pandit Vishnu Digamber Paluskar, has been an indefatigable worker in the world of Hindustani classical music and her brother Madhup Mudgal, a known classical vocalist in Delhi, helps her with her dance-music. Well trained at first in Kathak and Bharatanatyam, Madhavi Mudgal had become quite well known as a Kathak dancer, often partnering the handsome Durgalalji, but when she chose the graceful and highly lyrical Odissi, learning it from Gurus Hare Krishna Behere and keluchuran Mohapatra, she dedicated herself to it totally. She has performed not only in all the major dance 'estivals of India, but also abroad in numerous places like the U.K. Europe, the USSR, Sri Lanka, Japan, Algeria, Ghana, Kenya and Maurituis. All these experiences since the age of 11 have given her much paise and confidence. A tissome body, large expressive eyes and lyrical grace are her assets, while inner involvement with the theme and remarkable reposefulness, easy footwork and lightness of movements mark her dancing.

SUSHEELA MISRA

MADHUBALA

Hers is a face that decades - and untimely death - have not been able to erase. A large, moon-shaped face, partially covered with stray wisps of windblown hair, glistening cheeks, limpid eyes and the trademark crooked smile : Madhubala still stares out of the posters in your neighbourhood gift shop. And when the TV screens light up with her golden oldies like *Aayega aayega, Aaiyee meherbaan, Ek ladki bheegi bhaagi si* and *Pyaar Kiya to darna kya*, it does seem like yesterday once more.

In a film career spanning three decades (1942-1962) and a life that abruptly wound up at 36, Madhubala managed to create movie memorabilia like *Mahal, Amar, Mr and Mrs ' 55, Chalti ka Naam Gaadi, Howrah Bridge, Kala Paani* and *Mughal-e-Azam*.

Despite her faminine splendour, the actress never portrayed the docile, unquestioning, tradition-bound waif. She was the woman who drove into an all male garage in the dead of night, all by herself (*Chalti ka Naam Gaadi*), played a spunky, never-say-die journalist in *Kala Paani*

and *Jaali Note* or challenged the might of the monarch in *Mughal-e-Azam*.

MADHURI DIXIT (b. 1967)

Madhuri Dixit is one of the few Hindi film heroines who can gyrate and thumb to the raunchiest of Saroj Khan choreography and still bring an inviolate innocence to it. It was *Tezaab* that made her a superstar, and her success was reinforced with the hummable hit song *Ek do teen*.

Her sensual songs like *Choli ke peeche* in *Khalnayak* sent audiences into a frenzy. With the comic *Dil* and fiery roles in *Beta* and *Anjaam*, she was able to explore the range of her talent. Although her *Hum Aapke Hain Kaun* is one of the biggest grossing Hindi entertainers, she pines to perform in enduring classic like *Mughal-e-Azam* or *Pakeezah*. Her latest and much-awaited offering is *Gajagamini*, directed by M.F. Hussain - another tryst with our muse.

MADHURI PHALNIKAR BHADURI

Despite this indepth feel for the desert, Madhuri herself does not belong to these areas. Having grown up in Pune, a city noted for its colonial ambience, its many industrial units and its urban lifestyle, Madhuri was more at home with a bicycle than the sketch pad. On her way to school each day, the little scholar invariably dallied at Pune's tree-lined streets , the well kept gardens and the green spread of empty plots. A committed badminton star, who was seeded as the Indian national champion thrice, Madhuri's painting was far from a serious pursuit at that time. This backseat ambition was indulged in as a hobby that she could squeeze into as her high pressure badminton routine. Only, Madhuri was determined to pour into this pursuit a furious passion. A gragarious individual by nature, Madhuri was soon persuaded by friends to exhibit her amateur efforts. This maiden attempt logged a surprising sales mark and proved a turning point in her career.

"Badminton was now to take less importance. I had always played the game under the stress of having to win and having come back with the National Championship thrice, I felt there was no charm in it." The shift over to serious art meant joining an undergraduate course at univerity and then the round of serious showings. Gone were the real life copies of familiar landscapes and in its place were groves, textured with layers of mature artistry. No wonder the then Prime Minister Rajiv Gandhi conveyed his commendation for her and Madhuri caught the attention of nature lovers and environmentalists who like to see and preserve the environment in more than physical forms.

Being a natural at depicting nature, Madhuri felt, was not enogh. Madhuri went on to try experimental works and thus was born a series of canvses on abstract subjects and quite strangely, horses. These were symbols of power, physical strength and unbridled movement. Their colouration was a vivid evidence of the fact that Madhuri the artist was not static. The love for colour, the generative attitude and the search for a different matter made Madhuri home onto the subject of portrayals. instead of studied canvases of formal faces and people, Madhuri packed her sketch pad and pencil and stepped out of doors to watch the lifestyle of the Lambani people, a tribal group that migrates to cities of western India in search of jobs as unskilled labour. Their delicate bone structure, their distinctive attire and jewellery, was what motivated Madhuri. Before long, these inputs took shape in a major showing that uplifted her artistry to the heights of recognition. It was at this stage that corporate firms, in search of talent, chaced on her potential and Madhuri's works adorned the calendars of the Tata Industrial group. Collectors of contemporary art, too, began to acquire her works as part of their personal stock and Madhuri became a regular exhibitor at the metro cities of the country.

Realising that inspiration for her came from real life scenes, Madhuri began taking extensive tours of places that had captured her imagination. It was this personal whim that made her travel to the western deserts and come back armed with loads of sketechs of the main fort of the border town of Jaisalmer. Havin criss-crossed the desert in all sorts of ways, on camel back, train rides and even on foot, Madhuri had dynamic information stored in her mind and her sketch pad, to undertake the latest series of works. More than the pomp and splendour of regal life in this state of erstwhile land of maharajas and merchants, she preferred to present the life of its ordinary folk.

Having established a viable subject of expressiveness Madhuri poured into it a concentration of technical expertise. In them, one can spot the feedback of a miniaturist's art, the creative possibilities of knife work on canvas, the temperating and confronting of colouration in delightful but muted tones and above all, a balance of colouration in delightful but muted tones and above all, a balance of placements that defies description. As a result, her faces are living symbols of persons breathing a liveliness and emotional strength that only a person who feels and then pains, can instil.

At home, while she sits pouring over her canvas, Madhuri is an artist who forgets the hours. Following a twelve-hour schedule of painting is made an enriching experience for her as she switches on her cassette playe and allows the strains of a lilting ghazal to fill the air and soak into the senses. "It is a meditation turned to the canvas", she confides", she confides. "Thoughts come and go, a fleeting deer, the patter of the rain drops, ending up in a kind of dreamy romantic mood that touches me somewhere". It is this subtle linkage of fact and feeling that has made Madhuri's works rise above the ordinary and exude an emotional and evocative response that the eye sees, the mind feels and the senses soak inwards.

SUBHRA MAJUMDAR

MADRAS MUSEUM THEATRE

Madras Museum Theatre is situated on Pantheon Road, once the most fashionable of destinations where the Governor would arrive with his lady to preside over the evenings entertainment. As one observer notes "the dramatic urge" was so pronounced amongs the residents of Madras, that amateur theatricals were popular as far

back as 1778. A theatre called "The Playhouse" was built on the Island grounds. After many changes of place, the present Museum Threatre was opened in 1895. The Museum Theatre stands like a Victorian lady in a red velvet gown, lifting her scallpped petticoats high up above the ground. The U shaped curve of the front of the theatre has a double row of arched openings, one which allowed light and air into the wide verandah that circle round it, the other for the long tall windows that opened into the auditorium. The design of the theatre is said to have been modelled on the Aldwych theatre at London, a modified version of the Elizabethean playhouse the seating in a wide oval, going down in tiers, to the pit, where the governor sat. The Madras Amateur Dramatic Society founded in 1838 held performances regularly at the Museum Theatre from 1895 onwards.

GEETA DOCTOR

MAHAKOSALA : CULTURAL HERITAGE

Mahakosala forms the largest unit among the three component parts that now constitute the State of Madhya Pradesh. Its ancient name Mahakosala or Dakshina (south) Kosala, with its capital at Sripur (Present Sirpur in Raipur district) distinguished it from the North Kosala, having its seats at Ayodhya and Sravasti.

The river Narmada having its source at Amarkantaka, flows through parts of Mahakosala and then it enters the Malwa region of Madhya Pradesh. The ancient remains found on the banks of the Narmada have taken back the cultural history of this part of the country to hoary antiquity. The archaeolgical relics from the districts of Jabalpur, Narsinghpur and Hoshangabad, in the form of stone and copper tools, terracotta figurines and pottery pieces, have furnished a good deal of interesting material to reconstuct the early history of this region.

ANCIENT CAVES

A number of rock shelters, being the habitations of early cave-men, have been located at Raigarh, Singhanpur, Pachmarhi, Hoshangabad and Sagar, Most of these caves bear paintings and engravings. These have shed light on the mode of life of the cave-dwellers. An extensive site in the Abchand forest area of the Sagar district has been explored by the University of Saugar. The site being a continuous chain of low lying hills, stands on the river Gadheri. Quite a large number of shelters bearing paintings have been discovered here. The paintings are in red ochre, cream and white colours. The scenes portrayed are generally those of hunting, horse-riding, battles, dance and music. Various domestic scenes are also met with. The recent excavations conducted at Adamgarh (near Hoshangabad) rock-shelters have yielded interesting stone tools, which were used by the cave-dwellers at various stages. Such excavations are necessary at some other similar sites.

The number of historic remains of different periods in the Mahakosala area is quite large. The Mauryan emperor Asoka had one of his edicts inscribed at Rupnath, a place 30 miles form Jabalpur. In the Ambikapur district, several Mayryan Brahmi inscriptions have been discovered in the

Ramgarh caves. These inscriptions give an indication of the existence of halls for dramatic performances.

THE TOWN OF TRIPURI

Tripuri (modern Tewar near Jabalpur) and Eran in the Saugar district are well known sites in this area. They have yielded punch-marked and inscribed coins, which take back the history of these two places prior to the 3rd Century B.C. Names of rulers like Dharmapala and Indragupta belonging to 3rd-2nd Centuries B.C., are known to us from Eran. During the Kushana-Satavahana period (1st-2nd Cent. A.D.) several Buddhist monasteries were construted at Tripuri. The excavations conducted here by the University of Saugar have shown that Tripuri continued to be a great political and cultural centre till the 12th Century A.D.

ARCHAEOLOGICAL SITE OF ERAN

As a result of the excavation work conducted at Eran, a clear picture of the moat and mud defence wall, built in about 1500 B.C. around the old town of Eran, has been obtained. the basal width of the wall was found 154 feet. The recent excavations also revealed that the chalcolithic habitation at Eran was in the shape of a semi-circle. On three sides it was protected by the river Bina, on which the town stands the fourth side was protected by the construction of the mud defence wall. It was found that the people at Eran did not occupy the area adjacent to the river, but preferred to live at a distance of about 200 feet away from the river. A trench taken in the centre of the present Eran village was found to be rich in the structures built of bricks during the early historical periods.

These excavations at Eran have thrown a flood of new light on the early history of eastern Malwa and Mahakosala between the period 1900 B.C. and 600 A.D.

During the Gupta period several Brahmanical temples were built in this region. Eran became a very flourishing town during this period. From an inscription of the Gupta emperor Samudragupta we learn that he paid visits to this place. Chandragupta Vikramaditya, the illustrious successor of Samudragupta, completely uprooted the foreign Saka rulers, who had earlier established · their hegemony in Malwa for over a period of three hundred years. During the rule of the Guptas, everal temples were built and statues of the Hindu deities were made at Eran, the remains of many of which are still extant.

Here the Gupta rulers had to measure swords with the barbarian Hunas. The last Gupta inscription dated in the year 191 (510 A.D.) records that a chief named Goparaja came to Eran with King Bhanugupta, and after fighting bravely died in the battlefield. His devoted wife burnt herself on the funeral pyre of her husband. This inscription is the earliest epigraphical record referring to the custom of Sati in this country.

OTHER GUPTA SITES

Other notable Gupta sites in Mahakosla are Tigwa (district Jabalpur) and Rajim (district Raipur). At Tigwa stands a typical Gupta temple with gracefully posed statues of the river goddesses, Ganga and Yamuna, Rajim has produced some remarkably interesting sculptures.

During the early medieval period, from 600 to 1200 A.D., the Chandellas and Kalachuris were the two chief ruling dynasties in the Mahakosala area. The Chandellas, known as the great builders of the Khajuraho group of temples, had their centres at Kalinjar, Khajuraho and Ajaigarh. The political centres of the Kalachuris were at Tripuri and Ratanpur. The large number of temples and sculptural remains found at Sripur, Karitalai, Ratanpur, Sohagpur, Janjgit and Amarkantaka (to name only a few) bear eloquent testimony to the development of art and architecture during this period.

Saivism had now become the main religion of the people, Followers of the Saiva, Sakta, Vaisnava and Jaina faiths were numerous, as is borne out be literary evidences and the archaeological relics of the period.

During the Muslim rule, followed by the Maratha supremacy in certain parts of Mahakosala, several forts and fortresses were built by the ruling chiefs. The Gonds are particularly known to have built strongholds at various places of this region. The fort at Nadla is a typical example of the Gond architecture. Other forts of the late medieval period can be seen at Dhamoni, Garhpahra, Janjgir and numberous other places of Mahakosala.

K. D. BAJPAI

MAHAMAGHA FESTIVAL AT KUMBAKONAM

Kumbakonam (Kumbhaghona in Sanskrit) in the Thanjavur District of Tamil Nadu is famous as a sacred temple town an as the scene of the great Mahamagham festival when millions of pilgrims from all parts of country congregate for a dip in the holy Mahamaghan Tank in the town and in the river Kaveri. The *Rig Veda*, the *Yajur Veda*, the epics - Ramayana and Mahabharata-most of the *Puranas* and many a *Kavya* in Sanskrit and Tamil, speak of the sanctity of the waters of the Kaveri and the bath therein. Kaveri is the Vedic *Marud arudha* and Kumbakonam is one of the five important sacred ghats on the banks of the river. The *Mahamagham* bathing festival occurs once in 12 years, when the Sun is in the Zodiacal sign Aquarius (Kumbha). Jupiter is in Leo *(Simha)*, and the Moon is in the conjuction with the constellation Magham (often mentioned as Makha). *Kumbha Melas* are held at Hardwar (on the Ganga) once in 12 years, when Jupiter is in Aries; at Prayag (Allahabad) at the confluence of the Ganga, Yamuna and Saraswati. Similar bathing festivals take place at Nasik and Ujjain also once in 12 years when people gather in their millions to bathe at specified ghats of the Godavari. This *Mela* goes by the name of Pushkaram (recently celebrated in August 1979). While the *Melas* at the different places mentioned above are spread over a period of days, the *Mahamagha Mela* at Kumbakonam is concentrated on a single day, the conceourse of pilgrims being all the more.

The first Maha Kumbh of the new millennium has just concluded. Legend has it that a joint churning of the ocean by the gods and demons threw out, among other celestial things, a pot containing the Elixir of Life. The gods did not want to share this at any cost with the demons, as it would render them immortal. The demons tried deceit; the gods escaped with the pot, and in the melee, a few drops of the Elixir fell at certain spots on the earth. The Kumbh Mela (literally the festival of the pot) is held at these spots, and it is believed that a dip in the river near which the Kumbh is held will absolve on of all sins. Other interesting versions of this legend also abound.

The holding of the Kumbh Mela, which, for the layman occurs every twelve years, is dictated by the positions of three heavenly bodies - the sun, the moon and the planet Jupiter. The only catch is that Jupiter has an orbit peiod of 4333 days or nearly 11 years and 10 months which is not quite twelve years. This gap of exact twelve years has to be reconciled with the location of the sun and the Moon for determining the dates of holding of the Kumbh. Four main sites have traditionally been prescribed - Hardwar, Prayag (Allahabad), Ujjain and Nasik. However, there is no fixed order of rotation between these sites; rather, the site is determined by traditionally prescribed planetary combinations in the following manner.

1. When the new moon (amavasya) occurs with the sun and the Moon in Aries and jupiter in Aquarius, the Kumbh takes place at Hardwar.
2. When the new moon (amavasya) occurs with the sun and the Moon in Capricorn and Jupiter in Taurus, the Kumbh takes place at Allahabad.
3. If the new moon (amavasya) occurs with the sun and the moon in Aries and Jupiter in Leo, than the Kumbh takes place at both Ujjain and Nasik.
(condensed)

References

Aiyar G.V.J., South Indian Festival, London, 1921. Buck, C.H., Faiths, Fairs and Festivals of India, Calcutta, 1917 Sharma, B.N., Festivals of India, New Delhi, 1978.

N. RATHNASREE

MALINI RAJURKAR

Malini Rajurkar, 52, settled in Hyderabad, is a singer of repute and renown. Performing a music conferences or private 'baithaks' is a matter of practised ease for her. She immediately impresses the audience with her range, repertorie, soft renditions of 'Khayal", 'thumris' and 'tappas'. Publicity shy, Malini was born into a family steeped in the Hindustani music tradition.

Thus, after her marriage to Vasantrao Rajukar in 1965, Malini came to Hyderabad to discover a fairly dormant music atmosphere. However, the new bride was given total encouragement by her husband and in-laws. So, she practised for nearly six hours every day. Resisting her attempts for enter college as a music teacher or maths lecturer, Malini's husband prompted her to concentrate fully on perfecting her art. Get into practical performances, he advised. The break he was advising came a year later, in 1966, when, after hearing her perform at a friend's place in Hubli, the famous Gangubai Hangal recommended her name for the Sawai Gandharva festival at Pune.

"It was my first large and important conference", reminisces Malini. "After singing here, I overcame my hesitation and performed in a string of music conferences. The experience taught me three things: firstly, despite nobody knowing my Guruji here, I got recognition. So it's the artiste who matters. It's not so important as nowadays, to have financial backing. Thirdly, I followed the principle of not looking for the results, but the experience of performing before a live audience, which became my notivating force. Not the reviews or money that followed".

So what does it take to be a good vocal singer? Flexibility of voice and practice are very important, feels Malini, to become a good artiste. "You need hard work, sincerity, common sense, punctuality, politeness and self-introspection. Classical music brings out the 'sadhana' of an artiste. The combination of 'swara', 'shabd', 'taal', 'laya' can be achieved by any perfectionist, but it's the individuals devoted contribution that counts". She feels she owes her success to a large extent to all her near relatives and friends who helped her out in moments of need, her mother, who kept a close vigil during her scholarship years, and last, but not least, her husband. "I prefer to stay behind the curtain", claims Malini, 'rather than up-front. For me, 'sangeet' is not just a raga or 'swara', it is an orientation, a commitment".

FIRDAUSI HYDRIE

MALLIKA SARABHAI : INDIA'S PRIMA DONNA

Young, uncommonly beautiful and intelligent, Mallika Sarabhai is one of the most outstanding classical Indian dancers today.

However, as a performer, this multi-talented dancer defies straightjacket categorisation. Her innovative spirit pushes her art for beyond the frontiers of classical tradition and courageously ventures to creat new ingenious forms to suit the themes she want to portray. At the same time, apart from her classical training, she is a conscientious students of folk performative culture and utilises folk forms to enrich the texture of her performance. Today she distinctly stands out as one of the creative performers enriching the dance and theatre scene as whole.

The career of this beautiful dancer gradually evolved from being a trained classical dancer to film-maker, writer-publisher, theatre personality and ultimately she become consciencious activist and commentator on social issues through the medium of her performance.

The Darpana Akademi of Performing Arts located in Ahmedabad, the capital of the Indian state of Gujarat, was the institution where Mallika had her initial training in classical Bharatanatyam and Kuchipudi styles. This institution was founded by her illustrious dancer-mother Mrinalini in 1949 with the active support of her husband, Vikram.

Both, the institution and Mallika, grew together from strength to strength. Darpana became a leading dance institution and Mallika too a leading dancer.

That is why when the internationally famous theatre-director and the head of the International Centre of Theatre Research of Paris launched a grand project of staging India's magnificent epic, the *Mahabharata,* Mallika was his natural choice to play the role of Draupadi, one of the central characters of the longest poem in the world.

Mallika acted the lead role both in the French and English versions of the drama. The performances were staged practically all over the world including at the Avigon

Festival in France, Brooklyn Akademi of Music, New York, Releigh Studies, Los Angeles, Ginza Saison, Tokyo, and Tranway, Glasgow and the Perth and Adelaide Festivals in Australia. Mallika became an international name.

The drama was later made into a magificent film. And in the film too Mallika enacted the lead female role.

Mallika has a brilliant academic career behind her. She graduated from St. Zavier's college of Ahmedabad with honours in economics and after that joined the famous Indian Institute of Management in the same city acquiring post-graduate degree in Business Administration. She did her Ph.D from Gujarat University with Organisational Behaviour as her subject. Her education helped her understand social problems which soon started reflecting in her work as a dancer. Since 1977 she is a lead soloist at the Darpana Akademi of Performing Arts specialising in the Bharatnatyam and the Kuchipudi. She, is due course, won many international awards for her graceful dance performances which brought the flavour of India on international scene.

From her illustrious dance - teachers she learnt some very rare items and compositions enriching her repertory. Some are so rare that among all the classical dancers it is she who alone can performe them. In her classical performances she rejected the traditional items where the dignity of woman as a social entity was impaired. Instead, she presented the legends of powerful Indian goddesses of the Indian pantheon known as 'Shakties' or personifications of spiritual and physical power in female form.

Perhaps due to its long association with the temple Indian classical dance has retained its devotional flavour. Prominent among the modern dancers who used for themes other than the devotional is Mrinalini Sarabhai. She effectively used Bharatnatyam vocabulary to speak of other moods and themes of contemporary social relevance like environmental pollution.

Mallika continued the tradition of creative choreography by absorbing the trend of depicting social issues, so well enunciated by her own mother Mrinalini.

In her choreographic work she drew on many elements to create a new vocabulary. She did borrow from the classical dance tradition but also utilised the rhythms and movements of folk dances, she studied matrial art forms of South and North-East India and through her keen observation stylised everyday movements and gestures of the common man in the street. Out of this she created a new language to express her ideas and speak intimately with the audience about the issues concerning them all.

In recently years Mallika has managed to apply her artistic talents to bring about social change by launching purposeful project. With the active help of the dedicated band of well experienced Darpana performance she choreographed items which made people examine their traditional attitudes towards women. She went to schools with her programmes on environmental issues. She visited slum areas to create AIDS awareness and also toured rural areas to fight against social prejudices.

She has become the thinking dancer of India creating new awareness through her art.

During her performance as Draupadi in Peter Brook's *Mahabharata* she became aware of the need to make storing and positive statements about the images of Indian womanhood. This latter led her to create a unique programme 'Shakri', the power of women, in London which subsequently toured Britain, Holland and India. Its reappraisal of mythological, historical and contemporary female figures had a stunning effect on her audience.

Immediately after this she created yet another purposeful programme titled "Sita's Daughters", very hard hitting and funny too, exploring new forms and techniques to communicate with her audience. Here she used various theatrical devices and communication techniques such as masks, mime, meaning ful body language, narrative monolgue, music, dance and song to put forth the stories with her own interpretations.

She has thus created with her performative talents and thinking mind the theatre of social purpose, her precious gift to the nation.

Apart from her dance activities her multiple interests stretch to different fields. In order to highlight the rich heritage of Indian arts and crafts she started a publishing house, *Mapin*, and edited several books. This has produced many books of excellence and has set the standards of book designing.

Ahmedabad's Darpana Akademi of Performing Arts, of which she is Honorary Joint Director, is her laboratory. Here she coordinates the training of students in dance, theatre, puppetry and music and look after the work of Darpana Dance Company, Janavak Folk and Tribal Dance Company, and Darpana for Development, an organisation established to create and develop performing arts modules for developmental issues. Apart from this she look after a film unit, *'Chitakati'*, established to produce educational films and T.V. programmes. In 1993 she founded yet another trust, *Kartikarnti*, to promote interdisciplinary work in the fields of arts and crafts.

Mallika takes deep interest in the developmental activities of school children. To make children aware about environmental issues and to help them enchance their capabilities she has established an organisation called *Jagruti*. The activities of this organisation are spread over eight schools in Ahmedabad covering about twenty five thousand students.

Looking at the range of activities that India's Prima Donna is engaged in, one realises it is not easy to be a Mallika.

M. L. VARADPANDE

MALVIKA SARUKKAI : NEW DIMENSION TO BHARATNATYAM

Behind closed doors the sounds of ankle bells and the resounding notes of the drum beat indicate that a practice session is in progress. The magnetic draw of these enticing sounds lead to a dancer, engrossed with her role on stage. But even in that off stage concentrated stance, dancer Malvika Sarikkai impresses. The slim and somewhat fragile figure is barely past her mid thirties, but this classical exponent of the Bharatanatyam style of Indian classical dance has been dedicating herself to her art form for more than twenty-seven years and the time tested and committed approach to her art shows in her very nuuance and movement.

Initially, she had trained under farmed masters like Guru Kalyasundram, Guru Rajaratnam and Guru Kalanidhi Narayanan. Then had come about at stint with another equally brilliant style of classical dance,Oddissi, and under its best known master, Guru Kelucharan Mahaptra, Later on, Malavika had also trained under Guru Ramani Jena and finally, when she had taken the plunge on her own, Malavika's own dance from had been a distinctive choreography of both pure dance or *nritta* and stylied depictions or *abhinaya*. It was a style that was exploratory and precise, that did not mutilate even a single principle of the basic concept and yet was layered by energy, grace and innovation, both appealing and charming.

By the time she was twenty-two, Malavika was a world figure on the dance stage. She was the youngest solo dancer in the Queen Elizabeth Hall when the Festival of India was being held in London. Then had followed the Festivals of India at France, USA, Japan and more recently, Switzerland. Besides these mega international events, Malavika has even regaled audiences in colleges and dons at university towns. Of course the international landmark events like the Arts Festival of Adelaide, the TANZ 90 at Vienna and even the Munich Opera stage had dance recitals by her.

What then, one might ask, is so special of Malavika's performance? It is that she re-invented the traditional and the legendary, in a sensitised form, that keeps intact the significance of the essential myth but enhances it through revitalised individual techniques. Thus he dance appears to be yet another interpretation of age old art. Her lines remain well ordered and her rhythms vibrate her emotional temper strides the centuries and the entire effect is aesthetic and yet understandable.

This capacity to represent the traditional in an acceptable and yet contemporary garb, first came into the forefront in her work, "Krishna Ritu Krida". This dance number was replete with emotional content as it dealt with the many *dalliances* of Lord Krishna through a year long cycle of six seasons. Every season became of basis of revealing the omnipotence and dynamism is the Lord whereby Krishna becomes a symbole of renewal and of environment interaction between Man and Nature. Her later work, "Fireflies", was a dramatic multimedia piece. In it, audiences were regaled to delightful poetic inclusions, traditional images, thematic links and above all, the classical dance expression that gave access to the primal emotions of human life. It won her many accolades, as critics across the country dubbed her as 'pathfinder', and a modernite who had managed to reinstate classical dance in the hall of modern technology and not left it to stagnate in the dusty backdrop of tradition and ritual.

Instead of making these nocturnal lamplight bearers, that every Indian child knows as 'Jugnu', as. objects of visual appeal, Malavika has used them as a symbol of human desire. The idea of using fireflies to convey this yearning for love, was what struck her after she had seen a Japanese production. In it the lady had gone to visit her lover in the dark, carying a lantern of glowworms to light her way. Sister Priya had written a poem on this theme and then there was no holding back. Malavika at once set to work identifying ten conventional moods or emotions as listed in the classics to portray universal human love.

Within the framework of the traditional too, Malavika has proved her mettle. Her depiction of *Kaliya Mardana* or the killing of the demon snake Kaliya by Lord Krishna, is a masterpiece of structuring to implement contemporary ideas. The snake demon is none other than the hydra-headed menace of pollution and its control is the positivism evident in the Krishna concept. Again, the dance of *Mahadeva* or Shiva, is a contemporary look at the devastating effects of deforestation and denunciation. The acts of penance performed by the Lord as a saviour of mankind is what inspires the idea of taking a grip of this ugly situation and exert ourselves to end it. In addition to these adaptations of ancient forms, have been straight forward depicitions of the *Ramayana* narrated by Tulsi Das and the *Kamba Ramayana*, which too, examines the contents of the epic in another context. Puranic legends, the forms of Shiva dances and the Krishna themes received sensitive treatment at the hand of this explotative and inventive artist.

Like the dances that she performs and conceives, Malavika creates a spatial and conceptual accent by her very personality. Dressed in a becoming Kanjivaram Sari, she insists that a dancer's personality is another dimension of the dancer's being. Through the wonderful technique of gestures you achieve." - she expounds, "we take an experience and we work on that" is her other dictum. No, it is not a rigid imposition but a way of life where artificial restrictions fall away. One day of Malavika's dance regimen reveals that the fetters of tradition and unnecessary discipline just sloughs off and the spirit rings true, in a soaring sort of way, flying with the fireflies, curshing the Kalia and coming out the winner after the penance of true Saivite.

. **SUBHRA MAJUMDAR**

MANIPURI DANCE

A religious dance style (of the Manipur State) for invoking divine blessing; originally only Siva and Parvati were propitiated but in course of time Radha and Krishna were also invoked; men and women take part to the accompaniment of the *mridanga* and (chorus) singing; has a restrained lyrical quality and is refined, graceful, gentle and somewhat slow moving at times, the dancers swaying and making sinuous movements of the arms and hands; there is no attempt at *abhinaya* (facial mime or expression); the woman dancers wear a very beautiful and colourful costume known as *Kamil* (introduced by a king, Bhagya Chand); the long and wide lahngas (skirts) being attractively ornamented with small mirrors and stiffened to stand out as they reach the feet.

Manipuri survived sheltered valley of Manipur in the Assam Hills; kept aloof from foreign influences, main Indian trends; isolation broken 1920's, when Rabindranath Tagore visited the valley; Tagore invited leading Guru Atomba Singh to teach at his school at Shantiniketan. The supply movements of Manipuri dance, suitable for Tagore's lyrical dramas; he employed them in his plays, introduced dance as part of curriculum at his institution.

The Manipuri dancer wears a large, stiff, glittering with round pieces; a shimmering gauze veil; hair done up in high rolled crown, with chain of white blossoms; luminous cheeks and forehead decorated with dots of sandalwood paste.

Known for its faminity, Manipuri marked by slow swooning rhythm, dancer with her hips thrust back, head tilted on one side, turns and glides on if in a dream. The immobility of her face, like that of a mask, in sharp contrast with the other three schools of dance, in which the face and eyes are major source of expression.

The drummer, his naked torsoir, a white dhoti with red border, tucked up above his knees, dances, while he plays on the drum; he slaps and thumps, the drum rumbles and bowls and chuckles, his energic, electric movements are a msculine, counterpart, to the slow, undulating patterns woven by female dancer.

Chief of the 20th century exponent include Atomba Singh who preserved the tradition of *ras* dancing, and Amuli Singh.

References

Ambrose, Kay, Classical Dances and Costumes of India, London, 1958.

Bannerji, P., Dance in India, Allahabad, 1947.

Bowers, F., Dance in India, New York, 1953.

Devi, Ragini, Dances of India, Calcutta, 1953.

MANSARAM

Mansaram deserves to figure prominently among those who have proved mark Twain wrong (about the East being East and the West being West so that "the twain shall never meet"). After nearly three decades of working as an artist in the town of Burlington in Canada, Mansaram is both Canadian and an Indian; his expression is imbued with influences both modern and traditional; and his works are truly the products of an unusal marriage between art and technology.

When recently "Air-India", the official Indian airline, looked around for an artist to present the diversity and the range of attractions India offers to a foreign traveller, Mansaram was a natural choice. His series of eight posters depicting the east, west, north and south of India with all the splendour of its architecutre, people and places reveal the depth of his understanding of India. As Canadian critic Jeff Mahoney put it, these posters are "an almost cinematic spray of collage imagery: the colours are electric and the feel for the land and its people is telling and passionate". Dr. Stephen Inglis, Director (Research) of the Canadian Museum was direct : he called these posters "Simply spectacular".

Mansaram is a multimedia artist. He works in xerography, videography, colleges, mixed media and photography. Back in the sixties in Bombay, he began with water colours and oils. A product of JJ School of Art, Bombay, he was spotted fairly early for his promise and potential. In 1959 an art critic who assessed Mansaram's painting on Nepal, described him as "One of Bombay's least known and most gifted artists".

In 1963, he left for Holland for post-graduate study at the State Academy of Fine Arts in Amsterdam. Initially he reminded Stedilijk Museum director Sandberg of "a bird fallen from his nest", an apt description of someone who had left the topical Bombay for the rainy Amsterdam, with little realisation that a short stay in Holland would be a prelude to his settling down permanently in another western country, Canada. In Amsterdam, Mansaram perfected modern techniques; he especialized in colleges, a discipline that remains with him till now. "It is the only logical form", he said, "for the extra-rational experience of Indian art which, like our music, refuses to be constricted within the walls of a logical story or even a theme".

The one man who attracted Mansaram towards Canada was Marshall McLuhan, a professor of English at Univerity of Toronto and celebrated media guru in the sixties. Mansaram knew him by his writings only. He speaks of his first meeting with McLuhan in 1966 with such vividity as if he met him yesterday. He credits the Canadian communications experts for inspiration to use mixed media for his artistic expressions.

"Camera is my sketch book now", says Manasaram. The reach of brush and palette has been expanded by adding camera and photocopier to his repertoire. In his case though this is no victory of technology over art. The technical tools are just that-aids for aesthetic expression of what he observes, feels and imagines about the life and the world around him. He is certain that Rembrandt and Picasso, had they been alive today, would not have shied away from employing technology for creating and enriching their art.

Mansaram says that his creative mind is constantly making "new connections" from the images of the immediate environment, stored memory, TV pictures, photos and pictures collected over the years and even his dreams. A process of triggered reactions and creative actions follows as he uses a variety of tools available to him camera, copier, brushes, paint, scissors and glue. His paintings, photo-based works, collages, videos, lasergraphs, words and even sculptures show the bewildering range of stimuli to his mind and sensibilities as well as his impressive, artisic skills. Some of his favourite themes are birds, squirrels, other objects in nature and human forms.

His exhibits of the "Rear View Mirror" series at India Pavilion in Montreal in 1968 attracted considerable notice. It depicted the little worlds that were all in the Past." It is like driving a car and looking in the rear-view mirror. You see what you left behind", he said. His paintings did not have one frame: these were frames within a frame showing how it was possible for the visual stimuli from his oriental background to co-exist with those from the technological society to which he had migrated. The multi-frame format like the split screen technique in the cinema, revealed a stream of consciousness reflecting what he saw, heard and read. The series was a tribute to Time, to the past which Mansaram believes is never dead; "and even if it were, its ghosts and angels would continue to haunt and protect us", he adds.

The exhibition of Mansaram's hangings at the Dhoomimal Gallery in New Delhi (August 1972) represented an excellent illustration of the mosaic approach to the visual. With its emphasis on synthesis or composite character, his works conveyed a variety of visual reproductions. The following years saw Mansaram at his prolific best, with a wide range of productions that included the "Ordinary and Extraordinary", "Backyard", "Time and Space", and "Bllueprint" series.

His "Art of Textiles" exhibition at India House, New York, in October 1979 was an innovative collection of wall hangings and banners that showed the dynamism and creativity of modern Indian art.

Closer home, his exhibition of paintings in mixed media at the Indus Gallery in Karachi in March 1991 was another important landmark. His Rajasthani roots, the desi flavour of his personality and, above all, the underlying South Asian imprint on his works and their warms, earthy colours combined to evoke a positive response from his Pakistani admirers. Speaking to one of them, an art critic, Mansaram said: "My creations are my way of celebrating. My pictures depict the joy which surrounds us all".

But he is by no means a hedonist. As an expatriate artist, he has gone through many experiences of struggle, pain and alienation too. In fact, a touch of loneliness beneath his cheerful outlook is quite discenible. He visits India frequently" as a ritual", partly to work from his Mount Abu studio but mainly to nourish his roots that are deeply embedded in the soil of India.

Yet Mansaram is deeply appreciative and grateful for what Canadia has given to him over the years. In 1970 he described Canada as "a fusion of many cultures from which some day there will emerge a society that will lead the world". Till today he remains optimistic on this score.

The exhibition of his photo lasergraphs called "New York - New York" revealed his grip on the multi-dimensionality of this megapolis. If there is one city that truly fascinates Mansaram, it is the Big Apple. He is convinced that its people, skyscrapers, art galleries and museums and its charged environment compel you to refrain from thinking "rationally " and in "a linear way". By using colour copier and other media, Mansaram brought forth the complexity of New York, the special hold the very idea and image of New York has on one's psyche. Art critic Arundhati Subramaniam caught the core of this genre when she described it as "Captivating virtual reality".

During a recent interview at his Burlington residence with the author, Mansaram spoke about his art and life. The memories of his early childhood are dominated by the anguish he had experienced on hearing the tale of Prince Siddhartha abandoning his family and kingdom in the search of Truth. If life was nothing but pain, tears and death, why try to live, he remembers asking as a teenager again and again. Later, lectures by J.J. Krishnamurthy helped him shape his philosophy of life. He earnt to avoid the beaten path, to be unconventional, different. He chose Amsterdam for study when his contemporaries went to Paris, Rome or London. He came to Canada when there were very few Indian immigrants here. He continued to work on his art when money-making seemed the all pervading passion around him. "What", I asked him, "sustains you as an artist"? He pondered, paused and the replied : The joy of sharing my creations with others". Clearly he meant it.

He had also remembered an earlier promise made to me to describe his art in poetry. As I took leave, he gave me a paper that read :

"I am a globe - performer, and a nomad

My audience is where I happen to show my work,

I create my Art from the heart,

The heart is not confined,

to the boundaries of a country or countries,

It floats and roams around the Cosmos".

RAJIV BHATIA

MARATHI AND GUJARATI FILMS

Dadasaheb Phalke is credited with making the first successful feature film in India. It was Raja Harishchandra. Though the film was silent, one could call it 'Marathi' film for the mytholgical characters were attired in the style of the Marathi stage. And though men appeared as women, the women were attired in nine yard sarees. Similarly, later when Gujarati producers and directors entered the filed, the artistes, especially the female artistes, were dressed in Gujarati style. Moreover, while the Marathi producers included 'Marathi' titles in their silent films, Gujarati producers included Gujarati titles.

Indeed one can say that the silent films produced by Dadasaheb Phalke, Baburao Painter, Bhai G. Pendharkar, V. Shantaram and other illustrious Maharashtrian film makers bore the distinct stamp of Maharashtrian mode of living and customs, and the silent films produced by Dwarkadas Sampat, Nanubhai Desai, Mayashankar, MehtaLuhar, Chandulal Shah and other illustrious Gujarati film makers reflected Gujarati manners, customs and traditions. This distinction was specially evident in historical films made in Kolhapur and social films produced in Bombay.

Pictures like *Sunhagad, Baji Prabhu, Netaji Palkar, Udaykal*, which dealt with the exploits of Shivaji and his lieutenants, could be described as representative Marathi films of the silent era, and similarly pictures like *Mumbaini Sehani, Pati Patni, Gunsundari* could be classified as representative Gujarati films of the silent era.

Advent of Talkies

With the avent of talkies, the language assumed greater significance. In the begining, the Gujarati producers made bilingual films in Hindi and Gujarati while the Maharashtrian producers made bilingual films in Hindi and Marathi. Thus the first Marathi talkie, Prabhat's *Ayodheycha Raja*, had its Hindi version with same artistes participating in both the versions. And though the first Gujarati talkie film, Sagar's *Narsi Bhagat*, did not have a Hindi version, Ranjit's *Sati Savitri* was produced in Hindi and Gujarati simultaneously, with the same artistes appearing in both the versions.

Indeed during the thirties, barring such devotional biographies of saints like *Narsi Bhagat* in Gujarati and *Tukarama* in Marathi, most of the Gujarati and Marathi films had their Hindi version. But while during the pre-war era from 1932-to 1940, eighty seven pictures were made in Marathi, only ten pictures were made in Gujarati. As a matter of fact since the advent of sound till the end of 1969, it is worth nothing that while 4067 Hindi films were made, the number of Marathi films made for the same period in 447 and the number of Gujarati films made is 138.

Pre War Era

In the pre war era, the Marathi film made a vital contribution to film art through realistic, human progressive films like *Dharmatma Tukaram, Kunku, Savkari Pash, Chhaya and Manoos*. They set a New vogue in social satire and purposeful comedy through films like *Dharmveer* and *Brahmachari*. Most of these films barring *Tukaram* and *Savkari Pash*, which have been included among the most significant Indian films ever produced, had Hindi versions. *Duniya Na Mane* (Kunku), *Aadmi* (Manoos) are also recognised as two most noteworthy social films of the thirties. These thought-provoking Marathi films set a very high standard in thematic content as well as realistic presentation. In comparison the Marathi films, produced during the war and after the war did not create the same stir or the same lasting impression.

The Gujarati films of the thirties did not create any stir though some pictures like *Be Kharab Jan* based on K.M. Munshi's script provided scintilating satire. Even Chandulal Shah's ambitious production of *Acchut* in Gujarati and Hindi could not achieve the same impact which Bombay Talkies' *Achhut Kanya* or Prabhat's *Dharmatma* had achieved earlier. Comparatively some of the Hindi films made by Sagar based on K.M. Munshi's novels, as well as pictures like *Sadhana* and *Aurat* succeeded in projecting the life in Gujarat more realistically as well as artistically.

During the war, the regional language films did not make any headway. While no Gujarati film was made in war years, the production in Marathi was considerably reduced. Yet, the Marathi films of the forties like *Dnyaneshwar, Shejari (Padosi), Amrit Maza Bal, Ramshastri* kept up the progressive tradition of the thirties. In fact, *Ramshastri*, which also had a Hindi version, is regarded as one of the best historical films ever produced in India.

Post War Films

After the end of the war and advent of freedom, the films in regional languages got a new impetus. In 1947, the phenomenal success of *Ramjoshi* and *Jai Malhar* not only gave a new impetus to Marathi films but changed its entire pattern. In introducing the popular rural folk song and dance for the first time on the Marathi screen, it won for the Marathi film a new audience. Since the, successful Marathi film has always had rural backdrop, with the *Tamasha* dancer, village Patil and the violent feuds that rock the rural life as the basis for major themes. In the post was era, many social urban films were also produced. Directors like Raja Paranjpe, Datta Dharmadhikari, Anant Mane, Ram Gabale, Raja Thakur and writers like G.D. Madgulkar, Vyanketesh Madgulkar, Dinkar Patil and G.R. Kamat were responsible for such noteworthy films as *pedgaonche Shahane,Kuberache Dhan, Poodhde Paul, Dev Pavla, Oon Paus, Doodh Bhaat, Postalil Mulgi, Bala Jo Jo Re, Stree Janma Tuzi Kahani, Chimni Pakhare, Dhakti Jau* and *Sangte Aika*. Out of these *Sangte Aika*, which ran for over two years in a single theatre in Poona, proved that the rural drama with folk song and dances had greater appeal to the Marathi audience than the urban comedy or middle-class domestic drama. The most successful films of the last decade viz. *Ek Gaon Bara Bhangadi, Kela Ishara Jata Jata, Sawal Maza Aika* and others testify to this fact.

Artistically, the post-war Marathi film has not made much progress, expecially during the last decade. In the fifties we had some remarkable realistic films like *Pedgaonche Shahane, Oon Paus, Chimni Pakhare*. As a poet's biography Shantaram's *Ramjoshi* and *Amar Bhopali* were noteworthy contributions. But not a single historical of the status of *Ramshastri* was made. Among the purposeful social films, *Prapanch* made in 1961 is perhaps the most outstanding. This poignant film depicting the tragedy of a woman addled with too many children by far provides the most telling argument in favour of family planning. Even in rural dramas, of late there is a growing tendency to present the present day working of village panchayats and expose the malpractices prevalent in our rural life. *Santh Wahate Krishna Mai* and *Ek Gaon Bara Bhangadi* make a seathing exposure of the evils rampant in the rural administration run by the panchayat chief for his personal gain.

Unable to meet the economic competition of Marathi stage and Hindi films, despite various handicaps, the Marathi films is struggling to keep up its identity with about fifteen new films every year. The Government of Maharashtra is also helping it through award and though exemption of entertainment tax for a least three films every year.

There was a spate of production of Gujarati films after the war. In 1947, for instance, eleven Gujarati films were produced as against eleven films produced from 1931 to 1946. In 1948, 27 Gujarati films were made, 16 in 1949 and 12 in 1950. Thus sixty eight Gujarati films were made between 1947-50. Some of them like Prakash's *Narsi Bhagat*, Minerva's *Prithivi Vallabh* were dubbed from Hindi to Gujarati. It was the great success of V.M. Vyas's *Ranekdevi* in 1947 that inspired such a large scale production of Gujarati films. Vyas himself made about ten films in five years. Majority of the pictures were based on either devotional or mythological subjects; some of them like *Hothal Padmini* were either historicals or based on popular legends like *Jesal Toral*. As to the social pictures, they followed the pattern set by *Gunsundari*. Indeed, Ajit Pictures 'Gunsundari' produced and directed by Ratibhai Punatar was the biggest hit narrating as it did the trails and tribulations of an orthodox Hindu wife wronged by her husband and in-laws.

In the fifties, the production of Gujarati films declined. In 1951 only six films were made in Gujarati, in subsequent years the average was just two pictures a year. After the advent of Gujarat State, the production has picked up and now on an average six pictures are produced every year in Gujarat. The tax exemption as well as State awards give an impetus to the producers of Gujarati films. But most of them follow the same old pattern. Technically average, neither in choice of theme nor in presentation do they mark any departure. The most successful Gujarati films of the last decade are *Mehandi Rang Layo* starring Rajendra Kumar and Usha Kiron and *Akhand Saubhagyavati* starring Asha Parekh. Both of them present the routine domestic dramas. Indeed, Mehboob's *Mother India* shot in Gujarat and Sarvodaya pictures *Saraswatichandra* based on the first important Gujarati novel presents Gujarati culture and way of life in far more artistic and interesting manner than any Gujarati film. Now at least an effort to make an off-beat film in Gujarati has been made. Kantilal Rathod's *Kanku* has received plaudits from the press. It may prove a turning point in the artistic standard of regional films in Western India. At least one hopes it does and thus bring about a revolution in regional language films of Bombay.

V. P. SATHE

MASKED FOLK DANCES

Greatest number found Arunachal Pradesh, *Yak* dance performed, Ladakh, and in southern fringes of Himalays near Assam, dancers impersonating a yak, dances with men mounted on his back.

MASROOR ROCK TEMPLES

Himachal is rightly known as Devabhumi or the Land of the Gods. There seems to be no village or town where a diety does not reside or that is bereft of a temple. These temples are repositories of both religious feeling as well as immense sculptural and architectural treasures. There are some temples that are, due to their archaeological and historical importance, under the aegis of the Archaeolgical Survey of India (ASI). Historians, art lovers and tourists rather than pilgrims visit these temples more. The Siva temples at Baijnath, Jagatsukh temple near Manali, the Naggar & Mirmand temples in Kullu, Nirat in Mahasu, Sun Temple in Chamba and the Masroor temple in the Kangra valley are famous for their architectural and sculptural magnificance and have a special place among ancient temples of Himachal Pradesh.

The origin of these fascinating temples seems to be shrouded in mystery. By the sheer magnitude of architectural prowess it does not seem that they would have been commissioned by a local chieftain. Some scholars believe that Masroor may have been made the capital of the rulers of the kingdom of Jalandhar when they withdrew from the plains sometime in the eighth centruy AD. (in fact, the lower Kangra district is still known among the Gaddis as Jalandhara or Jandhara). Another fact that pints to this date for the Masroor temples is that their architectural and sculptural styles match those of the Elephanta temples (600-800AD) near Mumbai. Interestingly, the temples at Masroor were never completed and there are several unfinished carvings suggesting that Masroor was probably later abandoned and the headquarters of Jalandhara shifted to the more strategic Kangra fort. However, legend has it that the Pandavas created these temples during their incognito exile and when they were found out, they had to move - hence the incomplete state of the temples.

Architecturally, the Masroor temples present an intersesting view. At dusk when the sun goes behind the temples and throws them into a silhouette they seem like a family of elephants standing still in mourning. But in the early morning light they come alive - the frescoes and sculptures jumping out of the light sandstone colour reverberating in the morning sunlight. The immense

doorway and enterance to the *garbha griha (sanctum sanctorum)* is carved intricately. There is a steep flight of stairs to reach the top of the complex where the *Shikharas* stand. From here the view is beautiful. The pond below in front of the temple reflects parts of the temple. This pond, according to legend, seems to have been built for Draupadi (Pandavas' wife) for her daily ablutions and it never dries out even in the hottest of summers. Built for Draupadi (Pandavas' wife) for her daily ablutions and it never dries out even in the hottest of summers.

The sculptures at Masroor are magnificent. Wherever the rock was not hard and suitable enough to be carved out, loose sculptures were inset to fill the gaps. Most of the beautiful and complete sculptures have been shifted to the Shimla State Museum which has eight Masroor sculptures in its collection, characterized by suavity, grace and smooth plasticity. These sculptures include those of Ganesha, Durga, Siva, Surya and Varuna. In the Thakurdwara temple among the Masroor temple complex are three idols of Ram, Lakshman and Sita in smaller size. Most scholars are of the view that these temples were originally Shaivite. However, sometime during the middle ages when Vaishnava influence increased, the statues of Rama, Lakshman and Sita were installed. There are several carved panels on the temples with figural and decorative work. Today most sculptures stand eroded by the vagaries of nature.

To the right of the temple complex, stop the remaining portion of the immense rock, the Maharaja of Guler, an adjoining erstwhile state, built a medieval structure, possibly a 'resting lodge'. It has cupolas and arches so common after the amalgamation of the Hindu and Mughal styles of architecture in the middle ages. The view from here is breathtaking. Deep green mango trees and bamboo thickets away in the strong breeze that lashes the ridge every evening.
(Condensed)

DILEEP PRAKASH

MASROOR TEMPLE : FINE EXAMPLE OF ROCK - CUT ARCHITECTURE

The famous Masroor temple complex in Himachal Pradesh lies nearly 22 km from Kangra. The approach, however, is from the rear of the temple, through a flight of stairs that take you up, revealing a view of the *Dhauladhar* range. It lies to the north-east of the village, a rocky sandstone ridge, the main axis of which runs from north-west to south-east. An outcrop of sandstone rock, the highest central portion of which has been separated from the rest by two transverse and more or less parallel cuttings, it accentuates the crest of the hill. In the intervening portions of the rocks are sculpted a series of temples unique in the entire Himalayan region and comparable to the monolithic temples of Mahabalipuram, Ellora and Dhamnar caves. Standing 800 m or 2500 feet above sea level, these temples command a magnificent view over a beautiful, well-watered and fertile tract of land.

The Masroor temple has an adjoining tank-large and rectangular - hewn from sandstone.

It is nearly 50 m in length and is reputed to have water throughout the year. Possibly, it is linked to a subterranean spring. The remoteness and inaccessibility of the temples have protected them from the ravages of time and destruction at the hands of Muslim invaders, while their monolithic character has save them from devastation during the major earthquake of 1905, which destroyed most buildings in Kangra.

The Idols inside the temple are those of *Ram, Lakshman* and *Sita*. Perhaps Lord *Shiva* was originally worshipped here as indicated by the presence of the figures of *Shiva* on the top of the entrance. On the basis of its architectural and sculptural decoration the temple has been dated between the 8th - 9th centuries A.D. The monuments is a complex of shrines said to contain more than 15 *shikhara* type temples; to these, only about 10 are extant. In the centre of the complex stands the principal and most elaborately carved shrine - the *Thakurdwara* - enshrining black stone images of *Ram, Lakshman* and *Sita* facing east. This shrine faces a little to the north east while the two subsidiary shrines of decreasing size face a slighly outer angle. A similar arrangement of these secondary shrines appears to have formed the back of the moument so that the principal temple stood in the centre of eight smaller ones, the whole complex hewn out of a more or less rectangular mass of rock.

The principal shrine consists of a square *garbhagriha* (sanctum sanctorum), an *antarala* (veranda) and a rectangular *mandapa* (Pavillion). The magnificent doorway to the *garbhagriha* has five *shakhas* (vines) ornamented with graceful and dainty foliated patterns, bands of diamonds and figural sculptures. The tall pilasters of the *antarala* and the *mukhamandapa* are ornately embellished with diamonds, *ardhpadma* (halves of lotus flowers), a pair of *ghattapallava* (earthen pot and leaves) and other decorative motifs.

Above the cells or the main shrine, the almost level with the now lost roof of the *mandapa,* the rock is cut as a flat roof, broken only by the main and the other smaller *shikhara* (spires) which mark the sanctum of each of the eight smaller shrines. There is a marked difference between the heights of the main pinnacle and those of the surrounding shrines. From each side of the *mandapa* a staircase ascends to the roof terrace. From here the view of the mountains is glorious.

The complex, now partially dilapidated, is made of sandstone of verying fineness and strength. In some places the carvings are hard and well preserved and give an impression that they are a later production while in other places the sculptures are so weathered that only the faintest outlines are visible. But, the actual doorway of the shrine is in a small recess. The ornamentation and technique of the pillars, door and lintels is exceedingly beautiful.

It seems that there were four shrines at the four corners of the complex. Only one of them is better preserved. Two pillars support the roof of the veranda. The *shikhara* of this possesses *chaitya-style* window carvings. Although such temples exist in various parts of the country, the mouments at Masroor stand out as one of the finest examples of rock cut architecture.

MASTER ARTIST "BANNUJI"

The art of miniature painting that flourished under the patronage of the Rajput rulers, is one of the most beautiful arts of Rajastha Schools incorporating definite styles and individual features emerged in different kingdoms, the pre-eminent schools being those at Mewar, Jaipur and .the earlier capital Amber, Jodhpur, Bikaner, Bundi, Kota and Kishnagarh.

Raja Bihari Mal (1548-75 AD) who reigned from Amber was the first Rajput king to seek allegiance to the first Mughal emperor Babar and subsequent matrimonial alliances sealed a bond between the two royal lineages. The Jaipur rulers became powerful nobles at the Mughal court, resulting in a phase of relative political stability in their kingdom. Freedom of travel between the two kingdoms led to many interactions between painters of the regions.

Though miniature painting reached its zenith in the 17th and 18th centuries, a few families have nurtured the tradition through the generations. Carrying forward the traditions of court painters of Jaipur is Master Artist Ved Pal Sharma, a descendent of a renowned family of court painters. He lives in the heart of the Pink City, Jaipur. He is popularly known as Bannuji.

Barınuji's studio cum ling room has traditional floor seating, bric-a-brac, plenty of books on subjects ranging from Indian to Western, medieval and contemporary art while the walls are embellished with paintings. It is informally separated into a living room and workspace by low worktables. Bannuji's neat work space has lovely charm with a crowd of clam shells for holding colours like the old masters used, a bunch of brishes, containers and water and a whisk of peacock feathers among other quaint articles.

A tail man, Bannuji is soft spoken, with measured sentences and frequent pauses between his sentences. He traces his painting background to the time when his great grand father migrated to jaipur from Aligarh as a court painter during the rule of Maharaja Ram Singh II (1835-1880 A.D.). The tradition of miniature painting continued down the generations, induced young Bannu to take up the brush when he was just ten. The art drew him deeper as the year went by and he also realized the responsibility of carrying forward the tradition as one of the only surviving descendants of traditional court painters. He studied miniature paintings, observed his grandfather at work and practised hard to develop the fluidity of line that comes effortlessly to him now.

Bannuji's personal painting style is a blend of elements from different schools as they appeal to him, but the most noticeable are elements of the Kishangarh School. Women in Kishangarh painting have slightly exaggerated curved eyebrows, heavy lidded eyes, sharp nose, long neck and slim figures. But while working on paintings commissioned by connoisseurs from India and abroad, he employs styles as desired by the clients, creating beautiful miniatures like those of the centuries gone by such as Mughal miniatures true to their style. Each figure, animal bird or tree seems to convey an emotion and participate in the overall composition.

Like in the old days, Bannuji painstakingly makes colours from stones and oxides, with different shades being obtained by mixing colours. Silver and gold leaf are used for the decorative effect. Bannuji has trained assistants who work on grinding and obtaining the colours. Apart from the stones for extracting colours, is the smooth brushing stone on which the paintings are placed when the colours have dried. Bannuji gently strokes the reverse side with an agate burnisher, which sets the colour into the paper, makes the painted surgace smooth and infuses a mellow glow to the work. Bannuji tries to obtain old handmade paper to paint on, for, he says it is much stronger and smoother than the paper being produced today.

In the past two decades, many old paintings have come to him for restoration. Some with withered sections of the painting, others in pieces but with collectors confident that Bannuji could restore them to their original excellence. He matches paper that is like that of the painting. It is affixed to the frayed parts and carefully painted on, observing lines, colours and concepts of the rest of the composition. Apart from restoration, Bannuji also teaches many students from India and abroad.

Before he starts painting, Bannuji brushes his work place with the whisk of peacock feathers to dust the place ever so gently. He then adjusts the sheet and takes up a fine squirrel hairbrush, which he maintains is paramount for Indian miniature painting. Its fineness permits thin strokes indispensble for miniature painting. He gently touches the brush into one of the many clam shells, tests the colur and fineness of the stroke before starting his work. It is a painstaking process - single painting may take over a month and a restoration even more. He has made Raagmala painting to depict musical modes covering a broad range of images to depict a particular season, time of the day aspect of life, sentiments of lover or worship. These paintings seek to evoke a particular image or emotion in the mind of the viewer, as the eye absorbs the composition and details of the painting.

The white walls of his studio cheerfully reflect sunlight. Once Bannuji takes up his brush, he is absorbed in painting, heedless of time. With the ease of a master artist Bannuji concentrates on the minute detailing of the finery of the figure, bringing them alive with hundreds of deft strokes.

BRINDA GILL

MATHURA MUSEUM

The Government Museum at Mathura, popularly known as Mathura Sangrahalaya, is one of the oldest museums in India. Particularly famous for sculptures from Sunga, Maurya, Kushana and Gupta periods in ancient India, the museum presents a grand panorama of Indian art and culture spread over several centuries.

The Museum was established in 1874 by F.S. Growse, the then Collector of Mathura district, as Curzon Museum of Archaeology. It was subsequently shifted to a specially constructed building in the Dampier Park area, not far from the Mathura Railway Station.

Mathura finds frequent mention in ancient Indian literature as one of the seven great cities and as a flourishing centre of trade and commerce, art, culture and religion. All major religions of India Hinduism, Buddhism and Jainism - flourished in Mathura for several centuries as testified by archaeological excavations.

Several specimens of the art that flourished under different dynasties are preserved in the Mathura Museum. This profusion of artistic activity led to the emergence of a school of art that became famous in the annals of the country's art history as the Mathura School of Art. Several lovely pieces of sculptures carved out of red sandstone quarried at Sikri, near Agra, adorning the galleries of the Museum testify to the creative florescence of ancient Mathura. The most significant contribution of the Mathura School of Art is the creation of the first anthropomorphic or human image of Lord Buddha. An art historian wrote: "The sculptors of Mathura undoubtedly deserve credit for creating the earliest, entirely Indian representation of Buddha"

This was not a mean achievement. In doing so, the sculptors from the Mathura School of Art had broken a new ground. Till then in Indian art, Lord Buddha used to be represented by a symbol such as a Bodhi tree, a stupa, a turban, a lotus triratna or the *dharamachakra*.

Mathura Museum houses images of Lord Buddha from different periods of history. Seen collectively, these give the visitor an idea of evolution of Buddha image from it symbolic representation to the human form. There is an image from the 1st century AD of the seated Buddha. Carved in red sandstone, it was found at Katra Keshavadev mound. Another image, found at the Jamalpur mound, dates back to 5th century AD and depicts Buddha in a standing posture. The Gandhara gallery of the Museum housed a beautiful image from the Kushana period, which shows Buddha deeply engrossed in meditation. He has gone thin and his bones are visible, portraying prolonged austerities.

It is believed that the early images of Buddha or Boddhisatva were inspired by the grand images of *Yakshas*, examples of which can also be seen at Mathura Museum. *Yakshas* were folk deities. Their images date back to 4th-3rd century BC. In fact, *Yaksha* images are among the earliest sculptured stone images found in India. These early images depict the *Yakshas* as magnificent, tall, imposing and awe-inspiring. A colossal statue of a standing *Yaksha*, a excavated at Parkham village, is housed at Mathura Museum. It is at once an archaic example of Indian statutory art - primitive and powerful. Dating to 3rd century BC, it is an excellent example of early Indian stone art.

With so many *Yaksha* and *Yakshi* images around, no wonder we find an interesting image of Kubera, the mythical King of the *Yaksha* group of deities, among the exhibits at Mathura Museum.

Among the plethora of sculptures of gods, goddesses and mythical beings, there are some unique sculptures of historical personages. Among them is a standing, headless statue of Emperor Kanishka, with a single line inscription in Brahmi-Maharaja Rajatiraja Devaputro Kanishko. This statue dates to 1st century AD.

Mathura being the center of the Krishna cult, many examples of Krishna sculptures are housed here. A plaque dating to 1st century AD shows Vasudeva, father of Krishna, carrying him in a basket across river yamuna. Another sculpture, dating to 6th century AD depicts

Krishna holding Mount Govardhana on his palm. Equally interesting is a red sandstone sculpture of Krishna's elder brother Balarama.

The Museum contains a plethora of beautiful female sculptures of great antiquity. The relic mounds known as Stupas were surrounded by railings, the uprights of which were generally carved in high relief with representations of beautiful, youthful women of immense charme. The Museum house such railing pillars adorned with beautiful women in various postures. Found at Bhuteshwar, Naroli and other places, these beauties in red sandstone belong to 2nd century AD. Terracotta figurines of the Mother Goddess belonging to 4th - 2nd century BC are counted among valuable possessions of the Museum.

There is a unique headless terracotta figure made of baked red clay belonging to the 1st century BC. It is a considered to be that of Kamadeva, the god of Love.

Ancient India is said to have had temples dedicated to this god. Literary evidence is certainly backed by such archaeological findings.

According to an estimate, the Mathura Museum contains about 33,500 art objects. Apart from 4819 stone sculptures, 2690 terracotta figures and 329 bronze idols, the Museum has in its collection 312 miniature paintings, several gold, silver and copper coins and other objects of historical and archaeological value. The Museum also houses the art objects excavated at Sonkha and Govindnagar. It has 18 galleries, including one dedicated to Gandhara School of Art. The Gandhara collection includes the graceful blue sandstone sculpture of Kambojika, the chief queen of Mahakshatrapa Rajula (1st century AD). It is said that the king constructed a stupe and a monastery on the bank of Yamuna at Mathura.

With such a vast collection at its command, the Mathura Museum certainly ranks among the best anywhere in the world.
(Condensed)

PRABHAKAR BEGDE

MAURYAN ART AND ARCHITECTURE

Popular art is the expression of people's sensitivity which rests reveals the psychology of the society from which it emerges. Mauryan art is one such form which reflects the flory and sopistication of the third century B.C.

Indian art at its earliest finds anchorage in the pages of Mauryan history, finding expression in town-planning, cave architecture, monolothic pillars, stupas and chaitya halls. One wonders at the sudden outbrust of architectural activities during this period (323 BC - 185 BC). The only remains of similar activity date back to the Harappan age (2000 BC). The entire long period in between is a blank as far as architecture is concerned, although there are references to sculptures and architecture executed in clay and wood that must have perished down the ages.

Religion, on the eastern horizon of India, was on an altogether different footing. Worship of *Chaityas* was in vogue and it was one of the seven conditions of welfare of the state, laid down by Buddha. Buddhist texts refer to *Chaityas* of various forms. Some were merely a tree with a railing around and a gateway which was a habitation of a *Yaksha*. On the ancient Indian coins (punch marked coins), a most familiar symbol is a tree with a railing enclosure. These railings and gateways certainly provided ample scope for craftsment to display their artistic skills. Equally popular was the erection of commemorative *Stupas* over the deposits of bodily remains and they are considered among the oldest religious stuctures in India, Gradually, *Stupas* came to be identified with those of Buddha and his disciples. These *Stupas* and *Chaityas* certainly required the artists' layout and designing.

Greek accounts, the Arthashastra and Buddhist and Jain literature of the times throw good light on the Mauryan period. Several big cities, such as Takshasila, Maskavati, Sakala and Patliputra are mentioned in these sources. A strong sense of imagination is required to recreate the long lost Mauryan Patliputra that was once replete with multistoreyed wooden buildings and palaces surrounded by parks and ponds. According to the Greek choroniclers, Patliputra was a garden city. The royal parks were lined with evergreen trees, which neither grew old nor shed their leaves. This capital city had more than 570 towers and 64 gates and was surrounded by a wooden palisade with loopholes for arches. A ditch around the city served the dual purpose of defence as well as of sweage disposal. The city wall had gateways with draw bridges. Every street had its water courses serving as house drains that finally emptied into the moat. Any deposit that obstructed the passage was punishable by law. House owners were required to have fire prevention elements. The streets were provided with vessels of water and sand kept ready in thousands. Strong fortification and perfect town planning of Patliputra served as a model for later builders. Patanjali's *Mahabhasya* referes to *pusyamitra Sunga* building a city around Ayodhya (Sukosala) based on the pattern of patliputra.

Much of the wooden Pataliputra was dressed in stone during the reign of Ashoka. This change was so sudden that it prompted Fa Hien, the Chinese traveller who visited India between 400-415 AD, to believe that genni (demons) were commissioned to put up the massive stone structures;

The archeological site at Kumarahar in Patna is believed to be the Mauryan palace. The remains found include a hall with 80 pillars each polished to perfection. Patanjali referes to it as Chandragupta Sabha, while the Greek sources call it as Hall a Audience. Except for one column, others are in abfragmentary state. Arranged in eight rows, with ten pillars in each, the plan resembles the hall of hundred columns as Persepolis, Kautilya, the legendary minister of Chandragupta, probably urged the king to attend to public issues here for three hours each day. Within the Kumarahar complex are the excavated remains of Ashoka's charitable hospital. A little distance away is another Ashokan remain, the *Agam Kuan*, or the fathomless well, believed to be a part of the legendary hell created by the emperor before his change of heart and conversion to Buddhism.

Remains of Mauryan art and artefacts can be seen at several museums. The Patna Museum houses some terracottas and figures like the lion head, the torso of a Jain tirthankara and the Didarganj yakshi, the latter having been evaluated as one of the finest specimens of the Mauryan period. This five feet high statue displays the traditional features of an Indian beauty, and has heavyy ornamentation and drapery. All these figures bear the characteristic Mauryan high polich. The museum also houses the lion capital of the Rampurva pillar (put up by Ashoka), bearing the first six pillar edicts.

The Indian Museum in Calcutta also has a good collection of stone railings, pillars, cross bars from the Bharnut stupa, various sculptures like the two griffins from Patliputra, a naga head from Rajgir and a few other statues.

Some of the Mauryan sculptures can best be admired in the form of the mighty monoliths or the Saila Stambhas put up throughout the Mauryan empire, Scholars are divided on the question of their origin, utility and development. A section believes that such pillars were worshipped in India before the times of Ashoka. The Mahabharata describes a similar wooden or golden *yupa* established by Brahma and worshipped by Yudhishthra. The other extreme view is that these were the creation of Greek masons, invited to fashion these moumental pillars. While it is true that friendly relations between the Mauryan and Greek courts continued for generations, we can at best surmise that these pillars display a skilful synthesis of India, Achemenian, Assyrian and Hellenistic arts.

Some of these pillars have remained in stitu, like most pillars in Bihar. A few of them were tempting enough for inquistive monarchs like Firoz Shah Tughlaq (1351 - 88 AD) to carry them off to decorate their capitals. Yet others have been ravaged by time and weather, These Mauryan monoliths vary in style and artistic finesse that characterize the patience, skill and craftsmanship of the great builders. The most striking element is the sheen imparted to these tall, tapering shafts. "The stone is altogether as bright as jade;" attested the Chinese pilgrim Hieun Tsang in 7th century AD. The pillars are crowned with a so-called 'inverted lotus' or 'Persopolitan Bell' on which rests the circular or rectangular abacus, serving as a base for single animal figures such as of a lion, a bull or an elephant. Most of the pillars are inscribed with Ashokan edicts on account of his spiritual vigour and his solidarity with the Buddhist order.

The Lion capital of the Sarnath pillar (now displayed at the Sarnath Museum) has been adopted as the national emblem of India. The round abacus is carved with four animals - elephant, bull, horse and a lion, each separated by a wheel or Dharmachakra. Atop the abacus are four lions standing back-to-back. These were originally topped by another wheel, of which now only a few broken spokes survive.

The symbolism of the Lion capital has been variously explained. The Dharmachakra is universally accepted as the symbol of Buddha's dharma or the law of piety, while the lion stands for regal majesty and divine power. The four animals on the abacus depict the guardians of four quarters. The elephant guards the east, the horse is stationed in the south, the bull takes care of the west and the lion looks after north. Some interpret these animals as symbols of various events of Buddha's life. The inverted lotus or the Persopolitan Bell is translated as a symbol of enlightenment and creativity.

Stepped in age old burial customs, the stupas or the sepulchural mounds were originally erected amidst earthern platforms created over four cardinal points. The next phase witnessed the introduction of wood and the development of a solid dome, capped by a square box under the shadows of an umbrella. Later, circumambulatory passages were created around the stupa which was fenced by a massive railing with entrance gateways. The Mauryan era saw the replacement of the wooden structures by stone, and in the Sunga period, the stupas themselves were enlarged and decorated.

A series of caves on Barabar and Nagarjuni hills (24 kms from Gaya in the Indian state of Bihar) are also from the Mauryan period. They are not only India's earliest rock-cut caves but also highlight the skills of the ancient craftsment who exacated them, polished their interior hard granite walls and graced them with doorways with sloping jambs.

SHAHID AKHTER MAKHFI

MEENAKSHI TEMPLE OF MADURAI

Madurai is veritably the most ancient and sacred city of South India and vies with Varanasi in antiquity and a continuous relgious tradition. Madurai was thriving when the Augustans ruled over Rome in c. 25 B.C. , a fact testified by the coins found in excavations indicating the existence of Roman colony in the neighbourhood. The Pandyan rulers held away over the southern part of the country untill the 14th century A.D. when Madurai was virtually the haven for poets and scholars. The Nayaks who ruled over Madurai for nearly two hundred years left their imprint on everything from literature to architecture. The tall *gopurams* of Madurai temples testify to the illustrious heritage of the city, considered to be the abode of Lord Shiva who according to mythology spread nectar to protect the city perineally.

Not all Madurai history is mythological. The river Vagai has yielded megalithic finds and Roman coins. Excavations have exposed burial urns of the 3rd, 4th and 5th centuries B.C. In the Mahabharata, a Pandyan price is mentioned to have attended the Swayamvara of Draupadi, Sahadev, the youngest of the Pandava brothers, defeated the Pandyas. The world Pandya itself is surmised to have originated from Pandus of the Mahabharata.

The Meenakshi Sundareswarar temple at Madurai is decicated to parvati, Lord Shiva's consort, herein worshipped as Meenakshi, the fish-eyed goddess. In the dark sanctum of the goddess, the diamons on the nose-ring dazzles in the flickering light of the oil lamps.

The Meenakshi Sundareswarar temple complex covers an area of nearly 85,000 sq. mts. It is virtually a city complete in itself with a maze of pillared corridors that lead to sanctums and assembly halls. Bare footed pilgrims scamper along the west floors. Visitors linger on to look at the sculptures of yalis, the mythical beasts with bared teeth rampant in awesome striking postures. These sculptured yalis are typical of the later day Vijaynagar style accentuating grandeur through mammoth proportions.

The Aytrakkal Mandapam or Hall of Thousand Pillars, adjacent to the Meenakshi shrine, was built in 1560. It is an architectural contribution of Ariyanayakam Mudali, a minister of the earliest Nayak ruler. The exact number of pillars is 997, including the great musical pillars. The sculptures on these pillars cover a great range of human emotions and expressions, from stateliness and grace, pride and dignity; divine composure, lusty humour and earthy ribaldry. Musicians with instruments have a rare charm of their own. The thousand pillars in the hall symbolise the forest of *Kadamba* trees where Lord Indra found the Shivalingam. It is now a great museum of rarest bronzes and sculptures. A magnificent Nataraja stands at the farthest end of the museum.

You enter the Meenakshi Sundareswarar temple through the Ashtha Shakti Mandapam with sculptured pillars depicting various aspects of Shakti as well as scences illustrating miracles performed by Lord Shiva in Madurai.

The Potramaraikulam or the lengendary lily tank, a creation of Indira himself - so it is believed, lies in front of the Meenakshi shrine. In ancient pre-Christian era days of the sangam glory, this tank served another purpose. Scripts of authors were given a water test: Only meritorious work floated above the surface. The eastern and southern corridors over the tank contain some vestiges of the murals painted under the Nayak rulers. Efforts are being made to revive some original murals. Tlhe Oonjal Mandapham contains the swing on which the golden images of Shiva and Meenakshi are placed every Friday for the weekly *darshan* (glimpse)

The most outstanding feature of this temple is the height of its *gopurams*, soaring high over the city scape. The first story of each of these ten gateways is decorated with huge sculptures of deities. ranging between grand and grotesque in effect. These massive *gopurams* are rectangular towers, concave in profile and surmounted by hull-shaped roofs of the versara type. The southern *gopuram*, the most magnificent creation of the Vijayanagar architects, is nearly 60 mts. high, measuring 32.9 mts by 20.4 mts at the base. Bu 't in mid sixteenth century by Siramalai Sevvanthi Murthi Chettiar of a famous family from Tiruchi, the southern *gopuram* is really amazing for its sculptural decoration. Sometimes the visitors are allowed to climb up to the top of the tower for a spectacular view of the cluster of towers and a distant view of the two hills called Yanai Malai and Naga Malai (the Elephant and the Snake hill) and the sluggish stream of Vagai. Madurai city is dotted with countless shrines, big and small, and the lanes are always throbbing with pilgrims and visitors from the wee hours of the morning to midnight.

Besides the great Meenakshi temple which encapsulates the spiritual fervour of Madurai, the city has other attractions too. Notably the palace of the Thirumalai Nayak (1623-59). This grand structure was partly demolished by his grandson for his own palace at Tiruchy. Still the spectacular corridor with all tall Roaman columns and the splendid decoration in stucco stand in evidence of its magnificence. The *Swarga Vilasam* is an octagonal pavilion with a marvellous dome built without girders or rafters. It is sheer royal splendour. Many local festivals are celebrated here "in the courtyard. The *Mariamman Teppakulam*, a spectacular rectangular water tank with a many tiered pavilion at the centre, is the place where the annual float festival is held in January. The great Ganesha sculpture was unreathed at this site when it was being dug up for the tank by the Nayak.

(Condensed)

SURENDRA SAHAI

MIMI : A SENSITIVE ARTIST

Mimi Radhakrishnan is a veteran print-maker. Her exhibition at the prestigious India International Centre New Delhi was a retrospective of sorts. She showed a selection of her work that dates back to her student days at Shantiniketan and M.S. University, Baroda, where she studied under such luminaries as Somnath Hore and K.G. Subramanian. The 40 odd lithographs on display traced her growth as an artist, both stylistically and subject-wise.

Mini's early works like 'The Nymph' Boy on a Ladder and 'Neighbours' are introspective and personalised; scenes from her life as a girl and later, as a young wife and mother.

Broadening horizons and interaction with renowned western graphic artists like Carol Summers, Paul Lingren and Charles Stroh resulted in a perceptible change in her outlook and an increased sophistication in her technique. Says Mimi, "Previously most of my work was inward-looking and rather naive, but now it is a social comment on the times we live in." This can be seen in her 1993 black and white series, 'The Party' which is a tongue-in-cheek look at the superficiality and shallowness that abounds in high society, in her 1995 lithograph 'Towards a Field' warm earthen tones on a black ground are brilliantly highlighted by the vibrant red of the village girl's bundle. Mimi confesses to have drawn her inspiration from the tribals of Bihar for this work, which is marked by its stylised simplicity of form. In 'Admiration', a star-struck young girl gazes in awe at the object of her devotion, who is perhaps an actress or dancer of repute. Here too, Mimi shows a masterful understanding of colour and dexterity of line.

Mimi is married to eminent sculptor Radhakrishan and frequently serves as his muse. While the lithograph is her preferred medium of choice, she is just as proficient in other branches of graphic art like relief printing and intaglio. She dabbles in oils too. She has a number of state and national awards to her credit and has participated in several Indian and international shows.

About her future plans, Mimi says: "Lithography is essentially a Western art form and I would love to explore the medium further in Europe some day. It is also a much misunderstood art in India, often being confused with commercial graphic art: I would like to dispel such misconceptions through my work." Modest aspirations indeed, for one as talented and as committe to her art as he is.

SARAH NATHAN

MINARS AND MINARETS OF INDIA

Minars, like the dome, is one of the most immediate and characteristic feature of Islamic architecture. The Arabic term 'manara' literally means place where fire burns. In pre-Islamic Arab world *manaras* stood for an elevated place from where signals of fire or smoke were made. The fire nexus was soon extinguished to associate the *manaras* with signposts, boundary stones, watch towers and light houses spread throughout North Africa and Central Asia.

The manara or the *minar* entered the Islamic architectural lexicon a few decades after the demise of the

Prophet Muhammad. During his lifetime, his Abyssinian slave Bilal used to climb the highest roof and broadcast the call to prayer. Precisely for this reason the orthodox communities in Islam detest the idea of *minars* being introduced to the mosques. The Prophet's mosque at Madina had no such *minar* and moreover, it was looked down upon as ostentatious and unnecessary. After a certain height, the human voice becomes inaudible and therefore extremely tall *minars* for the mosques were unwelcome. Further it gave rise to invasion of privacy. The *mu'adhhdhin* (who recites the prayer call) could overlook people's homes. Interesting injuctions were issued in Arab countries, viz. except for the *mu'adhdhin*, on one else was allowed to ascend the *minar* and that too only during the prescribed prayer times; the *mu'addhins* were required to take an oath that they would refrain from peeping into neighbouring houses, at time *mu'adhdhins* were blind folded and beter still blind men were most preferred for this job.

The Caliphs of Islam were too keen to incorporate the *minar* as it offered an ideal platform for reciting the *azhan* (call to prayer). The minar further served as a closk tower which announced the precise time while addressing the azhan. During the month of fasting, *Ramazhan*, a lantern attached to the top of the *minar* indicated the time for commencement and conclusion of day's fast.

The first Islamic century witnessed the role of a Minar as a bare essential, the second century introduced refinement and later its development was varied and influenced by local masonic traditions. The approach to the structural problem of erecting a *minar* dictated the design and dimensions. The clergy once suggested that a *minar* should not occupy a space which could otherwise be used for prayers. This injunction compelled the *minars* to be erected on the walls of the entrance facade. Gradually, a variety of *minars* were invented - circular, octagonal, hexagonal, faceted, spiral or tapering, single or paired. In fact, they displayed all possible shapes that tower can possibly assume. The scope of their utility also witnessed a reasonable expansion. *Minars* came to be associated with tombs, milestones (*kos minars*), hunting towers (*shikargahs*) punishment pillars (*char minar*), etc.

Though the *minar* originated in the Arab world, the grandest of them all was however destined for India : the mighty Qutab Minar. It was begun in 1199 by Qutubuddin Aibek as a supporting minar to his equally grand Quwwat Mosque. He erected the first three storeys which are heavily indented with different styles of fluting. The *minar* 27 feet in diameter at the base which tapers to 9 feet at the summit. Qutbuddin's successor, Ilutumish added the fourth storey. The 238 feet high *minar* was damaged by earthquakces a number of times. After one such disaster, Firoz Shah Tughlaq rebuilt the fourth storey and further added a fifth stretch. The decoration of the *minar* consistes of inscriptional bands on its body written in bold Tughra characters. Inside the *minar* there is a spiral staircase of 379 steps leading to the top. Besides being the earliest *minar*, it proved to be the most successful and thereby triggering an explosion of *minars* that mushroomed throught out India. A smaller version of the awe inspiring Qutb Minar can be seen (now in ruins) in the shape of fluted *minars* flanking the central arch of Jami Masjid (*Arhai-din-ka jhopra*) at Ajmer. Erected around the same time as Qutab Minar, these minarets proved to be technically weak in absence of independent foundation and were therefore abandoned soon after.

Next few centuries witnessed the development of the gateway minars which found an ideal expression in Gujarat where it was firmly rooted in the ground with richly secuptured heavy buttresses from which they emerged. Throughtout Gujarat, we find the systematic use of *minars* as they come in a variety of shapes and sizes. Unfortunately, most of them (like the *minars* of Jami Masjid, Qutabuddin Shah's Masjid, Malik Alam's Masjid, Bibi Achut Kuji's Masjid, Bibiji Masjid, etc.) were damaged due to earthquakes or lightning. However, two of the most impressive *minars* can be seen welcoming visitors close to the railway station of Ahmedabad but there are no traces of the mosque to which they originally belonged. In Sayyid Uthman's mosque at Ahmedabad we find the earliest example in *minar* being shifted from the central facade to the corners. These corner minars are tall (six storeys) and heavy for the open mosque. It can be contrasted with the slim pinnacle like minarets with delicate traceries and carvings in Rani Sipari's mosque (Ahmedabad). The Junagarh mausoleum of Nawab Mahabat Khan's mother includes a pair of beautiful *minars* with the spiral staircases entwining the *minar* from outside. The best of tall and sleek *minars* can be seen among the monuments of Champanir, like the Jami Masjid, Nagina Masjid, Shihr-ki-Masjid, etc.

Gujarat, Khandesh, Rajputana, Bidar, Bijapur and Golconda developed their own *minars* with slight variations. Finally the Mughals picked up the thread and developed the corner turrets. Their lofty *minars* can be seen attached to Delhi's Jami Masjid, Agra's Taj Mahal, tomb of Itamuddaulah, to name a few.

Close to the Qutb Minar lies Alai Minar which stands as a mute witness to the whims and facies of the Delhi sultans. One such sultan was Alauddin Khilji in 1311 who wanted to excel and exceed the height of the Qutb. He had planned a minar that would dwarf the Qutb Minar by half.

Unfortunately, the Sultan died leaving his work unfinished and what we see is just the skeletal remains of what could otherwise have been most remarkable structure in the world;

Some of the most interesting and unusual minars are to be seen on the eastern frontier of medieval India. A late thirteenth century *minar* at Chota Pandua in Bengal is a curious five-storeyed *minar* that soars to 125 feet and tapers gradually from bottom to top like the *Chaubara* of Bidar. The minar presents an uneven outline of the structure constructed of five successive tiers, each smaller in diameter than the one below. The diameter at the base measures 60 feet which diminishes to 15 feet at the top. The *minar*, entered through a basalt (post and lintel) doorway, is believed to be a part of the mosque built by Shah Sufi Sultan.

Firoz Minar at Gaur (West Bengal) is another eastern jewel created in bricks that climb to a height of 84 feet through a spiral staircase. Standing on a twelve sided plinth (now covered with earth), the first three polygonal storeyes of the *minar* share the uniform diameter of 20 feet while the top two storeys are circular and diminishing in diameter. Unfortunately, the crowning cupola surmounting the sixth storey no longer exists. Corresponding to the entrance doorway, a similar opening is pierced on each storey. The *minar* is named after its builder Saifuddin Firoz (1487-90), the Abyssinian slave who set an unfortunate precedent that he who kills a king's murderer acquired the right to the throne. Firoz Minar, also referred to as Chirag Minar, served as lamp post like the Mughal tower, Ubh Diwal in Rajasthan.

Another interesting minar in West Bengal is the Neem Serai which closely resembles the Hiran Minar at Fatehpur Sikri. Both the *minars* are studded with elephant tusk-like projection giving rise to various stories. Neem Serai Minar, situated on a hill overlooking the two rivers (Kalindri and Mahananda) suggests that it served as a watch tower. The spikes may have been used to display the rebel heads. The sixteenth century minar gradually narrows as it reaches the top (now broken). Hiran Minar is believed to be Akbar's hunting tower (Shikargah) Another tradition considers it to be the precise spot where the favourite elephant of the emperor lies buried. It was a fashion in medieval days to crete a tower for just anything. Jahangir is believed to have erected a tower over the remains of his favourite antelope. At Bir, one encounters a *minar* that is believed to have been ordered by the Tughlaq emperor to mark the site where he buried his extracted tooth.

Chand Minar at Daultabad is another 100 feet high motivation that appears Turkish and can be seen from miles around. The 15th century circular *minar* is attached to a small mosque at the foot of the fortress and is divided into four storeys by wide balconies on brackets. A spiral staircase inside the tower leads to the top which is capped by a dome. Ek Minara at Raichur closely resembles the Chand Minar, except for the height which is 65 feet and is divided into two storeys by projecting galleries.

The Mughals were more interested in corner towers and smaller turrets atop the facade. The 130 feet *minars* at the corner of Jama Masjid in Delhi are one of the most illustrative Mughal minars. The builders of the Taj Mahal borrowed the idea of 'minars in mausoleums' from Salim Shah's (1545) incomplete tomb at Sasaram where the *minars* are seen for the first time in a funerary monument. Since then most of the tombs were fashioned with *minars* and some notable developments can be seen among the tombs of Itamud-Daulah, Akbar and Taj Mahal. The *minars* in Bibi Ka Maqbara (1678) at Aurangabad closely rival that of the Taj and are one of the last notable architectural creations by the Mughals.

The Char Minar (1593) is one of the earliest surviving monuments of the Qutb Shahis of Golconda which served as a model for their subsequent architectural development. The 186 feet high Char Minar is decagonal in plan and is divided into four sections by arched lanterns profusely ornamented with mouldings.

Gol Gumbaz (1656) in Bijapur is another example of *minars* being attached on all four sides. The seven storeyed octagonal *minars* are pierced in each of their faces with pointed arches placed in rectangular panels and crowned by a bulbous dome with seculptured lotus petals at the base.

One of the most impressive *minars* in South India can be seen in masjid-i- Ala built by Tipu Sultan at Seringapatanam in 1786. These two unsuals *minars* in an otherwise simple mosque are octagonal and separated by a galleried balcony and crowned by a masonry dome. The entire *minar* is broken up by a series of holes with a few arched openings.

Indian roads and highways were once dotted with *Kos Minars* that guided the travellers and most of the European travelogues mention these secular towers that varied in height between 11 and 50 feet. Some Europeans like Peter Mundy (1621-32) and William Finch (1608-11) describe the numerous skull towers that they encountered during their sojourn in India. One such tower, popularly called Char Minar, dating back to the thirteenth century, can be seen in Delhi.

SHAHID AKHTER MAKHFI

MINIATURE PAINTING

As the name suggests miniature painting was originally an illustration in a book and was therefore compact in scope and size. Eventually miniatures outgrew this strictly book format and became collector's items in themselves, either in albums or as individual pictures. The conventions, precision and richness of the original illustrations were nevertheless preserved and although distinct schools and styles developed within India, the basic characteristics of miniature painting remained largely unchanged.

Foremost among the major schools of painting were the Mughal and Rajput. Mughal painting was heavily influened by the arts of Persia and the early Mughal emperors employed Persian artists in the courts. Although Muslim rulers, they were relatively liberal in their attitude towards the subject matter for painting, Particularly with regard to the depiction of the human form. Whilst their principal themes were concerned with the activities of rulers and their courts, Mughal artists were open to the influence of' Pre-Mughal painting and contemporary Europe and included in their subject matter characters and events from both Hinduism and Christianity. The Rajputs were the Hindu rulers of a number of small kingdoms in Northern India, mainly Rajasthan. There were many sub-schools or Kalams of Rajput painting but they are all characterised by the stylisation of the figure, a rich variety of colour and the predomiance of Vedic and Hindu themes.

Bundi painting came into its own after the advent of Mughal power in India. In the absence of any clear dating of pictures before the end of the 16th century, it is believed that in the Rajput states the favourite theme of painting was illustration of Jain religious texts and a continuation of the Gujarat school of *Chaurapanchasika* (1500) style. Gradually the protruding eye of the Jain style and most other hard lines of the drawing disappeared and gave way to a style with flat heads in profile and exquisite colour schemes typical of the land of warriors, the martial clans who had an exalted sense of honour and chivalry, living and dying for it. The inter-woven and turbulent histories of Bundi and Kota, two small kingdoms in eastern Rajasthan, differ little from those of other Rajput states except that the initial success of Bundi (Kota split off from the ancient Hara kingdom only in 1925) and its later eclipse by Kota towards the end of the seventeenth century are relected in the paintings which have become famous far beyond the borders of the state of Rajasthan.

The strong character of Bundi painting asserted itself towards the end of the 17th century, after a fruitful assimilation of divergernt trends; hence the Mewar influence in the long oval shape of the eye, the Mughal in the rounded female face and male costumes, and the Deccani influence in certain facial types as well as the placement of the pavilion in the composition. The sumptuous greenery, nature's gift to Bundi, contributes the most distinctive touch, ducks frolicking in the pond, plantain trees and spiked flowering plants, painted in gorgeous colours of orange, red and green.

A row of trees at the top of the composition is a typical Bundi feature. The remarkable luxuriance and attention to detail forms the core of the distinctive Bundi painting.

Prior to their introduction to the Mughal painting, the Bundi artists worked on devotional themes centering around Krishna. The Ragmalas were a favourite subject. "Ragamala paintings", as Ebeling observes, "are visual interpretations of Indian musical modes previously envisioned in divine or human form by musicians and poets. They show most frequently romantic or devotional situations in a somewhat stereotyped, aristocratic setting. These paintings were created in albums containing most often 36 or 42 folios, organized in a system of families". Most of the scenes are portrayals of lovers in different moods and seasons woven around Krishna and Radha, the divine lovers.

The Chunar Ragamala of 1591 is the earliest dated portfolio from Bundi. The three pupils of Mir Syed Alim and Abdal Samad who painted the Chunar Ragmala set the trend in style. It was copied extensively at Bundi and might have been commissioned by Bhoj Singh (1587 - 1607) who served at Varanasi. Some scholars place it around 1625. In any case it establishes the close links between the new Bundi style and Mughal painting. The pre-Mughal painting in Bundi was based on conceptualisation and using flat colours in large areas, appealing primarily to sentiments. The Bundi rulers who had done stints of prolonged service at the Mughal courts were acquinted with trends in Mughal painting. The reddish brown tinge of the faces and the tall graceful and slightly - built female figure, part of the characteristic Bundi style, now showed a change for tall figures in pearl jewellery, men in long *jamas Patkas* and *churidars*, while women wear *ghagharas* (skirt) and a high *Choli* (Blouse). Shading under the armpits shows influence of the early Mughal style. Under the pronounced Persian influence the Bundi painter gives up over-simplification for a greater charm of face and subtlety of line. Also the grouping of figures and use of dramatic postures is noteworthy.

The most ambitious project on *Bhagwat Purana* was painted in 1640, noted for its bigger format and impressive design. Under Bhao Singh (1650 - 82) Bundi painting reached its apogee. The pallette is gorgeous with oranges and greens setting off areas of white. A contemporary Ragamala collection shows magnificence of colour schemes and composition.

The most distinctive feature of Bundi painting, however, is its excellence in drawing of elephants, wild and volatile in action, hunting and in chase. Compared to Bundi elephant drawings, Mughal paintings of elephants appear a tame affair. Bishan Singh (1773 - 1821) had a great flair for hunting and his passion for the big game more than compensated for his indifference to any aesthetical pursuits.

Bundi painting did not have a continued court patronage as rulers with aesthetic inclination were followed by rulers with boorish tastes. Hence we have periods of brilliance followed by periods of lack-lustre routine work. Towards the end of the 18th century there was introduced a new feature of broad borders of burnished red framing the composition. The lure of Krishna legend still continued. However, with the decline of the Mughal power at the centre, Bundi also faced decline.

There has not been much contradiction of the general belief that Kota painting is a continuation of the Bundi style and subject. The one noticeable change that took place in the early eighteenth century was in the flamboyant depiction of clouds. Kota miniatures are identified with pictures of hunting scenes - the earth - shaking confrontations of elephants and fastidiously observed details of tiger hunts.

To the years 1825 - 1835 belong a group of drawings of animals deer, lions, tigers, snakes and monkeys in a variety of attitudes. Quite clearly the Kota artist had seen the visiting British artists at work. Certainly at Kota the loves of Krishna or variations from *Rasik Priya* or *Baramasa* or *Bhagwat Purana* were no longer of much interest. Painting continued to be practiced under Chattar Sal (1866 - 89) but was devoid of any distinction. The Krishna legend had lost its magic but there was no other theme to replace it, nor was there any inspiration to do so. With the advent of the British on the scene, the splendour of the Kota painting became a thing of the past.
(Condensed)

SURENDRA SAHAI

MITHILA FOLK ART

As one draws and scribbles on walls with pencils or crayons, especially when no one was looking; Well, humans in very ancient times began painting the same way using colours from plants and flowers to paint on cave walls and floors. And so beautifully, that this tradition of painting was kept alive, sometimes by kings and rich nobles, more often by the common people themselves, in their own communities. These styles of painting have come down the generations and become a part of the folk art of our country.

To many art lovers in the world, India is like a vast museum with endless art galleries - both natural, man-made, ancient and modern, classical and folk. One such gallery is that of Mithila which has preserved the sophisticated Tantric drawings and paintings in the form of ritualistic art for thousands of years. Mithila, the ancient kingdom of Janak (of Ramayana fame), has ultimately found its cultural identity through this exclusive style of painting.

Drawings and paintings on floors, which are called "Aripan" or Alpana, as well as on walls, are traditionally an intergral part of any festivity in 'Mithilanchal' (broadly meaning the northern side of river Ganga in Bihar upto

Terai region of Nepal). All such paintings were made by the illiterate or semi-literate womenfolk belonging to the privileged classes of society. But the 1966-67 famine in Bihar changed the perspective for this traditional art when these women artists were told to draw on handmade paper for commercial purpose. Once shown to the people outside the region, the Mithila style of painting took the world by storm. And once it became a source of livelihood, people from other sections of the society were also drawn towards it.

Traditionally only natural colours prepared from flowers, plants and vegetable leaves and other domestic items are used in Mithila paintings. For example, rice paste mixed with water called 'Pithar' is used for white colour in Aripan. So is turmeric for yellow and *Sindoor* (vermilion) for red. Green colour is extracted from beans and bean-leaves, while black is prepared from lamp soot. Aripans are drawn by finger tips only but in wall paintings, fine bamboo stick with a cloth tied on its tip can also be used.

Most popular items of Mithila paintings are closely connected with Tantric patterns. Being an essential part of Mithila's socio-cultural life, this art continues to beautify the Maithili homes on the festive occasions. But at the same time it is now travelling throughout the world on pieces of handmade paper carrying the creative beauty of Mithila's traditional art.

Various themes, symbols and subjects from Ramayana, Mahabharata, and folk tales are used in these paintings. Creatures of water, land and sky, gods and goddesses, men and women, plants and plantets are all included in these paintings to create an universal appeal.

Mithila paintings are now becoming popular among art-loving people around the world. Gifted artists like the late Gariga Devi, Jagadamba Devi, Sita Devi, Godawari Dutta etc have made great contribution to help it get universal recognition.

Another gifted artist in this genre is Shashikala Devi. Born in a middle class family of a village in Bihar, Shashikala learnt the art from her mother, late Subhadra Devi, who was a versatile genius who would paint almost all types of Aripan and murals with perfection. Young Shashikala learnt only be assisting her mother. Now her murals adorn busy public places like Madhubani and Darbhanga Railway Stations and noted dancer Mrinalini Sarabhai's home at Ahmedabad.

She has held many exhibitions both in India and abroad, which have received rave reviews.

SATISH CHANDRA DAS

MODERN PERIOD

Late 19th century, traditional Indian paintings dying out, replaced variety of forms; all influenced by west. 20th century, reaction set in, Bengal School Glories of Indian art, re-discovered leading artist Rabindranath Tagore, theoretician E.B. Havell, Principal, Calcutta School of Art. Work sentimental, of considerable charm. Bengal school, reshaped contemporary taste; Made artists aware of heritage. Amrita Sher Gill inspired by post-impressionists; made Indian painters aware, new directions. Mid 20th

century, Indian paintings, part international scenes; artists paintings various forms; coming to terms with heritage, with emergence of modern culture.

References

Ghulam Yazdani, *Ajanta,* 4 vol
Moti Chandra, *Jain Miniature Paintings from Western India*
Karl J Khandalavala & Moti Chandra, *New Documents of Indian Painting*
N.C. Mehta, *Studies in Indian Painting* (1926)
Kar Khandalavala, *Pahari Miniature Painting*
Douglas E. Barret and Basil Gray, *Paintings of India*

MODHERA SUN TEMPLE

Many temples in India are exclusively dedicated to *Surya :* Martand temple in Kashmir, Matarmal in Almora, Osia in Rajasthan, Konark in Orissa and Modhera in Gujarat.

The Modhera sun temple is situated on the bank of the river Pushpavati, 30 kms from Mehesana and 125 kms from Ahmadabad in northern Gujarat. This is an ancient township, traceable to the Puranic age, when it was known as Dharmaranya. It is believed that Lord Rama performed here a *Yajna* (sacrifice) to purify himself of the sin of having killed a Brahmin - Ravana, the king of Lanka. Rama built "*Modherak*" which subsequently came to be called "*Modhera*". It became a pilgrimage centre for hordes of people who thronged to the place to pay homage to *Surya.*

The Modhera temple is the creation of the Solanki era in Gujarat when it was ruled by Bhima-I in 1026-27. This was the time when Somnath and the adjoining area was plundered by Mahmud Ghazni and reeled under the effects of his invasion. The Solankis, however, regained much of their lost power and splendour. Anahilvad Patan, the Solanki capital, was restored to glory. Royalty and traders jointly contributed to build grand temples.

The first view of the sun temple is breathtaking, with the pillared portico of the *sabhamandap* reflected in the massive tank. The weathered golden brown stone of the edifice has an overpowering grandeur. The temple follows the contemporary stylistic traditions, incorporating twin compartments - a shrine with the cells housing the presiding deity and the *mandapam* or *sabhamandap* (assembly hall). A narrow passage connects the two structures. The lower portion of both structures is ornamented with horizontal bands of sculputral decoration. The *mandovara* (upper wall portion) is covered with panels of large images of deities from the Hindu pantheon, placed in their carved niches and tabernacles. The *vimana* or the spire has horizontal bands of figurative and geometrical designs, all rising to the apex of the pyramid, the recreating in stone the mythological Mount Meru-abode of gods. Urusrimgas, miniature replicas of the shrine, cling to the central spire. Although the spires over the cells and *sabhamandap* were destroyed by the invaders and have survived only in the core pyramidal structure, an idea of their form can be had from the spires of the small temples built on terraces of the steps over the tank.

The temple interior is peristylar and consists of superbly carved pillars. Covered with lavish sculptural decoration, these pillars are examples of the perfect craftsmanship of the Solanki artisan. These pillars are geometrically arranged to create an octagonal space at the centre of the hall used quite frequently for ritualistic dance performances.

The *sabhamandap* is a small independent structure. The four entrances have ornamental *toranas* (decorative hangings over the entrance) which have a marvellous quality of intricte and precision craftsmanship. At the centre of the hall is the walnut shaped ceiling, with its numerous folds of floral girdles, upheld by two aisles of pillars arranged on diagonals of the square plan. Even at its dimly lit height, the astounding splendour of stonecraft shines brightly. It is a visual delight to stand under the 23 feet high ceiling.

The structure containing the sanctum is modest in size but a rare gem of architectural and sculptural decoration. At one time, the image of the sun, cast in gold, was placed at the centre of the sanctum to receive the first rays of the sun. The invaders removed the image for its gold and left the sanctum walls bereft of any decoration - a mere empty jewel casket. The structure is oblong in shape, 80 feet by 50 feet, with a single entrance over which the artisans have worked like jewellers. The slender columns at the porch are ingeniously crafted. On the exterior walls are the large panels of gods and goddesses, celestial maidens, nymphs and dancers, and of course impressive images of surya riding his chariot across the heavens. Very discreetly, the profuse erotic sculptural panels have been placed at inconspicuous angles to avoid unnecessary attention.

The entire structural complex at Modhera is aligned to the east, to the rising sun. *Kama Kunda*, the water tank, meant for ritualistic ablution before offering worship, is one of the most perfectly designed structures of its kind in the country. A regular well-patterned lateral formation of stone steps descends upto the bottom of the tank. The geometrical configuration of steps allows a direct or diagonal descent from all the four sides. On the small terraces on the steps are small temples with niches housing *Vaishnavite* deities. The dramatic play of light and shade on these steps creates a fascinating impact. On top of the eastern steps stands a magnificent *torana*, now surviving as ruined columns without their splendid superstrucutre, which leads into the *sabhamandap*. These columns, like every other inch of space on the temple structure, are loaded with sculptural decoration of an extraordinary beauty. Thus, the Modhera sun temple is a glorious example of Gujarat's rich cultural heritage.

SURENDRA SAHAI

MOHAMMED RAFI (1924 - 1980)

Virtually the voice of India, Mohammed Rafi articulated the joys and sorrows of millions of Indians through his songs. One of the three most popular Hindi film playback singers, ever with Kishore Kumar and Mukesh, Rafi made his debut in 1944 in the film *Pehle Aap*. He tasted success, however, the Mehboob's Anmol Ghadi in 1946, where he sang duets with Noorjehan. With the longest career span stretching from the 1940s to the 1980s, Rafi has sung for almost all heroes from Pradeep Kumar, Bharat Bhushan, Dilip Kumar, Guru Dutt, Shammi Kapoor, Dev Anand to Rishi Kapoor and Amitabh Bachchan. His career was somewhat eclipsed when Kishore Kumar became the voice of Rajesh Khanna, the super star of the 1970s. The music of composers like Naushad, S.D. Burman, Shanker Jaikishen and the poetry of Sahir, Kaifi Asmi would not have been immortialised without the melodious croonings of Rafi.

Mohammad Rafi (better known to music-lovers as 'Rafi'), a versatile play back singer, who breathed his last on July 31, 1980, is known for his famous Indian language songs. But very few may know about his English songs, that too, written by the Indian poet singer, Shri Harindra Nath Chattopadhyaya and tuned by Shanker Jaikishan team. Shri Suresh Chandvankar, Hon. Secretary of Society of Indian Record Collection (SIRC), writes about Rafi's pop hits.

Shri Chandvankar is working with Tata Institute of Fundamental Research, Mumbai.

MOHINI ATTAM

Historically, till a quarter of a century ago, only four dance practices were recognized as classical Kathakali, Bharatya Natyam, Manipuri and Kathak. But slowly, with the cultural renaissance which was sparked off by the Indian independence movement, realization dawned that there were other dance practices whose claim to be termed as classical could not be ignored. The three most noteworthy claimants are Kuchipudi, Odissi and Mohini Attam.

Mohini Attam is the Dance of the Enchantress. Its home is what we now call Kerala, created after independence by the amalgamation of the princely states of Travancore, Cochin and the malabar District of the former Madras State.

Mohini Attam, a lyrical and enchanting dance form, became the sole vehicle for feminie interpretation developed on the lines of the other classical dance styles of India. It is also a dance of sheer visual beauty, far removed from the ever-vigilant supervision of the temple and the grip of rituals. Devotional fervour is permissible but not mandatory. Religio-philosophical tenets are not allowed to interfere with the central idea of dance - its soul enchantment. The natural beauty of the Kerala landscape provides ample inspiration for its lyrical and lilting movements. Its rounded body movement, the distinctive heave of the torso and the soft walk create the sensation of the verdant paddy fields, the undulating plam fronds and the rippling back waters of Keral.

Some scholars trace Mohini Attam to the secon or third century A.D. (to the era of the great Tamil epic, Shilappadikaram). Whereas others maintain that it was created in the middle of the eighteenth century in the court of Maharaja Swati Tirumal of Travancore at his behest. Neither premise is correct.

Literary evidence shows that it was very much in vogue in the beginning of the seventeenth century A.D.

and thus must have had its origins before that. It is between 400 to 600 years old.

The symbolism behind the nam *Mohini Attam* is equally enchanting. The two elemental opposing forces of the univere are represented in the Hindu mythology by the *devas* (celestials) and *danavas* (titans or demons). In their eternal struggle for supremacy sometimes the *devas* or other times the *danavas* emerge victorious. But there is one eternal salvation available to either side in the form of *amrita* (ambrosia) which grants immortiality. This *amrita* can be acquired only by churning the *ksheerasagara* (milky ocean).

At a momentous juncture, both these opposing forces agreed to unite and churn the milky ocean. The dhurning itself created unprecedented upheavals and adjustments in the cosmic order. When at last the golden *kalasha* containing *amrita* emerged the *danava*, true to their creed, snatched it and refused to share it with the Devas.

An eternal calamity would descend upon the universe if the negtive forces of darkness achieved immortality. The *devas* rushed to lord Vishnu, the Supreme Sustainer, one of the Divine Trinity of The Hindu mythology. Whenever the universe is threatened with dire calamity it is Vishnu, the Sustainer of cosmic balance, who takes an *avatara* (incarnation) to resotre the cosmic order. At the behest of the *devas* and to maintain the realm of righteousness Vishnu appeared in the *avatara* of Mohini (the enchantress) to prevent the *danavas* from gaining immortality.

Mohini the most enchanting and bewitching form that Vishnu ever took danced her dance of enchantment and cast a spell over the *danavas.* She beguiled them into surrendering the golden *Kalasha* of *Amrita* to her and fed it to the *devas* and thus averted the awful calamity.

Here *amrita* represents all the knowledge, all that is good which guides life towards its ideal goal. This knowledge (amrita) gives immortality that is *reality.* Once this knowledge is re-instilled the cosmic order can be re-established.

Vishnu Mohini personified the sheer joy and pleasure of life. This lvoely illusion intoxicates the beholder by its enchanting beauty.

Mohini Attam is thus the dance that reflects the enchantment that is life, its enjoyment and relish that create an atmosphere of grace and beauty. But its virtue it casts a spell of enchantment on the beholder leading him towards knowledge along the path of enchantment and beauty.

The contemporary Mohini Attam dancer looks equally enchanting in her white and gold or white and contrasting colour costume. Simple but elegant gold jewellery and the distinctive bun on the side of the head encircles by a jasmine garland give her a rare elegance. Her sidelong glances and constantly fluttering eyebrows create to truly enchanting picture which is enchanced by soft stepping and undulating and sweeping movements of the arms and torso. The gentle but soulful *abhinava* (enactment or acting) sets Mohini Attam apart from the rest of the theatrical arts of Kerala like the magnificent but overpowering story - dance Kathakali and the ancient Sanskrit drama *Kudiyattam* with its elaborate and long drawn out performances.

The induction of the Sopana style of singing and *tala* cycles indigenous of Kerala today greatly enhance the lilt and grace of the dance itself. This style of singing can be best described as bhavea *sangeetam* (emotional music) which is ideally suited as an accompaniment to the gentle songs of love that predominates its repertoire.

Presented in its true spirit Mohini Attam shines as an epitome of extreme grace, good taste, dignity and above all high cultural values.

DR. KANAK RELE

MONASTERIES OF LADAKH

Ladakh is unsurpassable in its rugged and awe-inspiring beauty. Situated at an average altitude of 1400 feet above sea level, this eastern most district of jammu and Kashmir is a desert where snow clad mountains rise in sheer grandeur. Through it flow the mighty Indus and Zanskar. Faced with extremes of climate, the life of the people of Ladakh, who claim their descent from Aryans and Mongols is hard. Yet they have learnt to live in harmony with these inhospitable conditions and have evolved a way of life that is unique.

The dominant religion of Ladakh is Buddhism, with a small population of Muslims and Christians. Buddhism is the living religion of the people here, the practice of which has enables them to live in complete peace not only with other religions but also with the harsh Nature. It is manifest in the art and architecture of Ladakh. The monasteries, or the *gompas* as they are called, are beautifully designed and have the finest of sculptures, wood carvings, bronzes, gold and silver chortens, paintings done on silk scrolls and walls and scriptures printed out of hand made wooden blocks. In the monasteries the devout pray for the peace of the world.

Broadly 'speaking, there are two sects of priests or lamas in Ladakh. They are known as "Red hat Lamas" practicings the original Buddhism. They wear red hats at the time of ceremonies. In the 15th century, reforms were introduced in the monasteries. The Lamas who belong to the reformed order are known as "Yellow Hat Lamas", and they, besides other things, observe celibacy. Different *gompas* in Ladakh belong to these two sects.

The general layout of all *gompas* is the same. They are invariably built on hilltops, with prayer flags flying from rooftops. At the entrance of every *gompa is a verandah*, on the walls of which are painted the Wheel of life, the Lords of four quarters, and fierce looking guardian deities called *Dharmapals*. The Wheel of life depicts various stages, including hell, through which human have to pass before achieving *Nirvana* or the final salvation. In the main prayer hall are placed the images of Buddha or Boddhisattvas as the central figures of worship. Boddhisattava is a soul that has by its merits gained salvation, but borgoes it so that it could return to earth and help other worldly beings attain salvation and enlightenment. Then there are Avalokiteshwaras, the personifications of compassion, often shown with eleven heads and innumerable arms and hands; Manjushri, who personifies wisdom; and Maitreya, the Buddha to come. Buddha himself is one such Boddhisattave who returns to the mankind again and again in the course of ages to relieve him of his miseries.

At a much later stage Tantric element crept into Buddhism from Hinduism and implied the introduction of feminine principles along with the masculine ones, and a system of female deities along with their male counterparts in fierce forms were shown in a state of ecstatic union. In almost every monastery there is a dark chamber dedicated to such deities where women and children are not admitted. Monasteries contain chambers for the Head Lamas and dormitories for the novices.

As one nears a gompa, one comes across a neat stack of stones in the shape of a wall, on which are carved prayers in praise of Lord Buddha. Such walls are called Mani Walls and while walking one has to keep them to one's right. In the beginning and end of Mani walls are chessmen like structures called *chortens*. These are the burial monuments of Lamas.

Nowadays Leh is reachable from Manali in Himachal Pradesh. This 500 km long route passes through Lahaul and a long stretch of 300 km desert with hardly any habitation except for a few tourist encampments, till one reached Hemis, followed by Thiksey and Sey. As one nears Hemis, one suddenly comes across clusters of trees with a *chorten* there and a chorten there. Soon, the monastery nestling in the shadow of tall, barren cliffs of Zanskar range comes in sight. This *gompa* was founded in 1630 under the patronage of Sengge Namgyal. Hemis is the richest and largest of all Ladakh *gompas*. Every *gompa* celebrates its festivals in the form of dance drams or Devil Dance's in winter. Hemis, however, is the only *gomps*, which has its two day festival in summer and therefore attracts tourists from the entire world. Lamas robed in gowns of rich, brightly coloured broades, wearing bright coloured and grotesque masks of legendary or mythical characters perform the dances. A Ladakhi orchestra accompanies these dances. The dances are performed in the courtyard, while the two-storey *gompa* is packed with visitors. These dances originally celebrated the event of the killing of the cruel Tibetan king Landgarma by a monk. Now they symbolize the victory of good over the evil.

Hemis to Thiksey is a pleasant drive of about an hour. A cluster of houses rises tier upon tier culminating in the chambers of lamas and the *gompa* on the hilltop. The imposing two storey temple is pained red and houses an equally imposing image of Maitreya Buddha sitting in lotus position. The *gompa* is said to have been built in the middle of the 15th century.

Half an hour's drive from Thiksey brings one to Shey gompa, standing amidst the ruins of a fort on a hillock. It was at one time the seat of royalty and is situated in a beautiful locale. In the main hall a two storey high gilded image of Buddha stands. It is said to have been installed by King Deldan Namgyal. On a rock on the roadside, which is a part of the hillock, is a large engraving of the five Dhyani Buddhas, recognizable by their vehicles and seems to be very old. The other *gompas*, worth a mention, in the suburbs are Sankar, Spituk and the one in the Leh fort.

After crossing the Indus over a bridge the famous Alachi Gompa is situated unlike other *gompas*, which are perched on hilltops and are imposing structures, Alchi is a modest looking structure of mud and timber. But the art treasures of wall paintings and seculptures, which this *gompa* contains, are superb. This *gompa* is said to have been built by Rin Chen Zampo, the great Tibetan teacher who was educated in the monasteries of Bengal and Bihar, went thrice to Kashmir and spent 17 years in India. But inscriptions point to its having been built by a member of a Tibetan noble family in the 11th century. The wall paintings of this monastery, well preserved over the centuries, are remarkable in concept and workmanship.

This monastery which is called Ajanta of the North has six temples called Du Khang, Sumtsek, jampal Lhakhang, Lotsawa Lhakhang, Manjur Lhakhang and Lhakhang Soma. Of these the first two belong to 11th and 12th centureis while the rest were built in 12th and 13th centuries. The first two are important from painting and sculptures point of view. The paintings can be broadly grouped into the following heads: scenes from Budhha's life; figures of various Boddhisattavas; figures of Vairocana and the depiction of cosmic Buddha Vairocana in a mandala. One can see various influences such as Hellenistic, Persian, Tibetan, Nepalese, Central Asian and India on these paintings. Yet the style of Alchi paintings is altogether its own. The central figures in the temples are those of boddhisattavas Avalokiteshwara, Manjushri and Maitreya.

The Sumstek is a three story temple, which is something unique. The temple has three gigantic Boddhisattavas, which extend up through openings in the ceilings to the second storey. The three images in clockwise direction are Avalokiteshwara, Maitreya and Manjushri. The garments of these figures are painted with scenes from Buddha's life in miniatures. The walls are filled with figures and mandalas in such profusion that not an inch is left without a painting.

R. N. PASRICHA

MONUMENTS OF INDIA

The monuments of India, which constitute an important part of her cultural heritage, have no parallel in the world in regard to their variety, beauty and design. These represent an extraordinary diversity in character; each monument in its building techniques and of the people who built it. The continuity of past patterns of life into modern times is nowhere better illustrated than in India, represented by monuments and sites from prehistoric times upto the nineteenth century. In fact, each monument mirrors in itself a great power of assimilation, the traits of the Indian soil and the cultures emerging out of it.

There are about 5,000 monuments of national importance which are being looked after by the Archaeological Survey of India founded in 1861 with the primary objective of locating, preserving, conserving and studying the monuments and sites in India. It is carrying out its functions admirably ever since.

It was indeed a memorable day in 1972 in the sphere of international cooperation when the UNESCO General Conference adopted a resolution on the creation of a Covention concerning the protection of World Cultural and Natural Heritage. Its main objectives are to :

i) define the world Heritage in both cultural and natural aspects.

ii) enlist sites and monuments from the member countries which are of exceptional interest and universal value, the protection of which is the concern of all mankind.

iii) promote cooperation among all nation and people for keeping these universal treasures intact for future generations.

This UNESCO Convention was retified by India in 1977. Since then, India has been an active member of this forum.

The list of recorded World Haritage sites now stands at 378 which include both cultural and natural wonders, an endowment that is shared by all and the protection of which is the concern of the entire mankind.

India has already inscribed 16 cultural and five natural sites. The cultural sites include Ajanta Caves, Ellora Caves, Agra Fort, Taj Mahal, The Sun temple at Konark, Mahabalipuram Group of Monuments, Goa Churches and Convents, Khajuraho group of Mouments, Hampi Mouments, Getehpur Sikri etc. The natural sites are Keoladeo National Park, Mans Wildlife Sanctuary, Kaziranga National Park, Sundebans National park and Nanda Devi.

Let us have a brief look at some of the World Heritage monuments of India.

1) Ajanta Caves

The Ajanta Caves in the Indian state of Maharashtra are thirty in all, including the unfinished ones. After centuries of oblivion, these Caves were discovered in 1819 AD. They fall into two distinct phases with a break of nearly four centuries between them. All the Caves of the earlier phase date between 2nd century BC and 2nd century AD.

The Caves of the second phase were excavated during the supremacy of the Vekatakas and Guptas. A few paintings which survived on the walls of Caves 9 and 10, go back to the Satavahana period. The themes are intensely religious in tone and centre round Budhha.

2) Ellora Caves

The magnificent group of rock hewn temples of Ellora, representing three different faiths, Buddhist, Brahamnical and Jain, mark the culmination of the cave temple architecture in Western India. The entire group of 34 caves was excavated during the 5th and 13th centuries AD. The Buddhist caves (1 to 12) were excavated between the 5th and 7th centuries AD, when the Mahayana sects were flourishing in the region.

3) Agra Fort

The Agra Fort represents the first major building project of the Mughal Emperor Akbar, though remains of only a few buildings built by him now survive. Built on the site of an earlier castle during 1565-75 AD, the fort, apart from other important units, contains Jahangiri Mahal, Khaas Mahal, Diwan-e-Khaas, Diwan-e-Aam, Machchi Bhawan and Moti Masjid. Irregularly triangular on plan, it is enclosed by a double, battlemented massive wall of red sandstone, about two km in perimetre, interrupted by graceful curves and lofty bastions. Of its four gates the most impressive is the Delhi Gate on the west.

4) Taj Mahal

The Taj Mahal stands on the right bank of the Yamuna, about 15 km, from the Agra Fort and was built to enshrine the remains of Mumtaz Mahal, the consort of Mughal Emperor Shah Jahan. The construction commenced in 1631 AD and was completed seventeen years later at enormous cost and labour. The architect responsible for the construction was Ustad Ahmad lahori. Unlike other Mughal garden tombs, the mausoleum is situated at the northern end of a large rectangular area with its central portion divided off into a square garden. The entire portion is enclosed within a high boundary wall having broad octagonal pavilions at corners. A majestic gateway is in the centre of the southern side facing a spacious quardrangle.

Constant conservation work goes on at this world famous monument.

5) The Sun Temple, Konark

Kainapara of the Periplus (1st century AD), Konark is an important port on the Orissa coast. The most notable marvel of Orissan art is the stately Sun Temple. Built in 1250 AD, during the reign of king Narasimhadeva - I (1238 - 1264 AD), it enshrined an image of Sun (Arka), the patron deity of the region. The entire complex was designed in the form of a huge chariot drawn by seven spirited horses on twelve pairs of exquisitely carved wheels. The sanctum symbolised the majestic stride of the Sun God and markes the culmination of the Orissan architectural movement.

6) Mahabalipuram Group of Monuments

Mahabalipuram, the city of Mamalla, is named after the title of great Pallave ruler Narasimhavaraman-I (630 - 668 AD). It was a sea port during the time of Periplus (1st centurty AD) and Ptolemy (140 A.D.) and many Indian colonists migrated to South-East Asia through this port town. Most of the monuments like rock-cut chariots, scenes sculptured on open rocks like Arjuna's penance depicts the Mahabharata events. The five monolithic chariots are named after five Pandavas.

7) Goa Churches and Convents

The most comprehensive group of Churches and Cathedrals built from 16th to 17th century AD at old Goa comprise the World Heritage monuments. These include Church and Convent of St. Francis of Assisi, Chapel of St. Catherine, Basilica of Bom Jesus, Church of Lady of Rosary; Church of St. Augustine etc. The Church of St. Cajetan is modelled on the original design of St. Peter's Church in Rome.

8) Khajuraho Group of Monuments

Khajuraho, the ancient Kharjjuravahaka, formed part of the territory of Jejabhukti ruled by the Chandelas, a strong central Indian dynasty, in the 10th century AD. The Chandelas built this magnificent capital town with munerous tanks, scores of lofty temples of sculptural grace and architectural splendour. The local traditions lists eighty-five temples but now only twenty five are standing examples in various stages of preservation.

9) Hampi Monuments

Hampi, traditionally known as Pampakshetra of Kishkindha, is situated on the southern bank of the river Tungabhadra. Once it was the seat of the mighty Vijayanagara empire.

The monuments of Vijayanagara city, also known as Vidyanangara in honour of the sage Vidyaranya, were built between 1336 - 1370 AD, during the rule of Hariharal to Sadashiva Raya. But a large number of Royal buidings were built by Sri Krishnadeva Raya (1509 - 1530 AD). This period witnessed the resurgence of Hindu religion, art and architecture on an unprededented scale. Extensive remains of the palaces can be seen within innermost enclosure of the ancient Vijayanagara. though the largest extent temple is that of Pampapati in Hampi and extensively renovated, its magnificent entrance tower was built by Krishnadeva Raya.

10) Fatehpur Sikri

Fatehpur Sikri owes its foundation to Emperor Akbar whose two sons - Prince Salim, (Later on Jahangir) in 1569, and Prince Murad in 1570 were thought to have been born through the blessings of saint Shaikh Salim Chishti. The emperor, in the course of his visit to the saint in 1571, ordered the construction of buildings for his own use and asked the noblemen to construct houses for themselves. Within a year most of the work was finished and within the next few years, a well planned city with magnificent administrative, residential and religious buildings came into existence.

The Jami mosque was perhaps among the first buildings to be built, its epigraph gives AH 979 (1671-72 AD) as the date of its completion. The Buland - Darwaza was added some five years later.

11) Monuments at Pattadakal

Pattadakal was not only popular for Chalukyan architectural activities but was also a holy place for royal coronations. Temples constructed here mark the blending of the northern Rekhanagara Prasada and the Dravida Viman styles in temple building. The place has illustrious examples of the Chalukyan art.

12) Elephanta Caves

The name Elephanta given to the island called Gharapuri is derived from a massive stone elephant found on the island in the year 1804. It is the Puri, the island capital of Konkan Mayruas, who held sway over the western coast around 6th century AD.

There are in all seven caves in Elephanta of which the most important is the Mahesamurti cave which measures 39 metres.

13) Brihadisvara Temple, Thanjavur

This celebrated Saiva temple, appropriately called Brihadisvara and Daksinameru, is the grandest creation of the Chola emperor Raja Raja (985 - 1012 AD). Architecturally, it is the most ambitious structural temple built of granite. The Brihad Linga within the sanctum is eight-metre high.

14) Sanchi

Sanchi in Madhya Pradesh was· known in ancient times as 'Kaknadbot' and 'Bot Sri Parvat'. The monuments at Sanchi range from circa 3rd century BC to 12th century AD. It is famous for its magnificent stupa originally built by Emperor Ashoka and later embellished during Sunga times and added with four highly sculptured Gateways. The sculptured panels depict Buddha's life.

15) Humayun Tomb

The Humayun Tomb in New Delhi rises from a podium located in the centre of a four square garden (Char Bagh) and further divided by causeqays. The central octagonal chamber containing the Cenotaph is encompassed by octagonal chambers at the diagonals and arched lobbies on the sides, their openings closed with perforated screens. The tomb was built by Humayun's widow Bega Begum nine years after his death in 1565. ·It is the first mature example of the idea of garden tomb which culminated in the Taj Mahal, Agra.

16) Qutub Minar

In the final year of the twelfth century, qutb-ud-din laid the foundation of the Qutb-Minar, the tallest stone-tower in India, 72.5m in height. Possibly raised both as a tower of victory and as a *minar* attached to the mosque for the call to the faithful for prayer, it was completed by Qutb-ud-din's successor and son-in-law, Shams-ud-din Iltutmish (1211-36), who also enlarged the mosque including its screen. (Condensed)

MADHU BALA

MUGHAL ART : IMAGES AND METAPHORS OF FLORA AND FAUNA

The 16th and 17th centuries saw the mainfestation of art as an integral part of Mughal life. Although Islam did not encourage human figurative work, this did not prevent the exuberance of Mughal art from depicting the marvellous beauty of an imagined Heaven on earth.

Interestingly, Mughal art was never a vehicle for religion but was concerned only with beauty and grandeur, with no undercurrents of philosophical, religious or ritualistic symbolism. Flora and fauna from nature were used only to the extent that these could embellish the arts and enhance the architectural bravura.

Mughal painters never adhered to the linear and idealized forms of a Persian school and, following indigenous trends, emphasized realism in the depiction of birds and animals. Their inclination to graphic detail and accuracy in rendering the characteristic features and forms reflects their originality. These trends eventually combined with the upcoming European techniques to enhance the effect of chiaroscuro and to model physical features, thus prompting naturalism in art and lending the Mughal school and unique character.

Historically speaking, the first Mughal emperor Babar, thanks to his roots and ceaseless wanderings, was familiar with the fabled gardens, palaces, mosques and mausoleums of the Central Asian and Persian World. He set the tone for his newly founded empire where a palace or tomb no longer stood in isolation but was presented through gardens, tree-lined avenues and flower beds, stone-paved water channels, stone tanks and cascades are raised causeways.

The love of flowers and plants continued under Babar's able descendants : Humayun, Akbar, Jahangir and Shah Jahan. Humayun has literary records affirming his delight in nature, as depicted in the ornamentation of his turban or in the painting of a captured bird. During the reign of Akbar, painting touched a next high in the *Hamzanama* folios. These are filled with detailed depictions of flowers in bloom and various fowl and forest animals in verdant settings. The *Hamzanama* drew copiously from the earliest Islamic metal and glassware conventions with floral imagery and occasional animals heads portrayed as terminal motifs.

It was in the reign of the next emperor Jahangir that Mughal decorative arts reached a zenith of creative expression, featuring abundant flora and fauna imagery. The jade scent-vials, fashioned in the form of a flower bud, were among the earliest known floral shaped Jahangir vessels. The great court artist Mansure painted birds and animals, plants and flowers in profusion and these paintings had an overwhelming influence on the exterior and interior surgaces of buildings.

Shah Jahan, the next emperor, condified formal portraits of flowering plants as leitmotif to continue for the next two centuries. Naturalistic portrayals of noble animals were adapted to decorative arts, and hors and antelope headed dagger hilts made of jade or nephrite were a favourite with the Emperor. On the architecutral front, the Taj Mahal stood on the edge of the Char Bagh, with its central canal, causeways, flower-beds and tree avenues. Living fauna abounded in the Char Bagh and colourful butterflies flitted among the flowering plants.

Imperial painting and other decorative arts under the next emperor Aurangzeb and later Mughal emperors gradually suffered a qualitative degradation, primatily due to withering of imperial patronage caused by political instability and ultimately the cataclysmic raid on Delhi by the Persian King Nadir Shah in the early 18th century.

One fascinating aspect of this extended period of art history was the culling together from multiple cultural traditions in which mythical animals appeared. Thus the images of the Hindu patheon Ganesha, Hanuman, Jambavat, Garuda and the Gaja-Simba- found their way in the illustrations of Persian translations of Hindu epics and Puranas commissioned by the Mughals for religious understanding. Two particular mythical animals that appear in Mughal art from the period of Akbar to that of Aurangzeb are the dragon and the simurg, the latter a combination of the energy and features of falcon, ostrich, ringdove and unicorn. The other feature was the composite nature of art. Fantastic animals of a mixed kind, found in Indian arts dating from the 1st century BC, porivided the Mughal artist his inspiration. This is evinced in a Shahnama manuscript painted for Jahangir in the early 17th century.

Dr. UTPAL K. BANERJEE

MUGHAL GARDENS OF RASHTRAPATI BHAWAN

It is the only place in the world where a million seedings are tended by a set of fity-two pairs of hands. Termed as the Mughal Gardens of Rashtrapati Bhawan (President's House) they were not a historic legacy of the Mughal reign in India. One of the few surviving examples of formal garden layout in the world, this unique garden is located within the inner precincts of the Rashtrapati Bhavan, the official residence of the President of India Republic. Its unusual link-up with the grand masters of garden architecture in India history was on account of its inspirational ouevre. Like the historic gardens of Mughal times, this garden, too, was built at the insistence and wishes of a woman. She was the Vicerine, Lady Hardinge, who has altered their annual summer holiday plans for 1924, from a stay at Shimla to the balmy salubriousness of the Kashmir Valley. During her stay at Srinagar, she was impressed by the gardens that the Mughal emperors had designed, - in the elevated foothills of the lower Himalayas and which they had given a sense of exclusivity by this mountainous backdrop. It served as a surrounding wall screening it behind the regulatory purdah or veiled look.

A barren outcrop of sixteen acres on top of the capital's Raising Hill was earmarked for this garden. Work started on it in 1924 under the guidance of architect Edward Lutyens and in deference to the brainchild of the Vicerine, the place was construed according to the principles of Persian garden architecture, secluded from the private wing of the official residence. In faithful reproduction of the philosophy that dictates as Persian artistry, there was absolute symmetry in the construction of paths and terraces. Water was the source of all life in the garden and this was made to cascade in chutes, fountains and channels along a central artery, with the planting and grassy spaces enclosed into geometrical segments of squares, rectangles, hexagons and sunken pool. This segmenting is the keynote of its formality and remains intact even today.

As a slight deviation from the orthodox principle of garden layout, the garden at Rashtrapati Bhavan has its water sides fringed with herbaceous borders which are filled with seasonal planting each winter. This European input is just as well, for today, the beds are a source of colour and interest in the garden. Instead of a year-long look of sombre and light as in the traditional garden, this place becomes the centre of attraction during the winter bloom, when its doors are opened to the public at large. The red sandstone walkways along the garden not only create its subdivisions, but also provide vantage points for enjoying the sight, and thus trampling on grass or flowerbeds in virtually unheard of in this place of flowery splendour.

Although the garden can be divided into four main areas, with the help of water chutes that run in a north-south and east-west grid, it is the overall effect of the garden that attracts the visitor, to tarry and admire. Along the main driveway are a series of exquisite topiary worked maulsari and cypress trees. Their dark hued foliage is a reminder of the imminence of death, in mortal terms and make one ponder on this mystique amidst the joy of the plumb, stem rose plants. Intersperesed in between the sombre parade, they denote the colour and cheer of life. That they do not last forever is meant to indicate the transitory aspect of life and the juxtaposition of both evergreen and fleeting planting is but a reflection of the cycle of life and death on this earth.

But a visit to the Mughal Gardens is not an update on philosophy. Its trim and elegant looks has a behind-the-scenes, year-long maintenance routine. As the seasonal, that give the garden its characteristic importance, have to be nurtured in-house, the work for a nursery begins in September. The plantings in this garden are created around a specific colour and species outley. Besides, the soil conditions need careful study, so as to maintain the even height in growth, so srucial to visual harmony. Hence, the cultural practice of manuring, planting and tending is totally manual and in supervised schedules. The central rectangular garden is the focal point of planting, while the square beds skirting the main pool in the lower end of the garden are used for experimental introductions.

Besides rountine plantings each year, the gardens are replenished with varieties that then become a part of the garden's repertoire. In this way, the gardens have become a show-case for plump gazenias, giant-sized pansies, internationally-renowned varieties of chrysanthemums and dahlias of every hue and creed. The newest accent is on the cultivation of prized gladioli and one must watch and see the blooms take a stand and be counted, in this treasury of garden delights. In addition, the 250 varieties of roses in the place are its valuable standby. Today, the gardens have become a special landmark in the minds of the common man. Every year, just after the advent of the spring festival of *Basant Panchmi* (Feb-March) citizens of the country anxiously await the opening of the gardens for public visits. There is an air of festivity in the place when the gardens are thrown open to the public. Because the nation, the people and its First Citizen, take a justifiable pride in this glorious showpiece of Indian heritage.

SUBHRA MAJUMDAR

MUGHAL STYLE OF PAINTINGS

Indo-Persian Style, base essentially on school of Iran; affected individually by tastes of Indian rulers, influenced by local styles. 15th century onwards, important paintings are *Khamseh* of Amir Khosrow of Delhi; *Bostan* painted in Mandu; maniuscript of *Ne'mat - Namch*, painted for Sultan of Malwa, early 16th century. Its illustration deri/ed Turkmen style of shiraz; but clear features, local version of western style adopted.

16th century, new style, more vigorous, full of vital energy, profoundly moving, emerging. Earliest dated example is an *Aranyaka Parva Parva* of the Mahabharata, among finest of series illustrating *Bhagavata Purana* and *Caurapancasika* of Bilhana, scattered in collections all over the world.

Mughal style; exclusive creation of Akbar. Trained in painting, created large atelier; staffed with artists; recuited all over India.

Initial stages work confined, illustration of books on variety of subjects - histories, romances, poetic works, myths,

legends, fables of Indian, Persian origin. Manuscripts written by calligraphers; illustrations executed by groups of painters, including colourist; chief of the group, designer, sketched. Colourist work proceeded slowly. Colours used mineral; also consisted vegetable dyes; brushes, exceedingly fine, made from squirrels tail or camel hair.

Earlier paintings; illustrations of *Tuti-Nameh; Dastan-e-Amir-Hamzeh*; originally consisted of 1400 paintings, usually large size, (approximately 25 inches by 16 inches); of which only 200 survived. *Tuti-Nameh* shows Mughal style in process of formation; hand of artists of non-Mughal style recognisable; style reveals intense effort to cope with new demands.

Persian translations of epic, the *Mahabharata*, the *Ramayana* - Mughal painter revealed richness of imagination. Most painter Hindus, subjects close to their hearts; tolerant, sympathetic patron, they rose to heights. *Razm-Nameh, Mahabharata* in Persian, a master piece.

Imperial atelier, cultivated, intimate manner, illustration of books; poetic with less number of illustrations. Paintings by single master; works very refined, delicate, infinite attention to detail, filled with colour. A *Divàn* of Anwari, dated 1589; paintings very small, none larger than five inches by 2½ inches; delicately executed. On larger scale, same mood, manuscripts, of reign of Akbar: eg the *Babaristan* of Jami 1595, a *Khamseh* of Amir Khosrow.

Jehangir; keen interest painting; atelier of own. Tastes not same as Akbar; reflected in style of painting; underwent significant change. Preferred portraiture; elaborate works of his reign, great court scenes, showing Jehangir surrounded by courtiers.

Compositions lost movement, evident in works of Akbar's reign. Figures formally ordered, in keeping with strict rules of etiquette enjanced in Mughal court colours subdued, harmonious; brushwork exceedingly fine.

Many paintings preserved in albums; assembled for Jahangir, Shah-Jahan, eg The *Muraggah-e-Gulshan*; gives idea of Jahangir as patron, collector, connoisseur of arts, a person with wide range of taste, curious, enquiring mind.

Jahangir esteemed art of painting; honoured painters; favourite Abu-al-Hasan, designated Nadir-uz-zaman, whose spectacular picture, Jahangir looking at Portrait of his father ustàd-Mansur, designated Nadir-ul-Asr; his studies of birds, animals unparalleled Bishandas; Mansbbar; Daulat; important painters.

Attention shifted to architecture; painting in Jahangir tradition continued; style noticeably rigid; portraits lacking breadth of life; colouring jewel-like; outward splendour dazzling. Best work *Shahjahan-Nameh*. Govardhan, Bichitra outstanding painters.

From Aurangzeb's reign, few pictures survived, work nondescript, chiefly of array of lifeless portraits, mostly output of workshops, Gears Scenes, showing sathering of ascetics, holy men, lovers in garden, terrace, Musical parties, abundant. Show genuine quality, particularly during reign of Muhammad Shah (1719 - 48), devoted to art. Mughal painting, came to end, Shah Alam II reign. Artists occupied reveries of past Library dispersed, destroyed during the Mutiny, 1857.

MUHAMMAD AHMAD BANNE (b. 1918)

Instrumentalist; Hindustani, Sarangi of Sunpat gharana; studied with Ashiq Hussain and Gulam Sabir.

P. N. CHOPRA

MUHARE : THE IMAGES OF GODS

Diversity of lifestyle in various regions of India has led to the evolution of multitudinous expressions in religious practices. Worshipping in the Indian context has been mainly in the iconic form. The visual imageries of the gods as deities has been principally anthropomorphic, ranging from the well defined forms for the respective genders of the gods, where each aspect of the physical anatomy is ideally crafted, to other styles where the concentration is on the amply outlined facial characteristics. Discriminatory attributes may be reflected in the depiction of well grown mustaches for the male and not so marked torso with a pair of breasts for the female form. The rudimentary anthropomorphous images may just have punches to denote the eyes, the nose, the lips, the ears etc. These aspects of anthropomorphic physiognomy run parallel to the floral and faunal imageries for the ritual icons. Metal, stone, wood, clay, fabric, pigments etc are generally the mediums for the iconic expressions of the beliefs and cults.

Himachal Pradesh has astounding imageries of classical gods and folk deities in the metal form. The present state of Himachal Pradesh has been formed by merging nearly twenty former princely states. The area of Himachal formerly belonging to the states of Kangra, Chamba, Mandi, Guler, Kulu and Nurpur, located on the lower slopes of Dhauladhar ranges in the valley of the rivers Ravi, Beas and Sutlej, has been referred to in ancient Indian literature as Trigata. This area has a isolated tradition of images of gods, traditionally cast in gold, silver or *astadhatu* (an alloy of eight metals)and now also in brass and copper. These images are locally known as "Muhare". The iconic features of Muhare are the fusion of several epic traditions, local cults of the diversified chieftain, and the local heros. Religious belief in the Himalayan region have been dominated by Shiva Vishnu on the one hand and with benevolent man - eaters like Hariti and Hadimba (of the *Mahabharata* times) on the other hand. From among the local cults, the cult of snake worship (Naga cult) has been dominant. The physiognomic characters of the Muhare deities are those of the human form. The Naga Muhare, for example, is represented in a human form with a snake symbol to distinguish it.

Since the Muhare are installed as folk deities in local shrines in the interior villages of the Himalayan valley, there is an annual customary ritual to bring these deities out. Deified Mohare are ceremoniously brought out of their abodes, seated on wooden seats known as Palki, decked in fresh attires. They journey on the shoulders of their devotees to reach the towns of Mandi or Kulu, as the case may be. The journey from the village for each deity begins on different days depending on the distance of the shrine from the temple. Ceremonial jubilation hymns are sung at the campfires at each night halt, taken in the precincts of local temples. The whole journey is a kind of relay with every participant reaching the main temples in Kulu or Manali. Circumventing the principal Lord in sequential order, the deties take a round of the entire city in a procession. They take a rest at the main grounds of the town before heading back home.

Traditionally, the Muhare were made by the casting technique with the features retaining classical charcteristics. The advent of the Rajput influence in the area saw the introduction of the embossing technique for making the Muhare. At about the same time, the characteritics of the face were also influenced by the folk elements. A change in the metals used traditionally came about probably for two reasons: the high cost of gold, silver or the *astadhatu* and the increasing use of Muhare for non-cultic and decorative purposes. The facial features of the deities are elaborated by the simple metal repouse technique while the neck is left plain without any roundness. Symbols like rudimentary breasts for gender identification or the snake, sun etc. for the recognition of the deity are demarcated by the same technique. Restricting the construction of the image mainly to the facial features is because only the face of the deity is visible to the worshipper and the rest of the form is covered by costumes.

Several rituals are observed even at the time of making the Muhare deities. The person who commissions a Muhare approaches the Muhare maker with a minimum offering of a coconut, paddy and a new dress. The Muhare maker, before beginning the work, cleans his workshop by sprinkling holy water and takes a bath. The brass sheet is cut to the required size and treated with ritualstic reverence. After the sheet is fixed on the ral (the frame) it is always covered with a cotton sheet when the artisan is not working on it. When the Muhare is complete, it is given a ritual wash and kept wrapped in a cloth. It is delivered to the patron on a pre-determined auspicious day. A rich patron may hold a feast to mark the receiving and installation of the Muhare and provide new clothes for the maker and his family, and sufficient grain and pulses for a year. The total charges for a Muhare, therefore, are conceived in terms of originating a deity and not just a statue.

CHARUS S. GUPTA

MUKERJI, HEMANT KUMAR (b. 1922)

Vocalist; Rabindra Sangeet; composer and music director for films; concert tours, East Africa, Europe, Aden (1959); disc recordings.

P. N. CHOPRA

MUKESH MATHUR : SINGER

Born on July 22, 1923, Mukesh Chand Mathur was a cousin of film star Motilal, the well-entrenched debonair and dashing hero who introduced him to films. Handsome, ever-smiling and an enthusisastic learner, Mukesh first sought to become a hero and in fact got some leading assignments, like in *Nirdosh,* and a couple of other films. Comparatively insignificant as they were, all these films flopped and he was well advised to concentrate solely on his singing.

"Dil jalta hai" was his first breakthrough song which short Mukesh into prominence and established him as a promising and capable singer for many popular heroes and characters. He thus went on to sing successfully for a string of films. Impressed, maestro Naushad used his talented voice for evergreen songs in *Andaz* and *Mela* for Dilip Kumar and in *Anokhi Ada* for Prem Adib.

Raj Kapoor, then an aspiring connoisseur, who had learnt the basics of film music from the great R.C. Boral, and had basked in the inspiring presence of K.L. Saigal in his most formative years, chose Mukesh to be his singing voice in his very first independent celluloid venture, *Aag*, in 1948. Their like mindedness and mutual compatibility sonn turned their professional relationship into an eternal bond and it was Mukesh all the way who sang for Raj Kapoor in almost all his subsequent films, whether made under his own RK banner or by other producers.

Significantly, Mukesh recorded his last song for RK's *Satyam Shivam Sundaram* on the eve of his departure, along with Lata Mangeshkar, for a tour of Detroit (USA) where, unfortunately, he breathed his last after suffering a massive heart attack on August 27, 1976.

Paying rich tributes to Mukesh, Raj Kapoor said he had lost his voice and quoted from Mukesh's debut song for him in *AAG*, i.e. "*Zinda hoon is tarah ke gham-e-zindagi nahin; jalta hua diya hun magar roshni nahin*" (Alive I am but without a care for life; A burning lamp I am but not quite aglow).

Mukesh sang for Raj many mellifluous songs with perennial appeal like "*Awara hoon*" (A tramp I am) in *Awara* and "*Mera joota hai japani*" (My shoes are from Japan) in *Shree 420* which brought him international celebrity status and for which he was profusely feted and greeted.

He also recorded for Raj several other unforgettable numbers for films made outside the RK banner like *Sunehre Din, Chhalia, Baware Nain, Kanhaiya, Parvarish, Anari, Teesri Kasam* and many more. He sang a variety of melodious hits for other actors too as in *Aaram, Sheesha, Milan, Saranga, Sanjog, Sambandh, Kabhi Kabhi, Dewar* and *Haryali Aur Raasta*. He even rendered some meaningful solos of everlasting value by way of background melodies as in *Bombai Ka Babu* and *Bandini*, both under maestro S.D. Burman.

Mukesh produced Malhar for which he playbacked some scintillating songs under the direction of Music director Roshan. Spurred by his unfulfilled ambition of acting and undaunted by the earlier failures, he went ahead to produce, score music for and act in *Anurag* but the films did not take off. *Mashooqa* was another picture in which he acted with the then singing heroine Suraiya, but that film too met with a similar fate. He, however, did make a brief screen appearance as a tonga-driver in RK's *Aah*.

His drift to production and acting somewhat dried up the market for his playback singing as producers and music directors deemed him unavailable for their pictures. Nevertheless, after a gap he made a lucky comeback with Dilip Kumar - Meena Kumari starrer *Yehudi's* number "*Yeh mera diwanapan hai ya mohabbat Ka Saroor*" (It is either my craze or the intoxication of love). There was, of course, no looking back thereafter and he went on to enrich further his kitty of successful songs.

The variegated repertoire of about a thousand records bequeathed by Mukesh to his fans includes his ardently rendered *Ram Charit Manas* (story of Lord Rama) and a quartet of sweet *bhajans* (religious songs).

Endowed with a sweet voice, coupled with a pleasant timbre, Mukesh evinced special flair for rendering sad songs with such intensity as if to corroborate the axiomatic assertion that tragedy is a higher form of art than comedy and to confirm the veracity of P.B. Shelley's observation, "Our sweetest songs are those that tell our saddest thoughts".

Charming, friendly and liberal in his views, Mukesh was ever ready to perform or lend a helping hand for national and social causes. For quite a while he occupied the *numero uno* slot among our male singers. However, he continues to enthrall his countless fans even 22 years after death muffled his voice. He was indeed a gem of rare purity whose glitter will never fade.

B. M. MALHOTRA

MULIK, PUNKAJ KUMAR (b. 1905)

Vocalist; Rabindra Sangeet, light music, bhajan, kirtan, composer and music director of films; studied with Dinendranath Tagore, Durgadas Banerjee, publications : Ragalakshman, Gitamanjari; disc recordings.

References

Bandyopadhyaya, S., Music in India, Bombay, 1970.
India *Who's who* 1980, New Delhi, 1980.
Ministry of Information & Broadcasting, Aspects of Indian Music, New Delhi, 1982.
The Times of India Directory 1980, Bombay, 1980.

MUNIR KHAN (b. 1923)

Instrumentalist : Karanataka, mridangani; studied with Thanjavur V.S. Vaidyanatha Iyer; concert tours, Sri Lanka (1941), Europe and Egypt (1963).

P. N. CHOPRA

MUSEUM OF INDIAN AIR FORCE

The Indian Air Force Museum in New Delhi houses a distinctively rare collection of memorabila from Indian Air Force's aviation history.

Traversing through its well-laid out galleries and hangers is like taking a leisurely stroll into the aviation world of early 1920's and 30's to the more recent times. From the photographic history of the Indian Air Force, of its early days at Risalpur (now in Pakistan) to the mammoth B-24 liberator, a heavy bomber of World War II and in use in Indian Air Force between the period 1948 to 1971, the wreckage of a Sabre jet, wings of Canberra constituting the war toophies from battles won to radars for controlling surface-to-Air Missile (SAM) - the museum has it all.

Miniature models of aircrafts in use in various countires, paintings and photographs of IAF's rare moments pioneers of World War II, rare small arms, its inception and the ceremonial sword of the Jam Sahib of

Nawanagar which used to be presented to the pilot trainee who stood first in order of merit at the Air Force Academy are displayed in the galleries.

The main hanger boasts of about 15 different types of aircraft. These have formed the backbone of the Indian Air Force. It includes the only surviving Wapiti aircraft, which was used by IAF from 1937 to 1942 characterized by two parallel wings interconnected with supporting poles and wires, it reminds one of the famous movie. "Those Majestic Men and Their Flying Machines". Mystere, Hurricanes, MIG-21, Hunter Lysander, Spitfire, Vampire and Tempest, which wrought hell during Second World War, rest majestically - a testimony to their years of youth and glory when the sky was their only limit. A towering statue of Flying Officer Nirmaljit Singh Sekhon, next to a Gnat is a fitting tribute to a brave pilot who was awarded Param Vir Chakra for outstanding gallantry by a grateful nation in the 1971 war. The hanger also boasts of a Ford Saloon Car used by the Chiefs of Indian Air Force during the period 1969 to 1992 which now graces the museum.

As one emerges from the hanger and indeed from history, one is greeted by a massive B-24 Liberator, Canberra, M 14 and Sikarosky 55 helicopters looking immaculately groomed and ready to take off to where they always belonged - the sky.

The museum mirrors the history of Indian Air Force both during war as well as peace and is a fitting tribute to its thousands of men who have contributed immensely to the building of its glorious traditions, imparting it a sense of history.

A. MEHROTRA

MUSIC - A SURVEY

The word 'Carnatic' or 'Karnatak' is believed to have been coined by Vidyarana in the 15th century. He was one of the Prime Ministers in the Vijayanagar Kingdom and in addition to being an excellent administrator, he was also a musicologist. it extended from (present names) Andhra Pradesh to Tamil Nadu and Karnataka States. It denotes South Indian Music, as distinct from North Indian or Hindustani music. Scholars like professor P. Sambamurti and Shri R. Rangaramanuja Ayyangar and many other scholars have written treatises on the assumption that Karnatak music is the authentic music of India and have quoted and referred to the same Sanskrit texts.

Sanskrit texts like 'Naradiya Siksa; Natya Sastra, 'Dattilam', Sangita Makranda', 'Sangita Ratnakara', Raga Tarangini', 'Sangita Raja', 'Svaramelakalanidhi', 'Sangita Raja', 'Raja Vibodha', Sangita Parijata' and many other treatises are referred to by Hindustani and Karnatak or Carnatic music scholars. The fact that both find the material and the base for their respective streams of music is iteself proof that there is a broad similarity between the two. The manner of interpretation and shift of emphasis from structural bondage to free improvisation in Hindustani music is one of the main differences between the two; these brought in their wake a host of ancilary changes in alapana and tale, which ultimately resulted in two almost separate systems of music.

Karnataka music has also been influenced greatly by the old Dravidian (Tamil) music. Works like 'Silappadikaram', 'Pattupattu', 'Kalladam', 'Kamikagamam', 'Tolkappiyam' and 'Tirumarikanda Puranam' have reference to and description of the gramas (the two tone-system), of Ragas, musical forms, instruments and the concerts prevalent there in Hindustani music, the Dhruvapada, of offshoot of the Salagasuda Prabandha, began fading gradually from the 18th century onwards. The Khyal, incorporating almost all essential aesthetic qualities of the Dhruvapada, also added a few attractive graces of the Thumri. Also, the relegation of the rhythmic part in Khyal gayaki where almost all the essential aesthetic qualities of Dhruvapada, exist.

The introduction of Tabla is a very important phase in the evolution of Hindustani music. It opened up for the first time the immense possibilities of free improvisation to the accompaniment of rhythm.

In Karnataka music, on the other hand, a study of the structure of its present forms (Kriti, Kirtanam, Varnam, Padam, Javali) makes if fairly clear that this music is maintaining the ancient traditions of the Prabhandas more closely and rigidly than Hindustani music. Just as in Prabhandha Gana strict adherence to the structure of the composition is compulsory, so also in Karnataka or Carnatic music though to a lesser degree, adherence to the forms of the compositions even in improvisation in the naraval, or layakari bolupaj according to Hindustani music, while rendering Krits etc; is still required.

The evolution of Karnatak music from the time of Pandit Venkatamakhim, who introduced the seventy-two melas (present scales) for the classification of Ragas, has followed a different path from that of North Indian music. Ragas in the South are mostly named in Sanskrit, whereas in the north, the names are derivatives of the dialects of the regions without much intrinsic significance; many of them have no specific reference like Raga Puria, Marwa, Sohani, or Paraj. Bilawal from Velavali, Bagesri from Vageswari, Malkauns from Malava-Kaisiki etc. Other names are indicative of the regions in which the Ragas originated, such as Desi, Jaunpuri, Malavi, Gujrat, Gauda Malhar, and Bangal Bhairav.

It is a matter of wonder that these two styles of music, even though they have the same svaras, appear so different to the ear. There are several Ragas in both styles which have indentical svaras but which sound very different. Some pairs of similar Ragas, known to most music lovers all over India, are : Malkauns-Hindolam, Bhupali-Mohanam; Suddha Bhairav-Tod, Todi-Subhapantuvarali; Purya Dhanasari-Pantuvarali Yaman-Kalyani; Ahir Bhirav-Chakravakam; Ananda Bhairav-Suryakantam; Hindol-Sunadavinodini; Bhimplasi-Abheri; Nat Bhairav-Sarasangi; and Puryakalyani-Burikalyani.

Who do the same svaras sound different ? where is the essential divergence? A study of the two styles indicates the basic difference is in the articulation of the *gamakas* (graces). In Karnatak music, the oscillations of notes are much faster than Hindustani music; the amplitude of the oscillations on the other hand, is generally much less; and sometimes, strangely, the range of oscillation of the articulation note does not touch the concerned note itself. For example, in Karnatak Raga Todi, the Sadharana Gandhara (Komal Gandhara) oscillates from Rishabha to Madhyama. When the Gandhara is actually sung, the andolita Gamaka (Undulation) of this svara begins from Rishabha, touches Madhyama, and comes back. The Gamakas of South Indian Music, with their short amplitude and fast oscillations, are of clear reflection of a steady and clean image, just as the imagein a mirror. Gamakas Play an important role on the mood and emotional cantent of the svara both in Karnataka and Hindustani music. It plays an over all development in the improvisation, styles of music. (Condensed)

GEETHA RAVIKUMAR

MUSIC : SADHANA AND MUKTHI

Music of 'Nada Vidya' as it is known in India, is supposed to be of Divine Origin. The *Saptaswaras* are said to be found in nature itself and all *ragas* are formed by the fusion of these *swaras* - *Sa, Ri,Ga, Ma, Pa, Da, Ni.*

Each raga in Indian classical music has a *bhava* or state of mind to convey. Ragas like *Anandabhairavi, Ritigoula, Hindolam* and other such *Janya Ragas* or *Natabhairavi* convey us the state of *Ananda*, Ragas like *Sahana, Nadanamakriya, Pun-nagavavali Bhairavi, Mukhari,* etc. infuse *Karuna Rasa; Ragas* like *Madhyamavati* convey a *Samarasabhava* or *Shanthi Rasa*, which is why *kutcheris, Hari-kathas* and even *Bhajana Ghoshtis* end their sessions with *Madhyamavati raga.*

The Saptaswaras are said to have diffused from pranava Swara, or Omkara Nada, the seat of which is the Muladhara chakra at the end of the spinal cord. Nada, as it originates from Maladhara, is in the Anahata State (unvulnerable to physical ears). The *Sukshmanada* as it proceeds upwards goes through *Nabhi*, were it becomes *Aahata* (Vulnerable to physical ears). Then it proceeds towards *Hridya* (Chest Cavity) and then reaches *Kandha* or throat and again proceeds upwards and is brought our through the *Rasana* (Tongue) to the Atmosphere (*Antareeksha*).

The three *Sthayis* in music, the lower *Mandra Sthayi*, the middle *Madhya Sthayi* and the upper *Tara Sthayi*, are said to spring from the *Nabhi, Haridya* and *Shiras* respectively.

The *Saptha Swaras* are also said to be invoked from the five Faces of Lord Shiva. It is certain that music is not a commerical art, but a divine achievement.

Great *Nadapasakas* of the past are said to have performed miraculous feast with music. Tyagaraja is said to have brought a dead man back to life by singing "Shreerama Padhama" in raga *Amrithavahini*. However, this is dismissed by "Yukthi vadis" who ask why Tyagaraja did not bring all the dead around him back to life. The argument is specious, Banishing death was not the aim. It was to revive a life that came to an untimely end.

Tyagaraja merely reminded the Lord of His duty towards his bhaktha and a dead Man regained his life, by the flow of the undying mercy of Lord Rama.

Nadajyothi Muttuswami Deekshitar is said to have brought rains to a drought-affected area by singing "Anandamrithakarshini" in the raga. Amrithavarshini. Similarly, when Deekshitar visited Sholingur, and due to certain unavoidable circumstances, reached the temple at an hour when the temple was closed. The priest refused to open the temple, Deekshitar composed "Akshaya Linga Vibho" in raga Sankara-bharanam in an ecstasy, and soon the temple gates authomatically opened. Similarly, the gates of the Shree Venkateshwara Sannidhanam are believed to have opened themselves when Tyagaraja sang "Teradhi Agarda" in raga Gowlipanthu at Tirupati.

Music is also said to have cured diseases in the past especially when the ailment was incurable through normal methods. Naryanateertha was cured of his stomach ailment, by compasing "Krishna Leela Tarangini". Shudhamaddalam Thampiappan is said to have been cured of a dreaded stomach disease, by singing the Navagraha Krithis of his Guru, Muttuswami Deekshitar, at the famous Vaitheeshwaran Kovil.

Music soothes the human nervous system and gives inner peace. Although, very rarely, some people become fully submerged in this state of inner peace, and lose themselves completely. This state is called "Rasasamadhi".

The main hindrance to achievement of Bliss through music is the desire for monetary gains, or fame and popularity, which dominate most musicians, music students and teachers. This is but natural and not wholly condemnable. At the level of talent, music, like other skills, must get its price and rewards.

Then comes the role of *Sadhana*. *Sadhana* in a spiritual sense, means slow and gradual transformation of the individual soul (*Jeeva*) into a State of Nothingness, but Fullness, where the mischiefs and pranks of the Mind and Money are brought to a stand-still and no thought waves are produced. The mind becomes very thin and is practically eliminated and what exists is the State of *Satchit-ananda*. When this state becomes permanent and never ending, and the Body fades away and drops, then the man has achieved the Final Stage of *Moksha*, from where there is no question of coming back again. The *Jnana, Karma* and *Bhakthi Margas* are three methods by which the *Sadhaka* reaches this stage.

In music, *Sadhana* is an attempt to achieve this Stage of Bliss through deep involvement. The correct place, chosen for *Sangeetha Sadhana* is a natural surrounding, say a river bed or seashore, seated in a natural surrounding, the *Sadhaka* having the happiness of seeing the country of Nature is already equipped with the Armour of Bliss, with which he can protect himself from distracting thoughts. A temple can also be a place for performing *Sadhana*. The sight of the *Ishta Devata* brings all thoughts in one direction. *Sadhana* can be done in one's residence also, preferably in the *puja* room. Anyway, there are no hard and fast rule about. The palace and atmosphere; it can be where the individual can get the best type of concentration.

Sangeetha pithamaha Purandaradasa set up and choreographed the primary lessons of Carnatic Music, namely *Sarali Varisai, Janda Varisai, Melsthayi Varisai, Dattu Varisai,* and *Saptha Tala Alankaras.* He chose the *Sampoorna Mela Kartha Raga, Mayamalavagoula* for this. *Mayamalavgowala* and it's *Janya Ragas* like *Bowli, Bhupalam, Gawla, Saveri, Malahari,* etc. are specially effective if sung in the early morning hours. As these ragas are sung at sunrise, our Inner Sun (Athma Chaitanya) is also arisen and awakened.

The end of the Sadhana or the Lakshya is Mukthi itself. The constant Sadhana, as it is combined with Bhakthi, reaches a point when Anahata Pranava Nanda deeply engraved within the infrastructure of our subtle body, is vulnerable to our ears. Then comes the Total Identification of oneself with the Pranava Nada (the formless aspect of the Ishta Devata). When the Pranava Nanda, Ishta Devata and the Sadhaka become one, that is the Ultimate end or Mukthi. Saint Tyagaraja's Jeevan Samadhi at Tiruvaiyaru was of this type.

May the Gurujanas of yore, and the Trimurthis of Sangeetha bless us to develop Genuine and self-Lacking interest in Nada Vidya.

K. SASIKALA

MUSIC COMPOSERS

Puranadara Dasa Father of Carnatic Music, (A.D. 1480-1566) was the greatest of the Haridasas, who like the revered saints of Pandharpur, Jnandev, Namved, Sakhubai and Gorakumbhar, played a very important part in spreading Bhakti movement. Purandaradasa was born in Purandaragad in Poona District to a Madhava Brahmin, Varadappa - a diamond merchand by profession. Purandaradasa was regarded as an Avtar of Narada. He studies and mastered Indian music and to suit the conditions of his time, he systematised practical music by working many Lakshana Granthas, Geethas and Suladis - all about 50,000 pieces to enable the student of music to acquire the art with ease. Wide knowledge, rich experience and unbounded love for humanity are clearly noticeable in his songs.

Purandaradasa can rightly be described as the "Father of Carnatic Music" for it was he who laid the solid foundation of Carnatic music on which the musical Trinity later built so fine a structure. Purandaradasa enriched both Kannada literature and Carnatic music by his compositions which appeal to pandits and peasants alike. He rescued Carnatic music from the chaos and corruption of alien influences. No tribute to the genius of Purandandaradasa could adequately express our indebtedness to him for those masterly creations in his hands became the noblest embodiments of Bhava, Raga, and Tala. He composed many Gitas, Tayas, Prabhandas and ugabogas. The Alap Paddhathi is well pictured in his Kirtanas in the same raga. Few musicologist have made the same contribution to the pedagogy of music as Purandaradasa. The present system of Carnatic music as followed in the South by beginners is scrupulous fidelity is the one formulated by him.

The gradation of Swara, Alankara and Gitas in Raga Mayamalagowla and Mallahari from the bedrock of the teaching methods of Carnatic music. His music is as pure as his soul and his glory as a composer will shine for ever. He is the Marga Darsi to the Music Trinity.

2) *Syama Sastri* (Alias Venkatatasubrahmanya) (1763-1827) Syama Sastri made his life a dynamic offering to the Universal Mahasakti. Among the falaxy of musical celebrities, Syma Sastri, originally a Veda Desattu Vadamal Brahmin of Bodayana Sutra form Kurnool District, was born in Tiruvarur to Vishavanathayya in the year 1763. He was given sound education in Sanskrit and Telugu. But he was destined to be great in the field of music. Syma Sastri was a Devi Upasaka and he had the Darshan of Devi Kamakshi who inspired the rich musical compositions that came out of his heart. He initiated Tyagaraja and Muthuswami Dikshitar into the cult of Parasakti. He took upadesa from Sangita Saamy, an Andhra Sanyasi from Banaras, who taught him the higher aspects of music, the intricacies of Raga, Tala and presented him with some rare musical works. Further Syam Sastri gained much knowledge by his contact with Panehimiriam Adeppayya and Pallavi Gopalayya. He was essentially a rasika, for he maintained amicable terms with his contemporaries. He led the normal life of Grihastha.

As he was in affluent circumstances, he never made a living out of his musical profession. He was a mahapurusha who used to sign songs on Friday - which are noted for their sweetness, originality, richness of conception and abundance of feeling. Many of his Kirtanas brought on him the warmest admiration of music scholars and uncompromising critics of his time. He used to pay occasional visits to Thyagayya. He composed a Navaratna Malika in praise of Madurai Meenakshi. The famous kriti "Saroja Dhalanetree" in Ragam Sankarabharanam is one of nine gems. His contribution of music is of the highest order. He was a scholarly composer in every sense of the term. He was a creative artist to a high degree whose pieces exhibit an individual style. His Sahitya is extremely simple and elegant. In point of Sahitya, he stands next to Kshetrayya. Indeed his compositions are marcels of Swara-Varna Samyogya.

3) Among the illustrious masters of the art who have made their lasting contribution to the development and perfection to the development and perfection of music is Muthuswami Dikshitar (1775 - 1835). This great and high - souled person, who has left the indelibe impress of his personality on Indian culture and art is one of the Trinity of Carnatic music. He came in the line of distinguished musicians amongst whom were the immortal Venkatamakhin and Govinda Dikshitar. Belonging to Tiruvarur, (birth place) of Thyagayya and Syama Sastri, Muthuswami had a natural aptitude for Sanskrit and music in which he attained mastery. His compositions bear the marks of Mantrasakthi, Srividya, Vedanta etc. He was initiated into the cult of Devi Upasana by his Guru Chidmbarasami. He accompanied him to Banaras (Varanasi) for further studies.

During his long stay of seven years, he learnt the subtleties of Hindustani music which he used later in his compositions with great effect and enriched Carnatic music. Traces of this are visible in his Kirtans in Yamankalayan and Brindavani Saranga. On his return he went to Tiruttani and received the blessings of Lord Subrahmanya. It is said that the Lord himself became his preceptor and each of his songs bears the signature 'Guruguha'.

His first song was 'Manasa Guruguha', in Anandabhairavi raga. Then 20 songs followed in quick succession. From Tiruttani he went to Kanchi and learnt the Upanishads from Upanishad Brahman, a saintly personality. Inspired by Goddess Kamakshi, Dikshitar compossed two songs in Raga Manohari and Hindol on her. He also composed *Kirtans* on *Panchabhuta Devas* and *Navagrahas*. The Goddess Kamalamba at Tiruvarur was his favourite deity and he composed the *Navavarna Kirtans* on Her. His other compositions were on Nilotpalamba, Ganesh, Achleswara, Anandeswar, and Siddheswara, Rajagopal of Mannargudi, Ranganyki and Meenkshi. The last six years of Dikshitar's life was spent happily at Ettayapuram under the patronage of the local ruler. Like a true scholar. Dikshitar scorned delights and lived laborious days. By arduous training, and discipleship he added to his remarkable gifts, profundity of learning, wide culture and intense spirituality.

The slow, measured cadences of his compositions exhibiting in all their variety, fulness and beauty, the Ragas chosen for them, the perfect harmony of the Bhava, *Raga* and *Tala*, the symbolic attunement of the words to the Swarasthanas, the lilt of the verses and the resonance of particular letter - sounds when noted with the nuances of the *Raga* and the harmonious combination of the *Raga* with the words subtly indicative of the emotions or *rasas* underlying them make his compositions masterpieces. His style is grand and majestic and is the offspring of intellectual loftiness. His kirtans are replace with *Ragabhava* and are in *Vilambitkala*. The rare feature of his kriti is that the Dhatu is rarely repeated. He was a vainika and vocalist too.

Among his disciples are Veenai Venkataramana, T. Subramanya, Ponnayya, Chinnayya and Tiruvarur Kamalam.

4) Thyagaraja (1767 - 1847) is the greatest name in the history of South Indian music. Barring a few of his compositions, the majority of his *kritis* are not born of conscious effort; they just flowed our of his intense devotion to Sri Rama. He was the father of Carnatic music and wrote about 700 songs and two music plays of unequalled beauty.

Although Purandaradasa, Narayana Tirtha and others had already set up conventions and standards, Thyagaraja outshone them. He was the architect of the *kriti* from and, for the first time, introduced 'Sangatis' to develop the ragas in their logical sequence. His "Pancharatana *Kriti*" stand as monuments to his greatness as a composer. The *Pancharatna Kritis* were all composed in *Ghana Ragas*. He consciously chose Nata raga for the first among them, and more consciously chose to compose it in Sanskrit, to despel the criticism against him as a Vaggeyakara. Out of 700 of his compositions available to us there are 51 in Sanskrit. The composition 'Jagadaananada Kaaraka' with high sounding phrases are fascinating compounds consists of 108 adjectives for Sri Rama. It is in this unique composition we find his eminence as a scholar both in Sanskrit and in music, his deep devotion to Sri Rama and his indisputable ability as the greatest of the Vaggeyakaras of Carnatic Music.

The introduction of "Sangatis" as an integral part of kriti is the most outstanding feature of his music. The accent on sangatis is always to emphasise the latent meanings in the Sahitya or bring out the *ragabhava*. We can classify his 'Sangatis' as those which embelish the *Sahitya* and those which emphasise the *ragabhava*. The

delicate and finder shades of meanings implied in the Sahitya are powerfully portrayed by the *sangatis* employed. Examples for such Sahitya Bhava sangatis can be seen from many of his compositions, e.g. "Kaala Harana Melara Hare" in Raga Suddha Saveri and "Maarubalka Kurnnavemira maa mano ramana" in Raga Sriranjani.

5) Koteeswara Ayyar (1869 - 1938) was the grandson of the great Tamil composer, Kavi Kunjara Bharati. He was born in 1869, in Nandalur, Madurai District. He was a good singer, an erudite scholar in Tamil and a devotee of Muruga. He was the first composer of Kirtanas in all the 72 *Mela Ragas*. Through these compositions, he has established the musical possibilities of the so-called *apurva melas*, which some thought would remain only as scales and never rise to the stature of ragas. In each of these 72 pieces, there is the *raga mudra, chitta svara* and the composer's signature, *Kav ikunjaradasa*. These compositions are all in Tamil and have been printed in the work : "Kanda Ganamudam" Volumes 1 & 2. The first volume contains the *suddha madhyama Mela Kirtanas* and the second volume, the *Prati madhyama mela kirtanas*. He has also composed other *Kirtanas* in *rakti ragas*. His songs, 'Ini namakkoru' in Raga Bilahari is in praise of the great composer, Thyagaraja, is widely sung. He has composed *Varnas* in *Raga Saveri, Danyasi and Bilahari*.

6) *Muthiah Bhagavatar* (1871 - 1945), son of Lingamayyar, was renowned as a performer of Kalakshepamand as a musicologist. He was a good singer and performer on the Gottyvadyam and Mridangam. His *Harikathas* were exceedingly interesting and held large audiences spellbound. He has composed *Varnas, Kritis, Kirtanas* and *Ragamalikas*. His *Sahityas* are in Telugu, Sanskrit and Tamil. He has composed in rare ragas and in ragas in which his predecessors had not composed. His 108 Kirtanas in praise of Sri Chamundeswari are a set of scholarly compositions.

His compositions bear the signature Harikesapura or Harikesa. He hailed from Harikeswavanallur and appropriately enough he adopted the Svagramamudra. Some of his compositions have been published in notation. He was a Samasthana Vidwan in Mysore and Travancore. The Travancore University honoured him by conferring upon him the Honorary degree of D. Litt. He was the Master of the art of kalakshepa. His songs and Varnamettus are of perennial interest. He was a great Vaggeyakara and Lakshya-Lakshana Vidwan.

He was the only man who constantly delved into the mysteries of the Lakshana aspect of music and who had the capacity to demonstrate on the same.

7) *Papanasam Sivan* (1890) was born in Polagam in Tanjore District. He spent his youth in Tiruvananthapuram and there came under the influence of the saintly composer Nilakanta sivan. He drew his inspiration from Nilakanta Sivan's Tamil songs. Papanasam Sivan has composed in Tamil and Sanskrit. His compositions breathe the fragrance of bhakti and his renderings have a captivating effect. He adopted the signature "Ramadasa" (this original name being Ramaswamy Ayyar). His compositions have been published with notation in the

'Kirtana Mala - I'. Some of his songs clothed in attractive tunes are widely sungs.

8) *Amir Khusrau* (1234) created new Ragas such as *Sajagiri, Jhila, Sarpardha* etc. He had composed new songs in different *Ragas* which emerged into *Khyal* in the later years. Many writers say the '*Khyal*' was created or rather *Khyal* singing was developed by Amir Khusrau. He had innovated many new instruments, bringing many charges in playing the new instrument, such as Been sitar. He had combined the Persian melody with Indian Raga, and innovated new ragas, such as Sarparda, Sajagiri and Jhila. (9) & (10) *Sadarang and Adarang* have composed many khyals. The *Khyals* composed by Sadarang bring our *Shringara Rasa*. He had composed many khyals to please the Badshah Mohammad Shah. He was a famous Beenkar and had composed innumerable *Khyals* in different Ragas, which the Hindustani musicians sing today.

11) *Mia-Tansen* (1532 - 1595) was very much interested in music since his childhood and was tutored by Swami Haridas who effectionately him as "Tanna". He was the court musician of Emperor Akbar, the Great. Initially, he was a Dhruvapad Gayaka and composed many Dhruvapadas in different Ragas. He invented Ragas like Thodi, Darbari, Malhar, Sarang, which are called 'Mia Ki Thodi', 'Mia ki Malhar', 'Mia Ki Saranga'. He was a great Beenkar.
(Condensed)

GEETHA RAVIKUMAR

MUSICAL INSTRUMENTS

The importance of instruments in the music and musicology of a country cannot be over-emphasised. It is almost a dictum that there could have been no theory of music without musical instruments; for, it was only a musical instrument that lent itself to measurement and there were no means of measuring the voice directly. Only during the last century have we developed sound measuring instruments which can give us adequate information about musical sounds.

Again, due to lack of sound-recording apparatus, ancient vocal music has not been preserved for us in an audible form. But many ancient instruments are still available among the tribes and general fold of the country. Sculptures and paintings of instruments bear testimony to prevalence of ancient music. These enable us to visualise, as nothing else can, the musical history of our society.

Musical instruments also reveal ancient inter-cultural contacts. For example, the wall paintings of Quizil, Yotkan & Than Huang of Central Asia, the sculptures of Borobudur, Prambanam, Angkor Vat - all these bear testimony to close cultural relations between India and her neighbours.

With the intention of getting the learned and the lay interested in the richness of our musical heritage, the Sangeet Natak Akademi, New Delhi organised an Exhibition of Musical Instruments in Rabindra Bhavan,

from 19 to 23 August, 1962. The Exhibition was inaugurated by Sri Nityanand Kanungo, Union Minister for Industries. The Exhibition itself consisted of two sections - (1) Photographs and Drawings of Instruments and (2) Actual Instruments.

The Photographs and drawings were mainly the collection of Sri. Krishnaswamy of All India Radio, Vijayawada. He has been working for nearly a decade in this field and his collection comprises nearly 300 photographs and drawings. About 30 photographs of musical sculptures obtained from the Archaeological Survey of India were also exhibited.

These photographs bring home to us the wealth and beauty of our instruments and present a marvellous panorama from the harps of 2nd Century B.C. to the modern sitar and Vina. The strange ravana hatto takes us back to the primitive beginnings of the violin.

The actual instruments, about a hundred, presented an outstanding variety, representing stringed, wind and percussion instruments.

Musical instruments are generally classified under 4 heads: tat or chordophones, sushira aerophones, avanddha or membranophones and ghana or autophones.

TAT (Strings) : This famiy comprises all the stringed instruments we know of Stringed instruments are again of two broad groups - the harps and the finger-board instruments.

The general opinion of scholars is that stringed instruments have their origin in the hunter's bow. It is interesting to note that almost all harps and lyres have the shapes of a bow.

Harps are more ancient than the finger-board instruments. They have one string for each note to be played in the raga. Almost all the ancient vinas and the South Indian instruments yazh are of this group. There used to be vinas with even hundered strings - the satatantri Vina. The only survivor of these is the santur of Kashmir.

Dur to the changing styles of our music, these vinas (harps) have gone out of vogue and yielded place to the finger-board instruments. There letter instruments comprise a few strings stretched on a board and a raga can be played on only one string. There are no separate strings for each note, as in the harps.

Though such vinas existed from quite ancient times, they dominate the Indian musical world after about the 15th Century A.D. All our modern stringed instruments are of this group.

Here again, we think of two classes of instruments, the plucked and the bowed. To the former belong saraswati vina, rudra vina, Sitar, gottuvadyam, sarod etc. the strings are usually plucked with a plectrum. To the bowed class belong the sarangi, dilruba and esraj. Also, some of these instruments have frets on the finger-board-vina, Sitar, dilruba, esraj, etc., some do not - sarod, gottuvadyam, sarangi, etc.

The original tribal and folk instruments, which later developed in to modern concert instruments, can still be found in our villages. The ravana hasta vina or ravna hatto, it is said was the progenitor of the modern violin. A long journey, indeed, from the ravana hatto to a Stradivari;

Sushira (Wind instruments) : Some of the most ancient wind instruments are bone whistles. And our modern flutes seem to have been developed from these. It is said that ancient man has he wandered through the forest, listened to the wind blowing through the trees and holes in bamboos; thereby the thought of wind instruments.

Wind instruments are usually classified as (1) Air-reed: all flutes (2) mechanical-reed: clarionet (single reed), Shahnai, nagaswaram (double reed) and (3) lipreed: bugles, conches..

The longer flutes are better suited for low tones and Alap. For faster music shorter flutes are preferable.

As children we have played blowing across a rooled-up leaf held between the thumbs. The leaf acts as a reed. This is the same principle on which reed instruments work. One or two reeds are fixed to conical pipe and the player blows across the reeds.

In India we have only double reed instruments - the Shahnai and the nagaswaram. The European instrument clarionet has one reed.

Lip reed instruments - bugles, horns, conches and turahi do not find any place in our concerts. as it is very difficult indeed to produce sustained notes and graces demanded by our music on these.

Avanddha (Drums): The antiquity of drums goes back to Lord Shiva himself with his damaru. The dundubhi and Nagara echo ancient battle cries. From these and other tribal and folk drums have grown our modern Mridangam, Pakhawaj and tabla.

The speciality of these instruments is the loading of the membrane. A paste of iron powder (among other things) is applied on the membrane to form a permanent load. In the case of Pakhawaj and mridangam a temporary load of flour is applied to the left membrane. These loads mkae the sound more musical and eliminate much of the noisy part.

It was Dr. C.V. Raman, the eminent scientist, who poineered the investigations on the acoustics of these instruments and the peculiar sloping bridges of the Tambura and Vina.

Ghana: This class of instruments are struck with rods to produce sounds. They are not stretched like strings and membranes. Mostly they are rhythmic instruments - like kartal, ghatam, bells, etc.

Not many of this class are used for melodic purposes, except the Jal-Tarang and Kashta-Tarang. The former consists of a set of porcelain cups of varying sizes. Water is poured into these in different amounts for tuning. The cups are struck with wooden hammers.

Kashta tarangs or the xylophone is a set of wooden bars of different sizes fixed to a frame. On striking them various notes are produced.

The Ghatam is an earthern pot. Humble as it looks, it has found a place of pride in South Indian music concerts. One has to hear it to believe the uncommon richness of its sound and rythmic effects.

Memorable as are the separate aspects of the descipline of Indian music, they are always connected with the Indian mainstream. To cite an example, the Shenai (this Hindustani wind instrument has been discussed in our literary works from the thirteenth century onwards and is possibly linked with the zurna of Central and West Asia) is artistically similar to the Nagaswaram or the Nadaswaram (this Carnatic wind instrument has been commented upon in our literary classics since the fourteenth century). To cite another example, the Saraswati Veena (the Carnatic zither which was perfected during the seventeenth century at Thanjavur) and the Rudra Veena (the Hindustani zither which was popular until the latter held of the eighteenth century) belong to the same family. To cite yet another example, the violin (although there are sculptural evidences of violin - like instruments as early as the tenth century AD) was adapted by Baluswami Dikshitar into the system of Carnatic music during the nineteenth century.

Infinite and infinitely melodious are the resources of the wind instruments, the percussion instruments and the stringed instruments in the hands of maestros - the Hindustani Flute (Pannalal Ghosh), the Carnatic Flute (T.R. Mahalingam), the Shenai (Bismillah Khan), the Mridangam (Palghat Mani Ayyar), the Tabla (Aliah Rakha), the Sitar (Ravi Shankar), the Veena (Dhannamal) and the sarod (Ali Akbar Khan).

At this point, it would he interesting to refer to an apocryphal story relating to the thirteenth century Indian poet and musician Amir Khusrau, who is credited with the invention of celebrated Hindustani stringed instrument known as the Sitar. And according to one version, during a trip to South India, Amir Khusrau had broken the Carnatic musical drum Mrindangam into two parts or the Tablas: The Tabla is a Persian word and a general one that includes various types of drums. Here the point is not whether this story is true. or not; more importantly, it reinforces the theme of Unity in Diversity.

The Noble Prize winning American physicist Richard Feynman appears in the frontispiece to his popular work entitled. The Feynman Lectures on Physics as an artist playing a drum with both hands; Here one can make a jump in time to the ancient Indian era, to realize that the Indian contribution lay in widening the scope of the aesthetics of the drums. For if we have two hands, why not utilize two drums to play simultaneously, one with each hand? And this aesthetic reasoning had resulted in the construction of the Mridangam which is a two-faced drum as well as the invention of a pair of Tablas with one face each to play on.

It is well to note that the major youthful interests of the Indian Noble Prize winning physicist Professor C.V. Raman had centred round the physics and aesthetics of the mridangam, Tablas, Veena, Tanpura and the Violin. Not surprisingly, Raman detected musical overtones in the sound of the Mridangam and the Tablas. And Raman made a brilliant discovery in his teens that the heterogenous loading of their membrances can produce harmonics which can enable to maestros to make the Mridangam as well as the Tablas yield the near equivalent to the sound of stringed instrument.

The heritage of India is rich in musical instruments. We could make it richer by making new experiments and encouraging the handicrafts of instrument makers. With the coming of electronic techniques perhaps a new dimension in instrumentation can be opened up.
(Condensed)

B. C. DEVA
A. RANGANATHAN

MUSLIM ART

Beauty is a divine quality. It is an attribute of God. One of the names of God is, therefore, al-jamil (the beautiful) in Islam. But Islam has also been ill at ease with many things beautiful. For example, with painting and sculpture, music and dance. So, arts flourished, but under secular impulses. Religion had very little to do with the creative life of Muslims.

Today, in some countries, there is an effort to Islamise Muslim art, when art is moving away from religion all over the world. More so because Muslim art did not come out of a vacuum. It is composite inheritance - from Greek, Persian, Indian, Central Asian, Chinese and Roman.

The Hindu traced almost everything to a divine origin. This helped the luxuriant growth of his art. But Muslim art, being secular grew intermittently, thwarted often by puritanical forces.

When the Arbas overthrew the Sassanian Dynasty of Persia in the 7th century, they imposed a puritanical Islam on the conquered. Yet by the 10th century, the Caliph's power began to wane and Persian culture reasserted itself. Samarkand and Bukhara followed the Persian example. But they enjoyed this freedom for only a short spell, for during the 13th century, the Mongols under Chenghis Khan destroyed the main centres of Islam. This left Islam without a radiating centre. As a result, the regional genius began to grow. For example, the Turco-Mongol arts gained ascendance. Timur's empire - the first large state stretching from India to Volga, with Central Asia as its heart, Samarkand as its capital - became a major factor in the artistic development of the entire region. Timur was a patron of city planning and architecuture. So the 14th and 15th centures saw a renaissance of Islamic art in Central Asia.

In India, under the Great Mughals (branch of the Timurids) there was a parallel development. Indian Islam created its own distinct culture.

Calligraphy is the most unique creation of Muslims. But it was not without a precedent. The Greeks had illustrated and illumined scroll writings. But the Muslims raised calligraphy into a supreme art, more because it became an act of piety and dedication.

Calligrapy served to satisfy the artistic urges of Muslims. It was used extensively as a decorative art in architecture, carpets, textiles etc. Numerous variations of the Arabic script were created in the process. No wonder the beauty of the female body was compared to the beauty of letters; But writing also took on a sacred character. (There is no parallel to this anywhere in the world). In calligraphy, art and religion fused. In fact, tablets with the name of the Prophet became objects of worship.

Architecture comes second to calligraphy. It rose to great heights. With the use of ceramic tiles as a wall covering from the 12th century, it had no parallel anywhere in the world. By the 14th century, this art is glazing reached perfection. And the Mughals promptly transferred this art to India. But in India Muslim architecture mingled with the local traditions to produce a world's marvel the Taj Mahal.

Islam is not hostile to music and poetry. The Quran is both poetry and music. And the call to the prayer is almost always "sung". And so too the Muslim funeral oration.

However, Islam had reservations with regard to music. But this was more an Arab tradition, not of Persia, where music enjoyed a high status among the people, and the Sufis raised it to mystical heights. They said that music is the easiest way to God.

Jalal al-Din Rumi, the greatest Sufi mystic and poet, had a powerful influence on Islam. His Mathnavi is generally sung.

There was little Arab influence in India. The influence was Persian and Central Asian. The Mughals brought both, but more of the Central Asian elements (i.e. the traditions of Samarkand and Bukhara). However, the Sultanates, which preceded the Mughals, were not puritanical. Firishta, a Persian solider, who took to writing, has said that princes of Dlave Dynasty, founded in 1206 AD, patronised both musicians and dancing girls. Srivara, the great historian of Kashmir, has said that Sultan Zain-ul-Abidin (the most tolerant of Kashmir's Muslim Kings) was a great parton of arts, and he had musicians and dancing girls at his court.

Abul Hasan of the Shahi Dynasty was so pleased with the performance of a band of Brahmin dancers and actors of the village of Kuchipudi that he made a land grand of the whole village to the troupe in 1675, (Kuchipudi has since become a famous Bharatnatyam dance form).

The Great Mughals (1526-1856) introduced the grand life styles of Samarkand and Bukhara into India. They loved luxury and pleasure, art and literature. Their principal diversion was to witness dancing.

However, it was only during the reign of Akbar, Jahangir and Shah Jehan that arts flourished. While Akbar was a keen patron of writers and artists (the great singer Tansen flourished in his court), Shah Jahan was a great builder and calligraphist. Abul Fazal, friend of Akbar, writes in his *Ain-i-Akbari* (Account of Akbar's life and rule) that there were eight forms of dances during his time. And also of the night life of nobles. Salim (Jahangir), the eldest son of Akbar, fell madly in love with Anarkali, a dancer in Akbar's court. (She paid with her life for this). Jahangir was a perfect connoisseur of the arts, especially of painting, and a great patron of artists. A Dutchman of the Mughal court writes that many of these dancing girls came from Persia, but were not as good as the Indian girls. Shah Jahan loved music. But his supreme love was for architecture. The Taj Mahal remains his immortal work.

With Aurangzeb, there was a throwback to fundamentalism. He had little interest in art, he disallowed all festivals, Hindu or Muslim, banned music, painting and other arts. He compelled the dancing girls either to marry or leave his realm. But interestingly, he allowed his queens and daughters to enjoy both music and dancing. As for himself, he was for a time infatuated with a dancing girl Zinabadi. But his nobles had other thoughts. His own uncle, Shaista Khan, the commander of the army, used to take with him four hundred dancing girls when he went on military expeditions.

The Muslim kings and emperors patronised the Kathak form of dance, introducing many changes, particulary the dance dress, form of salute, delicacy of manners, etc. It thus become a secular art form.

The Muslims brought the Persian art of book illustration and illumination into India. But in painting pictures, they combined the Indian and Persian elements.

Later, they took to the more vigorous style of Samarkand, which gave India many of the action paintings - of huntings and battles. India must be grateful to many of the Samarkand artists who took up residence in Delhi and were responsible for the hundreds of exquisite portraitures. This was new to India, but used to flourish in Samarkand under Chinese influence. Indian paintings were largely religious and Hindu. About this Abul Fazl had said that it.

"Surpassed our conception of things".

We will conclude with a quotation from Ananda Commaraswami : "For the Mughal countries, life was a pageant, for the Rajput and the Brahmin, life was an eternal sacrament". We have of course come a long way from that.

M. S. N. MENON

MUTTUSWAMI DIKSHITAR

Muttusvami Dikshitar, the youngest of the Karnatak Music Trimurtis, was born on March 20, 1775 at Tiruvarur (Tamil Nadu). He lived for 60 years and merged with the cosmic spirit on the Dipavali day in the year 1835, the day predicted by him.

Though he was an *advatin* (a believer in the Supreme Being without attributes), he accepted and practised *sgunopasana* (worship of the deities), and composed *kritis* on almost all the gods and godesses of the Hindu pantheon and specifically on the presiding deities of many temples of South India.

Dikshitar was also a *Srividya Upaska* (worshipper of Mother Goddess according to *Tantra Sastra*), having received *upadesa* from Chidananda Yogi with whom he stayed in Varanasi for five years. Among his 480 odd compositions are several *samudaya kritis*, the most important of which being the *Navarana Kritis*. The *kritis* are in Sanskrit.

While the majestic and sublime beauty of the music of these *kritis* are the delight of the connoisseurs his dexterity in profundity of thought, fecundity of imagination and his erudition in *Mantra* and *Tantra* Sastras and the characteristic style of presenting them, having received reverential admiration from savants.

MYSORE DASARA

On Vijaydashami, the final day of the Dasara festival, there is a tourist bonanza with its elaborate Dasara procession and sparkling torch light parade. On the afternoon of Vijayadshami everyone in Mysore heads for the forecourt of the city palace while the less fortunate line the streets waiting for the traditional procession to begin. In wounds its way from the top of Chamundi Hill where Chamundeshwari, the presiding diety of the city, resides. A replica of the Goddess is taken on an elephant driven chariot in the form of a procession through the bazars finally to the forcourt of the city Palace.

Chamundeshwari, atop a brilliantly caprisound elephant makes her way to the dias where the chief guest of the occasion showers her with the rose petals. The elephant carrying the goddess and those accompanying her are bedecked with gold sequine and *zari*. As they approach the dias of the Chief Guest they raise their trunks in salute. In days gone by the elephant belonged to the royal Wodeyar stable and the Wodeyar of the day would greet the diety in the forecourt. Chamundeshwari then leads the procession through a town packed with tumulous crowds stopping occasionally to receive the homage of devotees. The deity is followed by a long group of musicians. The torch light parade arranged for the Dasara evening has a certain sophistication and finesse. The Chief Guest normally drives by in an open jeep, accompanied by the smartly uniformed Jawans of his escort on their prancing horses. As the evening sky darkens and the flood lights come on palace jawans give a fascinating display of their Prowess including jumping their horses through rings of fire.

The grand finale is the torch light drill, again by police jawans. Then the dark sky is again lit up with multi-coloured showers of lights from the fire works which mark the end of the programme. The city palace aglow and shimmering with a million tiny lights also add to the beauty and splendour of the occasion.
(Abridged)

SHUSHMITA DUTT

MYSTIC MURALS AND MINIATURES

Like her architecture and sculputre, Orissa has her own rich tradition of painting. The prehistoric rock shelters of Western Orissa prove paintings are more ancient as compared to the seculptural and architectural art.

The Orissa school of painting has three different streams and each has distinct quality. The tribal art, with all its contrasting and lively colours, has uniqueness attached to it. Plain strokes of the folk art, with red and white lines painted all over the wall of the hamlets, is a sure attraction. And the classical paintings has a class of its own which has retained its original flavour.

The line is the most important feature of the Orissan Painting. The merit of the painting is judged from the lines. Here they are bold, direct and drawn in black colour. Stylistically these paintings are linked with the pre-historic rock shelter painting, which provides and backdrop for a style which has evolved in later years.

The huge rock paintings on the caves in the dense forest of Sundergarh, Sambalpur and Kalahandi districts, speaks highly of the talents of the then artists. The colours used were haematite or oxides of iron, copper or lime. This tradition is sustained today in the form of mural painting done by tribals. The Saura Paintings still retain the freshness and vigour of rock paintings. The form and style of paintings, specially of animals and geographic patterns are visible in the Chita, Murja and Jhoti art. Mostly done by the village women, the themes of the paintings are birth, death, marriage and local rituals.

Jhoti, Chita and Murja, generally drawn on the walls or on the floor, aims at establishing a relationship between the mystical. throughout the year, village women perform several rituals to pray for fulfilment of their desires and for each occasion, a special motif is drawn and coloured accordingly. Murja is generally used to draw mandals and kothis during rituals. During the month of Kartika, Murja drawings are made near the "Tulasi Chauhara" to pay homage to the gods and goddesses. Jhoti is drawn with paste of soaked rice called pithau. The fore finger of the right hand is used as brush. At times the pithau is sprinkled on the walls resembling the paddy plant. The chitas are drawn on grain bins. It is believed that Chita on the person is a protective shield from the tortures of Yama. Tattooing is called Kuteri Chita. For women, it is a symbol of chastity.

The famous Saura paintings by the Langia Sauras, who mostly reside in Ganjam and Koraput districts, have still preserved the antiquity of painting in their pictorial tradition, their central theme is house. The painting is regarded as a little temple within the house. The spirit of the dead sits in it as a fly. The artists use the walls of the living rooms as canvas after they are freshly washed with red clay. They follow their instinct and inspiration while drawing these motifs. Orissa is the only place where a tourist can see a post-Gupta painting. In Sitavinji in Keonjhar district there are paintings on the ceilings of a huge boulder called Ravanachhaya. Most of the painting in the temples and *maths* in Orissa belong to the 19th century, like the murals of Emara *matha*, Bada Odia *math* and Raghunatha temple is Puri.

It is interesting to note that in Orissa, when temples are no longer built, making paintings have gained momentum. Unlike other parts of India where a sequential order can be evolved in the history of painting, from classical murals to miniatures, in Orissa all the branches of paintings had evolved side by side. Whether made with powdered rive, powdered leaves, shells, flowers petals, or mud, paintings have been a part of the Orissan tradition for a very long time.

SUNEETA MOHANTY

"N"

NAGARI

The 'city' or cultivated script; also called Devanagari the script of the city of the gods or the divine script; according to legent (or myth) Sanskrit letters are the eternal outlines of the sounds they represent. As the script was once also called Nagalipi (snake writing) it is supposed by some that it originated with the Nagas, an early Mongolian people of north-western India. Its earliest from was the Brahmi. Devanagari was probably not evolved till 1,500 years after the Vedas; when it was used for writing early classical Sanskrit and later its characters were used for the Indo-Aryan languages, in some of which the forms of the charcters have changed considerably. Its present form was probably perfected about the 2nd or 3rd century A.D. but the basic forms are thought to be derived from an earlier type of writing called Sriharsha, used in certain parts of north India. As evidenced by some stone inscriptions, the earliest examples of primitive Devanagari script are of A.D. 100, an improvement appearing in those of the 2nd century and that of 754. The earliest manuscript goes back to the 11th century. It was standarised in tl.e 7th and 8th centuries and kept on receiving modifications till about the 18th century.

P. N. CHOPRA

NAGARJUNA : (A.D. 100 - 200)

Buddhist philosopher born in a Brahmana family (in Andhra Pradesh); reputed author of *Rasaratnakara*, a treatise on alchemy, *Madhyamikasastra, Dwadasa Sastra* and *Sata Sastra*; travelled in India to disseminate his philosophy that mind could never grasp reality since mind and sense objects where unreal; all that exists was *sunyata* (void) or *nirvana*; everything is an illusive reality which cannot be conceived or explained; men is not capable of solving ultimate problems. Was a gifted metaphysician and dialectician. Became a Buddhist and founded the *Mahayana* (Madhyamika or middle path) system of Buddhism and is given a very high place by some Buddhist sects. The influsion of Brahamanical ideas into Budhism was also perhaps initiated by him.

DR. P. N. CHOPRA

NAGAUR FORT - (THE MURALS OF)

The princely city of Jodhpur, well known for its hilltop, imposing fortress - the Mehrangarh - is surrounded by a fortified wall having several entrances. One of these, known as Nagauri Gate, is named after an ancient town 135 kilometers on the way to Bikaner. Founded in the 4th century AD, Nagaur had been the stronghold of Nagvanshi Rajputs who, for many years, commanded this region of strategic importance in the defence of Rajputana. Nagaur fort, with its impressive battlements stood on the trade route from Delhi to Rajasthan, Gujarat and further south on the West Coast. With the passage of time the Pratihara rulers of Mandore, near Jodhpur, took control of Nagaur. They strengthened and beautified the fort and developed the walled city as an impregnable citadel. However, Nagaur fell to the invading forces of Mahmud Ghori of Ghazni in 1192. In the ensuing battle lasting for centuries between the Muslim Governors and the dispossesssed Rajput rulers, Nagaur changed hands many times till Sher Shah Suri occupied it for a brief spell. In 1556, the fort was taken by Akbar, the great Mughal, and later his grandson - Emperor Shah Jahan bestowed it upon his Rajput follower, Rao Amar Singh Rathore of Marwar. Nagaur and the adjoining territories remain an inheritance of the Maharaja of jodhpur (Marwar) till this day.

In its heyday Nagaur has witnessed many gory battles, but the township flourished and the fort prospered in a continuous process. However, now deserted for years and dilapidated, it has lost much of its old charm and grandeur. Amidst the ruins survive a few palaces and havelis (mansions) which are a repository of a very exclusive and sensuous style of art in the form of superb murals drawn in Nagaur's own distinctive tradition. In the inner complex of the fort stand these palatial buildings, with finely mortared interiors in white plaster of marble finish. The ceilings in most cases are profusely decorated with floral motifs and intricate geometrical designs in Abha Mahal, supposedly the residence of Rao Amar Singh Rathore, the walls and niche have elaborate paintings in soft colours, depicting battle scenes, beautiful maidens and celestial figures. In the vicinity stands the Baradari, the 85 pillared Hall of Public Audience, with a profusion of ornamentation on the walls, arches and the ceiling. The two storeyed palace of Hadi Rani, Amar Singh's beloved wife, is adorned with the finest murals. These depict vividly the way of life of the royal ladies: enjoying music, plucking floweres and fruits from trees in the gardens, swaying merrily on swings or bathing in the pool, the stately women in flowing skirts and glittering jewellery look charmingly alive in graceful postures. The delicate lines of figures drawn in sober pastel shades of colours pleasantly reflect the relaxed flow of life of the aristocracy. These superb murals bear ample testimony to the uniqueness of Nagaur style of paintings as distinct from the other traditional schools, though having some affinity with the arts of Chamba school of Himachal Pradesh.

In the Sheesh Mahal (Mirror Chamber), now short of much of its sparkle, plenty of evidence of the Mughal influence is noticed in the murals, most of which are faded or obliterated due to aging. Here, in the inner verandah one notices a cluster of portraits of royal women in charming head-dresses interspersed between the figures of serpents. These are many other fine specimens of the murals in the fort have almost been destroyed with the passage of time. Fortunately, in recent years this treasure house of Nagaur's rare are distinctive style of art has attracted the attention of INTACH (Indian National Trust for Art and Cultural Heritage), who have almost completed the long-needed, restoration and revival of a large majority of the murals.

DIPAVLI DE

NAINA DEVI

As usual, the little wooden gate was open, welcoming all. The pretty garden and the elegant drawing room were as inviting. The same original paintings, rose-wood framed, and gilt-edged mirrors hung on the walls. The rich carpets on the floor, crystal and silver knick-knacks on the side tables were the same. The same antique furniture was there but draped in white. However the beautiful Perisan vases did not display the usual riot of fresh, colourful cut flowers, but were full of fragrant Rajnigandha. The family, close friends, old and young artists, all were there, as usual.

The only absence was that of the hostess of the *mebfil* (gathering) Naina Devi, elegant in flowing chiffon and dainty diamond jewellery, short wavy hair framing her face, lit up by a radiant, welcoming smile.

This mehfil in her home had been arranged as a tribute to the maestro who had breathed her last in 1993. The presentations were brief and poignant. They recalled that the journey of Naina Devi had begun on September 27, 1918, when she-Nilina-was born in the palatial mansion of Keshab Chandra Sen, her grandfather. He was a social reformer and a contemporary of Raja Rammohan Roy and other towering personalities.

Famous writers like Manmatha Ray, actors like Atindra Chakravorty, classical maestros like Ustad Enayat Hussain Khan and Girija Shankar Chakravorty, film personalities and music maestros like Timiar Baran, R.C. Boral, K.L. Saigal and famous dancers of the time used to visit the Sen mansion. They were warmly welcomed, sumptuously entertained. Rare compositions were heard, plays enacted, and dance dramas created.

When the family moved to their house in Banaras for a few months, Nilina, imbibed and absorbed the folk traditions of classical music and dance.

In later years, she loved to recall the Burhva Mangal festival at the advent of summer. Wealthy connoisseurs, musicians and dancers would go out on private boats on the Ganges. Till late in the night, music flowed along with the river to the rhythm of the boats.

In an era, when it was taboo for girls of respectable families to dance and sing, the Sen sisters learnt music and dance, in fact dabbled in all the arts. Benita, the eldest had a flair for writing and produced stage plays; Sadhona became a Kathak dancer and danced her way into popular films. As for Nilina, fate had a surprise gift waiting for her, when Christmas eve free in Calcutta was at its magnificent peak.

In that colourful, glamorous gathering of the elite Indian and foreign families, the young Prince Ripjit Singh of Kapurthala, Punjab met the carefree and charming Nilina.

There was an instant romance and marriage, a swift transition from the family mansion in Calcutta to the royal palace in Kapurthala. At the age of fifteen Nilina Sen became Rani Saheba in the princely state.

After the birth of two sons and two daughters, there was a cruel blow. At the age of 29, she suddenly lost her husband.

Earlier in 1948, noted thumri exponent Sunil Bose, who was in All India Radio, had persuaded Kunwar Ripjit Singh to let his wife be recorded by Columbia Gramophone Co. Four discs were recorded by the young Rani under the name Naina Devi.

Leaving aside the trappings and veils of royalty, Naina Devi became a formal disciple of the Rampur *gharana* (School) Ustad Mushtaq Hussain Khan at Jaipur.

She specialized in *purab ang thumri* and *tappa*, based on the foundation of pure classical raga. In later years she firmly expressed the view that without training in *raga, thumri, Kajri,* or *Chaiti* (Classical Indian modes of singing) could not be sung.

In 1960, Naina Devi came to Delhi and founded her school Raag Rang in 1961. The idea was to support and encourage artists. Here there were no barriers, all were welcomed with equal warmth. Naina Devi managed Raag Rang on her own and collections from art lovers.

Naina Devi used to tell the budding musicians than "music is not taught, but learnt". A child growing up to the strains of a *tanpura* will be a better artist than one learning for an hour every day and forgetting about music for the rest of the day, she would say. She felt that the decline in musical standards was inevitable if the gurushishya (teacher - disciple) system was not revived.

A veteran musician Ustad Hafiz Ahmad Khan feels that Naina Devi's personality was shaped right in her childhood itself. In the aristocratic Keshab Chandra Sen mansion, there were no cultural barriers. A renaissance of art, philosophy and science took shape from the discussions, mehfils and seasonal festivals. There was lavish hospitality too. Naina Devi continued the style of gracious, elegant living all through her life.

In 1965, Naina Devi became Consultant for Music and Dance on Delhi Doordarshan. This ushered in a glorious decade both for the electronic media and the stage. In her series "Swar Aur Sangit", she presented grand old masters like Bade Ghulam Ali Khan, Shambhu Maharaj, Siddheswari Devi, Rasoolan Bai and Roshnara Begum.

In recognition of her contribution to music Naina Devi was awarded the Padamshri in 1974 by the Government.

MAITHILY JAGANNATHAN

NAKO - THE KINNERS' PRIDE

Nako is Himachal Pradesh is the confluence of the verdant and the vibrating Kinnaur and the land of desolate grandeur, Spiti, by its sheer location. Flanked on the east by Tibet and west by Sangla Valley, and as one moves northwards, by the exquisite Pin Valley, Nako with her population of just five hundred inhabitants is the largest village of the Hang-rang Valley.

Counted amongst some of the highest motorable villages of the world, Nako at 3670 mtrs above sea level in unique in itself. The entire village of stone houses with tin and thatched roofs presents an ambience of small, yet tidy community, content with what nature has provided the Nakoites with.

Surrounded by the majestic Himalayas, Nako appears to be ensconced by nature from all the four sides. The crystal clear water of the Nako lake and the ever luminous sky creates an illusion as if the sky is descending on earth to embrace her, particularly on the surface of the lake against the backdrop of moon-like rocky mountains.

The land belt in and around Nako, failling both in Kinnaur and Spiti region of the State of Himachal Pradesh, have often been referred to as the 'land of the fabled Gandharavas' - the celestial musicians and dancers.

Nako is situated on the India - Tibet route and its inhabitants are quite influenced by the Tibetan School of Buddhism, perhaps because of the proximity of their land to Tibet and also due to the interaction between the two communities in the ancient days. Religion plays an important role in the lifestyle of these people. One could see various 'mani points' in the village full of sculptured rocks and stones with Tibetan zodiacal signs.

Polyandry is still followed in these villages, not because of the influence of the mythoigoical heroes of the Mahabharata, who, as the legend goes, spent the last year of their exile in this area, but because of the tough terrain, vagaries of nature and the meagre resources available to the Kinnauries in the area. Primarily to keep their small land holdings intact, usually the eldest son marries and the younger brothers either become lamas (priests) or share the wife. The major crops of the areas are various fruits and barley. The local liquor called the Aangoori or Behmi is usually brewed with barlly and consumed by both men and women.

Surrounded by beautiful mountains with fruit-laden trees, exotic valleys, lush-green slopes and the gushing streams, Nako is ideal for a perfect holiday, full of rest and relaxation.

RAJ MITTAL

NALANDA : THE CITY OF KNOWLEDGE

Nalanda, like Rome, was not buit in a day. It took several centuries to evolve, diversify and extend its civilising influence not only to all corners of the country but to lands as distant as China, Japan, Malaysia, Java, Sumatra, Korea, Nepal and Tibet.

Originally a mango-grove called *Pavarika* in the village Bargoan in Bihar, the place was sanctified by the *Sakyamuni* (Gautam Buddha) himself when the Enlightened one broke journey here to halt and rest, not once but several times. It is said that Mahavira also spent fourteen rainy reasons here. Ashoka built a *Vihara* (monastery) here and Harsha made it possible for a thousand scholars to delve deep into a hundred disciplines everyday in its numerous halls and more numerous temples.

Contemporary eye-witness accounts testify that there were so many *Viharas* around Nalanda, Rajgriha and Vikramsila that the whole area was called *Bihara*. It is from this word that the present day Indian state of Bihar derives its name. The transformation or Nalanda *Vihara* into the Nalanda university was brought about as a result of assimilation of centuries of scholarship and culture in and around the main monastery. In other words, Nalanda had a rich heritage as a *Vihara* before it became an international centre of education and culture. Nalanda

stood for freedom in learning, thought, expression and action.

The heritage of Nalanda was both non-Buddhist and Buddhist. While the former included the *Vedas* and the *Puranas,* the latter consisted of works such as *Vinay, Pitaka, Dhammapada, Abhidhamma* and *Majhima Nikaya,* with excellent commentaries by scholars such as Nagarjuna, Maiteriya, Asanga, Vasubandhu and Dinnaga, who defined and refined Buddhism in its various facets and dispensations. Nalanda, therefore, honoured thought and men of thought in the best of Indian traditions.

Nalanda was a residential university like so many others in India in those times, such as Taxila, Ujjaini, Vallabhi, Vikramsila and Amravati. Yet, it was a university with a difference. The Gate Keepers of Nalanda were scholars of the highest repute, well versed in their subjects and drawn from the best in the country to examine the fresh entrants at the Gate itself. This was a novel method of 'Entrance Examination' which was very tough from all accounts. Seven or eight scholars out of every ten were unsuccessful. So the scholars came to the gates of Nalanda again and again, till they were selected. Merit alone was the criteria and even the Vice Chancellor had no discretion. There are records of instances where scholars either belonging to or patronised by royal families were rejected, in spite of the fact that the expenses of Nalanda were met with from royal grants of village revenues. There is evidence that the revenues of several villages were granted to Nalanda, for the maintenance of its hostels and the administration of its temples and *Viharas.*

Several Chinese scholars and monks visited, studied and taught at Nalanda. Their memoirs are a rich and authentic source for the reconstruction of academic life at Nalanda. According to one such scholar-monk, I-Tsing, the minimum age for admission to Nalanda was twenty years. This indicates that scholars who had already passed out from some other university were admitted to Nalanda to pursue higher knowledge. We also have the evidence from Hiuen Tsang, the Chinese pilgrim who came to Nalanda in the days of the "Good King" Harsha. He confirms that "learned men from different cities, who desire to acquire renown in discussion, come (to Nalanda) in multitudes to settle their doubts". The Gate-Keepers of Nalanda were in fact, the Gate-Keepers of India's knowledge, her culture and heritage. Anyone was welcome for an open discussion on any aspect of religion, philosophy, law and life.

Although the subject of theology was compulsory, Nalanda was not a sectarian or a religious university in the narrow sense of the term, imparting only Buddhist thought. Subjects other than Buddhism were taught as fervently. Almost all sciences, including the science of medicine were taught. So were the *Upanishads* and the *Vedas.* Panini's grammar, the science of pronunciation (Phonetics), etymology, Indology and *Yoga* were all included in the curricula. Surprisingly, even archery was taught at Nalanda. Hiuen Tsang himself learnt *Yogasastra* from Jayasena. When King Harsha requested Shilabhadra to send four learned scholars to Orissa to debate with the heretics, Hiuen Tsang was chosen to be one of them.

Hiuen Tsang, who stayed at the university for 17 years, first as a student and later as a professor under the Master, Shilabhadra, came to India via Gobi desert and entered Kashmir through the Himalayas. He mentions being received with honour throughout his journey in India till he reached Nalanda. His book is called '*Siyuki*' which he wrote on his return home.

At Nalanda, Hiuen Tsang was received at the Gate with a thousand lamps, his erudition and reputation having travelled faster than him. Here he studied to obtain the degree of Master of Law and became the Vice-Principal of this great University. The head of the University was called '*Pandita*' and Shilabhadra occupied this position when Hiuen Tsang came to join as a student. When Shilabhadra himself received Hiuen Tsang at the gate of Nalanda, it was the meeting of the two mighty minds of those times. In no time, the new entrant rose in the stimates of Shilabhadra who sent him out not only on difficult assignments but also on long and perilous journeys to Orissa and Kumarupa.

According to Hiuen Tsang's description, the daily schedule at Nalanda was packed with rituals. The day began with a call for the morning bath, which was compulsory for every inmate; at least it was obligatory to bathe at the prescribed hour. The bath was followed by the ablution of the holy image of Buddha, by furnishing heaps of flowers and incense. This was a fairly prolonged ritual accompanied by recitation of *stotras* and singing of hymns. After prayers and meditation the inmates had their meagre breakfast. Thereafter, they went to their respective halls for discussion. In the afternoon, another ritual called "*Caitya Vandana*" was held, wherein priests assembled at the main gate of the monastery and sang songs in praise of *Sakyamuni*. They could go out in the evenings and the night was meant for repose.

Knowledge of Sanskrit was essential for all entrants in spite of the fact that *Sakyamuni* delivered his sermons in Pali. Knowledge of Sanskrit meant complete mastery of Sanksrit Grammar, literature and correct pronunciation. On the authority of Hiuen Tsang, it can be soud that the entrants to Nalanda were supposed to be well-versed in "*Beda*" i.e. *Veda, Vedanta, Samakhya, Nyaya* and *Vaisesika*. I. Tsing also confirms this in his accounts.

The method of teaching at Nalanda was tutorial followed by discussions. Listening to the discussions was education and the discussions continued throughout the day and, indeed, the night. Nalanda scholars never tired of discussions; rather, they welcomed them. Hiuen Tsang was deeply impressed with the Nalanda discipline. In its existence of about 700 years at the time of his visit, there had not been a single case of any strike or disturbance or even commotion (except intellectual ferment) at the University. Besides, there were discourses open to all where all subjects from life to death were discussed. According to I.Tsing: "They arrange every day about hundred pulpits for preaching and the students attend these discourses without fail, even for a minute". There was no writing work for Nalanda scholars except the copying of manuscripts and texts. It may be recalled that both Hiuen Tsang and I-Tsing carried hung loads of such texts back to China upon their return.

Nalanda was an example of the *Guru-Shishya parampara*, a great Indian tradition. The authority of the Guru (teacher) over the shishya (student) was absolute, and yet, dissent was permitted in academic matters. The tradition, although going back thousands of years, flourished at Nalanda more than elsewhere.

Describing the *Guru-shishya* relationship, I.Tsing says : "He (Shishya) goes to the teacher at the first watch and at the last watch in the night. First the teacher bids him to sit down comfortably. Selecting some passages from *Tripatakas*, he gives a lesson in a way that suits the circumstances and does not leave any fact or theory unexplained. He inspects his pupil's moral conduct, and warns him of defects and transgressions. Whenever he finds his pupil at fault, he makes him seek remedies and repent. The pupil rubs the teacher's body. Folds his clothes and sometimes sweeps the apartment and the yard. Then having examine the water to ensure there are no insects in it, he gives it to his teacher. Thus, if there is anything to be done, he does all on behalf of the teacher".

No fees of any kind were charged at Nalanda for the studies. No price was paid for food or clothes or accommodation. There was no punishment of any kind. For the faults or the defects of the students, the teachers punished themselves. The teacher-pupil relation was like that of the father and his son. The greatest delight and the highest reward of the teacher came when his pupil outshone him. *Sakyamuni* had even laid down detailed duties and responsibilities of the teachers and the pupils, from early morning till night when the teacher went to sleep. In the words of Gautams the Buddha, "the pupil is also to act as a check, as it were, upon the preceptor, in keeping him streadfast in the faith".

The students and the teachers wore the same yellow robes, whose details are available in the Buddhist texts, "wrapped round the waist and back, and secured with a girdle; the under-garment wrapped round the loin and reaching below the knee". Food was simple and '*satvik*'. According to Shaman Hwui Li, the author of "*The Life of Hiuen Tsang*", all the provisions were contributed by two hundred house-holders from about a hundred villages.

As regards games and amusements, the students were allowed wrestling, and some sort of 'kabbadi' but the game of dice was strictly prohibited in spite of it being extremely popular in Indian society.

The fall of Nalanda at the hands of the Turks is a story too deep for tears. Like Nero, Bakhtiar Khiljhi, its destroyer in 1205 A.D., laughed while Nalanda burnt. The City of knowledge, which took several centuries to build, took only a few hours to be destroyed. Legend has it that when some monks fell at the feet of the invader to spare at least its world-famed library, *Ratnabodhi*, he kicked them and had them thrown in the fire along with the books. The monks fled to foreign lands, citizens became denizens and Nalanda was relegated to a memory.

Thus ended the story of Nalanda till it was re-told first by Hamilton and later by Alexander Cunningham. The excavations started in 1915 and continued for twenty years. Yet much remains to be done. At the Nav Nalanda Mahavihara, which stands close to this ancient site, *Sakyamuni* seems to beckon all men of knowledge to restore the flory of this greatest centre of learning of the yore.

PRANAV KHULLAR

NAND LAL

(B. 1902) - Instrumentalist; Hindustani, Shehnai; studied with Ram Dasji and Chhote Khan; disc recordings.

P. N. CHOPRA

NAND RISHI (NUR-UD-DIN)

(B. 1877) - Muslim Sufi mystical poet; patron saint of kashmiri Muslims; poems have been collected in 2 anthologies, Rishinama and Nurnama; though illiterate, his songs and lyrics were full of beauty; founded order of Rishis; had great influence on Hindus as well.

P. N. CHOPRA

NARADA PURANA

The Narada Purana is one of the 18 puranas and is placed the sixth in order by the Vishnu, Markandeya, Matsya, Skanda, Bhagavata, Agni, Varaha, Padma, Bhavishya, Brahavaivarta and Narada itself and the seventh by the Kurma, Linga, Garuda, Padma, Saura and Siva Puranas and the eleventh according to the Vayu Purana. The Padma Purana includes the Narada among the six sattvika puranas out of the 18 puranas. The Skanda Purana recognises the Narada as one of the Vaishnava Puranas. H.P. Sastri and P.V. Kane consider the Naradiya Purana as one of the three (together with Garuda and Agni) encyclopaedic puranas. The Padma Purana describes the Narada Purana as the 'Nabhi' (Navel) of Lord Vishnu.

The Narada Purana has 25,000 verses according to the Vayu, Matsya, Bhagavata, Agni, Nardiya, Brahmavaivarta and Devibhagavata and 23,000 according to the Vayu Purana.

The Narada Purana consists of two parts. Purva (former) and Uttara (Latter). The first part has 125 chapters and the second 82. The Purvabhaga is further divided into four padas (sections) viz. Bhoga, Moksha, Kriya and Charya.

Narada's glorification of Lord Vishu shows that he was a propagator of Vaishnavism. According to Narada, Brahma, Vishnu and Siva are only three manifestations of the Supreme God, Mahavishnu or Narayana.

These three manifestations perform the respective functions of creation, preservation and destruction of the Universe. Know as Janardana, Hari and so on, he is called Sarvadevasvara (God of all Gods), Nadarupa (whose form is sound), Pranava (mystic syllable OM) Sabdabrahma (verbum), Adideva (first God) and Chidrupa (whose form is chit, the universal spirit as identified with pure thought). He is Veda (sacred knowledge), Akshaya (imperishable), Ananta (endless), Visweswara (Lord of the Universe) and Paalaka (saviour) and there is nothing beyond Him.

Narada enumerates the ten incarnations of Vishnu viz : Matsya, (fish), Kurma (tortoise), Varaha (Boar), Narasimha (Man-lion), Trivikrama, Bhargava Rama, Dasarathi Rama, Krishna, Buddha and Kalki. According to Narada, Vasudeva Krishna is an incarnation of Vishnu. Narada Indentifies Radha-Krishna with the Supreme God and considers Him to be the main source of the Trinity.

Siva (Sambhu) is described as a prominent God though, when compared to Vishnu, he holds a lower rank. Vishnu Himself proclaims that Siva is his alter ego and one without beginning and end.

Siva is praised as the deity responsible for creation, preservation and destruction.

Epithets like Virupaksha (odd-eyed) Nilagriva (blue-necked), Pasunam Pati (lord of animals or beings), Panchasyadeva (five-faced-God) Dasabhuja (ten-armed), Umaapati (husband of Uma) and Siva (auspicious).

Narada described the greatness of Siva-linga and its worship. There is also a description of Tandava (dance) performed by Siva and Uma, Vinayaka and Skanda.

Among the members of Siva's family, only Lord Ganesa is dealt with in detail.

Brahma is Padmasambhava (lotus-born), Pitambaprapitamaha (great grandfather), Chaturanana (four-faced) and Lokavidhaanakrit (creator of the world). He is the one who had narrated all the 18 puranas, to his son Marichi for the benefit of all.

In the Narada Purana, among the mother goddesses, Radha figures as the most prominent deity associated with Lord Krishna. The other female deities are described as only reincarnation of Radha, viz. Lakshmi, Durga, Saraswati, Savitri and Devi and the other prominent female deities mentioned in the Narada Purana.

The Narada Purana mentiones that Mahalakshmi as the goddess of wealth occupying a lotus flower and being sprinkled with nectar through golden jars by four elephants. She displays Vara (Boon), Abhaya (Protection from danger), Abja (lotus flower) as Srak (garland) in her four arms. She is clad in silk and wears a crown.

The three-eyed goddess Durga, know as Vishnu maya, wearing a creacsent moon on her forehead and wearing ornaments, with one thousand hands displaying various weapons, wa born from Krishna's body. She was given in marriage to Siva.

Narada mentiones Durga's four incarntions, viz., Chhinnamasta Rama, Tripurabhairavi, Matangi and Dhumavati.

Devi is the greatest Sakti of Siva, creating the whole universe. She is Jagadambika and Bhubaneswari i.e., the Mother and the Mistress of the world. She is bright as the rising sun and has three eyes and lofty breasts. She wears the moon on her forehead and displays Vara, Paasa, Ankusa and Abhaya in her arms. She appears always with a smile.

The main contribution of Narada to the growth of Saktism in India is the elevation of Radha to the position of the Chief presiding deity of Saktism.

Narada's treatment of bhakti is an example of the popularity of 'Narada-Bhakti'. Bhakti is the Paramakarana (prime cause) of all kinds of siddhis (achievements) as aaloka (light) is of activities of the creatures. It is the destroyer of all the sins and is a daavanala (forest fire) to the Papaaranya (forest of sin).

In Jyotisha, Narada breaks new ground in the Puranic literature by giving an account of Ganita, Jaataka and Samhita spread over three chapters.

Narada deals with Varasramadharma, Dana (gift), Prayaschitta (expiation) Karmavipaka, Sraddha, Purtadharmas, description of various sins and narakas. Furthermore, Narada describes a number of vratas especially Ekadasi Vrata.

Regarding tirthas, Narada has given a detailed description of the holy places like the holy Ganga, Kasi, Purushottama, etc. is description of holy places is a valuable record.

In the Naradiya we find more emphasis on Acharas. It is stated that one who does not follow acharas is considered although he is a devotee of Hari and meditates of Hari. This shows that performance of duties is the most important factor. Furthermore, Narada attaches great importance to satsanga (i.e. association with the virtuous). The description of the greatness of Satsanga may be considered as a main contribution of Narada.
(Ccndensed)

DR. K. DAMODARAN NAMBIAR

NATIONAL EMBLEM OF INDIA

The national emblem or crest of the Government of India is the symbol of India's message of peace and goodwill to the world. The Lion capital with the *Chakra* (wheel), flanked by a horse and abull, was the royal insignia of the Mauryan Emperor, Ashoka, of the 3rd century BC. The original has been preserved at the Archaeological Museum at Sarnath near Varanasi in Uttar Pradesh.

This Maurya masterpiece, shaped out of Chuna sandstone, once majestically embelished the Ashokan pillar at Sarnath, a place of great reverence of Buddhists all over the world. Presently in ruins, Sarnath is situated about 1C Km north-east of Varanasi, a Hindu holy city located at the congluence of three rivers, the Ganga, Yamuna and the mythical Saraswati. Sarnath's archaeological remains still attract thousands of Buddhist piligrims, archaeologists, historians, students and tourists, both from India and abroad. it is one of the four holiest spots in the Buddhist legends, the place where Lord Buddha turned the wheel of the Law (*Dharmachakrapravartana)* after attaining Enlightenment. This has been manifested in the form of the lion capital which symbolizes the Buddha as the *Sakya-Simaha* (The lion of the *Sakyas,* the tribe that Buddha belonged to).

The pillar at Sarnath was primarily intended to commemorate the great wheel with twenty-four spokes. There are four animals carved in relief on the abacus of the wheel the elephant, horse, bull and lion - symbolizing the four quarters of the universe. One can interpret here the continuation of Vedic mythology, recalling that the *Rigveda* conceived the lion as the ing of the forest, the swift galloping horse as the vehicle of the Sun god and the bull as god Indra's vehicle.

The boldly designed, finely proportioned and well-balanced conception draws the admiration of the beholder and recalls the first sermon by Lord Buddha at Sarnath. A group of four lions surmounts the Sarnath capital, each facing a cardinal direction. The pose of their limbs and the tense muscular anatomy speak of the imagination of an accomplished master craftsman. Their faces and free-flowing manes, the blod contours of their rounded figures, their subtle modelling in relief manifest the unerring and confident hand of master artists of the Mauryan court.

The characteritic brilliant Mauryan polish gives the pillar and lion capital a lasting finish, the softness of jade and a dazzle still fresh despite a thousand years of exposure to sun, rain and dust. The skill of attaining a smooth glass finish is certainly the result of indigenous mastery of the stone-cutter's art, drawn from Indus Valley civilization tradition in the 3rd millennium BC to the Mauryan period in the 3rd century BC. The sculptures and pillars of Mauryan period display the highest quality and delicacy in their long-lasting polist, achieved through a method probably inherited by hereditary stone-cutters.

According to an expert, the high degree of polish resulting in a lustrous, crystal-like finish on a sandstone surface was probably obtained by the labourious application of agate (a semi-precious stone) file.

A. K. KHANNA

NATIONAL RAIL MUSEUM

About one-and half century ago, the first Indian train steamed out on its maiden journey. The 16th of April, 1853, was the golden day for Indian Railways when at 3.30 p.m. a large crowd cheered and waved to say goodbye to twenty coaches of the train and its 400 passengers; 21 guns thoundered to salute it. Covering a distance of 35 Km from Boribunder to Thana, it reached its destination at 4.45 p.m.

Today, the Indian railways is Asia's Largest and the world's second largest network. The advanced technolgies have ushered in a new era in the history of Indian Railways. However with the aim of preserving 'old beauties' a National Rail Museum has been set up in Chanakyapuri, New Delhi.

The first of its kind in the country, it is spread over an area of 10 acres. Inaugurated in February, 1977, the Museum consists of six display galleries and a large open area where the 'vintage beauties' are stationed. The erstwhile fast-runners now stand still as if passing their old age in complete relaxation and contemplation. The area evokes the atmosphere of a railway yard.

The museum serves a significant educational purpose. Various small exhibits - some working, some dummy models - show different aspects and working of railways. The vast open space where different models of actual engines and coaches are kept is no less interesting. Joy ride on a 'toy train' exhilarates the passengers - children as well as their parents - and one can have glimpses of various 'heavy-weights' of yester years. The locomotice and their contemporary carriages are stationed side by side to provide a proper perspective. On view are 42 vintage locomotives, 20 quaint carriages and saloons, a complete armoured train and saloons of erstwhile Maharajas and Nawabs in their original colours and livery besides two off-beat exhibits - a Hand Crane and a Crane Tank.

The most prized exhibits of the museum include the '140 year' old 'Fairy Queen' which is still working; the 234 -

ton 'Garrat Engine; Phoenix, the rail motor car; B-777, the tiny engine of Darjeeling Himalayan Railway; the four-wheel saloon in which King Award VII travelled in 1876, the Viceregal dining saloon; 133-year old Ramgotty; the saloon of the Maharaja of Mysore built in 1899 with extremely high quality trak wood and adorned with gold and ivory; Simla Rail car fitted with a petrol engine, and the unique Monorail. All these make the national Rail Museum a facinating place.
(Condensed)

TARUN PARMAR

NAUSHAD'S MUSICAL WIZARDRY

Among the music composers of our times for the Hindi Cinema in particular, Naushad Ali (77), may well be considered the pioneer. An admirer of his, in an attractive and informative souvenir, 'Naushad, A filmography writes in verse : "I think of naushad the music director. Who has swayed, swung and soothed broken hearts, battered minds had bruised souls....."

Naushad made a decisive impact on young minds by the lifting tunes he gave to film songs. Even as a boy who grew up in Lucknow, Naushad showed extraordinary interest in music and frequented a shop selling musical instruments. He used to experience the sounds they would emanate even when he would be cleaning them. The boy was one day found playing on the harmonium - and he was punished; The owner asked Naushad to take with him any harmonium of his choise and practise on it. An angry father threw the harmonium out of the house. But bound to music as the boy was, he would not give up. After some kind of musical training on instruments under Ustads, he made his way to Mumbai in 1937, when he was 18. He was lucky to get an entry into the film world, and after working as an assistant, became the music director of 'Kanchan' in 1941. Since then, his rise to fame as a maker of melodies was steady. He did the musical score for 74 films and 3 T.V. serials - a total of about 700 songs.

'Ratan' (1944) and 'anmol Ghadi' (1946), Mela (1948) and 'Dillagi' (1949) were among the 27 films for which he gave the musical tunes in the forties. Lovers of music in the South (who kenwno Hindi like this writer) hummed to themselves 'Ye Zindagee Ke mele....' and 'Dhartee Ko Aakaash Pukaare....' (Mela); Ankhiyaan milla ke..... Chale Naheen Jaanaa' and 'Aaee Deewaalee.... (Ratan); 'Mere Bachpan Ke Saathee' (Anmol Ghadi); 'Muralee waale Muralee Bajaa' and 'Too Mere Chaand Main, Teree Chaandanee*(Dillagi).

The film songs of the fifties, described as the 'Golden Period of Hindi Film Music', were great hits - Babul' (Chood Babul Kaa Ghar.........); 'Deedaar' (Meree Kahaanee'); 'Baiju Bawara' (all the songs were outstanding; the tragic story featured Bharat Bhushan and Meena Kumari); Mother India' (O Jaane Waalen....)". The sixties began with the historical romance 'Mughal-e-Azam'. And so the grand creative work has continued till this day.

Naushad has not only climbed to the peak of excellence in music composition but has helped others to climb to great heights of fame and fortune. The foremost of these is Lata Mangeshkar, who has gone into the Guinness Book for the record number of songs she has sung for the films. She has been rightly described as a miracle.

The Indian tradition looks upon music not merely as a means of entertainment but a spiritual 'Sadhana'. Naushad may not have set his listeners on the spiritual path but he certainly did on the romantic path. His music evoked wonder and awe at the mystery of human relationship. In contributing to the evolution of film music - both by way of giving tunes to songs and providing background music to scenes - Naushad has carved a secure niche for himself in the Hall of Fame. His life is a demonstration of what a gifted person con accomplish to make the lives of his fellowmen a little better than what they would have been otherwise in atension-torn, fear-haunted world.
(Condensed)

V.S.R.K.

NAUTANKI

Nautanki, another north Indian form of folk opera; recalling medieval romances, tales of heroes;

NAVARATRA - UTSAV

The nine-day propitiation of Durga or Mother Goddess commencing from the *Aswina-shukla pratipad* (September / October) till *navami* (from the first till the 9th day of the bright half of the Aswina month) is traditionally called Navaratra-Utsav.

Explaining why Durga has to be propitiated at this particular time of the year, the Devi Bhagavata says :

It means that the months Vasanta (Spring) and Sharad (Autumn) are like the two poisonous teeth of *Yama* in respect of humanity and therefore goddess *Chandika* or Durga should be propitiated to ward off those evils.

Puranas enjoin the observance of this festival by all four varnas in every city and village of the country with appropriate fasts i.e. with one meal at night or day after worship. The worshipper should sleep on bare floor. He must feed girl-children each day as explained hereinafter and make them happy by the gift of clothes and jewels. The goddess should be worshipped at all these times.

Goddess Durga may be propitiated either by Vedic mantras or the tantrik Navakshari after being duly initiated in it. The mode of workship is generally as follows : after sankalpa, the *Kalasa* or pot of holy water should be installed in which the Devi should be invoked with due mantras and worshipped in the sixteen-fold manner with appropriate *neivedyas* and *balis*. Then girl-children should be worshipped, the child of each day being a year older than the previous day. A child of one year, however, should be avoided. Thus girls from 2 years to 10 years would be ideal. They are respectively called (1) Kumarika, (2) Trimurti, (3) Kalyani, (4) Rohini, (5) Kali, (6) Chandika, (7) Sambhavi, (8) Durga (9) Subhadra. The prayer should begin thus:

The girls should be worshipped with flowers, akshata, etc, and be presented, as mentioned earlier, with new clothes, ornaments, mirror, comb, etc. It may be said that girls selected for this puja should be free from defects. The recital of Chandi is also prescribed as also performance of *havan*.

The worship of the horse and elephant too is recommended, particularly in royal households.

Devi as Saraswati should be invoked on the day when *Mula* asterism rules; she should be worshipped as such , on the day of Purvashada, i.e. on the next day, and *bail* or final worship should be performed on the day following. As a matter of interest to youngsters, the Rudra-Yamala has it:

Once Devi is invoked on a heap of books, one wishing to become learned, should avoid writing and reading for the day.

Again, should however one be unable to worship Devi on all the nine days, it is essential to worship Her on the 8th day at least. Says Devi Bhagavata :

Devi was born as Bhadrakali along with her ganas on Ashtami or the 8th day, and destroyed Dakshas Yagna: hence its sanctity. In fact by worshipping Her on the three days 7th, 8th and 9th, one gets the full benefit of observing Navaratri in full.

(May goddess Durga protect us all !

NISHKINCHAN

NAYIKAS - IN CLASSICAL SCULPTURE

The Natyasastra (2nd century BC - 2nd century AD) of sage Bharata classifies men and women, who are called *nayakas* and *nayikas*, meaning lovers and sweethearts, according to their physical and mental traits and emotional states and situations. It further classifies the emotions of a woman followed by a detailed classification of the stages of a woman, love, female go-betweens and the meeting place of lovers. Never before or after have the emotional states of men and women in love been analysed and classified with such precision. These classifications were derived from the typical social milieu of the classical age.

The nayaka-nayika bhava, i.e., the relationship between the lover and his beloved, it the most persistent theme in classical Sanskrit literature. Both kinds of srinagara (adornment of body and fact), sambhoga (love in union) and vipralamba (love in separation), have been beautifully rendered by Sanskrit writers, specially by Bhanudatta and Vishvanatha in their Rasamajari and Sahitya-darpan respectively.

Scholars have concentrated more on the nayikas of classical Sanskrit literature. They are divided into three main categories: the *swiya* (one's own woman), the *anya* or *parakiya* (another's woman) and the *samanya* or *sadharana* (a courtesan or a prostitute). The *swiya nayika* is further divided into three categories, namely *mugdha*, *madhya* and *pragalbha* or *praudha*. The *madhya* and *pragalbha* are further classified as *dhira*, *adhira* and *dhiradhira*. The *parkiya* nayika has two types : *Parodha* (another man's wife or woman) and kanyaka (an unmarried damsel). Thus, in all, sixteen basic types have been enumerated. But this is not all. The nayikas are further classified according to their mental and emotional states into eight categories. These, according to

Sahityadarpan, are the *Swadhinapatika, Khanadita, Abhisarika, Kalahantarita, Vipralabdha, Proshitabhartika, Vasakasajja* and the *Virahotakanthita*. The *Rasamanjari* mentions one more type of nayika called the *Pravatsyatpatika*.

The mugdha nayika is a sweet young lass experienceing her first encounter with the sentiment of love and whose basic characteristic is shyness. The madhya nayika has passed through the stage of bashfulness and is adept in the various aspects of love-play. The pragalbha nayika is one who is at the peak of her feminie and seductive glory, is adept in the art of love-making and, at times, can even dominate her lover;

The samanya or sadharana nayika is lowly and self-centered, one whose love is greedy and reserved only for the prosperous nayakas who shower her with money and gifts in exchange for her favours, which are devoid of any genuine feelings.

The khandita is that unfortunate nayika whose lover is involved with another woman; however, he returns to her after his tryst.

The abhisarika, who is intensely passionate and goes to meet her lover according to her pre-arranged tryst with him, has often formed a beautiful theme in literature. There are two types of abhisarikas, the Vadhu and the Veshya. The former moves stealthily, muting the sound of jingling bracelets and anklets. The latter dresses gaudily, decks herself in all her jewels and perfumes herself with flowers and garlands. The Vadhu is one of the two swiya nayikas, madhaya or pragalbha.

The Kalabantarita is a nayika who plays a sort of hide-and-seek with her lover who is seeking a tryst with her. Though she likes him, she pretends to reject him. In this sweet love-play, shyness is the dominant feeling.

A lovelorn woman awaiting her lover is a vipra labdha, she is dejected because he has not arrived at the appointed hour as promised, Kalidasa's Meghadhutam is entirely dedicated to the emotions of love in separation, Vipralambha. Here, the yakshi is suffering the pangs of separation from her husband who is away from her due to curse and she is awaiting the day when he will come back. She is also a fine illustration of the Proshitabhartika nayika.

The Vasakasajjika nayika is woman dressing in all her finery and decking herself with beautiful jewels. She may also be one who, though avoiding too many ornaments, is still anxious to appear attractive before her lover. But at the same time, irritated by her lover's delay, who is expected any moment, she instructs her companions and maids not to load her with ornaments. The best representation of a vasakasajjika is the painting from Ajanta of the Princess At her Toilette.

The other nayika who is eagerly and anxiously awaiting the tryst with her lover is the utka or utkanthita or virahotkanthita. As time goes by, she gets worried about the probable reason why her lover has not reached, as well as for his well being.

Sanskrit poets and dramatists have created various situations to depict these nayika with or without nayakas while illustrating the various aspects of sringara, the sentiment of love. Though some of these are best appreciated in literature, many of them examplary depiction in sculpture as well.

We find skilful and delightful female figures of the nayikas in different postures sculptured in Indian subcontinent (2nd century BC onwards) during the periods of sunga, Satvahana, Kushana Gupta, Chalukya, Rashtrakuta and Pala till it reached artistic zenith during the rule of the Chandelas, Eastern Gangas and Hoysalas. The Chandela sculptors delightfully explored feminine beauty in all its veriegated aspects to embellish the temple walls. The nayikas, asparas, urikshikas, ganikas and surasundaris on the outer walls of the Khajuraho temples depict practically all aspects of female activities, such as dressing, undressing, applying make-up, removing a thorn from a toe, writing a letter applying lac-dye, putting on anklets, wringing out wet hair, playing with a ball, and so on. The graceful female bracket figures of the Hoyasala temples are known as madanikas, or youthful damsels. These and the ones on the facades of Orissan temples are depicted in various playful mudras (postures).

PRABHAKAR BEGDE

NICHOLAS ROERICH ARTIST AND THE SEER

In the Kulu Valley, the ancient Kuluta, at Naggar, in the full view of the snowy peaks, amidst *deodars* and blue pines stands a large rectangular stone. The inscription reads : "On December the Thirteenth 1947 here was cremated the body of Nicholas Roerich - the great Russian friend of India - Let there be Peace". The stone stands like an altar fashioned by the sole hand of nature which gave it an almost perfect shape of a rectangle. It is a fragment of a rock which detached itself from a cliff nearby as if to provide a seal over the spot where the Bard of the Himalayas was cremated, to mark the place of his physical dissolution.

Our late Prime Minister Jawaharlal Nehru, inaugurating Father's Exhibition of paintings said:

"When I think of Nicholas Roerich I am astounded at the scope and abundance of his activities and crative genius. A great artist, a great scholar and writer, archaeologist and explorer, he touched and lighted up so many aspects of human endeavour. The very quantity is stupendous thousands of paintings and each one of them a great work of art. When you look at these paintings, so many of them of the Himalayas, you seem to catch the spirit of those great mountains which have towered over the Indian plain and been our sentinels for ages past. They remind us of so much in our history, our thought, our cultural and spiritual heritage, so much not merely of the India of the past, but of something that is permanent and eternal about India, that we cannot help feeling a great sense of indebtedness to Nicholas Roerich who has enshrined that spirit in these magnificent canvases".

It is difficult in this short space to give an adequate picture of a Man who lived such an extraordinary life and left such a vast heritage. I shall only dwell on some of the most important facets of his life.

Whenever I think of my Father, I see before me his serene and thoughtful face, his kind violet - blue eyes which at times would become quite dark. I can hear his quiet voice, he never raised his voice and all his countenance reflected of his character. It was the composure of a Superior Man, grave and yet kind, thoughtful with a remarkable and happy sense of humour.

In all his movements there was a measured harmony. He never hurried yet his output was prodigious. When he painted or when he wrote he did so with quiet deliberation. When he wrote in his large and clear hand-writing he never corrected or changed his sentences or words, least of all his thoughts. It was a continuous progressive effort towards a certain definite goal and that was true of his entire life. Under all conditions of life, in the most trying circumstances he remained calm and possessed and never wavered in his determination.

He held before himself the transcendental ideals of the great Italian masters of the Renaissance, Leonard davinci and Michael Angelo.

He was born in 1874 at St. Petersbourg in Russia and came from an ancient family of Scandinavian extraction. He simultaneously attended the academy of art and several faculties at the university, including the faculty of law in deference to his father's wishes.

He began his archaeological researches and excavations when only eighteen years old. In Russia, he was at the head of leading art and educational institutions for fortythree years. He painted thousands of paintings. Executed murals and mosaics for public buildings and churches, designed settings for Operas and Ballets. Wrote his books and essays on Art and Archaeology, his short stories, fairy/tales and poems, and conducted researches in Archaeology, History and Art. He assembled remarkable collections of Art and Archaeology, which were among the best in Russia.

Some of the settings he designed for the theatre like Prince Igor and the Sacre due Printemps produced by Diaghilev in Parts have since become classics of the state.

Recognition and fame came very early in life to my Father. When he finally embarked on his World travels he was only 43 and was already a world figure with a tremendous record of achievement:

Philosophy, the Great Oriental thought attracted him from his earliest days. The books on Sri Ramakrishna, of Swami Vivekananda and others were published in Russia at the beginning of the century. The poems of Tagore were beautifully translated into Russian by the Great Lithuanian Poet Baltrushaitis. At that time an exhibition of Indian Art was organised in Parise by the Russian Art Connoisseur Golubev. Father dedicated one of his articles to this exhibition and concluded it with the following significant words :

Beauty still lives in India;
Beckons to us the Great India Path

This 'Path' was to take him later to India to discover for himself and through him for other is the beauties of this land, to paint as no one has painted before him the grandeur, the sumblime beauty and inner meaning of the Himalayas. His studies in Philosophy and Oriental thought were a constant background in his quest for Self-Realisation.

He travelled far and wide not only throughout Russia, Europe and the New World, but also Asia and his extensive expenditions took him accross Central Asia. Mongolia, Tibet, China and Japan.

Father loved India, the Himalayas and dedicated to them many books, essays and thousands of his canvases. That

"Great Indian" path which beckoned to him from his days became a reality when he came to India. He could contact the very sources of the great philosophies, of ancient transcendental thought. He travelled throughout India and the Himalayas and finally settled at Kulu where he lived and worked till his death in 1947. Concluding one of his articles on India while on an expedition to Mongolia he wrote:

"O, Bharata all beautiful, let me send you my

heartfelt admiration for all the greatness and inspiration

fill thy ancient cities and temples, thy meadows, deobans,

thy sacred rivers and the Himalayas".

His greatest heritage left to posterity are his paintings and writings, His writings comprise some 27 volumnes besides innumerable essays and articles. His better know books are :-

Collected Works, Flame in Chalice; Altai Himalaya, Heart of Asia, Realm of Light, Fiery Stronghold, Shambhala, Paths of Blessing, Gates into the Future, Himalayas - Abode of Light.

His paintings number over 7,000 dispersed throughout the whole wide world in museums and private collections. In India Father's paintings are in many public collections, viz at the Kala Bhavan, Banaras; Trivandrum Museum, Allahabad Museum and Chandigarh Museum.
(Condensed)

SVETOSLAV ROERICH

NIFT - PREMIER FASHION INSTITUTE OF ASIA

Fashion is not something new to India. It was a well developed concept in Mughal era. The women of the court paid personal attention to developing fashion trends and groomed their progeny to carry the task further. The caste-bound social stratification had its own defined diversity of fashions for each group, but there was little scope for rearranging or altering the specified dress codes of different communities. When India became a sovereign state, and the princely states merged with the Indian Republic, court patronage to faschion disappeared.

Therefore a strong need was felt to establish a national centre to develop and train fashion designers who could explore and exploit the potentials of vast available reserves in the country and withstand healthy competition from established fashion leaders of the world.

Consequently, the National Institute of Fashion Technology, know in brief as NIFT, was established in 1986 with the staus of anautonomous body under the Ministry of Textiles. The initial collaborative support to establish the institute came from the Fashion Institute of Technology, New York, USA, which continues even today in the form of faculty exchange programmes.

Just four years after its inception, NIFT graduates were invited to various international platforms to participate in prestigious shows such as Air France sponsored Young Designers Contest, Asia pacific show, smirnoff Design Contest in U.K. and Makuhari Grand Prix in Japan.

NIFT entered into wide-ranging and long-term pacts with the Nottingham Trent University (NTU), U.K. and FIT, New York. To day NIFT as a fashion institute is capable of

organizing international conferences. One such conference "Texpressions" was organized in 1998.

A number of exhibitions, fashion shows, workshops, participation in the Festivals of India abroad, major international shows and competitions provide diverse interactive platforms to NIFT alumni.

NIFT has introduced a wide-range of course that allow the students to creatively handle various media such as fabric, leather, jute and other materials.

Dr. CHARU SMITA GUPTA

NIRMAND - THE TEMPLE -TOWN OF HIMACHAL

Nirmand, in the picturesque state of Himachal Pradesh, is a sprawling village where the mythical saint Parshurama is said to have established the sway of the Brahmins, the upper-caste Hindus. It is located on the left bank of the river Satluj, about 700 metres above its water level, perched as it is on the mountain top. The local Himachalis have a reason to be proud of Nirmand which is considered by them to be as sacred as Varanasi is for the Hindus inhabiting the rest of the country.

As one walks up and down the village from one corner to another, at almost every step one is greeted by a shrine, large or small. In fact the largest number of temples, both timber and lithic, are seen only in this holy centre of pilgrimage that attracts the multitudes from all over the country. Walking past clusters of miniature shrines made of stone with their curvilinear spires, and a *gomukh* spouting water, one is made aware of the religious significance of this place.

Numerous kings and emperors, among them an emperor of Kanauj, - one of the forebears of Harshavardhana (A.D. 606-647), were tempted to lavish bounties and endowments on stone temples, some of which were even erected by them, as early as the sixth century. Today, fragments of their architectural portions and sculptural reliefs are seen preserved here and there in the temple compounds, or reused in the residential dwellings of the local people.

Long before the emperors of the Gupta or post-Gupta dynasties, Nirmand is a pre-Harappan and Harappan site. Archaeological excavations conducted in the village have yielded Harappan period artefacts. The period of Rishi parshurama is believed to be a thing of hoary antiquity, belonging to the realm of myth and legend.

There are numerous Vishnu, Shiva and Durga temples all around that contain a large number of sculptures that may arouse the interest of lovers of antiquarian objects. The Thakurdwara, a small temple enshrining a life-sized stone statue of Vishnu accompanied by his consort Lakshmi, is well worth a visit. The statue carved in the Prathihara style dates from the tenth century, and is a competent example of the workmanship of the highly talented local sculptors. The figures of Vishnu and Lakshmi are slim, dainty and elegant, perfectly proportionate, and display none of the defects seen commonly in the Prathihara sculpture from other provinces.

DR. SUBHASHINI ARYAN

NIZAMUDDIN AULIA : THE ENLIGHTENED SAINT

Nazam'ud -Din Auliya transformed Sufism into an institution. Hitherto, Sufism had been aimed at individual spiritual salvation and training; he turned it into a mass movement. He also raised the Chistiya order to a pan-Indian position. It was mainly through the disciples of Nizam'ud-Din Auliya that this order spread far and wid in the various provinces of India.

Nizam'ud-Din Aulia was born in Badaun in Uttar Pradesh in 1244 A.D. (640-41 A.H.). His name was Muhammad but he came to be known as Nizam'ud-Din. His grandfather had migrated to india from Bujhara under the stress of the Mughal invasion of that region. His father died in his childhood. His mother, Bibi Zulekha, a lady of fervent piety, brought him up and moulded his thought and character.

At the age of sixteen, he came to Delhi to complete his education where, despite acute poverty, he pursued his studies with single-minded devotion. When there was nothing in the houst to eat, his mother would say, "Nizam'ud-Din, today we are the guests of God".

At the age of twenty, he left for Ajodhan (Pak Patan) and became a disciple of Saikh Farid'ud-Din Ganj Shakar. Three years later the Saikh appointed him his chief successor and directed him to settle in Delhi and work for the expansion of the Chistiya order.

Nizam'ud-Din Auliya was an erudite scholar of the "*Hadith*" with a deep insight into Islamic jurisprudence. He had his own peculiar ways of instruction. He did not advise any visitor directly, but referred to his problems indirectly and suggested remedies through ancedotes and parables.

He gave a revolutionary direction to religious activity by emphasizing that service to mankind brought greater spiritual reward than mere formal prayers. He believed in overcoming evil by good for the insolent and by non-violent and pacific ways towards those inviting retaliation. He took up the task of bringing happiness to the hearts of men. Such noble thinking endeared him to the people.

Laying great emphasis on renuciation, Auliya said that a man should renounce the world and not concern himself with anything pertaining to it. Prayers and fasting were of little concern to him, and a love of the world made them worthless.

He held in high esteem those holy men of any religion who showed a non-discriminatory attitude in the distribution of food. His own *langar* (community kitchen) was open to Hindus and Muslims alike. On one occasion, when Auliya was strolling with Amir Khusrau on the roof of the *Jamat-i-Khana,* he sighted a group of Hindus at worship. Greatly impressed with their devotion, he remarked to the Amir, "Every community has its own path and faith, and its own way to worship".

Nizam'ud-Din Auliya approach to religion emanated from his concept of God. For him, God was an all-embracing Reality present in his ethical, intellectual and aesthetic experience.

Nizam'ud-Din Auliya was a firm believe in pacifism and non-violence. Violence, he said, created more problems than it solved. He believed that in forgiveness and large-hearted tolerance lay the supreme talisman of human happiness. He addressed his disciples to be good even to their enemies and very often he would recite the following verse:

He who is not my friend, may God be his friend,
And he who bear ill-will against me.
may his joys (in life) increase.
He who put thorns in my way on account of enmity
May every flower that blossoms in the garden
of his life, be without thorns.

He breathed his last on 18 Rabi'ul Thani, 724 A.H. (1325 AD). He was laid to rest in an open space. Sultan Mohammad bin Tughlaq built a dome over the grave of the Auliya. In later period, it was renovated. The area where the tomb is located is now known as Basti Hazrat Nizam'ud-Din.

Throughout the centuries, people irrespective of their religion have paid respectful homage to his memory. His *khankah* is situated by the side of the river Yamuna behind the present day Humayun's tomb, in the area of Ghiyaspur. It now comprises of a hall in the centre with two small rooms on its sides. Food is still distributed to visitors and inmates round the clock.

NASIR RAZA KHAN

NORAH RICHARDS

Norah Richards, a famous cultural exponent of British origin, had a great attachment to India. She was born on 29 October, 1876 in Ireland. Educated in Belgium, Oxford and Sydney, Norah Richards visited India for the first time with her husband, Prof. Phillip Ernest Richards who taught English at Dayal Singh College at Lahore. She was credited with publications of plays including Sati (1914) and Bharat Varsha (1918). In 1935, she adopted the village Andretta in Kangara valley. She taught the native villagers to be practical and self sufficient and initiated them into "growing more trees an more food". With her heart in theatre, Norah not only encouraged an annual theatre festival involving leading personalities like Prithiviraj Kapoor, Zora Sehgal and Prof. Jayadayal, but also offered them pieces of land at throw away prices. She started the Saraswati Summer School for the local villagers to provide a meeting ground in natural surrounding for the mutual stimulation of those interested in art society, literature and drama.
(Adapted)

SOMA BASU

NUTAN : THE COMPLETE ACTRESS

Nutan, whom death snatched away from her family and her legion of fans in early 1991, was one of Hindi cinema's three top-notch female incons, particularly in the 1950s and the 1960s. She, like Nargis and Meena Kumari, was distinguished for her strong screen personality, versatility and intensely emotional acting. The cognoscenti, however, singled her out as the most perfect actress and indeed one of a kind. Ace filmmaker

Manmohan Desai described her as "the most versatile actress of the Indian screen. The best ever".

She first appeared as a child star at the age of nine in *Nala Damyanti* 1945); in which her mother Shobhana Samarth and Prithviraj Kapoor played the lead roles and which was directed by Nutan's father, Kumar Sen Samarth, who was a qualified cinematographer.

In 1950, Shobhana Samarth started her own production unit called Shobhana Pictures and produced her maiden film *Hamari Beti*. While the ever-popular hero Motilal and she played husband and wife, Nutan acted as their daughter. Her younger sister, Tanuja (mother of the current successful heroine Kajol), who was later known for her natural acting, also made her debut in the same film as a child artiste.

Nutan began to be noticed as an upcoming heroine and Ravindra Dave, the director of Pancholi Pictures, cast her in *Nagina* (1951) opposite Nasir Khan, Dilip Kumar's younger brother. The film, which was a suspense-filled thriller and for which C.H. Atma sang some memorable solos in the great K.L. Saigal's mould under the musical duo Shankar-Jaikishan, ran well throughout the country and Nutan's role was well appreciated.

By a funny coincidence, Nutan herself, who was still in her midteens, was denied an entry into the cinema-hall where *Nagina* was being exhibited as the then Central Board of Film Censors had accorded an "A" (Adult) certificate to the movie;

Later, in the same year, she featured in the much acclaimed *Hamlog* in which she played a lean and thin T.B. patient. *Sone ki Chioya* (1958) and *Parbat* followed. Meanwhile, the box office success of *Baarish* and *Paying Guest* (1957), in both of which she appeared opposite Dev Anand, catapulted her to the top. In 1963 she featured as the leading lady in two diametrically opposite roles, viz., *Bandini*, which was a serious film, and where she played a murdress, and *Tere Ghar ke Saamne*, a light-hearted entertainer.

Nutan was a veteran of over a hundred films including *Anari, Chhalia, Kanahiya* and *Dil Hi To Hai* (opposite Raj Kapoor); *Sujata, Milan* and *Khandaan* (Opposite Sunil Dutt); *Saudagar* (opposite Amitabh Bachchan) and *Karma* (opposite Dilip Kumar). She paired with Shammi Kapoor in *Laila Majnu*, Basant and Laat Sahab, with Kishore Kumar in *Dilli Ka Thug* and Bharat Bhushan in *Shabab*. Films known for her outstanding performances include *Main Tulsti tere Angan Ki, Saraswati Chandra* and *Maa Aur Mamta*.

She won the first Filmfare award for convincingly playing the role of a rebellious repressed girl in Amiya Chakroborty's *Seema*(1955). Bimal Roy's *Sujata* and *Bandini* also brought her the same award for her very sensitive portrayals of a low caste orphan and a wronged woman, respectively, who in a fit of rage kills her long lost husbands second wife. *Milan,* which was embellished by lilting songs sung by Mukesh and Lata Mangeshkar to the tunes of Laxmikant Pyarelal, also fetched her the coveted award.

Nutan also acted in her home production *Soorat Aur Seerat* based on an idea by her mother and directed by her husband, Rajnish Bahl. The film contrasted physical beauty which is skin-deep with the eternal beauty of the soul, as visualised by a blind man and later when he regains his vision.

Towards the end of her life when she was afflicted by the cancer and the premonition of an impending death haunted her, she turned more and more towards God and even composed and sang some 'Bhajans (devotional songs). Earlier, in *Chhabili* she had herself sung the song, "*Ae mere humsafar! Rok apni nazar*" (O my co-traveller ! rein in your glances).

She also earned further admiration from her fans for her role of *Kaliganj Ki Bahu* in the Doordarshan produced tele serial *Mujrim Haazir*.

Many of Nutan's roles whether as a heroine or as character actress, remain etched in peoples' memory. Truly, once saturated with the demands of a challenging role, she would come out with her best emotional self, displaying an unmatched competence.

B. M. MALHOTRA

"O"

OBJECTS D'ART - A UNIQUE COLLECTION

The city of Pune houses a number of private collections by the connoisseurs of art. among them is the award-winning private collection of Crystalware of Phiroz Hataria. Hataria's collection of over five decades speaks volumes for his love for collecting exquisite, priceless pieces of crystalware from world famous mastercraftsmen. There are gold salvers crested with faultless crystal grapes, gold hangers for things as mundane as shaving and tooth brushes, crystal bull, love birds, decanters, liquor glasses, fruit and ice bowls and bowls of various shapes and sizes which line up the immaculately organised, mirrored closets, each in itself a superb piece of craftsmanship. There are cuckoos and crystal parakeets, life-sized marble statues, icons, figurines and lamps from Italy; Ming and other vases from China, France and other countries. A 70-kg plus brass swan complete with lotus buds and flowers adores the central lobby of his residence turned museum. Golden pens, ink wells, telephones, bathroom fittings in gold and pristine glass all seek one's attention. Crystal spoons, ice buckets, paper weights, crockery and cutlery from Armani, Soga and other world famous dealers simply transport one into a world beyond the ordinary. The collection is something to be seen to be believed.

Hataria's love for things beautiful dates back to 1920s. Inheriting nothing from his father who was in business, he acquired the taste for collecting exquisite things.

ANIL MEHROTRA

ODISSI DANCE : THE NRITTA AND NRUTYA

The history of Odissi dance is largely the history of the Devadasis (dancing-girls) attached to almost all the important shrines of Orissa. A considerable number of inscriptions testify the consecretion of dancing-girls to the temples. The practice of consecrating dancing girls in honour of Gods was at one time prevalent throughout India and it began in Orissa with growth of Saiva temples at Bhubaneswar. The Magheswar Temple inscription (1045-1190 A.D) describes the consecration of dancing girls very eloquently.

Odissi claims to be 2000 years old and true inheretor of Natyasastra traditions. About 108 basic dance limits (Karanas) of Natya Sastra are found in Odissi. Odissa is a highly stylised dance, with strict rules governing every aspect of its rendering. As the dance once supplied the inner rhythms of harmony to architecture of Orissa which abounds with thousands of daning images, Odissi is full of sculpturesque poses known as *Bhangis*. Mostly these *Bhangis* are based on "Tribhanga" of three bend concept of Hindu iconography. This feminine pose is mostly approved with three bends in the body, the first caused by the crossing of the legs, the second by a curvature at the waist and the third by an inclination of the head to one side, generally to the left. Moreover in pure and decorative dance items of Odissi, where there is no meaning to convey, importance is given to the stance, the bodyline and the manner or performing. The movements are soft and lyrical. All these combine to build up the elaborate grace and charm, the fundamental characteristics of Odissi.

Odissi has a rich repertory and embraces both Nritta (Pure Dance) and Nrutya (interpretative dance). Generally both these elements are found together, though in different measures in the different items of the repertory. The items are *Mangalacharan, Batu, Nritya, Pallavi Abhinaya* and *Mokshya Nata*. In all these items the music is sweet and melodious, The Mardala, a drum, the Gini, a pair of cymbals and a flute provide the accompainment. The songs are in Sanskrit mostly from Geeta-Govinda on Oriya compositions of the poets of medieval period.

The three Gods, Srikrishna, his elder brother Balaram and their sister Subhadra are Worshipped at the Jagannath Temple. Which dates back to the eight century A.D.

Krishna is but Jagannath; let all remember that he is the Supreme Being i.e. the incarnation of God.

You having taken the ten forms or
incarnations of God Himself, O,
Krishna; I bow to thee.

The above are the exact words with which the Oddisi, as also Mahakavi Jayadeva prayed to his deity at the temple of Jagannath at Puri in the twelfth century A.D. The inspired poet, creator of the lyrical dance-drama Gita Govinda used to pray to Sri Jagannath, the Lord of the Universe, everyday, singing his own classical creation. In Gita Govinda, the subject matter is the heavenly love (Aprakrita Preme) of Sri Radha and Sri Krishna. Shrimati Padmavati, the saintly wife of poet Jayadeva, used to accompany the hymn of the poet-singer with inspired dance offerings in oddisi style. This convention is kept up even to this day when the Maharis (Devadasis) dance before Lord Jagananth's shrine to the accompaniment of the same song from the poet Jayadeva's immortal classic Gita Govinda. This ritualistic singing of Gita Govinda at the Sri Mandir of Puri was first introduced by Maharaja Narasingha Dev-II in the thirteenth century A.D. The accompainment of Mahari dancing also was his innovation.

The Gurus who are more prominent in the field of Odissi Dance are Guru Pankaj Charan Das, Guru Kelucharan Mahapatra, Guru Deva Prasad Das and Guru Mayadhar Rout. Most of the well known dancers are the disciples of these Gurus. Madhvi Mudgal, Protima Bedi, Sanjukta Panigrahi and Indrani Rehman are the principal dancers of 20th Centuries.

FOLK DANCES OF ORISSA

Orissa is the proud possessor of a large variety of folk dances which are of great beauty and variety. They are closely associated with fairs, fetivals, marriages and religions ceremonies in fact, with the whole life of the people. Besides the dances performed on auspisious occasion, there are dances to appease evil powers that bring misfortune and to please good powers that bring good fortune. There are also dances solely for self entertainment. Each is distinguishable by its variety of movement, form, gesture, constume and music. All the them menifest different styles derived from the local traditions and the social environment.

CHHOW DANCE

Mayurbhanj Chhow has a vast repertory of over hundred dances. Excepting the earlier dances with heroic characters, thematically it draws substaintially from the Ramayana and the Mahabharata. Many themes are also drawn from the Krishna legend. The dance is more famous for its group numbers sometimes having more than twenty characters at a time.

When Chhow was exclusively under the royal patronage, it was being presented to the audience only once in a year for three consecutive nights during the last three days of the Hindu New Year coming in Mid-April. But the undervelolped villages groups used to perform during festival which has the religious sanction.

As the dance is full of acrobatic stunts in which the dancerrs are required to balance their feet, the dance is held in the open ground specially prepared with soft earth and sand.

A performance of Chhow Dance beings with a musical prelude with intense drumming know as Ranga Vadya. This short piece of vigorous music charges the atmosphere and the dancers get inspired.

PAIKA NRUTYA-BATTLE DANCE

Most of the Paika villages of Orissa, spread all over the state have maintained the older tradition of Paika Akhanda the village gymnasium - where young people assemble in the evening after the day's work. Along with traditional physical exercises, they dance with sword and shield in hand to the acccompaniment of the countrydrum. The primary aim of this dance was the development of physical excitement and, consequently cour-age, in the dancing warriors.

GHOOMRA DANCE

Ghoomra is a typical drum. It is just like a big pitcher with a long stem made of clay. The mouth is covered with the skin of a *godhi* (a reptile). When played with both hands, it produces a peculiar sound quite different from other varieties of drums.

DALKHAI

Though Dassehra is the occasion of Dalkhai, the most popular-folk-dance of western Orissa, its performance is very common on all other festival such as Bhaijauntia, Phagun-Punai, Nuakhai, etc. This is mostly danced by young women of Binjhal, Kudi, Sama and some other tribes of Sambalpur, Bolangir, Sundergarh and Dhenkanal districts of Orissa in which men join them as drimmers and musicians. The dance is accompanied by a rich orchestra of folk music played by a number of instruments known as Dhol, Nisan, Tamki, Tasa and Mahuri. However, the Dhol played controls the tempo while dancing if front of the girls. (Condensed)

DHIRENDRANATH PATNAIK
K. C. PATNAIK

ONAM

Most important and grandest Hindu festival of Kerala; held in Chingam (August - September); according to the legend in the *Puranas*, Bali, the Asura king, promised Vamana (Vishnu in the form of a dwarf) every-thing as a sacrificial gift but Vamana asked only for a piece of land he could cover in 3 strides, to which Bali agreed; no sooner had the sacrificial water been poured on Vamana's hands than he became a giant and in 2 strides covered earth and heaven, leaving no space for taking the 3rd; seeing his predicament, Bali offered his own head for making the 3rd stride; Vishnu was so pleased that he made him king of the Asuras in Patal-loka (the nether regions); at Bali's request, he allowed him to come up to earth to see his people once a year and it is because the people of Kerala believe that Bali visits them on this day, that this festival is celebrated; when beautiful floral decorations are made to welcome him, feasts are prepared and games and other types of entertainment organised, the chief being the famous water festival, with its Vallumkali (snake-boat race) held at different places, the best being at Aranmulai and Kotayam; each long, graceful snake-like boat is rowed by 100 oarsmen to the beat and rhythm of symbals, drums and songs, the day ends with girls dancing round the traditional brass lamp and with much rejoicing.

B. N. SHARMA

OOTTUKKADU VENKATASUBBA IYER

Venkatasubba Iyer is believed to have lived in the latter part of the 17th century. He was born at Oottukkadu, a village 12 km south of Kumbhakonam in Tajnavur District of Tamil Nadu. He was a mystic, poet, vaggeyakara and a practiotioner of Yoga. He spent most of his time in meditation on the Divine Mother, and in singing and dancing in ecstasy before his favourite deity, the Kalianartana Krishna at the Oottukkadu temple. He was an adept in Natya Sastra.

He has composed a large number of songs in Tamil on Balkrishna which are known as Krishna *Ganam*. He has also composed songs on Muruga (subrahmanya).

ORCHHA - A MEDIEVAL SPLENDOUR

Situated 19 kilometers south of Jhansi, on the Jhansi Khajuraho highway in the Indian state of Madhya Pradesh, Orchha is the city of palaces, temples and monuments. This small stretch of land along the river Betwa has witnessed an interesting blend of aesthetics and spiritualism. Founded in the 16th century by the Bundela Rajpur king Rudra pratap, Orchha remained the capital of Bundelas till 1783. The structures built here during 16th and 17th century are in excellent state of preservation and speak highly of the fine workmanship of its proud creators. One can also see here some of the finest piece of the Bundela school of painting.

The city saw its golden period during the first half of the 17th century. Mughal Emperor Jahangir visited Orchha in 1606 and to commemorate his visit to the city, the famous Jahangir Mahal was commissioned. This spectacular building has a tiered structure crowned by innumerable chartries.

Adjacent to Jahangir Mahal is a rather simple looking Raj Mahal, built by king Madhukar Shah, a deeply religious person. The plain exteriors of this building are contrasted beautifully by the rich interiors which are decorated with bold, colourful murals on a variety of religious themes.

Another interesting palace here is the Raj Parveen Mahal. Named after the beautiful paramour of Raja Indramani, this small structure has an interesting legend attached to it. It is said that Akbar was so captivated by the beauty of Raj Parveen that he requested her to be sent to Delhi. The purity of her lvoe for Indramani, however remained unchanged and won her a reprieve from the great Mughal who respectfully sent her back to Orchha. This two-storeyed brick structure was meant to be a pleasure resort or the rulers of Orchha. The height of the palace was deliberately kept low to merge it with the surrounding trees.

The aesthetic sensibilities of the Bundelas are well reflected in the beautifully-laid out "Phool Bagh", a formal garden complex. The most remarkable feature here is a subterranean structure, used by the rulers as a summer retreat, and its ingenious water ventilation system connecting it with bowl-like structure called "Chandan Katora".

The droplets of water from the fountains of "Chandan Katora" filtered through to the roof, stimulating rainfall in the subterranean structure.

The most exquisite of Orchha's well paintings can be seen at the Laxmi Narayan temple. Walls and ceiling of the temple are full of murals which are in excellent state of preservation with the colours retaining their vividness.*

SANDEEP SAXENA

ORISSA : LAND OF TEMPLES

Orissa, the land of temples occupies a unique place in the realm of art and architecture. The magnificent temples of Orissa and their age-old tradition, reminds one of the rich cultural heritage of the State. It is a monument to the inherent aesthetic legacy of the people. An unbroken tradition of artistic development can be seen from the 7th century Parasurameswar Temple of Bhubaneswar, to the much later Sun temple of Konark. The Jagannath *dham* is one of the four *dhams* of India.

MUKTESWARA TEMPLE

The Mukteswar Temple (C 950 AD) at Bhubaneswar is a gem of Orissa architecture. Here the early architectural tradition blended with new architectural design, new art, new conceptions of cult images. A *torana* an arched gateway is a unique feature of this temple. The interesting feature of this temple are the fine interlacings of a minute design, resembling a *chaitya* window, which executed with unusual skill, takes the form of a very rich fret-work, rare in its appearance in Orissa. The temple dedicated to Lord Shiva Mukteswar, is carved with figures of ascetics in various poses of meditation and scenes from the stonehouse of Indian fables, the *Panchatantra*.

RAJARANI TEMPLE

The Rajarani temple (C 100 AD) is an essay in grace and poise and is particularly interesting in that it has no presiding deity. The name of the temple is supposed to be derived from th red-gold Sand-stone used and is intricately carved with figurines in various stages of daily chores.

LINGARAJA TEMPLE

The Lingaraja temple (11th Century AD) dominates the skyline of Bhubaneswar from as far away as 15 km and exhibits architectural skill of the Orissan temple at its best. This temple was constructed in 11th century at the site of an old seventh century shrine. Dedicated to Lord Shiva linga here is unique in that it is a Harihara linga-half Shiva and half Vishnu.

JANGANNATH TEMPLE AT PURI

Puri is the hallowed seat of the Hindu religious deities Lord Jagannath, Subhadra and Balabhadra. It is one of the most sacred places of Hindu pilgromage. It consist of four chambers - *Vimana, Jagamohan, Natamandir* and *Bhoga Mandap*.

The temple has four colossal gates and two large compound walls. The temple was built in 12th century by the Ganga King Chodagangdev. The Jagannath temple stands on a raised platform popularly known as Nilasaila. The Vimana rises to a height of 218'8" from the ground level.

Of the myriads of sculptural panels attention is drawn the panels of Bhoga Mandap and Nata Mandap such as rowing of boat with the goddess inside, Ganga and Yamuna with their Ayudhas and in the recently exposed surface of the Jagmohan and Vimana the 24 Avataras of Vishnu, Krishnalila scenes, etc. The Lakshmi temple with three chambers contemporary of the main temple, the Nursimha temple, the temple of Vimla and other temples and shrines give a panoramic picture of the Hindu world.

SUN TEMPLE AT KONARK

The sun temple of Konark known as the Black Pogoda, is the grandest achievement of the Kalinga school of architecture. It was built by Narasimha Dev in about 1255 A.D.

This crowning piece of Orissa architecture and sculpture is a poetry in stone. The *Mukhasala* or entrance hall continues to interest both devotees and visitors. The separated *Natamandir* here is a new architectural feature. The *Jaganmohan* and *Deul* are conceived as a huge *ratha* of the Sun god drawn by wheels arranged in pairs at regular intervals.

KHICHING TEMPLE AT MAYURBHANJ

Kichakeswari is the presiding deity of Khiching temple entirely built of cholorite slabs. Closeby, a plethora of temples - some abandoned while some others still living - which bear testimony to the master masons of Kalingan style. The museum at Khiching possesses rare and historically valuable specimens of art and sculpture.

BALDEV JEE TEMPLE AT KENDRAPARA

Kendrapara is an important place from the religious part of view. This sacred city is widely regarded as Tulasi Khetra and the presiding deity is Lord Baldev. It has been revealed from puranas that Lord Baldev killed the demon Kandarasura who was ruling at Lalitagiri and married his daughter Tulasi. Rasabali one type of sweet and potalipitha (cake) is the famous Prasad of this temple. (Condensed)

ORISSA HANDICRAFTS : MIRRORING A HERITAGE

Orissa is famous for its traditional crafts, cottage industries and cultural heritage. Most of these crafts, apart from being distinguished for considerable utilitatian value, are objects of artistic excellence. These items mirror the excellent standard of life, aesthetic sense of the people and above all the rich heritage of Orissa. These handicrafts have thrived for centuries.

Stone carving is an age-old craft and constitutes a major part of Orissan handicrafts. In the decoration of the ancient temples, the carvers acquired superb technical skill. The carved products include replicas of temples, images of gods and goddesses, the Konark wheel, horse and decorative figures like *alasa kanya* (indolent damsel), *salabhanjika* (lady leaning against a sal branch), *surasundari* (heavenly beauty), *lekhika* (lady writing a letter) etc.

Similarly, wood carvings of Orissa are equally popular. These are executed in a style blending folk and classical forms with a special feature of colour paintings on the wooden objects. A variety of decorative and utilitarian objects like toys depict animals and birds, real and mythical, ornament boxes, bowls etc. A combination of folk and classical styles makes these objects unique in the field of Indian crafts.

Chitrakars or folk painters of Puri and Raghurajpur paint *patta chitras,* an indigenous type of painting which detes back to a remote past. *Patta Chitra,* though basically a folk style, has been influeced by classical oriya sculpture forms. The subjects depicted in the Patta Chitra mainly cover major Hindu gods and goddesses. This ancient craft of palm leaf illustrations present delicate mythological figures.

PATTA-CHITRA PAINTINGS

Patta-Chitra painting on canvas is a unique contribution of the folk artists of Orissa. These paintings have to their credit the aesthetic beauty of the Odissi culture, tradition and the picturesque landscapes. Since ancient times, Puri in Orissa has remained the only centre of Pata Chitra paintings, which focussed on Lord Jagannath worshipped as "Vishnu Vaikuntha". Lord Jagannath depicted as the source of all "avtaras" (incarnations). As these paintings mainly have the designs of Lord Jagannath, Balabhadra and Subhadra, it is obvious that the techniques of the Pata paintings originated from the art of painting the "Trinity".

However, there are remarkable varieties of Pata Chitra paintings. These include Sri Jagannath "Pati", a painting based on different episodes of Ramayana, Mahabharata and other Puranas. Also are Pata Chitras bades on Orissa folklores, modes of worshipping the gods and goddess and erotic Pata Chitra. All paintings bear ample evidence of the keen sensibility of the sharp perceptibility of an artistic mind.

To prepare Pata Chitra painting, the painter sticks two pieces of cloth together by means of a paste prepared from tamarind seeds, thus forming a 'Pati'. A powder is prepared from a soft claystone found in abundance throughout Orissa. It is again mixed with tamarind paste and is brushed on the 'Pati' is dried, it is rolled up and from this roll, pieces of 'Paties' are cut and utilised for the chitras. The colours used in this art are made from natural ingredients such as China clay, soft clay or chalk, conch shells, red stone etc. The black colour is obtained from charcoal powder; sea-shells, available in plenty on the vast seashores of Orissa provide the white colour.

Pata painting thus prepared speaks the language of its crator. Though it depicts a world of myths and gods, it is till a world of folk imagination, a piece of art.

Masks and toys of papier-mache are made in Raghurajpur, Puri and Jeypore of Koraput. These items are painted in bright colours. Beautiful toys with detachable limbs like nodding tigers, different types of masks are made in papiermache. Various types of decorative articles like masks, colour flowers are produced.

The applique work of Pipli is a hereditary craft. Brightly coloured patches of red, blue, black, white and yellow clothes are stitched together to form a colourful and harmonious pattern. Samana (conopies) and Chhatris (umbrellas) bear testimony to the magnificent applique tradition. These applique works are in great demand. Temples and other religious instirutions extensively patronised this art.

At the same time, potters still make earthern pots to be used in various religious and social functions. They are made in various shapes and sizes and are adorned with fish and flower motifs and geometrical designs.

The Orissan terracotta items provide the perfect counterfoil to the amazing legacy of stone carving. Horses, elephants, boats in terracotta are made to meet the local demands during festivals.

The artistic works on non-ferrous metals are one of the most ancient handicrafts of Orissa. The types and varieties of brass and bell metal products cover a vast number of items. Viz pots, temple accessories, ornaments, decorative wares and curios are some of the popular items. the fine engravings on brass and bell metal utensils, bronze bangles and pots are important aspects of Orissan art.

The daily-use articles like combs, flower vases, pen stands and decorative items are made of horn. The horn is polished smooth and then shaped into various forms.

Tarakashi, the silver filigree of Cuttack is noted for its delicateness and intricate workmanship. This art is ancient. Made of silver threads as fine as spider's web, jewellery and decorative pieces are known all over the world for their superb finish, fine foils, texture, snow glaze, delicate artistry and elegant craftsmanship.

A rich yellowish variety of grass reed *kaincha* is called golden grass. Beautiful mats, utility articles and decorative items are woven from this golden grass by the female folk. The durability and flexibility of these products are some of their special features.

As the tribals, the indigenous people of Orissa, constitute a vital percentage of the state's population, their crafts have special significance. Pottery, cane, bamboo, beads, grass and wood items, plaster and papier mache, stone and theatre crafts, dried flower, lacquer, Santhal and saora paintings and metal ornaments are some of their well-known crafts.

Apart from these items Zari works, lacquer work, cloth garlands, glass beads, camphor garlands, jute carpets, rush mats, seashell beads, *pital mach* (brass fish) of Belguntha, wooden toys of Paralakhemundi, Ganjappa playing cards, lifesize bamboo - made animals of Jeypore, terracotta toys of Umerkote, wooden elephants of Dharamgarh, cane and bamboo products of Phulbani, metal casting Dhokra and metal flexible fish constitute the vast and vibrant world of Orissa handicrafts.

MANGALA PRASAD MOHANTY

"P"

P.V. NARASIMHA RAO (B. 1921)

Narsimha Rao began dismantling the licence raj immediately after he became the country's ninth prime Minister in 1991. His programme involved slashing government regulation and red-tape, abandoning subsidies and fixed prices, and privatising state-run industries. In short, bringing down the Nehruvian economic edifice.

Such reformist zeal was surprising in a Congressman who had worked loyally with three generations of the Nehru Gandhi family. He supported Indira Gandhi in her split of the Congres organisation in 1969 and subsequently headed various ministries-notably earning kudos as foreign minister during Rajiv Gandhi's tenure.

Hindu fundamentalism became a significant force in national politics during Narasimha Rao's tenure as Prime Minister. But what really earned him most notoriety were the various corruption scandals that rocked the Congress - the party lost control of several major state governments. Narasimha Rao resigned as party chief in September 1996, and the following year he was charged with corruption and bribery.

A scholar-intellectual who once was chairman of the Telgu Academy, Narasimha Rao is fluent in six languages, his translated Hindi verses and books and has written fiction in Hindi, Marathi, Telgu and English.

PADUKA : AN EXHIBITION WITH A DIFFERENCE

The Bata Shoe Company of India runs a beautiful museum in Totonto, Canada where shoes from evey part of the world are displayed. A large section of the museum displays Indian footwear called "Paduka", it is not just an ordinary exhibition but also seks to link the physical with the spiritual.

"Paduka" is the name of India's oldest quintessential footwear. It is the Sanskrit word which comes from the root 'pada', meaning to walk or to go. In the Vedic times, the word 'pada' was added to personal names or titles as a token of respect, like "Narayanapada", "Devapada". From 'pada' originated words like 'padakatka', which is a foot ring. 'padatala' the sole of the foot, 'padayatra' or jouney on foot, 'padaka' meaning small foot, and many more. In Sanskrit 'Padaka' means a sandal and 'paduka' means shoe or slipper.

"Paduka" is also known as "Kharawan" in various parts of India. For over 5000 years, "padukas" have afforded ritual protection to holy men, gurus and brides. In its simplest from the 'paduka' is made of wooden board cut in the shape of a footprint with a post and knob at the front, which slips between the big and second toe. This ancient design is ideally suited to the Indian climate. Open and airy, it keeps the sole raised above the sun-baked ground. Made of sturdy durable materials "padukas" protect the feet from rocks and thorns. When made of ivory, inlaid wood and silver, "padukas" become ornaments in a bride's trousseau, serve as a ritual object of veneration for devotees or become votive offerings from the faithful. In many homes in rural India, particularly in the north, women who work in the kitchen wear "padukas" or 'kharawan'. When they go out of the kitchen, they wear other footwear. The "Padukas" are not normally used in the toilets or bathrooms. Often the priests are seen to wear "padukas" in the temples. Hence, by the nature of their use, "padukas" have acquired a sanctity.

The Bata Shoe Museum's permanent collection of rare Indian footwear is enriched by sculptures and miniatures from the Nation Museum, New Delhi, and courtly costumes of the Mughal empire from private collections in India. (Condensed)

MEENA BHANDARI

PAHARI ARTS AND CRAFTS

The artistic talent of Pahari people of Western Himalayan region is not only to be found in the '*Pahari Miniatures*' - the relics of the past, but it is also a vital force behind the folk creativeness. Imbued with the innate desire to add gaity and colour to the life, they contributed towards the evolution and development of various arts and crafts in Himachal Pradesh viz., Folk painting, Clay Images, Jewellery, Embroidery, Pottery, Weaving, Wood Work, stone work and scores of other handicrafts of the day to day utility. Influenced by the traditional ideals and legendry beliefs, Pahari folk painting is mainly a manifestation of religious emotions. During their festivals, the women give expression to their religious emotions on leaf, floors, walls, paper and cloth.

Leaf painting is done on arvi (colocasia esculenta) Leaves on '*Bachhdwah Dwadshi*' and '*Kajali Tritya*'. Both these festivals are celebrated for the welfare of family and the material wealth. On another festival named '*Bahula Chauth*' painting is done on bamboo winnowing basket locally known as '*soop*'.

On these occasions, women paint in red vermilion, rice paste or makol (white earth) animal and human figures and heavenly bodies etc. in accordance with the legends associated with these festivals.

On '*Hoi Asthami*' the image of goddess Hoi is painted on the wall. Women paint the Goddess in different forms. However the Goddess is painted in a squares are suggested, signifying her supremacy over the mortals. Heavenly bodies are drawn as a symbolic of cosmic unity.

On the occasion of Diwali, from the outpost of the premises to the altar, the entire pathway is profusely decorated with '*Makol*', '*golu*' of rice paste and other pigments by women. Foot-marks to inward direction are drawn, bounded by curvilinear floral decorations. The people believe that Lakshmi - the Goddess of wealth would visit their places at mid-night. They keep the doors open with burning lamps along the entire pathway throughout that night.

The decorations done on the occasion of Diwali has much in common with '*Rangoli*' of Maharashtra, "*Mandana*" of Rajasthan and "*Alpana*" of Bengal in style and theme.

During marriage a connubial painting called "*Kauhara*" or "*Dehra*" is executed on the wall. Sometimes such painting is done on paper or cloth so that is can be preserved for future use.

In addition to these, the decoration of interior and exterior of their homes with '*Golu*' (greyish earth) or '*Makol*' in various floral designs is indicative of the crative genious of Pahari folk. The unique way in which cowdung decoration is done on the floor called '*hangaiyan*' is something outstanding. These all amply glorify the creative skill of employing the humblest of materials in a very artistic way in an attempt to diversting life of all drabness.

CLAY IMAGES

The preparation of clay images for propitiatory and decorative purposes has a continuous tradition. Women prepare propitiatory clay images on the occasion of '*Haritalika tritya*', a festival associated with Shiva worship. According to the '*Bhavishyotar Purana*', the festival was first of all celebrated by Parvati.

On the day of festival women perform puja to these clay images, later to be distributed among the children. In addition to these propitiatory images, terracota images for various decorative purposes are made by the '*Kumbharas*' (potters) throughout the Pradesh. These images are usually moulded.

In Kinnaur and Lahul and Spiti districts, images are made on different occasions as bas- relief tabloids of Buddha and other saints in different '*mudras*' are prepared by pressing dough against a wooden mould and fixed on the walls of monastries. These images are made on different occasions as a part of Lamaisric tantric ritual introduced from Tibet.

JEWELLERY

Pahari people, particularly women, have a instinctive penchant for Jewellery. Besides gold, silver, ornaments of beads, sheels, flowers and coloured threads etc. are used. In Chamba even bangles and rings of horse hair and bamboo were made till recently. Some of the ornaments of traditional origin which are still in vogue are '**tonal**; '**tampan**', '**Kuntai**' and '**Zutti**' etc.

Most of the Pahari jewellery is inspired by nature. Tree creepers, leaves, buds, birds and animals etc. all have contributed their bit to shape it. "*Dod-mala*', '*Jo-mala*' '*Jhungrooli*', '*Kan-phool*'and '**Kach**' etc. are some of such ornaments. Other ornaments like '**Chauki**', '**tabiz**', '**tilles**' and '**Pazeb**' etc. are partly or completely influenced by the Mughal style. Enamelling on the ornaments was introduced by the Persians.

There is a great diversity of design and use of jewellery in the Pradesh. In Kinnaur, though one finds a dazzling profusion of ornament on head, ears, nose and neck, very little is left for the waist and nothing by way of foot-ornament. Similarly in Lahul and Spiti women have ornaments for head only called '**berag**'. It is a piece of felt studded with turquoise, silver talisman and corals etc. It is worn around the neck and hangs like a protective flap over the braided hair. The ornaments are here made of silver only. Pahari jewellery is rich in variety and form. People prefer few but heavy ornaments. But light ornaments are being preferred in urbanished areas.

EMBROIDERY

Once embroidery was a flourishing household industry offering livelihood to windows and destitute ladies. Now, though the production is not as such women have taken to it as a spare time hobby. They not only exhibit their creative skill on '**rumals**' but also on purses, bedsheets, pillow covers and scores of house-hold articles.

Gujjar ladies beautify their '**kamiz**' with rich embroidery in a contrasting combinations of different colours, and inset-tinsel pieces. The '**rumlas**' are called '**thapra**' and are still used as gift covers during marriages. Ordinarily, one side of the cloth is finished and the other side is covered with coarse lining cloth. But at times similar finished effects were achieved on both sides in running stitches. These stitches are locally called '**dora tanka**'.

POTTERY

The aesthetic talent of people is visible in their simple and indispenable earthenwares of wide range and variety. The shapes and forms of the pottery articles have mostly remained traditionally unchanged. Yet artistic pottery articles viz. jars, bowls, smoking cups, etc. are produced by the potters. The pottery here is unglazed. Resinous glazing is attempted by few potters of Kangra but the effect is temporary. Kangra pottery is most popular and famous for its fine finish, symmetry and strength in the Pradesh.

The potter beautifies his pots with superficial use of geometrical designs and floral motives. Figurative designs are rarely used. These designs are drawn on lips, neck portion and along the spheric line of the angular projection before the pot is fired. The pottery is usually brick red, black and grey in colour.

In Kinnaur, the primitive method of pottery is still practised. The potter does not use potters' wheel but shapes his pots by hand on the mould. A pot is moulded in two pieces and later jointed together.

WEAVING

Of all the crafts, weaving is perhaps the most common and old craft of this region. With great variety of design, colour and purpose, this craft has been promising industry throughout the Pradesh. At some places it has emerged into a big enterprise affording employment to many skilled weavers. The stuff, the design and the brightness in the use of contrasting colours coupled with artistic treatment of the job, are some of the qualities which have earned world-wide reputation for this craft.

The designs in the shawls are necessarily geometrical square formations filled with contrasting colours. In '**pattis**' (tweeds) and blankets, however, stripped or checked designs are preferred.

Though weaving is an accepted craft of the Pradesh yet we find only simple and hollow or stripped designs on the products of the outer region. On the other hand, excellent designs of great artistic merit are executed on the woollen products in the inner part of the Pradesh.

The woollen products of Kinnaur, Kulu and Chamba are reputed the best for their superior stuff, workmanship and artistic treatment.

WOOD WORK

The antiquity of wood carving is evident from the 7th century wooden temple of Chamba. Excellent temples embellished with exquisite carved structural elements are studded throughtout Himachal Pradesh. These all aptly signify the tradition of excellent wood work in the Pradesh.

Presently, though the traditional grandeur of wood work is on the decline yet fine decorative and utilitarian wooden articles like carved wooden doors and windows, decorative human and animal figures, face masks, table lamps etc. are produced at many places. In addition to these carved products, household articles are also made out of wood turning on crude indigenous lathers. Some of these products are *Kunda* (a wooden bowl), kosi (milk pot) paru (lotus shaped pot with lid), Kalas (tumbler) '**dongri**' (a storange pot) and scores of other articles. Mostly walnut wood is used for the preparation of these articles. Some of the excellent wooden products are preserved in Bhuri Singh Museum, Chamba and in Himachal Lok Sanskriti Sansthan, Mandi.

STONE WORK

Like wood work, stone carving is also a very ancient craft of the Pradesh. In the outer parts secores of stone temples with richly carved structural elements can be seen. But with the changing trends, this craft has almost been eclipsed. Few of the good craftsmen are still available in Chamba, Mandi and Kangra who prepare stone-wares of household use only and rarely anything by way of art product.

Today though Pahari painting are no longer made large collection of the past master like Nainsukh, Purkhu of Kanga, Mahesh of Chamba are found in museums of Chandigarh, Surich, Boston, London and New York. (Condensed)

O. C. HANDA

PAHARI MINIATURE PAINTINGS

The terms Pahari denotes a wide area around Sivalik Hills running through Poonch, Jammu, Basohli, Nurpur, Kangra, Haripur Guler and the mid-Himalayan areas like Ramnagar, Bhadarwah, Chamba, Kulu, Tehri Garhwal and so on. The language of the people of Pahari region is Dogri and its various allied forms. It is known from the records that there were about 38 States in the Pahari region. Out of which Basohli, Jammu, Nurpur, Kangra Chamba, were prominent. The art of painting which flourished in those States till the end of the 19th century is known as Pahari paintings or Pahari Miniatures. Since the beginnings of the 20th century, hundreds and thousands of such art pieces have come to light and their place in the history of world art has been established.

In these states different styles of painting originate under the patronage of local rulers.

Locally, the word style is known as Kalam, and therefore the word *Kalam* is being used for each style or school originated in different centres.

BASOHLI KALAM : EARLIEST MINIATURES

The oldest miniature, known so far of Pahari painting, is of the Basohli Kalam. Basohli is a Tehsil headquarter of Jammu Province of the Jammu and Kashmir State, situated on a low spur over looking the river Ravi, about hundred and thirty-two kms. from Jammu by road.

The Basohli Kalam originated in Basohli only and the earliest paintings come to us of Kripal Pal's atelier. The portraits and paintings, illustrating Bhanudatta's *Rasamanjari*, called *Chittarasamanjari*, are now in the collections of the Dogra Art Gallery (67 in number). Lahore Museum, Srinagar Museum. The Boston Museum and in other private collections. One of the miniatures belonging to this set bears the colophon. The inscription disclosed the date on which it was presented to Raja Kripal Pal of Basohli by the artist, Devi Dass, in the year 1694 A.D. These are the earliest dated pictures on paper of rectangular size, rich in colour. Their male and female figures are of peculiar facial types. Red and Yellow borders overlapped by the architecture and trees; shining beetle wings are stuck in the painted jewellery to produce the effect of raised emeralds. A monster head projecting from the base of the pavilion and the use of pure colour producing brilliant effects are the particular features of these paintings. In these early miniatures. The architecture dominates the picture surface. The sky line is very high and shell like clouds are painted horizontally in the narrow space of the sky and the whole composition moves around the surgace connecting individual objects or elements into one whole. The tree groves are arranged in semi-circular movements which gives a great movement to the whole arrangement.

BASOHLI : SECOND PHASE

In the second phase of this kalam, that is Raja Medhani Pal period, one the Gita Govinda paintings in which the architecture has no traces. The facial formula changed a little and the whole drama is enacted in the open air where sorrows and shadows have no place. Instead of the complicated designs of the early phase, these are marked by a love for simplicity and effective brilliant colours. The female as well as the male forms become simple and much of decorative element also avoided. Instead of earlier facial expression which was passionate, wild, bold, expressive and full of intensity a more round, calm and simple form was achieved. The dresses are light and transparent, many vacant spaces on the picture surface are left to accomodate air in the open landscape. In relation to the figure, the delienation of a forest or groove by circular trees occupying the main picture surface are highly stylized forms. Animals, trees, human beings and other things are peculiar characteristics of these miniatures. Aesthetically, both the phases of Basohli Kalam were of a period of creative activity, experimentation and formulation of new ideas. After these two phases, this kalam could not keep its purity intact and got influenced by the Mughal and kangra Kalams. Artists remained active in the centres of the Pahari painting till Gulab Singh ennexed the state in 1846 A.D. into his kingdom.

JAMMU KALAM

In Jammu Balwant Dev (or Singh) and his painter Nain Sukh Jasrotia were the first to establish a Jammu Kalam in which indigenous element is nowhere evident. It is clear from the known miniatrues of this kalam that there was no school of Jammu till circa 1748, Nadir Shah's invasion in 1739 A.D. compelled the traders and artisans from the plains to take refuge in the hill states. At this time Jammu was ruled by Raja Ranjeet Deo (1735/1781 A.D.) who gave shelter to so many people coming from plains, The youngest brother of Ranjeet Deo. Balwant Deo, was the person who is credited with originating the Jammu Kalam. Dated and undated miniatures of this great patron are the earliest survivals of this Kalam and painter Nain Sukh Jasrotia was the main figure of his Court as far as the creation of these miniatures is concerned. Two other painters Vajan Shah and Didi are also known to have worked in the service of Balwant Deo. The earliest dated painting of Balwant Deo belongs to they year 1748. Most of these painters were evidently good portrait painters. The studies of Raja Balwant Deo and people around him like musicians, singers, dancers, courtiers, attendants and even the animals and birds are very high order and show the refinement and subtelety of the then existing Mughal portraiture. Balwant Deo appears in these miniatures in almost every activity of his life. He is whown smoking, holding a court, examining a miniature, inspecting a horse, shooting at ducks, inspecting a construction of building, writing a letter and getting his beared trimmed. All this record is sort of diary of his life.

JAMMU : DECLINE

The Jammu Kalam of this period is markedly a Mughal off-shoot mixed with the local environments. But no successor of Balwant Deo could continue his work and take it to further heights as it happended in Kangra, with the result that a downfall started. After the death of Brij Raj Deo the Sikh influence extended to Jammu. The artists were ten forced to leave Jammu. After a span of about 40 years Maharaja Gulab Singh could patronize the artists again. A great number of paintings were painted in Jammu from circa 1830 to 1910 A.D. of which a collection of about five hundred paintings can be seen in the collection of Dogra Art Gallery, Jammu. Masters like Nand Lal, Ruldoo, Harichand, Channu and Jagat Ram Chhunia were the painters of this last phase. The *Kalam* which was established during the period of Gulab Singh and his son Ranbir Singh could not reach excellence of the previous kalam. Their common style consisted of simple two figure compositions like Radha and Krishna sitting in an arched balcony with flat background and horizontally place lower portion of the window. Radha and Krishna painted by Ruldoo are the simplest folk belonging to a timeless space. Ruldoo's pupil Hari Chand was mainly a painter of portraits (some of his portraits are done in three dimensions, light and shade in which photographic effect is attempted) and groups of gods and goddesses. Jagat Ram followed his master Hari Chand. Sansar Chand, who is a living artist in Jammu, was a student of Jagat Ram.

KANGRA KALAMS

Kangra Kalam flourished in the hill of Kangra and got the patronage of Sansar Chand, who had maintained an atelier of artists. In these years the Kangra Kalam culminated in the form of a highly refined miniature style of painting. Influenced by Mughal School of Delhi and Lucknow the paintings of this period are impressive in composition, rich in tones and tints of colour and the brush has gained excellence in its treatment, which no other kalam in the Pahari painting could surpass. The greatest works of this period were a series of illustrations of

Bhagawat Purana, the *Gita Govinda*, the Satsai of Bihari (1775-80) School flourished from 1770 to the end of 19th century some of the finest works were produced between 1775-1820.

CHAMBA KALAM

The Chamba Kalam was influenced first by Basohli and they by Kangra, Kulu has its own indigeneous kalam which was after wards influenced by Kangra. Guler also could not escape the influence of Kagra. In the west of Ravi, Poonch, Reasi, Ram Nagar and Ram Kot (Mankote) were the idioms of Jammu Kalam.

TRADITION AND INDIVIDUALITY

If Pahari paintings are discussed in the background of available miniatures, it will become clear that the Pahari artist was not devoid of individuality. He also never strayed far from the tradition to which he belonged. Therefore most of the Pahari paintings are within the framework of certain rules which were handed over from generation to generation. The Basohli artist disclosed the spiritual struggle of the soul through the exotic loveliness of colour and passionate feminine graces. His women were creatures of a world in which love outpoured of every thing. His hot colours expressing the endless warmth of the soul which is engrossed with love and passions. All his objects in the painting are timeless in a design of his own creation.

On the other hand, the Kangra Kalam is marked by delicacy and endless mixing of tones where calrn and cool passions dwell in the abode of light and shadows. The human beings are engrossed with the love and fulfilment of desire. The object of their adoration, in the beautiful setting of Pahari landscape, always remains their beloved. Pahari painting is a record of the spiritual longing, aesthetic urges, physical passions and social customs of the Pahari people between 17th century to the beginning of the 20th century. (Condensed)

V. R. KHAJURIA

PAINTINGS - DECCANI STYLE

Flourished Deccan Plateau; last quarter 16th century; reminiscent of contemporary Mughal School. Homogenous style, evolved, combination of Persian, Turkish, Indian elements, with distinct local flavour. Style patronized by the Sultans of Bijapur - Ibrahim Adil Shah II of Bijapur - distinguised. Splendid portraits of him, more lyrical, poetic in concept found - eg wonderful series depicting *ragmala* survives. Of illustrated manuscripts, important are *Nujun-u-ulum* and *Tarif-e-Shahi*, painted around 1565, in neighbouring state Ahmednagar. The Sultanate of Golconda; produced work high quality - eg manuscript of *Divan* of Muhammad Quli Qutb Shah, series of distinguished portraits, end of 17th century. State of Hyderabad; founded 18th century, headed by grandee of Mughal Empire, great centre of painting work reflects Golconda tradition; increasing Mughal, Rajasthan traditions.

PAINTING : ON GLASS

Painting on glass necessitates a different procedure than painting on paper or on solid opaque surfaces like wood. The picture which is generally coloured in tempera (non-transparent colours often thickened with white) is begun first with the brush lines and details, which when finished will appear uppermost. Then the larger areas of colour are brushed in these are generally flat except for the face and body, or in drapery where a summary fulness is achieved by shading. The "shading" is really a kind of modelling with a smooth gradation of colour which shows the roundness of forms and is not related to light and shade. Thus the usual painting process is reversed; details especially the finishing lines are done first and the large areas of colour afterwards, Gold, leaf, small sequins and other shining particles are used to imitate jewellery. Sometimes portions of the picture are mirrored with mercury. In some places metal foil or gold paper is fixed behind the picture and the portions of the picture left bare are seen as gold. The picture is then mounted with its unpainted side foremost, so that it is seen through the glass. The technique requires a certain amount of skill and can be quite laborious.

The glass painting style is an amalgam of the old and the new; we may consider the works "traditional" because they adhere to patterns and inconography which were accepted by both patrons and artists, and they can also be innovative depending on the freedom exercised by artists with varying gifts.

Indian glass painting is at once highly electric and roubustly native. T hough one may find the language of these pictures limited but it is expressive, lively and intelligible.

SUDHAMAHI REGUNATHAN

PAINTINGS AT AJANTA

Found rock-cut cave temples; belong to 2nd or 1st century B.C; style reminiscent of relief sculpture, *Sanci*. Also, remains of painting of 5th century A.D; decorated on walls and ceilings of caves, monasteries. Themes Buddhist; illustrate major events of Buddha's life, the *Jataka*, various divinities of expanding Buddhist patheon. The style, expansive, free, dynamic; graceful figures painted by accompanied brush; given body and substance by modelling in colour, by schematic distribution of light and shade. Narrative compositions, reflect maturity of contemporary sculpture eg large images of *bodhisatvas*, in cave 1, combine rich elegance, with spiritual serenity.

Except large, magnificent painting of dance scene, found rock-cut cave Bagh - hardly any other work survives.

Caves temples at Badami, Sittanavasal; probably of late 6th , 7th centuries AD, already echoses of style of 5th century, which appears died out this time.

PAITHAN PAINTING

A number of these story-tellers are also known to practise in the north, in Rajasthan for instance, where itinerant entertainers captivate the rural audience with narration from the epics illustrated with picture scrolls. Some of these scrolls may be as much as 12 metres long and can hardly be assimilated at glance. Indeed, the earliest surviving folk art pictures of this kind among them the Paithan paintings which are of particular importance evince certain stylistic affinities with such large wall paintings as have come down to us. While the continous pictorial sequence of the narrative suggests a direct connection with the compositions of the early Buddhist reliefs at Bharhut and Sanchi.
(Summarised)

ANJALI SIRCAR

PAITHANI SAREE - THE BEAUTY OF YORE

A small village on the banks of river Godawari in the state of Maharashtra has the distinction of creating exclusive sarees famed for the uniqueness of style. The village is paithan and the saree, named after it, is known as "Paithani".

About 56 km from Aurangabad, this home of the Paithani saree has produced silken, gold embroidered and in rich, vivid colours, sarees that have stood the test of time for over 2500 years. First mentioned in ancient Greek records dating before Christ, the Paithani is still the most celebrated textile of Maharashtra. It conjures up visions of the grandeur and pomp of Maratha rule, during which time it reached the Zenith of its popularity. The Peshwa had a special love for this fabric. In the 18th century, the entire town used to be involved in the making of the Paithani saree. Although today there are not as many weavers as there once used to be, enough people are found in the town who are engaged in this activity for generation and are keeping the tradition alive.

Down the centuries, method of weaving the saree has remained exactly the same - on wooden looms and without the help of any mechanical device. Only, in the earlier years the weavers would just count the threads to weave in the design whereas today they have the codes written down on paper. It was highly prestigious to own a Paithani in the days of yore, and the width and richness of the 'pallu' (the hanging end of the saree) decided a person's social standing. The maximum length of the embroidered 'pallu' was 18 inches and the more motifs on them, the better. It was also almost mandatory for the moneyed to display new Paithanis at family weddings. For the bride, a Paithani 'shalu' (a special wedding saree more ornate than the others) was a must. Even couplets which describe the elegance of these sarees are common feature of the folk songs of Maharashtra.

Sarees in vivid colours - blue, purple, magenta and interspersed with gold threads take shape and designs on the looms. One of the toughest motifs to weave in 'bandimor' which is woven on the 'pallu'. It essentially consists of four peacocks arranged in a circle, and takes an expert weaver anything between 18 to 24 months to weave. "Asavali" (vive and flower) 'narali' (coconut), 'akruti' (square floral motifs) and 'kalas Pakli' (a petal form) are some of the other old and favourite designs that adorn the Paithanis.

The Mughal influence on design can be seen in the motif of 'totamaina (parrots), 'humparinda' (pheasant) etc. It is said that the Nizam of Hyderabad was also a great admirer of this art, and his daughter-in-law added the Ajanta motifs to the already existing designs.

Pune was the centre of fashion in those days and orders for the Paithanis were received from almost all parts of the country. The Peshwas insisted that more gold be woven into the Paithanis.

Old Paithanis were woven with real gold threads, but in the modern day version, silver threads are coated with gold. The Paithani saree should never be stored on a hanger. It is best preserved wrapped in fine white cloth and put away in wooden boxes.

SHALINI MITRA

PALACE OF RAM NAGAR

Palace of Ramnagar, about 110 km north of Jammu city is located in a picturesque set up having a back-drop of lofty mountains with their luxuriant forest studded slopes. The sprawing palace is built on an elevation just out side the town. It has a·treasure of fascinating flush frescoes. Though Ram Nagar area was under Raja Suchet Singh but it was granted this as a fiefdom by Maharaja Ranjit Singh in 1820s. He left a significant art and architectural bonanza. The palace shows simplicity and solidity reflecting the synthesis of Mughal and Dogra architecture. Monuments are entered through a magnificial doorway flanked by alcoves decorated with flated tapering pillars. The Ramnagar frescoes have the colours of Basohli miniatures and the refined look of Kangra miniature.

PALACE ON WHEELS - THE ROYAL EXPERIENCE

Palace-on-Wheels, a joint venture of the Rajasthan Tourism Development Corporation and the Indian Railways, is undoubtedly the best way to explore and capture the grandeur pomp and pageantry of Rajasthan's royal past. Relaunched in September last year on the broad-gauge section of the Indian Railway, this new-look train is absolutely brand new and ensures full conformt of its privileged passangers. It replaces the earlier Palace-On-Wheels which used to be run on the metregauge section.

Completely self-sufficient, its public spaces include two restuarant coaches and a bar coach with an attached library. Deep veneered wood encases large picture windows through which guests can see the coutryside-of-a thousand battles slide effortlessly past. Inside, the lights glow intimately and stained glass mirrors reflect myriad images.

Soft music plays in the background as master chefs serve up superb meals and the bartender mixes are layered across the windows in a manner reminiscent of palaces, in colours that are traditional.

The 14 coaches are named after former Rajput states. Each evokes visions of those royal kingdoms. Each coach has four coupes, done in colours most reminiscent of that state, and highlighted by its royal emblem. Of the four compartments, two each feature double beds, the other two twin beds. A third bed, for an additional person or an accompanying child, is in the form of a fold away bed on a higher tier. Each compartment has an attached bath with running hot-cold water and showers, built in wardrobes, overhead the night lights, piped music, reading lights etc.

The furniture with its inlaid motifs has been specially create for the Palace-on-Wheels. All coaches and corridors are fully carpeted.

At the end of each coach is a separate lounge where passanger can relax when they wish to move out of their bedrooms. Here they can unwind with a book or magazine, engage in conversation, or simply watch as the panoramic vista of the great Indian desert unfolds.

The Maharaja and Maharani restaurants offer seats arranged in groups of twos and fours near the windows. Chefs in the attached pantry prepare.

BHARAT BHUSHAN

PALACE PAINTINGS OF CHAMBA

The mural paintings of the Rang Mahal, Chamba, have been conserved in National Museum, New Delhi. These paintings of the Rang Mahal, have been refixed in a room in the museum that is an exact replica of the palace room that housed the paintings. A painted verandah of the palace that had murals on its walls has also been recreated by the side of the room.

A PALACE OF MURAL PAINTINGS

The Rang Mahal was started to be built in Chamba, a small hill town about 76 miles by road from Pathankot, by Raja Umed Singh in the mid-18th Century. However it could be completed by his great grandson, Raja Chharat Singh, in the beginning of the 19th Century. At that time Rang Mahal was the nerve center of activity in Chamba and was the residence of the Raja. Later, however, it came into disuse as the ruler moved to another palace. Neglect of the older palace and the heavy rains of the hills soon had an effect on the building and the paintings inside.

DILAPIDATED CONDITION

For long the art world did not know the existence of paintings in the palace and its Pahari murals. After the discovery of these paintings attempts were going on to preserve these murals. The entire building was in need of structural repairs. The Joints of the palace roof and the walls had given way, plaster was falling and the paint was flaking. Probably once the entire palace was painted but now, besides a few panels here and there, only one room and one verandah had paintings on its walls. The rest of the paintings were already lost for ever.

For technical help to save the remaining paintings, the Union Ministry of Scientific Research and Cultural Affairs appointed a committee came to the conclusion that the preservation of the building is almost impossible to save the paintings, the wholescale removal of paintings was called for. The first step was to draw a plan of the painting's layout on the walls to help in the final setting up at the museum later on.

For actual removal of paintings two different methods were used, because the plasters on which the paintings were done were of two different types. In one room a 1" to 3" thick layer of hard lime plaster was laid, on which the painting was done. In this class of paintings it was found that the paint was adhering well to the lime plaster which itself was durable and therefore the paintings had been removed along with the plaster. The method has been described as "*plaster-detachment*" method. In the other class of paintings, found in a verandah of the palace, a white steatitic earth, locally known as 'makol' had been used as plaster, which was not adhering well on the plaster. More-over, steatitic plaster has no binding strength and as such it was thought desirable to remove only the paint layer leaving the loose and deteriorating 'makol' plaster back. The method is known as "*paint-stripping*" method.

In '*Plaster-Detachment' Method* First, a protective solution is applied to the surface of the paintings and then, two layers of cloth are pasted with a light adhesive. A wooden board of the size of the marked wall-section to be cut and removed in placed against the wall. The wall-section is cut with a saw and slowly working with long pointed and sharpened tools an attempt is made to loosen the plaster completely from the back. When this is accomplished the wooden board is gradually tilted along with the plaster. All, the four walls of the room, were thus removed, one by one, in sections. These sections were then carefully packed and sent to the museum laboratory in New Delhi.

For providing fresh support the removed plaster-panel is kept on a rigid table, face down and with the help of electric grinding wheels and hand-tools scrapped and thinned to a thickness of about $1/_4$". Fresh plaster is then poured at the back to strengthen the section. After the block is fully dry the facing is removed. All these section are then joined together edge to edge form the complete walls. In this fashion the four walls of the Rang Mahal room were recreated in the museum. The painted wooden ceiling of the palace room was also removed and has now been refixed in the new room.

In '*Paint-Stripping Method*' also too cloth facings are applied to a marked out section of the wall-painting surface with strong adhesive. The facing is allowed to dray for four or five days. It is then peeled off. If the adhension between the facing and the paint is stronger than the adhension between the paint and the plaster, the paint is detached with the facing. The excess plaster coming off with the paint is scrapped and new support prepared by pasting together two cloth canvasses is joined at the back of the paint. Again all the sections were joined together edge to edge to recreate the walls. The cloth facing applied to the surface of the painting in the beginning was removed with suitable solvents.

Finally, the yellowed varnish present on the surface of the paintings was removed in order to bring back the colours of the paintings to their original shades.

PATIENCE AND PERSERVERANCE

The final phase of the transfer of the murals from the Rang Mahal is over now with the completion of the reserting of the walls and the ceiling of the room and verandah of the painted palace in the National Museum galleries. (Condensed)

O. P. AGRAWAL

PANDAVAGIRI TEMPLE AT AYYKUNNU

Situated about 20 Km from Thrissur is a magnificent hill temple, the origine of which, according to legend, goes back to the time of the Pandavas. Set against the backdrop g paddy fields and shallow water basings, the hill te affords a very beautiful view of the valley down below.

The diety in the main temple is Devi or Parvati. Legend has it that this temple was built by Parasurama. The Pandavas, along with Draupadi, are said to have visited this place during their stay in the forests. The Pandavas did penance (Tapas) here and the Goddess, extremely pleased, blessed them. Drauppadi was granted the boon of 'Dheerga Sumangali' and victory for her husbands in the battle with the Kauravas. Thus the place come to be called "Pandavagiri".

It is believed that there are several caves in the hill but no excavation work has been undertaken so far to find out these ancient caves.

Today the temple is well known for the powerful diety of Devi. People pray her for the early marriage of girls, wealth and prosperity, and freedom from incurable diseases. Childless couples offer worship for getting children.

The Devi idol faces west. There is an inner and an outer 'prakara' around the temple. The architecture of the temple with tiled roof is typical of Kerala. In the outer enclosure there is a temple dedicated to Lord Ayyappa.

The temple was in a dilapidated condition for a long time. A few years back with the active involvement of Swami Bhoomandanda Tirtha of Narayan-ashram Tapovanam, the villagers have rebuilt it. The fortress like walls, which surround the temple, have been repaired.

In the rear side, down the clopes, lie the Narayananshrama Tapovanam of Swami Bhoomananda Thirtha. The Ashrama is set in sylvan surroundings, full of coconut trees. Discourses, mainly on the Bhagavad Gita, publication of books and spiritual Sadhana by the Ashramites are among the important activites of the Ashram.

S. V. V. RAGHAVAN

PANDIT HARI PRASAD CHAURASIA

Pandit Hari Prasad Chaurasia India's ace musician of the bansuri or flute, was born in a mofussil town of Allahabad in the state of Uttar Pradesh. He chose to master the bamboo flute and bring it up to concert prominence, at a time when the classical climate featured the sitar and the sarod with greater fervour. Even more unconventional was his choice of a *guru* or teacher. While others had dedicated themselves to the better known exponents of the Maihar School, namely Pandit Ravi Shankar and Ustad Ali Akbar Khan, Pandit Chaurasia has pursued relentlessly the favour of being initiated into this music though its relatively unknown guru, Ma Annapurna Devi. She was the brilliant musician daughter of the founder of the Maihar School, Baba Allaudin Khan, but had preferred a reclusive existence. When she had tried to dissuade Chaurasia from her and asked him to turn to the luminary disciples of her late father, he had remained unshaken and even more resolute.

When he blows the first notes on his flute, the air is mesmerised with a certain euphoric quality. Through the plaintive and touching notes of the *bansuri*, he creates the closest equivalent to celestial sound and interprets this divinity through the teaching of classical music. There is *swara* or note, *raga* or melody and pure sound or *nada*, in the art. The encrustations of nuance and rhythm, as dictated by the tenets of his *gharana* or school of music, give it a rounding. Even though the family profession was wrestling and his father introduced him to this physical art, it was his neighbour, Pandit Rajaram, himself a musician of the Benaras School, who had come to his rescue. The reluctant wrestler son was allowed lessons in music as a concession and it was Rajaram who had obliged. This system had continued unbroken for a good eight years, when again fate had knocked at the Chaurasia doors. A chance listening in, at a flute recital of Pandit Bholananth's when he was a lad of fifteen, changed his life. It was the flute and nothing else, for him. When he was invited to play at a concert at Cuttack, in the eastern state of Orissa, the shy teenager had complied. A job at the local All India Radio station had followed.

The all India Radio years were years of grinding and relentless toil. "I joined there as an accompanying artist for big musicians at their concerts. It was now possible for me to practise for ten to fourteen hours a day. Back home, I could not practise for more than two hours" This happy chance to being with the flute gave the Pandit the necessary grounding but clearly, it did not help towards his ultimate goal of becoming a top class performer. He resigned his secure job at the radio and began to give solo concerts against billings. Together with regular practice, he now began to include a degree in innovative appeal and as the years advanced, the latter became the hallmark of this gifted flautist.

By the end of the sixties, his music had touched the heartstrings of the international music community. None other than the legendary violinst, Lord Yehudi Menuhin, had certified his quality. Back home, too, the humble *bansuri* had taken him places. It all began in 1984 when he was chosen as the national awardee by the Sangeet Natak Akademi, the country's premier institution for the arts. Six years later, the state organisation for the arts in Maharashtra acknowledged his contribution to Indian music by conferring on him the prestigious *Maharashtra Gaurav Samman Puraskar*. In the same year, he received from the President of India the *Padmabhushan* award, and this award was followed by a gamut of initations to regale audiences world-wide.

But all these honours and accolades have only made Hari Prasad Chaurasia a very genuine human being. Clad in a flowing dhoti and silk kurta, his forehead adorned with a red vermillion "Tika" his very first notes on stage turn the audience into a mesmeric non-being. As the music advances, the artist and listener proceed on a journey of esctatic experience.

As he rises from the stage to acknowledge the clappings and encores, a half smile of satisfaction escapes from the corners of his mouth. The *bansuri* is then carefully restored to its velvet case and the maestro goes behind stage. The next day will begin for him at 5 a.m., the Pandit's usual wake-up hour. The flute by his side lies encased but the mind and heart of the great maestro is already at work playing with his mental faculties on a *bansuri* that is seemingly silent.

SUBHRA MAJUMDAR

PANDIT KRISHNA RAO SHANKAR RAO PANDIT

(b. 1893) - M. Mus.; Hindustani, khayal of Gwalior gharana, dhrupad, tappa; studied with Shankar Rao Pandit; received Sangeet Natak Akademi award for Hindustani vocal music (1959); publications: Sangeet Sarga, Sar, Sangeet Alap Sanchari; disc recordings, Principal, Shankar Gandharva Mahavidyalaya, Lashkar, Gwalior.

PAINTING : AN OUTLINE HISTORY OF

Up to the 9th century A.D. presumably all early painting was on palm leaves or birch bark-both easily deteriorating, brittle materials; paper appears to have reached India, via Kashmir, from Central Asia, and was probably, of Chinese make in the beginning, in the 6th and 7th centuries. Indian-made paper can be assumed to have existed after the 7th century.

Then came the first illuminated manuscripts. There is a small gap, perhaps a 150 or 200 years, that may well be filled. The oldest manuscript illustration was sometime in 9th or 10th century, From that time onwards we have an uninterrupted series of illustrated manuscripts and miniatures, both on palm leaves and on paper. The thought that miniature painting was introduced into India from Iran, has been found to be untrue; long before the arrival of Iranian influences, Buddhist and Jaina manuscripts were embellished with illustrations.

The first illuminated manuscripts hail from, Bengal and Nepal in the East, and Gujarat in the West. Their style is vastly different.

In Bengal, during the Pala Kings, there was a late flourishing of Mahayana Buddhism. The surviving illustrated manuscripts, mostly on palm leaves are all Buddhist texts, and the illustrations are mainly Mahayana deities. The style of these little miniature paintings is entirely identical in character with contemporary sculpture. The contemporary mural painting viz. the Queen Maya in the lower leaf, giving birth to the Buddha Gautama, stands in the same twice bent pose as the latest Ajanta murals, with the personal ornaments equally rich.

The Gujarati Jaina miniatures are painted in adherence to a strict formal code of cliches; a hieratic art where everything is symbolical indication, not visual representation. Savage colours are used-very few in the beginning, increasing with the 15th century - for these savage faces, harsh noses, protruding eyes, angular bodies; every face nose and eye is the same. Variety comes in with patterned dresses.

Mughal miniature painting belongs to an altogether different world. First of all, because it does not spring from the people but from the Court; secondly because its subject matter is entirely restricted to court interests; thirdly, because even technically and stylistically it is, essentially, an importation.

Turing over the leaves of a Mughal Muraqqa (album), subjects usch as these are found. The Emperor receiving an embassy in Durbar; or accepting a gift from a Durbari, or hunting on horseback; or watching an elephant and a lion fighting etc.

It is this love of precise recording that made Mughal painting so ready to absorb some technical qualities of contemporary western art. Such as use of gentle shading, and also a much more realistic treatment of aspects of nature viz trees, clouds, animals etc.

Perhaps no subject excites the Craving for realism more than the painting of imperial pets; horses, goats, elephants, hunting hawks, various deer, cheetahs and so on.

In Mughal miniature paintings women hardly appear. But in non-Court painting women preponderate; the beauty of the female form is one of the major subjects of Rajput and Hill miniature paintings:

Here, we have a return to the ancient Indian ideal, expressed so superbly in the temples of Konarak of Khajuraho, and even in many of the mural paintings of Ajanta, the love of man and woman, is one of the most beautiful and most important things in life. Indian miniature painting, from the 16th century pictures of Malwa and Mewar to the early 19th century masterpieces of Kangra and Garhwal, sing the delights of human love. Often this human love is justified by showing the ideal lovers of Hindu mythology: the loves of Krishna and Radha.

The Mahabharata and the Ramayana, provide the subject matter of some of the finest miniature paintings of the Hindus, to whom these epics the myths and legends of the gods and heroes of their religion was as essential as the air they breathed.

Siva, Parvati, Ganesha, the goddess Durga, the battles of the gods, the churning of the Ocean, the sleep of Vishnu; these themses of religion and mythology give endless scope to the Hindu artist to branch out into subjects never attempted by his fellow-painters at the Imperial Court.

The miniature from Narasinghgarh, Malwa, Rajasthan, painted by Madho Das, about 1618, is an excellent example of the melting of a number of impulses; religion, because it is Krishna and Radha and the gopis: a love of music, because it is a picture of the musical mode, Megha Raga, played at the time of the rains; and human love.

From the little principality of Basohli in the Punjab Hills comes the passionate and primitive pictures. Here too heavenly and earthly love combine to create an image of human passion.

Even when the painter proceeds to illustrate the greate epics or legends, the earthly quality, the deep roots of this art in the lives of the ordinary people of India, can be instantly seen. Thus when Narada, divine messenger, commands Krishna for his victory over the demons, the Asuras, Narada is sitting in a Punjabi mud hut, with a straw roof, the cows are chewing their cud in the yond, huts of the village are seen in the background, and the bucolic world of the punjabi village is visualised as the setting of the great epics.

The climax of this joie de vivre, of this astonishing combination of heaven and earth, comes in the Pahari Paintings around 1800, indeed, well into the first quarter of the 19th century. In Rajasthan too, larger pictures of great charm and sensuous beauty are prouduced, but it was probably in Kangra that the ultimate in this direction has been achieved. (Condensed)

CHARLES FABRI

PARDAH

'Screen, curtain, veil', the seclusion of women, a custom observed by many Muslims and imitated by some higher caste Hindus.

P. N. CHOPRA

PARVEEN SULTANA - THE SINGING GENIUS

The classical maestro, Begum Parveen Sultana's singing genius, in her chosen field of Hindustani classical music, has no equal. She was first seen on the public as a budding singing star, barely in her teens, at the pretigious Sadarang Sangeet Sammelan in Calcutta. The front rows of the auditorium that day were occupied by the greatest names of the century. They had decided to grace the occasion for a variety of reasons: some personal, other curious and even critical, for the unknown beginner came to the podium without the requisite alchemy of a distinguished musical backdrop. Her guru or teacher, the late Chinmoy lahiri, was better known as a professional teacher rather than a performer and her musical lineage, so intrinsic to the quality of an Indian performer, boasted of no distinct school or gharana. Her primary start in the field had been inculcated by her father, a performer of sorts, but not an ustad or musician.

Her father, Ikramul Majid, was by profession an ivory merchant and by passion a practising musician. This devotion to the art had given off several sideshoots; it had made him strike a close acquaintance with master musicians then residing in Calcutta and his untiring efforts had led to the opening of a radio station at Guwahati, his home town in the eastern state of Assam. He had, of course, given a musical performance at this maiden occasion and while practising a hymnal number for it, the child Parveen had sat by him, in rapt attention, and later hummed the tune, in perfect raga outline before the astonished parent. There and then the decision to teach her music was taken and Parveen was to spend the next seven years under a rigid timetable of practice, school work, more lessons in voice culture that now spans the three octaves with amazing fluidity.

PATOLA OF SURAT

Choicest exports from textile centre at Surat, along the caravan routes to the markets of Samarkhand, Bokhara, Baghdad, Basra, Damascus, Rome; in 15th and 16th centuries.

Making, a complex process, threads of warp and weft separately dyed in partitions; hence patterns emerge on the finished product in weaving Patola *Pallus* used with silk sarees.

Pochampally; Bhandhani of Rajasthan, are tie and dye textiles, of similar family, symbolic of girlhood, love, material happiness. One of most treasured attire among bridal garments. Brilliantly colourful.

PATWARDHAN, VINAYAKRAO NARAYAN

(b. 1898) - Sangeet Praveen; vocalist and actor; Hindustani, khayal of Gwalior gharana, classical compositions; studied with Keshavrao Patwardhan, Vishnu Digambar Paluskar; received title of Sangeet Mahamahopadhyaya from Akhil Bhartiya Gandharva Mahavidyalaya, Mandal; elected fellow of Sangeet Natak Akademi (1965); concert tours, Nepal (1956), Europe (1964); disc recordings; publications, Raga Vijnam, Bala Sangeet and others; formerly Principal, Gandharva Mahavidyalaya, Pune.

G. S. DIXIT

PEACOCK

On the onset of monsoons Peacock, one of the most beautiful members of the pheasant family, spreads its lovely wings and dances to welcome the rain. The dance that has always mesmerised man, the dance that lures peahens, the dance that has placed this bird in an enviable position and it has occupied a prominent niche in Indian folklore, mythology, arts, crafts and literature. That this why it has attained the coveted position of the National bird of India.

Peacock has been fascinating man since time immemorial. It various qualities have been mentioned in Rig Veda, the oldest Sanskrit text. Closely associated with Indian mythology, it is considered to be the Vahan (Vehicle) of Lord Kartikeya, commander-in-chief of god's army.

The pictorial presentation of melodies in the Indian miniature paintings show deep friendship and affection between the nayika (heroine) and peacocks. Malhar Raag, Vasant Raag and Madhu Madhavi Raagini (all various modes of classical singing) invariably feature peacocks in a significant role. Natyashastra and Abhinaya Darpana, the treatises on Indian dances, are the sources of classical dance style like Bharat Natyam, Kathakali and Kuchipudi, Peacock dance forms a lively item of Kathak, expressed by 31 single and 27 combined hand gestures.

Many tribal dances also revolve around the theme of peacock. In Kar dance of Baiga people (Madhya Pradesh), gaily dressed men put peacock feathers on their large turbans while the women decorate their coiffeur with these feathers. Mauria tribals of Bastar (Madhya Pradesh), wear masks with peacock feathers in their headgear for Chherta dance. Kharia, Bimjhal, Oraon, Kol and Kisan tribals of Orissa perform Karma dance; while the nuptial dance called phul Basant is performed in Sareikala (Bihar) in the style of the peacock. Nagas of Manipur imitate the courtship dance of peacock in their harvest dance known as *Khamba Lim*. The Worli tribals

of Maharashtra put peacock feathers in a brass pot and dance around it. Lord Krishna always put feather of this bird on his head.

This beautiful birdforms a popular motif in folk embroidery, as well as on walls of home decorated by rural women. Wood carvers find it equally appealing; and so do the enamel jewellery makers. Rajput kings were proud of bedecking their palaces with this motif.

Not only Hindus but, the Mughals fancied it and reared it in their gardens. So much so that Shahjahan got made an exotic throne, named *Takht-e-Taus* (Peacock Throne), which was a splendid work of art and had a pair of peacocks studded with emeralds and other precious stones. Romans has peacock as their emblem. Christians hold it as an attribute of Christ and St. Barbara. An exquisite peacock is carved in the cathedral of St. Mark in Venice. The religious symbol of Zoroastrians is Malak-e-Taus, i.e. angel peacock. Muslims residing in Java consider this bird as a guardian of the gates of paradise.

Indian literature, postry in particular - ancient, medieval and modern - describes the intimate relationship of peacock with man. Calling it as a glorious bird of heaven, the ancient Sanskrit literature has described it as a friend and messenger of love. Writers have called its dance as a symbol of happiness.

Kalidas, the legendary poet, showered high praises on peacock. His great works such as *Kumar Sambhava, Meghduta, Raghuvamsa* and *Ritusambhara* depict an intimate bond in bless and sorrow between the peacocks and humans. In the subsequent master pieces of the literature of mediaeval period such as *Banabhatta, Bhavabhuti* and *Bharavi* peacock retains its important place. Peacock appears on sculpture also as a recurring motif on jars belonging to the Harappan civilisation (2500-1500 BC. Railings of Bharhut Stupa, dating back to 1st century BC, contain carvings of a number of peacocks. These are also carved on pilaser of Gwalior, belonging to Sunga period (2nd century BC). Since this bird forms a part of Indian, iconography, it has been sculpted in various periods - Sunga. Kushana, Gupta, Chola, Hoysala and Pala.

The peacock motif has also been favoured by the craftsmen. Be it shell-craft, sholapith, jewellery, embroidery, weaving, finligree, wood work, toys, stone ware or metal ware.

The blue peacock, *Pavo Cristatus* (Linnaeus), found mainly in India and Sri Lanka, is the size of a swan and is the most colourful among the well-known species of this bird. It has a fan-shaped crest of feathers on its head, a white patch under the eye, a long, slender blue neck and a spectacular bronze-green train of about 200 elongated feathers. The green one is known as the Burmese Peacock and is largely found in Maynmar and other parts of South Asia. The Ethiopian species has a double crest. The peacock has two other breeds the peacock cannot fly more than a hundred metres or so at a stretch. The female of the species is less attractive, with a dull brown colour and no train of feathers. However, she has the same crown on her head. It lays four to six eggs at a time, which incubate in about four weeks.

The peacock is not merely an object of beauty but has its own importance in the eco-system. It is protected under the Indian Wildlife Act (1972). (Condensed)

THAKUR PARAMJIT & BIMAL SAIGAL

PERFORMING ARTS

Indin cultural traditions have roots spread over millennia. Although cinema made its appearance at the end of the 19th century, music, dance and theatre have their known history over several centuries.

Indian music and dance have their genesis in the depaths of devotion to god and religious sensibilities. The Sam Vedic tradition of music is still prevalent in the South Indian temples in the disciplined chorus of many voices. The North Indian music was affected by Truk, Afghan and Mughal influences. The classical dances have gestures and movements as dedication to the divinity in a prayerful mood. The Sanskrit theatre has been built around religious stories and legends whose beginning has to be made with due invocations to the gods.

A deep religious sense of dedication has played such a vital role in all artistic sensibilities that the artists have relegated their own name to oblivion. Just as the artists have not left their names anywhere, so have they omitted to leave any records of date and time.

Further the art expressions and manifestations have always been holistic. Thus, dance mingles with music, music with sculpture and architecture: all in a complementary way. The Indian mindest views the visual and performing arts in their entirely. Finally, performing arts have served a specific purpose of Establishing communication among people and spreading education.

The folk music, folk dance and folk theatre, adds another prime purpose : participation of the people from audience. The illustrations can be called from Ankia Nat of Assam; Bhavai of Gujarat; Bayalata and Bhutnach of Mysore; Dashbatar of Tamil Nadu; Ytra of Manipur. West Bengal and Orissa, Krishnattam and Kudiattam of Kerala; shadow puppets of Andhra, Orissa, Karnataka and Kerala; string puppets of Rajasthan, Tamil Nadu and Orissa; rod puppets of West Bengal and Orissa; Mayurbhanj Chhau of Orissa; Seraikela Chhau of Orissa; Seraikela Chhau of Bihar; Purulia Chhau of West Bengal, Nautanki and Nagal of Uttar Pradesh, Nach a of Madhya Pradesh and many more.

The folk arts have always been very dynamic whose pattern and meanings have peripherally changed from time to time. For example, a large Bhavai group can show epic tales, family welfare plans and the poverty of chronic borrowers of money in a continuous sequence Secondly, folk traditions carry a large variety of themes. Thus, a Yatra troupe can have in its reportoire Puranic stories historical incidents and events based on contemporary politics.

Further folk traditions have an extraordinary sense of liveliness. The Tamasha troupe can canvey sarcasm and satire through relevant music in a metropolis, mofussil town or remote village with the same felicity using the local lingo and taking recourse to imagination with hardly any supportive props. The music dance and theatre in the folk-forms commingle with each other seamlessly.

Another seminal feature of the Indian music is its tala which is radically different from mere rhythm. Just as ragas have an organic existence, so have the talas; using their own syntax, with both articulation and silence. The lyrics of both North and South are dominated by a religious feeling, although Bengal, Maharashtra and Gujarat have

attempted to come out of this frame work. Many new instruments have been adopted like the violin, Guitar and mandolin from the west. Many new ragas have been created in the post-independence phase, by stalwarts like Baba Alauddin Khan. The early masters were Bade Gulam Ali, Faiz Khan and Abdul Karim Khan who created their own gharanas.

The unbroken tradition in India caters for all the dance movements of head, neck, chest-arm, waist, stomach and thigh, apart from those of eyes, eyebrows, eyelids, eyeballs, cheek, nose, lips, teeth, tongue, chin, face as well as footfalls, fingers and toes. Various sentiments and emotions, starting from 'Shrinagar' for love go upto laughter, compassion, anger, Bravery, fear, hatred, weirdness and peace. The abstract dance (Nrita) depicts sculptural poses without any narrative, while the mimetic dance (Nritya) interpress the epic stories or simple narratives of religious or countly tales.

From the South comes Bharatnatyam of Tamil Nadu with an uninterrupted tradition among the temple-maids (Devdasis) over centuries.

Kathakali of Kerala is one of the canonised forms and performed as a complete dance-drama enjoying immense popularity. The other mellowed form of classical dance is Mohiniattam, mainly marked for women dancers, whose undulating torso resembles the swaying coconut-leaves and the billowy waves of the coastal sea.

In Andhra, the Brahmin Bhagavatars had created yet another form of classical dance, named after Kuchipudi village, which used a tradition of singing and dancing to depict the epic tales.

In the North, the most popular and prevalent form is Kathak, with its roots in Uttar pradesh and Rajasthan.

The narrative uses a lot of scintilating footwork and devolves around the Radha-Krishna love theme, having found early patrons in the Mughal emperors and, later, in the Oudh kings like Wajed Ali Shah.

In the North-East, Manipuri classical dance receives boosting from the Manipuri music and Kirtana, composed around Radha-Krishna's themes, with variations found in the drumdande Pung-Cholam and martial arts Thang-ta.

Among the Indian performing arts, drama is the one most influenced by the Western theatre, although all the regions have had sustained folk traditions.

The mainstream Hindi theatre began later with Uday Shankar Bhatt and Upendra Nath 'Ashk', and has received contributions from Vishnu Prabhakar, Mohan Rakesh and other the principal architects have been the National School of Drama of Delhi and its repertory, Bharat Bhavan Rangmahal of Bhopal and Bharatendu Natya Academy of Lucknow.

Calcutta and Delhi have seen some remarkable street theatre created by Utpal Dutt and Safdar Hashmi. Mono acting has been another unique genre. (Condensed)

UTPAL K. BANERJEE

PERFORMING ARTS OF KERALA

Running along extreme south-west sea coast of India, the tiny state of Kerala is known for it rich natural wealth and colourful performing arts. Though Kerala strongly evokes the memory of its internationally famous majestic dance drama, the Kathakali, there are several other theatrical forms which predate Kathakali by centuries. At one end of the theatrical spectrum, there is the classical Sanskrit theatre of Kerala, the kuityattam, and at the other, numerous interesting dance-drama forms steeped deep into local customs, rituals and socio-cultural environment.

Most of these forms are confined to local temple premises and are not known much outside the state. A number of these dances and performances are associated with the cult of Bhadrakali which is quite ancient in origin. There are a number of masked and trance performances where dancers wear headgears rising up more than five meters in height. Mythological, divine, semi-devine and demonic characters who appear in different performances put on colourful make up and dazzling costumes befitting their station and inner qualities. The colour symbolism developed by these forms found its reflection in the majestic costumes and make-up of kathakali.

The basis of these performances is local and classical epic and puranic mythology, folk legends and tales, and other related story material. Dance and music is an important ingredient of these performances. Impressive array of musical instruments are pressed into service to create an atmosphere of awe and mythical mgnificence suitable for the themes taken up for enactment.

Most of these performances are ritualistic in character and offered to various deities to appease them. They are conducted for the general welfare of the community as well as an individual. Pure recreation is seldmon their purpose. The represent profound culture of the region with all its intricacies. To understand these forms is to understand the mystique of Kerala. (condensed)

M. L. VARADPANDE

PERFORMING ARTS PERSPECTIVE

Indian performing arts, covering dance, drama and music have been - like their counterparts of visual arts - more than individual arts. As exponents have noted, they are among the most powerful means of fusing the logical with the intuitive, the analytical perceptions with the sensory ones and the holistic understanding with linear thinking. They are the disciplines which, within themselves, deal with basic understanding of human experience and conceptualisation.

Like architecture, sculpture and painting, the performing arts, too, mainfest the principle of multiplicity and unity on the **spiritual, philosophical** and **aesthetic** planes. The innermost urge to communicate with the gods at a mystical level is expressed by the performer by making his art a dedication and a prayerful offering. At a **philosophical** level, the performing artist does not reflect life as it is, but reveals or re-creates - through finite forms and symbols - a vision suggestive of the infinite universabeing. He seeks again and again to transcend the reality of everyday living to a higer reality. At the **aesthetic** level, the artist attempts to achieve an experience of supreme bliss, second only to the absolute bliss (Brahmananda), a state of "release".

Rasa (the evoked state), as conceived in ancient aesthetics and practised by the artist, has two aspects. First is the state of bliss as experienced by the viewer (Rasika). The second is the sentiment and mood (Bhava), the permanent and transitory states, as has been the object of presentation. While the evocation or **Rasa** is the ultimate objective of all artistic experience and expression, **bhava** gives the performer a unique way of abstracting, and thus universalising the content of art. It is this aesthetic theory of **Rasa** which provides an underlying unity to the Indian arts.

The roots of the Indian music, dance and theatre traditions lie in the treatise of Bharata's Natya Shastra composed around the second century AD. As a compilation of practice and belief pertaining to the performing arts, this remarkably comprehensive volume deals with dance, drama, stage, music and elocution. The possible movements of every part of the human figure are distilled into those that can be put into choreography: movements of each single limb and organ of human body have an emotional quality, analogous to the emotional expression of the subtle intervals (sruti) in music. Like drama, the mime element of dance employs the entire human physique to speak in a language of movement as to evoke a mood, doing away with speech of the drama proper and employing only music for expression. While detailing techniques, movements and gestures of dance and drama, Natya Shastra also describes the stage, theatre architecture, make-up and costume. It speaks about both spiritual depths and aesthetic, even analysing the literary nuances of a text. The Natya Shastra has been a powerful, integrated encyclopaedia of the performing arts - a source of inspiration for directors, playwrights, actors, dancers, musicians and designers - and its relevance has not faded with time.

All the seven classical dance - forms of India, namely, Bharatnatyam, Kathakali, Mohiniattam, Kuchipudi, Odissi, Kathak and Manipuri, derive their authority from the Natya Shastra, and are all divided into pure dance (nritta) and expressional dance (nritya). Nirtta is a blooming of decorative patterns and an upholding of various parts of the anatomy, creating beautiful designs as seen in the miniature paintings. Nritya, however, uses face and hand-gestures to mirror emotions and stylised expressions from everyday life. Their symbolic language is imitative, descriptive, suggestive or even abstract, conveying a whole world of meaning. Their semantics suggest the sky and the earth, the seven seas and the underworld. A dancer may interpret the accompanying song or may take an imaginative flight with the associations that the words suggest.

Origins of music in India are deeply spiritual and devotional. Symbolically, most gods and goddesses of the pantheon are associated with music and rhythm. The creative energy of Brahma is defied as Saraswati, inseparable from her veena (lute), Shiva dances to the beat of damaru (drum) and Krishna enchants the world with the strains of his flute. All manifestations of godhead are traditionally propitiated with music and dance. Indian music can be traced back to the chanting of the Sama

Veda four millennia before and the primacy of voice and the association of musical sound with pravers have remained essentially unchanged. While nada is the sound of the Universe, anabata nada (sound produced without percussion) is not a matter of sense perception but a mystic experience in which sound and light are fused together in a direct perception of the Absolute.

Ancient music has always been nourished by such diverse streams as the relgious, folk, tribal and the courtly. The physical body of the music is to the musician what a writing tool is to the poet. The listner has to stay in tune with the highly-charged state of consciousness of the performer, rather than the physical condition of the sound that carries the music. The singing voice in Indian music is the earthy sound of the everyday speech, not a musical escape from it. All music in the traditional mode adopts the characteristics of intimate conversation. Raga, a central concept in all Indian music, has an intensity, a singleness of colour (not a rainbow) that the performer must create a new every time he performs, to suffuse the hearts of men. Each raga is an incipient melodic idea, with its own rules of ascent and descent in the octave, prescribed resting places, characteristic phrases and a distinct ethos of its own, evoking a state of feeling relating to the human condition and to nature. As Sheila Dhar describes, "Its expression and effect depend on its dynamics - on how it swerves towards or away from a tone or from silence; how it curves, dives, wafts, spirals, trails or plummets; on where it gathers its greatest weight and luminosity....." The Carnatic music, in particular, has an extraordinary feature the constant presence of classical music is part of the daily life. A Kriti can be a part of the daily prayer of a housewife while placing fresh flowers before the family deity; the same Kriti can be heard on a formal concert platform from a professional artiste.

Natya Shastra is still the companion of traditionalists as well as experimentalists on the contemporary theatre scene, besides Nandikeshwar's Abhinaya Darpana, Abhinav Gupta's Abhinava Bharati and Dhananjaya's Dasa Rupaka, in common with other performing arts. The classical Indian theatre in Sanskrit evolved into the modern language theatre well into the second millennium and continued in various parts of India, giving rise to a regional theatre identity influenced by local conditions of geography and politics. With the incorporation of folk traditions into the classical framework, an enriched theatre idiom found more access to the people. A similar process was visible in literature, where regional languages were gaining importance, influencing - in turn - the culture and symbols of theatre. The art of the actor is the process of communication and Indian theatre, through many languages, has been exploring both its roots and its thrusts in new directions.

The all-pervasive harmony is discernible not merely among the performing arts, but also spills into the graphic and plastic arts. The first example is the classic Geeta Govinda composed in Sanskrit by Jayadeva in the twelfth century. Its lyrical text, with its many-layered annotations, is found all over India and Nepal. Singers have sung it in designated (or improvised) ragas; dancers have danced to it in all the classical forms; painters have created masterpieces inminiatures and murals alike; manuscripts have illumined it lustrously and sculptors have been inspired by it in their work of adorning temples all over India. Another instance of unity is evident in the tenth century Chola temple of Brihadishwara, with its rigorous architectural aesthetics based on the Shilpa Shastra fully in tune with the santified texts of Agama Shastra, its individual niches and corners adorned by sculptured images, with their own prayers - chants,. invocation music and celebratory dance, and its halls and pillars resounding with daily, seasonal and special fairs and festivals. It is a living temple where all the performing arts blend seamlessly with the grand spectacle of Shiva's choreographic exuberance, blending with parnoramic images of the Nayanar saint-poets. Geeta Govinda and Brihadishwara both capture harmony in India's heritage.

UTPAL K. BANERJEE

PERIYAR - THE HEAVENLY WILDERNESS ON EARTH

India has seven principal mountain ranges. The Western Ghats is one of them. Uniqueness of the range is that it directly faces the Arabian Sea and, in fact rises from there itself, forming a 1600 - kilometer long great wall, averagely of 1200 - meter elevation, against the South-West monsoon. Consequently, sea-facing slopes of the Western Ghats are rewarded with high rainfall resulting in draping of the hills in luxuriant vegetation. True tropical evergreen rain forests are found here. From the other side of the Ghats originate rivers, which travel the whole Deccan Plateau, and via the valleys of the Eastern Ghats, drain in the Bay of Bengal. These Ghats harbour rich and varied biodiversity.

The world - famous Periyar - Tiger Reserve, in the Ldukki district of Kerala, is representative of the biogeographis region. A lake here adds to the beauty of the Reserve and has made some of the Periyar area easily accessible by motor-boats. One can have a look at the flora-fauna from the safety and confort of a boat.

This lake is over 100 years old, It was in 1895 that the Periyar river, the second largest in Kerala, was dammed, forming this unique lake of 26 square kilometer extent, submerging the valley intervening the hills in the region. Due to high altitude location of the lake, only the high hills stand tall, while the smaller ones are islands. The sun rays falling on the restless waters of the lake were reflected back as millions of twinkling stars. Azure sky was afloat with snow-white clouds. Hills around were pleasing lush green.

In the midst of the lake, is a building on a hillock, partially hidden in the vegetation. Brick-red tiled, sloping roof of the aesthetically designed structure merges harmoniously· in the surroundings. A flight of steps from the lake's edge leads to it. It is the Edappalayam Lake Palace, the then summer retreat of the erstwhile Travancore royalty.

Panorama of Periyar sped past. Not it would be moist deciduous. The Hills around are draped with blaze of various hues of red of blooming Terminalia Paniculata and Terminalia tomentose. Strangely, the colour of the blooms of the same species varied from pink to deep red. Perhaps it was due to varying ages of the trees and locations. The tops of these hills are carpeted with lush green grass and almost devoid of trees. At places there are densely forested hills covered with semi-evergreen forest, where huge evergreen species loomed high into the sky, towering over the associated deciduous species. The mosaic of epiphytes festooned the trees.

The rich floral community of the Periyal hosts equally rich faunal variety, though only some common ones like, among mammals, wild boar, sambar, elephant, gaur and among birds, cormorants, egrets, herons, kingfishers, orongos and some butterflies, moths, crickets, ants, wasps, bees, spiders, mantids etc. can be seen. Pariyar is famous for elephants. They are in plenty here. Elephants are least shy of all the animals at Periyar in the presence of human beings. Besides racket-tailed Drongo bird which are known to be such a perfect mimic of calls and songs of so many birds.

There are sparrow sized grey tit with conspicious white patch. Woodpeckers were aplenty in Periyar. So are Large, glossy, black and yellow spiders had huge woven webs from tree to tree. Many species of exotically coloured butterflies are also found. In Pariyar, there are butterflies with more than six inches wing-span.

Nilgiri langurs are shy and infrequently sighted. They are all black with greyish head. Another interesting sight is that of giant Indian squirrel, its long bushy tail dangling from a horizontal branch of a tree. It's indeed giant for a squirrel to be about a mater long. Furthermore, its, lustrous brownish-black coat, buff under parts and chestnut mid-back and head make it one of the most beautifuly animals. (Condensed)

PUSHP K. JAIN

PHAD PAINTING - CAPTIVATING COLOURS ON CANVAS

The staggering variety and array of artefacts and handicrafts, that contribute to the perennially irresistable attraction of Rajasthan, are incorporated with colour and beauty and imbued with a distinctive character that speaks of a rich and centuries old culture. One fine example of this unparalleled heritage are the vividly hued *phad* paintings where the very essence of a ballad is captured on canvas that depicts each scene with dexterous clarity. The methodically arranged figures are brought to life by the professional narrators, known as Bhopas, who hail from Marwar (Jodhpur-Nagaur). Their lyrical *prabchan* (narration) is aided by music from *ravanhatha*, a stringed instrument, considered a precursor to the violin.

The institution of *phad* painters, however, emerged with the association of *phad* with narration. Narrated and painted folklores have been and still are an important medium of communication in rural Rajasthan. There has been a long standing tradition of professional narrators and singers of folklore as well as the use of paintings and other artefacts as aids for their narratives. The study of *phad* also seeks to explore narration in its totality, that is oral art with visual components like paintings.

The art of painting a *phad* is almost 700 years old and originated in the princely state of Shahpur, 35 km from the district of Bhilwara. Due to immense royal patronage, the craft flourished and survived for generations.

The term *phad* is derived from a Sanskrit word *patta* for a flat surface for painting and in Rajasthani dialect it means a fold. The painting of a *phad* is religious in spirit and demands a ritualistic discipline. It must be steeped in folklore and the painter is required to work under the vigilant instructions of the Bhopas, adhering to the traditional norms. There is a close interaction between the painter and the singer, as the Bhopas depend on the painter to give expression to the ideas and demonstration of his skill, whereas the painter paints to fulfil the requirements of folk narration.

The *phads* that display the heroic exploits of gods and many Rajpur warriors are generally of five kinds : namely - Pabuji, Devnarayan, Krishna, Ramdal, (Ramayana) and Ramdeoji. Of these, the most legendary and popular is that of Pabuji, who is considered a demi-god in Marwar even today.

As the legend goes, Pabuji, the son of Dhandalji Rathore, the chief of Kolugarh, sacrificed his life at a young age of 25 years for the sake of Deval Charini, a cattle herd who was considered the reincarnation of Shakti. Revered as a great hero, adulatory verses are sung in Pabuji's praise by the Bhopas.

A traditional *phad* is approximately 30 ft. long and 5 ft. wide and the material used is local 'khadi' or canvas. Primarily only vegetable colours were used, which remained fast and fresh for a long time. Scarcity of these colours gradually compelled the artists to make the innovations and find substitutes, as otherwise it would have led to a complete stagnation of the craft. Hence the usage of water-proof earthen colours evolved. These colours are made by pounding the natural earthen colours with gum and indigo.

The painting commences with great flourish when the Bhopas arrive on an appointed auspicious day. The ritual offering of a coconut is made to the Goddess Saraswati - the Goddess of learning A free hand sketch is then made on the canvas, where various postures of human and animal figures are perfected. Floral trees adorn the empty spaces, thus filling up the entire piece. The figures are then painted in a light yellow colour initially, known as 'Kacha'.

The first stroke of colour is always made by a virgin girl from another family of good repute. The artist uses one colour at a time, filling it in wherever required. The colour orange is used for limbs and torsom yellow for ornaments, clothing and designs, grey for structure, blue for water and curtains, green for trees and vegetation and red prominently for dress. The subtle black out line brings linear expressions alive.

The *phads* that are made for the Bhopas are always signed the signature being near the largest central figure. The price of the *phad* however, is determined prior to beginning the painting.

After continuous usage for many years, the *phad* used to be immersed in the sacred lake of Pushkar. But now with their gaining popularity, this practice has been virtually abandoned. The inflow of tourists from outside the country have provided a new lease of life to these folk paintings and their creators, who even paint 'tukras' (small pieces of canvas), on popular demand, where sometimes only one figure is highlighted. No longer are the themes restricted to the aforementioned, as in Udaipur and Bhilwara, as *phads* are found that depict scense even from Mahabharata, with many variations.

Apart from being highly ornamental, the *phads* have a large utilitarian value·also, as they are solely responsible for importalising the ballads and folklores that would have otherwise melted into the inevitable oblivion.

ARCHANA SINGH

PHILATELY OF INDIA

India issued its first postage stamp on October 2, 1854. Since then the Indian Posts and Telegraphs Department has issued stamps each year in different sizes and shapes - squares, rectangles, diamonds - in vertical and horizontal formats. Stamps are also now being printed in multicolours.

Before independence in 1947, the Indian Postal Department issued almost all the stamps with the portrait of the then reigning British monarch, as on very rare occasions the stamps had some other picture that of the British monarch. After independence India began issuing stamps with different themes and designs. Collection of stamps and other philatelic items, according to the theme of its design or issue, became very popular among the philatelists. The theme "Indian tourism on philately" is one of the most remarkable ventures of the postal service.

Stamps in India have also been issued to commemorate certain important events. Like the annual conference of the Pacific Area Travel Association (PATA), India is 1966 and 1978; to mark the international Tourism Year in 1967 and the World Tourism Organisation Assembly session in 1983. Another stamp depicting your activities was issued in 1991 to mark the International Conference on Youth Tourism in New Delhi.

Besides depicting some important temples seen across the country, the philatelic material so far issued also displays some internationally-known monuments like the Taj Mahal in Agra, Gold Gumbaz, Bijapur, Hawa Mahal, Jaipur and many more stamps on wild animals, birds and butterflies, Indian trees and flowers, Himalayas and ecology are very attractive. The stamps showing Indian miniature paintings, Indian tribals, Indian bridges and Indian handicrafts povide a window to the Indian tradition and culture.

DR. MADJISIDAMA RAO NANNAPANENI

PHOTOGRAPHY IN INDIA

The invention of Photography was announced in Europe in 1839. As the presence of a small European population in India helped expose the country's cultural and architectural heritage, it led to the evolution of a fascination for India's pictures que natural and constructed beauties in their minds. The period 1850-60 was the golden age of amateur photography while during 1860-90, professional photography reigned supreme. By the end of the century, with much modified and simplified cameras, photography became a household affair and many took it up as a business. The first half century of photography in

India produced valuable prints of Indian life and people. During this period, Calcutta, Bombay and Madras were the centres for intense photographic docmentation of British India.

The Indian architectural heritage has always attracted artists and tourists. Much before the invention of the camera, many artists and draughtsmen had visited India to draw the serene glory of the country's magnificent architectural sites. After the birth of the camera during the first half of the 19th century, recording the beauty of monuments and important places was much in the hands of amateur photographers, who toyed with their lenses at leisure.

The 1850s and 1860s saw photographers like John Murray, Robert and Harriet Tytler and Edmund David Lyon adding a new chapter to the history of architectural documents by photographing known and lesser-known monuments of India. Dr. John Murray, a surgeon by profession, was an ardent admirer of Mughal architecture, and most of his works include monuments scattered in an around Delhi and Agra. The photgraphic blend of antiquity and architectural grandeur is further reflected in the works of Robert and Harriet Tytler, who were taught photgraphy by John Murray.

Edmund David Lyon was Particularly attracted by the intricate architecture of Ramalingeshwara temple, Rameshwaram, and the noble magnificence of the Dutch tombs at Surat.

Later, in the 1880s, another man appeared on the photographic scene, who soon earned the epithet 'Prince of Photographers'. He was Lala Deen Dayal, the first known India photographer and founder of the largest photographic firm in India, Deen Dayal's contribution was in many respects richer than many of the European firms' put together, mainly because he had an easy access to Viceregal tours and durbars, as well as to the core of India life, the villages. Several of his monumental photographs were takeh when he accompanied Sir Lepel Griffin in 1882 on his tour of Central India, and later appeared in Griffin's "Famous Monuments of Central India", London (1886).

Professional photography in India owes much to Samuel Bourne, who arrived in 1863 and formed a firm known as Bourne and Shephered, which is today one of the oldest surviving photographic businesses in the world. During his seven year stay in India, he produced a number of beautiful photographic series on the Himalayas and Kashmir. Bourne focussed on palaces and other buildings, besides doing landscapes and mountainscapes. India's high peaks clad in snow, the soothing sounds of silence which fill the air with soft lyrics and the rough, unusual textures of rocks have always tempted photographers to capture the divine beauty of mountains. One of his picture which excels in its technical values is view of Curious Gravel Formations on the Lagudarsi Stream at Kioto, Spiti. The technical excellence of this picture lies in the neatness with which the rough surface of rocks has been captured in the picture. Light reflects differently from the uneven surface of the rocks, giving it a contrast which heightens the dark shadows around the subjects, highlighting their harsh, cracky texture.

The Calcutta cyclone in 1864 attracted Pearson and Paterson to focus on the wrecked ships. Two titles - "The Wreck of the Brig Esmeralda of New York" and "Ships

Wrecked on the Hughli" are valuable contributions to the Photograhic history of Calcutta.

Frederick Fiedig's two hand-coloured salts prints - the Black Pagoda Temple, Chitpore Road, Calcutta, and Temple on the Coromandel Coast near Madras reveal the great interest Europeans had in India's traditional past and culture, and the fact that distances never bothered them. The day to day life of Bombay (now Mumbai) also made good thematic ground for European Photographers.

When Bourne left India, he handed over his photographic equipments to Colin Murray, who also inherited his style and fascination for picturesque beauty. "The Water Place and Udaipur" by Colin Murray is a natural scenic composition with a natural interplay of light and dark. He strongly believed in the beauty of a waterbody, and his works are proportionate compositions of architectural grandeur and nature. In another picture titled "The marble Ghat at Rajnagar", Murray delineates the intricate carving on the pillars on one hand and the rocky texture of a hillock on the other.

Other European photographers of the period were John Edward Sache and Friedrick Fiedeg. Their photographs of the Hooghly river are tributes to the mighty river, as well as the earliest photgraphs taken of the land.

ANITA VARMA

PHULKARI - THE PRIDE OF PUNJAB

Amongst the folk arts of Punjab, the embroidered women's headwear known as Phulkari occupies the place of pride. It has received world-wide appreciation because it is something unique and done for the pure love of it. The multicoloured kaleidoscopic patterns are a veritable feast for the eyes.

Phulkari literally means "flower work"; its intricate and original geometrical designs and patterns, balanced composition, pleasing and harmonious colour combinations make it a real work of art. But the most important thing is the technique of embroidery, which takes years of experience to perfect.

This embroidery is done on homespun, homewoven coarse cloth called *Khaddar* in dran stitch on the wrong side of the cloth. In leisure hours in the afternoon, women both young and old gather to have a session of phulkari.

As Tradition, Phulkari made by the young girls are for their personal use and not for sale. For, these have to be given at the time of her marriage as bride's trousseau. The richer the family, larger the number of Phulkaris given by the relatives.

The most favoured colour of the base fabric is red and all its various hues. This is because Phulkaris are mostly used during marriages and religious festivals. And red color is considered as auspicious by both Hindus and Sikhs. Other popular colours are brown, black and white.

Once a part of bride's trousseau, Phulkari is now being used as bed spreads, curtains and wall hangings. Artefacts like bags, pouches, cushions and even drasses are also being made out of it.

PUNEET KUMAR

PIETRA DURA

At first glance the Taj Mahal, India's most exalted monument, is perfect for its symmetry blend of architectural elements and setting. Closer up, its beauty is seen subtly enhanced by exquisite surface decorations which include calligraphy, floral *pietra dura* inlay work and marble carving. This beautiful yet restrained surface ornamentation elegantly creates a jewel-like quality of the mausoleum and the cenotaphs within.

Helena Blavatsky, the Russian founder of the Theosophical Movement, awed by the exquisite *pietra dura* floral work on the Taj Mahal, wrote in 1879: "some of them look so perfectly natural, the artist has copied nature so marvellously well, that your hand involuntarily reaches to assure yourself they are not actually real. Branches of White jasmine made of mother-for-pearl are winding around a red pomegranate flower of carnelian, or the delicate tendrills of vines and honeysuckles... Every leaf, every petal is a separate emerald, amethyst, pearl or topaz; at times you can count as many as a hundred of them in one single bunch of flowers, and there are hundreds of such bunches all over the panels....."

The ornamentation of the Taj Mahal directly reflects the refined aesthetics and involvement of its patron Emperor Shahjahan. Grief stricken of having lost his wife Mumtaz Mahal, who died giving birth of their fourteenth child, Emperor Shajahan spared no effort at building a masoleum in her memory. The tomb's surface decorations comprise tow separate decorative elements - one is hardstone carving and other pietra dura (Italian for hard stone) inlay. In hardstone carving, patterns were sculpted in shallow relief directly on the white marble, such as the exquisite floral sprays on the exterior dado. For *pietra dura* work, cavities were cut on the smooth marble surface into which thin sections of precisely carved hard and semi-hard gem-stones, selected for maximum textural beauty, were painstakingly inland. The term "Pietra dura" implies the requisite hardness and durability of materials used in this work, technically describing those stones that fall between the 6th and 10th degree of the Mohs scale of hardness, that is between feldspar and diamond. This inlay technique was refined to include laying unsymmetrical and curved pieces of stone into the marble surface, to produce free figures of scrolls and flowers. Intricate designs were inlaid with semi-precious stones such as lapis lazuli, onyx, jasper, topaz and cornelian, causing scholars to remark that the Taj Mahal seemed to have been built by Titans and finished by jewellers.

Pietra dura in its European context, developed in Florence in the sixteenth century. It is not certain whether the concept and skill travelled from Florence to India or was brought from Persia or developed independently in India. But questions of origin apart, the skill was painstakingly refined and combined with relief work in plain white marble, under Emperor Shahjahan, to become the glory of Mughal architecture - for marble inlay work was employed as a decorative element only on Mughal architecture in India. No expense was spared for the *pietra dura* decoration of the Taj Mahal and in the 1630's caravans travelled to far reaches of the Mughal Empire and beyond in search of jewels. White marble was mined at Makrana in the Indian state of Rajasthan; nephrite jade carried from Kadhgar and Khotan in Chinese Turkestan in Central Asia: lapis lazuli was brought from Badakshan in the mountains of north eastern Afghanistan; yellow amber came from Upper Burma; turquoise from Tibet; while carnelian, jasper, amethyst, agate, heliotrope, green beryl were procured from different parts of India...... In all, forty-three different types of gems embellished the mausoleum.

Traditionally Islamic artistic architectural ornamentation had taken the form of calligraphy and abstract geomatrical patterns to which were added floral motifs which stemmed from Emperor Jehangir's love for the beautiful blooms that so impressed him during his visit to the scenic vale of Kashmir in 1620 A.D. His powerful queen Empress Nur Jahan, patron of architecture, built a small two-storied marble mausoleum, the Itimad-ud-Daula in Agra, for her parents in 1627 A.D. It was profusely embellished with floral *pietra dura* work of semi-precious stones. Before this, inlay forming patterns had been executed on the gateway to Emperor Akbar's tomb near Agra, built by his son and their Jahangir, where less precious stone had been used. This imposing gateway, more profusely ornamented than the tomb within (dated to 1613 A.D.), was decorated with geometric designs and floral motifs formed from inlaid white marble and multi-coloured stones strikingly set on red sandstone.

Hundred of tourists visit the Itimad-ud-Daula everyday and of course thousands visit the Taj Mahal, admiring their stunning craftsmanship. Agra city has been fortunate to have kept alive this unique legacy of the Mughals.

Passed down the generations from father to son, uncle to nephew, the craft of marble inlay work still lives on; some of the direct descendants of the master craftsmen who worked at the Taj Mahal continue to practice *pietra dura* inlay work. From itinerant sellers of small inexpensive roughly finished boxes at monuments to exquisite, intricately crafted objects at Emporiums, marble inlay work is synonymous with Agra's crafts.

The entire marble inlay work continues in a slow, deliberate, painstaking fashion just as in the days of Emperor Shahjahan. In the first stop, the marble which has to be inlaid is coloured red and pencil markings of the pattern are etched on the red surface. Then semi-precious gemstones are shaped to the exact size of the pattern with the tips of the thumb and index fingures on the emery wheel. The wheel is necessary, for the speed of the operation can be controlled by a stick. For some flowers the petals are so fine - a bit thicker than a millimeter - that a hundred and fifty silvers compose the final bloom: The time taken to craft one petal is about fifteen minutes.

Stems may be no thicker than a strand of thread. At times the piece of stone crafted is so fine that the wheel cuts through the thumb nail and finger of the craftsman. It is the younger craftsmen who shape the precious stones for their fingers are nimble and soft. After the stones have been shaped they are placed on the pattern made earlier on the marble and if their shape is exact, the outline is then scraped with a pointed tip chisel onto the marble - a stage which is executed by the order craftsmen. With a flat tip chisel a cavity of about four millimeters is made and with a special glue, whose ingredients are a trade secret, the stones are stuck and bonded forever. With sandstone and silver oxide powder the inlaid marble surface is then

polished and smoothened for seven or eight hours: the red colour is washed off and the exquisite object is ready.

Marble being translucent, light passes through it beautifully lighting it up as well as the inlaid stones. Some table tops are so designed that the lights below create a magical glow. The range of objects includes boxes, tabletops, wall plates, coasters, trays, lamps, chess boards, decorative pieces generally in white marble but now black and green marble are also in demand.

The classical marble inlay patterns that grace the Taj and the Itimadud-Daula are often still reproduced by craftsmen but buyers from the west ofter request them to create bolder and bigger floral patterns. The marble is still obtained from Makarana in Rajasthan like the old days and semi precious stones inlaid on them.

Three hundred and fifty years ago Emperor Shahjahan, an astute connoisseur of gems, realised their artistic merit in *pietra dura* decoration. He appreciated the fine skill demanded by the process and perfected it, to build the world's most beautiful mausoleum.

BRINDA GILL

PILLAI, T.N. RAJARATHNAM - NADASVARAM WIZARD

Rajarathnam was born in 1898 at Tirumarugal. His elder sister's son was the famous Nadasvaram maestro "Kakkayi" Natarajasundaram Pillai. Rajarathnam's uncle, *Nadasvara Vidvan* Tirumarugal Natesa Pillai, was the Asthana Vidwan of Tiruvaduthurai Mutt. So, Kuppuswamy Pillai's family also moved to Tiruvaduthurai. The entire life of Rajarathnam was spent at Tiruvaduthurai. His father Kuppuswamy Pillai was himself a *Nadasvara Vidvan.*

Initially, Rajarathnam learnt vocal music under Trukodikaval Krishna Iyer and started giving vocal concerts when he was fourteen. Later, he was giving vocal support to Tiruppambaram Flute Swaminatha Pillai for sometime.

Natesa Pillai adopted Rajarathnam and entrusted Rajarathnam him to Kannuswamy Pillai for Nadasvaram tuition. In addition, he also learnt under Tiruvaduthurai Markandam Pillai. Thus, his training under the two stalwarts helped Rajarathnam very much.

Within a short time, he learnt all the intricacies of Nadasvaram playing and started giving concerts independently and very soon became popular in the music field.

He followed the 'Bhani' of some of the leading *vidvans* like Poochi Srinivasa Iyengar, Vaidyanatha Iyer, Veenai Dhanammal and a few others and won their high appreciation.

Rajarathnam Pillai was synonymous with the raga 'Todi'. He exquisite rendering had covered the entire gamut, charm, technical intricacies, artifices, shades and subtleties of the raga and revealed the total panorama of its swaroopa and soul that it is difficult of bypass his style (Bhani) altogether. Referring to Rajarathnam recital, musicologist R.R. Rangaramanuja Ayyangar says :

"The opening phases of Rajarathnam's Todi soared like a rocket in the placid, noght sky. The torrential flow of sound, chunks of melody gyrating in terrific speed, the expansive raga spreading out like a magic carpet, threw the crowd of listeners into hysteria".

He revolutionised the art by taking 'tanpura' and 'mridangam' in lieu of the othu (drone) and tavil. The option is significant from the viewpoint of melody, mellowness and mellifluence.

Rajarathnam broke the custom of the Nadasvaram players having 'tuft' and wearing khadi dhoti and shirt. Instead of 'tuft' he had cropped his hair and wore shervani and shoe.

Another tradition he broke was that of the Nadasvaram players standing while playing; they used to sit on a platform only at wedding concerts. Rajarathnam insisted upon a platform only at wedding concerts. Rajarathnam insisted upon a platform being erected for cutcheri of nya kind, including temple festivals. He started the practice from palayamacottai in 1929. But the made an exception. For the cutcheri held at Tiruvaduthurai Mutt Thula Festival, at mayuram, and Thai Poosam Festival at Tiruchendur, he played standing.

Rajarathnam had only three disciples 'Kakayi' Natarajasundram Pillai, Kuzhikkarai pichaiypa and Karukurichi Arunachalam who were privileged to be trained by him. Karukurichi became his chief disciple when Rajarathnam came to Tirunelveli in 1935 for a cutcheri. Among the many who had accompanied Rajarathnam on the tavil were : Ammanchatram Kannuswamy Pillai, Nidamangalam Meenakshisundaram Pillai, Malaikottai Panchapakesa Pillai, Pandanallur Rathinam Pillai, Tirumangalam Sunderesa Pillai, Kumbakonam Thangavel Pillai, Nachiyarkoil Raghava Pillai, Nidamangalam Shanmugavadivel and Yezhpanam Dakshinamurthy.

Two of the numerous titles conferred on Rajarathnam were "Madaswara Chakravarti" and "Nadaswara Everest". And these titles seemed to be pre-eminently apt as Rajarathnam ruled the Nadasvaram.

For musicians, whether established or in the making, his music always acted as a fountain of ideas to enrich their own.

He is among the illustrious artistes whose memory shall always be cherished for magnificent artistry. (Condensed)

N. V. R. SWAMY

PLASTIC ARTS

Think of Indian Art and one recaptures in one sweep Harappa and Mohenjo-daro. Bahrhut and Amaravati, Mouryan and Gandhara sculptures and the golden age of the Guptas; the great Medieval monuments of Ellora, Elephanta, Badami, Aihole, Pattadaka, Khajuraho and Konarak; of Ajanta, Bagh the Rajput and Jain miniatures; the splendid art of the Chola, Pandya and Hoyala trinity; and the Mughal and Deccani miniatures which are part of the immensely rich tradition though a little away from the core. Each phase with its distinct plastic concept and yet, remarkably connected by a social relevance and the magic thread of faith.

With modern Indus art one has to consider individual artists each one of whom is an entity with a unique expression and development. To mention only a few of them Nandlal Bose, Jamini Roy and Sher-Gil; Bendre, Hebbar, Hussain, Raza and Souza; Ram Kinker, Dhanraj, Bhagat, Amarnath Sehgal, Chintamoni Kar and Sankoo Chaudhuri, Sailoz Mookerjee, Paritosh Sen, Nirode Majumdar and Panikar, Laxman Pai, Biren De, Ram Kumar, Krishna Khanna, Swaminathan, Gujral and Padamsee; Santosh, Shanti Dave and Subramanyan.

The contribution of these artists and of many others, however, relevant it may be to the modern milieu, is essentially on an individual level. How different it must all seem against the grand edifice of anonymity characteristic of our tradition.

The contemporary artistic expression has sought little inspiration from home; on the contrary more from a far.

The Renaissance School or the Revivalist School, inspired by Abanindranath Tagore, who gathered around himself a most zealous and gifted band a artists, relied on an essentially romantic and nostaligic mood in an effort to recapture the lost heritage, which was basically in consonance with the prevailing tremendous national aspirations. The proliferation of its influence and the significance of its role is now a matter of the past. It was a brief and ineffective link.

Of the contemporary mood and manner, all the highly complex and multi-inspirational styles and tendencies, cover the last two decades. To start with one has to go back to the early years of the century to the principal art school at Calcutta, Madras, Lucknow and Bombay. These school manned by foreigners or westernised Indian evolved and pursued a pattern of art education of another civilization, one looked to the English and through the English to Europe.

Thus was the situation around the time of the close of the second world war. The war, or the end of it, unleashed quite a few new forces and new situations, political as well as cultural. Our art schools, for example, made the first efforts to administer the new approaches and new idea on a judicious scale. The doors of Europe thrown open again, wider than ever before, and the flood of the whole mass of literature, prints journals and composite volumes on significant areas of modern European art, all were absorbed eagerly. Those who are now well-known and who have to a large extent contributed to contemporary Indian art absorbed every thing that they could lay hands on right from 1900, more particularly of all that had happened in Europe between 1920 and 1945.

However more importance is laid now on technique and method, which dictate the expression, the mode has became more important than the mood, technique more than the image, the method overshot the conceptual element altogether. Our attitude took on a very segmentary turn significantly. The time-honoured over all concept of a work of art was abandoned. A picture became a picture on the strength of its mere linear quality or of colour or of strokes, movement, rhythm, form, construction, composition, etc. The detail, no longer part of the whole, determined the excellence of a work of art. Casting aside the literary and the communicative element, in an era of technical supremacy and the non-image cult was ushered. That we have gained technically, indeed taken great strides in this regard, is certain. But in this achievement, the individual, regional flavour has been lost.

At the same time our art today, whatever its purpose and nature, has been to an extent conditioned by life round, Environment conditions art inspite of oneself.

The entire canvas of contemporary artistic expression has one significant characteristic. Each successful work of art is a personal statement of the very private relationship the artist has with objective experience gained directly or indirectly. This is true on a universal scale and is much more so in the case of India which has a longer and more enduring tradition.

This freedom from convention has opened an enormous avenue of creative possibilities and, as a corollarym has also given rise to a good deal of "ill-digested" novelty as well. The introduction of new materials, extraneous to the realm of painting until recently, and the putting together of scrap, junk and tinsel are charcteristic of the present age. The contemporary Indian artists have admitted this into their vocabulary following in the steps of their Western counterparts. It may be that much of our abstract and experimentalist painting also gives evidence of the same kind of uncertainty, daring and sheer febrile outlook to a great extent. But amidst this mess stands out the achievement of some of our most gifted artists.

The bulk of our contemporary art has been derivative and eclectic. At its best, it is purely experimental; at its worst pastiche. But in the hands of the more serious, devoted practitioners it has acquired a significance that could only have evolved out of an intense personal conviction, genuine even if it be for the moment, irrespective of the multifarious sources of inspiration in the. mode and technique. (Condensed)

S. A. KRISHNAN

PLAYING CARDS (A-4)

Games have been popular in India since ancient times. Board games were depicted in the reliefs of Bharhut which date from the end of the 2nd century BC and dice games have played a prominent role in the epics and legends of gods and heroes. The Mahabharata, begins with a kingdom gambled away. Dice board games were popular in Buddhist monasteries.

Perhaps the earliest form of chess in India was the four-sided chaturanga. This too was played with dice. The classic form of chess also originated in India and travelled from there to Persia, eventually traversing the entire Islamic world to reach Europe. Playing cards first appeared in India around 1500.

The world of India playing cards is just as colourful, vivid and enigmatic as that of their European cousins, with whom they have much in common. The first mention of playing cards in Europe is exactly 600 years old if we go by the Julian calendar. In India, the oldest reference goes back to June 1527. The founder of the Mughal dynasty, emperor Babar, who ruled from 1526 to 1530 reports in his annals, "This evening...... Mir Ali Korchi was despatched to Tatta (in Sindh) to Shah Hussain. He is fond of the game with cards and had requested some which I have duly sent him". The word used for cards in this text is "*ganjifa*" or the Persian "*ganjafeh*".

THE PERSIAN "GANJAFEH"

There is still no indisputable explantation of "*ganjafeh*", which means both card game and playing cards. It is possible that it is derived from ganj (treasure); in fact this would make a lot of sense since there are coins in ganjifa card designs. "Ganjafeh" finds a brief mention in Persian texts of the 15th century. In the 16th and early 17th century card playing was a favourite pastime in the coffee houses of Isfahan only to be suppressed later. It subsequently faded into oblivion. Material evidence of Persian "ganjafeh" cards from the 15th or 16th century is thus not available. We know only of their relatives in India.

CARD GAMES OF THE EMPEROR AKBAR

After 1527 for a long time we have no mention of card games in India. The next reference is found in "*Ain-i-Akbari*", a book written by Abul Fazl Allami towards the end of the 16th century on the reign of the great Mughal emperor Akbar (1542 - 1605). Abul Fazl devotes a short chapter to the games - chess and ganjifa - played by Akbar. it is reported that the emperor played with a deck of 12 suits which had apparently been invented by the "**old wise men**". The emperor however, had not taken a liking to the game and had therefore changed it. The twelve suit game of the "**old wise men**" with the court or picture cards of a king (mir) and minister (wazir) and ten numeral or pip cards for each suit was basically a military game. In it we see the various corps of the old Indian armies including the cavalry, infantry, armoured soldiers, elephats, fortresses, even a naval fleet and finally a paymaster with "pots of gold". In addition there were five further suits: a suit each with women, gods, demons, animals and snakes. The last four are surely derived from Hinduism. The origin and age of this game is one of the biggest puzzles in reasearch on Indian playing cards. Perhaps the game has survived in the form of the twelve-suited Ramayana *ganjappa* played in remote parts of Orissa.

It is probable that the game mentioned in Abul Fazl's book was not a new invention but the description of an elaborate *ganjifa* game which was crafted by court artisans according to Akbar's instructions. The classic Indian card game of eight suits with 12 cards each, or a total of 96 cards, is called "*Mughal ganjifa*". It is still played in some regions of India.

THE CARDS OF THE HINDUS

In addition to the secular "*Mughal Ganjifa*" there were at least three different Hinduistic forms of *ganjifa* with mythological themes. There was the *dikpala ganjifa* with eight suits, the dasavatara with ten to twelve suits and the ganjappa already mentioned above. In all these games every suit had two court cards, that of a king and of a minister, and ten numeral cards. The link with *ganjifa* is therefore unmistakable. It is of course also possible that both had a common ancestor - perhaps the twelve-suited game described in the "*Ain-i-Akbari*". In addition to the games mentioned here there is also the chada of Mysore with Hindu themes.

INDIA AND THE WORLD OF CARDS

Into this complex scenario a further factor came into play. Around 1500 AD the European playing cards with four suits - the Italian and Spanish designs - were brought to India by Portuguese seafarers. Gradually these began to be imitated and played at the courts of the Indian princes. While four suits are the norm in Europe, there are often eight or more suits in Indian card games. There are also differences with regard to the court cards. In India there are merely two court cards, that of the king and the wazir. In Europe one the other hand there are at least three or more, such as king queen, knight and foot soldier.

Towards the beginning of the 16th century the game of ganjifa with eight suits and two court cards per suit came to the Mughal court in India via Persia or Central Asia. An older game on martial lines and clearly influenced by Hindu culture however, already existed there. Almost at the same time the European cards arrived in India via the sea routes. It is still unclear if and how the four-suited kanjafah with three court cards of the Mamalukes is related to the eight-suited ganjifa with two court cards of the Persians and Mughals in India. However, some link must have existed. Perhaps all these games have a common predecessor - possibly the Chinese playing cards. It is conceivable that the Mongols introduced these in western Asia in the 13th century where they were then adapted by the Turks who belonged to the military hierarchy of various dynasties in the Middle East. The "**money**" suit design of the Chinese cards would have been retained. It is also probable that chess, which was a popular game in Western Asia, played a significant role in this process. The fact that the names shah and wazir are common to both games and other indications point in this direction.

THE 18TH TO THE 20TH CENTURY

The cards in the collection of the Museum are from the 18th to the 20th century, only a few date from the 17th century. Ganjifa in its various forms was played at the many Muslim and Hindu princely courts, and was in fact a game of the aristocracy. They could well afford to have the card decks wonderfully illustrated and decorated by their court painters, often having them painted, cut or engraved on expensive materials such as ivory, mother of pearl or gold and silver. Valuable decks were also sent as presents from one court to another. Frequently this led to a mixing and erasing of local stylistic features. Even the English "**nabobs**" in the 18th century had beautiful ganjifa cards mad for them in Oudh (Awadh) and Bengal, such as the large ivory one from Murshidabad which belonged to the real founder of the British empire in India, Rebert Clive, and which is now displayed at the Victoria and Albert Museum in London. (Condensed)

RUDOLF VON LEYDEN

POCHAMPALLY SAREES AND ROOMALS

Pochampally sarees woven with elaborate process; every individual thread of warp and weft tied, dyed, to a pre-aranged pattern. Sarees have decorated 'Pullo'. Outstanding features designs produced with equal effects both sides; not possible among printed, lacquered designs.

The 'Telia roomals' (scarves) belong to same family; originally used turbans, lungees, dress materials, table cloths, curtains. Chirala, Pochampally noted centres for Roomals; commonly used in Iran, Iraq, Saudi Arabia, Africa. Colours used red, black, natural while of yarn.

POET-SAINTS OF INDIA

The eminent poet - saints - who gave a new and accessible creed to the Indian people, intimately in touch with the rhythms of their life - were instrumental in transforming the traditional concept of religion, replacing it with the concept of bhakti as the essence of faith and true way to God. In the process, they also succeeded in suffusing Indian literature with songs, poems and musical compositions written in the common man's parlance, with simplicity and directness in their message, and yet with levels of complexity reaching for beyond.

Not confining themselves to philosophical and spiritual matters, the poet - saints took up cudgels against formal orthodoxy, ritual practices and priest craft. They condemned sham and bigotry and preached that nirvana (salvation) was accessible to all. Once the atman (soul) unites with Paramatman (the Supreme), the aspirant is unified with God "like water mixing with milk, water merging with water, salt dissolving in water; with no duality whatsoever" (Dadu, 16th Century). Kabir's voice in 15-16th century was the same: "Jal mein kumbh, kumbh main jal hai, Bahar Bhitar pani" (The pitcher is in water, there is water in the pitcher; the water is everywhere).

The central idea of bhakti was, therefore, the passionate belief that one could be united with God through unconditional love and devotion.

Historically, the devotional movement was caused under the influence of Buddhism and Jainism, both of which stimulated Hinduism to what can be termed as a process of self-cleansing.

The devotional current spread to all parts of India and swept into all walks of life to make some much-needed corrections, for example in the caste system, and one finds the lowest becoming the revered preceptor of the highest. As as consequence, the great religious texts became available to the ordinary people in a language and diction that they could easily assImilate.

The devotional movement first flowered in the South. A tradition grew in the 7th century of Azbvars (Vaishnava poets) who included among the top twelve a king, a peasant, a member of the depressed class, a person belonging to a so-called criminal tribe and the poetess Andal, regarded as Meera of the South. Another tradition around the 9th - 10th century was Thevaram, the song-cycle contributed by Shaivite saints like Nayanar, Appar, Uniya Vacchar, Thirugyan Sammandar and Sundaramurthy. The tales and legends of Thevaram, poets are still extant in the inner-precinct paintings of the Brihadeshwara temple, as are Andal's songs.

The devotional movement gathered momentum by the turn of the millennium. Ramanuja, the great Vaishnvite teacher of south India, based his system on poetic intuitions rather than on the abstract logic of Shankara's monism. He infuenced the movement's spread to the north, as Ramananda of the 15th century Varanasi was a follower of his tradition. Among the poet-saints (and Ramananda's disciples) were Ravidas the cobbler, Kabir the weaver, Dhanna the peasant and Sena the barber, besides Sadna the butcher. Out of these Ravidas was the preceptor of the princess Meera, and Sena the teacher of the king of Bandhavgarh! Tulsidas, too, who wrote the Rama Charit Manas, accessible to every hearth and home in north India by the end of the 16th century, was deeply influenced by Ramananda.

The bhakti movement comprised two mainstreams. Philosophically, the more potent was the Nirgun (worship of the un-manifest), which linked with the Supreme and explained mysticism in metaphors of love. But more warm, humane, poetic and accessible to the common imagery was the Sagun (worship of the manifest). Some Nirgun poet saints were Premmargi (following the path of love), with a remarkable closeness to the Sufi poets. Other Nirgun singer-savants were Gyan-margi (following the path of knowledge), such as Kabir, Nanak, Eknath, Gyneshwar, Tukaram, Malleshwari and Ramlinga Adigal. The Sagun saint-musicians followed either Krishnabhakti-dhara (among whom were Jayadev, Sri Chaitanya, Haridas, Surdas, Meera, Vidyapati and Purandaradsa) or Rambhaktidhara (comprising of names like Tulsidas, Keshavdas, Bhaskar and Kamban).

Kabir, the weaver-poet-saint of Uttar Pradesh found Rama and Rahim as totally synonymous. Writing in dohas (couplets) and expressing his love form Almighty, his humanistic philosophy seared through the conventions of caste, creed and cult. His spiritual insights and thoughts were omcosove and found a place in the Sikh scripture Adi Granth. The blind poet Surdas, a contemporary of emperor Akbar and a mentor of Tansen, composed songs overflowing with pure, heartrending devotion in his works Sursagar, Sursarawali and Sahityalabari. Meera, the princes-poet, in the 16th century rebelled against the palace-orthodoxy by choosing a God-oriented ascetic life of prayer and devotion.

In Maharashtra, Gyaneshwar founded the mystrical edifice through his exquisite poetry. Namdeva and Eknath built up the edifice further and the glorious pinnacle was erected by Tukaram in the 17th century with some 4,600 abhangs (well-knit songs).

The movement reached its zenith in the 16th century when Purandaradasa and Kanakadasa, led by Vyasaraya, composed a large corpus of devotional songs.

Thyagaraja who lived in the 18th century composed about 800 songs, emphasizing Nadopasana (music with devotion). His music has an unmistakable spiritual impact on the listeners till today. If Puranadaradasa was the Grandfather of Carnatic music, Thyagaraja was the one of the Trinity, to other two being Muthuswami Dikshitar and Shyama Sastry.

Combining the framework of bhakti with the rich folk heritage of Bengal gave rise to the order of singers, poets and composers called the Bauls. Showing a remarkable affinity with the Sufis, the Bauls loved a simple life and were intoxicated with Truth in any form, Lalan Shah Fakir, a well-known Baul, stated with incomparable clarity: "Since you may never again get a human birth like the present one, Why not follow the dictates of your mind and strive for perfection?"

Sufism, from the 7th century onwards, held the mystic belief that the spiritual world could be reached only through love (ishq) of God and intellect had no access to it.

The development of Urdu poetry owes a lot to the Sufi saints. Amir Khusro, the famous disciple of Saikh Nizamuddin Aulia, was the first major poet to use Hindustani, and his dohas continue to be popularly sung by Qawwals. Sufi poetry written in Hindi added a new lyrical touch to mysticism. Indeed, Hindi established a bridge between Sufi poets and bhaktas - both seeking the higher reaches of reality. Both were radicals in that they rebelled against religious formalism and orthodoxy. The Sufi poets from Punjab and Sindh made use of endearing popular folktales such as Heer Ranjha to give expression to concept of love as a mystical notion. The great Punjabi mystical poet Bulle Shah depicted the longing soul of Heer as the lover and God as the beloved and all their ordeals as obstacles to their union.

By reaching out to the masses in their everyday language, the bhakti saints and Sugis created a veritable social revolution. By promoting a direct relationship between man and his God, the poet-saints and Sufis eliminated traditional clergy (as the Buddha did in the 6th century BC and Martin Luther in the European Reformation). They boosted the confidence of the poor masses regardless of their caste and helped integrate the diverse elements of the Indian subcontinent into a single functioning society. (Condensed)

UTPAL K BANERJEE

POILENG - A PECULIAR BUDDHIST RITUAL

The beautiful Indian state of Arunachal Pradesh, bordered by China, Bhutan and Myanmar (Burma) is inhabited by a mosaic of more than eighty tribes and sub-tribes, each with their own distinct cultural identity and language. Some tribes profess the Donyi Polo (religion), while other are Buddhist, with a few having converted to Hinduism or Christianity and some following their traditional animistic tribal beliefs. The Buddhists are again divided into the followers of the Mahayana sect in the north, where exists the largest 350- year old Buddhist Monastry in Tawang, and the followers of the Hinayana sect in its south.

The Hinayana Buddhists, known as Hinjang here, celebrate a peculiar festival called "Poileng" to honour their deceased monks. Hinjangs are spread not only over a large area of Arunachal but also in quite a few areas of upper Assam.

Attended by thousands of people, "Poileng" festivities entail a huge expenditure. And as this has to be borne by the village where the deceased monk or Bhonte had served, the ceremony may be deferred for a year or two till all the arrangements are complete.

Till the festival is held, the body of the monk is embalmed mummified, with the aid of special medicines and techniques perfected by the monks down the ages. This is then kept in a coffin.

As the day of the ceremonies draws near, young men and boys start constructing a carriage or rath, decorated very tastefully with multihued festoons and banners, all of which have some religious significance. The wheels of the *rath* are massive in size and are cut out of a single tree trunk. These wheels vary in number as per the status of the deceased monk, the highest number being eight wheels.

During the Poileng, special consecration rites and rituals are performed and the coffin is ceremoniously carried on the **rath**. People then pay their respects to the departed soul and jostle with one another to pull the rath as it is considered to be a privilege.

As the festival draws to a close, the coffin along with the Bhonte's mortal remains are consigned to the flames.

DR. TRIDIB KAKOTY

PONGAL

Pongal : (A preparation of sweet rice) : - Hindu festival celebrated at Andhra Pradesh, Karnataka (where it is called Sankranti and specially in Tamil Nadu; held in Pausa (December - January); is spread over 3 days and is biggest and gayest harvest festival of South India : the first day is· observed as a family feast; the 2nd (called Surya Pongal) as the day for worship of Surya when rice cooked in milk and jaggery is offered to the sun; on the 3rd day, Mathu Pongal, cattle are worshipped; they are bathed, their horns polished and flower garlands wreathed round their necks; a festival, Jallikathu, is held in Madurai; Tirichirapalli and Tanjavur on this occasion; bundles containing money are tied to the horns of ferocious bulls which unarmed people (mostly villagers) try to retrieve; everyone joins in the community meals at which the food is made of the freshly harvested grain, etc.,

B. N. SHARMA & SIVANANDA SWAMI

PRABHA ATRE

(Prabha is an academician, musicologist and a renowned singer)

"My Music, first of all, should identify with me and must have the qualities of both the head and the heart", says Dr. Prabha Atre. Her whole approach to music is intensely involved, but yet unassuming. She wears lightly her achievements as an academician, musicologist and musician.

After an initial phase with Vijay Karandikar, in Pune, she found herself under the tutelage of the late Suresh Babu Man and the late Hirabai Badodekar, from the illustrious Kirana 'gharana; who were to prove the guiding light to her musical career. In 1960, here association with Shrikant Bakre, a student of Ustad Amir Khan, exposed her to the late Khan Saheb's style.

After getting a job with all India Radio, she plunged headlong into a musical career. From then on there was no looking back. Her art and sensitivity clearly surface in her thinking and singing. Her doctoral thesis was on 'Sargam; an integral part of music theory. She has also penned a few books, "Swaramayee" published in 1984, which received the Maharashtra State Government Award in 1989. She was awarded the Padmashree and the Sangeet Natak Akademi Award.

Regarding innovation or any departure from the strict classical traditions, Prabha says, "I am not a blind follower of tradition. I like to see the logic behind issue. I have not deviated from tradition yet, I have taken a tangent from the traditional".

She feels classical music can be popularised, with a compulsory cultural training in schools and colleges. Which will help children develop a wider perspective of life and promote a better understanding of the classical arts. (Condensed)

S. SWARUP

PRADEEP - THE POET PATRIOT

It was indeed gratifying that in July, 1998, the Hindi screen's seniormost poet and lyricist, Kavi Pradeep (real name : Ramachandra Narayanji Dwivedi) was presented the prestigious Dada Saheb Phalke Award. The Award, which signifies the highest recognition by the Government of India for outstanding contribution to the growth and development of Indian cinema, came to him rather late in his lfie, just five months before he breathed his last on December 11, the same year. Yet he was elated by the honour, which he felt would have had a rejuvenating effect on his fast-deteriorating health.

The honour was bestowed by the President of India on the occasion of the 45th National Film Award ceremony in New Delhi. Standing ovation greeted the octogenerarian poet-lyricist as he was brought on the stage in a wheel-chair. His presence reminded nostalgically of the tumultuous decade preceding India's independence when our freedom fighters were inspired by this poet's patriotic and thought provoking lyrics.

Pradeep will be remembered not only for his impassioned and inspiring film songs but also non-film compositions, in particular the patriotic dirge: "*Ae mere waten ke logo ; Zarea aankh mein bharlo pani; Jo shaheed huey hain unki zara yaad karo qurbani* " (O my compatriots; Let tears well up in your eyes as you recall the supreme sacrifices made by Indian martyrs).

He wrote this song with a pained heart in the wake of the foreign aggression in October, 1962 and Lata Mangeshkar sang it for the first time in 1963 in New Delhi under the direction of music maestro C. Ramachandran. As the soprano notes of the song rose, the listeners, including the late Prime Minister Jawaharlal Nehru, could not help wiping tears from their eyes;

The song stired Indians no end and the composition acquired a new emphasis in the context of the recent Kargil conflict causing an uprecedented resurgence of patriotic fervour.

Writing of inspiring patriotic songs was indeed Pradeep's forte. Way back in 1942, when our nation, electrified by Gandhiji's 'Quit India' clarion call, was in the thick of the freedom struggle, he wrote :

Door hato ae duniyawaalon, Hindustan hamara hai
(Keep off, you colonisers, Hindusan (India) belongs to us;)

The film which featured this song, Kismet, ran continuously for three years and eight months at Calcutta's Roxy Theatre.

The British authorities suspected Pradeep of harbouring and airing strong anti-establishment views and of hobnobbing with active India freedom fighters. For some time, therefore, our young revolutionary poet had to remain incognito and incommunicado to avoid arrest or other action.

Earlier, in 1940, he had penned another inspiring number, "*Chal chal re naujawan.... aage badhe jana, aafat se ladte jana... aandhi ho ya toofan, phatta ho aasman*" (Keep marching ahead, O Youngman.... even in the face of thunder or turbulent challenges) for the movie Bandhan. The song enthused the youth of our countery like never before and remained on everyone's lips throughour the subcontinent for quite a long while.

He himself sang in his resonant and sonorous voice the famous song of the film Jagirit (1954), music for which was composed by Hemant Kumar and in which the poet-singer took children on a "Bharat darshan" (Tour of India) to see historic and important sites. He also paid a lofty tribute to Gandhiji for winning the country freedom by non-violent means.

These and other songs with a philosophic content, both written and sung by him for films like Nastik, Naagmani, Waman Aavtar, Do Behnen, Talaq and Sashera enjoy an undiminished popularity even to this day. His songs of this genre rendered by some other singers for such films as Marshal and Sambandhi are also equally popular. His devotional songs for Jai Santoshi Maa too became highly popular and were heard in almost every household and at temples and other celebratory functions.

Pradeep was also a distinguished recipient of the Sangeet Natak Akademi Award, the Sur Sagar Award and the National Integration Award.

It was in 1938 that the Young Ramachandra, who was born on February 6, 1914, and who had by then become a part-time teacher and an accomplished poet in Ujjain, moved to Mumbai. In that tinsel town, Himansu Rai, the founder of the erstwhile Bombay Talkies, straightway employed him as a lyricist for his company's films and gave him the name Pradeep, which he considered more appropriate for a poet. The prefix 'Kavi' (poet) was attached to his new name to distinguish him from the hero Pradeep Kumar, whose mail began to be mis-delivered to him and vice versa.

Patriotism, moral philosophy and essence of life constitute the leit motif of his compositions, though hendid write on other themes and situations as well. His repertoire comprises of around 1500 film and non-film songs. A good number of them will undoubtedly ensure continued appreciation of his genius.

B. M. MALHOTRA

PREMCHAND MUNSHI

World renowned novolict, short story writer and above all a pioneer of progressive literature; real name Dhanpat Rai, pet name Prem Chand; born on July 31, 1880 at Lamahi, a village 4 miles north of Varanasi; married a child widow after the death of first wife; lived in exteme poverty; passed Matric in 1904 graduated privately and rose to position of Deputy Insptector of Schools; under Gandhi's influence joined non-cooperation movement in 1920; started literary career as a free-lance journalist in Urdu; collection of his stories *Soze Watan* proscribed; switched over to Hindi in 1914; pioneer of writing fiction with a social purpose; portrayed real problems of urban middle class society and peasants; left behind about a dozen novels

and 250 short stories; some of his well known novels are Rangabhumi, Godan, premshram, etc.; his greatness lies in the fact that his writings embody the social purpose and social criticism rather than mere entertainment; died October 8, 1936.

MADAN GOPAL

PULAK BISWAS - INNOVATIVE PAINTER & ILLUSTRATOR

Pulak Biswa's preferred medium is rice paper mounted on paper or canvas. Retaining the creases and wrinkles of the paper, he visualizes and draws out the images that form in his mind. The forms are not totally abstract and the texture does not dominate.

In Pulak Biswas paintings, one notices the human figure dominating. The swarthy, lean bodies might remind one of the weariness and anguish of the everyday struggle of living. Underneath though one senses a perserverence that suggests hope, oras in the artist's own words, the indomitable spirit of the people. This aspect is especially clear in the steadfast gaze of the people he depicts. In some of the paintings, the eyes are painted with unusual clarity.

The colour washes of mainly ochres and reds show the earthiness of the hard working masses. The definite strokes indicate a minimalistic approach and help enhance the optimism that emanates from the painting.

Pulak Biswas, at the same time, is one of the top illustrators of mostly children's books.

As an illustrator, his career spans about forty years, Being a children's book illustrator, Pulak Biswas feels he gets as much freedom as he does while painting. He believes that one should not undermine children's intelligence as they can distinguish between a good and a bad illustration. It is an illustrator's responsibility to help visual growth of a child and to give it direction.

Pulak Biswas received the prestigious BIB Plaque (Bienalle of Illustrations, Bratislava) for his book '*Tiger on a Tree*!

The illustrations for 'Tiger on a Tree' are in black and orange against a white background. The strong graphic quality of the pictures creates powerful images on the viewers' minds. (Condensed)

SONALI BISWAS

PUNJAB : THE CRADLE OF GREAT CIVILISATIONS

The five major rivers, Jhelum, Chenab, Ravi, Beas and Satluj constitute the cultural and historical Punjab known variously as **Sapat-Sindhu, Panch Nad or Punjab**. But uptil the emergence of the independent and sovereign State of Punjab under Ranjit Singh around the beginning of 19th century, this Punjab or even a major portion of it was never united as a single political unit. It also kept changing its political affiliation as the balance of power shifted to the North-West or to the South-East. Even under Ranjit Singh the Anglo-Sikh Treaty of 1809 delimited the political boundaries of the sovereign State of Punjab at

Satluj in East and South-East. As a matter of fact it was only under the British regime that the whole of Punjab achieved an intergrated political identity. The independence of India in 1947 started a process of political fragmentation of the land of five rivers portioning off its major parts to the new State of Pakistan, Linguistic reorganisation of the Indian Punjab in 1966 viewed in this context was only a continuation of the splitting up of Punjabi personality and cultural identity. As a cultural entity the idea of the punjab conjures up visions of a cultural process: Of confrontation between the divergent cultural forces, of continuing dialogue between the native or naturalized elements and the incoming influences and of the resolution of tensions seeking expression in creative synthesis and newer tensions.

Till the sea-routes became operative for import of foreign civilizations and alien ideas converting the coastal areas as the modal points of cultural commerce it was the land of Punjab through which incoming civilzations and cultures established contact with the Indian culture. This process started with the dawn of the history of the Indian people in the shape of the successive waves of penetration of Indian sub-continent continuing intermittantly till the emergence of Punjab as a sovereign State in 19th century. With the tribes and marauding hordes came mystics and philosophers, theologians and thinkers as also well organised systems of ideas. This naturally resulted in cross-fertalization, not only in the genatic sense, but also in realms of history of ideas and consciousness. We come across in the Punjab the same phenomenon of cultural, religious, social, linguistic and literary pluralism which characterises the cultural history of India.

Eversince the first chaloclithic civilization of India arose and flourished in the Punjab traces of which are still to be found in the excavation of Mohinjo-Daro, Harrapa and Ropar, the land of five rivers has been the cradle of great civilizations, religious and faiths. Assimilation of outside influences to their history and tradition has contributed in no mean measure to the dynamism and catholicity of, the culture of the Punjabi people.

Another significant result flowing from this intermingling, has been that the Punjabi outlook on life has not sustained orthodoxies of faith, belief or behaviour. In the context of the history of Indian culture as a manifestation of two diametrical opposite movements: elitistic cultural movement, symbolised by Brahamanism and ritualism with Sanskrit as the vehicle for expression and communication, and the antielitist, peoples' movement, expressing itself in the form of Buddhism and Jainism and their various cults and Sikhism, etc., and articulating itself in the spoken languages of the people, Punjabi culture can be identified more with the latter than the former. The sway of Buddhism and varied cults shooting off from it in the years of its decline in the Punjab during the first seven centuries of Christian era, the emergence of Sikkhism in the medieval times as well as parallel growing influence of Islam, the anti particularist and anti-ritualist thrust of the teaching of the Sikh Gurus and the Sufi mystics, the wholehearted acceptance of the teachings of Arya Samaj by the Punjabi Hindus in the late 19th and early 20th centuries, all these developments provide eloquent proof in support of this contention.

A study of the course of Islam in the history of Punjab in some depth will reveal that the Sufi mystics of Punjab imbibed a great deal of Indian Ideas of immense love of God and they were deeply influenced in their acquisition of the non-islamic cultural notes and modes by the local traditions. The avid interest with which the Punjabi Muslims adopted music and paintings as the modes of self expression and achieved great perfection in these two media is self-revealling Similarly, the spirit of rebellion against the crippling orthodoxy, which is the levellaing element in the formation of Sufi mysticism, found in the liberal atmosphere of Punjab a very fertile gound to grow. Sikhism which is essential terms constitutes the Indian response to the challenge of islam also developed identical anit-ritualistic and anti-particularist tendencies at the same time as it assimilated the transcendental concept of God to the theory of immenence which in inherited from the Indian tradition. Sikhism was able to draw upon the idea of history from Islam which the latter inherited from its semitic origins.

The innovation and experimentation did not stop with ideas alone. The Sikh architecutre, especially the Sikh temple, enshrines the Buddhist idea of a lotus in a pool of pure water and the Islamic austerity and functional utility in a wonderful symphony. Similarly the Sikh music is a wonderful combination of the classical system of Indian music and the community singing so popular with devotional singers of the Sant Parampara as well as the Sufi singers.

This is primarily due to the catholicity of the Sikh Gurus Mardana, the Muslim, accompanied Nanak's song on the Rabab; communion was possible for them alike in the temple and the mosque, both had gone to Macca; Guru Arjan included in the collection of sacred songs the hymns of Muslim Sufi saints like Farid and well as those of Hindu saints of the devotional movement like Namdev.

Both the aspects, of pluralism as well as compositness in the cultural of the Punjabi people, are to be come across almost inextricably mixed up. In spite of constant interflow of ideas and concepts the relgious life in the Punjab remained by the large pluralistic with Islam, Hinduism and Sikhism as the major religious groups. However, in the realms of language and literature. the trend towards pluralism was very delicately balanced by a proclavity towards compositness. In the Vedic, Heroic and Buddhistic periods of its history Punjab's contribution to varied fields of numinous poetry, metaphysical writing, learning and scholarship was both unique and sublime. Mention of river Indus and other rivers of the Punjab in the Rig Veda clearly supports close affinity between the ancient sages of the Aryans and the land of five rivers. Similarly the immortal teachings of Shrimad Bhagwad Gita were also composed at Kurukshetra, an inalienable part of the historical and cultural Punjab. The great Sanskrit grammarian and scholar Panini was also an illustrious son of the Punjab who composed his unexcelled grammar of Sanskrit language **Ashtadhaiyee** at Takshila University which was a great seat of learning in the ancient Punjab. During the Buddhist period also Punjab gave birth to several scholars of Buddhist metaphysics and theology of whom mention must be made of Kumaral Budh, Asang and Vasu Bandhu; the writings of the latter are considered to have greatly influenced Shankaracharya in formulating his theories.

With the advent of Islam were introduced Arabic and Persian languages alongwith their unique literary traditions. The contact with Arabic and Persian languages created the ferment out of with evolved the modern speech of the Punjab : Punjabi. But in addition to exercising a decisive in fluence upon shaping the Punjabi language, Arabic and Persian Languages brought with them visions and echoes of distant lands which interflew most effusively into those of distant times preserved and procured by the local languages branching off from sanskrit. Bringing together of the memories of the distant lands and distant times gave birth to myriad new patterns of idioms, styles, images expressions, genres, and traditions which still retain a singular freshness and pregnant charm of emotion and thought. Sheikh Farid was equally adept at a dignified and elegant expression in Persian prose and poetry as well as being the progenitor of Punjabi poetic tradition. His compositions are deeply imbued in the topography, flora and fauna, the scenes and sights, the fears and hopes, of the people of Punjab. Similarly Guru Nanak dextrously welded Punjabi, Hindvi, Sadh Bhasha and even Persian for giving tangible forms to his inner most feelings and emotions. While the Sufi poets of punjab as well as other Punjabi poets of Muslim stream maintained a living contact with the Islamic traditions and the Arbic and Persian writings at the same time transforming the local patois into a viable vehicle for the most sophisticated and elevated expression, the poets of Sikh tradition maintained an identical balance between their cultivation of punjabi language and their assiduous nurturing in the Brij and Sanskrit traditions of classical writing and learning.

This basic diversity of backgrounds in spite of the essential unity prepared the ground for evolution of Urdu language and literature in the Punjab on the one hand and the most outstanding contribution of the Sikh poets in the development of Brij classical and scholarly tradition. We have such charming cultural phenomena as Punjabi literature in Gurmukhi and Persian scripts, Sanskrit and Brij literature in Gurumukhi script and so often and so on.

This simultaneous cultivation of different languages and literary traditions by the people of the Punjab found consummation in the modern periods in which the Punjab produced frontrank writers in Urdu, Hindi and English. Dr. Mohummad Iqbal, Faiz Ahmad Faiz, Saadat Hasan Manto, Krishna Chander and Rajinder Singh Bedi are some of the name whom any history of Urdu literature can afford to ignore only at the cost of its credibility. Similarly the achievements of Yash Pal, Agaye, Upendar Nath Ashk, Mohan Rakesh, to modern Hindi literature are most outstanding and significant. What English writing in India owes to such stalwarts as Mulk Raj Anand, Khushwant Singh and P. Lal cannot be questioned by any responsible critic.

Projecting these names against the background of the literary attainments of Punjabi writers starting from Sheikh Farid; Guru Nanak and other Sikh Gurus and Bhai Gurdas; Damodar, Waris Shah, Qadir yar and Mohummad Bakhsh amongst the Qissa poets; Shah Hussain, Bulleh Shah, Ali Haider and Ghulam Farid amongst the mystic poets and such other literateurs of modern era as Bhai Vir Singh, Puran Singh, Dhani Ram Chatrik, Mohan Singh, Amrita

Pritam, Gurbakhash Singh, Kartar Singh Duggal, Sant Singh Sekhon, Gopal Singh, Balwant Gargi and Harbhajan Singh, the literary achievements of the people of Punjab appear in the aspect of the rich mosaic interlaced with rare gems of most complex textures. One can only fainty perceive the grand design unfolding itself behind this multi-linguistic and multi-traditional activity. A clear perception of the earliest manifestation of that design is available in the Adi Granth (compiled in 1604 A.D.) which was conceived by Guru Arjun as a compendium of the religious insights of the people of the Punjab embracing the hymns of peoples of all creeds and faith and which because of its radical espousal of the ideas of religious coexistence and tolerance is unparralleled in the literary history of the Indian people. (Condensed)

ATTAR SINGH

PUNJABI THEATRE : NEW DELHI

Private, registered; branches at Calcutta, Chandigarh, Bombay; promotes Punjabi plays; provides theatre and plays for enjoyment and enlightenment; promotes social awareness, etc., though medium of stage.

MULK RAJ ANAND
H. N. DASGUPTA
BALWANT GARGI

PUPPET SHOWS

Puppet shows, a form of rural histonics; two or three foot high dolls made of wood and cloth performed on stage; human like, unseen hands from over the curtain adjusted their movements; master touch by means of strings. Episodes from epics with moral, adorning a tale rendered realistically by puppet layers. Playing the roles of traditional heroes and villians, the inanimate dolls dances, gesticulated, displayed their emotions, sang, entered into long discourses; the human voices behind curtains synchronised with puppet's gestures. The spectator witnessed good over evil; life over death; he himself gained immoratlity.

PURI BEACH

The beach at Puri is amongst the finest beaches on the 482 km long coastline of Orissa. The silver sands present the most fascinating vista.

The beach at Puri is picturesque but rough and not fit for swimming. However, some adventurous souls venture a few steps into the waters before shouts from the shore make them beat a hasty retreat. The sunrise at the beach is a spectacular sight but not before clouds give anxious moments to those gathered on the beach, particularly the photographers keen to capute the grand moment. The sky is aglow with the golden light heralding the sunrise. It is a kaleidoscope of rainbow hues spread across the sky, a marvellous sight as the golden disc rises over the waves. One feels like payinh obeisance to the sun god Surya, source of life and energy on earth.

A stroll towards the fishing village is an altogether different world with a few thatched huts on the sands. The fisherfolk are at work. Early in the morning before the beach gets crowded with people, these hardy men venture into the sea with their catamarans, pushing these small wooden contraptions into the forthy waves, a valiant effort amply rewarded with a catch of shrimps, sardines, whitebait, mackerel, barracuda and even the occasional hammerhead shark. The rich haul is emptied on the beach where an eager assembly of small raders swiftly auctions the days catch to reach the market.

Tranquillity deserts the beach as the sun rises higher on the horizon as more and more people, throng the beach, a veritable Mall on the sands.
(Condensed)

SURENDRA SAHAI

PUSHKAR FAIR

An important Hindu bathing festival, accompanied with a big fair, is held at pushkar Lake (11 km. north-west of Ajmer) where there is the only temple in India dedicated to the god Brahma (the Creator) where he is said to have performed a *yagya*; it is believed that without bathing in the sacred waters of the lake, the full benefit of visiting the other important places of pilgrimage can not be acquired.

B. N. SHARMA & SIVANANDA SWAMI

"R"

RABINDRA BHARATI UNIVERSITY

Rabindranath Tagore influence on the Bengali is perhaps more pervasive than that of Shakespeare on the Englishman. The grand scale in which his birth anniversary is celebrated annually all over West Bengal is an indication of this. It extends over as many as seven days or even a frotnight. The most popular method of celebration is a feast of Tagore's literature in the form of recitations, songs and dance from Tagore's own works. The Bengali takes delight in his songs and dramas and finds reading his books the best pastime.

But Tagore's influence is not confined to his people alone. He has received homage in the highest possible terms from men of distinction in the West and the East. His poems have a dynamic quality which has evolved through different phases into a lasting maturity. In their mature form his writings developed a new philosophy of life which has a unviersal appeal to men of all countries. This philosophy holds that man's ideal religion is the realisation of god in man which accepts service to humanity at large and particularly the underprivileged humanity as the best form of service to god. His literature is thus not only a rich store-house of refined joys but also the progenitor of a kind of humanism which elevates the mind and gives a direction and purpose to life.

The State Government thought of providing a fitting memorial to the greatest son of the land. Apart from forming a centenary committee for arranging for large-scale celebration and publication of a cheap edition of his works, it decided to found some memorial of permanent form. That is how the idea was conceived of establishing a University bearing his name in his ancestral home. Steps were thereupon taken for not only acquiring the entire ancestral home but also neighbouring premises for providing a sizeable area for the campus. The University was actually established on 8th May, 1962 being the first birth anniversary after the completion of the centenary year.

Rabindranath's ancestral home is situated at Jorasanko in Calcutta. It was here that he was born and brought up and he breathed his last. Even in the latter part of his life this continued to be his Calcutta residence. It is linked up with him through so many bonds of association. It is also associated with memory of a distinguished line of his predecessors who played a leading part in the resurgent cultural life of Bengal, in the nineteenth century. The "Thakur Bari" as it is popularly known thus became the nerve centre of Bengal's cultural life.

A house sanctified by so many associations deserves to be protected as a national property. It was principally this motive that actuated the State Government to take up acquisition of this property as well assurrounding lands. Himself one of the topmost exponents of writing as a form of expression, Rabindranath believed that other modes of expression like music, dance or painting deserve equal attention. It was, therefore, thought that the best use it could be put to was to locate a University there to be named after him which will specialise in teaching the fine arts and literature and particularly Tagore literature.

It was also thought appropriate that the ancestral home proper should be utilised for setting up a museum to exhibit objects telling the story of the cultural revival in Bengal in the nineteenth century as a result of the impact of Western culture. Those were the days when Bengal led India in different fields of life and the galaxy of her distinguished sons drew the tribute from Gokhale : 'what Bengal thinks today all India thinks tomorrow'. Their achievements could be fittingly the subject for exhibition in this museum.

What ordinarily escapes the eye is that, the two Universities Visva-Bharati and Rabindra Bharati are tied in a bond of common objective, both being interested in Rabindranath, though in somewhat different ways. While the Visva-Bharati is mainly interested in dissemination of knowledge and culture in the manner its founder wanted it to be disseminated, the main role of the Rabindra Bharati is to disseminate knowledge about Rabindranath. Naturally, therefore, there can be no clash of interest. With this end in view, the Unviersity has provided for representation of the Visva-Bharati both in the general body as well as the Executive Committee. The Rabindra Bharati has, for the same reason taken up specifically the task of disseminating knowledge about Tagore and research on his works.

The objective of the University as defined in the Rabindra Bharati Act (West Bengal Act XXIX of 1961) passed by the State Legislature is defined in the preamble as follows:

"Whereas it is expedient to perpetuate the memory of Rabindranath Tagore and, to that end, to establish, on the occasion of his one hundredth birth anniversay, a University at his residential house in Calcutta for the advancement of learning and culture particularly in the branches of music, the fine arts, dance and drama".

This is in keeping with the Poet's conception of education as a process of developing all his various faculties of self-expression which should include not only the language of words but the different fine arts. He has said, "A large part of man can never find its expression in the mere language of words. It must, therefore, seek for its other languages-likes and colours, sounds and movements."

The Act also authorises the University to carry on research work, to establish museums and to affiliate institutions teaching fine arts including dance, drama and music.

Government have completed proceedings for acquisition of not only the ancestral house of Rabindranath but also contiguous lands to provide a sizeable area for development and future expansion of the Unviersity. The total area of the campus including all these lands would be 10 bighas, 12 cottahs or a little over 3.5 acres. The Univesity has been already put in possession of part of these lands. The rest of the land is being made over according to a phased programme.

In 1962-63 the University set up two Faculties namely, (1) the Faculty of Fine Arts which includes dance drama and music and (2) the Faculty of Humanities. Under the former a three-year Senior Diploma Course has been started. Under the Faculty of Humanities has opened a one-year diploma course in Tagore literature to provide for deeper appreciation of Rabindranath's writings.

Steps have also been taken to set up a museum in the ancestral home proper for depicting the cultural history of Bengal in the nineteenth century. The nucleus of a museum has been already set up in the first floor of the building known as Vichitra.

(Condensed)

HIRANMAY BANERJEE

RADHA KRISHANGARH - THE MONALISA OF INDIA

A long chiselled nose, little quivering lips, tranquilising lotus eyes, bow-shaped eyebrows and a broad forehead on an elliptical fair face supported by a cylinderical tender neck. This is the "Radha Krishangarh", a historical personality of the 18th century, immortalized by an unknown miniature artist of the Krishnagarh School of Art in Rajasthan, India. Christened as "*Bani-thani ki Chavi*" (Image of a well made-up belle) this miniature portrait of a royal singer displays the Indian feminie fineries at their best and in the world of art is know as the "Mona Lisa of India".

Such a fascinating work of art remained buried in anonymity for nearly two centuries till it was brought to light in 1943 from the darkness of the royal 'toshakhana' (repository of precious articles), by an European art-lover, Eric Dickinson. Only after it was evaluated in glowing terms by renowned art critics that this Painting received world-wide appreciation and its deserving place among the best art creations of the world.

This 18th century painting is the high point of the Kishangarh School of Art in Rajasthan. The Kishangarh State near Ajmer develped a special style of painting under the patronage of the rulers of the time, which came to be known as the Kishangarh style. This painting is a tribute to a love story the passion of King Sawant Singh for a talented and beautiful commoner.

Sawant Singh was no ordinary ruler. Apart from being a caring administrator, he had a well gifted, romantic and maudlin personality. He was a fine painter, a sensitive poet and a linguist. He mastered Hindi, Sanskrit and Persian languages and composed about 75 verses under the pseudonym of 'Nagridas'. His compositions like *Utsav Mala, Bihari Chandrika, Rasik Ratnavali* and *Grisham Vihar* are cherished even to this day. A Collection of his poetry, compiled under the title '*Nagar Samuchaya*' became very popular.

Sawan was a prince when his step-mother Bankawat Ji visited the Moghul court at Delhi. She was so impressed by the golden voice and singing abilities of a teenaged girl in the royal court of King Muhammad Shah Rangila that she took her in own personal service and brought her along. The girl, then at the prime of her teenaged youth, not only wooed the hearts of all those who were ever privileged to listen to her devotiohal songs, rendered each day in Praise of Lord Krishna, but also mesmerized those who saw her shimmering self, covered with generous make-up and tasteful adornations from the forehead down to the toes. It was her fancy with the make-up that earned her the title of '*Bani Thani Ji*'. The physical charm and the traits of similar artistic frame of mind swayed the young Sawat Singh, who was already

married by then to the daughter of King Jaswant Singh of the Bhavnagar state.

Sawant's intense love for th singer faced tough resistance from every possible quarter and he was frustrated to such an extent that he gradually lost all interest in governance of the state and shunned his hitherto affluent lifestyle. Finally, in 1757, he abdicated his kingdom and moved on to the holy place of the Hindus - Brindavan - with his beloved. Brindavan is the place where Lord Krishna lived and charmed 'gopis'. While enjoying each other's company, both composed and sang holy hymns in Praise of Lord Krishna. *Bani Thai* alos sharpened here her poetic skills and wrote verses with the pseudonym 'Rasik Bihari' and rendered these in her golden voice to add to the religious fervour these in her golden voice to add to the religious fervour of the assembled devotees. In his verses in the praise of Lord Krishna, Sawant Singh portrayed himself as Krishna and his beloved *Bani Tahnai* as his paramour, Radha. Inspired by these very verses the artists of the State created minature paintings embodying their popular king and his paramour as the divine couple. While at Brindavan, 'Bani Thani' breathed her last in 1763. Such was the shock of her separation that Sawant Singh also left this world to join her only a year later in 1764. They have left behind a love story which is remembered and told till date in households of Rajasthan. In "Radha Kishangarh" is immortalized an un-crowned queen of the people's hearts.

BIMAL SAIGAL

RAGHURAJ KISHORE

Raghuraj Kishore, an accomplished artist, has spent a lifetime doing temple architectural drawings at world famous heritage sites. His works speak volumes for themselves. Apart from his contributions at Khajuraho and Angkor Vat in Cambodia, he has re-created Asia's biggest prehistoric rock shelter at the Bhopal museum of the Madhya Pradesh Archaeological Department, depicting the pre-historic rock shelters of Bhim Baithka. It is a thrilling experience to enter the gallery and feel for a moment as though one has been transported to Bhim Baithka itself.

However, Raghuraj Kishore is better known for his highly acclaimed work of preparing 'to the scale' drawings of *Kandariya Mahadev, Vishwanath* and *Laxman* temples located in the Khajuraho temple complex. It took him seven long strenuous years to do the detailed pencil drawings of each and every sculpture of these three most important temples at Khajuraho. He claims that the entire Khajuraho complex can be re-built on the basis of the drawing work done by him and his team at Khajuraho.

He spent his seven youthful years (1957 to 1964) in the heat and dust of Khajuraho doing the drawings. The work involved sitting face-to-face with each sculpture with pencil and drawing papers in hand. It took him 15 months to complete drawings of the 100 feet high *Kandariya Mahadev* temple, proceeding step-by-step to reach the summit. All this while, he was precariously perched on high scaffoldings which would shake even with a gentle whiff of wing. The same effort was repeated for the two other temples.

He was assigned the task of preparing 'to the scale' drawings of these Khajuraho temples by his parent organisation, the Archaeological Survey of India. Seven long years of proximity and in-depth work on the Khajuraho temples convinced him that the medieval sculptors of the place had followed a particular pattern in the design of the temples. To his understandings, the basic pattern followed by Khajuraho's builders a thousand years ago is that of a sitting female, and it is this posture which was kept in mind when the edifices were built.

The Government of India rewarded him for his stupendous work by including him in a Cambodia-bound team of archaeologists, temple architects and experts to assist the Cambodian government in the preparation of detailed drawings of the world famous *Angkor Vat* temple.

With many awards to his credit, he has many a time assisted the Madhya Pradesh Government in preparing its Republic Day tableaux. He has also helped put up yet another Bhim Baithka rock shelter replica at the Birla museum in Bhopal.

Holder of a diploma in fine arts from the JJ School of Arts, Mumbai, he was initiated into temple architectural drawings at the tender age of 14 by his late father, Mr. Ganpatrao Singh who himself was a draughtsman at the Scindia Palace temples in Gwalior. Settled in Bhopal, Raghuraj Kishore is still actively involved in preparing scale models of temple monuments, including the ones in Bhopal, Indore and Gwalior. Block prints of his Khajuraho temple drawings have been published in the book, "The Temples of Khajuraho" written by the renowned archaeologist Krishnadev.

DINKAR SHUKLA

RAJ KAPOOR : FILM ACTOR & PRODUCER

"I have always believed, and I say it again, that a showman and a politician run on the same platform... they sell drama". Raj Kapoor's confession matched his credo of cinema, for the showman consistently peddled dreams to the common man through his onscreen personae of Raju, the happy-go-lucky tramp.

His most persistent image, despite his versatility, remains that of the quintessential Indian who walks through the city squalor with threadbare Japaani shoes, the frayed English pantaloons and the made-in-India heart filled with spirited songs and unbridled optimism. Be it Awara, Sree 420, Phir Subah Hogi, Jis Desh Mein Ganga Behti Hai, Kapoor's Chaplinesque hero never abandoned his optimism and his desire to articulate the great Indian dream of progress, equality.

As a producer-director, he used R.K. Films, his production company, to make paeans on love. Love denied by class barriers: Bobby. Love strangled by moribund tradition: Prem Rog. Love thwarted in a market society: Ram Teri Ganga Maili.

Coupled with this sentimentality was the characteristic sensuousness of his films Vyjantimala's seductive song-and-dance in Sangam, Zeenat Aman's mini-skirts and half cholis in Satyam Shivam Sundaram or Mandakini's bathing splendour in Ram Teri Ganga Maili, this Dada Saheb Phalke Award winner made an art of erotica.

RAJA RAVI VERMA

Ravi Verma was born in the year 1848 at Kilimanoor, about 35 km north of Thiruvananthapuram. His family was closely related to the royal family of travancore and his original name was Ravi Verma Koil Thampuran. The title "Raja", which was prefixed to his name, was conferred on him by the British.

Raja Ravi Verma's incomparable contribution to Indian culture and aesthetics has not been properly evaluated. The vibrant characters of India religious and classical literature have mostly been enshrined only in poestic imagination and it was to Ravi Varma's credit that he brought them literally to life and made them a visual reality. Sages like Viswamitra, celestial beauties like Rambha and Urvashi, legendary characters like Shakunthala, Damayanti and Rukmangada come alive from the canvass exquisitely handled by the great painter. Some of his paintings were so arresting that no less a person than the great Tamil Poet Subramania Bharathi described them as surpassing the best in human conception. Later on, Bharathi wrote verses to the effect that Ravi Varma had gone to heaven to see the gods he had painted.

Ravi Varma's pictures have become intimately interwoven with the cultural life of thousands of Indian homes, especially in Tamil Nadu. Some of his most famous paintings include "Hamsa Damayanti", Shakunthala turning back to take a wistful look at he Lover, on the pretext of taking out a thorn from her foot, and Rukmangada's anguish at having to kill his son, in the episode of his "Ekadasi Vrata".

Ravi Varma got recognition and fame in the Prime of his life. Before he was 30 he was awarded the Viceroy's medal for his portrait of a Malayalee woman. Another picture of his, of a Nair woman, was exhibited at the madras Exhibition at the time of Lord Herbert and it figured later in an international show at Vienna. Since then his fame spread rapidly and extensively and Princes and Governors, Contemporary artists and connoisseurs from all parts of India became his fans. At the request of Sir T. Madhava Rao, Dewan of Baroda, a galaxy of 14 oil paintings on puranic episodes was drawn by him for the Maharaja's art gallery. These pictures were kept for about a month at Thiruvanathapurama for the public display before they were sent to Baroda. The Maharaja of Mysore also Patronised him and the painter showed his skill mostly in his pictures on the themes of the Ramayana and the Mahabharata.

Ravi Varma was mostly a self-made man though his maternal uncle taught him the rudiments of painting mostly in water colour. Early in life, in his studio at Kilimanoor, he had only a few plates of colours, some charcoal, a bit of canvas and some brush. But his arena widened vastly after he became acquainted with the British painter Theodore Johnson, who came to visit the Maharaj of Travancore. Thereafter, Ravi Varma took to oil painting and drew pictures of Hindu mythological characters and contemporary princes and dignitaries.

The artist was a great devotee of Mookambika Bhagavati and sincerely believed that his skill and renown were the result of the Goddess' blessings. Even during his last moments he was not only remembering his "Ishta Devata" but actually described her in detail to his son Rama Varma, who was by his side. Raja Ravi Varma died at the age of 59.

The Trivandrum Art Gallery, the Baroda Palace Picture gallery and the Jagan Mohan Palace of Mysore are some of the places where the great artists' works are accessible to the public. But many of his famous paintings have gone abroad.

(Condensed)

R. RAMDAS THAMPURAN

RAJASTHANI CULTURE - IMPACT ON INDIAN LIFE

Rajasthan, the land of heroes, has always been inspring our people in their determination for doing things of national interests. The inspiration for sacrificing every thing for the freedom of our motherland was first received by our people from the various heroic deed of the Rajputs and their families. The various *johars* committed on the fort of Chittor by Rajput women are unique examples of sacrifices for saving womanhood from barbaric hands. There are numerous examples for relinquishing everything and inviting poverty and hunger for the cause of the motherland.

Along with these acts of bravery and sacrifices, Rajasthan has equally been rich in the field of devotion, Meerabai, Sahjobai, Daduji and Bavji Chatur Singhji sang eternal songs of Bhakti. Meerabai has to revolt against Maharana Vikram of Chitoor because of his cruel behaviour. She renounced all worldly comforts in pursuit of her love towards Lord Krishna and went to Brindavan and Dwarka to be one with other devotees where she inspired thousands of Bhaktas. Meerabai's cult of worshiping God as her husband brought in a revolutionary change in the devotional poetry of India.

The romantic events of Rajasthan like those of Dhola-Maru, Ramu-Chandna, Moomal-Mahendra, Ujli-Jethva, Sudh-Budh, Savarlinga and several others have given us poetry of very high order. Their authors are not known, because they are all folk epics and have been composed from mouth to mouth. The collective imagination of the masses, the language of the verses, the use of imageries and their musical compostitions are a result of their several hundred years' incessant use among the people, with the result that this folk type of literature has an all India appeal. Several of these romantic episodes along with several others of romantic robbery, incidents in the manner of Rabin Hood and day to day love-affairs caught the imagination of the people and several folk plays came into existence. Rajasthan, at present, has about six or seven different styles of such folk theatres, all rich in their thematic compositions, colourful dance-forms and spectacular presentation.

The folk songs of Rajasthan, particularly, those of Jaisalmer and Barmer, mostly desert areas, are rich in a particular type of folk poetry and musical compositions. The Manganiyas and the langas of these regions, living mostly at the mercy of their patrons, whom they visit periodically with their typical sarangi, kamayecha and morchang, are the real masters of this typical folk poety.

Since nature has been unkind and cruel to the people of these areas and drought conditions prevail almost all the year round, these people has to develop not only their own ways of earning but their ways of entertainment also. In the absence of colour in nature, they created artificial colours in their own costumes and acquited proficiency in various arts and crafts.

The musical compositions of the Langas and Manganiyas of this region too have acquired and distinctive colour and variety, because of the void created in their life due to the atrocities of nature. These compositions, though folk in nature, are classical in their rendering.

The folk ballads of Rajasthan like the Pabuji, Randevji, Gajaji, Devanarain and several others are no more confined to the limites of Rajasthan. They have provided rich material for the study of Indian ballads and have revealed several mysteries of this particular style. They are sung by their traditional singers, know as Bhopas, for nights together and the pictorial cloth rapping forming background for their ballad singing, has now been accepted by all great artists as an art-form of international importance.

The classical music and the classical dance of India, owe a great deal to the state of Rajasthan. The rulers of different states of Rajasthan were the real patrons of these classical arts. Jaipur, Udipur, Jodhpur, Alwar, Kota and Bindu were their seats. The "Nom Tom" Gharanas of Dhrupad singing was developed by the Dagar family of Udaipur and Alwar. Rajasthat contributed a great deal to the develpment of the great Kathak art of dancing; it is said that it was first evolved there.

The heroic deeds of the Rajputs and the sacrificial nature of their women, an history says, have influenced the literature of almost all the North Indian States. Bengal perhaps was the foremost in this direction. Almost all Bengali writers used Rajasthan as their source - material for their Dramas and Novels. Dr. Rabindra Nath Tagore was a great admirer of Rajasthani poetry and used its salient features in the enrichment of his own literature.

Meerabai is considered as an embodiment of Indian Bhakti and here songs are sung in all Indian Languages. Even in dance forms like Bharat Natyam of remote South, her songs are used in various abhinayas. It was due to writers and poets of Bengal, Gujarat and Maharashtra that personalities like Rana Pratap, Maharana Kumbha, Rana Sanga and others could become national heroes. It is said that the greatness of the hero like Chundawat could only be realized after the publication of the Marathi novel "Rajasthan Ch Bhishm", 50 years back.

It was first though Gujarat and Bengal that Meerabai was accepted as a Bhakta. Historians like Pt. Gauri Shankar and Jadunath Sarkar were the first to bring this fact to the notice of the people that Meerabai rebellion was because of her conviction and her deep devotion of Lord Krishna. The Gujaratis, for a long time, though that she belonged to Gujarat and rendered all her songs in Gujarati. Several of their composers composed devotional songs in the name of Meerabai and felt greatly honoured.

The Jaipur Kathak style was an evolution of the art of story telling by Kathakars, through rhythm and bodily movements and was first confined to devotional affairs. It later caught the imagination of the rulers of Rajasthan and connosseurs of art and got their patronage. Several of them were engaged to perform this particular form in the temples managed directly by them. So it could retain its devotional nature to a great extent. The Lucknow schools of Kathak too had its origin in Jaipur. It is said that Kalika-Bindadin of Lucknow, the great Kathak exponents, had their heritage in the Kathaks of Jaipur. Their fore-fathers migrated from Rajasthan and got patronage from the Nawabs of Oudh. They gave a revolutionary turn to this devotional art and gave it an erotic colour because of their romantic nature. That is how the Jaipur bifurcated in Jaipur style. Lucknow style and Banares style.

The Rajasthani puppets, today, have perhaps the greatest impact on the art of Indian puppetry. The traditional Rajasthani puppetiers can no more be found in thier ancesteral home. They move in groups right from Kashmir in the North and cape Comorin in the South and have found new patrons for their performances every where. The new pupper enthusiasts are fortunate enough in having easy access to this traditional art-form for their contemporary compositions, because of its adoptability and lack of rigidity.

The Folk Dances of Rajasthan

The various folk dances of Rajasthan like the Ghoomar, Terahtal, Dandiya Ras and Kachigodi are no more confined to Rajasthan now. Due to the efforts of institutions like the Bhartiya Lok Kala Mandal and the Rajasthan Sangeet Natak Akademi, they have had easy access to several other parts of India. The folk dramas of Rajasthan too have wide impact particularly of the Malwa region of Madhya Pradesh, Haryana, and some parts of Gujarat and Western Uttar Pradesh because of linguistic similarities. The *Swang* of Haryana and the *Noutanki* of Uttar Pradesh were greatly inspired by the *Chidawa* style of folk drama. The *Bhawais* of Rajasthan and the *Bhawasis* of Gujarat are very closely linked. The Kuchamani Khyal and the Chidawa Khyal of Rajasthan, because of their frequent visits of Calcutta, Bombay and Madras to entertain their Marwari Patrons, have left a very deep mark on the Tamasha of maharashtra and the Jatra of Bengal. Several Rajasthani tunes and rhythms have been adopted by them. The Madhya Pradesh Manch has so much in common with the Turra Kalangi of Chittor and Rasdhari Khyals of Mewar.

The Molela Delities and Phad paintings

The Molela deities and the Ramdevji of Runicha Rajasthan are no more confined to Rajasthan. Their devotees claim to belong to all the states. They come on foot to obtain these images from the Molela villages and carry them to their respective places in ceremonial processions.

The Phad painting of Shahpura and Bhilwara of Rajasthan now have crossed the Indian borders and have attracted international attention. They are now prevalent more among the artists and art lovers, rather than their traditional performers, know as Bhopas. The ballad singing which used to be an integral part of these paintings in less singificant today because of extraordinary importance given to its painting.

The Rajasthan School of Paintings particularly, the Kishnagarh and Kota Kalam have influenced almost all the artists of India. The old paintings are in great demand and are sold fabulous prices. Several artists of Bengal and Uttar Pradesh adopted this style in their new composition.

The Rajasthan costumes and the jewellary have perhaps the greatest appeal these days for festivities and special Ceremonial occasions. Their colour and varied styles have attracted the attention of several fashion experts. The impact of Rajasthan and its culture on Indian life is indeed, varied and deep.
(Condensed).

DEVILAL SAMAR

RAJKUMAR SINGHAJIT SINGH

Born into a family of dancers in Manipur, Singhajit started learning the art of 'Pung' playing at the age of 10, followed by years of traditional training in dance from the famous Guru Amubi Singh, and in "Sankeertan" singing from Guru Chaoba Singh. Since 1954, he has been a distinguished Manipuri guru at Triveni Kala Sangam in New Delhi. An excellent dancer and guru, he has won praise also for his creative choreographic work and has already produced and presented over 27 Manipuri ballets since 1965. He has performed and given lecture demonstrations extensively around the world and has been honoured with the Sangeet Natak Akademi Award, Padmashri, Delhi Sahitya Parishad Award Manipuri Parishad Award and "Nritya Choodamani". He has also been conferred the D. Litt by the North Eastern Hills University. He and his wife Charu have dedicated themselves to enrichment and popularisation of Manipuri dance. Charu has been the leading female dancer of Triveni Ballet Unit. She, too, has travelled and performed extensively with her husband and won many honours.
(Summarised)

SUSHEELA MISRA

RAMAYANA : INFLUENCE OF

It has also been truly said: it (Ramayana) is not only a literary treasure but also a source of ennobling influence on the relationships between men as parents and children, husbands and wives, brothers and sisters, relations and friends, teachers and pupils and rulers and the ruled.

A unique feature of this epic is that each character who appears in it represents one aspect of human philosophy. It is like a diamond from which many splendid colours emanate. To mention a few: The main character, Rama, followed the path of duty and righteousness, in his attitude and conduct towards his friends, servants and devotees. Rama and Sita, the two central figures, are exemplifiers of right thought, right speech and right action under all circumstances. Sita represents compassion and grace. She sufferes most but preserves herself with heroism, love and devotion. She is the ideal wife and is the model for our womanhood. Lakshman's role is that of an ideal brother, so loving and so steadfast that he left the comforts of home and family life to look after the protect his brother and his wife. Bharata is the perfect embodiment of purity and selflessness. His role uplifts the heart and gives us a glimpse of the heights to which human nature can rise which cleansed by love and devotion. Hanuman is depicted as a great warrior and an ideal ambassador. He is a noble and heroic character. Vibhishana, the brother of Ravana, always stood for truth and honour. Ravana represents evil and his killing by Rama symbolises the victory of good over evil.

Ramayana, one of our classics, gives to our youth the fundamentals of culture. It is a literature which makes for fellowship and reconciliation. As long as the mountains stand and the riverse flow so long shall the Ramayana be cherished among men and save them from sin. (Condensed)

M. HIDAYATULLAH

RAMA DAAN

Ramadaan is a holy month in the Islamic Calendar. It is the month in which the Qur'an was sent down as guidance to manking. It is the month for much meditation and intense prayers, for acts of greater piety, charity, and for making resolutions about rightenous conduct. Above all, it is a month of fasting which is one of the main pillars of Islamic faith. Of course, fasting is prescribed in all the religions, though there are differences relating to the observance of fasting. According to Islam, all the prophets were directed to prescribe fasting.

In surah Baqura, Chapter 2 says: "O you who believe! Fasting is prescribed to you as it was prescribed to those before you, that you may (learn) self-restraint.

Verse 184 : (Fast) for a fixed number of days; but if any of you is ill, or on a journey, the prescribed number (should be made up) by days later. For those who can do it (with hardship), is a ransom, the feeding of one that is indigent. But he that will give more, of his own free-will, it is better for him. And it is better for you, that you fast, if you only knew.

Verse 185 : Ramadaan is the month in which was sent down the Qu'ran, as a Guide to manking, also clear (singns) for guidance and judgement (between right and wrong). So every one of you who is present (at his home) during that month should spend it in fasting; but if anyone is ill or on a journey, the prescribed period (should be made up) by days later. Allah intends every facility for you; He does not want to put you to difficulties, But (He wants you) and complete the prescribed period, and to glorify Him in that He has guided you; and perhaps; you shall be greatful.

Verse 186: When my servants ask you concerning Me, I am indeed close (to them); I listen to the prayer of every suppliant when He calls on Me: Let them also, with a will, listen to My call, and believe in Me: that they may walk in the right way.

All the above verses stress the importance of fasting. Ramadaan fasting enjoins one to go without food from just before sunrise up to sunset. Such fasting for 30 days helps one to develop good habits and exercise dietary control. For example, if somebody wants to give up drinking, he can do so because of the intense spiritual motivation for not drinking in the month of Ramadaan.

Similarly, if he was other bad habits such as smoking, eating without any restraint, drug addiction or gambling they can also be got rid of.

The importance of fasting is well known to physicians and psychotherapists. In the month of Ramadaan, an atmosphere of Taqwah or righteousness is created. That aids meditation and meditation can improve our thought process.

when we start thinking rightly, it leads to right feeling, and right feeling automatically follows right action. All these right thinking, feeling and doing are to be practised in the light of Quran and Sunnah.

The purpose of fasting is to restore spiritual and physical health. Fasting being a month-long exercise, it helps us to abstain from unnecessary foods drinks and sexual gratification which are disturbing by their very nature. Self-control and self-discipline promote piety and righteousness. For many physical illness, doctors ask the patients to fast, which helps eliminate toxins from the body. In old days, for many diseases fasting was the only treatment.

Fasting helps one to reform oneself because during fasting one constantly thinks of improving one's behavious better and becoming righteous in the eyes of Allah and to gain the reward after the death. Besides, a man becomes charitable-minded, and charity helps the persons to think of others; to think of others itself helps his near relatives, friends and the needy. In an extended way, if everybody thinks of charity, it covers the whole society and when the entire needy society is helped, it helps to remove poverty which is a crime in today's socio-economic life. Once the socio-economic problems are solved, man automatically thinks of higher things. A Muslim is supposed to give *Zakaat* i.e. a tax on his whole year's income and this tax revenue is spent only on the needy and the deserving. *Zakaat* means purification and it purifies the soul, mind and body.

Though fasting is compulsory in Islam, a person suffering from chronic diseases, stomach trouble or incurable illness is exempted from fasting. But the person who cannot fat can give *Fidiya*, that is he can feed the needy persons. A travelling person, whose health may be affected by fasting, is exempted from it but he must keep the same number of fasts at some other time. If the journey is short and would not disturb him, then he can keep the fast. Pregnant women, nursing or breast-feeding woman may or may not fast depending on their physical condition or on the advise of doctor. Of course, a woman in menses is exempted from the fast. There might be similar questions on fast which may be referred to one who has the knowledge of Quran and Sunnah.

It is seen that the man who parys regularly five times, keeps one month's fasting, gives *Zakaat* and performs Haj is usually happy and healthy. And he will have less psychosomatic tension or problems. Of course, all have to die one day, so aging problems and death cannot be avoided.

A Muslim should take full advantage of Ramadaan to make himself a better Muslim through fast, meditation, prayers and pious resolutions. All religions prescribe fasting.

ABDUL KARIM MOHAMMED NAIK

RAMESVARAM TEMPLE

(Completed 17th to 19th century) - One of the most outstanding and stupendous South Indian temples in the Dravidian (Pandya) style of temple architecuture; situated on an island near Adam's Bridge (which separates India and Sri Lanka); has two shrines within concentric walls and 4 massive gupurams (gate towers) on each of the 4 sides; the pillared corridors which surround the shrines extend to nealy 1,333 metres in length, the breadth varying from 5.2 to 6.4 m. and the height beign about 9 m.; the pillars (each 3.6 m. high), huge blocks of granite, richly carved and beautifully proportioned, stand close to each other along 210 m. long corridors, due to the immense length of which, the perspective dwindles to a mere pinpoint of light in the distance, the whole effect being one of remarkable grandness; the corridors are believed to mark the place where Rama (the hero of the Ramayana) performed his first act of worship after his rescue of Sita from Ravana's lanka and the temple is, therefore hallowed by his (legendary) association with site.

P. K. ACHARYA
STELLA KRAMRISCH

THE RAMAKRISHNA MATH AND MISSION

The Ramakrishna Mission Association was established on May 1, 1897 by Swami Vivekananda with a view of unite the lay and monastic followers of the Master in a common organized effort for the service of the humanity. In 1899, the Belur Math was started and this Association ceased to function as an independent organisation. The Math itself carried on the preaching, educational and philanthropic activities. But in 1909 it was again felt that a separate organisation was necessary and the Ramakrishna Mission was then registered under the societies Registration Act. The Governing Body consisted of the Trustees of the Belur Math and was responsible to the Association.

The Ramakrishna Maths and Mission Centres are monasteries to religious studies, worship, meditation and preaching and are scattered all over India and abroad. The monks of the Ramakrishna order get their spiritual training in these monasteries. These monasteries are affiliated to the Belur Math. All the Maths have timples or chapels where the presiding deity is Sri Ramakrishna. These Maths are financed by friends and devotees.

The Math and the Mission are two sister institutions and by no means watertight compartments. They are governed by the same group of monks and trustees. There are, again, many centres which are combined Math and Mission centres. Also, there are some Math Centres which carry on the activities normally undertaken by the Missions. The activities of the Maths and the Missions in India can be broadly divided into three groups: a) Spiritual and Cultural, b) Educational, and c) Philanthropic.

The Math and Mission centres, specially the former, spread the spiritual teachings and cultural ideals as illustrated in the life of Sri Ramakrishna. This is done through public lectures and classes, birthday celebrations of the Master and other great incarnations and prophets, celebrations of Hindu festivities like the Durga Puja etc., running of reading rooms and public libraries, and the publication of religious literature and magazines. Some of the centres have published a good amount of literature in various provincial languages, besides English, on the life and teachings of the Master and his disciples as also translation of standard Sanskrit work on philosophy and religion.

"Education", as Swami Vivekananda put it, 'is the manifestation of the perfection already in man'. To attain this goal of education, living with the guru (teacher), as of old, is quite essential. So, many of the Mission educational institutions forms an important feature in all of them. In addition to the college and school curricula, vocational training in various arts and crafts, like onework, carpentry, weaving, leather-work, etc. is given to the students in most of these institutions, specially in the residential ones. Sports and physical training are encouraged. In short, an attempt is made to help the students manifest the perfection already in them by making the environments suitable for building a health body, a healthy intellect, and a healthy mind.

In the education of girls, while all these ideals are stressed, particular care is taken to see that they imbibe all that is best in the Indian womanhood of the past, as seen in characters like Sita, Mira Bai, and others. Fine arts, domestic hygiene, cooking etc., from part of their education.

A number of Colleges, Higher Secondary Schools, Middle Schools, Junior Basic and Elementary Schools for Boys and Girls are being run by the Maths and Missions at various places in India and abroad.

The Philanthropic activities are to two kinds - permanent ones and temporary nature. The hospital, dispansaries, invalid homes etc. are included in the first category. The second category includes temporary relief works conducted by the Mission whenever there are famines, floods, epidemics, earthquakes etc. The hospitals and dispansaries are called 'Sevashramas' or 'Homes of Service'. A good number of them are located in the places of pilgrimage like Varanasi, Vrindaban, Hardwar and in the interior of the Himalayas and in distant villages. During 1961-62, there were eleven indoor hospitals with 979 beds which accommodated 22,157 patients and 66 outdoor dispensaries which treated 30,47,519 cases including old ones. The Mission hospitals at Varanasi, Vrindaban and Rangoon have separate Women's Sections and there is a Domiciliary and Maternity clinic at Jalpaiguri. The Mission also runs a number of Invalid Women's Homes.

For the works outside India are 11 Math and Mission Centres in East Pakistan, two in Burma, one each in Singapore, Fiji, Mauritius and Ceylon. There are 14 Centres - ten in U.S.A. one each in Argentina, England, France and Switzerland. These Centres are under the spiritual leadership of the monks of the Ramakrishna order.

In March 1962, there were 73 Mission Centres, 65 Math Centres and 22 Sub-Centres conducting activities of various types.

RAMLILA

North Indian feature; festival of Rama; organised in Ramayana by Tulsidas in 1574; celebration signifying victory of god Rama over the demon king Ravana of Lanka; whole of Ramayana read in 20 - 30 days, incidents acted simultaneously. The *dramatic personal* numerous; scenery real as far as it could be. Finally culminates on tenth day; Ravana is killed in battle; people are overjoyed; Rama's triumphal entry into Ayodhya; people shower flowers, chaplets on sacred group form stane terraces. Thus ends Ramalila also.

THE RANAKPUR JAIN TEMPLE

The maginificent Jain temple at Ranakpur is unique in that it stands on 1444 pillars but none of these obstructs the view of the Lord from any corner.

This treasure house of pillars is located in the remote and enchanting valley of the Aravali hills in Rajasthan, the land of many legends. The rivulet Maghai gives an added beauty to the temple. The forest around it lends solitude and grandeur to the overall ambience.

This three-storeyed wonder in marble, also called the Chaturmukha (Literally four-faced) Jain Temple of Rishabdeva, was given this shape by four devotees - Acharya Somasundarji Surjiji, Dharanashah - a minister to Kumba Rana, The Rana himself and the carefree, visionary architect Depaka. It is said that the temple took fifty years to complete at a total cost of Rupees 9.9 million in those days. In spite of the large area and tall pillars, about forty feet in height, there is perfect architectural balance and harmony in the shape. Artistic engravings and sculptures give it a feeling of ecstasy and divine bliss.

There are four engraved entrances to the sanctum sanctorum, which contains four statues of Lord Adinath on its four sides. Each statue is six feet tall. The same pattern has been repeated on all the three storeys. There are eight cellars forstoring the sacred images in troubled times.

The temple also has seventy-six smaller shrines, four assembly halls and four principal shrines, totalling eighty four. According to Jain mythology, a human being must undergo 8,4,00,000 births before being able to attain eternal salvation. The figure of eighty four shrines in the temple is a symbolic reminder of these 84 lakhs births and deaths.

JOGINDER CHAWLA

RANE, SARASWATI BAI SUNDARAO

(B. 1918) - Vocalist; Hindustani, khayal of Kirana gharana, light music; studied with Nattan Khan, B.R. Deodhar, Hirabai Barodekar; disc recordings.

S. P. SEN

RANGAMALA PAINTINGS

At the first glance, an Indian miniature painting, to the uninitiated, appears nothing more than a clutter and tangle of pastoral settings, dominated by a male and feminine figures, dallying in the glades. When someone points out that these scenes are not detached visions of artistic expression but provide the basic of Indian music, the viewer is likely to greet this suggesting with wry humour. Know as "*Ragamala paintings*", these masterly works are visual creations of emotional and perceptive concepts and depict the ragas or musical modes of Indian classical music. Miniature painters, employed at various medieval courts, discovered the potential of limitless self-expression in their depiction and today, these 130 known sets of "Ragamala Paintings" have added a novel dimension to the aga of music, as practised by its classical adherents.

The first floor gallery of National Museum houses a permanent exhibition of samples of thirty seven sets of Ragamala Miniatures, beginning with a representation of the earliest School of work dated 1595 from the Deccan school of art and considered a landmark find in this unique form of visual Indian music. This visible selection is only a drop in a vast treasury, for the Museum itself is the repository of more than 1100 such works and while all of them are not complete sets and other have been revaged and neglected beyond repair, their representative character and bulk, remain unrivalled in content. Only the Victoria and Albert Museum in London can be a close contender in the quality of Ragamala collectables now. Its growing importance has even led to the unearthing of stocks hitherto unknown as when quite recently, an entire set of forty four paintings was acquired by National Museum. It is the only known set of Deccani Ragamala works made by artists in either Gwalior or Aurangabad.

These pictorially articulate visions of an aural art first made their appearance in the Indian cultural comity in the fifty century. The artist drew his inspiration from a musical text written by the sage Narada, titled Narada Shiksha. But while the text dates back to the early beginnings of the art, its artistic depiction did not gain credence till almost hundred years later, when artists suddenly became aware of the relationship that governed sound and sentiment. It generated into a dynamic movement, fanned by patronage and fulfilled itself into figurative and pastoral scenes, making music the subject matter of art, through colour, mood, deific requirements and the presence of myth and reality. Artists at court fell to discovering aesthetic links behind the ancient musical treatises and thereby built up a sizeable collection of paintings giving voice to the cultural psyche of the people whose music they depicted.

The only strait jacketed hold this breakthrough in Indian art had to comply with, was the need to paint within the demands of an Indian ragas. But this raga could be drawn and painted in compositional placements of one's own making as long as it came out distilled from the individual artistic depths and yet remained anchored to a principle integral to Indian music. Many a time this idealisation was personalised, from an association with the krishna legend, but even the secular court and its patron was copy enough for the ragamala artist.

Of this raga factor, one needed to know more than just a passing knowledge of the art. As each raga was sung or played at a stipulated time of the day or night, the artist had to locate the scenic display according to this unchangeable abstraction.

THus the mist-filled aura of a dawn-break was essential to the painting of the morning raga, TODI. It was also a moment of pensive thought and the evocative element centred around the anguish that a young lady felt after holding a night long wait for a lover, who never returned. There is touching bereavement in her posture, as she sits alone, holding an instrument, within the forest glade, with only a pair of deer for company Even these creatures, known for their timidity, are overcome with sympathy for the afflicted "rasika" or devotee of the arts and listen enthralled as she sings out her heart to the serene notes of the raga TODI.

Besides the vocabulary of musical theory, the ragas were also a salute to the beauty of the seasons. As there were a group of six changes in the wather and each one distinct from the other, the artists found a rich source for productivity in this changing world. Again, personal preferences seemed to make one season more popular than the other, as the welcome showers of the rainy season and the first flush of spring, gained greater favour among them. The many forms of the *rag Malhar* provided, the ideal narrative for the painter's brush. He painted the prancing rain drops, the threatening dark clouds, the flourishing spread of greenery and the lush atmosphere dotted with peacock and peasant, making metaphor and imagery enjoy a field day. In the centre of this grandeur were a group of happy maidens, enchanted by the gaiety of the season, as they swayed in rhythm and danced to the beat of the drum, or the strike of the cymbals. It was also a time of dalliance, in the arms of the Lord Krishna, who too joined in the merry-making infectiousness, as the Lord is believed to be, whenever he is in the company of a true devotee. The association of the eternal lovers, Radha and Krishna are centre-stage, where Radha is the embodiment of a true devotee and the sublime ecstasy what a true devotee experiences, in the workship of the beloved lord.

Within the precincts of palace courtyard and bedchamber, too, the Ragamala painter found inspiration as he emphasised the containment of the night *raga Deepak*. Outside, a starlit sky peeped through the intricate stone trellis-work of the latticed verandah. The Prince and his beloved embraced in the silence of their opulent surroundings. A maid in waiting stood sentinel at the door and above, the minarets of the palace, glistened in the moonlight. The musical instruments in the room were silenced, for it was past the hour of civilised waking and besides, the strains of this deep Raga transcended beyond the obvious and audible into the inner depths of profoundity. It was the inner experiences of complete consummation that the raga had created in the listener.

These impactful drawings and paintings also had a utilitarian aside. If one browes closely through the display, after the first flush of awe at their meticulous detailing, one realises that most of them are centred around court life of that time. The raiments of the figures, the architecture of the land, the features of the faces come into sharp focus, under the painter's lyrical eye. This thematic painter's lyrical eye stance has given the works a certain uniformity, a decided formalism and a feel of glory and grandeur that merges delightfully with this music. The gossamer veiled women with pinched noses, full breasts, doe-like eyes and graceful stances, are not just an art form but become a basis for understanding the gravity of this plastic art.

Yet within this uniform diffusion of compositional selection, there are encouraging differences. These are due to the different schools of art. The influence of the Persian upon the Indian folk, or the workmanship of one court artist on another, have given the Ragamala troves its varied content. The schools of Mewar or Udaipur or Jaipur in Rajasthan have taken cognisance of their desert landscape and architecture and masters like Amuru Sataka have indulged themselves in bright colours for heightened effect. In the guardianship of a royal patron like Jai Singh, the Maharaja who founded the city of Jaipur, it is a question of verse writing at the head of the painting, so that the name of the raga and its character are expressed in spirit and in letter. The hill kingdoms of Kangra and Kumaon are marked by fine drawing, while the plateau regions of Malwa and Bundelkhand specialise in attractive brush work. The crowing glory of this series is the Provincial Mughal works, attributed to the reign of the emperors Akbar and Jahangir. Sure enough it is not the women's dresses that attract attention but the trend setting jama (dress) worn by the emperor himself, which is highlighted in the apparel of Lord Krishna in these Works. Coupled with this regal modelling, there are historical personages portrayed against the backdrop of a palatial setting. Sourt musicians like Tansen and his revered teacher Haridas, provide an audience for their regal patron Emperor Akbar, thus providing a contrast of kingly court against a spartan heritage.

Since no mention of music can be complete without a recognition of its mythical source, there is a gold embossed Tanjore painting of Nataraja, the dancing form of Lord Shiva. The legendary drum that beats to the rhythm of eternal time, the perfect balance of the figure and the fiery ring of cosmic power surrounding the deity, are all there to view and understand. On the opposite and of the scale are the ancilliaries that speak of the raga division as a family of six male ragas with five wives each and having eight sons making up a sizeable total, of ragas and raginis.

SUBHRA MAJUMDAR

RANGOLI

"Rangoli", a Hindu tradition for thousands of years, is employed to beautify entrances to homes, whether a modest hut or a modern building. The preparation starts by first cleansing and sweeping the porch and then decorating it with colourful Rangoli. In Rangoli, the artist draws various forms, portraits and scenes of daily life and other multi-dimensional displays. It is know by different names in various parts of India such as "Rangoli" in Maharashtra. , "Sathia" in Gujarat, "Chalk" in Uttar Pradesh, "Sanja" in Madhya Pradesh, "Kolam" in Kerala and Tamil Nadu, "Mggu" in Bengal and "Mandana" in Rajasthan. It is in fact a symbol of unity in diversity. This art form is of a transient nature because a slight wind could destroy the creation. (Condensed)

SRI CHAND

RASA TRADITION IN MANIPURI

COMPOSITE INDIAN CULTURE

Indian culture represents a remarkable synthesis of various Aryan and non-Aryan elements. Strange, Perhaps, is the word for this harmonious blending. The Vedic Aryans who were basically a nomadic and pastoral community, were not, I suppose, great lovers of music or of what is known as *Sangeeta*, even though we have the evidence of the ancient rishis singing *Samagana*. The dancing figurine discovered as a part of Mohenjodaro culture and civilisation represents almost a symbol - a symbol of non-Aryan fascination for fine arts which might have created an impact on the minds of the contemplative Aryan rishis. The Taitriya Upanishad speaks of Rasa as the *Brahmanraso-vei sah*. But this concept of *Rasa* finds supreme espression only in the *Natya Sastra* of sage Bharata, recorded possibly in the 1st century A.D. This fifth Veda, as it was called, contained all the elements from the four Vedas and was primarily menat for all classes of people including the women and the sudras. The close association of this *Natya Sastra* with Lord Shiva and his associates like Tandu speaks about the predominantily non-Aryan tradition as Shiva was positively a non-Aryan god. Even the sage Bharata had to struggle so hard for it. Abhinaya Darpana of sage Nandikesvara, which is supposed to be an authority on Rasa and Sangeet (with Bharata, on Rupakas, after Raj-sekhara), is no exception to this. But in the peculiarly synthetic experience of the Indians, all roads lead to the Brahman. Hence we have the traditional *Rasa brahmavada, nada brahmavada* and *rupabrahavada* of the Indian aestheticians, and even *tala brahmavada*. To the devout Vaishnava drummers of Manipur, tala represents the Lord, the Shri Guru. Because Time has no beginning and no end (*anadi ananta kala*) and *tala* represents only a captured fragment of it (*khanda kala*). The Indian believe, of course, that all these are fragments of the lord (*mamaeva amsha*) after the Gita. There is unity in diversity : *Vahusyamaham Ekopi*, after the Shruits.

THE MUSICAL TRADITION

The Sangeeta tradition of India is distinctively a puranic concept and represents a synthesis of tantric and brahmanic cults. It gives an accent on Nada as Brahman-Nadabrahmavada. The *Vishnu Purana* says that all songs are a part of Him, who wears a form of sound. And the same purana speaks of *Kirtana* as sung aloud on matters relating to the name, leela and attributes of the lord. This is the *samkirtana* tradition of India which finds eloquent expression in the Bengal School of Vaishnavism in the 15th century A.D. when Shri Krishna Chaitanya and his followers became great lovers of music and introduced the name of *Hari-nama Kirtana* with all the devotees singing the dancing in ecstasy. This tradition finds its source in Naradasamhita which beautifully sums up in the oft-quoted lines:

"I do not dwell in heaven, nor in the heart of Yogis.

There only I abide. O Narada, where my lover sings".

Strictly speaking, there is nothing like a Rasa tradition in Manipuri sangeet. There is only the great impact of the Bengal School of Vaishnavism with its inevitable

Samkirtana on the sensitive minds of the artistic Manipuris. This samkirtana was practically reborn, so to say, with regional complexion and depth of feelings and became a major cultural event which attained maturity in the 18th century A.D. during the reign of Rajarshi Bhagyachandra (1764 to 1789 A.D.) To the devout Manipuri vaishnavas, samkirtana is a great yajna - mahayajna. The *padavali* or *leela kirtana* of Bengal, specially that of Thakur Narot - tamadas in Bengal in the 16th century assumed the form of Nata kirtana in Manipur. Because there is *abhinaya* for the Kirtana - both *Tandava and lasya*. And according to *Govinda Sangeet Leela Vilas*, the authorship of which is attributed to Rajarshi Bhagyachandra, whoever, male or female, sings the glories of the lord with the accompanying abhinaya is called Nata Kirtana. This *Natakirtana* (known popularly as Nata Pala) i a must for all the various religious ceremonies and festivals of Manipur life — Hindu ceremonies like Kanavedha, Upanayana and Shraddha ceremonies etc. To watch this Kirtana with all its rituals and exquisite music and dances presented strictly offer the 8 divisions of time (Asta Kala) during a day of Lord Krishna's *leela* with Radha and the Sakhis, is a fascinating experience. Apart from the songs set to particular ragas and raginis pre-sented with abhinaya and cymbals on the hand, the Manipuri *Mridanga (Pung)* has its own ragas and *sancharas* which are almost endless in number and which are presented within the pattern of its characteristic style of prayer and worship. And when the Bhaktas relish the rasa (Rasasvadana) of the entire Kirtana, they become deeply moved and start weeping and crying and even rush to the performers and lie prostrate before them as a sign of deep appreciation.

MANIPURI RASALEELAS

The well-known Manipuri *Rasaleelas* (pronounced as Raasleelas) represent only a fragment of this vast Samkirtana tradition. The entire pattern of the movements and the exquisite costumes were conceived by Rajarshi Bhagyachandra in his dreams when Lord Krishna came to him and asked him to find out the tree in a particular forest, out of which His image would be carved. This story reflects the extreme piety of the Manipuri Vaishnavas who considered themselves blessed enough to watch the real performance of the eternal Rasaleela at Vrindavan. As a form of *Natya* and as distinguished from *Rupaka,* this *Rasa* or *Rasak* is strictly after the tradition of Gargacharya, the teacher of Lord Krishna and here songs and dances predominate. *Rasa Prakash* of Garacharya speaks of Rasaka being subdivded into six viz. Maha, Vasanta (Manju), Nitya, Nirvesh (Kunj) Gopa and Tala, all of which are now performed in Manipur on appropriate occasions. All these leelas cover almost the entire gamut of the life of Shri Krishna starting from the childhood pranks and exploits (Gopa Rasa). His play and apparent separation from the *gopis (Tala Rasa)* and ending with His eternal play with them at Vrindavan on fullmoon nights, either at Autumn, after the Shrimad Bhagavatam (Maha Rasa), at Ashvin Purnima (Kunja Rasa). The classification of Natya into Rupaka and Rasaka is distinctively a Vaishnavic concept and has been the efforts of the various gurus of Manipuri songs and dances to compose a series of leelas in the form of dance-drama, where dialogue assumes a secondary importance. This may be considered as an extension and illumination of the Samkritana tradition. But all these leelas relate to a single theme: Lord Krishna and His play with the gopas and gopis at Vrindavan, strictly after the Bhagavata tradition.

Thus we find that Manipuri tradition of Samkirtana does not mark much of a departure from the Vaishnavite tradition of Bengal school. It only struck deep roots in the artistic soul of the people and found expression in various Rasaleelas and Nata Kirtan performances which became poetry to be seen (Drishya Kavya). Much of the dance and music heritage of ancient Manipuri culture was integrated with the classical tradition of India in whic the various slokas from the Bhagavata Purana and from vaishnava Padavalis were profusely used and sung in various ragas and reginis which were composed during the height of Sanskrit learning.

But the only way to understand and appreciate this Vaishnava tradition is to have a clear knowledge of Vaishnava Bhakti-rasa, without which much of the Krishna-leela as conceived by the Bhaktas shall remain unintelligible. Some of the orthodox rhetoricians like Jagannath refuse to consider Bhakti as a rasa and are prepared to give it the status of Bhava. But to the Vaishnava, Bhakti is the Rasa, perhaps the only Rasa, relating only to the love of Krishna (Krishnarati) around which all the other rasas move and have their being. Bhakti is "a psychological entity, a literary-erotic emotion transmuted into a deep and ineffable devotional sentiment, which is intensely personal and is yet impersonalised into a mental condition of disinterested joy". There is also the testimony of the Bhagavata itself which speaks of Bhakti as the Bhagavad-rasa and the Bhakta as the Rasika. Bhagavat itself is Rasa, after the sruits. This conception of Bhakti finds elaborate treatment in the two works of Rupa Goswami viz, Bhakti rasamrita Sindhu and Ujjavala Nilamani, which was further supplemented by six sandarbhas of Jiva Goswami. The Vaishnavas recognise only 5 categories of Bhaktirasa viz. Santa, Dasya, Vatsalaya and Madhurya, and the last one which exists only in the relation of Krishna with the gopis and for which even the Vedas craved, after Padma Purana is called Bhaktirasa - raj.

We have, on the authority of Jiva Goswami, that the gopis are nothing but the aspects of the Bhagavat-Krishna's highest energy of bliss (Hladini shakti) and the Lord simply enjoys His leela which is inscrutable. The gopis are Krishna's own and yet they appear as belonging to others in the prakata leela. Of all the gopis, Radha is the greatest beloved of Krishna and Chandravali assumes the role of a rival heroine in the Krishnaleela. But the well known biographer of Chaitanya, Krishnadas Kaviraj (1615 A.D.) equates Chaitanya with Bhagavan and introduced Chaitanya worship as a cult. Krishna in His Chaitanya-leela combines the roles of Krishna and Radha with a view to enjoying the bliss both as a subject and on object. Hence Chaitanya's adoption of the complexion and feelings of Radha as well as those of Krishna. This view holds a particular fascination for the Manipuri Vaishnavas and every Samkirtana performance should begin with a dedication to lord Chaitanya or Gouranga which is known as Gourchandrika or Gourachandra. This indentification of a prophet or a guru with the lord himself almost on a

mystic level, is a peculiarly Indian phenomenon, I suppose, and holds true for the devotees at least.

It is now evident that the Vrindavan leela of Shri Krishna emphasises the *madhurya* aspect of the lord. Here Krishna becomes a friend, a son or a lover and becomes very near and sweet to the devotees. The epic figure of Vasudeva-Krishna with his wisdom and statesman-like qualities is transformed almost beyond recognition. The puranic life of Krishna as recorded in the Bhagavatam has been brought to the foreground. As Dr. S.K. De puts it: "The ancient epic spirit of godly wisdom and manly devotion is replaced by a new spirit of mystical and theological fancy, of tender rapture over divine babyhood and of sensuous and erotic passion of ecstasy over the loveliness of divine adolescence and its god is moulded accordingly".

LEELAS - A RELIGIOUS HISTORY

It is with difference that apply a sort of analytic and itnellectual approach to this religious phenomenon. All these interpretations move, perhaps, on the periphery of understanding which, on the part of the devotee, should be an integral experience. Dean Inge writes somewhere that "myth is the poetry of religion, and poetry, not science, is the natural language of religion". What we generally consider as Vrindavan leela myth or allegory is not at all a mere symbol or divine allegory to the devout Vaishnavas. The entire leela is a fact of religious history and the puranic world to them is manifestly a matter of religious history. The miss this spirit is, perhaps, to misunderstand the entire religion. And there are certain points at which the method of the analyst ought to be replaced, as Arthur Waley wrote in a different context, by those of a poet. The devout Manipuri Vaishnavas still believe al these aspects of Vrindavan leela and they weep and cry at the various Rasaleelas and Samkirtanas of Manipur. And it needs, perhaps, a lot of samskara to appreciate and understand properly the fundamentals of Bengal School of Vaishnavasim. The scholarly interpretations and analytic approach do not matter so much. One must have the eyes to see and the ears to listen in such matters pertaining to spiritual experience. This is the knowledge which most of us have lost in the knowing of it. What is myth to us is a reality to the Vaishnava and this makes a great difference.

E. NILAKANTA SINGH

RASAYANA (RAJUVENATION THERAPY)

Ayurveda is the ancient science of life. The Rasayana branch of Ayurvede deals mainly with the prolongation of life, besides keeping the body in a perfectly healthy condition.

Rasayana Therapy is a unique speciality of Ayurveda, dealing with the aspects of rejuvenation. It is included in the eight major branches of Ayurveda. According to Ayurveda, the term Rasayana is defined as the measures/means to improve the quality of dhatus (Vital Component) so as to prolong the age provides nourshment to vital components stability to youthfulness, longevity and optimum strength.

Thus, by virtue of the above qualities, Rasayana theraphy plays a very important role in the maintenance of positive health and also in curing diseases. This view is further supported by the statement of Charka in which he has emphasized the various beneficial effects of Rasayana such as long life, improvement in memory, sharpness of the brain, positive health, yourthfulness, good complxion, excellent voice, strength of the various sensory facultities of the body, command of languages, and brightness of skin luster. These qualities, if achieved by a person, he may be considered as a healthy and the Rasayana individual theraphy helps to achieve the same in the best way.

VAIDYA SURESH CHATURVEDI

RAVI SHANKAR (1920)

With time, Ravi Shankar's following has not only grown bigger but also younger. That perhaps is a measure of the sitarist's ability to infuse the pulse of the times into timeless *ragas*. Ravi Shankar, born in Banaras (Varanasi) to the diwan of Jhalawar, began his career at the age of 10 as the youngest member of the Paris-based dance troupe of his elder brother Uday Shankar. Those formative years, when he was amidst the best of the cultural world and formed a friendship with Yehudi Menuhin, laid the foundation of catholicism in Ravi Shankar's music, which was reinforced by his training under Allauddin Khan of Maihar. The *Senia gharana* maestro not only gave him his treasure trove of *ragas*, but also his daughter Annapurna Devi.

Ravi Shankar's music took him through Bombay, where he gave the score for films like *Dharti Ke Lal, Anuradha* and *Neecha Nagar*. However, the theme for *Pather Panchali* stands out in his film compositions. With these, the classicist, who had also composed the evergreen music for *Saare Jahan Se Achha*, proved that innovation was not beyond his pale. This aspect was never more apparent than when he teamed up with Western classicists like Menuhin, Andre Previn, Zubin Mehta, Jean Pierre Rampal and Philip Glass.

However, it is his association with the Beatles that led the West to take notice of not only the sitarist but Indian classical music as a whole. "George Harrison became my student and I a cult figure", says the maestro who has given the world musicians like Vijay Raghav Rao, Vishwa Mohan Bhatt and, now, daughter Anoushka, besides a number of sensitive ragas.

His contributions have been celebrated through a plethora of awards that range from the Grammy to the Megasaysay, from the music equivalent of the nobel to the *Bharat Ratna*.

RAVIDAS JAYANTI

Celebrated in North India in *Magha* (January - February) in honour of birth day of Ravidas born in first quarter of 15th century A.D. at Sergobardhenpur (near Varanasi) ; given his name as was born on *Ravivar* (Sunday); was a great saint and was said to have performed many miracles; life was spent on banks of the Ganga in meditation of God; was a Sudra so is worshipped by Harijans; many people of other castes also go to his temples to worship him; on this day a huge procession accompanied with music is taken out through main streets of town terminating at his temple where he is worshipped followed by rejoicing and feasting.

C. H. BUCK
B. N. SHARMA

RELIGION AND CULTURE - IMPACT OF ISLAM ON INDIAN SOCIETY

India inherits an ancient civilization which is the result of diverse forces operating for many millenniums. Many races - greeks, Sakas, Pallavas, Kushanas, Huns and others - that from time to time found their way to this coutnry contributed consciously or unconsciously to its evolution. It is, therefore, endowed with that dynamic character which explains its exceptional vitality. We possess the will to assimilate whatever appears to us good in the life and thoughts of the peoples with whom we happen to come into contact. The advent of Islam, however, presented a challenge at the outset to the process of synthesis and fusion that had been going on for centuries in the past. Unlike the earlier invaders, Muslims came to India with a well-defined faith. Simple and clearcut, Islam had nothing in common with the elaborate, ritualistic and absorptive Hinduism. Its well-defined social system, philosophy, laws and a strong monotheistic outlook made its absorption in Hinduism impossible. Throughout the medieval ages, the problem, as Jawaharlal Nehru put it, was how these "two closed systems, each with its own strong roots, could develop a healthy relationship".

For seven centuries the struggle for supremacy went on. On the one hand, there was the "influence of Islam and the philosophy of life represented by it. On the other hand, there has been the pervasive influence of Indian culture and civilisation". The initial clash was inevitably followed by rapprochment, fusion and mutual adjustment.

The Iranian-Arab culture, which the Turko-Afghan conquerors brought with them, was a composite culture, Arabs having absorbed the ancient civilzations of Iran and Egypt and the remnants of the Graeco-Roman civilization. Characteristically enough, the Arabs had accepted in course of time some of the ancient traditions and legends of these countries as part of their own national heritage.

The idea of the brotherhood of Islam and of theoretical equality among its adherents, belief in one God and complete surrender to His will, which are the characteristics of this religion, made a deep impression on the minds of some of the Indian thinkers and reformers of the period. The contact of Islam with Hindusim in south India led to the revival of anti-caste and monotheistic movements. The south became the "home of religious reform" from the 8th to the 10th century. The Vaisnava and Saivite saints started schools of *Bhakti*, and scholars like Sankara, Ramanuja, Nimbaditya, Basava, Vallabhacharya, and Madhava formulated their philosophical systems. These impulses for re-awakening and religious revival were transmitted to the north chiefly through Ramananda of Banaras, who was a distinguished pupil of Ramanuja. About 1450 the mystic weaver Kabir "assailed at once the worship of idols, the authority of the *Quran* and *Shastras* and the exclusive use of a learned language". It will, however, be incorrect to say that these monotheistic and anti-caste movements among the Hindus in the Middle Ages though strengthened by Islam had originated in it. Indeed the *Upanishads* (8th century B.C. - 6th century B.C) had propounded the idea of the oneness of God. And as Sir Jadunath Sarkar, the Indian historian, remarks," all the higher thinkers, all the religious reformers, all the sincere devotees among the Hindus from the earlier times have proclaimed one and only one supreme God behind the countless deities of popular worship and have declared the equality of all true adherers and placed a simple sincere faith above elaborate religious ceremonies. They have all tried to simplify religion and bring it to the doors of the commonest people". So what really happened after the Muslim conquest was a "re-emphasis on the essential monotheistic character of the idea of God and the superiority of the path of devotion over ritualistic sacrifice and mere book of knowledge and wisdom". Thus stress was laid on the subordination of rites and ceremonies, pilgrimages and fasts and the multiplicity of gods. The *Bhakti* movement served two main objects. It rescued the Hindu religion and enabled it to withstand the onslaught of Islamic propaganda and proselytism. it also brought about an understanding between Islam and Hinduism and fostered friendly relations between the two communities.

Many a sect arose which tried to harmonize Islam and Hinduism and to find a common meeting ground for the devout of both the creeds in which their differences or ritual, dogma, and external marks of faith were ignored. Ramananda, Kabir, Nanak, Dadu and Chaitanya were some of the leaders of the *Bhakti* movement, which practically covered the whole of India. Muslim sufis and mystics were close to Bhakts. Mainly an off-shoot of Vedanta of the Hindus, sufism rapidly spread in India from the time of Akbar and produced a large mass of literature. It tended to bring Hindus and Muslims closer.

The impact of Islam also led to the devlopment of regional languages. Sanskrit ceased to be a living language even on a limited scale by the end of the 13th century when a major part of this country passed under Muslim rule. For over three centuries (1200 - 1550) the Hindu intellect in north India was almost barren and no work of merit was produced. The peace and prosperity of Akbar's reign, however, gave a literary stimulus and there was a sudden growth of vernacular literature throughout the country. A number of good works were produced in Bengali, Marathi, Punjabi, Sindhi and eastern Hindi. Vidyapati's songs in Maithili, Chandi Das's in Bengali, Mira's Poems in Rajasthani, and Eknath's in Marathi were not only popular but recognised literary works. Arabised Persian mixed with Turkish being the language of the Muslim invaders, many of their words found their way into the regional languages. Marathi, for example, had 35% words of persian origin in 1830 and the percentage in Punjabi and Sindhi was still higher.

Hindus were not interested in recording events, because they "despised this world and its ephemeral occurrences" Only four biographies have been preserved in Sanskrit and in all of them "facts lie buried under a mass of flowers of rhetoric, tricks of style and round-about expression". Dates are completely ignored. The dry, methodical and matter of fact Muslims, on the other hand, kept a regular record of their campaigns and achievements in whatever part of the world they went to. Their advent in india led to the production of a large number of chronicles and autobiographies, which serve as source material for the history of the period. Hindu writers naturally initated their style, and thus was introduced, as Sir Jadunath Sarkar writes, "a new and very useful element into Indian literature".

The contact of Islam was beneficial in another way. Contrary to the Hindu practice of making a secret of their productions, the Muslims believed in copying and illuminating and circulating their works on a large scale. The introduction of *Kagaz* (paper) also helped this process. Many of the older Indian works were translated under the patronage of Mughal rulers like Akbar, and freely circulated, which led to the diffusion of knowledge.

In the domain of fine arts, the richest contirbution of the Muslims, Sir Jadunath Sarkar writes, is the Indo-Saracen School of painting. As the painting of human figures of anything that has life is forbidden in Islam, the earliest Muslim paintings to reach India from Khurasan or Bukhara showed "complete Chinese influence, especially in representing the human face, rocks, sheets of water and dragons". Intense individuality, proper spacing and symmetry were the characteristics of this art. The only specimens of Hidnu art, which had escaped the ravages of time and invaders, are those in the Ajanta caves which depict the full throngings of life, power, glory, love and youth, and on the same canvas are exhibited tranquility, which lies in a life of detachment, devotion, piety and faith.

The style of architecture which the Turkish invaders brought in India was not exclusively Muslim or Arbian. It was in fact the product of fusion of the style of architecture of various countries such as Transoxiana, Iran, Afghanistan, and Northern Africa with that of the Muslim Arabia. They had developed a good taste and also talent for refinement in architecture. In India they were greatly impressed with the skill of Indian masons and architects whose style they also adopted sometimes unconsciously. Indian architecture had some unique features, such as flat roofs, corbel brackets, tapering domes, wide caves, narrow columns, and decoration and ornamentation. Moreover, the emphasis of Indian architectural style was on solidity and grace. The synthesis of these two architectural styles led to the evolution of a new school of architecture which is known as Indo-Muslim or Indo-Iranian. The Taj Mahal is a living monument of the perfect synthesis of these two cultures, while Fatehpur Sikri and the tombs of Akbar and Itman-ud-Daulah remain specimens of an imperfect fusion. The influence of this style is visible not only in the monumental art of India but also in utilitarian works - houses, streets and bathing places (*ghats*) and even in places of worship.

Music was a well-developed art in idnia. Islam, which had a sort of religious disliking for it, had not much to contribute, excepting some of the inventions which are attributed to the poet, literature and mystic of the time, Amir Khusrau. By combining the Indian *vina* and the

Indian *tambura*, he was bale to produce the *sitar*, a very popular Indian musical instrument. *Tabla* is nothing but a modification of the Indian *mridanga*. A fusion of Hindu and Iranian systems led to the evolution of lights songs like *qawalis* - a counterpart of the religious music of the *Bhakta*.

The cultural influence of Islam is also visible in dress, diet, in the celebration of fairs and festivals, in the ceremonials of marriage, and in the manners of the court. *Achkan* and *salwar*, the popular northern Indian dress, owe their introduction of Muslim influence. Hunting, hawking, *chaugan, nard* or back-gamon, and many other games assumed a Muslim character in form and technique. The Muslims, generally leading a more luxurious life than the Hindus, were responsible for setting new fashions which were copied by the richer classes. They were accustomed to sumptuous dinners and sometimes as many as 100 dishes were served on their tables. Abul Fazl enumerates these dishes in his famous work *Ain-i-Akbari*. It naturally led to the introduction of new articles of food and new styles of cookery, which in course of time became completely Indianized.

The immediate result of the Muslim conquest was the rigidity of the caste system. A large number of conversions during this period, sometimes prompted by the desire to have a more affluent life and a higher social status, but often by force and coercion, produced a strong reaction. Brahmans, the priestly class among the Hindus, who had lost their former privileges of exemption of taxes, etc. found in this an opportunity to consolidate their hold by making the caste system rigid.

Purdah, or the strict veiling of women, was another impact of the advent of islam in India. Hindus adopted *purdah* as a protective measure to save the honour of their womenfolk and to maintain the purity of their social order. The tendency to imitate the ruling class was another factor which operated in favour of its introduction among the Hindu ladies.

The above review of the impact of Islam on different aspects of life in India shows correctly how that Hindus reacted to a culture very different from their own. Some features of it which added richness and variety to their life were more easily assimilated. They tended to accept in varying degrees those others which impinged on their established pattern of living but not seriously. Where the differences were radical and irrsconcilable, they were content to be allowed to follow them quietly side by side with the unacceptable ways of their rulers. Only the forces of time could evolve a pattern of integration in such cases.

We cannot, therefore, say that culture during the medieval times was something entirely new or radically different from the culture of the preceding or succeeding ages. Indian culture in all ages has been fundamentally the same and the new strains have only added to its fabric. They only add richness to it. Take, for example, the dress or the mode of life of the indian people. Great political upheavals and economic and military revolutions have hardly brought about any radical change in the dress of the mass of our people. Although some new elements, such as shirts and skirts, *achkans* and *salwars* have added to the variety and colour of our costume, the indispensable *dhoti* and graceful *sari* have continued to be as popular today as they were in the days of the Buddha and

Mahavira. A person may take pride in his European apparel, but he too relapses at times to the garb of his ancestors when homely comfort or religious conventions so demand. So too with food and drink, mode and style of living, and habits. Seldom have our people except the *elite* taken to European diet. During the Mughal age not many except the nobility and high-ups among the Hindus adopted the food of our rulers. Many of the upperclass and middle-class Hindus, no doubt, borrowed something of the Mughal dress, language and vocabulary, besides the Mughal mode of life and behaviour, but the masses continued to follow their traditional path. At the same time social customs and personal laws still continued, in varying degrees, to be influenced by religious creeds.

P. N. CHOPRA

RICE STRAW PICTURES : FASCINATING INNOVATION

India has a great tradition in art. In common with the rest of the country South India has magnificent examples to augment this tradition. Rice straw picture is one such art from Kerala. It is inspired by its surroundings.

The credit to conceive this exquisite art goes to K.V. Victor, a native of Kerala. Revered as the 'Father of straw pictures the people of Kerala believe that the created this art from literally out of nothing but by sheer imagination. Seventy year-old Victor developed this art some 25 year ago. While strolling down a street he found a farmer playfully placing straw stricks on the ground - thus forming various figurative designs. At that particular moment it crossed Victor's mind that these straw designs could be put across a paper or cloth. Thus a new art from was born, the art of making pictures from rice straw.

Beautiful in their looks and striking in contrast, rice straw pictures are to be seen to be believed. The golden hued straw, shining with the slightest of light falling on it against the black background is just fascinating. Whether it's a picutre of galloping horse crushing grass under its hoofs or an elephant tearing off heavy tree stems with its long trunk, or a scene from Mahabharata depicting Lord Krishna explaining the mysteries of iife and death to a bewildered Arjuna, it is nothing but sheet beauty. So is the picture of Taj Mahal, complete with all its details and splendour.

Each and every straw that goes into the making of these picutres is exquisitely cut and chiselled to fit into various curves. At one place it takes the shape of a floating cloud and at another it is the rambling waves of water and swaying trees at beaches. Everything is so alive is the story of India's civilisation and culture".

In his will, he poetically epitomised the binding national symbol of the Ganga in the following words : "The Ganga, especially, is the river of India, beloved of her people, round which are interwined her racial memories, her hopes and fears, her victories and her defeats. She has been a symbol of India's age long cultural and civilisation, ever changing ever flowing and yet ever the same Ganga". No wonder then that the mendicant, the merchant, the prince, the preceptor and the conqueror have, over the ages, been drawn to the Ganga. And so it was in recent history when the Danes, the Dutch, the French, and the British who coveted the riches of the east, sailed up the Ganga, the principal focus and core of the sub-continent.

The Ganga is one of the ten mighty rivers of the world. It meanders across the length and breadth of India for some time 2525 miles covering the entire area north of the Vindhayas till she merges with the ocean in the Bay of Bengal. Its origin lies 4000 metres above the sea level in the Western Himalays, to the North of Uttar Pradesh amidst a deep icy cavern resembling the mouth of a cow. This is known as *gaumukh* which attracts a large number of pilgrims. The Ganga basin which spreads across eight states, sustains some 37 per cent of India's population. The Ganga basin is extensively cultivated and forms 47 per cent of the total irrigated area in the country.

The Ganga has been a major channel of communication since ancient times. During the British rule, one of the favourite pastimes of the Europeans was to cruise along the Ganga to beat off the unbearable heat. The Viceroy, Lord Wellesley, had a special boat which was "richly ornamented with green and gold and it would carry 20 people with ease".

Today, the Ganga is in trouble; it is polluted by three main Sambars, tart and thick, can be made with tamarind, dal and buttermilk. Some kind of vegetable is usually boiled along with the base. It is mixed with just enough rice to absorb the juices and dollops of ghee, so that neat little balls of rice to absorb the juices and dollops of ghee, so that neat little balls or rice can be popped into the mouth. The next course, the rasam, is watery and soupy. Wet the rice completely with rasam, is watery and soupy. Wet judicious combination of tamarind and tomatoes, rasams have a piquant, tangy taste which lends itself to drinking it straight.

The last course is always the soothing, gentle curd rice so good for the stomach. Made with homemade yogurt, it is the perfect way to end a satisfying meal.

"Dakshin" is an ancient Sanskrit word meaning "south". It symbolises what this cookbook is all about - the best and the most delicious of south Indian vegetarian cuisine. Filled with tempting recipes and evocative photographs this book presents the finest cooking from this region. It will go a long way in further popularising South Indian dishes which are light, with low fat and friendlier on the stomach.

Also, it drives home the benefits of vegetarianism - the concept that is gaining currency throughout the world.

P. K. ARORA

RIVERS OF INDIA AND THEIR CONTRIBUTION TO CULTURE

Indian rivers have played a significant role in the development of culture. During the pre-and proto historic times, the archaic cave men lived on river bank. The nature of their material life is known to us mainly on the evidence of stone tools and rock-paintings, which have survived to this day. A large number of painted rock-shelters have been discovered in the river-valleys of Chambal, Narmada, Betwa, Mahanadi and Godavari.

The world-famous proto-historic culture flourished in the Indus Valley during the 3rd and 2nd millannia B.C.

The discovery of this culture in the year 1921 brought to light the fact that in those early times India did not live in isolation. She had innter-relations with Egypt, Mesopotamia, Iran and the Bahrein area. It is the riever *Sindhu* (Indus) which gave the name *Hindu* (later India) to this country. The Indus and its tributaries of Punjab are, time and agin, referred to in ancient Indian literature. They are also mentioned by the Iranians, Greeks and Romans. The early Vedic texts were composed on the banks of these rivers.

Another important Vedic river was Sarasvati, which flowed through Punjab, Haryana and Rajasthan. It was a sacred river; on its banks were performed numerous Vedic religious rites. The later Vedic literature was largely coinposed on its banks.

In ancient times north India was known as *Aryavarta*. The area between the Himalayas and the Vindhyas, east of the river Sarasvati and West of Prayaga (Allahabad) was called Madhyadesa. The river Ganga and Yamuna were the chief rivers of this region. Their tributaries - Gomati, Sarayu, Sone, Chambal, Betwa, Ken, etc. contributed largely to the advancement of various facets of culture on their banks during the ancient and medieval periods. Ganga and Yamuna were deified as river-goddesses. From the Gupta period onwards these two goddesses are usually carved on the entrance door-jambs of temples almost throughout the country.

The association of Sindhu, Ganga and Yamuna and of their several tributaries with the Himalays bestowed to these rivers a religious sanctity. The same was the case with the mighty river Brahamputra of the north-east, which like Ganga meets the ocean *Mahodadhi* (now know as Bay of Bengal).

The relics of cultural heritage, beginning from the pre-historic times of the late medieval period are preserved to this day on the banks of these rivers. They are in the form of stone tools, seals and sealings, metal artifacts, pictorial art-forms and objects of architecutre & sculpture. This evidence, along with the literary and epigraphical source-material, has been extremely useful in the study of our past history.

The chief river of Central India is Narmada, also known as *Reva* and *Makalasuta*. On the bank of this river were situated two well-known historical cities, Mahishmati (Maheshwar) and Tripuri (Tewar, dist. Jabalpur). The excavations conducted at these sites have revealed several stages of habitation on the banks of Narmada during the early epochs of history. Other important rivers flowing through Madhya Pradesh and the contiguous regions are : Chambal, Betwa, Dhasan, Ken, Tons, Sone, Mahanadi and Indravati. These rivers have played significant role in the shaping of the material culture of the people of the region. Important towns like Ujjayini (Ujjain), Vidisha, Padmavati (Pawaya), Dasapura (Mandsaur), Mahishmati (Maheshwar), Airikina (Eran) and Tripuri (Tewar) grew up on the banks of these rivers and of their tributaries as great political and cultural centres.

The plentiful plethora of rock paintings in Madhya Pradesh can be assigned to a considerably vide range of period, from the pre-historic times to about c. 1400 A.D. Madhya Pradesh can claim the credit of having the largest number of painted rock-shelters, spreading into the longest stretch of time, in the entire country.

The colours used in the paintings are usually red, ocher, yellow, green and blue. The scenes portrayed in most of the shelters show various types of animals, birds, snakes and other reptiles, rivers, trees, hunting scenes and animal fights. Domestic life is also represented in the paintings through the scenes of music, dance, fire-worship, honey-collecting, etc.

The rivers Narmada and Tapti flow from the east to the west, and join the Western ocean proviously known as *Ratnakara* (present Arabian sea). Like Ganga and Yamuna, the river Narmada was also deified. Her images were made during the early medieval period. Their number is, however, limited.

The valley of Mahanadi (flowing through the areas of Madhya Pradesh and Orissa), has preserved valuable relics. Like the major rivers of Punjab and Madhyadesa, the Mahanadi was used for navigation.

South India has also quite a good number of rivers. The chief among them are Godavari, Krishna, Tungabhadra and Kaveri. They find occasional mention in Indian literature, epigraphs and foreign accounts. In the extensive regions bounded by Yamuna in the north and Godavari and Krishna in the south various songs (*gathas*) were sung by the common folk. These ballads of love and religious poetry throw welcome light on the life, particularly of the common people.

Archaeological field work conducted in the banks of several Indian rivers has revealed tangible evidence pertaining to the evolution of Indian culture in its variegated forms. This material has also indicated the inter-state relations and those with other countries, which existed in the past.

The rivers have contributed immensely to the diffusion of Indian culture far and wide. Their role towards integration of the country is eloquently proved from the evidence now available to us.

K. D. BAJPAI

RIVERS OF INDIA REGARDED & MOST SACRED

India is a coutnry that not only nurtures the resources nature has bestowed upon it, but also worships them for the all-round prosperity they bring in their wake. Rivers are one such gift which are considered highly sacred throughout the length and breadth of the country. This is primarily because these mighty rivers have perennially been a source of livelihood to millions of people living in areas lying along their courses. No wonder people see in them a manifestation of divine female power (*Shakti*).

The two sacred-most rivers of north India - Ganga and Yamuna - are revered as goddesses. In fact Ganga is considered as the holiest of all great Indian rivers. Originating at a high altitude in the Himalayas, it runs for ever.... Since it is a snow-fed river, its waters are pretty cold throughout the year. Devotees traverse long distances to partake and procure the ""Gangajal" (water of Ganga), as it is almost thought to be divine. Because the Gangajal procured from the "Har ki Pauri" in Hardwar perennially remains fresh; In mythology, Ganga is depicted as a beautiful young woman, holding a lotus in one hand, cascading down the tresses of Lord Shiva. A dip in its holy

waters is said to absolve one of all one's sins. The other sacred river, Yamuna, merges into Ganga at Prayag (Allahabad) where it is also joined by the mythical Saraswati, leading to the *sangam* (confluence) of three great rivers.

Brahmputra is the mighty river that dominates the landscape of north-east India. Emanating from the Mansarovar region in the Himalayas, it incessantly gushes down with a massive force through the dense forests of north-eastern states of India, particularly Assam. Brahmputra may not be revered as much as the Ganga is, but she is considered to be more beautiful. Despite its masculine-sounding name, Brahmputra is essentially feminine and exceeds Ganga by a good 450 kilometers in length. The most unique feature of this great river is its navigability at an astounding altitude of ten thousand feet; Like the Ganga, its waters too are snow-fed and are generously rainfed, thus making in flow throughout the year.

Mahanadi is the lifeline of the eastern Indian state of Orissa. It traverses some of the richest mineral tracts of India throught the Eastern Ghats. Its huge expanse and force have been shackled at various points on its run by numerous dams. This river carries and discharges the greatest amount of water in the country during the monsoons.

Narmada undoubtedly is India's most breathtakingly beautiful river. She is also the most feminine in her movements, as she slithers through thousands of kilometers of hostile terrain. Her dazzling blue waters flow serenely during her entire run of 1,247 kms. from Madhya Pradesh to Gujarat. This river is believed to be as holy and revered as the Ganga. There is a saying that Saraswati makes Kurukhetra holy, Ganga makes holy Hardwar and Kashi (Varanasi), but Narmada makes sacred whatever she touches;

Yet another important river Godavari voyages across the Maharashtra plateau into the state of Andhra Pradesh. Fed from the Sahyadri ranges, Godavari truly bifurcates south from the north of the country. The river sustains thousands of villages and feeds acres upon acres of paddy fields of Andhra Pradesh. However, Godavari has not been accorded the status it desrves among the pantheon of Indian rivers. This ancient river runs 1450 kms through the Eastern Ghats to reach the Bay of Bengal. Her drainage basin is one of the largest in India.

Cauvery is the last of the great Indian reviers. It is often referred to as the Ganga of the south. South Indians worship her as the living goddess and is venerated in multifarious ways. Babies are christened after this river, localities and roads are named after here and it is not uncommon to have a new businees venture called by her name. In terms of living culture, Cauvery leads all other Indian rivers, including the Ganga. This river runs through some of the richest south Indian lands, watering the fields and blessing the people on its course. Emanating from Talakaveri in the south Kanara district of the Indian state of Karnataka, Cauvery runs all over that state and parts of its neighbouring state of Tamil Nadu, spreading prosperity all around.

SUMATHI GURURAJ

ROCK PAINTINGS OF BHIMBETKA : A PEEP INTO TRIBAL LIFE

The region of Gondowana, comprising the entire Deccan plateau, is encircled by the Vindhya hills on the north and by the Sahyadri ranges in the west, extending to the Western Ghats in the further south and to the Eastern Ghats. This is the mythical abode of the *Rakshasas* mentioned in the Ramayana. Anthropological evidence also suffests that prehistoric human beings first emerged in this region, now in the Indian state of Madhya Pradesh.

Bhimbetka, just 46 kms away from the state capital Bhopal, offers the visitor a glimpse into the environment that has been so propitious for the growth and development of the neolithic cave people. Here we find cave paintings from the neolithic period, estimated to be 24000 years before the present times. The anatomical and geological analysis of the skull of the primitive man discovered in this area, and the red and yellow stones have provided concrete evidence as to their age. There is evidence to show the presence of a hill strem flowing through the plateau in those times, as well as the presence of non-cornivorous grazing animals. The easy availability of water and the animals as food must have helped the cave people flourish over thousands of years. Their painting skills can be seen in several caves.

The rock painting fall into three distinct periods - those from 10,000 BC, those form 5,000 BC and those from 2,000 BC. However, scholars hold varied views on the age of these paintings. There are more than 700 caves spread over a radius of 9 kms. and the sevices of a knowledgeable guide are recommended for those seeking more than a cursory glimpse of the rock paintings.

The life depicted in the cave paintings is one of tension, perhaps of fighting. In some, the warriors of the times are seen on horseback with arms resembling spears and shields. Obviously, these people used metals - either iron or copper. According to some scholars, these cave people belonged to pre-Dravidian and Aryan ages. However, it appears more plausible that they belonged to the following periods :

1) **Upper Paleolithic :** Paintings from this period are in the form of linear representations of huge figures of animals such as bisons, tigers and rhinoceroes.

2) **Mesolithic :** In addition to animals, we find human figures and hunting scenes. There are depictions of communal dances, birds, musical instruments, mother and child, pregnant women, men carrying dead animals, men drinking and burials taking place.

3) **Chalcolithic :** The drawings from this period indicate that the cavemen came in contact with the plains people of Malwa, a neighbouring area.

4) **Early Historic :** There is depiction of religious symbols, tunic like dresses and the existence of some sort of scripts from different periods -s ome religious beliefs are also presented, like tree-gods and chariots.

5) **Medieval :** The paintings from this period are chematic, In some caves, armed men and groups of animals are seen. Tehre is even a scene depicting the killing of a man. In the oldest cave paintings, no mystic linkage with death has been found, hence killing of humans appears to be natural. Depiction of blood and killings is also observed to a lesser extent in other caves, showing children, females, dancers, singers, boiling meat on pots, honey cornbs, fish and other eatables. Wild boars and buffaloes are a regular feature of the paintings, and occur in a large number of them. The cave painter took all pains to depict the mass pictures which can be termed as totems where varieties of weapons are seer. painted in gradually reducing size but their impact on humans is visible. The arrows are tipped with sharp stones. The paintings of female archers are also to be seen, and lead us to conclude that mass hunts were organized.

The instruments for the paintings, as some scholars suggest, are wooden branches of date palm trees, which were crushed in the manner and form of present day paintbrushes. The colours used were made from vegetable extractions, soils and mixtures and pastes made with animal fats. It is a marvel that the colour paste thus made has remained intact for thousands of years without fading.

From the cave paintings, it is also observed that the cave man had a clear perception of death. In one painting, a human figure is seen in between a bison, chasing him in hot pursuit, and a crab like figure awaiting him in the cave he is rushing towards for seeking shelter. This symbolic representation, according to some scholars, is the march or list of death;

The authenticity of these cave paintings is a matter of heated debates. However, the existence of these cavemen is beyond any doubt. They were in existence prior to the emergence of the Dravidian and Aryan civilization in India. These people were the docile primitive tribes who lived in the Malwa region of Madhya Pradesh. This is borne out by the fact that even today one fourth of the local population are triblas. It has been assumed by a large number of scholars that the motifs and style of these cave people and that of the contemporary tribals in Madhya Pradesh are one and the same.

In can be surmised that the extinction process of these cave people would have been caused by the plains people, growing in strength and number and advancing upon them with better equipment and weapons. Not able to resist the incursions, the cave people would either have been killed or taken away as slaves. With the passage of time, they lost their identity and most likely merged into the mainstream. All this is guess work but there is certain evidence of confrontation in the neighbourhood in the centuries to follow.

The central point in our triangle is Bhopal, the capital of the Indian state of Madhya Pradesh. It derives its name from "Bhojpal" or "Bhojpur". A city by the name of Bhojpur still exists about 28 km from Bhopal. It was founded by the legendary Parmar king of Dhar, Raja Bhoj (1010-1053 AD), Raja Bhoj engaged in an intense fight with the Chalukyas of Kalyani. Prior to this, he engaged in another fierce fight with the Chandellas, who defeated him. It is a surprise how Raja Bhoj saved his kingdom after a severe defeat at the hands of the Kalacharis. However, till the last days of his reign, he continued to fight and attack another dynasty of the Chalukyas, only to be defeated once again. Thereafter, he fell sick and died. His palaces were totally destroyed and relics of his time lie buried under the soil.

However, an unfinished Shiva temple, "Bhojeshwar temple", still remains. It stands on a simple square plinth, 66X66 ft. It has no re-entrant angles usual in such buildings. The richly caved dome, though incomplete, has a magnificent, soaring strength of line and is supported by four pillars. These, like the dome, have been conceived on a massive scale. Yet they retain a remarkable elegance because of their tapering form. Divided into three sections, the lowest is an octagoan with facets of 2.12 ft, from which rises a 24 faced section. Richly carved above, the doorway is plain below, throwing into sharp relief the two exquisitely sculpted figures that stand on either side of the pillar. On the other three sides of the structure are balconies, each supported by massive brackets and four intricately carved pillars. The lingam in the sanctum sanctorum rises to an awe-inspiring height of 7.5 feet with a circumference of 17.8 feet. it is set upon a massive platform, 21.5 feet square and composed of three superimposed lime stone blocks. The architectural harmony of the lingam and the platform creates a superb synthesis of solidity and lightness. This half-finished temple has earned the reputation of "Somnath of the East". The temple, which was in a ravaged condition, is presently under competent restoration and reconstruction by the Archaeological Survey of India (ASI).

To the west of Bhojpur once existed a vast lake, presently, nothing of it can be seen except the remanants of a maginifcent old dam to contain the waters. The site was selected with great skill as the dam consisted of hills, with two natural gaps of about 100 and 500 yards respectively. These gaps were covered by earthen dams laced on both sides with enormous blocks of sandstone, set without mortar. This great work has been ascribed to Raja Bhoj. The embankments thus created held up a vast expanse of water in an area of about 250 square miles. This lake was destroyed by Hoshang Shah of Malwa (1405-34 AD), probably to reclaim a vast area of fertile land to ensure a huge revenue. Legend has it that it took an army of Gonds (a local tribe) three months to cut through the dam, and it took another three years to empty. However, the entire exercise proved to be an ecological disaster as the lakebed took another thirty years to dry up and it altered the climate of Malwa region.

However, water has not been scarce for Bhopal. The city has two lakes, the larger one being 8-9 miles long. The founder of the city was Dost Mohammad (1708 - 1740 AD), an Afghan soldier of fortune who fled from Delhi after the death of Aurangzeb. It is said that the Gond queen Kamalapati sought help from dost Mohammad after the murder of her consort. Legends narrate how the queen would recline in her lotus barge on moonlit nights and drift across the lake.

Bhopal now forms the nucleus of tribal culture of the State. Under the aegis of Human Resource Department of the Government of India, a Tribal Museum has been set up in Bhopal, where specimens of huts representative of the major tribes of India have been constructed in their original form. The huts contain specimens of tribal arts. The artistry of these tribes can thus be seen in one place. One cannot but help notice of the similarity in the creative impulses between the paintings of Bimbetka and those found at Warli. It confirms the continuity of India culture in form, manner, spirit and intent.

B. P. MAITI

ROERICH DEVIKA RANI - FIRST LADY OF THE HINDI SCREEN

Complimented by critics with the sobriquet, "First Lady of the Indian Screen", Devika Rani, the star heroine of early Hindi talkies, could be easily distinguished from her contemporary actresses by her graceful beauty, velvety voice, sophistication and elitist background. She was a grand-niece of the Nobel Laureate Rabindranath Tagore, being his sister Sukumari devi's grand-daughter. Her father, Col. M.N. Chaudhuri, was the first Indian Surgeon-General of Madras (Now-Chennai).

Born on March 30, 1908, at Waltair (Chennai), Devika completed her schooling in early 1920s. As she evinced a keen aptitude for arts, her enlightened parents sent her to England to study at the Royal Academy of Dramatic Arts and the Royal Academy of Music in London. She won scholarships at both these institutions. She also took a degree in architecture, did a stint with Elizabeth Arden in the art of make-up and after due specialization, worked as a textile desinger at a well known art studio.

While in London, she met Himansu Rai who had gone there with a law degree from India to study for the Bar at the Inner temple. He had, however, gravitated to cinema as a filmmaker. Devika agreed to design the sets of Rai's maiden production, *Light of Asia* (1926), which he made in collaboration with Emelka Film Company of Munich. The film was mainly shot in India at authentic locales, but its post-production work was completed in Germany, where the company provided finance, equipment and technical personnel, including director Franz Osten, who later joined Rai when he set up the Bombay Talkies in Mumbai in 1934.

Rai then made *Shiraz* (1928) for the famous U.F.A. (Universal Films A.G.) of germany and British Institutional Films of England, followed by *A Throw of Dice* (1929) with the same German company and Bruce Wolf of the U.K. Devika joined Rai as an assistant art director and costume designer for this latter film. In Germany, she also studied filmmaking, including holding the make-up tray for Marlene Dietrich. Working closely together in their common pursuit of the art of cinema, particularly during the shooting of *A Throw of Dice* in India, Himansu Rai and Devika Rani - the two kindred souls-developed a mutual amorous relationship which culminated in their marriage. While the romance was set in Rajasthan, the marriage was solemnized in South India. Thereafter, Devika travelled with the film on the Continent and featured in a mime show, which was a curtain-raiser for the movie.

All the above-mentioned three silent movies, co-produced by Rai, had him in the leading roles opposite Sita Devi, an Anglo-Indian girl whose real name was Renne Smith. These films were well appreciated by the audiences in Europe, though Indian filmgoers considered the treatment and execution of the movies more foreign than indigenous.

While still abroad, Himansu Rai co-produced Karma (Fate) in English and Hindi, based on a story by Dewan Sharar and directed by J.L. Freer Hunt. In this film Rai again played the hero making his last screen appearance, while Devika made her debut as a heroine. They played royal heirs, who aspired to modernise their respective kingdoms. The English version of the film, in which princess Sudha Rani of Burdwan also appeared in a key role and which included scenes of Maharajas, elephants, tigers etc., earned exuberant acclaim in London and other European cities, as did the Hindi version in India. The British press was particularly profuse in its praise of Devika for her delicate glamour and exceptional loveliness of face, voice and diction. The film ran in London for eight months and won the *Daily Mail* prixe. Its success catapulted Devika to great international fame and as an inevitable corollary, when a year later Rai founded the Bombay Talkies, she was the first favourite heroine of its pictures. With its latest machinery and foreign technical staff the studio could rightly pride itself on its unmatched excellence.

Devika Rani is best remembered for the Bombay Talkies 'classic, *Achhut Kanya (1936)*, which was based on a story titled, 'The Level Crossing' by Niranjan Pal and which was directed by Franz Osten and music for which was scored by Saraswati Devi. In this film, Devika appeared as a low-caste, untouchable girl in love with a high-caste boy (Ashok Kumar). The film's theme of bridging the vast chasma between castes was quite bold for its time and both the leading artistes gave eloquent performances. Devika, in particular, carried the day with her smart looks and charming speech. As that was the era of singing stars, Devika also crooned a couple of songs in the film, including the memorable duet with Ashok Kumar, "*Main ban ki chidiya banke ban ban doloon re*" (Being a free little bird I fly everywhere). The film was a huge success and audiences accepted Devika as a prime heroine richly endowed with beauty and talent. It also established her and Ashok Kumar as the most popular romantic screen pair in the first decade of Hindi talkies.

Earlier, they had acted together in *Jeevan Naiya* (1936), which was Ashok Kumar's debut film. After *Achhut Kanya*, they also appeared as leading artistes in the company's next four films, which too tackled some contemporary social issues. *Janam Bhoomi* (1936) depicted an idealist urban doctor shifting to the countryside to serve the rural poor. *Izzat* (1937) dealt with preservation of the identity and traditions of an aboriginal tribe, while *Prem Kahani* (1937) again highlighted caste biases. *Savitri* (1937) was the only mythological turned out by the company, but with a different and sleek approach. Devika also worked with Ashok Kumar in *Mamta* (1936), *Nirmala* (1938), *Durga* (1939) and *Anjaan* (1941). Her films with some other heroes included *Jeevan Prabhat* (1937), *Vachan* (1918) and *Hamari Baat* (1943).

Himansu Rai being at the helm of the Bombay Talkies, was totally involved in the process of filmmaking right from the story idea to the final editing. He deftly combined artistic aspirations with commercial considerations. The prolonged strain of hard work resulted in a nervous breakdown, which caused his death in May, 1940. After him, the reins of the company came into the hands of Devika, who displayed a rare understanding of a complex business. Under her baton, the company went on to make successful films like *Punar Milan* (1940), *Jhoola* (1941), *Naya Sansar* (1941), *Basant* (1942) and *Kismet* (1941). The huge success of *Kismet*, with its record continuous run, paradoxically caused a split in the Bombay Talkies, with S. Mukherji, a senior partner, forming a new company named, Filmistan.

Thereafter, control of the Bombay Talkies passed through several hands till its closure in 1954 when a businessman bought it to convert the studio into an industrial estate. Devika Rani, after selling her interests, retired from the screen and married Svetoslav Roerich, the famous painter of Russian origin, in 1945. The couple first took residence in their sylvan retreat in the Kullu Valley and later in their sprawling estate near Banglore.

Svetoslav continued to wield his painting brush with inspired creativity and produced extraordinarily exquisite portraits and sceneries. A portrait of Devika Rani painted by him with a special labour of love stood out as his best work at an exhibition of his paintings inaugurated in New Delhi by the then Prime Minister Jawaharlal nehru in 1960. A larger-than-life painting each, of Jawaharlal Nehru and Indira Gandhi, done by Svetoslav adorns two panels on the inner circular walls of the historic Central Hall of India's parliament in New Delhi.

Svetoslav's father, Nicholas, was a great painter too. At his death he had left behind a very large number of his most artistically executed paintings and many other artefacts of great value. These and the family's other precious heirlooms, priceless jewellery and huge immoveable property constituted an enormous wealth which led to unsavoury disputes after the couple died childless. Svetoslav passed away on January 9, 1993, and Devika followed him on March 9, 1994. At her funeral Devika was given full state honour.

Earlier in 1958, the President of India has honoured Devika with a "Padma Shri". In 1970, she became the first recipient of the prestigious "Dadasaheb Phalke Award". Nationalist leader and poetess Sarojini Naidu described Devika as "a magical flower of romance". This magical flower, which cast a spell on generations of Devika's fans, will continue to stir and inspire many more for a long, long time.

B. M. MALHOTRA

ROY, JUTHIKA

(B. 1912) - Vocalist : bhajan; studied with Kamal Dasgupta, Vishnadev Chatterjee; concert tours, Sri Lanka (1948), East Africa (1955); disc recordings.

S. P. SEN

RITU BERI : THE NAME SAYS IT ALL

Ritu Beri - prima donna of the Indian fashion scene creates waves internationally with each of her latest collections. Feeling the pulse of the fashion-conscious the world over, she has the uncanny sense to create trendy garments which instantly capture the attention of both the glitterati and the not so rich.

The very mention of her name conjures up images of lavishly mounted fashion shows which display her skills as a fashion-designer par excellence. No wonder, over the years, she has emerged not just as an "ethinic designer" but as a cosmopolitan manistream designer with a capacity to attract every woman;

But it is not just women alone whom Ritu Beri appeals; even men are drawn to Ritu Beri label because she has been able to create stunning collections for them too. For well over a century, men's wear has centred around shirts and trousers only. And now with designers like Ritu Beri focussing their attention on the male wardrobe, men have been able to shake off their stagnated predicament and step out into the fashionable ethinic wear or the executive wear, which has painstakingly been turned into a more relaxed and colourful option. These efforts have yielded rich dividends for the designers. For, the ready to wear male garments industry has proved to be far more productive than the yield from women's wear.

With a sense of history, Ritu Beri has set up the "Ritu Beri Fashion Fraternity" which seeks to promote promising young fashion designers. By so doing, she has not only created a niche for herself in the history of fashion in India, but has also taken a big leap in creating a pool of skilled fashion designers who will keep her banner flying for decades to come.

For the 1996 Olympics at Atlanta, Ritu Beri was selected to design the special collection to be worn by the Indian contingent at the opening ceremony. This collection was hailed as "sporty, having a sophisticated Indian touch, truly befitting the occasion". For Ritu Beri, this was both - "a great honour and a big challenge". Because she had to creat a combination of "western design with a distinct Indian appeal". And this she accomplished with great elan;

Besides being a fashion designer of international repute, Ritu Beri is also a 'caring' human being who has desplayed a deep regard for the well-being of animals too; she recently launched a unique collection, suitably called "Caring Means Sharing". This collection comprises T-Shirts, caps, mugs, stuffed toys, postcards etc. The funds raised through the sales of this product line will help bolster the efforts of "People for Animals" - an organisation which has many centres for animal care throughout the country.

"Caring Means Sharing" is a dream project for Ritu Beri. Says she: "The best way I could help the hapless animals was to use my creativity to bring forth a collection which conveys the message that we must respect the animals and fight animal abuse". He message is also conveyed in the choice of material she uses for her products Leather substitutes and fake fur ensure that the creation of products do not require killing of animals.

Now when India has celebrated the Golden Jubilee of her independence, how could Ritu Beri lag behind. To mark the occasion, she designed and presented a fashion extravaganza in New Delhi which took the viewers on an "unusal cultural journey through the various eras of fashion" in India.

In recognition of her infinite designing talent, Ritu Beri has been conferred innumerable awards both in India and abroad. She has held fashion shows not only in India but in various other countries as well including USA, UK, China, Mauritius, Kenya and many more.

BHARAT BHUSHAN

"S"

S. K. BHATIA (DR.)

Melvin Jones Fellow Lion Dr. S. K. Bhatia : born 10th Dec., 1941. Edu. M.BA, Dip. Lib. Sc., Dip. Journalism. BAMs, E.M.P.M.R.S.H. (London)

Started career as Librarian in PG DAV College (D.U.) which he left in 1968. He served as Secretary General of Delhi University and College Libraries Association (also founded by him. He joined Orient Longmann Ltd. as Public Relations Officer.Joined Lalvani Bros. (Wholesaler) as Asstt. Manager. In 1975 he joined D. K. Publishers & Distributors as its Gen. Manager and in 1985 starated his own Publishing House in the name of Reliance Publishing House and has published more than 400 titles till now. He is also the Chairman of International Instt. of Education, Information and Technology.

Applied Art - Design and Drawing Handicraft & Printing	S. K. Bhatia
Bharatreehrui's Niti Shatak	S. K. Bhatia
Bharatreehuri's Vairagya Shatak	S. K. Bhatia
Chanakya's Niti Darpan	S. K. Bhatia
Dictionary of Dreams H.B.	S. K. Bhatia
Dictionary of Dreams P.B.	S. K. Bhatia
Dictionary of Idioms	S. K. Bhatia
Dictionary of Learning for Children	S. K. Bhatia
Dictionary of Letter Writing Spellings	S. K. Bhatia
Dictionary of Library & Information Science	S. K. Bhatia
Dictionary of medical Terminilogy	S. K. Bhatia
Dictionary of Mythology	S. K. Bhatia
Dictionary of Quotations of Famous Authors	S. K. Bhatia
Dictionary of Thesaurus	S. K. Bhatia
Directory of Indian Book Industry	S. K. Bhatia
Directory of Libraries in Delhi	S. K. Bhatia
Directory of Universities and Colleges of India	S. K. Bhatia
Directory of Universities and Colleges of India with CD	S. K. Bhatia
Encyclopaedia of Sex for Teenagers	S. K. Bhatia
Encyclopaedia of Herbs, Condiments & Spieces	S. K. Bhatia
Encyclopaedia of Misticism & Occultism	S. K. Bhatia
Encyclopaedia of Sex and Love Technique	S. K. Bhatia
English - English Dictionary for Youngsters	S. K. Bhatia
The Practical Guide to English	S. K. Bhatia

His forthcoming titles are 'Encyclopaedia of Sex for Teenagers', 'Directory of Universities & Colleges of India, 6th ed.', 'Directory of Indian Book Industry' (2nd ed.) 'Director of Business Management Insts. in India, 'Directory of Libraries in Delhi 5th (ed.).

SABEER BHATIA

Sabeer Bhatia, whose Hotmail changed the way people send email, is the only Indian pretty close to 'Billdom'. Arguably the first Indo-Greek venture, Hotmail started with three subscribers in 1995 and now has 22 million of them in 230 countries.

Bhatia grew up in Bangalore and went to the US in 1988 to get a bachelor's degree at the California Institute of Technology and a master's in electrical engineering at Stanford. After graduation, he put in a stint at Apple Computer for a year and another at the now-defunct Firepower Systems. But his big moment came when he decided to start Hotmail with his Apple and Firepower colleague Jack Smith in 1996.

The latest in a line of second-generation entrepreneurs who have taken the experience and money they earned building their first businesses to launch new ventures, Bhatia's new passion is Arzoo (Passion in Urdu).

It's an e-commerce firm that he says will change the way people buy and sell on the Internet. Since the current Web shopping interface leaves much to be desired, Arzoo may just turn out to be Bhatia's next multi-million dollar winner.

SABIR KHAN (b.1925)

Instrumentalist : Hindustani, sarangi of Senia gharana; studied with Haji Mohammad Khan, Bahadur Khan; concert tours, Afghanistan (1955 and 1959), Pakistan (1960).

SACHIN TENDULKAR (b.1973)

It is not often that sporting prodigies go on to achieve predicted greatness. Sachin Ramesh Tendulkar is a shining exception. He has not only reached epochal heights as a batsman of exceptional caliber, but has even bettered the expectations his cricket-crazy country had when he first strode on to the Test arena as a precocious 16-year-old in 1989.

A decade later, Tendulkar is not only the best batsman in the world but is also hailed as the most saleable cricketer around, In India, he enjoys incredible popularity, the ultimate icon of millions of youngsters.

Tendulkar has become a legend through the sheer weight of his performances on the field. His record in Tests as well as one-dayers is stupendous. Tendulkar has 21 hundreds as well as 21 fifties in Test matches with a fantastic average of around 57. His one-day statistics is equally impressive with 8,000 plus runs which includes a world record 23 hundreds besides 44 fifties. In addition, he is a useful bowler who can break partnerships with his assortment of swing and spin bowling.

Tendulkar's technique is impecable, he packs tremendous power and strength into his short, stocky frame, and his ability to time the ball is exemplary. He has all the shots in the book and more, and appears to play them with conviction against any kind of bowling on any kind of surface.

One wonders how many marks Tendulkar will leave in his name by the time he decides to call it a day. For he is still only 26 and has a fair distance to go, his back problem notwithstanding.

SAHIR LUDHIANVI :
SOUL-STIRRING URDU POET AND FILM LYRICIST

Sahir Ludhianvi, one of the brightest stars in the dual firmament of literary world and Hindi cinema during the three decades of qualitative creativity spanning 1950s to 1980s, enjoyed great popularity among his fans spread across and beyond our subcontinent. As an enlightened Urdu poet with progressive proclivities and leftist learnings, he vehemently opposed feudalism, championed the cause of the exploited workers, protested against iniquitous treatment meted out to women and castigated the society for its hypocrisy and indifference to the pervasive misery and suffering of the poor.

Sahir, meaning magician, charmer or enchanter, was the nom de plume Abdul Hayee (that's how he was indeed christened) chose as he embarked upon his career as a poet while he was a student. Born at Ludhiana on March 8, 1921, he was the first son of a rich and proud landlord, Fazal Mohd. and his wife Sardar begum. Fazal Mohd's marriage with Sardar Begum was his eleventh one as he had not begotten a male issue from any of his previous ten marriages.

Serious discord, however, surfaced between husband and wife as Fazal Mohd. Looked down upon and considered the lineage of his spouse as much below the status of his family and, therefore, wanted to keep his marriage with her under wraps. He also wanted her to cover her face with the traditional veil. Sardar Begum objected to these dictatorial commands and separated from him and moved to the care of her brother along with her son, who was only six months old at the time.

She filed a case in the court to claim Fazal Mohd's immovable property for her son. The case lingered on for about twenty years and consumed all her cash and jewellery as expenses. When Abdul Hayee was in the fifth standard at school the court, after ascertaining his wishes, rejected Fazal Mohd's appeal for grant of the custody of his son to him and instead decreed that the boy continue to live with his mother.

Sahir wrote his first poem in 1937 which his school teacher poet found technically in order but undistinguished otherwise. Undeterred, the budding poet continues flirting with the muse while studying at Government College, Ludhiana, and later at Dayal Singh College, Lahore, from both of which institutions he was expelled for his political activities. He gave up his studies before completing his graduation and went the whole hog to pursue his political and literary activities.

He published the first anthology of his poems titled, Tal Khiyaan (Bitternesses) in 1944. The same year some of his poems containing anti-imperialist and revolutionary thoughts were confiscated by the then British rulers. He remained in Lahore for some time before moving to Mumbai in 1945. During his stay in Lahore and in Delhi he edited a few Urdu periodicals and wrote more poems.

The second collection of his poems, Parchhaiyaan (Shadows) was published in 1955 and his third poetical work Aao Koyee Khwab Bunein (Let's Weave A Dream) in 1971. Gaata Jaaye Banjaara is a collection of the lyrics that he wrote for a number of films.

An early composition of his, Taj Mahal, rated as an all-time popular poem, shook the literary world when it presented an altogether new point of view :

Ek shahenshah ne daulat ke sahara lekar
Hum ghareebon ki mohabbat ka udaaya hai mazaaq

(By using his enormous wealth (to build the Taj Mahal), an emperor has ridiculed the love of we the poor).

The most interesting things about this couplet is that Sahir had neither visited Agra nor seen the Taj Mahal.

A good verse, in Sahir's view, had to be beautiful, true and useful. He also wrote:

Duniya ne tajjarubaat-o-hawadas ke shakal mein,
Jo kuchh mujhe diya hai woh lauta raha hoon main.

(I am returning (through my poetry) only that which the world has given me in the shape of experiences and accidents).

His poetry, therefore, not only accorded with his declared norm but also gave ample glimpses from his own life.

In Mumbai, Sahir came in contact with many writers Like Krishan Chander, Saaghar Nizami, Kaifi Azmi, Jan Nisar Akhtar and Josh Malihabadi. Following their example, he too decided to write for films. However, there being no ready opening, he had to start with fair-writing the drafts of Krishan Chander's stories at a monthly remuneration of Rs.150/- Thereafter, he wrote a few film songs, which an established lyricist used under his name and paid Rs.500/- per song to Sahir.

On a fateful day, his tryst with music director S.D. Burman opened the door for his progress as a film lyricist. His first song, "Thandi hawayen, lehra ke aanyen" (Cooling winds, blow enchantingly) set to music by Burman in Naujawan (1951) proved an instant hit. Thereafter, Burman and Sahir worked in tandem and the lyrics of Baazi name of the lyricist also got included in the credits of the film and the practice was adopted henceforth by the industry to the satisfaction of many other lyricists. Among the playback singers, Lata Mangeshkar had already given a lead by having her name included in the credits of Raj Kapoor's Barsaat (1949).

Burman and Sahir continued to produce emotion-soaked songs in many films including Sazaa, Jaal, Taxi Driver, Pyaasa, and Munimji. However, a clash of egos between them led to their parting company. Sahir them collaborated with O.P. Nayyar for Naya Daur, which was a roaring hit. While the music director attributed the success of the songs to his film tunes, the poet insisted on the superiority lyrics. Sahir opposed the music directors wanting lyricists to fit words to their pre-composed tunes. Shair also demanded to be paid more (even by a token one rupee) then the music director, a proposal that did not find favour with the producers. Hence, the self-confident and self-respecting Sahir started working with some other well established as well as new music directors like Roshan, Ravi, N. Dutta, Madan Mohan, Khayyam and Jaidev. The songs produced by the new teams were also great hits due to both Sahir's sparkling poetry and their melodious rendition by the singers in the scintillating tunes created by the singers in the scintillating tunes created by the music directors. Roshan provided music for Taj Mahal, Dil Hi To Hai, and Barsaat Ki Raat ; Ravi for Gumrah, Humraaz and Waqt; N. Dutta for Dhool Ka Phool and Sadhana, Madan Mohan for Ghazal and Railway Platform; Khayyam for Phir Subah Hogi, Shagoon and Kabhi Kabhi; and Jaived for Hum Dono and Mujhe Jeene Do.

The classic Pyassa (1957), which was based on Sahir's life story, was a great hit epecially because of its soul-stirring poetry and Guru Dutt's sensitive performance. "Yeh duniya agar mil bhi jaaye to kya hai? (What if one could even gain this world?) and Jinhen naazhai Hind Par Woh Kahaan Hain) where are the ones who are proud of India? Knocked on the conscience of the audiences as also to the society at large. Trishul (1977), another successful film too took a chapter from Sahir's life. The role of an aggrieved and defiant son played by Amitabh Bachchan under Yash Chopra's direction was nothing but a dramatized version of Sahir's own feeling of hurt and unfulfilled ambitions.

Sahir gave to films many other significant and haunting numbers such as "Raat bhar ka hai mehman andhera" (Darkness is a guest just for the night, "Tu Hindu banega na Musahlman Banega/Insaan ki aulaad hai insaan banega" (You will grow up to be neither a Hindu nor a Muslim but a human being as you are the child of human being). "Woh Subah kabhi to aayegi" (That morning will dawn someday), "Aurat ne janam diya mardon ko / Mardon ne use bazaar diya" (Woman gave birth to men / And men sold her in the market), "Saathi haath badhaana" (Partner, lend a hand) and "Chalo ik baar phir se ajnabi ban jaayen hum dono" (Let us be strangers once again).

Through his poetry Sahir painted a dismal picture of the society with its glaring black spots and stirred the national conscience, calling upon the leaders in power to rectify the wrongs. By asking, "Where are the ones who are proud of India?" he was obviously, though obliquely, referring to Jawahar Lal Nehru, the then Prime Minister of India. However, contrary to a general impression, Sahir was not opposed to Nehruvian Socialism or his other policies. He was, in fact, a great admirer of Nehru and devoted and dedicated to him a whole poem eulogising him for his outstanding contribution and support to secularism pacifism and socialism.

Sahir remained a bachelor till the end of his life, though his name came to be associated with a few female celebrities. His mother passed away in 1976 without realizing her wish to see her son married and settled as a family man. Ardently devoted as he was to his mother, his sole emotional anchor, her death dealt him an unbearable blow so much so that he became a virtual recluse, distancing himself from the literary and social swirl around him. He breathed his last on October 25, 1980. Ironically, one of his last famous songs was the kabhi kabhi (1976) assertion, "Main pal do pal ka shair hoon" (I am a poet of a moment or two).

Sahir was a recipient of many honours and awards, including Padma Shree, the Maharashtra Urdu Academy Award, Maharashtra State Literary Award and Soviet Land Nehru Award. He was also honoured by his former college at Ludhiana, and the city renamed one of its important roads as Sahir Ludhianvi Marg. The Maharashtra Government also appointed him Justice of Peace and a special Executive magistrate.

With his significant and potent poetry Sahir ignited the imagination of the country's youth and instilled in them a healthy opimism, as exemplified by his following verse: "Na munh chhupa ke jiyo hum na sar jhuka ke jiyo / Sitamgaron ki nazar se nazar mila ke jiyo" (We neither hide our face nor bowed our heads / we looked straight into the eyes of the tyrants). He rephrased this verse for an inspiring song in Humraaz (1967) as :

Na munh chhupa ke jiyo aur na sar jhukak ke jiyo,
Ghamon ka daur bhi aaye to muskara ke jiyo.

(Do not live hiding your face or bowing your head; even if a phase of sorrows comes, live with smile.)

B. M. MALHOTRA

SAIR-E-GUL-FAROSHAN (PHUL-WALON KI SAIR)

Flower festival of Mehrauli (New Delhi); originated by one Muhammad Shah 'Rangila', falls in Bhadrapada (August-September); celebrated jointly by Hindus and Muslims with great enthusiasm; huge hand-fans of different kind are made specially for occasion and are decorated with flowers and are carried by people in procession accompanied with music and song.

P. N. CHOPRA

SALABHANJIKA
WOMAN AND THREE MOTIF IN INDIAN SCULPTURE

The role of a women in nature has been poetically expressed in the motif on 'Salabhanjika' or Woman and tree' and depicted in the 2nd century B.C. sculptures at Sanchi, Bharhut and Bodhgaya. It is a theme that frequently occurs in ancient and medieval sculpture.

In the beginning, 'Salabhanjika' was the name of a garden sport played by women. Under a blossoming Sala (tree), women stood in a particular pose under low bending boughs overladen with flowers, These women came to be known as Salabhanjika.

According to Pali accounts, the Buddha's mother Maya Devi was standing in this pose when the Buddha was born. In course of time, the word Salabhanjika became conventional term for a woman standing in this pose. On the stupa gateways of Bharhut, Sanchi and Mathura, the female figures carved between the horizontal architrave and upright pillars festooning the corners became known as torana-salabhanjika. The most celebrated early sculpture of a slalabhanjika is at Sanchi. On the eastern gateway is a beautiful female figure swaying majestically from the branch of tree.

The woman-and-tree motif found its most elegant expression in the red sandstone Mathura sculptures of the Kushana period. The leaves and flowers of the Ashoka tree were most popular. The delicate beauty of these nymphs and dryads has a charm of its own that connot be matched by the sculptures of self-standing female figures in classical Indian art. The tree in blossom lends charm to the beautiful female figure. Beauty of nature combined with the beauty of the female form is the basis of the worship of mother earth. The threefold fixation or the tribhanga pose of the female figure with her sensuous curves further elevates the aesthetic quality of the salabhanjika.

PRABHAKAR BEGDE

SALARJUNG MUSEUM

Nawab Mir Yousuf Ali Khan Salarjung III, owner of the largest collection in the world, from the fantastic collection emerged the Salarjung Museum at Hyderabad; a sailent feature of Museum in its international character and the collections pertaining to each country are arranged in one or more rooms; Eastern section includes exquisite collection from China, Japan, Burma, Egypt, Persia and India; Green Celadon of the Ming and Sung Periods, lacquered furniture and bronzes and old ivory carvings, inlaid screens and carved furniture form Niko and glazed painted pottery from Satsuma highlight Japanese section, miniature paintings from Persia preserved in their forceful subtlety and carpets from Bokhara, Shiraz and Tabriz oriental Manuscript section containing the Holy Quran caligraphed by Yaqoot-al-Mostasani and bearing the seals of Jahangir, Shahjahan and Aurangzeb are treasures by any standard; among other interesting section of museum are the Indian textiles, bronzes, miniature paintings, Jade room and representative Western Section; collection includes porcelain Wedgewood pottery and cut glass items from England, France and Germany a representative collection of European paintings and sculpture including originals of Lansdeer, Laighton, Canaletto and Chardin; among marble statues veiled Rebecca by Benzoni has attracted much attention as also the wooden sculpture by and anonymous Italian sculptor depicting good and evil from Geothe's Faust; among other numerous items are collections ranging from wall clocks to walking sticks; Salarjung library has an extensive collection of Oriental manuscripts in Urdu, Arabic and Persian and is a treasure house for the student and scholar; over thirty thousands English volumes cover a wide range of subjects including museology, art history, natural history and aesthetics.

M. N. UPADHYAYA

SALMAN RUSHDIE (b.1947)

Salman Rushdie's allegorical tales have raised some very real storms. His third novel, the Satanic Verses (1988), forced him into hiding after Iran's Ayatollah Khomeini issued a fatwa to execute its author for blaspheming the Prophet, and a $ 6 million bounty was placed on his head.

Rushdie gained both critical acclaim and popular success with Midnight's Children (1981), and allegory about modern India that examines historical and philosophical issues through surreal characters, dark humour and a melodramatic prose style.

Rushdie continues to publish while in hiding-imaginary Homelands (1991) is a collection of essays and criticism, while East, West (1994) is a collection of short stories.

SAMBALPURI SARIS

Sambalpuri saris have a charm of their own; they are not only adored for their vibrant colours and intricacy of designs and patterns but for their life span, fadeless colours and gracefulness.

Sambalpuri saris carry a combination of bandha and woven patterns (tie and dye). The pallu is weft Ikat and the woven patterns mostly display stylised fish, elephants, etc. calligraphic bancha saris some times have puzzles, secret messages and poetic renderings.

Unlike patola of Gujarat and Ikat of Andhra Pradesh, the Sambalpuri Saris do not focus much on weaving. To create designs on sari, the artist just prepares blueprints of designs and motifs to be woven as per his imagination. Working on the blueprint, he ties the portions of thread where certain colours are not required. Later on, the uncoloured portions are coloured with the desired hue. This way various motifs are created on the sari. As the motifs are born of the tie and dye, hence process, and not of weaving, hence weaving holds little importance in this art of fabric designing.

The importance of Sambalpuri sari lies in the meager quantity of thread it uses. Nevertheless, beautiful saris, curtains, bedspreads, wall hangings, tablecloths and handkerchiefs are created for the buyer. Though the origin of this art is obscure the 'Bhulia' community is said to be its custodian....

Concentrated in areas like Baragarh, Sonpur, Balangir, Barapali and Sambalpur of Western Orissa, this respectable community has alive the tradition of Sambalpuri sari weaving from generation to generation.

This art of weaving had almost become obsolete when crusader Padamshree Krutartha Acharya led a co-operative movement for its resurrection. He established many outlets/showrooms in Orissa and other parts of India, which offer the best and original Sambalpuri material. Sambalpuri saris and other stuff have found connoisseurs among some profile customers like the late Prime Minister Indira Gandhi and Queen Elizabeth-II of England.

During the last about five decades, Sambalpuri products have also won international acclaim for master craftsmen like Padmashree Kunja Behari Meher, Padamshree Jadunatha Supakar, the late Radhashyama Meher and Surendera Kumar Meher who created Sambalpuri masterpieces.

MANOMAYEE PUROHIT

SANCHI, ABDUL QADIR KHAN

(b.1917) – Vocalist : Hindustani, khayal of Agra gharana; studied with Fayyaz Hussain Khan.

SANGEET NATAK AKADEMI

On 28th January, 1953 the Sangeet Natak Academy was inaugurated by the first President of India Dr. Rajendra Prasad. Maulana Abul Kalam Azad, the then Union Minister for Education emphasized in his opening address that it would be the "aim of this Academy to preserve our traditions by offering them in an institutional form..... to promote research in the field of Indian dance, drama and music, and for this purpose to establish a library and museum, to encourage ... exchange of ideas and enrichment of techniques..."

The Academy has since functioned as an autonomous organization, and is funded by the Department of culture of the Ministry of Human Resource Development, Government of India. It has three constituent units, the Jawaharlal Nehru Manipur Dance Academy (JNMDA) at Imphal, the Kathak Kendra in Delhi and the Rabindra Rangshala on the Delhi ridge.

The academy also established the National School of Drama and the Asian theatre Institute in July 1959. Eventually they merged and separated from the academy in 1975 and became autonomous organizations the same year.

Over the years the Sangeet Natak Academy had built up a large archives of audio and videotapes, photographs, slides and films on the performing arts. Thus, there is invaluable archive material on the tribal, folk and traditional performing arts from different parts of India. Traditional music, dance and theatre have been extensively recorded at various festivals covering diverse regions such as Bhuj. Somnath, Kerala, Nagaland, Assam, Karnataka, and Tripura.

The academy has also produced a number of films including Ustad Bade Ghulam Ali Khan and Ustad Allauddin Khan, Ramayana in Kutiyatam and Kathakali, Folk and Tribal Dances of India, Chayanatak, Tanavernam and Bhootaradhana. Eminent masters in various disciplines, including dance gurus and eminent musicians Pankaj Charan Das, Kelucharan Mohapatra, Birju Maharaj, Vempani Chinna Satyam and several others have been video-filmed.

The academy also houses the "Gallery of Musical Instruments it was inaugurated by Yehudi Mehunin, the distinguished violinist, on 13 February, 1964. Apart from the instruments the collection includes a substantial variety of masks and headgears, costumes and art facts from various parts of the country. The Gallery also provides information on musical instruments and other objects in its connection to researchers and visitors.

The academy's library has a small but specialized collection of books on music, dance and theatre consisting of over 20,000 volumes in English and Hindi and regional languages.

Almost ever since its inception, the academy has organized several All India theatre Festival and seminars. Since 1994, workshops have been organized for directors introducing them to new concepts and methodologies in theatre at home and abroad.

Puppetry is also promoted and various events have been organized such as an international exhibition of puppets and symposia on puppet theatre where delegates from different countries have participated.

The publishing program of the academy includes books and monographs on the performing arts and the quarterly journal Sangeet Natak.

The Sangeet Natak Academy fellowships and awards are given to outstanding artists in the fields of music, dance and theatre in recognition of their contributions to the performing arts.

(Condensed)

GAYATRI MANCHANDA

SANSKRIT MANUSCRIPTS

Manuscripts form as precious a part of our cultural heritage as the stone-monuments or other artistic antiquities or historical documents. For understanding the history and culture of the country, the literary treasures enshrined in the manuscripts cannot be ignored. For nearly four thousand years, Sanskrit has been continuously active and perhaps no other language coming from antiquity has put forth such an enormous amount of literature. Only a part of this has come into print, the rest being available only in manuscripts. While oral transmission and memorizing were the most ancient form of preservation, the writing down of texts began quite early. The early writer used any material that was available cloth silk or cotton (patta), plank (phalaka), leather and parchment therefrom (carman), metal (tamra-patra), clay-tables, rock (sila) and bark and leaves of trees (tvak and patra). Specimens of old documents on all these materials have come down to us. Not only have edicts, inscriptions and grants been engraved on rock and copper-plate, but even literary works poems, plays and songs have come down in rocks and copper-plates. But on a large scale, ancient literature has been preserved on palm-leaves in the south and some other parts of India, and birch-bark in Kashmir, and paper which came to be used in the mainland of India much later, say from about tenth century. How these old manuscripts in different materials were made, the wiring implements. Pagination, binding preservation, paleography, calligraphy, illumination – all these form a fascinating story. Although a palm-leaf manuscript lasts longer and keeps better in the long run than the modern paper-printed book, there has been regular loss of manuscript decay.

The primary placed of preservation of manuscripts was the vary place of their production namely the houses of scholars, and the schools where they taught and the temples and religious Maths where some the them stayed. The destruction of some of these places, resulted in the loss of manuscripts. The kings who patronized writers had also libraries of manuscripts in their places. In ancient India, the live institutions of scholarly contacts, like debates and visits to courts and places of pilgrimage, led to the migration of manuscripts from one corner of the country to the other. Appayya Dikshitar's works written in Tamilnad are found in Kashmir and the great Kashmirian Classics are today preserved in Kerala. During the centuries immediately following Christ, there was the expansion of Indian culture in Cambodia, Siam and Indonesia and Sanskrit works including Dharma Sastras and Puranas travelled to South-East Asian countries. During the great era of Buddhistic expansion, Central Asia, Tibet and China became literary provinces of India. Sanskrit manuscripts were taken by sarvants to these regions where they were preserved in the original or translated into the local languages. There are thus 1,467 Sanskrit works in Chinese and 4,446 in Tibetan translations. Not only religious and philosophical works, but even medicine, grammar, poetics and drama were taken and translated. There are in these translations numerous Sanskrit classics of which the originals have been lost in India. The Sanskrit manuscripts have been excavated by European scholars and today one has to go to Leningrad, Stockholm and Berlin to study these.

In the last three centuries, Sanskrit manuscripts flowed towards European and American universities, museums and libraries and private collections. There are about 50,000 Sanskrit, Prakrit and Pali manuscripts in Europe. There are Sanskrit manuscripts in Japan also.

In India, of course, it is not possible to make even a rough estimates of the manuscripts lying scattered in every known and unknown place, in public and private custody. With the founding of the modern Indian Universities and institutions for research in the last hundred and fifty years, a new enlightened interest in manuscripts has developed. A consolidated alphabetical inventory of Sanskrit works and their authors, giving reference to all their known manuscripts in the different libraries of the world have been compelled. Accordingly, between 1891 and 1903, the German Sanskrit Theodore Aufrecht compiled three volumes of his catalogue catalogorum based on 98 collections and catalogues and extending to 1,195 pages of folio size. The new catalogue catalogorum of Sanskrit manuscripts of the Madras University is one of the few major research projects of India, and from the point of view of its basic value to all research, it is the most important of Indian research undertakings. To the Indian collections, we have to add those in Nepal; and then there are also the Buddhistic Pali collections in Ceylon and Burma.

In the universities of India, only, some of which have so far interested themselves in manuscripts, there are already nearly one lakh of manuscripts, the Tranvancore University alone possessing a rich collection of about 30,000. In the traditional Sanskrit colleges and Pathasalas of the country, there are more than one lakh, the Banaras Sanskrit college, now the Varanasi Sanskrit University, alone having 70,000 which is the biggest single collection of the country. Taking research societies and institutes, they have among them more than two lakhs of manuscripts. In the libraries and Museum again, these are Nearly one lakh, while Hindu Temples and Maths have about a quarter lakh, the Jain monasteries, in Rajasthan and Western India particularly, have an incredibly large number of well-preserved and important collections. In Rajasthan, there are two laks and in Ahmedabad City along the Jain Mandirs possess about 60,000 manuscripts may be found. Private number of manuscripts, in Cochin alone, pandit families possess 5,000 manuscripts and in place like Banaras, there are even individual family collections going upto this number, and there are of course numberless manuscripts is complete without a survey of Nepal where there is large concentration of manuscripts in public and private possession, some of these being very important; Nepalese manuscripts are as valuable for textual criticism as Kashmir and Malayalam manuscripts. Dacca and Lahore, now no longer with us, the two universities have about 5,000 and 6,000 Sanskrit manuscripts respectively.

The organising of a department for surveying manuscripts is not a mere matter of safeguarding one class of Indian antiquities. The systematic survey of manuscripts will throw up several outstanding Sanskrit classics of early creative periods as Sanskrit literature in all branches of knowledge which have gone into oblivion and whose different systems of ancient Indian thought,

branches of literature, and criticism, and arts and sciences. One need mention only the example of who the discovery of the manuscripts of Kautilya's Arthasastra revolutionised the ideas about ancient Indian culture or of the fragments of Asvagosha's dramas in central Asia took back the antiquity philosophical works from their Chinese and Tibetan renderings enables us today to understand better the earlier phases of Indian systems of thought like Samkhya, Vedanta and Nyaya. (Condensed)

V. RAGHAVAN

SANSKRIT UNIVERSITY OF VARANASI PLATFORM FOR INDOLOGISTS

Sampurananand Sanskrit University, the first institution of its kind in India, came into being in 1791 at the initiative of Jonathan Duncan, the then Resident of East India Company and Lord Cornwalis, India's Governor General. Pandit Kashinath was the first principal of the college. The college was run with governmental assistance and there was provision for obtaining additional funding in case of natural calamity or disaster.

Initially, a faculty was appointed to teach the Vedas, Vedanta, Nyaya, Philosophy, Puranas, Poetry, Astrology, Ayurveda and theology. Lord Cornwalis was the visitor of the college and the Resident occupied the second highest position.

Duncan's idea perhaps was not only to support Hindu philosophy and an ancient language but also to train people who could assist the judiciary in the litigation among Hindu citizens on the basis of the Hindu Holy Scriptures. On this score, theology was introduced as multi-disciplinary subject comprising the entire gamut of Vedic and Puranic literature.

At the outset there was only on teacher for the classes of all the four Vedas. In the year 1800, the faculty strength rose to four. For some reasons, the teaching of Vedas was stopped in 1828. This provoked a lot of resentment among the elite. However, much later, Yajurveda was reintroduced in 1922 and still continues as a principal subject at the Sampurananand Sanskrit University.

Though the subject of Puranas was approved from the early days of the Sanskrit College, it enjoyed little importance in the curriculum. The College administration displayed a casual attitude towards the growth and development of the subject, possibly due to paucity of funds. Fortunately, one Gauri Shankar the promotion of a course called Puranic Studies, Which brought some renowned scholars to the classroom.

Since Persian language was widely used in the Indian judiciary, it was introduced as a subject at Sanskrit College in 1913.

The foundation stone of its magnificent main building was laid by the King of Varanasi on November 2, 1847. Actual construction began in 1848 and the whole work was completed in 1852. European Gothic architecture made the building unique and perhaps the only one of its kind in entire contemporary Varanasi and it s adjoining districts. The entrance is inscribed with several famous quotes from the Hindi, Sanskrit, Persian and English languages respectively.

Earlier, the glory and progress of this college commenced in 1844 under the stewardship of the famous British scholar of Sanskrit, J. Muir. He organized the curricula in a scientific manner. His essays on a wide variety of subjects are still preserved in the college. However, Muir resigned in January 1846, and Rind Wallis took over. He was an efficient principal although he knew little of Sanskrit. He was replaced by Dr. J.J. Ballayntyene in February 1846. He was a highly spirited administrator and great scholar of Sanskrit who made his mark in the history of the college, working till 1861 and doing his best to enhance the statues of Hindi.

During 1846-48, the innovative discipline of English – Sanskrit had been introduced. This entailed the study of English Literature to help analyze texts of great authors of Sanskrit. It was not only language that was studied, but there was comparative study of the thoughts of classical Indo-European authors considered to have contributed philosophically and otherwise to mankind.

German Indologist Dr. G. Thibaut who had a deep interest in Sanskrit, Philosophy and astrology became its Principal in 1880. He authored a number of titles in various areas of philosophy and got recognition wherever Indology and Sanskrit were taught.

Dr. Ganganath Jha, a great scholar of philosophy, was the First Indian to be appointed Principal of the college in 1918. He was there for five years till 1923. He is credited with publishing classical Sanskrit texts and their English translations.

In 1937, Dr. Mangaldev Shastri took over. Incidentally, it was at this time that Dr. Sampurananand was made the Uttar Pradesh Government's Minister of Education. He was a reputed scholar who had high respect of Sanskrit and allied subjects. He, under the Chairmanship of Dr. Bhagwandas, another noted scholar, formed a committee to establish linkages of Sanskrit education with other areas of knowledge. The committee drafted a brilliant report, which, though implemented rather belatedly in 1950-51, helped transform the curricula at the college into a highly progressive one. Following its implementation, Sanskrit was accepted as a modern and useful subject throughout the country.

On March 23, 1958, Dr. Sampurananand, now the Chief Minister of Uttar Pradesh in independent India, visited Varanasi and elevated the college to a university – the Varanasi Sanskrit University. Dr. Adhitya nath Jha, the then Chief Secretary of Uttar Pradesh and son of Dr. Ganganath Jha, the first Indian Principal of the Sanskrit college, was appointed the first Vice Chancellor.

On December 1, 1974, after the death of Dr. Sampurananand, the Institution was renamed Sampurananand Sanskrit University in his honour.

The University has an impressive museum with sculptures that date back to 900/1200 A.D. It also has a pillar of Ashoka's period made of Chunar sandstone, brought to the Sanskrit College campus in 1853. For astronomical studies, the university has an impressive Vedhshala (observatory) which has the look of the Jantar Mantar in Delhi. It invites astronomers from across the country and abroad for research.

Sampurananand University has come a long way by offering a platform to scholars of Sanskrit and Indology, inspiring them to help develop these areas of knowledge and learning.

PRANAV KUMAR VANDYOPADHYAYA

SANT RAM (b.1929)

Instrumentalist : Hindustani, tabla of Delhi Gharana ; studied with Banarai Dass ; concert tours, Afghanistan (1950), Nepal (1960).

SAPTARSHI, P.D.

(b.1912) – Instrumentalist : Sangeet Visharad ; Hindustani, violin; studied with Krishna Rao Shankar Pandit.

SARATHI, CHATTERJEE : THE VOICE THAT RESOUNDS

For Sarathi Chatterjee it has been music all the way. Born into a family that worships music, he grew up with the sound of music reverberating in the four walls of his home. Sarathi was first tutored by his father, Prof. A.K. Chatterjee, a representative of the "Kirana Gharana" (a family tradition of music) and a disciple of Pandit Narain Rao Joshi, Prof. Chatterjee especially specialised in the singing of Khayal, Thumri and Bhajans. Sarathis's mother, Shefali Chaterjee has mastered Rabindra Sangeet and Bengal folk music.

Sarathi received further 'talim' from the celebrated vocalists Pandit Rajan and Sajan Mishra of Benaras Gharana. Sarathi; blended elements of the Benaras Gharana into the Kiran' 'Gayaki'. This synthesis of the two great traditions has produced a unique musical expression and experience. His traditional treatment of ragas has won acclaim "for not filuting the purity by even a fraction".

Sarathi is also an accomplished performer of the more romantic styles of singing such as 'thumri' and devotional music like 'bhajans' :
(Condensed)

SHALINI MITRA

SARI : THE WOVEN ELEGANCE

The very mention of sari conjures up images of elegance so exclusive to the Indian women. This rectangular piece of unstitched cloth draped in an artistic manner by women in Indian peninsula is almost synonym with the Indian woman.

The most remarkable feature of a sari is its innate adaptability, which gives its wearer flowing grace and touch of elegance. Its unparalleled fusion of colour and art reflects Indians rich cultural heritage.

Sari seems to have originated from infinity and would perhaps end only in infinity. Every fold of sari unfolds a phase of rich Indian heritage. The epic Ramayana mentions that Sita wore sari, while the other epic

Mahabharata also says that Draupdi too, like other women of the times, wore sari. Historical date reveals that in the initial stages of the Christian era, an unstitched garment was worn in India with the pleats tucked in at the naval; it was accompanied by closefit choli or bodice and a scarf-like over garment. This has marked resemblance to the present-day sari. The weaving techniques of some varieties of sari, like Baluchari are indeed centuries old.

Initially sari was a simple piece of fabric of solitary colour but with the passage of time, border and palluv have become indispensable to it. This unstitched stretch of fabric can be characterised into various parts, specially to understand its draping on the body. The inner end-piece or more commonly, it is tucked in an underskirt called petticoat. The body or the base of the sari occupies the major chunk of the total sari length. Palluv is the outer-end-piece of the sari; drape of the sari ends with it.

Palluv may be arranged on the shoulder in layers or without them. The length of this flowing end of the sari can be adjusted according to the need. At times, the palluv is taken from the shoulder to cover the head, which is edges of the sari and delineates the contours of the flow of the sari, both in falls and around the girth. Commonly, palluv and the borders are the most decorated parts of a sari.

Draping of a sari is done differently in different regions of India. Though with the breaking down of geographical barriers and widening of the social sphere the most popular styles of sari are "Ulta Palluv" (traditional style). These drippings are with pleats, which are tucked in at the navel. Palluv is then taken on the left shoulder in "Ulta Palluv" and on the right shoulder in "Seedha Palluv". Different styles are still restored to on auspicious occasions and festivals and they are unique in themselves. In one front of the body from the right shoulder. The left end corner of the Palluv is tucked in at the waist giving it a touch of neatness. The pleats are tucked in the front of the petticoat.

The Bengali way of wearing a sari is a cross-wise adjustment where corners are doubled and tucked in from both sides at the back. The palluv may be held on the right arm or simply rested on the shoulder with the weight of the keys, which are tied to the end of the palluv.

Marathi style of sari is worn without a petticoat. Sari is secured around the waist by trying a knot. Palluv is taken on the shoulder and rest of the fabric is adjusted in pleats and tucked. One of the pleats is taken at the back, bifurcating the Sari in the trouser style and is tucked at the back. This drapeit requires a 9-yard sari as compared to 5.5 – 6.0 yardsrequired for the traditional draping.

A drape common in south India, particularly in Tamil Nadu is "Madisar" style. This is worn by Iyer Brahmins. In this style, sari is secured with a knot and the pleats come at the back. According to tradition, this draping cannot be worn by unmarried girls. Sari here can be 9 – yard long or even longer as required.

Complementing the various kinds of drapes are the innumerable varieties of saris. Some of them are Kanjivaram, Patihani or Banarsi. Most of the varieties take their name from the places there they are made. Saris made of natural fiber like silk and cotton are preferred for auspicious occasions. Ideal pure silk sari weighs between 30 gm to 60 gm while a cotton sari is judged by its count, 120 by 120 is considered good. The increase in the count

makes weaving tedious and time consuming, as the thread has to be made finer. In Kanjivaram and Paithani, 24-carat gold thread is used in weft to create designs while sari is still on loom. The motifs made on the sari are generally traditional and geometrical. The bandhani sari from Rajasthan is dyed with pure vegetable colours for its bright, ethnic and beautiful look.

Sari has enjoyed the trust of Indian women from time immemorial. It's perhaps this undying faith which has kept the looms working and saved the art of sari weaving from extinction. Sari gives its wearer a special advantage to conceal as much as reveal within the set norms of decency. Though contemporary Indian women have taken to western wear, but when she wants to be charmingly feminine, she trusts none but sari.

MEENU GUPTA

SARISKA – A SANCTUARY OF RARE BEAUTY

Passing through Sohna, Nuh and Ferozpur Jhirka in Haryana, and Nagaon and Ramgarh in Rajasthan, one reaches Alwar, 180 Kms. away from Delhi.

Sariska is 36 Kms. from Alwar. Alwar has Siliserh and some other landmarks. Siliserh is a big and beautiful lake 16 Kms. away, set in the midst of Aravali hills where an old palace by the lakeside has been converted into a hotel.

On way to Sariska as one drives from the entry point to the Kalighati checkpoint 10 kms. away on the metalled road, one comes across jungles of exquisite charm. The hills and cliffs of lime and quartzite are extremely beautiful. In March-April, the trees have shed their leaves. The naked trees exposing their slender anatomy of branches look rhythmic. Dhak trees laden with red flowers seem to set the woods afire. Wild animals such as boar, herds of chitals, sambhars, chowsinghas and neelgais foam under trees and occasionally cross the road. Groups of monkeys and langoors occupy the middle of the road. Their famales can be seen suckling and caring their young ones. Peacocks in their best flutter about everywhere. In the sanctuary speed of vehicles in restricted and even speaking aloud is prohibited so as to avoid disturbance to animals.

After Kalighati, the valley narrows down further, and near the ancient temple of Pandopole, which is about 10 Kms further, the view is breathtakingly beautiful. One crosses a number of dry streams, which must be gushing with water during the rains. Pandavas of the Mahabharat fame are said to have come to this forest during their exile.

At the sanctuary, an open jeep is available in the evening for tiger sighting. It is exciting to drive the serpentine track ascending and descending alternately through a jungle of rare beauty. Near water paints, which are numerous and well maintained by the forest authorities, one comes across peacocks, sambhar, deer, chitals, and chowsinghas. As one goes deeper, the jungle becomes denser where, if luck favours, one may come across a tiger. At sunset the woods become dark and quiet. One may or may not sight the big cat, but one is always delighted with the rare beauty of the woods and wild animals moving freely in their natural habitat.
(Condensed)

R. N. PASRICHA

SATYAJIT RAY : THE ARTIST

"One of the world's greatest filmmakers designed two international award-winning typefaces and bizarre posters, " wrote an art critic about Ray's diversity of interests, when covering an exhibition of his works a few years ago.

Satyajit Ray, despite his obsession with the downtrodden while making his films, could pursue his more ambitious but less recognized leanings for fine arts, notably drawing and painting.

His grandfather Upendra Kishore was an eminent author-composer as well as a printer-publisher, specializing in children's literature. His father was also a writer-poet and founded a children's magazine, Sandesh, in 1913. However, he passed away in 1923 and after various disruptions, Satyajit Ray was able to revive Sandesh in 1961.

His family sent him to Santiniketan around 1941, where he learnt oriental art and calligraphy. Ray himself admits that he owes a lot of his maturity in fine arts, including that required for his film-making, to his two year stint at Santiniketan. It was here that he learnt to look at Nature and respond to its silent rhythm. His doubts about Indian Schools of painting were also reconciled here. Nandlal Bose taught him how to feel sincerely and deeply about objects.

In 1943 Ray joined an advertising firm, D.J. Keymer, as a junior visualiser and became an art director with the same firm in 1950. While working with Keymer he had developed the art of interpreting words and concepts visually. He could use the text and type along the pictures to form a totally integrated design. The discipline of working within a limited space as he did in his advertising firm found its finest expression in the sketches of the frames for his films later. In fact, for his first film Pather Panchali (1956) Ray had designed the entire publicity material – slides, posters, booklets, hoardings, and the credit titles as well.

Ray may be accredited to have brought to Indian advertising this sophisticated approach – an originality that broke away from western perceptions and maintained an Indian environment. Yet, the appeal was universal. Even as a freelance designer (with signet press) in the late fifties, the variety of letter types that he could introduce, both in Bangla and English, showed his amazing grasp over the art of typography. His innovations like Ray Roman and several other fonts using the Bangla alphabets (notably those used on Sandesh and Anandmela covers) influenced a new generation of young designers, which, in turn helped elevate the general level of graphic art, especially in west Bengal and what is now known as Bangladesh.

In fact, Ray said about himself, "Although I trained for three years at Santiniketan under Nandal Bose, I never became a painter. Instead, I decided to become a commercial artist and joined an advertising agency. But, in time, I realized that an advertising agency was subservient to the demand of its clients; its artists seldom enjoyed complete freedom. "And indeed, his approach to freedom was one of modernizing our inherent culture, transforming its raw material to meet the demands of a contemporary dialogue.

Passion for refinement and sensibility was eternal for him. More than his genius, in the long run, his extreme versatility stood him out. That a man could be a film-maker, designer, painter, writer of note, music composer, song-writer, book-illustrator and an acknowledged authority on the art of printing is indeed bewildering.

A. CHOUDHARY

SAVITA DEVI

Savita Devi was born on April 7, 1942 in a well known musical family of the Benaras 'Gharana'. Her mother, the legendary Siddheshwari Devi imparted all her musical learning to Savita; 'Thumri', 'Dadras', 'Chaiti', 'Kajri', 'Tappa', 'Hori' of the Purbhanga style made famous by Siddheshwari Devi.

Although the legacy of her mother's singing is evident in her style, Savita Devi's speciality, is that whether she is singing a 'thumri or khayal', she maintains the separateness of the two forms. Her style is her own, an improvisation of her mother's yet distint and a reflection of her own musical creativity. Her sonorous voice glides emotionally over 'thumris' and 'dadras' rendering them with a special dimension, Savita regards her music as an offering to the gods.

Today Savita heads the department of instrumental music at the Daulat Ram College, New Delhi. Her 'riaz' lasts three to four hours a day and she had a hectic schedule, which often exhausts her, but she is candid about the fact that there is little choice. Being a single parent has been hard (she separated from her husband Kishen Maharaj some years ago), and has necessitated earning a living. Although she would have loved to spend the best part of the day, mornings doing 'riaz' this has not been possible.

Savita Devi has set up the Siddheshwari Devi Academy of Indian Music in the memory of the late mother. A great concern of hers is to carry forward the legacy of music and to achieve this, she is doing extensive research in the 'thumri' style of singing, the idea of this being to develop new and more pleasing ways of presenting old compositions.

RITU BHATIA

SCULPTURE

Earliest examples of Indian sculpture go back to Neolithic times when different sorts of tools (axes, chisels, hammers, etc.) were made of volcanic traprock, smaller ones (found in the Vindhya region) being made of beautifully coloured or translucent stones (agate, chalcedony, jasper, carnelian, etc.); primitive articles of polished stone have been found in numerous megalithic sites (in south India) associated with pre-historic burial chambers, some excavated in rock below ground level. From Indus Valley Civilization (5,000 – 2,000 B.C.) sites come some distinctive specimens: beads (of gold, lapis lazuli, turquoise, jadeite, carnelian, etc.), beautifully published and perfectly bored, small seals of limestone and steatite with finely carved forms of realistic (Indian) animals (some mythological), threes and some human figures, with some distinctive pictographic script (undeciphered); male torso in red structure, stone figurines, a small stone dancing figurine, an exquisite bronze dancing girl and a bust (of a priest) with a shawl with a trefoil pattern. Next outstanding examples of sculpture appeared in the Mauryan period under Ashoka (276-232 B.C.) such as the simple yet beautiful 'piety pillars' (upto 17 m. in height and about 50 tonnes in weight) with a highly polished, glasslike luster, the remains of one such being the lion capital of Sarnath the national emblem of Independent India, the beautiful bull of Rampurva and a huge elephant carved out of a rock at Dhauli bearing an inscription of an edict of Ashoka; from about 200 to 100 B.C., sculpture of deities of forests and trees (Yakshas and Yakshis) began to be made in sandstone with the same beautiful highly – polished surface of which some fine examples are the Parkhan statue (Mathura museum), 2 Yakshis some other figures and the (headless) torso of a tirthankara. From the 2nd to 1st century B.C. (early classical period), great achievement in sculpture was attained in the carvings of Buddhist stupas and chaityas – those on the columns, gateways and railings of Barhut which represent Jataka stories and scenes from the Buddha's life, of Sanchi with its scenes from the Jatakas, the Buddh's life and realistic and charming scenes of everyday life; of Bodh Gaya, particularly on its stone railing; and of Amarvati, on its medallion panels (the finest in India, possibly in the world) which are full of symbolic motifs; the rock-cut Buddhist cave caityas (chapels) at Bhoja (75 B.C.) Bedsa (A.D. 100- 200_ and Karle (120) also have many sculpture of bulls, horses, elephants, female and male figures, etc., the caves themselves being the earliest examples of rock-cut caves, there are more than 1,200 rock-cut temples and monastic halls in India (mostly in the western Ghats) – Ajanta has 29, Nasik 23 and Kanheri 109, During Kushan period (2nd to 1st century B.C.), due to influence of Hallenistic sculpture, Gandhara school of sculpture came into being with its realistic scenes of daily life, some pieces having Greek deities as subjects; most famous examples of this type are statues of Buddhas with delicate and beautiful drapery and expression of peace on face; when Mathura became eastern capital of Kushans, it already had a strong art tradition; from 300-150 it produced large, primitive stone images and votive tablets on a commercial basis which were supplied from Central Asia to Patna and Sanchi; from early years of Kanishka's reign dedicated satues of Buddhas and Bodhisattvas, Jain tirthankaras, Hindu deities, etc., began to be produced in and Mathura sandstone and larger than life size 'stone portraits', such as the (headless) Kanishka statue (Mathura Musuem), deep-cut ornamental relief were also made showing western influence (the style becoming known as that of the Gandhara school). With the Imperial Guptas (320-490), the somewhat inferior work of the Mathura school was perfected resulting in masterpieces such as Sarnath Buddhas, the wonderful Sanchi torso of a Bodhisattva (Victoria and Albert Museum) and the colossal copper Buddha of Sultanganj (Birmingham Museum) executed about 450.

The Dasavatara temple (Deogarh, district Jhansi), a superb little stone structure (of the Nagar style of the Gupta period), though little is left of it, still has the wonderful carvings on the doors and niches intact and is a magnificent specimen of Gupta art, as are some wonderful carvings in (ruined) temples (Hindu and Jain) at Chirgaon.

To Chalukya times (500-800) belong the cave temples of Badami and the temples at Pattadakal and Aihole, the sculptures being freely and forcefully executed. Under the Rashtrakutas (750-950) were produced some of the most magnificent rock sculpture of India as at Elephanta.

From some centuries beginning with the 8th, Hindu fervour for cutting pillared halls and images, etc., in the living rock, reached its climax in Ajanta, Ellora (where there are 12 Buddist caves also); the huge images of the Kailash temple are carved in high relief with superb dynamism vitality and originality which must have taken a century to complete; the Jains carved colossal free- standing statues and bas-reliefs of their tirthankaras and saints, one side of the rock-bound road winding up to the Gwalior fort has huge Jain statues carved in the rock face, the highest being 19 m. high; at Sravana Belgola (Karnataka) is the free standing 19 m. high stone image of Gomatesvara, a Jain saint, carved in 983.

Some of the best examples of stone sculpture are in the Orissan temples of Puri (750), Bhunbaneswara (8th to 10th centuries) and Konark (13th century) – the sculptures of (female) figures, animals and the friezes of musicians, elephants, etc., the horses and wheel of the god's chariot are of the finest and technically superb. Under the Pala and Sena kings of Bengal (730-1125), Buddhist images of high merit were made in black, polished stone but their outstanding work was done in metal casting. In the time of the Chandella rulers (800-1204) were erected the Khajuraho groups of temples with remarkable carvings on the friezes and female figures in erotic poses. Beginning a bit later but of this period also belong the exquisite marble temples of the Jains at Dilwara (Mount Abut) and Girnar with richly ornamented motifs on ceilings, walls and pillars. The south Indian Chola temples of about the same period, particularly at Tanjavur, incorporate excellent sculptured carvings, the bronze sculpture of the Chola rulers is famous, particularly the figures of Shiva in the Tandava dance pose and some statues of goddesses and lam- bearers. During 1100 and 1345 came the richly carved and meticulously fine workmanship of the sculpture of the Hoysala style of temples, the most famous being at Belur and Halebid (Karnataka) with their wonderful female figures and animal frieze-said to be unmatched elsewhere. In the 15th century some of the most remarkable sculptured workmanship was executed in the temples of Vijayanagar kingdom (1350-1565), particularly at Hampi though it became over embellished and began to show signs of decadence. From the mediaeval period onwards this art declined as royal patronge and encouragement of individual enterprise ended, the Muslim rulers conforming to the Islamic injunction of not making a replica of any living creature. In modern times some excellent individual sculptures have arisen but no distinctive school or style has been evolved.

P. N. CHOPRA
K. M. MUNSHI

SCULPTURE – INDIAN CLASSICAL – ESSENCE OF

Indian sculpture, vibrant and pulsating, provides an eloquent commentary on the behavioural patterns of society during various periods of Indian history. Apart from free-standing stone sculptures entire rock surfaces provided large canvases for depicting life in all its colours. In few countries is the art so intimately intermingled with the life and political adventures of the people. Temples of the classical period could be aptly described as 'architectonic sculptures having a beautiful inter-relationship between architecture and sculpture. Themes ranging from religion to mythology to literature has been variously and vigorously depicted. This unique relationship between the people and their art and literature together formed a classic fusion which evolved its own distinctive melody and rhythm that is at one awe-inspiring and exciting.

Indian civilization has always been dominated. by metaphysical preoccupations and continuously emphasizes on the spiritual. Indian philosophy is a vehicle of attaining alavation (Moksha) from ignorance (avidya). Indian sculpture, however realistic it may be, is highly symbolic. The aim of symbolism is to resolve the conflict between the material and spiritual worlds. The complete synthesis of Indian thought, feeling and imagination has proved exceedingly favourable for art in its plastic linear forms, assimilating in it the truths and values of the metaphysical order. Religious philosophy, translated into symbolism, was adopted most conspicuously in both religious as well as secular art and architecture.

Indian philosophy expounds two metaphysical nations. One, the belief in the transcendent reality or being (atman/brahman) into which are fused the values of goodness (Shivam) beauty (Sundaram infinitude (anantam), silence (santam) and beatitude (anandam), and two, the idea of absolute value and statues of man as 'being' (tat) and 'becoming' (sat). Art in India has evolved techniques that make for the synthesis of the mundane and sublime as seen on the temple walls. Here, more than anywhere else, the stones are evocative even if their meaning is mysterious and esoteric.

Hindu and Buddhist art share a common symbolism Buddhists are like Hindu art depicts joy, beauty and serenity. The Buddhists have used Hindu deities like Surya and Indra in their art. The use of mudra (postures) in forming a symbolic language is also common to both. Water is one of the most important symbols for both, denoting the life-giving energy that also swallows all creation in the end. Elephant is another motif, which could be traced through Hindu as well as Buddhist art. The white elephant in particular, which symbolizes rain, fortune, longevity and abundance, is important to both. Again, the naga, serpent, is a motif common to both Hindu and Buddhist art and is frequently depicted in an attitude of pious devotion on the portals of shrines. The lotus is another common symbol and the Lotus Goddess, Lakshmi, adorns early Buddhist monuments. She stands on a lotus in her hand flanked by elephants dousing her with water. Zimmer, the noted scholar of Indian art, says "It is extremely important to observe that the Buddhist and Hindu representation of such popular divinities do not differ from each other, either essentially or in detail, for Buddhist

or Hindu art as also Buddhist of Hindu doctrines were basically one. India aesthetics – Hindu, Buddhist or Jain were based on the doctrines and conventions that were transcendental and intellectual in character, idealistic in aim and purpose".

The central idea clearly discernible in Indian classical art is that beauty in iherent in spirit, not in matter. The Sukraniti, one of the old Indian treatises, clearly lays down that while making images of gods, the artist should depend only upon spiritual vision, and not upon the appearance of the objects as perceived by the senses. The vishnudharmottara, a fifth century treatise, clearly lays down that "the painter should study the picture and mood of nature and depict the seasons he sees around him by the flowers and fruits on trees and the joy or happiness of men animals and birds". Thus, though the Indian art forms are philosophical, they are realistic in their minute observation.

The Gupta age ushered in a glorious chapter of cultural fulfillment. Just as it crystallized the Kavya (Poetry) in literature and formulated patterns of Puja (worship) and festivals, so did it codify and systematize the canons of Indian art.

These canons were clearly based on idealism as also realism or naturalism, which meant an artistic reproduction, which, was perfect objective and accurate. Though the classical form crystallized during the Gupta period, it continued to evolve in its expression, reaching its artistic zenith in art of Chandela and orissan Schools.

In the art philosophy of India, the underlying religious ideals are contained in the doctrine of the 'three paths' leading to salvation – the way of work (Karma–Marga), the way of faith (Bhakti-Marga) and the way of knowledge (Gyana-Marga). The path of faith along with that of work was ideal for Indian artists who followed both with religious zeal. The combination of these two ways of attaining salvation in art has not parallel in the history of world art.

This art activity was not the preserve of the royal or the noble classes alone. Inscriptions from different places like Bharhut, Sanchi, Mathura and other places offer evidence regarding donors, their ranks, social status and the regions they came from, as also their part in making either the whole monument or a specific part.

Both Bharhut and Sanchi represent a phase or Indian religious evolution in which the widespread folk-cult of the Yaksas and Yaksis, the turelary gods and godlings of forest and village life, of trees and serpents and fertility were included in the ambit of art and played a supportive role to the main religious theme.

Subsequent period saw the emphasis slowly shifting to 'literary' theme such as the Jataka Tales. These tales were immensely popular as is evident from the sculptures of Sanchi, Bharhut and elsewhere. In the centuries that followed, literature dealing with both spiritual and the secular, provided these for some magnificent sculptural embellishments. The secular aspect of life was dominated by Srinagara, the erotic sentiment, glorified equally by classical writers and sculpture.

There is a beautiful relationship between Indian sculpture and literature. Srinagara was predominant theme in India literature and the mithuna motif depicting amorous couples represents Srinagara in sculptural form. The prtrayal of Mithuna gradually acquired as artistic and sensuous character. These sensuous themes skin to the nayakanahika bhava, i.e. the relationship between a lover and his beloved. Of Sanskrit and Prakrit poetry fulfilled the demands of the discerning. The Vishnudharmottara makes a very significant observation. It says, "it is very difficult to understand the rules of painting without the knowledge of dancing, and the art of dancing is difficult to understand without the knowledge of music. Without music dancing can not exist at all. This shows the inter-relatedness of all forms of arts. The inter-relationship between sculpture and performing arts is amply illustrated in the Chola sculpture. Postures of dance are evident in the contours of the limbs. The gopuras (towers) of Chidambaram, temple are rich and valuable not only form the aesthetic point of view but also as an effective commentary on dance modes. The Sun Temple of Konark is another notable example where dance, music and the musical instruments are beautifully translated in the sculptural form.

Natural and human sentiments also had a role to play in the creation of art. The seasonal changes of the Indian landscape, poetically rendered by Kalidasa in his Ritusamhara are accompanied by melodies of the procession of seasons: spring, summer, rains, autumn and winter.

Indian sculpture of classical period embodies the story of its people, their myths, beliefs, aspirations and the type of environment they sought to create for themselves. But there is one strong and common factor that dominates the Indian sculptures everywhere: Srinagara, the sentiment of love.

(Condensed)

PRABHAKAR BEGDE

"SCROLLS – NARRATIVE" OF ANDHRA PRADESH

Long before the Indian villagers gathered around the community television sets for information, or went to the cinema halls, they had both entertainment and education provided to them by the wandering minstrels who with the aid of narrative scrolls told stories from Indian epics, the Ramayana and the Mahabharata. These scrolls were brightly painted in folk style and in minute detail elucidated the lives and tribulations of the epic heroes, all of which was sung or explained to the villagers who had gathered around the village temple or under banyan tree.

In the Telangana region of Andhra Pradesh, the tradition of narrative scroll painting still exists which continues to be used by the wandering performers to tell stories to a community whose interest is clearly diminishing because of the onslaught of television and cinema, but who nevertheless continue to patronize the performances.

All over Telangana, once, there were several families doing that but now only one family is painting these scrolls, and this is Dhaniyalakata Nakasi Chandriah's family who practice the art in Cherial in Warangal district, thus giving the scroll painting the name "Cherial Painting".

Chandriah, on his father's urging, not only gave up his tailoring business and took up paining but done much to popularise the art by participating in Festival of India in Germany and erstwhile USSR, where he demonstrated his traditional folk art. He was even given the National Award for the best craftsman by the Government of India.

There are traditions of narrative scroll painting in Bengal, Bihar, Orissa, Rajasthan and Gujarat, but those from Telangana are unique in that they illustrate the origin of a particular community and eulogise the stories of its heroes. The scrolls occasionally depict tales from Indian mythology but stories of heroes of the community are cleverly interwoven into these stories.

Hyderabad's well known art collector Jagdish Mittal, who was one of the first persons to discover these paintings and assess their value in terms of their historical importance, feels "the Telangana scrolls are refined. To my mind they are the most sophisticated folk paings in India. He says the Telangana scrolls surprinsingly do not appear to have been influenced by the Muslim court painting prevalent in this region between the 17th and 19th century, and stylistically bear resemblance to the Kalamkari temple hangings and the wall paintings of Lepakshi.

The Telangana scrolls vary in length, from eight ft to 30 ft most of the scrolls are vertical in format with the story told in panels that are depicted horizontally. Each panel depicts one of or two scenes of the story. A few scrolls are done in the horizontal format, and these are divided into horizontal parts with the story depicted on both sides.

Each performance begins with an invocation to Lord Ganesha the destroyer of all obstacles, who is invariably depicted in all scrolls in the first panel itself.

The scrolls is usually fixed on the wall or in its absence on two bamboo poles, and the narrator tells his story by unrolling the scroll from the top so that the visuals match the story he is narrating. Usually two or three members of the same family assist the main performer who sings or narrates the story. The narration is accompanied by the sound of drums and cymbals.

The scrolls are held sacred. Preserved and passed on from one generation to another. When there is no performance, the scroll is rolled up in two layers of cloth, and kept away in attics. When a new scroll is acquired ceremonies akin to the birth of a child are performed, and when the scroll has to be discarded (because it is damaged or frayed) it is immersed in the river.

SHADOW PLAYS

Shadow plays of two kinds; one of projecting on a white screen silhouette shadows of dolls acting and dancing; this art mostly in hands of troupes, who travelled from village to village; gave shows in street corners; rewarded with aims the village spectator gave. A number of dolls, an earthen lamp, a white upper cloth, a drum paraphernalia of wandering artists; this kind of shadow play now extinct.

The other, still current – Andhra shadow play; Puranic characters ornamentally painted on flat leather strips, thrown against white screen from behind well lit stage; manipulated to move, act, dance by means of long, thin, bamboo sticks. Background music crude, rhythmic sense is strong. Story interspersed with long interludes of foisterous fun, racy anecdotes, sending audience roaring with fun and laughter.

The Encyclopaedia of Indian Culture

SHANNO KHURANA

SHANNO KHURANA'S speciality is the 'Khayal'. She starts with a slow 'Khayal', 'Vilambit', and likes to end with a 'Thumri' or a 'bhajan'.

She has performed in All India Radio for nearly 40 years. She is one of the few people in her field with a sound technical background and years and years of learning. "It hasn't been easy, there is a lot of pain in that kind of rigour, but it was worth every minute of it...

She began her career after she was noticed in the 1940s at the 'Piloo Ke Thumri' singing competition, held at Lahore. The chief music producer of Lahore station was in the audience. When the show was over, he asked her if she would like to sing on the radio. She agreed, even though she lived 20 miles away from the city, at the airforce base where her husband was dentist. Fortunately he supported her decision.

In 1946, a few months before the partition, her husband decided to resign from the Airforce and started practice in Delhi. Soon after their move Shanoo began performing on the AIR.

It was Thakur Jaidev Singh, a well known musicologist and philosopher, who became the chief producer, AIR, who initiated Shanoo into taking here music more seriously. He raised a question about the notes in the Multani raga, which she used to sing. She didn't know the answer. This made her realise that there was so much about music she did not know. Thakur, who recognized here potential, told her, "To a certain extent you have made a name for yourself but you must do musicology – learning music randomly, from one guru or another isn't good enough".

Shanno began studying music. In the course of her M.A. and Ph.D. she travelled far and wide to learn rare ragas from masters. She learned to listen keenly and analyse music. Thakur suggested she became a disciple of Ustad Mushtaq Husain Khan, of the Rampur 'Gharana' who was known as a master of all forms of music: 'Dharupad', 'Khayal', 'Tarana', 'Tappa', 'Thumri', and 'Saaz'.

Six months later, while she was singing here guru started weeping. He told her she had a beautiful voice and that he was ready to take her as his 'Shishya'. And so began shanno's arduous path towards becoming one of India's finest classical singers.

"Being women we have had to struggle double hard... all the Ustads would say, "What do you want to learn music for? You a middle class woman from no real Gharana" why don't you go home and relax? "All these reactions strengthened Shanno's desire to create a platform for women musicians. "If women are taking up architecture and engineering as professions, why not music? "In 1982 she did a survey of women musicians in the country and compiled a list of artistes who had received their training from great masters, and had studied musicology. She set up an organization called 'Geetika' and began organising an annual music festival for women. So far she has managed to locate women who perform forms like the 'Dhrupad' and 'Dammar', which were traditionally a man's domain.

(Condensed)

RITU BHATIA

SHANTI HIRANAND

Shanti Hiranand is a prime artists keeping alive her late guru, Begum Akhtar's traditional style of 'Ghazals', 'Thumri' and 'Dadra'.

Her devotion to Begum Akhtar is apparent when she talks about her. Although Shanti Hiranand was already performing on Radio Lahore at the age of 11, it wasn't until she met the 'Queen of Ghazals', Begum Akhtar in Lucknow in 1952, that her decision to make music her career, came about.

Begam Akhtar, a legendary name in light classical music had a powerful influence on Shanti's life: "She had a magnetic personality, and I was completely fascinated by her. I wanted to be like her. I was part of her life and family, and literally lived in that house for 10 years. I wanted to please her and complied with every wish of hers. I was her shadow".

Born in the cultural city of Lucknow, Shanti acquired mastery over Urdu language and poetry, necessary in the rendition of 'Ghazals'. She practiced regularly with her Guru for 10 years. In 1962 at the age of 28, Shanti married a man who supported her decision to be a musician. This and the subsequent birth of their son, all added richness to her life and music; "I have enjoyed everything in my life – being a mother, cooking for my husband, running a house, standing in the rain, travelling. Each experience has been relevant, each has it's own place. Music and 'riaz' also continued. I never believed in compartmentalizing my life".

Shanti has been singing on All India Radio for the past 46 years and has performed in prestigious all India conferences such as the ITC Sangeet Sammelan, Delhi; Center for Performing Arts, Bombay; Sahitya Kala Parishad, Delhi, etc. Some of the awards she has received are the Sahitya Kala Parishad award and the Kalyani Kala Kendra award.

Shanti's voice rings with a spirituality and intensity reminiscent of her teacher's. A few months before her death, the Begum told her audience at Vadadra; "If you want to hear my music after my death, hear it through Shanti's singing". Clearly this prophecy is being fulfilled. Shanti's haunting melodies and rich voice hold her audience spell bound. Seldom, it is said, has an artiste imbibed so much of her mentor.

SHARAN RANI

(Referred to as the 'cultural ambassador of India' by the late Jawaharlal Nehru, she was the first classical musician to take Indian classical music to other countries).

The sarod is synonymous with her name. At the age of 62, Sharan Rani has been on stage for 50 years, in India and abroad, is the recipient of numerous honours, the prestigious Sangeet Natak Academy award and 'Padamshri'.

She considers her music a 'Sadhna' a form of meditation. "My pulse rate drops dramatically when I am playing". Rigorously trained under the great maestros Ustad Allauddin Khan and Ustad Ali Akbar Khan, Sharan Rani has achieved the rare distinction of being the only woman sarod player in the country. The difficulty of its sitting posture and the way it needs to be held while being played, have earned the sarod a reputation of being a difficult instrument, 'essentially a man's.' 'This is not apparent when you watch 'Sarod Rani' as she is popularly referred to, play. Her fingers seem to flow, reflecting her amazing technical command over the instrument.

Her life would not be regarded as normal by an outsider. She rarely answers the phone, has a couple of friends and does not socialise at all. Her day begins and ends with her sarod. In her Bengali cotton sari, her 'bindi' and thick glasses Sharan Rani looks like any housewife you might se haggling over vegetables., or frequenting a sari shop. When she begins talking you realise there are two things she has never done. In fact she has never even attempted to fit into the roles most women are conditioned into accepting. "I was interested only in music, everything else in my life seemed incidental as long as I could play...."

Sharan Rani can be described as a true feminist; as woman who has flouted all conventions. She was wilful even as a teenager determined to have a musical career at a time when women were supposed to enjoy music at home and not perform in public. She was a source of great worry to her parents. She was aware, right from then, that hers' would not be an easy job." But I knew I had to find a way".

She married at the age of 30, a love marriage to businessman Sultan Singh Backliwal, also a scholar and art expert, who understood and accepted her devotion to the sarod. "He knew I was not interested in anything domestic and told my mother-in-law not to expect me to cook anything", she laughs, "Every time I had to cook, I'd end up burning something".

Her contribution to the world of music has been immense. "Ma" to a number of students, she follows the "Guru-Shishya parampara tradition and is involved in passing the musical traditions that are hers' to her disciples. Besides this, she has composed many unique 'bandis' and ragas, her latest raga being the 'Raga Radhika Priya', 'Alam Manjari ' and 'Har Gauri'.

Sharan Rani has donated her rare collection of over 300 musical instruments to the National Museum, New Delhi, where they are exhibited in the 'Sharan Rani Backliwal Gallery of Musical Instruments'. Besides many pieces of exceptional beauty and national importance, the Sharan Rani collection embraces a very large number of old Indian musical instruments, almost all types of instruments used in classical Indian music. There are also many folk and tribal instruments in the collection, collected from 'Gallis', 'Mohallas', 'Darbars' and homes of musicians, 'fakirs' and others, each with a unique life history. The Sharan Rani collection of similar instruments from the various states of India as well as of very periods provides an opportunity for a comparative study of the instruments.

RITU BHATIA

THE SHAWL – KASHMIR

More than its natural beauty, the art-crafts of Kashmir make an irresistible appeal to art lovers. Kashmir art-wares are as far-famed as its scenic spots. From the very ancient times Kashmir had a romantic attraction to the outside world. Chinese philosophers and Greek scholars visited the land in the early years of the Christian era; Ashoka and Kaniska ruled over this territory for a time; Saivism and Buddhism thrived side by side; people led a quiet and contented life. Though the living conditions have changed, the arts and crafts are still practised.

The ancient history of Kashmir is lost in the mists of antiquity. The only historical record of her past is Kalhana's Rajatarangini. The Ashoka and Kanishka ruled over the land is evident from monuments and inscriptions; that the Greeks influenced her arts is obvious form the architectural remains of the temple of Martand and Pandrathen;

Chinese and Persian arts have played considerable part in influencing the arts of Kashmir. It was to that great and good king, Zain-ul-Abidin, who ruled this valley for half-a-century, in the fifteenth century that we owe the introduction of Turkish and Persian master-craftsmen into Kashmir for the promotion and development of here carpets and shawls. So is the tradition, at any rate, among the shawl and carpet makers there. The most famous of Kashmir's artcrafts is the well-known and world-famous shawls, woven out of the soft wool of the Himalayan and Tibetan lambs and goats, dyed with soft delicate shades of colour and embroidered with leaf, flower bird and animals designs, Renowned from ancient times for their unparalleled softness, fitness and warmth, Kashmir shawls bear witness not only to their highly developed aesthetic sense.

The Kashmir shawls are of two kinds: hand-woven. The former is called kani and the latter amli. The loom-woven shawls are manufactured by a patch-work process, strips of shawls are woven first and then sewn together to obtain the desired patterns. The sewing is so fine that the stitches are invisible. Very often the border stitches are done in silk with an additional woollen waft to give the necessary strength and weight. In the case of amli shawls, a plain pashmina is covered over by an elaborate pattern needle works, profusely embroidered in floral and other motifs, and they are very artistic and also costly. The so-called Ring-shawls, which are the pride of Kashmiri weavers, are made of Shahtosh wool and are woven entirely by hand. Another costly and artistic type of shawl is the jamawar, noted for its varied designs, and which are often made into chogas and achkans.

Kashmir shawls are generally made of two kinds of woolen materials, one imported from Europe and other country-made. The important materials used to come mostly from France in pieces of thirty yards and of various widths, white in colour and the texture varies from rough surface to finer ones. They are first washed before they are sent to the dyer. The country-made materials are sometimes mixed with silk to get a better surface effect. When the yarn is silk and wool but country-made, it is called rampuri; when it is mixed with cotton, it is called garbhi. The latter is not generally used for embroidery.

The real country-made is called asli, and is made of finest fleece from the wild goats of the higher Himalayan regions, especially from Tibet and Yarkand. The women-folk spin the yarns in their cottages, which later are worked on pit-looms.

Asli is of two colours, one the natural colour (dark brown or rat colour) and the other is dyed in various shades or bleached in sulphur for white. When this yarn is combined with some foreign yarn it is called reffletani. In the olden days only vegetable colours were used mixed with the soft waters of the Dal Lake; now imported chemical colours are very much in vogue and are mixed in boiling water to make them fast. The third stage is embroidery. Both silks are and wool are used for the purpose, nowadays artificial silk is also used and this is generally done on machinery in bright colours of common use. And they are the cheapest. They are called Machini Lohis. A better variety than this is what called Charhashia, which is made of wool. Sometimes with rough designs and sometimes with fine designs, of many colours, mixed with silt and cotton threads. Often imported border designs from Germany and Belgium are used, and at the corners little native embroidery is done. It is commonly believed that the entirely needle – worked shawl, known as amli, was not native to the valley and was a new technique introduced over hundred and fifty years ago. It is in these embroiderers, known as rafugars.

The most striking and attractive features about these shawls are elaborate designs in harmonious colours that one sees embroidered on them. First, the outlines of these designs are printed by wooden blocks in black colour, then embroidered with needle and thread. This is done by men only. Gold thread embroidery is sometimes the work of women. There are designs where more than one artist is at work, like in Mughal paintings, and this joint-work never spoils the pattern or the colour scheme. Designs are of varied nature, but mostly leaves flowers, creepers, birds and even the serpentine curves of the river Jhelum as it flows through the city of Srinagar. The Chinar leaf motif is one of the prettiest and commonest of them.

Some of them have such appropriate and attractive names: Kandukar is betel leaf design, made of big and rough stitches; one corner finely executed and the rest three crude and rough. Chhatkingri is slightly finer in stitches but of the same betel-leaf pattern. When all the corners are embroidered equally fine and with the same design, it is called eksar; when all the corners are not equally embroidered, it is called farukdhar. Tirkar is design in many colours, round flowers and rich in colours. In this also are eksar and farukdhar. Margolikar, generally done in black thread, is usually narrow with delicate running designs of many kinds. Kalamkar is of different designs of various shades of colours, the sun-flower being the common motif. Then embroidered on one side it is called ekrookha and when on both sides, dorookha. Cotton threads are generally used in such embroideries. The flower-pot design with sprouting bloosoms on white ground of fine and rough cloth is called gamlekar. There are other varieties of this type, which are known as chinikar gulabchini, mohurkar, zulfikar, Ashakmashuk, Leila Majnu, all of which are generally done in black. Black-brown or blue-black, with little red sprinklings here and there on white ground.

Zemindar, ambker, andaker are of bright colours with rich embroidery almost covering the whole of the background and worked with cotton threads. Jugnikar is usually of leaf-green colour, with fine needle work designs of variegated flowers done in wool and cotton threads.

Another motif of fine workmanship and close stitching, where leaves are shown in clusters of five is known as ekrookha. The dorookha shawls are also on many varieties with beautiful designs embroidered on both sides. Ekrookha is used for coating choga, etc., while dorookha, for chadder or shawl. Small bordered ones with fine needle work are called charhashia and big bordered ones in many colours are called paledar. Asli, as already referred to, is real Kashmir work, woven or embroidered, whose borders are at times separately woven and then attached to the cloth in such a fine way as not to be visible, sometimes the whole piece is completely embroidered. There are other kinds of dorookha shawls with embroideries of two different patterns on either side, and at times even the colours on both sides are not the same. Taulia shawls are plain on one side and embroidered, while the reverse side is like Turkish bath towels. Shikarkar is the name given to shawls with birds and animal motifs; even human motifs and calligraphy were used in Kashmir shawls. Zari shawls are made of imported cloth of heavy texture with bright deep red, deep blue, deep green and bottle-green colours. The gold thread is attached for embroidery with yellow thread, and the designs are generally in concentric circles and sometimes flowers are embroidered. The borders are wide, and after the embroidery is done they are beaten with a wooden club to give them polish.

In the production of a shawl more than a family is engaged in, each with his or her allotted task. The rafugar gives the finishing touch by processing them through a wooden contrivance known as charak before they are sent to the market.

There are other kinds of embroidery, which are distinctive and peculiar to Kashmir. There is the kasida, which is widely done on shawls, scarfs and on silks. In this embroidery there is no wrong side. Sowzini is also well known and is commonly used for shawls. Chikindozi and Falakdozi are two other kinds of embroidery popular among Kashmiris. Dyes for colouring the yearn were all prepared in olden days from Natural vegetables herbs, such as nuts, chamaihaldi, jaman, bark, kasumba, kesar, naspal, basma, ratanjot harar, bahera, amla, dandasa, rund, majoo, hermal mehundi, indigo etc., which they could procure easily and at very cheap rates. Chemical colours have completely replaced the natural dyes, and with it started the decline of the real beauty and value of Kashmir shawls.

The Kashmir shawl industry in the valley reached its zenith during the Mughal period, when it was almost considered as a court art. Such was the patronage given to this industry both by the Mughal emperors and the nobles of their court. Not only the royalties in India but also even the royalties in Europe vied with one another in collecting rare shawls and treasuring them as heirlooms to their progeny. Such was the appreciation and demand in Europe that textile manufacturers in France, England and other European countries got some of these Kashmir designs copied and started manufacturing shawls to meet the growing demand of the European market. Thus came to be born the well-known Paisley shawls, the best of them can easily be mistaken for real Kashmir shawls. Made by the cheap jacquard method, these shawls began to compete keenly with the genuine ones, as they could be made cheaper and in large quantities, with the result that the western markets were practically closed to real Kashmir shawls, and the weavers and embroiderers in the valley, at least a good number of them, had to take to other professions. Facing lean days at home, some of them migrated to the Punjab and carried on their trade under trying conditions. Bulk of the shawls sold in Indian market as Kashmir shawls were reality manufactured at Lahore and Amritsar by the settlers from the valley, and those settled in the Himalayan valleys produced other types of woolen shawls but of simpler and bolder designs. (Condensed)

G. VENKATACHALAM

SHEELA SUBARWAL – ART FOR A CAUSE

In her beautiful sun-lit studio, overlooking a lush three-lined garden, Sheela Subarwal is putting finishing touches to water colour painting. At 72, when most women would be content to put their feet up and relax, she spends upto five hours a day painting here. "Art is my religion", she says disarmingly.

Sheela's early training in pre-partition Lahore under the celebrated B.C. Sanyal stood her in good stead when she moved to Calcutta. Soon she was exhibiting with such greats like Rabindranath Tagore, Jamini Roy and Ramkinkar Baij in India, U.S.A. and the summer salon in London.

Sheela has been and will always be a traditionalist, who makes no bones about her disdain for abstract art. While more than proficient in her portrait and flower studies, it is her stylised folk-art paintings of the Santhal tribe in particular that are her forte. Brilliant contrasting colours and rhythmic lines characterise such works as "To the market" and "Gossip". Her exquisite watercolour wash paintings like "Mother and Child", done in the style of the Bengal School, are also particularly arresting. (Condensed)

SARAH NATHAN

SHIRALI VISHNUDAS

(b.1907) – Sangeet Praveen; vocalist; Hindustani, khayal of Gwalior Gharana, sitar of Senia Gharana; studied with Vishnu Digambar Paluskar, Ashtewale, Alauddin Khan; concert tours: UK, USA, Canada, Burma, Egypt, Palestine, Sri Lanka, Malaya (1929-38), USSR (1956); publication: Hindu Music and Rhythm; formerly music composer and director Uday Shankar's dance troupe and Films Division, Government of India; disc recordings.

SHIRDI SRI SAI BABA : MAN OF MIRACLES

Mystery surrounds the birth and parentage of Sai Baba. All that is known are a few remarks dropped by Baba himself and these, often symbolical, do no always appeal consistent. However, it does seem that his birth took place about the middle of last century in the Nizam of Hyderabad's state. Probably in the village of Parti. Apparently his parents were Hindu Brahmins, but a tender

age Baba seems somehow to have come under the care of Moslem Fakir, a saintly man and probably a Sufi, who became his first guru.

After four or five years, either through the death of the fakir or for some other reason, Sai Baba came into the charge of a noted government official at Selu named Gopal Rao. This remarkable man was not only rich and liberal but also pious, cultured, and deeply religious.

He was a warrior-saint with powers both temporal and spiritual. When he first saw the young Sai Baba he recognised him, it is said, as an incarnation of the great saint, Kabir. Gopal Rao was therefore happy to have the boy live at his residence and take part as a constant companion in the activities of court, field and temple. Thus the child received from Gopal Rao, his second guru, a training and education of the highest, though not of the bookish, kind.

But after some years the warrior-saint decided that the time had come for him to leave the earth. Accordingly, at the time fixed by himself for departure, he sat in the midst of a religious group performing rituals of worship and by his own yogic power left his body. But before being so he pointed westward and bade the young Sai Baba to travel in that direction to his new abode.

Sai Baba went westward and eventually came to the village of Shirdi, in the Bombay presidency (as it was then). He was not at first made very welcome there. Arriving at a Hindu temple on the outskirts, he was attracted by its solitary calm and wanted to live in it. But the priest in charge took him for a Moslem and would not let him put a foot inside the temple.

Sai Baba took up temporary residence at the foot of margosa tree. He left Shirdi and returned several times; then eventually in the year 1872 settled down permanently in the village. A dilapidated Moslem mosque of Shirdi became his home. Here he kept a fire burning constantly, and oil lamps lit the interior of the mosque throughout the night. This was according to the view, common to both Hindus and Moslem that places of worship should be lit up at night.

A few people recognised Sai Baba's divine qualities and came to pay him homage, (among the first was the priest who had driven him away from the Hindu temple) but most of the villagers regarded him as a mad fakir and of no account. In the tradition of holy men of India, he depended on charity for food and other material needs. These were few, but he did need oil for his earthen lamps. One evening the shop-keeper who supplied Baba with oil, gratis, told him untruthfully that he had no supplies. Perhaps this was a joke to amuse the village loiterers. Anyway a group of them, together with the oil-monger, followed the mad young fakir back to his mosque to see what he would do without his religious light and may be to have a good laugh at his expense.

Water jars are kept in mosques for people to wash their feet before entering the sacred precincts. In the dusk the villagers saw Baba take water from the jars and pour it into his lamps. Then he lit the lamps and they burned. They continued to burn, and the watchers realised that the fakir had turned the water into oil. In consternation they fell at his feet, and prayed that he would not put a curse on them for the way they had treated him. But Baba was not what they thought. He was not a sorcerer resenting their contempt, and ready to seize an advantage. His nature was pure love. He forgave them and began to teach them.

This was the first miracle Sai Baba performed before the public and it was the match that lit the fire which became a beacon drawing thousands of men to him from a far., Many became his devotees. He used his miraculous powers to cure their ailments, to help them in their day-to-day problems, to protect them from danger wherever they happened to be, and to draw them towards a spiritual way of life.

A great many found their sense of values changing. Some surrendered themselves entirely to the divine will which they saw in Baba, gave up their wordily liver, and came to live at Shirdi as close disciples. Sai Baba taught them according to their needs and capacities. Learned pundits who thought him illiterate found that he could discourse on spiritual philosophy and interpret the sacred writings of India more profoundly and clearly then anyone lese they had ever known. But always he led his disciples along the Bhakti marga, the radiant pathway of divine love, self-surrender and devotion.

The fire he kept burning always at the mosque was to provide a ready supply of ash. This he called udhi, and used it for many kinds of miraculous purposes, particularly for curing ailments. The miracles he performed cover the full range of siddhi, or supernormal powers, as expressed in such spiritual and yogic classics as Srimad Bhagavata and Patanjali's Yogo Sutras. Many times he proved to his devotees that he knew what they were thinking and saying and doing when hundreds of miles away from him.

Baba gave visions to people, as for instance, the visiting high Brahmin who was hesitant to go into the Moslem mosque. From outside the mosque the Brahmin saw Sai Baba as the God-form he worshipped, Sri Rama. So convincing was this vision of Rama that he rushed in and fell at Baba's feet. Other types of Miracle include the giving of protection at a distance – protection accident, plague, ill – fortune and imminent death.

By the end of last century, in spite of India's primitive communications at that time, Sai Baba's fame was snowballing rapidly. The high peak was reached by about 1910 when an endless stream, of visitors began to flow in from Bombay and other places. Pomp and ceremony were thrust upon the rugged, unsophisticated old saint; loaded down with jewellery, seated in a silver chariort with fine horses and elephants, he was taken in a grand and colourful procession through the streets.

Baba, it is said, disliked all this show, but he submitted to it to please the people. Yet despite the royal treatment and the riches offered him, he continued to beg his food as of old.

When in 1918 Sai Baba died at Shirdi, he had just enough money to pay for his burial, and no more. Sai Baba's Samadhi (tomb), the mosque where he lived for over forty years and where the sacred fire is still kept burning, and other spots associated with him in Shirdi are today the Mecca of thousands of pilgrims – Hindus, Moslems, Parsees, Buddhists and Christians. (Condensed).

HOWARD MURPHET

SHIV NADAR (b.1945 —   )

Globally, Shiv Nadar is recognised as a man of vision and enterprise. His story is not very different from several other well-known names in the world of information technology (IT). His group, HCL, was an attic startup in 1975. Today, the group's yearly revenue is around $ 700 million and it has 30 offices in 19 countries outside India.

An electrical engineer from Coimbatore, Shiv Nadar worked as a systems analyst at Cooper Engineering and as a senior management trainee at DCM in 1968 before setting up HCL at a time when India had just 250 computers.

He was among the few IT experts who had the vision of a networked world, and in 1997 Time Magazine complimented Nadar for that foresight by saying "The world has caught up with Nadar's vision of a networked future, and the results are shaking up enterprises, economics and governments around the world".

Similarly, Geoffrey James in his work Giant Killers placed HCL in the same strategy league as Microsoft, Hewlett-Packard and Compaq.

SHIV KUMAR SHARMA : WIZARD OF SANTOOR

India is known for its unique blend of the ancient and modern; the sublime and the real; and the continuity with change.

This combination is aptly reflected in this artist of the national and international fame, Pt. Shiv Kumar Sharma, whose elevating music has touched countless hearts in and outside India.

Pandit Sharma's matchless mastery of the santoor – his chosen instrument – was savoured by each member of the over 500 – strong audience at a prestigious auditorium in Toronto recently. It was a fabulous recital, with Ustand Shafat Ahmed Khan accompanying the artist on the tabla and the artist's on the tabla and the artist's son – Rahul – on tanpura. On this occasion, the Raagmala Music Society of Toronto, a premier cultural organisation of Indo Ganadians in Greater Toronto Area (GTA) arranged a special function to formally honour the artist for his life-long contribution towards projecting and popularising the classical Indian music around the world. The rich tributes paid to him confirmed the special appeal of Pandit Sharma's music.

Born in 1938, Shivji was blessed with the love and foresight of his father, Pt. Uma Dutta Sharma, who saw in him the potential of a great musician. Like several other famous artistes, Shivaji was introduced to music – first vocal then the tabla from the early age of five years. He pursued these interests under the supervision of his father who himself was a respected exponent of classical music of the Benaras tradition. In his case, music and academic studies went hand in hand. In due course of time, Shivaji obtained a Bachelor's degree in English literature and Masters in Economics.

Fondly known as 'Shivaji, he is well known for his pleasing manners, humility and sincerity. It may be useful to recall the struggle, the hard work and the triumph of this great musician of our times.

While studying at School and college, the young Shive Kumar's heart really was set on acquiring an unrivalled expertise in music. He began with his love for the table and mastered this art.

Then in a stroke that made history, he shifted to the Santoor. He did this under the guidance and supervision of his father who had the confidence about the potentialities of the santoor came to India from Iran. Its origins are, however traced to the shat tantri veena (100 stringed lute) or the pinaki veena which is mentioned in India's oldest religious work – the Rig Veda. Hence my earlier reference to the combination of the ancient and the modern in Shivaji's work.

Pt. Shiv Kumar Sharma has justfiably won acclaim for the important, innovative modifications he made to the santoor. This had the effect of raising it to the status befitting classical music. It was no easy task. Musicologists and experts had dismissed the santoor as "a dead instrument", pronouncing firmly that it was good merely for folk music. Though his hard work spanning now over 40 years. His first concert was at Haridas Sangeet Sammelan in Bombay in 1955 – Shivji proved those experts wrong, much to the lasting joy and benefit of his admirers. Today, he has created "a global village of listeness across the world who make it a point to attend his concerts.

Shivaji has won many accolades and awards. India's Sangeet Natak Academy bestowed on him the Padmashri in 1991. The University of Jammu conferred the honorary degree of Doctor of Letters on him in 1994. In 1985 he was honoured as the honorary citizen of the city of Baltimore of U.S. In 1987, The President of India gave him the Padmashri in 1991. The University of Jammu conferred the honorary degree of Doctor of Letters on him in 1994. In 1985 he was honoured as the honorary citizen of the City of Baltimore of U.S. In 1987, the Ameer Khusro Society of America gave him a special award for being an outstanding artist in creative instrumental music.

He has given numerous concerts in various parts of the world. He has been a popular broadcaster. He has released many cassettes and CDs and has composed music for films. The film 'Silsila' comes to one's mind for its impressive music which Shivji produced in collaboration with the noted flautist, Hari Prasad Chaurasia. This duo has rendered great music for many more films.

Pt. Sharma was once asked if the santoor had a long-term future. His response was a categorical 'Yes' he referred to the works of his disciples based in India, Japan and Germany. He also looked lovingly at his son, Rahul, who has been training under his watchful eyes and shows promise.

Shivaji has often spoken about his philosophy of music and its impact on human beings. Classical music is capable of expressing human emotions such as happiness, sorrow, devotion. As he plays various ragas, the santoor becomes a tool in his hands through which he communicates with his listeners. He believes in the universality of the music.

Real music, he says, goes beyond the grammar and technicalities touching every sensitive soul. "When I pay santoor, I get divine bliss which I share with my audience". Another significant theme in his music relates to harmony. "Like the synchoronisation of sur and tall, I would like to see my neighbours, my city and country (and indeed other countries) in complete unison"says Shivji who has become synonymous with the 'santoor' of which he truly is "the grand master" and the wizard.

SHIVARATRI AT MANDI

The seven-day Shivaratri fair of Mandi – a State fair is the consummation of a synthesis of Shaiva and Vaishnava cults. The feat of synthesis was achieved at Mandi by the then Raja of the erstwhile state of Mandi. Vaishnavism, was imported into Mandi by Raja Suraj Sen (1637) – 1648 A.D.). Despite several marriages, the Raja was childless. He consulted astrologers, religious teachers and those well-versed in the 'Shastras' (religious texts). They advised him to install Shri Madhorao, the regal aspect of Lord Vishnu and to abdicate the state to him to act as his regent. The town of mandi or for that matter, the entire Mandi and Kullu valley are Shaiva and Shaivism is the main cult of the people. This may be the reason that on Shivarathri Shri Madhorao, seated in the palanquin borne by the "Sevadaras" and flag bearers, pays his obeisance to Baba Bhutnath, an aspect of Lord Shiva at the nearby shrine of Bhutnath.

In the erstwhile state of Mandi, the entire polity hinged on the smooth working of the relationship between the Raja and the 'devatas' and devis' of this region. The deities held 'jagirs' bestowed upon them by the Raja. The entire village looked to the authority of the deity for religious and other worldly affairs. It may be any function in the home, fair or festival, community lunches and controversial matters. The people obeyed the deity and the 'gur' was the spokesman of the deity. The 'kardar' (general manager), 'Pujari' (priest) and other functionaries helped the deity to hold together the entire village in harmony and unity. These deities further obtained their power and authority from the Raja. It was at the time of Shivaratri fair that all 'devatas' and devis' with their paraphernalia and orchestra (pahari baja gaja) would come and meet the Raja who, in turn, would acknowledge their position and status equal to the present 'jagirdars! This is how the bonds between these mountain deities and the Raja were strengthened. The Shivaratri fair thus affords a peep into the ancient polity, strong and united.

There are huge crowds in colourful attire at Mandi during the fair. The first 'mela' (fair) after Shivaratri is dedicated to Shri Jagannath, Paddal; second to Goddess Siyamakali, Tarna; third to Shri Ramchander and Jalpa Devi, Paddal; fourth to Siddhakali and Bhuvaneshwari Devi, Seri; fifth to Shri Triloknath and Sheetala Devi, Purani Mandi; Sixth to Bhimakali, Bhuli and seventh to Baba Bhutnath, Chohatta. Shivaratri fair thus affords an occasion to worship and to express gratitude for having good living and abundance to these local deities whom acted as our protectors and guardians.

The night before the seven day Shivaratri fair begins, there is the 'Jag' (Camp Fire) of the 'deuloos' (volunteers of the deity) at the palace of the Raja Sahib of Mandi. The (gur) oracle of the deity moves with the sword and burning sticks in hand. He utters the 'Bhaka' (Genesis of the deity) and goes round 'Githa'. There are sacred and divine things of Shivaratri 'Mela' and one should also try to get at the real essence of Shivratri fair. President Radhakrishnan was so right when he said we can not understand things human unless we understand things divine".

Dr. NEELAMANI UPADHYAY

SHOBHA GURTU

Every time a young Shobha Gurtu (Nee Shirodkar) stopped by to pay her respects to the late Begum Akhtar, the Begum was known to remark about the similarity in their voices. In fact, so charmed was the begum that occasionally she even called for her 'Sarda' (her name for Shobha) to accompany her on-stage.

And while these remain particularly cherished occasions, there were other equally memorable moments with acknowledged maestros, like Pt. Ravi Shankar and Kishan Maharaj, that have added much excitement and richness to Shobha Gurtu's early professional life, making her a virtual living legend.

Born in 1927, in Belgaum, to talented Goan Singer-dancer mankabai Shirodkar, Shobha Gurtu's childhood years were spent in an ambience best described as inspiring. Not surprisingly she decided, early on in life, as to what her future vocation would be. In the years to come, Gurtu's training, in keeping with the 'Guru Shishya Parampara', was under the tutelage of the musicians, Nathan Khan Saheb and Gamman Khan Saheb who inculcated her into the 'Purabi' style of singing, made famous by the inimitable Begum Akhtar and the equally formidable Siddheshwari Devi.

Whatever the Khan Sahebs taught, I learnt, there was little room for questioning. One's Guru was to be respected. But I must say they treated me like a daughter. 'Bahut Lagan se sikhate the'... "she racalls, a trifle misty-eyed, seated in a sparsely decorated little flat on World seaface.

Back in the present, Gurtu claims that her career has had almost no downswings. 'Bhagwan ki daya hai... meri awaz meri den hai... logo ne hamesha taarif hi ki hai'. In fact', she adds, "everything fell into place on its own. I started out with small soirees, then went on to small time concerts, moving on to accompanying the greats and finally ot solo shows as well as radio and TV performances".

Gurtu acknowledges her gurus for having helped her tone her rich and sensously evocative voice. "Their training has brought me here. Even today when I perform on stage I think first of God and then my Gurus. And my music just flows", she adds.
(Condensed)

RITU BHATIA

SHOBHA SINGH ART GALLERY

Sardar Sobha Singh Art Gallery is situated around the idyllic surroundings of village Andratta in Kangra Valley in Himachal Pradesh. It houses the 100 odd works of the renowned painter Sardar Sobha Singh. These works mostly on religious and traditional themes adorn the walls of the gallery which attract the art connoisseurs and critics from far and wide. The gallery was established in 1950s. Apart form a hall which contains his famous works, the other room open to visitors is Sobha Singh's study. Spartan in décor and neatly laid out room, it instantly instills a feeling of warmth and tranquility. A combination of simplicity, elegance and richness, the room has overflowing bookshelves relièved by pictures and works of arts on the walls and an unfinished painting of Guru Ravi Das on the easel.
(Condensed)

SHOVANA NARAYAN – THE KATHAK VIRTUOSO

Kathak is the acknowledged classical dance from of Northern India. Rooted in Hinduism, it enacted and interpreted familiar classical mythology and folklore with a familiar code of gesture and expression. Born in the temples, it drives it name from Kathakars, members, in times gone by of hereditary guilds of myths and storytellers who recounted and interpreted tales (or kathas) from Hindu mythology involving song and dance as these rhaposdists reached the points of ecstasy in their devotion. The bhakti movement brought in an element of romanticism. Portrayed through the popular tale of Radha and Krishna, human emotions of devotion, yearning, grief and joy were given prominence, Evolving further from the temple to the court in the Mughal period, Kathak was given a new impetus.

Kathak is primarily a dance form communicating simplicity of thought and emotion through a highly complex vocabulary of evocative gestures, controlled vitality and intricacy of footwork. It subtly explores a range of moods with delicacy and balance, extending the limits of art representing a grand fusion of cultures.

Shovana Narayan, having studied under the great masters Birju Maharaj and Kundan Lal brings out the beauty and emotion embodied in the Lucknow school with its emphasis on expression and man's feelings, as also the Jaipur School, with it technical brilliance and strong expression.

In 1986-87 Shovana Narayan experimented with duets, with Western Classical bellet dancers. "I have underscored parallelism between certain movements of the ballets, as in Spanish Flamenco, and Kathak. But I have not mixed the styles. I have introduced new theme, relevant issues... We, classical dancers, don't temper with the traditional framework, we do not mix styles but we innovate on themes".

Hindi feature films, give the impression that Kathak is a favourite dance of the nautch girls. To this Shovana says, "See initially all dance forms had a bad reputation in India. It was thought that only a nautch girl was supposed to dance in front of customers to lure them. In fact all dance forms went through a period of degeneration. Two social cultural reformers Rukmini Arunandale and E. Krishna Iyer started a cleaning process. An effort of revivalism was initiated. It was in the early 20th century that the dances were given appropriate costumes, the items were formalised dancers were given due encouragement and respect.

Besides being a well known Kathak dancer Shovana is also a senior civil servant in the Government of India,

"When I was sent to learn dance I was just a three year old kid and my first guru was the famous dancer and actress Sadhana Bose who called me a babe in arms. It takes a lifetime to learn any dance," say Shovana.

While being strongly grounded in the centuries old traditions of Kathak dance, she ahs successfully added new dimensions to it through innovative use of contemporary themes and poetry.
(Condensed)

SEEMA BURMAN

SHRINES TEMPLES AND MOSQUES IN KASHMIR

According to Kalhana, who is the main source of information about ancient Kashmir, there were shrines here, there and everywhere. With the coming of Muslims in about twelfth century, many of the temples disappeared and mosques sprang up instead in abundance. Both temples and mosques fall into two categories – Archaeological and Devotional. There are springs also, which fall under either category.

It is after the rise of Buddhism that Hindus began to build temples. The Kashmir classical style is fundamentally different from any other style of Hindu architecture. Writes Sir A. Cunningham:

"The Architectural remains of Kashmir are perhaps the most remarkable of the existing monuments of India as they exhibit undoubted traces of the influence of Grechian art. The Hindu temple is generally sort of architectural pasty, a large collection of ornamental fritters huddled together, either with or without beeping, while the Jain temples, usually a vast forest of pillars, are made to look as unlike one another as possible by some paltry difference in their petty details. On the other hand, the Kashmirian fans are distinguished by the graceful elegance of their outlines, by the massive boldness of their parts, and by the happy propriety of their decorations".

"They cannot indeed vie with the severe simplicity of the Parthenon nor with the luxuriant gracefulness of the monument of Lusicrates, but they possess great beauty, different indeed, yet quite their own".

"The Kashmirian architecture is characterised by its lofty pyramidal roofs, its trefoiled doorways, covered by Pyramidal pediments, and the great width of its intercoluminations suited equally well to rainy and snowy climates. There is no doubt that the Kashmirian style was well known to the Greeks. A Kashmirian pillar has a base, a shaft and a capital. The trefoils arch of Kashmir is very original and interesting as may be seen from the remains of some old monuments".

ARCHAEOLOGICAL

Under this category come temples like Avantivarman, Martand, Pandrethan and mosques like Pathar Masjid, Pari Mahal and so on.

Archaeological are of the opinion that the temple (174'x 148') at Avantipura were built in the 9th century by king Avantivarman who had his capital 18 miles away from present Srinagar. The balconies alternate angular and rounded flutting, set off the natural contrasts of massive stones of which they are built. Its carvings stand as they stood in Avantivarman's time but now a body without a soul. The two temples known as Avanti Swamin and Avanti Sura were dedicated to Vishnu and Shiva.

The Temple of Martand dedicated to sun between 1500 to 2,000 years old appears to be the ruins of a grand old temple 63 ft. long enclosed in a quadrangle of columns and arches forming cloisters all round it. There are about 84 carved pillars. It is a dream in stones designed by Titans and finished by jewellers. In comparison it looks fairer than the site of Parthenon or Taj or St. Peter of Escurial.

The temple at Pandrethan has one of the largest moats. Cunningham says that is was probably built in 921 A.D. by Meru during the reign of Kind Partha. It was Ashoka's Srinagar. The domed roof of the temple is a fine piece of sculpture. There are series of arches in the retaining wall.

A temple and some tablets have been unearthed during recent excavations at Harwan which look like the oldest mountain monuments as belonging to the Kushan period when Kashmir was closely connected with Central Asia. Nagarjuna held Buddhist congregations here.

The temples at Taoer, Devasar, Didha Matha, Bandi, Bhunyar, Fatehgarh etc. also need a mention.

Nut Jahan built the Mosque known as Pathar Masjid for offering prayers in it. Jamia Masjid was build in 1404 A.D. This is the stronghold of Mir Waiz of Kashmir. Rebuilt in 1479, 1618, 1674, 1841 and 1912 it commanded unique influence among Muslims before 1947, particularly in 1931.

The Ziarat at Hazaratbal on the Dal Lake attracts crowds of Fridays. Prophet's hair enshrined here are exhibited on rare occasions. It is being rebuilt at a huge cost.

The Pari Mahal (Sash-I-mah) designed by Dara Shikoh stands on an isolated crag and with almost perpendicular sides towards the top. Once used for astronomical observations it has stood for cenuries, weather worn, sad, alone and untenanted.

Other mosque like Ali Masjid, Akhun Mullah Shah, Hassanabad, Patna Chhuk etc. also need a mention.

DEVOTIONAL

Under this category come temples like Hari Parbat Shankaracharya, Shodashyar, Bijbihara and mosques like Shahe-Hamdan, Makhdoom Saheb, Chrare – Sharif etc.

Hari Parbat stands on Dal Lake and is located in the center of the city. Apart from its monumental value, it is a symbol of secularism as Hindus, Muslims and Sikhs have shrines round it.

The temple of the top of Shankaracharya hill is supposed to have been built during 2,629 – 2,564 B.C. Tradition says that the lingam was placed inside the temple by a goldsmith in the year 54 of the Hindu era. The temple commands a fine view of the city that lies prostrate at its foot.

The temple of Shodashyar stands on the bank of the Jhelum in Sonawar. Once this temple was connected with the temple on the top of Shankaracharya Hill by a long staircase. That there existed some affiliation between the two temples cannot be ruled out. A philanthrophist from Hyderababd rebuilt it in the early twenties.

The temple at Gaddar is the only temple of recent construction which is not dedicated to Shiva. Its roofing is in gold plates and was the royal temple of Dogra rulers who were not Shaivyas. The palace having shifted and the Dogra rule having been liquidated the temple presents a grim look.

Makhdoom Sahen mosque is built at some altitude on one side of the Hari parbat fort. There is a tank also in the compound which is filled up with water by people who carry it in jars from long distances when there is a drought or excessive rain – It looks on Mulla Khan.

Charar-e-Sharif mosque lies about 14 miles towards southwest of Srinagar. It commands influence second only to Hazratbal. Once every year, the flag is carried in procession from this shrine to Shah-e-Hamdan in which thousands of Muslims participate.

SRI AMARNATH AND SPRINGS

The celebrated cave of Amarnath situated in along glacial gorge high among the eastern mountains is visited by thousands of Hindu pilgrims from Kashmir and different parts of India on the full-moon-day of the month of Sawan (July-August) every year. It contains a self-formed Lingam of Ice (the emblem of Shiva) which increases and decreases with the waxing and waning of the moon.

The lingam is not impregnated with any matter but it is composed simply of pure water turned into ice. Not is it an ice spring, for an Amavas day the ground is dry. The pilgrimage is mentioned in Book 1:267 of the Rajatarangini in the accounts of Kind Nara who reigned in Kashmir in 1048-1008 B.C. which proves that even before the time of Kalhana, (the author of the book who lived in the 12th century of the Christian era) it was annually visited by pilgrims.

Trisandhya spring in Brang remains dry all the year round except in the month of Baisakh-jeth (April-May). The water first flows continuously and then at intervals.

The spring at Wasuknag remains quite dry for six months of winter but flows with water for six months of summer.

The spring at Pavansandhya, 5 miles to the east of Verinag ebbs and flows continuously as though it breathes pavana or air like a living creature.

There is a spring at Brang between Anantnag and Verinag and the fish therein are blind in one eye. Another is at Wayyar (Wular). There are similar spring at Anantnag and Sadar-quatahal. Tsurnag on the top of the Sarhal Mountain makes whirls like the potter's wheel.
(Condensed)

GWASHALAL KAUL

SHRUTI SADOLIKAR

SHRUTI SADOLIKAR – KATKAR has something of a philosopher within her. Though born into the family of an illustrious musician (her father the late Wamanrao Sadolikar), she never had a godfather to further her career in music. "My father was never easy with his praise". Her informal association with music began at the age of six as a companion to a friend of hers, who was learning from her father. However, Shruti continued to learn from her father till his death. In the meanwhile, Ustad Gulubhai jasdanwala, a disciple of Ustad Alladiya Khan, took her under his wing and thereby began her formal tutelage under the Atrauli Jaipur 'Gharana'.

Speaking of her musical career Shruti says, "I have been lucky to get good gurus at an early age, even during my school days and received the right exposure at the right time. And then I was lucky to get good programmes and a good audience. Whatever I have achieved the credit goes to my parents and gurus'.

Shruti has a masters degree in music from the S.N.D.T. University.

Regarding the current music scenario, when one has to give your best in a short time when performing on A.I.R. and Doordarshan, Shruti feels, "During my father's time 'mehfils' used to go on into the night. Now at conferences we are expected to give our best in as little as two hours. We bear in mind, that we have a time limit to sing an entire 'khayal'. And yet we manage it.

Speaking about the attempts made to link Hindustani and Carnatic Music, particularly in instrumental music, Shruti feels this confluence of music, "Jugal-bandi", the very thought means that both should be together. You can't have two flows. Then you can't enjoy either. "Jugal-bandi" of two artistes of the same system but may be from two different gurus, can also give two angels and that may be more enjoyable".

Shruti feels classical music can be popularised by educating the public. Speaking about its future she opines, "Music flows to find its own course like the Ganga. It will flow into eternity, may be changing its course, a little here or a trifle there but will never cease to flow".
(Condensed)

S. SWARUP

SIDDESHWARI DEVI

(b. 1908) – Vocalist: Hindustani, thumri, dadra, kajri, etc; studied with Sayaji Maharaja, Bare Ramdas and Inayat Khan; concert tour, Afghanistan (1965); received Sangeet Natak Academy award for Hindustani vocal music (1966); variously honoured by many State Government; disc recordings.

SIKKIM – THE SUBLIME

The tiny jewel-like Indian State of Sikkim is flanked by Nepal and Bhutan. To its north lies Tibet and girdling it to the south is the west Bengal district of Darjeeling. Dominating both the landscape and legend of this state is the mightly massif of the landscape and legend of this state is the mightily massif of Khangchendzong – known to the outside world as Kanchenjunga. It is the third highest peak in the world – towering at 8603 meters. But to the people of Sikkim, it is a guardian deity, a country god whose benign watch fullness ensures peace and prosperity for the land.

The divine statues of this massif has been made enduring by its widespread worship by all the communities of Sikkim - Lepchas, Bhutias and Nepalese alike. So sacrosanct is the mountain that successive mountaineering expeditions have climbed to within meters of the peak, but left the summit inviolate in deference to local beliefs.

Sikkim derives its name from the Lumbu world Sukhim which means the 'New House'. Lepchas refer to it as Nye-Maeel, 'the paradise' and for Bhutias it is the beloved Bemyul Denzong – the 'hidden valley of rice'; all apt descriptions of this enchanting land.

The river Tista rises in North Sikkim originating in Tsochmy Lake. Its foaming waters are augmented by Lachen Chu and Laching Chu as it rushes furiously to embrace the mighty Brahmaputra. The Rangit is born in West Sikkim in the bosom of Rathong Glacier – 'the turbulent one'. These and other no fewer swifts – flowing rivers make the valley fertile and hold out the promise of large-scale hydro-electric generation.

Great topographical variety is encountered in Sikkim, with elevations ranging from 240 meters (786 ft) to 8450 meters (28,000 ft). Sharp ridges, awesome ravines and deep precipices cover most of the area. The fluctuation in elevation has resulted in sharply varying climatic condition. While the terai region to the south is warm and humid in summer and pleasantly cold in winter, altitude and temperature has endowed Sikkim with exceptional botanical riches. Within its 7300 square kilometers is encountered the entire gamut of climate, ranging from arctic to alpine to sub-tropical. Nowhere else in the world does such a relatively small area offer such an infinite variety of vegetation.

While the floral world of Sikkim includes primulas, gentians and blue poppies, it is truly dominated by the amazing proliferation of orchids and rhododendrons of differing sizes and colours. The total number of orchid species for the whole world is estimated at over 5000; of these, Sikkim alone has more that 600 species, both the epiphytal which attach themselves to rocks and trees and the terrestrial, which grow on the ground.

More than 30 species of rhododendrons grow here on trees in the sub-alpine region and in bushes at higher altitudes. The rhododendron has rightly been described as the glory of Sikkim. Flowers, some scarlet, others pale pink or white, grow on trees over 40 feet tall as well as on bushes barely two inches above the ground.

Sikkim is a bird watcher's delight. Perhaps in no other part of the world does an area of this size carry such a large profusion of species. Over 550 species of birds soar in the Sikkim sky.

Though there is an ethnic diversity startling for so small an area, but tolerance and harmonious co-existence are the characteristics of Sikkimese society. The ethos of Sikkimese life, the Buddhist – Hindu culture, is shared by all, and shared beliefs have laid the foundation for an integrated community. The Lapchas, the Bhutias – whose ancestors followed Khyebumse into Sikkim and the Nepalese themselves and melang of diverse ethnic groups including Limbus, Rais and Chettris, live together in their mainly agricultural land. Ironically today it is the Nepalese who form the majority of Sikkim's population. The first Nepali settlers were sharecroppers; it is they who introduced terrace farming to Sikkim, and with their initiative and skills, have made great contributions to the state's development.

Given the historical and cultural links between Sikkim and Tibet, it is not surprising that Tibetan Buddhism has deeply imprinted itself in the land, and particularly amongst the Bhutias. Social life revolves around the monastery whose monk plays a crucial role in giving direction to existence and meaning to daily toil. Till recently, one male member from nearly every Bhutia family entered the monastery. The Lepachas adopted Buddhism in the seventeenth century, and amongst the Napalese there are both Buddhists and Hindus.

In the terraced fields of the valleys and uplands, rice, barley, buckwheat and millet are the principal crops and provide staple items of food. Orange, ginger and cardamom are important cash crops. The Sikkimese – Lepchas, Bhutias and the Nepalese alike relish Chhang, which is a mild beer drink prepared from fermented millet. The traditional way to serve is in a tongba, a bamboo container with a hollow pipe used as a drinking straw. Chhang drinking is an integral part of social get-togethers and religious festivities in Sikkim.

ASHOK DILWALI

SILKS

India renowned for silks, from South India, Bengal, Assam, Benaras, colourful, elegant designs; admired at home, abroad.

South Indian silks used in any kind of costume; specializing in contrasting colours; noted for pullos, borders. Amazing variety produced by master craftsmen, heavily designed or lighly patterned.

Gadwal best known among cotton textiles; zari combined with borders, pullos. Designs featuring milkmaids or 'Golla Bamas' blended with motifs, striking floral patterns. Other leading cotton-centers, Coimbatore; canjeevaram, Irkal, Surat, Venkatgiri.

SILVER FILIGREE OF ORISSA

The craft of filigree captures the fineries of the Indian handicrafts in the snow-white purity of silver; set in intricately designed aesthetic forms and figures. It is a unique craft practiced in very few places in the world.

Silver filigree or "Tarakashi" in India is native Cuttack city in Orissa, a state in the eastern region. The Cuttack filigree is internationally acclaimed for its marvellous craftsmanship, delicate artistry and an excellent finish.

Filigree items are crafted in pure silver stretched into very fine wires and thin foils. These wires and foils are artistically assembled in an elegant framework of delicate designs of decorative pieces, jewellery and even utility items like spoons, knives, fruit bowls, nuttrays, boxes, purses, cuff-links and ashtrays. Decoration pieces include models of ships, famous Indian monuments, scenes from Hindu epics, photo-frames, and animal and bird figurines.

Filigree is distinguished from other ornaments and jewellry by its exquisite finish, texture and snow gloss.

The intricate process of filigree craft commences with the preparation of a framework with silver wire. The inner textures are superbly crafted separately with fine strands and foil bits to the desired shape and designs and are beset in the main framework. The whole pattern is fixed on a mica sheet with a paste and then soldered finely. The final creation is given a finish and cleared in soapnut water.

The finale is achieved with a smear of a mystical powdery polish which renders it the ostentatious snow gloss to cast a spell on the beholders.

BIMAL SAIGAL

SIMILIPAL – A MAGICAL WILDERNESS

Similipal is the richest watershed area in Orissa, giving rise to many perennial rivers like the Budhabalanga in the north, the Khadkei and the Kairi-Bhandan in the northwest, the west Deo in the southwest, the Salandi in the south, and the East Deo and the Sanjo in the east.

Due to unique geological and geomorphological qualities and average annual rainfall of about 2000mm, the region holds large reservoirs of subterranean water. Crystal clear pools, cascading rapids and gorgeous falls are typical of Similipal.

Talking of falls, two or them – Joranda and Barheipani are just spectacular and perennial. At Joranda, water cascades 493 feet into an inaccessible rocky gorge. It's only possible to have a top down view from the adjacent hills. Vegetation down there is least interfered with and almost pristine. Wild bananas grow there. Barheipani on the other hand has a much greater height, 1308 feet, but the waterfalls with two intermediate breaks. Barhei in Oriya means rope. The fall is so named as the waterfall weaves like a rope.

The combined effect of all the elements is that the summer at Similipal is milk, though at times temperatures rise to 42 C and the winter rather harsh with temperatures falling to 3C. Several broad valleys are effeced by forest. Her trees are stunted with hardly any canopy and are scattered far and few in the extensive grasslands. These are good grazing for cheetal, sambar, bison and elephant, Naturally animal sighting is good at these forest pockets.

Sighting of the animals is also assured at artificial saltlicks like the one at Chahala and Jenabil forest rest houses. Salt licks are spots where the soil has high salt content. There are several natural salt licks, in addition to which artificial ones have been created. These are regularly frequented by cheetal, sambar, barking deer, wild bear and elephant, early in the morning and late in the evening.

Similipal Tiger Reserve is in the Mayurbhanj district of Orissa. It is a 2750 sq. km vast tract of forest out of which 845 sq. km forms the core. The rerrain is hilly, the view from the highest peak Khairiburu at 1165 meters or Meghasani at about 1100 meters, is that of lush green spread all around an enveloping valley rising up the hill slopes to the top hill after hill – even at the highest of summer.

There were 95 tigers in Similipal according to the 1993 census. But the sighting of this great cat is rare due to its secretive and solitary nature combined with the character of forest. One can make out the presence of this super predator by occasional alarm calls of barking deer, cheetal or sambar and its conspicuous pugmarks on tracks.

The Muggar or crocodile was almost extinct from the river systems of similipal by 1979. The crocodile management and breeding center at Ramtirtha on the outskirts of the reserve at Jashipur has released 422 muggars into the Budhabalanga, the Khairi, the west Deo and the East Deo rivers. "Regular monitoring has revealed the crocodile sighting, on an average, works out to three cross at every two km".

A major attraction of similipal is the large variety of orchids found here, 86 species have been identified so far. Arboreal orchids are epiphytes – plants that grow on the plants without parasitizing them. They store water in their thick fleshy steam, leaves and roots. They collect much of their nutrients from the falling organic debris. Most of the orchids at Similipal exotically coloured and shaped, bloom during May and June. Generally 4-5 species bloom at a time for few days while others patiently wait for their turn. An orchid blooming into foot long handing chains, called foxtails, consisting of several hundred tiny, translucent, mauve coloured flowers in the first week of June is a captivating sight.

Similipal is a tribal belt too, it's common to find people with bows and arrows even on National Highway 5 and National Highway 6 which encircle the reserve area. (Condensed)

PUSHP K. JAIN

SOLAR ECLIPSES

Eclipses being a part of solar phenomena did engage the attention of the ancient seers in a manner that marvels us. They had not only discovered the laws governing the occurrence of eclipses but the effects they produce on terrestrial phenomena.

To the pseudo-scientists of his days, who when they asserted that the ancient Hindus thought that the eclipses were supernatural phenomena and that the solar and lunar globes are being swallowed by Rahu and Ketu – the brilliant astronomer and astrologer Varahamihira posed the question; "If Rahu has a form, travels in the zodiac, possesses a head and has a circular orb, how come it that he whose movement is fixed and uniform seizes the two luminaties who are situated 180° away from him.

Varahamihira says: "In her own eclipse the moon enteres the shadow of the earth and in that of the sun, the solar disc. Therefore, it is that the lunar eclipse does not commence at the western limb nor the solar at the eastern limb".

Some local scientists talking about solar eclipse on October 24, 1995 went out of their way to say that eclipses are only physical phenomena and it was "superstitious" to observe any rituals during their occurrence. They also says that "abhishekams and installation of Idols" etc., in temples were no good and a waste of money.

In other countries, scientific associations mostly confine themselves to the study and observation of the eclipses from an astronomical point of view.

In national astrology, solar eclipses are prominent features indicating most important and far-reaching event. The operating causes at an eclipse are the combined influences of the planets holding certain relative positions at the time and this is not limited to a few hours for the major planets move slowly into configurations.

All celestial phenomena produce their effects not instantaneously but in large portions of time and space. If one carefully study all the total solar eclipses that have occurred during the last one hundred years and take stock of the historical series of effects, one will not fail to appreciate the importance of eclipses.

It is refreshing to note the following observations of Soviet and Japanese scientists on the effects of eclipses.

"The position of the sun, the earth and the moon on a straight line could cause very strong earthquakes. This conclusion was drawn by staff members of the Soviet Magnetic Observatory, Vladivostok, as a result of processing information received by means of magnetometres on the night of March 24-25* (* The reference is to the 1978 March 24 and 25 total lunar eclipse).

"The brief pulsations, which arose soon after the end of the lunar eclipse were unexpected in the recording of the variations of the magnetic field.

"Since disturbances of such a kind do not arise in the magnetic field of medium latitudes, it was resolved that the earthquake was reflected on the instruments. This was confirmed by reports of earth tremors in various parts of the world on the night of March 24-25".

The Japanese biologist Meki Takata of Toho University asked himself the question: Wouldn't the moon eliminate the effect during eclipses, by placing itself between the sun and the earth? Dr. Takata found that "during total solar eclipses, as the moon brings to cover the sun the flocculation index of book starts to decline reaching its lowest point when the eclipse was complete". Takata concedes "man is a living sun-dial".

On June 2, 1954, at the time of a solar eclipse, physicist Maurice Allan noted at the exact moment the eclipse began, the pendulum's level of oscillation changed suddenly. His explanation was there must be a cosmic force which the moon screens from us.

In India, studies conducted after the February 1980 eclipse by Rewa University reveal:

"The belief that water exposed to a solar eclipse was unfit for human consumption was proved true in environmental and biological experiments carried out during the last week's solar eclipse.

"The experiments also confirmed, that Kusha grass and Tulsi (osmium sanctum) leaves had a purifying effect on water, as mentioned in Indian Literature.

The experiment, according to Dr. Rathore, Dean of the life Sciences Department of Rewa University, shows that Kusha grass was more useful than Tulsi to preserve the quality of water.

The studies were conducted on the water collected from different sources, and its physico-chemical properties studied".

This would cover all materials of human consumption. That is shy the traditional practice of placing Kusha needs in kitchen, water storage vessels, bathrooms etc. is not to be dismissed as a superstition.

Some astronomers have also found the immediate effects of the eclipses: "Dogs begin to howl like wolves, birds to roots, animals run to places of safety, thunder storms develop, some human beings become aggressive, blood pressure rises; some babies might develop deformities if pregnant women are exposed to the eclipses".

Dr. Chari hit the nail on the head when he explained that, during the eclipse, a high amount of radiation of x-rays and gamma rays takes place which can cause mutations in the foetus and hence pregnant women should avoid exposure to the eclipse.

He said one of the reasons why elders fast during the eclipse could perhaps be linked to the Russian scientists belief that bacterial growth is accelerated during the eclipse.
(Condensed).

DR. B. V. RAMAN

SOME FAMOUS SIKH SHRINES

Sikh history originates form Nankana Sahib. Gurur Nanak Dev, the founder of Sikh Faith, was born here in 1469. The name of the place at the time was "Rai Bhoi di Talvandi". The landlord contemporary of Guru Nanak Dev was Rai Bular, who himself became a devotee of the Guru. It was renamed Nankana after the Guru. It is located in what is called Nilanwali (Forest where nilgais abound), and is about 75 kilometers west south west of Lahore. Nankana Sahib is in Sheikhupure district of Pakistan and is connected to the district town by rail and road. There are several shrines connected with the memory of Guru Nanak Dev's childhood and early youth here. Later Guru Arjan Dev and Guru Hargobind also visited nankana Sahib and a Gurdwara was also raised subsequently in their honour.

During the Sikh rule, these Gurdwaras were richly endowed with liberal land grants (over 7,000 hectares). The management was in the hands of udasi and Nirmala priests until the Shiromani Gurdwara Parbandhak Committee took over during the Gurdwara Reform Movement of 1920-25. The Gurdwaras had to be abandoned in the aftermath of the partition in 1947. They are now looked after by the government of Pakistan. Nankana Sahib is one of the three places which can be visited periodically by bands of Sikh pilgrims with the approval of the Government of Pakistan, the other two being Panja Sahib near Hasan Abdul and Lahore.

Gurudwara Panja Sahib at Hasan Abdul has an importance of its own.

Hasan Abdul is a small town and a railway station along the main Lahore-Peshawar railway line in Compbelpore (or Attock) district. Close to it is a spring of cool, clean water which according to tradition was created by Guru Nanak Dev. It is said that the Guru arrived here at the end of his tour of West Asia. At that time the only source of water near this place was reservoir at the top of the nearby hill where lived a Muslim divine Wali Kandhari. The guru sent Mardana thrice to the Wali in order to drink and fetch some water, but every time the latter refused to oblige saying that he would not help a Muslim (Mardana was a Muslim) who followed a 'Hindu' Guru. Guru Nanak then asked Mardana to remove a stone nearby from where water sprang forth. At the same time water in Wali Kandhari's reservoir began to ebb until it was completely dry. Wali Kandhari, infuriated by the 'Hindu's' miracle, rolled down a rock towards the latter. Guru Nanak Dev, sitting unruffled, merely extended this right arm towards the rolling rock and not only the rock stopped dead, but his open palm made an imprint on it as if it was made of molten wax. Wali Kandhari, impressed by the miracle came down and bowed to the Guru asking his pardon and blessing.

Gurdwara Panja (Palm) Sahib was established during the reign of Maharaja Ranjit Singh, the foundation of the beautiful three-story building, designed after the Samadhi of Maharaja Ranjit Singh in Lahore, was laid on 14th October, 1932 by five eminent holy men, Panj Piare. Built with gray sandstone, its exterior is spotted with protruding domed bay windows. The central fluted dome is surrounded by several symmetrically placed big and small domes. Unlike the Maharaja's Samadhi in Lahore, it has porches covering entrances to the sanctum which stands within the Sarovar that receives water gushing forth from around the rock bearing the sacred Panja Sahib or the palm-imprint of the Guru. Several other buildings for staff and pilgrims and other ancillaries were added subsequently. Guru Ka Langer at Panja Sahib was famous for the quality of food and service at all hours of day and night. Congregational fair used to be held on Baisakhi (Mid-April) and on 30th October until 1947. Now only organised bands of pilgrims occasionally visit Panja Sahib with the permission of the Pakistan Government. One of such regular visits coincides with the Baisakhi festival. (Condensed)

MAJ. GURMIKH SINGH

SOOD, K. (B. 1919)

Sangeet Prabhakar, Sangeet Vusharad; instrumentalist : Hindustani, Jal Tarang; studied with Janardan V. Pathe.

H. RIPLEY

SOUTH INDIAN CINEMA

Indian cinema has its inheritance primarily from two sources. First, primitive silent cinema which never reached a stage of cinematic development comparable with that in Europe of 1920's, secondly, Indian Folk drama of 1930's which, in general, was a distorted version of ancient Sanskrit theatre the classical Indian drama. Ancient Sanskrit. drama was a combination of dialogue, melodrama, song, mime, and dance. It had elements of ballet and opera. It was the kind of theatre from which different genres had not yet separately crystallised. Although classical theater became almost extinct since it had lost court patronage due to various political and other factors over many centuries, the folk theatre survived. Many crudities had crept into it. All these elements dance, opera, melodrama, pattern, descended on the screen with cinematically disastrous results, which rare exceptions of poetic beauty. This was the common starting point for regional Indian cinema in the 1930's. it is from this common beginning that different regions made different strides.

While the development of theatre and the background in other arts have significantly contributed to the difference in the qualitative development of the regional cinema, the economic factors have also played a dominant role in shaping the cinema of the different regions.

In south India, Malayalam film has the smallest of the four language film-markets. With less finance at stake and much less controls imposed by the sources of finance, the Malayalam film enjoys a measure of freedom which is unknown to the film-makers of the other three languages. Two kinds of Malayalam films are produced. One is either neo-realist or pseudo-realist while the other is mutilated local James Bond. In Kannada as well as Telugu, the formula is either religion or sex, with family drama taking a close third place.

With highly stylised expressions of Kathakali for the backdrop, the Malayalam film has surprisingly restrained acting. With a fantastic range of nuances and subtleties of Bharatanatyam on the stage, the Tamil film is still in the grip of essentially melodramatic and stylised acting. The better kind of Malayalam film is more visually conceived than the rest of the South Indian cinema. The impact of training in the Film Institute of India at Poona has had a direct bearing in the development of recent Malayalam cinema, whereas the students of Poona are unable to get into the fringes of the Tamil film Industry. The reaction of young creative filmmakers to the commercial domination of South Indian cinema has shown itself by near total break from all that conventional cinema has been like. It has not merely affected the system and the form, but also the content and the philosophy. Merely because commercial cinema in South India has always had a happy ending, the optimistic undercurrent by which all problems on the screen are eventually solved in a satisfactory manner, the new film maker reacting against all convention is depicting a depressingly pessimistic view of life on the screen.

In an broad generalization, there can be no doubt that the Malayalam film is closer to depicting truth than cinema in the other three regions. The Tamil film is beginning to have an atmosphere of material reality but spiritual and psychological vacuum. The décor, the costumes and the material atmosphere, in general, in the Tamil film traditionally used to be rooted in neither time nor place, with an absolutely weird and fantastic atmosphere prevailing, this is so with the bulk of the Tamil films produced even today but there is a significant improvement in some of them.

Culturally, these films continue to remain in their elementary hero-heroine-villain pattern. With unrealistically perfect and imperfect characters occupying the screen, problems are not depicted as being born out of social and psychological reality but out of villainy. In the depiction of love, for instance, the hero and the heroine will sing a duet song, and dance, this moment one the Marina Beach in Madras, the next moment in Kashmir and the third moment on the walls of a river dam, the fourth near a waterfall. They will chase each other in stylised form and make use of public parks for their secret love not to be realised by their parents. On the other hand, the comedian in the film, very often a domestic servant, in the kitchen garage or in the kitchen garden, Ironically, however, the fantastic unreality of the love of the leading pair is meant to be taken seriously by the audience while the down-to earth love in the garage is meant to be laughed at.

In short, barring exceptions in the Malayalam cinema, some of which have sense of maturity, the South Indian film is yet either clean enough or decent enough for children not mature enough or bold enough for adults.
(Condensed)

S. KRISHNASWAMY

STAMP – THE ART OF DESIGNING

Stamps act as window to the cultural and historical heritage of a nation, its commerce, trade, flora and fauna. C.R. Pakrashi, a philatelist and a stamp designer for many years, describes a stamp as the "mini ambassador of a country".

Philatelists the world over spend a lot of time and effort in collecting and preserving stamps which may appear as the most mundane of things to a common man. But even a serious collector may not be aware of the significance of the designs in each stamp, and appreciate the work behind it. Pakrashi a commercial artist reckons, "Though there are a number of philatelic clubs and many children as well as adults are interested in stamp collection common awareness about stamps is lacking. "Nevertheless, designing stamps, especially a commemorative one, is very often a challenge and very much a creative exercise as these stamps are always associated with important events of personalities. The design must convey the essence of the subject and its ethos or the achievements of the personality, in the most artistic way". Pakrashi describes stamp designing as a very "fascinating and involving form of art".

To design a stamp well, one has to study the subject and do a lot of groundwork before putting down one's ideas within that limited space. Understandably, it is not an easy task. "A stamp designer has to be a commercial artist with knowledge of the printing process, and also possess an understanding of history and various other subjects", states Pakrashi, a lot of research work is required in the libraries and museums to collect as much information as possible so that the design can convey the message in a definite language. The stamp should be communicative as well as attractive.

One can acquire expertise in this specialised art from through active involvement and of course, experience Pakrashi describes the whole exercise as a very satisfying experience that more than compensates for the effort".

It is this creative urge that has motivated many a well-known artist to design stamps, and Styajit Ray's design on Tagore centenary or M.F. Hussain's work with the new famous slogan "Mera Bharat Mahan" are a couple of such examples. Pakrashi took the first plunge by participating in an all India exhibition held to commemorate the 2500th Buddha Jayanti celebrations in the country. "It was a symbolic design where both the 'Bodhivriksha' and an arch typifying Ajanta's caves have been used", reminisces Pakarshi.

His design was awarded the first prize. It was a twoanna denomination stamp issued in 1956.

"Stamp designing has been a life-long involvement, a hobby practiced with dedication and seriousness all these years since 1959", says he.

He has over fifty designs to his credit. Many awards and accolades came his way. A letter from Stanley Gibbons, world's biggest stamp auctioneer, collector and publisher of philatelic journals, acknowledges his contribution with a much coveted compliment: "Your record of active stamp designing would, indeed he difficult to surpass.....

Some of his more important designs include Gandhi Centenary, Jai Bangla, Asian Games '82 (series of three stamps). Congress Centenary (series of four stamps), Quit India Golden Jubilee, J.R.D. Tata First Death Anniversary and 50 years of United Nations (again a set of two) stamps.
(Condensed)

SUMITRA SENGUPTA

STEPWELLS OF GUJARAT : ARCHITECTURAL MARVEL

Gujarat is home to hundreds of step-wells scattered through out the state. In fact, constructing a well was held to be a pious deed that absolved one of sins and certainly earned more merit than mere sacrifices for the builder. Almost each village or town boasted of at least one Vav. For centuries, these Vavs served their purpose. Today, many of the stepwells have withered with time. However, some of the Vavs have survived as structures and continue to supply water while some are venerated for their spiritual presence.

A typical well is made up of the Mandapa or the entrance pavilion which forms the main approach at the ground level; the kuta or the flight of steps leads down to the water or Kund at the bottom. Most of the wells are decorated with sculptures on all available surfaces. One wonders at the engineering skills with which so many pillars and lintels are made to support the five or seven storeys and that too with everything under the surface of the earth.

The earliest among the stepwells in Gujarat are nested among the Junagarh hills – Navghan Vav and Adi – Chadi Vav. The two step-wells appear to have been patiently carved out of soft rocks and these stupendous projects have been executed to get depths – a marvel even by modern standards. However, in the long list of structurally crated step wells one has to revert to Dhank where sixth century Jhilani and Manjushri Vavs can be seen. Almost five centuries later another stepwell sprang up near the famous sun temple at Modhera. The lateral formation of steps is punctuated with a number of miniature shrines at all levels.

Rani ki Vav in Patan is the most magnificent of all stepwells created in 1032 A.D. by Rani Udaymati. She was the queen of the most powerful Chalukya king Bhimdeva whose reign is marked with manifold building activities. A greater part of this vav remained buried for years while the exposed portions were dismembered to embellish another stepwell – Bahadur Singh ki vav in the same village. Though in ruins and dilapidated to a great extent, the remaining part of Rani ki vav continues to impress for its grandeur in dimension and profuse ornamentation.

Almost the entire Hindu pantheon seems to have been chiselled on the walls of the well, besides the sculptured niches and corridors that gradually diminish as the well draws nearer at a depth of nearly 285 feet. Vaishnava sculptures depicting Lord Vishnu in various forms can be seen. The most pictorial among them is one that shows him reclining on the couch of Sheshnaga (Lord of Snakes). Female figures (Apsaras / Devanganas / surasundaris) are in abudance. Possibly they are the best symbolic representation of the reproductive powers of nature. For instance, a scene depicts a devangana standing under a mango tree, holding her left breast which suggests fertility and maturity just like the mango and the mango tree.

In decorating the Rani ki vav, some of the sculptures can be interpreted as religious and they are often compared to sculptures in Modhera Sun temple, Buddhist Stupa in Sanchi, Vimal Vasahi temple of Mt. Abu and even Khajuraho. Some of the images are simply erotic conjunctions like the monkey pulling away a female attire or the damsels themselves undoing their lower garments while scorpions climb their thighs. The artists have also included combats, weapons and warriors confronting opponents in the shape of man or animal.

A little distance from Rani ki Vav are some interesting outlines of medieval waterways. It was early 12th century when Jayasimha Siddha Raja excavated artificial lakes. The largest among them was Sahasarlinga Tank which must have been an immense reservoir, as is evident form the surviving remains of the brick embankments and the giant sized sluiceways. In the nearby museum one can see the various statues recovered while excavating the Rani ki Vav and the Sahasarlinga waterways.

Mata Bhavani Vav is Asarva, on the outskirts of Ahmedabad, is another step well assigned to the Chalukyan period and dedicated to Amba-Bhavani (Names for the Mother Goddess). It is noted for its religious significance rather than its architectural appeal. The well is simple and modest in make with minor ornamentation in the galleries leading to the stretch of steps that travel down to the pool of water. However, some pre-medieval carvings and sculptures can be admired on the parapets that house the Canopied roofs, niches and friezes.

Asarva is famous for another step-well popularly called Dada Harir ki Vav. This Vav brings us to the early 16th century reign of Sultan Mehmood Begarah (1458-1511), the most outspoken among the Gujarat sultans. Bhai Harir Sultani was the superintendent of the royal harem and she had planned the Vav along with her mausoleum and mosque amidst a sparawling garden interspersed with fruit-bearing trees. The vav is reached through a flight of steps that remain uniform throughout the descent. The pool at the bottom leads to the shaft of the well which is divided by an arched doorway. Besides, there is a narrow spiral stairway leading to the well. Being a Muslim monument, it is bereft of figurative decorations, which have been replaced with floral motifs. The Hindu influence is evident from a few animal figures. Inscriptions in both Sanskrit and Persian tell us about the cost of construction which was 329,000 Mehmudis – gold coins of the Beghara era. Besides other details and obeisance to the Creator, the epigraph reads, "this well was built at a place where four roads meet, crowded with good men, who come from four quarters. As long as the moon and sun endure, may the sweet water of the well be drunk by all men". However, the water in this vav has dried up over the centuries.

Adalaj Vav, 18 kms from Ahmedabad, closely resembles Dada Harir Vav in its size and layout but is richer in ornamentation although it was built just prior to it. As per local legends, this step well is a commemoration of unrequitted love. Water can still be seen in the well and it is attributed to the living spirit of Rudha Devi, the beautiful wife of Veer Singh.

Helical Vav in Pavagarh is another interesting and unusual well attributed to Visvakarma Vastushastra where the entrance staircase leads to a spiral stairway which further culminates into the well. In face the spiral stairway gradually becomes the wall of the well and a timid soul should avoid these steps that make one dizzy with the sight of the water getting closer with each step. At Wankaner Palace one finds a more recent (1935) stepwell built in sandstone but worked out with a marble surface. It reflects the palatial outlook and the purpose was simply to provide a summer escape by lowering the temperature down below.

SHAHID AKHTER MAKHFI

STUPA

Most typical movement of Buddhist faith; consists domical mound, with sacred relics enshrined. Origins traced to mounds, raised over buried remains of dead, found in India, before rise of Buddhism. Regular architectural forms; mound provided with a parasol surrounded by miniature railing on top; raised on a terrace; whole surrounded by large railing consisting of posts, crossbars, coping – all secured by tenous in technique appropriate to craftsmanship in wood.

Along stupas, roofless shrines enclosing a sacred object as a tree as an altar erected; temples of brick, timber with domicle roofs constructed on plans that were circular. Structures perished, ideas of their shapes obtained from excavated foundations. Remains of structural building excavated at Bairat and Vidisa; wood and brick shrines with timber domes, and vaults existed. Eg a temple at Sanchi was apsidal in plan; perhaps had barrel – vault roof of timber.

Hall at Kumarahar Patna, had high wooden platform, on which stood eight rows of ten coloumns each, which supported a second story. Mauryan architecture had Iranian influence transformed substantially to suit Indian environment.

Stupas progressively large, more elaborate; railings initiate wooden construction, carved; eg. At Bharhut, Sanchi-II, Amravati; period with elaborate gateways consisting of posts supporting from one to three architreves. In due course, attempt, to give height to the stupas, by multiplying terraces that supported the dome, by increasing number of parasols on top.

In Gandhara, south eastern India sculptured decoration extended to stupa proper; drums, domes, railings, terraces decorated with figural, ornamental sculpture.

Large number of representational building – rich source of information; depicts walled cities with massive gates, elaborate multi-storied residencies, pavalions with a variety of domes; consistent use of arched windows, doors, important elements of architectural décor; All these found on relief sculpture sites of Barhut, Amravati, Sanchi and Mathura.

SUBRAHMANYAM CHANDRASEKHAR
(1910 - 1995)

Subrahmanyam Chandrasekhar, the internationally renowned astrophysicist whose youthful work on "White Dwarfs" in 1930 won him the Noble Prize for Physics in 1983, died of heart failure at the University of Chicago Hospitals on August 21, 1995. He was 84 and had spent 59 pears as a Faculty Member of the University of Chicago. His work ranged across Stellar Structure, Stellar Dynamics, Radioactive Transfer, Magnetohydrodynamics, General Relativity and Black Holes.

Subrahmanyam Chandresekhar was born at Lahore on October 19, 1910. His father C.S. Ayyar, a member of the Indian Audit and Accounts Service, was an authority on Grammar of Carnatic Music. And his uncle (his father's younger brother) was Sir S. V. Raman, the first Asian scientist to win the 1930 (Noble Physics Prize for his work on the "Scatering of Light".

Chandrasekhar's career as a Research Scientist began in the wake of a meeting he had with Arnold Sommerfield in 1928. This meeting which inspired him to write a celebrated paper – Compton Scattering and the Fermic Dinac Statistics – was mentioned in the Proceeding of the Royal Society of London in 1929. He secured record marks in the Physics Honours Course of the Madras University in 1930. These distinctions got him the Government of India Scholarship which was tenable at Trinity College. Cambridge, Chandrasekhar's career at Trinity College, Cambridge, was particularly distinguished for his distinctions include the Sheep Shanks Exhibition Prize and fellowship of Trinity College in 1933. But the year 1936 also marked his association with Yerkes Observatory and the University of Chicago for the rest of his life. And he was Morton D. Hull Distinguished Service Professor of Theoretical Astrophysics from 1952 to 1986, when he gained Emeritus Status.

Combining Einstein's Special Theory of Relativity and the then new Quantum Mechanic in 1930 – (Chandrasekhar was then 19 while voyaging through the Mediterranean Sea) he demonstrated that if the mass of the star exceeded a certain critical mass (greater than approximately 1.4 times of the mass of the sun) the star would not become White Dwarf. It would continue to collapse under the extreme pressure of gravitional forces. Sir Arthur Eddington was not able to grasp the far-reaching consequences of an elegant application of Einstein's Special Theory of Relativity, which was at the core of Chandrasekhar's discovery. The iron lay in the theory – subsequently known as the Chandrasekhar limit – had contributed to the mathematical underpinnings governing the astrophysics of Black holes as a logical extension of the General Theory of Relativity, which was verified by Eddington on 29th March, 1919. However, viewed in historical perspective it is clear that the Chandrasekhar limit had postulated the state of White Dwarfs as well as implied the existence of Neutron Stars and Black Holes.

In his well-known autobiography entitled a Mathematician's Apology Prof. G. H. Hardy – a great mathematician who was Ramaujan's mentor at Cambridge and a friend of Chandrasekhar (both of them were fellows of Trinity in the thirties argued that mathematics was a "young man's game" with Galois dying at 21, Abel at 27 and Ramanujan at 32.

But Chandrasekhar proved that mathematics is not necessarily a young man's game. In fact his famous style, known as the Chandrasekhar Style, enabled him to switch disciplines.

Chandrasekhar's creative career spanned nearly 67 years – from 1928 to 1995. His most recent work, Newton's principia for the common Reader, Oxford, 1995, reveals yet another facet of this mathematical genius – a reare sensibility which inspired him to translate the archaic mathematical languae of Newton's classic. The Principia into the idiom of modern mathematics. And in the process of translating this work in the modern mathematical idiom, Chandrasekhar had also made a major contribution to the history of ideas.

Adopting his famous style, when Chandrasekhar wold change his field of specialization, he would write the definitive work in that field at the end of each such period. His memorable volumes such as an Introduction to the Study of Stellar Structure (1939), principles of Stellar Dynamics (1942), Radiative Transfer (1950) Hydrodynamic and Hydromagnetic Stability (1961) and the Mathematical Theory of Black Holes (1983) had led to such distinctions as the 1944 fellowship of the Royal Society, the 1947 Admas Prize of Cambridge University, the 1953 Gold Medal of the Royal Astronomical Society, the 1962 Royal Medal of the Royal Society of London, the 1968 Padma Vibhushan Award of the Government of India, the 1983 Noble Prize for Physics and the 1984 Copley Medal of the Royal Society of London.

It is not only for his mathematical brilliance that Chandrasekhar was celebrated. He was even more celebrated. He was even more celebrated for his literary sensibility which was evident in such elegant pieces and expositions such as the Jawaharlal Nehru memorial lecture entitled Astronomy in Science and in Human Culture, the Oppenheimer lecture Einstein and General Relativity Historical perspectives, Beauty and the Quest for beauty in Science and Einstein's General Theory of Relativity and Cosmology. Furthermore, in his Shakespeare, Newton and Beethoven, Prof. Chandrasekhar says that "on reading Shelley's A Defense Poetry, the question instantly rises why there is not a Defense of Science written by scientist of equal endowmen? In trying to answer this question, one could think of at least three works – Whitehead's Science and the Modern World, G. H. Hardy's mathematician's Apology and chandrasekhar's own Truth and Beauty – a significant contribution to what C.P. Snow termed as the dialogue of the two cultures, Science and Literature.

Prof. S. Chandrasekhar will live alongside Kepler, Galileo Lenoardo Da Vinci, Newton, Einstein and Dirac in History's Hall of Fame. (Condensed)

RANGANATHAN

SUBRAMANIA IYER MUSIRI

(B. 1899) – Vocalist; Karnataka; film actor; studied with N.N.Iyengar, K.C. Iyer and Sabesa Iyer; honoured with title Sangeeta Kalanidhi by Madras Music Academy, Isai

Peraringar by Tamil Isai Sangam, Sangeet Natak Academy Award for Karnataka vocal music (1957) and elected its fellow (1968); court musician of Travancore and Devasthana Vidvan, Tirupati; formerly Principal, College of Music, Annamalai University and Central College of Karnataka music, Madras and Dean of Faculty of Fine Arts, Kerala University; disc recordings.

SUFI TRADITION IN PUNJAB

Sufi is a Persian word; it means "Pure" and it also referes to garment made of wool. The Sufis got their name from the loose woolen gowns they wore. Four Sufi sects were active in India, Namely Qadiri, Chishti, Suhravardi, Naqshabandi, From the 11th century onwards Sufism Filtered into Punjab – at that time the region extended from Peshawar to Delhi. By the 14th century they had a mass following. Lahore and Multan were their prominent centers.

The Sufis were an esoteric offshoot of Islam but that did not prevent them from assimilating the language, idioms and traditions of Hindu India in their parables and sermons. Thus, Islam, a religion born in Arabia, become "acclimatised" in India.

The Suhravardi cult could not establish its roots but the other three sects wee very popular. Sirhind became the center of the Naqshabandi sect. Even emperor Jahangir was awed by the popularity of Hazrat Mujaddid Alif Sani, the chief of the Naqshabandis. When Hazrat Mujaddid opposed Akbar's Din-e-Ilahi, the Afghans started looking upon him as their saviour and political leader. Jahangir imprisoned in the fort of Gwalior or suppress dissent but be had to release the saint in view of the violent reaction.

Protest against the Mughals became the prominent note of the Naqshabandis. Hazrat Adam Banuri, a disciple of Hazrat Mujaddid, alarmed Shahjahan by parading the strength of his disciples in Lahore; consequently, he was banished from India.

As the Naqshabandis were dead-set against the Mughals on the political level, they sided with the Sikh Gurus, it was due to the sympathy and affinity of the Afghans with the Sikhs that the Afghan Nawab of Malerkotla opposed the decision to wall up alive the sons of Guru Gobind Singh. In recognition of this, Banda Bahadur left the Dargah of the Hazrat and the garden around it unscathed when he levelled Sirhind.

There is reason to believe that Guru Gobind Singh was well acquanited with the Naqshabandis, certainly he was a master of Persian. It is likely that the prominence given to the sword in Sikhism and a accepting the Guru as supreme leader is a legacy of the Naqshabandis. Other prominent centers of the Naqshabandis were Jahankhelan in Hoshiarpur district and Jagraon In Ludhiana district. Jahankhelan was the seat of Hazrat Qadir Baksh and Hazrat Sain Mohkam Din lived in Jagraon.

Ghuram in Patiala district was a prominent center of the Chishtis. The seed of the Chisti sect was sown in Punjab by Hazrat Miran Bhik. Like the Naqshabandis, the saints of the Chishti order also endeavoured to create harmonious relations between Hindus and Muslims. Miran Bhik, for example, was devoted to Guru Gobind Singh. His prominent disciple, Hazrat Hafiz Musa, made the village of manakpur in Ropar district the center of his activity.

Hazrat Shah Khamosh, a prince of Hyderabad (Deccan) relinquished rank and comfort to sit at the feet of Hazrat Hafiz Musa. Shah Khamosh caused to be built the "Deccanion ki Masjid", and "Deccanion ki Haweli" and Deccanion ka bagh". The presence of these southern style structures make Manakpur unique in Punjab – although the dust of oblivion now lies thick upon them and the whole village.

The prominent centers of the Qadiri cult were Ludhiana and Batala. Hazrat Mohammad Fazili in Batala and Hazrat Sayyed Mohammed in Ludhiana were the prominent saints of this cult. It was the consequence of the endless effort of hazrat Fazili that a large community kitchen and an orphanage were established in Batala.

That Sufi philosophy was highly esteemed by the people of Punjab is seen from the inclusion of baba Sheikh Farid's poetry in the Guru Granth Sahib. Mian Mir who laid the foundation stone of the Darbar Sahib was also a Sufi. It was due to the influence of Sufism that the dyers of Machhiwara made Guru Gobind Singh "Uchch da Pir" to save his life although they had to hoodwink their own community to achieve this.

At the time of partition Punjab was totally mutilated and it was inevitable that the shady tree nourished by the life-blood of the Sufi saints was reduced to a stump... but the roots were so deep that it could not be completely killed. To this day Hindu and Sikh devotees visit the Dargahs of the Sufi saints to offer prayers.

Every Vaishnava devotee visiting the Vaishnava Math in Raikot (Ludhiana district) pays his obeisance to "Sain ka Takia" situated outside the abbey. In the same way, at Hathan (Sangrur Dsitrict) the 'dia' is not lit at the "Vaishnava Dwar" until the chiragh is lit at the grave of Hazrat Kamali, situated at the gate of the temple.

DR. NARESH

SUNIL GAVASKAR (1949)

What makes a great player stand out from an ordinary one is the ability to defy the law of averages. What makes a charismatic one is the courage to be himself. What has made Sunil Manohar Gavaskar, the archetypal opening batsman, is a combination of both. The Little Master's consistency was remarkable – he hardly ever had a lean trot in his 17 year international career. His historic 1971 debut in the Caribbean , where he scored 774 runs in just four Tests, marked him out as a batsman destined for greatness. It was a promise realised in full measure.

Among his records are the maximum number of Test centuries (34); becoming the first member of the 10,000 run club in Tests, the only player to score a century in each innings on three occasions; and the only Indian to score 1,000 runs in a calendar year thrice.

What Gavaskar lacked in flamboyance, he more than made up through determination, self-belief and concentration. He has been equally astute off the field, standing out as India's most successful player even in his post-cricketing days.

SURAJKUND CRAFTS MELA

Surajkund Crafts Mela held in the state of Haryana near Delhi has emerged as one of hest known cultural events in the country. In has been attracting thousands of domestic and foreign tourists for the past nine years, after it was launched as an annual fair. The 10th Crafts Mela held in Fabruary 1996 focussed on some of the finest handloom and handicrafts traditions of the country.

The Theme State of this Mela was Himachal Pradesh, a state with beautiful locations, traditional folk-craft and weaves, mountains, rivers, temples and a rich cultural heritage.

The Nicha Gate of Himachal Pradesh formed the master motif of the Crafts Mela. The Nicha Gate is monument with intericate carvings and elaborate tantric paintings aimed at warding off evil spirits from a village.

Every year a state is selected as the Theme State to highlight various attractions of that particular state. Besides crafts from other states are also exhibited.

The first Crafts Mela was started way back in 1987. The Theme State concept was started in 1989 and Rajasthan was the first such state.

The Surajkund Crafts mela provides an opportunity to witness some of the most fascinating aspects of folk theater in India. At the specially designed open-air-theater called 'Natyashala' artists from Zonal Cultural Centers perform before large gathering. Over the years, artists like Mallika Sarabhai, Sonal Mansingh, sharon Lowen, Prabha Bharti, Habib Tanvir, Manjit Bawa, Reshma of Pakistan, Teejan Bai and Gulabo have performed here.

L. K. BAKSHI

SURJIT AKRE : PAINTER OF EVERDAY LIFE

Post-independence India has produced many women painters who have established themselves nationally and internationally, and are a well-known name in the field of fine arts today. Akre Surjit, who has been painting for the last twenty years in one such painter. She has exhibited her works in most of the prestigious art galleries in India and has participated in several major exhibitions abroad.

She was born as Surjit Kaur in the small town of Taran-Taran in Punjab, she spent most of her life in Delhi where her parents migrated when she was quite young. Her keen interest in drawing and painting was not particularly liked or encouraged by her traditional parents, who wanted her to get married and settle down after finishing her studies. However, fate had willed otherwise; she was destined to be a famous painter.

The opportunity to fulfill her dream of becoming a painter was a godsend. As soon as she obtained a diploma in Commercial Art, her father was posted to Moscow and the family moved to the Russian capital. There she studied oil painting under Prof. V.N. Oreshnikov from 1977 to 1985 at the prestigious Repin Institute of Painting, Sculpture and Architecture. It is but natural that her works during this period shows a clear influence of Russian culture, environment and surroundings.

She held her first solo exhibition in St. Petersburg (Moscow) in 1985, and again in New Delhi in 1986 and 1989. In the last twenty years Akre Surjit has exhibited her work in most of the prestigious art galleries, holding several solo shows. Her paintings are in prestigious collections such as at the National Gallery of Modern Art, New Delhi.

National Museum, Chandigarh; and in the galleries of Air India, ONGC and Lalit Kala Academy, among others.

During her long career, Akre Surjit has painted nature profusely, done excellent portraiture and nude studies. Over the years, she has evolved her distinct style, full of rich texture, simple figures shorn of unnecessary detail. Her strong, uncluttered compositions effortlessly portraying the emotions, aspirations and frustrations of ordinary people around her, copying with their daily life and its problems. Being a woman and having herself faced several of those problems faced by ordinary Indian women in their daily lives, she is determined to raise and depict them through her medium of expression which she creates so effectively and sensitively in her paintings. Her distinct Indian content, style and use of hues is reminiscent of the most famous Indian name in this field – Amrita Shergil. (Condensed)

N. K. SAREEN

A SURVEY OF INDIAN ARCHITECTURE

A study of the evolution of architecture in ancient India would at once reveal that the symbolism and embellishments used in different monuments varied according to the requirements of the times.

Almost no monument found in India dates Prior to the Mauryan period. This is because prior to the mauryan times, the builders did not used stone, and their buildings did not survive for us to know, see and talk about, With the Mauryans, wood and stone came to be used extensively. The rockhewn shrines of the Barabar hills in Bihar, throne in the interior of Bodh Gaya, some portions of the stupa umbrella at Sanchi and Sarnath are all products of this period. The stupa, which was a burial mound to begin with, evolved into a revered structure. Emperor Asoka raised stupas in the honour of Lord Budha all over India.

In the Sunga period, architecture relied on stone and extended outside the boundaries of their empire. The rock cut architecture, started by the Buddhists to build cave retreats for their monks, was soon adopted by Jains and Hindus. In the south stand magnificent examples of rock cut temples at mammalapuram (also known as Mahabalipuram). These immense monolithic structures are carved out of a series of boulder-like granite rocks. On the sea coast, some fifty mile south of Chennai, one finds seventeen temples, none of them very large, carved from the outcropping hillocks of granite, built under the patronage of the 2nd century BC while the latest date to the 7th century AD. The splendid Sculpture and lovely frescoes adorning these caves make them one of the most glorious monuments of India's past. Even more impressive are the later cave temples of Ellora crowned by the mammoth Kailasnatha temple. The Elephanta cave – temples styled on the lines of the Ellora caves are famous for their sculpture, especially for the great trimurti (trimverate form) of Shiva. The cult of cave-temples spread far an wide, but it was under the Satvahanas that the largest artificial caves came to be excavated in western Deccan, at Ajanta. In fact, cave-temples and monasteries are to be found all along the route followed by Buddhism in its spread over India.

In Gupta period that followed, the brick temple architecture gained prominence. The flat roofed temples of the Gupta period evolved from the tradition of stupas and rock-cut temples, but used brick and stone for construction. This marked a new style of architecture that lasted for more than 400 years and is popularly known as the Indo-Aryan temple style. The general pattern is a tower with rounded top and curvilinear outline. The temples at Khajuraho, Madhya Pradesh, are fine examples of this style.

Historian distinguish between the Northern and Southern styles of temple architecture in India. Following the Northern styles, Orissa architects developed temple architecture to take it to new heights. With lavish exterior decoration and varvings, Orissa temples are built in a series of four halls; the Hall of Offering, the Hall of Dancing, the Assembly Hall and the sanctum sanctorum.

The Southern or Dravidian style usually takes the shape of a rectangular, truncated pyramid. The earliest ones are from the Pallave period (600-850 A.D.) Later on, in the Chola period (900-1150 AD), the art of temple building was perfected. The finest example is the Brihadeesware temple built by Rajaraja the Great (985-1014 AD.). Another masterpiece is the temple at Gangaikondacholapuram built by Rajendra I. The Brihadeeswara temple was probably the largest that was built in India at that time. This massive structure has been designed in such a way that its shadow does not fall on the ground at any given time of the day all round the year. And as if that is nothing, on the tower of the temple, 216 ft. high, rest the dome or kalas, made of black granite. This is estimated to weigh at least 80 tons; It is said that to get it to the top, a ramp was built from a village about four km away, running all the way to the top of the temple. The heavy Kalas was rolled up the ramp and placed on the tower.

The modest tower of the Pallava period was replaced by domed final. This marked the next phase of Southern style of temple architecture, culminating in the vision of beauty that stands at madurai, the Meenakshi temple. By now the Pandyan rulers had taken over. Gradually, however, influences traveled across the sub-continent and the diving line between the Northern and Southern style became rather thin.

The amalgamation of styles can be seen at the magnigicent ruins of Hampi, the capital of the old Vijayanagara empire. Peppered with brilliant decorative imagination, the Vijaynagar architecture combines the ornate Hoysala style of Karnataka with Pandyan features.

The Rajputs in north India combined the religious and the secular in their styles. They developed a distinctive style of architecture that blossomed into a magnificient schools by the 11th century AD.

With the beginning of invasions, northern India witnessed several distinctive style of arcitecture, brought in by te successive rulers. In Delhi, the Sultanate architecture is varied and distinct for the period of each dynasty. However, utilization of local mesons and craftsmen by the Turkish rulers led to a new fusion between the exterms

simplicity of Islamic architecture and the highly ornate Indian architectrure. Qutub Minar built by Qutubddin Aibak marks the beginning of this trend. The Tughlaks were great builders too, and the Tughalakabad fort, not in a state of ruin, is till aweinspiring. Their buildings were massive yet simple. They introduced the dome and the arch in Indian architeture.

This combination of two distinct styles gave rise to a very individual school sherein the different styles adapted them selves according to the new impetus.

The lodis (Sikander Lodi, 1451-1526 AD) introduced the concept of double domes built one upon the other, leaving some space in between. They have left behind the Lodhi Gardens in Delhi, housing the nausoleums of several kings, as their legacy.

The Mughals were also great builders and architects, as well as good planners of gardens. It was under the Mughals that architecture reached the painnacle of its glory and the process of synthesis between Islamic and Hindu architecture was completed. Some of the finest architectural creations belong to the Mughal period. Humayun's Tomb, the first important building of the Mughal period, is a fine example of synthesis of Indo-Persian traditions. Akbar developed a standard style with a pleasing balance of Indo-Islamic and Rajput styles, as in Fatehpur Sikri, Shah Jahan raised architecture to the level of poetry with lavish use of white marble and pietra dura work using semi- precious stones, creating the Wonder of the world –Taj Mahal his decision to shift the capital to Delhi brought about a flurry of construction activity in the city. He personally supervised the site on which the Red Fort stands today. Added to that, he built the Jama Masjid, the largest mosque in India today.

Synthesic of Islamic style of architecture can be seen in the monuments of the Ahmed Shah dynasty. Ahmed Shah, who was a convert to Islam, continued to use the styles of his ancestor, and adopted medieval Hindu and Jain styles of architecture, combining them with the dome and the pointed arches. The Jami Masjid at Cambay and Broach are the finest examples of this styles.

SUDHAMAHI REGUNATHAN

SVATI TIRUNAL

Swati Tirunal was the Maharaja of the erstwhile state of Travancore. He was a master of more than a dozen languages. He was a Padmanabha-dasa in the complete sense of the term. Besides being an able ruler with vision, he was an outstanding poet in Sanskrit, a connoisseur and patron of literature, music, dance, drama, sculpture and painting. He is, however, better known as a versatile 'Vaggeyakara' (composer) in several languages and forms of music, Kritis constitute the bulk of his musical works; the rest are Padam, Bhajan, Varnam, Svarajati, Tilana and the Hindustani musical forms of Dhrupad Khyal and Tappa. In addition, there are about 50 songs in his two Upakhyanas and one Prabandha.

As a part of the navarati celebrations, Svati Tirunal started the suctom of conducting music cencerts in the evening. These concerts were held in the Navarati Mandapa in the Fort Palace in Trivandrum. This practice continues to this day. He selected nine of his compositions for being Sung as the main item in each days concert and for this purpose, he assigned a kriti each for each day. These nine kritis are the famous Navaratri Kritis.

The Musicians elaborately render the assigned kriti – with raga alapana, tanam, and the kriti (including neraval and swaraprastara) and a layavinyasa on the percussion instrument(s). He died at the young age of 33.

SWAMI CHINMAYANANDA (1916-93)

Balakrishnan, who later came to be known as Swami Chinamayananda, was born in Ernakulam. After his schooling in Kerala, he joined Lucknow University for his master's degree in English literature.

Swami Tapovan Maharaj of Uttarkasi and Swami Sivananda were among the personalities who influenced Swami Chinmayananda in his spiritual walk. A world-renowned authority on the scriptures of India,. Specially the Bhagwad Gita and the Upanishads, he worked relentlessly for 40 years to bring about a spiritual revival in India. He organised a series of jnana Yagnas every year in prominent cities, beginning with Pune. He founded the Chinmaya mission, which is engaged in spreading the knowledge of Vedanta besides overseeing numerous cultural, educational and social service activities. He represented the Hindu religion at the Parliament of World Religions in September 1993 in Chicago. He wrote about 30 books dealing with religion.

The Yogi attained Mahasamadhi in San Diego, California.

SYAMA SASTRI

The period of the Musical Trinity of South India constitute the Golden Age of Karnatic music. Sangita Kavitvam or Musical reached the acme of perfection in their hands. Their composition are characterised by a new style, vigour and expressiveness. Each song of there is in a separate tune and they have analysed and presented the varied facets of ragas. Prior to their time, a composer wrote tens of Sahityas for one and the same tune. Amongst the Trinity Tyagaraja (1767-1847) was the most versatile and prolific and Muthuswamy Dikshitar (1776-1835) and Syama Sastri (1762-1827) though not so prolific, have enriched the repertoire of South Indian music with compositions of extraordinay beauty and charm.

Syama Sastri was a scholarly composer. He was held in great esteem by his two brilliant contemporaries Tyagaraja and Muthuswamy Dikshitar.

Syama Sastri's like those of this two brilliant contemporaries is full of colourful, thrilling and inspiring incidents. His short period of apprenticeship under the great Acharya, Sangita Swamy proved a blessing to him. It was from him that he learnt the secrets of the science of rhythm, its ramifications, and its employment in practical music. His apprenticeship under Panchimiriham Adiyappiah, the celebrated composer of the Viribona Verna (Bhairivi raga – Ata Tala) and the Guru developing a reverential regard for his disciple are thrilling to read. It is happened that one day as the disciple was conversing with

Adiyappiah, a bit of betel leaves juice slopped from his mouth and fell on the vastram (cloth) of the Guru. Syama Sastri felt a shudder at this act of sacrilage on his part and ran to fetch a pail of water of cleanse and remove the stain from the cloth of his Guru. Adiyappiah stopped his pupil from cleaning his cloth and said "This is Devi's anugraham" (blessing). I have been only waiting from this for a long time".

Though Syama Sastri was younger than Adiyappiah by 32 years still the fact that he was a devotee of Devi and had received her blessings was a powerful factory in making Adiyappiah develop towards his disciple a regard bordering on reference.

The historic musical context between Syama Sastri and Bobbili Kasavayya and how the former sang a pallavi in Sarabhanandana tala as a counter to the Pallavi in Simhananda Tala sung by Kesavayya and emerged victorious are fascinating to read. Sarabhanandana Tala comes to be known for the first time through his Pallavi. An avatara of this tala takes 19 ¾ matras or 79 aksharakalas. Besides some of the shadsangas like the drutavirama, laghu virama, laghu druta and laghu druta virama figures amongst the 24 angas of this tala.

Syama Sastri was a high creative artist. His composition are of sterling worth. They are in common raga like Todi, Dhanyasi, Bhairavi, Kambhoji, Sankarabharanam and Kalyani and in uncommon ragas like Kalagada, Karnataka, Kapi, Manji and Chintamani. He had adopted an attractive style in his kritis his sahityas are principally in Telugu and a few are in Sanskrit and Tamil.

He is the architect of the musical form Svarajati. This was originally a dance form. Sastri converted it into an attractive musical form by eliminating jati passages. His three svarajatis Rave Himagiri Kumari (Todi raga – Adi tala); Kamakshi anudinmu (Bhairavi Raga - Chapu Tala) and Kamakshi in Padayugame (Yadukulakambhoji raga-chapu tala) stand unparalleled both for the delineation of the raga bhava and the fecundity of the musical ideas. In the Bhairavi Svarajati the commencing notes of the eight charnas will be found to be in the ascending order of pitch: sa, ra, ga, ma, pa, dha, ni· and sa. He has incidentally illustrated herein the nature of the arohana sthayi paddhati of raga alapana... In the Yadukulakamboji Svarajati, the last tarana is concluded with a makutam (crown-like ending) of three phases of variable magnitude: Khanda (5), Misra (7) and Sankirna (9) R G S / M G R S N D P / M G R S N D P M G. This entirely complex grouping fits in very nicely into the texture of the composition and forms a fitting finale. These three svarajatis form a ratna trayam (3 gems).

Sastri has given the modern shaping to the Anadabhairvi raga. Anandabhairavi raga is an old raga. There are folk tunes and also lullabies in it. A persual of the medieval compositions in Anandabhairavi will reveal the fact that many strange phrases which are now considered taboo occur in them. The Gita 'Kamala Sulochana' contains many Arsha prayogas i.e. phrases which will no more be considered as appropriate for Anandabhairavi. Bhadrachala Ramadas has also introduced in one of his songs in Anandabhairavi raga, the phrase sa ri ga ma ga ri sa in the tara styai. Ramaswamy Dikshitar, the father of Muthuswamy Dikshitar, has introduced the Prayoge pa ri sa in the Chtta Swarga to his

Kriti Amba ni Saranamu Jochchiti. Paidala Gurumurthi Sastri has introduced the phrase P N N S in his gita Pahi Sri Ramachandra in his raga. Syama Sastri steered clear of the track and gave the picture of Anandabhairavi as it ought to be with the emergance of the raga Abheri, the phrase pa ni sa has no place in Anandabhairavi. Syama Sastri's kritis (-) oh; Jagadamba (2) Pahi Sri Giri Raja Sute (3) Mariveregati and (4) Himachalatanaya Brochuta and the Varna Samini Rammnav, Sarasakhi Ivele" (Ata tala) are splendid composition in this raga and mirror to us the varied and colourful aspects Anandabhairvi. Anandabharivi has been considered as his sotthu i.e. a shis property. The polished nature of his music is one of the attractive freatures of his compositions. Some of his compositions apart form their high entertainment value have also a lakshana value. In the art of composing swara Sahityas, Sasrti stands without a parallel.

He delighted in incorporating rhythmical beauties in his compositions. There is not even the slightest suggestion of any artificial element in the introduction of those rhythmical beauties. The key phrase in the field of rhythm is Ta tim gina tom, a phrase of the magnitude of 5 aksharakalas. The kriti 'Meenalochana Brove' in Dhanyasi raga and which belongs to the group Navaratnamalika starts after the pause of a Ta Tim Gina Tom. This is a very unusual feature in a musical composition. In his kritis, we find many words constituted of 5 syllables, (Ta dhingi na tom) and coming off naturally. As examples of such words may be mentioned (1) Anudinamu (2) Sarasamukhi (3) Japamudanu (4) Durusuganu (5) Tarunamishi (6) Krupasalupu (7) Varamosagu (8) Machimalanu (9) Saranamani (10) Padayugame (11) Pogadutaku (12) Kamalayuga (13) Samayamidi (14) Gatiyanuvenu (15) Mahima-vini (16) Kamalamukhi.

Syama Sastri has popularised the Viloma type of Chapur tala. The normal Chapur tala takes the sequence 3 plus 4. His composition Mari Vere Gati in Anandabhairavi is in his normal Chapur tala. The viloma Chapur tala takes the sequence 4 plus 3. His Composition Ninu Vinaga mari in Purvakalyani Raga and Triloka Mata Nannu in Pharaz raga are very good examples.

He has composed a few kritis which are suggestive of two rhythms. That means the composition can be reckoned in either of those two rythms and without loss of musical effect. It is, however, clear that one of the rhythms was intended as the inherent rhythm and the other as the suggestive rhythm. The inherent rhythm is the Sthapita Tal Tala and the suggestive rhythm is the Suchita tala. Taking the composion Samkari Samkuru in Saveri raga as an example, the Rupaka tala will be the Sthapita tala of this song and Adi tala (Tisra Gati) will be the Sachita tala of this song. That the compose intended both these rhythms is clear from the fact, that the Pallavi and Anupallavi conform to the Rupaka Tala on their very face both these rhythms is clear. From the fact that the Pallavi and Anupallavi conform to the Rupaka tala on their very face and the Caharan confirms to the Adi tala (Tisra Gati) in equally clear manner.

No other composer has composed songs answering to the rhythmical beauties referred to above. It is no wonder that this illustrious contemporary Tygaaraja had a great regard for him.

Svaraksharas occur in many places in his kritis. Svarakshara is the beauty signified by the concluence of the svara syllable and the identical or like-sounding syllable in this sahitya. It is structural beauty. This is a dhatu-matu-samyukta alankara. As examples may be mentioned the following :

(1) In the Kriti Devi Brova Samayamide in Chintamani raga in the first charana we find the phrase: Nidosudu gada. Herein Nida is the svarakshara part.

(2) In the Kambhoji Kriti Devi ni,
In the phrase Padasarasa Padasa occurs as svarakshara Atita-anagata complexities are also seen his kritis.

(Condensed)

P. SAMBAMOORTHY

"T"

T. RUKHMINI

(T. Rukhmini plays perfect tunes on her violin and also sings as this gives her a total synthesis of tune and rhythm)

T. RUKHMINI showed an extraordinary interest in dance and music at a very tender age. She could pick up perfect tunes or perform intricate dance steps while she listened to the radio. Encouraged by her parents and brothers, she developed on interest in the violin. She took preliminary lessons from 'vidwan' R.R.Kesavamuthy. Further embellishments came through advanced training under Dr. Semmangudi Srinivas Iyer and the violin maestra Sri Lalgudi Jayaraman. She preferred singing along with the violin as this gave her a total synthesis of tune and rhythm.

The first major concert that is always fresh in her memory is that of the violin support she gave to the flute maestro late Sri T.R. Mahalingam at the town hall, Bangalore when she as just 16. Ever since she had been providing violin support to almost all leading 'vidwans' and 'vidhushis' like Semmangudi, Chembai, Mali, M. S. Subbulakshmi, D. K. Patta Mal and M.L.Vasanthakumari to name a few.

She started practising vocal music alongside so as to enable her to provide appropriate violin support at vocal music concerts. This led to full fledged vocal concerts on the public platforms and over AIR. To improve her vocal music she took futelage under the doyen of Carnatic music Sri Srinivasa Iyer. Today she is an 'A' class AIR vocal artist and has participated in several national programmes, music conference and sung on Doordarshan.

She has been felicitated with many awards and titles. She received the first prize in instrumental music at the Youth Festival in 1954 and won the music Academy Awards five times. The title of 'Tantrivilas' was conferred on her by the Sur-Singer Samsad in 1983 and the 'Kalaimani' award by the Tamil Nadu Eyal Isai Nataka Mandram in 1992.

She has travelled widely in the US and Europe on concert tours giving support to great ' vidwans'. She is the first woman to have accompanied the great T.R. Mahalingam for his recitals. She was invited to Paris by D' Autome where she provided violin support to D.K. Jayaraman, D.K. Pattammal and Yesudas.

T. Rukhmini stands apart from other musicians in certain aspects. A science graduate, she has a certain refinement which comes from years spent buried in books. When she was a child she remembers travelling to concerts along with her books. She led a highly productive disciplined life where her violin practice and studies co-existed under the watchful and protective eye of her parents – who finally groomed her to became a musician of high caliber.

N. C.

TABO : AJANTA OF THE HIMALAYAS

Tabo has invariably been described as the Ajanta of the Himalayan region since time immemorial. This adage is true in more ways than one. The interiors of the famed temple and Monastry to Tabo are profusely embellished with wall paintings and sculptures. The thematic content, as at Ajanta, is Buddhist. However, Tabo is not a rock-cut structure. In these remote parts, ordinary clay is a widely used construction material for all kinds of structures, sacred as well as dwelling units from a distance, the Tabo chos-khor enclosed within a wall enclosure convery the impression of cluster of ordinary buildings. No one can ever imagines that they house such a stupendous treasured-trove of paintings, sculptures and illuminated manuscripts. The sole credit for their preservation goes to the monks who like there.

According to prevailing tradition, this monastery site, located in the Spiti valley, owes its existence like many others in Kinnaur, Lahul-Spiti and Ladakh, to the famous Buddhist monk Richen-bzangpo, commonly referred to as the Great Translator (Lotsava). In the book under review, the author has challenged this widely held belief based on inscriptions from the temple itself. Klimburg-Salter surmises clearly that the sacred structure was founded by Ye-Shes-od, the Tibetan king, as per one inscription and renovated forty-six years later, according to a second inscription.

In ancient times, i.e. from 10th – 16th Century A.D. the Poo Thsil (district) of Kinnaur, Lahul-Spiti and Ladakh formed part of what was known as the western Tibetan empire. Before the advent of Buddhism, the tribal inhabitance of these areas had their own religious practices and rituals. In spite of the official religion, Buddism, they continued to practice the same rituals besides worshipping the Buddha. This is affirmed by a portrait of a Goddess belonging to the pre-Buddhist era, which still survices one one of the walls of the Tabo monastery, where she figures along with her retinue.

The trail to Tabo and other Buddhist sites was blazed by A.H.Francke in the first decade of the present century and then by Giuseppe Tucci in the 1930s, and many scholars have since raised their pens to write about these monasteries tucked away in not-so-inaccessible remote Himalayan valleys. Salter, too, has devoted 18 years to this brilliant expose and her publication coincides, more or less, with the centennary celebrations at Taboo (1996).

The seven chapters in the book unfold the artistic mystery of this shrine in a most competent manner. The first few pages contain useful information for those interested in visiting Tabo. The introductory chapter sheds a revealing light on the geo-political or historical setting. Before discussing analytically the pictorial and sculptural wealth lying hidden inside the monastery, Salter devotes a chapter to analyze the proposed chonology for the first one hundred years of this valuable structures. For this, she explores the evidences furnished by epigraphs, archaeology and art history. She first critically examines the paintings and the cells sculptures of clay. The immense significane of the earliest paintings and sculptures lies in their Kashmiri style. This is curious, for images in Kashmiri style are also available at other Buddhist temple in this region. The core chapter contains exhaustive and enriching imputs by Salters's colleagues. An interesting chapter highlights the textile designs. Parallels have been drawn to numerous Buddhist temples and monasterirs that lie on the way to Taboo. If one chooses to go via Kinnaur, The Poo tehsil, Nako, Charang and numerous unheard-of hamlets have temples and monasteries richly decorated with wall paintings and shelter remarkably well-preserved sculptures in wood, bronze and clay some in pure Kashmiri style. For those interested in Epigraphy and history of the western Tibetan Empire. There are two chapters at the end.

In spite of the repainted images and repairs undertaken time and again to preserve the Taboo monastery in good shape, the wall paintings and the clay sculptures have remained more or less in their original, Printine glory.. Besides the resident monks who have played an active and vital role in the conversation of these precious paintings and sculptures, Nature has had its own hand. The dry and cold climate of Spiti valley has been largely responsible for preventing them from decaying and vanishing.

The volume under review will remain a kind of milestore, an invaluable chapter in the glorious history of the artistic heritage of the western Himalayas.

SUBHASHINI ARYAN

TALAT MAHMOOD

May 9, 1998, will go down as a sad day in the history of Indian Music, as it was on this day when the man with a golden voice, Talat Mahmood, passed away.

Talat Mahmood's keen interest in music was evicent from his childhood itself, although his father was strongly opposed to his becoming a singer. Ultimately, defying all odds, he went ahead to pursue his passion and took proper coaching in this field.

A stroke of luck took him to Calcutta and when he was just 20, his first song "Tasveer teri dil mera behla na sakegi" (Your picture alone will not be enough to gladden my heart) was recorded. This proved and instant hit and took Talat to unprecedented heights of fame. He never looked back after that.

The 50s were the age of melody for the Hindi films. Music directors competed with each other in producing lilting numbers. During this period, Talat held his away as the most outstanding male playback singer. Who can forget those memorable melodies from "Aarzoo", "Anhonee", "Footpath", "Patita", "Shikast" and "Taxi Driver". There was something wonderful and haunting about Talat's voice.

Although Talat sang for all the top heros of those days, but somehow his voice was uniquely suited to the screen's tragedy hero Dilip Kumar. When Talat sang for Dilip Kumar number like "Koi nahin mera iss duniya mein" (I do not have anyone in this world to call my own) (Daag), ("Sham-e-gaam ki kasam" (I swear by the sad evening) (Footpath), "Mera jeevan saathi bichad gaya" (I have been separated from my life partner) (Babul), "Yeh hawa, yeh raat, Ye chandni" (what a breeze, what a moonlight nigh) (Sangdil), it appeared as if time had stood still.

Dilip Kumar himself had once remarked that the became the "Tragedy King" because of Talat's voice. In Dilip Kumar's words, Talat was not only a great singer but a gentle, cultured and sophisticated being His

contemporary, Manna Dey on his first meeting with Talat said that at the very first sight he became jealous of Talat as he was not only having a golden voice but had an equally charming personality. Very few people know that President Nasser of Egypt and King Zahir Shah of Afghanistan were his fans.

Talat worked with all the top music directors of his time like Naushad, Sajjad Hussain, Shankar-Jaikishan, S.D.Burman, Khayyam and Salil Chaudhary. He was awarded "Padma Bhushan" for his artistic endeavours.

Talat Mahmood also acted in a few films like "Lawaris", "Dil-e-Nadaan", "Ek Gaon Ki Kahani", "Malik" and "Sone Ki Chidya". But there was indeed something heavenly about his voice.

SHUBHA

TAMASHA

Marathi stage till middle of 19th century imbued with national awareness, historical playes of Mahratta heroes from Shivaji downwards written and presented, banned by alien government, Marathi dramatists invented subtle devices, ideas put in allegorica: fantasics or farcical domedies. Tamasha, an indigenous form of folk dance-cum-drama, exempt from pre-censorship, a medium to convey what was probifited on convertional urban stage, informed by subtle political propoganda, it fired rural India with a longing for freedom.

TAMTAS OF ALMORA

Metal and fire-tools and hands---- serious faces bent over work, Tamtas of Almora renowned for their skill with copper, along with bronze and gold, find mention in the earliest Vedic text, the Rig Veda. As such Hinduism attaches sanctity to copper utensils. Tamta is a corruption of the word "tamrakara" meaning coppersmith.

Almora is situated on the Himalayan ranges running through western Uttar Pradesh. It was the cultural and political capital of the Chand rulers of Kumaon, the region that today comprises the districts of Nainital, Almora and Pithoragarh.

Copper mines were a major source of revenues for the Kumaori Kings. Tamtas claim their ancestors came from Rajasthan during the reign of the Chand rulers. There seems to be some substance in the claim because copper is mined presently in only two other places in India, Ghatshila in Bihar and Khetri in Rajasthan.

A Tamta household throbs with activity throughout the year. Their workshops lie sprinkled in Tamturea, the colony of coppersmiths. They make vessels of all shapes and sizes. Very simple hand-made tools liketongs, hammers and cutters are used in the craft.

At Tamtura the workday starts early in the morning and continues late into the evening. Like in other hill communities, women play an important role here too. Along with doing household chores they go to forest to gather bakhet, the bark of pine used as fuel in the furnace.

Tamtas are gradually adapting to the changing market patterns. While previously their art had more or less religious overtones, it is now getting increasingly secularised.

Water filters, flasks and vessels bear out this change. Water filters and flasks have been a hit for water stored in a copper container is considered good for digestion. (Condensed)

MANISH PANT

TEEJANBAI

The rhythmic movements, spontaneity of action and effortless emotive rendering characterises Teejan Bai's "enactment" of the epic Mahabharata. Although this epic has been the subject of innumerable adaptations, both of the celluloid and on stage, Teejan Bai through her Pandwani Style has lent a totally new dimention to its dramastic narration. Pandwani is a ballet from of singing in which the performer "enacts" the scenes and events from Mahabharata to the accompaniment of Music.

Teejan Bai's inimitable rendering in both verse and prose of the great Indian epic has won her accolades not only in India but the world over. The strumming of her 'ektara', the shuffling of her feet, the rustle of the saree, the gestures and grimaces add lusture to her solo shows. She has performed in Festivals of India's in Switzerland. Moscow and Paris where she mesmerized the audiences who were simply enchanted by her movements and gestures, even though they did not understand a word of what she was singing.This speaks volumes about her unique style.

Teejan is a born singer and here first training was provided by her maternal grandfather, Brijal Pardhi, who himself was a folk singer of repute in the Chattisgarh region of Madhya Pradesh. "I used to hear my grandfather and would try to copy him. I do not exactly remember when I started singing but my first stage appearance was when I was fifteen, in a village near Durg. I performed for 18 days continuously. It was the beginning. Then started going from village singing devotional songs".

Her big break came when she was invited by the former Prime Minister, the late Mrs. Indira Gandhi, to perform in Delhi. Since then she has not looked back.

While on stage she plays her "Tambhura" which she uses as "Bhima's gada" (Mace) or the "Bow of Arjuna", as the scene demands. She effortlessly transforms, in just a matter of seconds, from projecting the coyness of Draupadi to the extreme anger of Bhima (Mahabharata characters). Since here is a one woman theatre, every part of the body and every contour of her face tellingly convey the message she wants to convey to her audience, derived from the different episodes of the epic.

She is now employed as an artist by the Steel Authority of India (SAIL) at its Bhillai plant, so that she can continue with her efforts to keep her art from alive. (Condensed)

TEEVRA SHARMA

TEMPLE FOR GANESHA

There are very few temples in this country dedicated to Ucchishta Ganapati. At Tanjavur in Tamil Nadu, there is a separate temple for this deity at Srinivasapuram built by a scholar in Tamil and Sanskrit who turned a sanyasin in his last years.

The construction of this temple is unique in many respects. The supporting deities are placed around the central figure in the sanctum sanctorum so that they occupy the position of their respective places in the Ganesa Yantram. In the inner circles are placed the Saptha Mathas – Brahmi, Maheshwari, Kaumari, Vaishnavi varahi, Indrani and Chamundi. The outer ring are installed the Ashta Digpalakas, Durga, Sanga Nidhi and padma Nidhi at the gate posts as Dwarapalakas, under each is placed the respective Yantra of the deity.

It is said that long ago there was an Asura (Demon) named Vidavan. He was very proud of his learning and intelectual powers and instead of seeking new knowledge and peace which are the aims of learning, he sought power. He wished to conquer the world but realized that the Devas, who were powerful and immortal, would oppose such a move. He decided as a first step to perform the difficult penance to Laord Brahma and get from him the boon of immortality.

On the solpes of the Himalayas, he did penance for many years. Brahma appeared before him and asked him for any boon he desired. The Asura demanded immortality which was refused. The Asura thought for a moment and carefully chose a boon, and asked Brahma that his slayer may be one who, with his consort, appeared before an assembly without any clothing and conquered him in a disputation. Brahma granted him the boon without, perhaps, realising the motive of the demon.

Having got the boon, the demon began to act in ruthless manner. The Devas went to Brahma and asked him to withdraw his boon. But Brahma pleaded his inability to do so. They all went to Shiva who directed them to Vishnu.

Vishnu suggested that an Yagna be performed to create a couple who could undertake the task of killing the demon as per the boon of Brahma.

A big Yagna was performed on the slopes of the Vindhya Hills. The great Trimurtis Siva, Vishnu and Brahma took part in it. From the sacrificial fire too celestial beings arose with brilliance and power equalling the light of ten million suns. One had the head of an elephant with four hands holding various weapons and the other was a female (Devi) in brilliant blue colour. Lord Siva prayed of the former that he should be his son. The great Sage Matanga prayed to the Devi that she be his adopted daughter and be called Neela Saraswathy.

The Devas, now jubillant that the end of their troubles was in sight, explained to the celestial beings their plight. The marriage of these two was celebrated in the Ocean of Milk. Lord Ganapati directed that an assembly may be convened and the Asura be asked to be present for the disputation.

The Asura was informed of this. He immediately understood that his end was drawing near. He went to the assembly hall trembling. There was a blaze of light so intense in its brilliance that no one in the assembly could bear it and every one had to close his eyes. The Asura also felt his eyes blinded, his tongue-tied and his limbs trembling with fear. Lord Ganesa with his weapons hit the Asura and he fell with a shriek. When the Devas heard the shriek, they knew that the demon was dead.

They prayed to Ganesa to reduce his brilliance so that they could worship him. Lord Ganesa with his consort agreed to withdraw the brilliance to a kind light and blessed the Devas and promised that whenever they prayed to him, he would remove all their troubles.

Hence the figure of Ucchishta Ganapati came into existence and although very rare, there are stone images in ancient temples built by the Pallavas and Cholas in remote corners. A temple for this deity alone in the sanctum sanctorum is very rare.

The temple at Srinivasapuram is situated in Giri Road, Tanjavur, just a couple of kilometers from the Bus Stand. Nearby is the Santhashramam where the Swamiji resided and directed the daily rituals in the temple.

N. RAMAKRISHNA

TEMPLE JEWELLERY OF TAMIL NADU

Tamil Nadu is not only famous for its charming country-side but also for its beautiful temples and glittering jewellery that adorns the womenfolk since time immemorial. They are very fond of studded jewellery, especially diamonds, rubies and emeralds studded in gold or silver and gold-plated ornaments. There are four different kinds of workmanship widely prevalent in Tamil Nadu. There are known as embossed or "Repousse" work, Gem setting, Crustari or Crustation of semi-precious stones and beads prepared with gold, silver, glass, pearls, precious and semi-precious stones.

Tamil Nadu has a rich selection of armlets, neck jewellery, hand jewellery and jewellery which adorns fingers, toes, hands, waist, hair, nose, ears and feet. The traditional names are Nettippatam for forehead, Thirukkupoo for knotted hair, Jimiiki and Mattal for ears, Oddi-yaanam (Odyan) for the waist and Tharivala and Kattikkapu for hand. Among neck ornaments, coin necklace, mango garland, addigai and long necklaces with very artistic and beautiful pendants are very popular. All necklaces have a central hanging (Padakam) in various shapes such as the peacock, swan, lotus, garuda, parrot, snake and other birds and floral designs with a pearl edging.

Nattippattam, Jimiiki, Mattal, odyan, Thirukkupoo, Tharivala and many other types of ornaments, along with Surya-Prabha and Chandra Prabha used by the Devadasis (Temple dancers), are now used by the Bharata Natyam dancers. This traditional jewellery is also known as "Temple Jewellery". The origin and significance of temple jewellery go back to the earliest times when Devadasi system came into vogue. The development of the Temple Jewellery was concomitant with the evolution of the Devadasi system and the dance styles.

Devadasi, literally meaning a servant of god, was a dancer who was married to the god. As she was the wife of the god, she was supposed to adorn herself with traditional jewellery made with precious and semi-precious stones set in gold leaf. Her hair was made into a single long braid and decorated with flowers or gold jewellery.

"Surya – Prabha" and "Chandra – Prabha" is set just behind the Nettipattam, a forehead ornament. This jewellery is striking with the white and red shining against the black hair. Jewelley enhances the personal charm of the Devadasi.

The coloured precious and semi-precious stones of temple jewellery have a symbolic meaning. Red, with its Many hues, is symbolic of love and belongs to Lord Brahma, the creator of the Universe. White stands for purity, truth and knowledge. It is also the colour of Lord Shiva.

Yellow, which reflects spring time and the fertility of rich harvest, is the colour of Lord Vishnu, the protector of the Universe. This colour being the colour of gold, also symbolizes the goddess Lakshmi, bestower or health, wealth and prosperity. Generally, in temple jewellery, rubies and diamonds are studded in gold – a synthesis of the red, white and yellow- the representation of Lord Brahma, Lord Shiva, and Lord Vishnu.

The motifs of flower and birds that are used in pendants also have symbolic meanings. Parrot is said to be the vehicle of Kamadeva – the God of love and passion and represents romanticism. Among the flowers, lotus is very popular. This flower spreads out its petals at dawn and therefore it symbolizes the sun and the universe.

BIMLA VERMA

TEMPLE OF MARTANDA – (KASHMIR)

In the early and medieval history of Kashmir, religious fervour among rulers and subjects seems to have been very strong. Different faiths were patronised by the rulers. Buddhism, Vaishnavism, all flourished.

There are instances when undeterred by narrow religious considerations, kings and queens have patronized different faiths, other than their own, and bilt temples for them.

Foremost among them is the temple at a village – Ranbirsingh pur called the temple of Martanda, dedicated to the Sun God.

Kashmir kings had always shown great reverence towards the sun God. The magnificent temple of Martanda stands on a hillock overlooking the valley. The grandeur and majesty of the structure matches the view it commands.

It is a massive structure with thick walls and the row of fluted pillars gives it an impressive appearance. The sculptures on the pillars, though bold and heavy, are still beautiful. The main shrine and a vast courtyard must have been surrounded on all sides by smaller shrines. A tank has been excavated in the courtyard in front of the central shrine. During excavation large posts were also unearthed. A Siva lingam in two pieces also came to light. There was excellent provision for drainage inside the temple. Gold, silver and copper images had been housed in the temple.

There are some interesting episodes connected with this temple. One of the kings, Kalasa by name, in an inexplicable mood removed and destroyed the copper image of Surya (sun), called Tamraswamin from this temple. Later, he repented and fearing the fury of Surya, he took refuge in this temple and also offered a gold image by way of propitiation.

King Harsa of Kashmir who belonged to the Lohara dynasty, is remembered in history for his destruction of temples and images of gods. Even he who was so thorough in his acts of destruction spared two divine images. One was the image of Ramaswamin of Srinagar and the other was the main image of Surya Vishnu of this famous temple of Mardanda.

(Condensed)

KOMALA VARADAN

TEMPLES AND SHRINES

Perpetual flames and snow , abundance of sandstone and deodar wood , heavy rains in certain areas and yet no rain in others , settlement of half dozen of centuries in between , founding of principalities by Rajput adventurers from Rajasthan, contacts with the Mughal Durbar, Vaishnava revival in art in the eighteenth and nineteenth centuries , Nadir Shah invasion of Delhi in 1739 which pushed some master painters from there to the patronage of the hill chieftains, spells of Kashmiri rule in the eigth and eleventh centuries in some of its western parts, contiguity to Tibet , Maharaja Ranjit Singh's devotion for Jawalamukhi and Kangra temples , deification of dead ancestors and personification of natural forces have resulted in rich diversity in temple forms, functions and decorations in Himachal Pradesh.

CAVE TEMPLES

Percolating water in a limestone hillside at Tilokpur on the Dharamsala- Pathankot road has created a natural cave with a stalagmite and a stalacite. The stalagmite is regarded as a Swayambu Shiva Lingam and the cave temple of shiva. Near the stalagmite is a small image of Shiva with the Ganga flowing down from it's matted hair.

A man-made scoop at Chakmoh, eighty four miles from Dharamsala, is worshipped as the original temple of Baba Balak Nath commonly known as Doet Sidh (the Sidh of the lamp).

It is said that Baba Balak Nath , when persued by Jogis, disappeared in this hollow. A fire (dhuna) is kept constantly smouldering in it. Numerous Doet Sidh Shrines with or without a sloping shed on them lie scattered in lower Himachal. Doet Sidh padukas (stone slab inscribed with a trishul between two footprints) representing Baba Balak Nath are placed inside them.

INDIGENOUS PENT- ROOFED TEMPLES

The earliest shrines, which are most numerous, are dedicated to male and female family and tribal ancestors ('Jathere','Jatherian','Kuljan') and objects of nature. Most of the temples of gods and goddesses ('Devghars', 'Deohar' and Dehars') in inner Himachal fall under this category.

They are pent-roofed structures. They vary from ordinary sheds covered with grass, reed or local tiles to three-storeyed substantial structures roofed with slates or Pine-fir shingles.

Village temples of Lahaul have sloping roofs with trifoliated pediments. They are the remnants of the old Mundari temples which the Mundari inhabitants of the area constructed before they were supplanted or suppressed by the Mongoloids.

SNAKE – BITE CURE SHRINES

Scions of Rajput houses from Rajasthan who established their ruling dynasties in Himachal brought along with them the worship of Guga, a twelfth century Chauhan houses in lower hills. Guga, his sister Gugri and Guru Gorakhnath and companions are represented as horse-mounted persons in stone or clay.

Snake-bite cure earth and water is the chief feature of Guga shrines. Others which offer this treatment are at Nagni Nurpur and at Shibo-Ka-Than and Tripal near Bharmar and Jawalamukhi Road stations on the Kangra valley Railway.

In Central Himachal, the sloping roofs of such temples are either straight at their ends or curved. Wooden bobbins hand from their vaves and look like tassels. Timber-bonded stone walls, in which there are alternating layers of stone and deodar wood, are quite common. There roof rests on wooden posts and this makes the verandah or the circumambulatory path round the sanctum cello.

In Pangi temples, the wooden sleeper roof is sloping on both the front and the back and an iron trident is stuck at its top. A large number of bells hang in front of the verandah. Brass vessels are pegged to the ridge-piece of the roof of Shririgul temple on Churdhar in Sirmur.

A substantial portion of these temples in Middle and Higher Himachal is made of deodar wood which has always lured carvers to show their deft workmanship on it.

Bigger temples have many functionaries in proportion to the resources and respect they command. Important among them, in a Kulu temple for example, are the Kardar (manager,) the Pujari (priest) the Gur (oracle or interpreter of the god), the Bhandari (watchman), Jathali(messanger), musicians, load-carriers, flower men, torch carriers, standard-bearers and blacksmiths.

Musical instruments, god's masks and his 'rath'(palanquin or chair in which the god is carried) are kept in the temple stores.

He-buffaloes, rams and he-goats are offered as sacrifices to the presiding deities. Horns of the sacrificed animals are hung round the Chamunda temple door at Devi Kothi (Chamba).

BIJLI MAHADEV

A sixty .feet high white mast in front of the Bijli Mahadev temple in Kulu attracts lightning which strikes the Shiva lingam inside the temple and shatters it to pieces. The priest then collects these pieces and places them in position by rubbing them with parched barley and butter. This joins them in such a way as to give the impression that the lingam was never broken. This is said to happen once a year.

CHAMBA WOODEN MASTERPIECES

The best representatives of the pent roofed temples are those of Laxna Devi at Bharmour, Shakti Devi. at Chhatrabari and Kali Devi at Mirkula (all in Chamba Distt.). The Shakti Devi and the Laxna Devi temples belong to the later Gupta period and were constructed during the region of Raja Meru Varma (c. 680 A.D.) of Chamba. The Mirkula temple was constructed by Queen Surya Mati of Raja Anant Dev (1028 – 1063 A.D.) of Kashmir.

Their fame rests on the exquitist work-manship of the carvings done on their pediments, doorsides, roof-panels and Pillars in Gandhra and Kashmiri Styles (Mikkula being in the purely Kashmiri form). The subjects carved include flying gandharavas, navgrahas, river goddesses Ganga and Yamuna, four Lokpalas, fourarmed Brahma, three-faced Vishnu and Mahishasur-mardini Durga. A special feature of the Mirkula temple are the depictions connected with the Buddha on the northern panel of the roof of the mandapa.

The Laxna Devi image is that of fourarmed Mahishasur-mardini in brass. It is three feet four inches high and stands on a nine-inches high pedestal. The Shakti Devi image is also four-armed and made of brass. It is studded with ornaments and wears a dainty crown. It stands on a inverted foliated lotus.

Both these images are slim, tall and of very fine workmanship. They belong to the later Gupta age.

The eight-armed Mahishasur-mardini image at Mirkula is of silver and is not of high workmanship. It is a swelled-up figure with a big head and thin legs and arms. Its crown has been fashioned in the Tibetan form.

PAGODA TEMPLES

Main temples in Pagoda style are those of Harimba Devi at Manali, Tripura Sundari Devi at Nagar, Trijugi Narayan at Dayar, Ad Brahm at Khokhan (all in Kulu Distt.) of Parashar in Mandi district and of Maheshra of Shungra in Kinnaur.

These temples have pyramidal tiered roofs and the style was introduced in Himachal in the ninth century. It is also believed that the Shakti Devi Temple at Chhatranhari was originally a pagoda temple.

Harima Devi temple with its impress of wieldness is the most well known of these. Its roof has three layers. Wooden bobbins hang from the roof layer projecting over the temple door. Carvings done in it resemble those at Mirkular. Sagar Manthan and Parbati combing the hair of Shiva are depicted on the wooden panels of the pediment, and navgrahas, floral motifs, animals, birds, gods and goddesses on the Entrance door. The mask of the goddess bear an inscription of the year 1418 by Raja Uddharn Pal of Kulu. Another inscription on the door-way shows that the present temples was built by Raj a Bahadur Singh of Kulu in the year 1553.

Ad Brahm Temple at Khokhan is one of the few temples dedicated to Brahma in the country.

THE FIRST SHIKHARA

The first attempt in the shikhara style in Himachal was the marvellous rock-cut fifteen temple-cimplex at Masrur, 22 miles from Dharmsala. It was a complete vimana in the early Nagara style (early eighth century A.D.) It was hewn out of an eighty feet high, two hundred feet long and a hundred feet broad piece of free-standing rock on a 2500 feet high sandstone ridge.

The height of the main temple (Thakurdwara) which formed the central part of the scheme, from its base to the top of the Shikhara, was eighty feet. Oher temples were constructed to heighten its effect.

The temple complex is now in ruins except some parts of Thakurdwara, but whatever is extant gives enough evidence of its architectural and sculptural excellence. The figures, chiselled out of sandstone, show suavity, grace and poise of Gupta classicism. They are well-proportioned, smoothly drawn, round limbed, brimming with youthfulness and beautifully finished.

Besides fifteen shikharas and a flat roof, it had four, gopurams-like structures which link it with the south Indian styles of temple architecture. First century B.C. coins of the Audumbras of western lower Himachal also show storied pavilions in relief resembling the storied towers of Dravidian temples.

Sir John Marshall called Masrur "a unique group of monuments" and Mr. Hargreaves described it of a "type rare in Hindustand".

BASHESHAR MAHADEV

The eleventh century Basheshar Mahadev stone temple at Bajaura (nine miles from Kulu) has four ardh-mandapas round the sanctum cella and above each one of them is a miniature temple triplet crowned by the "trimurti". The relief sculptures of Ganesh, Vishnu and Durga which are placed in the ardh-mandapas facing south, west and north respectively are each five feet and three inches high with a flaming halo behind. They are slim in design, delicate in feature and frame and qualitatively very superior. The best one is that of Vishnu along with the river goddesses Ganga and Yamuna on the sides of the temple door facing east.

VAIDYANATHA TEMPLE

Shiva vaidyanath sone temple at Baijnath (41 miles from Dharamsala) was constructed in the beginning of the thirteenth century. There is a walled enclosure around it. Portico-pillars are classical in proportions and nicely carved. There are beautifully balconies in its northern and southern walls. Its roof rests on four pillars and is divided into nine sections. There are two stone inscriptions in late Sharda script in the mandapa which detail the history of the construction of the temple and give a pictorial description of the Binwa stream which flows below it. Beautifully carved images are placed in the recesses on the outer walls of the temple, the best being that of Surya which stands on marble pedestal.

AVILOJITESHVARA TEMPLE

Boddhisatva Avilokiteshvara temple at Triloknath (in Chamba) was constructed during the reign of king Lalitditya of Kashmir (724-61 A.D.). It has a carved façade and stands on straight carved pillars. The three feet high six-armed carved marble idol of the Avilokiteshvara is seated crosslegged in 'padamasan' and has the figure of Amitabh on its head. The image is of the twelfth century A.D. and is in the northern Tibetan style. Lights are constantly kept burning in front of its.

MANDI SHIKHARAS

TRIFOIL arches decorate the facades or porches of the Shikhara temples at Mandi. A special feature of the image in the Triloknath temple (Mandi) is that it is of three-faced Shiva and in it both Shiva and Parvati have been shown seated on the Nandi.

The stone idol in the Ardh-narishwar temple at Mandi represents half-Shiva and half-Parvati. Their mounts, bull and lion, have also been carved on a single stone slab. The idol is beautifully and profusely carved.

CHAMBA SHIKHARAS

Chamba town has ten shikhara temples, most of whom have idols wrought in the local idiom of the tenth century Parthiara style. Laxmi Narayan is the earliest of these. It has a white marble brough from Vindhayachal which is studded with costly ornaments and precious stones. The brass idol of Shiva and Parvati in the Gauri Shankar temple is earlier than the Laxmi Narayan idol. Hari Raj temple is richly carved. Champavati temple was constructed by Princess Champavati after whom Chamba is named. It contains a stone image of Mahishasur-Mardini.

Bharmaur has two shikhars temples, whose of Manimahesh and Narsingh. In front of Manimahesh temple stands an "ashtdhatu" Nandi, five feet ten inches long and five feet high, on a thirteen inches high pedestal bearing an inscription indicating that this Nandi was made by Gugga during the resign of Meru Varma. Though the Narsingh temple was got constructed by Rani Tribhuvanrekha of Chamba in the tenth century, yet the "asthdhatu" idol of four-armed lion-faced man belongs to the reign of Ajay Varma (c 760-80 A.D.).

Durga and Shiva temples at Hatkoti are the most respected ones in upper Mahasu. The eight armed godden Mahishasur-mardhini Durga image is eight feet high and bears an inscription.

Shikhara temples at Masrur, Baijnath and Kangra have ardh-mandapas and naddapas besides garbh-grihas. Such temples in Kulu and Chamba districts had no mandapas. Their garbh-grihas are fronted by ardhmanpas and some are even withouit them. The chamba shikharas have protective coverings of wood over their tops to dram down snow. Such parasole on the 'amalka' stone are found in Kulu also.

JAIN TEMPLES

There are two small Jain temples in the ruins of Kangra fort. In one of them only the pedestal of a Trithankara image no remains. The other contains a seated image of Adinath which bears an obliterated inscription of 1466 A.D.

DOMED TEMPLES

Domed and flatroofed temples abound in Lower Himachal only. They were mostly constructed in the eighteenth and nineteenth centuries. They are in the Moghul-Sikh style of the period. Kosks, simple or ornamented domes, foliated arches and arched windows projecting out of the walls' are the chief features of these temples. Domes are glided or of brass or copper.

Bajreshwari Devi temple in Kangra which was destroyed by the 1905 earthquake was the best example of a gaudy domed temple in Himachal. Devi temples at Jawalamukhi, Chintpurni and Renuka are also in the domed style.

Jwalamukhi is one of the fiftyone Mahashakti Pithas. After Daksha Yogna-Bhanga, Shiva placed the burnt dead body of Sati on his shoulders and started wandering about in a state of madness. To save the world from the destructive wrath of Shiva, Vishnu started cutting the limbs of the dead Parvati one by one and the places where they fell became sacred centers of Shakti worship. The tongue of Sati fell at the place where the temple of Jawalamukhi is situated. The flames that come out of the openings in the earth's surface at the places are regarded the manifestations of the fallen tongue of Sati and are worshipped as Jawalamukhi Devi (Godess from whose mouth flames come out). Ther is no idol inside the temple.

The dome of the temples was got gilded by Maharaja Ranjit Singh in 1813 and Kahwar Naunihal Singh presented carved silver doors to it in 1840.

Chief fairs at Jawalamukhi are Chaitra and Asuj Navratras.

At Chintpurni (50 miles form Dharamasala). The Devi is worshipped as Bhagawati chhinmastika- the headless from in which she killed Nishumbha, Main fair at Chintpurni is held during the first ten days of "Shukul Paksh" of Shrawan (August). Shrawan Ashtmi is the most auspicious day.

The new Renuka Ji temple lies on a bank of the Renuka Lake. The lake is regarded as the manifestation of Renuka ji (wife of Rish Jamdagni and mother Parshuram) who jumped to death init. On the Deo-uthani Ekadshi in Kartika, thousands come to take their holy dip in the lake.

Chintapurni and Renuka Ji temple buildings have nothing special about them.

FLAT-ROOFED TEMPLES

Most of the flatroofed temples are dedicated to Rama and Krishna. Since they belong to the period when the Pahari paintings were created walls of some of them were decorated with paintings depicting personalities, scenes and events from the Ramayana, the Mahabharata, the Bhagwat Purana and Shiv Purana.

Such frescoes exist in about a dozen temples today. Chief among them are Narbadeshwar at Sujanpur Tira (fifty miles from Dharamsala), Ram Gopal at Damtal (four miles from Patahankot) and Brajraj Swami at Nurpur.

Brajraj Swami was constructed in the first half of the eighteenth century. Tempera paintings in its gracefully depict the deeds of Lord Krishna against the intrigues of Kansa in their proper sequence. These were done by the painter Golu of Nurpur. The special feature of these frescoes is that the whole of the painted surface has unity of theme (i.e. depicts one subject only).

According to local tradition, the black marble image of Lord Krishna known as Brajraj Swami was brought by Raja Jagat Singh (1619-46 A.D.) Nurpur from chitor and is the same image which Mira Bai used to worship.

Narbadeshwar temple was got constructed by Suketan Rani of Raja Sansar Chand of Kangra in the beginning of nineteenth century. It contains best frescoes in Kangra Kalam. They are vividly composed, magnificiently drawn and delicately coloured and are highly appealing to the eye. Gold touched paintings round the halo are particularly attractive.

Damtal temple was originally built in the sixteenth century. Faded and erased frescoes in its verandah present glimpses from the lives of Rama and Krishna mainly. There is a painting of the Nurpur hero Raj Bir Singh also. Frescoes in a room on the upper storey of the temple are of a later date than their verandah counterparts. Though they are richly and glowingly done, yet are inferior in work-manship to those in the verandah.

IN TIBETAN STYLE

Bhima Kali temple at Sarahan (Mahasu) and Chandika Devi temple at Kothi and Usha Devi temple at Nichar (both in Kinnaur) are among those which bear the impress of Tibetan architecture. Bhimakali temple is a big stone-built structure with a number of rooms and doors and corridors and is pyaramidal in shape. The temple idol is that of the Kali manifestation of the Devi standing over a headless demon. It is three and half feet high wrought in silver and placed in the upper storey of the temple. The temple has an image of Usha Devi also.

Chandika Devi of Kothi is the most powerful goddess in Kinnaur. Its temple contains carvings in wood and its door is of carved silver plates. The idol is of pure gold and is placed in a 'rath' which is swung up and down at the time of worship.

Temples of Maheshras (the three sons of Banasur, the father of Usha Devi), exist at Shungra, Kathgaon and Chhugaon. The Chhugaon temple has fine wood carvings.

These temples have beautiful door tings and knobs.

Human sacrifice used to be offered at Bhimkali temple, Prushuram temple at Nirmand, sun Temple at Nirat and Dattattareya temple at Dattnagar (all in upper sutlej valley).

Narbada or Kaika festival, which is celebrated in a number of temples in kulu and Mandi originally used to be a Narmedh or Narbadh (human sacrifice) rite.

CHANDERVERKAR

TEMPLE AND TOMBS OF JAMMU

Jammu city is called the city of temples. But is equally a city of Muslim Pirs whose tombs lie dotting various parts of the city. There are also several mosques in the city. This pattern of juxtaposition of temples and tombs is visible throughout the Jammu Province in its various towns, most remarkable feature of the religious life in Jammu is that more Hindus than Muslims visit these tombs and worship and make offerings. On certain days of the year festivals are held at these tombs when the fervour of the thousands of Hindu devotees is, indeed, beyond description.

Of the temples in Jammu city, there are not less than a hundred of these cyclopean structures scattered in various parts of the city. Indeed, almost every hundred or two hundred years in any direction will bring in sight one or more such new soaring towers ending up in a golden Kalsa. Chiming of bells and singing of bhajans in praise of the Almighty early morning in them creates a spiritually soothing mileu accompanied by the simultaneous Azans from the mosques in the city. Add to them the singing of shabads in several Gurudwaras by the Sikhs and there is the most exhilirating secular mozaic of life.

RAGHUNATH TEMPLES

Excepting one or two temples in the Jammu city, the rest were built in the second half of the 19th century or even later and are similar in style. Nevertheless some of them are over powering by their lofty masts and spaciousness and also by the numerous sculptures in them. That is so especially in the case of the famous Raghunath temples, a group of seventeen imposing shrines built in the center of the city whose golden turrets are visible from miles around gleaming in the sunlight. Its extravagant sculptures have verily been called Mythology in Marble. Another single towered Shiva Mandir built on a double flight of steps is the most imposing of these religious sites. Of the ancient temples in Jammu city one very interesting temples is a cave shrine devoted to Shiva held very sacred by Hindus. It is about hundred feet long, floored with marble slabs and located on the river Tawi bank amid jungles and rocks.

An important aspect of some of the Jammu city temples is that a few of them have excellent frescoes done in a old Pahari painting style. Two of them are especially profusely painted on the entire interior surface. The them of the frescoes is generally drawn from the scriptures. Best of these painting marvels, however, are to be found in the Sui Simbli and Buraji temples about sixteen miles from Jammu city.

TEMPLES AT BABOR AND KIRAMCHI

Most important of the Jammu temples from architectural and sculptural angles are those at Babor, Kiramchi etc., all over a thousand years old. This is indicated by their architecture, though authentic history of all them is missing till now.

The vast ruins of the six stone temples of Babor are especially inviting; its lavish and exquisite sculptures, gigantic beams and slabs, fantastically carved, fluted and monolithis pillars and pillasters present a rich cultural heritage. According to Dr. Vogel, the Archaeological Superintendent in Northern India in the early 20th century, Babor was for a short period the capital of the Dogra rulers of Jammu in the twelfth century. There are, however, several moot points about this assessment and, moreover, as said above there are no authentic historical records available till not about any of the ancient shrines of Jammu. I am also refer here to the opinion of the prominent geologist, Frederic drew, who was in the employment of the Jammu and Kashmir Government, and who wrote in his book Jammu and Kashmir Territories (about 1870) that Babor shrines are of great solidity, of what age I know not" he added "the material of these buildings is slightly calcareous sandstone which is found among the strate near. It has stood well against weathering and its toughness may be know from the huge beams used in the construction as much as 14 feet long". No mortar or any other binding materials have been used in their constructions.

Formerly one had to approach Babor after trudging at least 20 miles in a very difficult country side but now for some years Dhar-Udhampur National Highway passes right through them.

There is a group of five stone temples at Krimchi. There special feature is their luxuriant and sizzling carving. Most intricate designs, as also replicas of the shrine themselves, are done with a masterly touch in these carvings ; each design accomplished on many stones and all so sombined as to show one perfect whole. Moreover, these caved replicas have been conceived in an ascending order so as to give an illusion of greater height to the temples then they actually are.

Here may be referred some important single shrine mostly of hoary age scattered here and there in the Jammu Province which also represent important landmarks in the cultural heritage of the place.These are the Shiva Shrine at Billawar, Basik Nag temples of Bhaderwah, Sukarala Devi Shrine,Sudh Mahadev temple, Sarthal Devi, Fort Temple of Udhampur,Purmandal and Utterbani temples. All these present a striking array of artistic achievements of the maestroes in the distant and near past.

MOSQUES

Speaking of the Islamic landmarks of Jammu city there are no doubt many mosques here, a few of them quite impressive and centuries-old, but the real attraction in that regard is in the several tombs spread in the city and over greater part of the province. To mention a few important of them : Pir Roshan Shah, Pir Buddan Shah, Panj Pir, Pir Mitha etc., etc., in the city and tombs Baba Faiz Bakash, Saint Fridon, Saint Israr etc. in the countryside. Generally speaking none of them is a lofty structure , but their white shining minarets do stand out from their surroundings imparting an impressive serene and trancendental touch to the Jammu landscape. The tomb of Baba Faiz Bakash has great architectural beauty and it's ornamentation instinctively attracted all and sundry. These tombs are generally speaking centuries old; that of Pir Roshan Shah is said to have been built in the 8th century, rebuilt and overbuilt several times later on.

The pious lives of these great Pirs in their eternal sleep in these tombs and the great deeds attributed to them and the unbounding faith for myrid devotees in those boble souls to do good to them (devotees) and relieve their sufferings mark them out as significant sites in the culture of Jammu. The inspiring scenes of communal intermingling on these sacred spots and the religious chores performed there bekon us all to higher and nobler values in life.

SURAJ SARAF

TEMPLES AT BANSBERIA (WEST BENGAL)

Innumerable temples of brick and stone are found strewn all over west Bengal, most of them belonging to the late medieval period. The style of temple architecture that developed all over Bengal during the period beginning from the late 15th century onwards marked a clear distinction from that of the early periods. A peculiarly new style, better known as 'Bengali style' with three clear varieties, Chala, Ratna and Chandani or Dalan evolved during this period. Chala or hut-style having curved cornices, imitating bamboo-huts of rural Bengal, became very popular. A variety of Chalas like Do-Chala (two roof surfaces), Char Chala (four roof surfaces) etc. can also be found. Ratnas (i.e. pinnacled temple towers or towers placed above the elongated Char Chala) and Chandni or Dalan (i.e. one – storeyed square of rectangular building) arrested the attention of Bengal architects for quite some time. Terracotta decorations and stone sculptures upon the surfaces of brick as well as stone temples, depicting puranic and legendary scences, made them more popular among visitors and devotees.   Temples throughtout Bengal, more or less, belong to these three styles, except the Rekha variation, which is akin to the Orissan temple style.

The Hamsesvari temple at Bansberia, however, is in a class of its own. A small town in the Hooghly district of West Bengal, Bansbéria is quite wroth a visit by those who love temple and their architecture.

The temple dedicated to the goddess Hamsesvari has a magnificent structure displaying a peculiar architectural skill hitherto not seen in any of the temple styles of Bengal. This sturdy edifice does not strictly fall in any of the conventional styles.   The shrine, however, has thirteen turrets and hence may be stylistically called, 'Trayodasa – ratna' or thirteen – pinnacled temple which is a Ratna type. But the turrets are not characteristics of the conventional type; they resemble actual lotus buds with petals marked distinctly and from a distance, appear to intertwined.

For the first time one witness here a symbolic representation of human anatomy. The five vital nerves in the human' body, namely IDA, PINGALA, SUSUMANA, BAJRAKSHA and CHTTRINI, are represented by the five staircases of the temple. A meditator intending to achieve spiritual emancipation is required to awaken these five nerves one by one by resorting to certain processes. The thirteen turrets resembling lotus buds are symbolic representations of the thirteen stages of the mind, which is shut to the light of knowledge and wisdom. These are twisted together in a string – like formation, symbolizing the knots that can be made to untangle and open step by step through meditation. The thirteen stages of the mind are like the lotus buds that can made to bloom by practicing severe austerity.   The supreme spirit or BRAHMA comes to reside in the highest stage when all knots of the said nerves are opened, and ultimate spiritual realization comes when one reaches the stage symbolized by the topmost lotus bud which blooms once this stage is reached and the meditator achieves his goal.

The sanctum sanctorum or 'garbhagriha' is the inner apartment of the edifice where the presiding deity, goddess Hamsesvari is installed. It is preceded by an open hall where devotees assemble. The sanctum and the audience hall are built of sandstone, though the turrets around it are made of brick. The ceiling of the audience hall is decorated with frescoes depicting flowers and foliage motifs in a graceful style.

The construction work of the temple was first taken up by king Narisimha Deva in A.D. 1799, but on account of his sudden death, it was withheld for sometime before being resumed. The building was completed by this queen Rani Sankari in A.D. 1814. An inscription indicating the date of foundation was placed above the main entrance to the temple. His grandfather Raghu Deva was a pious king of the Bansberia Raj.   Ramesvara Dutta, the father of

Raghu Deva, was the most prosperous ruler of the Raj and won from Emperor Aurangzeb the title of Raja Mahasaya in A.D. 1679.

Raja Narisimha Deva, who was an expert tantric and spent eight years in Banaras, intended to erect a unique edifice to enshrine Hamsesvari. To fulfil his object he brought skilled architects from Banaras to construct the building. But he could not live to see it completed. The work was consummated later at the hands of his worthy queen Sankari and remains till date a unique example of temple architecture.

PRANAB RAY

TEMPLES OF KUMAON

A medieval center of Lakulisa Saivism, Jageswara is regarded as one of the most sacred tirthas (pilgrimage centers) in Kumaon region. The Linga (phallus), now warshipped as Jageswara or Yogeswara is locally considered to represent one of the twelve Jyotirlingas. The Mahabharata and other scriptures have references to this celebrated tirtha.

Jageshwar temple, after which the valley is named, is situated is a narrow valley hemmed in by high mountains covered with pine, oak and cedar trees. Two streams, Nandini and Surabhi, flow down these hills and culminate in Jataganga near this sacred place. Verdant and dense groves and murmur of rivulets invest it with sanctity and enhance the beauty of this place. The grand temples, is famous not only for its exquisite craftsmanship but also for its pristine beauty of being located among think deodar woods.

The structural activity at this site can be broadly divided into three principal periods: early Katyuri – from 8th to 10th C.D., late Katyuri- 11 – 14c. A.D., chand – 15 to 18c. A.D. of the numerous temples of this group, the Mrityunjaya temple seems to be the oldest – dating to about the 8th c., while the temples of Jageshwara, Navdurga, Kalika, Baleshwara and a few minor ones belong to the subsequent two centuries. The temple of Surya Navagraha and Neelkantheshwara belong to the late Katyuri age. The oldest in the series and built during the Chand period are five small temples assignable to the reign of Gyan Chand 1374-1419 A.D. four of such temples to the south-west of Mrityunjaya built in pairs bear typically the double shrine pattern.

Jageshwar is the only place where Shiva is worshipped in the form of Mrityunjaya. Apart from historical, cultural and religious values attached to this place, jageshwara attracts people for its peaceful surroundings and virgin scenic beauty. It is situated 34 km. to the east of Almora. The main road from Almora to Pithoragarh runs along Jageshwar.

ADYA SHARMA

TERRACOTTA FIGURINES IN INDIAN ART

The word 'Terracotta' stands for figurines of clay usually baked or burnt clay. It is one of the most ancient forms of plastic art. Clay, the medium of terracotta, is one of the easily obtainable and bountiful gifts of nature to mankind. Due to its cheapness and its being quite handy, man at the very threshold of civilization began to make ceramics, dolls and deities in clay.

In several countries of the ancient world this art became quite popular. Mention may be made of ancient Greece, Egypt, Iran, Mesopotamia, Elam, Crete, Mycena, Cyprus, China Polynesia and India. Terracotta art in its rich and varied form is known from these countries. A continuous stream of terracotta figurines through all the different ages is seen in India. They have their peculiar local characteristics and the different trends therein may be distinguished.

Three Methods

Terracottas were made entirely with the help of hands and moulds. The technique followed slit in the preparation of terracotta figurines of the pre-historic and historic sites of the country roughly falls under the following three divisions.

1. Figurines modelled in soft clay by the hands and roughly pinched to the desired shapes : The rendering of human form is crude and conventional and no separate parts of the bust are made, but we find appliqué decorative ornamentation affixed in their first stage.
2. Figurines built up with clay and carefully modelled except the face, which is pressed out of a mould.
3. Figurines and reliefs made from moulds completely: These are usually to be seen in the round, but circular or rectangular plagues are pressed out entirely from their moulds. The original model was first prepared in wax or clay. From this a mould was taken by squeezing clay on the model. The mould was baked and copies could be readily taken from it. After drying in the sun the figurines are given preliminary heat of fire.

Paint was applied in most of the terracotta figurines, generally of red, pink, light yellow or black colour. The colours must have been applied either by means of a brush or dipping the whole piece in the pot containing colours.

Early Terracottas

The history of terracotta figurines in India extends over a period of three thousand years. At Harappa, Mohanjodaro and other chalcolothic sites terracottas have been found in large numbers. Historical sites such as Tamluk, Pataliputra, Sravasti, Vaisali, Rajghat, Kausambi, Jhusi, Mathura, Sankisa, Ahichchhatra, Taxila, Rupar, Eran, Tripuri, Pawaya also have yielded countless terracotta figurines.

Apart from a few brick temples of the Gupta and post-Gupta period, some of the old temples in Bengal, that have defied the ravages of time, have terracotta panels all over their walls. In most cases, they portray the stories from the Vaisnava and Saivapurans.

Terracotta figurines discovered in the Indus valley are in human forms, both male and female, and in the form of animals. In the human figurines the eyes are large and round affixed separately, the nose is prominent and formed by pinching the clay together and the lips are thick affixed separately. The breasts are not considered large but are separately affixed while the arms are held at the sides. The female figurines wear a broad girdle (mekhata) but are otherwise nude. By way to ornaments large earings are worn, and necklace is some figurines.

Animal figurines of the Indus valley representing the antilope have been found at Chanhu-daro. The horns, the tail and eyes of this animal are prominently indicated. Among other animals represented in the terracottas of this age, the bull occupies a very important place. Bulls are humped as well as non-humped. Other animals are crocodile, dog, horse,lion, monkey, pig, ram, rhinoceros, sheep. The birds represented are cock, hen, parrot, peacock etc.

Between the Indus valley and the Mauryan age, the center of culture shifted from the Indus valley to the Gangetic plains. In the Mauryan period, which is one of the most glorious ages exhibiting the successful efforts for the development of plastic art, terracotta art was developed. The western artistic influence also entered in the Mauryan period.

Mathura, Bulandi Bag (Patna), Sarnath, Bhita, Basarh, maski and Koratgi are some of the find places of this terracotta art, which fall in two groups of human (male and female) and animal figurines.

In the Sunga period art shows definite indigenous traits. In this period terracottas began to be partly cast and partly modelled. They were often painted red, pink, yellow or black. Besides the terracotta figurines of male and female, animal and bird figurines are also found. The plaques of this period are in the three dimensions. The terracotta figurines of the period have been found at Lauriya Nandagarh, Kausambmi, Mathura, Bhita, Sankisa, Nagari in Rajasthan and Taxila in the North West. In the Boston Museum of Fine Arts there is and inscribed terracotta figure of this period.

Patronage given by the Satavahanas and the Kusanas to various expressions of art contributed to the development of art during their reign. The main characteristics of the terracotta figurines during this period can be divided into three categories: (a) Those works in which Hellenistic influence is prominent. (b) Those in which there is a mixture of Hellenistic and India motifs and (c) Those which are solely representative of India elements.

Among the sites where terracotta figurines of this age have been found in North West are Shah-Ji-Kidheri, Taxila and Jaulion, Ushkar near Baramula (Kashmir). In north India mention may be made of Bhita, Sankissa, Mathura, Kausambi and Besnagar. A few artistically rich pieces have recently been discovered from Tripuri also. Satavahana terracotta figurines are also known from the site of Kondapur in Andhra Pradesh.

In the Kusana period two school of art flourished in India viz. the Gandhara school and the Mathura school. The plastic art of India including terracottas, derived either from the Gandhara or the Mathura School.

Gupta Period

The terracotta art of the Gupta period, which was the golden age of Indian History. Terracotta figurines belonging to this age have been found at Mahasthana, Rangamati, Mathura, Kasia, Sahet-Mahet, Rajghat,

Achichchatra, Kausambi, Bhita, Bhitargaon, Sankisa, Besnagar, Eran and Pawaya. The mould system of the sunga period continued right up to the Gupta period.

The human types, both male and female, of the Gupta age are remarkable for the great variety of styles. The faces are charming with sharp pointed nose, full round breasts. Both male and female figurines show minimum of ornamentation. Kalidas and Bana, two celebrated literary figures of this period, refer to artistic practices in clay indicating the popularity of this form of art.

Dr. V.S. Agrawala describes the following male hair – styles:

1. Chhatrakara – The hair crowns the head of a semi-circular parasol with locks arranged like ribs close to each other, all radiating from a topknot. On the two sides the spired locks (alakayali) descent in three or more receding horizontal tiers.
2. Chattrakara with parting simanta: The hair is arranged parasol – like with locks above and on the sides.
3. Trefoil styles, in which the hair is arranged in two sides masses with or without parting backed by a crest.

Among female heads the general style is the foil with two side appendages and a crest (Sikhanda) in the center. Other are :- (1) Honey-comb style and (2) Trefoil style.

With a plain flat bend in the center. The side masses and the topknot a common feature of all female heads. (3) Simanta with chatula central parting of hair adorned with jewels. In some specimens the crest jewel is shown behind a raised roll of hair on the head. And (4) Bharamarka style: The combed space above the forehead is beautified by an ornament represnting a bee or Bhrama a without spread wings from which this style was known as Bhramaraka.

The Medieval figurines (7th to 12th Century A.D)have been found at Dah-Parbatiya and Kundilnagar (Assam), Sobhar, Raghurampur, Paharpur and Bangesh in Bengal, Nalanda in Bihar, Sarnath and Sahet Mathet in U.P and Avantipur in Kashmir. In the Medieval period we generally get plaques.

The terracotta figurines served various purposes. Some of these were worshipped as household deities while a few served as motive offering. Some must have been prepared purely for decorative purposes and served as the playing toys of children.

In Egypt and Mesopotamia terracotta figurines have been found in the graves. Ancient people believed in the continuity of life after death and hence stored the necessities of life along with the dead in the grave for use in the next birth.

The terracotta figurines furnished valuable information about the religious social and the artistic ideals of the past.Terracotta art is largely concerned with representations of the scene of every day life. As such its social importance appears to be considerable. Rajghat has yielded a fair variety of terracottas representing scenes from everyday life.These figurines depict daily life and persuits of the common people in many facets.

GROUPS OF TERRACOTTA

The rich treasures of Indian terracottas preserved in several museums in India and Abroad can be divided into several types or groups for convenience of study.

Female Figurines (Mother Goddess) : Terracotta of very crude, grotesque and rough workmanship have been discovered from many ancient sites. We generally call these "mother goddess" and the typical features are elaborated head-dress and jewellery, prominent breasts and wide hips, often represented nude and standing. Dr Stella Kramrish calls them 'timeless ' or ' ageless'. In India the mother goddess is called by various names such as Aditi , Indarani , Maya, Padmasri or Vasudhara. Star type small figures have also been found from various ancient sites. Their legs and hands which have pointed ends are stretched sideways. Most of the figurines have no eyes and the nose-ridge is usually made out of pinching the clay.

Mother and Child or Ankadharini : In the National Museum , New Delhi ,a beautiful Ankadhari woman is shown seated in European fashion on a high pedestal. She carrries, a child in her left lap while with the right hand she is pressing her breasts to shower the milk in plenty. She wears an elaborate head-dress with three floral bas decorations, heavy double earings, necklace and other jewellery which are all applied by hand. This specimen is from Mathura and belongs to the Mauryan period (4th-3rd century B.C)

The Dampati Scenes are depicted in the terracotta from Ahichchhatra, Kausambi and other sites. In these figurines generally the female wears the Sari supported by a gridle and a Pataka the two ends of which fall down in front. Her right hand is set at the hip and the left is flung across the neck of the male. The husband wears a Dhoti and puts a scarf on his chest. He fixes his right hand on the gridle of the female.

The Mithuna Type:- This is one of the important motifs of India art from very early times in which the couple is shown sitting on a cushioned couch. The female sits on the lap of the male. She feigns her left hand across the neck of her beloved while with the left she holds one of her earings.

Bachanalian Scenes-such Terracotta plaques show drinking couples. This subject is quite common in the Kusana art of Mathura. In the Allahabad Museum there is a good terracotta plaque showing this scene. A male and a female are seen sitting on stools. The male holds a Madhupatra (cup) and the female a madhughata (wine jar) respectively in their hands. The male is taking the wine cup towards his lip.

Votive Tanks. – Several specimens of votive tanks have been found at Ahichchhatra and Kausambi. They consist of a wall enclosure with lamps and birds and dwarf musicians squatting inside against the wall with shallow cups placed in front of them.

In the Gupta period the images of Vishnu, Surya, Ganesha, Kartikeva, Mahishasurmardini and Lakshmi are found among the terracotta plaques. Among some other main terracottas, mention may be made of serpent goddess (Mansadevi) the Yaksas, scenes of bird-playing (Suka-Krida), scenes of music and dancing.

Through all the ages of the history terracotta figurines have thrown considerable light on the dress, ornaments and hair styles of the contemporary people. We usually find the male generally wearing a dhoti and the upper part is left bare. In some figurines a scarf over the shoulders. A few male types wear sleeved coats, closed in front by cloth fasteners. Heavy turbans are also seen in several examples.

The females wore saris, jackets, skirts, and tunics, sari being the most popular apparel. The sari is supported by beaded girdle of patakas, a portion of which comes down in front. The folds of the sari are beautifully indicated.

Heavy jewellery adorned the males and females. A large variety of earings, necklaces, torques, armlets, bangles and girdles are found on the bodies of various figurines.

The ancient tradition of fashioning clay images is still honoured all over India, though the influence of machine-made wax figurines, objects made of plastic and plaster of Paris, with rough cotton pieces, has led to the degradation in the moulding of clay, and the original primitivism of design is nearly destroyed. On the occasion of festivals, specially around Dasahra, Deepavali and other minor festivals like Mahalaksmi, Haritalika, Gan-Gaur, Ganeshpuja, Jagaddhatri, Saraswati and opportunity is provided for an extensive exhibition of these objects arranged in a colourful manner.

SUJIT KUMAR BHATTACHARYA

TERRACOTTA FOLK ART OF INDIA

India is one of the most religious countries in the world and her pantheon is very rich ; this could be very well seen from the representations of the Mother – goddesses in the from of Gramdevata. When there is a festival in village people offer various clay-animals, human figurines, balls, votive tanks, Garba, Ghumat, Bamboo-sticks etc. to these Gramdevata. These animals are called "Ghoda" but actually they are figurines of horse, elephant, tiger, rhinoceros, cow buffalo and camel. Sometimes they are offered as "Sawari" (vehicle) and sometimes they are offered as 'Bhog' (Sacrifice). When people get their vishes fulfilled, they hang thses clay horses on the branches of trees also.

Gramdevata

The Gramdevata is a tutelary or protecting mother of a particular place or locality. Especially in rural areas this cult of the goddesses is very popular. There is hardly a village without the shrine of the Gramdevata. All people however, can adore her near a water-side in a forest, or in stones, wood or clay temples. Sir Monier William has described the important Mother-Goddesses in India such as: Sitala, Khodiyar, Becharaji, Untai, Ambaji, Kalka, Thakurani. Moreover some more familiar are Bhathuji. The more popular names of the Goddess in South India may be mentioned as under: Kollapuri-amma, Kuskur-amma, and the Seren Kanniyamar, Bhadrakali, Durgamma, Aiyanar, Karappan and Muttaiyan.

Adivasis

We find more elaborate descriptions of Gramdevata in the Smriti-Purana Samuchhaya, Gramdevata Pratista and Yogini Tantra. This crude form of religion comprising animism, magic, polytheism, mythology, ghost-beliefs, and other which exercise sway over the mind of the rural population, who have not yet come under the influence of

Hinduism. In fact the rural religion sees spirits practically behind all phenomena and creates a phantasmagoria of numerous uncanny words of spirits. These tribes are now concentrated in Vindhyan complex comprising the Satpuras, Mahadeohills, Gavaligarh, Maikal range, Huzaribagh range, Chhota Nagpur, Singhbhum, and Manbhum, Aravallis hills, Sahyadris, Mysore area. This cult draws most of its votaries from the lower tribes particularly from Bhils, Dangs, Gonds, Santals, Uraons, Baigas, Gadabas, Murias, Worli, Toda, Kurumbar, Kadar, Puliyan, Muthuvan, Savaras, Baiga, Chenchu Reddi, Irukus and Yenadis. Their common daily enemies are evil spirits and epidemics of cholera, smallpox and fever, childlessness and cattle diseases, failure of crops and rain.

Belief in India

People want to ward off evils, dangers and diseases and pray for health, success and happiness. They have always to devise means. At the base of all the religions lies a mass of primitive beliefs. The early stage of religion, superstition is the means by which he explained things to satisfy these inquisitive primitive minds. The simple explanation given by the local people is that a person in distress vows to offer a horse or an elephant or a tiger or a rhinocero to god-lings or Gramdevata. When his wishes are realized, he offers as substitute this trumpery donation. Moreover it is an act of prudence to secure their goodwill as an insurance against possible misfortune. Their attitude finds expression in a well-known proverb of Kathiawar which says 'Pay reverence once to a benign God, for he may do you good, but twice to a malign power in order that He may do you no harm'. It is a common practice to offer substitution of these kinds of clay horses, elephants, tigers and rhinocero all over India. Thus when an animal could not be procured for a sacrifice an image of it is offered as a substitute. We have common examples of substitutions of the same kind; on the same principle, women used to give cakes in the form of phallus to a Brahmin. Some give silver cow to Brahmin as a donation instead of a living cow. Some people cut the gourd at the junction of four roads. In the days of the Navaratri perforated pots with lamps and flowers are offered to deity. Even Muslims offer the Ghodas made up of rags to their tombs and Pir-bawa. Sindhis offer these clay images called Ghoda when they worship Goddess Laxmi on the new year. In North India and Gujarat people offer these miniature of figure of animals to Goddess Sitala when there is epidemic or cholera. People have the same custom of offering clay horses, elephants to tutelary deity in Bihar and Bengal. The gurdian deities of villages in Madras are Aiyanar, Karappan and Muttaiyan. It is a belief that they ride every night for driving away evil spirits. So figurines of elephant horse and tigers are provided for them to ride on. These figurines are not common as we find elsewhere, but, if are really imposing big figures. They are sometimes made of wood also. In Maharashtra people worship clay horse and bulls on the last day of Shravan and it is a big festival all over the province. These figurines are reminders to the deity of the help expected whether given before or after the help is received. Moreover people used to offer (maduparaka) honey, ghee, milk and (vasana) cloth, (Naivedya) food and flowers, perfume and dipa. It is worth nothing that the worship is carried on generally by non-Brahmin priests, exorcist, Bhuva and Bhagatas.

Parallel Belief in Asia

It seems from the early times that people of Egypt, Mesopotamia, Iraq and Palestine have been accustomed to place their graves some objects to help the dead person on his long and tedious journey of his life. Oswal Siren has described the terracotta dug up from the early tombs of the Han period, the majority of the figurines were of remarkable effigies of animlas, principally illustrated in the representation of camels, horses, bulls and other domestic pets. Even to-day horse-worship is still mixed up with the creed of the Buddists of Yunan who probably derived it from India. Moreover even the Japanese believe that certain objects should be kept with the dead body-they are useful to them in the long journey. Similarly for a living horse, horse of baked earth afterwards substituted. The clay figurines of various types have been found from the tombs of the Nkados and Princes. The Japanese farmers offer the clay images of animals to their local deity to protect their crops and cattle from the evil spirits as we find the Indian farmers do. Afterwards they started offering wooden effigies of horses and did it to such and extent they constructed a special building called EMADO (Horse) picture gallery, for the public worship. The custom of omen of horses is also quite common in Germany, and they consider horse as a holy animal as we consider cow in India. These clay horses are known as Vytaka or Dymka in Russia and are offered to commemorate the dead persons of the family.

Terra-Cotta Folk Art

Folk art is a symbol of social and religious life, It reveals the inner beauty, the design and the value that lie deep in the community. The traditions, religious beliefs, and culture of a society are perfectly mirrored through these terra-cotta votive offerings. Their colour and shape suggest the aesthetic taste of the people in the daily life. Folk art is a collective aspiration and expression of the people who generally live in rural areas. It is deeply rooted in the soil and closely associated with the popular customs and beliefs. These clay animals are intimately linked with their myths, rituals and superstitions. It is difficult to trace the origin and development of this ageless folk votive terra cotta but the earliest terra-cotta art traditions in India can be traced back to the Indus Valley Civilization about 2500 B.C. It has preserved itself ever since as one of the most handy medium of popular art and traditions.

The mystery of these votive dedicating clay images of animals lies partly in the fact that they suggest rather than state. They are the vernacular expression of figural images. These are not made primarily for aesthetic reasons but purely for religious purposes, Therefore, these symbols speak the same truth as philosophy and myth. They may in a general way, be described as hieratic or perhaps best of all as traditional. They suggest a greater freedom of movements though they are primitive in appearance and technique. They are bold in creations and simplified in form. Distortions are made to make them more conventional and vital. The colour and shape of a figurine depend upon its convention and proportions. The potter (artist) does not care for anatomical and realistic forms of animals. But their certain parts of body are made more elaborate, for example the ears of elephant, the legs of horse and horns of rhinocero.

Generally these clay animals considered as poor man's sculpture are of uncommon interest, for rarely do we find in the plastic art of the primitive people of the country expressions of such vitality and elemental simplicity.

Like all true primitive art the aesthetic adventure of the people as found in terra-cotta is an unconscious one dictated by urging that know no outward moulding and refinement. However, forms powerful and mature emerge from the vast store-house of their unconscious as a stream of unbroken imagery. This are of the people concerns itself with clay horses, human figurines, votive tanks balls and Garba and with those disembodied deities and spirits that guard alike seeds end crops, diseases, death and fertility. The great mysterious nature-cycle is the altar on which they lay their offerings.

These votive animals, like all other production of folk art, are brilliantly decorative and sincerely ingeneous. They vary from place to place but are both technically and stylistically are clearly of classical descent. Even if the potterwoman does not introduce any new detail, these figurines are usually very expressive, corpulent, dignified. A dashing horse-man, tiger, a long-legged horse and elephant and common figurines. The artist produces a please a pleasing effect. The artists uphold their native traditions, especially in their manner of handling them. Life itself, however, is always suggesting new themes but the problem is how to remain faithful to these traditions and yet keep pace with times. These terra-cotta provide data for the Archaeologists Anthropologists and Art Historians. This art is on the decline these days and conscious efforts to stem the engulfing tide are needed to preserve it. It is in imminent danger of being overshelmed by superior by superior socio-economic forces of modern civilization.

Technique

In the villages the potters work generally at the Diwali time in the month of Aso. They prepare bodies on the figurines are modelled in various sizes entirely by hand. Their features and adornments, head, eyes, ears, legs, tails, neck are prepared separately from strips of wet clay. Afterwards all these parts are applied to model by the appliqué technique. The technique is crude in practice, the potters are completely conscious of the medium, so that sometimes they make short tails,, short trunks of elephant, to avoid their breaking down. These figurines are lightly fired and subsequently decorated with white and red local pigments.

AMBALAL J. PATEL

TERRACOTTAS OF AMBIKA KALNA

A mere 82 Kilometers away to the north of bustling Calcutta lies a quiet, small township Ambika Kalna in the district of Burdwan. In its heyday Kalna was a flourishing port of Bengal on the right bank of the river Bhagirathi or Ganga. For many centuries river Ganga. For many centuries river Ganga had been the principal waterway of west Bengal, serving as the only channel of communication between the trading north Indian cities and the Bay of Bengal. As an important port in the lower Gangetic plain Kalna was known to the Greeks and Arabs. During the reign of the mighty Gupta dynasty it was a part of the Kama subama kingdom, and was later known as the 'Rath' land of the sovereign Sen kings of Bengal. The region had been the scene of many bloody encounters between the Mughal emperors of Delhi and the Pathan Sultanate of Bengal in the 15th and 16th centuries when the port of Kalna played an important role.

Ancient Kalna finds a mention in the folklores and ballads associated with Chand Saudagar – the celebrated Bengali merchant who sailed from here with his fleet of cargo ships across the seas the seas to Indonesia, Bali, Sumatra and Cambodia, since olden days Kalna had also been an important pilgrimage center en route the holy shrine of Puri, the above of Lord Jagannath. The importance of Kalna suffered a setback with the advent of railways in the 19th century, when along with other river ports Kalna too lost much of its glory and went into oblivion.

But for one reason Kalna is distinct from the other suburban towns of West Bengal : it is a treasure trove of some remarkable terracotta temples, perhaps superior to the much celebrated shrines of Vishnupur in many ways. Raised between 1739 and 1849, the temple complex of Kalna presents a sublime synthesis of the wide range of architectural forms and terracotta art, rarely monotonous or redundant. The superb burnt-clay friezes and the tiered pinnacles or 'Ratnas' adorning the temples are reminiscent of the various influences that penetrated Bengal at different times. In the alluvial land of teh region, easily available materials like mud, bamboo and thatch have been used to shape the massive 'duel', 'Bangla' and 'chala' type of vaults in the regional style. The intricately carved terracotta figures moulded from clay are life like portrayas of people and the contemporary society, sometimes suavely depicting scenes from the epics, done with great mastery.

The temple complex of Kalna is the creation of the Burdwan royal family and is located near the rajbari (palace). The first temple built by Rani Brojo Kishori is dedicated to Lord Krishna and goes by the name 'Lalji' (son-in-law) being located on the pilgrim's watery way to the holy Puri Dham, Kalna had developed a cultural affinity with art heritage of orissa. This is evident in the architecture of the temple, resembling the Orissan shrines with multiple ornate spires called 'Ratnas'. With its Panchavimshati Ratna (25 pinnacles) the Lalji temple is a three storeyed structure. The comices projecting above the walls are adorned with floral motifs. Stucco figures of mermaids and birds showing European influence. The base friezes of finely carved terracotta tiles depict scenes of everyday life, of dances and dramas, hunting and fighting. The brackets at the corners are supported by figures of horse riders, acrobats and warriors.

Facing the Lalji temple stands the imposing octagonal Dolma ncha. Nearby is seen another Panchvimshati temple named Krishana Chandra. The lively terrocotta figures here portray families, processions, boat riding etc.

The best preserved is the shrine of Pratapeshwar built in 1849 by the widow of Raja Pratap Chand, in her husband's memory. Thought small in size, this Shiva temple has four arched doorways elaborately adorned with the finest terracottas, depicting events of the Ramayana. The entire façade is covered with titles of equisite beauty portraying musicians, ascetics, wrestlers, mermaids, men and women, in different moods and posture. All the figures are highly expressive and pulsating with life and vigour. The finely moulded clay figurines of the friezes show synthesis of the contemporary styles of Bengal and Orissa at its best.

Though not in terracotta, the 'Nabo Kailash' built by Raja Tej Chand, comprising 108 Shiva temples in two concentric circles, is highly interesting, particularly for the orientations of the alternate Linga icons of black and white marbles.

DIPALI DE

TEWARI LAXMI GANESH DISSEMINATING "HINDUSTANI MUSIC"

In the North Indian Classical music traditions, the human voice is regarded as the most precious and subtlest of all instruments, designed to praise the Creator with music in what is known in India as the Language of God. Some are gifted with this special power of devotion. Such a one is Pandit Laxmi Ganesh Tewari. The sings in the Gwalior style of Khyal which, in the 18th century, developed out of the ancient from known as Dhrupad.

"All through my life", Tewari said in a recent interview, when he was interrupted in his office when happily at work in the cyberspace, "I have tried to combine the three main aspects of my life: Performance – which is my worship... whether I am giving concerts or not, I sing; I would never leave that, it is very important to me.

"The second aspect is my scholarship- the work which I have been doing in India, and lately in Trinidad, and now in Fiji. I have been collecting old songs for a quarter of a century, listening to traditional stories from old musicians, from people in Indian communities around the world who still remember the old ways.

"The third aspect, "he concludes, "is my teaching". Which he has now done at Sonoma state university in California for twenty one years.

Much of his research work has been made public in the form of books, CDs and articles. Soon to be published is a book about his guru, Dr. Lalmani Misra, and a book about the folk music of India. This letter will include a transcription of the melody, a translation of text, and a brief comment on or explanation each of the almost unimaginably many and varied songs of the area in Uttar Pradesh where Tewari was born and brought up. They will be classified according to ceremony such as songs sung at childbirth, weddings, devotional songs, of different caste groups and songs sung in different seasons. Over 300 songs will be included in this collection. When asked if he planned to do collections from other regions, he chudkled, "There are a prodigious number of songs in India, this book may be enough for a lifetime". However, he is already at work on the monumental task of a 1600-2000 page transcription of the Alha (a legendary tale of valour of two brothers, Alha and udal) as sung by Jai Sing of the village of Bidokhar in Uttar Pradesh to be published in Hindi.

Depending primarily upon publications to disseminate the vast and precious knowledge that he is collecting and preserving, Tewari leads a life that anyone inclined towards intellectual rigour, nomadism, and being-in-love-with-what-they-do will look upon with awe and envy, His vigorous enthusiasm for every for everything from research in remote Turkish villages, to being in touch with the world vie Internet, Keeping a large and beautiful garden of flowers and fruit trees, as well as his deep devotion to singing is truly inspiring.

He sings all the time, practicing in the morning, which he prefers, and in the evening. "People on campus", he laughs, "claim they can hear Tewari coming, for he always comes singing". He gives six or eight concerts in a year, and has just released a new CD entitled Morning Glory.

Accompanied on table by Pandit Swapan Chaudhuri, on sarangi by Pandit Ramesh Mishra, one of India's fines sarangi players, and on tanpura by Carolyn Tewari, Tewari sings Raga Ahir Bhairav and Kabir's Bhajan (devotional song) 'Sahib bain' with flawless intonation in this fine new recording. His voice, caressing, light yet full, brings out all the subtle pleasure of calmness, serenity and peacefulness inherent in this early morning rags. Swapan Chaudhari one of the world's greatest tabla players, moving from slow Ektal in the first bandish, to fast Teental in the second, is both superbly subdued, and elegantly dramatic. One dreams deep thoughts to the gentle beat of drum, the haunting call of Ramesh Misra's sarangi, the beauty of Tewari's voice until the heart is quickened by the evocation of the sun's rising.

Tewari, born in Kanpur, Uttar Pradesh, India in 1938, moved to Varanasi in 1958. There, in strict guru-shishya-parampara (Tradition) he lived and studied with his guru Dr. Lalmani Misra, the director of the College of Music at Banaras Hindu University and Pandit Madhav Vaman Thakur. Studying also with progressor B.R. Deodhar, he completed his music degree in 1967.

At Wesleyan University in the United States, after doing field research in Turkey and in his native Uttar Pradesh, he completed his Ph. D. in Ethnomusicology in 1974. That same year, he began to teach at Sonoma State University in California.

From his doctoral studies he produced his first three folk music records: Turkish Village Music, Nectar of the Moon: Vichitra Veena Music of Northern India and Folk Music of India: Uttar Pradesh. Since then he has made numerous recordings and CDs. His scholarly articles appear relgularly in international journals such as South Asia journal of Research from London's School of Oriental and African studies, South Asia Journal of the University of Western Australia, Asian Folklore Studies from a Nazan University in Nagoya, Japan. His book. A splendour of worship: Women's Fasts, Rituals, Stories and Art, was published by Manohar Publications of New Delhi.

Eager to have this extensive knowledge about folk music available to others for use and study, he donates his original materials to the great archival collections, including the Archives of Traditional Music in Berlin, the Archives of both Columbia and Indiana Universities in the United States, and to the main archive in New Delhi, at the American Institute of Indian Studies. Shortly, he will be sending his research material from Turkey to the Wesleyan Archives.

He attends many international music conferences, and occasionally teaches as a visiting professor in India, as well as at such schools as Dartmouth, the Manhattan School of Music, the University of Hawaii, and the Ali akbar College of Music in San Rafael. The student he taught, both musicans and music scholars, now number in thousands.

Today, Tewari, enjoys not only a remarkable reputations as a scholar, but is regarded as one among the great Hindustani musicians, including such luminaries as Ali Akbar Khan, Ravi Shankar, Lakshmi Shankar, G.S.Sachdev, Salamat Ali Khan, Swapan Chaudhari, Zakir Hussain, and Chitresh Das.

In addition to his University duties, for eight years Tewari has driven 110 miles each way, twice a month, to teach several special groups and individual singers in San Jose. Known among his students as a person of rare patience and delicate discernment, many regard him as one of the finest teachers of our time.

"The music is not something you can do today, expecting to get a "fruit" a few years down the line". Tewari says softly. "You must constantly work at it to get the fruit to taste sweet, to make the sound beautiful. Nor is it an art you can put aside for a while. But if you have the dedication, it will slowly and surely become a medium of mediation".

Asked about the future of Indian music, he replied: "I see it flourishing around the world in two different ways: both as a pure form, and as fusion music. The practical American mind feels it must be able to earn money at what it has studies so hard to accomplish. Thus there is tendency to mix Indian music with Western music. I do not object to that.

"All over the world", he said, "the interest in Indian music is growing. There are major centers of it, not only in America, but in England. London has many great Indian musicians in residence, also Berlin, Toronto, the Netherlands. In every country there is the both study of pure classical music, as well as music that is fused with Eastern jazz and classical.

The tendency of the new generation of immigrants and second generation Indians in America, and in many parts of the Western world, is to add Indian Classical music as a form of worship to their already successful business lives".

JAN HAAG

THANJAVUR PAINTING

It is the opulence of brilliant colours and dotted with precious gems that has brought out the monumental Thanjavur paintings form the Hindu temples of South India to the modern art galleries thus enriching the connoisseurs' enviable collection.

Thanjavur paintings are the product of highly conservative South Indian civilization and are expression of the artists' religious devotion. These were created to adorn the temple walls.

A typical Thanjavur painting depicts a sacred Hindu deity. It is gilded and beset with precious and semi-precious stones. These paintings are figurative and their characters are plump and robust with mounted chins and chubby cheeks. Though gold is the basic binding colour,

the colour schemes are often rigid with the usage of pure colours and no allowance is given for any colour mixing to create shades. Red and blue or red and green combination are common. Body colours are generally white or yellow. Thanjavur paintings are large sized and are usually framed. Some of them are as large as murals and are meant to be viewed from a distance.

The iconic painting are usually done on wooden planks of a jack tree. To this wooden base is mounted a card-board sheet with a special glue made from tamarind seeds. Over this card-board, layers of cloth are pasted. A lime paste is then repeatedly coated on the surface and is smoothened with a polished stone or a shell. Sketching is done with a brush on the smoothened surface and the gold foil or gems are stuck on the drawing with the help of an adhesive paste made by adding glue to the unboiled lime-stone, ground finely. This paste is also used to level the surrounded areas to bring the surface to one plane and to render more support to the embedded gold foils, gems and coloured glass pieces. Colouring of the rest of the details is done in the last to complete the highly decorated and ornamented figures.

Among the relatively less popular but exotic style of Thanjavur paintings are murals portraiture, painting on glass, ivory, leather mica and playing cards and the painted wooden shrines. But it is the iconic paintings from Thanjavur which have generated much interest for centuries not only in India but world-wide.

These gilded icons which once radiated a glow on the serenity of the dimly lit shrines and inspired faith in devout Hindus are still mesmerizing a new-cult of admirers of this art cutting through the barriers of religion.

BIMAL SAIGAL

THANKA PAINTING

Thanka painting is very popular in Tawang Hills of Arunachal Pradesh generally displayed through the exquisitely painted wood carvings on doorways. The legend of "thumb pun zbi (four prosperous brothers) which is repeated fairly frequently on most doorways is the story of four animals- an elephant, a monkey, a rabbit and a bird, who jointly cooperated in nursing the seeds to grow into a tree and shared the prosperity. The story imparting the lesson of unity, prosperity, integrity and respect, is a symbolic representation of Budhist though. Artists specializing in thanka painting usually us thumbs pun zbi theme. These artists used to make use of special colours made of powdered precious stones and vegetables dyes in their paintings. Now they have switched to ordinary fabric or oil prints. These themes are commonly painted on archways on either side of the entrance and sometime on the walls of the front porch or verndah.

THE TRADITION OF LAMPS IN INDIA

Lamps are an integral part of Indian culture. They weave their own magic irrespective of whether they are in the form of a mere candle or the traditional all filled wick lamp. The poetic beauty of the flickering flame cannot be described in words.

The origins of the lamp can probably be traced back to the time fire was discovered. Fire holds an irreplaceable place in man's life. In India, it came to be associated closely with the Hindu religion and form of worship. Therefore, it is but natural that the objects in which ceremonial fire was lit or kept also aroused feelings of recerence. These objects were, therefore, considered equally important and were made with the utmost care. In the beginning, natural substances such as stones, shells, tree-products etc. Must have been used. There paved the way to their present beautiful shapes, with craftsmen giving the lamps more depth and meaning. We find in India a gamut of beautiful lamps made of all sorts of material-clay, terracotta, porcelain, brass, bronze, silver and at times even dough. There is literature on lamp making. Norms exist regarding its size, lighting and measurements. Festivals of lamps are celebrated and rituals are prescribed for their worship. Even dances center around lamps.

Most importantly, there are different types of lamps used for different purposes. The lamp is considered a woman and is symbolic of Goddess Lakshmi (goddess of wealth) and is referred to as Deepalakshmi.

The earthen lamp or "mitti ka diya" is the most common, easily available and seen lamp. Made on the potter's wheel from clay, thousands of these are turned our every year for use by people. A good diya has to be soaked in water before use. The single diya is the most common lamp. However, the potter often lets his imagination run riot to churn out different types of diays. Some are just attractive domes with openings to hold the lamp so that so that only the eight flickering can be seen while the dome protects it from wind. Some are a bunch of five diyas-one in the middle, surrounded by four others.

Porcelain lamps shaped like diyas are also made these days, as are the ones in terracotta and clay. Designer diyas hold a place of their own. They come in all sizes. The diya is held stop an elephant or a babkura (Horse): there are hanging lamps in the shape of pigeons or birds wherein the chain is hooked onto the bird's beak and the body of the bird houses the place for filling oil or wax.

The place of price is taken by lamps made of various metals, Lamp in olden times were made of commonly available metals including gold and other precious metals and stones. The tradition continues in the temples, where exquisitely made lamps can be seen. Temples in South India have an amazing diversity of lamps. Gujarat also has its own repertoire of lamps. Some temples have niches in the walls where lamps can be placed. Others have huge lamps at the entrance. The lamp is in the form of a huge pillar, carved intricately. Plates at equal intervals hold the oil and the beaks of the wicks. The circumference of the plates is the widest at the bottom and gets progressively smaller as one moves up. The top is decorated with a lion or a peacock. The base has figures from Hindu mythology. Such pillar lamps or deepstambhas are mostly cast in bronze.

Different lamps are made for different purposes. An aarti deepa, used at the time of prayer, is different from the one used to light the sanctum. The aarti deepa usually has a handle attached to it for holding it.

The arrangement of the lamps is also artistic and varies according to place and occasion. These are either placed in circles or in rows.

Lamps thus play an important role in everyday life in India. Lighting a lamp near a Tulsi plant is ritual followed by people almost all over the country. Diwali, essentially a festival of Lights, is all about lamps lighting up life and chasing away darkness. Plentry and abundance to the family. Electricity has not been able to replace the traditional and emotional significance of a humble lamp in the lives of the people of India.

CHITRA BALASUBRAMANIAM

THEATRE IN INDIA --- AMATEUR ENGLISH DRAMA

In the old days, there were amateur dramatic clubs in the more important cities of India. These clubs were made up almost entirely of Englishmen and Englishwomen, and their performances were part of the social doings of the town during appropriate seasons. Acting of plays in the English language by Indians was confined largely to college and school productions. Even here, only some of the urban colleges attempted any regular production of plays in the English language. Certain of these institutions have had a long tradition of play-production in English, and have some good production of play-production in English, and have some good production to their credit.

Oddly enough, it is after independence that there has been a real spurt in the acting of English plays by various groups all over the country. There are now a large number of dramatic clubs or societies, some related to the British High Commission or the American Embassy, and some consisting of mixed groups of Indians. Americans and English people and some purely Indian groups. In larger cities like Bombay, there are regular theatrical groups which have attained an almost semi-professional character. This spurt in dramatic activity in the English language appears to be part of the large stimulus, given to artistic activity throughout India after independence.

Production of an English play by an Indian group has several difficulties to overcome. First of all, there is the problem of the selection of suitable play, many Indian groups are ambitious and like to attempt to perform some of the more famous plays of contemporary times. But the selection of a play is not an easy matter. For one thing for an amateur group, selection of plays must depend on the reading of large number of plays by members of the group. The does not usually happen. Very often it is by the reputation that a play has already attained or by the accident of someone having read a play that it gets selected for acting. Then again, many modern plays expect a stage which has many theatrical virtuosities. Not many Indian theatres are sufficiently well fitted to make possible the performance of some of the these very modern plays; and so in selecting a play it is necessary to consider the limitations of the stage and the theatre in which the play is to be presented.

Yet another problem is the suitability of a play from the point of view of the actors and actresses available to the group. Many of the plays in the English language are so related to the conditions of life in England or America today that the presentation of them on the Indian stage by Indians is fraught with many difficulties. Situations and circumstances are often unfamiliar to Indian audiences. There is the problem, of course, of looking like modern Europeans. In the old days when Shakespearean or eighteenth century plays were the usual ones to be acted, particularly by university groups, there was not quite the same problem of looking the part. In a sense constume-plays provide a kind of universal disguise, which makes it possible for almost anyone to take part in such plays. Also, a play in poetic language is in some ways easier to act because there is a certain universality in poetry and problem of accent, etc, do not present the same difficulties as in doing a play in contemporary English Requiring the accent of contemporary English – speaking people. Of course, poetic drama has difficulties of its won, but they are of on entirely different kind. So in selecting a play amateur groups often find it convenient to do a play which has a sufficiently universal interest so that the demands of time and place are not as paramount as they might otherwise be.

When a group has selected a play there arises the question of a producer. Often in the amateur groups, the selection of a play is in fact made by someone who offers to produce it. In this sense the problem is solved. But frequently when the group may have a feeling for a particular play it finds it difficult to find someone to put the play on the boards. The production of a play requires from the producer a great deal of understanding and initiative, and in modern plays this understanding includes at least in imaginative capacity to enter into the life of the people who are portrayed in the play. Equally the exacting demands of stage setting and décor may tax all the knowledge and ability of whoever may undertake to be the Stage Manager.

Then comes the question of casting persons in the various parts. Many amateur groups, of which I have had some knowledge, have consisted of persons generally interested in the drama but not necessarily endowed with a great deal of dramatic talent. A group may have as many as 30 or 40 members in it, but it is often difficult to kind eight or ten persons from amongst the group who could take part in a play. Since in may of the plays, the parts require particular physical characteristics or sizes and shapes, even the eight or ten people in a group who may willing and able to take part in a play may not be all equally suitable. One finds that very often at the time of putting a play on the boards, a group has to look around for outside persons who might be willing to take part in that particular play. This means that the dramatic group or society is in fact to a very considerable extent only a nominal group and for the actual production of a play one has to look widely outside the group. This involves various problems of loyalty and relationship, which are part of the difficulties of the amateur theater in India.

Since amateur theatrical groups are made up of persons many of whom have only a limited interest in the drama, they tend to break up into separate groups on the slightest provocation; and very often the same persons may be members of more than one theatrical society. This greatly complicates the problem of selecting actors and actresses to play parts in a production. Sometimes, two or three different groups may attempt to produce a play at or about the same time, and there is frequently a scramble to get hold of the few talented actors and actresses that may be available to all them. Each new society comes into being in order to achieve something that has not been achieved by the already existing groups or in order to have a character that the new group hopes will be different from that of the older groups. But the increase in the number of groups only complicates the situation. Then it occurs to someone to set up a co-ordinating society and such a co-ordinating society then attempts to bring together these various groups and in some measure regulate their activity. But it has been the experience in India to find that the new co-ordinating body itself becomes a play-producing body and then there is need for yet another co-ordinating body, and so on.

A further complication in the situation sometimes arises by the entry into the amateur theatrical world of persons who are not wholly amateurs in the sense that their interest in play production is purely for the love of it, but who are interested in drama as at least a partial source of income. Since there are no professional groups in India producing English plays, such persons cannot hope to set up a professional body. So they have to enter the amateur world and see if they can pick some profits for themselves out of the amateur theatricals. This also causes difficulties of various kinds, and instead of helping in the better production of plays, often they serve to dissipate the energies of the few willing and available actors and actresses and bring about dissensions in the groups.

Another difficulty that an amateur group has to overcome before it can produce a play is to find sufficient funds to equip the stage and make the necessary costumes for particular production. Since there are not many regular theatres in India, in many places producers of play have to ring up a make shift stage and this involves enormous amount of labour and much ingenuity. Even when there are reasonably well-equipped stages, rents are high and the investing of fairly large sums of money in the production of a play is a matter of serious difficulty to many groups. Even the seemingly simple matter of getting enough copies of the plays or script is not easy for many of the theatrical groups in our country.

But in spite of these various difficulties it is my impression that the standard of amateur production of English drama in India has gone up very considerably since independence. In Bombay, Delhi and other places, one may expect to see a number of good productions during a year, and some of the best known modern stages successes are presented by amateur groups in these places.

If dramatic production is to be encouraged, it will be necessary to lend assistance to amateur groups in various ways. The following are some of the needs as I see them.

We must have a number of reasonably well-equipped theatres in all our larger cities and towns. There must also be a theatrical library in which it should be possible to find an adequate supply of actable plays as well as literature on the business of the stage. Then there should be some central body, which should have funds at its disposal from which loans could be advanced to theatrical groups to enable them to put up plays. If a town has more than one theatrical group, it should be possible to build up what might be called a costume and property bank, so that from a common pool various societies could borrow material according to their needs. Of course, every play will require special constume and equipment, but a stock of things will be a great convenience. Encouragement should be given to amateur actors and actresses in the from of prizes and other awards for good performances. Amateur societies should also, if possible, be enabled to go on tour to at least the neighboring towns and perform plays there so that they have the opportunity of wider contact and of a larger criticism of their work. Movement of this kind may give an opportunity to actors and actresses to see performances by other groups and there will be not only a certain kind of healthy competition but also the stimulus of mutual criticism.

SAMUEL MATHAI

THEATRE – ASPECTS OF MODERN INDIA

A mere representation of historical fact cannot be a subject matter for a drama. It can not be merely a narration of facts. It should be a powerful incident in the life of a human being. What could that incident be? The society has framed a code of conduct for the smooth and harmonious functioning of the individuals. This code has collective sanction of the individuals forming the society for its impartial enforcement. The society and the individual are interdependent but not independent. But, the individual at a particular stage of development tries to go in advance of the society. He wants to execute his own ideas independently. He tries to disobey the laws of the society, setting up a plea of circumstances. The society tries to control him. Thus arises a conflict between the society and the individual, which generally constitutes an important subject matter of drama.

The individual guided by his intellect, tries to create his own code of conduct which he calls principles. But his instincts and sense of humanity sometimes get in conflict with his principles, giving rise to a conflict within his own self. This conflict within the individual is another powerful theme of drama.

'RASA' – THE OBJECTIVE OF DRAMA

Having secured a theme, the dramatist chooses his own characters in his own imaginative world and puts powerful dialogues expressing his ideas through the characters. These dialogues whether in the form of prose of poetry, should be powerful and correctly express his thought. At this stage the characters are mere fantasies; their body consists of dialogues. They are note real human beings; they are ideas merely. The script of the play is interpreted by the director. He chooses his caste with due consideration to suitability of the roles and sets the rehearsals. The actor not only memorises the dialogues but also portrays the emotions behind the dialogues. He rehearses to such an extent that after some time the dialogues become natural to him. He projects across the footlights to the audience, the feelings of the character created by the author, through his on expression, gesticulations, speaking of the dialogue, outward manifestation of his emotions and sentiment, like tears, laughter, paleness etc. The actor does not really

feel but appears to feel as approximates to reality as is possible. Acting is the concealment of one's own self under an assumed individual. Thus the actor creates a felling in the mind of the spectator that it is exactly a reality that is happening at the moment. The actor succeeds when he makes the spectator forget his own surroundings and makes him resonate sympathetically with due emotions and sentiments of the character created by the author. This is known as 'rasa'. The spectator, without reference to his own real existence, falls in tune with the ideas and the sentiments of the characters created by the author and represented by the actors.

The Indian drama always portrayed this idea. Bharata has conceived it in 'Natya Sastra':

The drama should be full of ideas and should have a variety of characters. It should be full of situations and should interpret the mental reaction to those situations. It should try to be true to nature.

INDIAN DRAMA – THE PAST AND THE PRESENT

India is proud of Kalidasa, Bhasa, Bhavabhuti, Sudraka and several others. They built the edifice of drama on strong foundations. In spite of the vicissitudes in the wake of political exploitation perpetrated in our country since several centuries and the consequent intermixing of the various outside cultures with ours, we can still look for inspiration to our great dramatists of the past. There were theatres ; the people enjoyed the plays of the great dramatists. There was royal patronage to these dramatists. The plays were of high calibre and rooted deep in the Indian culture. It is, therefore, no wonder that they survived the onslaught of barbarity.

With the dawn of Independence the nation has dedicated itself to revive and rejuvenate our arts. The institution of the Sangeet Natak Academy, among others, amply bears this out. But our efforts in this direction seem to be west-oriented. Wanton imitation of the west is to be abhorred. The west is not be condemned merely for the sake of it. It has its own good qualities. In spite of the tremendous advancement is science; the west has not ignored the revival of culture. Their spectacular material progress has, in fact, kept pace with their cultural progress. But out Indian culture is entirely different from the western culture, we have a tradition of our own, bequeathed to us by the saints and the sages of the past. Our way of life and attitude to life are entirely different. We believe in self realization through the elimination of the baser elements in us. Our ideal is the dedication of one's own self to the welfare of the others. The type of culture that we need to nurture should have its roots firm in our ancient traditions and its branches sprawling out to receive from all quarters sunshine and air so vital to its growth. And this applies with equal force to drama which reflects culture of the time.

DRAMA – ITS ENDURING VALUE

The play should never be used as a vehicle of propaganda. It is neither heard nor seen when it is merely a piece of propaganda. The play should carry a message to the higher sense of human beings through the portrayal of emotions and sentiments. It should be a piece of beauty giving delight but not amusement to the spectator. Mimicry is not acting for it offers mere amusement. The actor on the other hand takes the spectators to a different plane where they forget their own real lives and converse in mute with the characters presented on the stage. The ideas of the author are conveyed to the spectator through the actor. They are driven home at least for the moment and are swallowed like a sugar-coated pill. Bharata has said that the drama should correct the manners of the society, When it has gone to bad ways.

The influence of drama in spectators is marvellous. If has shaped their characters many a time. Gandhi ji has said in his biography that he was very much influenced on seeing the drama of Harishchandra. It is not merely an amusement but a piece of delight. It has gone through all ages, races, countries and all forms of religions. The stage is the most effective source of in fluence on man. To the thoughtful and reading man, it brings light, fire, colour and the vivid instinct which are beyond the reach of study. To the common indifferent man immersed in business and socialities of daily life, it brings vision of glory and adventure of emotion and of broad human interest. It gives him glimpses of the heights and depths of character and experience setting him thinking and wandering in the midst of amusement. Thus we see the drama is the reflection of cultural activities of human life. In a country where drama has flourished once, its temporary decay there is indicative of a set-back in the cultural advancement of society in that country.

The drama should never be neglected. It should live as long as the society exists. It is a lesson, It is a corrective; it is communication with the past, an estimate of the present and a direction to the future.

B. K. RAO

THEATRE : NEW DIRECTION AND PERSPECTIVE

The Indian theatre is, today, at an exciting point in its development. During the decade now closing, it has gone through many changes, both objective and subjective. Almost in all the language areas today there are more theatres, more groups, more plays and playwrights, more directors, actors, designers, and above all more audiences, than were there even about few years ago. Subjectively, there has been a decisive shift in the attitudes about the theatre which, today, tends to be regarded more and more a creative act rather mere entertainment, a search for identity rather than mere self-exhibition. More and more, the theatre, people now strive for suggestive simplicity rather than a spectacle, for an evocative environment rather than elaborate naturalistic detail. Popularity is no more the primary and supreme value in the theatre and is being replaced by the attempt to create a genuine desire and hunber for a deeper experience among the spectators. Also, the audiences are beginning to the theatre now not for socialising, but in search of something more abiding and worthwhile. Obviously, these changes are still only symptomatic indicating some kind of beginning of a process rather than an accomplished fact, but the new direction is unmistakable.

PLAYWRITING

The most meaningful and decisive change perhaps, has come about in play-writing. Today Indian theatre has a much bigger repertoire which is all-India in character. During the last few years the Bengali plays like Evam Indrajit and Baki Itihas by Badal Sarkar, Marathi plays like Shantata, Court Challo Ahe and Gidhare by Vijay Tendulkar, Kannad plays like Tughlaq and Yayati by Girish Karnad and Suno Janamejaya by Adya Rangacharya, Hindi plays like Ashadh Ka Ek Din and Adhe Adhoore by Mohan Rakesh are being performed in various theatre. Centres in original as well as in translations. This has given a new sweep and dimension apart from variety, to the entire theatre scene. Theme-wise, these plays try to probe deeper and at many levels into the condition of man today in our society. They are neither simple entertainment nor mere thesis plays presenting this or that social or individual problem. Instead, they try to explore the basic human relationship and their contradictions, their ironies and absurdities, and the consequent predicament of man today.

Apart from these plays which are being staged, often simultaneously, at such distant centers as Bombay, Calcutta, Delhi, Madras, Bangalore, Jaipur etc., the work of many new playwrights emerging in any Indian languages has given a new meaning and significance, and hence a new perspective, to the theatre everywhere. In Hindi, for example, Dhramavir Bharati's Andha Yug, in the fifties attempted a vehement and powerful exposure of the futility and absurdity of was as a solution to social and individual antagonisms, and has been one of the most significant contributions to the post-war Indian drama. Now, Trishanku (B.M. Shah), Shuturmurg (Gyandev Agnihotri), Marjeeva Hatya Ek Akar (Lalit Sahgal) and Draupadi (Surendra Varma) are some of the other recent Hindi plays by younger writers which have further strengthened and enriched the Hindi theatre. Similarly Koipan Phool Nu Nam Bolo To (Madhu Rye) in Gujrati, Sultan (Elkunchar), apart from the work of the established playwrights like P.L.Deshpande and Vasant Kanetkar in Marathi Bandi (G.Shankar Pillai) in Malayalam. Banahansi (Manoranjan Das) in Oriya, and the work of Lokenath Bhattacharya in Bengali and Lankesh in Kannada – these all have made the theatre more varied and interesting related to significant human experience rather than to the trivialities of life.

FLEXIBILITY IN DRAMATIC FORM

Inevitably, these and many other plays written recently have explored the dramatic form in different ways. The rigid three-act frame of realistic drama has gradually become much more free and flexible, making and imaginative use of many non-realistic conventions and devices, both Western as well as Indian, such as chorus, narrator or commentator, Sutradhar, court-room scene, play within a play, flashback, montage apart from the use of music and recitative dialogue, unreal or surrealistic character, simultaneous action, exploration of myth and ritual, etc. The new play-wright, in his struggle to express the complex and tangled experience of modern life, has used all these elements freely. There is an intense search for a dramatic form which can articulate and define this experience effectively in all its contradictions and dimensions. It is primarily this search which has led also to a new interest in the Sanskrit and traditional or folk theatre. Habib Tanvir's experiments in producing Mrichchhakaik and Mudrarakshas in Urdu or English. Sombhu Mitra's recent production of Mudraarakshas in Bengali, Shanta Gandhi's productions in Hindi or Madhyam Vyagyoga and Bhagwadajkam and plays like Jasma Odan (Bhavai) and Amar Singh Rahod (Nautanki), and many other such attempts have underlined the significance of relevance of our own theatre tradition for new creative work.

This struggle of the Indian drama for a fresh creative expresson has been further strengthened by the presentation of the significant Western plays in translation. Authors like Sophocles, Shakespeare, Ibsen, Strindberg, Chekhov, Gorky, Pirandello, Brecht, camus, Sartre, Becket, Miller, Tennesee, Williams etc., have been staged in new translations, occasionally also adaptation of the Western plays is not new here, this process has continued right through the last hundred years or more of the modern Indian theatre. But today the Western play is being staged in our country either because it is in some way vitally related to our life today, or because it is a classic and expresses the abiding concern of mankind, which is certainly indicative of a new maturity and seriousness in our theatre.

MORE SOPHISTICATED PRODUCTIONS

It is evident that such an extension in the writing and translation plays could not be possible, or even necessary, without a corresponding development in staging. In fact, during the past few years, the production of plays in various centers and languages has acquired considerable sophistication and aesthetic awareness. The increase complexities and responsibilities of play production has brought about the decisive emergence of the 'director' as one of the most important elements in the art of the theatre. Producing a play is no more merely a spontaneous act of some enthusiastic and talented actors, but a creative orchestration of many skills, arts as well as the artists, requiring not only considerable planning, organization and coordination of various elements, but also a vision and the capacity to perceive interpret and then to reach across to the audiences the meaning of a dramatic work. Accordingly, while the directors like Sombhu Mitra, Utpal Dutt, E. Alkazi, Habib Tanvir, Satyadev Dubey, Shayamanand Jalan etc., have acquired national eminence for their outstanding work, a number of other people are emerging as talented and competent directors in various language, including such names as Shanta Gandhi, Vijaya Mehta, Arvind Deshpande, Ajitesh Banerji, Rajinder Nath, Mohan Maharshi B.M.Shah, Om Shivpuri, Kamalakar Sontakee, B.V. Karant, Shama Saidi etc. In the work of most of these people there is striving for truth, for a kind of fidelity to life without recourse to the usual theatrical clichés. Some of them, while retaining some of the flavour of the theatre of their region, wherever that actively and vitally exists have revealed a distinct sense of individual identity, a style which would at one by expressive of themselves as well as the wider reality.

EMPHAIS ON TOTAL DESIGN

In actual staging also there is now a greater emphasis on the total design of a production, on simplicity and aesthetic quality of décor, on imaginative patterning of light, of colours, masses, levels and spaces, on a creative choreography of movements. Accordingly, the designing and execution of sets, furniture, costumes, lighting, and make-up are becoming specialised jobs requiring training and continuous participation. The productions have, increasingly, displayed a bold imaginative use of the various elements of the theatre. The symbolic, architectural quality of Sombhu Mitra's production of Tagore's Raktakarabi, the epic dimension of Alkazi's production of Gyandev Agnihotri's Shuturmurgh, the lyrical rendering of ordinary everyday life in Habib Tanvir's production of Angar, the evocative simplicity and spontaneith of the tragic humour in Arvind Deshpande's production of Vijay Tendulkar's Shantata, Court Chaloo Ahe are certainly new landmarks in the modern Indian theatre. Our producers are experimenting with all kinds of staging techniques and devices, both Western and Indian including central or arena staging, multiple setting, or bare stage with only levels or extensions of the stage with only levels or extensions of the stage into the auditorium among the spectators, audience participation through various devices, the same actor doing many roles, use of the narrator or singer of miming of properties and a change of locale, use of masks, etc. These methods, though sometimes introduced in a self-conscious or contrived manner, often relieve the productions of the banality and triteness resulting from a pointless verisimilitude, and helps in making the performance a sensitive creative act for the players and exciting experience for the spectators.

Similarly, acting is no more mere fun or self-exhibition undertaken casually or as a hobby. That it is a serious creative activity, requiring not only dedication and concentration but hard work and training, is being generally recognized even among the most elementary groups. Acting in our plays, therefore, has become more restrained, natural imaginative, free from the usual claptrap and hamming either of the film or the commercial theatre variety. In fact, the virtuosity, range and imaginative portrayal by an actress like Tripti Mitra is probably comparable to the best anywhere in the world.

AUDIENCES

This rapid survey of some of the major artistic factors of our theatre brings us inevitabley to the question of the audience, that peculiar and rather tricky element of the art of the theatre, which is completely independent of the playwright, actors or director, but without which they cannot function. Unlike all the other arts, the theatre is inconceivable without an audience. And yet the factors which influence the presence of the audience in a performance are often very intangible, generally beyond the control of those engaged in the theatre creativity. It is undoubtedly one of the most complicated questions of the theatre anywhere , and very much more so in our country where its growth has been interrupted and distorted for many reasons. For instance, numerically, there are today more spectators for theatrical performances than there ever were. During the last few years the commercial theatre has registered a new advance in some areas. In Calcutta, there are now seven regular theatres compared to the four only a few years ago, and they have quite good houses for their four performances every week. In Marathi, the new spurt in the commercial theatre has been simply fabulous. It is run by contractors who engage actors for a specific play, paying them a fixed sum for every performance. Some of these plays have a run of hundreds of a nights, bringing substantial money not only to contractor but also to the actors and playwrights. Usually there are more than a dozen such shows on in Bombay, played to crowded houses. These temporary companies also tour around different towns in Maharashtra where they are even more popular. In Tamilnadu, the Sabhas, which until recently patronized only dances and music recitals, have now become interested in dramas also, particularly by casts consisting of film stars, and the popularity and demand for the playwright-actor like Cho is simply staggering. Three or four commercial theatres are also functioning in Cuttack and Puri in Orissa.

The situation in the rural or semi-urban theatre forms like Jatra, Tamasha, Nautanki etc. is also interesting. It is said that some of the Jatra actors and actresses get thousand of rupees as salaries and Jatra companies are so well off that they maintain well-appointed modern offices in Calcutta. For the Tamasha, there is a regular theatre house at Poona where regular performances are put up every night, and so on. Thus it would appear that, as far as the commercial theatre or the theatre of entertainment was concerned. there was no shortage of spectators.

But this is only partly true and is misleading in many ways. For, the modern commercial theatre does not exist every where, and in a number of regions and languages there are few spectators for drama as such, and for any serious and artistic play people have to be persuaded and coaxed to come to see it. It is also interesting to note that, while in some regions a flourishing commercial theatre with its entertainment bias lures the audiences away from the serious theatre, in some others, they are uncertain and erratic because there is no regular commercial theatre to create a theatre-mindedness,

COMMUNITY AND THEATRE

This is closely related to the fact that the community at a large is not vitally involved in the theatre. The theatre gets very little or no help from any official or unofficial source, like the Central or State Governments, municipality or other local bodies, Academies etc. These bodies are either indifferent to the theatre or use their resources to further some narrow objectives There are no private trusts or foundations interested in the promotion of these arts—except, of course, the Centre for the performing Arts at Bombay set up by the Tatas, which is socially too high-brow and also West-oriented, and Kala Mandir at Calcutta established by the Birlas, which does not seem to know at all what really to do.

DRAMA DEPARTMENTS IN UNIVERSITIES

The theatre does not find any mentionable place in our Universities either, where not only future actors, directors and playwrights but also serious and genuine audiences could be created and nurtured. In fact, an active drama department in the universities could become a very vital and infections nucleus of the theatre for the entire community.

This is proved by the result of the activities of the National School of Drama at New Delhi. It has, during the twelve years of its existence, not only trained a substantial number of actors, directors and technicians, but has also provided some of the most exciting theatre to the Delhi audiences, and has contributed vitally towards an all-round improvement in their taste as well as the standard of play production in the city. But our universities seem to be saddled with such unimaginative academicians who are not interested in the theatre. At present except the Rabindra Bharati University at Calcutta, M.S. University of Baroda and Andhra University-whose performance in the field, unfortunately, has not been very creditable – no other university has any drama department. It would be futile, under the circumstances to expect any provision for the theatre at the level of the secondary education. And this is so not because of lack of resources so much as that of imagination and understanding. For, both the Central and State Governments spend very much larger sums for the publicity theatre though song and Drama Division and such other agencies. This imbalance and lopsidedness is probably typical of the place of arts in our thinking and planning.

THEATRE IS ALIVE

And yet the theatre struggles along. In spite of all its inner contradictions and weaknesses, and in spite of all the apathy and indifference of the community and the shortsightedness of the powers that be, the Indian theatre today is alive and restless with a new energy. The most hopeful feature is that it is beginning to be dissatisfied with itself, and no more wants to remain a pale slavish copy of the Western Fashions which it has so far generally tended to be. Instead, it has started groping for its own individual identity, to shape its own distinctive personality which its has so far lacked. The long, varied, myriad-coloured traditional theatre people, not for any blind revivalist purpose but for a creative imaginative use to express the shattering complex experience of life today. A whole new generation of the younger playwrights, a actors, directors, technicians is coming forward, who have not only the competence but also the determination to make the theatre one of the most vital activities and an exciting experience both for the individual as well as community.

N. C. JAIN

THIRUNELLI TEMPLE IN KERALA

. Thirunelli, a land of incomparable scenic beauty with the fast flowing rivers and green-clad Brahmagiri hill regions, has been one of the major pilgrim centers in Kerala. The historic Thirunelli temple has been referred to as the "Kasi" of South India.

This temple located in the valley beneath the Brahmagiri hill in Wynad, north Kerala, is dedicated to Mahavishnu. Nearly 143 Km. away from Kozhikode, Thirunelli temple and its surrounding holy spots draw numerous devotees from various parts of South India. Private and State Transport buses bring in pilgrims from distant Kozhikode and Guruvayoor.

There are many legends associated with temple. One says that the temple was dedicated by Brahma to Mahavishnu. Once Brahma was deslighted beyond measure with his place with its grove of lovely trees and flowering plants, among which stood a 'nelli' (Gooseberry tree) beneath which was an idol Mahavishnu having four hands bedecked with numerous fine fewels. To Brahma's surprise, the idol suddenly vanished from sight. Being overtaken with grief and surprise at this sudden disappearance, Brahma engaged himself in deep contemplation. After some time the idol reappeared and Brahma heard the·following words uttered by an invisible being: "The image that you have seen is that of Vishnu".

Brahma then made a temple, consecrated Vishnu there in and entrusted its protection to two pious Brahmins of the village. Brahma also ordained that visits to and prayers at this temple would rid people of their sins. Brahma also decreed that the performance of ceremonies here would give salvation to departed soulds. It is believed that Parasurama, the legendary founder of Kerala, had worshipped at Thirunelli to rid himself of the sin òf having committed matricide. He decreed that those who came to Thirunelli and offered Bali (rituals for the dead) at the sacred Papanisni rivulet here would get mental solace.

Papanasini springs from the Brahmagiri peak and flows by the side of Thirnuelli temple. A major center of pilgrimage, the river has special religious significance as devotees believe that a bath in its waters washes off the sins. Immersion of the mortal remains in its water confers 'Moksha' (Salvation), it is believed.

Brahmagiri, the peak from where the river originates, is believed to have been the place for a yoga conducted by Brahma. In papanasini, the devotees conduct rituals for the forefathers on a huge rock called "Pinnappara". Legend runs that the huge rock belonged to an Asura who was cursed by Vishnu, turning him into a rock.

The rocks from Thirunelli in Gaya are the remains of the Asura. With his legs at Thirunelli, his torso in the river Godavari and his head at Gaya.

Padampurana mentions that offering rituals for the dead at Papanasini river would lead the departed solus to Salvation Pinnappara, devotees believe, is a sacred place where numerous sages and legendary heroes like Jamadagni, Parasurama and Sri Rama had offered 'pitu tarpana'. Papanasini is one of the seven holy Teerths (others being Panchatheertha. Rnomochini Teertha, Gunnikateertha, Satabindu, Sahasravinda and Varaham) But today only three teerthas, namely Papanasini, Panchateertha and Gunnikateertha remain unspoiled.

Panchatheertha is situated on the way to Papanasini river from the temple. At the center of Panchatheertha lies rock of five feet diameter. On which are sculptured Foot-prints, Samkhu, Chakra, Gada and Padma, symbolically representing Mahavishnu. It is belived that Vishnu had stood on the rock for giving directions to Brahma.

Gunnikateertha, situated a km away from the temple is also believed to have been the abode of Siva as a 'Swayambhu' and from here Siva went to Kottiyoor, 60 km away to kill Daksha. A small care adjacent to Gunnikateertha is believed to have been the place where the sage Agastya meditated.

Pilgrims travelling by foot for a out three km from Papanasini through the jungle can have a darshan of three other holy spots. They are Garudanpara, Patala and Pakshipatala.

P. K. DEVAN

TIE AND DYE TECHNIQUE

The yarn tied-dyed; cloth to undergo the process in Bandhaini. Rubber bands used to resist colour; to protect part of cloth not to be dyed.

Gorgeous sarees, dress materials made; in full tie and dye; also with tie and dye pullo, border only; the main body of saree sometimes contain "chiiki" designs, small lines in disturbed arrangement. Ranging up to one hundred and twenty counts; Textile pleasing. Used as curtains, dress materials, table cloths, scarves, sarees, blouses. Tie and die of Pochampally colourfully striking; won admiration all over India, including South East Asia; the Middle East; the continent; the U.S.A. silks also being tied-dyed; gives name striking effect.

TIRUPATI : VATICAN OF THE EAST

Tirupati – the abode of Lord Sri Venkateshwara (the birthless one), also called Sri Balaji in the North, is a very popular pilrgrimage center of India. Known for its sanctity, power and its much-fabled riches, the temple is what every devout Hindu wishes to visit at least once in his lifetime.

Located in the southernmost part of Andhra Pradesh, Tirupati usually represents both the temple-town at the foothills and the main pilgrimage center called Tirumal of Sri Balaji, nestling at 3000 feet uphill.

The temple is one of the oldest in the country; its recorded history goes back to at least 2000 years, placed somewhere between 57 BC and 78 AD when, as the legend goes, a local chieftain called Tondaman discovered the idol of Sri Balaji in a huge ant-hill on the hills, where he built a small temple and started daily worship. Over the centuries the original structure has grown enormously as one sees it today with the grateful additions made by puissant dynasties and victorious monarchs that include the Cholas, Pandyas, Pallavas and the Vijayanagaras. Their benefactions to the temple in the form of valuable jewellary are preserved even to this day in the treasury of the Lord.

The Temple structure is an architectural wonder. Though small in size compared to the other famous temples of the south, it is never the less a marvel and draws more people from all walks of life and from all parts of the country and abroad throughout the year. A staggering 20 million people are said to visit the shrine every year.

The image of deity is profusely bejewelled from tip to toe in precious metals and stones worth millions of rupees. Even the Vimana (tower) above the sanctum sanctorum and the huge pillar in front of the deity wrapped in sheets of gold that shine brilliantly against the lush green hills behind. Both from its religious point of view and for its legendary riches, the temple of Lord Sri Venkateshwara is considered to the second richest religious institution in world after the Vatican City.

Going up the hill by road or on foot (climbing 3500 steps) is an experience by itself. The sylvan hills and the breathtaking valleys offer unforgettable scenic beauty all along.

RAMCHANDER PENTUKAR

TISSUE CULTURE

Biotechnology has made significant strides and gained high visibility in scientific field during a short span of time. It has opened up new research vistas and offered new tools and technologies to develop novel organisms, biological systems, commercial products and processes, thus emerging as a very promising multi-disciplinary field with unbound potential to resolve varieties of problems related to agriculture, health, industry, environment, energy and other important sectors. With the application of biotechnology, safer and more effective vaccines, quicker and reliable immunodiagnostics and vital hormones have been developed; high yielding elite varieties of plants resistent to various pests and environmental stresses have been generated; methods for fast multiplication of plantation and horticultural crops have been worked out and highly productive strains of important industrial micro-organisms have been engineered. Also developed are safer and more economical methods of biologically controlled waste treatment, pollution control, mineral extraction etc. These have arrtacted the attention of not only the scientific community but also planners, governments and members of the general public and over the world.

In India, during the last ten years, many centralised service oriented research facilities have been established, many new programmes of manpower development introduced to evolve inter-institutional and industry-institutional collaboration and to generate highly trained and skilled manpower at various levels. It has strengthened the base of biotechnology and a given a big momentum to research and development activities and achieved breakthroughs in aeas like plant tissue culture immuno-diagnostics, immuno-contraceptives and other vaccines, embryo transfer technology, industrial microbiology, DNA finger printing, biological pest control, aquaculture and in other applied and basic aspects of modern technology.

What is tissue culture ? Tissue culture or micro propagation is a rapid method of vegetative multiplication under disease-free controlled conditions. To start tissue culture, young buds are taken from the donor plant, surface sterlised and place in an artificial medium containing all pre-requistes for plant growth. Then in controlled evnviroment the growth of this culture is directed towards the production of a large number of true to type shoots, which can either be rooted in vitro in sterile medium of established potting mixture and then hardened in green house for use.

The process can be well illustrated in cardamom cultivation, in Western Ghats of South India. Here cardamom is cultivated in an are of 82,000 has distributed all over the Ghats. It is a predominantly cross pollinated crop propagated through seedlings and rhizomes. Seedillings are not true to type whereas rhizome propagation is time consuming and helps in the spread of viral diseases. Production of large number of planting units in shorter time frame can be done using tissue culture technology. Similarly tissue culture is done on a number of other plants ranging from bananas to orchids.

What is the need for tissue culture? The reasons are simple. Seedlings are heterogeneous and show variation with respect to yield and qualitative parameters. Tissue culture plantelets are true to the selected mother plants. Besides tissue culture technology enables the production of a large number of genetically uniform planting materials of a high yielding clone in shorter time frame. The planter can identify high yielding mother plant with superior quality from his own plantation for multiplication through tissue culture. Planting of high yielding uniform tissue culture plantlets lead to an increase in unit productivity by eliminating poor qualities among seedling population. Tissue culture helps in faster multiplication of hybrids or any other type of superior plant. And these plants are disease-free Last but not the least, tissued culture plantlets can be produced throughout the year.

Tissue culture plays a key role of in the production of horticultural foliage and plantation crops. It is useful for the rapid introduction of the elite varieties of plants who have higher yields, increased vigour and better health. Plant tissue culture is actively pursued in universities, research laboratories and private companies by the scientists. India has one of the largest groups of tissue culture scientists in the world.

The Indian tissue culture industry has the potential to garb a sizeable chunk of the growing international market for flowers and other plants. Each medium-sized tissue culture unit can earn foreign exchange worth 20-30 million rupees and there is enough potential for 100 such units in the country.

MEENA BHANDARI

TREASURE OF INDIAN ART

German scholars have always taken interest in the study of Indian religion, philosophy and art. India's rich and ancient cultural heritage has attracted art lovers and historians from all over the world. The museum of Indian Art, Berlin, is one of the famous centers of Indian art objects. Its origin can be traced to the formation of a comprehensive Institute of Asian Arts, a precursor for several museums in Berlin – the Museum of Far Eastern Art, the Museum of Islamic Art, and the Museum of Indian Art – all of which exist side by side with the Ethonological Department.

The collection of Indian Art objects at the Museum of Indian Art, Berlin, can be traced to the 16the century. It was originally a private collection, meant to be viewed by noble visitors. In the middle of the 17th century, Wilhelm V. Humbolot initiated the idea of displaying the collection for the general public and thus a Museum was developed. During World War II, a large number of art objects were moved to safer places. The present Museum of Indian Art, Berlin was founded in 1963 and is one of the seventeen state museums founded under the Prussian Cultural Foundation, the largest and the most important cultural authority in Germany, established in 1961.

The objects d'art include sculptures in stone, metal and terracotta, relating to Buddhism, Hinduism and Jainism; miniature paintings based on Raagmala series and art pieces in jade. Buddhist sculptures depict different stages of Lord Buddha's life, his previous incarnations and Boddhisattvas relating to compassion and re-incarnation. A well-known easily identifiable by a small image of Buddha Amitabh in his crown and lotus in his hand. Important titles include Boddhisattva Avalokiteshwara, Buddha Amitabh, Buddha (Khushana Gandhara School 1st to 2nd century AD), and veneration of a stupa (Sanchi, circa 50 AD). When Buddhism travelled to Tibet, it was not accepted in its original form and was blended with Tantra Mandalas, the center of enlightment, were used as means of tantric meditation. Eash mandala is considered to be the paradise of a particular God or Goddess and is unique in its characteristic configural arrangement and colour treatment. The schematic diagram known as mandala has a central part symbolizing 'sunyata' (nothingness) where the particular deity rests and other deities occupy the surrounding places.

Buddha (Kushana Gandhara) is a departure from traditional images of Buddha. Kushana rule had two centers of art – Gandhara and Mathura, At Gandhara, the sculpture were carved out of green or grey schist and have foreign influence and the Buddhist form is derived from Greek art while at Mathura, the mottled red sandstone is used and Buddhist form is purely Indian.

The history of Indian art is available from the 3rd century BC during Ashoka's reign (276-236 BC), whose dedicated efforts to popularize Buddhism include his range eighty four thousand stupas to enshrine holy relics of the Buddha and to mark sacred Buddhist sites. Much earlier (circa 2300-1750 BC) people living on the banks of Indus produced artifacts in terracotta, stone and metal. However, from 1750-3000 BC, people concentrated more on literary pursuits and creative art took a back seat. In the 3rd century BC, art again appeared and though it was more religion-oriented, its motifs take it back to Indus valley civilization. The ringstone of Maurya dynasty (3rd century BC) is another rare collection in the Museum of Indian Art, Berlin. Besides Buddhist sculptures, Hindu icons were also made in the Gandhara style and three – headed Shiva is a rare depiction of Hindu deities of this period. In 320 AD, the political power shifted to the plains of north India as the power of the Kushana kings weakned and a new dynasty, the Gupta dynasty, emerged. The art during this period had influence of Kushana style at Mathura, 'River Goddess Ganga' and 'Krishna as a child', both in terracotta are rare pieces of this period. In Bengal and Orissa two schools of art developed. The sculptures of Orissa have their origins in the Gupta period. Both Buddhist and Hindu deities originated at medieval monasteries and temples in Bengal, Orissa and Bihar. Skanda Kartikeya from Orissa, Brahma and Dancing Ganesha from Bengal and Surya from Bihar are also in the collection of this museum. 'Chamunda' with fierce fangs, demonic demeanour, along with Lord Shiva and Surya (10th century, from Bihar) symbolizing solar energy, are impressive artifacts from his period. Bronze casting technique was also prevalent and metal and stone sculptures were created simultaneously. Vaikunta Vishnu (Kashmir, 5th-7th century AD) is the famous four-headed Lord Vishnu. The influence of Gandhara art (seen as a moustache) is there and his attributes have taken human form. Another medium displayed in the Museum is jade, famous for its unparalled versatility. During 17th – 19th centuries, jade jewellery, sculptures, decorative and luxury items were in vogue and they are duly represented here.

ANITA VARMA

TRICHUR POORAM : FESTIVAL OF PACHYDERMS AND PARASOLS

Come summer and lakhs of people congregate in Trichur, the cultural capital of Kerala, to witness Trichur Pooram, the spectacular festival of color, light and sound, caparisoned pachyderms and the breathtaking display of pyrotechnics. Transcending all barriers of caste, race and religion, Trichur Pooram has carved a special inche in the cultural millieu of Kerala and attained the status of a national festival. Unmatched in its pomp and pageantry, this post harvest festival has been acclaimed as the King of festivals.

The genesis of this most awaited cultural extravaganza can be traced back to the days of Sakthan Thampuram, the erstwhile king of the Kochi Royal Family who organized it almost 200 years ago to appease the denizens of Trichur who could not participate in the Pooram of Arattupuzha, another temple close by owing to heavy downpour. He ordered for a separate festival in summer and to facilities the celebration, the vast expanse of teak forests around Vadakkunthan temple in Trichur was cleared at his behest.

The Trichur pooram is a thirty hour long show starting at 6 am on the Pooram day and ending at 12 noon the next day. It consists of processions taken out from various temples in the vicinity of Trichur. All the temple processions congregate at the sprawling Pooram maidan around the 1500 year old Vadakkunathan temple and pay respects to Lord Shiva, the presiding deity of the temple who is supposed to host the other deities participating in the festival. It is the layout of the main temple, the vast Pooram maidan and the circular road around it, that enhances the magnificence and splendour of the festival.

The essence of the festival is the veneration of Lord Vadakkunathan by the deities of Thiruvambedi and Parmekkavu temples. The two processions starting from these two temples deserve special mention, each of these processions comprises of specially selected elephants with their foreheads adorned with glittering fold grit "Nettippattoms" (a large fringes cloth into which are sewn around 600 gold plated pieces of farying sizes and the central elephant carrying the presiding deity of the temple to which the festival is dedicated. The gold head dress adorning the elephants, together with the specially trained people atop the elephants with multicoloured silk parasols, flaunting circular peacock feather fans and swinging yak tail bunches is an awesome sight.

In front of procession, there will be a display of Chanda Melam, an orchestra of instruments like Chenda, Kurum, and Kuzhal (windpipe) elethalam (cymbal) and Kombu (conch) some processions are accompanied by Panchavadyam, a music ensemble comprising of Thimilia, Maddalam, Edakkam, Elathalam and the Kombu. The highlight of the orchestras is the famous "Elanjithara Melam", a performance under the shade of the Elanji tree in the precincts of the Vadakkunathan temple. With 200 artists playing on different instruments, the Elanjithara Melam" is unique in temple festivals. Entranced by the magic of the pulsating orchestra, spectators wave their hands in tune with the rhythm and dance with delirious joy and ecstasy.

The most interesting feature of Trichur Pooram is :Thekkottirakkam" (moving towards the south) followed by the magnificent "Koodikkazcha" (the fabulous durbar of the caparisoned elephants). The grand event of the durbar is the enchanting "Kudamattom" or the pageantry of changing multi-coloured, mirror-studded parasole by the rival temples of Paramekkavu and Thiruvambadi. Mammoth crowds converge all around the maidan to have a glimpse of the much awaited umbrella display in the glorious evening sun which goes on for half an hour. The silk umbrellas held atop the array of gaily-decorated elephants keep changing. One brilliant colour following another in a spirit of competition between the rival temples. Both sides compete with each other in waving the yak tail bunches and feather fans on the top of the elephants in unison with the beating of drums in front of the procession. The sheer variety, the colours, the patterns and the unison with which the umbrellas are displayed is a magnificent spectacle, sending spectators into raptures.

As darkness descends, the processions return to the respective temples and later rejoin at the maidan. At night the ground is illuminated by torch lights. In the dead of night one can have a glimpse of the long array of caparisoned pachyderms amidst the dancing from the "Trishuls" (tridents) of blazing torches which assume an ethereal dimension and give the procession a fairy tale like splendour.

After the procession the stage is set for the greatest show, the "Vedikkettu" the non stop pyrotechnics which start at dawn creating a wonderwork of light and sound, color and brilliance, clouds and shadows. This great night spectacle in one of the high points of the festival as most spectators measure the success of the festival by the exellence of fireworks.

This spectacular display of pyrotechnics signals the end of the Pooram festival. The two deity-carrying elephants circle the huge lamp outside the temple and then link their trunks in the gesture of farewells, a befitting finale to the long hours of pageantry to honor the goods and goddesses of Trichur.

SUSHEELA NAIR

TRICHY SANKARAN : THE MRDANGAM MAESTRO

Performer, university teacher, author, music composer and researcher, soloist and accompanist, Trichy Sankaran is a multi-dimensional personality.

Though based in Toronto for over two decades, Sankaran's roots are deeply embedded in India's soil. By engaging in a life long mission to bring the vast richness and depth of percussion instruments, Carnatic mrdangam and kanjira, as well as Carnatic vocal music to lecture rooms and concert halls in North America, he has been quietly bridgins a link between East and the West. The mrdangam is a double-headed barrel drum from south India. Like the north Indian tabla, It has a dark tuning spot in the center of the skin which is made of iron fillings and rice paste. Considered to be a very sophisticated drum, the mrdangam is the capable of many different textures and tonal subtleties.

Sankaran's love for his chosen instrument-mrdangam – began very early. He started playing at age seven, under the supervision of his cousin. From age nine his guru was Palani Subramania Pillai, Sankaran is quick to point out that palghat Mani Lyer and Palani Subramania Pillai together brought mrdangam to "the biggest status", like Alla Rakha achieved this for the tabla in the north.

Sankaran has also taken interest in north Indian music through his Jugal-Bandis – music combination of different styles with north Indian artists such as Zakir Hussain, Sharda Dahni and Vilayat Khan.

Sankaran's work caught the media attention in adequate measure. Canadian. Broadcasting Corporation (CBC), Doordarshan of India and other TV networks interviewd him. Newspapers found that Sankaran played with "an amazing verve and dexterity, producing endlessly varying sequences of tome and rhythm". The Indian express stated : "His mrdangam cooed like a cockoo, trotted like a mare and, on occasions, roared like a lion".

The Gladstone observer of Australia found him to be a drummer who "leaves audiences and fellow performers speechless with his lyrical and evocative style of mrdangam". The New York Times simply called him" a fabulous musician" whose "unfailingly inventive handling of rhythm, texture and even pitch and his tireless execution riveted attention".

Sankaran is a gifted artist who has brought the Indian music closer to music lovers in Canada. He has been described by his freign students as a "musical ambassador who shows by example the potential for a Truly unified world music ..."
(Condensed)

RAJIV BHATIA

TRIVENI KALA SANGAM

Triveni Kala Sangam is a renowned cultural spot near Mandi House in New Delhi. It is a meting place for culturally active minds as well as a place where students have been alike to pursue a dream. It was started in 1951 with Sundari K. Shridharani as founder and honorary director Triveni has seen of the best talents in the country at its doorsteps. Pandit Ravi Shankar has taught here as did Guru Sikkal Ramaswamy from the south to teach dance to Indrani Rahman, Yamini Krishnamurthy and chandralekha to name a few. Its art department is considered one of the best in the country and its students have exhibited at prestigious shows in India and abroad. The three teaching departments – dance, music and painting form the basis of Triveni. Other activities include short term courses in art and culture. It has three exhibition galleries, an open air theatre a chamber theatre, a sound proof recording studio, a book shop, library and a photography unit.

TULA FESTIVAL AT MAYILADUTURAI

The Tula festival at Mayuram or Mayiladuturai is celeberated for one full month at Mayiladuturai during the month of Arpisi – from October 17 to November 15, 1991.

Thousands of pilgrims flock to Mayiladutural on the Kadamugham Day to take their bath at the Rishabha Theertham (Cauvery) Ghat. During the thirty days, the first day and the last ten days are important when the Mayil Puja and Tirukklyanam will be celebrated. There is a big tank inside the temple called the Brahma Theertham.

The first thing that attracts a visitior to the place is the famous and ancient temple dedicated to Mayuranathar. Belonging to Tiruvavaduthurai Adhinam, this temple covers an area of about eight acres. The inner prakarams of the temple of Mayurananthar and Abhayambikai are noted for their workmanship in stone.

The Maha Kumbhabhishegam of Sri Mayuranathar temple was performed by his Holiness of Tiruvavaduthurai Adhinam in 1961 after extensive renovations.

The other temples of interest are the Pancha Vishawanatha Swamy temples at the Big Bazaar, Pallkkarai, Vallalrakoil, Thimmayappanayakan Ghat and in the north street near the north temple well. The Ayyarappar temple is yet another temple under the management of Tiruvavaduthurai Adhinam. The Punugesswarar temple at Kornad is also a noted shrine.

The Maha Lakshmi Durga Devi temple at Dharampuram Adhinam is a famous temple dedicated to the Goddess with 18 arms known as Ashta Dasa Bhujaa. There are temples dedicated to Vana Durga, Chokkanathar, Gnanapureswarar and Dharam-pureswarar at Dharmapuram.

The Medha Dakahinamurthy temple at vallarlar Koil is a unique one on the banks of the river Cauvery and attracts a large crowd on Thursdays when he is adorned with Golden Kvacham. Every year a Maha Abhishekam is done to this Lord Also.

The other small temples of interest are the Durgai temple and the Mariamman temple at Senthangudy and many other newly constructed Vinayakar temples in many parts of the town and extensions. The parimala Rantganathaswamy temple at Tirundalur is a noted Shrine dedicated to Lord Ranganather.

N. RAMAKRISHNA

TURMERIC CURATIVE : PART OF INDIAN CULTURE

Ivividly remember, many years ago, when I saw ten-inch long spike of turmeric (Curcuma longa, Linn) flowers, the first thought was, "Ah' it's bouquet". As a reflex action I had immediately take the photo. The spike was almost unnoticeable, being near the foot of the short stem of about three feet high perennial herb, overshadowed by very large tufted leaves.

Turmeric, known as Haridra is Sanskrit, in fact, is extensively cultivated all over India, more so in the states of Maharashtra, Tamil Nadu and West Bengal. There are several varieties, each known by the name of the locality where grown. The short and thick rhizome of ovate, oblong or pyriform shape of this herb is the tumeric of commerce.

The brownish – yellow rhizomes consists of central bulbous portion with finger like lateral offshoots, They are separated and broken into convenient sizes. After removing dirt and fibrousroots, the rhizomes are subjected to the process of 'curing'. This involves cooking them in

water and drying uniformly. Later, 'Polishing' is done by rubbing or trampling to remove the outer skin. The final product is the attractively coloured turmeric we come across in the markets.

Turmeric is intricately interwoven in the Indian culture, particularly among the Hindus. It is one of the auspicious items in their religious ceremonies. Anointing a bride with turmeric paste is a compulsory wedding ritual for the Hindus. The herb is also a normal consituent of condiments and curry powders. It is a universally recognized organic dye.

Besides all this, importance of turmeric lies in its medicinal properties. It finds a high place in the Indian Systems of Medicine.

Juice of the fresh rhizomes is applied to wound, bruises and leesh-bites. This juice is also used as antiparasitic for many skin affections. Turmeric paste is applied to smallpox and chickenpox to facilitate the process of scabbing. The paste is used in ringworm, eczema and other parasitic skin diseases like the juice of fresh rhizomes. In cases of pemphingus and shingles, affected part is coated with mustard oil on which turmeric powder is dusted for cure within 3-4 days. Application on paste of turmeric and red sanders wood (pterocarpus santalinus) in buffalo milk removes freckless from face. According to 'Susruta-samhita' taking 40 gm turmeric with urine for a month is useful in leprosy.

Milk in which turmeric rhizomes have been boiled and sugar added, is a popular drink for treatment of cold. Mixture of clarified butter and turmeric powder relieves cough. Simply inhaling the fumes of burning turmeric in the cased of catarrh and coryza causes a capious mucous discharge and procides instant relief.

Turmeric powder and lime paste is applied to inflammed joints. Clarified butter mixed with turmeric powder, rock-salt and honey is useful in some poisoning cases. Exposing scorpion sting affected body part to the smoke of turmeric powder sprinkled over burning charcoal provides relief.

Application of an ointment made of turmeric, hemp leaves and onion with warm mustard oil or linseed oil is a great relief in painful and protruding piles. Paste of turmeric powder with latex of Euphorbia nerifolia (common Milk Hedge) is also a useful ointment in piles.

Several standard turmeric formulations like Haridrakhanda for obstinate skin complaints, Haridradi Ghrta for jundice and Haridradi Taila (oil) for wounds are available easily.

Modern day research has found that water extract of turmeric possesses significant anti-inlflammation activity. In another experiment, it was observed, application of turmeric powder over septic as well as aseptic wounds in rats and rabbits substantially acclerated the healing process.

In an clinical study at Vaidrbha Ayurvedic College in Mahrashtra state of India, powders of turmeric and Achyranthes aspera (Rough Chaff) long with latex of Euphorbia nerifolia were coated on surgical linen thread as described in 'Susruta-samhita' and was applied to nineteen patients of fistula uncer. The treatment resulted in faster improvement in the patients.

An ulcer on the right lower leg of a woman was successfully treated with dressing of turmeric powder along with oral administration of several herbs at the Ayurvedic Health care centre in South Australia.

Doctors at Sitapur Eye Hospital in Uttar Pradesh state of India, in controlled study of the corneal ulcer, observed that the use of herbal eye drops made of turmeric and several other herbs, along with conventional allopathic treatment, recovered faster than those who received the allopathic treatment alone.

These are but few examples, Several other clinical studies and research projects have confirmed many of the suggested medicinal properties of turmeric in the Indian Systems of Medicine. Today, healing properties of turmeric are recognised the world over.

SOME OTHER SIMILAR MEDICINAL PLANTS

Curcuma amada, Roxb, (English: Mango Ginger. Sanskrit: Karpura – Haridra) – Tubes are useful in prurigo. Rhizomes paste is applied in bruises and skin diseases.

Curcuma angustifulia, Roxb (English: Indian Arrowroot, Sanskrit: Tavakshiri) – This chief source of Indian arrowroot is also of many medicinal uses. Water in which tubes are boiled is useful in cases of dysentery, dysuria, gonorrhoea and useful in typoid, ulceration of bowels and bladder.

Curcuma aromatica :

Salisb. (English: Wild Turmeric. Sanskrit: Vana Haridra) : This has similar uses as Curcuma longa.

Curcuma zedoaria :

Rosc. (English: Round zedoary. Sanskrit:
Juice of the tubes is given to treat worms in children. Juice of leaves is given in dropsy. Root is chewed by Indians to clean sticky taste in mouth and to clear throat.

PUSHP K. JAIN

"U"

UDAY SHANKAR

Modern Indian ballet, started by Uday Shankar, Went to England chosen by Russian ballerina Anna Pavlova, to be her Partner, ballet, *Radha* and *Krishna*, studied 4 major styles, classical dance, created new ballets, with complex music, choreography, used classical and folk rhythms, employed western stage techniques, presented ballets with skill, polish, Ballets include, *Shiva Parvati*, *lanka Dehan*, *Rhythm of life* (1938), labour and Machinery (1939) employed contemporary social, political themes.

Shanti Bardhan, junior colleague, Uday Shankar, produced on Panchtantra, based on ancient fable, four friends used masks mimed movements of animals, birds.

Narender Sharma, Sachin Shankar, both pupils, Uday Shankar, continued tradition, Menaka, Ramgopal, Mrinalini Sarabhai, Mallika Sarabhai, Anand Shankar, experimented modern themes through *bharata-natyam*, *Kathakali* style.

UMAID BHAWAN PALACE: THE INSIGNIA OF JODHPUR

The enchanting and stately silhouette of the fifty-years-old pink sand stone palace, Umaid Bhawan, looms large over the sun-city of India, Jodhpur, in the state of Rajasthan. Build by the 36th ruler of jodhpur, Maharaja Umaid Singh, this sprawling palace happens to be one of the largest Private residences in the world. However, in present times, most of the 347 rooms in the palace have been converted into a five-star hotel managed professionally by the ITC- welcome group chain of hotels. Owned by the former maharaja Gaj Singh of Jodhpur, Umaid Bhawan is considered to the one of the premiere palace hotels in India.

The palace was originally conceived as a massive famine relief project as the region of Jodhpur is prone to droughts.

A 26-acres site on Chittar Hill was choses for the palace whose foundation was laid on 18th of November, 1929. Three thousand labourers worked for 13 years to build this splendid edifice. The main building materials used is the locally available pink sandstones. These were first masoned by hand the dressed stones joined without use of morter.

The basic plan of the palace reveals three distinct areas, delineated from each other. On the one side was the *zenana* (women's quarters), on the other the kitchen, storerooms, staff quarters and administrative offices, while in the central section were the public areas consisting of the main entrance, Darbar Hall (Hall of Audience), followed by the state dining hall and private entertainment rooms of the Maharaja, the royal apartments and the main suites. The overwhelmingly impressive exteriors fully complement the plush interiors of the Umaid Bhawan. Entrance through three large wrought gates, bearing the royal insignia; elegant, sweeping marble staircases leading to what are now the Maharaja's privates apartments and some of the Hotel's more ostentatious luxury suites, and a circular lobby areas leave the visitor breathless. Cool and finely manicured green lawns surrounded by vividly coloured bougainvillea bushes provide an ideal place to relax. One can also lounge in the elaborate white marble Baradari (Pavillion).

The palace also houses a mini auditorium, a ballroom, a conference hall, library, a bar and a restaurant, shopping arcade, a billiards room, a smoking room and a TV lounge. There are facilities for tennis, squash, an indoor swimming pool and a health club in the basement. The throne room, with its specially commissioned murals depicting scenes from the Ramayana are well worth a look.

Umaid Bhawan palace has been called the "JAZZ Age Palace" mainly because its interiors have been done in the classic Art Decostyle, much in vogue in Europe and USA of the 1930s.

SANJAY SINGH BADNOR

URBAN PAINTINGS

The artist who chooses to take on the city is looking for recognition from the galleries, curators, critics, publishers who keep their eyes of artists in the city. The represent the process by which the history of art is written. Indian artist working place since the middle of that century have left a significant collection of urban painting. Among the metropolis, Calcutta, Bombay and Delhi drew the attention of artists who made these mega cities as the focal point of their -canvas. Somenath Hore adopted Calcutta which is widely reflected in his "work" Paritosh Sen, one of Calcutta's most articulate painters has also painted vividness of Calcutta's life with master's brush. The other prominent artists who have set up their easels before the city are Ramkumar, Prbhaker Barwe, Nalini Malani and Bikash Bhattacharjee. Some of these artists have responded to the city simply because it was the front of them while others felt a need to respond to the political and social activities going on around them.
(Condensed)

USTAD MUSHTAQ ALI KHAN

Ustad Mushtaq Ali Khan (1911-1989) was a unique musician who strode the Hindustani music world like a colossus for over five decades. He was a true representative of the prestigious Senia Gharana and was the seventh in succession from Masit Sen, inventor of the Masit Khan's instrumental a which are in slow or medium speed. The maestro's distinctive trait was that he lived for an ideal and never compromised it for public applause – Although he was born at Varanasi, he lived most of the time amongst Bengalis and even his hand written notes were in the Bangali script. He was a secularist to the core, had a Hindus wife and celebrated Sarasvati Puja in his home every year. (Summarised)

USTAD NISAR HUSSAIN KHAN

With the death of Ustad Nisar Hussain Khan at Calcutta in July 1993, the Indian classical music lost one of its brightest stars as also one of the last links with old traditions, Malikarjun mansoor Krishnnarao Shankar Pandit, Kumar Gandharva and Zia Mohiuddin Dagar. Born in 1909 at Badaun in Uttar Pardesh, he was a musician's who during. His long innings enriched coffers of Indian music with such desciples as Ghulam Mustafa Khan, Hafeez Ahmed Khan, Akbar Hussain Khan, Rasheed Khan and his own sons, Sarfraz Hussain and Zulfiqar Hussain. He was the luminous star of the Rampur Sehaswan Gharana, an off-shoot of the Gwalior gharana.

Nisar Hussain Khan's musical training started at the age of five under the wings of his grandfather Haider Khan. When he was 11, he had a chance to visit Delhi as also to sing at a festival mehfil there in the presence of Saujaji Rao, the Maharaja of Baroda, who was a great patron of music. Maharaja tool a fancy for the child and took him along to Baroda where he started learning from his father Fida Hussain Khan. Years later, he graced the court of Baroda. Among his favourite ragas were Darbari, Malkauns, Gaur Sarang, Desho, Tilak, Kamod, Desh jhinjhoti and Gaur Malhar. Honours and awards were showered upon him in plenty which included the Sangeet Natak Akademi Award and Padma Bhushan.

PRAKASH WADHERA

"V"

V. S. RAHI : A GIFTED PAINTER

Virendra Singh Rahi is one of India's very senior, respected and renowned traditional painters who firmly believes in preserving, promoting and enhancing our cultural heritage through his drawings and paintings. At the ripe age of seventy, he is busy painting a series on *Bhagwad Gita*, one of the best known religious texts on human relationships and social behaviour. He is also working on another series of pain tings on *Geet Govinda*, a poet's treatise on love.

Being the Vice President of the All India Fine Arts and Crafts Society (AIFACS), New Delhi, Rahi has been a dedicated art teacher and adviser on the subject to the Government of India. He has also written on art and literature and contributed poetry to various publications, newspapers and magazines during his long and illustrious career.

Virendra Singh was born in August, 1929, in Hamirpur in Uttar Pradesh. He is the youngest of seven children of Thakur Gopal Singh, who despite being a *Zamindar* (Landlord) had literary leanings. He along with his wife, had also actively participated in the freedom movement of India.

Young Virendra Singh endowed with a good height and excellent physique, frequently participated in wrestling bouts. Thakur Gopal Singh's patriotic zeal compelled him to ask his youngest son to join the Indian Army, however Veriendra Singh never liked the idea an spent most of his time on drawing and spoiling the walls of his house. Rahi now recalls that while his mother encouraged him to follow his favourite subject, his father always discouraged him. Moreover, nobody in those days had ever heard of any professional painter in India. It was either a pastime for the rich and famous like Raja Ravi Verma or it was simply a menial job of signboard writing. Rahi recollects that it was his love for art, fuelled by his wanderlust, that really forced him to rebel against his father and run away from home in search of fulfilling his own dream and lead his life the way he wanted.

He was only fourteen or fifteen when he first landed in Ajmer in Rajasthan and then in Jaipur doing odd jobs, sometimes even working as a labourer to support himself Undeterred to support himself. Undeterred by his financial problems, Rahi pursued his goal single – mindedly and soon joined the Maharaja College of Art, Jaipur. He completed his diploma in fine arts in first division and also received a gold medal from Maharani Gayatri Devi for one of his paintings submitted at an all – India exhibition held in Jaipur. His teacher Shailendra Nath De was so impressed by his work and dedication that he recommended his to Nandlal Bose, the best known art teacher of Viswa Bharati University at Shantiniketan.

Under Nandlal's guidance, Rahi mastered different styles of painting and passed his diploma in fine arts and handicrafts from Shantiniketan in first division in 1953. He also held his first one – man show in Shantiniketan the same year. It has been more than four decades since Virendra Singh Rahi came out of Viswa Bharati University and there has been no looking back for him. He has won many awards and prizes and held several one – man and group shows all over India.

Rahi, who now lives in Delhi, is a very contented man who proudly declares, "My life has been full of struggle and great fulfillment simultaneously. I paint for humanity and I have thoroughly enjoyed my work, God has been very kind to me and at my age, while many people have already called it a day, I still draw and paint with the same gusto and it gives me as much pleasure and enjoyment as it used to give me fifty years ago".

N. K. SAREEN

VALLI : THE COMMITTED DANSEUSE

When you talk to the sylph-like and doe-eyed Alarmel Valli, you are convinced of her commitment to *Bharatnatyam*, the classical dance form.

The excitement of having at last met a complete dancer is confirmed when you watch her on the stage. As Valli sweeps the stage with her technically perfect movements joyous abandon that comes from mastering the grammar of dance, an *abhinaya* (enacting) that goes beyond mere facial gestures-all of which leave the audience breathless-you realize How a disciplined mind and body and a creative spirit can transform dance.

The 37 –year old Valli is considered to be one of the finest exponents of the difficult and vigorous Pandanallur style of Bharatanayam taught to her by the two greatest teachers of the style, Guru Chockalingam Pillai and Guru Subbaraya Pillai.

Valli says the classical performing arts, whether dance or music, are timeless in their universal appeal. "After a good classical dance or music performance, you feel uplifted and happy despite the turmoil around you ".

Valli who has performed in the United States, France, England, Germany, Egypt, Iran and other countries is a living proof of the classical arts transcending barriers and reaching across to peoples of different cultures.

When Valli performed in a small town is Italy, and Italian peasant woman told her that though she did not understand Valli's dance, watching it was enriching. In Holland, Valli had a man come up to her crying and thanking her for showing that the body could be used to seek the divine.

The knowledgeable and the critics have gone even more ecstatic about Valli's dance. John Russel, the well-known New York critic watching her performance at the New York Festival of International Arts in 1991,exclaimed that valli is that rare thing, a solo performer who puts all others out of mind'.

In Cairo critics raved that 'human feelings of all kinds were crystallized in the bends and curves of her body'.

"Wherever I go I make friends," says Valli, an extrovert, who brings to her performance an openness and friendliness. Which is why her performances are unique; she brings to the stage not only valli the technically perfect danseuse, but Valli the person with varied interests that include English, Tamil and Sanskrit poetry, her knowledge of languages (she speaks French and a little Italian),Her love of history and ancient cultures, her knowledge of music, her interest in films and theatre and her interest in aesthetics.

Valli feels since she is constantly evolving and growing as a person, no two performances of hers are ever alike.

In her childhood, Valli was so weak that no one thought she would become a dancer. She even did not come from a family that was traditionally involved in the classical arts, as many families in Madras are. Her family was more involved in the academic field. So, when Valli's mother took her to the Pandanallur gurus and put her under vigorous training under them, there was opposition in the family. But her mother's persistence and Valli's own dedication paid off (she would get up at four in the morning, dance with her gurus, go to school and again practise in the evening). She was presented her *arangetram* (sort of certification of being a dancer) when she was only nine. Not only that, she was asked by her gurus to assist them in choreography when she was only 14.

"It was my good fortune to learn dance under gurus like Chockalingam Pillai and his son Subbaraya Pillai. They were disciplinarians and perfectionists. They never once demanded money. They just wanted somebody who would carry on their style with commitment. I was equally fortunate to have a mother who was so strict and who had the eye to spot my talent", says Valli in humility.

T, Mukta, music, she says, gave an added dimension to her dance. "Dance is music in motion. When you understand music, it is much easier translate the oral experience into a visual one", she says.

Dance has been such a commitment and obsession for Valli that marriage has not fitted into her scheme of things so far. It is not as if she had deliberately chosen to remain single. It is just that with dance, the tours and performances, there has been little time for anything else.

"You can only be part-time wife if you are a committed dancer. Dance takes so much out of you that little is lift to give after that. My life is full as it is. It can't be any fuller", says the winsome dancer.

RATNA RAO SHEKAR

THE VEDAS – A UNIQUE FOUNTAIN OF WISDOM

For long centuries the Vedas remained an uncharted and unknown ocean for the West. This was not because of the difficulties of language. Western scholars had mastered more difficult languages like Greek and Latin when they wanted to know the philosophies of Greece and the laws of Rome. It was largely a case of their reluctance to accept that there was something worthwhile to know from the East. However, the doors to the vast wisdom of the vedas got opened by the 19th century and the west then realised with a great wonder and excitement what a great treasure-house they had gained access to.

Arthur Schopenhauer, the great German scholar, proclaimed with great elation that access to the Vedas was the greatest privilege that the 19th centuries might claim over all previous centures. He went on to say "In the whole world there is no study so beautiful and so elevating as those of Upanishads. It has been the solace of my life. It would be the solace of my death. Emerson was so

Overpowered by the majesty and magnitude of Vedic thought that he was moved to decribe it as "sublime as night and a breathless ocean". "It contains every religious sentiment, all the grand ethics which unites in turn each noble poetic mind".

Perhaps no Western philosopher had been so much influenced by the wisdom of the Vedas as Max Muller. The Rishis of the Vedas provided the answers which he had been seeking for the questions which had been baffling his mind for long. Referring to these Rishis he declares with great sense of gratification. They have revealed to me a whole world of thought of which no trace existed anywhere else and they helped me to throw the first faint rays of life and reason on perhaps the darkest period in the history of religion, philosophy and mythology ".

Max Muller's was not merely an interest in Sanskrit Literature. It was a genuine interest in India's spiritual heritage. The more he delved into vedic literature, the more he was captivated by its spiritual energy. He says "If I were to ask myself from what literature, we have in Europe... may draw that corrective which is most wanted in order to make our inner life more perfect, more comprehensive more universal, in fact, more truly human, a life not for this life alone, but a transfigured and eternal life, again I should point to India".

These statements of profound admiration and wonder at the wisdom of Vedas were not the off-the-cuff observation of novices in philosophical or religious thought, but were the spontaneous outpourings of some of the greatest minds of the Western world in the 19th century based on indepth studies and comparative analysis of different religions and philosophies.

Unfortunately, it cannot be said that the Vedas have been understood by most people in the land of their revelation in the sense that they have been understood by these masterminds of the west. Several misconceptions about the Vedas still persist.

Many who have not cared to study them seriously, dismiss them as the mumbo; jumbo created by the priestly castes in order to retain their intellectual domination over the rest of the society. Some others treat the Vedas as just a compendium of rituals and Mantras and think that conformity to rituals is the be-all and end-all of Vedic wisdom. Very few people seem to be having the patience or the intellectual training to understand the essence of the Vedas as wisdom based on intense spiritual experience.

Religion for the Hindu is an experience not just a theory of God. The religious genius, according to Dr. Radhakrishnan, is not a pedant or a pundit, not a sophist or a dialectician, but a prophet, sage or a rishi who embodies in himself the spritual vision. In another context, Dr. Radhakrishnan says "religion is not the acceptance of academic abstraction or celebration of ceremonies but a kind of life or experience. It is insight into the nature of reality or the experience of reality (Anubhava)". It is unfortunately this character of the Vedas which is often being missed by many who claim to be Vedic scholars in our country.

Keeping this aspect of the Vedas in view, I wish to refer to two important features which, in my opinion, distinguish the Vedic thought from most other religions and philosophies. The first is the unique concept of "finality and change" and the second is the universality of truth and unity of God.

It will be an over-simplification to say that Hindu religion was born with Vedas, because the vedas were not born or created at any point of time. The Rishis did not created the Vedas; they only discovered them. The truth and wisdom explained in the Vedas were there long before the Rishis discovered them through their experience, just as America was there before Columbus discovered it. As Swami Vivekananda explained to his Western audience, the truths of the Vedas existed before the Rishis, just as the law of gravity existed before Issac Newton discovered it. The Vedas were discovered through spiritual experience and not created by the intellect or imagination of a group of persons in a particular month of a year. That is way they are described as without beginning or Anadi. And what is without a beginning is also without an end. Ananta What is Anadi and Ananta is Nityatva or final.

However, this concept of finality of the Vedas has been misunderstood by many scholars in our country and outside. The Hindu view of the finality of the Vedas is very different from what is understood by that term by other religionists. The Hindu believes that while the truths revealed in the Vedas is very different from what is understood by that term by other religionists. The Hindu believes that while the truths revealed in the Vedas are final, they are capable of being re-experienced. The Vedas teach man highest truths that he can know and help him reach the highest goal. Truth obviously cannot have an addendum or a corrigendum and in that sense the truths revealed by the Vedas are eternal or final. But the belief of the Hindu is that God has never finalised the revelation of his wisdom and love and that he continues to reveal his wisdom and love without limitation of ages. In other words Hinduism is a spiritual force which continues to be in the process of evolution and growth, though always retaining its roots firmly in the truths revealed by the Vedas.

What all followed the Srutis namely the Smrutis were not writings on clean slates, but a continuation of the truths already revealed. Take the case of the Itihasas. There was no full stop after the Vedas, nor the beginning of a new philosophy or religion with the Itihasas. Instead the Itihasas are the logical develop from the Srutis of Vedas. The two topics, the Ramayana and the Mahabharata are as sacred to the Hindus as the Vedas themselves, but their sacredness is not because they revealed a new philosophy or religious thought but because they explained and established the truths of the for the benefit of the ordinary people.

Through the various episodes and characters of the epics, the epics made the Vedas relevant to the lives of the common people centuries after the Vedas were discovered. Some of the characters of these epics Rama Laxmana Sita, Hanuman Krishna, Yudhishthir, Bhishma-lived the truths of the Vedas in actual life. In fact the lives of some of them can be described as Upanishads in action. We see in them the highest manifestation of excellence and the highest expression of perfection, whether it was a prince's commitment to duty, or of a younger or a son's devotion to a father, or a wife's devotion to a husband or a disciple's reverence for his Guru. These noble characters of the epics remained absolutely faithful to the Upanishadic truths in all

circumstances and during the most difficult crises of their lilves. In their lives we find the eternal wisdom of the Vedas and at the same time the power of change and continuity. Change is not nonconformity. As Dr. Radhakrishanan says, it is only in a savage society that change is looked upon with suspicion, and maintenance of status quo is treated as sacred. Progress and change are the lifeblood of civilised societies and these have indeed been the main strength of the Hindu civilisation over the last several milennia.

Another great source of strength of the Hindu religion has been that at no time in its history has it claimed exclusivism in access to truth. The proclamation of the vedas: "That which exists is one sages call it by different names", marks the highest level of sublimity in philsophy and religious thought Swami Vivekananda quotes this sentence about half a dozen times, In his talk on "Vedic Ideals" and declares that "Tremendous results have followed from this one verse". He says that this truth has given the theme to all subsequent thought in India and will be the theme of the whole world of religions.

If different beliefs and faiths could coexist in perfect harmony within Hinduism itself, it was because of the acceptance by the Hindu of the fundamental truth that all paths lead to one God.

The Hindu's respect and tolerance for all religions outside Hinduism, also is based on the doctrine "That which exist is one; Sages call it by different names" When Lord Krishna says "Whosoever wants to reach me through that", He was only elaborating the basic Vedic philosophy of universality of truth and unity of God. The Gita explains this most beautifully:

"I am in every religious as a thread through a string of pearls. Wherever thou seest extraordinary holiness and extraordinary power, raising and purifying humanity, know that I am there".

The fact that such ideas could be articulated for the guidance of humanity so many hundreds of years ago, makes the Vedas really unique in the history of the civilisations of the world. In all ancient civilisation we find the struggle for supremacy among different concept about God. The supremacy of Zeus over other Gods. The same story is seen in the ancient civilisations of Babylon and if the Hebrews. The Jehova of the Hebrews was depicted as a God who would not tolerate the slightest deviation from his peoples' loyalty to him. But for the Hindu, truth is to be respected whenever it is manifested and God is one whatever may be the name by which different people choose to call Him or the manner in which different people worship Him. This indeed has been one of the important reasons for the strength and vitality of the Hindu civilisation which has survived unbroken over several millenia.

P. C. ALEXANDER

VEENA SAHASTRABUDDHE

Ten years ago Veena Sahastrabuddhes was an unknown voice. An efficient housewife who quietly pursued music as a hobby. Today she has made her mark as one of the most effective and successful musicians of her generation. The climb from an unknown housewife to the crowd-pulling classical singer has been meteoric. Her prerecorded cassettes brought out by Rhythm House have been instrumental in bringing her into the national limelight. She has managed to work our a formula of a musical style which combines the slow and appealing 'alaaps' of Kishori Amonkar and racy 'taans' of Kumar Gandharva. Veena also sings 'bhajans' in a manner reminiscent of Kumar Gandharva.

VELAVADAR NATIONAL PARK : THE GRASSY PARADISE

When one visit Blackbuck National Park- Velavadar (Gujarat), Oscar Ostlund's words that "nature is the mirror through which you may see some concert glimpses of the ineffable Being that men call God", echoed in my ears. How else can we explain the presence of a mesmerisingly flat grassland and otherwise bushy and dry terrain?

When the plains of India simmer in the blazing heat of the summer sun, this park, about four hours' drive from Ahmedabad, presents a soothing change to the visitors with its 30-45 cm tall, dry grass. The first shower s of the mansoon change the attire of this 34-08 sq. Km area to a colourful lush green. This is one national Park which virtually places wildlife at its doorstep. Tourises are surprised because the moment they drive in, blackbucks almost receive them in hordes.

This park falls in the Bhal region of Gujarat and before India attained independence, valavadar was part of the princely state of Bhavnagar. It was used as grazing ground by the cattle of Maharaja. As blackbuck was also present in the area in large concentrations, Maharaja indulged in hunting with the aid of cheetah. Hunting was permitted only in particular seasons under strict rules and regulations. After independence, hunting continued unabated and finally for the conservation of the unique biodiversity of this grassland, the area was declared as a National park in 1976.

Blackbuck, popularly known as *Kaliyar* in Gujarati and *Krishana sara*, *Krishna mruga* as well as *Saranga* in Sanskrit, is commonly seen in this part of Indian and is considered sacred by most of the communities. Tourists traversing this part of Gujarat by road frequently spot blackbuck loitering around in the fields. Farmers respect the presence of this herbivore and both the animals as well as homo sapiens tolerate mutual interference.

The connection between man and blackbuck dates back to thousands of years. Since antelope is considered a sacred animal in Hindu mythology, even a glimpse of this animals is considered auspicious by many Indian communities.

Besides blackbuck the park is well knowan for its graceful cranes-Sarus and Demoiselle, painted and white Storks, white Black Ibis, Spotbilled Duck, Pintail, Partridge, Red wattled Lapwing and the winter migrants, Harrier. In monsoons these are replaced by much awaited Lesser Florican. It is amazing how these dainty birds detect the probable arrival of monsoons, for, in 1994, they reached just two days before rains. In 1995-96 their arrival was six and four days before the first showers.

This time I reached Valavadar after the first bout of the monsoons. During my crisscrossing of the park, I can across a herd of chital and blackbuck crossing the road. All of a sudden a blackbuck leapt in the air, as if imitating a ballet dancer and seemed to hang in the air for a fraction of a second before landing gracefully to leap again, Immediately, ten other blackbucks of different sizes could be espied jumping. I was awestruck and wished the time would freeze.

I had not yet got out of the enigmatic trance when just some feet away an 18 to 20 cm tall bird leapt in the air." It is my lucky day", I mumbled, for this was none other than the shy and difficult to spot Lesser florican cock trying to attract a mate by his winsome courtship leap.

NEERA

VENKATA RAO CHINTALAPALLI

(b. 1871 – Vocalist : Karnataka, violin; studied with K. Srikantaiah, Karur Devudu brothers, M.G. Pillai and K.C. Iyer; received title of Sangeet Kalanidhi of Madras Music Academy (1962), Madras Music Academy (1962)(, Madras Sangeeta Nataka Sangam Award (1967), Sangeet Natak Akademi Award for Karnataka instrumental music (1967).

VERMA, MANIK (b. 1926)

Vocalist. : Hindustani, khayal, thumri of Kirana gharana.**Error! Bookmark not defined.**

VICTORIA MEMORIAL : CALCUTTA'S LANDMARK

Queen Victoria's Memorials in marble presents a some what calm, very unlike Calcutta image. Its imposing structure stands out in the midst of what used to be the white town, the nucleus of British India and now the heart of West Bengal. At the south eastern end of the maidan, this white structure provides solace and a touch of tranquillity. While the open space called the maidan, draws the aggressive workout friends, joggers and riders in the morning, the green patch of the memorial has regular visitors: the elderly strollers and youngsters. It is functioning as the lungs to the body of the city. In the memory of Queen Victoria, who died in 1901, this memorial was built on the suggestion of Lord Curzon who also proposed that the structure be entirely European in design.

The architect of this historical edifice, Sir William Emerson, who was the director of the British Institute of Architecture, opted for some thing that was different from the 'native'. colonial style and took inspiration from St. Peter's in Rome and St. Paul's in London. But it required time to convert 80,000 tons of Makrana marble into a city's landmark. Fromlaying of the foundation stone by the Prince of Wales. Sometime in 1906. It was a long wait till the end of 1921, when the Duke of Windsor formally opened the memorial. Since then, the streams of visitors haven't stopped to this museum.

A visitor can wade through the royal relatives and governor generals represented in bronze, marble as well as on canvas. There are some special items of interest such as the writing desk and a rosewood piano used by the queen, along with photographs and letters. On prominet display is a painting by a Russian artist Verestchagain, of 'The entry of king Edward VII into Jaipur in 1876'. A few natives like Dwarkanath Tagore are also represented on canvas, together with British administrators and scholars.

The museum house a good collection of weapon, daggers, swords, shields, rifles and pistol. Even big guns are displayed, besides books and paintings. Till 1770, there were no paintings of India done by British artists. But its national gallery now has portraits of freedom fighters Mahatma Gandhi, India's first President Rajendra Prasad and first Prime Minister Jawaharlal Nehru.

The main central hall has the sculpture of the Empress, a work done by Sir Thomas Brock, showing Victoria as a young woman. This part of the museum has friezes and panels on the wall depicting important events from her life.

One section of museum is exclusively devoted to the 300-year old history of the city – the Calcutta gallery. It gives an insight into what made Calcutta into what it is now, and glimpses of the treasure it had.. from Kalighat painting to personal articals of Rabindranath Tagore and many of those who were part of the erstwhile Bengal legend.

Come evening, and the visitors are greeted by the horse-drawn buggies, called 'Victoria', to make them around at a leisurely place. All nostalgic reminders of the colonial past that made Calcutta the city of the elite.

As the evening sun goes down, the northern part of the memorial's facade holds the attention, suitable caught by the creative sound and light show. Meanwhile the illuminated Victoria Memorial which has a three – tonne heavy, six-meter tall bronze Angel of Victory, yet again reiterates its claim to being the most important landmark of the city of Calcutta.

KAMAL SAHAI

VILAYAT HUSSAIN KHAN

The great master of the Agra school of music, Vilayat Hussain Khan, gave his last performance in the National programme of music of AIR on 12th may, in which he sang Maru Bihag Raisa Kanada and a Holi in Kaphi. Vilayat Hussain was noted for many things. He had a precious collection of rare Ragas. He knew at least 60 to 70 authentic compositions in various rare Ragas which he ungrudgingly recorded for AIR.

He was the one musician who very orthodox and traditional rendering of the Ragas. He would always stick to the intrinsic purity of the version of each Raga as he had received it from his ustad.

He was one of the few teachers of music in this country who taught rare pieces of his pupils without any reserve whatsover. He trained hundreds of pupiles who are spread far and wide in the country. These are the living monuments of his learning.

He was also a great composer. He composed as many as 63 songs in various Ragas and all of them are of exquistic quality both from the point of view of text and reading.

He wrote a book entitled "Sungitagyon kak Sansmaran" i.e. the "Reminisences of the Great Masters of Music".

THAKUR JAIDEVA SINGH

THE VINA

The study of Indian music should find a prominent place in the scheme of Indological studies. The genius of India is fully reflected in her sangita. Indian music is one of the major system of music the world. It has a long and noble pedigree. The frequenies mentioned for the notes of the Shadja grama, (the primordial scale of Indian music), the classification of the notes to vedi, samvadi, anuvadi and vivadi and the Dhruva vina and chala vina experiment described in Bharata's Natya Sastra all testify to the fact that in the history of world music. Indians are earliest people to have definite ideas of tone system, to-nal relationships and consonantal and dissonantal notes. The Indian solfa system _Sa ri ga ma pa dha ni_ is the earliest in the history of world music. It is mentioned in such an early work as the _Narada Parivrajaka Upanished_. The western solfa system _doh, ray, mi, fah, soh, la, si_ dates only from the time of guide d' Arezzo (10th Cent. A. D.)

The vina is the national instrument of India. In the celebrated vadya trayam. Vina, venu, Mridangam, the vina is given the first place. It is the instrument par excellence for rendering Indian Music. It is associated with the Goddes of learning, Saraswati. The history of the vina is in fact the history of Indian music. It is highly complex instrument and takes 12 years for one of to attain mastery over it. The practice of VeyiSadhakam ie. Playing a thousand time a day at a stretch, the scale in three octaves and in three degree of speed is of interest from the point of view of comparative music instrumentation. Certain styles of play like the Chakra bandhan are also of interest from the point of view of instrumental technique.

The vina is referred to in the vedas. In early literature vina meant only a stringed instrument and not the fretted instrument as at present. Thus there were vinas whose strings were plucked and played as the harp, vinas were in the strings were struck and played as the Satata-antri vina and vinas were in the strings were set in vibration with a bow as the Dhanur vina. There are two main stages in the development of the vina- the open strings stage and the – stopped strings stages.

MELODIC SYSTEM

Indian music is the perfection of the melodic system and all aspects of melodic expression have been fully explored here. Where in the west, a melody is conceived with a harmonic conscience, here. Whereas in the west, melody is conscience, here in India the melody is conceived with the object of presenting the various facets of the raga. In the use of hundreds of ragas and rhythms and in use of quarter-tones, one- third tones and delicate graces, Indian music stands without a parallel. There are many concepts in Indian music which have never occurred to the occidental mind. The concept of Raga and the concept of manodharma sangita are our gifts to world music. In a concert of Indian music, one hears not only the composition of the great composers but also the music improvised on the spot by the performer. It is this improvisation based on a sound, logical and aesthetic basis that has kept Indian music alive all these centuries. The performer of the mridangam (drum) in India provides a rhythmical harmony. He not only provides a cross-rhythmical accopaniment to the music of his principal but also performs solo, expounding a chosen tala for half an hour or more.

Tirujnanasambandar, the most prolific author of the Tevaram hymns in Tamil, is the youngest composer in the history of world music. As a boy of three he sang extempore his first song *Thodudaiya seviyan*. He lived in the 7th century A.D. his brillian contemporary, Sankara pays a handsome tribute to him in sloka 75 of his Saundarya lahari. Andal (10 Cen. A. D.), the author of Tiruppavai in Tamil is the earliest woman composer known to world music.

OPEN STRINGS STAGE

The earliest stringed instrument is the Jya or the bowstring. When strings of different lengths were tied to the bow and played it became the yazh or the harp of the ancient Tamil literature. The strings of the harp were tuned to a particular scale and played. The instrument was played on open strings. The tonal volume was amplified by tying the strings to a boad-shaped resonator. The modern western harp is a highly improved and enlarged version of the ancient yazh but it has a forntal pillar and a mechanical device to increases the pitch of all the strings by a scmitone simultaneously.

The idea of having all the strings stretched from end to end on a single resonating chamber was next tried. This resulted in the svaramandali and the satatantri vina. Both the instruments were played on open strings. The former was plucked with finger nails and played. The satatantri vina has a trapazoid resonator and four contiguous strings were tuned to a single note and played. The instrument was struck with two thin sticks and played.

STOPPED STRINGS STAGE

The idea of producing all the notes on a single string instead of a number of strings dawned on man. He straightened the arm of the harp and placed crude frets on the boat-shaped resonator. This instrument is the Kudjyapi which still survives in the Philippine Islands. In this instrument the long open string served to sound the key note. In the other string, the meru or the first fret was placed at the mid-point so that the segmented string on the right and left gave the note of the same pitch. The idea of dvigunatva was perceived. The gandhara grama was the popular scale of that period and the frets were naturally placed at the positions which give the notes of the gandhara grama. The F sharp of the ga grama was replaced by the stable note, Panchama. The gandhara grama in this revised version, is actually the South Indian Todi raga or the North Indian Bhairavi raga. This is the scale heard when the notes from E to E are sounded on the whote keys of the Piano. Transilient scales from this gandhara grama can still be heard in the traditional music of Japan and in the music played in the temple of Tooth in Kandy, Ceylon on festive occasions. The Rig as sung in South India still conforms to the notes of gandhara grama. The two-stringed Kudyapi vina is the Nakula.

Man then attempted to shorten the length of the instrument. The boat-shaped resonator gave way to the Kachchapi type of resonator and with a short finger-board with a few frets on them. The Kachchapi vina resulted and this is represented in many ancient sculptures and paintings.

The idea of having a separate dandi with frets mounted on them and with distinct resonators marked the next stage and the Kinnari resulted. The three gourds of the Kinnari were later replaced by two gourds one at either end of the dandi and this is the sitar of Hindustani music. The Vina represented in the Halebid sculpture did not have frets for the full two octaves. The last stage in the Evolution of the Vina is represented by the South Indian Tanjore Model Vina. Herein the main resonator was of jackwood and the secondary resonator on the left was of gourd. Twenty – four frets were placed on the finger-board. With four playing strings one could play music ranging over a compass of 3½ octaves on this instrument.

It should be noted that the strings in the Vina are kept in medium tension and played and not in full tension as in the case of the Violin.

Although there are only 12 frets for the twelve semitones of the octave, the subtle quarter-tones in between the semitones were played by deflecting the strings. The three side strings served as a drone – coupling. They also served to merk the rhythm. Thus the Vina is a self-sufficient and complete instrument and one could play complete music on it without the aid of any accompaniment. The varieties of left hand technique and right hand technique developed in Vina play are worthy of study by all votaries of instrumental music, eastern or western.

THE FINAL SHAPE

When the Vina in its final form emerged, the frets were removed and the instrument was played by stopping the strings with a piece of cylindrical wood held in the left hand. This is the Gottuvadyam or the Mahanataka Vina and this is one of the most delightful instruments of Indian music.

The Vina is not only a top-class concert instrument, but also helped man to understand the laws of vibration of stretched strings, the nature of svayambhu svaras (harmonics), the geometrical progression of the octave notes, the vadi-samvadi relationships of notes etc. This it served as an acoustic meter. When the 24 fretted Vina was evolved in Tanjore, it became easy for the musicologist Venkatamakhi to enunciate the scheme of 72 melakartas or hepta tonic scales based on the 6 patterns of lower tetrachord, and upper tetrachord, with F natural for the first 36 melas and F sharp for the next 36 melas.

Although India had been in contact with Western music for over two centuries, still Western music never invaded Indian homes. This is proof of the life, vitality and greatness of Indian music. This is not the case with other Asian countries.

P. MOORTHY

VISHNU (PT.) NARAYANA BHATKHANDE

With the twentieth century a new era and new forces were released in all fields – political, social, cultural – of national life. The credit for the upliftment of music goes to two "vishnus" – Pandit Vishnu Narayana Bhatkhande and Pandit Vishnu Digambar Paluskar. While mentioning the work and achievements of one, the other name comes before as automatically. Both these stalwarts worked against heavy odds. Music and musicians had no place in the society. Those who still pursued this art, did so only at the risk of losing their social status. In the same way the musicians themselves were not readily prepared to part with their hard – earned knowledge. One had to waste years and years to get a few crumbs of the art. There were no schools, no syllabus, no notation system and no literature on music. There remained a vast gulf between the theory and the practice of the art. Actually, the theoretical aspect was totally ignored by the artists. There was no possibility of knowing the Lakshnas of a Raga. Sometimes even the name of the Raga was not disclosed to the students. In such a gloomy state of affairs (Pandit) Vishnu Bhatkhande started his work. Some princely states were still patronising the noble art. Under their Patronage musicians practiced music, free from the worry of earning their livelihood. Most of our 'Gharanas' flourished in one or the other state. Many of our reputed performers – vocalist as well as instrumentalist – were the product of these traditions. The main difficulty was that this system worked in a very limited sphere. It was beyond the reach of a commoner to get the facilities of learning from these Ustads with – out the personal favour of the ruler. For others even the opportunity of listening was rare, as admission to the concerts held in palaces and courts was restricted to a privileged few. Vishnu Bhatkhande had to work continuously for years to make this treasure accessible to all.

Vishnu Narayana Bhatkhande was born in a Maharashtriyan Brahmin family at Bombay on 10 August 1860. From early childhood he started learning music. He graduated from Bombay University in 1885. Later, he took his degree in law and started his career as a legal practitioner at the Bombay High Court. He studied all the available books on music in Sanskrit and other languages into he time he could spare from his legal profession. In 1904, he set out on a countrywide tour. He visited many centres of musical learning. He was able to collect a number of Rages and compositions from different Ustads. It was not an easy task to make them part with their closely guarded treasure. Often, he had to spend large sums of money. At other times he had to handle the situation tactfully. Mohammad Khan of the famous Manrang Gharana allowed him to record about four hundred Khyals in different Ragas. Vishnu Bhatkhande got access to some rare an valuable manuscripts and other works in different public and personal libraries.

Vishnu Bhatkhande remained at the Bar till 1910. After that he left this profession for good an directed all his time an energy towards music. He had the privilege of learning various styles of music from celebrated exponents like Deojibuva Belawalkar (Dhrupadiya) and Wazir Khan of Rampur. He also learnt Sitar from swami Vallabhdas. Vishnu Bhatkhande published five parts of the *Kramik*

Pustaka Malika which contains hundreds of compositions in different ragas collected by him during his tour.

However, the most important achievement of Pandit Vishnu Bhatkhande was the editing and writing of books on the theoretical aspect of Hindustani Music. Keeping in mind the blind faith which people had reposed in the ancient shastras in Sanskrit language, he wrote a book *Lakshya Sangeet* in Sanskrit. He quoted shlokas from this book as reference in his other works. In the four parts of his famous Marathi book Hindustani *Sangit Paddhati* he critically analysed different aspects of Indian music, such as swara, Shruti, Mela, Grama, Moorchina, Raga – Raginis, Raga Lakshna, and various Ragas. For the classification of Ragas, he introduced the system of ten Thatas or scales in place of the old Raga – Ragini system. He himself composed songs in various Ragas and Talas. *Lakshangeets* were a unique type of compositions introduced by him, which in their song-compositions conveyed useful data about the raga and thus grew popular with students. He has described about 125 Ragas in his book "Abhinava Raga Manjari " in Sanskrit verse from. Besides, he edited several treatises on music The first all – India Music Conference at Baroda in 1916 was organised through his initiative. Later, its sessions were held at Delhi, Banaras and Lucknow. These conferences were not confined to music concerts alone, but they provided a forum for musicians and musicologists to exchange views on controversial issues. Efforts were made in right earnest to study different versions of Ragas and standardise them. At the Lucknow session of the Conference decision was taken to set up an institution for teaching music. Thus the famous Marris Music College which was later renamed as Bhatkhande Sangit Vidyapith took shape. Panditji had already started similar music institutions at Gwalior and Baroda with the help of the rulers of these states.

Pandit Bhatkhande's work can be broadly summarised as follows. Collection and sompilation of valuable data on music, writing and editing of various works on music; evolving a simple notation system; establishing music institutions; and, organising concerts and symposia.

During his whole life he worked very hard for the cause of music. Even those, who may differ with him on some aspects or details of his observations, readily acknowledge him as one of the greatest scholars of the times and one who was the first to give a code, a body of laws to Hindustani Music during the modern period. Among scores of his disciples, names of Pandit S.N. Ratanjankar and Dr. R.L. Roy are worth mentioning. The illustrious life of Pandit Vishnu Narayana Bhatkhande came to an end on 19 September 1936, but his name will ever be remembered with deep gratitude by posterity.

VINAYA CHANDRA MAUDGALYA

VISHWANATHAN ANAND (B. 1969)

He's the king. Viswanathan "Vishy" Anand single – handedly put Indian on the world chess map. And yet, despite all his stupendous achievements and his current world number – two position, perhaps the best compliment over paid to him was by the arrogant, aloof, acerbic Gary Kasparov, who said of Anand "He's nice."

Vishy is a gentleman sportsman. He plays with lightnings speed, and yet remains modest about his genious. His quest for excellence has never got in the way of his genteel manner. And no defeat has landed a blow on him from which he could not cheerfully recover. Even after a crushing defeat at the hands of Kasparov in the in the world championship title – duel, Anand retained the wry sense of humour that is so much part of his character.

There are those who believe that the best is behind Anand. And that his lightening reflexes have been slowed by age and pressure. And that the sparkle in his game has been dimmed by the solidity and experience he has gained. But Anand is not content to rest on his laurels. And his tremendous enthusiasm for the game remains undiminished.

But, Anand is much more than just a chess champion he is an ambassador for sport.

VISUAL ARTS SINCE INDEPENDENCE

Abroad review of last 50 years in the development of contemporary Indian art shows that the Indian artist, by and large is still hovering between tradition and experiment.

Historically speaking, we had been exposed to western influences since 1600, the year of the setting up of the British East India Company. But we became overly dependent upon the achievements in European art since 1900.

With the background of the western academic traditions epitomized in the works of Raja Ravi Verma and others, the post-independent period is an important one In the history of contemporary art in India. It signifies the long struggle of the Indian artist to synthesize the traditional and modern values and make a mark on the international scene.

One can certainly admire and appreciate the creative endeavours of most significant artists of early decades in giving a creative thrust to their visual and plastic expressions. For example, the revival of national artistic aspiration in the works of Abhinindranath Tagore, Gagandraneth Tagore, Rabindranath Tagore and Nandalal Bose, followed by landmarks set by Jamini Roy and Amrita Shergil. Rabindranath Tagore, who gave a meaning to his works through the sheer vitality his consciousness, stands out as a unique painter.

The artists in the post – independence period have been, on the one he and, eclectic, experimenting various mannerisms under the influence of Euro-American art movements, and on the other, obsessed with a deep search for roots. The tension between desire for the new and the self-consciousness towards the past has coloured the most diverse art styles in India during this period.

Whereas a few groups of artists in the late forties and fifties such as the Calcutta group, (Gopal Ghose, Nirode Majumdar, Rathin Moitra, Pran Krishna Pal and Pradosh Das Gupta), Bombay's Progressive Artists' Group) (M.F. Husain, S.H. Raza, H.A. Gade, S.K. Bakre, F.N. Souza and K.H. Ara) and Delhi' S Shilpi Chakra B.C. Sanyal, K.S. Kulkarni, D.R. Bhagat and Kanwal Krishna – (I too an associated with the group expressed their revolutionary attitude, some desired their creative efforts to be linked to the past).

Consequently, despite the insularity of the visual culture, a dialogue is going on between innovation and tradition. The contradictions of these existing attitudes, both in visual and plastic arts, are apparent in works and aspirations of artists of this period and have given birth to most influential trends, the modernistic and the traditionalistic. The latter was, of course, invented by a single artist, Jamini Roy, who longed for the past in an ominous way.

The tension between desire for the new and self consciousness towards the past has coloured the most diverse style in India through the last over 50 years.

However, one notices some striking contributions made during this post Independence period by some of our best know eminent artists.

For example, Bhabhes Sanyal, at 95, reflects in his oeuvre the art scene in the country of his time. His works reveal him as a man in love with life. Being constantly creative in his thought and work, he has developed a personal form of landscape painting in highly spirited brush strokes the life, sometimes expressing anguish, sometimes emotions of joy.

Binode Behari Mukherjee and Ram Kinker Vaij made unique contributions, in their own individual way, exerting to get away from their dependence on mere traditional or western modern mannerism and sought their own creative insight.

Whereas N.S. Bendre, a versatile painter, passionately experimented in different styles and techniques for self-expression K.K. Hebbar tried to bring out the active life spirit within the rustic village folk; the poor and ordinary people of his surroundings. Hebbar's basic preoccupation was to discover the rhythmic significance of art – a traditional ideal.

M.F. Husain combines the tradition of bright colour palette linked to Rajput painting and German Expressionism, lending his work an international flavour. He portrays a bleak social environment, often using distorted or deformed human figures, horses and objects.

He is involved in a revival of the public murals as a means of reuniting the artist with the community a point of view which is shared by Satish Gujral, a multifaceted creative personality, painter, sculptor, muralist and architect.

Satish Gujral symbolizes a great leap forward in experimentation for synthesis. He is a powerful expressionist, who has created images in dramatic contrast of light and dark when painting and lending similar vitality to his sculpture whether using contrasting materials and textures or creating symbolic reliefs in 'Brunt Wood'. His works, wherein the native and mexican art traditions intermingle to produce a spectacular aesthetic effect, seem to burst forth towards the viewer with great dynamic force and envelop his mind. The same is true of his more recent paintings, inspired by 'Qawali' music and rendered in aesthetic values, characteristic of Indian miniature paintings.

Other artists who stand out for their valuable contribution to the present day art scene include F.N. Souza who strikes an aggressive note in treating the human figure and distoriting the human figure and distorting it ruthlessly, as dis Picasso, for intensity of expression. He alternates between religious and erotic themes with a certain touch of sarcasm. Tyeb Mehta also distorts the human figure violently, but seems to reassemble its fragmented parts more carefully to invent an expressive figuration that suits his pictorial representation.

Krishen Khanna is eclectic enough to create works that hover between a figurative and an abstract conception. His recent tendency is towards creating an art that breaks away from the traditional notions to achieve an even more radical position. In contrast, Bikash Bhattacharjee and Jogen Chowdhury percieve art as an agent of social reform and revelation and Ram Kumar continues to pursue creating abstract harmonies and a poetic world out of landscapely forms and colours.

K. G. Subramanyan and Gulam Sheikh deploy traditional pictorial techniques as a means to express a dramatic and paradoxical point. Whereas Subramanyan has painted highly artistic and spontaneous images out of commonplace themes, infusing them with metaphors and wit, Gulam Sheikh presents lyrical generalization of the crowded impressions of life and surroundings. And A. Ramachandran's paintings are marked for their narrative quality and Indian flavour with a Crétain sense of romanticism.

J. Swaminathan's paintings reflect a belief in the renewal of cultural values through association with the exceptional talents of the tribal artist. He, however, remains a modern artist both conceptually and pictorially using symbolic elements of tribal art as an element of aesthetic prehension.

In the works of 'tantrist' painters Biren De, G.R. Santosh, S.H. Raza, Om Prakash and Prafulla Mohanti, there is subtle reflection of a central issue in seeking the metaphysical reality. Inspired by 'Yantran' and 'mandalas', they express a spiritual aestheticism using symbols of universal energy and divine nature a strong trend seeking a national identity.

S.L. Prasher, in his paintings, sculptures and murals, attempted to project the vital life force – the 'Prana Shakti'

For relating his approach to traditional insights. He defined his work as 'Pranantrik' and the individuality of his work had accrued from it. Some other artists like Manjit Baba, Jatin Das, Sunil Das, Sunil Das, Anjolie Ela Menon, Gogi Saroj Pal, Arpana Caur, Jai Zharoria and Amitava das, among others, are actively engaged in their creative endeavours for synthesizing the traditional and modern aesthetic values in their own individual manners.

Unlike paintings, the renaissance of Indian sculpture did not involve any revival movement. It was an absolutely new beginning initiated in an academic/ realistic approach which it accepted as a model, mainly sculpting formal portraits and monuments.

It was only during the early years of the post – independence period that some sculptors became conscious of the great heritage in the field of sculpture and turned to it for inspiration, more for their thematic content rather than the formal approach. The works of D.P. Roy Chowdhury and the like, such as G.R. Mhatre, S. Phadke, G.R. Talim and S. Pansare were different from the later creations, during the late 40s and after, of sculptors like Ram Kinker Vaij, Pradosh Das Dupta, D.R Bhagat,

Sankho Chaudhuri, Janaki Ram, A.N. Sehgal, Satish Gujral, Meera Mukherjkee, Nagji Patel Somnath Hore and Mrinalini Mukherjee to mention some.

They worked on definite ideas using significant, symbolic forms in a variety of media. Their sculptures, pervaded by an artistic disposition, are far from simple revivalism, however.

Ram Kinker's sculptures show a fundamental urge to express through the three dimensional media in highly emotional and telling forms that are maintly rooted in the cubistic approach.

Both Das Gupta and Bhagat shared Ram Kinker's ideas, his open attitude and responsiveness. Whereas Das Gupta created massive forms of female figures, Bhagat – a pioneer in using different craft media and techniques gradually changed from naturalistic form to vigorous geometric form, basing his content on Indian religious and philosophical themes.

Sankho's schulptures, though in lyrical stylization, are marked by simplicity, characteristic of Brancusi, Gabo and Moore. He occupied himself with highly stylized perforated bronzes. In contrast, Sehgal's strong reaction to the negative aspects of society is effectively communicated through his sculptures. His intent seems to inform and persuade others for a human cause. The result is a poignant expression in plastic form.

Satish's sculptures are images of dynamic energy, concealing the recognizable, the logical or intelligible, to create form language that evokes mystic feelings in whatever media he chooses to work with, multimedia, 'brunt' wood or black marble (as in his most recent works).

The graphists or printmakers in present day India represent the tremendous outburst of multifarious tendencies in their creative expression, utilizing a variety of print – making media and techniques with striking competence.

Among the graphic artists, I may mention just a few who have made an outstanding contribution to its development. For instance. Kanwal Krishna who started as a painted of Himalayan landscapes in a powerful style of handling water – colours, was a pioneer and a great revolutionary in style and technique while handling the graphic media like etching etc. He reconstructed the Himalayan landscape and presented it with a new and specific sense of feeling and form.

Krishna Reddy is a master of technical innovations, particularly in the controlled use of the viscosity of inks. He is quite a technical virtuoso who is very influential in the west. His images rendered in techings are like diagrams of amplified resonance illuminated by sparkles of colour and light. And while Anupam Sud's techings are heightened in autobiographical sense with a certain ironic vision, they equally show a technical competence.

In short, we may say, that the post-independence period is characterized by a freedom of expression, diversity of aims and deviation to formalistic principles embodying contemporary aesthetic values. Although the influence of Picasso and Moore is still prominent, but no less popular are the deliberately loud and attention seeking works of younger artists under the impact of pop and surrealists, as against the growing search for the roots in the indigenous arts.

P. N. MAGO

VYAS NARAYANRAO G.

(b. 1920) – Vocalist : Hindustani; Khayal of Gwalior gharana; studied with Digambar Pulaskar; disc recordings.

"W"

WATER BALLET

Through colourful illusions, compounded with difficult "mudras" and expressions in water, the aquatic ballet has taken the new age dance world by stone. Conceptualised by Calcutta's Indian Life Saving Society. Popularly known as the Anderson Swimming Club, such an aquatic feat has taken the dance form to a different height. The recent enactment of a dance drama written by Dr. Sunil Das and Choreographed by Sudarshan Roy, *Alor Pakhi* has brought the crowling glory to the traditional Tagorean dance – drama forms. The combination of water, whether in the form of ripples or waves with sound and light creates a vibgyor of illusions. So, the most integral aspect of such a dance is the theme and story telling. The theme of Alor Pakhi centres around man's quest for the ultimate truth. A bird seller wanders from village to village bartering freedom for birds. He meets a young lad and tells him about the Bird of light. Together they wander off in search. They hazard social barriers, difficult terrains, natural onslaught and finally reach the land of demons. The beautifully blended sequences of the conflict with the demons clearly reflects the concept of the good ruling over the evil. (Summarised)

SOUMYAK GOSH

WEAVING ART OF ASSAM

Assam, meaning unequal or unrivalled, indeed lives upto its name when it comes to the state's exclusive handloom products. A land traversed with hills, valleys and plains in the north – eastern region of India boasts of a fine heritage of exquisite craftsmanship and vibrant colours. Assam's handloom sector contributes handsomely to the state' economy.

Almost every home in Assam hums with the sound of the loom as weaving is taken up not as a commercial venture but as a labour of love. Woven into myriad colours and contours, Assam's handloom products are inexorably linked with its geographic conditions and historic connections. Interlaced with lyrical motifs, the designs mostly depict natural scenes, animals and flowers. The patterns are sometimes geometric but seldom ornamental.

Designs and colours of the textile products vary from region to region, mainly because of several ethno-cultural groups that distinguish themselves in their own, respective creations. The population of Assam is a broad racial inter-mix of people of Mongolian, Indo-Burmese and Aryan origin. The hilly tracts are mostly inhabited by tribes like Babo-Kachari, Tiwas, Chutias, Dimasa Kachari, Karbi, zemi Naga, Hamar, Garo, Rabha etc.

Each ethno-cultural group has its won interesting predisposition to a specific colour. Green is the favourite of the "Pathi" group among the Rabhas, while the 'Randanis' prefer brown and orange. Changes in condition and environment also influence the choice of the colours and designs. The highlanders' clothes and patterns are usually sharp coloured while people in the plains use light shades.

As one goes downhill, these contrasts tend to dissolve into a serene smoothness.

The Assamese use black, red yellow and white on fabric. Red yellow are considered sacred colours. White being the dominant colour, the Assamese bride wears white silk which signifies purity. The silk is woven into a pattern with either red or multi-coloured floral and geometric motifs.

Not only design and colours but the texture of the textile and the choice of loom also very from tribe to tribe. Zim Nagas, Dafala, Nishis, Karbis and Hamar prefer the loin or vast loom while the others opt for the convenient shuttle loom.

The eight point star motif, a familiar design, has a wide appeal not only among the Assamese and various ethnic groups, but is used in Thailand and Vietnam as well.

The traditional assamese male dress in "dhoti" (loin cloth) "engasula" (shirt) and a "gamocha" (long scarf) around the neck; while women wear "mekhla" (sarong) and "riga" (long narrow scarf) which shows a Tibeto-Burmese influence.

The dress of the Bodo-Kacharis, inhabitants of areas above the valley of Assam differs from that of the Assamese : Kachari women are expert weavers in creating ornamental designs in mostly geometric, striped, diamond and floral patterns

Influence of early Hindu culture is very apparent in many motifs of the Chutia ethnic group in the form of temples and geo-ornamental designs.

The Zemi Nagas from the north Cachar hill district use rich colour contrasts and spear motifs in their dresses. Besides black vermillion, orange and other shade of red are also used. Their men wear flowing robes 'denipal' hanging down from their left shoulder. These Nagas have acquired expertise in making beautiful shawls and "puans" (lower garment for women) on their loin looms.

Most of the Assamese tribes lay great stress on weaving" as on obligatory duty of their womenfolk. In fact, girls are trained in the art of spinning and weaving from the very childhood. They are supposed to artistically design their wedding dress. Every year on the occasion of 'Bihu' festivals females given their beloveds a 'bibaun' (scraf) which is usually women with a floral design. Magb Bibu, Bobag Bibu or Rungoli Bibu are such occasions when Assamese women instinctively transform the 'bibuan' into a spiritual creation.

The girls of Rabha tribe are expert weavers at their throw shuttle and fly shuttle looms, preferring bright colours and blending matching colours on a single colour background.

Rearing 'endi' silk worms is one of the major cottage industries which fetches a family a substantial income. The cocoons are sold in the weekly markets. Karbi tribe of Mongoloid origin is famous for rearing 'endi' silk worm.

Assam's people and its various tribes have significantly contributed to the weaving arts of the state. Presenting and preserving of this heritage is a matter of pride and honour not only for the state but for the whole nation.

SHALINI MITRA

WOMEN IN TRIBAL SOCIETY

India has a rich tribal heritage comprising special institutions, religions, dresses, languages, and different levels of economic development. The position of women in tribal societies also varies because the treatment given to her differs from one tribal group to another. It is difficult to analyze the position enjoyed by women in tribal society, in terms of superior and inferior status as there may be quite a good many in between depending upon women's role in a particular society. Lowie has remarked that diametrically opposite views are current among the educated laity regarding women's place in Primitive society and a general sweeping statement must not be accepted wholesale.

In all ancient civilization the status of women was high. The comparatively lower position of women in the later Vedic period was accompanied by a decline in social values and norms. This though is true only of patrilocal societies. The present paper discusses the position of tribal women in patrilocal societies which require the wife to live in her husband's residence. We have also to examine in this connection the type of inter-relations that exists between husband and wife in the family in a tribal society. Such an analysis will show the degree of hold a husband exercises on his wife and the economic spheres in which they are free to work.

B. Malinowski observes that the status of women in a tribal society can only be studied "after taking into consideration the mutual duties between the sexes and the safeguards provided for the protection of each sex against the high-handedness of the other". The social status of women is determined by her different roles as a daughter, a wife and a mother. In this sense the position of women in the social sphere Lowis s a fluctuating one.

Lowis points out that status may mean four things; the actual treatment obtained, legal status, opportunities for social participation and character; and these determine, each in a specific sense and manner, the status of woman in society. The role of women in tribal society can be determined by the rules observed by her in the daily activities of the society, i.e. the role played as her in marriage and family, the degree of economic participation, the opportunities for social participation enjoyed and rituals observed.

The attempt here is to analyse the position of women in tribal society with particular reference to the Bhil tribe of Rajasthan. The information about women in different tribal societies has also been given to make the analysis comparative and more meaningful.

FAMILY

The Bhils have a patrilineal society and as such have all the characteristic that go with it, such as the system of partilocal residence, final authority resting with the males and nomenclature and in heritance being traced through the male line of blood. This sets certain limitations upon the Bhill women; she cannot inherit her ancestral property, has to change her residence after marriage and is thus automatically deprived of her parental protectation. Marriage is a social necessity and any idea of remaining unmarried through out life meets the opposition from the Bhil Society at large.

A Bhil woman, like the woman of any other tribe or caste, passes through three important stages of maidenhood, wifehood and motherhood. As an unmarried daughter she is reared in her parental house where she is socialized in accordance with the norms of Bhil culture. In her childhood a tribal girl has to assist her mother in domestic affairs. At the age of seven or eight she nurses her younger brothers and sisters during the absense of her mother. By the time the reaches the age of 12 or 13, she is able to do all the household work with full responsibilities.

After marriage she has to change her residence from her parental village to the village of her husband and has to face the problems of adjustment in a new social setting. During her married life she is kept under critical observation by her parents – in – law who watch her performance of her social, economic and religious functions, both within and outside the home.

In her husband's house, she has to get up early in morning and her first duty is to bring water from a distant well, spring, river etc. Then she prepares food for the entire family after she has cleaned the utensils. After finishing the morning meal, she looks after young children. She hardly gets any time during the day.

If widowed she is faced with the problem of economic dependence. She may however, go in for remarriage Nata either with the younger brother of her deceased husband or any other person of her choice. She may even decide to remain a widow throughout the rest of her life.

ECONOMIC PARTICIPATION

The impact of Bhil women can be felt in every act that is performed in the farms or in the forests. She is a constant companion of her husband in agricultural pursuits. The division of labour between the males and females has fallen very heavily on the shoulders of the woman. The bhil daughters begin to share the economic burden from the age of five to six years. She collects wood from the jungle and grazes the cattle, and also helps in the fields. Apart from looking after household duties, she cleans the cattleshed and removes the cowdung: It is for these reasons that a Bhil daughter is thought of as an economic asset and at the time of marriage her parents demand dapa or bride price perhaps to compensate the loss.

Her participation in agricultural activies is important. Women help I manuring, sowing, inter-culturing, irrigating, harvesting etc. They also protect the corps against birds and stray animals. Besides they take care of cattle with the help of their younger children. The Bhill woman supplements the income of the family by working as a casual labourer during off-seasons. She is more industrious than the man in all the subsidiary occupations.

Tribes like Kadar, Bhuyes, Kharias, Bihors, Chenchus etc, Practise food gathering, i.e. they collect edible roots, stems leaves, and tubers from the forests. It is generally the duty of women to collect these edibles while men tend to specialise in hunting.

About the Chenchus it is said that the only division of labour is between the exes and even this is less marked compared to many other primitive races. Among the Chenchus "Husband and Wife" writes Furer Haimendoff" are for all practical purposes partners with equal rights and their Property is jointly owned,. Nominally everything belongs to man except those personal belongings a wife acquired from her parents".

Among the partilocal Tharus of the Nainital tarai in Uttar Pradesh, Women's status is high. It may seem a paradox to us that in a patriarchal society which the Tharu have today, women still enjoy a dominant position in their community. The property is owned both by men and women and the latter spend their income without any advice from their menfolk".

SOCIAL OPPORTUNITIES

A Bhil girl has a wide measure of freedom before marriage. She can dance and sing and can laugh and joke with any man without any reservation.

Tribes like Nagas, Muria, Mundas, Hos have yough dormitories where young boys and girls plays and dance and sleep at night. They can also have physical relations during the course of training in the art of love. No such youth institutions exist among the Bhils. Bhil girls are prohibited from having sexual relations but by and large they otherwise enjoy wide freedom.

After marriage the Bhil girls are subject to many restrictions and are expected to observe a strict moral code. The restrictions imposed on women at different times vary during the daily routine, menstruation period and days of pregnancy. The Bhil daughter-in-law has to observe *Purdah* in her presence of her father-in-law and also the other male relations of the husband.

Girls of the Grasia tribe of Rajasthan have a relatively freer married life. According to P.C. Dave, "If they are forced to marry a particular man they do not like, they have their way by running away from the husband's house and securing the divorce later. If they are charged of infidelity or any social irregularity by the husband, they have full freedom to explain their case personally before the panchas".

Speaking about the women of the Maria Gond tribe of Bastar, W.V. Grigson says, "As a girl a Maria has considerable freedom both in premarital sexual life and in the choice of a husband and she is fairly free to leave her husband if he ill-treats her or if he cannot beget a child".

Bhil girls are not married early. Generally, marriage takes place after puberty. Bhils observe strict exogamy in regard to gotra. It prohibits girls to marry within the village and with a boy of the same gotra.

Marriage by capture is also prevalent among the Bhils of Rajasthan. In Such cases the person who has eloped with a girl may be a bachelor or widower or even a married one. When the whereabouts of the run-ways girls are located, the parents of the firl collect a party of friends and relatives from the village and take "Jhgra" by informing the man that the girl should be returned to them or compensation should be paid to them in lieu of Ijat.

The members of the opposite party also collect their relatives and negotiates with the girls' side though a middle man, known as Jhagadati, Generally a settlement, despite the chaotic situation, is reached and the terms and conditions of payment are settled. The amount settled as compensation to the parents of the captured girl is very high in case the girl was married one. This may range from Rs. 700 to Rs. 900 for married girls and Rs. 300 to Rs. 400 in the case of unmarried girls. Dapa or bridge price in negotiated marriage also range from Rs. 300 to Rs. 400.

Widow remarriage Nata is the general rule rather than an exception. There is also a system of levirate marriage whereby the younger brother of the deceased husband marries his widowed bhabhi, which means Economic services continue to be available to the same family.

The Bhil society has provided for divorce in case the couple is not able to lead a cooperative and happy life. The grounds for divorce are sterility, ill-temper and adultery. A woman may seek divorce due to lunacy, drunkness, Extravagance, and adultery. The right of divorce is enjoyed Equally both by husband and wife. Divorce is symbolised by tearing breadthwise the border of a new sari of the women concerned. The women is handed over this torn sari with a rupee tied in it. By relatives or panchas. After this she becomes free to marry any other man she likes. If a man leaves his wife, the wife may remarry and her second husband has to pay a sum of money to her first husband. If the woman is divorced, she will have to pay back the bride-price to her divorced husband.

RITUAL AND RECREATION

Among almost all the tribes of India, a belief in the supernatural or mystical forces is about all that exists by way of religion. The tribal woman is not allowed to take actual part in religious activites. The place of a Bhil woman in the religious life of the tribe can be judged from the number of rituals, rites, caremonies, associated with child-birth, marriage and death as well as those connected with various agricultural operations.

Agriculture being the main economic pursuit of the Bhils, their fairs and festivals are influence by the different stage of agricultural operations. There fairs and festivals provide recreation where the women, wearing colourful dresses, participate in songs and dances. In these fairs, cases of elopement are quite common.

Writing about the status of woman among tribal people of India, D.N. Majumdar points, out that "Mere absence of rights does not indicate subservience, just as the existence of there does not warrant their exercise". Even the tribal woman whom competent authorities have credited with freedom and latitude in inter-sexual relations suffer from cruelty and desertion and even if divorce is an escape, few take recourse to it. He further observes that the status of women in India can be understood more in the context of Indian ethnology than in that of religion or Brahaminism.

Women in tribal societies occupy in important place in their home. Their influence is much stronger than that of the males in rearing and socializing the children. In her own home she is not a liability but an asset as the division of labour is equitable. Socially she has more or less in equal status and has her own place. She is free to present her grievances before the panchas. But in the religious sphere she is not allowed to observe rituals and rites connected with the various aspects of the life of the tribal people.

To conclude in the words of Lowie, "Neither superstitious sentiments nor man's physical superiority have produced greater debarment of primitive woman, that she is generally well treated and able to influence masculine decisions regardless of all theory as to her inferiority or impurity; that is precisely among some of the rudest people that she enjoys practical equality with her mate".

N. N. VYAS

WORLD OF PICHHVAIS

Large colourful paintings with lot of rhythm and vibrance adorn the walls of lounges of posh hotels, airports and the living rooms of several art lovers in our country. These are called "Pichhvai", painted in Rajasthan, which is not only the land of chivalry, colour and romance but also home to fascinating arts and crafts.

According to a legend, an ancient holy image of Krishna was rescued by Rana Raj Singh in 1691 during the persecutions of Mughal Emperor Aurangzeb. About 65 kilometres from Udaipur, the wagon carrying the icon suddenly came to a halt. This was taken as a nomen and a temple was built to house the image which is worshipped as Shrinathji.

The worship of Shrinathji, a form of Lord Krishna, has been popular in Rajasthan since 17th century. Nathdwara, where the temple was built is a renowned centre of pilgrimage for the Vaishnavas, the devotees of Krishna and Vishnu alike. Over the years, Nathdwara has also come to be linked with, and become favour for, what is popularly known as the "Pichhvai" in local parlance.

Literally, speaking, the word "pichhvai" means something 'hung at the back'. The "Pichhvai' is a painted cloth-hanging which is suspended behind the idol of Shrinathji in this well-known shrine. The them of these "Pichhvais", as a rule is the image of Lord Krishna as represented by the idol fashioned out of black stone.

The tradition of painting on cloth dates back to the days of antiquity in India. Pieces of cloth painted in water colour pigments were hung on walls in Indian homes and temples in the absence of wall paintings. The art of painting "Pichhvais" originated in Mathura and Vrindaban where the painters have been portraying the image of Krishna on cloth-hanging through the centuries. In Mathura, one can still find painters working on "Pichhvais" although the tradition there has more or less declined because of lack of patronage.

At Nathdwara, this art form survived because the "Pichhvais" were made not only for sale to the pilgrims, but also for its constant use inside the temple of Shrinathji where "Pichhvais" embellished the interior of the sanctum sanctorum housing the main image. When the temple gates are thrown open to devotees, the "Pichhvais" are changed on each occasion. The themes of these paintings very so as to suit the particular occasion or ceremony for which they are intended. Temple "Pichhvais" are made by artists attached to the temple purely out of a sense of devotion, for, according to popular belief, such activity earns the artists salvation.

A number of 'Pichhvais' display a complete departure from conventional depictions and instead of the image of Shrinathji, feature the Raslila, Krishna's dance with his gopis (partners). The painters of the "pichhvais" lent a dramatic touch to this theme by introducing interesting changes here and there. Among other motifs common to most Pichhvais" are rows of well-fed cows including calves with upturned heads as though held spellbound by the magical notes of Krishna's flute. The best collection of "Pichhvais" is preserved in the Shrinathiji temple.

B. N. ARYAN

WOVEN WONDERS OF BENGAL

The excellence of Indian textiles as well as the glorious heritage of India weavers have been acclaimed the world over for thousands of years. Intricacies of spinning, dyeing and weaving cotton yarns were even well-known to the flourishing people of the Indus Valley civilisation. Excavations at Mohenjodaro have unearthed ancient implements of spinning and weaving as well as fragments of dyed cotton fabrics, dated to 1750 B.C. Cotton apparels have been described in the Vedas, the two Indian epics and in the Buddhist scriptures, and icons too have depicted them visually. Gandhara sculptures and the immortal frescoes of Ajanta caves vividly present are glimpses of contemporary clothings woven from cotton and silk. While India's textile exporting centre, Calicut, had given the famous 'Calico' to the world – in the medieval days, cotton fabrics made by Bengali weavers too became a legend in Europe and in the Middle East, for their finest textures and lightness. Known as the 'muslin' or 'mul mul', the featherweight textiles of Bengal were celebrated in the international market as 'woven wind' and 'wonder gossamer', fetching fabulous price. Under royal patronage the city of Dhaka, then capital of Bengal, became the production centre of muslin during the Mughal rule. The fabric was so fine and transparent that, as the legend goes, once emperor Shahjahan express hi displeasure towards the inadequate and indecent dresses worn by his daughter princess Jehanara, even though she had draped herself in six folds of the muslin ; A five – metre length of muslin sari made by the Bengali Weavers in those days could easily pass through a tiny finger ring.

The marvel of muslin and the famous Jamdani sari, however, ended in the eighteenth century with the British seizing control of Bengal under the East India Company. It is said that to protect the interests of the textile mills of Manchester, the muslin weavers of Dhaka were physically persecuted and coerced to stop weaving delicate fabrics. The art – heritage of fine weaving, thus came to an end and remained crippled for nearly two hundred years and the artistic muslin was almost dead and forgotten, only some specimens having been preserved in private collections or in museums.

With the partition of India, many skilled weavers migrated to India from Dhaka and settled down in West Bengal, around Shantipur in Nadia district and Ambika Kalna of Burdwan, both traditionally renowned centres for hand-woven cotton textiles. These talented and industrious artisans doon revived their ancestral occupation and the art of exquisite weaving once again flourished in a and the art of exquisite weaving once again flourished in a widespread area of West Bengal. Today, finely woven, feather-touch delicate saris in exotic designs and colours are being produced in the vast weaving belt comprising Shantipur, Phulia, Samudragarh, Dhatrigram and Ambika Kalna, each centre producing superb cotton fabrics in its own unique weaving style. Dhatrigram produces jacquard and plain Jamdanis (needle embroidery), while Kalna is famous for 'Tangails' and gorgeous Jamdanis. Phulia and Samudragarh specialize in a combination of jacquard and Jamdani works and Shantipur is known for it is superfine dhotis (cheaper cotton saris) and jacquard woven saris. The produce of these centres is being marketed through cooperatives and various undertakings. The Kalna Chamber of Commerce and Small Industries Corporation organizes weekly sari 'Heat' (oper market) offering the individual weavers as well as the weaving industry, opportunities to have a direct interface with the actual customer, fetching better remunerative prices avoiding middlemen. On every Saturday weavers from different centres scattered over far away villages assemble at Kalna sari heat with cartloads of their creative works – exquisite cotton saries in sensuous colours and varied designs. Prices very between Rs. 200 to 2000 a piece and above, depending upon the quality and labour involved, the weaving time for each sari being a period of seven days to almost a year.

. In one such Haat, we came across Rabindranath Saha, a gifted weaver who made a sensational revival of muslin. With his innovative skills and perseverance he designed a special loom to weave fine muslin from delicate cotton threads of 200 counts. This was a scoring over the usual 80 to 120 count thread considered to be the finest. He presented this very special muslin sari to the former Prime Minister, the late Mrs. Indira Gandhi in early 1984. Encouraged by her appreciation, Saha then set out to produce still finer muslin of 400 count. This too he achieved after twelve years of painstaking efforts of modify his loom, spinning implements and replacing the traditional wooden shuttle with one made of soft cane. The finest of threads, almost invisible, could be spun from a superior variety of cotton grown in Thrichur district of Kerala. A 1000 – metre length of this gossamer yarn weight just four grams. The entire length of muslin that the weaved measuring 1.26 X 5 metres, weighing a mere 110 gms. Easily passed through a finger ring that Saha had been wearing.

DIPALI DE

"Y"

YADAV RAM KISHORE

It is a happy experience to come across an artist in whom authentic tradition, with its concern to ensure that vision has a secure springboard for its flight in a solid base of craft skill, speak with a modern voice. This is what Ram Kishore Yadav seeks to do.

It was in commercial art that Ram Kishore Yadav graduated, from the Delhi College of Art. Given his temperament, it is a lucky coincidence that he specialised in applied art. Art is not a gesture where the meaning is clear only to the artist who makes the gesture. It fails if it does not communicate. This clarity of communication is an absolute and peremptory requirement in applied art. Fine art too has to communicate.

In the seventies yadav sought to reflect rural life and the urban environment in his oil paintings. Some of these are delightful, like the one showing a peasant couple with their cart taking rest on a road. In his paintings of the urban environment, he used arches and angles to give an accented geometricism to the architecture and some of the lit interiors are fine patterns of light and shadow. But some of the paintings indicate that capturing the anomie of big cities was among his intentions. Here however success was not unqualified and he soon realised that if he was to reach deeper meanings, he had to change directions.

The quest in seeking new direction commenced in the early eighties and has continued, with slow but sure evolutionary gains. The technique changed, forging closer links with the craft tradition which has always been exacting in its demands. Copper and aluminum sheet, with forms in low relief against a ground treated with repousee and related techniques for varied textural effects, are mounted on wood board pasted over the canvas which is painted to complete the design. The palette shows subtle understanding of contrasts and harmonies in juxtaposition with the native tints of the metals. The execution is always tidy and elegant. The work came to resemble low relief sculpture and the refinements he introduced as time went by further accented the resemblance, for he began to use solid, moulded and cast metal forms in addition to sheet metal raised to relief by repouse. The relief also became progressively more detailed and finer, revealing delicately done miniature forms when looked at close while, from a distance, they merge into a decorative graining or texture. This is essential a feature of mural art and all these works have the monumental feeling of the mural in spite of their relatively much smaller dimensions. They also retain the overall decorative quality of the mural.

In the new phase, Yadav began by tapping the possibilities in the Indian astrological tradition. Several decades ago, K.C.S. Panikkar also had been fascinated by the purely visual possibilities of the zodiacal and nativity charts. But he had confined himself to the structural strength of the geometric design and the piquant beauty of calligraphy (in Malayalam script). Yadav also uses calligraphic forms, but sparingly, single alphabets rather than phrases or sentences, and alphabets evokes mystery because it seems to belong to a script as yet undeciphered, like for instant the script of the Indus valley civilization.

Yadav then moved to variation on traditional forms like those of Siva and Ganesha. Here, the image with the greatest potential for meaning he has been able to create is that of the sun. He creates great halations of light around the orb and crowds the disc itself with forms of teeming life. A perception, primarily aesthetic, has finally helped Yadav towards an integral sensing, integrative on many planes.

In a world torn by tragic and needless conflicts, Yadav reaffirms this in compositions where he has integrated the symbols of various religious, the Pranava, the cross and the crescent. This, at present, may be summative and notational but as he gains further life experience, he is sure to gain the visual richness in his creations inspired by the sun, and the flora and fauna which emerge from that fount of all life. Yadav has exhibited his works in all the major and prestigious galleries in India and abroad, particularly in US and Germany. These have won him many laurels.

KRISHNA CHAITANYA

YAJNAVALKYA : THEY MAKE US PROUD

In the 12th century BC- six centuries before Mahavira and the Buddha, centuries before Confucius and Plato, 1200 years before Jesus Christ, there lived in this land a sage called Yajnavalkya. He was a native of Videha, the Kingdom of the Janakas (land of Sita of Ramayana, the easternmost settlement of the Aryans, which was most prolific in thinkers and scholars- of Gautama (of Natyashastra fame), Kanada (propounder of the Vaisesika system of philosophy), Jaimini (founder of the Mimamsa system) and Kapila (founder of the Samkha system). But Yajnavalkya stands above them all as the author of the basic priciples of Hindu philosophy, which have remained unaltered to this day. Hailed as the father of Indian philosophy, he represented the highest ideals of Vedic thought.

Yajnavalkya appears almost at the end of Vedic age (2000) BC-1000 BC. It was during this that the *Samhitas, Brahmanas and Upanishads* came to be written. We only know that were the works of numerous sages and kings. But, unfortunately, most of them are mere names of us, almost mythical. But Yajnavalkya is the first historical personage to emerge from this hoary antiquity. He was a friend and contemporary of Krti Janaka of Videha (not the father of Sita), who is placed by historians in the 12th century BC. And we know from *Brihadaranyaka Upanishad* that Janaka called a Congress of scholars to debate certain philosophic issues and that Yajnavalkya defeated them all, carrying away the king's prize of 1000 cows adorned with gold coins on their horns.

Yajnavalkya was challenged by no less than eight scholars, including his own teacher Uddalaka Aruni and Gargi, a woman. The Brihadaranyaka gives a detailed account of the contest, in which many of the philosophic questions of the time came up. Yajnavalkya gave a profound discourse on the Absolute or *Atman*, after which, it is said, "Uddalaka held his peace".

And then came the final challenge from Gargi, Saying "I have armed myself against thee, O Yajnavalkya, with two questions she wanted to know more on the nature of *Brahman*. On this, Yajnavalkya describes *Brahaman* as limitless in time and space, but in whom exist time and space. *Brahman* is devoid of the attributes of matter, such as gross or subtle, great or small...(it is) without taste, smell, eyes, ears, speech, understanding, without light or breath.... The *Brahman* is unseen, but all-seeing, unheard but all-hearing, unperceived but all-perceiving, unknown but all-knowing. On this Gargi told the assembled scholars: " No one, I am sure, can ever even dream of defeating him in any argument concerning Brahman". Here is a no personal god, no gods or goddesses of popular Hinduism. And all this over three thousand years ago; No one has been able to improve upon this description of God.

Gargi wanted to know then the importance of rituals and sacrifices, to which Yajnavalkya replied, " of a truth, of Gargi, he who does not know this Imperishable one, and sacrifices and distributes alms and who does penance wine thereby only finite good". Thus he reduced the importance of rituals and sacrifices at a time when the priests were trying to make them supreme.

The fame of Yajnavalkya as the greatest philosopher was thus established. Soon we see him teaching some of his own teachers. At least he takes up the task of instructing the king himself, who was considered one of the foremost scholars of his time. One day Yajnavalkya asked him: "Whither will you go after death?" The kind had no answer, Yajnavalkya's treatment of the matter has baffled scholars throughout the ages. Deussen says in his book "Philsophy" that we have no better reply to give even today. And this was his reply. "The soul after death goes nowhere where it has not been from the very beginning, nor does it become other than that which it has always been".

On another occasion king Janaka wanted to know that serves man for light, to which Yajnavalkya replied that when external light such sun, moon or fire fails, then shines the inner light of man's Self or Atman.

Explaining the nature of *Karma*. Yajnavalkya says : "A person consists of desires. As is the desire, so is his will, as is his will, so is his deed and whatever deed he does, that he will reap. But as for the man who does not desire, who, freed from the desire the Self only, he goes to *Brahman*. If a man understands the self thus, saying "I am He ", What more could he wish or desire ? Knowing this, the people of old did not wish for offsprings". Deeper, finer, nobler words were never uttered by human lips, says Deussan.

Towards the end of his life, Yajnavalkya renounced the world as was the custom among Hindus, and became a mendicant. But before the left his family (he had two wives – Maitrayi and Katyayani), he had a long discussion with Maitrayi (she was herself well – versed in Vedic and Upanishadic philosophy) to remove some of her doubts.

Explaining his understanding of immortality, Yajnavalkya told Maitreyi : "After death, there is no consciousness". She wanted him to unravel this paradox. He said, "where there is duality, there one sees the other, smells, hears, comprehends and knows the other, but when everything has become to him his own self, how should he smell, see, hear, understand or know any one at all ? How should he know the knower ? So after death, when the Atman (Soul) merges with Brahman, it becomes immortal. It cannot have a consciousness of its separate existence."

Thus did Yajnavalkya's teaching supply the basis upon which Hindu philosophy has evolved and expanded throughout the ages. They may be summed up in the three propositions : (1) The *Atman* is the knowing subject within us the light of lights. (2) That *Atman,* as the knowing subject, can never become an object and is, therefore, itself unknowable. Empirical predicates cannot be ascribed to it. (3) The *Atman* is the sole reality. "There is no second outside of it, no other distinct from it", Duessen explains it like this :" There is not, and never can be, for us reality outside of the Atman (soul) (a universe outside of our consciousness)". This is a fundamental position of Upanishadic philosophy.

M. S. N. MENON

YAMINI KRISHNAMURTHY

It was in the sixties that the tall willowy and beautiful Yamini came to centre stage and has been a key figure on the panorama of Indian classical dance ever since. She has grown in stature and today, she is own of the immortal exponents of Indian dance. Having had the applause throughout a splendid career spanning three decades, she now rests on her laurels. But her passion for dance continues. Sitting back relaxed on the lawns of her flat in South Delhi Yamini looks dignified and content. The elegance of a dancer is unmistakable in her bearing. A loner by nature, she is a moody person with a stron individuality. At the same time, she is witty.

Born in Madanapalle, a small village is the Rayalaseema district of Andhra Pradesh, Yamini was a stubborn child used to having her own way. "As a kid I was very tomboyish. I never played with dolls. I used to climb trees and played the games the boys played", she laughts, fondly remembering her childhood.

Little Yamini's innate artistic spirit was kindled at the Chidambaram temple in Tamil Nadu. "I was just four when I went to the temple with my father. The temple towers are replete with the dancing postures of Lord Shiva. The beauty of the dance postures made a deep impression on me and it was then that I was inspired to become a dance. I wanted to dance like Him".

Curious about a little girl who was obsessed with dance, Gauriammal, a Davadasi, volunteered to teach her dance. She found an over enthusiastic disciple in Yamini. Recalling the happy memory of her first Guru, Yamini said, "she was very authoritative but a lovable lady. She used to call out to me for dance lessons as and when she pleased and I had to drop everything else and get ready to dance and get ready to dance. She was totally immersed in dance and music. I learnt 'Abhinaya' (acting) from her".

Recognising his daughter's unrelenting passion for dance Pro. Krishnamurthy enrolled her into Rukmini Devi Arunandale's Kalakshetra in Madras. Thus commenced the formal training marking the beginning of a glorious tryst with dance

Yamini's genius glistened while still in her teens. Fierce dedication and extraordinary talent was a powerful combination in moulding the doe-eyed beauty into a danseuse extraordinary. Initially based at Madras, Yamini moved to Delhi in the late sixties. She performed regularly in India and abroad.

The most striking aspect of Yamini's dance was the dynamic charisma of per personality. Like an empress commanded the stage with tremendous self – confidence. She exuded a vibrant energy that made the audience come alive to her performance. There was a brilliance in her immaculate precision in timing and her immaculate precision in timing and her masterly control on line. Her movements were grammatically accurate, yet she had the awesome capacity to lift the dance above mere technique which held the audiences spell-bound. How did she feel while performing? "Before a performance I go into a creative tension. An in built inspiration comes to me that is charged by looking at the audience. There is a thread of communication that runs from me to the audience and I never lose hold at my end. I take the audience along with me when I dance. In fact, what really sustains me is the audience.

While Bharatnatyam is esoteric and ritualistic, Kuchipudi is sensuous in appeal and romantic in temperament. Yamini is exceedingly comfortable and exceptionally skilled at both. Sonali Mansingh, the reigning queen of Odissi, says, "Yamini blazed a new trail in Bharatnatyam. She has a different style altogether. She had a lot of fire and her lines were marvellous. She is enormously gifted".

The trailblazer speaks : "I have brought in a freshness, a brisk and complex rhythmic element into dance. I have brought in freshness, a brisk and complex rhythmic element into dance. I have created a lot of new compositions. And before I took up Kuchipudi, it was known as folk art. I revived it and made it so popular that it became a rage in the sixties.

The spirit of Kuchipudi is synonymous with Yamini. Her chiselled features, large lustrous eyes, fluid grace and sculpturesque poses added a charming lyricism to the dance form. "Nobody else could bring out the erotic element in Kuchipudi as beautifully as Yamini used to", asserts Leela Venkataraman, the noted dance critic. Sonal Mansingh points out that "she had a log of sensuousness and her physicality was very strong".

Yamini's supermacy at 'Abhinaya' the expressive mode of dance is legendary. At one moment there was tenderness, at another fury, at yet another ecstasy. The 'Navarasas' (nine forms) fitted across her face with characteristic finesse and expertise. The expertise was not learnt, it was inborn. Yamini's communicative artistry is unsurpassed till today.

The guiding light in her life was her late father Krishnamurthy. A Sanskrit scholar and a professor in English Literature, he was a great source of inspiration and knowledge of Yamini. He was my artistic Guru, I learnt so much from him effortlessly. I lost him in 1984. I don't' think any other death will affect me anymore.

The two different styles of the Kancheepuram and Tanjore schools of dance combine in Yamini, for her noted Gurus were Ellappa Pillai of Kancheepuram and Kittappa Pillai of Tanjore. "They introduced new insights into dance and taught me an innovative approach of complexity and authenticity".

Reflecting on the performance that she enjoyed most she gushed: "I inaugurated the Chindambaram Festival in the early eighties. I felt so happy and energetic dancing In my favourite temple. I also opened the Khajuraho Dance Festival in 1978. Dancing in these two temples was just like dancing in the heavens".

"It was an exhilarating experience to dance at the Amphitheatre in Athens. It was massive structure and we didn't need a mike. I was popular dancer in France, USA and England but the country that really loved me most was Italy".

At 26 Yamini became the youngest to receive the covered title "Padma Shri' for her outstanding contribution to classical dance. She was also the recipient of the Sangeet Natak Academy Award in 1977 for overall excellence and lifetime contribution, besides getting many other awards.

When asked to name the greatest of all dancers, she flashed a beautiful smile, looked heavenwards and calmly replied. "Lord Shiva himself".

SUREKHA RAO

YEHUDI MENUHIN

Every now and then, in the field of music, we come across the unaccountable phenomenon of a child showing incredible technical mastery and artistic maturity far beyond his years. There is no way of explaining this except as an attribute of genius or as a "gift of the Gods". The supreme example of this is Mozart who astonished the world as a little boy, not merely by his wonderful mastery of two instruments–the piono and the violin-but also by his achievement as a composer. The most remarkable example of such a phenomenon in the twentieth century is Yehudi Menuhin.

As he grew up, Yehudi Menuhin fulfilled all the expectations that he had aroused by developing into one of the major creative and interpretative forces in the world of music. What is more, believing in the common heritage of man, he began to devote his great talents to further human relations and international understanding. In this he reached out to all peoples of the world, transcending narrow man-made barriers.

Yehudi Menuhin was born on April 22, 1916, in New York. His parents were Russian emigrants. He started his serious musical education while still a child. Of the many teachers who shaped his playing of the violin and his musical thinking the three most important are: Louis Persinger, the American violinist and, George Enesco, the great Rumanian composer and violinist and Adolf Busch. He made his debut at the age of seven as a soloist with the San Francisco Symphony Orchestra conducted by Alfred Hertz. The New York debut followed shortly afterwards. In 1927 he appeared in Paris with Paul Paray. In his Berlin debut in 1929 he played in one single evening the Bach E Major, the Beethoven and the Brahms concertos with the Berlin Philharmonic Orchestra, Bruno Walter conducting. Before long he had won the hearts of every capital in Europe, trailing clouds of glory wherever he went. Soon he began to appear with his sister Hephzibah in violin and piano sonatas, giving distinguished interpretations of piano and violin literature which have become memorable musical experience in the last four decades. The first round the world concert tour was in 1935, when Yehudi Menuhin appeared in 63 cities giving a total of 110 concerts.

Throughtout this early period his parents did all that was humanly possible to ensure that Yehudi Menuhin had a normal childhood. then, on the advice of his father, at age of nineteen, he retired for two years to study and " to get to know himself." He emerged from his self-enforced retirement with a newer and deeper awareness of music and of his own role as a musician. Soon he found himself fully booked up, year after year, and appeared as a soloist with every outstanding symphony orchestra in the world with such conductors as Toscanini, Furtwangler, Bruno Walter, Koussevitsky, Stockowaki, Mitropoulous, Beecham, Montieux, Ormandy, Dorati.

During the Second World War Menuhin gave more concerts than any other living concert artist – for the Allied Armed Forces, the Red Cross and civilian charities. He flew in bombers across the Atlantic, the Pacific and the Arctic oceans, often giving two an three recitals in a day in trying conditions in camps, hospitals, ships. He was the first concert artist to play in liberated Europe after the war giving innumerable benefit concerts in Berlin, Bucharest, Budapest, Moscow, Prague, Vienna and in several Displaced Persons Camps.

By now the world had come to realise that he was not only one of the greatest musicians of his day, but a humanist with a strong sense of social justice cutting across nations and classes, races and religions. Music he believed, is so close to humanity that one must go to humanity to develop oneself as a musician. He recognised that his gifts and the unique position that he had been able to achieve impose on him an immense responsibility which was to be of service to others. And he had brought injustice and oppression, racial, economic, political, whether it was apatheid in South Africa or political oppression elsewhere. In all such cases, he was not just a liberal arm – chair intellectual who spoke brave words. He took a firm stand and stood committed, often risking his career, his future, even in his life. This had won him the esteem and affection of young and old all over the world because he is clean, totally unselfish and incorruptible in an age of expediency and bent morals.

He was the Director of two Festivals – Windsor in England and Gstaad in Switzerland. He has founded a school where he had brought to the teaching of music much advanced thinking and techniques. He had developed a deep and passionate interest in the music of the East which he was never tired of championing. And today he was the President of the International Music Council.

In the ultimate analysis Yehudi Menuhin will be judged as a musician because that was his true vocation and that was the discipline through which he had realised himself, India had become a part of his life, not just Yoga and the fascination of Indian music, but in his own words, "the serenity of India, its deeper sense of values, its timelessness, its genius to make sense and create order out of chaos".

V. K. NARAYANA MENON

"Z"

ZAKIR HUSSAIN

This legendary custodian of the tabla is none other than Ustad Zakir Hussain, who invariably creates international waves with his art each year and who unfailingly returns to concert audiences in India, to enchant music lovers of all categories. When he plays abroad, the young maestro generates interest as both soloist and fusionist and recently, after the Atlanta Olympics meet, as a composer. To his fan following in the country, he is a priest and a traditionalist who strictly adheres to the principal of the classical tabla. Even before he unfolds the protective covering around his instrument, he has a word with his audience, Winning over their confidence by disclosing exactly what he will play and how the tabla, generally regarded as an accompanying instrument, is actually a melodic device, capable of speaking in a language of deep-set evocation.

While a great deal is known about his music, his heritage and the numerous awards that have been conferred on him, the Ustad himself likes to handpick the Padmashri, conferred on him by the President of India, as the one closest to his heart. He recalls that he was on stage accompanying the legendary sitarist Pandit Ravi Shankar at a function in the St. Xavier College, Mumbai. His father, Ustad Allah Rakha, was sitting in the front row of the audience when one of the organisers came and whispered message in his ear. Immediately, his father's face lit-up and the massage was duly conveyed to the revered Pandit on the stage.

A non-plussed Zakir watched helplessly Pandit Ravi Shankar stood up and lifted his accompanist and declared to the hall that Zakir was now a Padmashri awardee. Amidst riotous raptures that followed, a found father and dedicated guru, Ustad Allah Rakha, addressed his son by the coveted title of 'Ustad' and declared him a deserving progeny.

But the beginnings of this child prodigy were no startling trail lazer. In fact, it meant a rigorous assessment of his potential. "I was barely seven when I had to play for about thirty five or forty minutes as an accompanist Ustad Ali Akbar Khan. Probably I did not realise what I was capable of doing it. For immediately thereafter the routine (of tabla lessons) started. It was to be woken up at around two or three in the morning and tabla practice with my father, and while the house slept, this used to go on till it was time to leave for school. It meant barely four or five hours of sleep and then practice and studies…"he rolls on.

Such a dreary routine of learning and developing a skill alongside would have guaranteed to be a soul-killing affair, were it not for the astute input of a creative man that the senior Ustad instilled. When the duo sat to play, in complete seclusion, he made it a point to impress his disciple's mind with the value of his heritage.

Together with the technique of tabla taps young Zakir's mind was ignited with a plethora of legends and incidents woven around the world of classical music, the tabla in particular. "It was the discovery of an entire tradition and not just the family one. The mystical world opened up and a belief in the existence of what one might call fantasy, germinated. It was this understanding that egged me on to achieve something…"

With paternal backing on a firm footing, the time arrived for the young musician to present himself as a professional. Again, the start was non-descript and had plenty of comicality. It was my first professional assignment and I was a boy of eleven. As a fee for my effort, dinner was packed for me and I proudly brought it home saying, "Look got food," feeling that I had become a man. I felt that now I could look after my mother and sister". However, at that time the entire musician clan was considered second class as a profession and as for the tabla players, they were virtually third class. The renowned dancer, Sitara Devi, chose him as her accompanist a year later. "I was given a hundred rupees as fee, but this money was not half as exciting or important for me as the food parcel I had brought home".

When the billings opened up further, contrary to expectations, the story of his trials still continued. As migrant to the US, he had thought things would be different. "I thought I would make fast buck there but things turned out to be different. I had imagined that everybody loved Ustad Allah Rakha and Pandit Ravi Shankar. What I had not realised was that besides the two them, they knew of no other Indian performer. For the new arrivals, the road to fame was still a distant dream. It was only twenty or twenty-five dollars a week, eating a pot of vegetable curry. wearing tron sneakers, travelling by bus and giving tuitions to people living at the other end of town".

"A concert where I played, there were barely forty or fifty people, and I soon realised that my other musician friends could not help much as they too were struggling in their own fields. But they made me aware of my 'incredible tradition". "I began to see India in a new light and soon realised that everybody there wanted to listen to me, learn, watch, assimilate and find out what I had to offer them. In the process I began to enrich my own knowledge of my tradition and even managed to evolve my own style of playing. Now when I play with western groups, there is a balance of things. It is seventy percent India and thirty percent is letting my hair down. Just why I still continue to play such music is because it helps me find out more, through fusion, through music for films and even through teaching the art, "he surmises.

But all this changeover and adjustment for the artist has not been a single-handed venture. Wife Antonia Minnecola, an Italian from Bronx" as husband Zakir prefers to introduce her has been his lodestar. "It was a date for a hamburger which became the auspicious beginning of this relationship that is now twenty two summers old". It was while she was a student of Kathak dance at the Sitara Devi Dance Academy that they had met. Today, the relationship endures for different reasons, "We both love art, tradition and creativity", he declares, "and in order to be creative we exist on equal footing and do not encroach on each other's creative fields". She runs a record company that records traditional classical music and world music of the ethnic category, making the Hussains a family that is totally Indian at heart and yet able to melt into any environment without making a crossover.

From that feeble start to a time of cultural adjustment, the tabla wizard has traversed many miles. Has he reached a level of personal satisfaction where he can sit back and enjoy the laurels he has so painstaking earned? " I am learning all the time. Professionally all around me there are tabla players who are just as good in fact, even technically superior. Perhaps in my case it is this striving to get it across to my audience in a package of proper proportion, that gives me a sense of enjoyment. Since I enjoy myself and am not afraid to let go, I refuse to set goals for myself".

PHAL S. GIROTA

ZARDOZI - INDIAN ART OF GOLD EMBROIDERY

Zardozi is a living art which is mainly practiced in Uttar Pradesh, Rajasthan, Gujarat, Madhya Pradesh and Maharashtra with a few centres in Jammu and Kashmir, Punjab, Bihar, Andhra Pradesh, Karnataka and West Bengal. The national capital of Delhi too is an important centre of Zardozi art.

Zardozi is the sheer magic of nimble finger and imaginative designs, envisaged by the ensemble of lustrous metallic wire which was traditionally a silver wire coated of plated with gold, silk threads, beads and stones. The luster of gold has been successfully retained in the polypropylene wire.

The tradition of gold embroidery still continues to flourish despite many ups and downs. In the contemporary times innovative uses of traditional skills have given Zardozi a new lease of life and the number of its patrons is increasing fast. If Indian bride looks so beautiful and dazzling, at least half of the credit goes to Zardozi bridal outfits having meticulous embroidery in colourful patterns.

Though the history of Indian gold embroidery can be traced to the vedic period and we find it repeatedly mentioned in early historical and literary records, there is however a total absence of early material. Definite evidences of the large –scale production of Zardozi textiles are found after the advent of sultanate rule in India. This tradition continued to flourish under Muslim rule. Portuguese and later Britain's East India company flooded European markets with Zardozi fabrics. Under British rule the art of Zardozi lost royal patronage but still it managed to survive and continued to flourish in independent India.

M. L. VARADPANDE